Glass Art

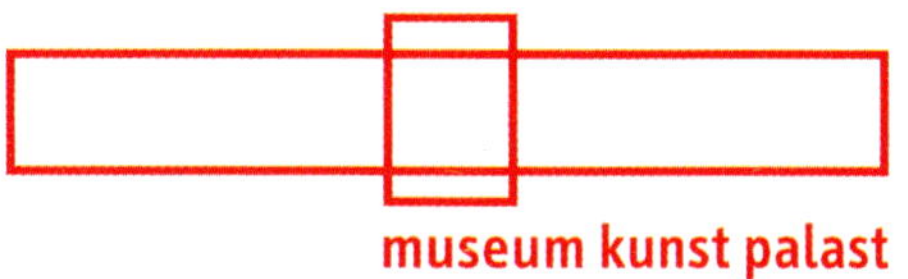

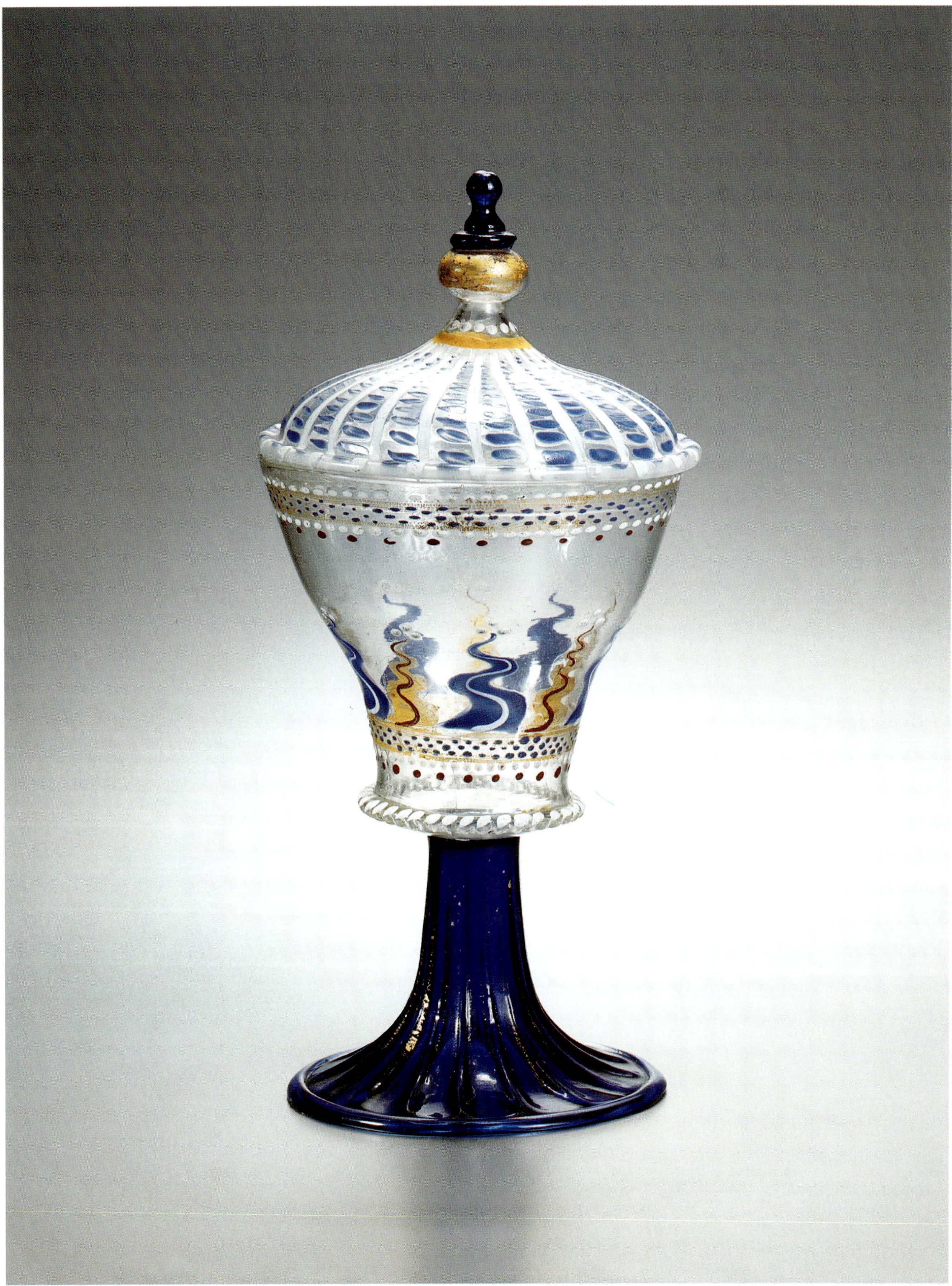

Helmut Ricke

Glass Art
Reflecting the Centuries

Masterpieces from the Glasmuseum Hentrich
in museum kunst palast, Düsseldorf

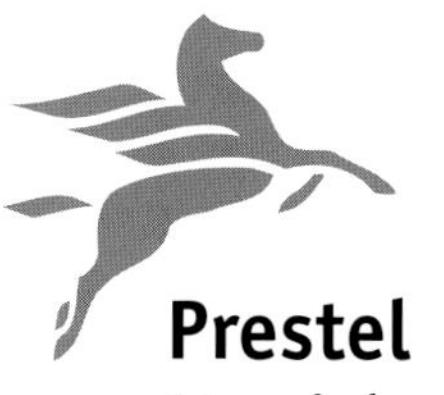

Prestel
Munich · Berlin · London · New York

The English translation has greatly benefited from funds provided by the
Ministerium für Arbeit, Soziales und Stadtentwicklung, Kultur und Sport
of the German federal state of North Rhine-Westphalia as well as from the
support of the Europäisches Übersetzer-Kollegium Straelen e.V.

Front cover: Cat. nos. 36, 551, 508, 231, 124, 298, 149, 379, 91
Frontispiece: Covered goblet with enamel painting, Venice, ca. 1500,
H with cover 25.7, without 17.9, ∅ foot 10.9, ∅ bowl 12.3 cm,
cover: H 8.9, ∅ 12.7 cm, acc. no. GL 1999-32

The Deutsche Bibliothek – CIP Einheitsaufnahme and the Library of Congress
Cataloguing-in-Publication data is available

Prestel Verlag
Königinstrasse 9, 80539 Munich
Tel. +49 (89) 38 17 09-0; Fax +49 (89) 38 17 09-35

4 Bloomsbury Place, London WC1A 2QA
Tel. +44 (20) 7323 5004; Fax +44 (20) 7636 8004

175 Fifth Avenue, Suite 402, New York, New York 10010
Tel. +1 (212) 995-2720; Fax +1 (212) 995-2733

www.prestel.com

Translated from the German by Claudia Lupri, Cologne
Editorial direction by Curt Holtz, Munich
Copyedited by Michele Schons, Munich
Typeset by Bernd Hüller, Munich
Designed by Monika Hagenberg, Düsseldorf; Rainald Schwarz, Munich
Photographs by Walter Klein, Düsseldorf; Helmut Dahmen, Landesbildstelle Rheinland;
Horst Kolberg, Neuß; Gabriel Urbanek, Prague
Drawings by Manfred Böhm, Düsseldorf
Maps by Martin Günther and Berend van Laar, Düsseldorf
Printed and bound by Passavia Druckservice GmbH, Passau
Lithography by REPRO LUDWIG, Zell am See, Austria

Printed in Germany on acid-free paper

ISBN 3-7913-2793-3 (Hardcover edition)

Contents

Preface

Since its discovery glass has enjoyed a special status. As the first "artificial" substance, it attests to the extraordinary technical skill attained by human beings, who showed that they could harness the physical givens of nature to produce a new material. To this day, it has retained its fascination: a substance of transparency, color, and brilliance produced by the mysterious interaction of such simple ingredients as sand and ash with fire.

Glass has accompanied humankind since the second century BC. Initially it was a highly valued luxury material for decorative objects, inlays for sculptures, or vessels for precious ointments, yet, with the invention of glassblowing, it increasingly served to enrich objects of everyday life, while continuing to be an artistic medium.

Glass has always reflected the circumstances of life, the culture, the historical situation, and the mentality of the people who have made and used it. A testament to nearly 4,000 years of cultural history, it reveals what human beings have been able to achieve with and wrest from this exacting material.

Only a few specialized collections in the world have the means to illustrate with superb examples the entire history of artistic glass design. The collection of the museum kunst palast (Kunstmuseum Düsseldorf until 2001) belongs to this small circle, surpassed only by a few others like the Corning Museum of Glass in the state of New York and the Victoria & Albert Museum in London. Since 1990 the Düsseldorf collection of nearly 9,000 glass objects has borne the name Glasmuseum Hentrich in honor of its most important benefactor, the Düsseldorf architect Helmut Hentrich.

Instead of introducing this collection with a standard catalogue of selected works, we thought it would be more interesting to take advantage of the fact that it covers all periods of glass art. Using pieces in the collection as examples, we decided to outline the history of this art in a survey. We were not as concerned with describing at length the complex and often overlapping developments as in summarizing them in short, manageable chapters. The selected works speak for themselves.

Thus a small handbook has emerged, with a comprehensive appendix, including maps showing the dissemination of glass throughout history and its most important centers as well as illustrations and descriptions of the most important glassblowing and decorative techniques. Also included are a glossary of technical terms; a section on reproductions, imitations, and forgeries; as well as a selected bibliography for further reference.

To avoid overloading the illustrated sections, references to the older literature on the individual glass objects have been omitted. They can be found in the collection catalogues of the Glasmuseum Hentrich, cited in the bibliography. Comparative pieces are mentioned only in the plate commentaries in connection with objects made in very small quantities. The literature cited in the plate commentaries includes only those works that refer explicitly to the piece in question.

Publications of this nature are always based on the achievements and knowledge of many. My predecessors, the curators Elfriede Heinemeyer and, in particular, Axel von Saldern, laid the groundwork for this book. I could not expand much on the latter's work on ancient and Islamic glassware. The texts on glassware of the periods of historicism and Art Nouveau owe much to the publications that Helga Hilschenz-Mlynek wrote as a free-lance collaborator for the Kunstmuseum Düsseldorf in 1973 and 1985. Many pieces from these periods, however, could be classified anew or more accurately. The present volume also includes many new acquisitions of Helmut Hentrich, gifts from other benefactors, and purchases made with museum funds. Much of the glassware of the 1950s and "new glass" up to the present is published here for the first time.

I found support for my work from many sides. In particular I wish to thank Anne-Marie Katins for her careful editing of the manuscript, Eva Schmitt for her valuable suggestions on the subject of glass, Susanne Frantz for her assistance with the translation and my wife, Ute Ricke, for her patience—and for producing the index. The often unduly tried translator of the German texts, Claudia Lupri, mastered her task highly professionally, with unflagging commitment and thoroughness—and this despite the fact that this volume was expanded far beyond our initial expectations. I owe her my special and sincere thanks.

H. R.

The Glasmuseum Hentrich at the museum kunst palast in Düsseldorf
History—Acquisitions—Perspectives

Helmut Ricke

Often it takes just a small step to achieve big effects. A few years ago, the opportunity to rearrange the glass collection of the Kunstmuseum Düsseldorf, today the museum kunst palast, arose. The result surprised everyone. For the first time the various parts of the collection—previously scattered throughout the museum—were presented in a large complex of rooms on the ground floor as an impressive entity, revealing the international significance of this collection to all.

The museum can now show approximately one-third of the some 9,000 glass pieces constituting its permanent collection. In addition, the Grüner Saal of the nearby Tonhalle offers the opportunity to hold temporary exhibitions of pieces drawn from the museum's holdings, or of works on loan, arranged thematically. Thus this large, indeed momentous, collection of glass, which has flourished behind the scenes for many years, became conspicuously visible.

The Glasmuseum Hentrich occupies a special position amongst comparable collections in Europe. More unified and comprehensive than most, its strength lies in its diversity and breadth, highlighted by an extraordinarily large number of exquisite pieces. A large collection of glassware previously belonging to Düsseldorf's former Kunstgewerbemuseum (Museum of Applied Arts) provided the basis for its development. This institution, stamped with the spirit of historicism, saw its primary responsibility in making aesthetically and technically exemplary works of previous epochs available to the regional craft industry as models. For this reason, in addition to a few superb pieces, many glass objects were acquired to illustrate the various blowing and decorating techniques or because they were considered typical products of a given period. Most of these pieces were acquired as gifts with funds provided by the Gewerbeförderungs-verein (association in aid of industry), the body responsible for the museum, whereas others were transferred from the storage of Berlin's Kunstgewerbemuseum.

In 1927 the collections of the Kunstgewerbemuseum, which in the meantime had been closed, were transferred to the newly erected buildings of the Kunstmuseum Düsseldorf. With this incorporation and in accordance with the concept of the new institution,

the restructuring of the glass collection, according to aesthetic and art-historical considerations, could begin. An important step towards achieving the museum's current international standing was to secure Roman and medieval vessels from the Josef Lückger Collection, Cologne, in 1936 and 1949, and, in particular, the acquisition of the Johannes Jantzen Collection, Bremen, in 1940. With the latter's nearly 200 fine glass objects from the Middle Ages, the Renais-

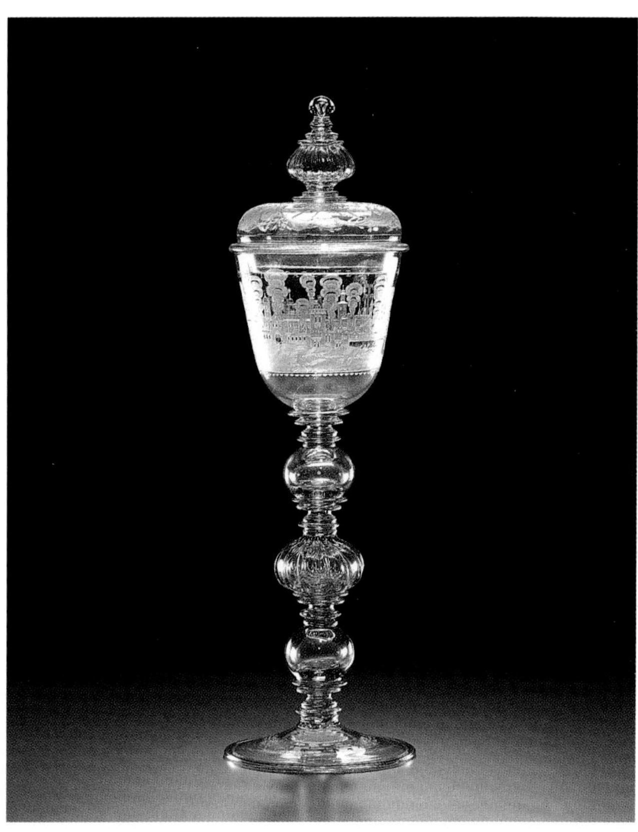

Covered Goblet with Aeneas Fleeing from Burning Troy

Attr. Johann Hess, Frankfurt, ca. 1670
H with cover 39.6, without 30.7, ⌀ foot 11.8, ⌀ bowl 10 cm
Cover: H 10.5, ⌀ 11 cm   Acc. no. GL 1999-33

sance, the Baroque, and the Biedermeier periods, artistically designed glass was finally established as one of the major focal points of the Kunstmuseum Düsseldorf.

Following occasional subsequent additions, the collection was substantial, but had no distinctive image in the early 1960s. Its primary focus lay in the area of European glass from the Middle Ages to the Biedermeier period, supplemented by Roman glassware of mostly Rhenish provenance, forming an important regional point of interest. Missing, besides outstanding ancient pieces, were primarily Islamic glassware and examples illustrating the development of glass-making since the mid-nineteenth century with highlights of Art Nouveau, Art Deco, the 1930s to the 1960s, and contemporary glass.

In exactly these areas lay the strength of the extensive collection amassed by the Düsseldorf architect Helmut Hentrich over a period of three decades, which he generously transferred to the Kunstmuseum Düsseldorf in the form of annual gifts from 1963 until his death, in 2001.

In 1966 the deliberate expansion of the glass collection began with the gift of the Hentrich Collection, the brisk commitment of the then director, Wend von Kalnein, and the appointment of the art historian Axel von Saldern, widely renowned for his research in glass, as the head of the Department of Sculpture and Applied Art (Plastik und Kunstgewerbe). For the first time the collection was exhibited as a unified whole and considerable sums of money could be spent on the acquisition of important glass objects or whole collections.

After von Saldern's appointment as director of Hamburg's Museum für Kunst und Gewerbe, in 1971, it was possible to continue uninterruptedly to the present the work he had begun. Thus the past 35 years reflect the inevitable consequences for the museum, and therefore the city of Düsseldorf, resulting from the unique opportunity afforded by the Hentrich Collection gift. The principle task in these years—apart from the suitable presentation of the collection—was to build it up to the point of creating the most comprehensive survey of glass art over the centuries and to document it in catalogues. In addition, since the 1970s the author has striven to realize an exhibition concept that, besides being thematically attractive, would contribute to glass research. These efforts, which should be understood as a program for the future, were accompanied by the methodical expansion of the library and the establishment of a documentation center on the history of glass art as well as close contacts with glass centers in Europe, the United States, and Japan.

Although the funds available for the expansion of the glass collection have always been limited, together with the gifts of Helmut Hentrich and other benefactors as well as the help of the Düsseldorf Museumsverein, the collection could nevertheless be well rounded off during these years. Between 1970 and 2000, approximately 4,000 additional glass objects entered the Kunstmuseum, 2,100 of which came from the Hentrich Collection alone. Moreover the Hentrich gift from 1963 to his death totals an impressive 2,800 glass objects.

Museum funds were used primarily to established a comprehensive collection of contemporary glass art. The acquisition of outstanding individual examples of early glass was equally important. The goal was to

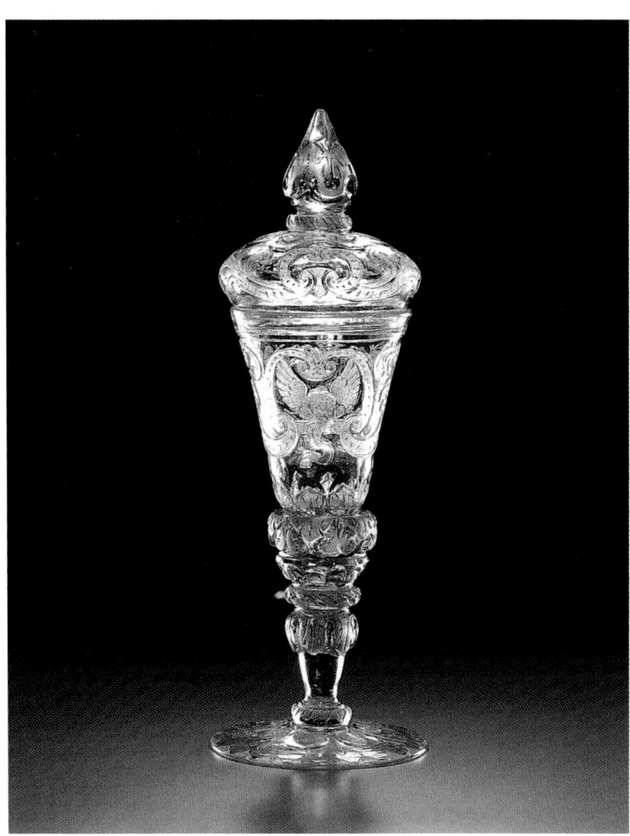

Covered Goblet with Relief-Cut Decoration

Workshop or follower of Friedrich Winter,
Silesia, Hermsdorf, Hirschberg Valley, ca. 1705–15
H with cover 30.6, without 21.2, ⌀ foot 10.9, ⌀ bowl 9 cm
Cover: H 10.4, ⌀ 9.9 cm   Acc. no. GL 1999-34

provide the collection with certain highlights and to fill the gaps in the larger developments.

The most important addition in the area of pre-Roman glass was a bowl from the Achaemenian Empire, Persia, from the late fifth century BC, very likely shaped on the turning wheel and bearing a complicated decoration of lancet-shaped leaves (cat. no. 5). Owing to its excellent state of preservation, it impressively illustrates the formal idiom and working techniques employed before glassblowing was invented. A unique piece is another, slightly later bowl with a plate-shaped cover, found in Greece but perhaps produced in a Persian workshop (cat. no. 6). Such fortunate acquisitions as these cannot, however, disguise the fact that the list of *desiderata* in the area of pre-Roman glass remains long. This is especially true of Egyptian glass of the 18th dynasty. The collection's three ornamental earplugs (cat. no. 1) fail to represent this period adequately. Early works from the Mesopotamian region illustrating the emergence of independent glass vessel designs are likewise still missing.

Roman glass, owing to the more than 300 vessels from the Hentrich Collection, supplemented by the

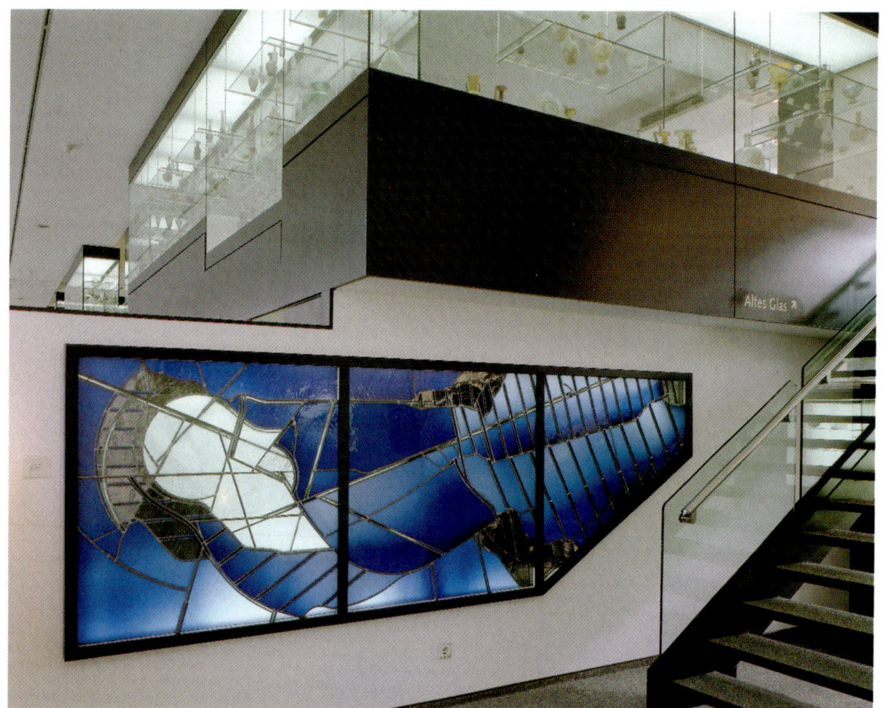

Ludwig Schaffrath (b. 1924), *Ago Wan II*

Glass picture on two levels. Made in 1985 for the stairway leading to the "Early Glass" department

objects from the Lückger Collection, is well represented. Only a few fine examples clearly showing the extraordinary achievements of Roman glass artisans were missing. Noteworthy amongst the new acquisitions are mold-blown pieces from both the early and late imperial periods (cat. nos. 15, 38) and a Syrian snake-thread bottle of the third century BC (cat. no. 33), which is an exemplary precursor of the extensive Rhenish production in this technique. Characteristic examples of Roman luxury glass items are still missing; two small millefiori bowls of the first century AD point the way for further acquisitions (cat. nos. 20, 21).

The glass of the Caliphates of the Middle East is as broadly documented as that of Rome thanks to the Hentrich gift. In 1981 an anonymous gift of 37, primarily early, Islamic glass objects supplemented the collection. Purchases were concentrated on specific shapes and unusual pieces executed in complicated techniques. Also worth mentioning is an early free-blown rose-water sprinkler of the seventh/ninth centuries, which survived its time underground without damage (cat. no. 54), as well as a dark blue bottle decorated with diamond-point engraving—one of the few reconstructible vessels of this rare group made in the ninth century (cat. no. 64). A pitcher with applied thread decoration of the eleventh/twelfth centuries documents the emergence of Islamic glass modeled on Roman prototypes (cat. no. 77). A four-

teenth-century two-handled bottle with the remains of extraordinary gold and enamel decoration (cat. no. 83) attests to the high quality of the last great phase of medieval Islamic glass design. As a precursor of medieval European vessels, a Persian prunt beaker of the tenth/twelfth centuries occupies an important place in the history of glassmaking (cat. no. 80).

Two vessels from about 1300, unique for their near perfect state of preservation, document the existence of a highly developed medieval glass art in Central Europe before the dark green *Waldglas* (literally, "forest glass") enjoyed popularity in the Late Gothic period. The well-nigh colorless glass, combined with a delicate light blue, provides a new basis for our previously fragmentary idea of hollow glassware of this time. The large footed bowl, its substance nearly completely intact (cat. no. 91), as well as the beaker with a decoration of extremely finely worked looped threads (cat. no. 89), belong to the few completely reconstructed vessels of this kind.

As to the future development of the museum's collections, a broad range of possibilities is opening up in the field of medieval glass, since our knowledge is growing almost daily. The acquisition of one of the enameled Venetian beakers of the late thirteenth century that have come to light in various places in Europe in recent years is highly desirable. A colorless prunt beaker of this period is also still missing. For the time being, an extensive loan generously made by the Krefeld collector Karl Amendt in 1988 serves to fill these gaps (cat. nos. 87, 88).

A large decorative vessel in the shape of a mosque lamp (cat. no. 124) attests to the close relationship between Venetian glass of the fifteenth century and the late phase of medieval glass in the Middle East. This is a unique piece to date. The glass vessel with gold and enamel decoration illustrates characteristic features of late medieval Islamic glass, which is underrepresented in the collection. The acquisition in 1993 of an extremely rare, late fifteenth-century Venetian agate-glass pitcher on a silver mount (cat. no. 125) was equally significant. Unfortunately it was stolen just seven years later.

The purchase of a goblet from the workshop of the Frankfurt glass-engraving family Hess (cat. no. 148) and a Zechlin covered goblet from the Zanthier Collection, on long-term loan, could fill the gaps in the museum's collection of engraved glasses of the Baroque period, which is comprehensive thanks to the Jantzen Collection. In addition, it was possible to acquire two pieces from the Swedish factory in Stockholm-Kungsholm—an early covered beaker of the seventeenth century and a covered goblet of the first half of the eighteenth century (cat. no. 171)—as well as two goblets from Russia (cat. no. 172). These are two areas of Baroque glass rarely represented in European collections. The most recent acquisitions in this area are eight glasses from the former Otto Dettmer Collection in Bremen: primarily covered vessels from the sixteenth to the nineteenth century (frontispiece and illus. pp. 8, 9, 11, 12, 14), representing some of the finest glass of this period. These pieces partly compensate the loss the Glasmuseum Hentrich suffered owing to a spectacular theft in February 2000 (cat. nos. 111, 125, 145, 147, 150, 183, 201, and five glasses not illustrated here); we hope that the illustrations in this book will contribute to their recovery.

Historicism—often misunderstood or misjudged—was insufficiently represented in Düsseldorf as in other large collections for a long time. The largest

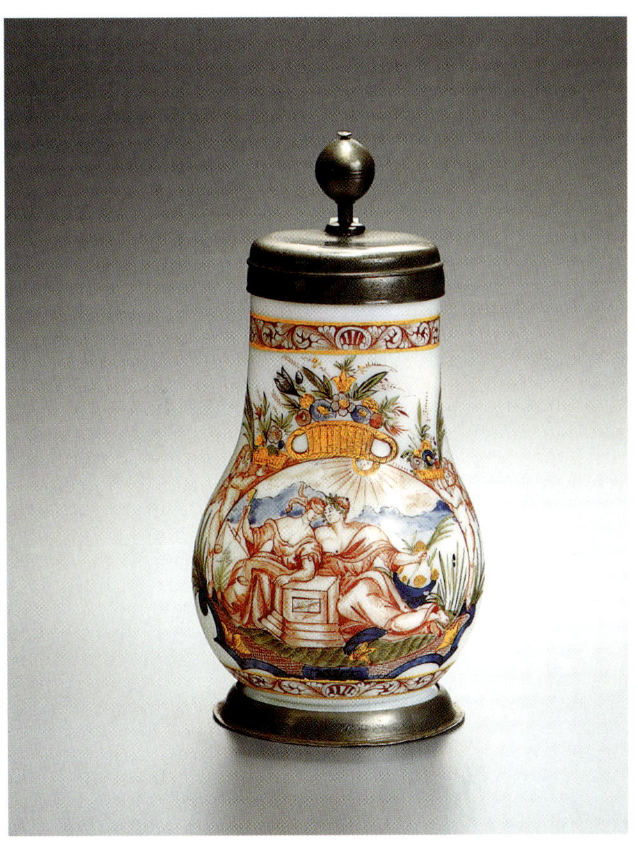

Milk-Glass Pitcher with Pewter Mount and Allegorical Depiction

Southern Germany, ca. 1750
H with mount 22.8, without 17.8, ∅ with handle 14.1,
∅ without 11.3 cm   Acc. no. GL 1999-36

growth in this area occurred, not entirely to the satisfaction of the museum, owing to the revised attributions of glassware previously considered older. Particularly noteworthy amongst the new acquisitions are glassware from the distributor Salviati in Venice and firms in Murano (cat. nos. 191–95), a monumental enameled goblet and plate by Lobmeyr in Vienna (cat. no. 199), and a large bottle by Joseph Brocard based on an Islamic prototype (cat. no. 217). These objects were purchased with the support of the Museumsverein and other benefactors of the Kunstmuseum.

Two fortunate purchases were made that, in view of the collection's strength in Art Nouveau, were long overdue. First the museum acquired a large group of Chinese glassware of the eighteenth and nineteenth centuries, which illustrates the profound influence East Asian glass exerted on French Art Nouveau (cat. nos. 209–13). Then a small collection of Indian glassware from the Mogul period (cat. nos. 203–8) was assembled. In the meantime it includes all major types and, apart from its intrinsic value, is interesting on account of the link it forges with the exotic late phase of historicism.

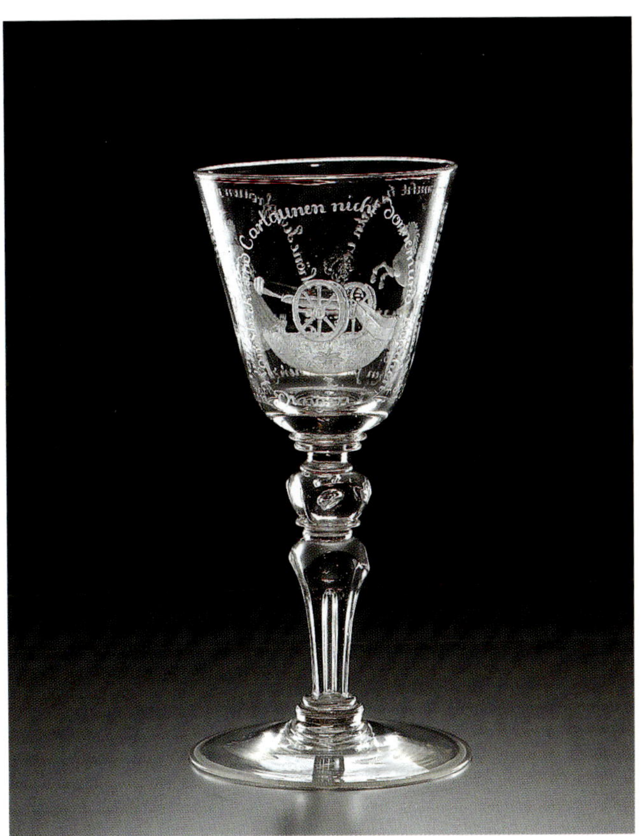

Goblet with Jocular Verse and Corresponding Depictions

Attr. Georg Ernst Kunckel
Thuringia, Gotha, ca. 1740
H 23, ∅ foot 11.5, ∅ bowl 12.3 cm   Acc. no. GL 1999-35

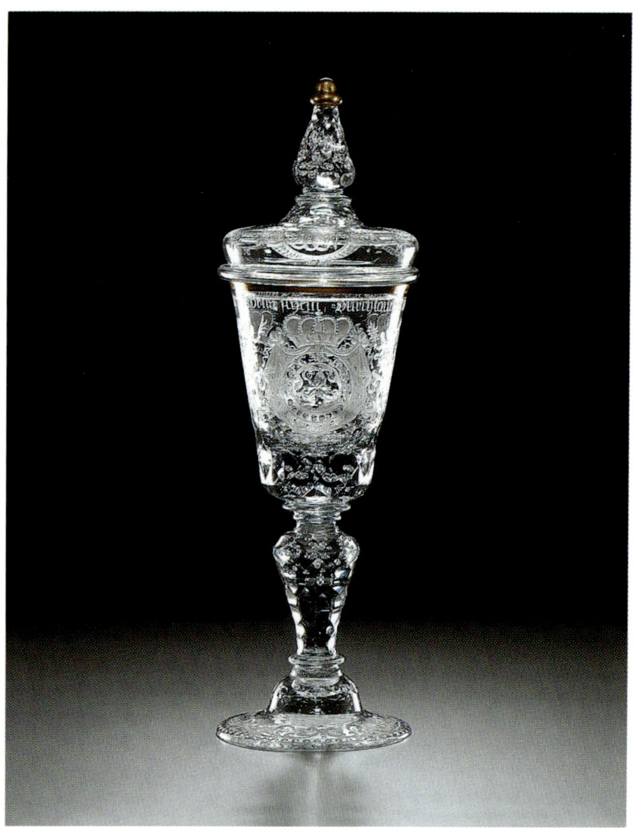

Covered Goblet Commemorating the Birth of Duke Augustus Frederick of Saxe-Meiningen

Attr. Johann Heinrich Balthasar Sang
Lower Saxony, Brunswick, 1754/55
H with cover 33.3, without 23, ⌀ foot 10.4, ⌀ bowl 9.6 cm
Cover: H 11, ⌀ 10.5 cm   Acc. no. GL 1999-37

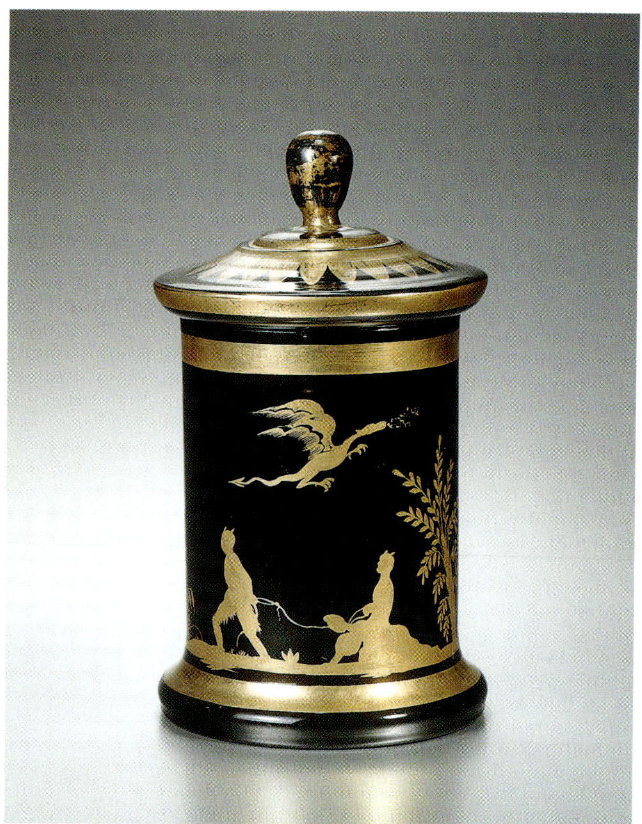

Covered Black-Hyalith Vessel with Gilt Painting

Glasshouse of Count von Buquoy in Gratzen (Nové Hrady), southern Bohemia, ca. 1830
H with cover 23.8, without 16.2, ⌀ standing base 13.6, ⌀ mouth 11.5 cm
Cover: H 8.6, ⌀ 13.8 cm   Acc. no. GL 1999-38

The Hentrich gift constitutes most of the recent acquisitions made for the Art Nouveau collection. The French glass objects from 1880 to 1940 alone number 564 in the collection catalogue published in 1985. A major focus is the work of Emile Gallé and the Ecole de Nancy (cat. nos. 222–59). Even larger is the number of Bohemian, German, and American glass pieces from this period. To a large extent, they still require in-depth scholarly attention. Glass of the Jugendstil, Art Nouveau, and Art Deco periods is so well represented in Düsseldorf that it can be strengthened only in details.

Further acquisitions include an important relief panel by the *pâte-de-verre* artist Henri Cros (cat. no. 277), several *pâte-de-verre* works by Albert Dammouse (cat. nos. 279, 280), a large window designed by Henri van de Veldes for the Villa Possehl in Travemünde, and a pictorial window designed by Barlach Heuer and realized by François-Emile Décorchemont. Unfulfilled wishes include fine examples lying beyond the museum's means, such as an important lamp by Louis Comfort Tiffany, but also a selection from the broader pro-

duction of American glasshouses. The same is true of glassware from Britain, which is underrepresented in the collection at present.

An extensive addition came in 1972. With the assistance of the Museumsverein, 113 outstanding glass pieces by the leading Bohemian Art Nouveau manufacturer, Johann Lötz Witwe, were acquired from the Barlach Heuer Collection, Paris (cat. nos. 308–11, 313–16). Subsequent to this purchase, another 75 Lötz glass objects and several important French pieces by Gallé, Daum Frères, and Décorchemont augmented the collection as long-term loans from Barlach Heuer. In addition, the Gerda Koepff Collection of 118 exquisite Art-Nouveau glass works came as a permanent loan and bequest. Since 1981 the approximately 150 extraordinarily fine glass pieces by the French Art-Deco manufacturer Schneider from the Ursula and Michael Kiffe Collection, Münster, have also supplemented the collection as permanent loans (cat. nos. 271, 273, 274). The daughter and widow of the artists, respectively, donated a large collection of works by Maurice Marinot and André Thuret, studio-glass artists of the 1920s and 1930s who contributed to the development of modernism (cat. nos. 290–92, 294).

The museum was able to acquire a collection of Venetian glassware of the highly productive years between the World Wars, rare outside Italy, on account of the support of Udo van Meeteren in 1975 (cat. nos. 371–73). Donations by Venetian companies and artists followed (cat. nos. 387, 388, 390). The Kunstmuseum subsequently continued in this vein by making purchases with museum funds (cat. nos. 375, 386, 389) and recently Helmut Hentrich has also dedicated himself to the glass art of Murano in addition to the work of René Lalique. Furthermore, the museum received glassware from Murano, but above all a large collection of postwar Czech glass, thanks to a donation of the Steinberg Foundation in Vaduz.

Efforts to secure works from the remaining European glass centers were also intensified. Funds from the Hentrich Gift enabled the financing of many of these acquisitions. Special attention was given to German glass of the 1920s to the 1950s (cat. nos. 361–70) as well as to designs from the circle of the Vienna art scene (cat. nos. 334, 339, 340) and northern Bohemian decorating workshops (cat. nos. 335–39). A long-term loan from the Pfohl family estate, approximately 30 pieces designed by the glass artist and designer Alexander Pfohl, who worked at the Silesian Josephinen-hütte and the Glass School in Haida (present-day Nový Bor), effectively supplemented this part of the collection (cat. nos. 358–60).

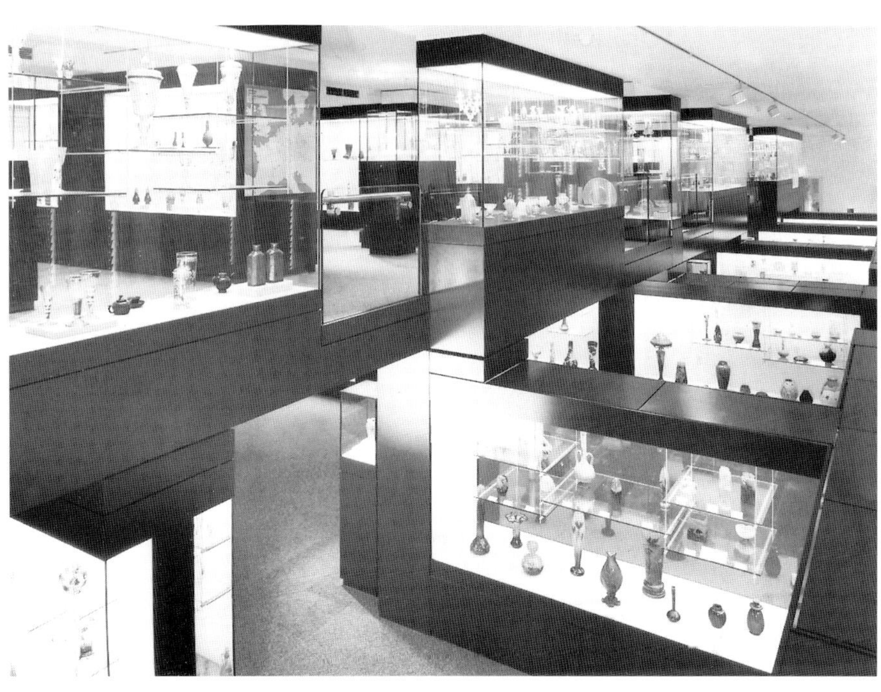
Displays in the museum kunst palast

Dutch glass of this category had previously not been well represented (cat. nos. 413–18). A donation of over 500 glass pieces from the Leerdam and Maastricht factories by the Dutch couple Tymen Knecht and Helen Knecht-Drenth in 1997 largely filled the gap.

Important goals have yet to be reached regarding the glass of Scandinavia. First results in this direction—besides regular acquisitions of works by the large factories Holmegaard, Orrefors, and Kosta—led to another donation of the Steinberg Foundation, as well as a collection of Swedish glass objects received on permanent loan from the Smålands Museum in Växjö in exchange for two late medieval vessels (cat. no. 399).

Recently, increased attention has been paid to utility glass and industrial design, building on this strong category in the Hentrich Collection. Pioneering designs by Wilhelm Wagenfeld (cat. no. 369), Andries Dirk Copier (cat. no. 413), Elis Bergh (cat. no. 392), or Gerda Strömberg (cat. no. 399) forge a link between the first design generation from about 1900 (cat. nos. 346, 349, 350) and the designers of the large glasshouses in Germany, Austria, and Scandinavia during the 1950s and 1960s (cat. no. 410). The museum has been given many glass pieces in this category from the companies that produced them and continues to receive numerous other gifts from the collectors Annemarie Rath, Dülmen, and Wilfried van Loyen, Düsseldorf.

This category received an important addition through the acquisition of the collection of the Städtische Galerie Schloss Oberhausen in 1992. The museum director at the time, Herbert Griebizsch, acquired the approximately 700 contemporary glass pieces between 1961 and 1963 as a new focus of the museum. After its founder's premature death, the Oberhausen museum was given a new focus and the glass was put in storage. Owing to this acquisition, the Glasmuseum Hentrich can now offer a broad survey of glass design in the decisive years around 1960. All important European factories are represented with typical examples. Of particular significance is a group of seven works made by Erwin Eisch in 1961/62, which can be regarded as the incunabula of international studio glass (cat. nos. 449, 450).

Since the 1970s, building up the collection of contemporary glass art has been given particular emphasis, continuing from objects acquired earlier to those

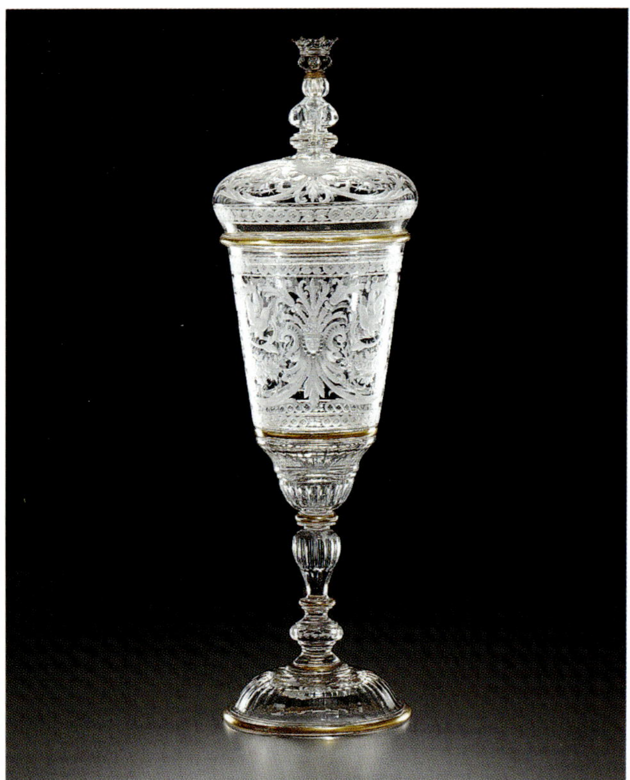

A particular attraction is a group of 18 works by the German-Swedish artist Ann Wolff, which she entrusted to the Kunstmuseum on permanent loan (cat. nos. 507, 508). Many of the works were acquired in connection with exhibitions organized by the museum. Others were purchased with the financial support of the Museumsverein or Stadt-Sparkasse Düsseldorf at international exhibitions that the Kunstmuseum was involved in organizing, and thus had the opportunity to select works in advance.

The acquisitions and donations of the museum's munificent benefactor Helmut Hentrich have contributed fundamentally to shaping the collection. He has continued to be able to create new focal points and thus has significantly helped determine its structure. Consequently the name "Glasmuseum Hentrich," which the glass collection of the Kunstmuseum has borne since 1990, is apt.

of the present. In the meantime it includes more than 400 vessels, sculptures, and objects by leading artists from Europe, the United States, and Japan (cat. nos. 419–558). The collection is wide-ranging: It follows the various movements of glass design of our day and illustrates those achievements that carry on the craft traditions in vessels as well as the diverse attempts to use the specific characteristics of glass to create non-functional art objects.

As in the past, the museum's scholarly work will continue to be linked to large temporary exhibitions, which attempt to evaluate critically and convey the achievements of glassmakers of the late nineteenth and twentieth centuries. Moreover, contemporary developments will continue to be observed.

The glass museum's guidelines for the future are clear. They ensue from the paths already taken. It is hoped that the opportunities for publishing permanent collection catalogues and documentation will improve. Currently no institution in Germany is attempting to collect production catalogues and other written documents on the history of closed factories, etc. The museum has a considerable basis, but since it has not been possible to evaluate and systematize the documents, they cannot yet be made accessible to the public. If it takes its increased responsibility to the glass collection seriously, the museum cannot evade this task in the long term.

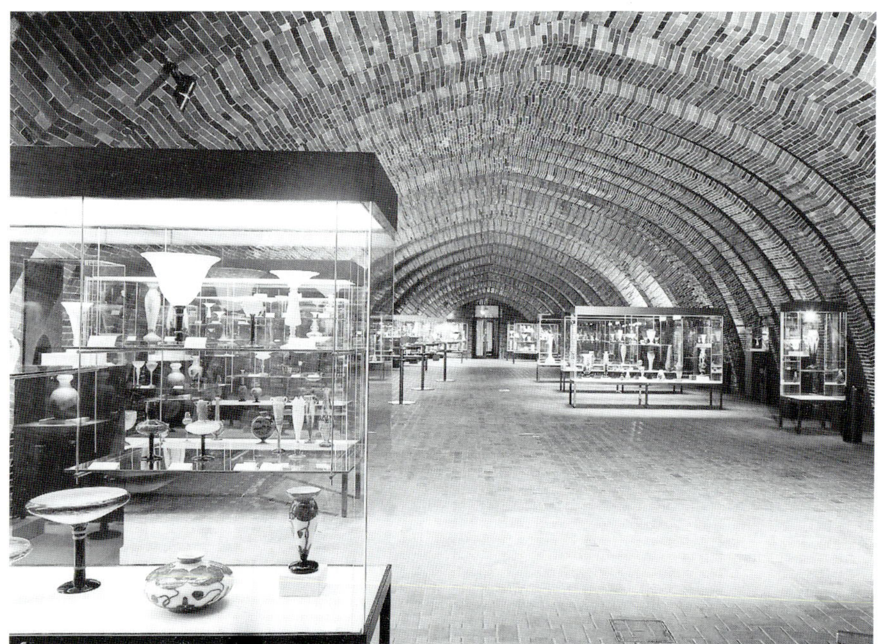

The Grüner Saal of the Tonhalle, the concert hall close to the museum, where temporary exhibitions are held

Catalogue

Abbreviations and Symbols Used in this Volume

∅	max. diameter	exh. cat.	exhibition catalogue
acc. no.	accession number	fig.	figure
attr.	attribution, attributed to	H	height
b.	born	illus.	illustration, illustrated
c.	century	incl.	includes, including
ca.	*circa*, about	L	length
cat. no(s).	catalogue number(s)	Lit.	literature
cf.	*confer*, compare	n.d.	no date
cm	centimeters	n.p.	no place, no page
coll.	collection	p.	page
coll. cat.	collection catalogue	pl.	plate
d.	died	no(s).	number(s)
D	depth	vol.	volume
e.g.	*exempli gratia*, for example	W	width

Pre-Roman Antiquity

The origins of glassmaking—and indeed of civilization itself—can be traced back to the ancient empires of the Middle East. Around the middle of the second millennium BC, the first vessels consisting exclusively of glass were made in Mesopotamia, and shortly thereafter in Egypt. Building on the age-old knowledge about glazes, a new material, comprising sand, soda, lime, and coloring metal oxides, was developed. It was initially used for small pieces of jewelry (cat. no. 1), for beads and inlays in statuettes, then increasingly for containers made to hold precious oils and fragrances. Transparency, which is taken for granted today, is not a characteristic of these works. Of greater interest to the early glass artisans was the ability to reproduce at will the ribbon and color structures of the highly valued semiprecious stones found in nature and to lend the material any desired form.

This attitude towards glass hardly changed in the next millennium. The core-formed unguentaria (toilet bottles) of the sixth to fourth centuries BC, made in the Mediterranean, in Egypt, and in the Phoenician cities of the Levant, bear witness to this (cat. nos. 2–4).

The first vessels of colorless glass sought largely to imitate the effect of rock crystal, that is, of a natural mineral. This required knowing how to decolor glass, which is naturally a greenish color because of the high concentration of iron contained in almost all types of sand.

Artisans working in the glass workshops of the great Persian empire of the Achaemenids at the time of the heavy conflicts amongst the Greek city states were already acquainted with these methods. They had also learned to apply pottery techniques to glassmaking. According to the most recent research, it is likely that they produced vessels of considerable size—admired even by the Greeks—on a turning wheel. In contrast to previous beliefs, cutting techniques were used for only a small portion of their lavish relief decoration (cat. no. 5).

The Greeks do not seem to have developed their own distinctive glass art in the classical period of the fifth century BC. Instead artisans obviously concentrated on the period's magnificent ceramics. They used glass for colored inlays in sculpture—especially for the famous monumental statues of deities in large temples, as the excavation of Phidias's workshop at the Olympian Zeus temple documents.

It was only in the satrapies of the declining empire of Alexander the Great, strongly influenced by the culture of the East, that glass began to play an important role again. Unguentaria and bowls continued to be the dominant vessel forms in the Hellenistic states in the third and second centuries BC. Particularly in Alexandria a veritable industry of diversiform luxury glass items emerged (cat. no. 7); this was to have a profound effect on the glass art of early imperial Rome.

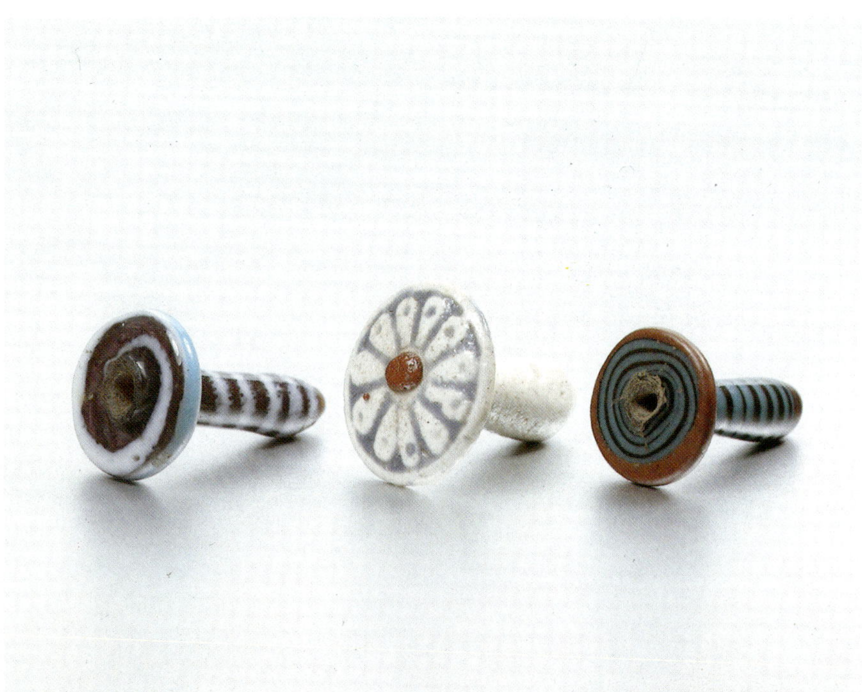

1 a–c   Ear Ornaments

Egypt
Probably New Kingdom, 18th–19th dynasty, mid-14th to mid-13th c. BC
L 2.6, 2.5, 2.3; ⌀ 1.6, 1.9, 1.5 cm

Formed over wire or small metal rods, around which colored glass threads were coiled. On **a**, hollow openings were closed with drops of glass. A pattern was embossed on the head of this pin with colored glass powder. Heads of **a** and **b** broken off and glued.

Acc. no. 17025 (acquired in Cairo in 1896)
Gift of Max Trinkaus

The production process corresponds to that of beads. See Goldstein, *Pre-Roman*, 1979, 78ff.; Saldern, *Cohn Collection*, 1980, cat. no. 30, who speaks of the pins as being "probably Hellenistic"; and Stern and Schlick-Nolte, *Early Glass*, 1994, 136f., no. 8.

Lit.: Heinemeyer, *Glas*, 1966, cat. no. 1

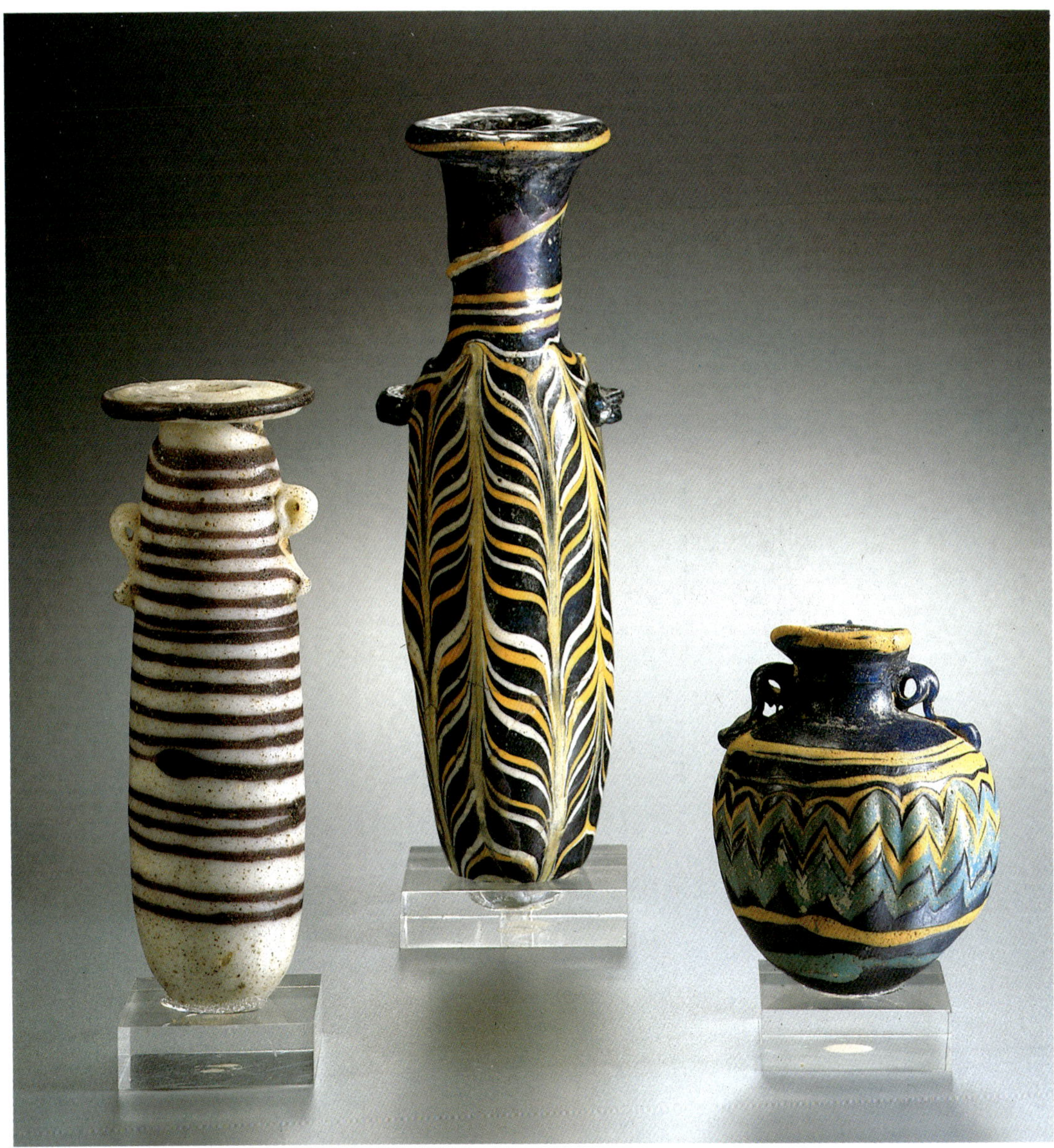

<table>
<tr><td>

2   Alabastron

Eastern Mediterranean
probably 6th/5th c. BC
H 9.5, ⌀ mouth 3.2 cm

Core-formed. Spiral thread marvered flush
with the surface, applied twice. Surface
rough, corrosion layer removed. Mouth partly
restored.

Acc. no. P 1971-63
Gift of Helmut Hentrich

One of the earliest examples of the second
group of core-formed vessels, made in the
Mediterranean several centuries following the
first group of unguentaria, created in Egypt's
New Kingdom. See, for example, *3000 Jahre*,
Lucerne, 1981, cat. no. 58.

Lit.: Saldern, *Antike und Islam*, 1974, cat.
no. 1; Ricke, *Ausgewählte Werke*, 1980, 1;
Ricke, *2500 Jahre*, 1987, cat. no. 2

</td><td>

3   Alabastron

Eastern Mediterranean
Ca. 4th/3rd c. BC
H 15.5, ⌀ mouth 3.5 cm

Like cat. no. 2. Thickened rim. Lugs. Double
spiral threads dragged up and down four
times to create a feather pattern.
Broken and glued, cleaned, partly restored.

Acc. no. P 1966-45
Gift of Helmut Hentrich

Lit.: Saldern, *Antike und Islam*, 1974, cat.
no. 3; Ricke, *2500 Jahre*, 1987, cat. no. 3

</td><td>

4   Aryballos

Eastern Mediterranean
Probably 4th/3rd c. BC
H 5.8, ⌀ 4.6 cm

Like cat. no. 2. Double spiral threads dragged
up and down 12 times to create a feather
pattern, traces of pulling discernible in relief.
Surface slightly roughened owing to corro-
sion; cleaned.
For the later core-formed vessels generally
see Saldern et al., *Sammlung Oppenländer*,
1974, cat. nos. 101ff.; Goldstein, *Pre-Roman*,
1979, 124ff.; *3000 Jahre*, Lucerne, 1981, cat.
nos. 42ff.; and Stern and Schlick-Nolte, *Early
Glass*, 1994, 204ff., cat. nos. 45–62.

Acc. no. P 1965-153
Gift of Helmut Hentrich

Lit.: Saldern, *Antike und Islam*, 1974, cat.
no. 9; Ricke, *2500 Jahre*, 1987, cat. no. 4

</td></tr>
</table>

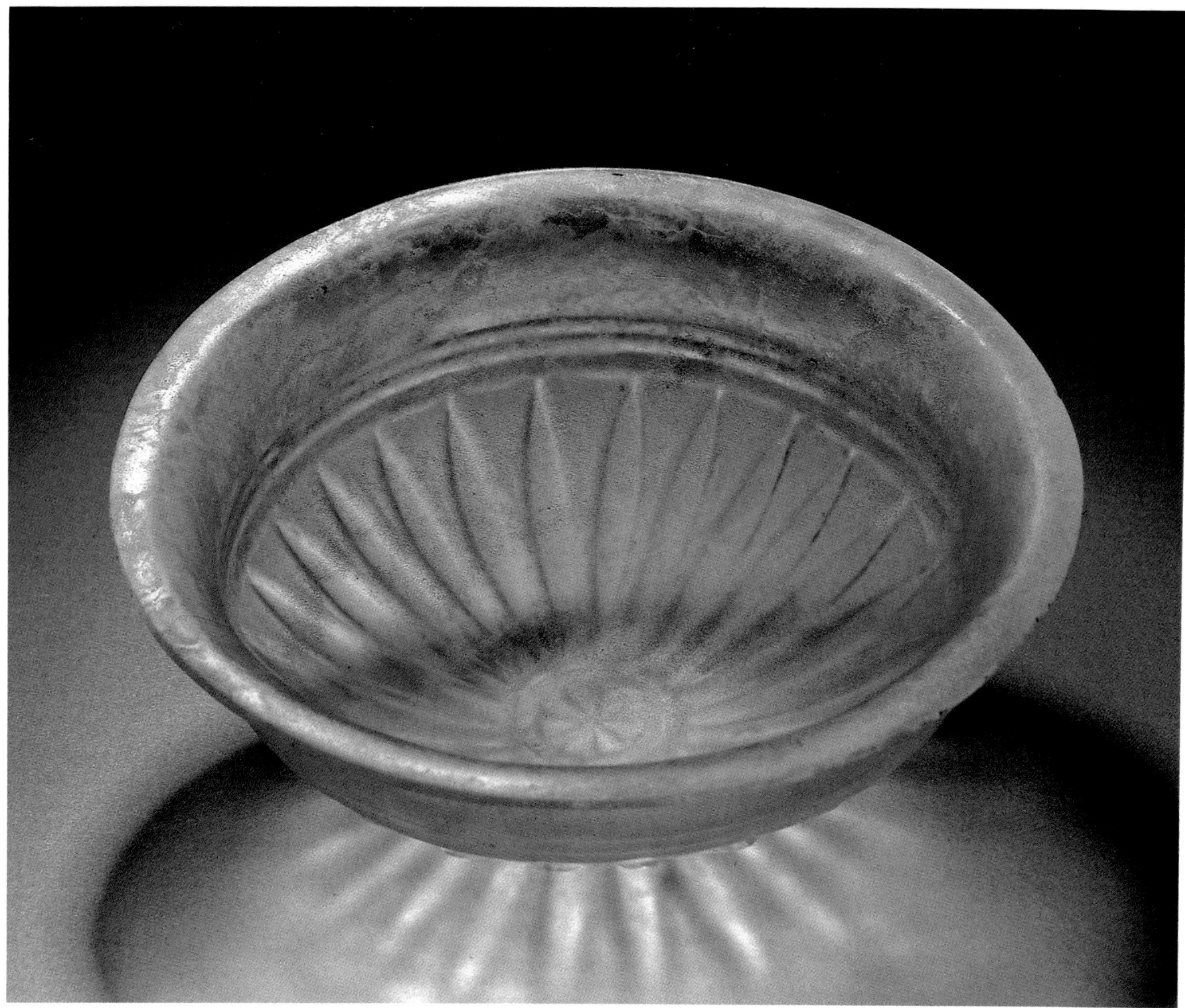

5 Bowl

Achaemenian Empire, Persia

Late 5th/early 4th c. BC
H 5.8, ⌀ 16 cm

Colorless, slightly yellowish decolored glass, mold-pressed on the turning wheel or form-melted; 24 lance-shaped leaves, offset with a double cut ring below the rim. Under the base, an eight-rayed cut rosette. Corrosion layer almost completely removed, acid-cleaned.

Acc. no. P 1973-12

Extremely rare glass from the circle of Achaemenian court art in the ancient great Persian Empire. Only six examples of this type are documented at present, the piece in Düsseldorf being the only one still intact. Found together with another bowl of different type, today in the Museum für Kunst und Gewerbe, Hamburg. For Persian glassware of this period see Goldstein, *Pre-Roman*, 1979, 118ff. See also Stern and Schlick-Nolte, *Early Glass*, 1994, 166–69, cat. no. 24.

Lit.: Saldern, *Antike und Islam*, 1974, cat. no. 12; Helmut Ricke, "Eine achämenidische Glasschale: Neuerwerbung des Kunstmuseums," *Düsseldorfer Museen, Bulletin* 6, no. 2 (1974): 197–99; A. von Saldern, "Two Achaemenid Glass Bowls and a Hoard of Hellenistic Glass Vessels," *Journal of Glass Studies* 17 (1975): 37ff. figs. 3, 4; Ricke, *Ausgewählte Werke*, 1980, 2; Ricke, *2500 Jahre*, 1987, cat. no. 1; Lierke, "Turning Wheel," 1993, 324f., fig. 3

6 Bowl with Cover

Persia or Greater Greece
4th–1st c. BC
H bowl 4.4, ∅ 17.6 cm
H cover 1.8, ∅ 18.8 cm

Colorless glass with yellowish tone. Presumably core-formed on the turning wheel or mold-pressed. Cover of flat glass plate slumped over model. Cut edge. Corroded, cleaned. Cover fragmentary.

Acc. no. P 1984-31

The bowl can either be seen in connection with Persian-Achaemenian glass art of the fifth and fourth centuries BC or was created in the Hellenistic greater Greek region during the following pre-Roman centuries. Since there are no comparable pieces, place and time of production cannot be determined at present. A remote similarity can be seen only in a series of much smaller, painted, covered bowls of the first to second centuries AD, found in graves in Cumae, Campania. See L. A. Scatozza-Höricht, "Phlegräische Glasfunde und die Verlagerung von Glashütten aus dem östlichen Mittelmeer nach Campanien," *Archäologischer Anzeiger* 3 (1990): 425–33. Their intended function also remains a riddle. Since glass was highly valued in the centuries before the introduction of glassblowing, the bowl may have been used in a burial cult or sacrificial rites. A purely profane use as a vessel for cooling or keeping food warm by filling the lower section with ice or hot water is, however, also conceivable.

Lit.: Ricke, "Neue Gläser," 1985, 45, fig. 3; Ricke, *Museumsarbeit*, 1988, 71, fig. 47

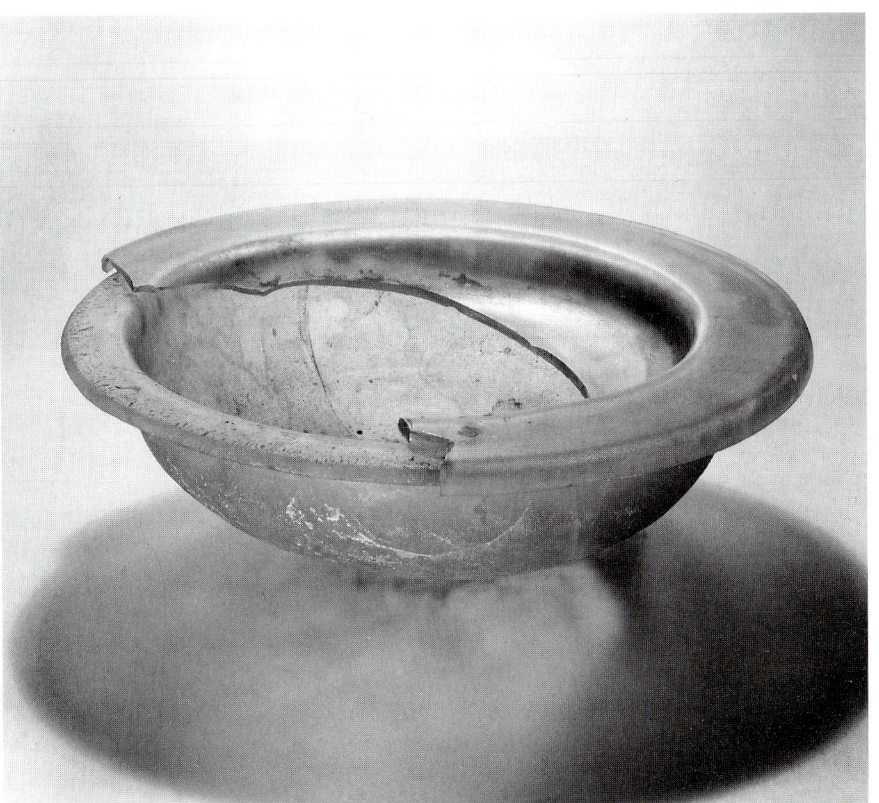

7 Bowl

Eastern Mediterranean
Hellenistic, ca. 2nd c. BC
H 8.6, ∅ 14.7 cm

Presumably core-formed on turning wheel or mold-pressed. Grooves. Numerous vertical cut lines; under the rounded base, hexamerous rosette. On the inside, faint horizontal scratches, presumably production traces. Corroded, deposits in part loosened or removed, the freed surfaces iridescent. Glued.

Acc. no. P 1966-63
Gift of Helmut Hentrich

Part of a large group of similar bowls based on metal prototypes. See also Stern and Schlick-Nolte, *Early Glass*, 1994, 252–55, cat. no. 66.

Lit.: Saldern, *Antike und Islam*, 1974, cat. no. 13

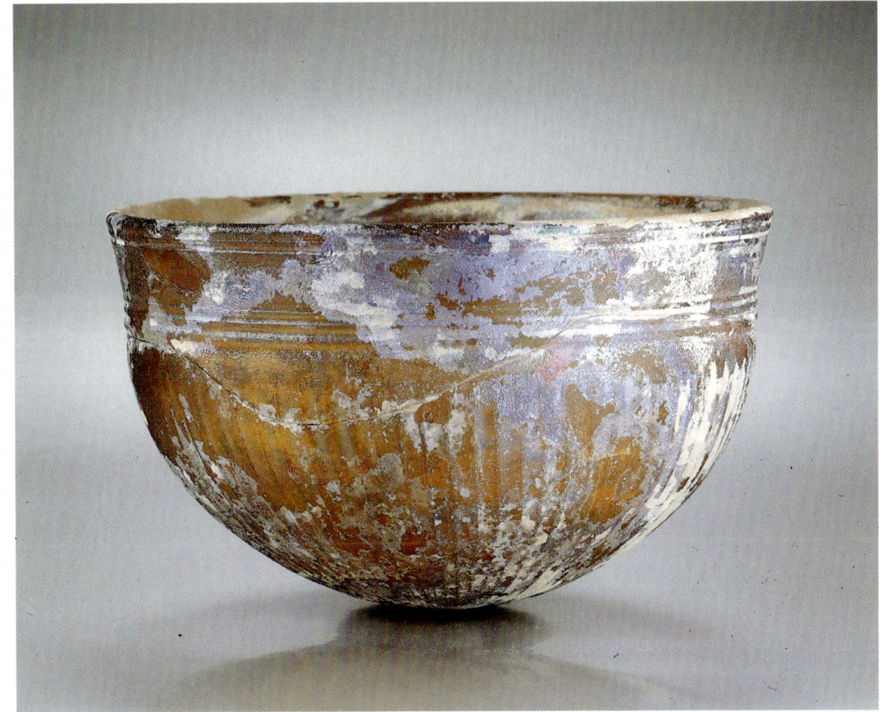

The Roman Empire

The rise of the Roman Empire to a leading power in the ancient world was accompanied by an undreamt-of upswing of glass production in the Mediterranean region.

Initially glass retained its status as a luxury material. From the earliest years of its development it had been considered equal to precious stones and such metals as gold and silver. The colored glass bowls pressed into a turning mold or shaped over a turning core, taken over from Hellenistic culture, the millefiori and mosaic-glass plates and bowls (cat. nos. 16, 17, 20, 21), the vessels with gold decor enclosed within the doubled glass walls or with agatelike ribboning continued to be very popular. At the same time, however, the step from luxury to mass production, from decorative object to vessel for daily use, was taken.

The prerequisite for this was the Syrian glassmakers' discovery at the beginning of the first century BC that glass can be blown with the help of a metal tube if it is melted to attain the consistency of a thin liquid. Thus the path was paved for the production of a large variety of vessels for different uses—from the simple bottle to the urn holding the ashes of the deceased (cat. no. 26).

Starting with the leading Syrian glassworks, in Sidon, Tyre, etc., glass as a manufactured product spread across the entire area of Roman rule. With mass production, glass increasingly became a trade item—of no minor importance in convincing the "barbarians" from the border areas of the superiority of Roman civilization. The safe and well-planned network of streets in the world empire ensured that the new forms glass took and the newly developed techniques were quickly disseminated and adopted. In addition, large quantities of raw glass ingots produced in specialized factories in the Levant have been excavated throughout an area coextensive with the former Roman Empire. For this reason it is generally very difficult to determine a specific place of production of Roman glassware. Wherever suitable raw materials were to be found, the same, or at least very similar, glass forms with hardly any variation in quality were made. This is true of the heartland Italy, where numerous workshops producing high-quality wares existed, as well as of Spain or the region along the shores of the Black Sea, and presumably also of the North African coastline.

Because of their particularly well-suited sand and large deposits of natural soda, the centers of glass production remained, however, in Syria, Mesopotamia, and Lower Egypt. Moreover, the Rhineland with Cologne as its center and the Gallic provinces began to play a major role in the second century AD.

The introduction of glassblowing caused a complete reorientation regarding form. Glass artisans must have immediately realized the potential of the new material. At the beginning they probably blew into a clay mold, since this method was familiar from mold-melting and working with molten metals. They decorated the glass surface with ornamental or figural reliefs in a wide variety of ways (cat. nos. 12–15). The increasing mastery of the technique of glassblowing was accompanied by the growing desire to make free-blown objects. Above all, simple bottles and flasks were produced (cat. nos. 8–11). The combination of these two basic techniques, called optic-blowing, belonged to the glassworks' standard repertoire even in this early phase. In the following centuries it became a common method of making utilitarian objects with particularly lively designs (cat. no. 34).

From the first and second centuries AD, nearly all small vessels and utensils in the Roman household were made not only of wood and baked clay but also of glass. Besides the large number of extant unguentaria for storing fragrances and medicinal ointments, there were beakers and bowls in all shapes, the popular ribbed bowls—some core-formed on the turning wheel, some blown and worked up with pincers (cat. nos. 17, 23–25)—pitchers, plates, pouring and measuring vessels, lamps, inkstands, and much more. Even vessels technically very difficult to produce have been found. A mixing vessel consisting of three compartments for different liquids within its spherical wall (cat. no. 32) or playfully designed bottles in the shape of birds or other animals (cat. no. 29), for instance, were precursors of the humorous joke glasses of the Renaissance.

The astounding number of completely intact extant glass utensils is due to the ancient custom of supplying the deceased with provisions and the most important utilitarian objects to accompany them on their journey to the next life. Having been buried in damp soil, the surface of the glass is often severely deteriorated. During this process the glass surface is leached, layers separate and lift from the ground, enabling air to penetrate them. This creates an iridescent shimmer seen on many Roman objects found underground, lending them an additional appeal.

Whereas color characterized the appearance of Roman glass—in keeping with the Hellenistic tradition—in the early imperial period (1st c. BC–1st c. AD), from the second century AD the transparency, lightness, and shiny surface of the material came to be emphasized more and more. Usually it was left in its natural hue; typical are vessels having a blue-green coloration of varying intensity. Finer glassware was decolored with manganese oxide. It was also used in higher concentrations to achieve a violet melt.

Furthermore, an increasing tendency to apply rich details and colored accents can be observed. Different colored glass was used for handles, looped ribbons, and eyelets (cat. no. 36), or for threads wrapped around the lip to emphasize the rim of the vessel's mouth. Decorating with freely applied threads gained in popularity (cat. no. 45). The most impressive vessels of this type are probably the so-called saddle-flasks, ointment vessels with complicated handles and freely applied, wavy bands (cat. no. 44).

Glassware adorned with applied, often strongly colored, threads should be seen within the context of this decorative tradition. Snake-thread decoration seems to have originated in Syria (cat. no. 33). This type of embellishment reached its undisputed climax, however, in the glassware of Rhineland workshops, as in the world-famous *Meisterstück*. The flat bottle decorated with extremely delicate snake-threads is displayed in the Römisch-Germanisches Museum in Cologne today. The tendency to apply richer ornamentation is also reflected in the growing popularity of cut and engraved decoration in the late imperial period (cat. no. 41). Mold-blowing was taken up again and developed in new directions (cat. no. 38), clearly surpassing the designs of the early period of glass-blowing.

The so-called shellfish beaker, apparently a specialty of the Rhenish workshops, represents a climax in glassmaking of the later imperial period. Small shells, snails, fish, and the like were blown separately, formed with pincers, and melted onto the walls of simply shaped vessels. They thus give the impression that the vessel has a second, perforated wall. This principle was carried to perfection in the *diatreta*, or cage cups. The technique used to produce these is currently the subject of fierce debate.

Generally it can be said that most methods of glassmaking and glass decoration that were of any significance in the middle and late imperial periods in the Roman territory were already known by the first century AD.

With few exceptions, this statement can be extended to include the subsequent development of European glass art, into the nineteenth century. Until the methodical natural sciences were established, in the second quarter of that century, glassmaking technology and color melt compositions underwent only minor changes. Roman glass art continued to be exemplary and much of Venetian glass art from the early sixteenth century was based on the revival of such techniques as thread-glass decoration, agate-glass melt, mosaic glass, or the so-called millefiori glass—Venice's contribution to the renaissance of antiquity in Italy (cf. pp. 78ff.). A more recent attempt to revive Roman techniques was made by the glassblowers of historicism (cf. cat. no. 191 and appendix, cat. no. F 2). Some of the techniques of early imperial Rome, however, continue to baffle glass technicians today.

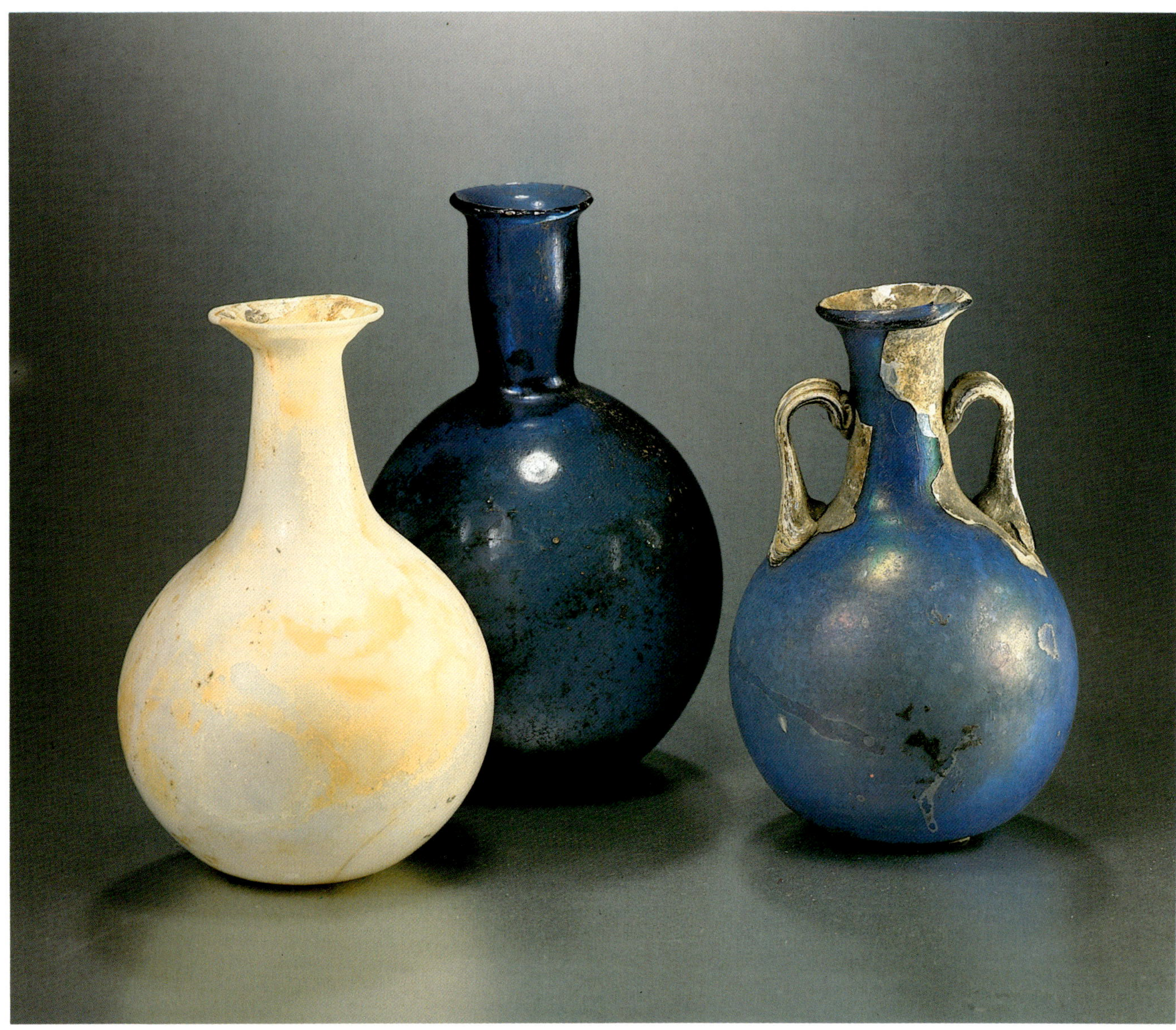

8 Small Flask

Roman Empire
Middle East or Italy
1st c. AD
H 7.4 cm, ⌀ 5.1 cm

Free-blown and shaped. Slightly corroded,
cleaned.

Acc. no. P 1980-53
Gift of Helmut Hentrich

Extremely thin-walled vessel. Possibly made
from a glass tube. Flasks of this type were
relatively common and came in a variety of
colors. Like lamp-blown objects they do not
bear any pontil marks. This fact coupled with
the extremely thin walls suggests that they
were made at an oil lamp. A definitive
answer to this question has not yet been
found.

Lit.: Ricke, *2500 Jahre*, 1987, cat. no. 11

9 Small Flask

Roman Empire
Middle East or Italy
1st c. AD
H 8.5 cm, ⌀ 5.5 cm

Like cat. no. 8. Slightly corroded, cleaned.

Acc. no. P 1949-53
Formerly Josef Lückger Collection, Cologne

For this group of glassware see M. Spaer,
"Some Egg Shaped Glass Vessels and Reflec-
tions on Early Glass Blowing," *Israel Museum
Journal* 6 (1987).

Lit.: Saldern, *Antike und Islam*, 1974, cat.
no. 169; Ricke, *2500 Jahre*, 1987, cat. no. 12

10 Small Flask

Roman Empire, presumably Middle East
1st/2nd c. AD
H 7.3, ⌀ 4.6 cm

Like cat. no. 8. Corroded. Remains of heavy
deposits, iridescent.

Acc. no. P 1966-34
Gift of Helmut Hentrich

Lit.: Saldern, *Antike und Islam*, 1974, cat.
no. 180; Ricke, *2500 Jahre*, 1987, cat. no. 13

11 Unguentarium

Roman Empire, Syria (?)
1st c. AD
H 14.8, ⌀ 2.3 cm

Light blue glass, free-blown and shaped.
Applied opaque white spiral thread.
Corroded, heavy deposits, in part loosened or
removed; iridescent.

Acc. no. P 1973-18
Gift of Helmut Hentrich

Common type of utilitarian glass, probably
for fragrances. Presumably made at the lamp;
cf. cat. no. 8.

Lit.: Saldern, *Antike und Islam*, 1974, cat.
no. 86

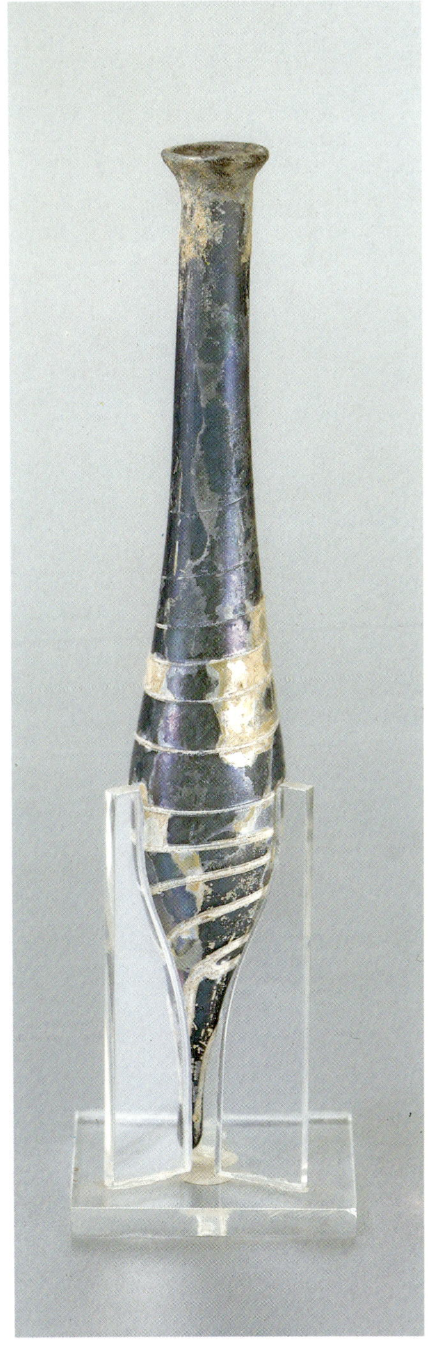

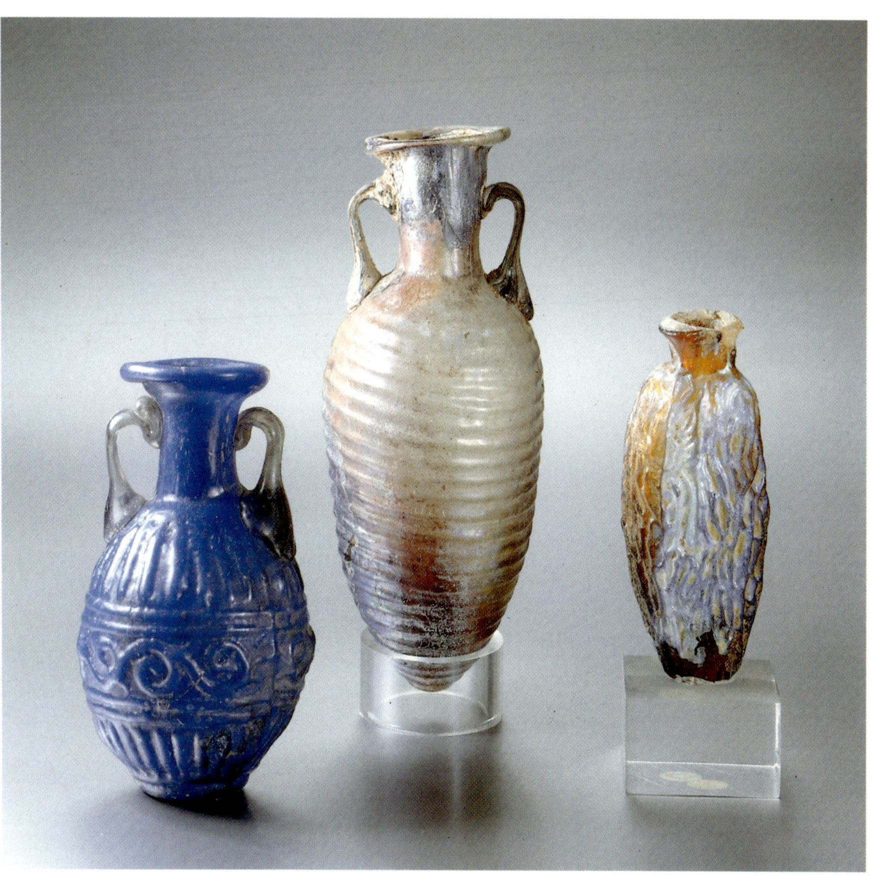

12 Two-Handled Flask

Roman Empire, Syria (?)
Probably late 1st c. BC–early 1st c. AD
H 7.8 cm, ⌀ 4.4 cm

Blown into a two-part mold, shaped. Slightly
corroded, deposit remains. Glued.

Acc. no. P 1973-53
Gift of Helmut Hentrich

Vessel from the early period of glassblowing.
Belongs to the group of so-called Sidonian
relief glassware, made in Sidon, Syria, but
also at other manufacturing sites in the
Roman Empire.
Is documented in several colors; in the
course of the first centuries AD increasingly
transparent.

Lit.: Saldern, *Antike und Islam*, 1974, cat.
no. 39; Ricke, *2500 Jahre*, 1987, cat. no. 6

13 Two-Handled Flask

Roman Empire, Syria (?)
1st c. AD
H 11.2, ⌀ 4.6 cm

Acc. no. P 1973-32
Gift of Helmut Hentrich

Like cat. no. 12. Examples with embedded
opaque white blobs are also known.

Lit.: Saldern, *Antike und Islam*, 1974,
cat. no. 40

14 Date Flask

Roman Empire, Syria (?)
1st c. AD
H 6.9, ⌀ 2.8 cm

Blown into four-part mold, shaped.
Corroded, light deposits, in part removed;
iridescent. Mouth slightly restored.

Acc. no. P 1971-79
Gift of Helmut Hentrich

Probably the most common type of glassware
in early imperial Rome, imitating a shape
drawn from nature. Particularly popular in the
Eastern provinces of the Roman Empire.

Lit.: Saldern, *Antike und Islam*, 1974,
cat. no. 45

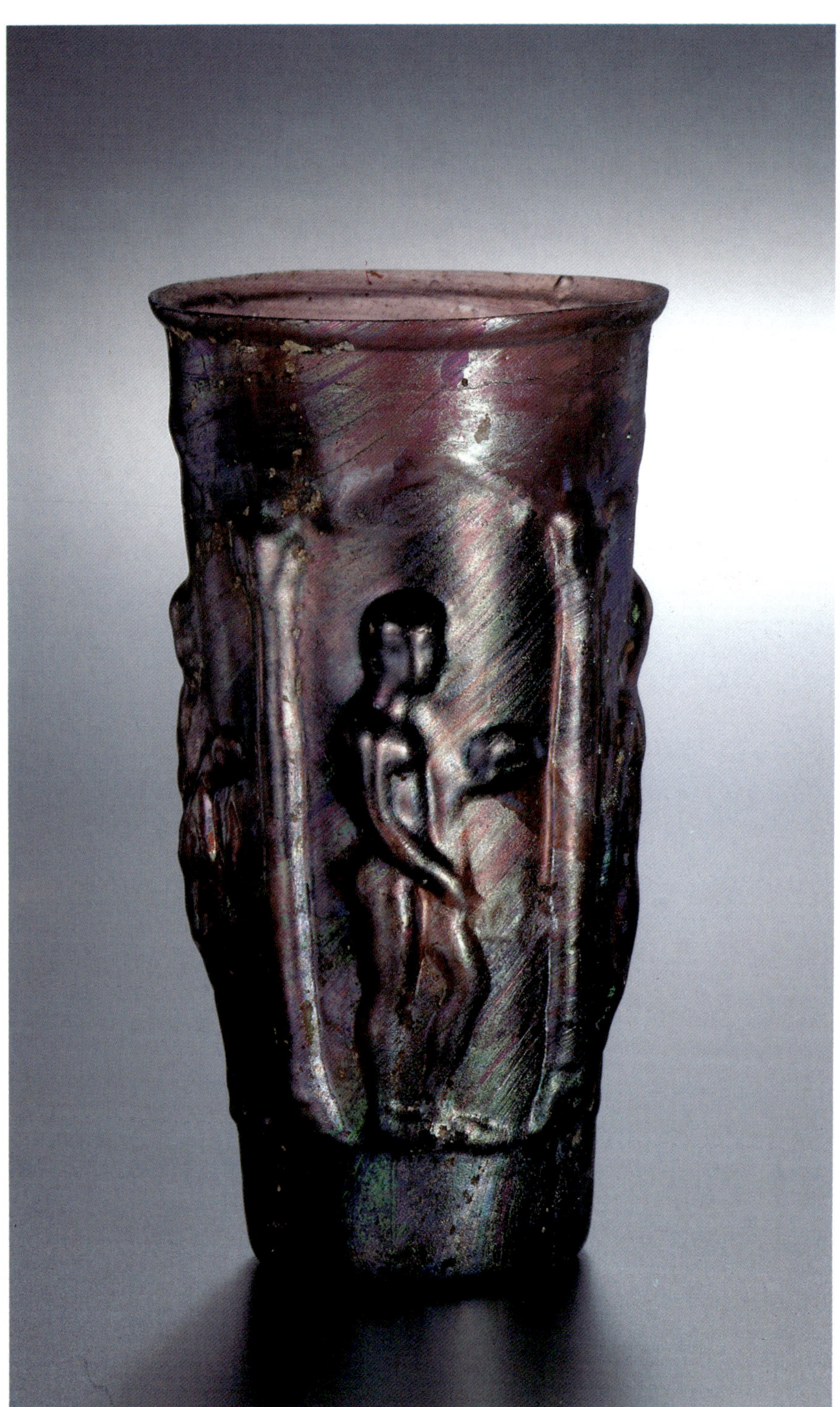

15 Beaker

Roman Empire, Syria
2nd half of 1st c. AD
H 12.2, ⌀ 6.8 cm

Blown into four-part mold, rim of mouth neither fused nor cut.
Slightly corroded, heavy deposits, for the
most part loosened or removed, underneath
strongly iridescent.

Acc. no. P 1970-1

Depicts one female and three male figures,
presumably as personifications of the four
seasons. The God Hermes and hero Heracles
can be identified with some certainty. The
other two figures could be interpreted as
personifications of the seasons (Diana?,
Hymen?).
For the latest research on beakers of this type
see Saldern, *Cohn Collection*, 1980, cat. no.
46; *3000 Jahre*, Lucerne, 1981, cat. no. 274;
Glass of the Caesars, 1987, cat. no. 85. The
Düsseldorf beaker is the only documented
example in manganese violet.

Lit.: Saldern, *Antike und Islam*, 1974, cat.
no. 50; Ricke, *2500 Jahre*, 1987, cat. no. 7

16 Plate

Roman Empire
Middle East (Alexandria?) or Italy
1st c. BC–1st c. AD
H 2.3, ⌀ 14.2 cm

Mosaic glass, mold-melted.
Corroded and cleaned. Glued, parts of well
and ledge restored.

Acc. no. P 1966-30
Gift of Helmut Hentrich

Shallow mosaic-glass dishes of this type are
relatively rare; see, for example, Goldstein,
Pre-Roman, 1979, cat. no. 45; for similar but
probably earlier pieces see Grose, *Toledo*,
1989, 189–94.

Lit.: Saldern, *Antike und Islam*, 1974,
cat. no. 16

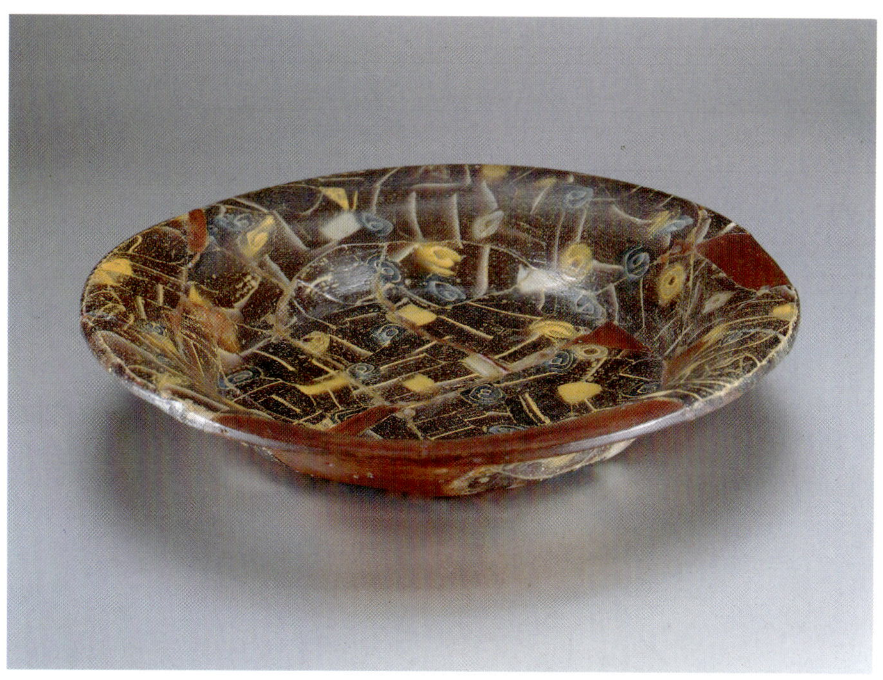

17 a, b   Ribbed Bowls

Roman Empire
Eastern Mediterranean (Alexandria?) or Italy
1st c. AD
H 3.2, ⌀ 11.2 cm

Slabs consisting of fused mosaic-glass pieces
formed over a turning core. On the inside of
17a: a concentric ring cut below the rim,
another one in the center. In **17b**: an additional ring in the center.
Heavily corroded, deposits, partly cleaned.
17a: glued, strongly iridescent on the outside. **17b**: piece broken off along rim, heavy
deposits on the inside.

Acc. nos. P 1966-224, 225
Gift of Helmut Hentrich

Rare variations of the common monotone
blue-green ribbed bowls, which belong to the
first mass-produced objects of Roman glass
art. Cf. in this volume "Production of a
Ribbed Bowl" under "Techniques," p. 359,
and Lierke, "Rippenschalen," 1993, 218–34.
See also Stern and Schlick-Nolte, *Early Glass*,
1994, 72–79.
For further examples of colored mosaic glass
see, for instance, Saldern et al., *Sammlung
Oppenländer*, 1974, cat. no. 328, and *Glass of
the Caesars*, 1987, cat. no. 27.

Lit.: Saldern, *Antike und Islam*, 1974, cat.
no. 17; Ricke, *2500 Jahre*, 1987, cat. no. 8

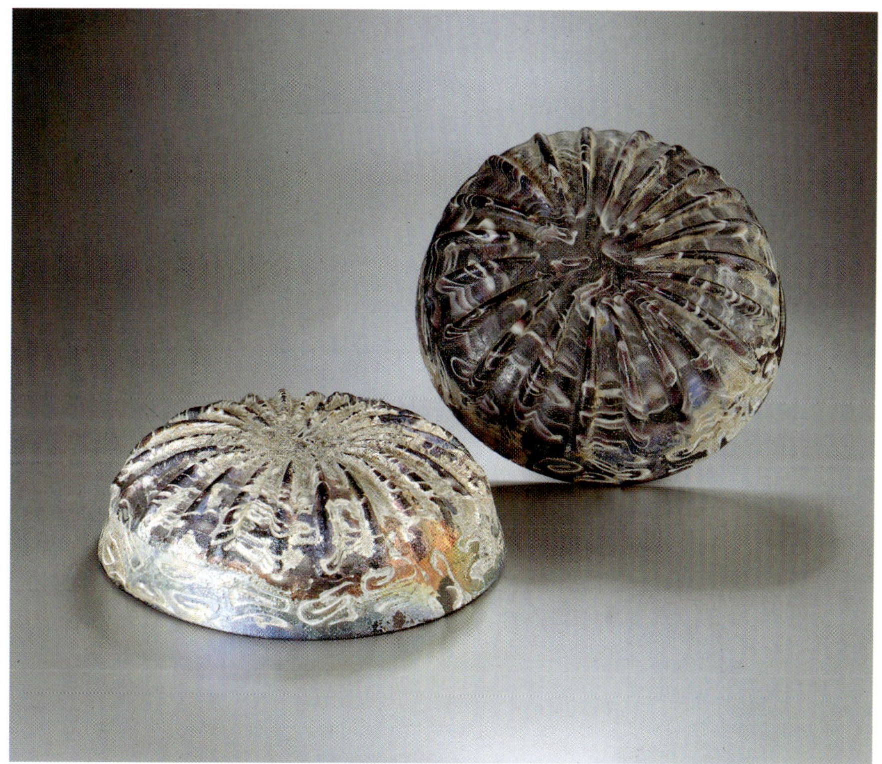

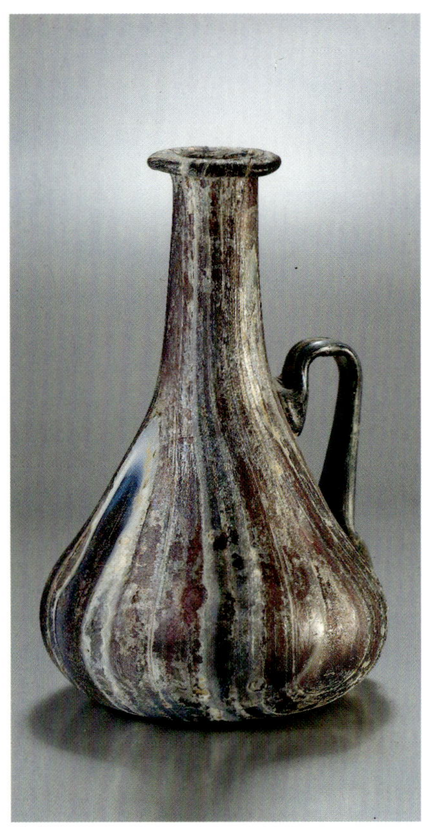

18 Handled Flask

Roman Empire
Eastern Mediterranean or Italy
1st c. AD
H 9.9, ⌀ 6.5 cm

Fused canes of colored glass free-blown and shaped. Rim of mouth folded inwards. No pontil mark.
Heavily corroded, deposits; slightly iridescent. Glued, below the handle part of wall restored.

Acc. no. P 1965-195
Gift of Helmut Hentrich

Glass of this type, intended to recall such semiprecious stones as agate or onyx, was particularly widespread in Italy, but many examples also came from sites in the Middle East.
The technique—preformed canes of glass had to be fused together before the vessel could be blown—suggests that these small bottles were worked at an oil lamp; cf. cat. no. 8. Examples with handles are rare. Spherical or teardrop bottles are more common. See, for example, Saldern et al., *Sammlung Oppenländer*, 1974, 129ff.; for the method of production see Grose, *Toledo*, 1989, 261, 262.

Lit.: Saldern, *Antike und Islam*, 1974, cat. no. 19

19 Flask

Roman Empire
Eastern Mediterranean
1st c. AD
H 15.2, ⌀ 6.5 cm

Ribbon glass, preformed canes of glass fused and free-blown. Two rings cut below the mouth.
Slightly corroded, remains of deposits; iridescent. Broken and glued, slightly restored.

Acc. no. P 1971-73
Gift of Helmut Hentrich

Ribbon glassware of this thick-walled type—definitely not worked at the lamp—belongs to the luxury glass production of early imperial Rome. Only isolated pieces are extant.

Lit.: Saldern, *Antike und Islam*, 1974, cat. no. 20; Ricke, *2500 Jahre*, 1987, cat. no. 9

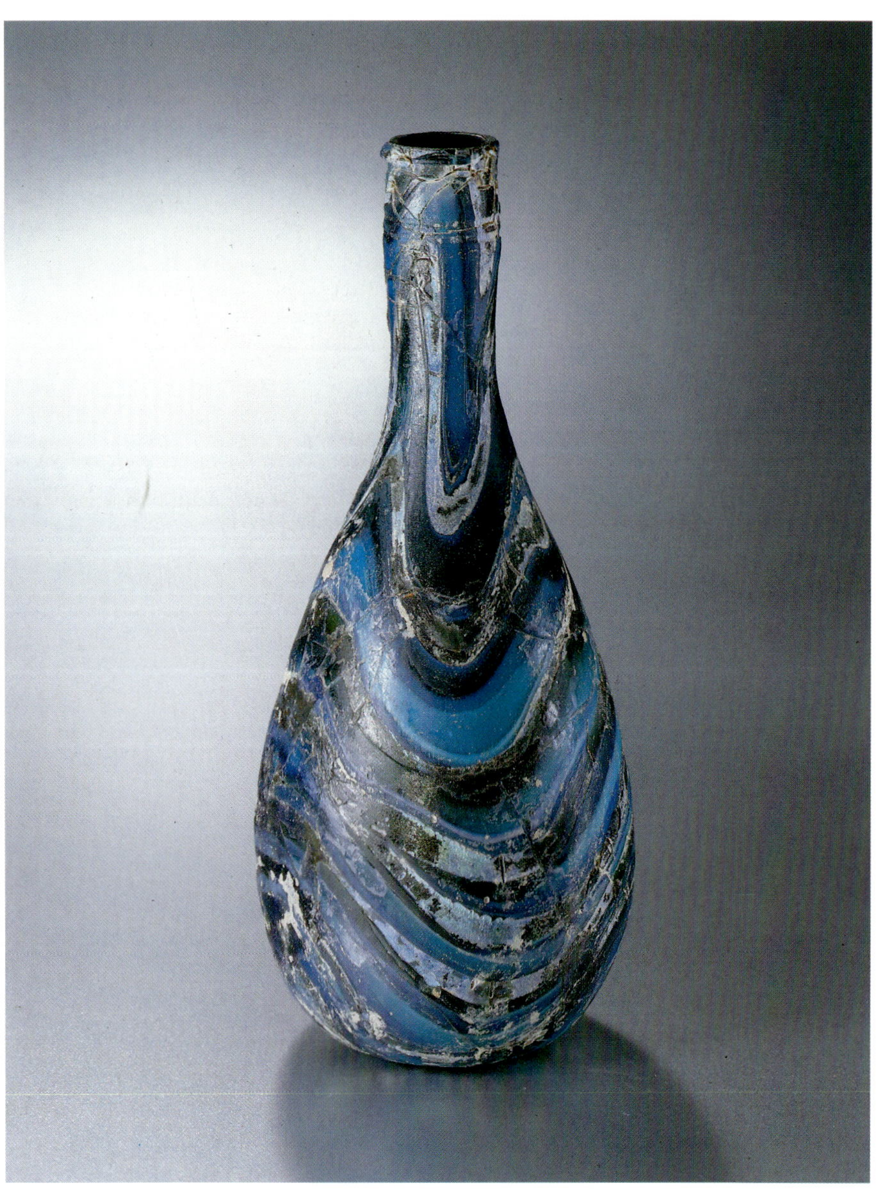

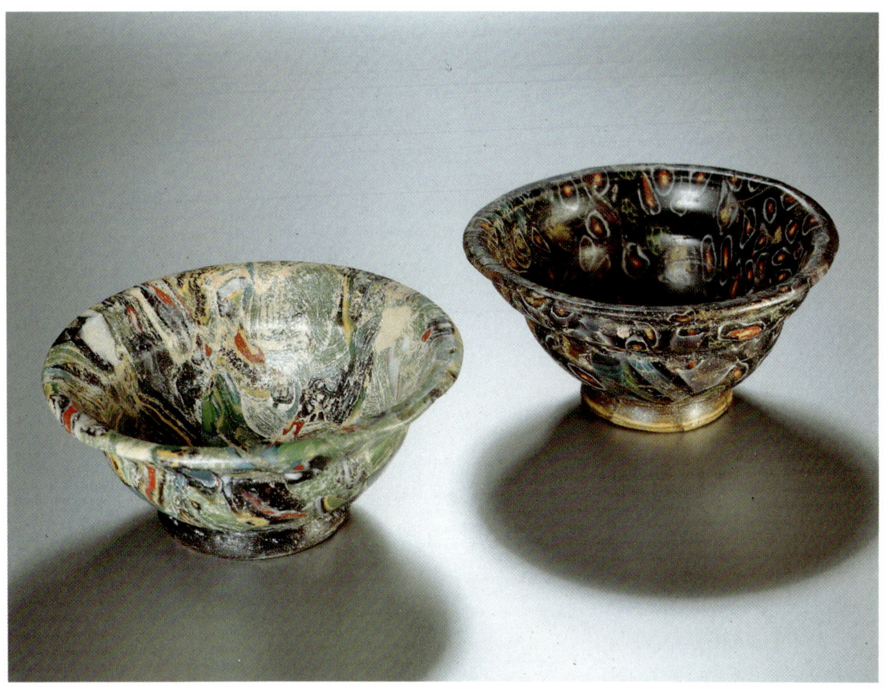

20 Bowl

Roman Empire, presumably Italy
1st c. AD
H 3.1, ⌀ 9.3 cm

Millefiori technique, core-formed on the turning wheel. Cut surface.
Slightly corroded, cleaned.

Acc. no. P 1976-18

A common shape in luxury glass of early
imperial Rome. Bowls of this sort, usually
referred to as acetabula or patella cups, were
made in large numbers in other materials as
well, above all in *terra sigillata*. Millefiori
pieces of similar patterns and color combina-
tions are documented in other bowl shapes of
the first century.
The combination of shapeless, irregularly patterned pieces that give the impression of
being remainders of the production of other
bowls is unusual. Similar glassware is rare.
See, for example, P. La Baume, *Glas der
Antiken Welt 1, Wissenschaftliche Kataloge des
Römisch-Germanischen Museums Köln* 1
(Cologne, n.d.), pl. 44,4, cat. no. H 3.

Lit.: Ricke, *2500 Jahre*, 1987, cat. no. 10

21 Bowl

Roman Empire, presumably Italy
1st c. AD
H 4, ⌀ 8.9 cm

Millefiori technique, core-formed on the turning wheel. Applied foot-ring. Cut surface.
Slightly corroded, cleaned. Wall partly
restored.

Acc. no. P 1976-17

For further examples of this group see, for
instance, Saldern et al., *Sammlung Oppenländer*, 1974, cat. nos. 314ff.; Goldstein, *Pre-
Roman*, 1979, 144ff.; *3000 Jahre*, Lucerne,
1981, 63ff.

Lit.: –

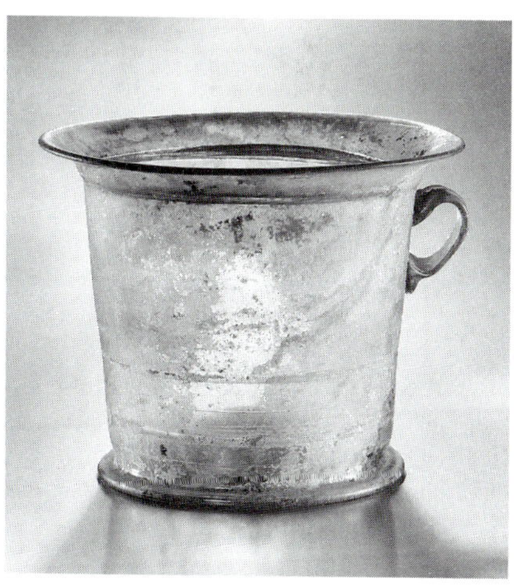

22 Modiolus

Roman Empire, probably Syria or Italy
2nd half of 1st c. AD
H 12.3, ⌀ 15.4 cm

Mold-blown and shaped. Tooled collar in the
wall below the mouth, similar fold used as
foot-ring. Concave base. Five cut rings, alter-
nately faint and strong.
Corroded, deposits.

Acc. no. P 1966-32
Gift of Helmut Hentrich

Cups of this type are documented in clay and
metal as well as in glass. They probably
served as measuring cups; see T. E. Haevernick, "Modioli," *Glastechnische Berichte* 51
(1978): 328–30, with 105 documented examples; see also Saldern, *Cohn Collection*, 1980,
cat. no. 115.

Lit.: Saldern, *Antike und Islam*, 1974,
cat. no. 243

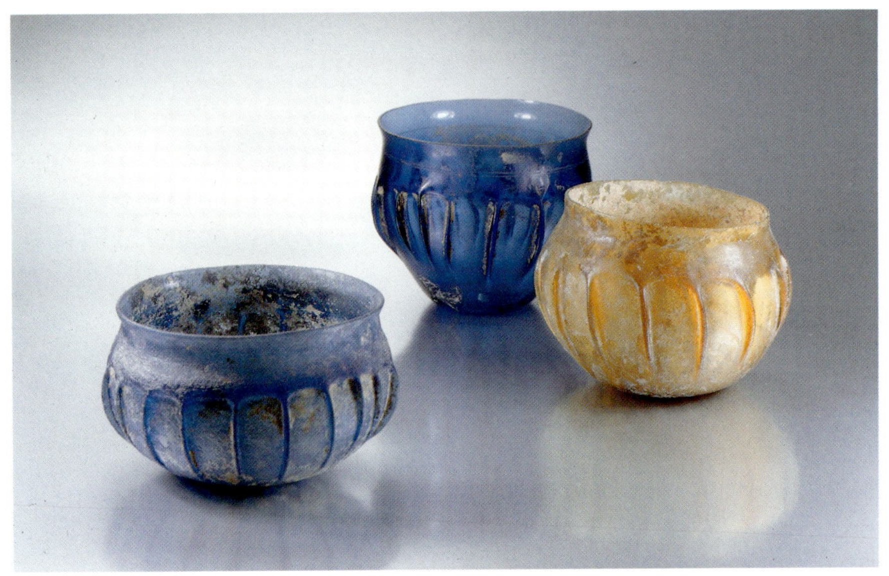

26 Cinerary Urn

Roman Empire, presumably Rhineland
Late 1st–2nd c. AD
H 31.5, ⌀ 20.5 cm

Light blue-green glass, material of the cover
somewhat stronger in tone. Mold-blown and
shaped, cover (belonging originally to this
urn?) free-blown and shaped.
Slightly corroded, cleaned on outside.

Acc. no. P 1949-3
Formerly Josef Lückger Collection, Cologne

Cremation burials were very common in the
Roman Empire. Vessels of this type are known
from the north and west as well as from the
eastern provinces and from North Africa.

Lit.: Saldern, *Antike und Islam*, 1974, cat.
no. 144; Ricke, *Ausgewählte Werke*, 1980, 3

23 Delicate Ribbed Bowls

Roman Empire, Italy
2nd half of 1st c. AD
H 5.5, ⌀ 8.8 cm

Blown, 19 ribs pinched out of the plastic body.
No pontil mark. Rim of mouth slightly cut.
Heavily corroded, remains of deposits.

Acc. no. P 1966-21
Gift of Helmut Hentrich

Common type of bowl, made in various colors, often with a white spiral thread coiled
around the body. In contrast to the mold-
melted ribbed bowls (cat. no. 17), these were
made with pincers at the furnace. Similar
examples in, for instance, Saldern et al.,
Sammlung Oppenländer, 1974, 100ff.

Lit.: Saldern, *Antike und Islam*, 1974, cat. no. 36

24 Delicate Ribbed Bowl

Roman Empire, probably Italy
2nd half of 1st c. AD
H 7.6, ⌀ 9 cm

Like cat. no. 23, 17 ribs. Cut ring below the
mouth. Almost no corrosion, light deposits.

Acc. no. P 1970-531
Gift of Helmut Hentrich

Lit.: Saldern, *Antike und Islam*, 1974, cat.
no. 35; Ricke, *2500 Jahre*, 1987, cat. no. 14

25 Delicate Ribbed Bowl

Roman Empire, Italy
2nd half of 1st c. AD
H 6.5, ⌀ 7.5 cm

Like cat. no. 23, 13 ribs.
Corroded, cleaned on outside, inside heavy
deposits.

Acc. no. P 1966-20
Gift of Helmut Hentrich

Lit.: Saldern, *Antike und Islam*, 1974, cat. no. 37

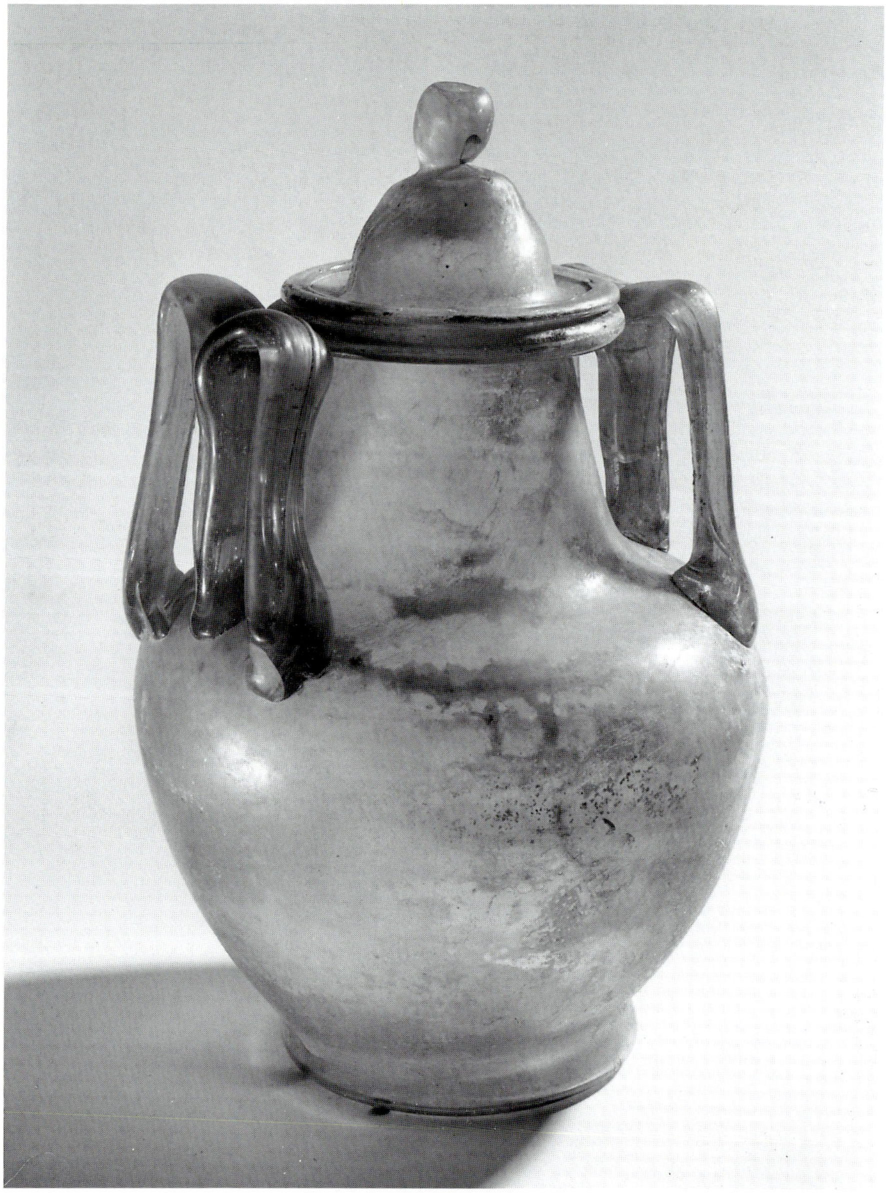

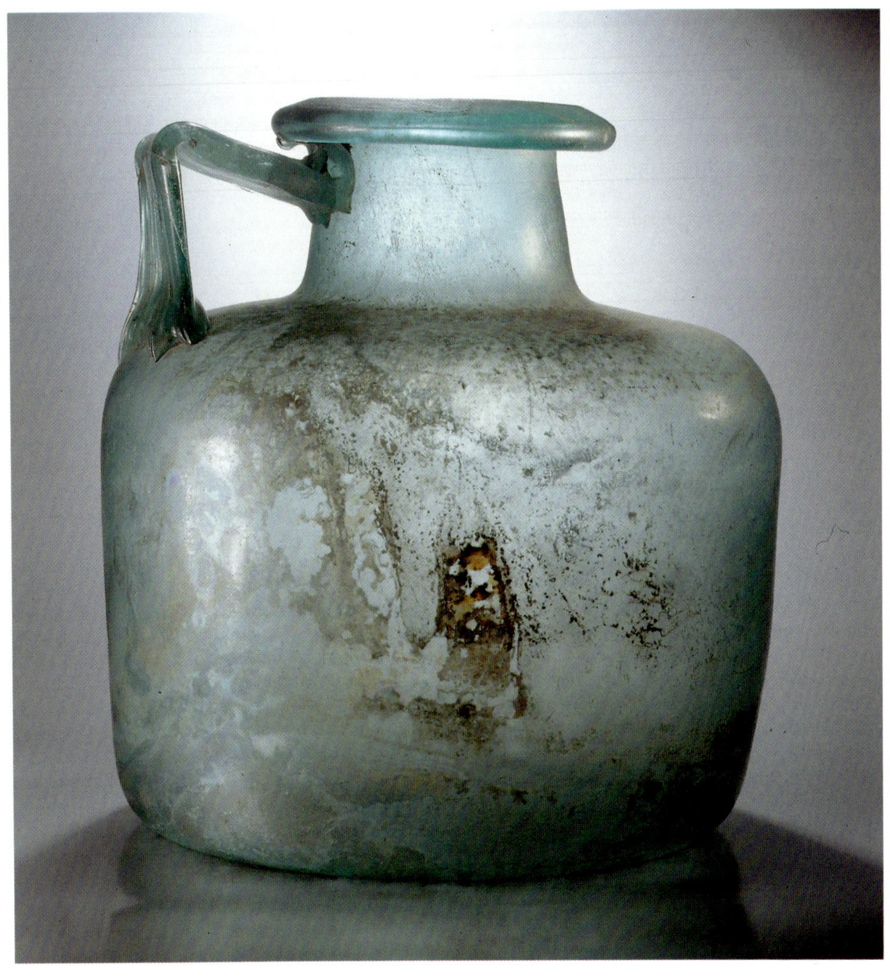

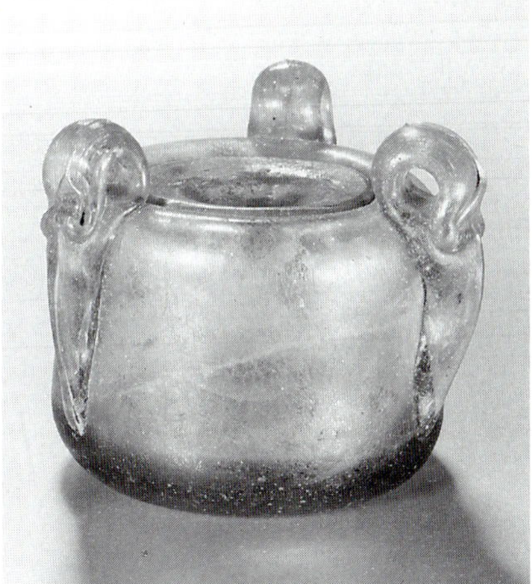

28 Inkstand

Roman Empire
Rhineland or Eastern Mediterranean
1st/2nd c. AD
H 5.9, ⌀ 6.9 cm

Pale green tone. Mold-blown and shaped,
mouth thickened, applied dolphin handles.
Slightly corroded, cleaned.

Acc. no. P 1949-72
Formerly Josef Lückger Collection, Cologne

Since securely localized examples of such
inkwells are rare in the Rhineland, this piece
cannot be definitively attributed to Rhenish
glassworks.

Lit.: Saldern, *Antike und Islam*, 1974,
cat. no. 240

27 Handled Bottle (Cinerary Urn)

Roman Empire, presumably Rhineland
Late 1st–early 2nd c. AD
H 24, ⌀ 22.5 cm

Light blue-green glass. Mold-blown and
shaped. Base slightly concave, folded rim,
ribbed handle.
Slightly corroded, cleaned on outside.

Acc. no. P 1949-69
Formerly Josef Lückger Collection, Cologne

Large storage vessel. Also documented as
cinerary urn, for example in the Rhineland
and in England. See *Glass of the Caesars*,
1987, cat. no. 39. For localizing the example
shown here to the Rhineland, cf. cat.
no. 26.

Lit.: Saldern, *Antike und Islam*, 1974,
cat. no. 147

29 Zoomorphic Flask

Roman Empire
Eastern Mediterranean, Syria (?)
Probably 2nd c. AD
H 7.3, L 17, ⌀ 4.7 cm

Pale blue-green tone. Free-blown and shaped.
Pressed down at the bottom to form a standing base.
Slightly corroded, cleaned. Glued and slightly
restored.

Acc. no. P 1966-339
Gift of Helmut Hentrich

A rare variation within the large group of
zoomorphic vessels, in which birds predomi-
nate. To date only five similar pieces have
been found.

Lit.: Saldern, *Antike und Islam*, 1974,
cat. no. 337

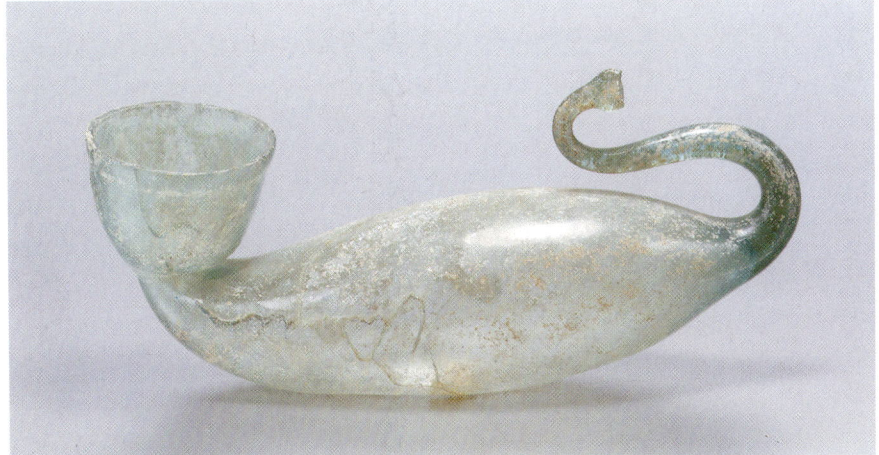

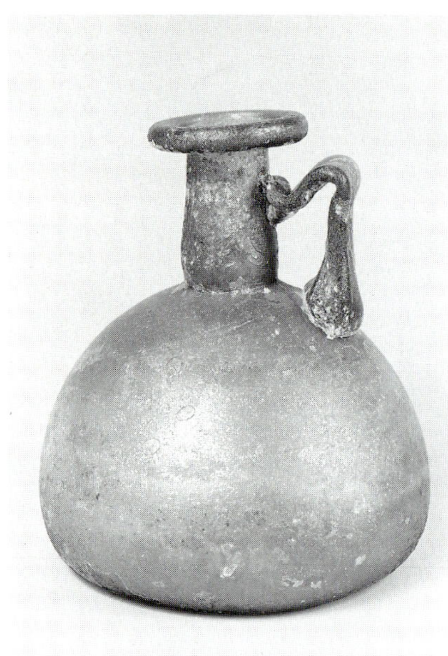

30 Handled Flask

Roman Empire, Eastern Mediterranean
Ca. 2nd c. AD
H 15, ⌀ 13.1 cm

Olive green tone. Free-blown and shaped.
Rim of mouth folded inwards.
Slightly corroded; strongly iridescent.

Acc. no. P 1965-187
Gift of Helmut Hentrich

Lit.: Saldern, *Antike und Islam*, 1974,
cat. no. 194

31 Flask

Roman Empire, Eastern Mediterranean
Ca. 2nd/3rd c. AD
H 14, ⌀ 11.2 cm

Pale blue-green. Blown and shaped. Concave
base, rim of mouth folded downwards.
Heavily corroded, deposits, on the outside
mostly loosened or removed; on the inside
strongly iridescent.

Acc. no. P 1965-186
Gift of Helmut Hentrich

Very common type of utilitarian glass of early
and middle imperial Rome. Produced in
numerous variations; also see Saldern, *Antike
und Islam*, 1974, cat. no. 173.

Lit.: Saldern, *Antike und Islam*, 1974,
cat. no. 174

32 Triple-Bodied Flask

Roman Empire
Eastern Mediterranean, Syria (?)
2nd/3rd c. AD
H 16.3, ⌀ 13.4 cm

Colorless, slightly yellowish glass. Mold-
blown from three pieces using three blow-
pipes and shaped. On the inside, the adjacent
walls of the three hollow bodies were fused
together.
Corroded, slightly iridescent. Glued and
slightly restored.

Acc. no. P 1966-78
Gift of Helmut Hentrich

Two and three-part handled bottles—for
holding different types of wine or for mixing
water and wine directly while pouring—were
not everyday utensils in the Roman household. The small number of extant pieces documents the exclusivity of such glassware,
necessitated by the complicated production
process.

Lit.: Saldern, *Antike und Islam*, 1974,
cat. no. 182

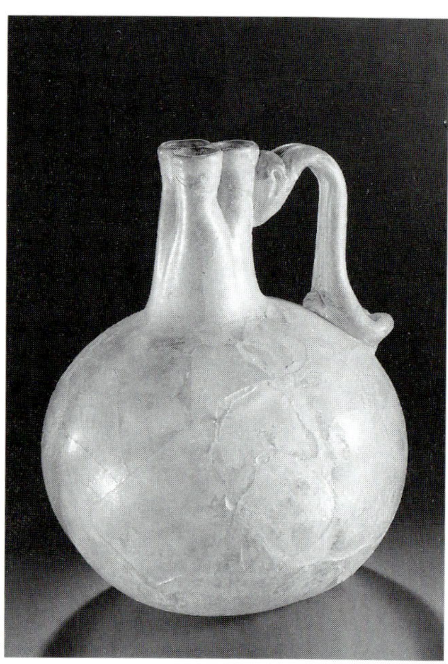

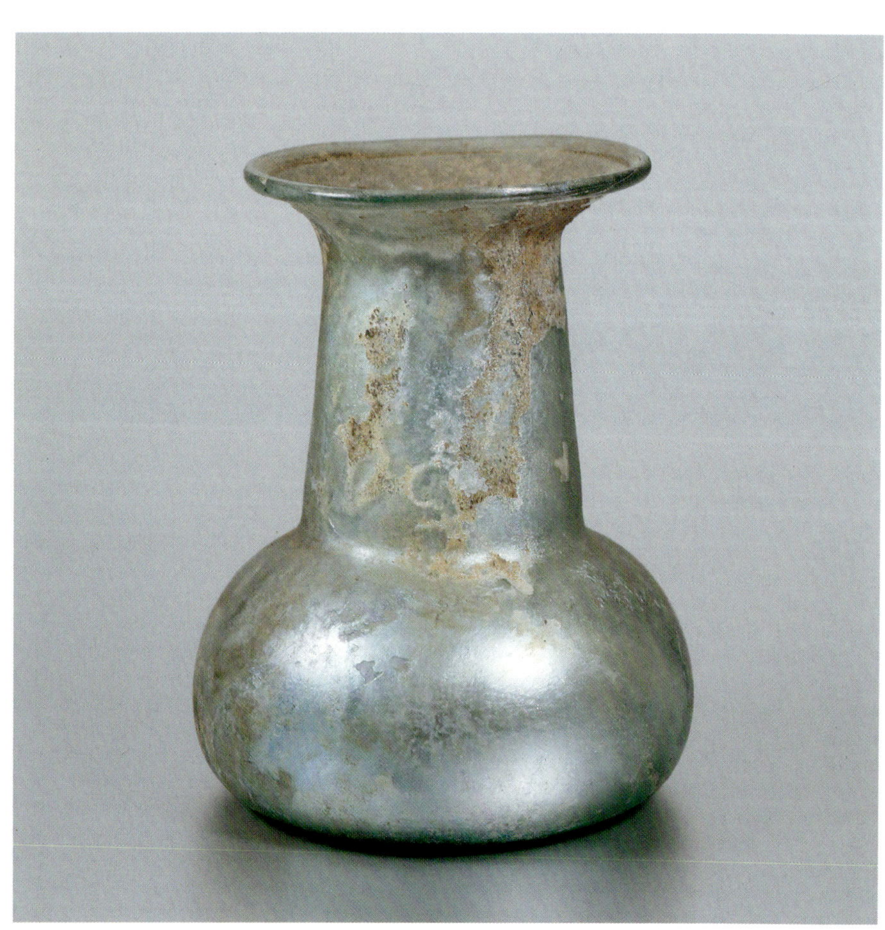

33   Snake-Thread Bottle

Roman Empire
Eastern Mediterranean, Syria
1st half of 3rd c. AD
H 21.7, ⌀ 7.5 cm

Mold-blown and shaped. Decoration of freely
applied opaque yellow threads, wall indented.
Slightly corroded, cleaned. Glued and slightly
restored.

Acc. no. P 1970-3

Glassware with snake-thread decoration is
generally considered a specialty of Roman
glassworks in the Rhineland. Syrian glassware
of this type, extant only in small numbers,
was made earlier and presumably inspired the
Rhenish production.
Only six extant vessels and a few fragments
of such Syrian snake-thread glassware with
bird motifs are documented, of these, only
two with colored thread applications. For a
close parallel in monochrome design see
Saldern, *Cohn Collection*, 1980, cat. no. 84.

Lit.: Saldern, *Antike und Islam*, 1974, cat.
no. 89; Ricke, *Ausgewählte Werke*, 1980, 4;
Ricke, *2500 Jahre*, 1987, cat. no. 22

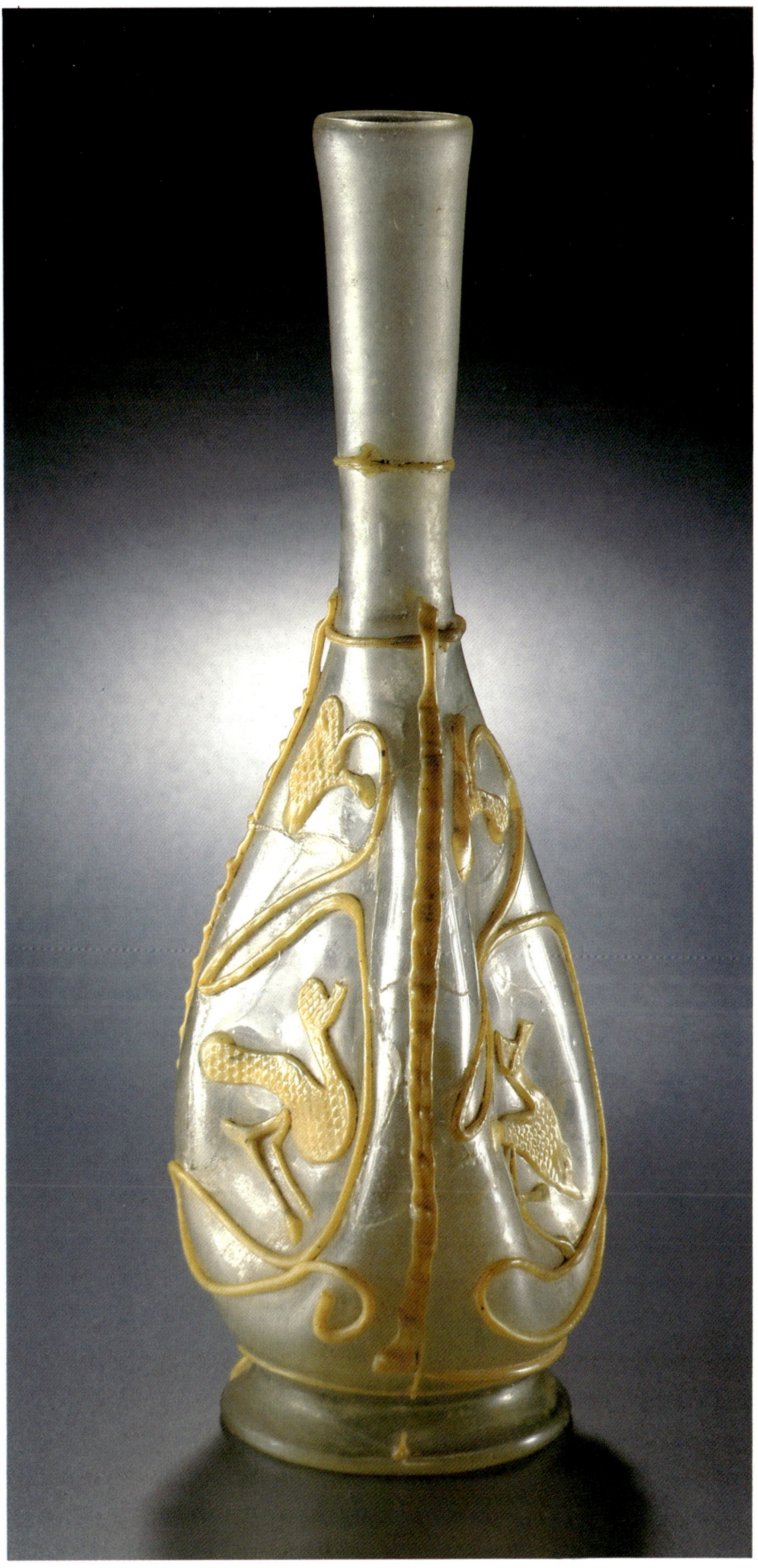

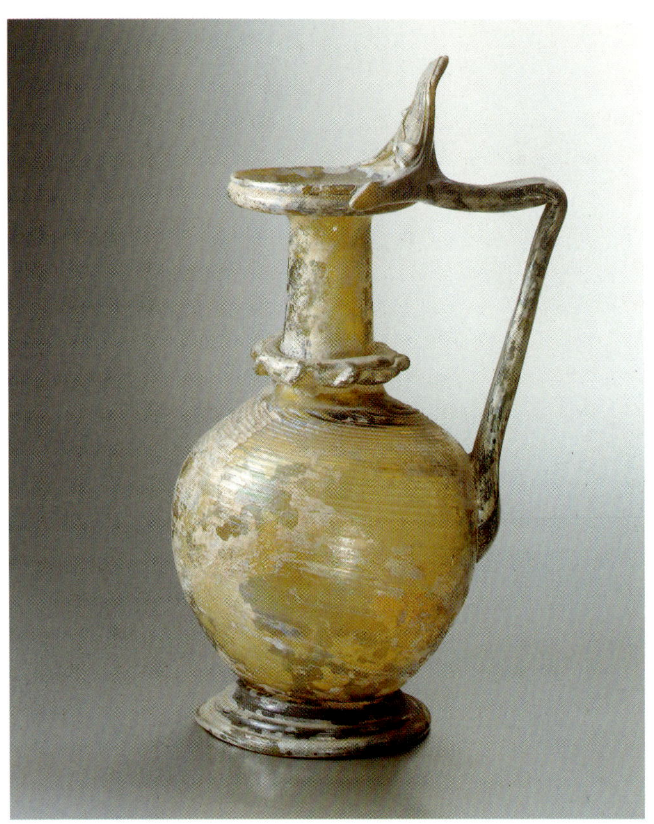

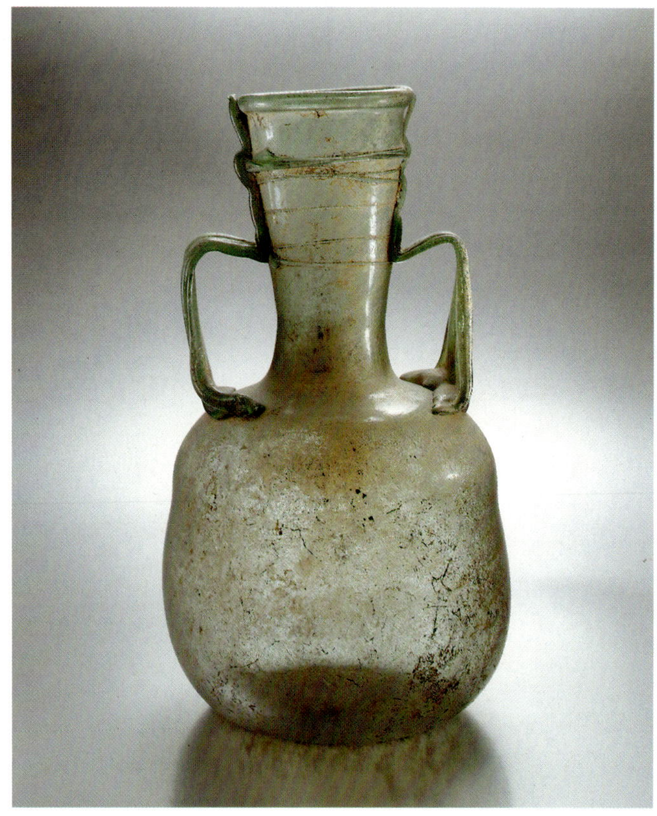

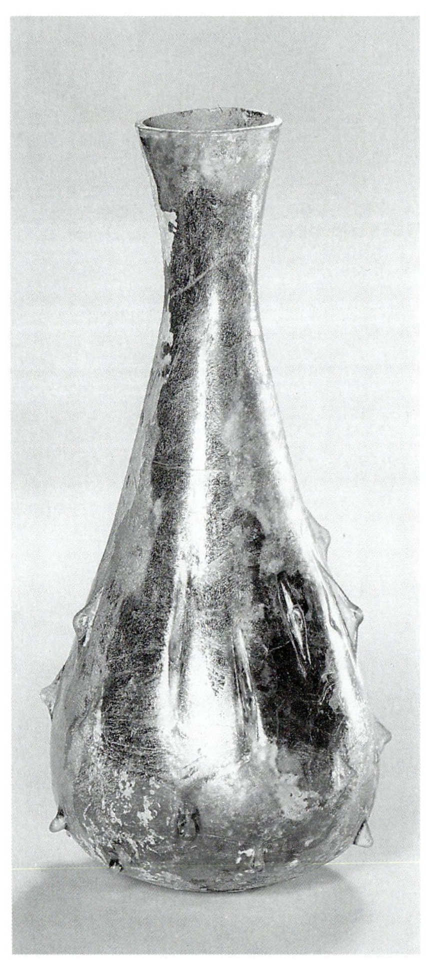

34 Pitcher

Roman Empire
Eastern Mediterranean, Syria (?)
3rd c. AD
H 24, ⌀ 11.2 cm

Slightly brownish yellow. Optic-blown, shaped. Pushed-up bottom. Trailed thread below mouth. Coiled foot.
Slightly corroded, deposits for the most part loosened. Slightly iridescent.

Acc. no. P 1966-331
Gift of Helmut Hentrich

Exceptionally well-preserved example of a large group of Syrian pitchers, their appeal arising from the lively embellishment with freely applied, striking detailing.

Lit.: Saldern, *Antike und Islam*, 1974, cat. no. 55

35 Bottle

Roman Empire
Eastern Mediterranean, Syria
Probably 3rd c. AD
H 18, ⌀ 8 cm

Colorless, light blue-green tone. Free-blown and shaped, pincered decoration. No pontil mark.
Slightly corroded, most deposits on the outside removed, strongly iridescent on the inside.

Acc. no. P 1966-18
Gift of Helmut Hentrich

An example of simple but effective furnace-worked ornamentation.

Lit.: Saldern, *Antike und Islam*, 1974, cat. no. 114

36 Two-Handled Bottle

Roman Empire
Eastern Mediterranean, Syria (?)
3rd/4th c. AD
H 33.6, ⌀ 18.4 cm

Light blue-green glass. Free-blown and shaped.
Slightly corroded, remains of deposits, cleaned on the outside.

Acc. no. P 1973-64
Gift of Helmut Hentrich

Extremely large, intact example of a common type of utilitarian glassware of late imperial Rome; see Saldern, *Antike und Islam*, 1974, cat. no. 231.

Lit.: –

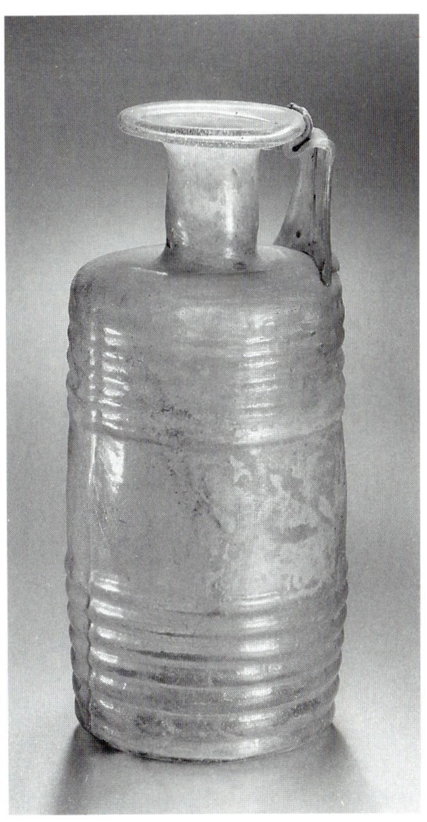

37 Barrel-Shaped Pitcher

Roman Empire, Rhineland or Gaul
Late 3rd/early 4th c. AD
H 18.5, ⌀ 8.1 cm

Colorless, slightly greenish. Blown into two-part mold, handle freely applied, folded rim. Mark on the bottom *CEBEIYLLICI* and three concentric rings as part of the mold. Slightly corroded, iridescent.

Acc. no. P 1949-51
Formerly Josef Lückger Collection, Cologne

Belongs to the group of so-called Frontinus pitchers. These barrel-shaped vessels are one of the few types of glassware securely identified as having been produced in the northern provinces of the Roman Empire, most notably in the Rhineland.

Lit.: Saldern, *Antike und Islam*, 1974, cat. no. 53; Ricke, *Ausgewählte Werke*, 1980, 3; Ricke, *2500 Jahre*, 1987, cat. no. 26

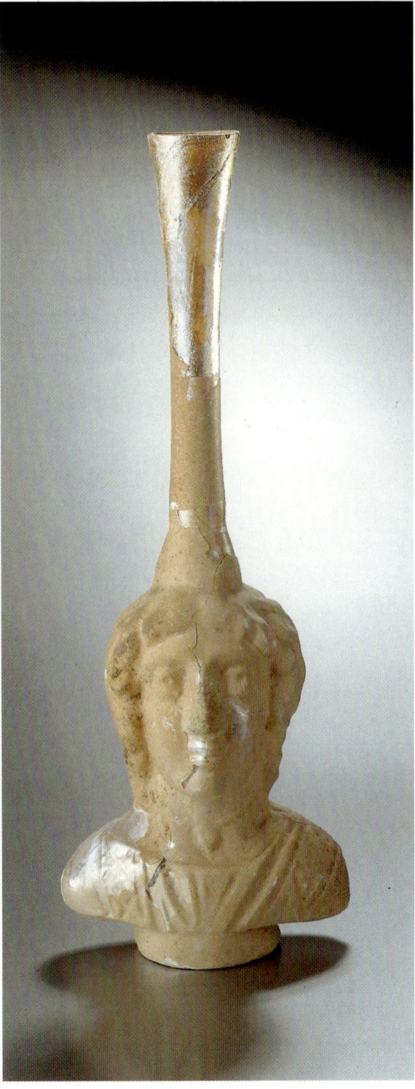

38 Head Flask

Roman Empire
Eastern Mediterranean, Syria
3rd/4th c. AD
H 26.2, W shoulder 9.4, ⌀ head 6.5 cm

Colorless glass, slightly yellowish tone. Blown into two-part mold, shaped.
Heavy deposits, in part raised, underneath strongly iridescent. Nose restored.

Acc. no. P 1970-2

Head flasks belong to the most popular mold-blown vessel types of late imperial Rome. Amongst the numerous examples from the Middle East this exceptionally tall piece is without parallel.

Lit.: Saldern, *Antike und Islam*, 1974, cat. no. 48; Ricke, *Ausgewählte Werke*, 1980, 4

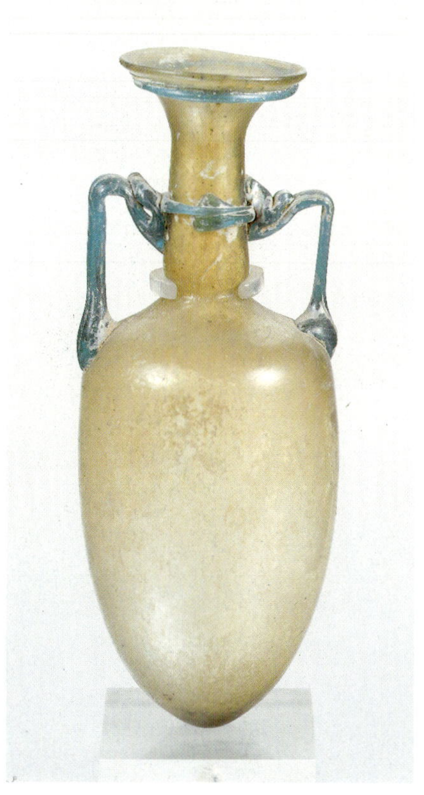

39 Amphora

Roman Empire
Eastern Mediterranean, Syria (?)
3rd/4th c. AD
H 18.3, ⌀ 7.3 cm

Pale olive green. Mold-blown, shaped. Handles, neck ring, and thread below the mouth turquoise blue.
Slightly corroded, cleaned; slightly iridescent.

Acc. no. P 1965-74
Gift of Helmut Hentrich

A common vessel shape from early imperial Rome with precursors in the pre-Roman period. Presumably intended to be placed in small metal stands.

Lit.: Saldern, *Antike und Islam*, 1974, cat. no. 205

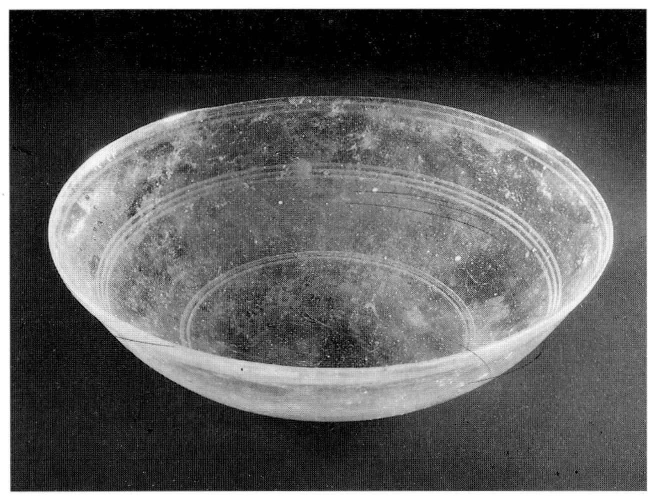

40 Dish

Roman Empire
Eastern Mediterranean or Rhineland
3rd/4th c. AD
H 4.8, ⌀ 22.1 cm

Colorless. Free-blown, cut from a spherical
shape, no standing base. Cut rings.
Slightly corroded, cleaned.

Acc. no. P 1949-9
Formerly Josef Lückger Collection, Cologne

Thin-walled, colorless dishes cut from globular forms were semi-luxurious utilitarian
glassware. They were often decorated with
concentric cut rings or with ornamental or
figural engraving.

Lit.: Saldern, *Antike und Islam*, 1974,
cat. no. 257

41 Plate

Roman Empire
Eastern Mediterranean, Egypt (?)
Presumably 4th c. AD
H 4.3, ⌀ 26.8 x 19.1 cm

Colorless, pale blue-green tone. Free-blown,
dilated. Foot-ring formed from the glass
bubble. Engraving underneath.
Slightly corroded, deposits removed, some
remaining in the hollows of the engraved
decor.

Acc. no. P 1966-336
Gift of Helmut Hentrich

Engraving was one of the rarer decorative
techniques of late Roman glassmaking.
Numerous fish motifs have been documented,
not necessarily bearing any relation to early
Christian symbolism.

Lit.: Saldern, *Antike und Islam*, 1974,
cat. no. 241

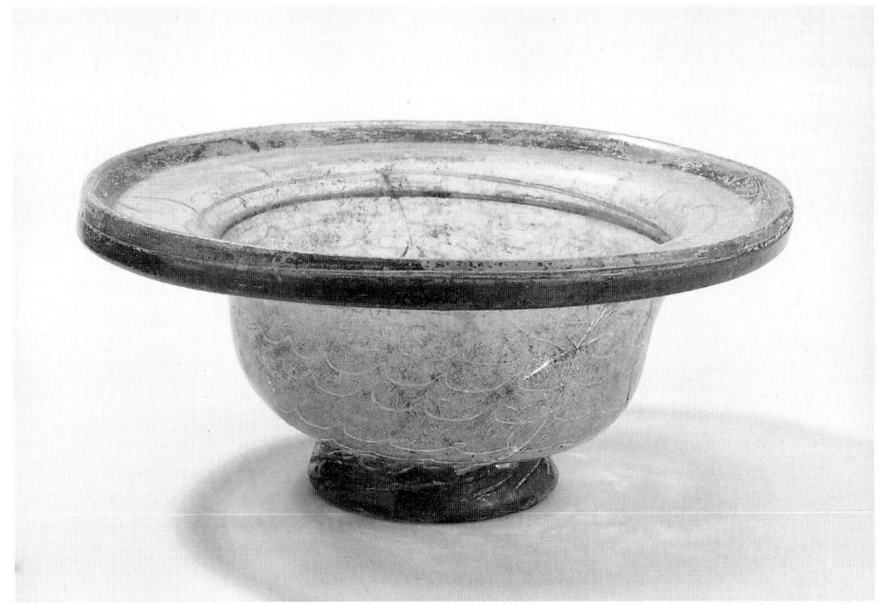

42 Bowl

Roman Empire, Eastern Mediterranean
Presumably 4th/early 5th c. AD
H 11.2, ⌀ 26 cm

Colorless, pale olive tone. Mold-blown,
shaped. The attached foot-ring, a thread,
triangular in profile and used to strengthen
the rim, as well as the thread running
around the edge of the rim are dark blue.
Thin opaque white threads were spun around
the wall, combed into wavy lines.
Corroded, deposits, numerous cracks. Glued,
slightly restored.

Acc. no. P 1973-66
Gift of Helmut Hentrich

For late imperial Roman standards, a very
carefully worked piece in a complicated technique.

Lit.: Saldern, *Antike und Islam*, 1974,
cat. no. 113

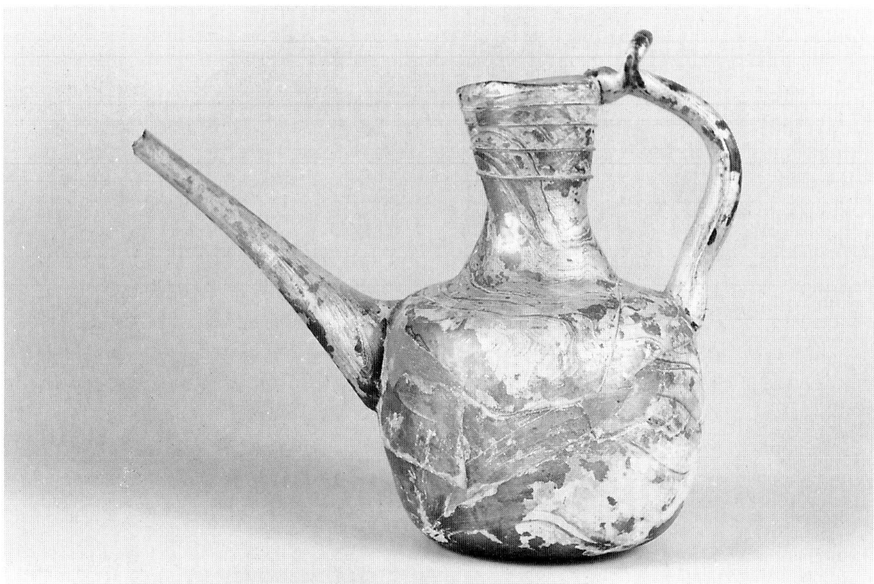

43 Pitcher

Roman Empire
Eastern Mediterranean, Syria (?)
Presumably 4th/5th c. AD
H 15.9, ⌀ 10 cm

Light blue-green. Free-blown and shaped.
Corroded, deposits, strongly iridescent. Glued
and slightly restored. Mouth of spout slightly
damaged.

Acc. no. P 1971-76
Gift of Helmut Hentrich

Presumably used to fill oil lamps.

Lit.: Saldern, *Antike und Islam*, 1974,
cat. no. 234

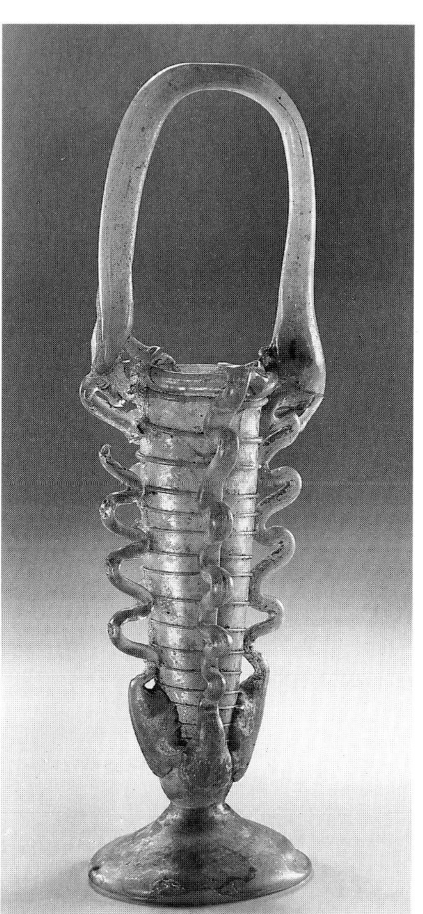

44 Saddleflask

Roman Empire
Eastern Mediterranean, Syria
4th/5th c. AD
H 21, ⌀ 5.8 cm

Light blue-green. Free-blown and shaped.
Applied threads and handle. Foot attached.
Corroded. Glued, small flaws and restoration.
One of the four wavy vertical threads was
attached later.

Acc. no. P 1966-15
Gift of Helmut Hentrich

The hanging unguentaria, inappropriately
described since the 19th century as saddle-
flasks, belong to the most common vessel
types of late imperial Rome. They generally
consist of two tubes, more seldom of one or
four. Special emphasis was placed on the
design of the handles, often consisting of
several parts, and on the rich thread decoration of the walls. Examples on a foot are relatively rare.
For several examples see, for instance,
Saldern, *Cohn Collection*, 1980, cat. nos.
99–102; for a particularly lavish piece see
Glass of the Caesars, 1987, cat. no. 77.

Lit.: Saldern, *Antike und Islam*, 1974,
cat. no. 103

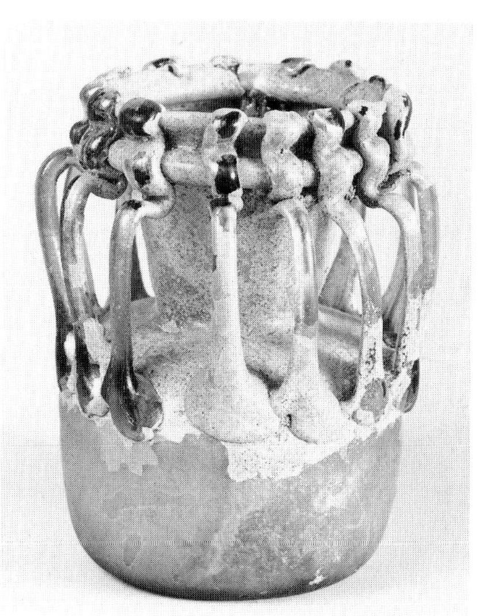

45 Vase

Roman Empire
Eastern Mediterranean, Syria (?)
Probably 4th c. AD
H 8.2, ⌀ 6.8 cm

Greenish glass. Blown, shaped. Fourteen freely
applied ornamental handles. Pushed-up bottom, neck with tooled collar below the mouth.
Corroded. Heavy deposits, partly loosened,
underneath slightly iridescent.

Acc. no. P 1965-202
Gift of Helmut Hentrich

A particularly richly embellished example from
a large group of Syrian vessels with ornamental handles. Usually these small vases have
only two or three handles, but are further
decorated with zigzag threads. For a variation
see, for example, Saldern, *Cohn Collection*,
1980, cat. no. 96.

Lit.: Saldern, *Antike und Islam*, 1974, cat. no. 97

The Sassanian Empire

With the divided Roman Empire's decline of power, the new great Persian empire formed under the leadership of the Sassanids began to rise to power in the Middle East in the fifth century AD. Building on the age-old technical knowledge of Mesopotamia and the new impulses of Roman working methods, a remarkable flowering of glass art occurred between the Tigris and the Euphrates rivers.

While late imperial types of glassware continued to be produced in Syrian cities, albeit in ever decreasing quality, the luxury glassware made in complicated processes in the Sassanian centers of power, probably above all in court workshops of the capital, Ctesiphon, is amongst the greatest achievements in glass history.

Besides colored utilitarian glassware (cat. nos. 49–51), which—like the court vessels—reveal a for-mal idiom independent of Roman glass, Sassanian glassworks also produced thick-walled, almost color-less glassware. The effect of the largely unassuming dishes and bowls is primarily determined by the strik-ing reliefwork. Whereas relatively simple wheel-cut decoration (cat. no. 47) relied directly upon Roman prototypes, the thorn-disk decoration and relief pat-terns of grain-like motifs represented a novelty in glass design. This type of ornament was modeled on beaten or cast metal works of the East.

The forceful impulses of this new glass art really flourished only after the Sassanian dynasty came to an end. The onslaught of Islam, fundamentally reor-ganizing the entire Middle East, signified not the end but the beginning of another remarkable upswing in the region's glass design.

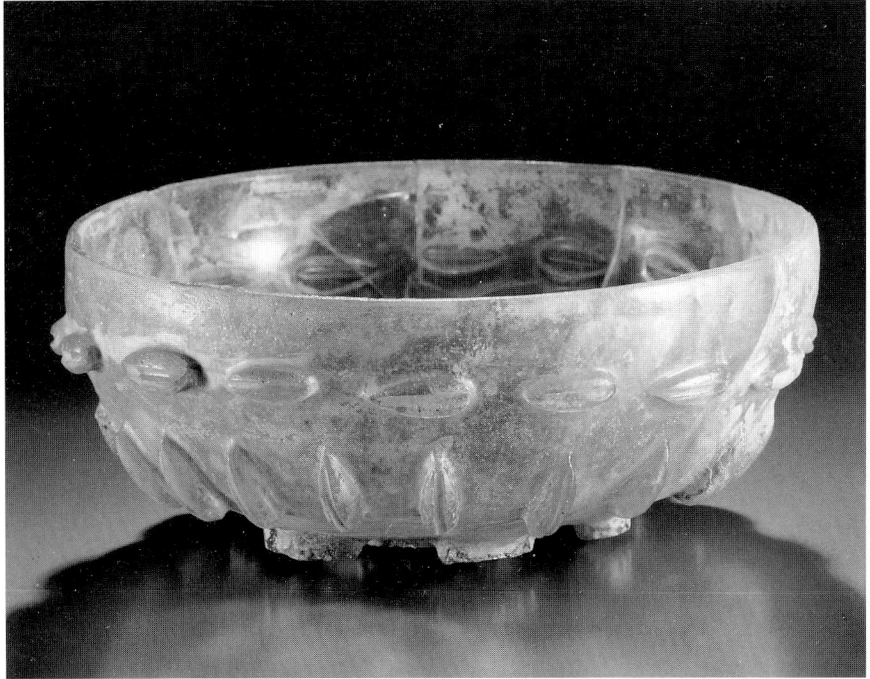

46   Dish

Middle East, Iran or Iraq
(reportedly found in NW Iran)
Ca. 4th/5th c. AD
H 5.8, ⌀ 14.7, H of relief max. 0.5 cm

Colorless, light green tone. Probably mold-blown or mold-pressed and mold-turned; cut. Decoration: two rows of grain-shaped motifs, 16 below the mouth, 19 in the middle; 6 kid-ney-shaped motifs around a central double disk under the bottom.
Corroded, deposits, partly removed. Glued and restored.

Acc. no. P 1966-5

The dish, of which no comparable piece is documented, links Roman glass art with that of the Sassanian Empire. For the relationship between the relief decoration and glassware of the early and middle imperial period see Saldern, "Sassanidische und islamische Gläser," 1968, 33ff.

Lit.: Saldern, *Antike und Islam*, 1974, cat. no. 270; Ricke, *Ausgewählte Werke*, 1980, 5

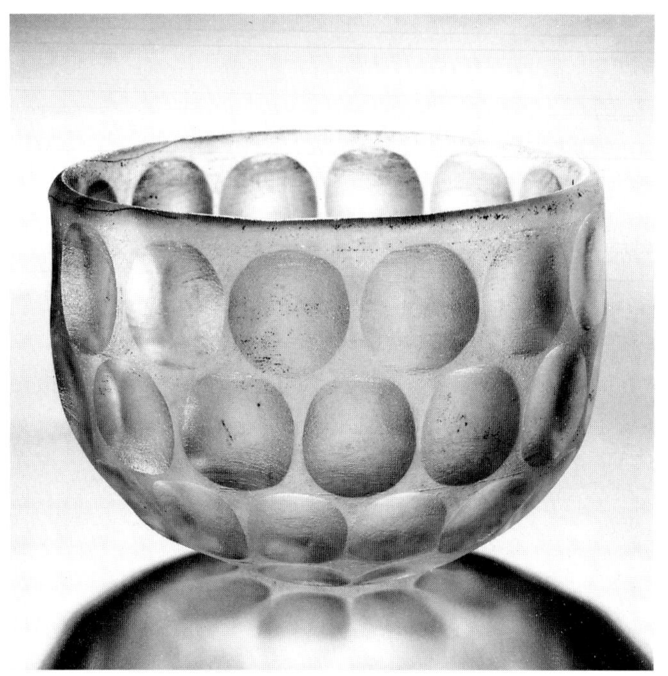

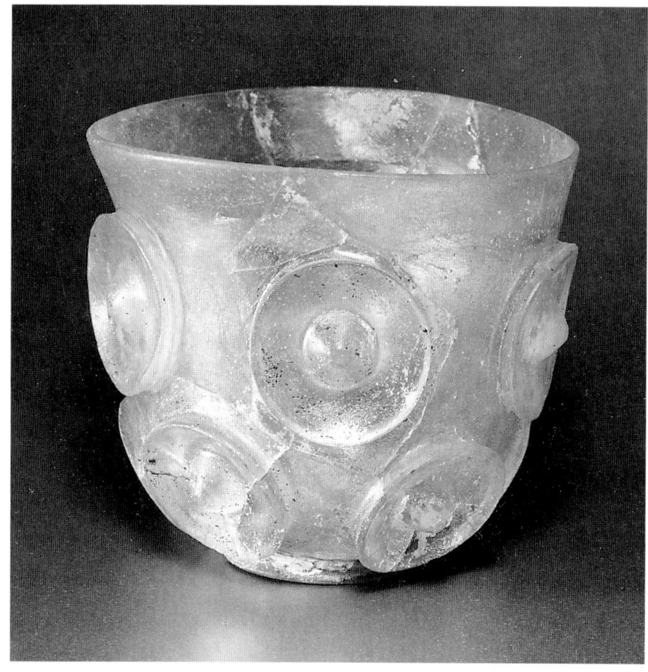

47 Bowl

Middle East, Iran or Iraq
(reportedly found in NW Iran)
Probably 6th c. AD
H 7.5, ⌀ 10.9 cm

Colorless. Probably mold-blown or mold-
pressed and mold-turned. Cut decoration:
3 rows with 14 circular recesses each and
1 row with 9. Cut decoration over large area
at the bottom center.
Corroded, acid-cleaned.

Acc. no. P 1966-4
Gift of Helmut Hentrich

A common type of Sassanian glassware.
Examples have been found primarily in Kish
and Ctesiphon, Iraq. It was possible to date
this type with a dish that came to Japan and
was found in the grave of Emperor Ankan
(d. 535). See Saldern, "Sassanidische und
islamische Gläser," 1968, 33ff. See also
Fukai, *Persian Glass*, 1977, 38ff. and fig. 3.

Lit.: Saldern, *Antike und Islam*, 1974,
cat. no. 271

48 Bowl

Middle East, Iran or Iraq
7th/8th c. AD
H 11.2, ⌀ 13.3, ⌀ ornamental disks 4.5,
H cones 0.9 cm

Colorless, light yellow tone. Probably mold-
blown or mold-pressed and mold-turned. Decoration: two rows of five relief disks each,
strongly profiled ring in the bottom center.
Only about one-third original. Connecting rim
and wall fragments secure reconstruction.
Fragments corroded, cleaned; iridescent.

Acc. no. P 1966-6

In spite of its fragmentary state of preservation the glass conveys an impression of the
high quality and technical perfection of late
Sassanian/early Islamic court art.
Only a few pieces of this type are extant; the
two most important are in the cathedral in
Halberstadt, Germany, and in the treasury of
San Marco in Venice. See Saldern, "Sassanidische und islamische Gläser," 1968, 33ff.

Lit.: Saldern, *Antike und Islam*, 1974, cat.
no. 274; Ricke, *Ausgewählte Werke*, 1980, 5

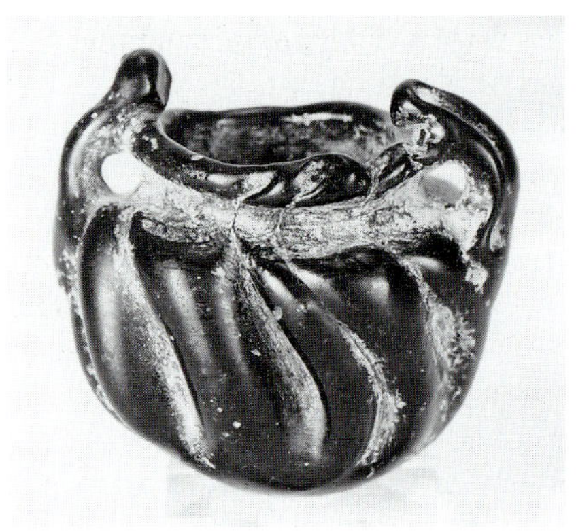

49 Bowl

Middle East, presumably Syria
Ca. 5th–7th c. AD
H 5.1, ⌀ 5.4 cm

Opaque black. Free-formed, nine notches.
Hardly corroded, remains of deposits.

Acc. no. P 1971-78
Gift of Helmut Hentrich

This small vessel is one of a large group of dark opaque glassware. Precisely where and when these objects were created has not been determined, though they were certainly made between the late Roman and early Islamic periods.

Lit.: Saldern, *Antike und Islam*, 1974, cat. no. 278; Ricke, *2500 Jahre*, 1987, cat. no. 31

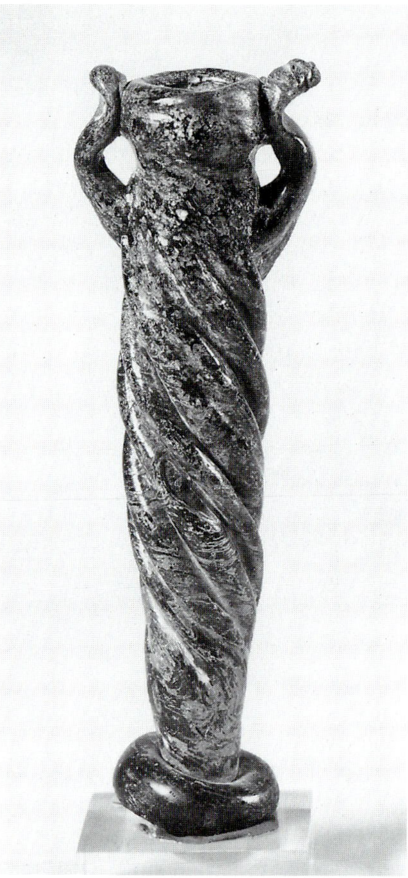

50 Unguentarium

Middle East, presumably Syria
Ca. 5th–7th c. AD
H 10.2, ⌀ 2 cm

Opaque blue glass. Free-formed, seven notches.
Corroded, deposits.

Acc. no. P 1966-36
Gift of Helmut Hentrich

See cat. no. 49. For similar small vessels see, for example, *3000 Jahre*, Lucerne, 1981, cat. nos. 479–82, with further literature.

Lit.: Saldern, *Antike und Islam*, 1974, cat. no. 279; Ricke, *2500 Jahre*, 1987, cat. no. 32

51 Bottle

Middle East, Iran, Iraq, or Syria
6th–8th c. AD
H 10, ⌀ 11 cm

Free-blown.
Heavily corroded, rest deposits; iridescent.

Acc. no. P 1973-74
Gift of Helmut Hentrich

A very common type of utilitarian glassware of thick-walled, robust material. Besides purely spherical bottles, numerous examples with variously pressed profiles are extant. Along with intensely green glass, glass appearing opaque black or brown was used.

Lit.: Saldern, *Antike und Islam*, 1974, cat. no. 367; Ricke, *2500 Jahre*, 1987, cat. no. 33

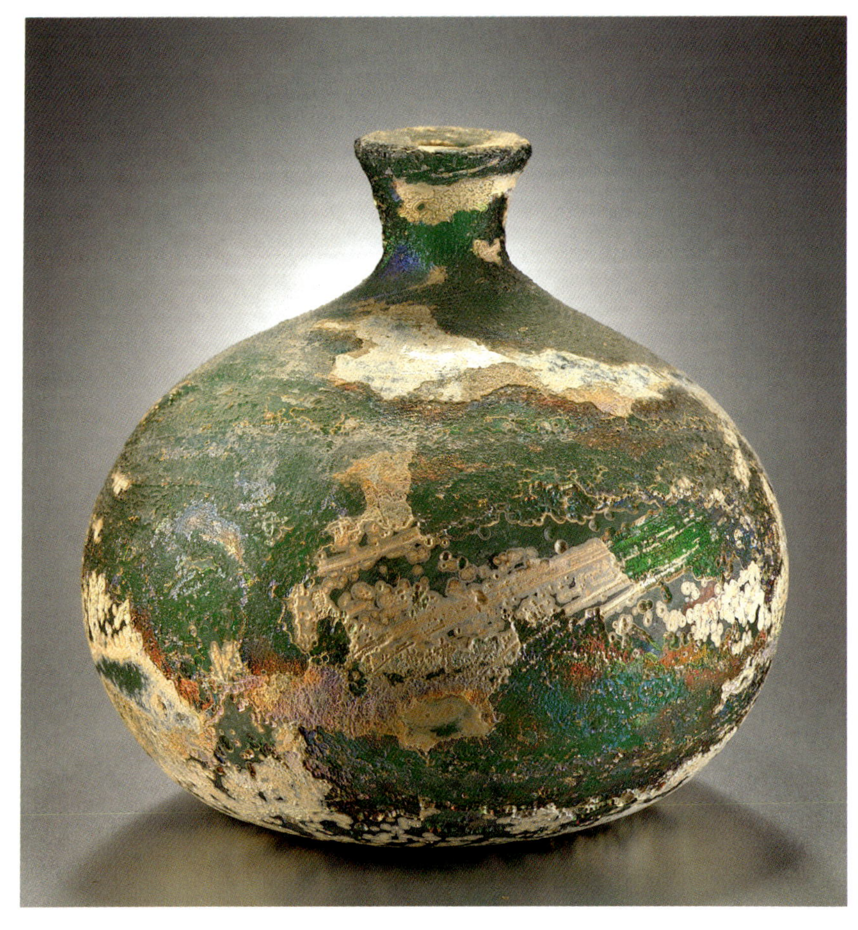

Islam

Many of the glass types that emerged as characteristically Islamic vessels had direct precursors in Sassanian glass art. Islamic glass developed in the old centers along the Mediterranean coast, the Euphrates, and the Tigris after the Arabian conquest around the mid-seventh century. It is seldom possible to date with any certainty individual glass vessels to the time before or after the Arabian conquest. This is true of the characteristic oriental oil lamps (cat. no. 52) as well as of the equally typical perfume sprinklers (cat. nos. 54, 78). The oil lamps are the precursors of the large mosque lamps of the fourteenth century, which came to epitomize Islamic glass art (cf. cat. no. 124). The sprinklers continued to be used in the East until the nineteenth century (cat. no. 215), spreading as far as India (cat. no. 207). Typical Islamic pitchers with pear-shaped bodies, narrow necks, and small spouts (cat. nos. 56–58, 77) also had precursors in Sassanian glass art.

Thus unbroken continuity characterized the development of Eastern glass art during the formation of the Islamic empires, for the Arabian conquerors largely refrained from destroying the advanced local cultures. Instead they cleverly used what they had to offer. A second, though much less formative, component was the late antique tradition concentrated in Syria and Egypt. It also contributed to the evolving, distinctively Islamic conception of form and decoration. Thus Sassanian glass art changed gradually, indeed imperceptibly, into Islamic glass art during the seventh and eighth centuries.

At present, only a very rough outline of dates is available for classifying medieval glassware of the Middle East chronologically and historically. Glassware that can be precisely classified, coming from excavations subject to strict scientific controls, is extremely rare. Respective care must be taken in dating archaeological finds. A span of two centuries continues to be standard for describing the period of an Islamic glass object.

Not until very recently has interest in Islamic history been awoken in those countries harboring archaeological sites. Over decades European archaeologists removed the more recent cultural layers, unseen, to examine the older ones usually lying below.

As to the variety of shapes and decorative techniques, medieval Islamic glass is certainly equal to Roman glass. The quantity of household glass utensils used also seems to correspond to Roman custom. As in ancient glass, a broad range of mostly free-blown or optic-blown vessels for everyday use are clearly distinguishable from the lavishly designed court glassware.

In utilitarian glassware, besides the pitchers mentioned above, colored bowls stand out. They have straight, later increasingly conical, walls (cat. nos. 59–61, 72, 73). Glass plates seem to have been even more common in the Islamic world than those in the Roman Empire. Bottles are often spherical with a long, tapering neck or have a sharp-edged profile with disk mouth (cat. no. 65). It is not uncommon for these vessels to be adorned with simple engraved or cut decoration. Beakers usually have simply straight or slightly inclined forms. Examples with stems and separately worked feet are rare (cat. no. 62), but gained in popularity as precursors of European footed beakers and goblet types developed from the early sixteenth century.

Glassmakers were technically skilled in partial and complete casing as well as in such complicated processes as fusing together pieces of contrasting colors (cat. no. 55). The emphasis on ornamental decoration, so typical in Islamic culture, supported the development of decorative techniques used only sparingly in Roman glass art. This is true, for example, of engraving glass with a diamond, a technique that came to acquire particular importance in Venetian glass art from the sixteenth century.

Even though diamond-point engraving produced high-quality decoration (cat. no. 64), the preferred decorative technique in fine Islamic glassware was cutting—usually in a manner similar to engraving. The production of this type of luxury glass seems to have been centered in workshops in what is today Persia and Iraq. Egypt, ruled until 1171 by the Fatimid dynasty, was also important. The lavish cut decoration of both regions bears witness to the development of diversiform Islamic ornamentation during the early Middle Ages. The very pure glass usually has a slightly yellowish tone.

Besides simple circle and disk shapes (cat. nos. 68, 70), Persian and Mesopotamian pieces have ornamental designs covering nearly the whole vessel (cat. no. 67). This development reached its peak with relief decoration carved almost entirely from an extremely thin wall (cat. no. 66).

Besides glassware whose outer walls bear decoration, another type of vessel emerged in which the very form was determined exclusively by means of cutting, thus acquiring a highly sculptural character (cat. no. 69).

In utilitarian glass, relief decoration consisting of many small parts increasingly took hold after AD 1000. Glassmakers adapted the forms underlying cut glassware by simpler means. Optic-blowing (cat. nos. 74–76) made new designs possible.

The thirteenth and fourteenth-century vessels from the Syrian centers as Aleppo and Damascus mark the end of medieval Islamic glass art (cat. nos. 81–83). Decorated with gold and enamel painting, these glass objects represent a significant link to glass art of the West.

Medieval Islamic culture came to an end with the Mongol conquest around 1400. Tamerlane's pillaging and the devastation of the large cities in the Middle East caused the destroyed empires to suffer for centuries. The old-world cultural focus shifted from the East to Europe. In the realm of glass art, Venice replaced the Syrian centers.

Islam's influence, however, had asserted itself in European glass art much earlier. Even in the high Middle Ages simple beaker forms betrayed their Eastern origins (cat. nos. 88–90) and glassware made in Islamic countries was highly valued by Europeans. Aristocratic families counted enameled and gilded glassware, brought from Palestine to the Occident by crusaders, amongst their most precious possessions. The famous so-called Hedwig Beakers were set in mounts as precious reliquaries or goblets and even landed in the treasuries of such Western churches as those in Magdeburg, Minden, Namur, and Cracow.

Venetian glass art profited from the fall of the Eastern empires around 1400, but remained largely independent of the late medieval Islamic tradition with regard to form. Glassmakers adopted only technical aspects of the decorative techniques, above all the combination of enamel painting with fired gold leaf. Local prototypes supplied in rich measure by the goldsmith's art of the late Gothic period, on the other hand, provided the vessel shapes (cf. pp. 78ff.).

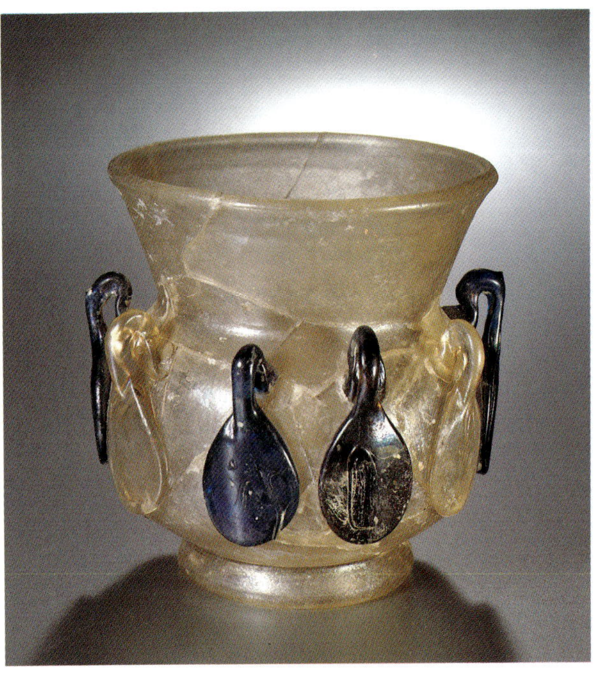

52 Lamp

Middle East, Iran
7th–9th c. AD
H 11, ⌀ 10.9 cm

Mold-blown, shaped. Nine freely applied eyelets for chains, alternating in colorless blue and brown. Tubular wick-holder in the vessel's interior.
Slightly corroded, most deposits removed. Glued, slightly restored.

Acc. no. P 1967-11

The colored applications make this an extremely rare example of a Sassanian/early Islamic oil lamp. Its shape continued to be widespread in subsequent centuries, up to the development of the large 14th-century mosque lamps. For a similar but less colorful piece see Saldern, *Cohn Collection*, 1980, cat. no. 176.

Lit. Saldern, *Antike und Islam*, 1974, cat. no. 321; Ricke, *Ausgewählte Werke*, 1980, 6; Ricke, *2500 Jahre*, 1987, cat. no. 36

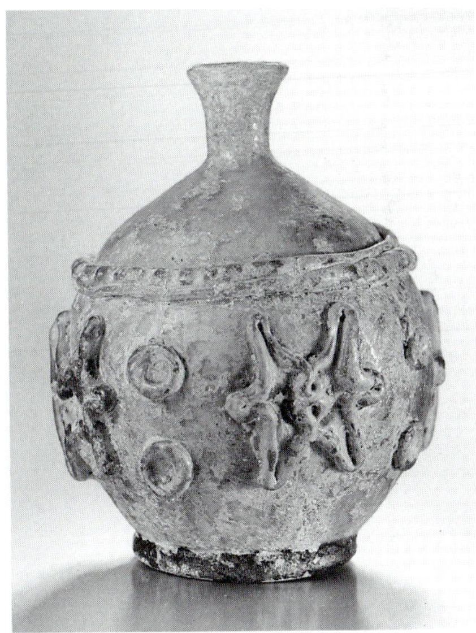

53 Globular Bottle

Middle East, presumably Iraq or Syria
Probably 7th–8th c. AD
H 9, ⌀ 7.2 cm

Colorless, light yellow tone. Free-blown and
shaped; applied relief decoration: five stars.
Heavily corroded, deposits, partly removed.

Acc. no. P 1973-71
Gift of Helmut Hentrich

Belongs to a larger group of glassware having
various shapes, but nearly identical decoration. Date and provenance have not yet been
secured in controlled excavations. For further
examples of similar pieces see *3000 Jahre*,
Lucerne, 1981, cat. nos. 513–24.

Lit.: Saldern, *Antike und Islam*, 1974, cat.
no. 332; Ricke, *2500 Jahre*, 1987, cal. no. 37

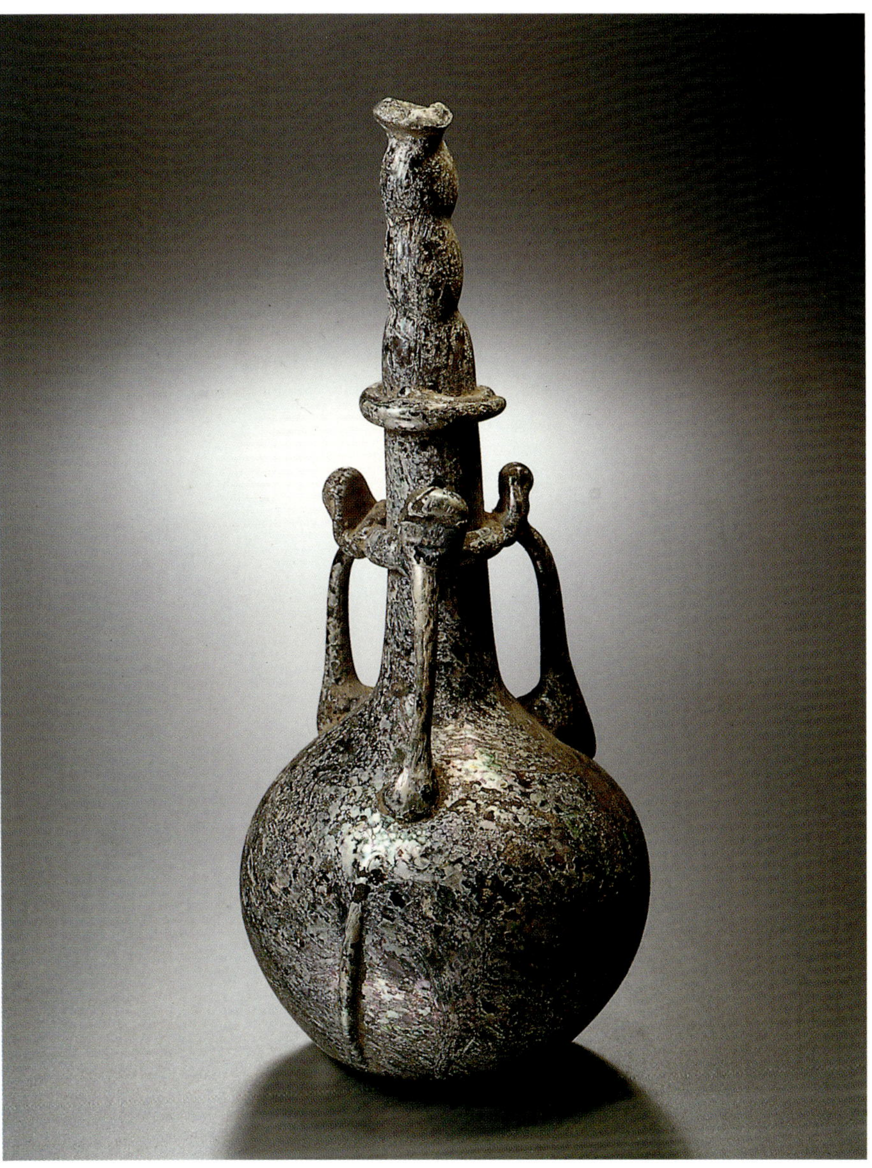

54 Perfume Sprinkler (*Omom*)

Middle East, presumably Iran or Iraq
7th–9th c. AD
H 21, ⌀ 9.9 cm

Colorless, light yellow tone. Free-blown and
shaped.
Heavily corroded, nearly complete layer of
deposits; strongly iridescent.

Acc. no. P 1976-19

Early, completely intact example of the rose-
water sprinkler, which continues to be found
under the name *omom* in Islamic glass art up
to the 18th and 19th centuries. Its type also
influenced Indian glass of the Mogul period.

Lit.: Ricke, "Neue Gläser," 1985, 46f., fig. 5;
Ricke, *2500 Jahre*, 1987, cat. no. 39; Niewöhner, *Sultan*, 1994, 90, no. 58

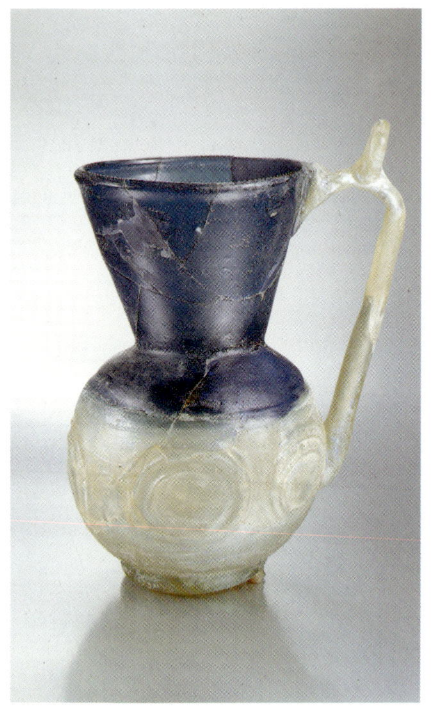

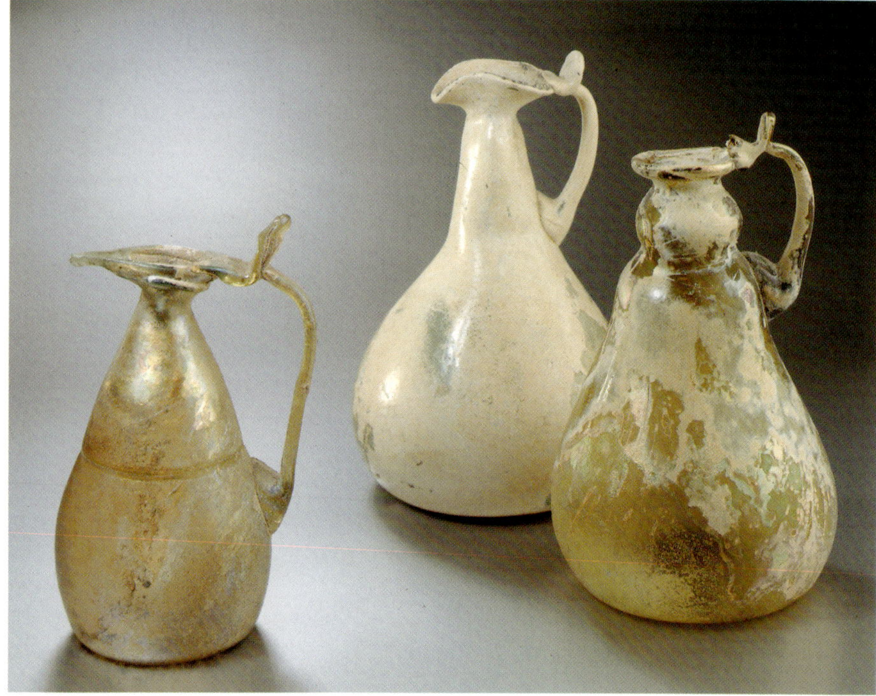

55 Pitcher

Middle East, presumably Iran
8th–10th c. AD
H 16.6, ∅ 9.5 cm

Lower portion: mold-blown (decoration: six oval layered disks); upper portion: mold-blown and shaped. Parts fused in hot state. Corroded, deposits removed. Glued, restored.

Acc. no. P 1971-90
Gift of Helmut Hentrich

Part of a small group of two-colored vessels in the combination colorless-and-blue or colorless-and-violet. More common than pitchers are bell-shaped bottles or globular bottles with cylindrical necks. See Saldern, *Cohn Collection*, 1980, cat. no. 180. The laborious technique of joining two pieces of blown glass, which became popular as *incalmo* in 16th-century Venice, is also documented north of the Alps as early as the 10th century. See Baumgartner and Krueger, *Mittelalter*, 1988, cat. no. 11. For Hellenistic, but not blown, two-colored vessels see A. Oliver, Jr., "Late Hellenistic Glass in the Metropolitan Museum," *JGS* 9 (1967): 17–19. For a monochrome variation see Kroeger, *Nishapur*, 1995, no. 141.

Lit.: Saldern, *Antike und Islam*, 1974, cat. no. 307

56 Pitcher

Middle East, presumably Iran
7th–9th c. AD
H 13, ∅ 6.3 cm

Colorless, light green tone. Probably mold-blown, shaped. Constriction halfway up owing to tooled bulge. Bottom concave. Heavily corroded, deposits, removed on exterior; interior strongly iridescent.

Acc. no. P 1966-95
Gift of Helmut Hentrich

Early, fully developed example of the pear-shaped jug typical of Islamic glass art. This type continued to be used in countless variations and sizes up to the 12th century.

Lit.: Saldern, *Antike und Islam*, 1974, cat. no. 586

57 Pitcher

Middle East, presumably Iran
7th–9th c. AD
H 13.6, ∅ 7.3 cm

Colorless, pale blue-green tone. Free-blown and shaped.
Heavily corroded, nearly complete layer of deposits.

Acc. no. P 1966-44
Gift of Helmut Hentrich

Variation of the pear-shaped pitcher; cf. cat. no. 56.

Lit.: Saldern, *Antike und Islam*, 1974, cat. no. 390

58 Pitcher

Middle East, presumably Iran
7th–9th c. AD
H 14.2, ∅ 8.1 cm

Greenish glass. Free-blown and shaped. Pushed-up bottom.
Heavily corroded; deposits, partly removed.

Acc. no. P 1971-55
Gift of Helmut Hentrich

See cat. nos. 55, 56.

Lit.: Saldern, *Antike und Islam*, 1974, cat. no. 390

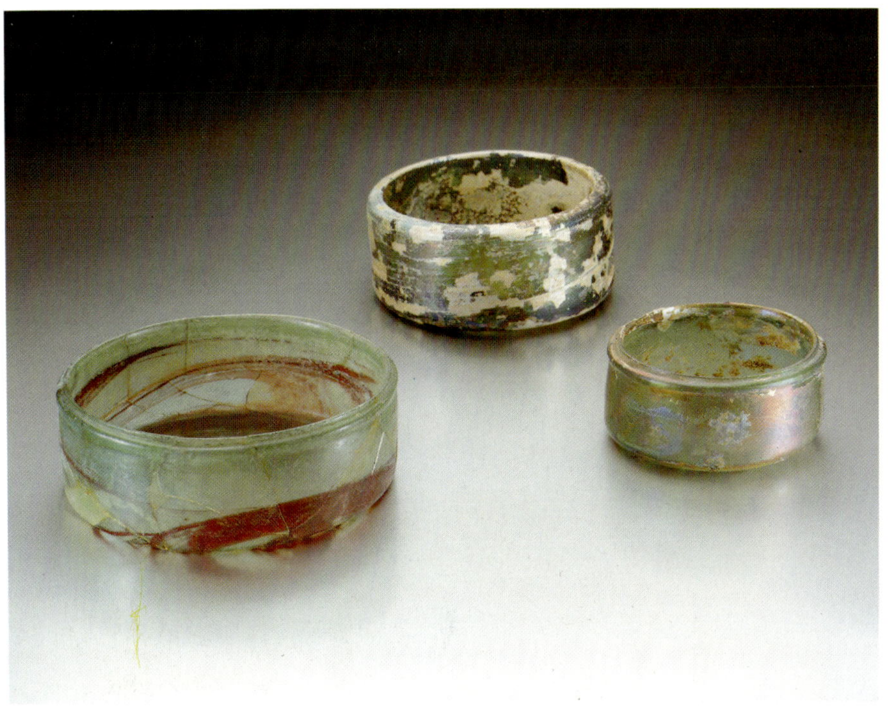

59 Bowl

Middle East, presumably Iran
Probably 8th–10th c. AD
H 3.7, ⌀ 11 cm

Green with dark red streaks. Mold-blown,
shaped.
Slightly corroded, most deposits removed.
Glued, restored.

Acc. no. P 1971-82
Gift of Helmut Hentrich

Most common type of small glass dish for
daily use in early Islamic glass production.
Made in numerous sizes. Most common colors
are green, blue, brown, and black. Red-
streaked examples are unusual.

Lit.: Saldern, *Antike und Islam*, 1974,
cat. no. 354

60 Bowl

Middle East, presumably Iran
Probably 8th–10th c. AD
H 4.3, ⌀ 9.7 cm

Green. Mold-blown, shaped.
Heavily corroded, deposits; strongly iridescent.

Acc. no. P 1966-66
Gift of Helmut Hentrich

See cat. no. 59.

Lit.: Saldern, *Antike und Islam*, 1974,
cat. no. 356

61 Bowl

Middle East, presumably Iran
Probably 8th–10th c. AD
H 3.5, ⌀ 7.4 cm

Like cat. no. 60.

Acc. no. P 1965-167
Gift of Helmut Hentrich

See cat. no. 59.

Lit.: Saldern, *Antike und Islam*, 1974,
cat. no. 355

62 Footed Beaker

Middle East, presumably Iran
Probably 9th/10th c. AD
H 13.2, ⌀ 5.8 cm

Colorless, light yellow tone. Mold-blown,
shaped. Collar and stem with foot were
worked separately. Three staggered rows with
ten small applied prunts each.
Slightly corroded, deposits; slightly iridescent. Glued, restored at the mouth.

Acc. no. P 1973-55
Gift of Helmut Hentrich

Developed from a simpler type of beaker,
without a foot. Very common in Iran. See
also Saldern, *Antike und Islam*, 1974, cat.
no. 326, and Saldern, *Cohn Collection*, 1980,
cat. no. 185.

Lit.: Saldern, *Antike und Islam*, 1974,
cat. no. 325

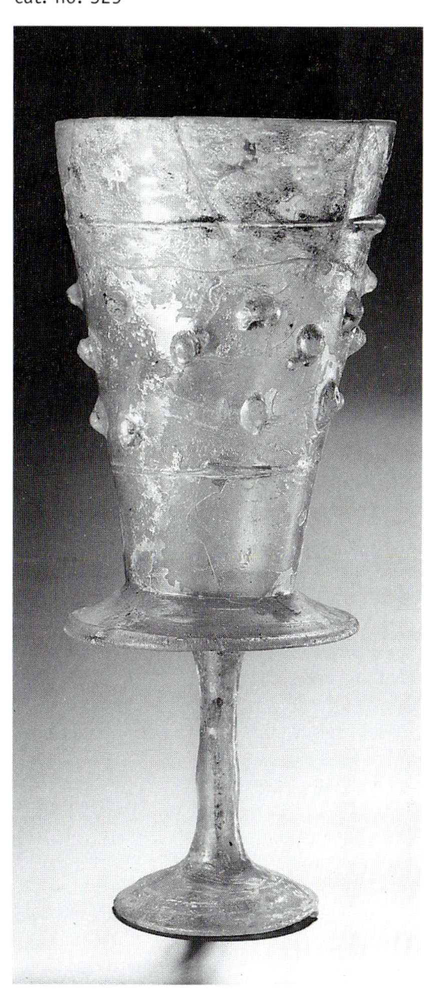

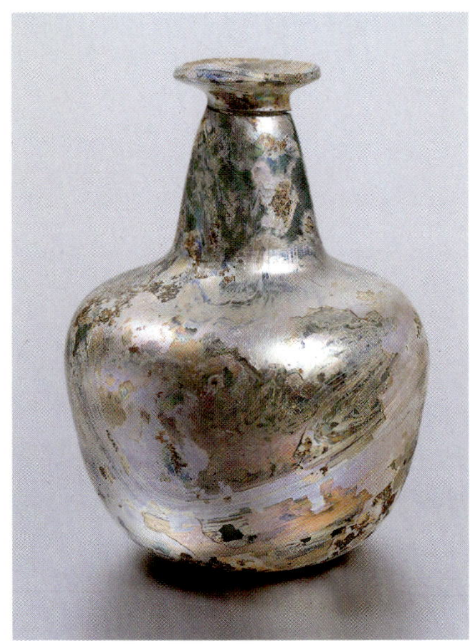

63 Bottle

Middle East, presumably Iran
9th/10th c. AD
H 11.3, ⌀ 8.4 cm

Greenish. Free-blown or mold-blown, shaped.
Corroded; strongly iridescent. Glued at the
neck.

Acc. no. P 1971-100
Gift of Helmut Hentrich

Secured excavations in Sāmarrā' and Nishapur
date this common bottle type to a relatively
narrow time span. It was also used for
engraved and cut decoration.

Lit.: Saldern, *Antike und Islam*, 1974,
cat. no. 360

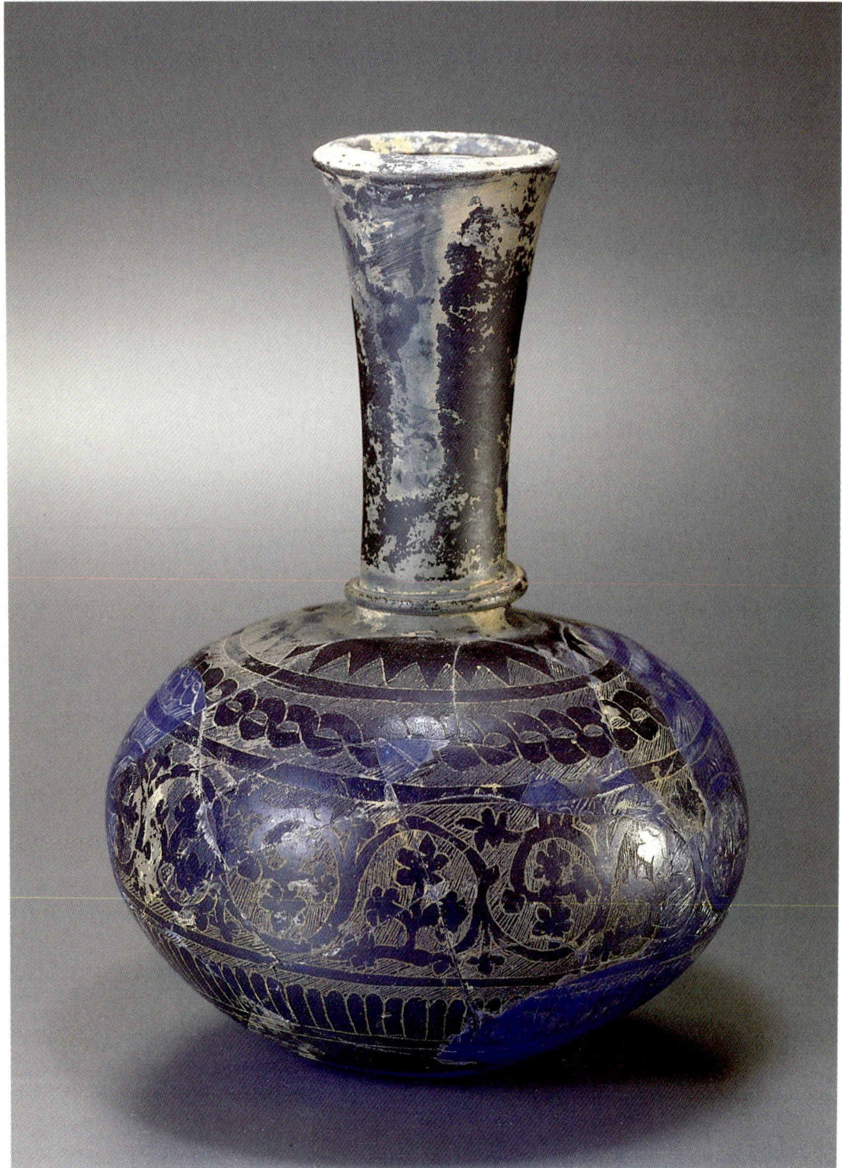

64 Bottle

Middle East, Iran (reportedly found in
Nishapur)
9th c. AD
H 18.6, ⌀ 13.2 cm

Dark blue glass. Mold-blown, shaped.
Diamond-point engraving.
Slightly corroded, remains of deposits.
Glued, large portions of wall restored.

Acc. no. P 1974-19

Within the small group of vessels and
fragments with diamond-point engraving, this bottle is one of the few that
could be completely restored owing to
the extant fragments.

The unusual ornamentation derives from older
types of decoration in textile art.
For this type of decoration see also Kroeger,
Nishapur, 1995, nos. 164/65, and Stefano
Carboni and David Whitehouse, *Glass of the
Sultans*, exh. cat. (New York: The Metropoli-
tan Museum of Art, 2001), 160–67.

Lit.: Ricke, *Ausgewählte Werke*, 1980, 6;
Ricke, *2500 Jahre*, 1987, cat. no. 43;
Niewöhner, *Sultan*, 1994, 16, no. 1

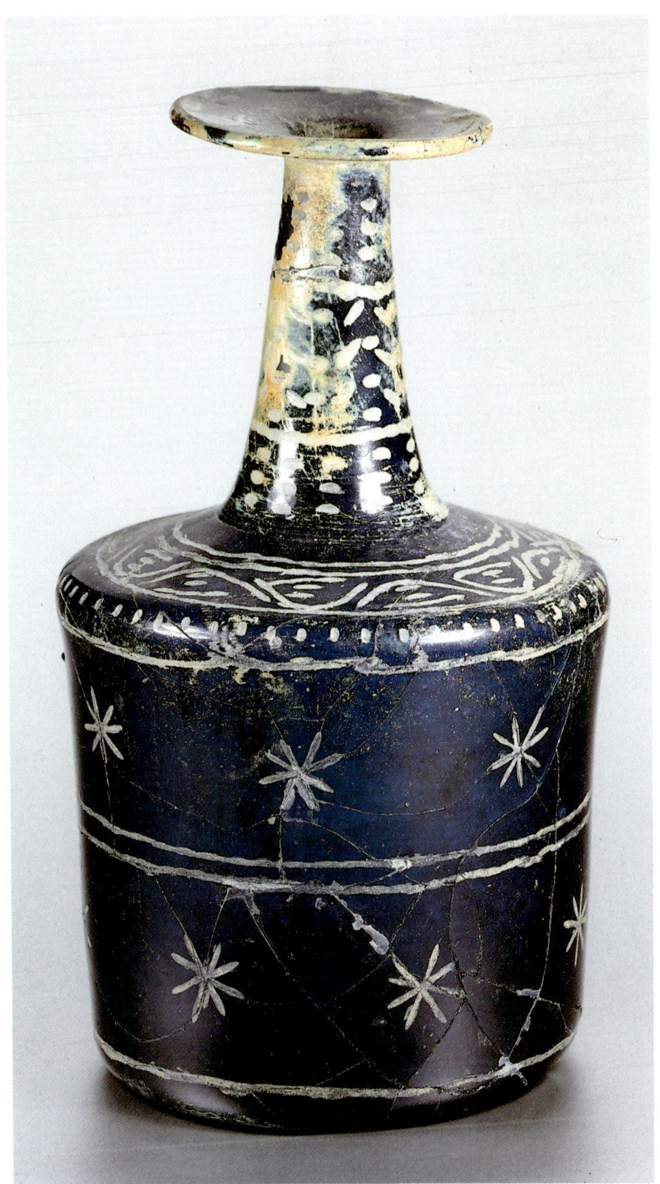

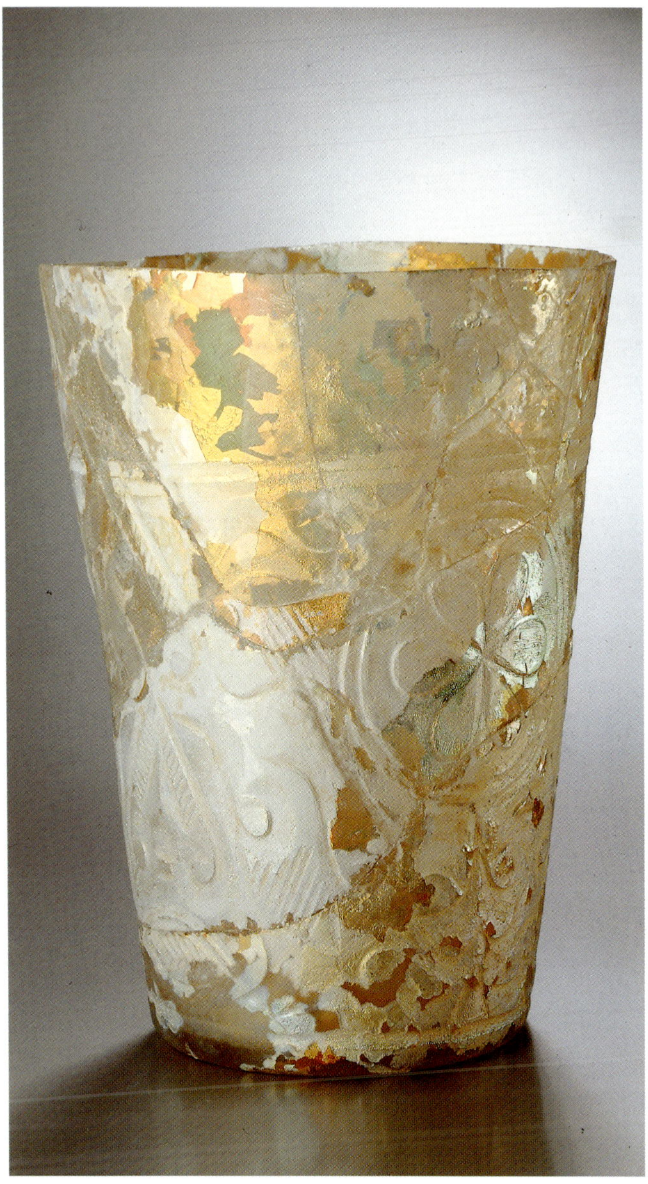

65 Bottle

Middle East, presumably Iran
9th/10th c. AD
H 26.2, ⌀ 15.1 cm

Almost opaque dark blue. Mold-blown,
shaped. Roughly engraved or cut decoration:
on the wall, two staggered rows of eight
stars each.
Partly corroded. Glued.

Acc. no. P 1964-35

Common bottle type, also documented in
other colors, various sizes, and without decoration. See Saldern, *Antike und Islam*, 1974,
cat. no. 360. A more richly cut example is in
Kämpfer, *Viertausend Jahre*, 1966, no. 58.

Lit.: Saldern, *Antike und Islam*, 1974, cat.
no. 407; Niewöhner, *Sultan*, 1994, 81, no. 53

66 Beaker

Middle East, Iran
9th/10th c. AD
H 14.6, ⌀ 11.2 cm

Colorless, light yellow tone. Mold-blown,
shaped. Relief-cut and engraved decoration:
two leaf rosettes on front and back, volute
and arrow motifs.
Heavily corroded, whitish deposits, partly
loosened; strongly iridescent. Glued.

Acc. no. P 1970-4

An example of the Islamic art of cutting,
particularly rich in detail and of excellent
quality. See also Kroeger, *Nishapur*, 1995,
no. 222.

Lit.: Saldern, *Antike und Islam*, 1974,
cat. no. 401

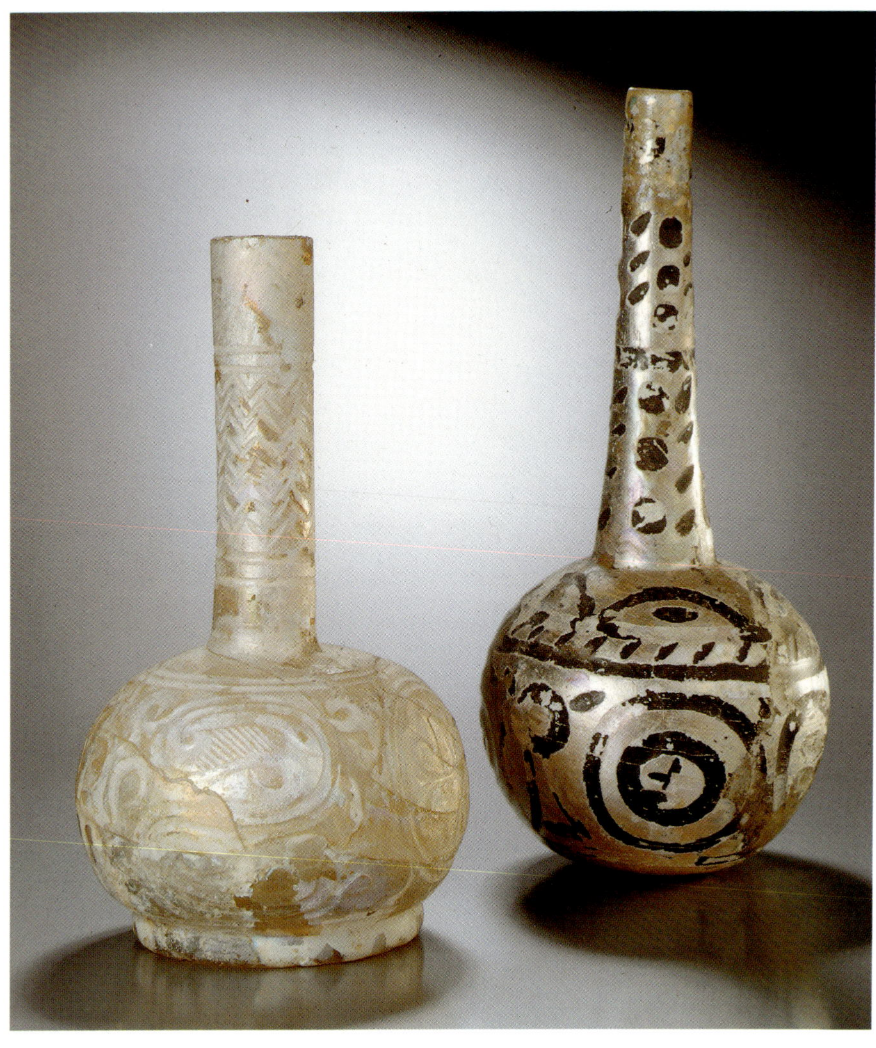

67 Bottle

Middle East, presumably Iran
9th/10th c. AD
H 16.6 cm, ⌀ 9.5 cm

Colorless, light yellow tone. Mold-blown,
shaped. Rich decoration cut and engraved:
two double rings with four inscribed leaf
motifs alternating with S-shaped, wavy foliate spirals and filler motifs. Small star
rosette under the bottom.

Acc. no. P 1971-105
Gift of Helmut Hentrich

For a comparable piece see Kroeger, *Nishapur*,
1995, no. 225.

Lit.: Saldern, *Antike und Islam*, 1974, cat.
no. 411; Niewöhner, *Sultan*, 1994, 80, no. 52

68 Bottle

Middle East, presumably Iran
9th/10th c. AD
H 19.9, ⌀ 9.2 cm

Colorless, light yellow tone. Mold-blown,
shaped, slightly pushed-up bottom. Cut decoration.
Strongly corroded, whitish deposits, black
around the cutting. Glued, mouth partly
restored.

Acc. no. P 1973-41
Gift of Helmut Hentrich

The cutting on this bottle was executed in a
cursory manner. Comparing it with the laborious relief-cut technique of bottle no. 67
clearly illustrates how different the quality in
decoration of the same common bottle type
could be.

Lit.: Saldern, *Antike und Islam*, 1974,
cat. no. 410

69 Molar Flask

Middle East, presumably Iran
9th/10th c. AD
H 7.8, ⌀ 3 cm

Thick-walled blue-green glass. Blown. Decoration cut from the body.
Heavily corroded, deposits partly removed;
iridescent. Two feet slightly restored.

Acc. no. P 1973-78
Gift of Helmut Hentrich

Belongs to a small group of glasses cut in a
highly sculptural manner. Dating secured by
finds in Sāmarrā'. For a larger group of these
vessels see *3000 Jahre*, Lucerne, 1981, cat.
nos. 606–14.

Lit.: Saldern, *Antike und Islam*, 1974, cat.
no. 419; Ricke, *2500 Jahre*, 1987, cat. no. 45

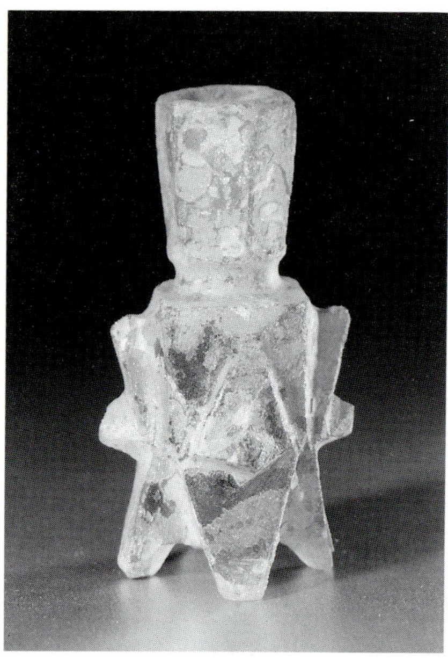

70 Bottle

Middle East, presumably Iran
9th/10th century
H 13.8, ⌀ 8.8 cm

Colorless glass with light green tone. Mold-blown, shaped. Cutting covers nearly the whole surface.
Slightly corroded, deposits; strongly iridescent.

Acc. no. P 1973-51
Gift of Helmut Hentrich

The decoration of simple, round, cut facets, almost inevitable when working with flat engraving wheels, can be observed continuously from Roman glass art to that of the Sassanids. A variation is the honeycomb pattern with overlapping round facets.

Lit.: Saldern, *Antike und Islam*, 1974, cat. no. 413

71 Small Box

Middle East, presumably Iran
9th/10th c. AD
H 5, L 11.5, D 4.9 cm

Colorless glass with light yellow tone. Mold-blown, shaped. Cut decoration executed in a

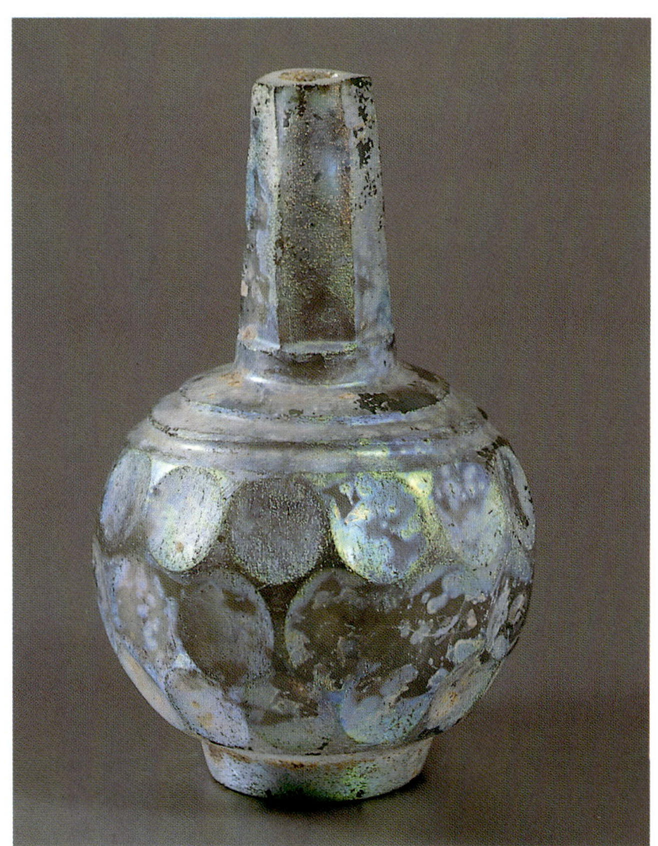

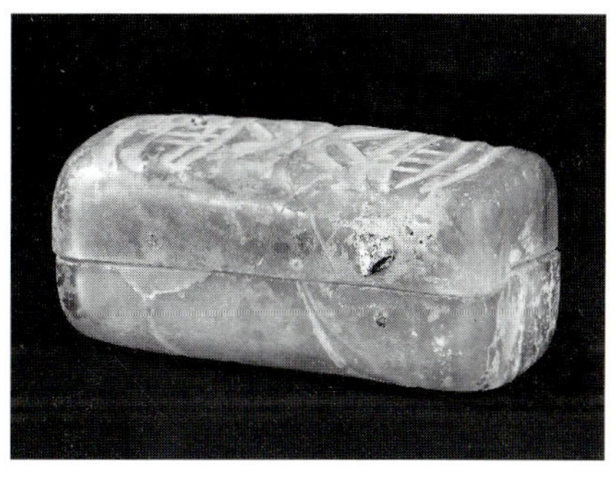

cursory manner. Under the bottom: four ovals with two horizontal cut lines each. On the lid: star motifs flanked by two pointed ovals divided horizontally in three.
Corroded, remains of deposits. Glued, small areas restored. Remains of metal mounts for the opening device, presumably a leather hinge.

Acc. no. P 1966-333
Gift of Helmut Hentrich

Possibly a container for writing utensils. Small glass boxes of this type are documented only in limited numbers.

Lit.: Saldern, *Antike und Islam*, 1974, cat. no. 423

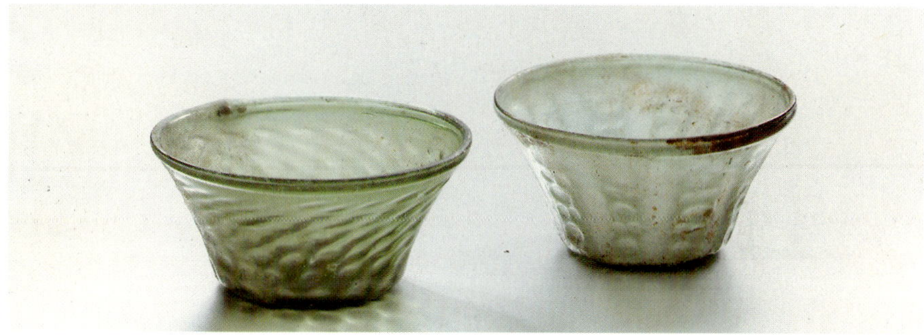

72 Bowl

Middle East, presumably Iran
10th–12th c. AD
H 4.5, ⌀ 9.7 cm

Light green glass. Optic-blown and shaped. Thickened rim, pushed-up bottom. Optic decoration changing from a honeycomb pattern at the bottom to diagonal ribs towards the top. Only slightly corroded, hardly any deposits.

Acc. no. P 1965-112
Gift of Helmut Hentrich

Besides the earlier bowls with vertical walls (cf. cat. nos. 59–61), the most common type of bowl in Islamic glass art. Usually green and undecorated, but also made in various other colors (usually blue) and different types of decoration.

Lit.: Saldern, *Antike und Islam*, 1974, cat. no. 316; Niewöhner, *Sultan*, 1994, 32, nos. 17/18

73 Bowl

Middle East, presumably Iran
10th–12th c. AD
H 4.9, ⌀ 9.5 cm

Greenish glass. Optic-blown and shaped. Thickened rim, slightly pushed-up bottom. Relief decoration: ten vertical bands alternating with circles and double circles. Corroded, cleaned.

Acc. no. P 1966-59
Gift of Helmut Hentrich

See cat. no. 72.

Lit.: Saldern, *Antike und Islam*, 1974, cat. no. 315

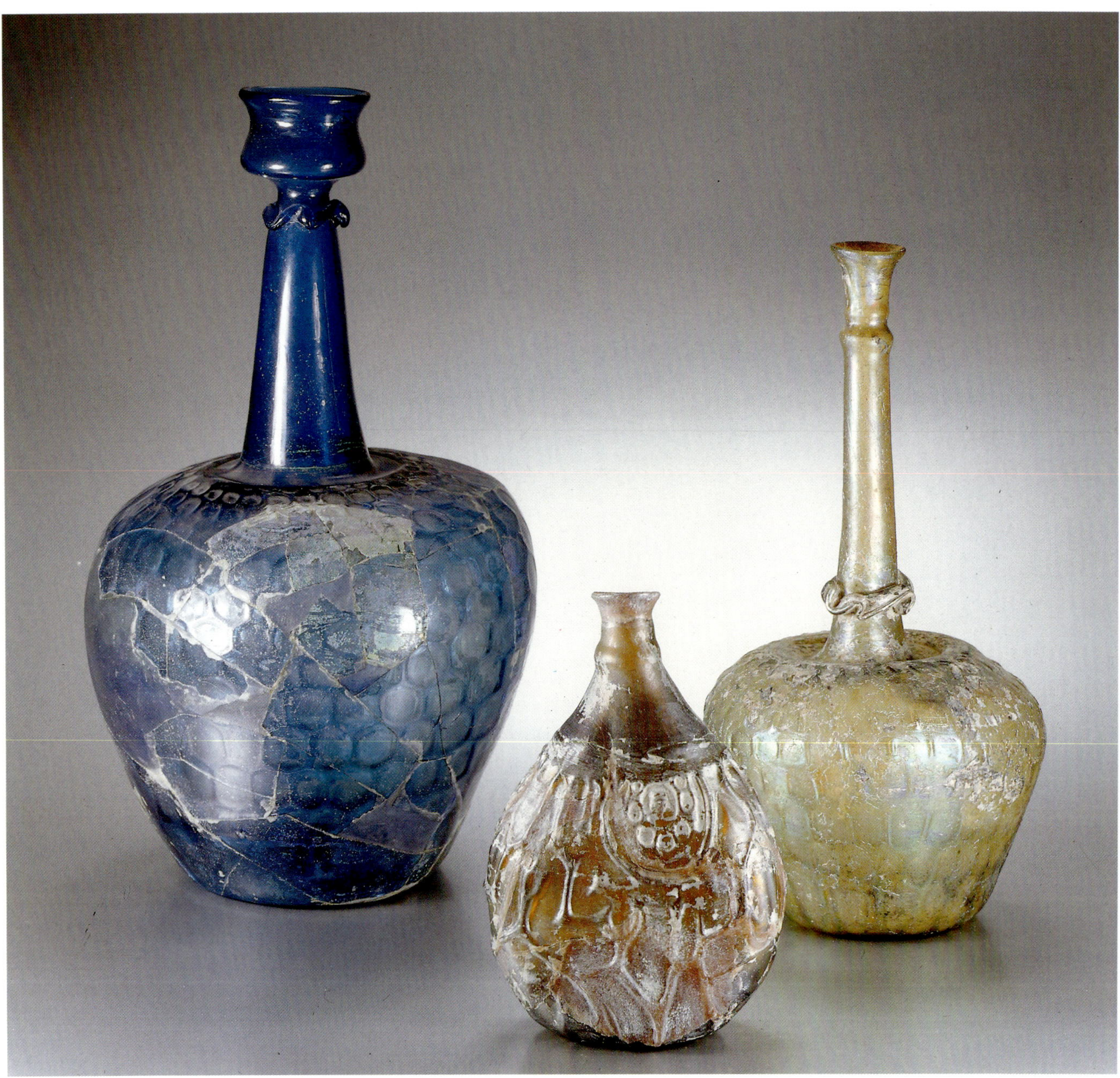

74 Bottle

Middle East, presumably Iran
10th–12th c. AD
H 29.4, ⌀ 16.9 cm

Optic-blown, shaped. Bottom concave. Honeycomb pattern.
Slightly corroded, deposits. Glued, about one-sixth of wall restored.

Acc. no. P 1970-533
Gift of Helmut Hentrich

The honeycomb pattern is the most common type of decoration in Islamic optic-blown glassware.

Lit.: Saldern, *Antike und Islam*, 1974, cat. no. 293

75 Bottle

Middle East, presumably Iran
10th–12th c. AD
H 14, ⌀ 9.6 x 4.4 cm

Optic-blown, shaped. Pushed-up bottom. Slightly corroded, deposits. Glued, about one-fifth of wall restored.

Acc. no. P 1971-80
Gift of Helmut Hentrich

The optical pattern of a honeycomb with three wheel motifs was very common, but was usually not used for vessels with an oval cross section. See Saldern, *Antike und Islam*, 1974, cat. nos. 290ff.

Lit.: Saldern, *Antike und Islam*, 1974, cat. no. 299

76 Bottle

Middle East, presumably Iran
10th–12th c. AD
H 23.3, ⌀ 12 cm

Optic-blown. Pushed-up bottom. Corroded, deposits partly loosened.

Acc. no. P 1965-200
Gift of Helmut Hentrich

See cat. no. 74. For a direct parallel, and other examples of this type of optic-blown bottle, see Saldern, *Cohn Collection*, 1980, cat. no. 165

Lit.: Saldern, *Antike und Islam*, 1974, cat. no. 291; Niewöhner, *Sultan*, 1994, 17, no. 3

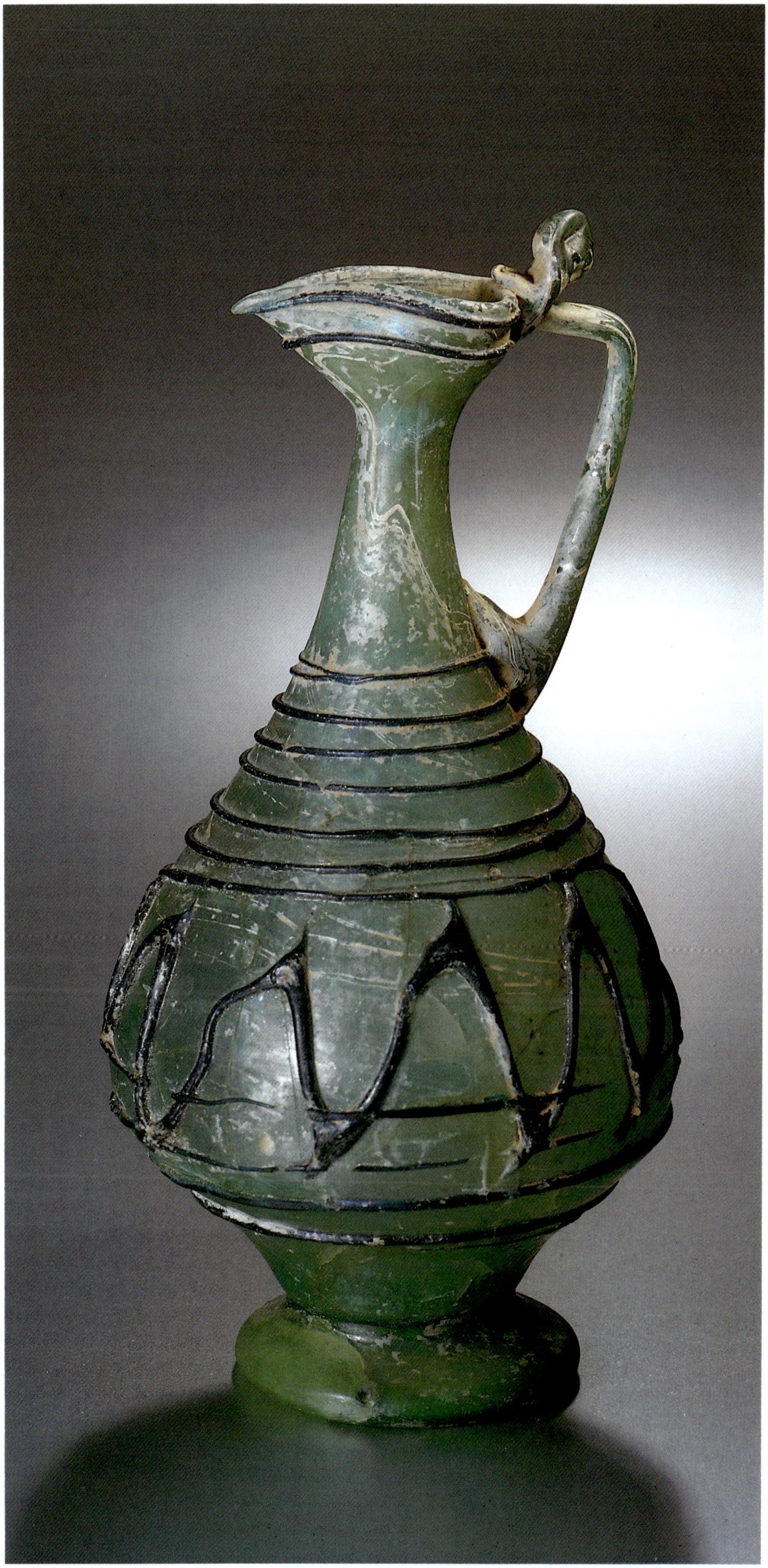

77   Pitcher

Middle East, presumably Iran or Iraq
10th–12th c. AD
H 20.7, ⌀ 10.5 cm

Mold-blown, shaped. Freely applied threads.
Slightly corroded, deposits mostly removed.
Part of foot restored.

Acc. no. P 1974-18

A later variation of the Islamic pear-shaped
pitcher. Cf. cat. nos. 56–58 In contrast to the
highly sculptural thread applications of early
Islamic glassware (see, for example, Saldern,
Antike und Islam, 1974, cat. nos. 327ff.), the
thread decoration on this bottle recalls late
Roman prototypes.

Lit.: Ricke, *Ausgewählte Werke*, 1980, 6;
Ricke, *2500 Jahre*, 1987, cat. no. 46

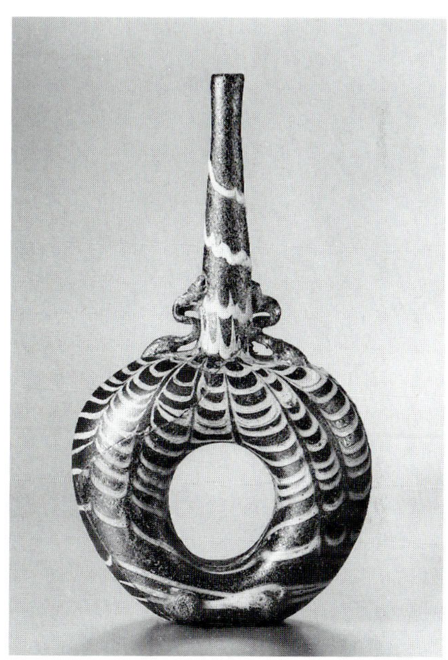

78   Perfume Sprinkler (*Omom*)

Middle East
Presumably 10th–12th c. AD
H 12.6, ⌀ 7.1 cm

Violet glass appearing brown-black. Free-
blown and shaped, white encircling thread
decoration combed into a feather pattern.
Four small button feet.
Corroded, cleaned. About half of body
restored.

Acc. no. P 1965-77
Gift of Helmut Hentrich

A variation of the rose-water sprinkler; cf.
cat. no. 54.

Lit.: Saldern, *Antike und Islam*, 1974,
cat. no. 342

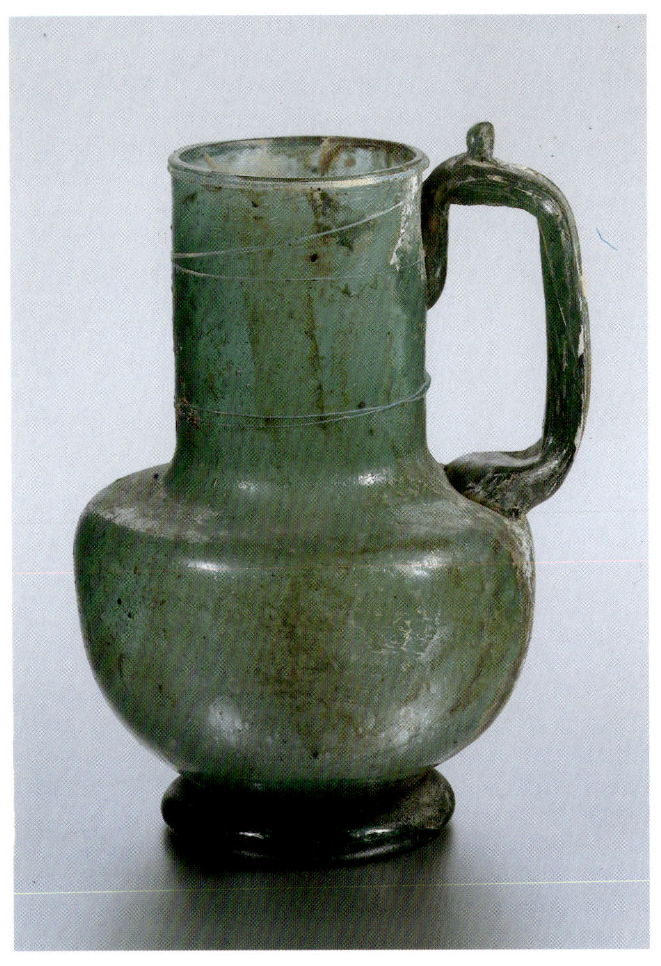

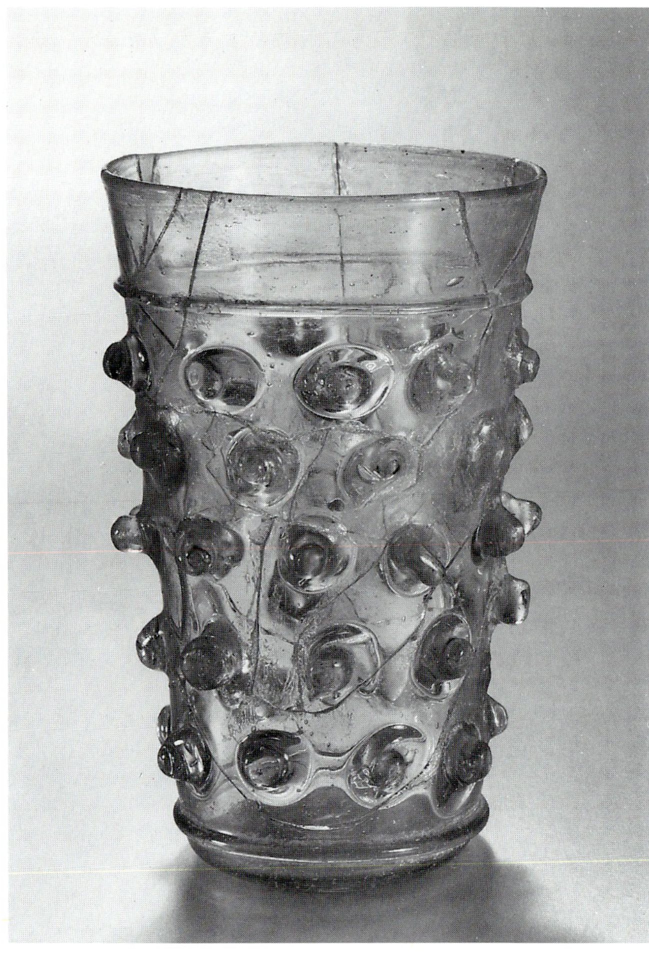

79 Pitcher

Middle East, presumably Iran
10th–12th c. AD
H 21.4, ⌀ 14 cm

Mold-blown, shaped. Handle freely applied.
Slightly corroded. Deposits removed.

Acc. no. P 1966-79
Gift of Helmut Hentrich

Rare shape in an unusual turquoise tone.

Lit.: Saldern, *Antike und Islam*, 1974,
cat. no. 394

80 Prunt Beaker

Middle East, presumably Iran (reportedly
found in Nishapur)
Probably 10th–12th c. AD
H 10.7, ⌀ 6.9 cm

Colorless, light yellow tone. Mold-blown,
shaped. Bottom slightly concave. Four rows
of nine prunts each, below these, one row of
eight.
Slightly corroded, cleaned. Glued, about one-
eighth of wall restored.

Acc. no. P 1980-1

No comparable pieces have been found to
date. It links Islamic glass design with the
central European prunt beaker (*Nuppenbecher*)
of the high Middle Ages, attesting to Eastern
influences in the north. Cf. also cat. no. 88.

Lit.: Ricke, "Neue Gläser," 1985, 48, fig. 7;
Baumgartner and Krueger, *Mittelalter*, 1988,
cat. no. 166

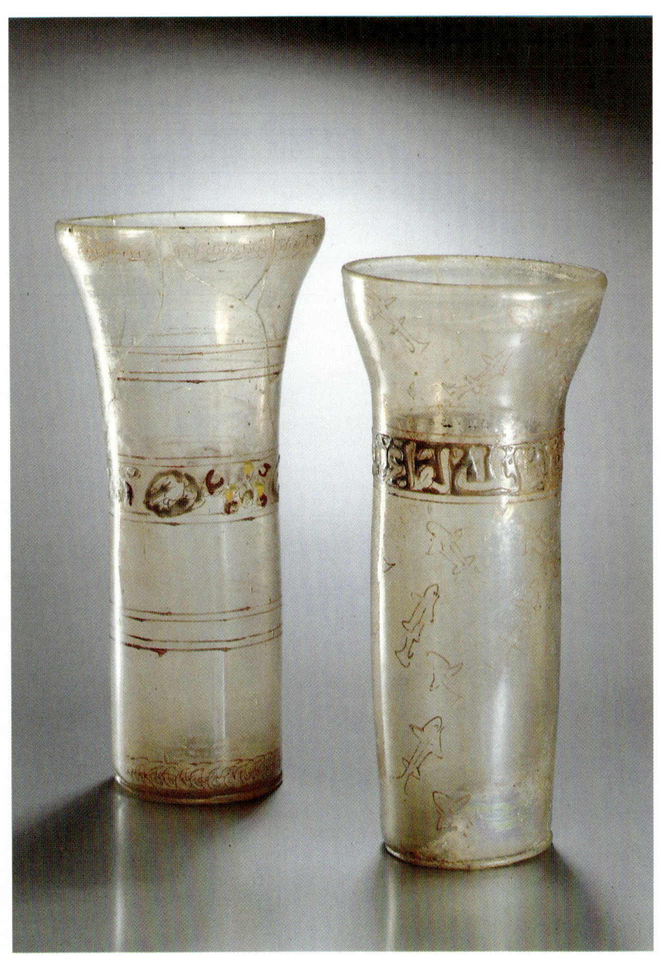

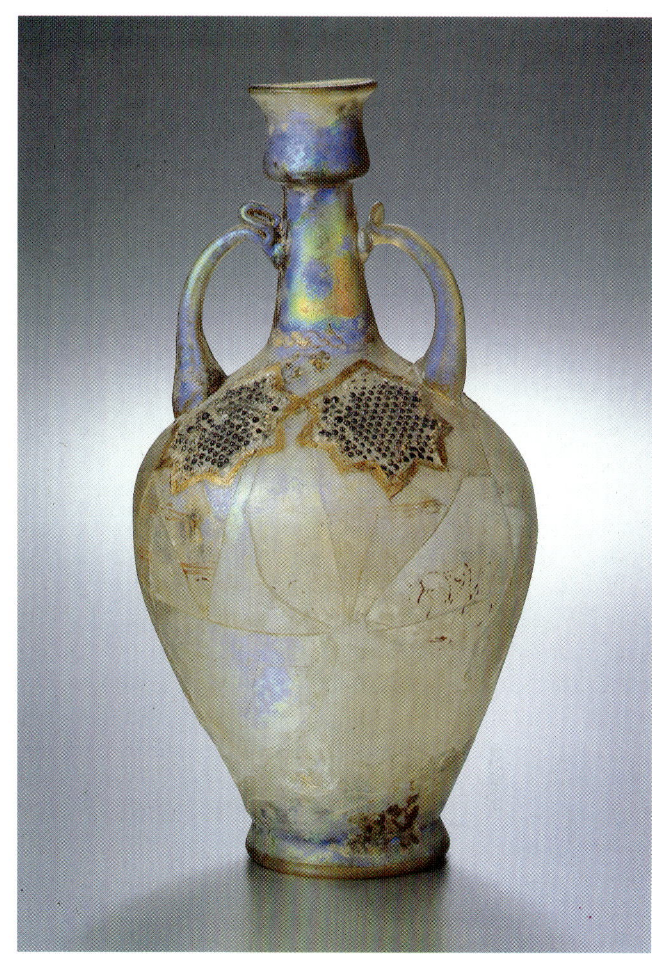

81 Beaker or Lamp

Middle East, Syria
Presumably Damascus (or Aleppo?)
Late 13th/early 14th c. AD
H 19.7, ⌀ 9.6 cm

Mold-blown, shaped. Pushed-up bottom, added foot-ring. Enamel and gold painted decoration. Enamel painting well preserved. Gold strongly rubbed. Decoration: braid ornament above the foot and below the mouth. In the main frieze, four medallions with birds of prey between cursorily painted arabesques. Slightly corroded, cleaned. Glued, slightly restored.

Acc. no. P 1973-67
Gift of Helmut Hentrich

Lit.: Saldern, *Antike und Islam*, 1974, cat. no. 426

82 Beaker or Lamp

Middle East, Syria
Presumably Damascus (or Aleppo?)
Late 13th/early 14th c. AD
H 18.6, ⌀ 8.5 cm

Like cat. no. 81. Enamel decoration: fish outlined in red. Kufic script consisting of the blank areas in the red-painted band. Translated it reads: "For the great and noble *Sultan*, our Lord."

Acc. no. P 1939-17
Formerly Staatliche Museen Berlin

The two beakers represent the most common type of Islamic glass art before the Mongolian conquest in 1400. The cursory manner in which the decoration is executed indicates that this type of glassware was made in large numbers.

Lit.: Saldern, *Antike und Islam*, 1974, cat. no. 427; Ricke, *2500 Jahre*, 1987, cat. no. 50; A. Shalem, "Fountains of Light: The Meaning of Medieval Islamic Rock Crystal Lamps," *Muquarnas* 2 (1994): 1–11, fig. 8

83 Bottle

Middle East, Syria (Aleppo?)
14th c. AD
H 23.3, ⌀ 12.5 cm

Mold-blown, shaped. Foot added. Enamel and gold painted decoration.
Corroded, cleaned. Glued, parts of wall restored. Enamel and gold decoration extant only in fragments. Composition of decoration: Delicate rope-like band on the neck; below, on each side of the vessel, two stars outlined in gold, with raised enamel dots; below, narrow frieze with extremely delicate characters; then, broad band with stylized vine scroll decoration and another banderole. Three concentric lines separate the individual ornamental zones. All details were originally outlined in red.

Acc. no. P 1974-8

Besides the many extant oil lamps, beakers, and long-necked bottles of late medieval Islamic glass art, the two-handled bottle occupies a special position. Its composition derives from the ancient amphora type, translated in details and proportions into the Islamic concept of form.

Lit.: Ricke, *Ausgewählte Werke*, 1980, 7; Niewöhner, *Sultan*, 1994, 83, no. 55

The Middle Ages

Glass utility glassware continued to be highly valued north of the Alps during the early Frankish reign. Large numbers of vessels for daily use (cat. no. 85) certainly also continued to be produced in the former Roman centers of the Rhineland, as objects found in the region's graves indicate. A considerable number of the developed vessel types drew directly on late Roman techniques and detailing. The claw beaker (*Rüsselbecher*) of the sixth/seventh centuries with its complicated composition is one example. Others, such as glass drinking horns, footless tumblers, and bell beakers (cat. nos. 84, 86), incorporated their own traditional forms and took Frankish drinking habits into consideration.

It is generally believed that the ancient world fell into decline during the turmoil of the Migration Period and that Western Christian culture gradually formed under the Carolingians in medieval times. This view would seem, however, to find no correspondence in historical writing on glass art. Instead, writers assume that after a gradual decline of late Roman glass culture simple glass production dropped to the lowest technical level in the Frankish empire under Carolingian rule.

These ideas have hardly any justification in view of more recent research. As documented by newer finds from Viking graves in Scandinavia, glass art reached an astonishing new peak during the Carolingian and Ottonian periods—parallel to the "renaissance" of antiquity in all other areas of art. Complicated thread-glass techniques were used as often as gold-leaf decoration and several types of colored glass, which glassmakers even knew how to fuse seam to seam.

The remoteness of the places where this glassware was found also explains why early medieval glass art continues to be underestimated to this day. The pagan tribes of the north maintained the custom of depositing goods in the graves of the dead for a longer period than the Christianized Franks, whose luxury glass was thus irrevocably lost.

The lack of significant glass finds from the early Middle Ages was long attributed to the clergy's assumed hostility to glass. Allegedly they wanted glass used only for windows of sacred buildings. These ideas were applied, unconfirmed, to the high Middle Ages. It went so far that the few extant examples of enamel painted beakers of the late thirteenth century (cat. no. 87)—clearly illustrating a highly developed formal and decorative idiom—were ascribed to Christian artisans assumed to have been active in workshops dependent on Islamic glass art in the crusader countries of Syria and Palestine.

Today it is almost certain that many of these so-called Syro-Frankish beakers were painted in Venetian workshops. Owing to vigorous trade in the Levant, the Serenissima had always maintained close ties with the East.

Numerous other glass vessels found in recent excavations also reflect Eastern influences. *Nuppenbecher*, like the extremely thin work from the Amendt Collection (cat. no. 88), have precursors in Persian glass art (cat. no. 80). In addition, vessels with painstakingly applied decorative blue threading impressively contradict the hypothesis that no highly developed glass art existed during the period of the knights, minnesingers, and court poets.

Thus it becomes increasingly clear that the production of such high-quality and technically complex glassware was not restricted to the Mediterranean or even exclusively to Venice. It must be assumed that in numerous regions in the north colorless, hollow glassware with colored decoration was produced parallel to colorless, colored, or even cased colored flat glass for the churches of the period. The role Venice played in this period has yet to be determined. The lagoon city should therefore by no means be thought of as the only place where fine glass was produced in the Middle Ages. Important impulses would also seem to have come from the north.

With cities flourishing and a bourgeoisie fast eclipsing the age of the knights, the most common types of glass vessel shifted increasingly from luxury goods to utilitarian wares. Artisans preferred strong green tones for the glass body—not for lack of skill, but as a conscious choice. The walls were of a functional thickness and usually decorated with prunts for a firm grip. The so-called *Waldglas* (literally, "forest glass"), its most common types being the *Kuttrolf* (cat. no. 92), the *Maigelein*, the *Rippenbecher* (ribbed beaker), and the *Krautstrunk* (cat. nos. 95–97), epitomizes a period in which glass became part of daily life.

These glass types were made primarily in the forests of the low mountain ranges of Germany, most notably in the Spessart.

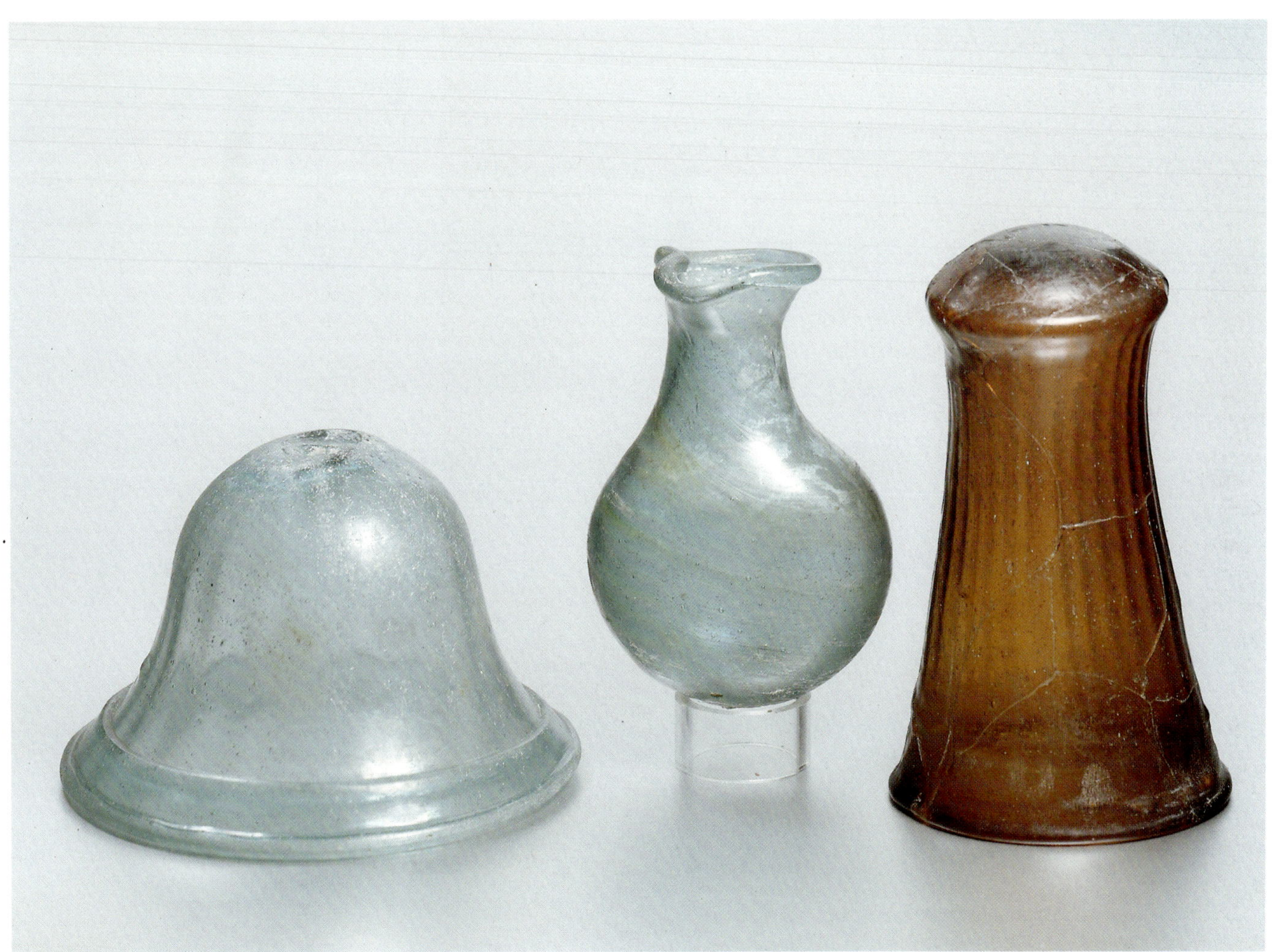

84 Tumbler

Frankish Empire, presumably the Rhineland
6th/7th c.
H 8.2, ⌀ 11.3 cm

Optic-blown, shaped. Rim of mouth folded
inwards, no standing base, slightly pushed-up
bottom.
Slightly corroded, slightly iridescent.

Acc. no. P 1934-112
Formerly Rheinisches Landesmuseum Bonn

A particularly common type of Frankish dish
in the Rhineland. The Rheinisches Landesmuseum in Bonn has the largest collection.

Lit.: Heinemeyer, *Glas*, 1966, cat. no. 78;
Saldern, *Alte Gläser*, 1968, cat. no. 8

85 Bottle

Frankish Empire, presumably the Rhineland
5th/6th c.
H 6.6, ⌀ 3.7 cm

Free-blown, shaped. Rim of mouth folded
inwards, no standing base.
Slightly corroded, deposits. Slightly iridescent.

Acc. no. P 1934-111
Formerly Rheinisches Landesmuseum Bonn

Simple utilitarian vessel; type directly
derived from Roman bottles with cloverleaf
mouth. Not very common.

Lit.: Heinemeyer, *Glas*, 1966, cat. no. 76

86 Bell Beaker

Frankish Empire, presumably the Rhineland
6th c.
H 12.5, ⌀ 7.4 cm

Optic-blown, shaped. Rim folded inwards, no
standing base.
Slightly corroded, slightly iridescent. Glued,
minimally restored.

Acc. no. P 1989-20A

Like the tumbler, very common in the
Rhineland during the Frankish period. Many
shapes exist, some even have thread decoration. The standard color is green, though
brown also exists, but is rare.

Lit.: –

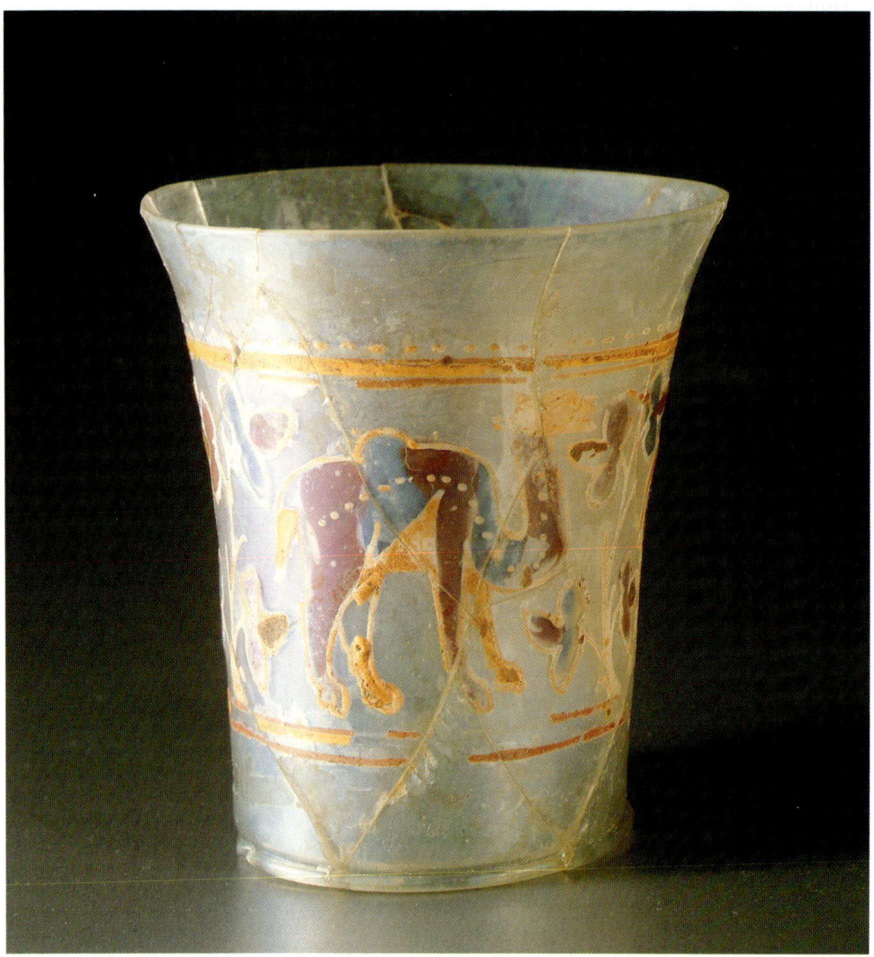

87   Beaker

Europe, presumably NW Mediterranean
(Murano?) (reportedly found in a town along
the Middle Rhine)
2nd half of 13th/early 14th c.
H 8, ⌀ 7.7 cm

Colorless, light yellow tone. Probably mold-
blown, shaped. Thread wrapped around the
bottom to serve as a standing base. Pushed-
up bottom.
Enamel-painted. Decoration: encircling band
showing three dromedaries separated by plant
motifs with four trifoliate leaves.
Slightly corroded, thus enamel colors somewhat altered. Glued, slightly restored; somewhat iridescent.

Acc. no. L 1989-1
On loan from the Karl Amendt Collection,
Krefeld

One of the best-preserved pieces from the
small group of high medieval enamel-painted
beakers, which for a long time were considered imports from the East (so-called Syro-
Frankish glassware). The dromedary motif
cannot be taken as proof of that provenance,
since it recurs in European architectural
sculpture and small works of art.
Although recent evidence increasingly points
to such glassware having been made north of
the Alps as well, we can assume this piece to
have originated in one of the documented
workshops in Murano.

Lit.: Baumgartner and Krueger, *Mittelalter*,
1988, cat. no. 92

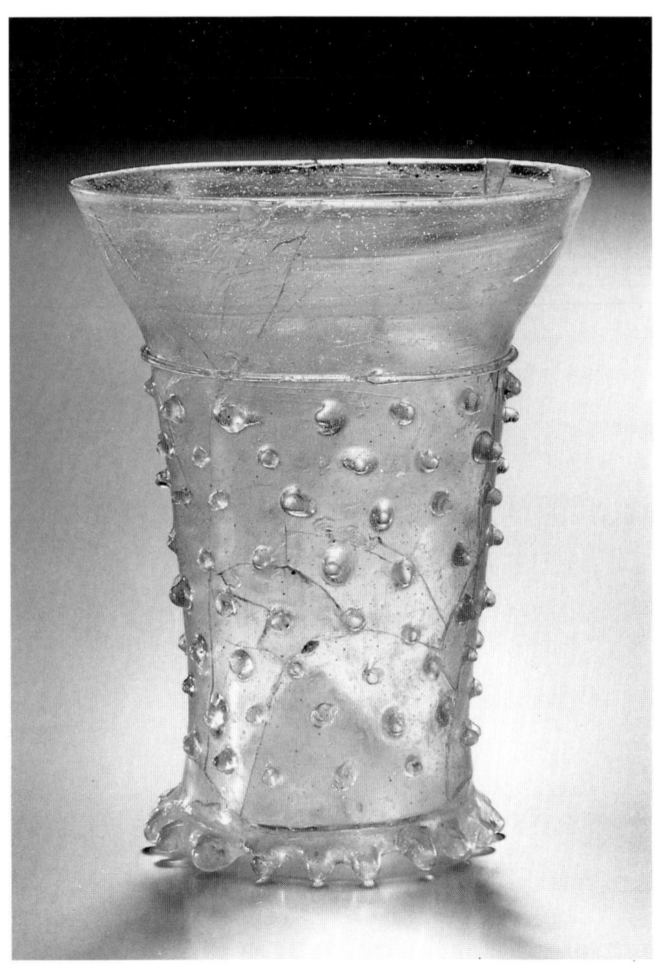

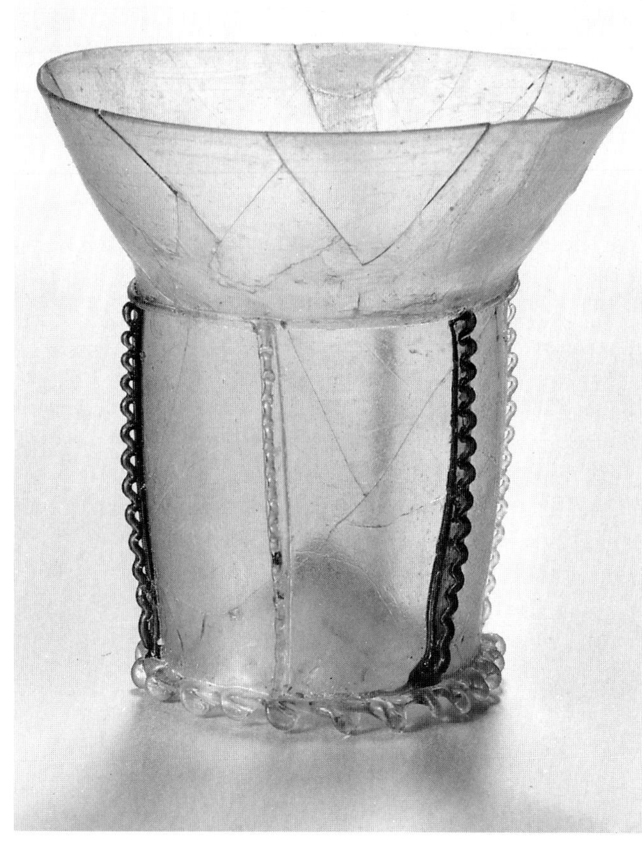

88 *Nuppenbecher*

Probably Germany (reportedly found in Speyer)
2nd half of 13th/early 14th c.
H 10.7, ⌀ 8.7 cm

Colorless. Probably mold-blown, shaped.
Small feet drawn from foot-ring. Delicate
prunts applied in 8 rows of 13 each.
Slightly corroded, cleaned. Glued, pushed-up
(?) bottom and portions of wall restored.

Acc. no. L 1989-2
On loan from the Karl Amendt Collection,
Krefeld

The finest prunt beaker known from the high
Middle Ages. Similar quality is otherwise
known only from fragments. Very probably
made north of the Alps.

Lit.: Baumgartner and Krueger, *Mittelalter*,
1988, cat. no. 168

89 Looped-Thread Beaker

Probably Germany (reportedly found in Speyer)
2nd half of 13th/early 14th c.
H 10.1, ⌀ 9.8 cm

Colorless. Probably mold-blown, shaped. Pincered foot-ring, pushed-up bottom. Freely
applied looped-thread decoration, alternatingly colorless and light blue.
Slightly corroded, cleaned. Glued. Wall slightly, lip heavily restored.

Acc. no. P 1979-7

The looped-thread decoration is one of the
highest technical achievements of glass art
in the high Middle Ages. It was executed
with a precision equal to the best Roman
snake-thread glassware of the Rhineland.
Only a few fragments made by this decorative
technique have become known. The Düsseldorf beaker is the only piece that could be
reliably restored.

Lit.: Baumgartner and Krueger, *Mittelalter*,
1988, cat. no. 155

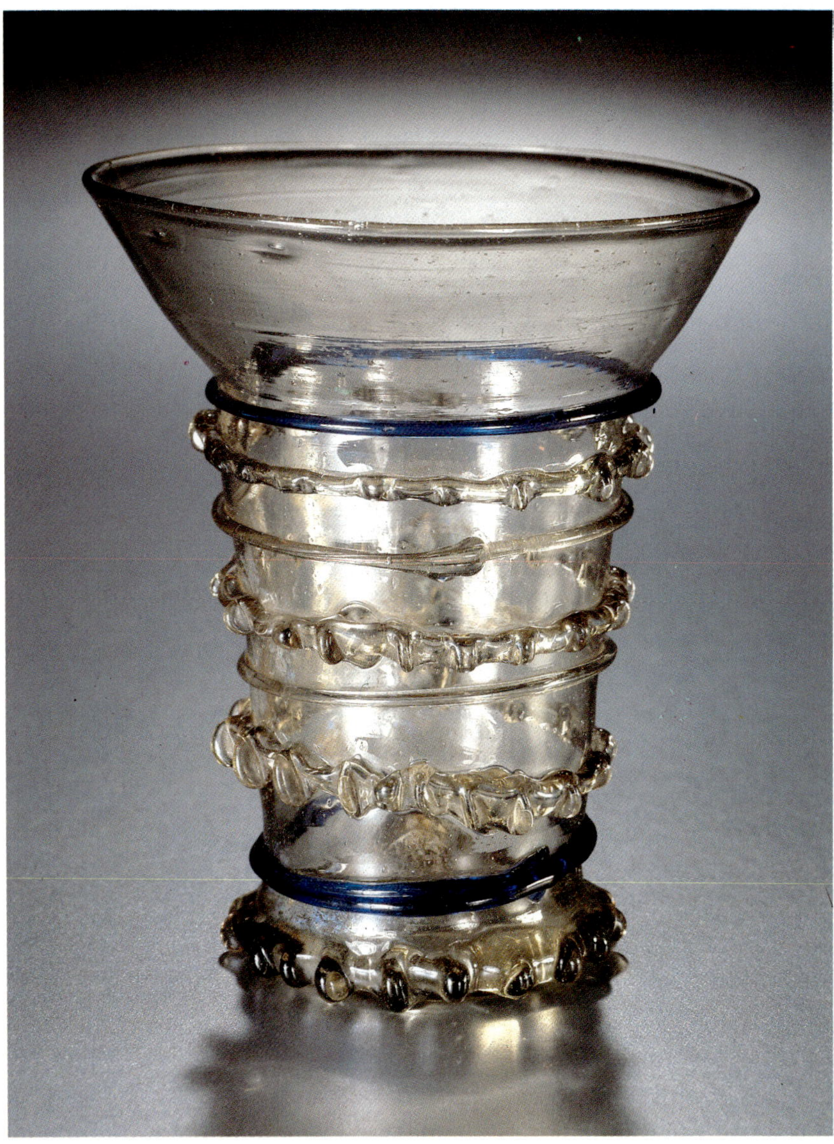

90 Beaker

Probably Germany
2nd half of 13th/early 14th c.
H 10.3, ∅ 9 cm

Colorless, light gray tone. Probably mold-
blown, shaped. Small feet pulled from foot-
ring. Concentrically applied threads, dark
blue at top and bottom, alternating between
smooth and pincered.

Acc. no. P 1940-59
Formerly Johannes Jantzen Collection, Bremen; previously Miller von Aichholz Collection

The beaker is one the few completely intact
glasses of the high Gothic period. It was
never underground and probably served as a
reliquary (remains of soiling). Its shape
recalls that of Islamic vessels; this type is
also known to have been adorned with prunts
and looped threads.

Lit.: Heinemeyer, *Glas*, 1966, cat. no. 117;
Ricke, *2500 Jahre*, 1987, cat. no. 52;
Baumgartner and Krueger, *Mittelalter*, 1988,
cat. no. 150

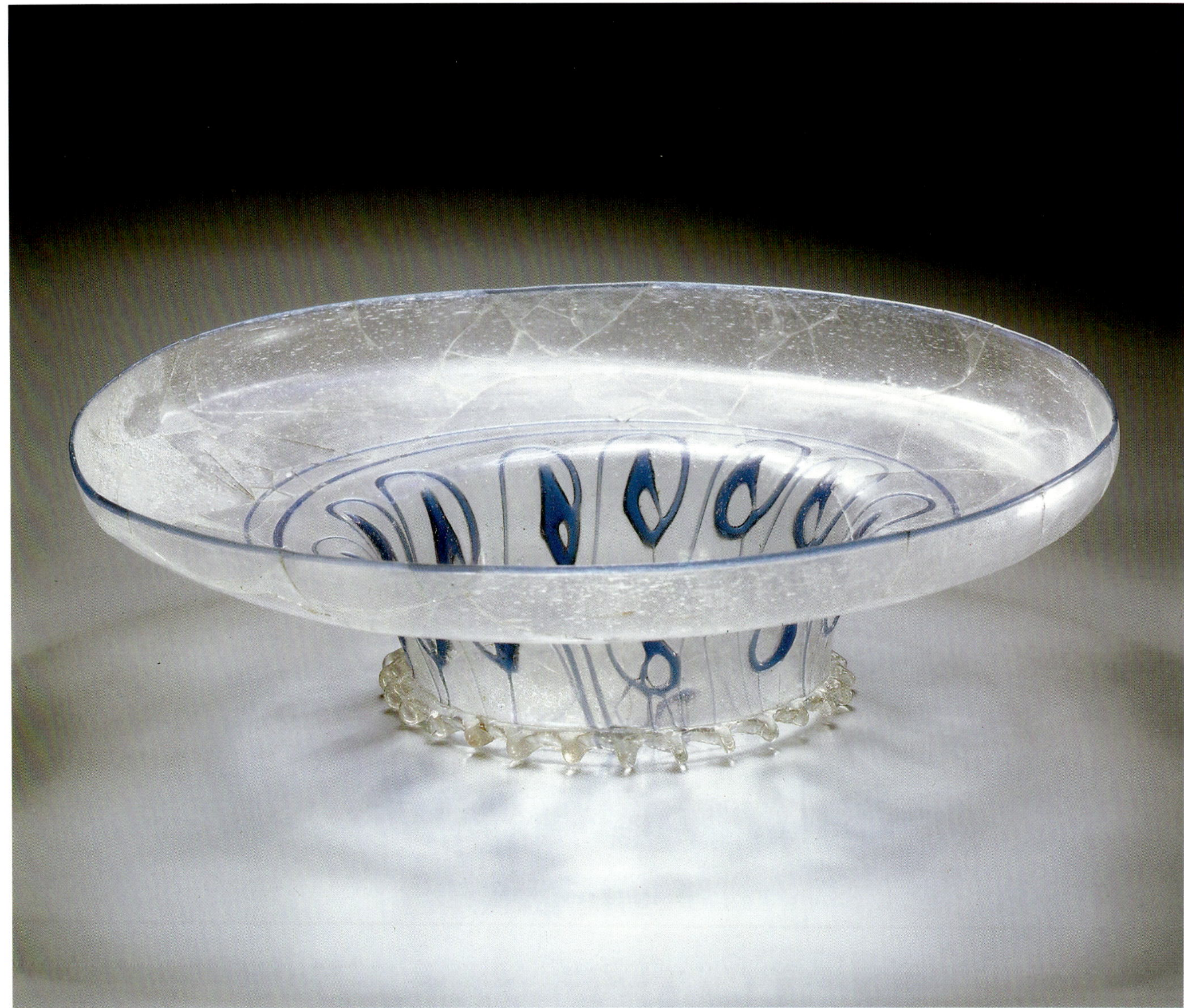

91 Footed Bowl

Probably Germany (reportedly found in Mainz)
2nd half of 13th/early 14th c.
H 7.4, ⌀ 25.6 cm

Colorless. Probably mold-blown, shaped. Pushed-up bottom. Pincered foot-ring. Freely applied light blue thread decoration. Slightly corroded, cleaned. Glued, wall slightly restored.

Acc. no. P 1985-297

The best-preserved and largest dish with volute thread decoration known to date; otherwise known only in fragments. See Baumgartner and Krueger, *Mittelalter*, 1988, cat. no. 320.
The glassmaker's assurance in freely applying the decoration illustrates exceptional skill, for he applied the decoration very quickly and in one step, almost in a single thread.

Lit.: Baumgartner and Krueger, *Mittelalter*, 1988, cat. no. 319

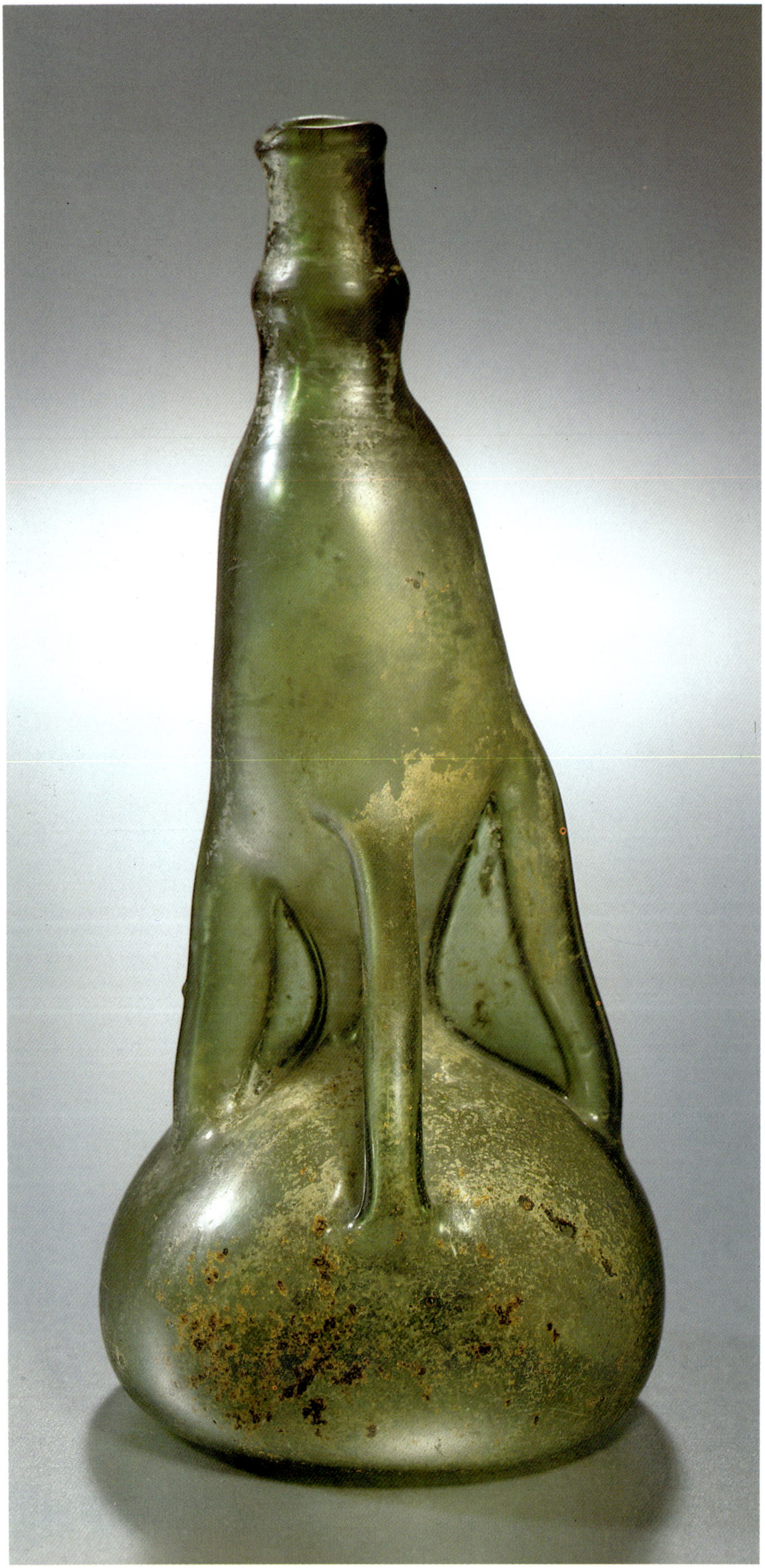

92 *Kuttrolf*

Germany
14th/15th c. (or earlier?)
H 18.8, ⌀ 8.6 cm

Free-blown, shaped. Slightly pushed-up bottom.
Slightly corroded, cleaned. Brownish deposits and decomposition on the interior.

Acc. no. P 1940-43
Formerly Johannes Jantzen Collection, Bremen; previously Emden Collection, Hamburg

Vessels with walls squeezed into tube shapes have been known since Roman times. The bottle represents the first of its kind, on which later variations with twisted necks were based; cf. cat. no. 116. There is no evidence to support the traditional dating to the 14th/15th centuries. Finds consisting of colored lead-glass fragments from the 13th century—see Baumgartner and Krueger, *Mittelalter*, 1988, 161ff.—may suggest an earlier date for the green glass.

Lit.: Heinemeyer, *Glas*, 1966, cat. no. 81; Baumgartner and Krueger, *Mittelalter*, 1988, cat. no. 381

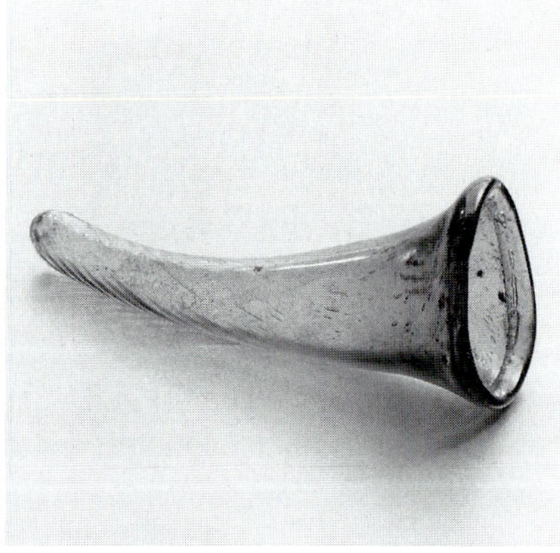

93 Small Horn

Germany
14th/15th c.
L 9.6, ⌀ 4.1 cm

Dark blue-green glass. Optic-blown, shaped. Folded rim.

Acc. no. P 1936-33
Formerly Josef Lückger Collection, Cologne

Unique piece, no comparisons to determine provenance and date. Presumably used as an inkwell.

Lit.: Heinemeyer, *Glas*, 1966, cat. no. 82; Baumgartner and Krueger, *Mittelalter*, 1988, cat. no. 553

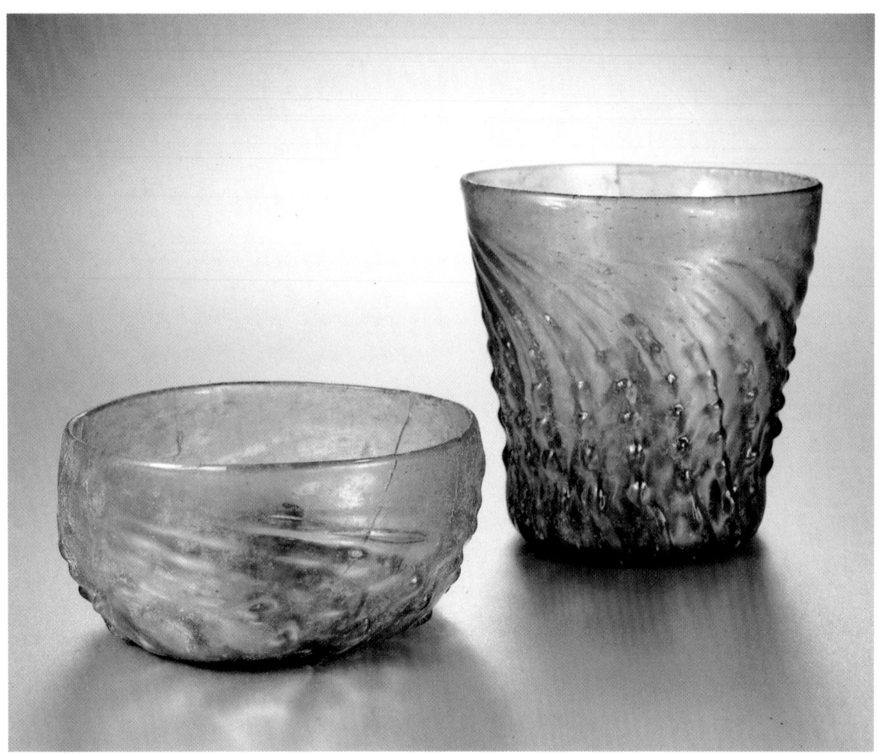

95 *Maigelein*

Germany
15th c.
H 4.2, ⌀ 8.9 cm

Optic-blown, shaped. Pushed-up bottom.
Slightly corroded, cleaned; slightly iridescent.
Glued.

Acc. no. P 1936-19
Formerly Josef Lückger Collection, Cologne

A very common type of late medieval glassware, particularly in the Rhineland. The tran-
sitions to bowl and beaker shapes are fluid.
For type, dating, and related forms see
Baumgartner and Krueger, *Mittelalter*, 1988,
cat. nos. 357ff., and Hess and Husband,
Getty, 1997, cat. no. 2.
The term *Maigelein* occurs only from the
19th century in connection with this dish
type. Apparently it originally designated
metal dishes.

Lit.: Heinemeyer, *Glas*, 1966, cat. no. 98;
Ricke, *2500 Jahre*, 1987, cat. no. 54

96 Cross-Ribbed Beaker

Germany
15th c.
H 8.3, ⌀ 8.3 cm

Optic-blown, shaped. Bottom pushed up to a
very narrow point.
Slightly corroded, cleaned.

Acc. no. P 1936-67
Formerly Josef Lückger Collection, Cologne

See cat. no. 95; see also Baumgartner and
Krueger, *Mittelalter*, 1988, cat. no. 359.
The glassmaker created the cross-ribbed decoration by blowing the piece into the rib
mold twice. To produce the diagonal ribs, he
twisted the glass bubble to the right after
the first blowing, to the left after the second.

Lit.: Heinemeyer, *Glas*, 1966, cat. no. 104;
Ricke, *2500 Jahre*, 1987, cat. no. 55

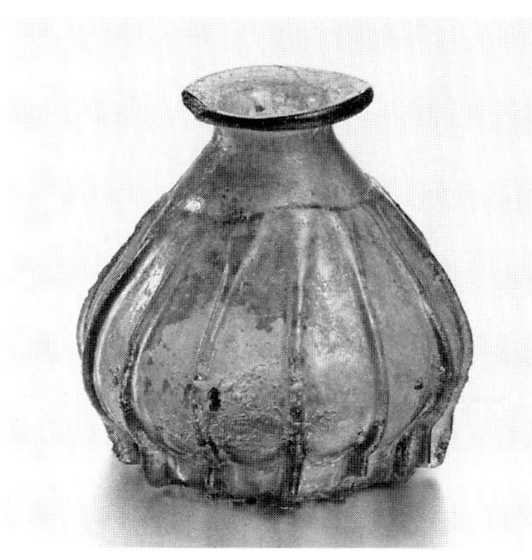

94 Small Ribbed Bottle

Germany, Rhine-and-Meuse Region
14th/15th c.
H 5.1, ⌀ 5.2 cm

Light green, optic-blown in mold with 14
ribs, shaped. Bottom pushed up into a point.
Slightly corroded; iridescent. Small piece broken off edge, crack in bottom.

Acc. no. P 1936-21
Formerly Josef Lückger Collection, Cologne

Ribbed bottles were very common in the high
and late Middle Ages. The typical ends of this
vessel's ribs, however, link this type with
beakers and stemmed-foot glassware of the
14th century.
Probably used as an inkwell.

Lit.: Heinemeyer, *Glas*, 1966, cat. no. 83;
Baumgartner and Krueger, *Mittelalter*, 1988,
cat. no. 306

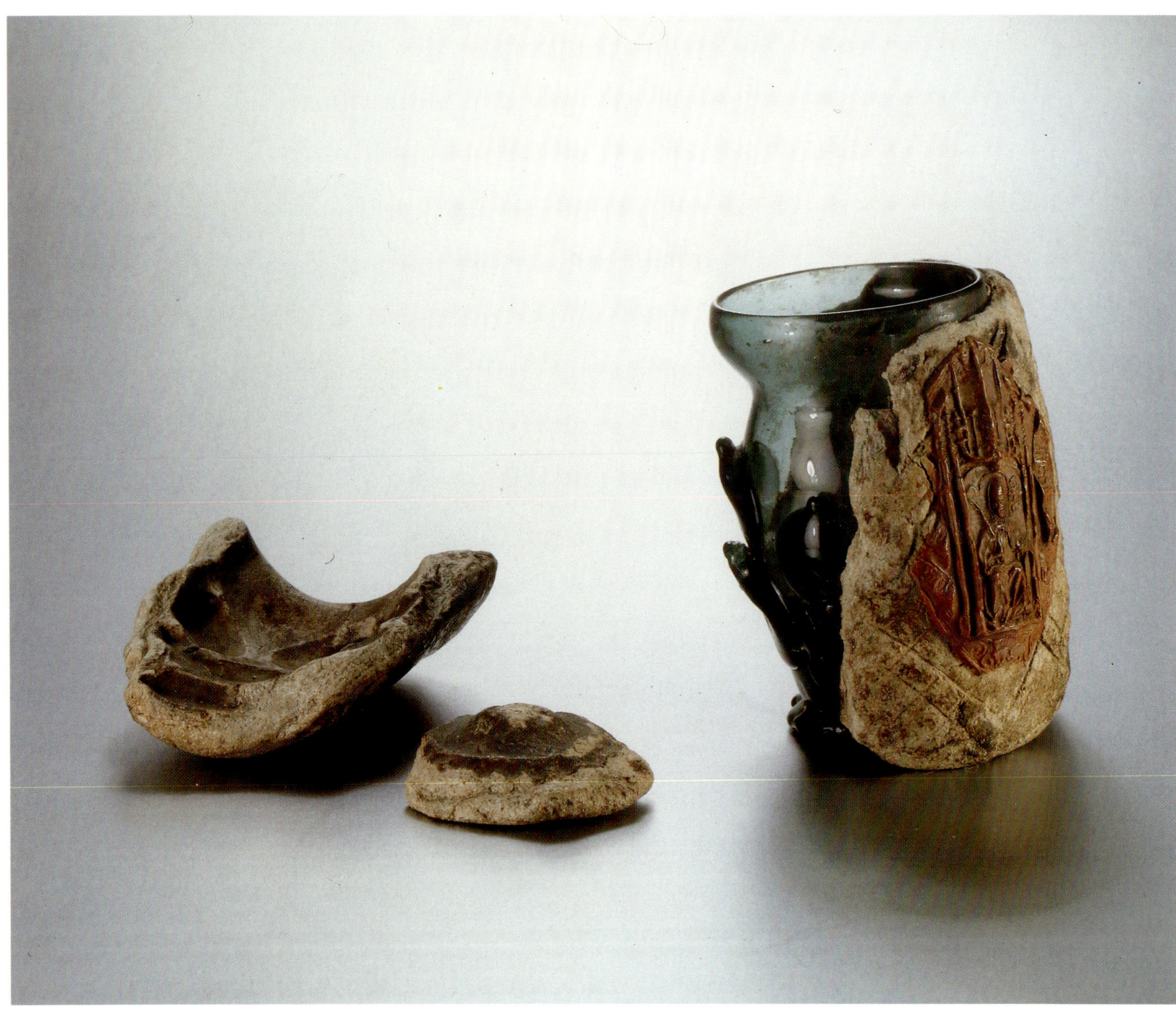

97 *Krautstrunk* as Reliquary

Probably southern Germany or Bohemia
Ca. 1500
H glass 8.5, ⌀ 5.7 cm

Intense blue-green glass. Probably mold-
blown, shaped. Two staggered rows of eight
prunts each. Slightly soiled.
Partly in the original wax casing, other parts
preserved separately.
The casing carries the seal of Konrad Rein-
hard, suffragan bishop of Brixen (Bressanone,
Tyrol), who was in office between 1481 and
1513.

Acc. no. P 1940-44
Formerly Johannes Jantzen Collection, Bremen

The *Krautstrunk*, so called because it recalls a
"cabbage stalk" stripped of leaves, belongs to
the group of vessels that determine the common conception of late medieval glass.
Compared with other types, such as the
Maigelein, these beakers are quite rare, as the
fragments found in the refuse pits of urban

housing reveal. That these beakers often
functioned as reliquaries explains the relatively large proportion of intact glasses from
this period. They were built into altars when
the church was consecrated and were thus
protected from damage over the centuries.
The seal on the wax covering is valuable in
dating the piece. Its usefulness in determining the container's origin, however, is limited. There were no Tyrolian glassworks in the
late Middle Ages. The sovereign gave preference to metal smelting and the region's
scarce firewood was used exclusively for
working the rich ore deposits mined there. It
was somewhat later that workshops producing in the Venetian manner were established
in Hall and Innsbruck.

Lit.: Heinemeyer, *Glas*, 1966, cat. no. 113;
Saldern, *Alte Gläser*, 1968, cat. no. 14; Ricke,
Ausgewählte Werke, 1980, 11

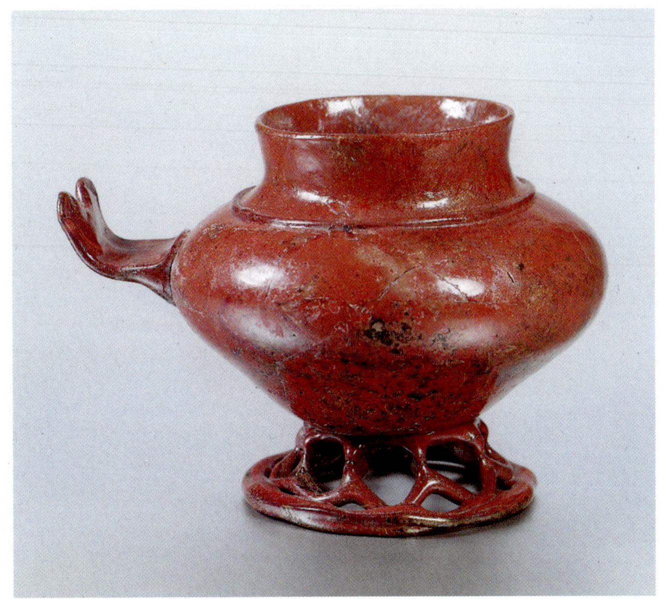

98   *Scheuer*

Germany
1st third of 16th c.
H 11, ⌀ without handle 12.4 cm

Opaque sealing-wax red. Probably mold-
blown, shaped. Foot, made of partly pincered
threads, and handle freely applied.
Slightly corroded (brown spots). Glued, about
one-third of wall restored.

Acc. no. L 1989-40
On loan from the Karl Amendt Collection,
Krefeld

The *Scheuer* is one of the rarest vessel types
of the Middle Ages. Isolated pieces are documented as early as the 13th/14th centuries.
See Baumgartner and Krueger, *Mittelalter*,
1988, 231ff., 381ff. Around 1500 such vessels, with the characteristic bent handle,
became more common—not only in glass but
also in other materials, such as metal, wood,
and clay.
The *Scheuer* from the Amendt Collection is
the only piece in opaque red glass and with a
net foot known to date. This type of foot
became a common decorative element on
drinking vessels from about 1500.

Lit.: Baumgartner and Krueger, *Mittelalter*,
1988, cat. no. 475

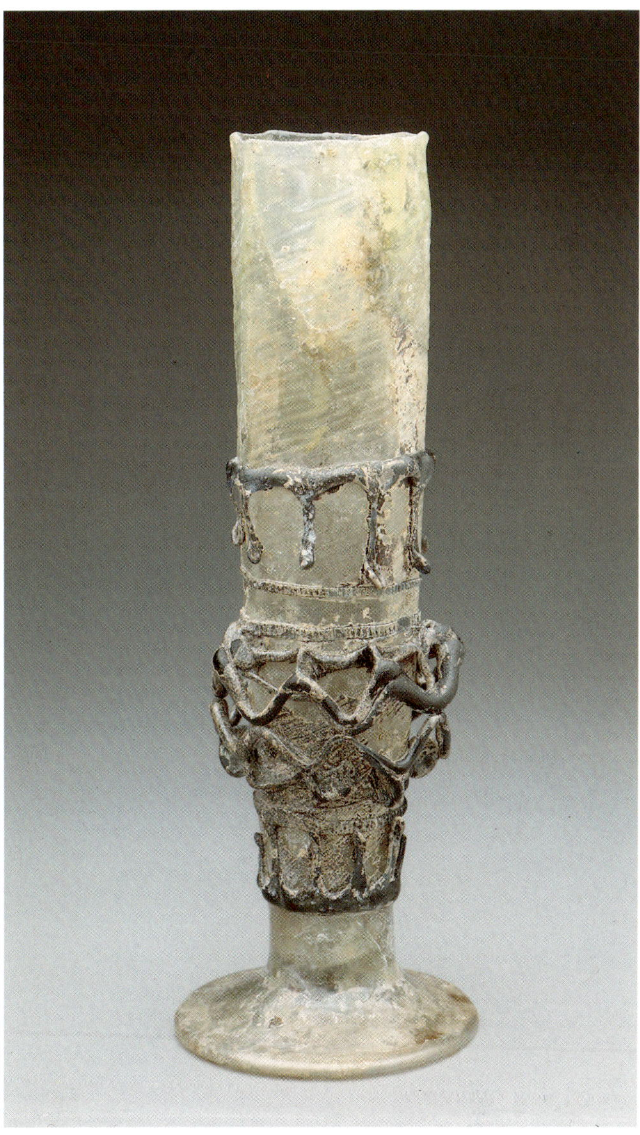

99   *Stangenglas* with Thread Decoration

Germany
1st half of 16th c.
H 23.1, ⌀ 8 cm

Colorless, greenish-yellow tone. Optic-blown
in a fine-ribbed mold, shaped. Foot and
mouth like cat. no. 102. Dark blue applied
thread decoration, in parts standing free
from wall.
Strongly corroded, partly cleaned. Glued,
slightly restored.

Acc. no. LP 1978-44
On permanent loan from the Museumsverein

Only fragments of such glasses were previously known. Dating is based on other securely
datable vessel types with similar freely
applied thread decoration.

Lit.: Baumgartner and Krueger, *Mittelalter*,
1988, cat. no. 508

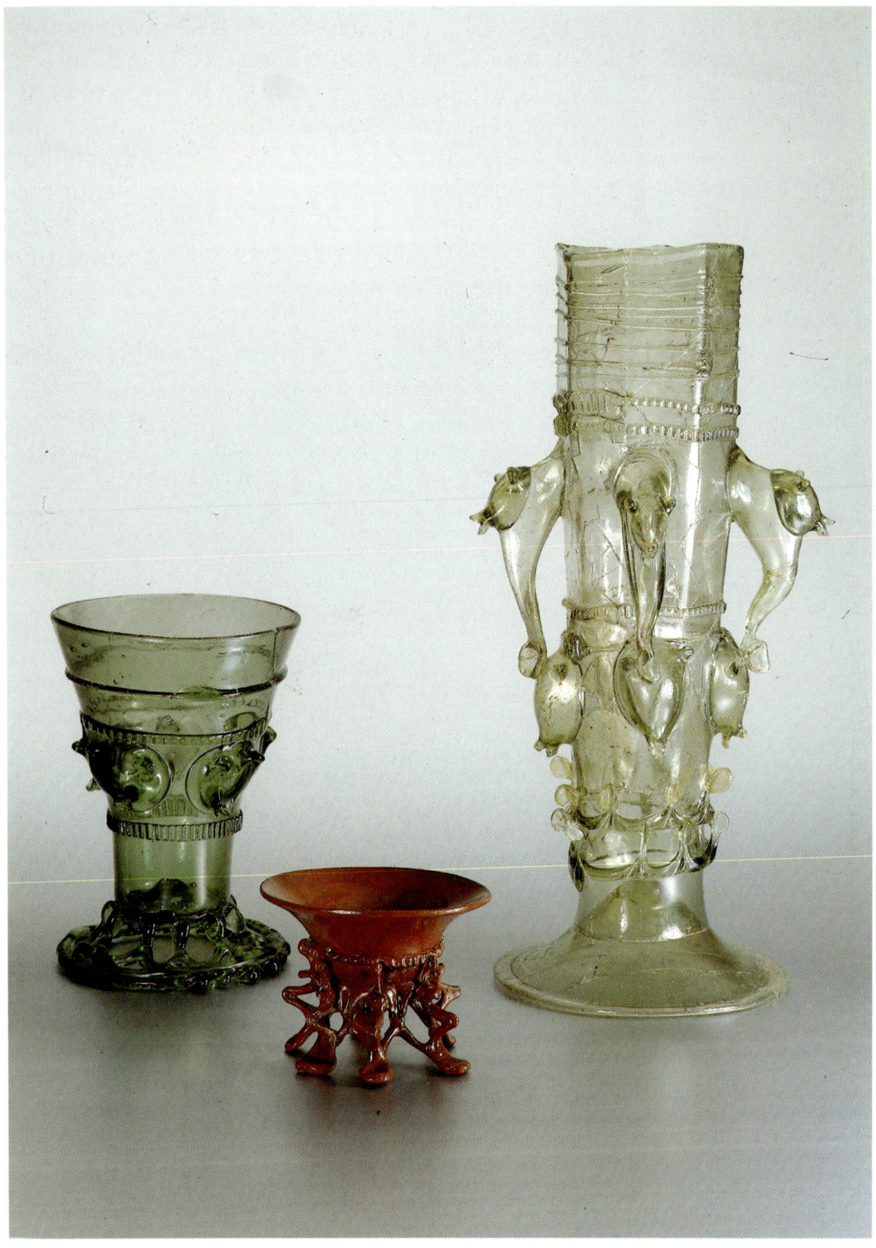

100 Standing Cup

Germany, presumably the Rhineland
(reportedly found in Andernach)
Early 16th c.
H 12.7, ⌀ 9.2 cm

Green glass. Probably mold-blown, shaped.
Pushed-up bottom. Freely applied foot made
of threads. Five zoomorphic prunts.
Glued, parts of mouth and upper wall
restored.

Acc. no. L 1989-41
On loan from the Karl Amendt Collection,
Krefeld

No other pieces with this shape are known to
exist. For feet made of a network of threads,
cf. cat. no. 98. The first animal-head prunts
on vessel bodies are documented about 1480.
See Baumgartner and Krueger, *Mittelalter*,
1988, 352ff., 399ff.

Lit.: Baumgartner and Krueger, *Mittelalter*,
1988, cat. no. 436

101 Small Bowl

Germany (?) (reportedly found in Aachen)
15th/early 16th c.
H 5.5, ⌀ 7.8 cm

Opaque glass in sealing-wax red. Probably
free-blown and shaped. Foot made of pincered threads.
Glued, restored.

Acc. no. L 1989-42
On loan from the Karl Amendt Collection,
Krefeld

No comparable pieces are documented with
regard to the shape of the foot and the type
of bowl.
The vessel might have served as a container
for spices or salt.

Lit.: Baumgartner and Krueger, *Mittelalter*,
1988, cat. no. 523

102 *Stangenglas* with Zoomorphic Prunts

Germany (reportedly found in Aachen)
1st half of 16th c.
H 26.3, ⌀ 10.9 cm

Yellow-green glass. Mostly free-blown. Foot
shaped from glass bubble and pushed up.
After applying a gob of hot glass to the vessel's side, the artisan blew the four groups of
animal-head prunts and trunks from the
inside out, through the wall. He formed the
mouth over an eight-sided clay core.
Slightly corroded. Glued, restored.

Acc. no. L 1989-43
On loan from the Karl Amendt Collection,
Krefeld

Particularly lavish design. Trunks and animal-
head prunts were known from Roman and
Frankish glass art. Their combination with
other types of decoration is without parallel
in this form. Fragments of similar glasses
were found during the excavation of the
Thuringian glassworks Volsbach.

For this type of glassware see also Henkes,
Glas zonder glans, 1994, 82–84, cat. nos.
20.4–7.

Lit.: Baumgartner and Krueger, *Mittelalter*,
1988, cat. no. 507

The Renaissance and Baroque Periods
Colored and Enameled Glass of the North

Analogous to the increasingly complex Gothic tracery in churches and manifold drapery in the period's figural painting and sculpture, *Waldglas* (literally, "forest glass") of the late Middle Ages became ever more sophisticated around 1500 and in the early sixteenth century. Glassmakers embellished beakers with netlike thread-feet and prunts expanded to form hollow-blown animal heads (cat. no. 100). This development reached its peak and conclusion in the slender *Stangenglas* of the sixteenth century, which had imaginative, often decidedly bizarre, elephant-trunk-shaped and animal-head prunts (cat. no. 102). Roman and Frankish claw beakers signaled a new way of seeing. The period was freed from its medieval bonds and the past began to be understood as a source for contemporary design.

The use of sculptural elements, a tradition rooted in the German late Gothic period, became increasingly widespread. It found expression in freely applied thread decoration detached from the wall (cat. no. 99) as well as in the popular joke vessels (cat. nos. 107, 119). Their manifold embellishments testify to the glassblower's inventiveness and skill. This kind of glassware—together with the period's large *Stangengläser* with prunts, ring beakers (cat. no. 106), and *Bandwurmgläser* (literally, "tapeworm glasses")—carried on the tradition of the *Waldglashütten* (forest glasshouses) without interruption, sustaining its significance into the late seventeenth century. As joke glass, the *Kuttrolf* took many forms (cat. no. 116). It became a common drinking bottle for brandy. The gurgling sounds emanating from it while drinking or pouring heightened the pleasure of imbibing. The *Römer* became a widely used drinking vessel (cat. no. 117). Its prototype, the *Berkemeyer*, having a stem with applied prunts and an unadorned funnel mouth, established a direct link to glass art of the late Middle Ages.

In addition there was a variety of simpler drinking glass shapes. One outcome of this development was the so-called unbreakable glass with its characteristic raspberry-prunt decoration (cat. no. 118). Glassmakers made playful use of the stability and robustness of potash glassware fused in the *Waldglashütte*, while at the same time taking into account the growing fascination with ornamentation and decoration accompanied by diamond-engraved inscriptions.

Adding surface decoration to mold-blown glass finished at the furnace was an increasingly visible trend from the mid-sixteenth century. The possibilities provided by hot decorative forms, such as prunts, threads, trunks, etc., were largely exhausted and the demands made of representative glass decoration grew. The necessary impulses for this change in taste no doubt came from the glass art of Venice, which had taken on the leading role in European glass design unchallenged. From 1500 to the mid-seventeenth century, luxury glassware made for the court or for the tables of cultivated patricians was synonymous with Venetian glass.

Glass art developed largely along two lines during this period, with the northern glassworks that operated in the tradition of the *Waldglashütten* decidedly maintaining their autonomy. They took over Venetian enamel painting as a decorative form, but adapted it skillfully to local types of vessels and found an independent, often crude pictorial idiom with its own subjects.

At the beginning of this development were simple depictions of coats of arms, usually on the narrow *Stangengläser* or the period's conical standing cups. From the last quarter of the sixteenth century, shapes and depictions were further developed. A subject that was common in Venice in the fifteenth century—mementos of family events (cat. no. 103)—became increasingly widespread. Beakers and plates were adorned with anecdotal, allegorical, or symbolic motifs. Sometimes artisans adopted Venetian glass shapes directly (cat. no. 113) and employed such decorative techniques as diamond-point engraving (cat. no. 110).

The Renaissance emphasis on the profane, aided by an economic upswing in Germany in these years, led to the enjoyment of the pleasures of the table. Thus Germans soon fell into disrepute, having been viewed by their neighbors as excessive eaters and drinkers, which is amply illustrated by the size of contemporary drinking glasses. From the late sixteenth century, the dominant northern vessel type was the large, usually greenish, *Humpen* holding up to three liters. Even if these glasses were generally not meant for just one person, but instead were passed around the table or given to guests as a "welcome" drink, the repeated imperial decrees against excessive drinking, above all against the requirement of the ancient code of honor to "drink to someone in return," reveal that these vessels did not have merely a representative function.

This type of glassware, richly decorated with painting in opaque enamel colors, was made chiefly in the glasshouses of Bohemia, which were increasingly gaining in significance, but also in Hesse, Franconia, and Thuringia. The large, often straight, forms were ideally suited to the two-dimensional painted decoration.

What the glasses have in common is the naive pleasure in narrative and the folk-art character of the depictions. They indicate that the customers came from the artisan or middle classes in the cities or from the lower aristocracy.

This circle of prospective customers also explains the immense popularity of *Humpen,* whose decoration affirmed the owner's allegiance to the unity, authority, and order of the Holy Roman Empire. The large number of *Reichsadlerhumpen* (imperial eagle beakers; cat. no. 108) and *Kurfürstenhumpen* (electors' beakers; cat. nos. 121, 122) that have come down to us document their owners' sympathies with a strengthened centralized imperial authority instead of the territorial rulers and their increasing claim to power. In the first half of the seventeenth century, during the Thirty Years' War, the owner of such a glass thus also documented his imperial, hence Catholic, position. After the Peace of Westphalia in 1648, which finally decided the fate of the empire in favor of the electors' particularist interests, this type of loyalist display soon lost its political impetus. The subject remained so common, however, that glass painters at the factory of Count Kinsky in Kreibitz (Chřibská), Bohemia, were still required to make a *Reichsadlerhumpen* with its many colors and details as their master examination piece in 1669.

The range of subjects depicted on German enamel glasses was broad. In keeping with their use, profane motifs were most common, but a large variety bearing religious subjects are documented as well (cat. nos. 114, 115). In contrast to the many pieces with worldly themes, glassware with biblical depictions was generally commissioned for specific occasions. The only exception is the relatively common *Apostelhumpen,* with which the owner drew attention to the fact that he was a Christian. In addition there were depictions of the four evangelists, scenes from the Old and New Testament, and, though considerably rarer, from the lives of the saints. Amongst the secular themes, depictions of hunting scenes, usually drives with stretched

nets, dominate after armorial glasses, *Reichsadlergläser,* and *Kurfürstengläser.* Many glasses also allude to historical events.

A large group of glasses treats mythological or allegorical themes, often in reaction to and commenting polemically on happenings of the day (cat. no. 109). These and most other depictions in enamel painting were usually not based on original designs by the painters. Enamel painters working independently or with glassworks were simple artisans who drew on the rich graphic production of the period, woodcuts or copper engravings, to develop their themes. The artistic skill of the painter is evident in fine detail, but above all in his ability to transfer the two-dimensional image onto the rounded glass. Ambitious painters sought to achieve a continuous depiction around the entire glass, no longer limited by the boundaries of the graphic sheet. In this approach, enamel painters paved the way for the glass cutters of the Baroque, who were confronted with the same problems in their work from the late seventeenth century.

The great age of enamel painting in Germany was the last quarter of the sixteenth and the first half of the seventeenth century. It represented, in contrast to the "welsch" (southern, foreign) luxury glass of Venice, a glass art indigenous and intrinsic to the north. With the consolidation of princely power, demands made of the representative function of glass art changed. Increasingly the nobility and glass cutters at the courts of absolutist sovereigns, and no longer the bourgeoisie, determined the forms and decoration of glass art. With few exceptions, amongst them the *Hofkellereigläser* (court cellar glasses) of Saxony's electors (cat. no. 123), glass decoration by enamel painting was restricted to the realm of peasant utility glass. There it remained up to the close of the eighteenth century and, in the Black Forest and Alpine countries, into the nineteenth century.

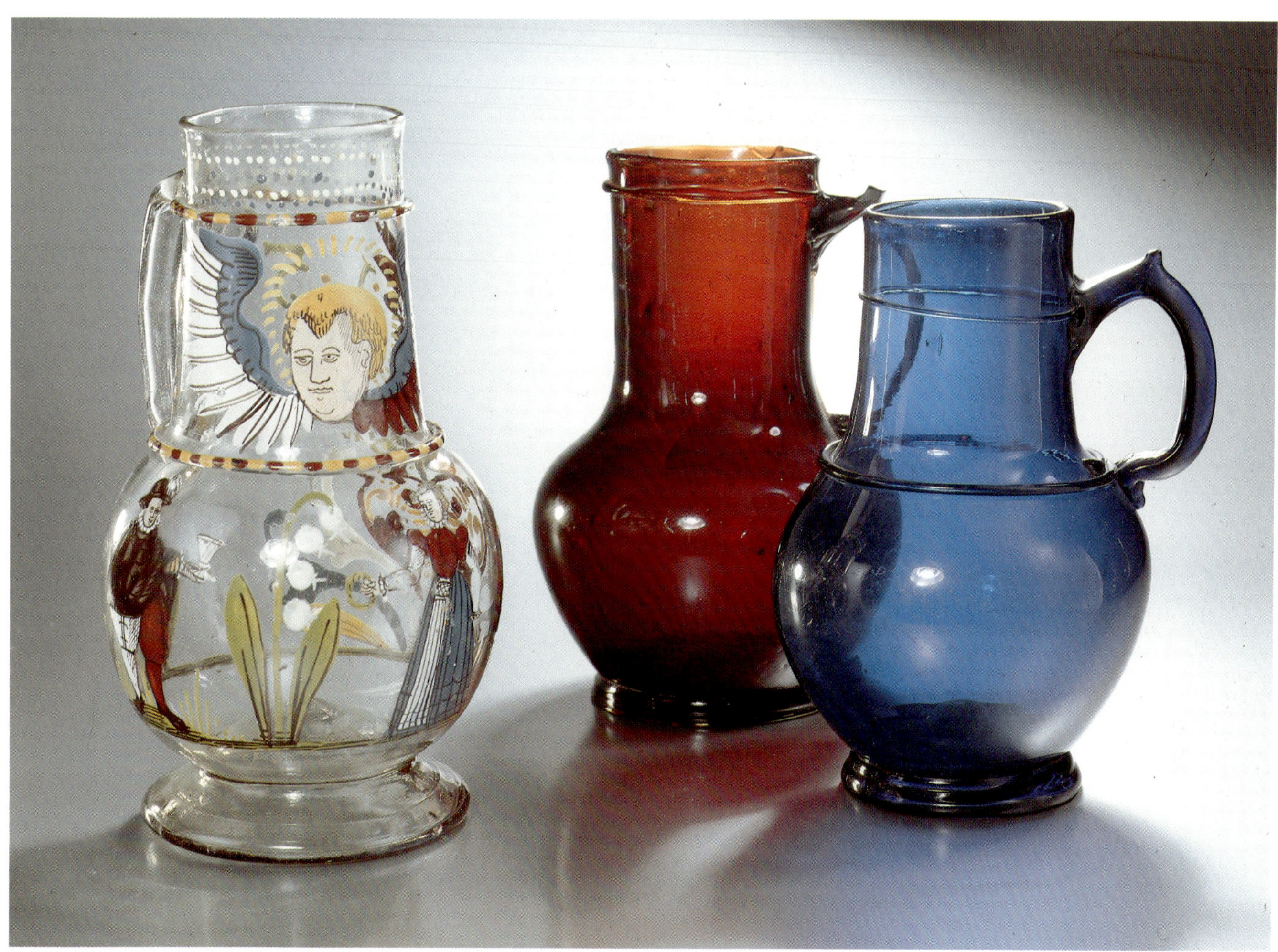

103 Pitcher

Bohemia
Dated 1577
H 16.5, ⌀ 9.4 cm

Colorless. Mold-blown. Foot shaped from the glass bubble and bottom pushed up. Handle with small pincered thumbpiece.
Enamel painting: bridal couple, the man presenting a glass, the woman a bridal wreath, between lilies of the valley and vine scroll decoration. On neck: a large cherub. On the opposite side, the annotation *1577*.

Acc. no. P 1940-71
Formerly Johannes Jantzen Collection, Bremen; previously Passavant-Gontard Collection, Frankfurt

Early example of a marriage pitcher with folk painting. See cat. no. 111; see also Saldern, *Enameled Glass*, 1965, 172.

Lit.: Heinemeyer, *Glas*, 1966, cat. no. 155; Ricke, *Ausgewählte Werke*, 1980, 12

104 Pitcher

Southern Germany or Bohemia
Late 16th/early 17th c.
H 14.1, ⌀ 9.8 cm

Brown glass. Mold-blown, shaped. Folded foot-ring. On wall below handle: an (unintentional) thin thread curves from top to bottom. Cut thumbpiece.

Acc. no. P 1965-856
Gift of Helmut Hentrich

Common shape for utility glass.

Lit.: –

105 Pitcher

Southern Germany or Bohemia
Late 16th/early 17th c.
H 13.9, ⌀ 9.1 cm

Blue glass. Like cat. no. 104. No pincered thumbpiece.
Small piece missing on folded thread below.

Acc. no. 13795
Formerly Franz Bock Collection, Aachen

Lit.: Heinemeyer, *Glas*, 1966, cat. no. 302

106 Ring Beaker

1st half of 17th or 1st half of 19th c.
H 18.6, ⌀ 8.8 cm

Light brown glass. Bowl mold-blown, shaped.
Coiled foot. Thick thread at base of bowl,
drawn out and pincered. Three eyes with
freely worked rings.

Acc. no. P 1936-90
Formerly Josef Lückger Collection, Cologne

Popular drinking glass of the 17th century
that has come down to us in countless examples and variations. See Klesse and Saldern,
Sammlung Biemann, 1978, cat. nos. 13f., and
Baumgärtner, Bremen I, 1987, no. 14.
The dating of this glass is not certain. The
large number of extant pieces would make
the 19th century a possibility. See Ritsema,
Amsterdam I, 1993, 324ff., nos. 458–61. For
secured pieces see Henkes, *Glas zonder glans*,
1994, 165, no. 39.2.

Lit.: Heinemeyer, *Glas*, 1966, cat. no. 139;
Saldern, *Alte Gläser*, 1968, cat. no. 16, with
references to other pieces

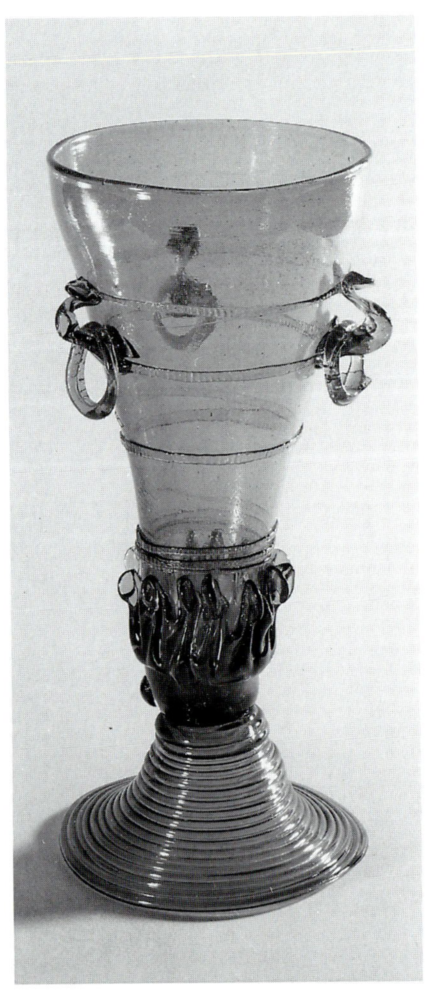

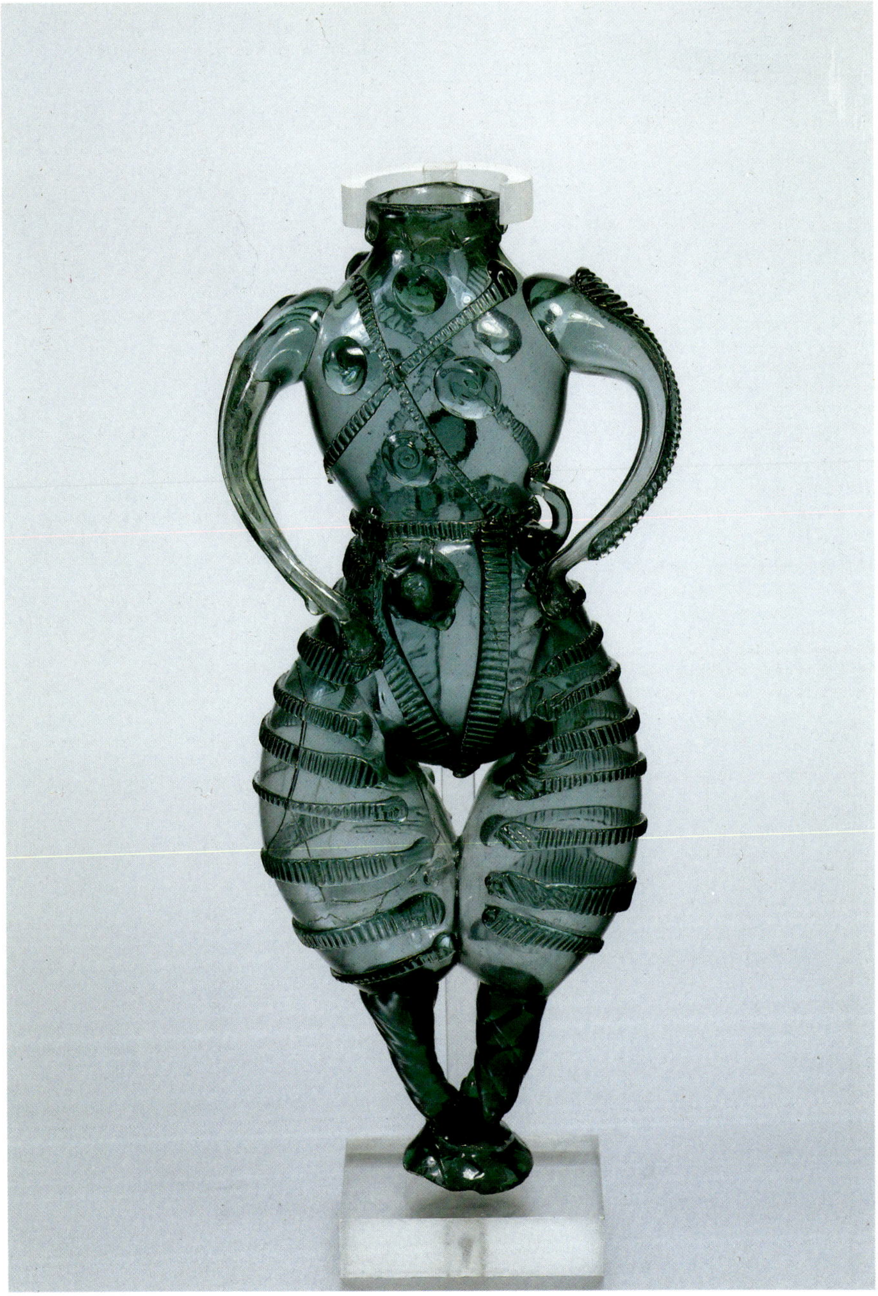

107 Bottle in the Shape of a *Landsknecht*

Germany
Late 16th/1st half of 17th c.
H 24, W 11.6, D 6.3 cm

Green glass. Free-blown and shaped. Broken
and glued, right arm restored. The separately
worked head with suction tube is missing, as
is the foot. The dark lacquer interspersed
with gold foil, applied to the vessel's interior
in the 19th century to hide the damage, was
removed recently.

Acc. no. 1939-10
Formerly Karl Thewalt Collection, Cologne

Belongs within the context of anthropomor-
phic joke vessels, which were very popular in
the 17th century. Only one comparable work
is documented, making the reconstruction of
the fragmentary glass possible. The intact
piece at The J. Paul Getty Museum, Malibu
(Hess and Husband, Getty, 1997, cat. no.
14), stands on a wide funnel foot. A silver
pendant sword belongs to the piece. The
head ends in a suction tube typical of the
more common goblets having a deer on top;
the nose is open, making it possible to suck
the drink. Female figures are more common
than male figures, made usually as doubled
Sturzbecher (somersault glasses). See Klesse
and Reineking, Cologne, 1973, no. 246, and
Ohm, Bauer, and Gabbert, Frankfurt, 1980,
nos. 271f.

Lit.: Heinemeyer, *Glas*, 1966, cat. no. 142;
Prohaska-Gross, "Landsknechtsglas," 1997, 78

Bohemia
Dated 1592
H 31, ⌀ 12.5 cm

Glass with greenish tone. Probably free-blown
and shaped. Folded foot-ring. Enamel paint-
ing: the imperial eagle with shields repre-
senting the constituent parts of the empire
(in the Quaternion System).
Circumscription above the eagle:
*DAS.HEILIGE.RÖMISCHE.REICH.MIT.SAMBT.SEIN
EN.GLIDERN.*
1592 on the winged shoulders, the shields of
the electors and the Holy See with marks.
Left: *TRIER CÖLN MENTZ POTESATZVROM*
Right: *BEHMEN PFALTZ SACHSEN BRANDEN-
BURG*
The shields on the wing feathers from top to
bottom, left wing: *CÖLN REGENSPVRG
COSSENITZ SALTZPVRG*
Marks on the side: *4 BAVREN
AUGSPVRG METZ ACH LVBECK*
Marks at the bottom: *4 STETT
LVNDBVRG WESTERBVRG THVSSIS ALWALTEN*
Marks at the bottom: *4 SEMPER.FREI
NIRNBERG MAIDBVRG REMECK STRAMBVRG*
Marks at the bottom: *4 BVRG GRAVEN
MERCHEN BRANDENBVRG MEISCHEN BADEN*
Marks at the bottom: *4 MARG GRAVEN
BRAVNSCHWEIG BAIEREN SCHWABEN
LVTRING*
Marks at the bottom: *4 SILLI*
Right wing, from left to right: *BRABANT N
SACHSEN WESTEREICH SCHLESWIG*
Marks at the bottom: *4 VICARI
DVRING EDELSASS HESSEN LEVCHTENBVRG*
Marks at the bottom: *4 LANTGRAVEN
CLEVL SOPHY SCHWARTZBVRG ZILLI*
Marks at the bottom: *4 GRAVEN
ANDELAW WEISENBACH FRANBERG STRAM-
BECK*
Marks at the bottom: *4 RITTER
BAMBVRG VLM HAGEHAW SCHLETSTAT*
Marks at the bottom: *4 DORFER
MAGDABVRG LVTZELBVRG ROTENBVRG
ALTENBVRG*
Marks on the side: *4 BIRG*

Acc. no. P 1940-72
Formerly Johannes Jantzen Collection,
Bremen

See p. 64.

Lit.: Heinemeyer, *Glas*, 1966, cat. no. 157

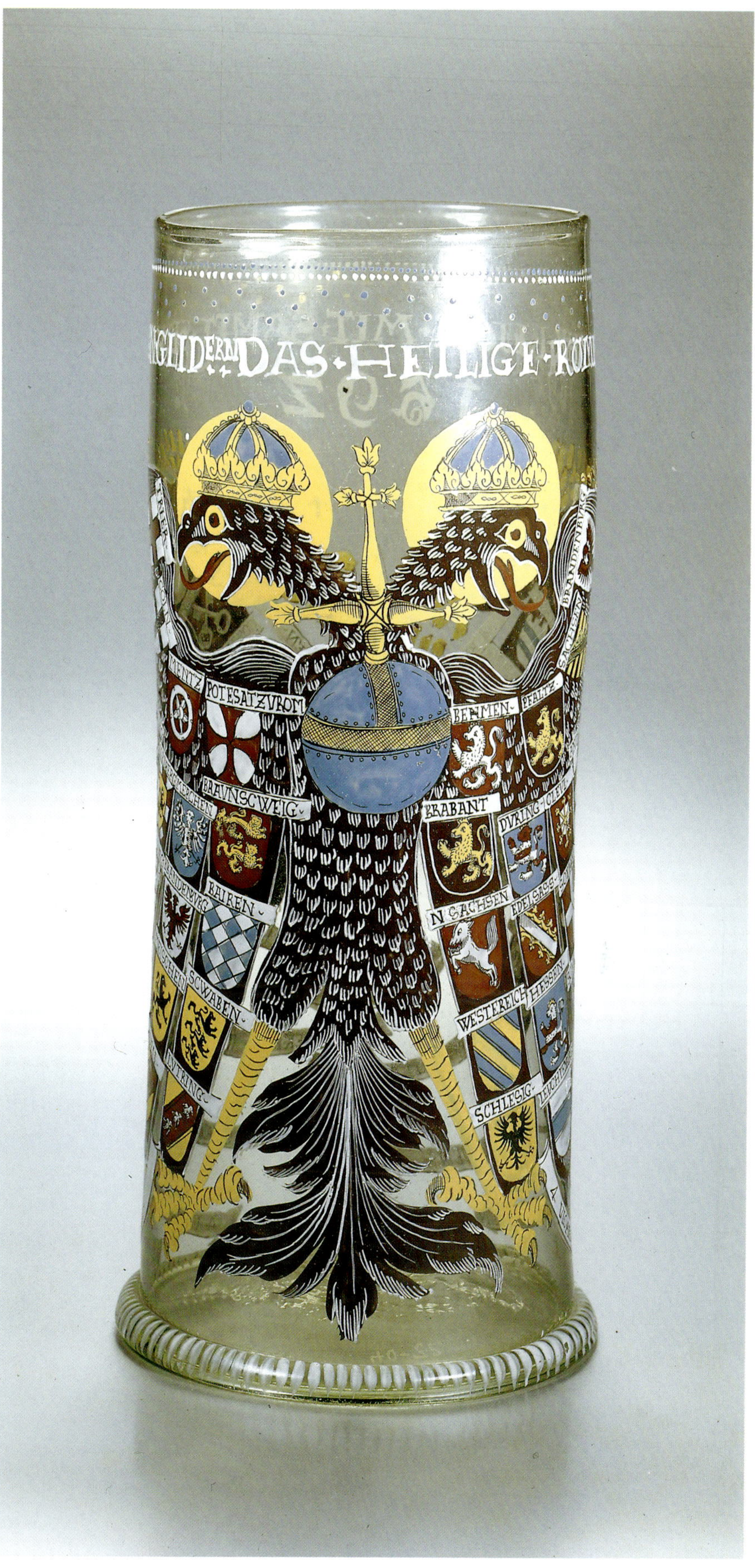

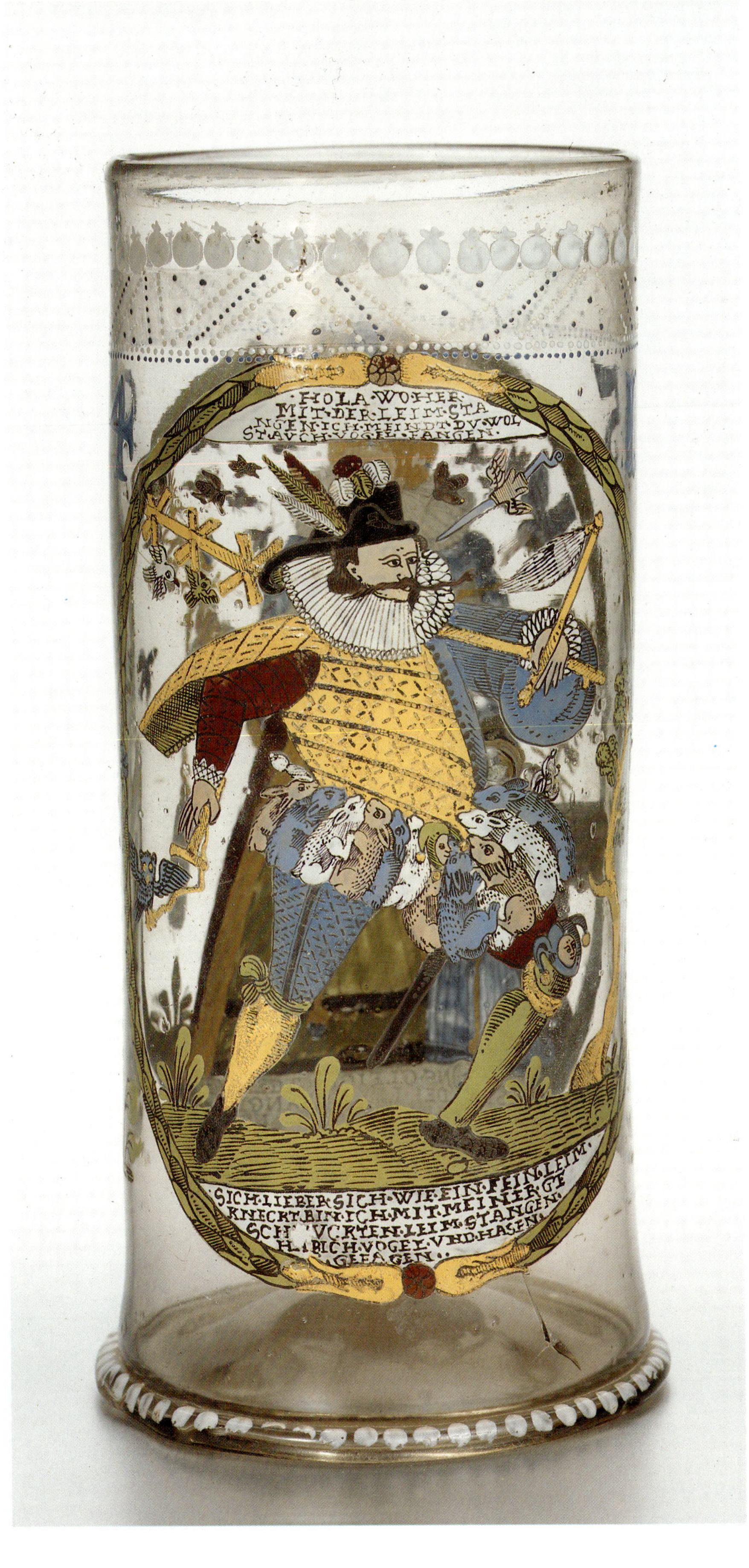

109 *Humpen*

Bohemia
Dated 1594
H 27.6, ⌀ 13.5 cm

Colorless, light green tone. Probably free-blown and shaped. Folded foot-ring. Decoration in enamel painting: a bird-catcher and his family, fitted out with lime-twigs and countless attributes, personify foolishness and human foibles.
Inscriptions near the bird-catcher, at the top:
.HOLA.WOHER./MIT.DER.LEIM.STA/NGEN.ICH.MEINDT.DV.WOL/ST.AVCH.VOGEL.FANGEN.
At the bottom:
*.SICH.LIEBER.SICH.WIE.EIN.FEIN.LEIM/KNECKT.BIN.
ICH.MIT.MEINER.GE/SCH[M]VCKTEN.LEIM.STANGEN./H[A]BICH.VOGEL.VND.HASEN./GEFAGEN*
⌀sic.].
Inscription near the woman bird-catcher, at the top:
.IA.MEIN.HANS./WIL.MIT.ZV.FFILT.DEN./GLICH.VND.GLEICH.SICH./GERN.GESELT.DRVM.WOLEN.WIRS./WAGEN.VND.ES.NIMANDEN.SAGEN.
At the bottom:
.MEINS.GLEICH.GEGEN.VBER./STAT.DER.LEIM.STANGEN./BRAVCH.MICH.GELRNE/DT.HATT.
Inscription left of the daughter:
MVTTER.SOL.I./CHS.AVCH./ALSO.MACH/EN.MVS.IC/H.DIESER.NART.[probably *Narretei*] *L/ACHEN.*
Small, star-shaped crack in the wall below the bird-catcher. Enamel painting lightly rubbed, in the yellow areas bubbly. Flaws in the inscription under the bird-catcher and in the skirt of the woman.

Acc. no. P 1940-73
Formerly Johannes Jantzen Collection, Bremen

The depiction of the "lime-twig man" derives from a copper engraving dated 1588 and made by an artist using the monogram KCNBF (Staatliche Graphische Sammlung, Munich, acc. no. 138719). It is a kind of satirical genre painting that enjoyed increasing popularity in prints from the 16th century and became a frequently featured motif in enamel painting on glassware.

For the complex iconographic relationships in this specific depiction of fools—hunting customs of the period, dispute about "welsch" (southern) and Spanish fashion (the depicted man follows half of each), hares, birds, and bumble bees as symbols of foolishness in reference to sexual excesses—see W. Harms, *Deutsche illustrierte Flugblätter des 16. und 17. Jahrhunderts* 1 (Munich, 1980), 118ff., with further motifs of the bird-catcher. For references to the source used for the *Humpen* see B. Schomberg, "Studien zu den 'Emblemata Saecularia' des Johann Theodor de Bry (Frankfurt 1596)" (master's thesis, Bonn University, 1988).

The painter of the glass probably added the counterpart depiction of the woman freely. A graphic source is presently not known.

For a *Humpen* with the same subject but by another artist see Ritsema, Amsterdam I, 1993, 233, no. 370.

Lit.: Saldern, *Enameled Glass*, 1965, 111, fig. 159, 109; Heinemeyer, *Glas*, 1966, cat. no. 155; Saldern, *Alte Gläser*, 1968, cat. no. 27; Ricke, *Ausgewählte Werke*, 1980, 12

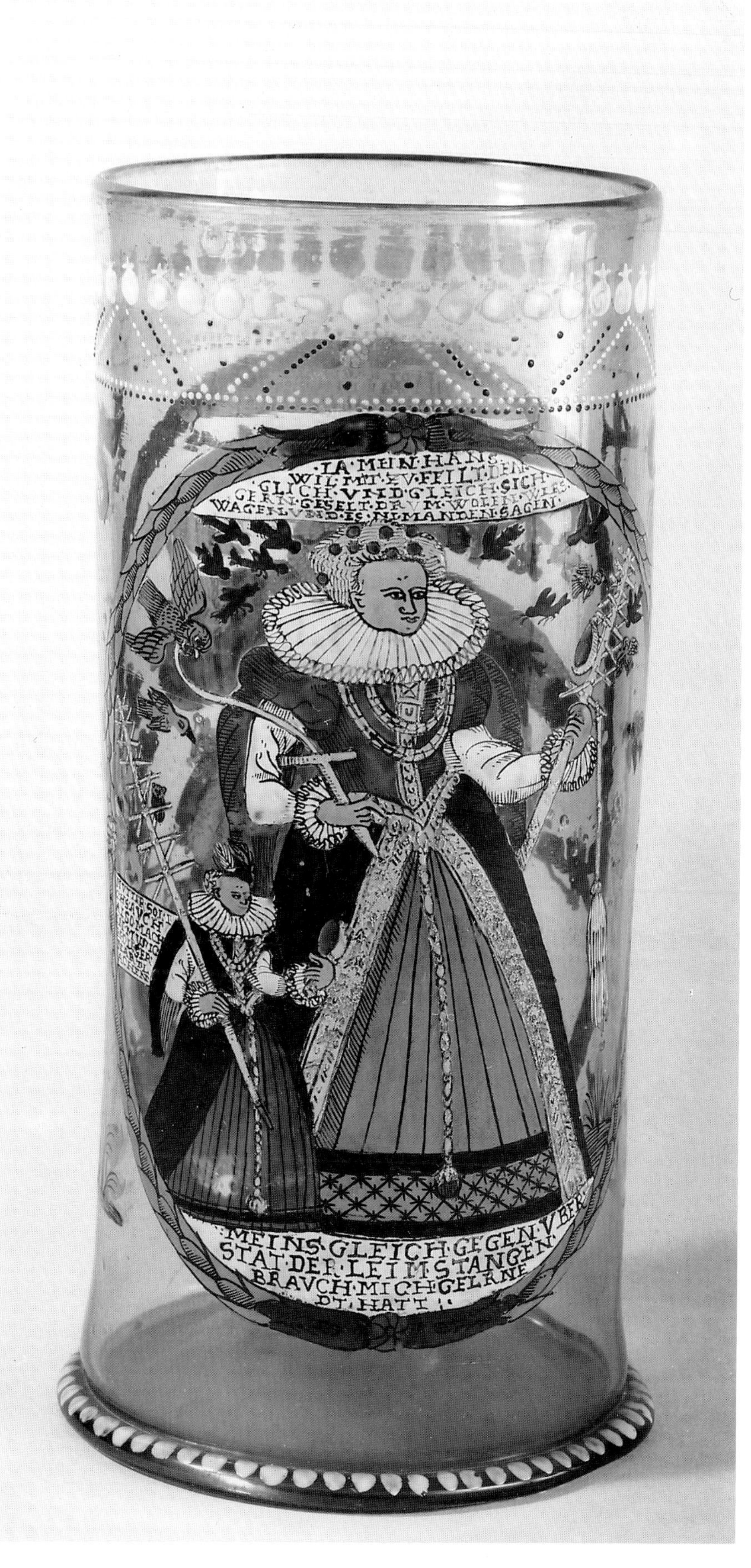

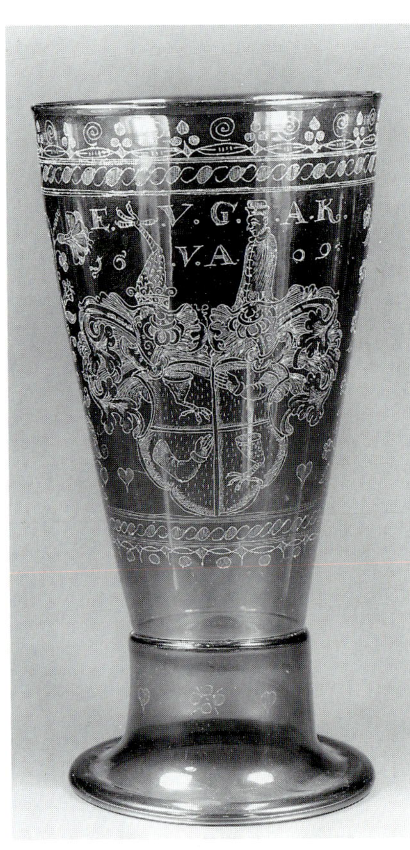

110 Standing Cup

Austria, Bohemia, or Silesia
Dated 1609
H 26.4, ⌀ 13.3 cm

Mold-blown, shaped. Foot blown separately and attached. Foot-ring folded downwards. Decoration in diamond-point engraving: coat of arms of Wolf-Nikolaus, Baron von Grienthal, and his wife, Apollonia, Baroness von Oedt, flowering vines, and the letters *.M.V.G.G.V.E.* and *.E.V.G.A.K./V.A.*

Acc. no. P 1940-63
Formerly Johannes Jantzen Collection, Bremen; previously, E. Herzfelder Collection, Vienna

Wolf-Nikolaus von Grienthal obviously had the standing cup made on the occasion of his being appointed regent of the Lower Austrian estates in the year 1609. It is one of a large group of diamond-engraved glassware in cobalt blue. There is an especially large number of extant plates. For other pieces from this group see R. von Strasser, "A Diamond-Engraved Service of the Early 17th Century," *Journal of Glass Studies* 13 (1971): 84ff. The glasses were made in the Venetian tradition in terms of form as well as decoration.

Lit.: Heinemeyer, *Glas*, 1966, cat. no. 287; Saldern, *Alte Gläser*, 1968, cat. no. 23

111 Beaker

Bohemia
Dated 1599
H 12.8, ⌀ 8.8 cm

Mold-blown, shaped. Folded foot-ring. Decoration in enamel painting: bridal pair in contemporary costume, the man presenting a goblet, the woman a bridal wreath. Between them appear lilies of the valley as a symbol of affection. Inscription on the reverse: *Gott und dich liebe ich 1599.*

Acc. no. P 1940-75
Formerly Johannes Jantzen Collection, Bremen

Common beaker shape, which has come down to us with various types of painted decoration. See Saldern, *Enameled Glass*, 1965, 164, fig. 296, 168, fig. 304, 170, fig. 311; Klesse

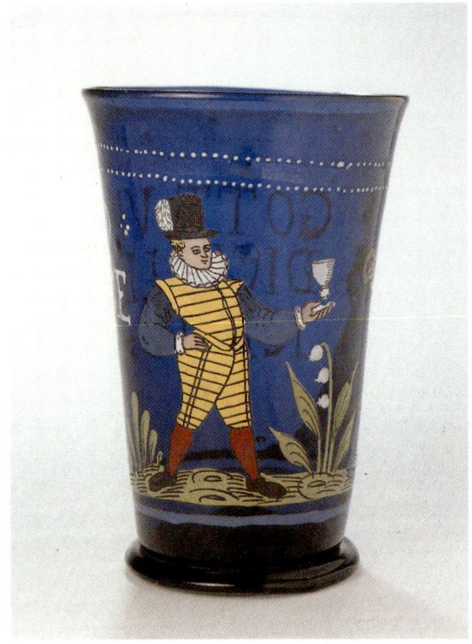

and Saldern, *Sammlung Biemann*, 1978, cat. no. 269, and others.

Lit.: Heinemeyer, *Glas*, 1966, cat. no. 161

112 Plate

Bohemia
Ca. 1600
H 2.6, ⌀ 20.1 cm

Free-blown, dilated. Narrow applied foot-ring. Enamel painting in white and yellow.

Acc. no. P 1940-77
Formerly Johannes Jantzen Collection, Bremen

Closely related to plates in the Biemann Collection at The Art Institute of Chicago, formerly Mühsam Collection, amongst others. See Klesse and Saldern, *Sammlung Biemann*, 1978, no. 273.

Lit.: Heinemeyer, *Glas*, 1966, cat. no. 163; Baumgärtner, *Sächsisches Glas*, 1977, 45, and fig. 15, where the author claims the piece was produced in Saxony

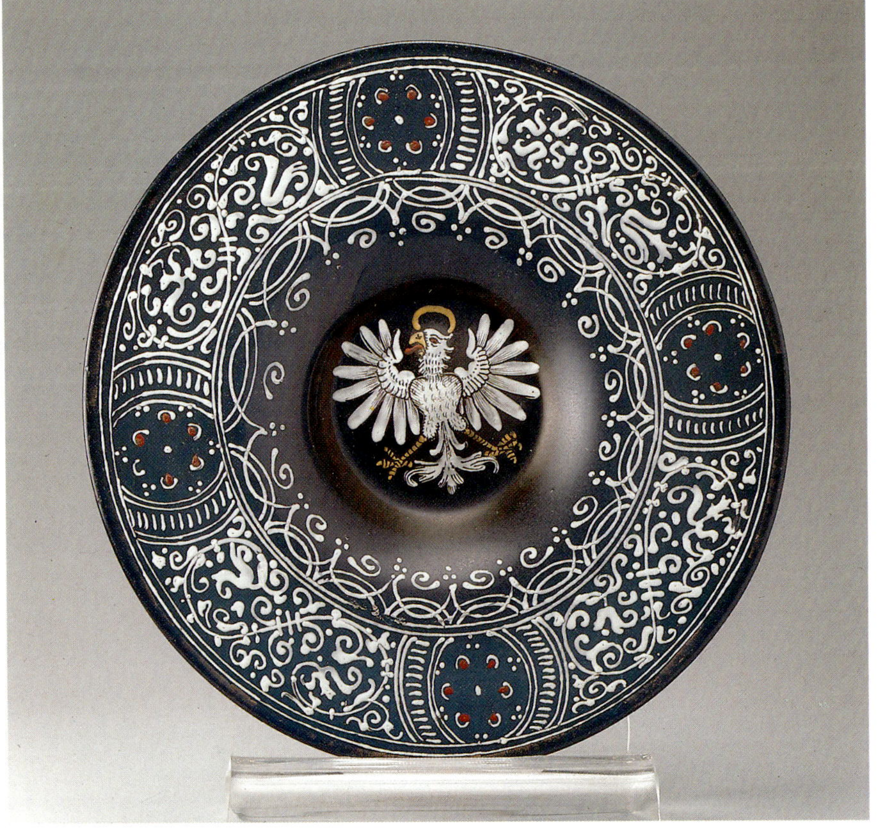

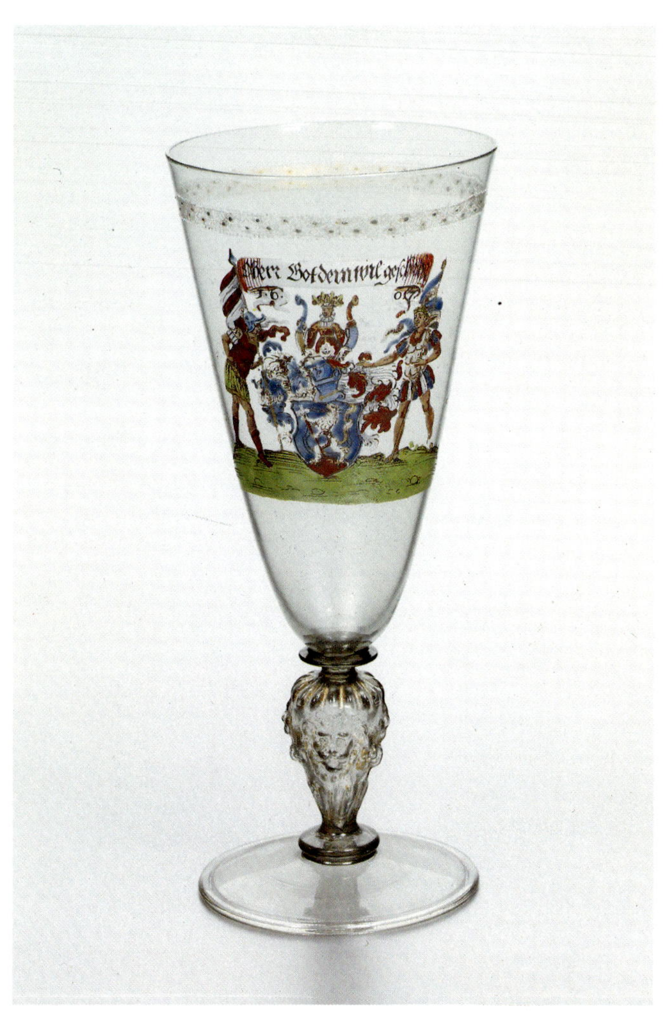

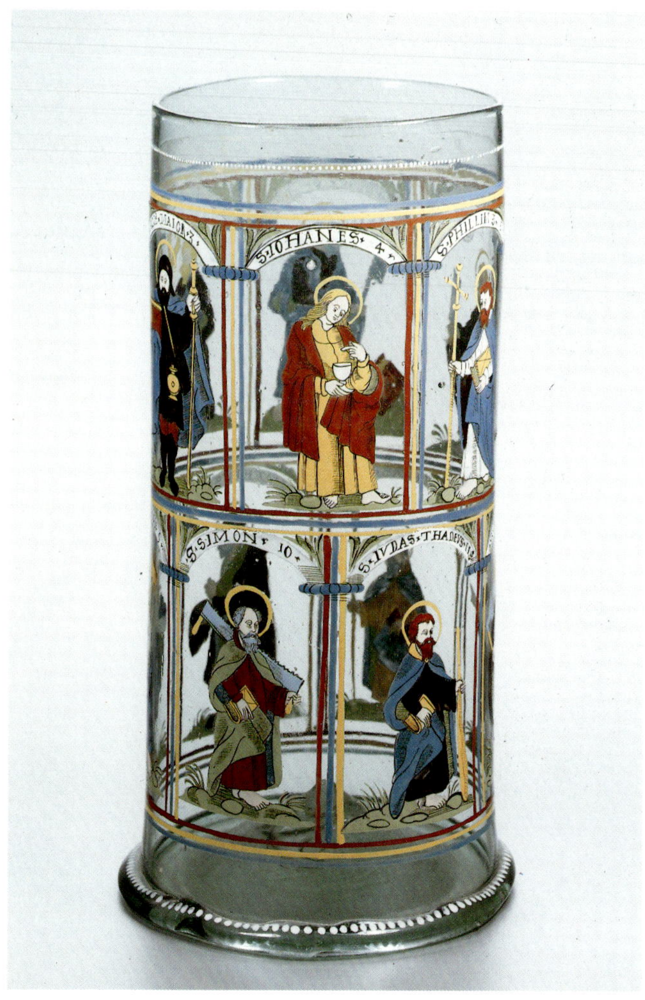

113 Goblet

Southern Germany
Dated 1607
H 25.7, ⌀ 11.5 cm

Mold-blown, comprising three separately
worked pieces. Stem with four lions' masks
and flowers. Foot folded downwards.
Enamel and gold painted decoration: an
unidentified coat of arms. Inscription: *O herr
Got dein wil geschehe 1.6.0.7.*

Acc. no. P 1940-31
Formerly Johannes Jantzen Collection, Bremen

Closely linked to Venetian sources of the
16th century. Glasses of this type were made
in *Weissglashütten* (glasshouses specialized in
white or clear glass) in southern Germany
and probably in Bohemia. They produced luxury glass for the nobility and patricians from
the towns in the period around 1600. For a
similar glass see *3000 Jahre*, Lucerne, 1981,
cat. no. 660.

Lit.: Heinemeyer, *Glas*, 1966, cat. no. 169;
Saldern, *Alte Gläser*, 1968, cat. no. 25

114 *Humpen*

Bohemia
Dated 1611
H 31.7, ⌀ 14.1 cm

Greenish glass. Probably free-blown and
shaped. Folded foot-rim.
Enamel painting: the 12 apostles, identifiable
by their attributes and the marks.
Top row: *S.PETRVS.1 S.ANDREAS.2. S.IACOB
MAIOR.3. S.IOHANNES.4. PHILLIPVS.5.
S.BARTOLLOMEVS.6.*
Bottom row: *S.THOMAS.7. S.MATHEVS.8.
S.IACOB MINOR.9. S.SIMON.10. S.IVDAS
THADEVS.11. S.MATHIAS.12.*

Acc. no. P 1940-80
Formerly Johannes Jantzen Collection, Bremen

Enamel-painted *Humpen* with depictions of
religious subjects were less common than the
popular armorial glasses, *Reichsadlerhumpen*,
Kurfürstenhumpen, hunting scenes, etc. For
Apostelhumpen see Saldern, *Enameled Glass*,
1965, 86ff., where the woodcut on which the
Düsseldorf glass is based is also illustrated,
p. 88, fig. 93, and Baumgärtner, Bremen I,
1987, no. 63.

Lit.: Heinemeyer, *Glas*, 1966, cat. no. 171

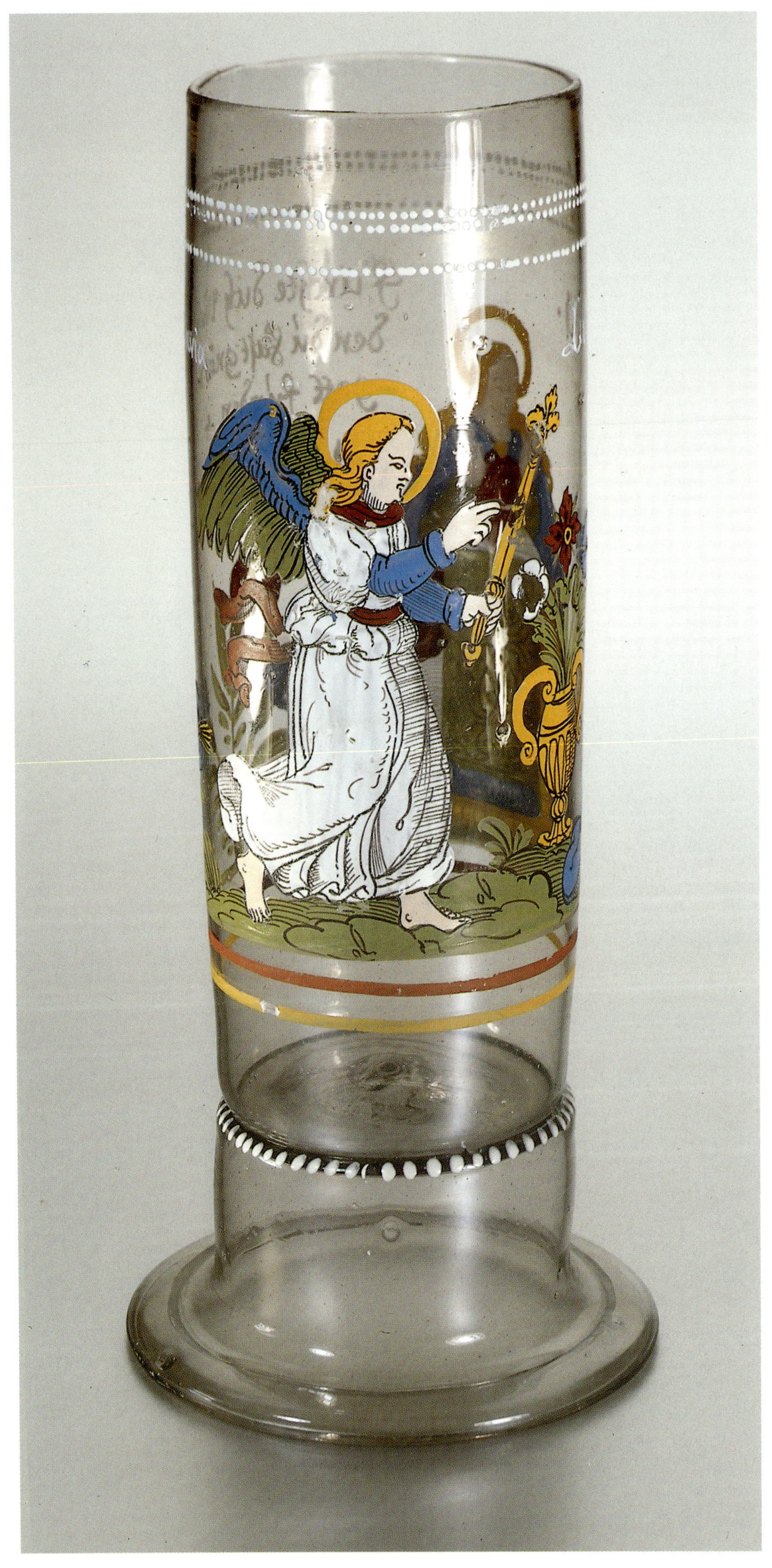

115 *Stangenglas*

Bohemia
Dated 1613
H 25.8, ⌀ 10.6 cm

Colorless glass. Mold-blown, shaped. Two
separately worked pieces fused together. Foot
folded downwards. Enamel painting: the
Annunciation scene accompanied by the
inscription: *Fürchte dich nicht Maria / den du
hast gnade bey / gott funden / 1613/ Luce.1.*

Acc. no. P 1940-81
Formerly Johannes Jantzen Collection,
Bremen

Rare subject in the popular enamel painting
of the early 17th century.
This kind of *Stangenglas* with a raised cylindrical foot was amongst the most expensive
vessel types of the period. Its origins can be
traced back to the 16th century. Numerous
armorial glasses of the mid-century took this
shape, but had a flaring foot.

Lit.: Saldern, *Enameled Glass*, 1965, 91, fig.
109; Heinemeyer, *Glas*, 1966, cat. no. 172;
Ricke, *2500 Jahre*, 1987, cat. no. 64

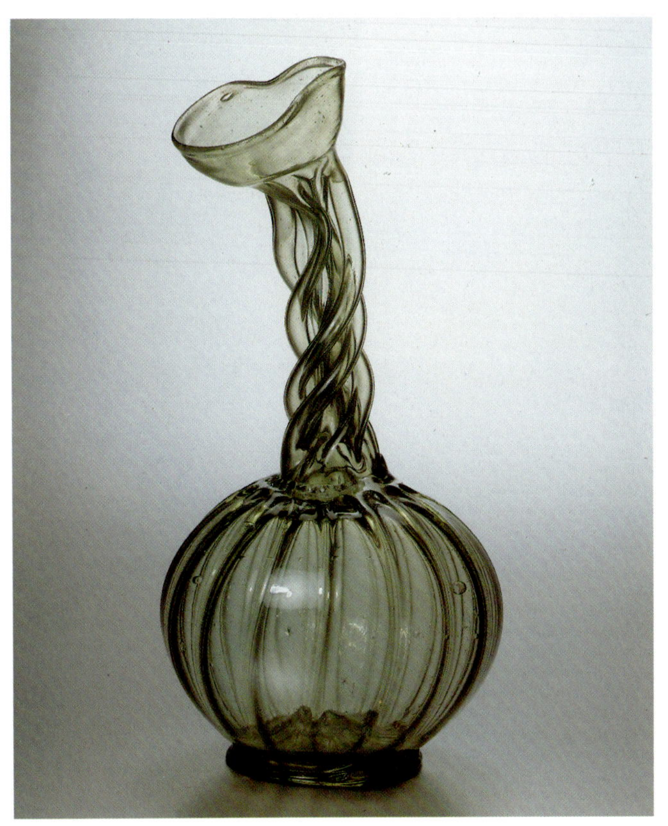

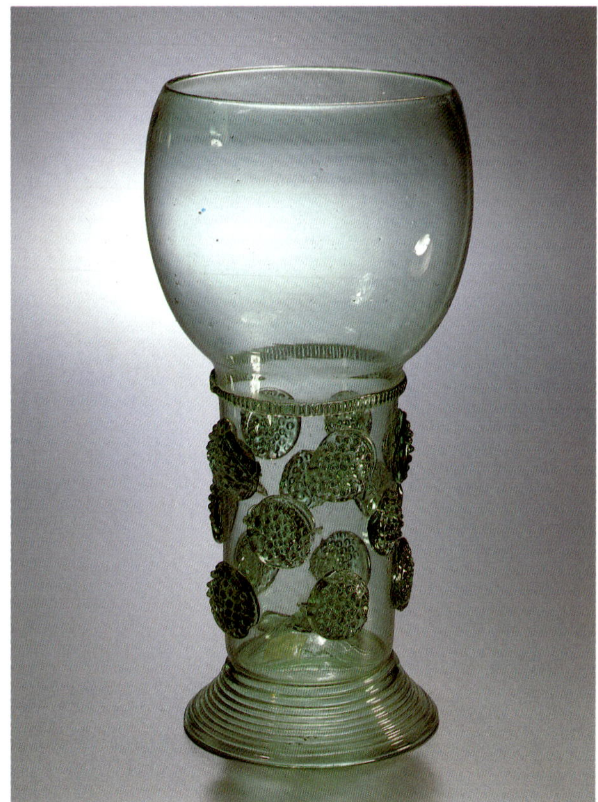

116 *Kuttrolf*

Germany
1st half of 17th c.
H 21.3, ⌀ 10.5 cm

Yellow-green glass. Optic-blown, shaped.

Acc. no. P 1940-53
Formerly Johannes Jantzen Collection,
Bremen

The medieval *Kuttrolf* with its complicated
construction, usually with a strongly contorted neck, is extant in numerous variations.
See Klesse and Reineking, Cologne, 1973,
nos. 183ff.; Baumgärtner, Regensburg, 1977,
nos. 54f.; Rückert, Munich, 1982, vol. 1,
nos. 253ff.; and Baumgärtner, Bremen I,
1987, no. 11. A very similar piece to the
present one is at the Gewerbemuseum Nürnberg, acc. no. G 3365. This type of "gurgling
bottle" served as a drinking vessel for brandy.

Lit.: Heinemeyer, *Glas*, 1966, cat. no. 133

117 *Römer*

Germany (Spessart?) or The Netherlands
Mid-17th century
H 19, ⌀ 9.8 cm

Light green glass. Mold-blown, shaped. Foot
decorated with trailing. On the stem are
three staggered rows of five raspberry prunts
each.

Acc. no. P 1940-18
Formerly Johannes Jantzen Collection,
Bremen

The term *Römer* originally described a large
variety of forms. See A.-E. Theuerkauff-
Liederwald, "Der Römer," *Journal of Glass
Studies* 11 (1969): 114–55.
Common drinking vessel for wine, frequently
depicted in Netherlandish still lifes of the
17th century. For this subject see especially
Grimm, *Glück und Glas*, 1984.

Lit.: Heinemeyer, *Glas*, 1966, cat. no. 146;
Ricke, *2500 Jahre*, 1987, cat. no. 69

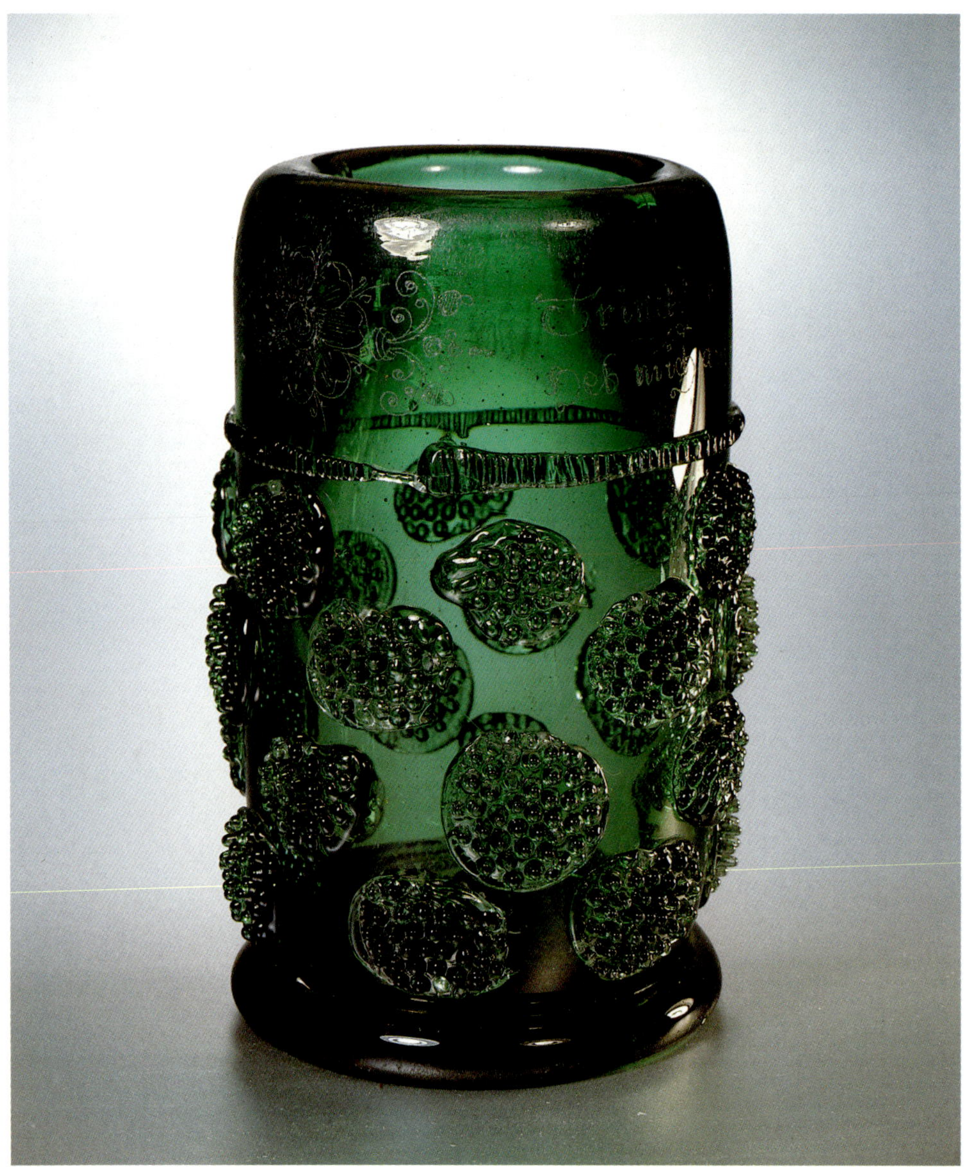

118   "Unbreakable" Beaker

Germany
Dated 1659
H 13, ⌀ 8.8 cm

Dark green glass. Mold-blown, shaped. Folded
foot-ring. Raspberry prunts, stamped with
relief ornament, in four staggered rows of six
each. Diamond-engraved inscription: *Trinckh
mich auss unnd würff mich Nider / Heb mich
auff unnd vill mich wider Ao. 1659.*

Acc. no. P 1936-96
Formerly Josef Lückger Collection, Cologne

Popular type of beaker in the second half of
the 17th century. The saying, which refers to
the robustness of the thick-walled vessel,
always indicates a year. The known pieces
usually bear dates between 1643 (The J. Paul
Getty Museum, Malibu, Hess and Husband,
Getty, 1997, cat. no. 13) and 1664. Comparable pieces in Saldern, *Alte Gläser*, 1968, cat.
no. 17. A cruder piece with a relatively late
date for this group is in Grimm, *Glück und
Glas*, 1984, no. III 58 (archaeological find
from Holland). Unlike the others, this piece
is presumably not from the same workshop.

Lit.: Heinemeyer, *Glas*, 1966, cat. no. 130;
Saldern, *Alte Gläser*, 1968, cat. no. 17; Ricke,
2500 Jahre, 1987, cat. no. 67

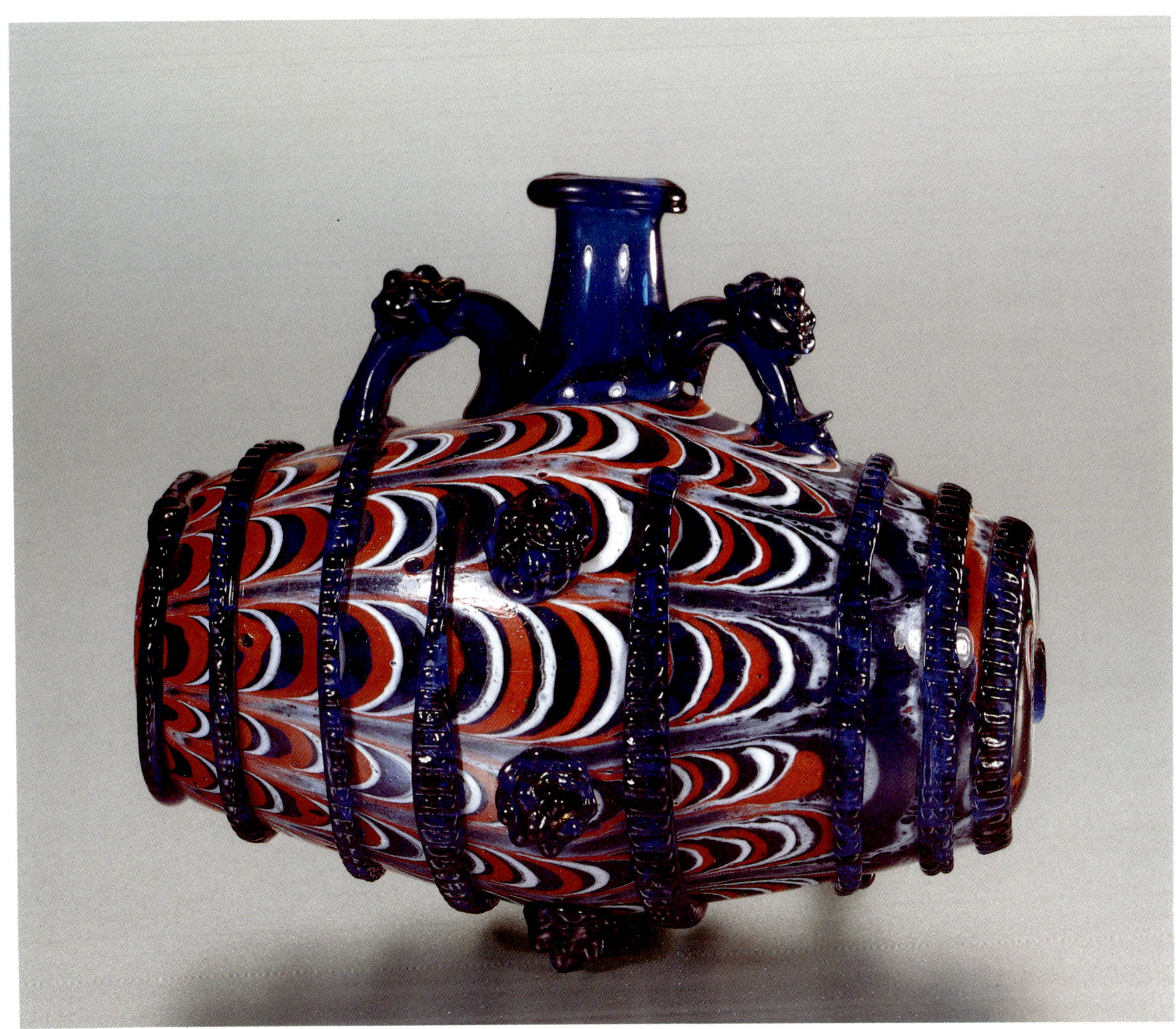

119   Barrel Flask

France, Auvergne (?)
17th c.
H 9.1, L 10.8, ⌀ 7.3 cm

Mold-blown, opaque red and white threads combined into a wave pattern. Freely applied decoration. Traces of gilding on the eight raspberry prunts.

Acc. no. P 1940-35
Formerly Johannes Jantzen Collection, Bremen; previously Merkens Collection, Cologne

Comparable pieces at the Musée des Arts Décoratifs, Paris; see also D. P. Lanmon, *Glass from Six Centuries: Wadsworth Atheneum* (Hartford, CT, 1978), cat. no. 16. A lavishly decorated example of the barrel-shaped joke vessel common in 17th-century Europe. The Cologne-Ehrenfeld glassworks used this piece as a prototype for one of its models. See Ricke, "Rhein und Saar," *19. Jahrhundert*, 1981, 226, fig. 17.

Lit.: Heinemeyer, *Glas*, 1966, cat. no. 143; Ricke op. cit.; Ricke, *2500 Jahre*, 1987, cat. no. 70

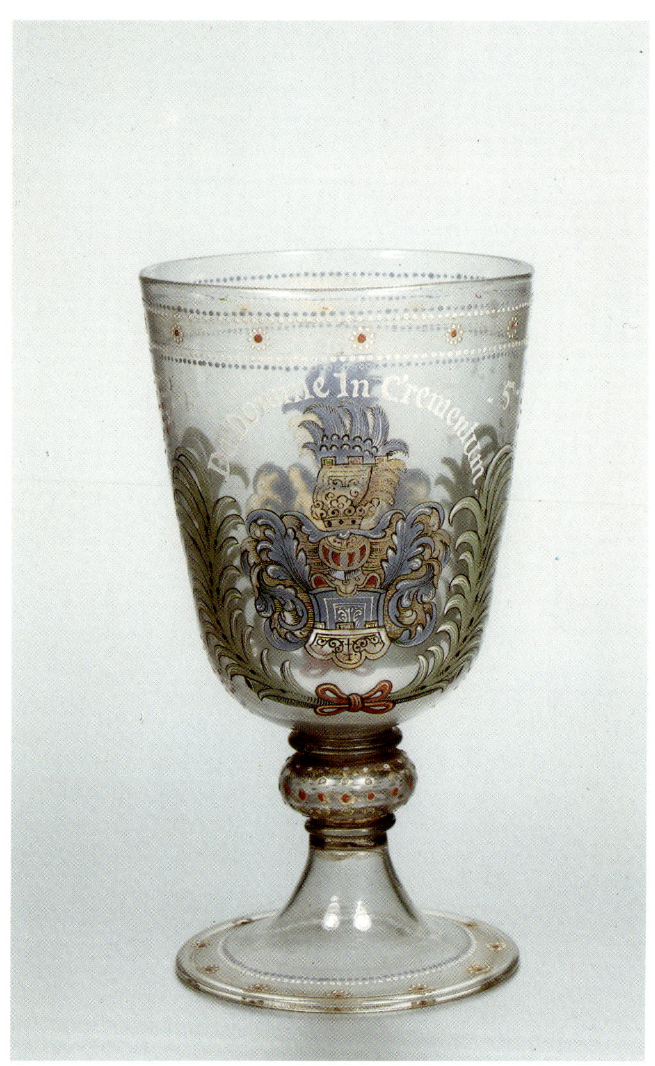

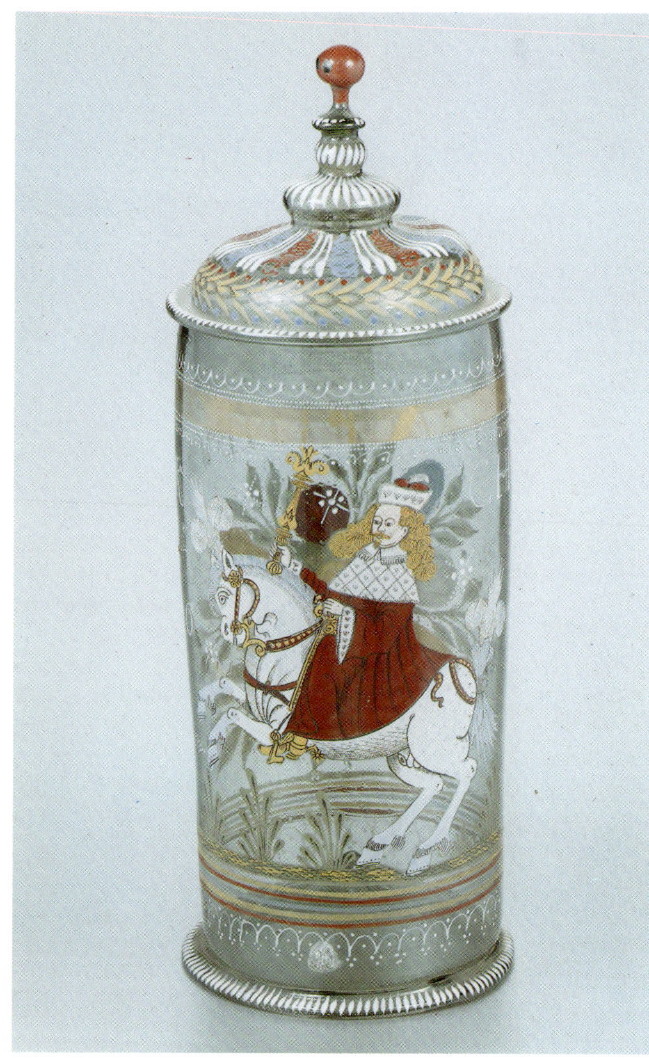

120 Goblet

Saxony
Dated 1645
H 20.1, ⌀ 11.6 cm

Colorless, light gray tone. Mold-blown, shaped.
Three separately worked pieces fused together.
Enamel painting on the front and on the
reverse: the coat of arms of the city of
Bautzen and the inscription *Da Domine In
Crementum 1645*.

Acc. no. P 1940-82
Formerly Johannes Jantzen Collection, Bremen

Determining the authenticity of this glass
has not been without controversy. Doubts
arose, however, only as a result of the false
assumption that it was made in 1545 (a mis-
print in Heinemeyer, *Glas*, 1966). This error
recurs in the subsequent literature. The goblet's shape is not unusual, however, for 1645,
the actual date of production. The enamel
painting would not seem to contradict this.

Lit.: Heinemeyer, *Glas*, 1966, cat. no. 153;
Baumgärtner, *Sächsisches Glas*, 1977, 38 and
fig. 1

121 *Kurfürstenhumpen*

Brandenburg, Marienwalde (?)
Dated 1658
H 34.5, ⌀ 12.9 cm

Glass with greenish tone. Probably free-blown
and shaped. Folded thread as foot-ring. Cover
does not belong to goblet.
Colored enamel painting: the elector of Brandenburg mounted on a horse. On the reverse: a
spray of flowers and plants and the mark *CHUR
BRANDENBURGK*.

Acc. no. P 1940-85
Formerly Johannes Jantzen Collection, Bremen;
previously Ermelinghof Manor Collection

Conceptually linked to the *Reichsadlerhumpen*
and *Kurfürstenhumpen* of the period. Its attribution to the glasshouse of the Brandenburg
electorate in Marienwalde rests on the image of
the prince. It is also possible, however, that the
Humpen was originally part of a set of several
glasses depicting the electoral college. In that
case a Bohemian or central German provenance
would be more likely.

Lit.: Heinemeyer, *Glas*, 1966, cat. no. 183

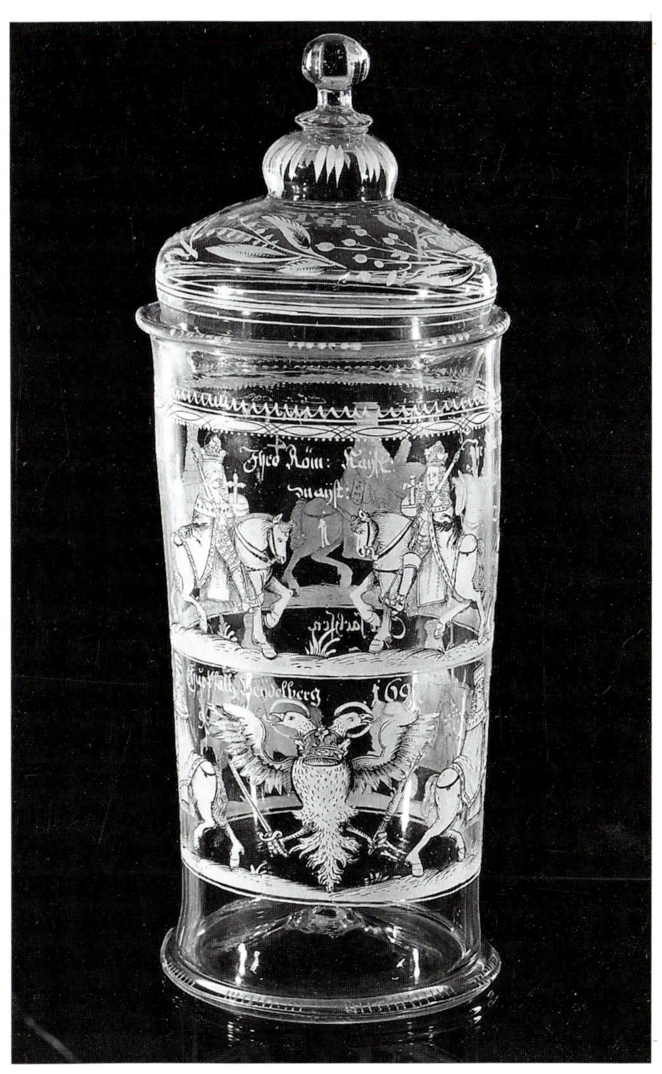

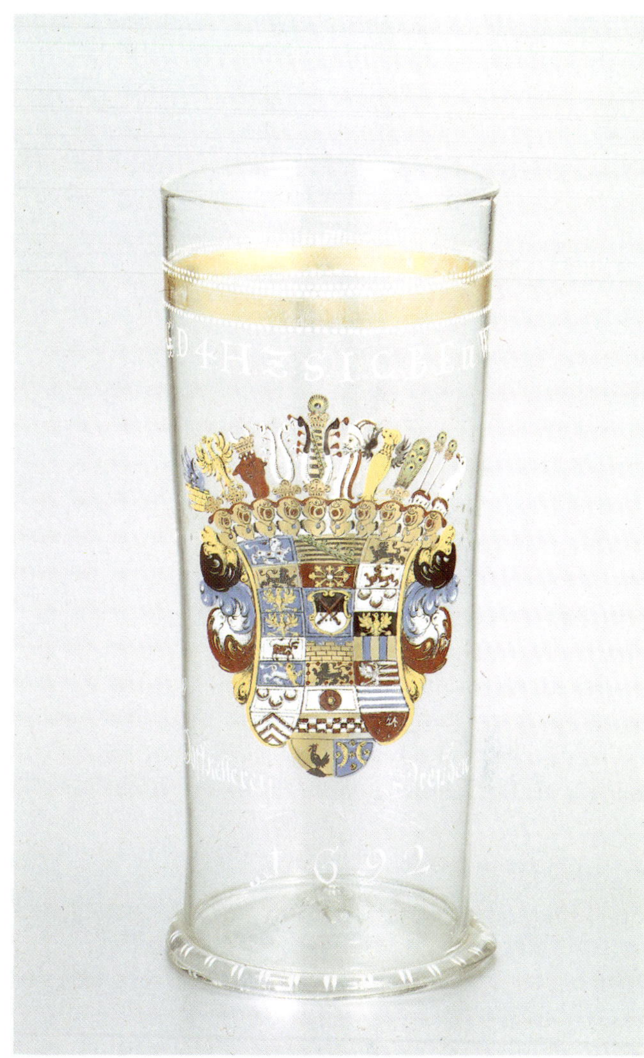

122   Covered *Kurfürstenhumpen*

Thuringia or Saxony
Dated 1691
H with cover 38, ⌀ 14.6 cm

Colorless glass. Probably free-blown and shaped.
White and black opaque enamel painting depict-
ing the emperor, the king, and the seven elec-
tors of the German Reich, who can be identified
by the accompanying marks. Top row: *Ihro Röm:
Kasl: Mast: 1 Ihr Röm: Königl: Mast. 2. Chur
Maintz 3. Chur Cöln 4. Chur Thrier 5.*
Bottom row: *Chur Beijeren 6 Chur Sachsen 7 Chur
Brandenburg 8 Chur Pfaltz Heijdelberg 9 1691*

Acc. no. P 1940-86
Formerly Johannes Jantzen Collection, Bremen

Late example of enamel painted glassware representing the empire. Only a few comparable
pieces are documented. See, for example, Rückert, Munich, 1982, no. 195. Based on the painting on the foot-ring, Rückert is against attributing the group to Franconia, contrary to previous
opinion.

Lit.: Saldern, *Enameled Glass*, 1965, 76, fig. 73;
Heinemeyer, *Glas*, 1966, cat. no. 187

123   *Hofkellereihumpen*

Saxony
Dated 1692
H 26, ⌀ 11.7 cm

Colorless glass. Probably free-blown and shaped.
Folded thread as foot-ring. Enamel painting: the
coat of arms of the Saxon electorate. Above:
J.G.4.H.Z.S.J.C.B.E.u.W.C. (Johann Georg der 4.,
Herzog zu Sachsen, Jülich, Cleve, Berg, Engern
und Westfalen, Churfürst). Below: *Hoffkellerey
Dressden 1692.*

Acc. no. P 1940-88
Formerly Johannes Jantzen Collection, Bremen

The traditional form of the Saxon *Hofkellereiglas*
(literally, court cellar glass), in use from the
first half of the 17th century until the early 18th
century with few changes. See Rückert, Munich,
1982, no. 180. Other types appear in Klesse and
Saldern, *Sammlung Biemann*, 1978, cat. nos.
312ff., and Saldern, *Enameled Glass*, 1965,
200ff. For a parallel piece of the same date see
Baumgärtner, Bremen I, 1987, no. 67.

Lit.: Heinemeyer, *Glas*, 1966, cat. no. 188

Venice and "Façon de Venise"

Since the late Middle Ages the fame of Venetian glass-ware has rested on the thinness and purity of its colorless glass mass. Since the fifteenth century Murano glassblowers have known how to fuse *cristallo* or *cristallino*, names that conjure up the purity of rock crystal. Venetian glass must have been produced in large quantities as early as the high Middle Ages. In 1292 the *signoria*, the island republic's council, felt compelled to banish the constantly growing glasshouses to the offshore island of Murano for fear of fire.

There are no reliable sources or verifiable facts about the early period of Venetian glass art to date. Firm ground is gained beginning in the second half of the fifteenth century, when the highly valued enam-eled and gilded glassware of Murano became an inte-gral part of late medieval culture.

The Islamic origins are not discernible in the design of the extant pieces. The large decorative ves-sel in the shape of a mosque lamp (cat. no. 124) is unique. Its exceptional status becomes clear against the background of the production range around 1500, which tended to be based on prototypes found in late Gothic goldsmith art (cat. nos. 125, 126).

As the leading glassmaking center in Europe, Venice maintained its position unchallenged from 1500 to the second half of the seventeenth century. In quick succession Murano glassblowers developed a large number of complicated new glass techniques and started reusing processes known in antiquity. The revival and improvement of the millefiori technique seem to have marked the beginning of this develop-ment. To make the mosaic bowls, Venetian glass arti-sans no longer melted the prepared patterned glass slices into molds. Instead, they picked up the disks with a hot gob of glass and subsequently blew them into the shape of a vessel (cat. no. 127).

The next step was to take up and modify ancient thread techniques. Glassware decorated with embed-ded, usually opaque white, filigree-glass canes were soon amongst the most sought-after products of Mura-no glassworks in the sixteenth century. One peak in this development was the invention of the *reticello* or network-glass technique (cat. no. 134 and "Tech-niques," p. 359).

In spite of repeated attempts to secure a monopoly on their glassware, Venetians were not able to prevent the founding of glasshouses working in a Venetian manner ("à la façon de Venise") north of the Alps. As early as the first half of the sixteenth century inter-ested landgraves and clever merchants established the first *Weissglashütten* (glasshouses specializing in white or colorless glass) in the north. They were either run by masters from the glassmaking city Altare near Genoa, Murano's rival, or by itinerant Murano glass artisans who were not deterred by the Draconian fines of the *signoria*. Since the recipes, shapes, and techniques employed by these glassblow-ers were Venetian, today it is virtually impossible to distinguish between glassware created in Murano and products made "à la façon de Venise" in Austria, Ger-many, or The Netherlands.

Only slowly did vessel types emerge that enabled, within the framework of the Venetian formal canon, an independent regional development—particularly in the efficient glasshouses of the southern Netherlands, in Liège and Antwerp (cat. nos. 132, 133). Such trends are most readily visible in the so-called winged glasses, also referred to as "verres à serpent," or drag-on-stem glasses (cat. no. 135), in Dutch sources. Their characteristic form cannot be easily localized to Venice. The theory that the two-part stem motif of these decorative goblets, sometimes also called "Impe-rialgläser" in German sources, developed from the Habsburg double eagle, supports the assumption that this type was made in the north.

Artisans often created hybrids, combining Venetian techniques—such as crackling the surface by plunging the hot glass into cold water (ice glass)—with forms from the north (cat. nos. 129, 131). Apart from pieces made in Flanders, such glassware came primarily from southern German glasshouses.

Generally Venetian blowers relied on the sponta-neous forms made directly at the furnace for their effects. Decoration by enamel painting and gilding became less common in the sixteenth century. Only the delicate line decoration of diamond-point engrav-ing (cat. nos. 128, 130) continued to be used over a longer period for its form-enhancing effects.

In the seventeenth century glassmakers attempted to heighten the attractiveness of Murano glass with ever more lavish thread decoration and three-dimen-sional applications (cat. no. 138). In addition, they increasingly used more color accents. Venetian glass-makers were not, however, able to satisfy the growing desire to use glass as a means of conveying allegorical meaning or individual statements during the Baroque period. Attempts to keep up with the development in the north by engraving glasses in the Bohemian man-ner were not successful. The crisis in Venetian glass art was obvious by the late seventeenth century. Despite several earlier attempts to overcome it, the crisis ended with Antonio Salviati's immense success at the World Exhibitions in the second half of the nineteenth century.

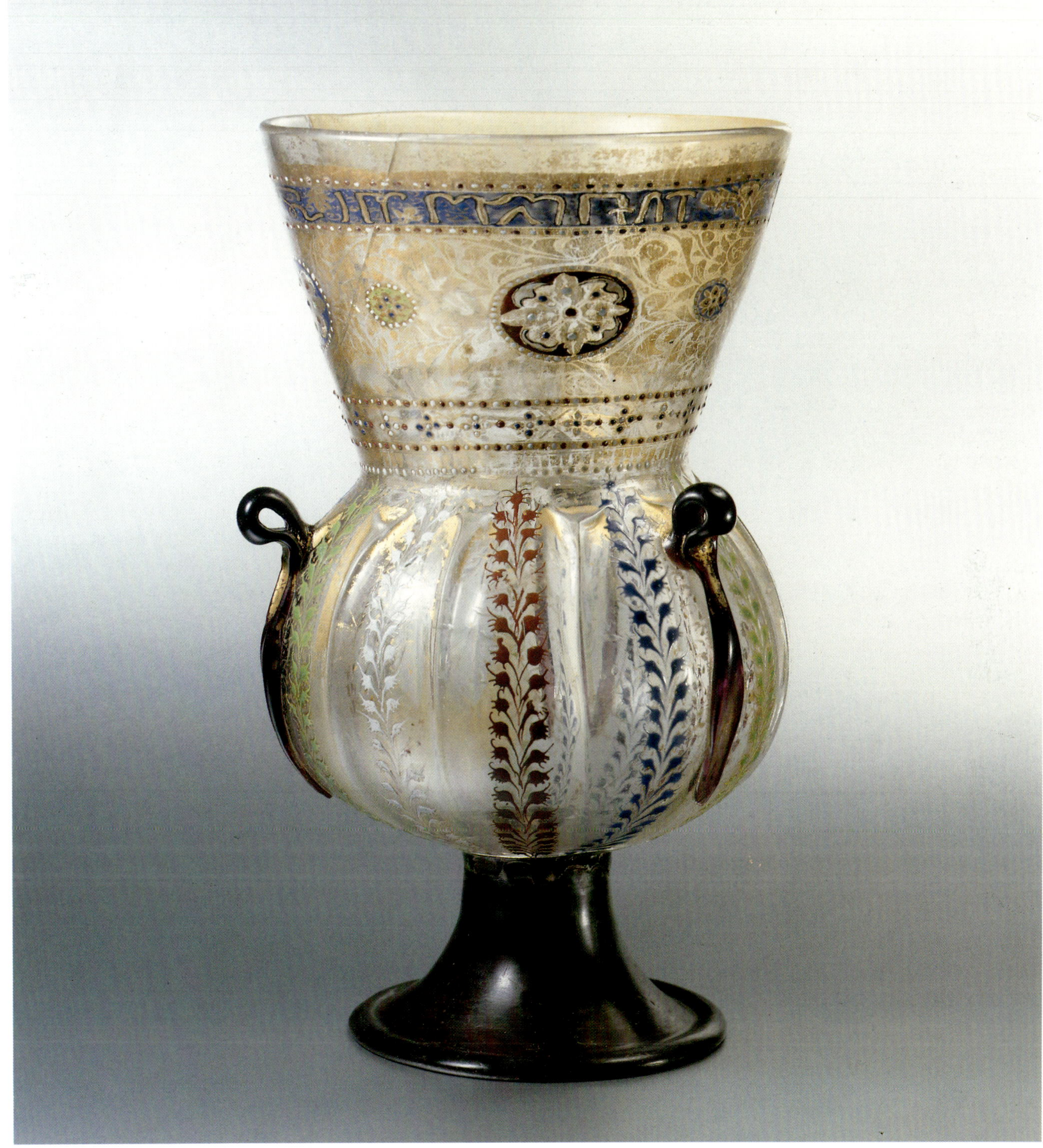

**124 Decorative Vessel in the Shape of a
     Mosque Lamp**

Venice
Ca. 1500
H 30.6, ⌀ mouth 18.4 cm

Colorless glass, manganese-violet foot and
loop handles. Optic-blown and shaped.
Twelve wide ribs. Enameled and etched gold
decoration.
Broken in several places, glued. Body restored.
Foot reconstructed.

Acc. no. P 1978-1

The pseudo-Kufic inscription under the mouth
makes no sense, proving that the glass came
neither from an Islamic workshop nor was
made in Murano for the East. As a decorative
vessel in the Islamic style, the large lamp is
a unique piece. It illustrates the influence of
Syrian enamel and gold painting, which came
to an end after the Mongolian incursions
around 1400, on the flourishing glass art of
Venice.

Lit.: H. Ricke, "Halb Orient, halb Okzident:
Eine venezianische Moscheeampel für das
Kunstmuseum," *Düsseldorfer Hefte 23*, no. 18
(1978): 11; Ricke, *Ausgewählte Werke*, 1980,
8; Stefano Carboni and David Whitehouse,
Glass of the Sultans, exh. cat. (New York: The
Metropolitan Museum of Art, 2001), 304f.,
no. 152

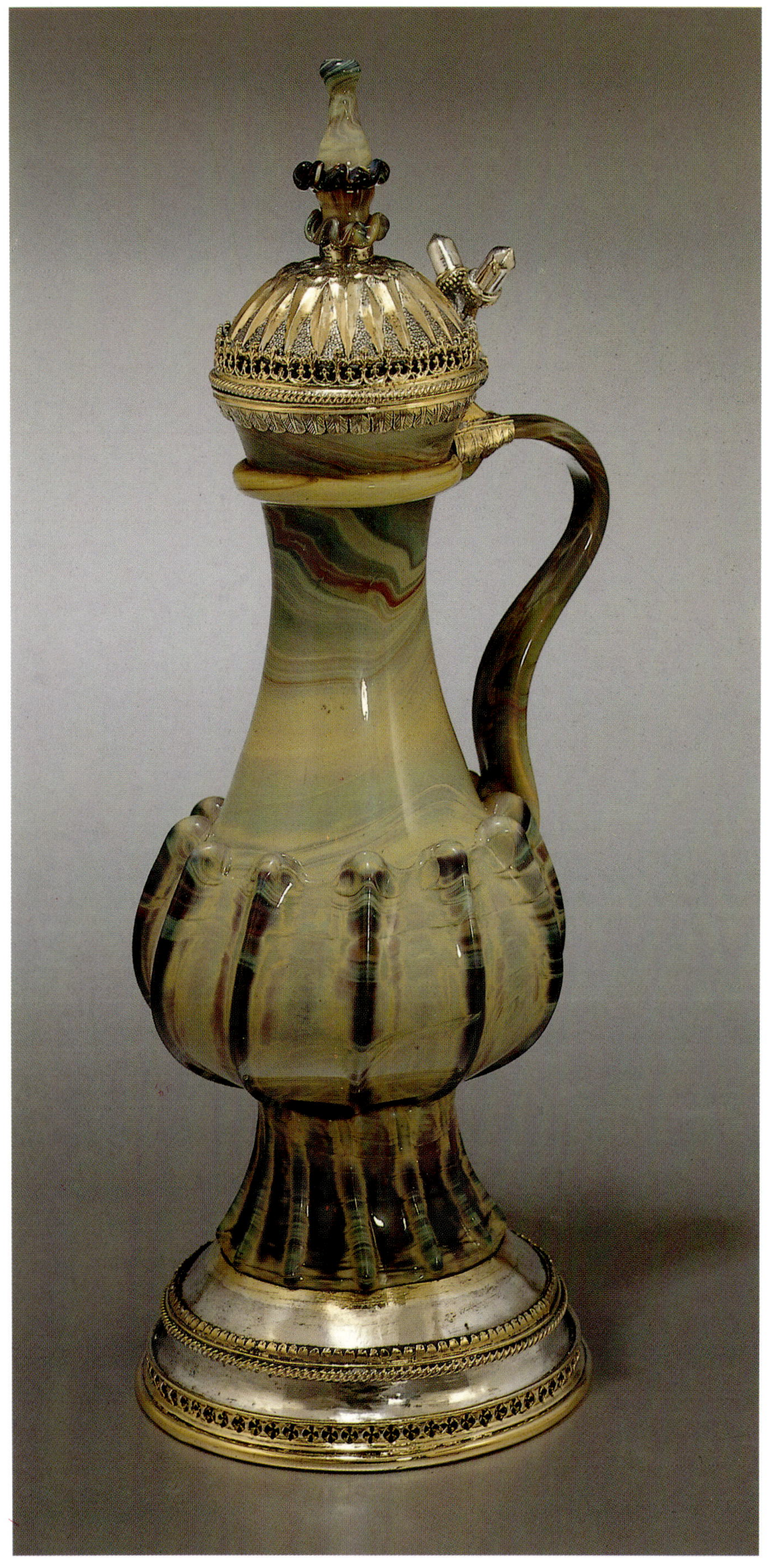

125 Ribbed Pitcher

Venice
Late 15th c.
H with lid 36.2, without 27.5 cm
⌀ body 12.1, mouth 7.5, foot 12.9 cm
Mount: silver, partly gilded, ca. 1520–30

Agate glass (*calcedonio*), dark red when light shines through it. Blown; fused from two parts. Lower portion of vessel body covered with another layer of glass and shaped in a 12-part skeleton mold; the added foot also has 12 ribs; freely applied handle with tripartite fluting.
After foot and lid were damaged, set in partly gilded silver mount, completely covering mouth and foot. The extant finial of the original lid was worked into the mount.

Acc. no. P 1992-23
Formerly Collection of the Princely Family of Salm-Reifferscheidt, Castle Dyck

Acquired with the support of the Kultusministerium des Landes Nordrhein-Westfalen and the Stiftung Kunst und Kultur des Landes Nordrhein-Westfalen

Agate or chalcedony glass was one of the most highly valued products of Venetian glasshouses in late medieval times. It is made by repeatedly shaping and working, cooling down, and reheating the glass mass colored with various metal oxides. See, amongst others, Dreier, *Venezianische Gläser*, 1989, 54ff., no. 26, and Theuerkauff-Liederwald, *Venezianisches Glas*, 1994, 73ff. Only a few late Gothic agate-glass pouring vessels are documented; most are without ribs and have elegant, slim spouts, recalling Islamic pieces. See, amongst others, the *Schnabelkanne* (pitcher with beak-shaped lip) in Ohm, Bauer, and Gabbert, Frankfurt, 1980, 60, no. 106, and cover image. Ribbed pitchers, in contrast, are much rarer. A direct parallel is a pitcher at the British Museum in London. It is somewhat larger, but more compact in its proportions. See H. Tait, *The Golden Age of Venetian Glass*, exh. cat. (London: The British Museum, 1979), 105, cat. no. 167, color plate 9 on p. 81.
The mount heightens the slimmer and tauter effect of the Düsseldorf pitcher. The lower half of the silver foot-ring is an additional socle made for the vessel by a goldsmith. The original foot rim must have been at half the height of the present foot-ring.

Lit.: Cat., *Kunsthistorische Ausstellung* (Düsseldorf, 1902), no. 833; O. von Falke and H. Frauberger, *Deutsche Schmelzarbeiten des Mittelalters* (Frankfurt, 1904), 138, pl. 126; R. Schmidt, *Das Glas* (Berlin and Leipzig, 1922), 82; exh. cat., *Grosse Kunst des Mittelalters* (Cologne: Schnütgen-Museum, 1960), 68, no. 102; H. Kohlhausen, *Europäisches Kunsthandwerk 2: Gotik und Spätgotik* (Frankfurt, 1970), XII, XXXVII, fig. 67

126 Goblet

Venice
Late 15th/early 16th c.
H 16, ⌀ 17.2 cm

Colorless glass. Bowl mold-blown, shaped;
foot optic-blown in 12-part mold, shaped,
upwardly folded foot rim. Enamel painting
and gilding.

Acc. no. P 1940-27
Formerly Johannes Jantzen Collection, Bremen

Very rare as goblet type, but in its construction related to common Venetian goblets and
standing cups of the period around 1500.

Lit.: Heinemeyer, *Glas*, 1966, cat. no. 214;
Saldern, *Alte Gläser*, 1968, cat. no. 19; Ricke,
Ausgewählte Werke, 1980, 9; *Mille anni*, 1982,
cat. no. 120

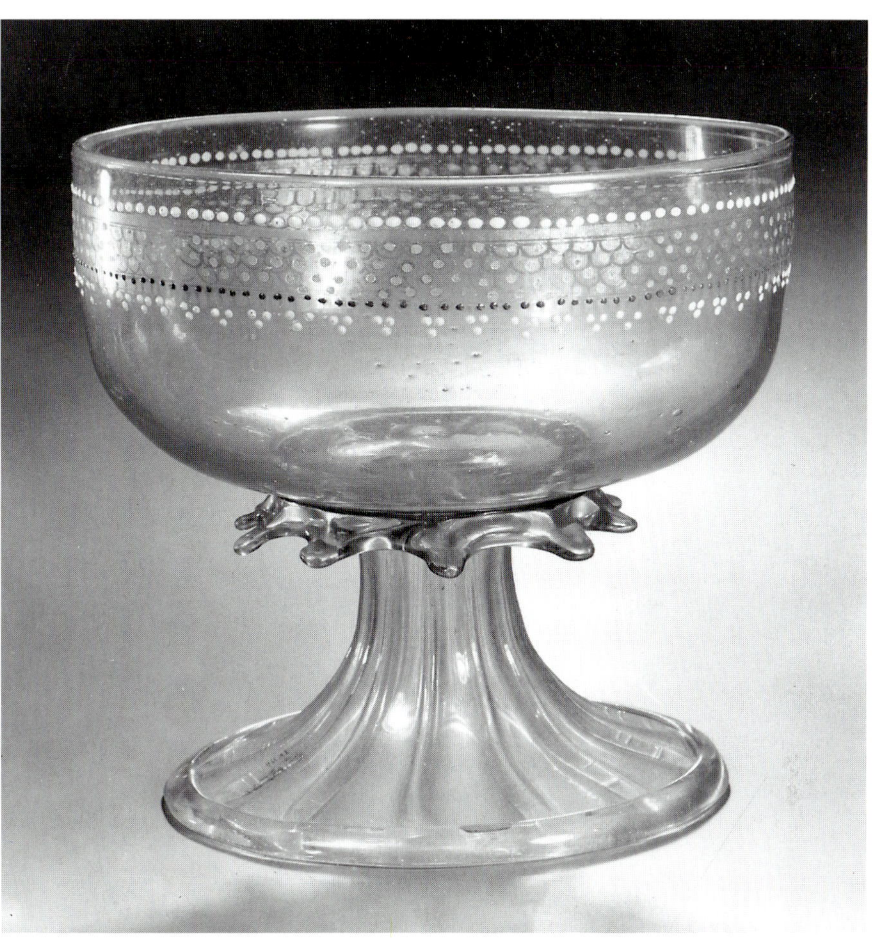

127 Millefiori Bowl

Venice
Late 15th/early 16th c.
H 7, ⌀ 10.1 cm

Multicolored millefiori disks partly underlaid
with gold, on manganese-violet ground.
Optic-blown in mold with 31 ribs, shaped.

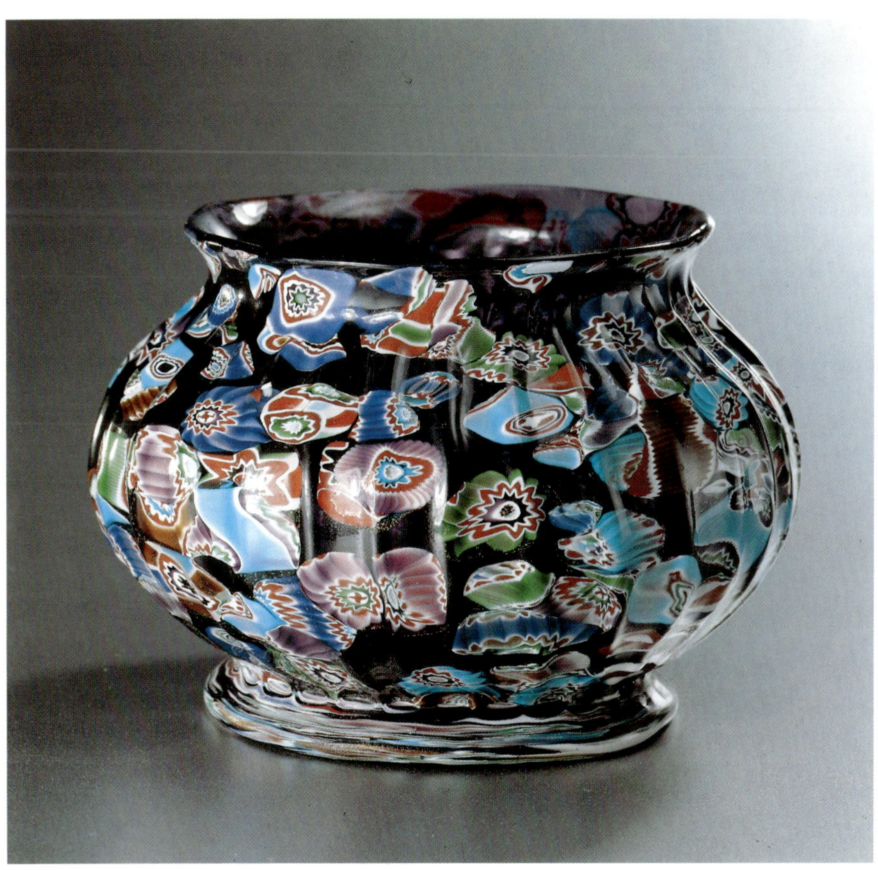

Folded, trailed foot-ring, marbled by stretching a millefiori slice.

Acc. no. 17786
Formerly Karl Thewalt Collection, Cologne

The glassmaker resorted to Roman millefiori
design. The Düsseldorf bowl is amongst the
extremely rare early examples of this technique. In contrast to the ancient mold-melted dishes, the Venetian pieces were made by
rolling the prepared patterned slices in a
glass matrix and then blowing the vessel into
shape.
Comparable pieces are illustrated in, for
example, H. Tait, *The Golden Age of Venetian
Glass*, exh. cat. (London: The British Museum,
1979), 104f., nos. 164–66.
For the revival of the ancient millefiori technique in Venice see P. Hollister, "'Flowers
which clothe the meadows in spring': The
Rebirth of Millefiori c. 1500," *Annales du 8e
Congrès de l'Association Internationale pour
l'Histoire du Verre* (Liège, 1981), 221–33.

Lit.: Heinemeyer, *Glas*, 1966, cat. no. 230
(222); Saldern, *Alte Gläser*, 1968, cat. no. 20;
Barovier Mentasti, *Vetro Veneziano*, 1982, 41;
Mille anni, 1982, cat. no. 104; Ricke, *2500
Jahre*, 1987, cat. no. 57

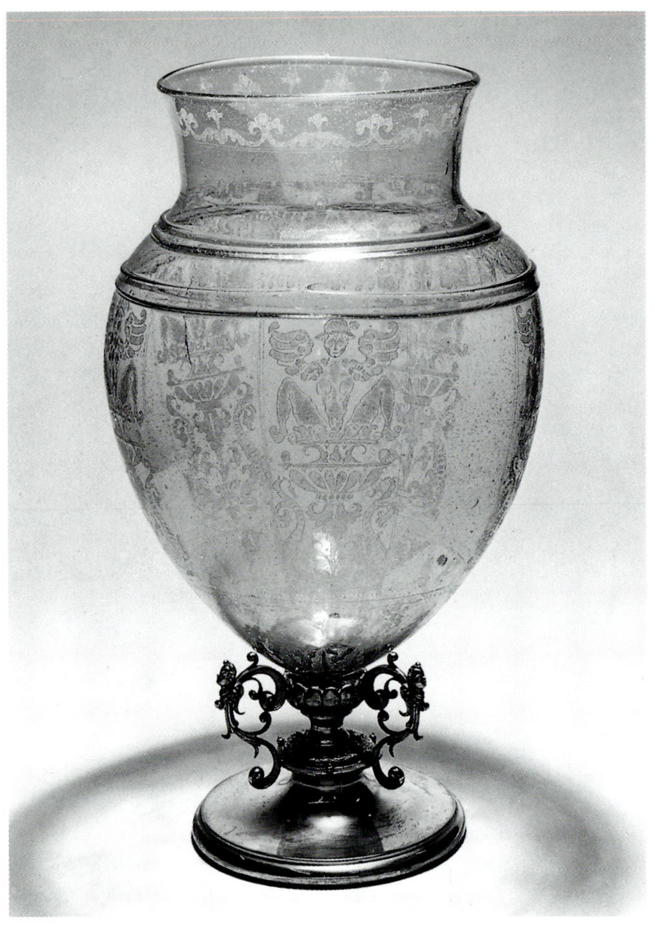

128 Goblet Vase

Façon de Venise, presumably Hall in Tyrol, or
Innsbruck, Court Glasshouse, ca. 1570–90
H 37.5, ⌀ vessel body 22.1 cm

Colorless glass with light gray tone, having countless small bubbles and impurities. Mold-blown and
shaped. Decoration: diamond-point engraving.
Metal mount does not belong to vase.

Acc. no. 13296

One of the largest extant goblet vases of its kind.
Its shape and slightly gray tinge speak in favor of
it having been made in the Tyrol *Weissglashütten*
of Hall or Innsbruck. This manner of diamond-
point decoration was rather unusual for Tyrolean
glassworks, but in the 16th century itinerant decorators from Venice presumably worked there. Its
motifs of winged creatures and ornamental detail
are comparable to those on a covered goblet with
baluster stem at the Kunstsammlungen der Veste
Coburg, though the latter is smaller and of different proportions. See Theuerkauff-Liederwald,
Venezianisches Glas, 1994, 270f., cat. no. 256.
The Düsseldorf piece could be restored with a
similar foot and corresponding cover.
On glassware from Hall and Innsbruck see
E. Egg, *Die Glashütten zu Hall und Innsbruck im
16. Jahrhundert* (Innsbruck, 1962).

Lit.: Heinemeyer, *Glas*, 1966, cat. no. 284; Ricke,
Ausgewählte Werke, 1980, 13

129 Ice-Glass Beaker

Façon de Venise, The Netherlands
Late 16th–1st half of 17th c.
H 18.3, ⌀ 11.3 cm

Colorless glass with light gray-brown tone.
Mold-blown and shaped; slightly pushed-up
bottom; folded, milled foot-ring. Hot gilded,
subsequently cooled off in water, fully blown,
and reheated, thus smoothing the surface.

Acc. no. P 1972-4
Acquired with the support of the Gerresheimer
Glashütte, Düsseldorf

Part of an extensive group of beakers, usually
somewhat larger and often adorned with a
row of concentric lion's-head prunts half-way
up the vessel's body. See, amongst others,
Dreier, *Venezianische Gläser*, 1989, 77f., cat.
nos. 104–8, and Hess and Husband, *Getty*,
1997, cat. no. 48. Cf. also the beakers in
Henkes, *Glas zonder glans*, 1994, 169ff., esp.
cat. no. 40.2, which, however, is not gilded.
Most closely related is the beaker in the sales
catalogue of the Glasgalerie Kovacek, *Glas aus
5 Jahrhunderten* (Vienna, 1994), 10f., no. 3,
which, like the work in Düsseldorf, has gilding throughout the wall.

Lit.: –

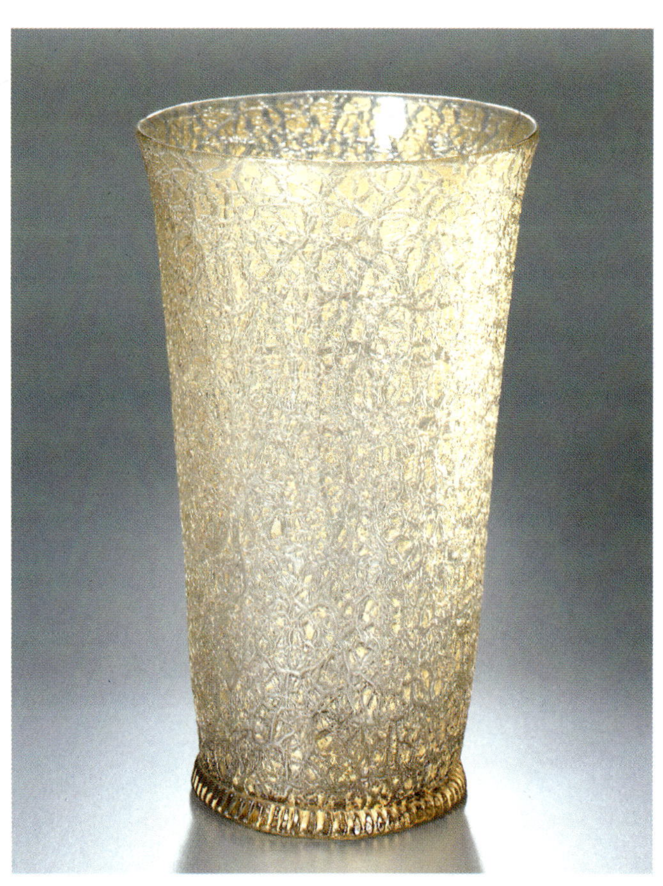

130 *Stangenglas*

Hall in Tyrol
Ca. 1570/80
H 41.8, ⌀ foot 13.3 cm

Colorless glass with light gray tone. Cylinder probably free-blown and shaped. Fused from two separately worked pieces. Foot rim folded broadly downwards. Mold-blown and shaped cover; tooled application. Diamond-point decoration: scrollwork with leaf-and-tongue pattern.

Acc. no. P 1940-62
Formerly Johannes Jantzen Collection, Bremen

Characteristic type of *Stangenglas* of the second half of the 16th century. Only rarely extant with cover. Current research does not confirm the traditional attribution to the archducal Venetian-style glasshouse in Hall without qualification.

Lit.: Heinemeyer, *Glas*, 1966, cat. no. 283

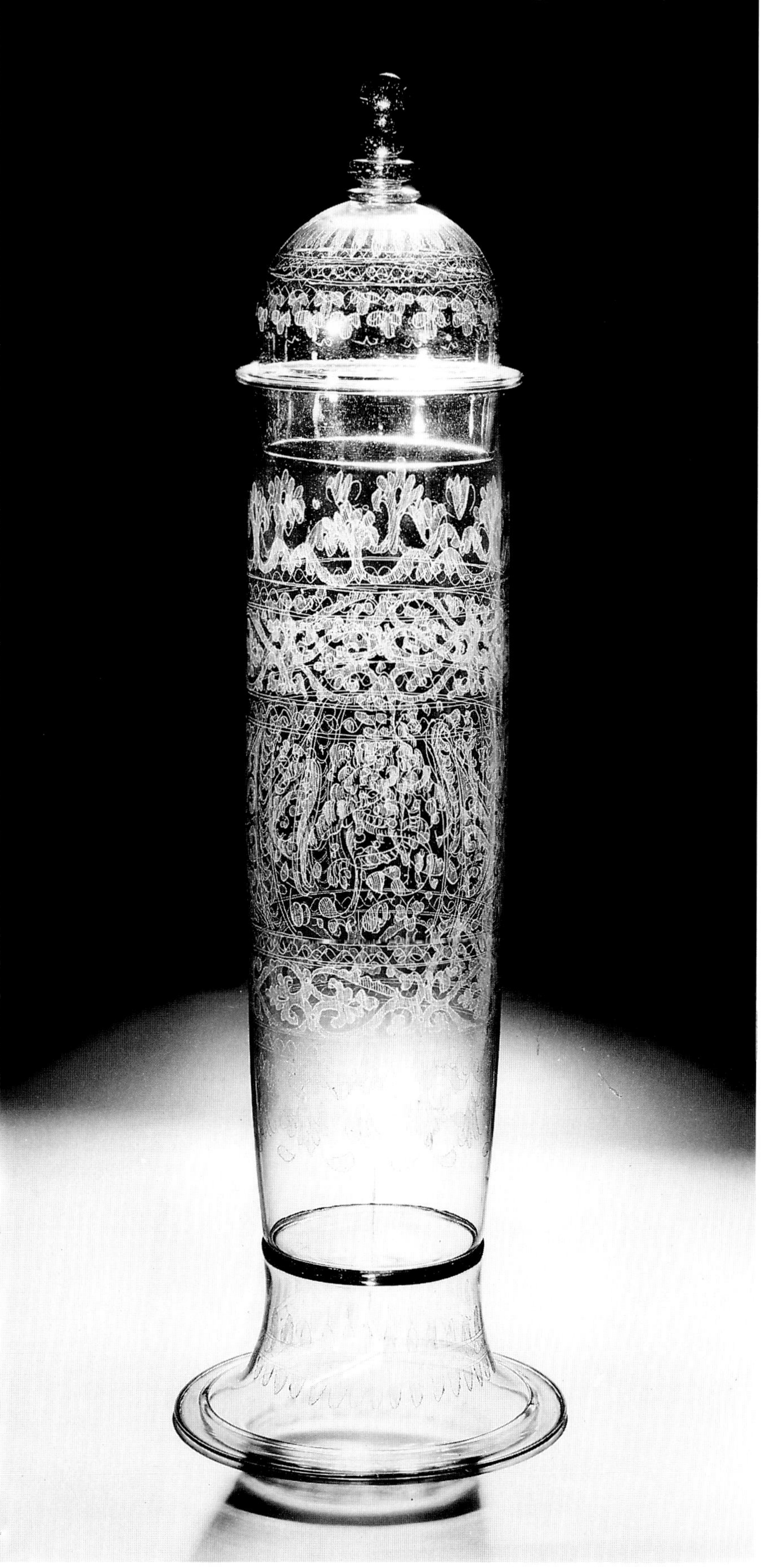

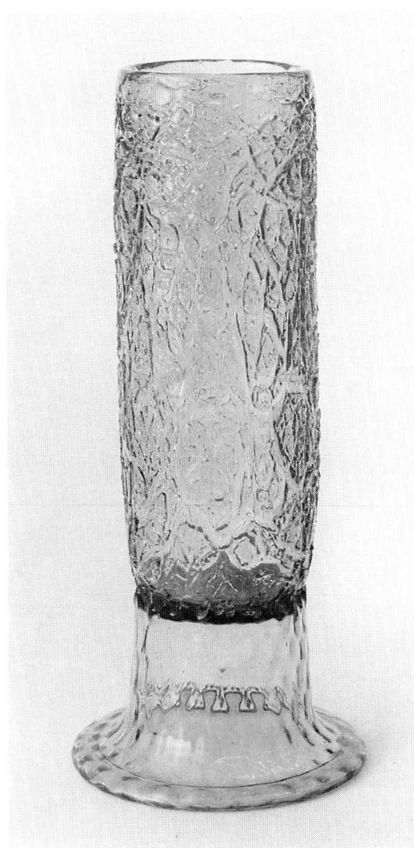

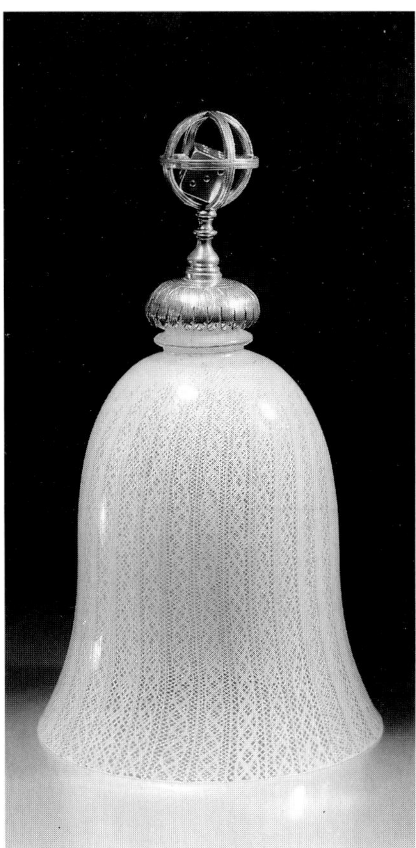

131 *Stangenglas*

Façon de Venise, probably southern Germany
Late 16th/early 17th c.
H 27.1, ⌀ 11.6 cm

Colorless, gray tone. Fused from two separately worked pieces. Upper portion probably free-blown and shaped, plunged into cold water, and reheated, thus smoothing the surface. Optic-blown foot. Foot rim folded downwards.

Acc. no. 17663
Formerly Kunstgewerbemuseum Berlin

The developed form of Stangenglas on a high cylindrical foot (cf. cat. no. 115) was rarely made in the ice-glass technique. The crackled surface of the glass is unusually coarse; it is therefore very different from common ice-glass beakers, which are usually localized to Antwerp. See, for example, cat. no. 129.

Lit.: Heinemeyer, *Glas*, 1966, cat. no. 231

132 *Sturzbecher*

Façon de Venise, The Netherlands
1st half of 17th c.
H 19.2, ⌀ 10.7 cm

Made of fused filigree-glass canes. Massive node. Silver mount—celestial globe containing a die.

Acc. no. P 1940-33
Formerly Johannes Jantzen Collection, Bremen

Joke vessel for drinking games. "Somersault" beakers and handbells with mounted silver knops were particularly common in The Netherlands, which had the most productive *façon de Venise* glasshouses. See, for example, Saldern, *Meisterwerke*, 1968, cat. no. 108, with a similar mount and a Netherlandish owner identified by the inscription *ICK BRINGT U MIJN LIEF*. See also Dreier, *Venezianische Gläser*, 1989, no. 48; Ritsema, Amsterdam I, 1993, 64f., nos. 80, 81; and Theuerkauff-Liederwald, *Venezianisches Glas*, 1994, 194ff., nos. 175–77.

Lit.: Heinemeyer, *Glas*, 1966, cat. no. 242; Ricke, *Ausgewählte Werke*, 1980, 14

133 **Covered Goblet**

Façon de Venise, probably The Netherlands
Mid-17th c.
H 40.3, ⌀ 12.7 cm

Colorless glass. Optic-blown in 14-part ribbed mold, shaped. Body: fused from three pieces; cover: from two pieces. Foot folded downwards.

Acc. no. P 1940-15

The vessel linked the late 16th-century flute glasses *à la façon de Venise* with the Baroque *Hohlbalusterpokale* (goblet having a stem with one or more hollow knops) of the second half of the 17th century. See also Theuerkauff-Liederwald, *Venezianisches Glas*, 1994, 326, no. 321.

Lit.: Heinemeyer, *Glas*, 1966, cat. no. 224

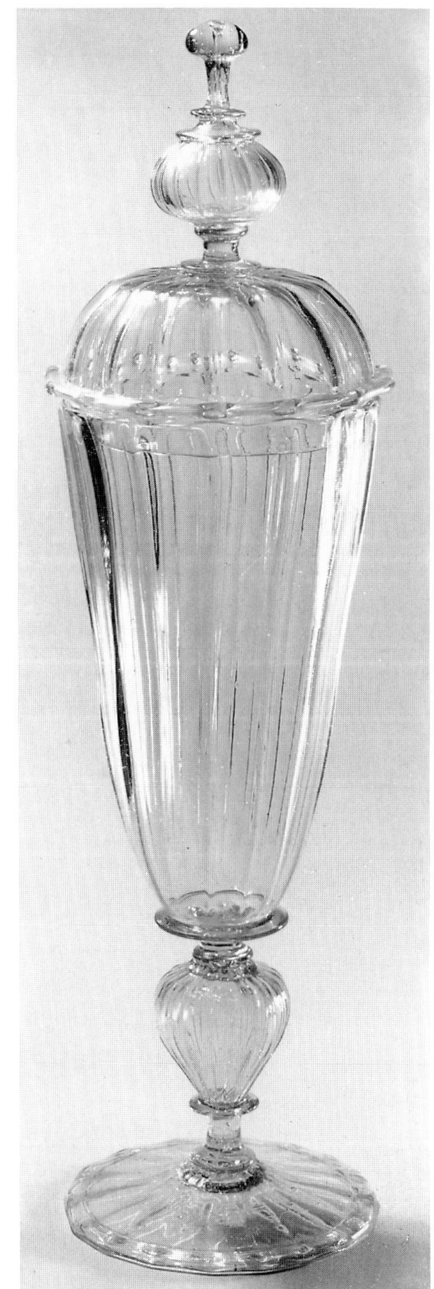

134 Network-Glass Tazza

Venice or *Façon de Venise*
1st half of 17th c.
H. 11.2, ⌀ 17.6 cm

Colorless with white embedded threads.
Fused from three separately worked pieces.
Each of these consists of two pieces fused in
such a manner—typical of the *vetro-a-reticel-
lo* technique—that small air bubbles became
trapped inside the wall (cf. "Techniques,"
p. 359).

Acc. no. P 1940-32
Formerly Johannes Jantzen Collection, Bremen

The *reticello* technique is the most complicated
amongst filigree-glass methods.

Lit.: Heinemeyer, *Glas*, 1966, cat. no. 247

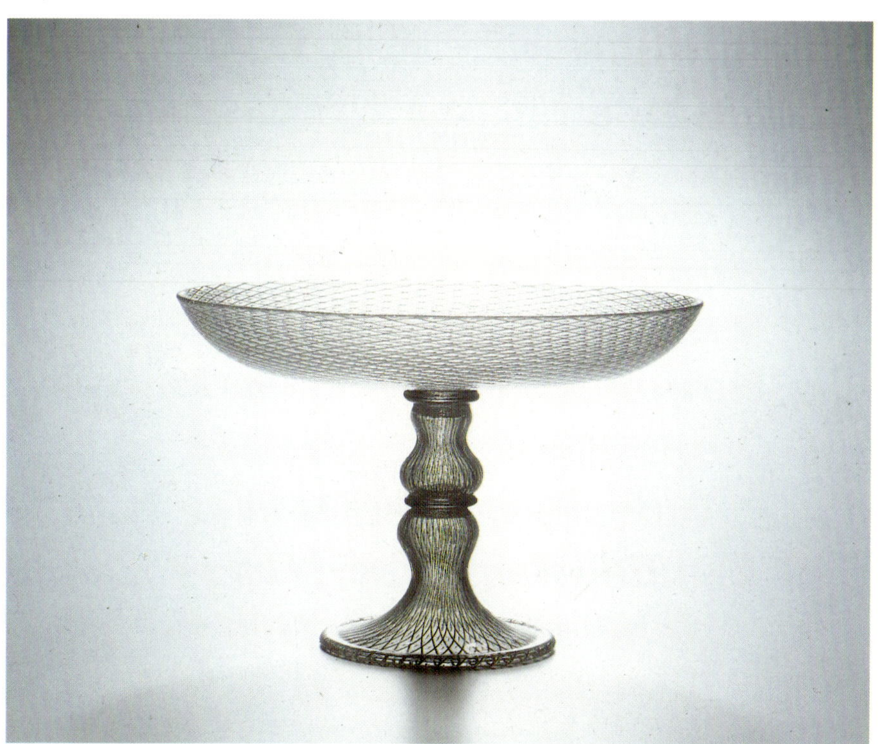

135 Winged Glass

Façon de Venise
Germany or southern Netherlands
17th c.
H 14.9, ⌀ 10.6 cm

Colorless. Free-blown bowl and foot, stem
shaped from prefabricated cane with inlaid
white thread decoration. Pinched wings.

Acc. no. P 1940-17

Lit.: Heinemeyer, *Glas*, 1966, cat. no. 271

136 Snake-Thread Glass

Façon de Venise
Germany or southern Netherlands
17th c.
H 21.9, ⌀ 9.1 cm

Colorless. Free-blown foot and bowl, stem
shaped from strongly contorted, prefabricated
cane. Pinched heads attached.

Acc. no. P 1940-41
Formerly Johannes Jantzen Collection, Bremen

Lit.: Heinemeyer, *Glas*, 1966, cat. no. 272

137 Winged Glass

Façon de Venise
Germany or southern Netherlands
17th c.
H 21.8, ⌀ 8.5 cm

Colorless glass. Blown bowl and foot, stem
shaped from prefabricated cane with white
and yellow inlaid threads. Blue pincered
wings.

Acc. no. P 1940-16

Winged glasses and snake-thread glassware
can rarely be localized to Venice itself.
Presumably Flemish glasshouses developed
this type of goblet, which often appears
in 17th-century Dutch still lifes.

Lit.: Heinemeyer, *Glas*, 1966, cat. no. 269

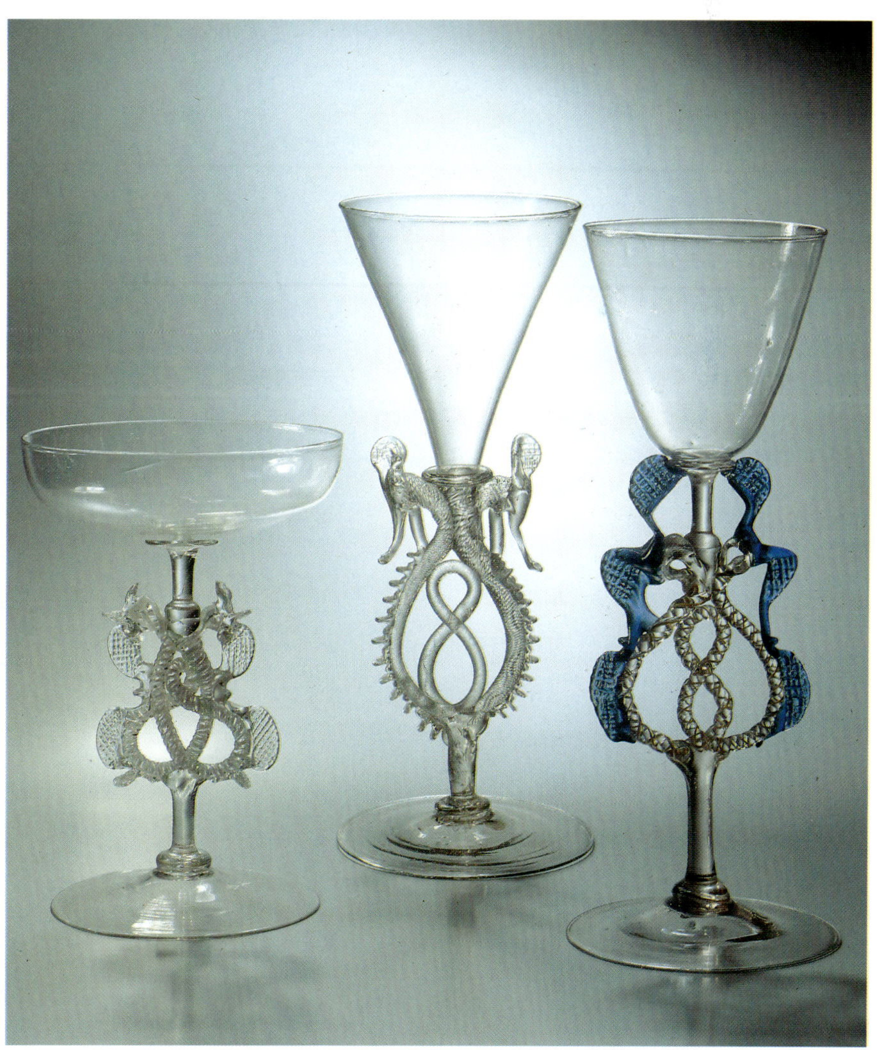

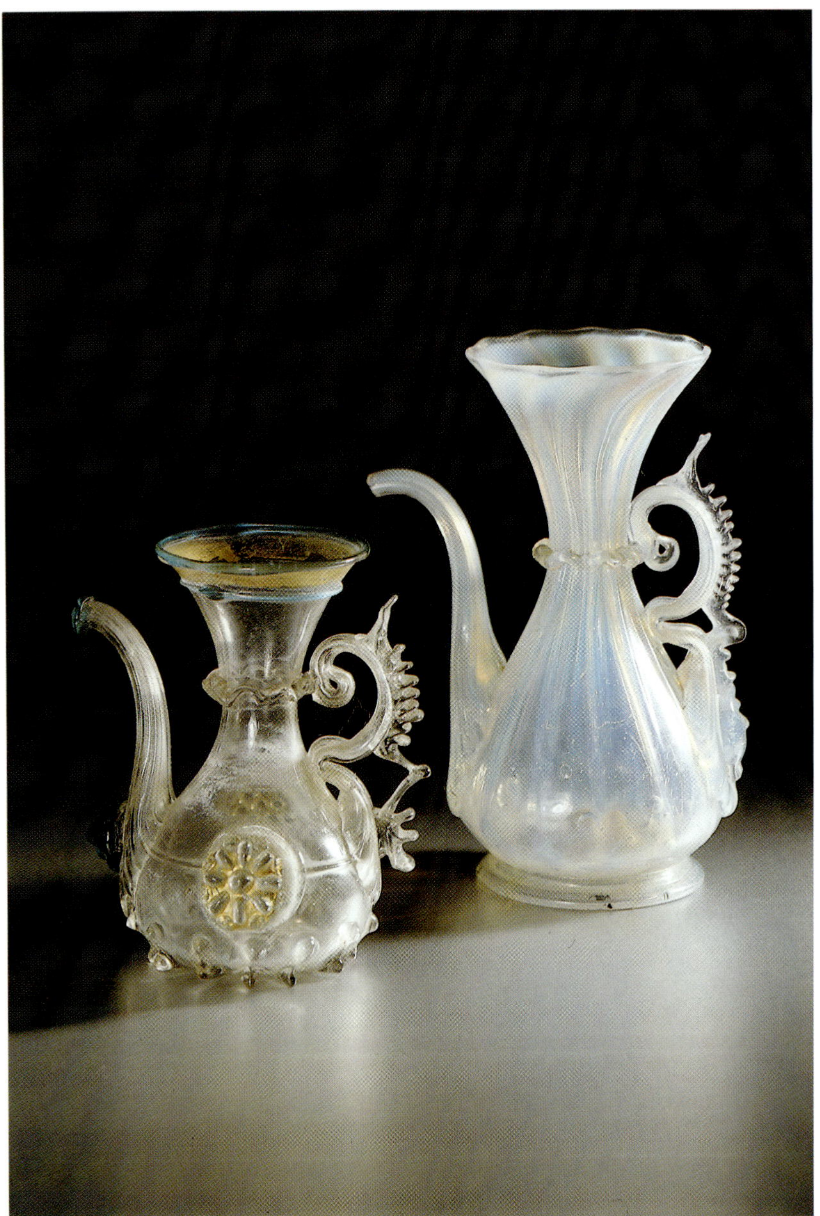

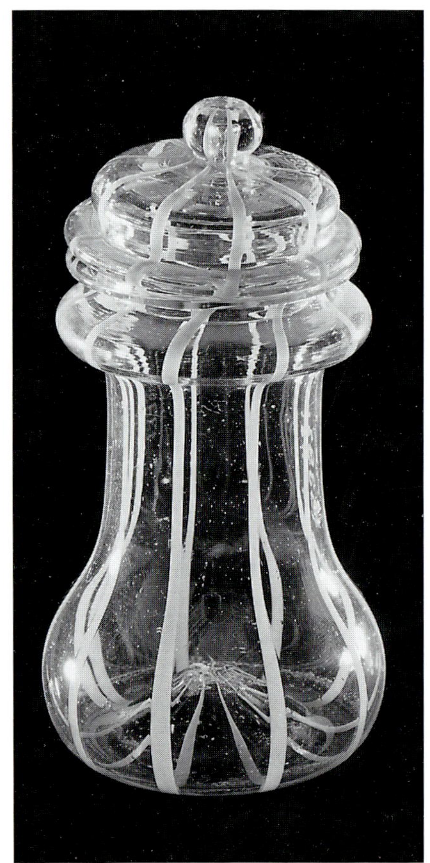

140 *Albarello*

Venice or *façon de Venise*
17th c., presumably ca. 1700
H 12.6, ⌀ 6.8 cm

Colorless, slightly bluish tone, with white
embedded threads. Mold-blown, shaped.
Exactly matching cover.

Acc. no. 13381
Gift of O. Wuppermann, Düsseldorf, 1888

Apothecary jar. Usually without cover. The
common type has no thread decoration.
On the vessel and its function see A.-E.
Theuerkauff-Liederwald, "Gläserne Albarelli:
Aus der Sammlung venezianischer Gläser Herzog Albrechts von Sachsen-Coburg-Gotha,"
Kunst & Antiquitäten 2 (1984): 28–35, esp.
fig. 5. Another piece with thread decoration
is in Saldern, *Cohn Collection*, 1980, cat.
no. 200. See also Theuerkauff-Liederwald,
Venezianisches Glas, 1994, 367–79.

Lit.: Heinemeyer, *Glas*, 1966, cat. no. 259

138 Small Pitcher

Venice or *façon de Venise*
17th c.
H 7.2, ⌀ 6.6 cm

Colorless. Optic-blown, shaped. Colorless and
blue glass applications. Gilded.

Acc. no. P 1936-93
Formerly Josef Lückger Collection, Cologne

For this type of small pitcher see Dreier,
Venezianische Gläser, 1989, 113ff., nos.
115–20, and Theuerkauff-Liederwald,
Venezianisches Glas, 1994, 386–408.

Lit.: Heinemeyer, *Glas*, 1966, cat. no. 238;
H. Ricke, "Venedig und der Norden: Europäische Glaskunst im 17. und 18. Jahrhundert,"
in exh. cat., *19. Westdeutsche Kunstmesse*
(Düsseldorf, 1988), 12–14

139 Small Pitcher

Venice or *façon de Venise*
17th c.
H 10.2, ⌀ 7.4 cm

Whitish opal glass. Optic-blown, shaped. Foot
of flattened folded trail.
Strain-cracking in the bottom and in lower
portion of wall.

Acc. no. 17662
Formerly Kunstgewerbemuseum Berlin

Lit.: Heinemeyer, *Glas*, 1966, cat. no. 241; H.
Ricke, "Venedig und der Norden: Europäische
Glaskunst im 17. und 18. Jahrhundert," in
exh. cat., *19. Westdeutsche Kunstmesse* (Düsseldorf, 1988), 12–14

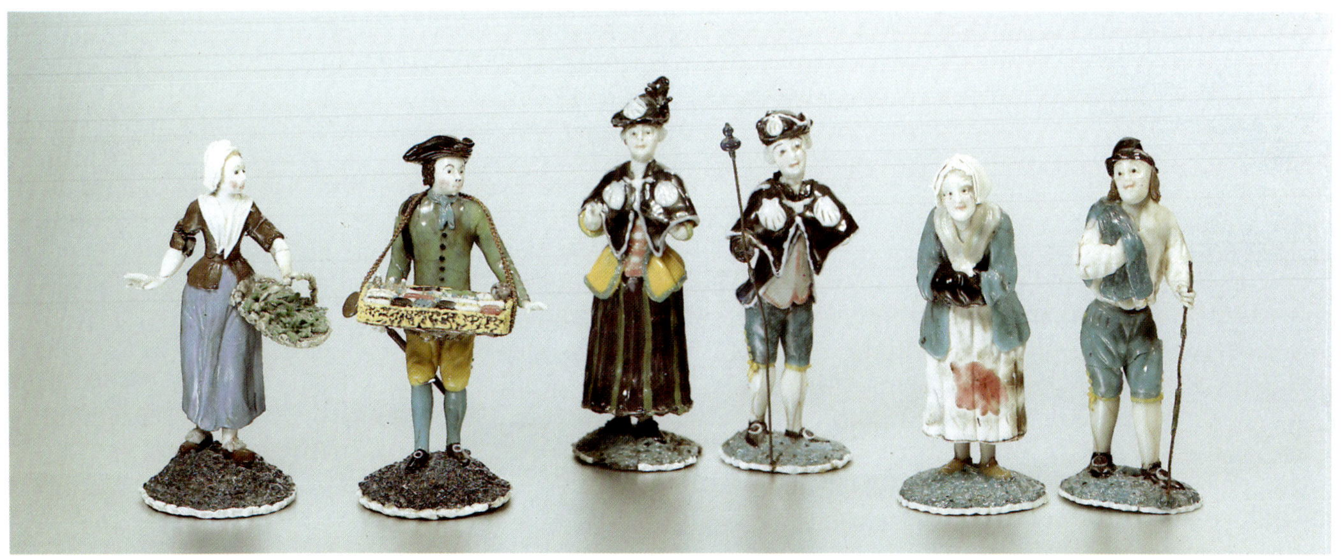

141 Three Pairs of Figures

France, Nevers (?)
2nd half of 18th c.
H 8.7–9, ⌀ bases 3.6–4.1 cm

Opaque colored glass. Lampworked.

Acc. nos. 17956-17961
Acquired in Constance in 1905

The three couples—a peasant man and woman, a cavalier and a lady in pilgrim's dress, male and female street vendors—were carefully worked around a wire armature. Nevers was a well-known center for this type of work in the 18th century, but Paris and Venice are also possible places of origin. The costumes date the Düsseldorf figures to the Rococo period. A similarly worked pair of beggars is illustrated in Charleston, *Masterpieces*, 1980, 162, no. 73.

Lit.: Heinemeyer, *Glas*, 1966, cat. no. 279; Saldern, *Alte Gläser*, 1968, cat. no. 24; *Mille anni*, 1982, cat. no. 362

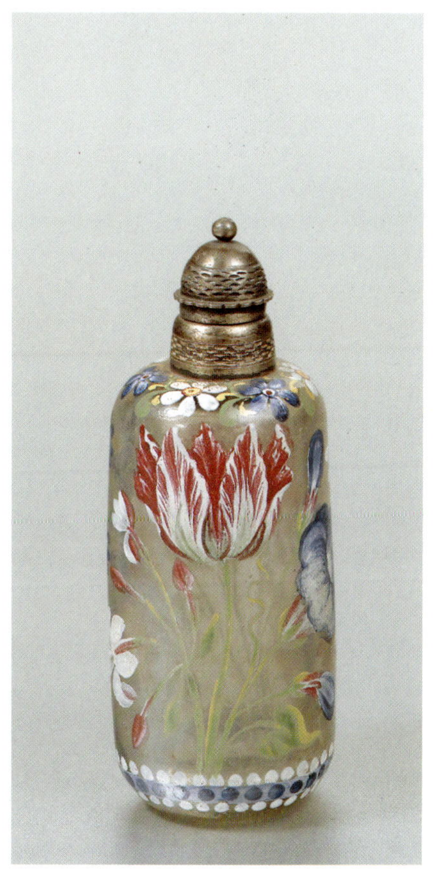

142 Flacon

Venice
Workshop or circle around Oswald Brussa
2nd half of 18th c.
H 8, ⌀ 3.2 cm

Colorless glass. Mold-blown, shaped. Enamel painting: large rose and tulip surrounded by lilies of the valley and other flowers. Silver screw cap, traces of gilding.

Acc. no. P 1940-90
Formerly Johannes Jantzen Collection, Bremen

For the workshop of Oswald Brussa see Barovier Mentasti, *Vetro Veneziano*, 1982, 169ff., and Klesse and Saldern, *Sammlung Biemann*, 1978, cat. no. 366. For a similar small bottle see O. Drahotová, *European Glass* (London, 1983), 48.

Lit.: Heinemeyer, *Glas*, 1966, cat. no. 193

The Baroque
The Era of Glass Engraving

Rock-crystal engraving culminated in the sixteenth century. Particularly in the north of Italy, lapidaries created crystal vessels with rich figural scenes in an ornate framework. These were highly prized objects, kept in princely *Kunstkammer* and *Wunderkammer*. It seemed only logical to use the effective technique of engraving with rotating copper wheels on glass, a material much easier to cut. Around 1600 Munich court artists, and shortly thereafter the imperial court artists of Rudolf II in Prague, took this step. Caspar Lehmann was the first to be granted permission to practice the new art.

To begin with, however, the thin and brittle glass of the Venetian-type vessels severely circumscribed the efforts of glass engravers. Georg Schwanhardt the Elder, a pupil of Lehmann who had settled in the imperial city of Nuremberg, had to content himself with a flat, unpolished intaglio at first (cat. no. 143). Soon, however, glasshouse masters of the leading production regions sought to improve their melt to create a robust crystal-clear glass that remained unclouded even when blown to a thick wall. Particularly in Bohemia, glassworks succeeded admirably in accomplishing this by the mid-seventeenth century. By repeated washing, roasting, and grinding, they carefully refined all raw materials and used new purifying agents and chalk instead of the cruder lime to stabilize the glass. Thus it was gradually possible to create crystal glass that was clearly superior to the as yet unrivaled Venetian *cristallo*. This made way for the development of the art of glass engraving, which culminated around 1700 and was an important aspect of Baroque glass until the mid-eighteenth century. The focus of artistic glass production in Europe shifted from the south to the north.

The full potential of glass engraving was initially exploited in Nuremberg. After Georg Schwanhardt, several other highly skilled glass engravers, including Hermann Schwinger (cat. no. 145), Hans Wolfgang Schmidt (cat. no. 144), Heinrich Schwanhardt (cat. no. 146), and Paul Eder (cat. no. 147), made Nuremberg—with painstakingly detailed landscapes and figural scenes, heraldic emblems and devices—the center of German glass art for nearly fifty years. Equal to Nuremberg glass engraving was its *Schwarzlotmalerei*. Independent decorators around Johann Schaper painted richly shaded miniatures onto small beakers (cat. no. 150).

Bohemian cutters and engravers also knew how to exploit the potential of the new glass. The circle around the so-called Master of the Koula Beaker (cat. no. 152) attempted to surpass the Nuremberg glass engravers in diversity of detail and subtlety of polishing. The engraved depictions developed increasingly in depth, the thick-walled Bohemian crystal glass being best suited for the task. The next step was almost inevitable. Where decorators were previously satisfied to draw or model the engraved depiction onto the glass, they now began to work the ornamental and figural motifs on the vessel's wall in relief. The Silesian glass cutter and engraver Friedrich Winter (cat. no. 153), who erected his water-powered engraving mill in Hermsdorf in the Hirschberg Valley under the patronage of Count Schaffgotsch, perfected this technique.

For the coming decades glassmaking and decoration by cutting and engraving was concentrated in this region as well as in neighboring northern Bohemia with its Erz- and Isergebirge, and in the Bohemian Forest in southern Bohemia. New factory-like glasshouses produced raw glass and often had decorating workshops. It was more common, though, to have specialized cutters and engravers decorate the glasses in their own homes.

Thus the Bohemians developed their typical system of contracting work out, based on a division of labor. A financially powerful glass dealer had the raw glassware produced and passed it on to home workshops, where various artisans, each with a different area of expertise, successively worked on the same glass. In these specialized vocations, the work of the cutter was principally distinguished from that of the engraver. The various types of cutting were further divided up and carried out by different masters. In the same way, there were engraving specialists for landscape depictions, figures, and decorative applications.

With this kind of division of labor, it is virtually impossible to link individual pieces to the names of specific glass engravers. By and large, the glassware created in this system was of a high quality (cat. nos. 154, 155). The factories, usually run by the local nobility, had a similar system to the home workshops. Here the division of labor also rationalized the production and increased the quality of individual pieces. A typical Silesian enterprise of this kind was the Schaffgotsch manufactory in the Hirschberg Valley, where numerous excellent glass engravers were active. The perfection with which different types of glass engraving were executed secured Silesian products a prominent position amongst high-quality factory ware in the first half of the eighteenth century.

Only very few highly skilled masters stand out from the mass of anonymous production and are known by name. One of the most important was Christian Gottfried Schneider, who worked in Warmbrunn (cat. no. 160). A series of extant paper rubbings of engravings carried out by his workshop make it possible to identify his style.

Besides in Bohemia and Silesia, engraved glasses were also made—though on a much smaller scale—in other traditional glass production regions, most notably in the Thuringian Forest and the Hessian Weserbergland. The masterpieces of glass engraving were not, however, mass-produced in factories. They emerged from the courts of greater and lesser sovereigns and princes of the German Reich who, in seeking to display their power, competed intensely with one another.

Particularly successful in this sector was the Landgrave of Hesse at his residence Kassel. The city had already had a Venetian glasshouse in the sixteenth century; now Kassel took the lead amongst German glass centers owing to the celebrated glass engraver Franz Gondelach.

The Brandenburg-Prussian court glass factory in Potsdam attained even greater significance with the early work of Johann Kunckel, the period's greatest glass technician. He founded the factory in 1678 and headed it until 1694. Gottfried Spiller, under Frederick I, Elector of Brandenburg and later King of Prussia, was celebrated in early eighteenth-century texts as the most capable glass engraver of his time. On glassware up to 10 mm thick, Spiller, who maintained close personal ties with the Silesian Winter family, elevated engraving to a degree of relief-like sculptural modeling that no other engraver had achieved before (cat. no. 164). By combining intaglio and relief carving— an aesthetically problematic endeavor (cf. cat. no. 157) —Spiller also brought glass engraving to previously unattained heights. The composition of the particularly clear Potsdam crystal glass, probably still based on Kunckel's recipe, facilitated his work. Its chemical structure offered the copper wheel little resistance. On the other hand, it made the glass particularly susceptible to slow self-destruction. In the so-called glass disease (crizzling) the material exudes alkali.

The most important bequest of Johann Kunckel was his method of making massive gold ruby glass. This highly valued, glowing, dark red glass was known in antiquity already and experimentally rediscovered by other chemists in the seventeenth century. Thanks to Kunckel it was possible to free the melt from incidental results, providing glass engravers with a new, effective material for practicing their art (cat. nos. 165, 167). The rare covered beakers in marbled gray-brown and typical Potsdam shapes may also derive from Kunckel's experimental work (cat. no. 166). They were created parallel to the massive sealing-wax red glasses from the circle of Saxon court glasshouses and

anticipate the fashion of Lithyalin glassware in the Biedermeier period (cat. nos. 185, 187).

Glass engraving played a special role in the small central German principalities. The most competent representative of this art, besides Andreas Friedrich Sang in Weimar and Samuel Schwartz in Arnstadt, was Georg Ernst Kunckel, active at the Gotha court from 1721. His finely engraved portraits and coats of arms are virtually unsurpassed (cat. no. 169). Kunckel generally used the typical Thuringian goblet shape with hexagonal or tetrahedral pseudo-faceted stems.

The undisputed center of glass art in this region was, however, the Dresden court of Augustus the Strong (cat. no. 168). He employed several glass engravers known to us by name. Unfortunately it is not yet possible to identify definitively and ascribe their excellent relief and intaglio engraved works.

In the north the factory in Lauenstein and Osterwald, belonging to the kingdom of Hanover, attained more than local significance (cat. no. 170). Continuing the tradition of Hessian glasshouses, it produced goblets of heavy lead glass with the characteristic conical feet and distinctive stem shapes. Other production sites in Europe, from Sweden to Russia (cat. nos. 171, 172), remained formally more or less closely tied to one of the leading centers. Only England, where no significant glass engraving emerged, represents an exception. Original English shapes, however, characterized the appearance of glass engraved by the many German decorators active in the northern Netherlands.

Diamond-point stippling on Dutch glasses (cat. nos. 173, 174)—their shapes still strongly linked to England—mark the final stage of glass decoration in the eighteenth century. The intimate, playfully light quality of these glasses is in the spirit of the Rococo. At the same time their small size, demanding a close-up view, anticipates the collection and showcase culture of the Biedermeier period.

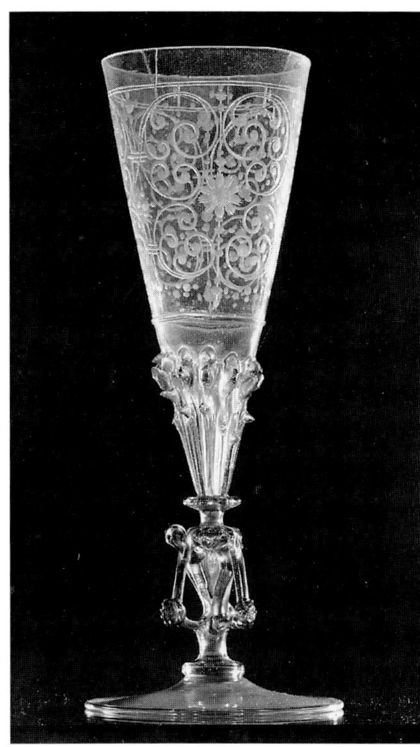

143 Flute Glass

Glass: Venice or *façon de Venise* (The Netherlands)
Ca. 1630
Engraving: Georg Schwanhardt the Elder
Nuremberg, ca. 1635–40
H 17.9, ⌀ 6 cm

Colorless glass. Bowl and foot blown separately and shaped. Stem shaped from three canes. Pinched applications and small raspberry prunts. Flat intaglio engraving.
Broken and glued. One of the three projections on the stem restored. Crizzled.

Acc. no. P 1940-99
Formerly Johannes Jantzen Collection, Bremen

Early engraving by Schwanhardt on thin glass *à la façon de Venise*. For the glass type see Barovier Mentasti, *Vetro Veneziano*, 1982, 135, fig. 127. For Schwanhardt see R. Schmidt, "Zum Werk Georg Schwanhardts d. Ä.," *Schlesiens Vorzeit in Bild und Schrift* 9 (1928): 106–10, and Meyer-Heisig, *Nürnberg*, 1963, 26ff.

Lit.: Heinemeyer, *Glas*, 1966, cat. no. 316

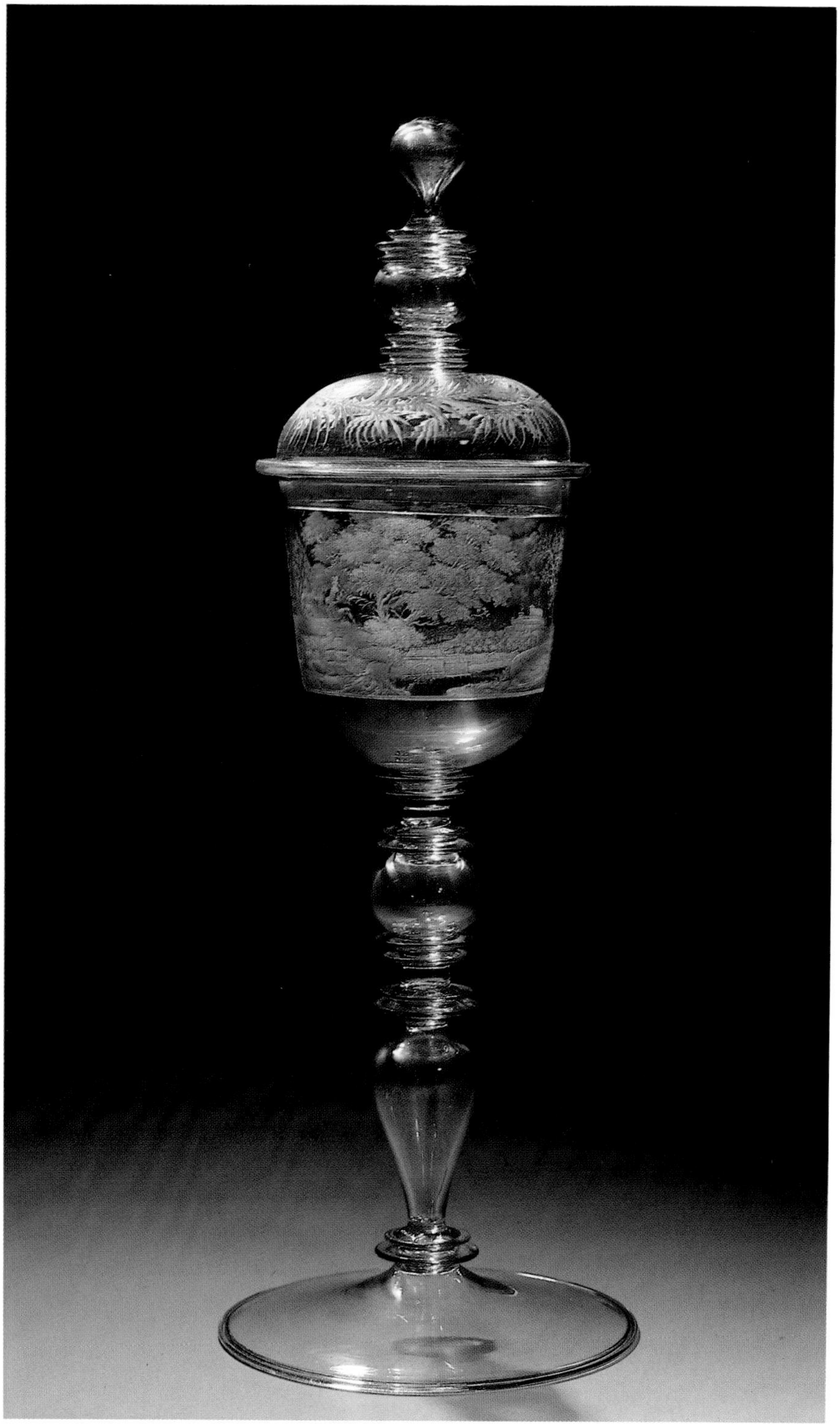

144 Covered Goblet

Hans Wolfgang Schmidt
Mark on tree stump: *HWS*
Nuremberg, ca. 1680/90
H with cover 44.1, without cover 30.6,
⌀ foot 15.3 cm

Colorless glass. Comprising several separately worked pieces. Foot folded downwards. Cover does not belong to goblet. Encircling decoration in finely detailed, unpolished intaglio. In the background: landscape with shrubs, mountains, town, river, and palace. In the middle: water mill, angler at a pond, and figures on a bridge over a small brook. In the foreground: flute-playing shepherd with dog and herd, trees.

Acc. no. P 1940-103
Formerly Johannes Jantzen Collection, Bremen

One of Schmidt's major works. He helped define the Nuremberg concept of landscape in glass engraving. For work by Schmidt see Meyer-Heisig, *Nürnberg*, 1963, 62ff.

Lit.: Heinemeyer, *Glas*, 1966, cat. no. 322; Saldern, *Alte Gläser*, 1968, cat. no. 29; H. Ricke, "Venedig und der Norden: Europäische Glaskunst im 17. und 18. Jahrhundert," in exh. cat., *19. Westdeutsche Kunstmesse* (Düsseldorf, 1988), 12–14

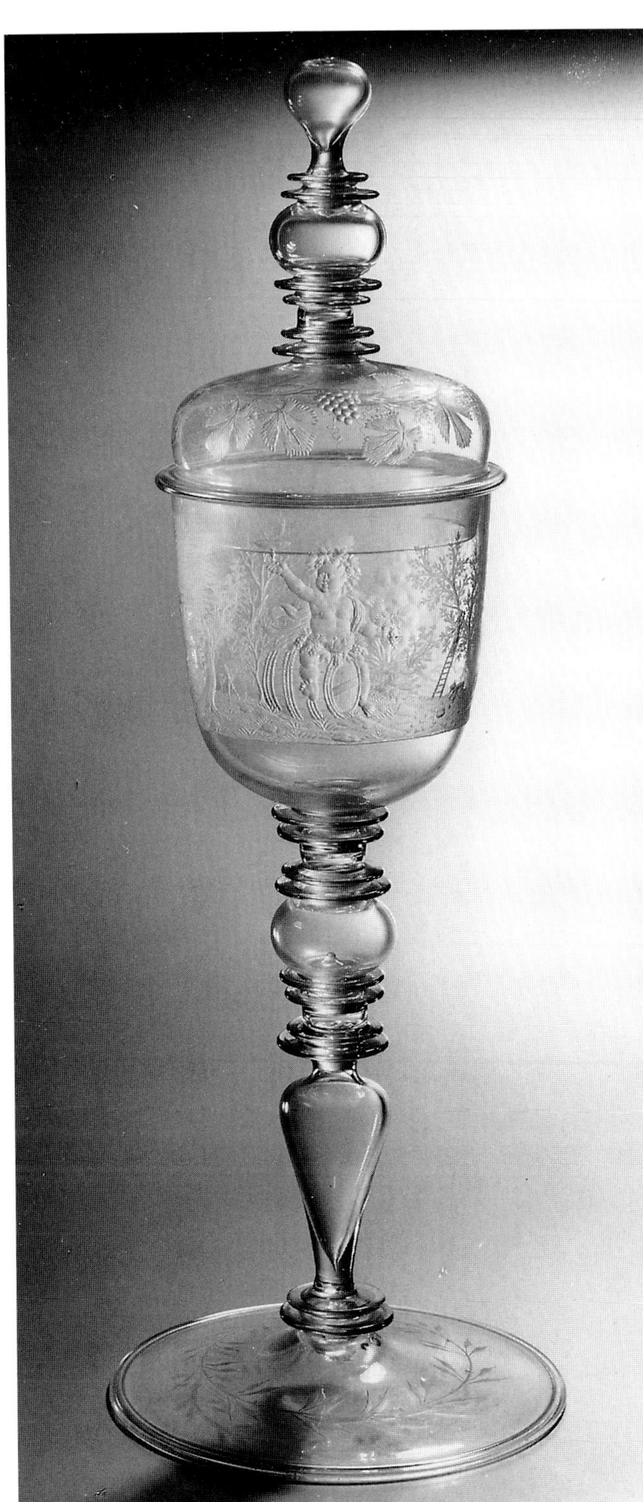

145 Covered Goblet

Attr. Hermann Schwinger
Nuremberg, ca. 1670/80
H 38.4, ⌀ foot 13.5 cm

Colorless crystal glass. Goblet and cover
assembled from several separately worked
pieces. Foot folded downwards.
Decoration in partly polished mat intaglio:
allegory of autumn with apple harvest to the
right; allegory of winter (putto in front of
fire) with trees bare of leaves and ruin to the
right. Staffage figures in the background.
Vine foliage encircles foot; on cover,
grapevine and mistletoe, corresponding to
the seasons.

Acc. no. P 1940-102
Formerly Johannes Jantzen Collection,
Bremen

Introduces the Baroque allegories of the seasons to glass decoration. For Hermann
Schwinger see Meyer-Heisig, *Nürnberg*, 1963,
54ff.

Lit.: Heinemeyer, *Glas*, 1966, cat. no. 319;
Ricke, *Ausgewählte Werke*, 1980, 16

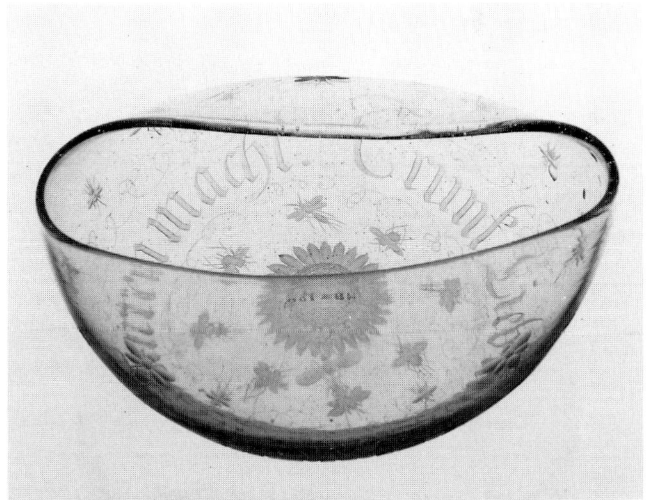

146 Bowl

Attr. Heinrich Schwanhardt
Nuremberg, ca. 1680/90
H 4.7, ⌀ 11.7 cm

Colorless crystal glass. Free-blown and
shaped. Decoration in mat intaglio and diamond-point engraving: vine scrolls and
insects. Inscription: *Trunk Lieb und Nacht viel
Narren macht*. Sunflower in the pontil mark.

Acc. no. P 1940-100
Formerly Johannes Jantzen Collection, Bremen

For Heinrich Schwanhardt, whose strengths
include calligraphic work, see Meyer-Heisig,
Nürnberg, 1963, 49ff.

Lit.: Heinemeyer, *Glas*, 1966, cat. no. 318

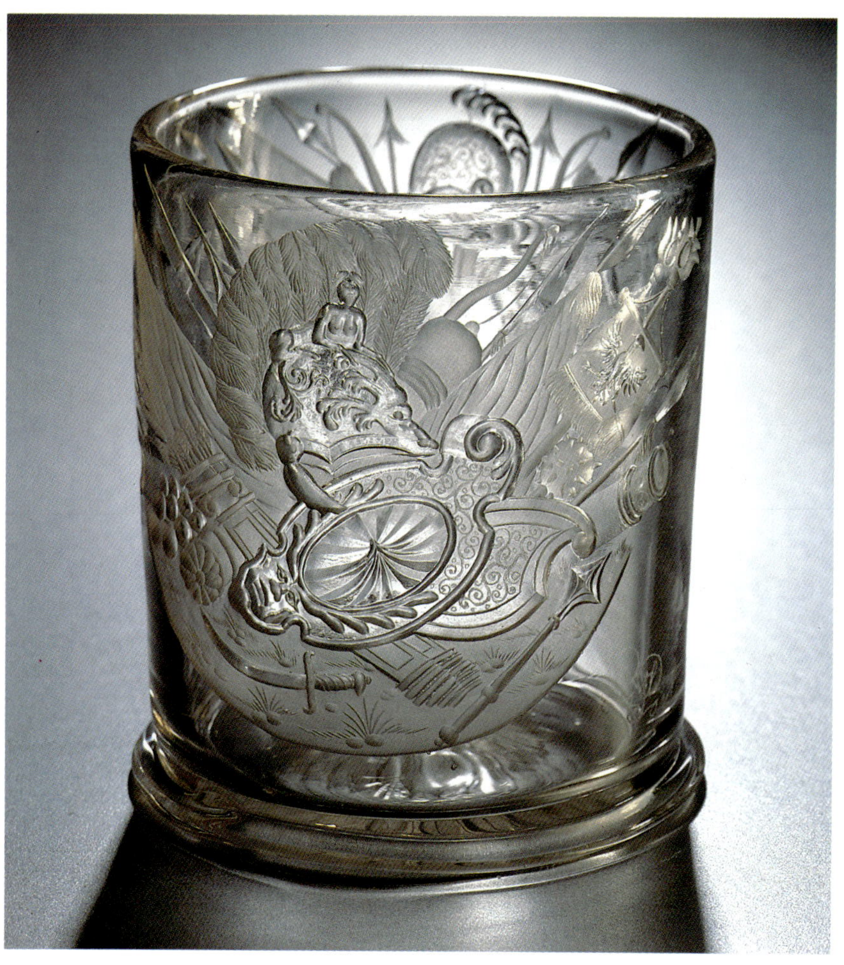

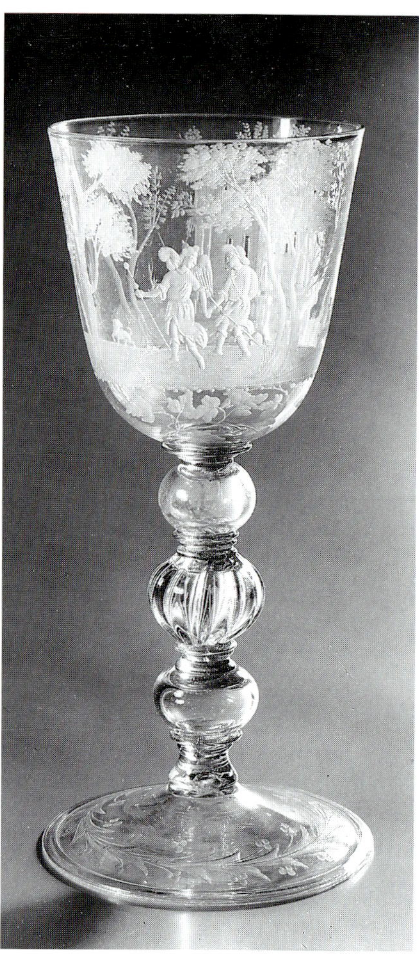

147 Beaker

Paul Eder
Diamond-engraved mark on wall: *Paulus Eder fecit*
Nuremberg, ca. 1700/10
H 9.5, ⌀ 8.6 cm

Colorless crystal glass. Mold-blown, shaped. Foot-ring with double profile. Decoration in partly polished mat intaglio and diamond-point engraving: weapons and standards as symbols of victory. On the underside of the base, ornately cut rosette to hide the pontil mark.

Acc. no. P 1940-105
Formerly Johannes Jantzen Collection, Bremen

For Paul Eder see Meyer-Heisig, *Nürnberg*, 1963, 66ff.

Lit.: Heinemeyer, *Glas*, 1966, cat. no. 325; Ricke, *2500 Jahre*, 1987, cat. no. 78

148 Goblet

Circle of the glass-engraving Hess family
Frankfurt, ca. 1680
H 22.4, ⌀ 9.8 cm

Colorless crystal glass. Mold-blown and shaped; middle knop optic-blown. Comprising several separately worked pieces. Decoration in mat intaglio: forest with ruins, staffage figures depicted on foot and on horseback. In the middle, the angel with Tobias carrying fish.

Acc. no. P 1988-25
Formerly Jobst von Zanthier Collection, Schmachtenberg

For the work of the Frankfurt glass-engraving Hess family see G. Pazaurek, "Der Frankfurter Glasschnitt und die Familie Hess," *Der Kunstwanderer* 10 (1927).

Lit.: Ricke, *Museumsarbeit*, 1988, 73, fig. 50

149 Beaker

Southern Germany
Third quarter of 17th c.
H 22.6, ⌀ 17.5 cm

Very pure, dark green glass, light blue tone.
Probably free-blown and shaped. Five staggered rows of six prunts each. In gilded mat
intaglio: hunting scenes with hunters on foot
and on horseback, wild boar, deer, fox, dogs.

Acc. no. 17783
Formerly Karl Thewalt Collection, Cologne

The intense colors and robust prunt decoration of late medieval utility glassware were
taken up again in the 17th century in monumental, representative vessels, which seem to
have been particularly popular in The Netherlands. The glass mass of these large beakers
was carefully purified as a rule; sometimes
they were decorated with diamond-point
engravings or inscriptions. See Kämpfer, *Viertausend Jahre*, 1966, no. 105. Engraved
examples are rare.

Lit.: Heinemeyer, *Glas*, 1966, cat. no. 141;
Saldern, *Alte Gläser*, 1968, cat. no. 18

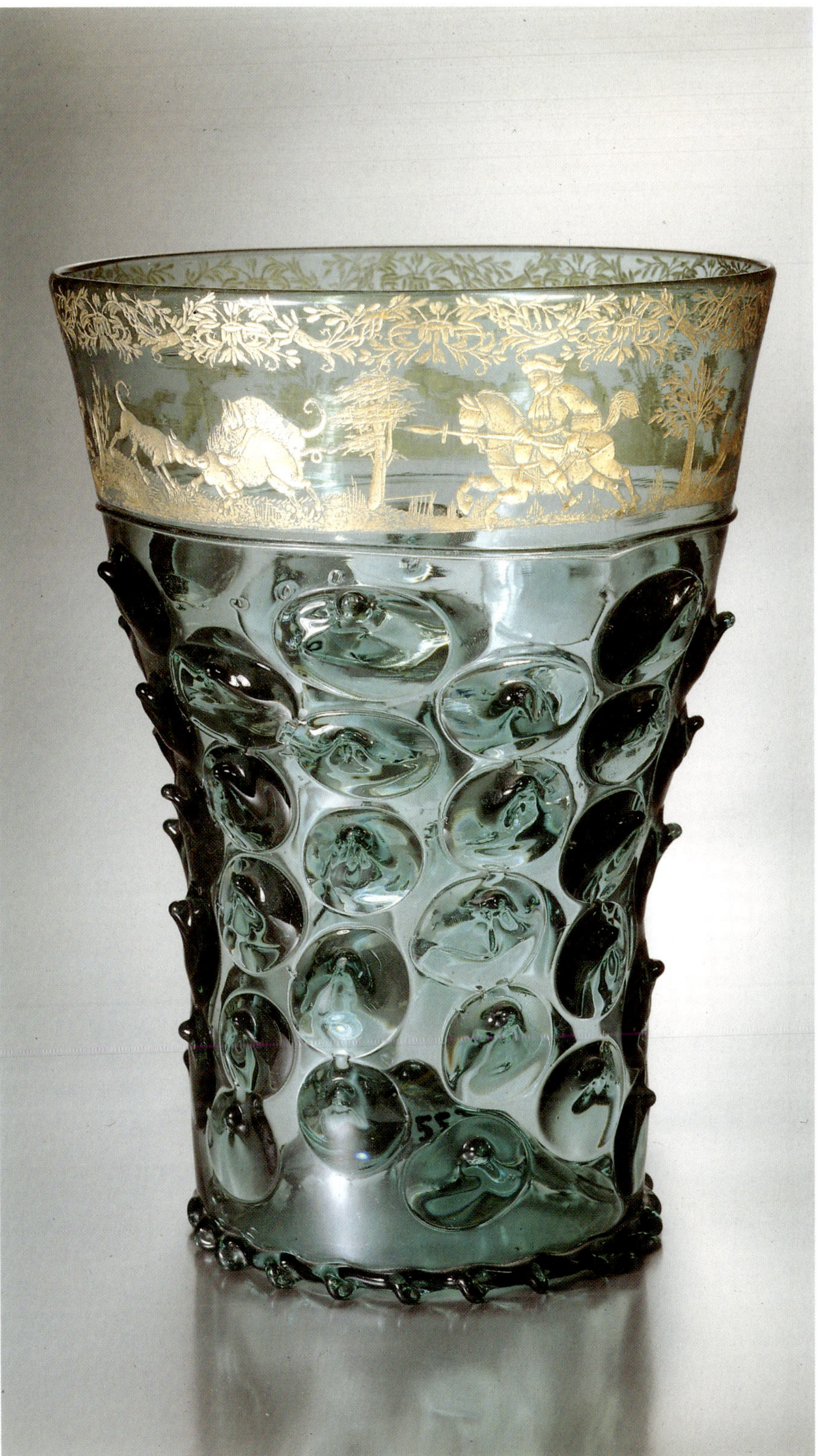

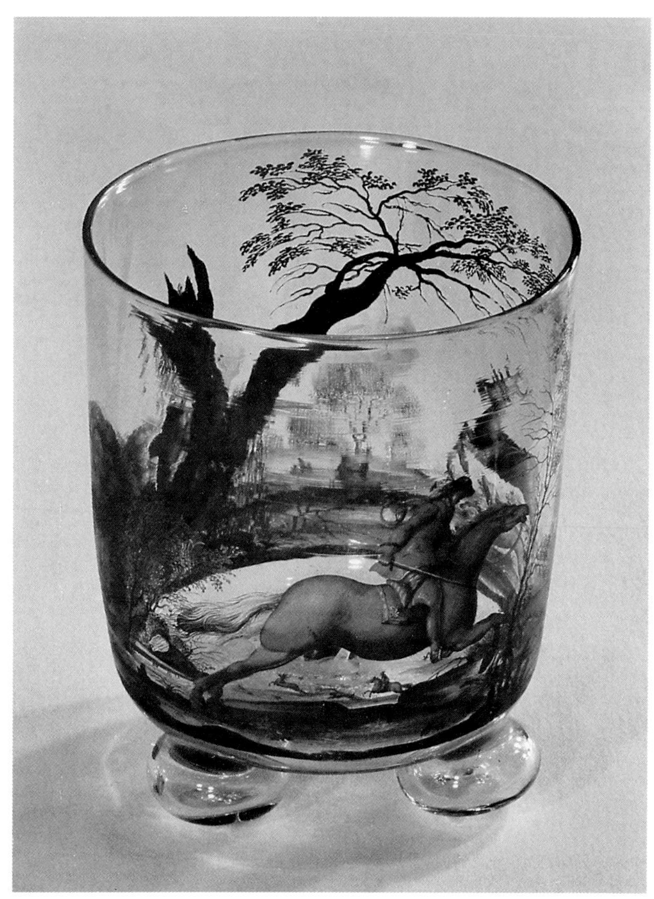 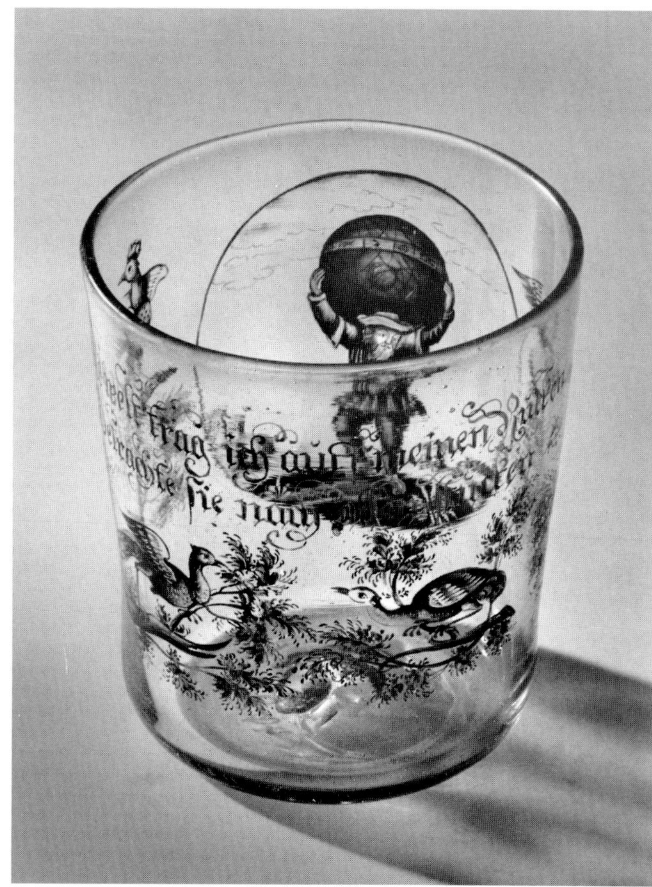

150 Beaker

Johann Schaper
Nuremberg, ca. 1665–70
H 10, ⌀ 9.1 cm

Colorless crystal glass. Mold-blown. Three
applied hollow feet. Decoration in etched
Schwarzlotmalerei (black enamel painting):
stag hunt on horseback.

Acc. no. P 1940-94
Formerly Johannes Jantzen Collection,
Bremen; previously Reichenheim-Oppenheim
Collection, Berlin

An almost identical and signed stag-hunt
beaker, which was at the Berlin Palace during
World War II before it was lost, confirms the
attribution to Schaper. See G. Mariacher, *Il
vetro europeo dal XV al XX secolo* (Novara,
1964), 292, and Bosch, *Hausmaler*, 1984,
no. 48.

Lit.: Heinemeyer, *Glas*, 1966, cat. no. 205;
Ricke, *Ausgewählte Werke*, 1980, 16; Bosch,
Hausmaler, 1984, no. 49 (with documenta-
tion of graphic source)

151 Beaker

Nuremberg or Silesia
(Circle of Ignaz Preissler?)
Dated 1697
H 8.5, ⌀ 7.8 cm

Colorless crystal glass. Mold-blown. Painting
in black enamel and brown-violet: Atlas as an
old man in contemporary rustic costume. On
the reverse, rich foliage and birds. Inscription: *Die Welt trag ich auff meinem Rukken /
betrachte sie nach allen stucken.*

Acc. no. P 1940-97
Formerly Johannes Jantzen Collection,
Bremen

The beaker was made in the tradition of the
Nuremberg *Hausmaler* around Johannes
Schaper, but also has features linking it to
the work of the younger Ignaz Preissler. See
R. von Strasser, "Ignaz Preissler: Frühe
Arbeiten, weniger bekannte Meisterwerke und
die Nachfolge," *Journal of Glass Studies* 29
(1987): 81–112.

Lit.: Heinemeyer, *Glas*, 1966, cat. no. 207;
Bosch, *Hausmaler*, 1984, no. 345 (with documentation of graphic source); Strasser, op.
cit., 90, figs. 15, 16

152 Bottle

Master of the Koula Beaker
Silesia, Riesengebirge, ca. 1685/90
H 15.4, ⌀ 11.1 cm

Colorless crystal glass. Blown in octagonal
mold. Sides cut and polished. Decoration in
polished and unpolished intaglio: mythological scenes—Apollo and Cupid, Ceres and Bacchus (?), Orpheus amidst the animals, Nep-
tune and Amphitrite—alternating with
surface-covering fruit and flower motifs.
Gilded silver screw cap. The Nuremberg
inspector and master mark *I.P.* can perhaps
be ascribed to Jakob Pfaff (master 1675, d.
1708).

Acc. no. P 1940-108
Formerly Johannes Jantzen Collection,
Bremen

For the circle around the Master of the Koula
Beaker see esp. O. Drahotová, "Der Kreis um
den Meister des sog. Koula-Bechers," *Tschechoslowakische Glasrevue* 20 (1965): 340ff.,
and S. C. Bauer, "Ein neues Glas aus der
Umgebung des Koula-Bechers," *Festschrift für
Peter Wilhelm Meister* (Hamburg, 1975),
150ff.

Lit.: Heinemeyer, *Glas*, 1966, cat. no. 338;
Ricke, *2500 Jahre*, 1987, cat. no. 79

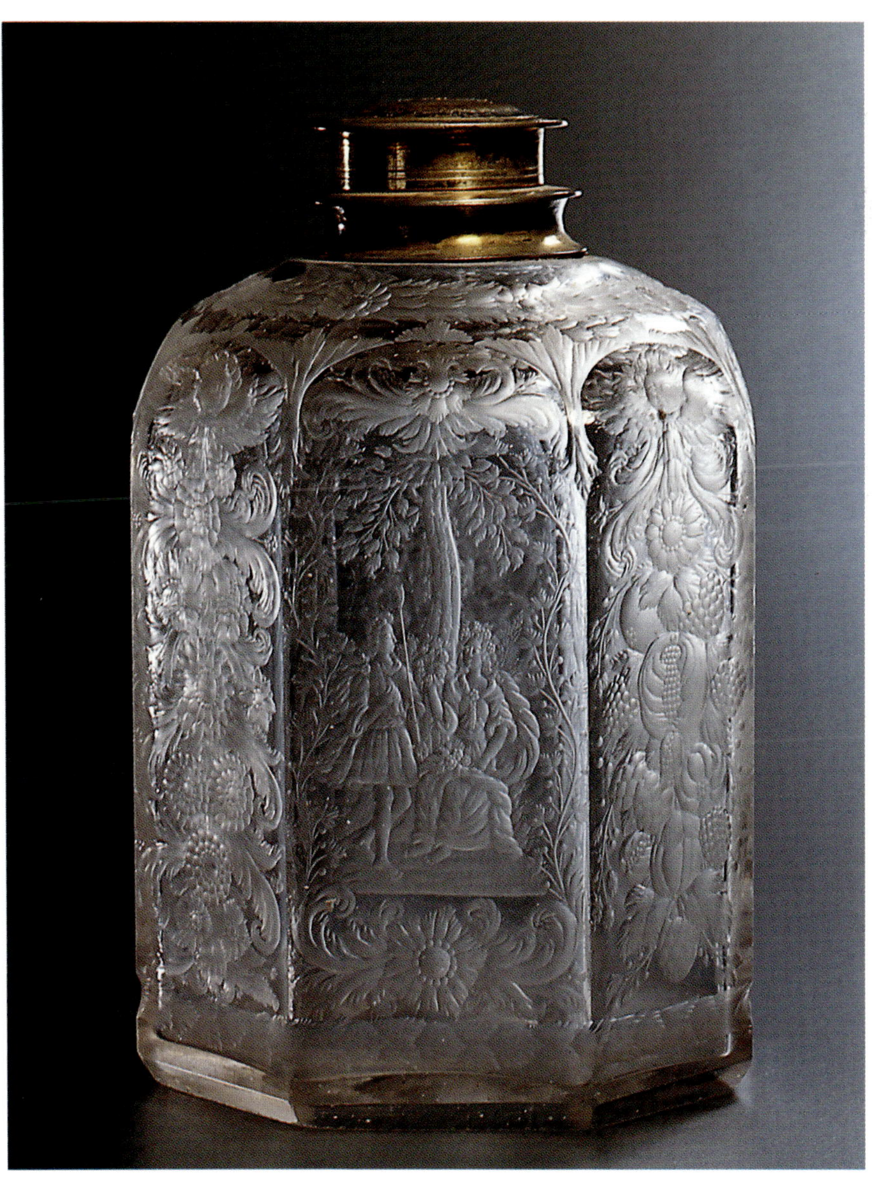

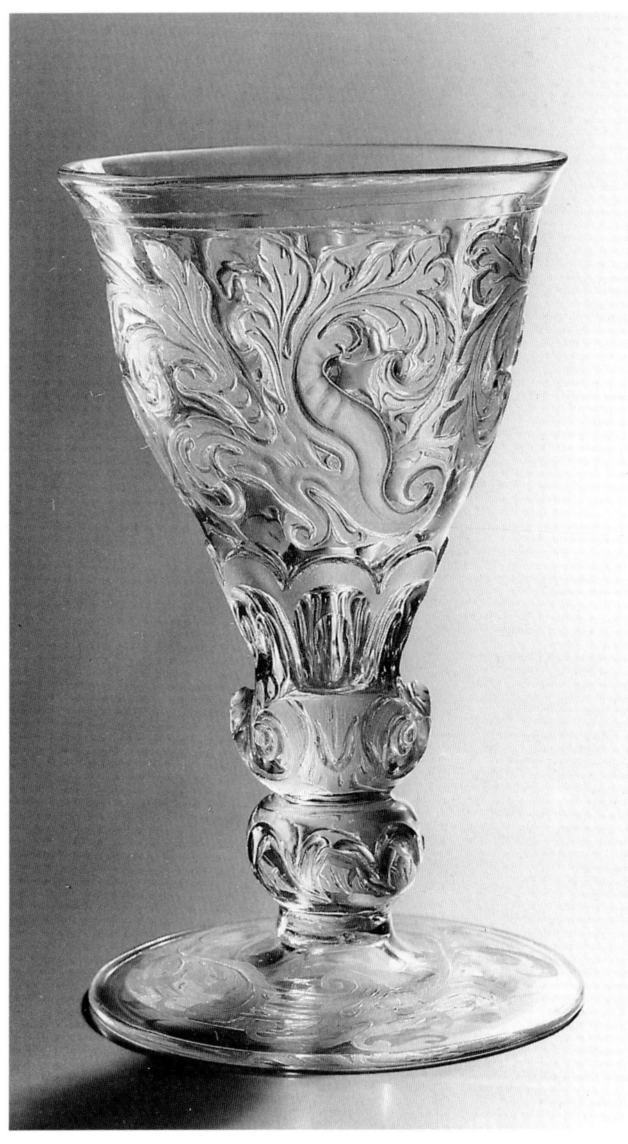

153 Goblet

Friedrich Winter
Silesia, Hermsdorf, Hirschberg Valley
Ca. 1690–92
H 16.7, ⌀ 10.4 cm

Colorless, thick-walled crystal glass. Mold-blown,
shaped. Decoration in elaborate intaglio and relief
carving, partly polished: acanthus foliage emerging
from a dolphin's head. On the foot, repetition of
the dolphin motif in flat, unpolished intaglio
engraving.

Acc. no. P 1940-115
Formerly Johannes Jantzen Collection, Bremen

For Friedrich Winter see, for example, Saldern,
Meisterwerke, 1968, cat. nos. 191–94; in more recent
literature, see esp. Rückert, Munich, 1982, vol. 2,
nos. 768f., 253ff., for comparison with the Düsseldorf work, esp. pl. 226; and Klesse and Mayr, *Wolf
Collection*, 1987, 72ff., cat. nos. 102, 103.

Lit.: Heinemeyer, *Glas*, 1966, cat. no. 345; Saldern,
Alte Gläser, 1968, cat. no. 30

154 Beaker

Bohemia
Ca. 1710/20
H 13.4, ⌀ 10.6 cm

Colorless, thick-walled crystal glass. Mold-
blown. Wall cut in 12 facets and polished.
Decoration in polished and unpolished
intaglio engraving. On the front: Hubert wor-
shipping the stag. On the reverse: the arms
of alliance, flanked by Prussian eagles with
crowned monogram *FR*, referring to Frederick
I, crowned king of Prussia in 1701. Another
coat of arms, on the underside of the base;
both have yet to be identified.

Acc. no. P 1940-112
Formerly Johannes Jantzen Collection,
Bremen

For the beaker type and engraving see Ohm,
Bauer, and Gabbert, Frankfurt, 1980, cat.
no. 378.

Lit.: Heinemeyer, *Glas*, 1966, cat. no. 333

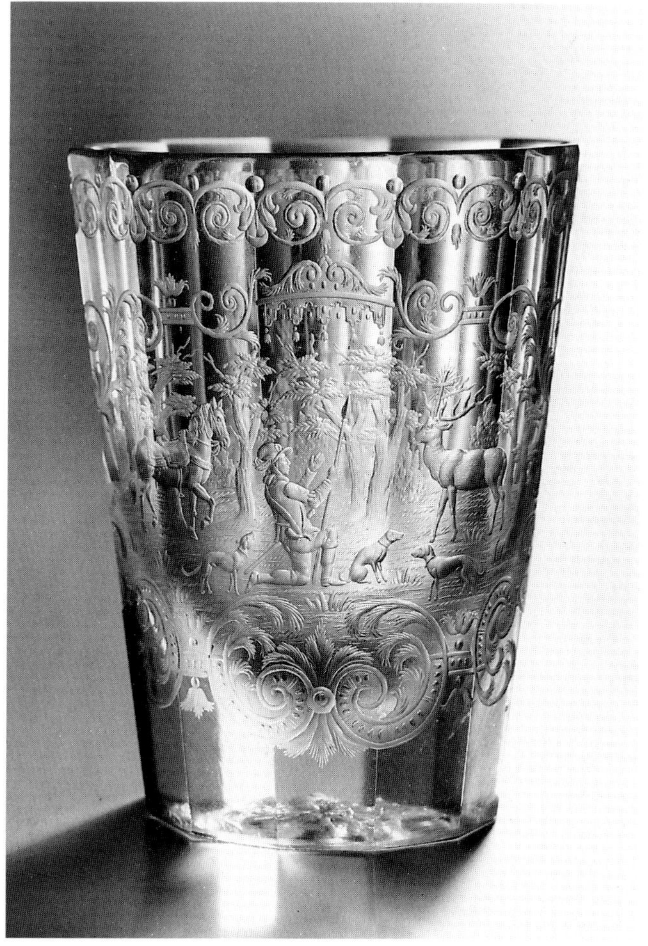

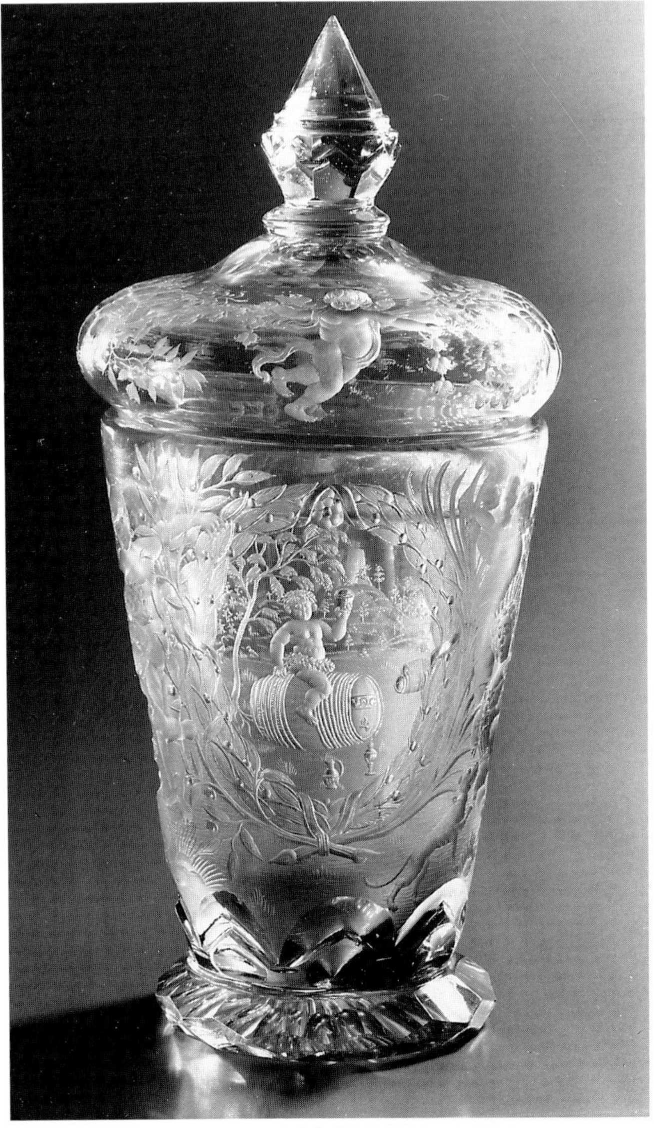

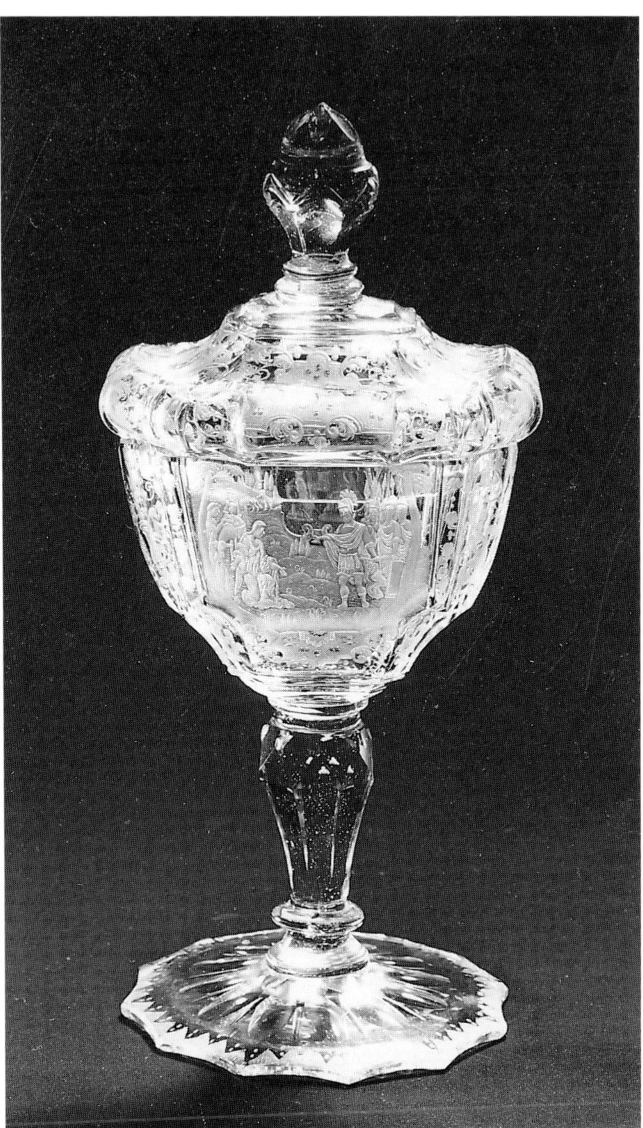

155 Covered Beaker

Silesia, Hirschberg Valley
Ca. 1715/20
H 21.2, ⌀ 9.9 (beaker), 10.7 cm (cover)

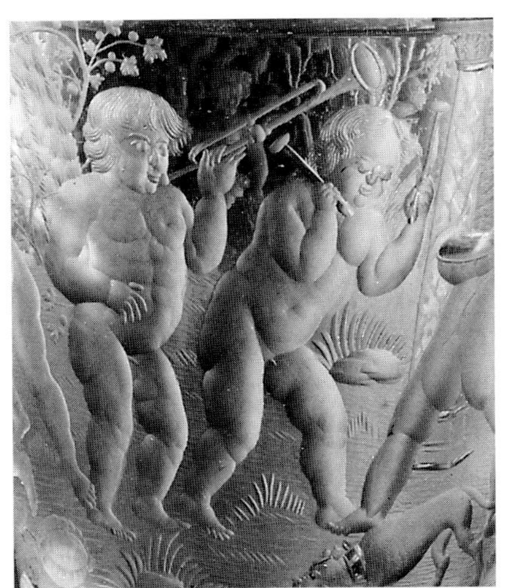

Colorless, thick-walled crystal glass. Mold-blown, shaped. Foot worked separately. Rich decoration in polished and unpolished intaglio engraving and polished cutting: Bacchus straddling a keg with a wreath of leaves around his waist, mark *UNG*. To both the left and right, three boys with flower baskets, one in each group breaks twigs off a wreath of leaves to decorate the baskets. On the opposite side, three boys blowing trumpets and beating drums. On the cover, two putti with flowering vines.

Acc. no. P 1940-116
Formerly Johannes Jantzen Collection, Bremen

The beaker documents the influence the figural style of Gottfried Spiller's Potsdam court workshop exerted on the Silesian region, to which family ties existed through Friedrich Winter. See also Klesse and Mayr, *Wolf Collection*, 1987, cat. no. 111.

Lit.: Heinemeyer, *Glas*, 1966, cat. no. 347

156 Preserve Jar

Silesia, Hirschberg Valley
Ca. 1730/40
H 18.7, ⌀ 8.3 (jar), 9.1 cm (cover)

Colorless crystal glass. Mold-blown, shaped. Cut and polished. Decoration in mat intaglio. Two figural scenes: generosity of Scipio (?), Alexander and Darius's wife (?); and bridal scene (?) depicting a kneeling woman being crowned with a wreath.

Acc. no. P 1940-118
Formerly Johannes Jantzen Collection, Bremen

Not a very common type of vessel, usually with elaborate engraved decoration. See Rückert, Munich, 1982, vol. 1, cat. nos. 277, 278, and Klesse and Mayr, *Wolf Collection*, 1987, cat. no. 107. For a simpler example, see Baumgärtner, Bremen I, 1987, no. 129.

Lit.: Heinemeyer, *Glas*, 1966, cat. no. 352

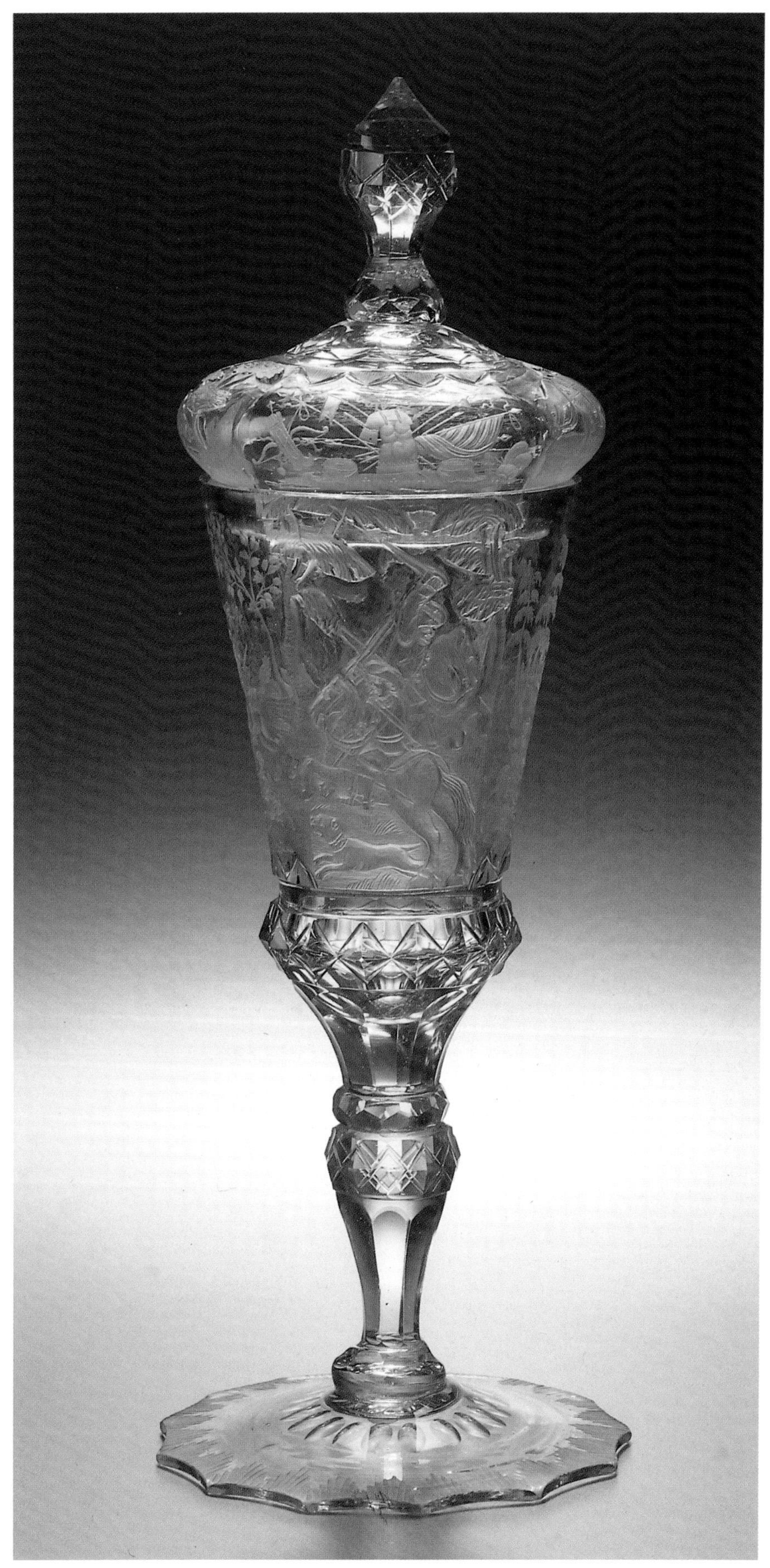

157 Covered Goblet

Silesia, Hirschberg Valley, Hermsdorf (?)
Dated 1729 on the collar of a dog
H 32.2, ⌀ 10.2 cm

Colorless, thick-walled crystal glass. Mold-
blown, shaped. Polished cut. Decoration
alternating between intaglio and relief carving: four depictions of equestrian battles. On
the cover: two saddled horses in relief carving, separated by trophies in intaglio.

Acc. no. P 1940-117
Formerly Johannes Jantzen Collection,
Bremen

Modeled on Friedrich Winter's works of relief
carving. Presumably one of the latest pieces
from this group made largely in the second
decade of the 18th century. See esp. Klesse
and Mayr, *Wolf Collection*, 1987, cat. no. 106.

Lit.: Heinemeyer, *Glas*, 1966, cat. no. 348;
Saldern, *Alte Gläser*, 1968, cat. no. 31; Ricke,
2500 Jahre, 1987, cat. no. 88

158 Covered Goblet

Silesia, probably Warmbrunn
Dated 1731
H 35.3, ⌀ 14.4 cm

Colorless crystal glass. Mold-blown, shaped.
Bowl and cover cut in 14 facets and flutes.
Decoration in mat intaglio engraving, partly
polished: allegorical figures of Devotia and
Justitia shooting at a castle. Inscription with
chronogram: *DeVotIonIs Iterate oCCUpatUM a
IUstItia* (1726). On the reverse, Habsburg
coat of arms in an aureole, alluding to
Emperor Charles VI, and the socled coat of
arms of Abbot Innozenz Fritsch of the Grüssau
monastery (in office 1727–34). A "ray of
grace" leads from the imperial arms to the
abbot's arms, then continues to the castle's
main building. Next to the abbot's coat of
arms is a putto with winged helmet and the
staff of Mercury. On the socle of the abbot's
arms, inscription with chronogram: *sUb Inno-
CentIo / prIMo. abaate / grÜssoViensl. / Defen-
sore Castel. / perpetUo VIrente.DeVotIonIs
Iterate oCCUpatUM a IUstItia* (1731).
Front and back view linked by allegories of
Abundantia and Fortitudo.

Acc. no. P 1940-119
Formerly Johannes Jantzen Collection, Bremen

The scene refers to the imperial fief of Bolken-
hain Castle secured for Grüssau monastery.
The occasion of the chronogram 1726 is unknown (Abbot Innozenz Fritsch was appointed only in 1727). 1731 is the year the fief
was secured.

Lit.: Heinemeyer, *Glas*, 1966, cat. no. 360

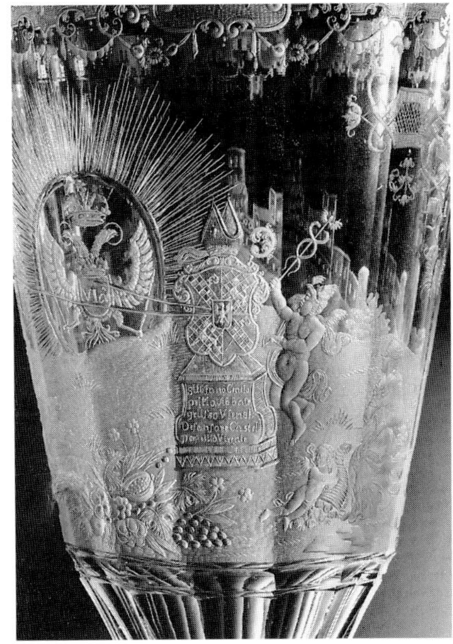

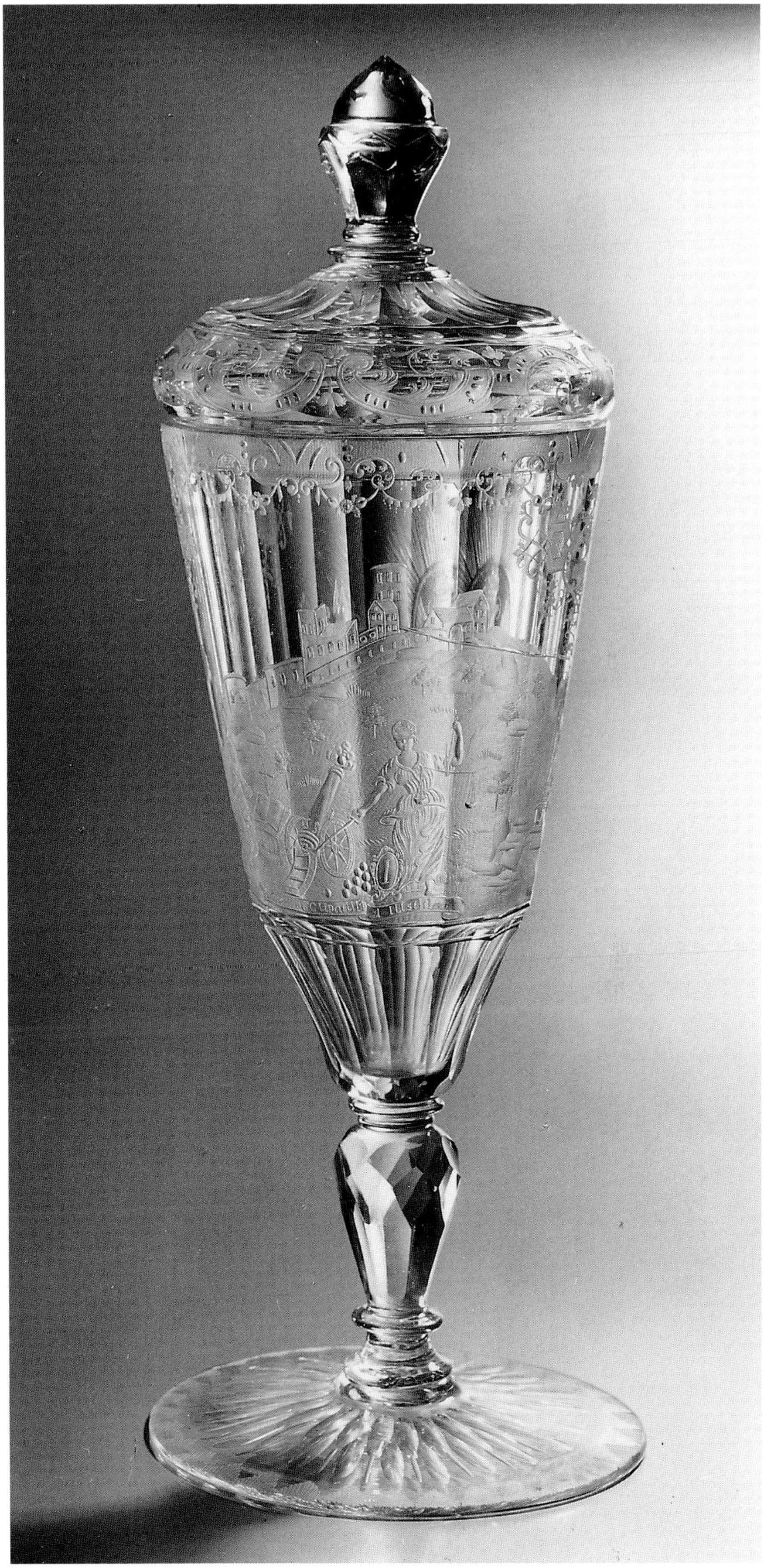

159 Preserve Jar

Silesia, Hirschberg Valley
Ca. 1740
H 13.4, ⌀ 9.8 cm

Colorless crystal glass. Cut and polished. Decoration in mat intaglio, partly polished. On one side, carriage with inscription: *Vivat Negotiae*. On the other side, a ship with inscription: *Das glück kombt offt gantz un verhofft*. Gilded.

Acc. no. P 1940-127
Formerly Johannes Jantzen Collection, Bremen

For this common type of vessel see Rückert, Munich, 1982, vol. I, cat. nos. 775f., and Klesse and Mayr, *Wolf Collection*, 1987, cat. nos. 123ff.

Lit.: Heinemeyer, *Glas*, 1966, cat. no. 367 (illus. switched with 366); Ricke, *2500 Jahre*, 1987, cat. no. 91

160 Covered Goblet

Attr. Christian Gottfried Schneider
Silesia, Warmbrunn, ca. 1740/50
H 26.18, ⌀ 8.6 (bowl), 9 cm (cover)

Colorless crystal glass. Mold-blown, shaped. Bottom of bowl cut and polished in 10 facets. Decoration in partly polished mat intaglio: a pastoral scene with large figures. On the reverse, large palmette with chinoiserie figures and landscape. In the spandrels at the top, small flute and lute players. At the bottom, trophies. On cover rim, landscapes.

Acc. no. P 1940-122
Formerly Johannes Jantzen Collection, Bremen

For C. G. Schneider see F. A. Dreier, "Stichvorlagen und Zeichnungen zu Gläsern Christian Gottfried Schneiders," *Journal of Glass Studies* 7 (1965): 66–78, Klesse and Saldern, *Sammlung Biemann*, 1978, cat. no. 123, and Klesse and Mayr, *Wolf Collection*, 1987, 85f., and cat. no. 119 (footed beaker with similar pastoral scene).

Lit.: Heinemeyer, *Glas*, 1966, cat. no. 371

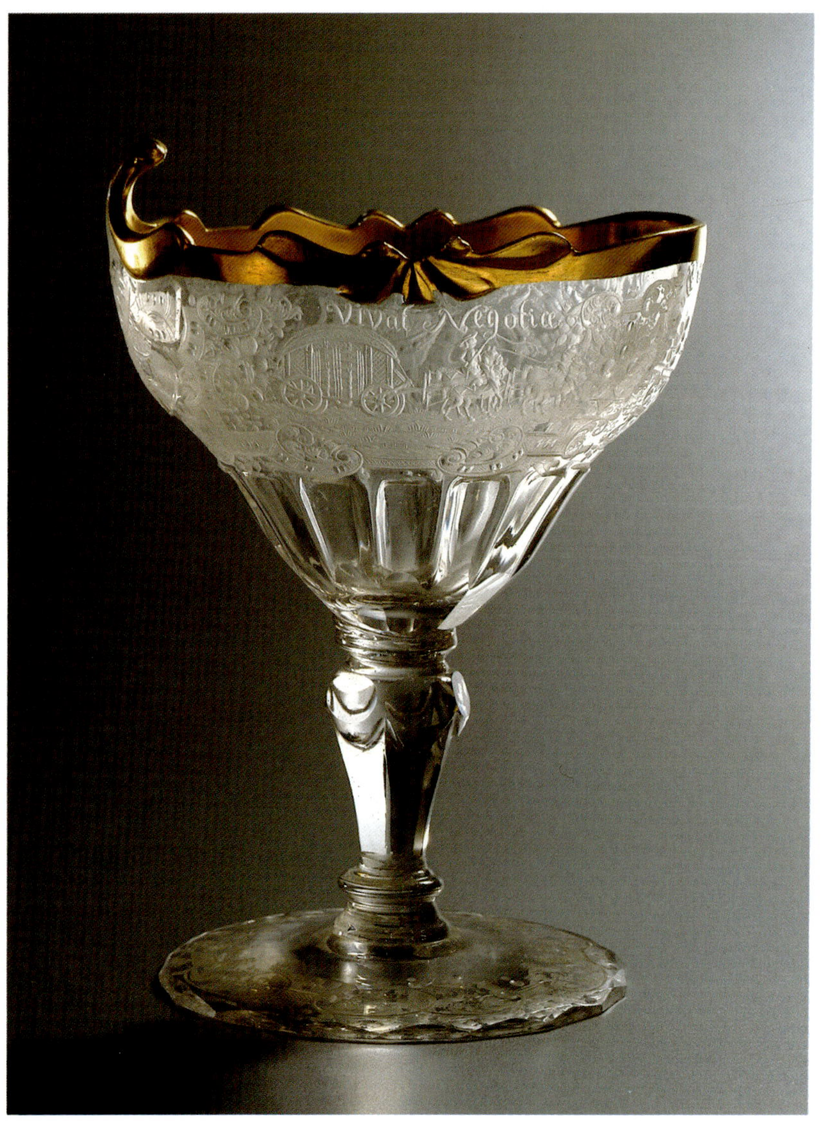

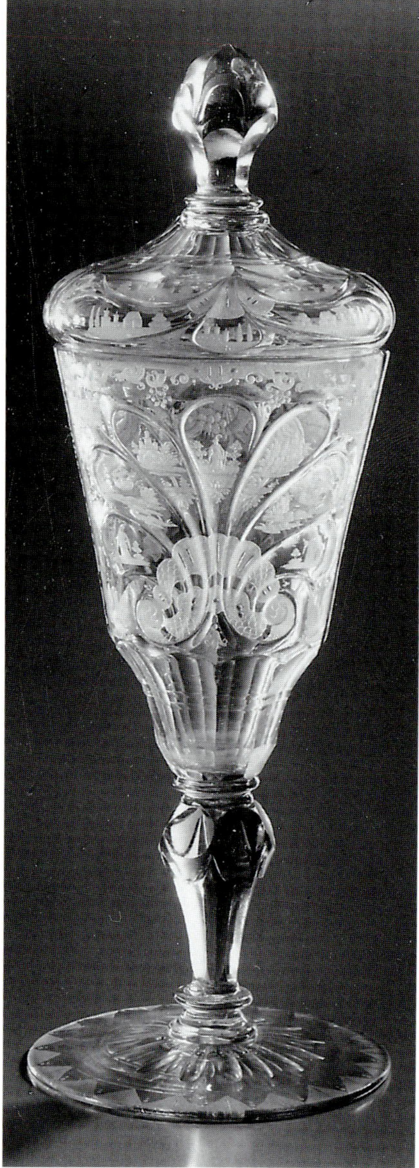

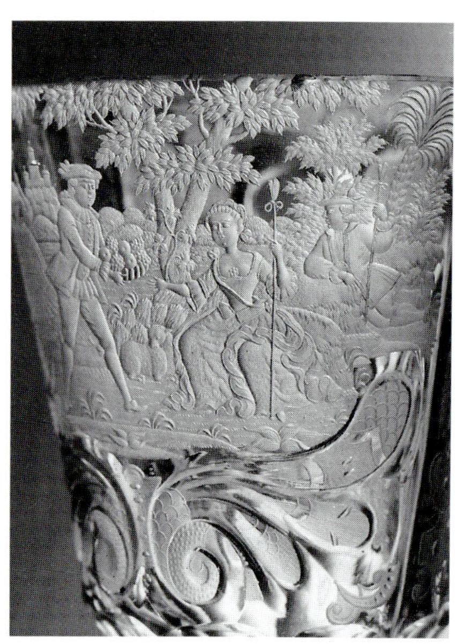

161 Covered Goblet

Silesia, Hirschberg Valley
Ca. 1740/50
H 25.2, ⌀ 8.4 cm

Colorless crystal glass. Mold-blown, shaped.
Cut and polished. Decoration in partly polished mat intaglio: on one side, a horse-drawn
cart in front of a town; on the other, a har-
bor with two ships; above that, mark: *Floreat
Commercium*.

Acc. no. P 1940-126
Formerly Johannes Jantzen Collection,
Bremen

Goblets of this type seem to have been popular presents or complimentary gifts in commercial circles. Perhaps they were also important for export to The Netherlands. Cf. cat.
no. 156 and Klesse and Saldern, *Sammlung
Biemann*, 1978, cat. no. 127, with further
examples. See also Ohm, Bauer, and Gabbert,
Frankfurt, 1980, cat. nos. 395, 397. A particularly beautiful piece is in Baumgärtner,
Bremen I, 1987, cat. no. 150.

Lit.: Heinemeyer, *Glas*, 1966, cat. no. 90

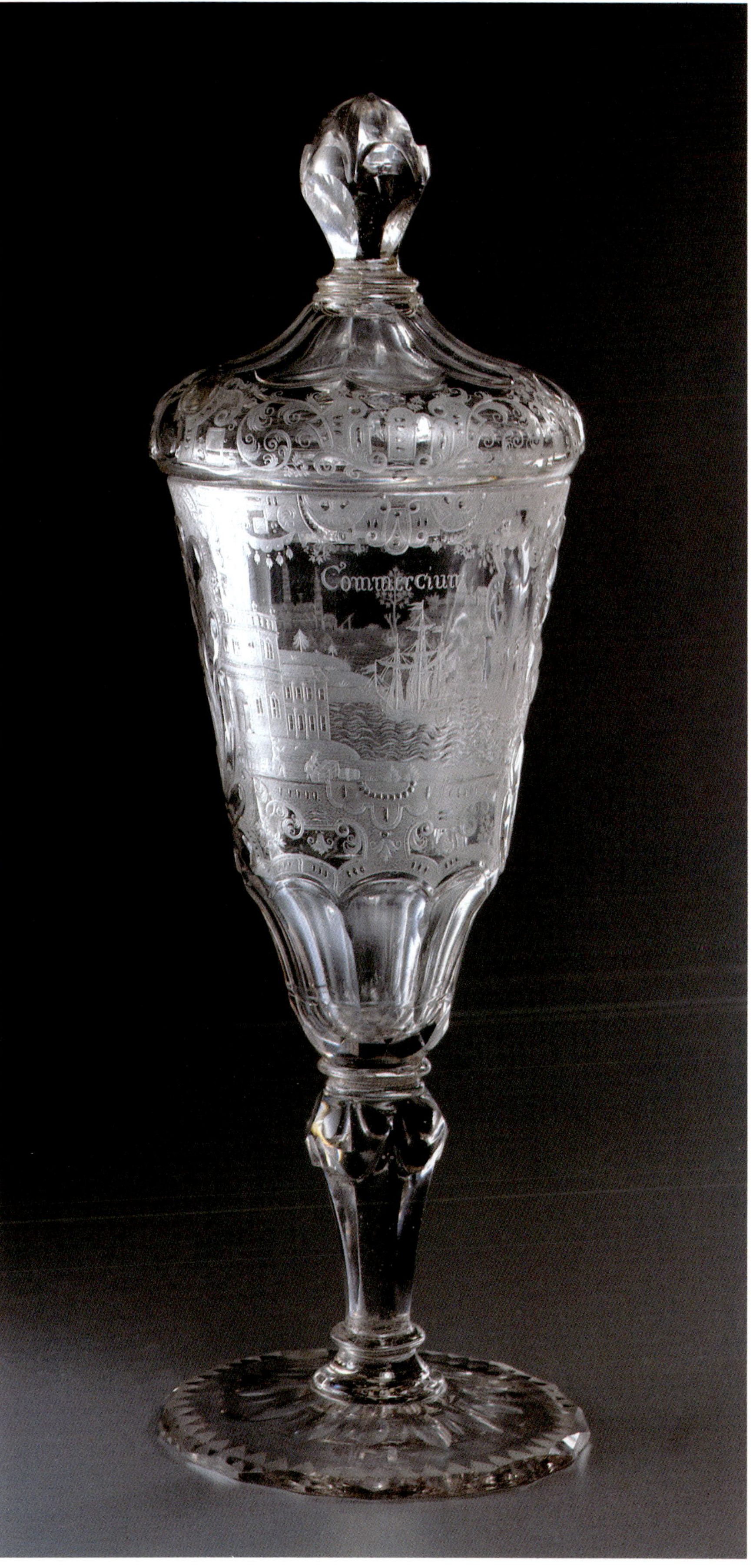

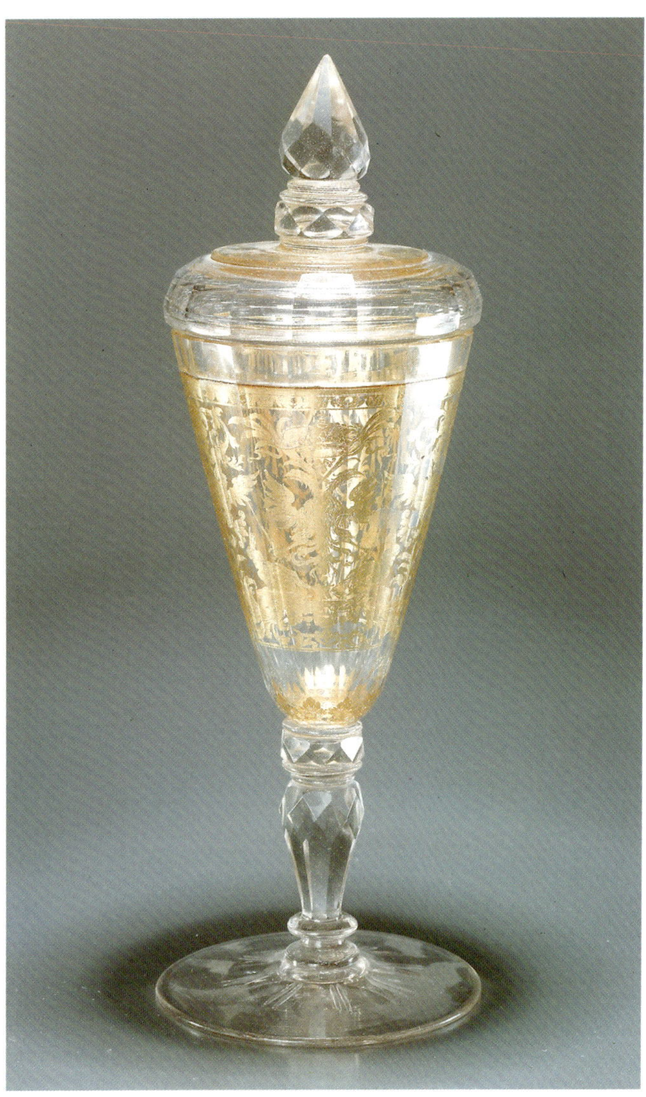

162 Covered Goblet

Bohemia
Between 1742 and 1745
H 24.7, ⌀ 8.9 cm

Colorless crystal glass. Mold-blown, shaped.
Cut in 16 facets. Bowl and cover double-
walled, decoration in applied etched gold leaf
between the walls. In the bowl, crowned
double eagle above fettered Turks; on opposite side, bust of an ancient ruler with laurel
wreath under a baldachin held by putti,
flanked by leaping deer and birds on acanthus wagon. Front and back linked by Indians
and hanging birdcages. On the cover, vines;
inside cover and bowl, Bavarian rhombs.

Acc. no. P 1940-147
Formerly Johannes Jantzen Collection, Bremen

The decoration probably alludes to Emperor
Charles VII, who, as Elector of Bavaria, held
the imperial throne from 1742 to 1745.

Lit.: Heinemeyer, *Glas*, 1966, cat. no. 429;
Saldern, *Alte Gläser*, 1968, cat. no. 36

163 *Zwischengoldglas* Beaker

Bohemia
Ca. 1730/40
H 9.8, ⌀ 7.3 cm

Colorless crystal glass. Mold-blown, shaped.
Cut and polished in 18 facets. Double-walled
with decoration in gold etching and lacquer
painting between the walls—depiction of one
of St. Francis Xavier's miracles: In front of
the vigilant Japanese ruler, a crab recovers a
crucifix, which had fallen into the water,
from the ocean floor. The ruler appears under
a baldachin, next to him an old adviser. Two
archers. The saint kneels at the shore; in the
background is a European ship.
In the gold border at the bottom, etched
mark: *S. FRANZISCVS XAVERIVS*. In the base, a
gold etched monogram of Christ in an aureole
underlaid with red lacquer.
Some seeds, in these areas decolorization of
the lacquer painting. Colors slightly decom-
posed.

Acc. no. P 1940-151
Formerly Johannes Jantzen Collection, Bremen

Religious themes were quite common on
Zwischengold glassware. Depictions of
St. Francis Xavier and other Jesuits as well as
scenes from their lives seem to have been
particularly popular. See, for example, Heinemeyer, *Glas*, 1966, cat. nos. 422, 423.

Lit.: J. Jantzen, *Deutsches Glas aus fünf
Jahrhunderten* (Düsseldorf: Kunstmuseum
Düsseldorf, 1960), cat. no. 121

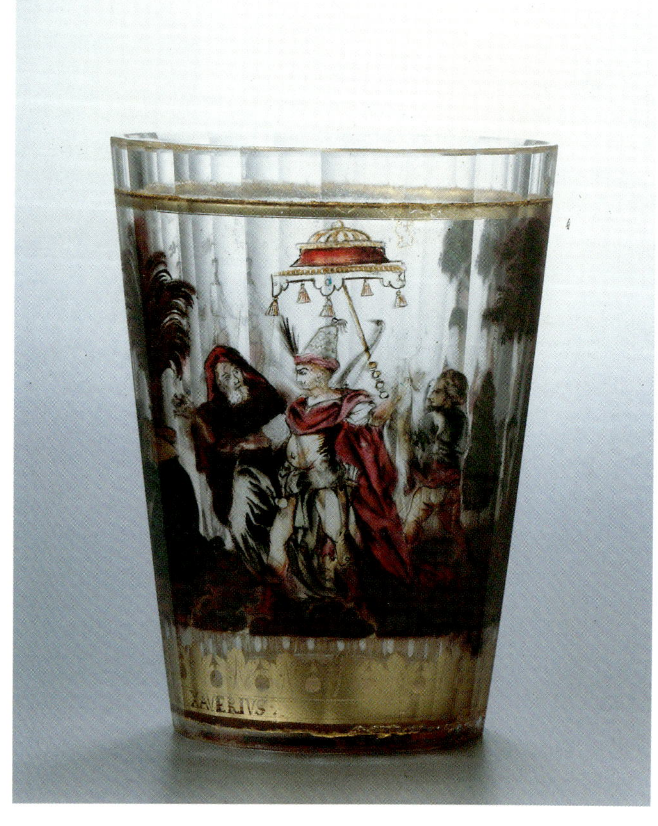

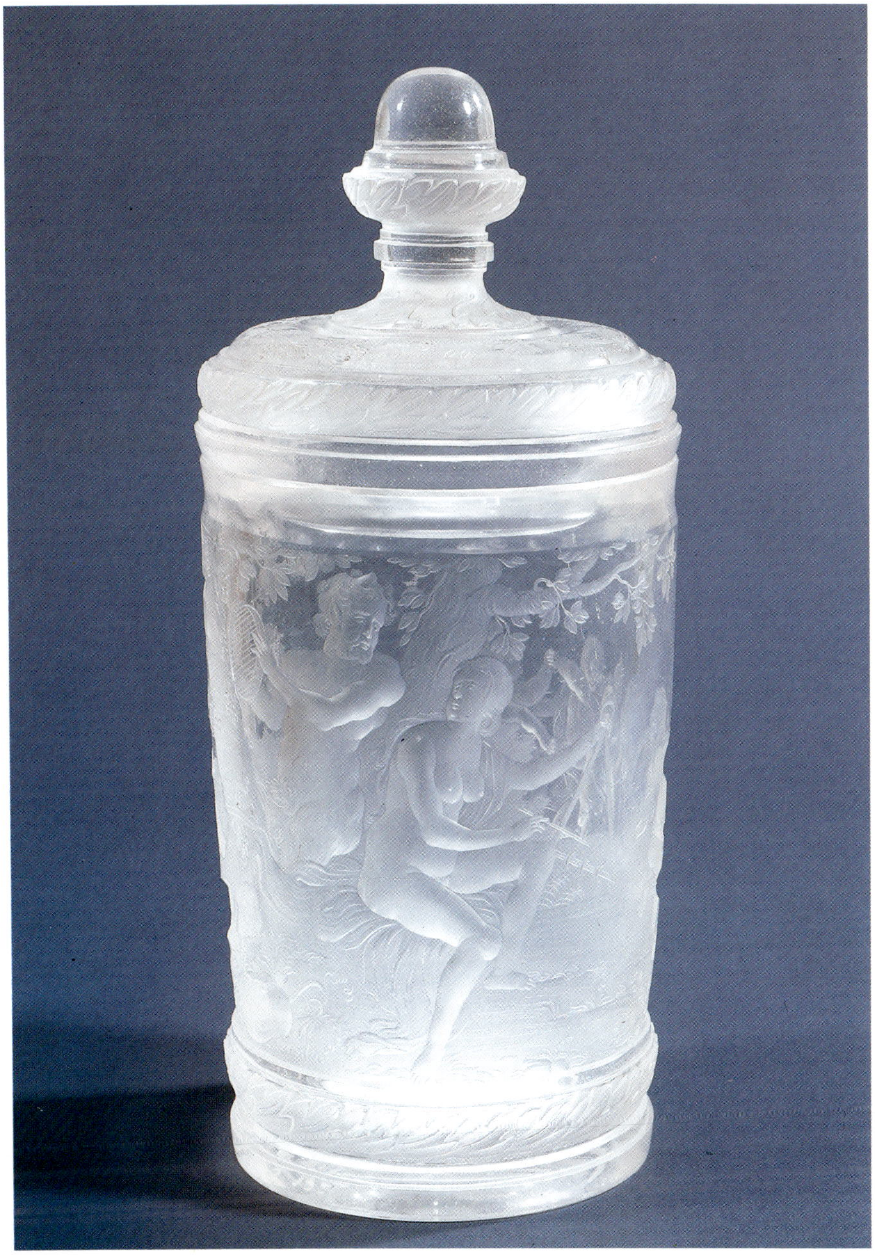

164 Covered Beaker

Gottfried Spiller
Brandenburg, Potsdam
Ca. 1700
H 26.7, ⌀ 12.6 cm

Colorless crystal glass. Mold-blown, shaped.
Cut in horizontal rings and polished. Wall and
cover decorated in relief carving and intaglio
engraving: encircling the wall, bacchanalian
scene with a satyr playing music, maenads,
as well as dancing putti and a boy faun; a
putto with wreath and a bunch of grapes,
straddling a goat (Bacchus as boy?), two
other putti under trees. On the cover, vine
foliage and grapes interwoven with fruit
vines in intaglio engraving between relief-
carved laurel friezes.
Slightly crizzled.

Acc. no. P 1940-132
Formerly Johannes Jantzen Collection,
Bremen; previously Reichenheim-Oppenheim
Collection, Berlin

Probably the most elaborate and, owing to
its sculptural modeling, finest of the few
extant covered beakers by Spiller. See
Charleston, *Masterpieces*, 1980, 140, no. 62,
and Klesse and Mayr, *Wolf Collection*, 1987,
92f. and cat. no. 128. As to the theme, the
work closest to the Düsseldorf beaker is a
piece at the Victoria & Albert Museum, London. See W. B. Honey, *Glass* (London: Victoria
& Albert Museum, 1946), 87, pl. 45A.

Lit.: Heinemeyer, *Glas*, 1966, cat. no. 382;
Saldern, *Alte Gläser*, 1968, cat. no. 32; Ricke,
Ausgewählte Werke, 1980, 17; Keisch and
Netzer, *Preussen*, 2001, 73, 77

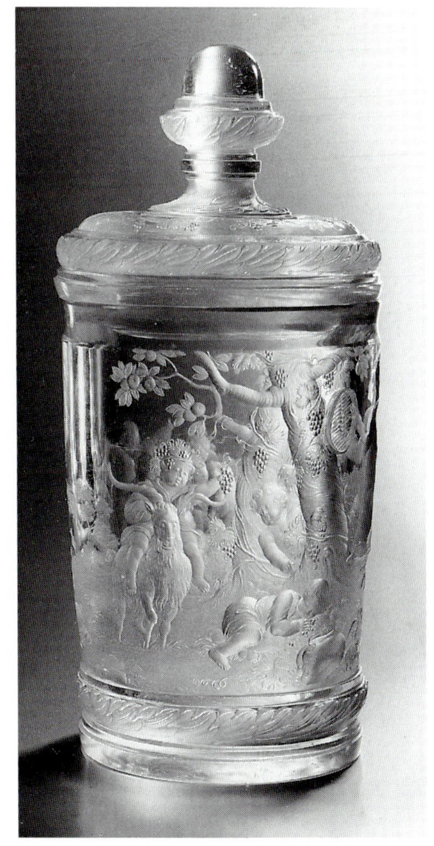

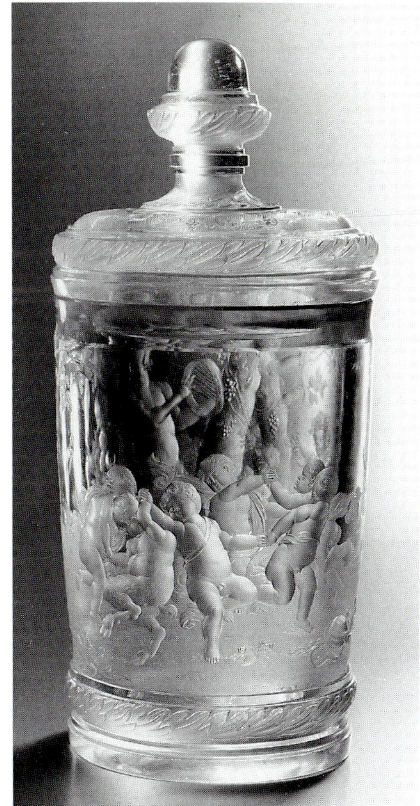

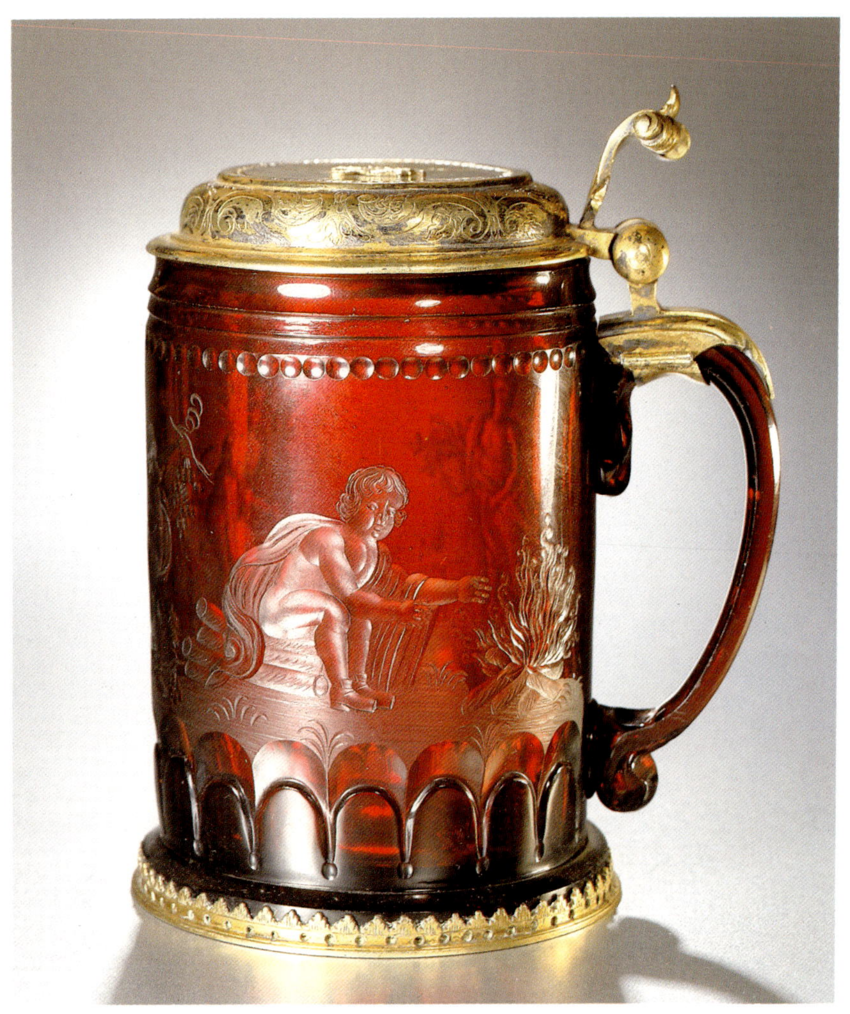

166 Covered Beaker

Brandenburg, Potsdam
Ca. 1700/1710
H 18.5, ⌀ 10.5 cm

Brown-gray marbled opaque glass with green-ish, blue, and yellow inclusions. Mold-blown, shaped. Wall cut in 14 facets and polished.

Acc. no. P 1940-133
Formerly Johannes Jantzen Collection, Bremen

The beaker has variously been associated with Johann Kunckel's experiments at his glasshouse laboratory on the Pfaueninsel in the Havel, but must have been made after his sojourn at the Brandenburg court. For Kunck-el's colored glassware see R. Schmidt, *Brandenburgische Gläser* (Berlin, 1914), 58ff.

Lit.: Heinemeyer, *Glas*, 1966, cat. no. 385; Saldern, *Alte Gläser*, 1968, cat. no. 34

165 Mug with Lid

Circle of Gottfried Spiller
Brandenburg, Potsdam
Ca. 1710/20
H 14.6, ⌀ 12.1 cm

Massive dark red, gold ruby glass. Mold-blown, shaped. Decoration in polished cut-ting and intaglio engraving: putti as allegori-cal figures representing the four seasons. Lid silver, gilded; engraved. Applied Minerva bust in silver relief. Gilded silver foot-ring.

Acc. no. P 1940-135
Formerly Johannes Jantzen Collection, Bremen

Part of the Potsdam glasshouse's gold ruby production initiated by Johann Kunckel. A similar piece is in the collections of the Stiftung Preussische Schlösser und Gärten in Potsdam; see Keisch and Netzer, *Preussen*, 2001, 105, fig. 8.

Lit.: Heinemeyer, *Glas*, 1966, cat. no. 384; Ricke, *2500 Jahre*, 1987, cat. no. 84; Keisch and Netzer, *Preussen*, 2001, 270, no. 210

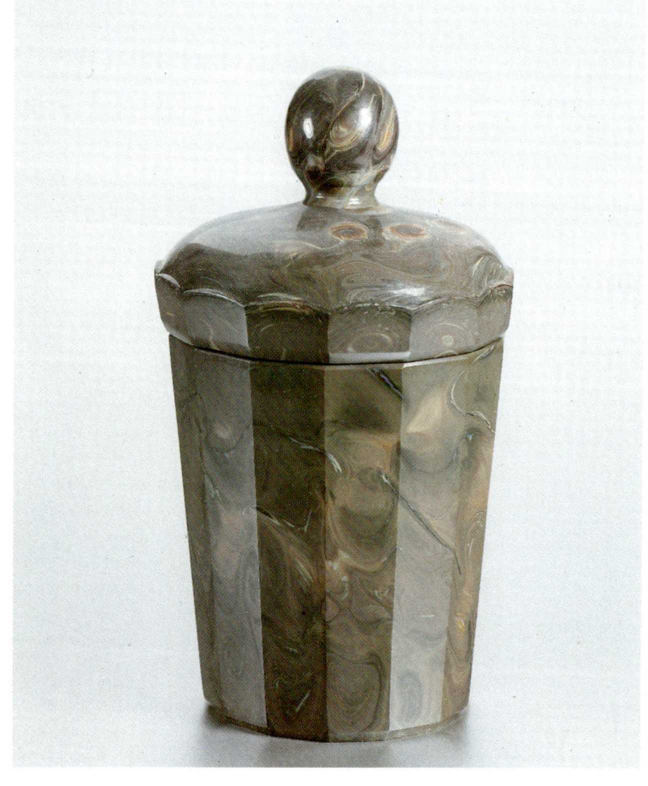

167   Covered Beaker

Brandenburg, Potsdam, or Bohemia (?)
Ca. 1710/20
H 25.6, ⌀ 13.3 (cover), 12.6 cm (beaker)

Massive gold ruby glass. Mold-blown, shaped.
Wall cut in 16 facets and polished. Decora-
tion in mat intaglio engraving: medallions
with allegorical depictions of the four sea-
sons with inscriptions.
Rose: *ivncta arma decori.*
Lily: *candore omnia vincit.*
Hunting horn: *ducit et excitat agmen.*
Theater stage: *Naturam superat.*
Chip off rim of mouth. Cover does not belong
to the beaker; presumably freely restored in
the 19th century.

Acc. no. P 1940–134
Formerly Johannes Jantzen Collection, Bremen

For the sources of the four-seasons medallions see S. le Clerc and S. M. Kraus, *Devises
pour les tapisseries…* (Augsburg, 1690), and
G. E. Pazaurek, "Französische Stiche als Vor-
bilder für geschnittene Gläser," *Belvedere* 13
(1928): 106f., illus. opposite p. 109.

Lit.: Heinemeyer, *Glas*, 1966, cat. no. 383;
Saldern, *Alte Gläser*, 1968, cat. no. 33

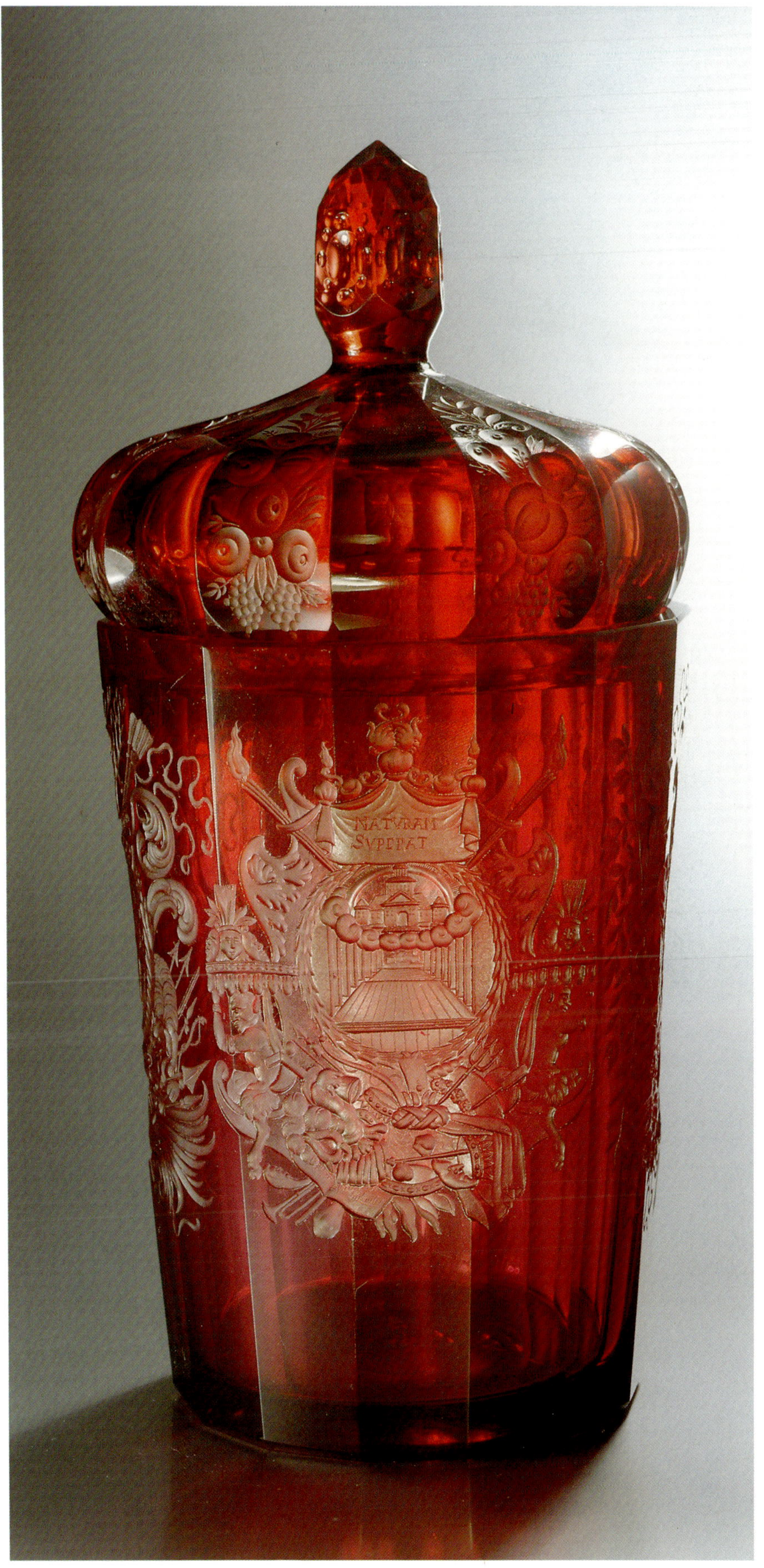

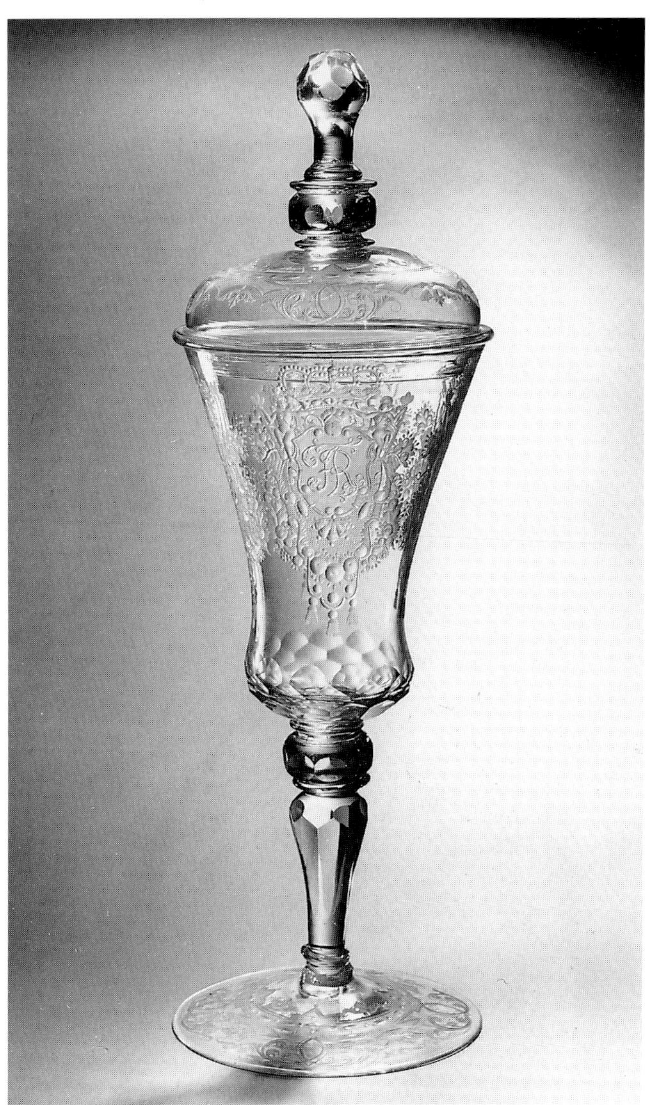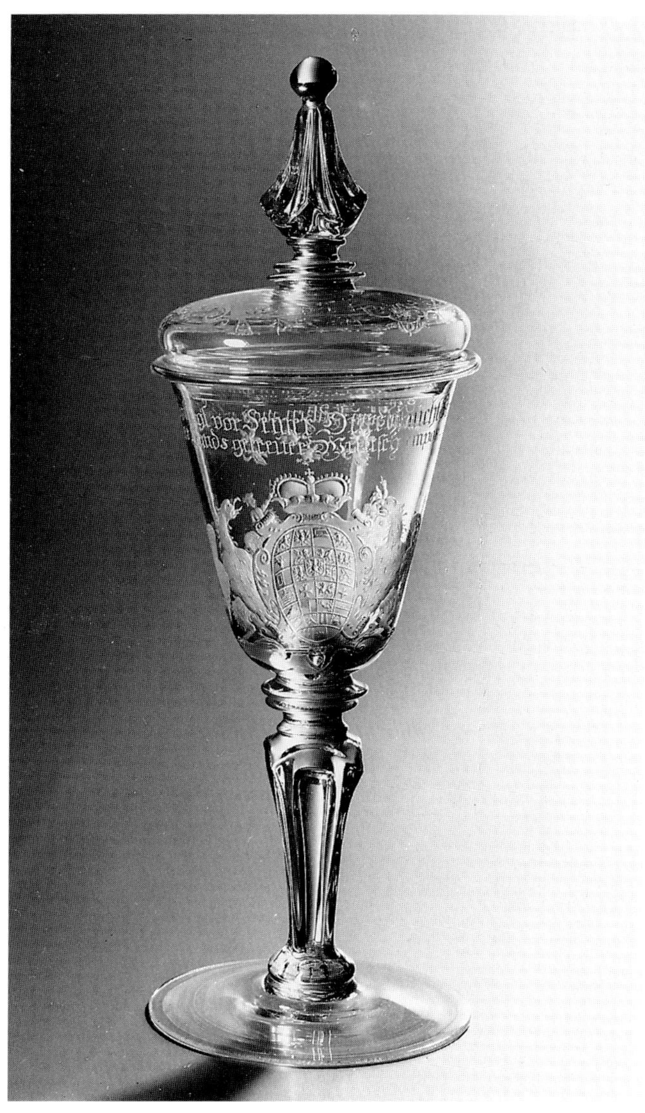

168 Covered Goblet

Saxony, Dresden Court Glasshouse
Ca. 1720/30
H 36.1, ⌀ 12.1 cm

Colorless crystal glass. Mold-blown, shaped.
Bottom of bowl and finial on cover cut and
polished. On the bowl, in partly polished mat
intaglio: richly decorated cartouches with the
initials *FAR* for Augustus the Strong, *CE* for
his wife, Queen Christiane Eberhardine, *FAK*
for Frederick Augustus III, Elector of Saxony,
and *MJ* for his wife, Maria Josepha.
On foot and cover wide interlacing with vine
foliage.

Acc. no. P 1940-139
Formerly Johannes Jantzen Collection,
Bremen

The earlier attribution to Johann Georg
Kiessling cannot be upheld in view of recent
research. See G. Haase, "Die Glasschleifer
und Glasschneider auf der Dresdener Hütte,"
Jahrbuch der Kunstsammlungen Dresden
(1985), 85–104.

Lit.: Heinemeyer, *Glas*, 1966, cat. no. 389;
Baumgärtner, *Sächsisches Glas*, 1977, fig. 90;
Ricke, *Ausgewählte Werke*, 1980, 18

169 Covered Goblet

Georg Ernst Kunckel
Thuringia, Gotha, ca. 1741
H 29.2, ⌀ 10.1 cm

Colorless crystal glass. Mold-blown, shaped.
Pseudo-faceted, four-part stem and corresponding finial on cover. On the wall of the
bowl, in partly polished mat intaglio: coat of
arms of Brandenburg-Ansbach and Sayn-
Wittgenstein-Altenkirchen. On the opposite
side, falconers on horseback and inscription:
*1. Wie Falken sich Zum steigen schicken wann
sie Zum Beitzen was erblicken.* Above the coat
of arms: *2. So steigt vor Seiner Durchlaucht
Flor des Lands getreuer Wunsch empor.*

Acc. no. P 1940-137
Formerly Johannes Jantzen Collection, Bremen

The glass alludes to the agreement made between the ruler of Sayn-Wittgenstein-Altenkir-
chen and the margrave of Brandenburg-Ansbach.

Lit.: Heinemeyer, *Glas*, 1966, cat. no. 393;
Ricke, *Ausgewählte Werke*, 1980, 18

170 Covered Goblet

Lauenstein and Osterwald
Ca. 1750/60
H 30.8, ⌀ 10 cm

Colorless, thick-walled crystal glass. Mold-blown, shaped. Foot folded broadly downwards. Stem, bottom of bowl, and cover cut and polished. Encircling the bowl: landscape in mat intaglio with inscription: *Die Landes Wollfarth*. Gilded.

Acc. no. P 1940-141
Formerly Johannes Jantzen Collection, Bremen

The goblet shows the characteristic conical foot of Lauenstein glassware, occurring similarly in products of Hessian glasshouses. The folded feet of the glasses in this group are anachronistic for the mid-18th century.

Lit.: Heinemeyer, *Glas*, 1966, cat. no. 397; Ricke, *Ausgewählte Werke*, 1980, 18; Ricke, *2500 Jahre*, 1987, cat. no. 93; A. von Rohr, *Lauensteiner Glas 1701–1827: Ein Beitrag zur Wirtschafts- und Kulturgeschichte Niedersachsens*, exh. cat. (Hanover: Historisches Museum Hannover, 1991), 75, cat. no. 41.12

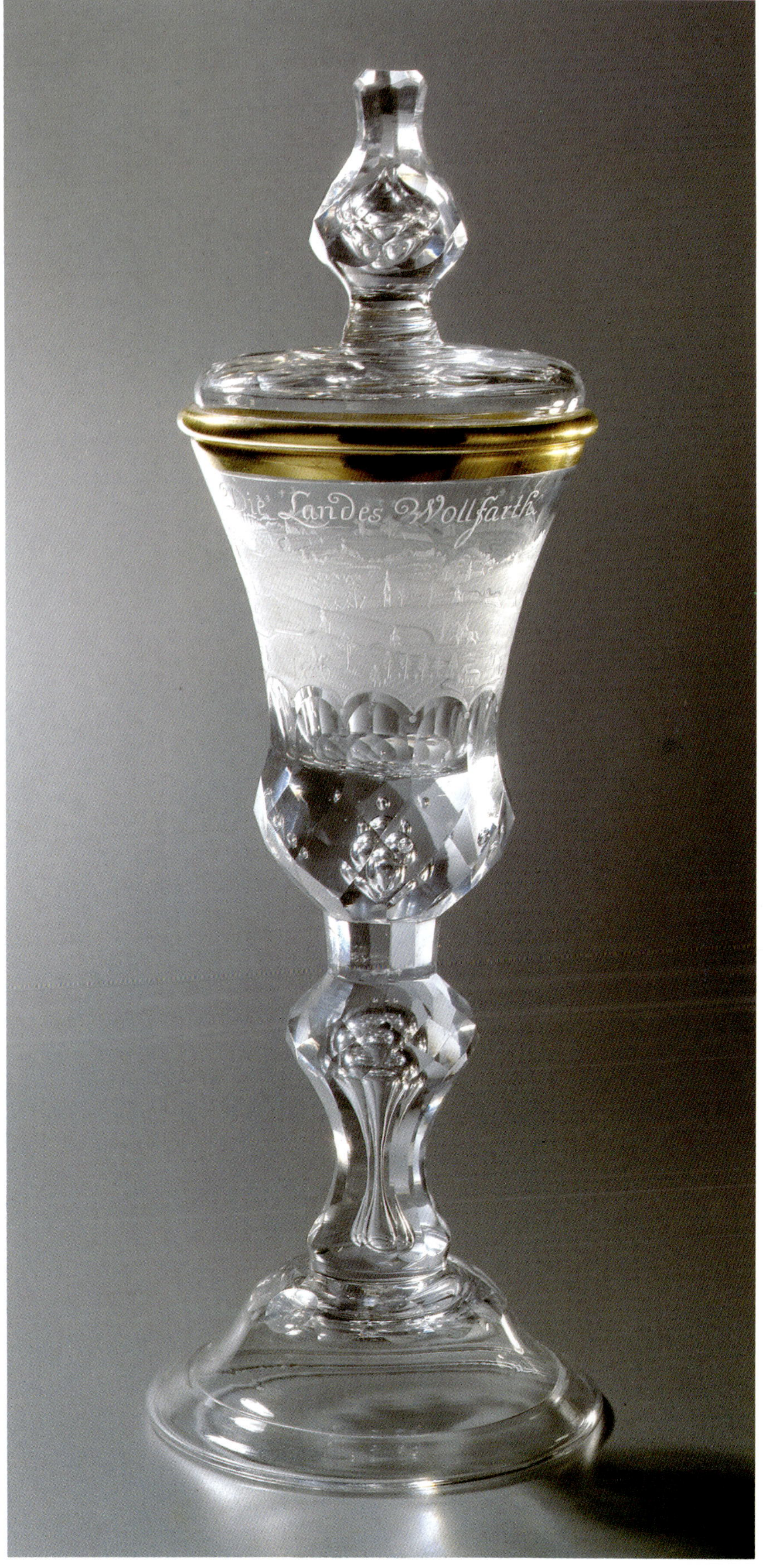

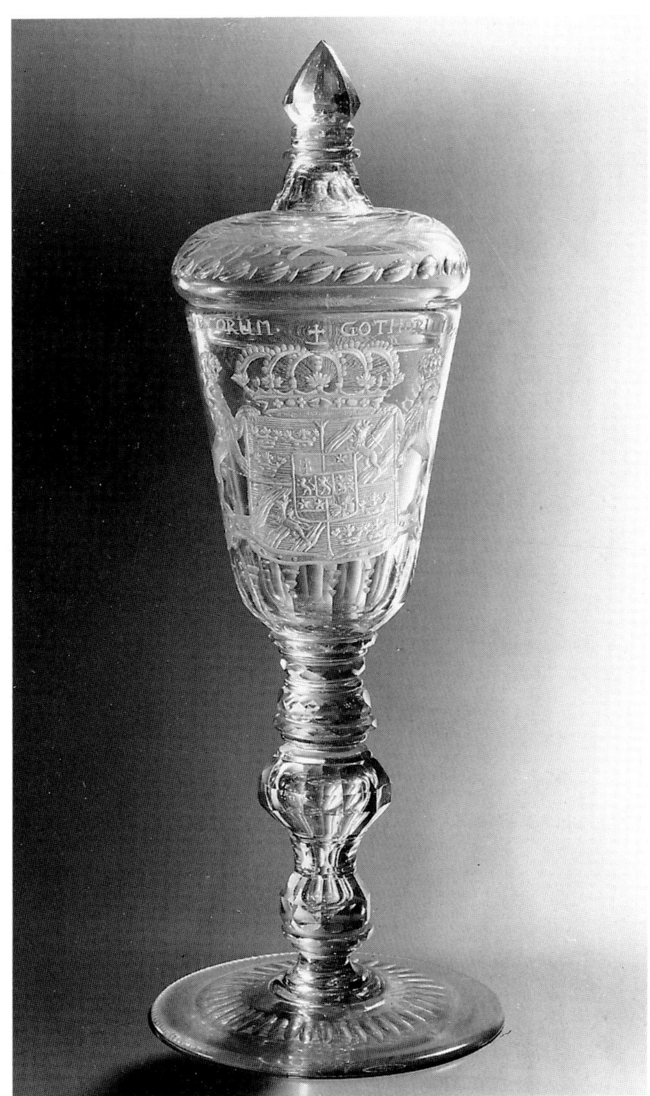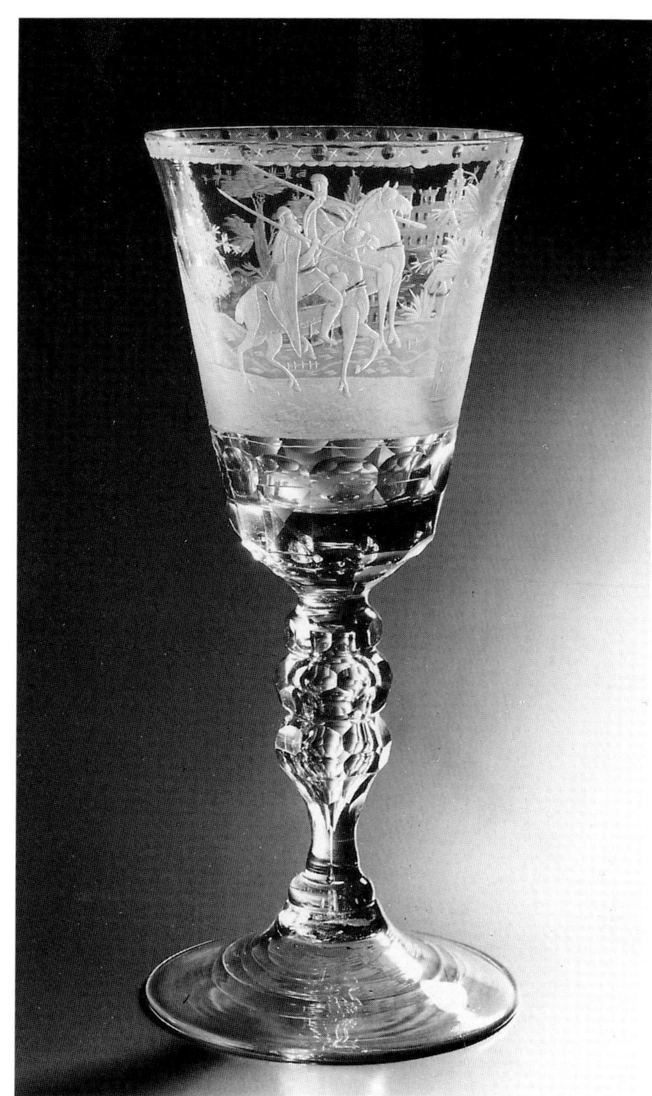

171 Covered Goblet

Sweden, Stockholm-Kungsholm
2nd quarter of 18th c.
H 32.3, ⌀ 12 cm

Colorless crystal glass with light gray tone.
Foot, stem, bottom of bowl, and cover cut
and polished. On the bowl in mat intaglio:
royal Swedish and Hessian arms of alliance
with king's crown, flanked by lion rampants.
The inscription *FRIEDERICUS.DEI.GRATIAS-
SUE.CORUM.GOTHORUM.VANDALORUMQUE.REX*
refers to Frederick of Hesse-Kassel, king of
Sweden from 1720 to 1751. On the reverse
appears a shining sun; on the cover, crossed
laurel and palm branches.

Acc. no. P 1976-53

Whereas the original works of the glasshouse
in Kungsholm in the late 17th/early 18th
centuries embraced Venetian shapes, Swedish
glass of the subsequent period drew on
Bohemian and central German sources. The
close ties to Germany, supported by the king,
furthered this development. For the development of glass art in Sweden see H. Seitz,
Glaset förr och nu (Stockholm, 1933).

Lit.: –

172 Goblet

Russia, Petersburg Court Factory
Ca. 1760
H 22.6, ⌀ 10 cm

Colorless crystal glass with light golden tone.
Mold-blown, shaped. In the thick base of the
bowl, seven tears (pegged air bubbles). Stem
and bottom of bowl cut and polished. On the
wall, in partly polished mat intaglio: encircling scene with two lancers, cavalier with
lady, and palace.

Acc. no. P 1976-54

Empress Elizabeth of Russia was a great supporter of the Petersburg Court Factory. Specialists from Saxon glasshouses took part in
establishing the works. For a long time, therefore, Russian Baroque glassware remained formally dependent on the production of Saxon
glasshouses. See Baumgärtner, *Sächsisches
Glas*, 1977, fig. 143. For Russian glass see
R. Šelkovnikov, *Russkoe chudožestvennoe
steklo* (Leningrad, 1969).

Lit.: –

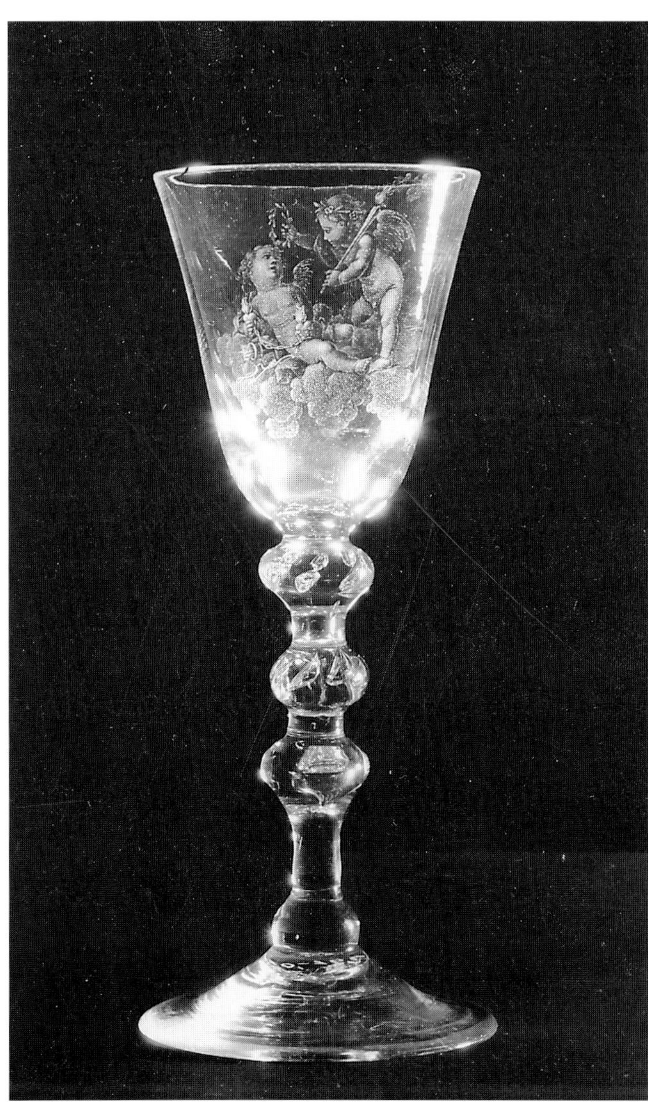

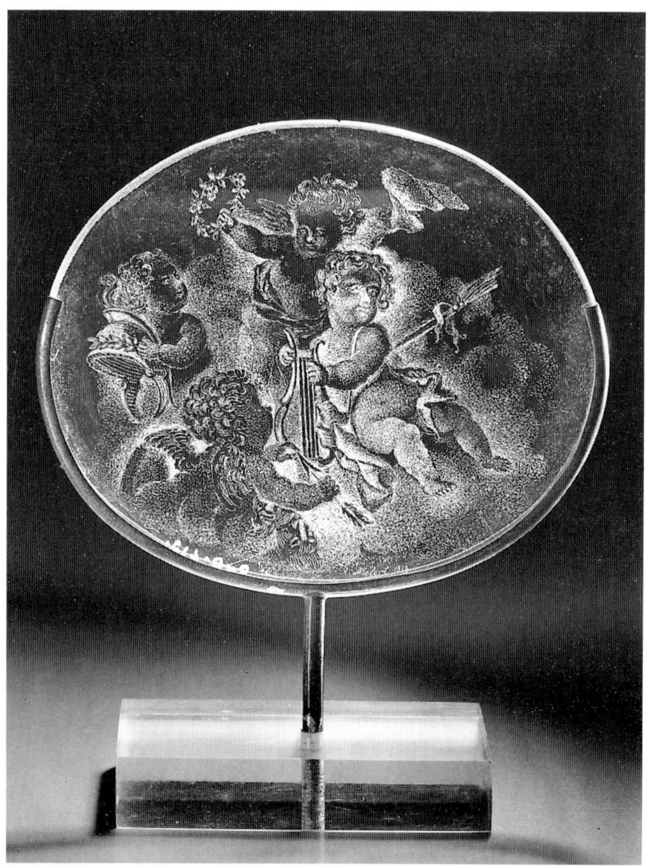

173 Flute Glass

Glass: England, Newcastle upon Tyne
Ca. 1760/70
Decoration: The Netherlands, circle of David
Wolff
Ca. 1770
H 19.4, ⌀ 8 cm (foot)

Colorless crystal glass. Mold-blown, shaped.
Diamond-point stippled decoration: allegory
of love—two putti with laurel wreaths on
clouds, one with a burning heart bound in
chains, the other with a burning torch, as
well as quiver, bow, and arrow.

Acc. no. P 1940-162
Formerly Johannes Jantzen Collection,
Bremen

For more recent research on David Wolff see
Klesse and Mayr, *Wolf Collection*, 1987, 117ff.
and cat. nos. 172ff.

Lit.: Heinemeyer, *Glas*, 1966, cat. no. 412

174 Medallion

Andries Melort
Diamond-engraved mark, lower right: *Melort
1839*
Holland, Breda
1839
H 6.7, W 8.2 cm

Colorless, flat, thin glass tablet. In diamond-point stippling: allegory of music and
drama (?).

Acc. no. P 1940-215
Formerly Johannes Jantzen Collection,
Bremen

Andries Melort worked as a silversmith and
glass engraver in Breda and Dordrecht. He is
one of the last representatives of Dutch
"stipple engraving." See J. van Haastert, "De
silversmid en glasgraveur Andries Melort
(1776–1849)," *Jaarboek van de Geschieden
Oudheidskundige Kring van Stad en Land van
Breda "De Oranjeboom"* 30 (1977), 62–79.
Melort worked in Breda from 1836 to shortly
before 1849.

Lit.: Heinemeyer, *Glas*, 1966, cat. no. 418;
Haastert, op. cit., fig. 42

The Biedermeier Period

After the elector of Saxony succeeded in having the first European porcelain produced in his factory in Meissen, many other sovereigns founded similar factories at their courts from the mid-eighteenth century. In a very short time glass lost its significance as a material used to make fine utilitarian objects and as a medium on which rulers had themselves portrayed. It also lost favor amongst the general public, which now preferred porcelain. The new, fashionable beverages of coffee and hot chocolate further reinforced the use of the latter material. Artistic glass design, determined for nearly a century by the tastes of the nobility, stagnated and gradually fell out of favor.

The political upheavals following the French Revolution, however, marked a new beginning. The rise of the bourgeoisie created a new market, new types of glass, and a multiplicity of new decorative forms. Already in the last decade of the previous century, Rococo, perceived as too playful and decadent, fell into disdain. Impulses generated by, for instance, the excavations of Pompeii and Herculaneum encouraged the development of a new formal canon drawn from antiquity. In glass art, producers also began to prefer the simple and pure forms, which provided suitable backgrounds for small and detailed, painted or engraved depictions. A new middle-class glass art emerged: the most important object was the collector's item for the glass cabinets that graced the living rooms and parlors of the period.

The themes of the glasses reflect—typically for the restoration period—a retreat to the private sphere. Dedications to friends, tokens of love, flower motifs with encoded names, and portraits of family members or of important personalities were popular subjects. The contemplative nature of the Biedermeier period had its counterpole in the numerous glass souvenirs bearing depictions of landscapes, townscapes, and views of famous buildings. They signal a yearning for the remote, for travel to distant lands ("wanderlust"), and Romantic dreams of freedom.

The works of two artists mark the beginning of the period's glass art. Both drew, with different results, on *Zwischengold* decoration, a technique used by Bohemian workshops in the second quarter of the eighteenth century (cat. nos. 162, 163). In their refinement, grace, and delicacy, Johann Josef Mildner's double-walled beakers with gold engraving and portrait medallions set into glass still evoke the spirit of the eighteenth century (cat. no. 175). Johann Sigismund Menzel, in contrast, used the new goblet forms of the day. His silhouettes on a gold ground drew on a form of eighteenth-century representation that complied with the bourgeois conception of personal reticence and modesty in self-portraits (cat. no. 176).

Transparent enamel painting adapted from porcelain painting became the most popular decorating technique at the beginning of the new century; the transparent ground brought out its qualities even more effectively than porcelain. Samuel Mohn (cat. nos. 177, 178), active in Dresden, and his son Gottlob Samuel, who moved to Vienna in 1811, are counted amongst this technique's most skilled practitioners. The circle around the porcelain painter Anton Kothgasser in Vienna (cat. nos. 182, 183) produced a broad range of painted *Ranftbecher*. These glasses have helped shape the image of the Biedermeier period as a time of self-sufficient domesticity, of contemplative regard for the world of small things, and of a heightened sentiment in human dealings.

Apart from painted glassware, glass engraving also came back into favor. Artists such as Franz Gottstein, Emanuel Hoffmann, Franz Anton Pelikan (cat. no. 189), or the so-called Master of the Rising Sun (cat. no. 184) were on a par with the great masters of the eighteenth century. But none reached the heights of Dominik Biemann, active in Franzensbad and Carlsbad, whose portrait engravings are unsurpassed to this day (cat. no. 188). His miniature portraits are masterpieces of intense expression: he scaled the mat engraving with the utmost care, taking the sculptural effect of every shadow into account.

The rise of the natural sciences, in particular chemistry, stimulated the development of new types of colored glass and decorative methods. The colored cased beaker, mostly having painted ornaments and a decorative border cut down to the inner layer, emerged as a new collector's item. The continued development of the opaque, stone-like glassware of the Baroque period should also be mentioned in this context. The black and sealing-wax red Hyalith glass from the factories of Count von Buquoy in southern Bohemia (cat. no. 187) or similar articles from Count von Harrach's glass factory in Harrachsdorf, decorated with scattered flowers or gold painted chinoiserie scenes, enjoyed great popularity. Joseph Wenzel Zich in Schwarzau and Joachimsthal sought to achieve more of a cut marble effect with his special "stone" glasses (cat. no. 186). At the same time Friedrich Egermann in northern Bohemian Blottendorf near Haida developed new staining methods to color crystal glassware. The red stain obtained with copper compounds and numerous firings proved to be promising. More elaborate and stunning were the so-called Lithyalin glasses of this great experimenter, who achieved extraordinary color effects by cutting and staining on an opaque red ground or on a casing of copper ruby (cat. no. 185).

175 Beaker

Johann Josef Mildner
Mark etched in gold on wall at bottom:
Mildner fec: à Gutenbrunn. 1795.
Lower Austria, Gutenbrunn
1795
H 10.5, ⌀ 7.4 cm

Colorless crystal glass. Mold-blown. Two
beakers placed inside one another; the outer
one has a separately inserted bottom. The
exterior of the inner beaker is gilded, the
interior of the outer beaker gilded, etched,
and underlaid with red lacquer. A portrait
medallion, separately gold-etched and painted from the inside, is set into the outer
beaker. The bottom of the inner beaker is
gilded and has an etched mark underlaid with
red lacquer: *Heribert noble de Farcis.*
A gold-etched inscription is under the inserted
bottom disk: *Es lebe der Kaiser, mein Mädchen
und ich, der Kaiser für alle, mein Mädchen
für mich; ich aber für beide, dem Kaiser zum
Dienste, dem Mädchen zur Freude. Verfertiget
zu Gutenbrunn, am Rande des grossen
Weinspergerwaldes.*

Acc. no. P 1940-170
Formerly Johannes Jantzen Collection, Bremen

Technically one of the most complicated of
the extant Mildner glasses, which usually
have only medallions worked into a single
beaker and a border on the rim or a foot-
ring. See Klesse and Mayr, *Wolf Collection,*
1987, cat. nos. 218ff. The portrait painting
shows Mildner at his peak.
For Mildner see Pazaurek, *Biedermeier,* 1923,
311–44 (Pazaurek and Philippovich, 1976,
292–326), and G. E. Pazaurek, "Die Gläser der
Warmbrunner Menzel-Werkstatt und J. J.
Mildner," *Belvedere* 8 (1925): 57–70;
Baumgärtner, *Porträtgläser,* 1981, 104ff.; and
Strasser and Spiegl, *Sammlung von Strasser,*
1989, cat. nos. 245–51.

Lit.: Heinemeyer, *Glas,* 1966, cat. no. 430;
Saldern, *Alte Gläser,* 1968, cat. no. 37; Ricke,
Glasprobleme, 1979, 55

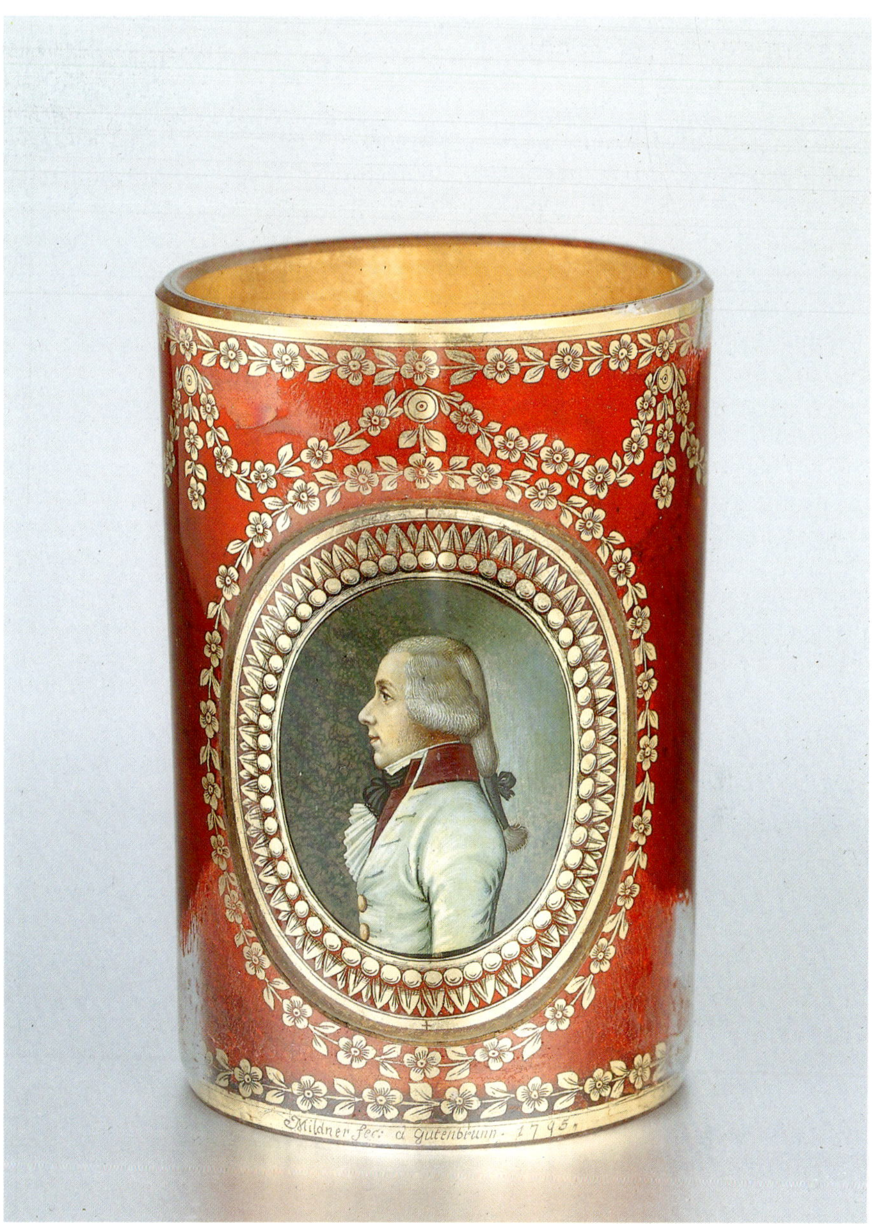

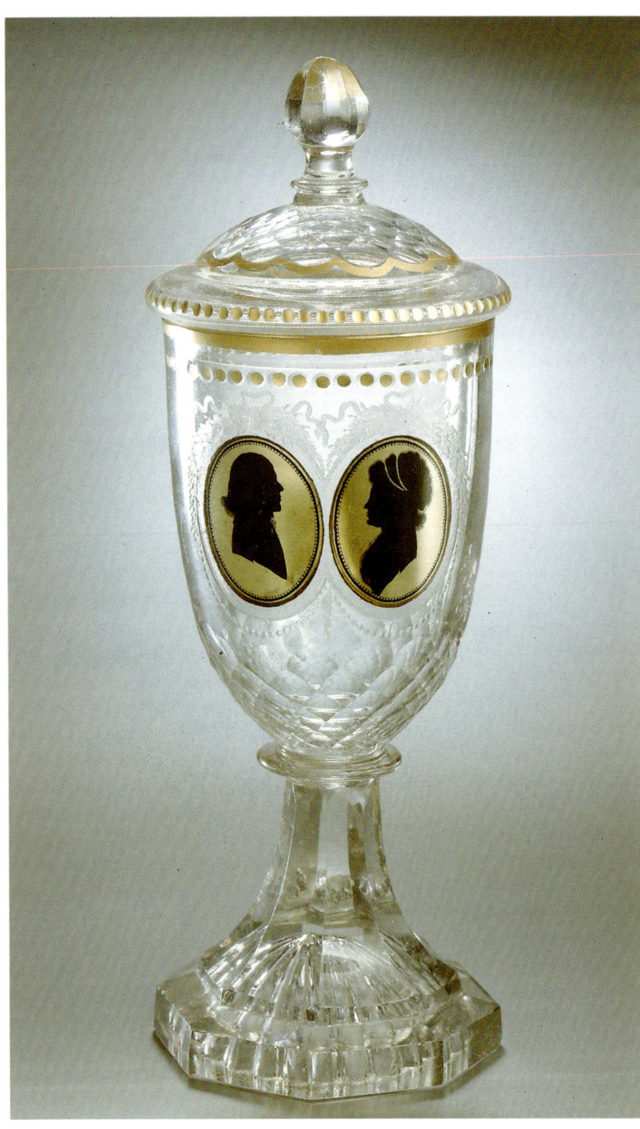

176 Covered Goblet

Johann Sigismund Menzel
Silesia, Warmbrunn
Ca. 1790–95
H 26, ⌀ 9.7 cm

Colorless crystal glass. Mold-blown, shaped. Foot and cover
richly designed in a polished cut. Engraved foliate wreaths,
gilding.
Two medallions worked into the wall; on the reverse, black
silhouette painting underlaid with gold.

Acc. no. P 1940-168
Formerly Johannes Jantzen Collection, Bremen

For similar glassware by Menzel see Pazaurek, *Biedermeier*,
1923, 314, fig. 277, and essay in *Belvedere*, op. cit.,
no. 172. See also Schenk zu Schweinsberg, *Bildnisgläser*,
1970, 16, no. 301 (identical to Baumgärtner, *Sammlung
Heine*, 1977, cat. no. 243); Klesse and Saldern, *Sammlung
Biemann*, 1978, cat. no. 169; Charleston, *Masterpieces*,
1980, 170f., no. 77; Baumgärtner, *Porträtgläser*, 1981,
107ff.; and Strasser and Spiegl, *Sammlung von Strasser*,
1989, cat. nos. 242–44.

Lit.: Heinemeyer, *Glas*, 1966, cat. no. 434

177 Covered Beaker

Samuel Mohn
Mark in black enamel at the bottom of wall:
M 1808
Dresden
1808
H 13.1, ⌀ 7.4 cm

Colorless crystal glass. Mold-blown. Edges
and finial on cover cut and polished. On the
wall, silhouette of a boy on yellow-stained
ground and life-size fly. On the reverse, a
bouquet of flowers on mat ground. Above
that the mark: *Kindliche Dankbarkeit*.

Acc. no. P 1940-172
Formerly Johannes Jantzen Collection,
Bremen

For a similar early beaker by Mohn see
Schenk zu Schweinsberg, *Bildnisgläser*, 1970,
40, no. 324 (identical to Baumgärtner,
Sammlung Heine, 1977, cat. no. 246). For
Mohn see Pazaurek and Philippovich, 1976,
158ff., and Baumgärtner, *Porträtgläser*, 1981,
125ff.

Lit.: Heinemeyer, *Glas*, 1966, cat. no. 435

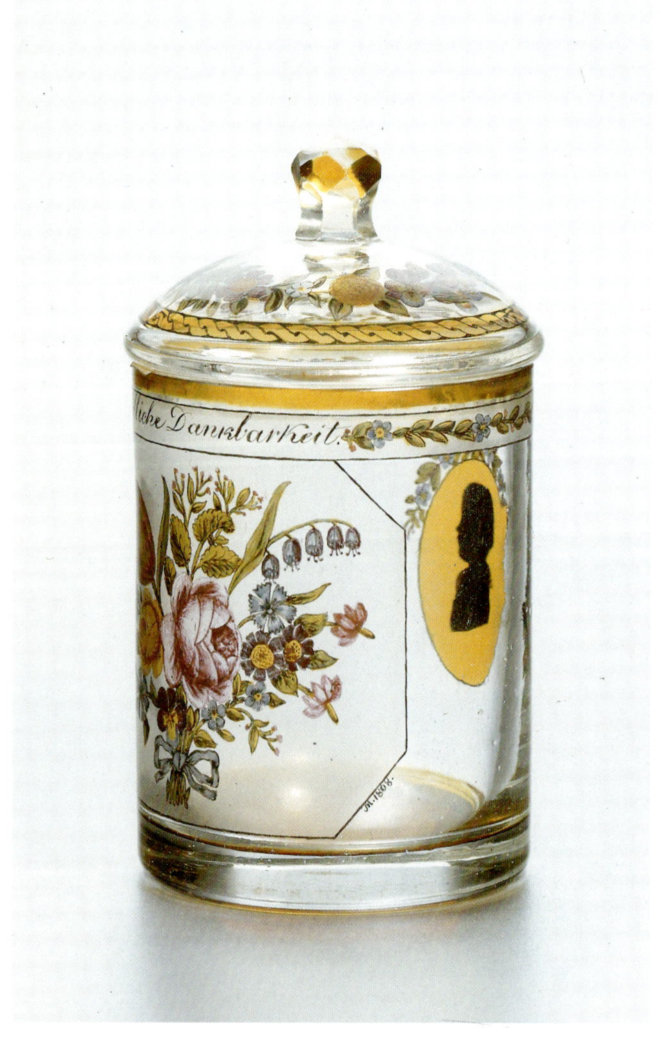

178 Footed Beaker

Samuel Mohn
Mark: *S Mohn fec.*
Dresden, ca. 1813/14
H 16, ⌀ 8.8 cm

Colorless crystal glass. Mold-blown. Polished cutting on foot and bowl. Decoration in transparent enamel painting and yellow stain. Encircling inscription above the standing base: *Zum Andenken der Freundschaft widmet von Seydlitz.* On the reverse, monogram *v.Z.* in laurel wreath on the ribbon of the Iron Cross. To the side, a life-size fly.

Acc. no. P 1940-174
Formerly Johannes Jantzen Collection, Bremen

The depiction of Mars as warrior in a defensive pose, the inscription, and the medal ribbon suggest a connection with the War of Liberation and the Battle of the Nations near Leipzig.

Lit.: Heinemeyer, *Glas*, 1966, cat. no. 439; *Biedermeier*, The Hague, 1972, cat. no. 25; Ricke, *2500 Jahre*, 1987, cat. no. 99

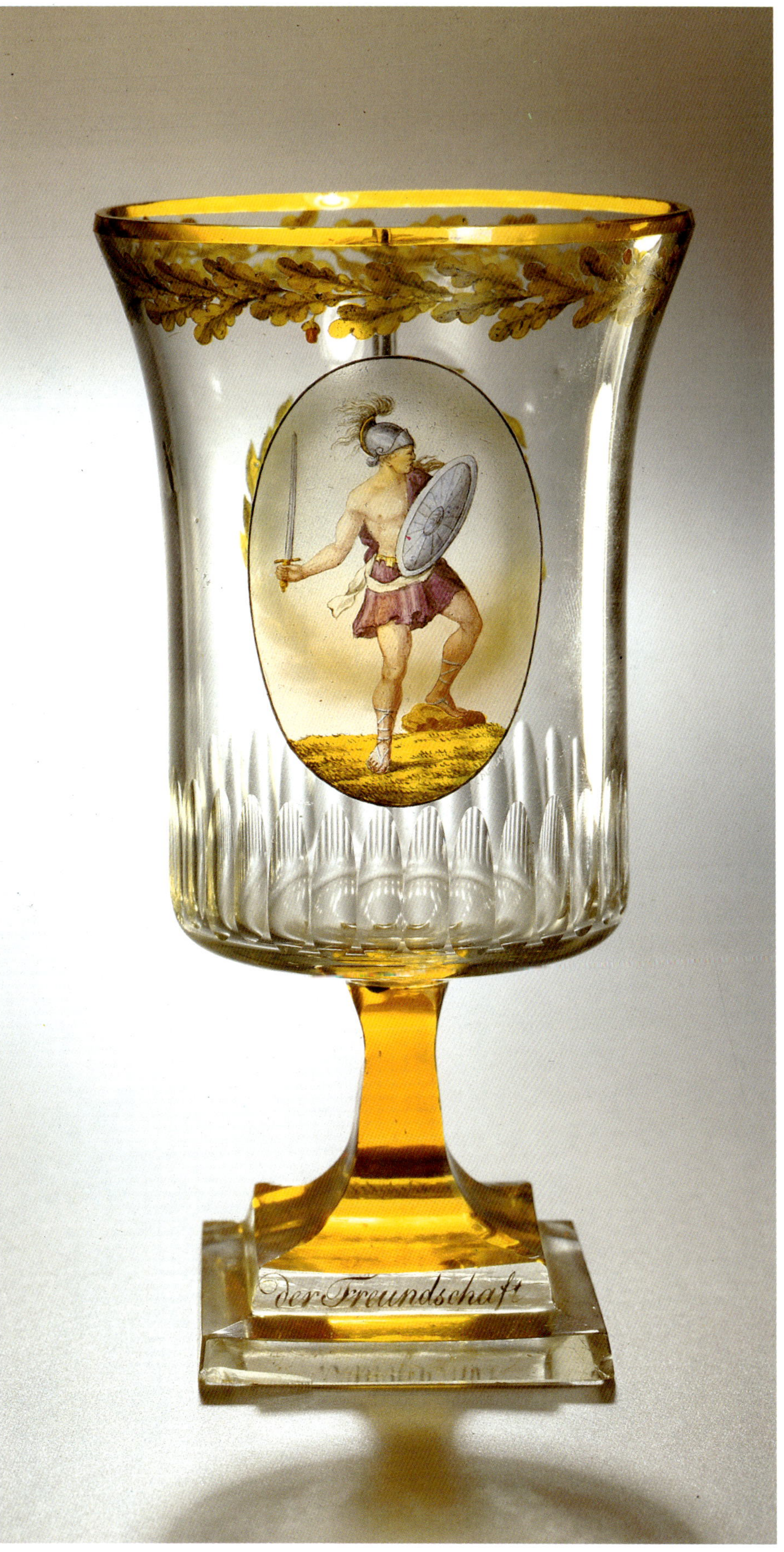

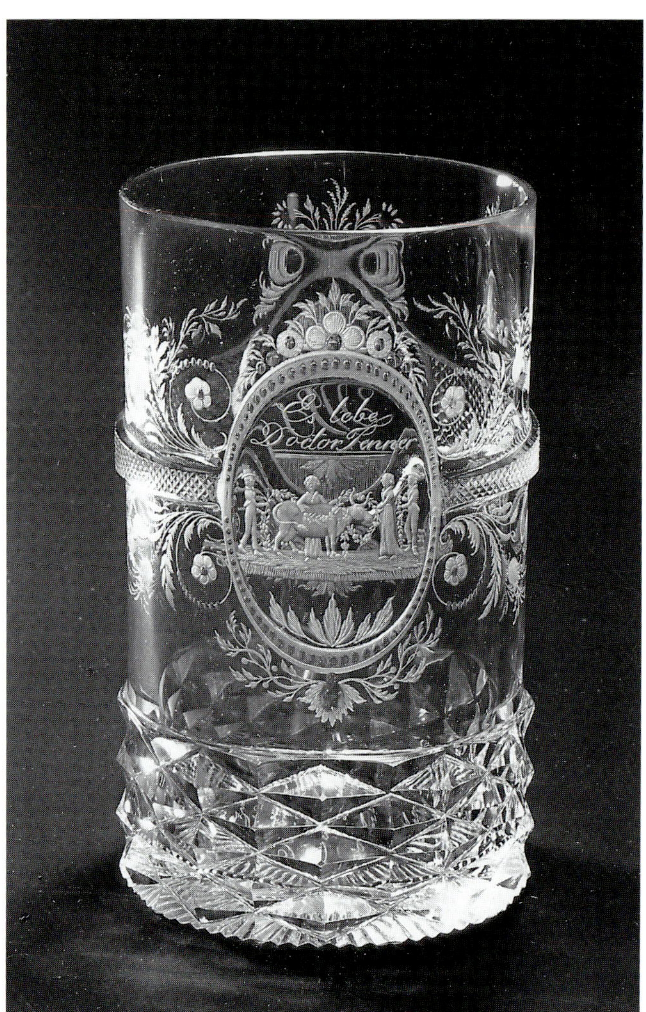

179 Beaker

Northern Bohemia
Dated 1812
H 11.2, ⌀ 7.1 cm

Colorless crystal glass. Mold-blown. Rich polished cutting and engraving (vertical wheel-engraving). In mat engraving on the front is a cow being wreathed and the inscription: *Es lebe Doctor Jenner*. On the reverse, the monogram: *DB*. Inscription in a cut aureole underneath the base: *Zum Andenken von D H Ano 1812*.

Acc. no. P 1940-191
Formerly Johannes Jantzen Collection, Bremen

The English surgeon Edward Jenner developed the smallpox vaccination with the help of cowpox, which is harmless to human beings and inoculates against smallpox. The glass was presumably dedicated to him to mark an occasion on which his vaccination cured someone afflicted with the disease.
For glassware in vertical wheel-engraving see Pazaurek, *Biedermeier*, 1923, 147–51 (Pazaurek and Philippovich, 1976, 149–53), and Spiegl, *Biedermeier*, 1981, 39ff.

Lit.: Heinemeyer, *Glas*, 1966, cat. no. 457; Ricke, *2500 Jahre*, 1987, cat. no. 98

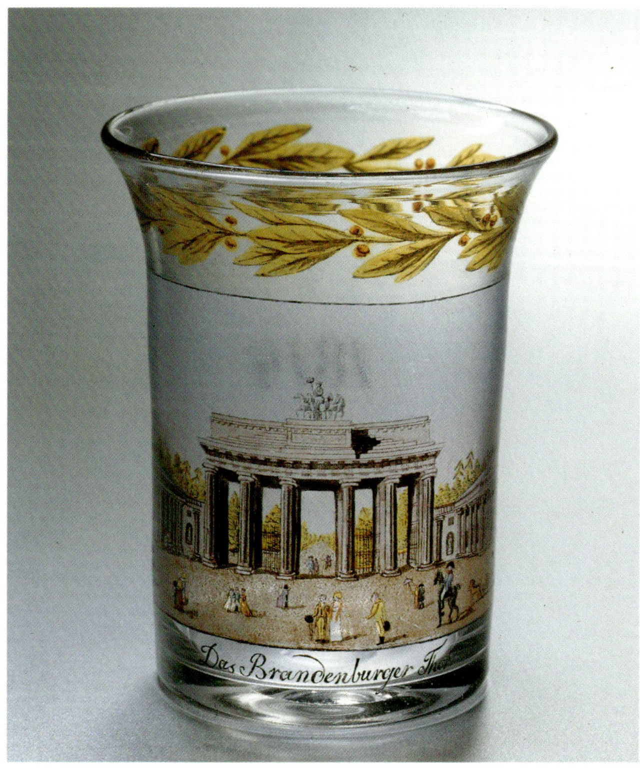

180 Beaker

Carl Moritz von Scheidt
Mark: *C: Mo: v.Scheidt, pin: Berlin 1814*
Berlin
1814
H 9.9, ⌀ 8.4 cm

Colorless crystal glass. Mold-blown. In transparent enamel painting a depiction of the Brandenburg Gate. Marks: *Das Brandenburger Thor* and, on the reverse, *1814* in large numerals. The beaker with the unusually emphasized date could have been made to commemorate the French returning the statue of a chariot drawn by four horses, which had been confiscated by Napoleon. The image shows the quadriga restored to its traditional place.
For a similar glass dated 1815 see Schlosser, *Das alte Glas*, 1977, 308, fig. 254.

Acc. no. P 1940-180
Formerly Johannes Jantzen Collection, Bremen

For von Scheidt see Pazaurek, *Biedermeier*, 1923, 166, 169ff. (Pazaurek and Philippovich, 1976, 165ff.).

Lit.: Heinemeyer, *Glas*, 1966, cat. no. 442; Himmelheber, *Biedermeier*, 1988, cat. no. 255

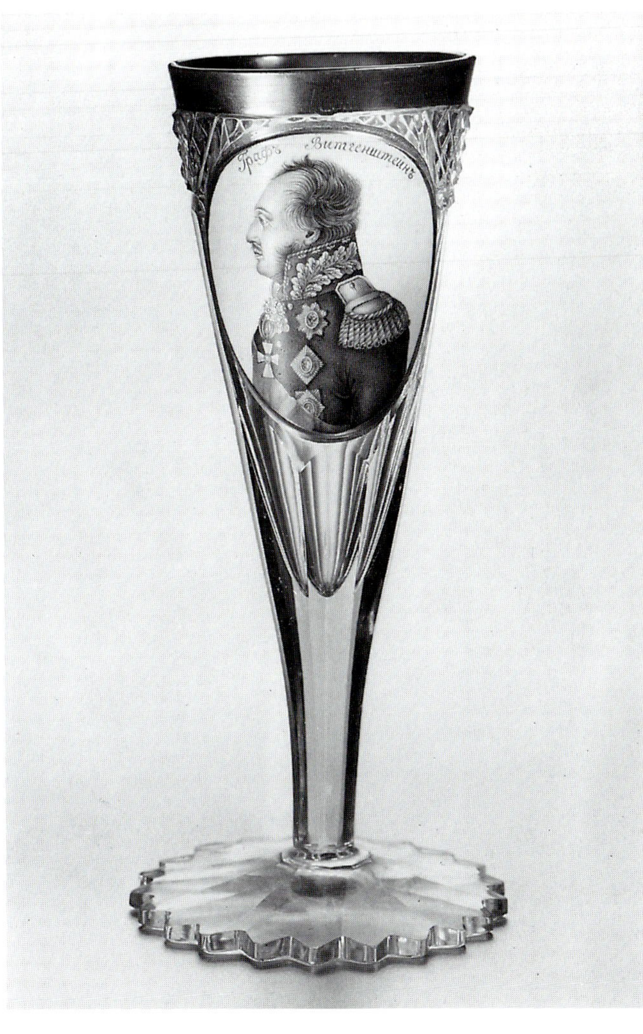

181 Flute Glass

Bakhmetev Glasshouse
Russia, Moscow
Ca. 1815–20
H 17.5, ⌀ 7.8 cm

Colorless crystal glass. Mold-blown. Applied milk-glass medallion. Rich polished cutting. In gray-brown detailed painting, portrait of the Russian field marshal Count Ludwig Adolph Peter zu Sayn-Wittgenstein-Berleburg (1766–1843), identified by the Cyrillic mark: *Graf Vitgenštejn*.

Acc. no. P 1973-3

Part of a large group of Russian glasses made at the Moscow Bakhmetev Glasshouse in the early 19th century. Many of the glasses made by this factory refer to Napoleon's Russian campaign, the burning of Moscow, and France's defeat in the War of Liberation. See B. A. Šelkovnikov, "Russian Glass in the First Half of the Nineteenth Century," *Journal of Glass Studies* 6 (1964): 101–22. Cf. esp. the somewhat more ornately cut and painstakingly painted conical goblet fig. 20, signed by the painter A. Vershinin. The stylistic similarity is, however, much too vague to justify an attribution of the Düsseldorf glass painting to Vershinin. The depicted count played a decisive role in the final phase of the Napoleonic Wars as commander-in-chief of the Russian forces.

Lit.: "Recent Important Acquisitions," *Journal of Glass Studies* 16, no. 31 (1974): 130; Ricke, *Museumsarbeit*, 1988, 74, fig. 51

182 *Ranftbecher*

Anton Kothgasser (workshop?)
Mark: *A K*
Vienna, ca. 1815
H 10.6, ⌀ 7.8 cm

Colorless crystal glass. Mold-blown. Rim, foot, and base star cut and polished. Portrait of the field marshal Karl Philipp Prince Schwarzenberg (1771–1820). Rim gilded, traces of gilding on foot.

Acc. no. P 1940-181
Formerly Johannes Jantzen Collection, Bremen

According to Heinemeyer the portrait is based on a painting by François Gérard from the year 1814, today at the palace of Versailles (acc. no. 4909). Compare the beaker with the portrait of the Prussia king Frederick William III in Strasser, see below, p. 62, fig. 42, and Strasser and Spiegl, *Sammlung von Strasser*, 1989, cat. no. 258.
For more recent research on *Kothgasser* see in particular Strasser, *Kothgasser*, 1977, and W. Spiegl, "Kothgasser, Mohn und die Wiener Porzellanmanufaktur, Teil 1–3" *Weltkunst* 6 (1983): 703–14; 7 (1983): 871–81; 9 (1983): 1241–47.

Lit.: Heinemeyer, *Glas*, 1966, cat. no. 44; Strasser, op. cit., 61 and fig. 43, 63; Strasser and Spiegl, *Sammlung von Strasser*, 1989, 134, fig. 136

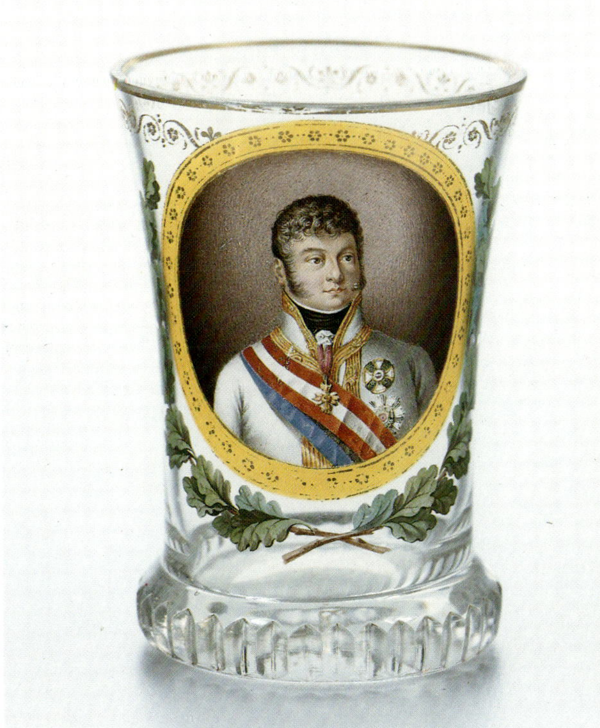

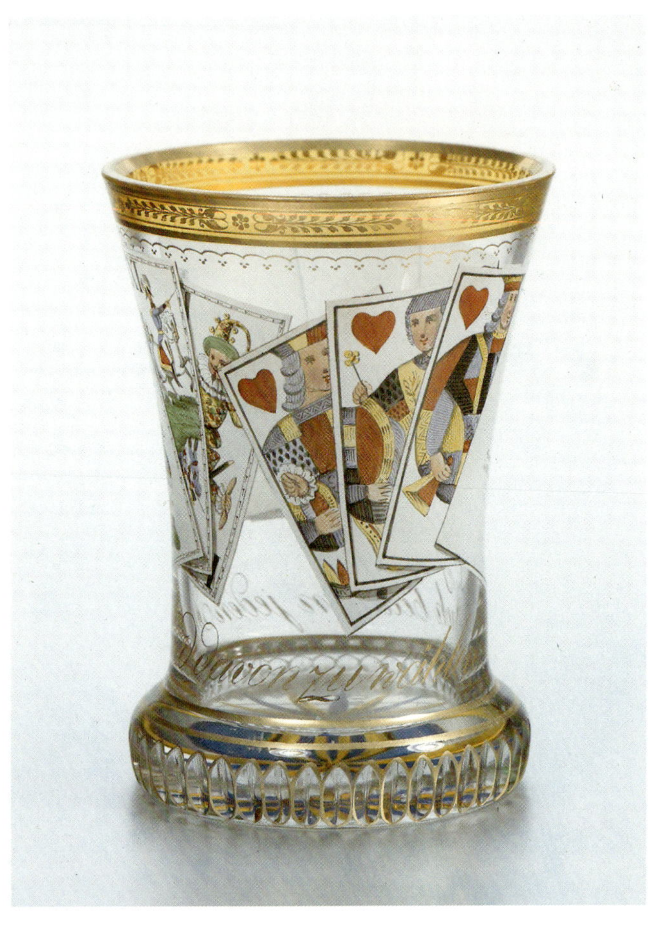

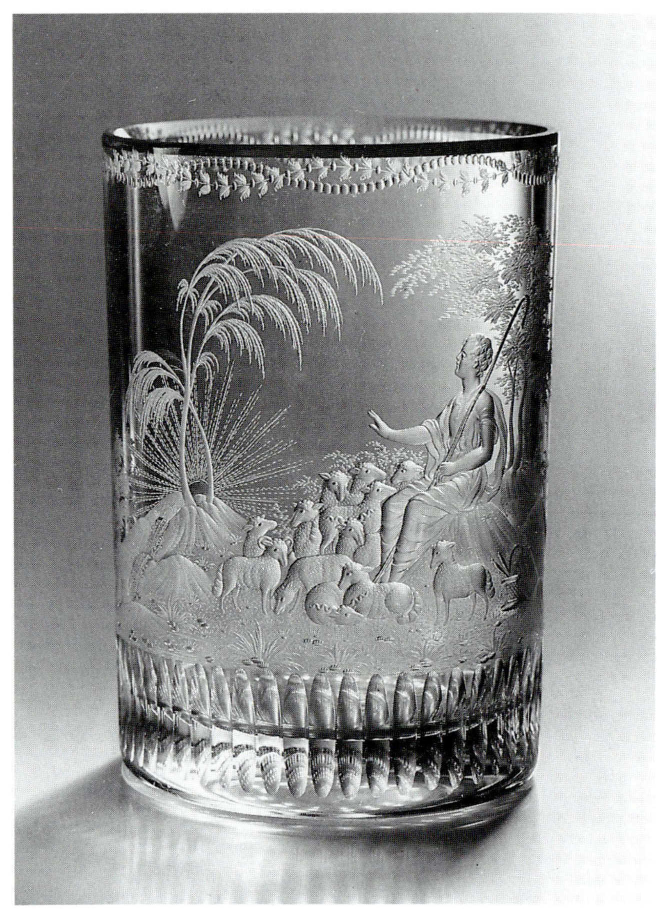

183   *Ranftbecher*

Anton Kothgasser
Mark as framed round stamp in black cursive writing
over the heart of the ace of hearts and duplicated
under the heart as couplet: *Anton Kottgasser in Wien
1822*
Vienna, 1822
H 11.8, ⌀ 8.8 cm

Colorless crystal glass. Mold-blown. Rim, cogwheel
base, and 16-point base star cut and polished.
The star is colorfully painted and the notches of the
cogwheel base outlined in gold.
On the wall a lucky constellation of cards—jack,
queen, king, and ace leading to three further aces,
in addition the "Trull" of the tarot. Inscription
painted in gold: *Nach belieben jeden Abend davon zu
wählen.*

Acc. no. P 1958-2
Formerly Johannes Jantzen Collection, Bremen

A particularly richly designed example of the popular
card glasses of the Kothgasser production, which
made the giver's good wishes for the receiver clear.
For such glasses see Pazaurek, *Biedermeier*, 1923,
217 (Pazaurek and Philippovich, 1976, 213ff.), and
Klesse and Saldern, *Sammlung Biemann*, 1978, cat.
no. 178. See also Strasser, *Kothgasser*, 1977, 50f.,
55.

Lit.: Heinemeyer, *Glas*, 1966, cat. no. 446; *Biedermeier*, The Hague, 1972, cat. no. 32; Ricke, *Ausgewählte Werke*, 1980, 20

184   Beaker

Master of the Rising Sun
(Hieronymus Hackel?)
Northern Bohemia, Meistersdorf
Ca. 1820–30
H 11.4, ⌀ 7.9 cm

Colorless crystal glass. Mold-blown. Rim and
base area cut and polished. On the wall in
partly polished mat engraving: shepherd with
his herd.

Acc. no. P 1940-196
Formerly Johannes Jantzen Collection, Bremen;
previously Herzfelder Collection, Vienna

For the work of the Master of the Rising Sun,
to whom several glasses with this subject are
attributed, see Pazaurek, *Biedermeier*, 1923,
60 (Pazaurek and Philippovich, 1976, 58), and
in summary Baumgärtner, Bremen II, 1988,
no. 26; see also Spiegl, *Biedermeier*, 1981,
87ff.

Lit.: Heinemeyer, *Glas*, 1966, cat. no. 462;
Biedermeier, The Hague, 1972, cat. no. 16

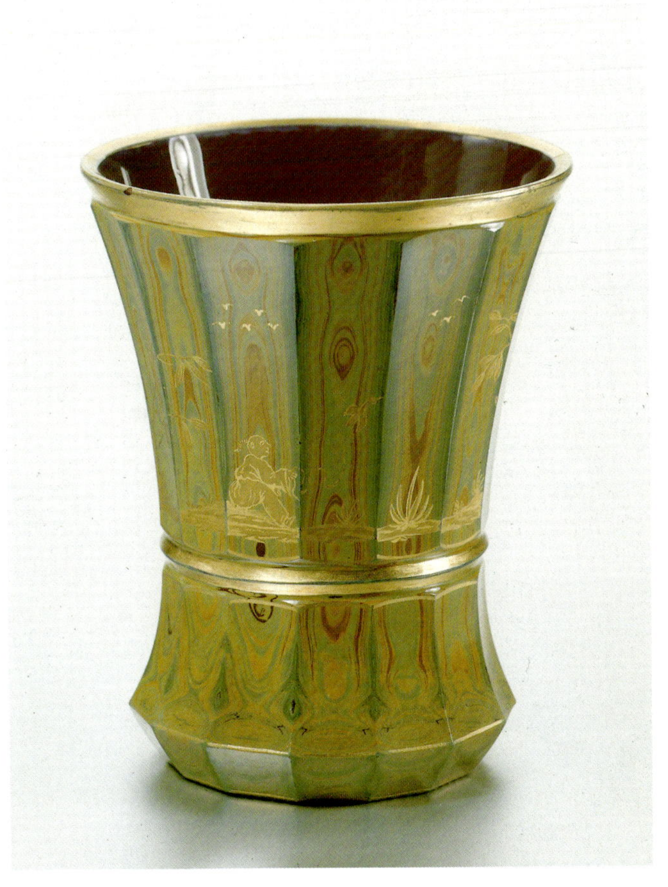

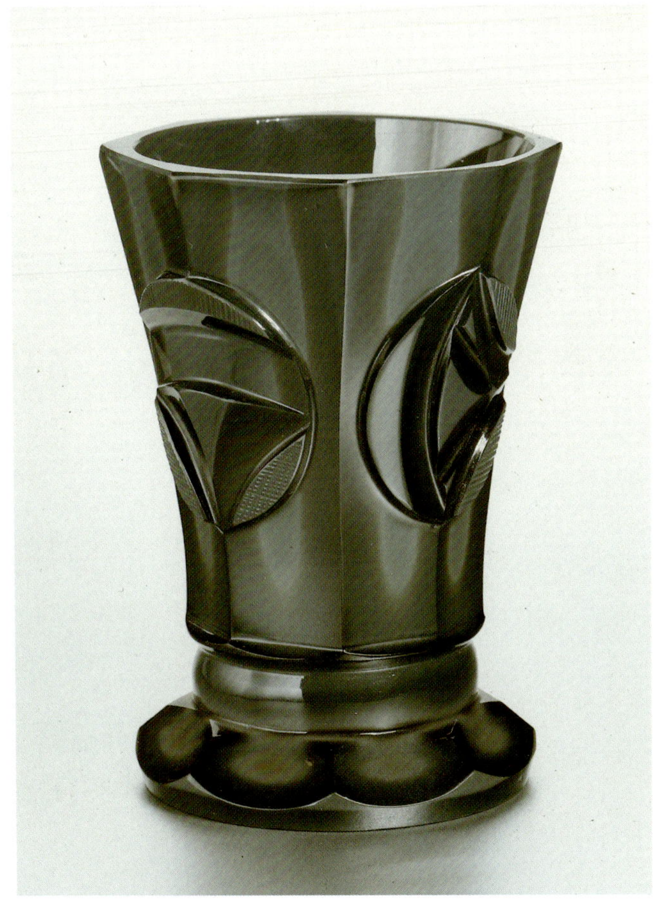

185 Beaker

Friedrich Egermann
Northern Bohemia, Blottendorf near Haida
Ca. 1830–35
H 11.2, ⌀ 9.2 cm

Sealing-wax red opaque glass. Mold-blown.
Cut. Lithyalin marbling created with various
silver and color stains. Chinoiserie scenes
painted in gold.

Acc. no. P 1940-206
Formerly Johannes Jantzen Collection,
Bremen

For Egermann's Lithyalin glasses see, for
example, W. Spiegl, "Das Geheimnis des
Lithyalinglases," *Weltkunst* 12 (Munich,
1981), 1796–99, and 13 (Munich, 1981),
1968–71 (cf. in particular illus. p. 1968,
left), and Spiegl, *Biedermeier*, 1981, 117ff.,
esp. figs. 135, 139.

Lit.: Heinemeyer, *Glas*, 1966, cat. no. 485;
Biedermeier, The Hague, 1972, cat. no. 62

186 Beaker

Attr. Joseph Wenzel Zich
Northern Bohemia, Schwarzau and
Joachimsthal
Ca. 1835
H 11.8, ⌀ 8.7 cm

Gray-brown marbled Lithyalin glass. Mold-
blown. Cut in eight facets and polished. Four
disk motifs with various interior details cut
in relief.

Acc. no. P 1940-208
Formerly Johannes Jantzen Collection,
Bremen

For Zich see A. B. Busson, "Die Waldviertler
Glashütten zu Joachimsthal und Schwarzau
in der 1. Hälfte des 19. Jahrhunderts,"
Weltkunst 10 (Munich, 1978), 1144f., and 11
(Munich, 1978), 1324–26.
See also Pazaurek and Philippovich, 1976,
268, and Strasser and Spiegl, *Sammlung von
Strasser*, 1989, cat. no. 307.

Lit.: Heinemeyer, *Glas*, 1966, cat. no. 489;
Biedermeier, The Hague, 1972

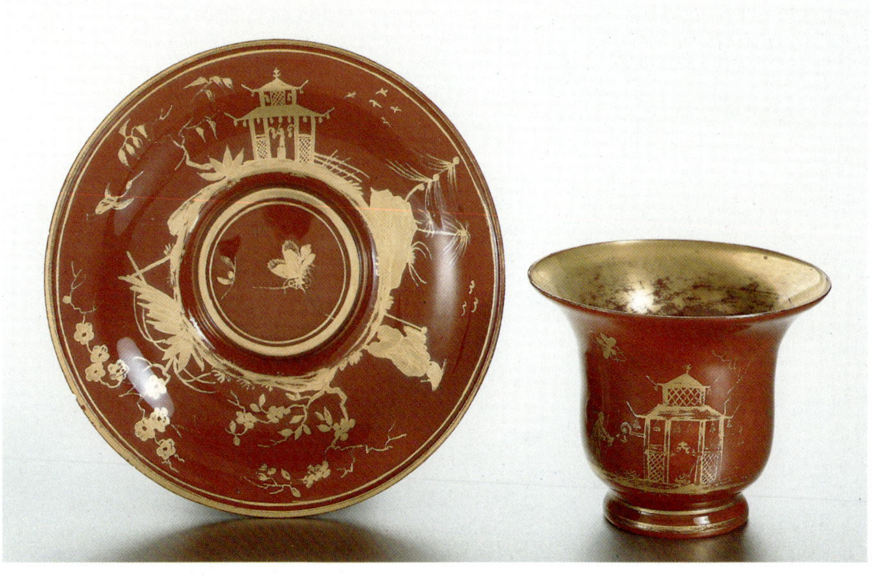

187 Cup and Saucer

Glasshouse of Count von Buquoy
Southern Bohemia, Nové Hrady (Gratzen)
Cup: H 8.2, ⌀ 10.5; saucer: H 2.3,
⌀ 16.2 cm

Opaque sealing-wax red Hyalith glass. Mold-blown, shaped. Interior of cup gilded, on exterior slightly rubbed chinoiserie motifs. On cup and saucer, Chinese landscape with pavilion, staffage figures, flowering twigs, birds, and a fly painted in gold. Decoration of this type was more common on black Hyalith glass. See, for example, Strasser and Spiegl, *Sammlung von Strasser*, 1989, cat. no. 306.

Acc. no. 17335
Formerly Kunstgewerbemuseum Berlin

For red and black Hyalith glass from the glasshouse of Georg Franz August Longueval, Count von Buquoy, see Pazaurek, *Biedermeier*, 1923, 265ff. (Pazaurek and Philippovich, 1976, 253ff.), and Baumgärtner, Bremen II, 1988, no. 87. For the history of the Buquoy glasshouse see M. von Buquoy, "Die Buquoyschen Glashütten," *Deutsche Kulturlandschaft an Moldau und Maltsch: Der südböhmische Heimatkreis Kaplitz-Hohenfurt-Gratzen*, vol. 1 (Munich, 1987), 374–79.

Lit.: Heinemeyer, *Glas*, 1966, cat. no. 484; Saldern, *Alte Gläser*, 1968, cat. no. 38

188 Portrait Medallion

Dominik Biemann
Mark engraved on bust at base of arm: *BIMAN*
Northern Bohemia, Franzensbad
Ca. 1830–35
H 13.2, ⌀ 7.8 cm

Colorless crystal glass. Shaped. Cut in many parts and polished. Portrait of Grand Duke Charles Frederick of Saxe-Weimar (Grand Duke 1828–35).

Acc. no. P 1940-198
Formerly Johannes Jantzen Collection, Bremen

For the work of Dominik Biemann see esp. Pazaurek, *Biedermeier*, 1923, 94–105 (Pazaurek and Philippovich, 1976, 97–108); S. Pešatová, "Dominik Biemann," *Journal of Glass Studies* 7 (1965): 83–106; and Baumgärtner, *Porträtgläser*, 1981, 83ff.

Lit.: Pešatová, op. cit., 98, fig. 10; Heinemeyer, *Glas*, 1966, cat. no. 467; Saldern, *Alte Gläser*, 1968, cat. no. 40; *Biedermeier*, The Hague, 1972, cat. no. 18; Ricke, *Ausgewählte Werke*, 1980, 20; K. Pittrof, *Dominik Biemann: Böhmischer Glasgraveur* (Stuttgart, 1993), 68f., nos. 1–14

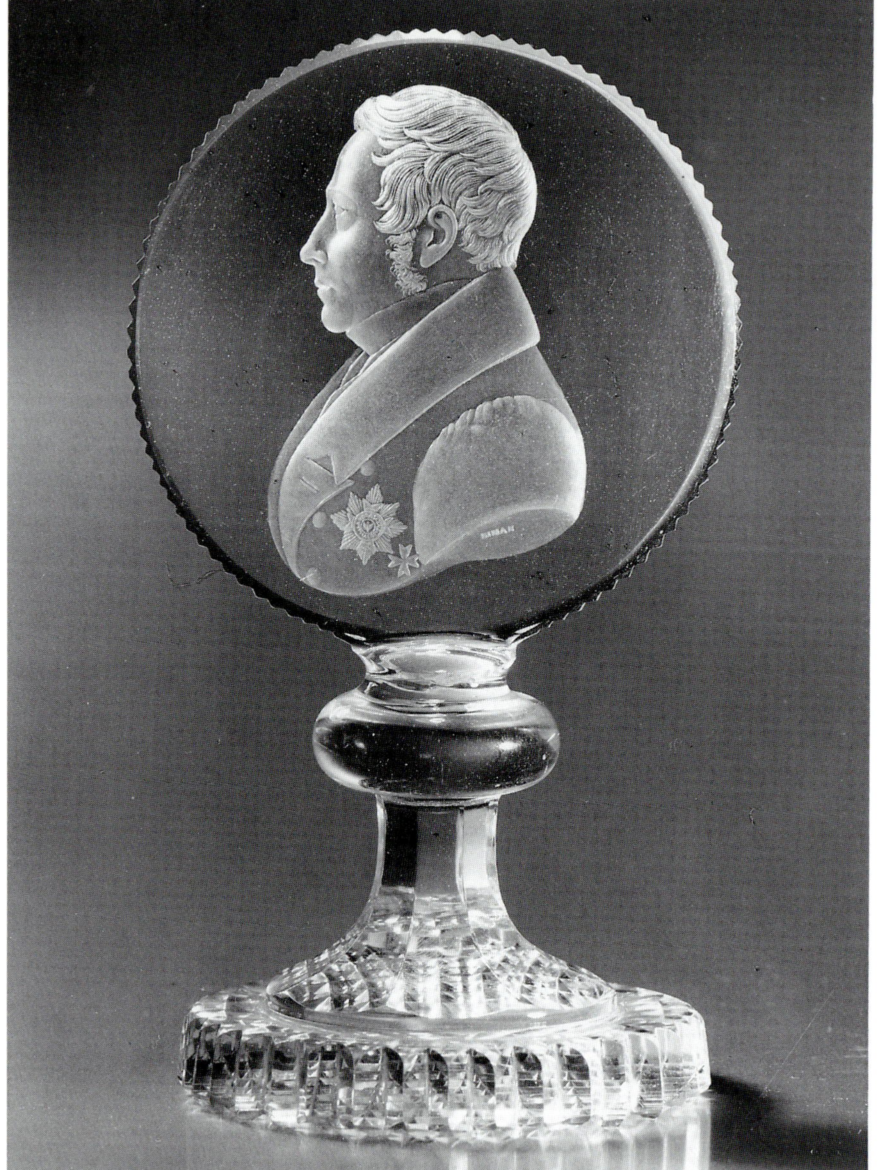

189 Covered Goblet

Attr. Franz Anton Pelikan
Northern Bohemia, Meistersdorf
Ca. 1830–35
H 32.3, ⌀ 13.2 cm

Colorless crystal glass. Mold-blown. Cover,
foot, and bottom of bowl richly cut and polished, eight-faceted stem. Encircling the
bowl in mat partly polished intaglio: wild
boar hunt with three men on foot and six on
horseback; numerous dogs. Forest landscape.
Engraved and polished dedication on a tree
trunk: *Elvirs an Suckow*.

Acc. no. P 1940-199
Formerly Johannes Jantzen Collection,
Bremen

The composition is based on a copper
engraving by Johann Elias Riedinger from the
second quarter of the 18th century. See
Klesse and Saldern, *Sammlung Biemann*,
1978, 65, fig. 155; there, too, is a stylistical-
ly similar goblet with an almost identical
depiction, cat. no. 226. Another version is at
the Württembergisches Landesmuseum; see
Schack, *Glaskunst*, 1976, 238, fig. 131. For a
different version at the Prague Museum of
Applied Arts see Spiegl, *Historismus*, 1980,
87, fig. 101. This glass is probably one of the
earliest in a series of variations and identical
with the goblet made by Pelikan for the exhibition of Bohemian industrial products.

Lit.: Heinemeyer, *Glas*, 1966, cat. no. 469;
Biedermeier, The Hague, 1972, cat. no. 21;
Klesse and Saldern, *Sammlung Biemann*,
1978, 64, fig. 153

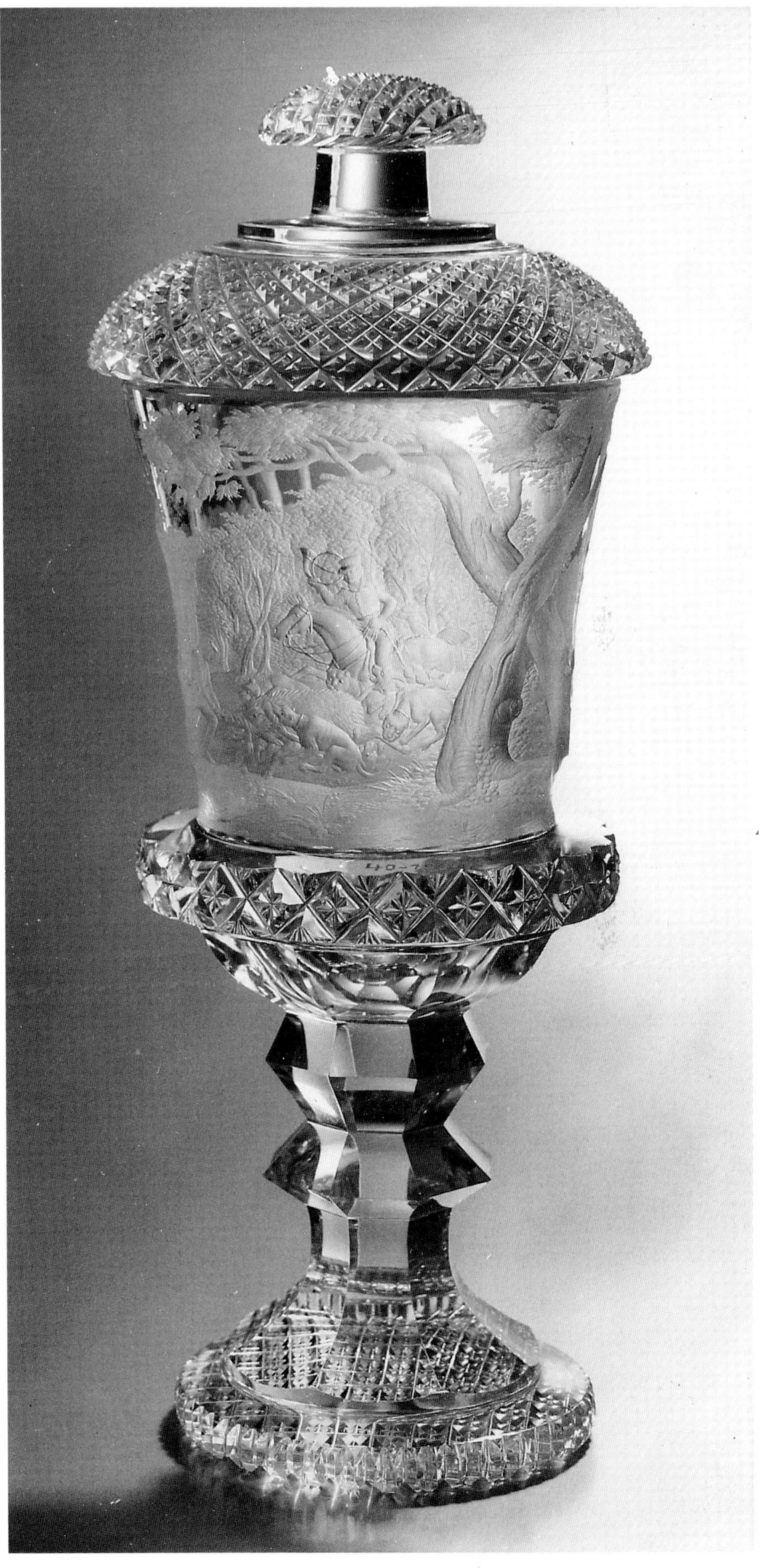

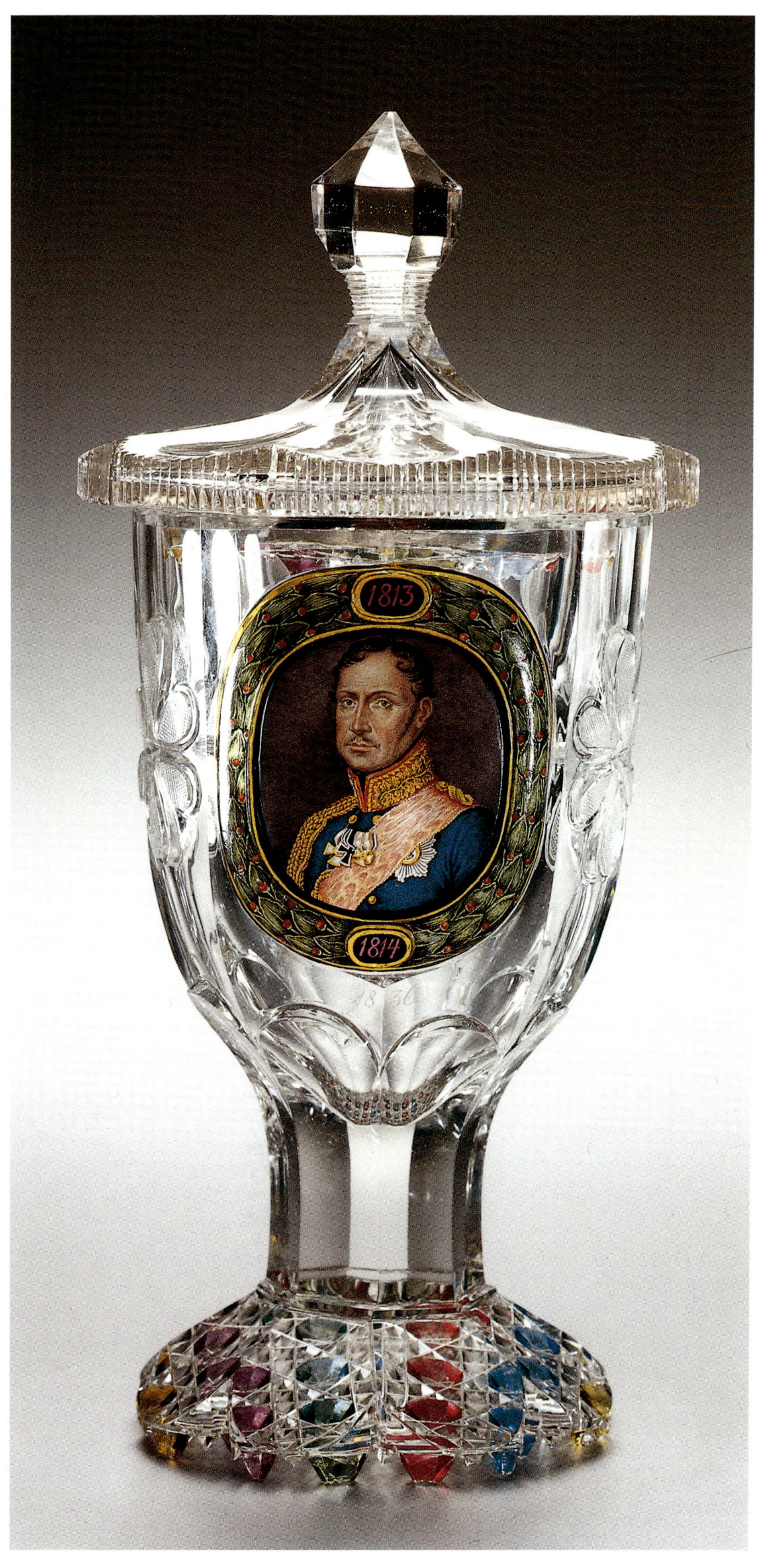

190   Covered Goblet

Bohemia
Dated on the bowl in mat engraving: *1836*
H 25.5, ⌀ 12.1 cm

Colorless crystal glass. Mold-blown. The
whole surface lavishly cut and polished.
Rich diamond cutting under bottom of foot
and cover. The cut-out stones are painted
with transparent enamel and assembled in
rows in the sequence yellow, violet, blue-
green, red, blue, yellow. On the bowl,
between relief-cut rosettes, is a portrait of
King William III of Prussia in transparent
enamel painting.
Below the medallion appears the date 1836.

Acc. no. P 1940-187
Formerly Johannes Jantzen Collection,
Bremen

The dates 1813 and 1814 in the frame of the
portrait medallion were probably in memory
of the leading role Prussia had in the War of
Liberation.

Lit.: Heinemeyer, *Glas*, 1966, cat. no. 471;
Ricke, *2500 Jahre*, 1987, cat. no. 106

Historicism

The term "historicism" used to denote the period between 1860 and 1890 has generally gained acceptance in art. Until a few years ago, it was dismissed universally, without distinction, as an unproductive and retrogressive period of stylistic copying and bad taste. Since then, our appreciation of the art of this period has grown. We are increasingly able to see the arts and crafts of historicism as resulting from the dedicated battle against early mass production's negative side effects. Arts-and-crafts' associations of the second half of the century were committed to the renewal of artisanship—drawing on the well-established to create something original. Still missing at first was a new design approach, a unified style. As a measure of one's own work, previous periods were consulted. For the first time, the arts and crafts were viewed from a historical perspective.

An intense scholarly examination of history characterized the second half of the nineteenth century throughout Europe. The principles of historical research were formulated and the first large reference works and comprehensive surveys went into print. The enthusiasm for history, closely allied with the founding of the European national states, determined the quality of life for large segments of society. Historicism, as a style, had found its expression in the revival of art from the past. It thus became the legitimate expression of a period that like none before had become aware of the significance and formative power of history. Thus the German middle class, in accordance with the nationalist mood of the zeitgeist, cultivated its own style of home furnishing. It recalled the former greatness of the German Reich and was thus primarily oriented towards "old German" culture. Glass—preferred in the form of enameled glasses of the 16th and 17th centuries—played an important role in this regard.

The most direct approach to works of the past is to copy them. This played a less significant role in the art of historicism, however, than is generally assumed. Artistically more relevant was transformation. The works of the Viennese firm J & L Lobmeyr (cat. nos. 199, 200) or the decorative goblets of Antonio Salviati in Murano (cat. nos. 193–95) exemplify the intense efforts to find new expressions in a discourse with the past. The free handling of the selected shapes by the two leading companies for historicist glass art shows the high qualitative potential arising from historicist artworks despite all limitations.

Always tangible, apart from the search for an independent design, are the efforts to surpass selected prototypes in glass purity and color and in technical perfection whenever possible. This aspect was particularly important in the production of the Rheinische Glashütten in Cologne-Ehrenfeld. The company was famous for the range of green hues it used for its old German services of drinking glasses and decorative vessels. Besides copying originals from large European museums, numerous new designs in the spirit of late medieval *Waldglas* were created under the artistic leadership of glassworks director Oskar Rauter. A kerosene lamp with thread decoration and sixteenth-century raspberry prunts (cat. no. 198) is one of the rather curious results. A large selection of glasses in the Venetian style was also offered for sale. A number of glasshouses attempted to produce these glasses. They were thought to embody the spirit of the Italian Renaissance, which was after all also exemplary for much of the period's architecture.

In Venice itself the revival of native glass art was taken up with great zeal. It aimed less, however, at the classical beauty of sixteenth-century shapes than the virtuoso transcendence of rich detail in seventeenth-century Murano glassware (cat. nos. 193–95). Apart from that, Venetians tried to revive ancient mosaic-glass techniques and developed them to miniature portraits in colored glass canes worked at the lamp (cat. no. 192). The work at the lamp experienced a significant upswing owing to the introduction of illuminating-gas burners. Several glassblowers, including Friedrich Zitzmann in Wiesbaden as one of the most productive, variously re-created dragon-stem glasses in the Venetian style. The Thuringian C. H. F. Müller, working in Hamburg in the 1860s and 1870s, probably produced the most outstanding works of this type. He offered a total of 26 different "imitation Venetian dragon-stem glasses." With this he caught the lively interest of fraudulent dealers, before he freed himself of these entanglements and sought the collaboration of professional craft designers (cat. no. 196).

England, forerunner of the Arts and Crafts Movement from the first World Exhibition in London, went its own way during historicism as well. In its substance, much of the spirit that would determine the subsequent epoch of Art Nouveau and Jugendstil could already be felt in the "material historicism" of vases by Webb & Sons (cat. no. 201), recalling rock crystal, or the cameo-glass vase attributed to Stevens & Williams (cat. no. 202).

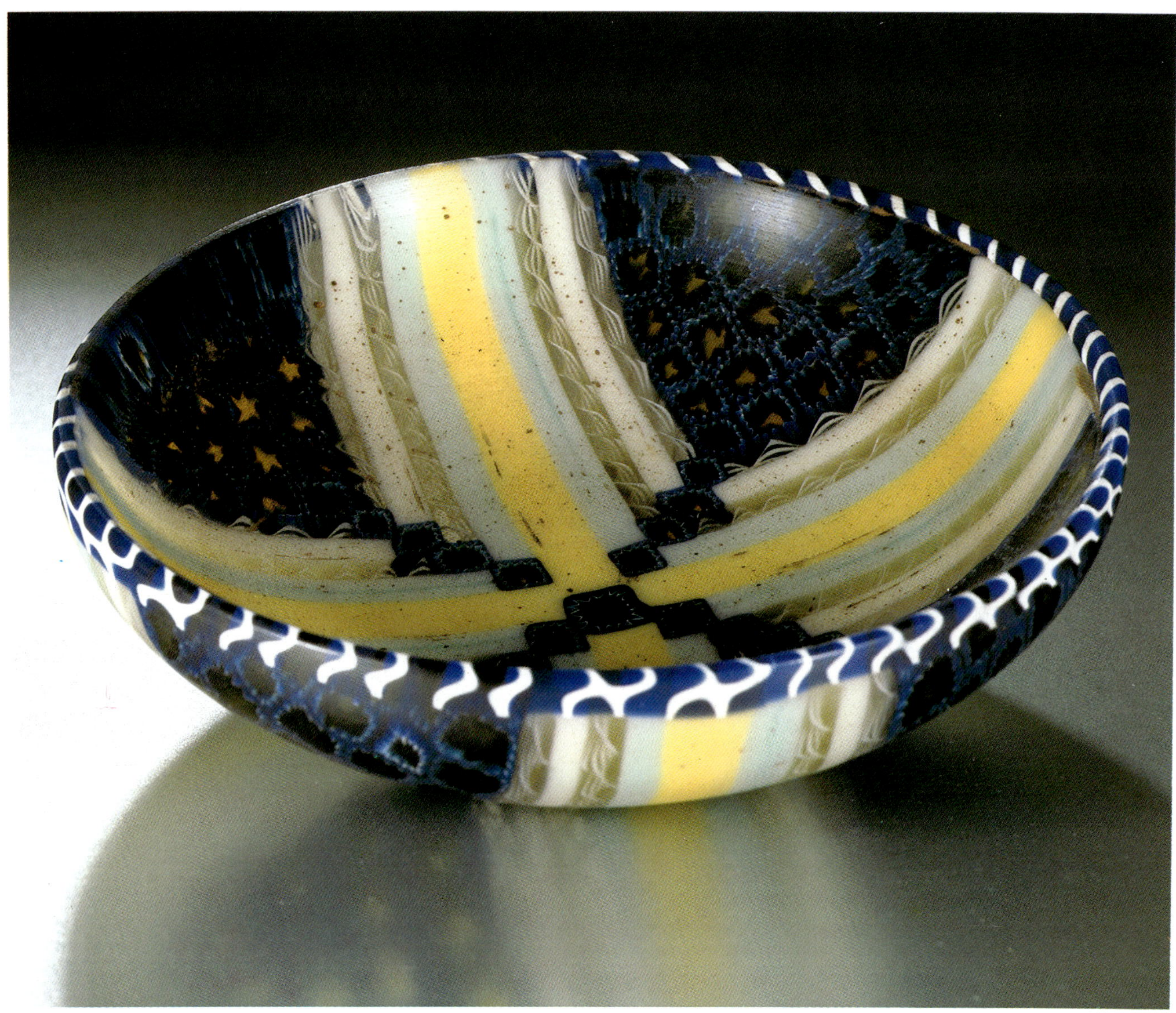

191   Dish

Vincenzo Moretti for Salviati & C., Murano
Ca. 1880/90
H 3.4, ⌀ 12.9 cm

Mosaic glass. Made from sections of preformed colored glass canes with patterns
fused in a mold.
Cut and polished on both sides.

Acc. no. P 1975-85
Acquired from the Salviati-Camerino-Tedeschi
Collection, Venice

Development of mosaic-glass technique based
on revived ancient methods.
For Moretti's work see G. Sarpellon, *Miniature
Masterpieces: Mosaic Glass, 1838–1924*
(Munich and New York, 1995), 91–136; see
also Barovier Mentasti, *Vetro Veneziano*,
1982, 211ff.; for the museum dish in particular see fig. 213.

Lit.: Ricke, *2500 Jahre*, 1987, cat. no. 108

122

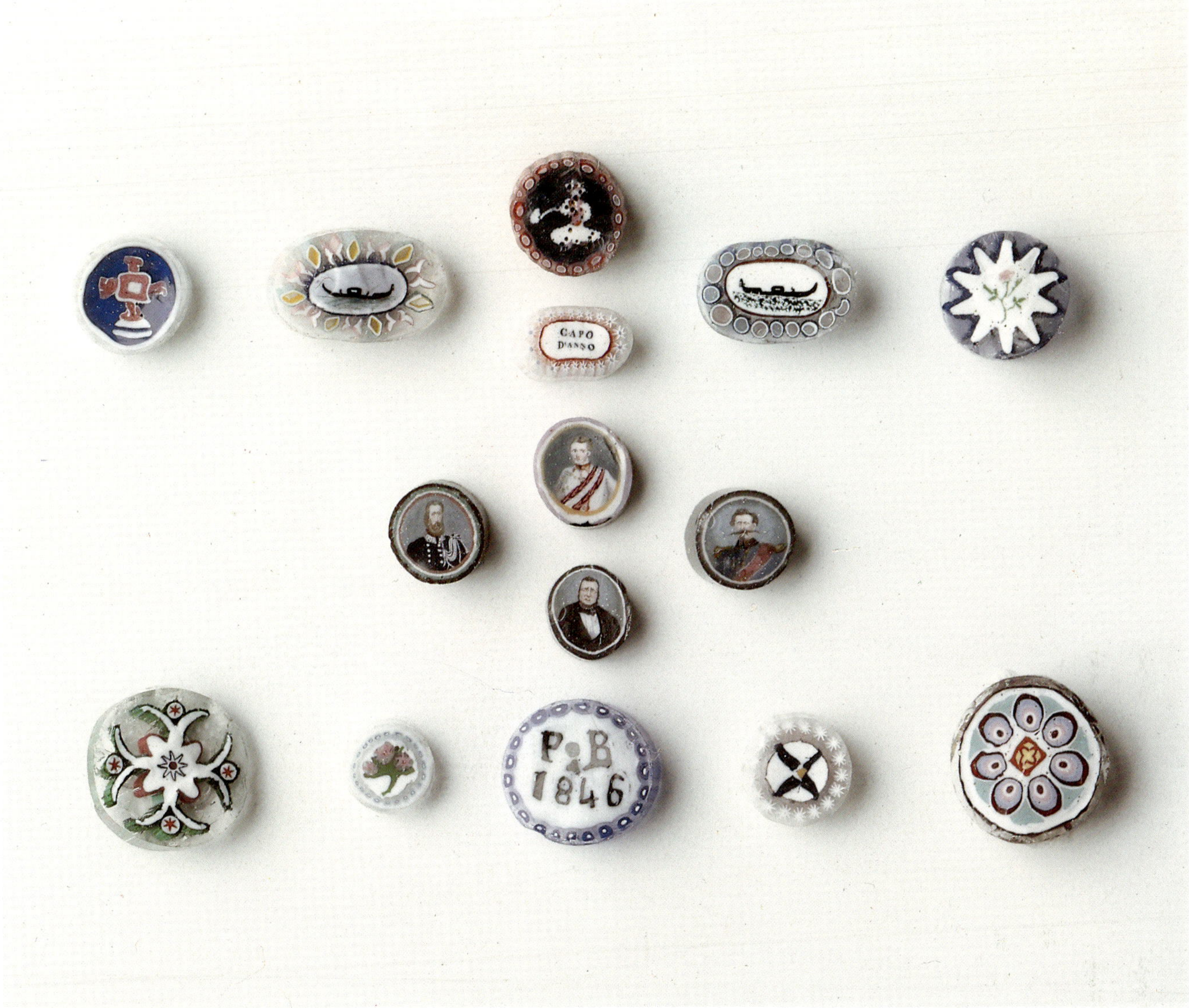

192 Mosaic Sections

Giovanni Battista and Giacomo Franchini,
Venice
Between 1845 and ca. 1862
⌀ 0.3 to 0.9 cm

Sections cut from mosaic-glass canes. Decoration of preformed colored glass canes made
with the help of a burner in the lamp technique.

Acc. no. P 1978-11
Gift of Salviati & C., Venice

The millefiori and miniature-portrait mosaics
by father and son Franchini represent the
absolute height of what is possible with this
technique. See V. Zanetti, *Lavori alla lucerna
di Giovanni Battista e Jacopo Franchini di
Venezia* (Venice, 1867), and esp. G. Sarpellon, *Miniature Masterpieces: Mosaic Glass,
1838–1924* (Munich and New York, 1995),
33–90.

Most of the ornamental sections can be dated
to the 1840s and early 1850s. In the main
they can be connected with Giovanni Battista
Franchini (1804–1873). His son Giacomo
Franchini (1827–1897) became known prima-
rily for portraits.
The four portraits in the Düsseldorf collec-
tion, made around 1862, represent: top:
Franz Joseph, Emperor of Austria; left:
Giuseppe Garibaldi; right: Napoleon III,
Emperor of France; bottom: Camillo Benso,
Conte di Cavour. (Because of unclean breaks
on the portrait surfaces, Franz Joseph,
Garibaldi, and Napoleon III are shown in mir-
ror image.)
The original pieces fused at the lamp had a
much larger diameter than the finished slices.
After repeated heating they were stretched,
thus reducing the depictions in the canes'
cross section to miniatures.

These types of mosaic-glass section were
embedded or fused into vessels, box lids,
pieces of jewelry, and the like.

Lit.: Ricke, *2500 Jahre*, 1987, cat. no. 109

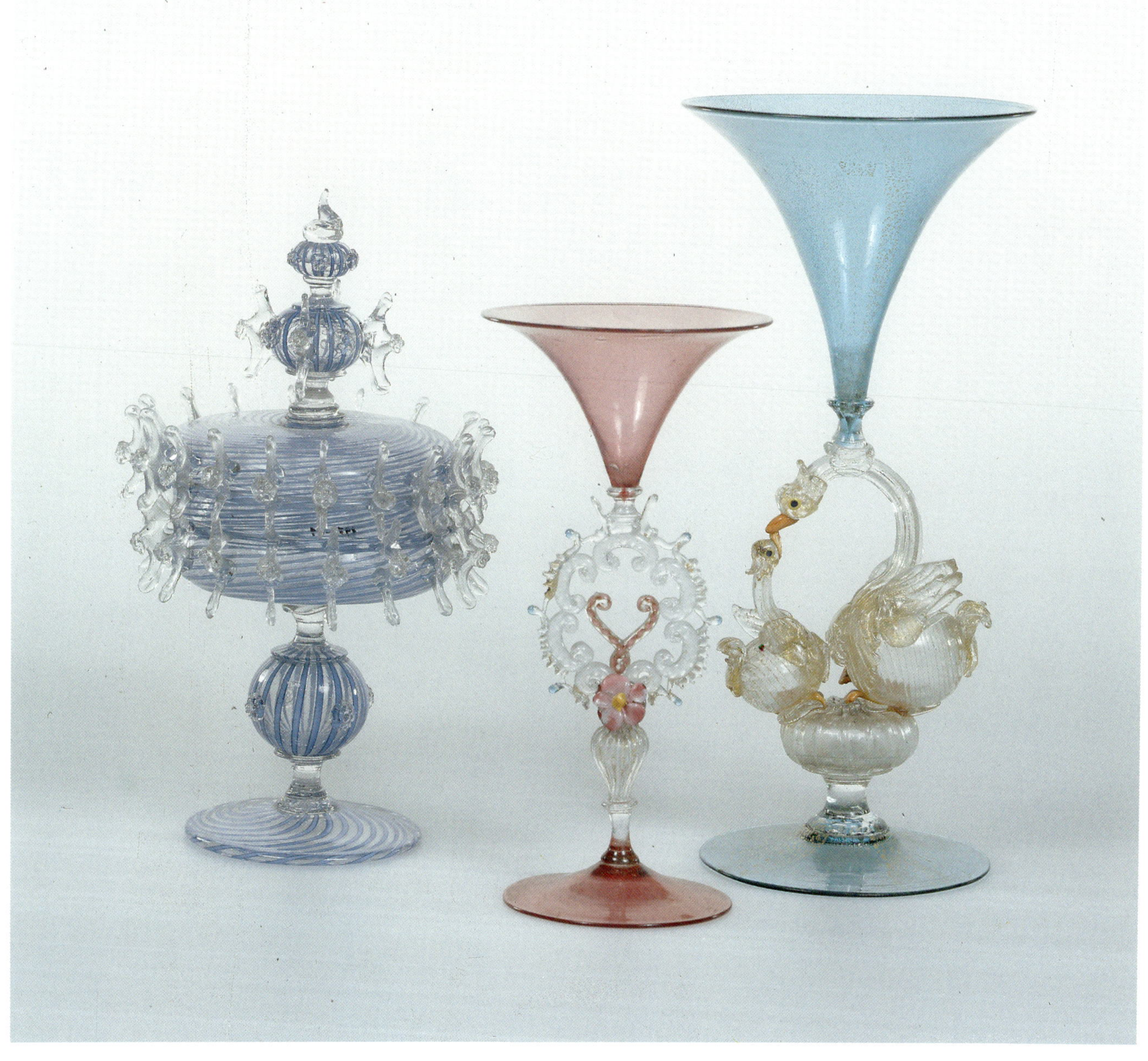

193   Decorative Goblet

Giuseppe Barovier
for Salviati & C., Venice
Ca. 1880
H 21.6, ⌀ 14.4 cm

Filigree glass, mold-blown and shaped freehand. Applications.

Acc. no. P 1975-81   Acquired from the
Salviati-Camerino-Tedeschi Collection, Venice

G. Barovier created numerous designs of this
type for Salviati. See, for example, Barovier
Mentasti, *Vetro Veneziano*, 1982, 202; see
also Barovier Mentasti, *Murano '800*, 1978,
fig. 43, cat. no. 200.

Lit.: Ricke, *Museumsarbeit*, 1988, 74, fig. 52

194   Decorative Goblet

Salviati & C., Venice
Ca. 1870/80
H 18.4, ⌀ 9.2 cm

Optic-blown, free-blown, and shaped; decorative motif of the stem made from preformed
filigree canes.

Acc. no. P 1975-76   Acquired from the
Salviati-Camerino-Tedeschi Collection, Venice

For similar glasses see Barovier Mentasti,
Vetro Veneziano, 1982, 191. Antonio Salviati
had already shown decorative goblets of this
type at the Paris World Exhibition.

Lit.: Schlosser, *Das alte Glas*, 1977, pl. XXI,
preceding p. 368

195   Decorative Goblet

Giuseppe Barovier
for Salviati & C., Venice
Ca. 1880–1900
H 25.2, ⌀ 11.5 cm

Optic-blown, free-blown, and shaped. Torn
gold application.

Acc. no. P 1986-35
Gift of Helmut Hentrich

For the attribution to Giuseppe Barovier see
Mille anni, 1982, cat. no. 462, and Barovier
Mentasti, *Murano '800*, 1978, 17, fig. V, cat.
no. 29.

Lit.: –

196 Decorative Goblet

Design by Fritz Keller-Leuzinger or Robert
Bichweiler based on an idea of Carl Heinrich
Florenz Müller, Hamburg
Executed by Carl Heinrich Florenz Müller
Ca. 1880
H 38.3, 23.3 without cover, ⌀ foot 8.5 cm

Blown and shaped at the lamp from tubes
and preformed glass and filigree-glass canes.

Acc. no. 12659 (goblet)
Acquired from the Liège art trade, 1888
Acc. no. B. 926 (cover)
On loan from the Musée du Verre, Liège
(originally belonged together; separated at
sale in 1888)

The decorative goblet was long considered an
authentic Venetian work from around 1600. It
belongs to a large group of historicist glasses
in the Venetian style, which the Thuringian
glassblower C. H. F. Müller made at the gas
burner in his Hamburg workshop. Most models by Müller exist in an earlier version,
which he designed and which bear a close
resemblance to the originals from the 16th
and 17th centuries. These types of glass
often caused confusion in the art trade. To
avoid being accused of forgery, Müller con-
tacted the craft designers Keller-Leuzinger
and Bichweiler. They reworked the designs to
conform more closely to the 19th-century
conception of form. For Müller's work see
H. Ricke, "Lampengeblasenes Glas des Historismus: Die Hamburger Werkstatt C. H. F. Müller,"
Journal of Glass Studies 20 (1978): 45–99.

Lit.: Heinemeyer, *Glas*, 1966, cat. no. 219;
Ricke, op. cit., 93, cat. no. III 5a

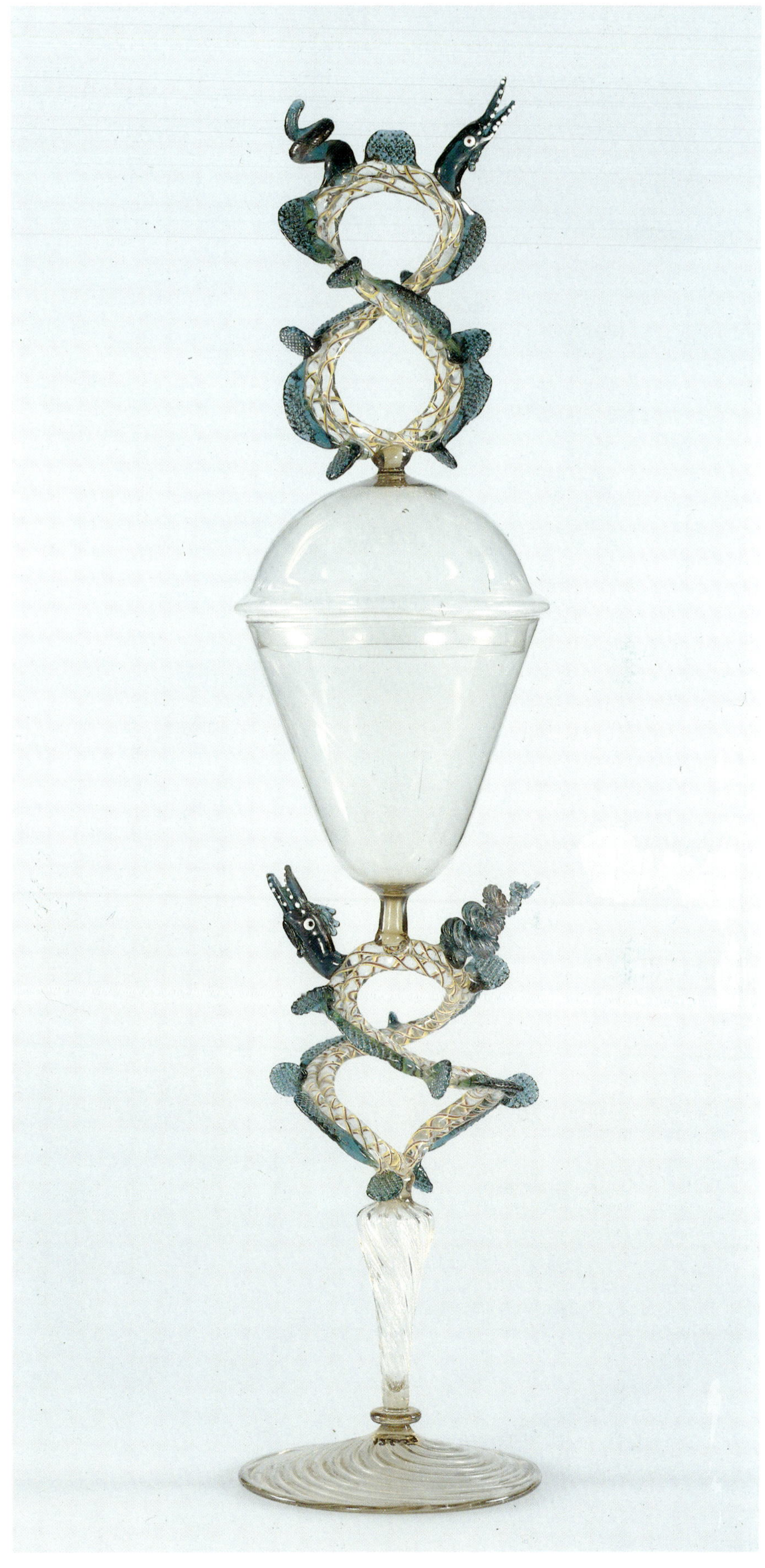

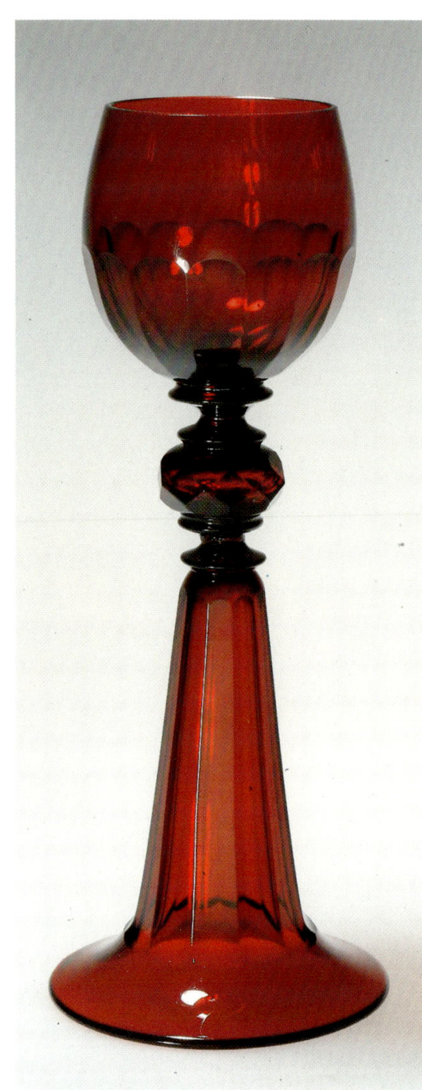

197 Goblet

Rheinische Glashütten AG, Cologne-Ehrenfeld
Ca. 1888
H 20.1, ⌀ 7.9 cm

Gold ruby glass, mold-blown and shaped. Cut in 16 facets and polished.

Acc. no. P 1964-14 A
Gift of the Oskar Rauter Estate, director of the glassworks in Cologne-Ehrenfeld

Listed in the first supplement to the *Preis Courants* (current prices lists), November 1888. See *Ehrenfelder Glas des Historismus: Die Preis Courants der Rheinischen Glashütten-Actien-Gesellschaft in Ehrenfeld bei Cöln. Abtheilungen für Kunsterzeugnisse* (1881 and 1886, supplements 1888 and 1893; repr., ed. by W. Schäfke, Cologne, 1979), 185, no. 454. In contrast to most other products from the Ehrenfeld glassworks, the shape of this glass was not based on historical prototypes.

Lit.: Heinemeyer, *Glas*, 1966, cat. no. 509; Ricke, "Rhein und Saar," *19. Jahrhundert*, 1981, illus. preceding p. 221

198 Kerosene Lamp

Rheinische Glashütten AG, Cologne-Ehrenfeld
Ca. 1895
H 20.8, ⌀ 10.4 cm

Light olive-green glass, mold-blown. On underside, as part of the blown vessel: *SYSTEM Dr. G. JAEGER Gesetz Gesch*. Intense green applications: eight prunts under the wavy ribbon on the body, three on the neck of the cover.

Acc. no. P 1964-11 A
Gift of the Oskar Rauter Estate, director of the glassworks in Cologne-Ehrenfeld

An attempt by the Ehrenfeld glassworks to apply shapes and decorative techniques originally developed for its art glass to practical objects. The result—an "old German" kerosene lamp—is not very convincing. The model does not appear in the price lists published up to 1893. Thus, it must have been made towards the end of the art-glass production in Cologne-Ehrenfeld, when the glassworks were forced to find new paths to commercial success.

Lit.: Heinemeyer, *Glas*, 1966, cat. no. 511

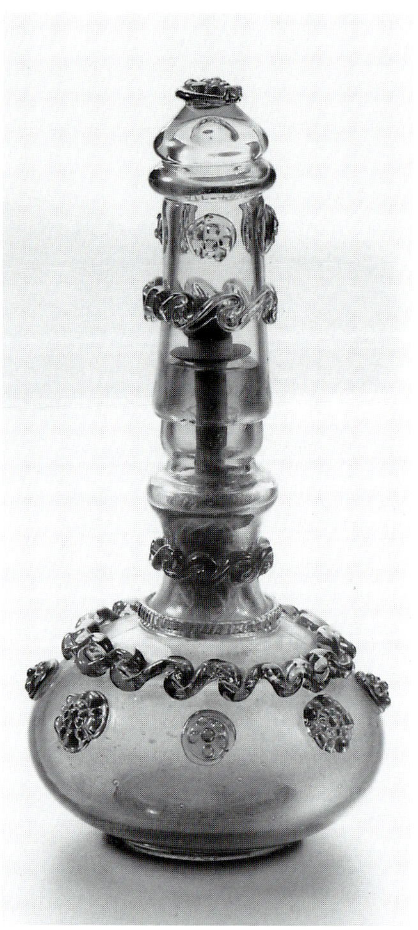

199 Monumental Goblet and Dish from the "Parsifal" Series

Mark in gold under the goblet foot and on the dish's decorative border: *JLLW* (ligated)
Designed by Richard von Kralik
for J & L Lobmeyr, Vienna
Blank by Meyr's Neffe, Adolf
1889
Goblet: H 68.3, ⌀ 14.5 cm
Dish: H 3.2, ⌀ 45 cm

Goblet: colorless, thin, inner casing of Rosaline Glass. Mold-blown and shaped; applications. Edge of cover tooled; foot folded downwards.
Dish: free-blown, inflated. Folded rim.
Both pieces are decorated in gilded enamel painting.
On the goblet: In the manner of a medieval patron, King Titurel holding a model of the grail temple. (The goblet cover reproduces the temple's shape.) On the reverse, columned architecture with Christ and personifications of worldly and ecclesiastical power; above that, the dove of the Holy Ghost. Circumscription on the edge of the goblet's bowl: *DEM.HEILIGEN.GRALE.WEIhT. ZUR.STEL.DEN.TEMPEL. KÖNIG.TITUREL.*
On the bowl in the center: head of Lucifer as archangel accompanied by the circumscription: *ZUERST.TRUG.LUCIFER.DEN.GRAL. ALS.KRONKLEINOD.VOR.SEINEM.FALL.*
Five scenes from the bottom left:
The Fall of Lucifer: *ALS.LUCIFER.SANK.VON. DEM.TRON.DA.FIEL.DER.GRAL.AUS.SEINER. KRON*

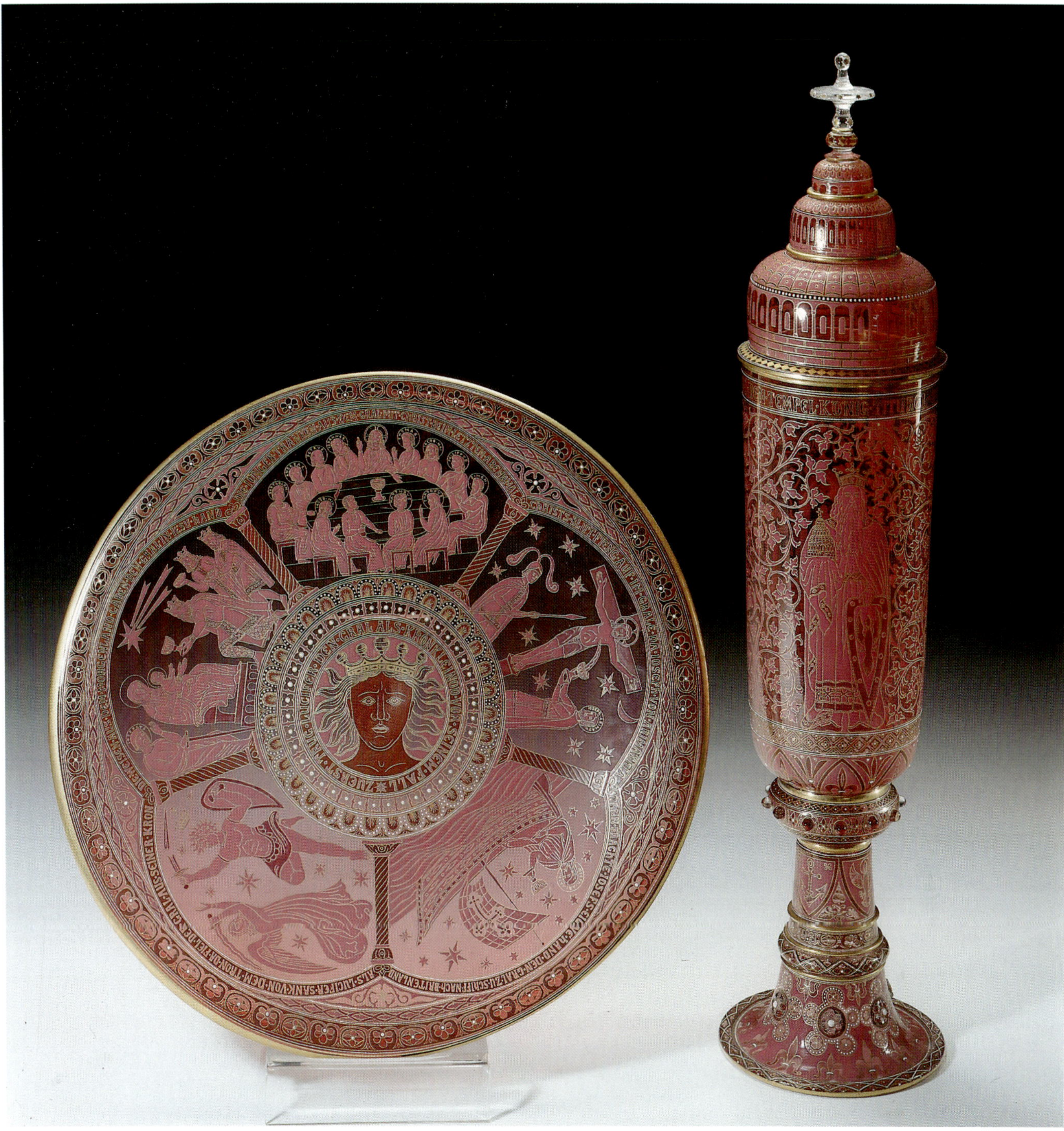

The Adoration of the Magi:
DIE.WEISEN.AUS.DEM.
MORGENLAND.GABEN.DEN.GRAL.IN.IESU.hAND
The Last Supper:
DIE.IÜNGER.TRANKEN.AUS.DEM.GRAL.
MIT.ChRIST.BEIM.LETZTEM.ABENDMAHL
The Crucifixion:
CHRISTS.BLUT.FIENG.AUF.IM.GRALE.DA.JOSEPH
.VON.ARIMAThIA
The Journey of Joseph of Arimathea: *DANN.*
BRACHTE.JOSEPhS.EIGENE.hAND.DEN.GRAL.ZU.
SCHIFF.NACH.BRITENLAND

Acc. no. P 1975-77

The poet Richard von Kralik, related to the
Lobmeyr family, created a few lavish glass
designs for the Viennese company. The most
convincing are his "Minnesinger" series
(see, e.g., Spiegl, *Historismus*, 1980, 48,
fig. 43) and the "Parsifal" series. To the latter belong, besides the Titurel goblet and
grail dish, various types of drinking vessel
and pitcher.
The depictions on the monumental glassware
illustrate Kralik's own grail poetry, in which
he attempted to unite the various medieval
traditions.

With painting done in the manner of early
medieval book illumination and verses kept
deliberately in a naive, natural style, Kralik
tried to evoke the spirit and times of the
saga in question.
For Lobmeyr see also cat. no. 334.

Lit.: Ricke, "J. & L. Lobmeyrs 'Parcivalserie':
Ein Schlüsselwerk historistischer Glaskunst,"
Bulletin VIII/1 (1976): 276, 277; Ricke, *Ausgewählte Werke*, 1980, 21; *Der Gral: Artus-
romantik in der Kunst des 19. Jahrhunderts*,
exh. cat. (Munich: Bayerisches Nationalmuseum, 1996), 152, 153, cat. no. 6

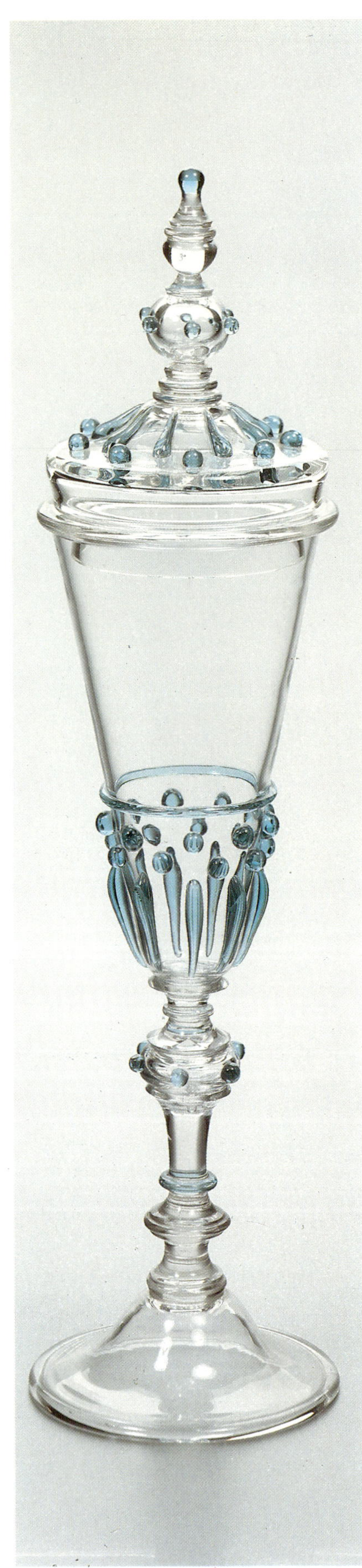

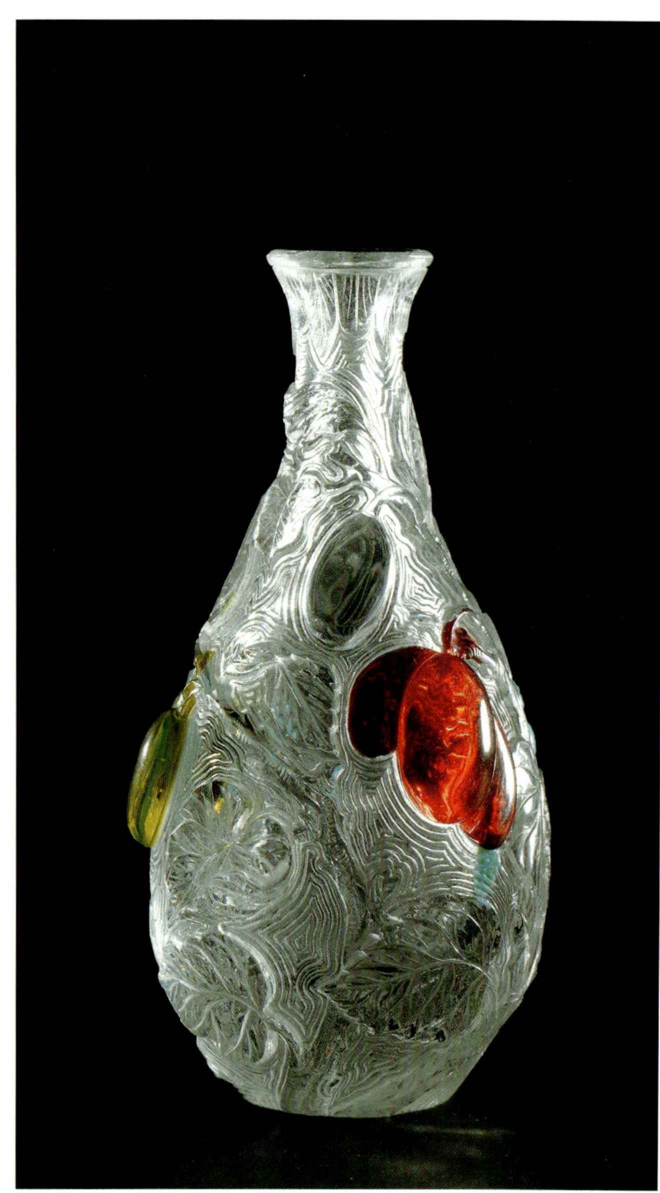

200 Covered Goblet

Designed by Ludwig Lobmeyr
For J & L Lobmeyr, Vienna
1880/81
H 34, ⌀ 9.5 cm

Colorless crystal glass. Mold-blown and shaped
from various parts; foot folded downwards.
Light blue applications: at the base of bowl
staggered rows of six drops and pearls each,
on the cover nine each. Six pearls on the finial.

Acc. no. 102
Acquired from the manufacturer, 1883

Typical of the original line, largely independent of direct prototypes, made by the Lobmeyr company in the second half of the 19th
century. The designs are documented in vol.
VII of *Lobmeyrsche Werkzeichnungen*, today at
the Museum für Angewandte Kunst in Vienna.

Lit.: Heinemeyer, *Glas*, 1966, cat. no. 504

201 Vase

Thomas Webb & Sons, Stourbridge, England
Mark etched into the border cartouche on the
underside: *Webb*
Executed by W. Fritsche
Ca. 1885
H 14.7, ⌀ 7.3 cm

Colorless crystal glass with embedded colored
glass, free-blown and shaped. Etched, cut,
and polished decoration: branches with fruit
and leaves. A few blossoms in turquoise and
light green, fruit in red and yellow.

Acc. no. P 1970-84
Gift of Helmut Hentrich

Rare example of the Webb company's "rock-
crystal" glass, which is amongst some of the
finest English luxury glass of the late 19th
century.

Lit.: Hilschenz, *Jugendstil*, 1973, cat. no. 77

202 Vase

Attr. Stevens & Williams,
Brierley Hill near Stourbridge, England
Ca. 1880/90
H 32.2, ⌀ 15.8 cm

Brown-orange inner casing covered by a thick
colorless glass layer with opaque white overlay. Relief decoration worked from the surface
in cameo technique: flower and leaves of the
lady's slipper and star flower rosette. Acid
frosted.

Acc. no. P 1986-40
Gift of Helmut Hentrich

John Northwood introduced the cameo technique to English glass art. The decoration
was not made with the rotating wheels of the
glass engraver but with glyptic engraving and
carving tools. The large glasshouses Webb &
Sons and Stevens & Williams increasingly
used this technique from about 1880. Some
of the glass pieces, such as the one shown
here, anticipate the style of Art Nouveau.

Lit.: Spiegl, *Historismus*, 1980, 208, fig. 245

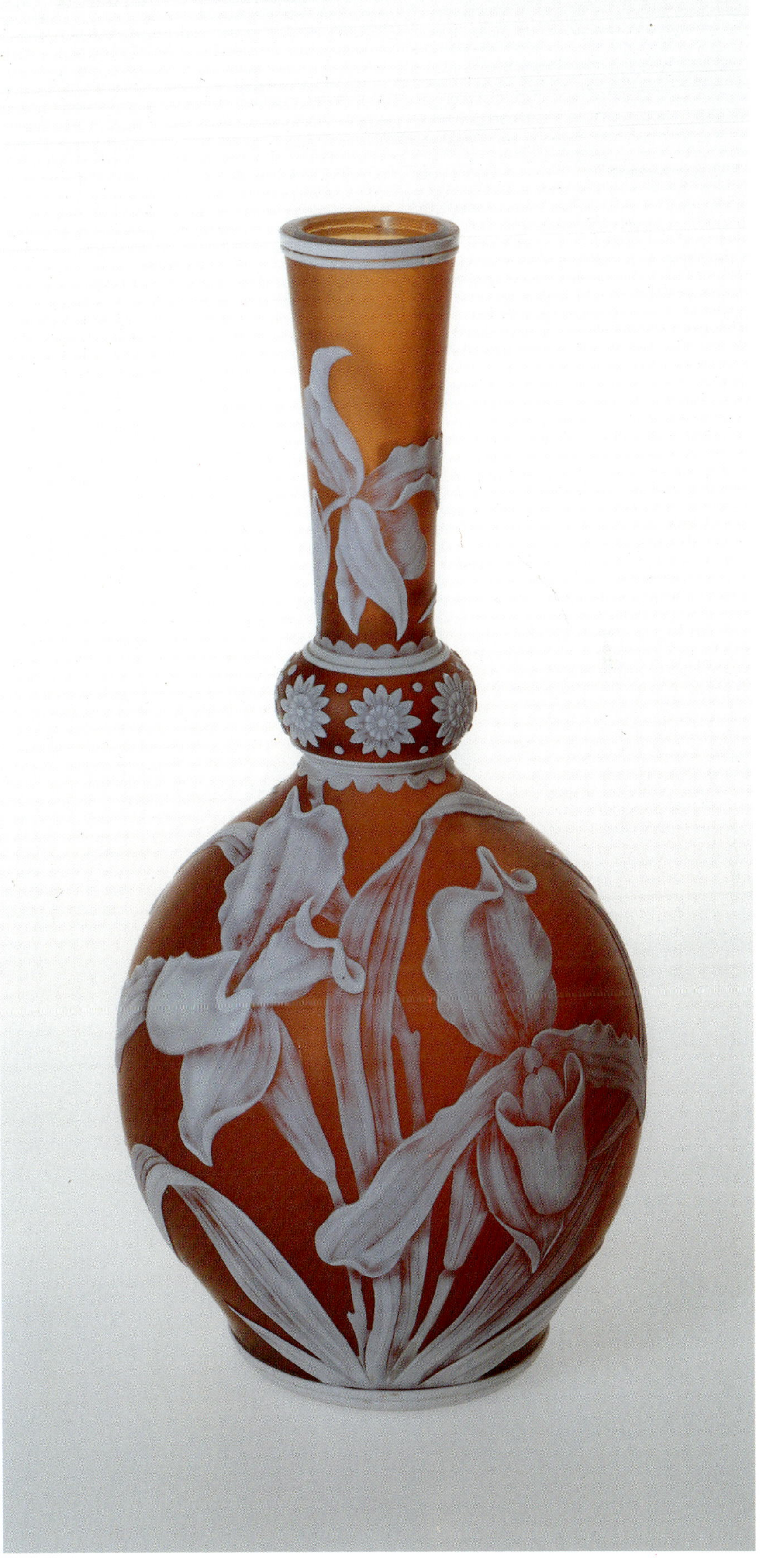

India—China—Persia

In the final phase of historicism, after exploring all styles and epochs of European art, artists became fascinated with art of the Far and Middle East. Lobmeyr in Vienna and Brocard in Paris (cat. no. 217), just to mention two of the most important workshops, were keenly interested in Syro-Islamic gold and enamel painting of the fourteenth century. The less well-known glass art of India also inspired reproductions (cat. no. 218). The glass design of China became even more important. From the time Emile Gallé was able to study the Berlin collection of A. von Brandt, the former Prussian ambassador in China, it became a lasting source of inspiration. With the rose-water sprinkler, finally, Persian glass art of the eighteenth and nineteenth centuries gave Art Nouveau an appealing vessel shape that delighted Tiffany and prompted the Bohemian manufacturer Lötz to produce numerous variations.

In India, glass art began to play a more important role with the consolidation of the Mogul reign in the seventeenth century. Numerous decorative possibilities were coupled with a limited number of forms bound by function. The most common type was the hookah base, a container for the water pipe. The smoke from the burning tobacco passed through the water for cooling and purifying before being inhaled. Thick-walled colorless glass with polished cut decoration or gilded cut-like engraving (cat. no. 205) was often used for these glass objects. Blue, emerald green, and cloudy jade hues dominate in colored glass, jade serving primarily for plates and dishes. Hookah bases are either nearly globular or bell-shaped. Vases, often also used as hookahs (cat. no. 203), are rare and sometimes decorated inside and out with enamel painting. Common are perfume sprinklers (cat. nos. 206, 207), which often derive from Persian prototypes. Perhaps the most appealing Indian vessels are the small, square bottles decorated with figurative scenes in enamel painting (cat. no. 208), the depictions often having literary sources.

In Indian glass art, numerous influences combined to form a new whole. Besides influences from the neighboring Persian-Islamic cultural sphere, those from Venetian glass art (cat. no. 207) also had a considerable effect. The Dutch East Indian company also left traces in the form of square bottles. The extent to which the English colonial and protecting powers participated in shaping the appearance of glass on the subcontinent by importing blanks produced for the Indian market still needs to be more closely examined. The same is true of the documented imports from The Netherlands. Bohemian glass exports, for which the East played an important role, should not be omitted either. Wherever the blanks were made, the characteristic appearance of Indian glassware of the Mogul period were created by means of decorative cutting, engraving, painting, and gilding. This work was carried out, with few exceptions, in India.

China has a glass tradition going back centuries before Christ. The material was, apparently, not especially important until the eighteenth century, however. Even after the upswing of glass production, in the Ch'ing period, the material's transparency, so important to Europeans, played a subordinate role in China. Glass was seen firstly as an easily shaped substitute for highly valued semiprecious stones, above all jade. This corresponded to the way Chinese glassmakers treated the material. Like in gem cutting, they worked the decorative motifs from the glass wall by sculptural means and then, as a rule, cut and polished the whole surface (cat. nos. 211–13).

Chinese glass techniques were highly developed by the eighteenth century. Chinese artisans had mastered casing (overlay) in various colors at a time when such methods still caused immense difficulties in Europe owing to the colored glass's varying coefficients of expansion. The center for these differentiated techniques was the workshop at the Peking Imperial Palace, which was founded in 1680 by Emperor K'anghsi and remained active until the late eighteenth century. Thereafter, most Chinese glassware seems to have been blown or cast at the traditional glass center of Boshan, which had already delivered blanks to the imperial palace.

Persian glass art of the eighteenth and nineteenth centuries reveals characteristics of a late period. A relatively limited number of shapes determine its appearance. The pieces were by and large crudely worked and, if decorated at all, then with cold colors (cat. no. 215). Measured against the high Islamic glass culture of earlier centuries, the glass objects are exactly what they appear to be—simple products for everyday use.

Only the rose-water sprinklers with an often elegant design are convincing in both shape and execution (cat. no. 214). The fascination of Europeans in the late nineteenth century—numerous museums of applied art of the time acquired glassware of this type—no doubt lay chiefly in the appeal of the unaccustomed, exotic shapes.

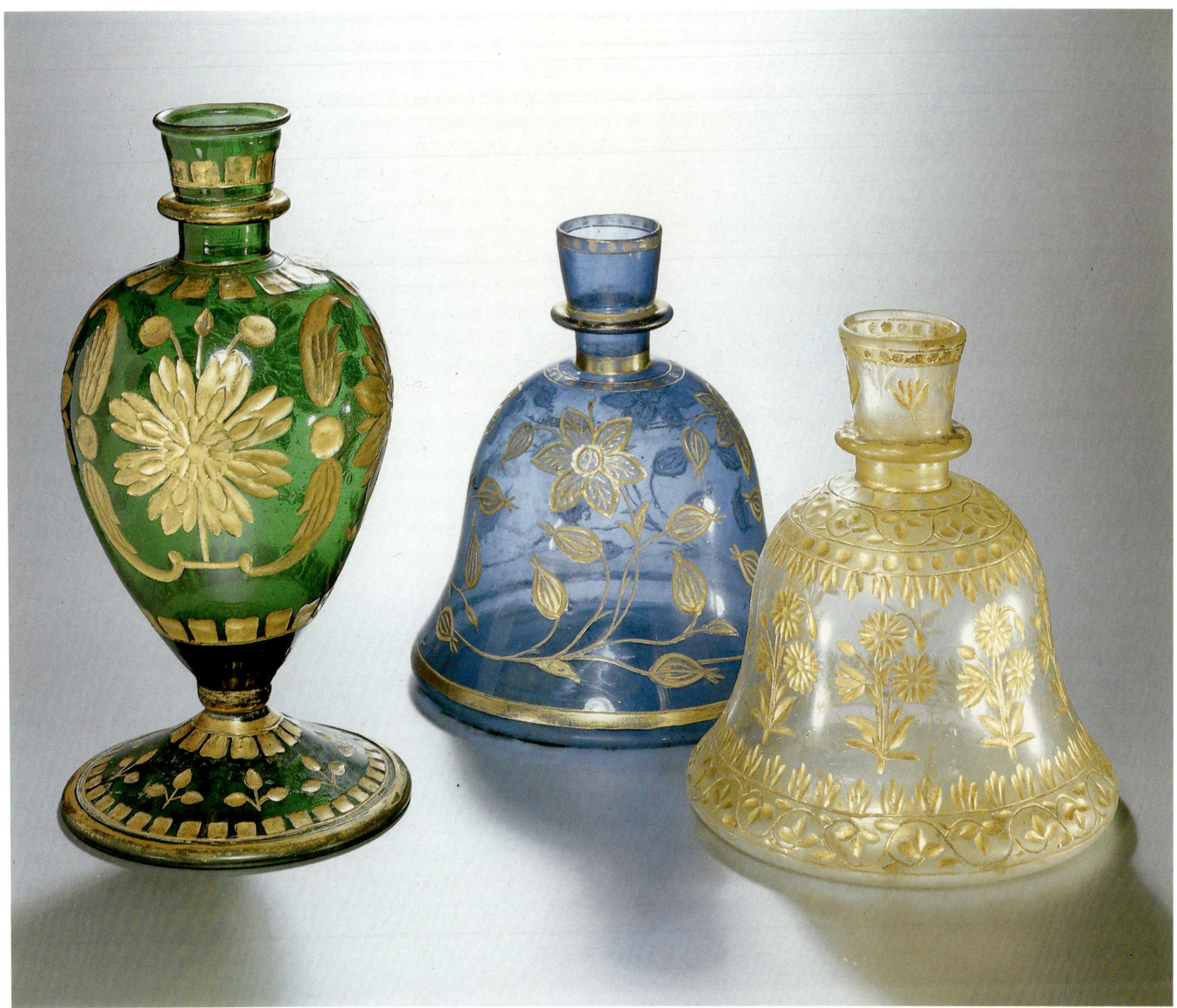

203 Hookah or Vase

India
Mogul Empire
1st half of 18th c.
H 24.9, ⌀ 12.3

Massive green glass. Mold-blown and shaped.
Foot worked separately and fused.
Decoration in gilded mat intaglio: four flow-
ers with stylized leaves.

Acc. no. P 1981-297

Special type of vase-like hookah container;
possibly used as a vase.
For the shape see Dikshit, *Indian Glass*, 1969,
pl. XXIX A.

Lit.: Ricke, "Neue Gläser," 1985, 53, fig. 13

204 Hookah

India
Mogul Empire
1st half of 18th c.
H 17.9, ⌀ 16.8 cm

Massive light blue glass. Mold-blown and
shaped. Decoration in gilded mat intaglio:
flowering vine repeated four times.

Acc. no. P 1981-296

For this very common shape see Dikshit,
Indian Glass, 1969, pls. XIVff.

Lit.: Ricke, "Neue Gläser," 1985, 53, fig. 13

205 Hookah

India
Mogul Empire
1st half of 18th c.
H 17.1, ⌀ 15.6 cm

Colorless glass. Mold-blown and shaped.
Decoration in gilded mat intaglio: flowering
plant repeated ten times.

Acc. no. P 1985-298

For shape and decoration see Dikshit, *Indian
Glass*, 1969, pl. XII B, D.

Lit.: Ricke, "Neue Gläser," 1985, 53, fig. 13

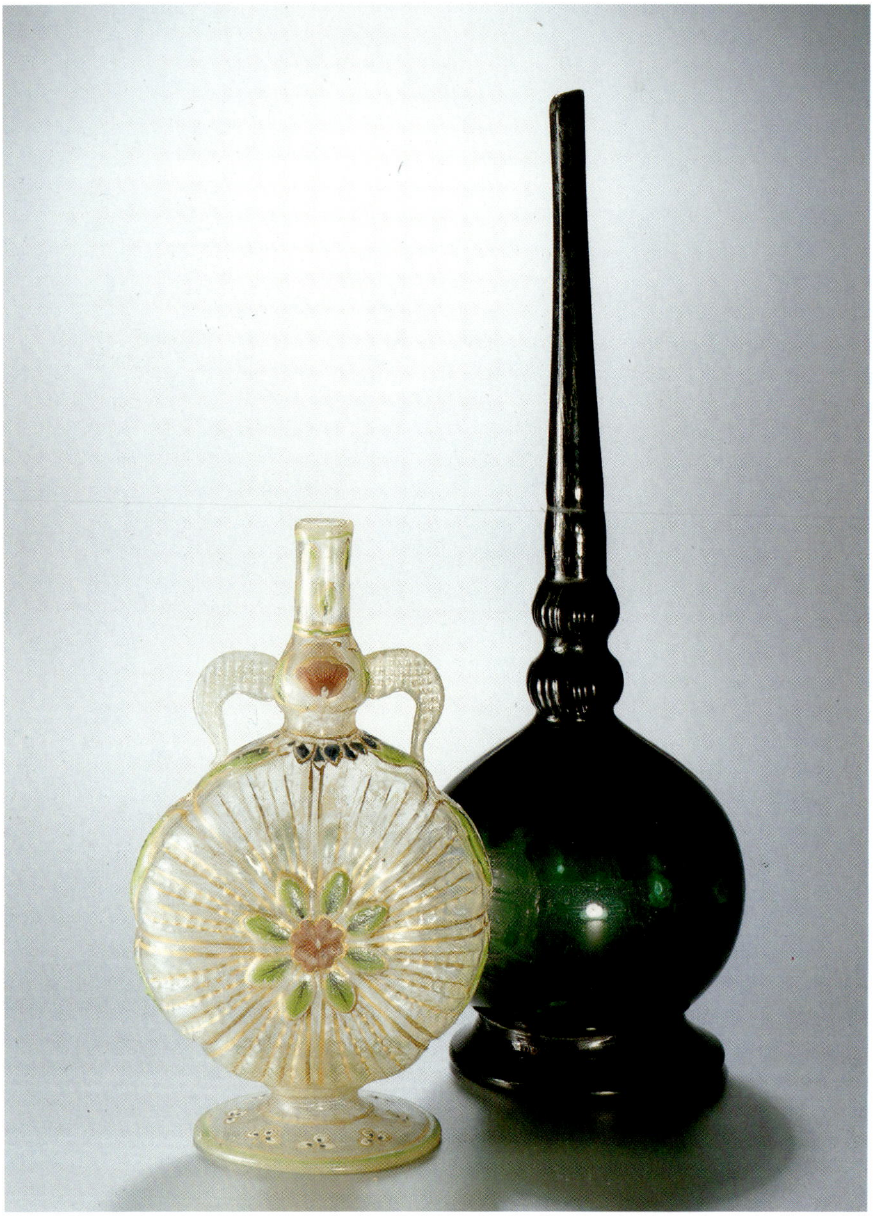

206 Perfume Sprinkler

India
Mogul Empire
2nd half of 17th c.
H 12.6, ⌀ 7.7 x 4.5, foot 5.3 cm

Colorless glass, light yellow tone. Body blown
in two-part mold. Foot worked separately and
fused. Freely applied pincered handles, the
left one restored. Painting in colored enamel
and gold.

Acc. no. P 1981-298

Influenced by the shape of Venetian prototypes. An unusual shape amongst the extant
rose-water vessels.

Lit.: Ricke, "Neue Gläser," 1985, 53, fig. 14

207 Perfume Sprinkler

India, Kapadvanj
Mogul Empire
1st half of 18th c. (?)
H 21.3, ⌀ 7.6 cm

Massive green glass. Optic-blown in ribbed
mold, shaped.

Acc. no. P 1980-24

The shape derives from Islamic *omoms*, espe-
cially Persian prototypes.
For similar Indian examples see Dikshit,
Indian Glass, 1969, pl. XLI B.

Lit.: Ricke, "Neue Gläser," 1985, 53, fig. 14

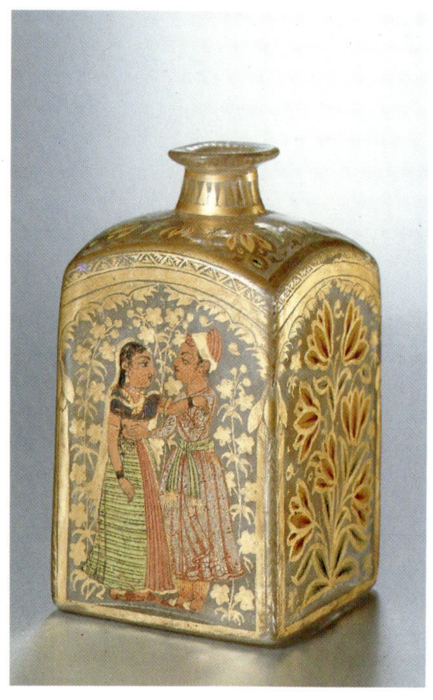

208 Square Bottle

India
Mogul Empire
18th c.
Blank from The Netherlands (?)
H 9.9, W of one side 5.6 cm

Colorless, light gray tone. Mold-blown and
shaped. Enameled and gilded decoration: on
the front, lovers; on the sides, stylized flowering plant; on the reverse, woman with dog
(gazelle?) watching the couple.

Acc. no. P 1989-50
Gift of Helmut Hentrich

Bottles with gilded and enameled painting
belong to those products of Indian art that
even the West has treasured highly for as
long as they have been made. The depictions
usually derive from contemporary Indian book
illumination. Mostly the bottles were made in
sets of six and placed in fitted cases, corresponding to the 18th-century "Flaschenkeller"
of German or Dutch provenance. The Netherlands also made this type of bottle for export
to India and the Dutch East India Company
brought large quantities of blanks into the
country. It is not possible today, however, to
distinguish the European from the Indian
glassware.
For similar bottles see, e.g., Schack,
Glaskunst, 1976, 196, fig. 28, 28a; Ohm,
Bauer, and Gabbert, Frankfurt, 1980,
nos. 102–4; Saldern, *Cohn Collection*, 1980,
cat. no. 195 a–g.

Lit.: Ricke, "Neue Gläser," 1985, 51, fig. 10

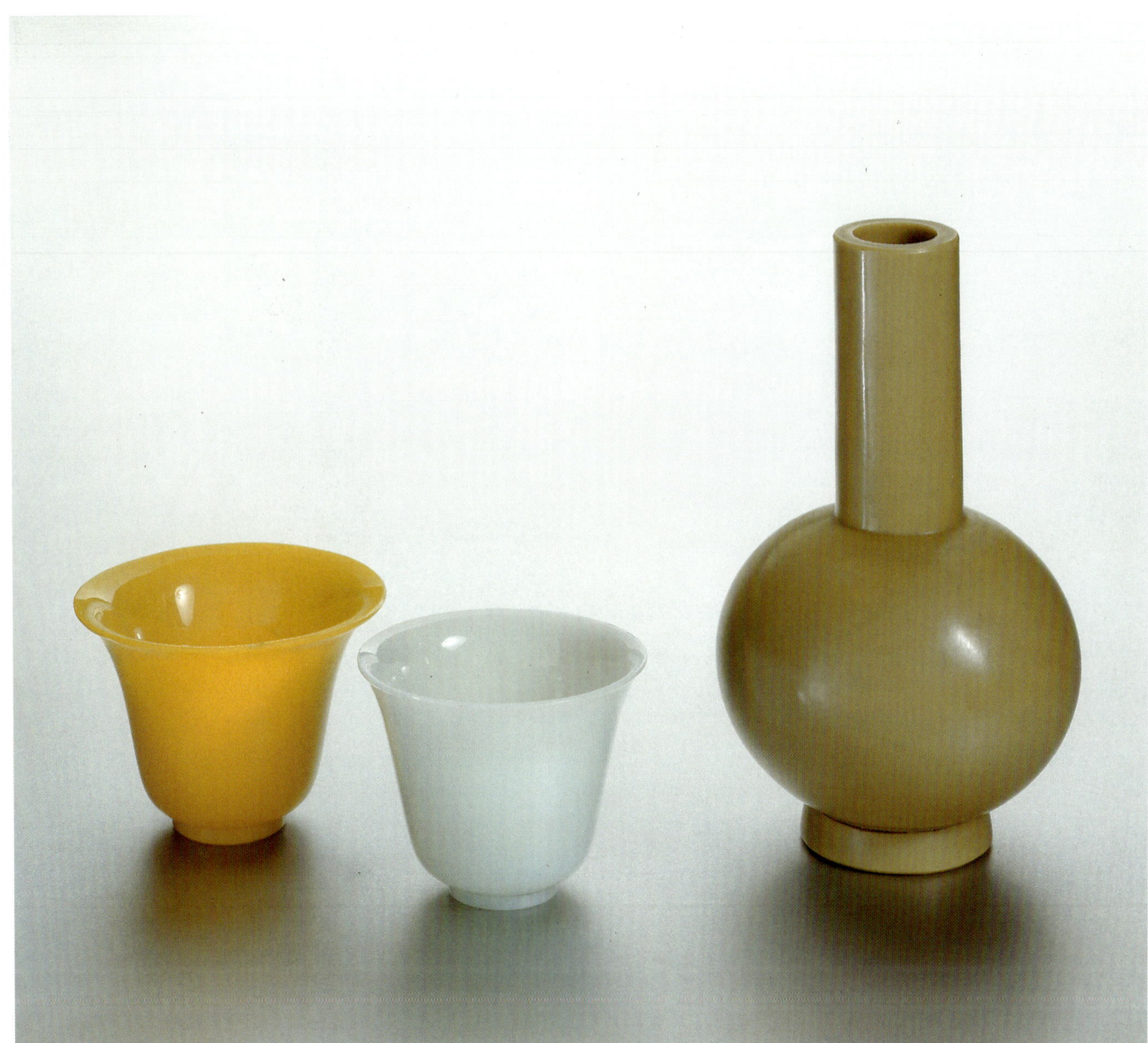

209 a, b Bowls

China
Ch'ing Dynasty
2nd half of 18th c.
a: H 6.8, ⌀ 9.3 cm
b: H 6.6, ⌀ 8.2 cm

Opaque yellow and white glass. Mold-blown
and shaped. Standing base ground flat.

Acc. no. P 1971-34, 38
Formerly W. Henrich Collection, Frankfurt

The shape is derived from Chinese porcelain
art. It strongly influenced European porcelain
and glass design in the 18th and 19th centuries.

Lit.: –

210 Vase

China
Ch'ing Dynasty
2nd half of 18th c.
H 17.7, ⌀ 10.8 cm

Thick-walled, opaque yellow-green. Mold-
blown and shaped; standing base and mouth
ground.

Acc. no. P 1971-32
Formerly W. Henrich Collection, Frankfurt

Lit.: –

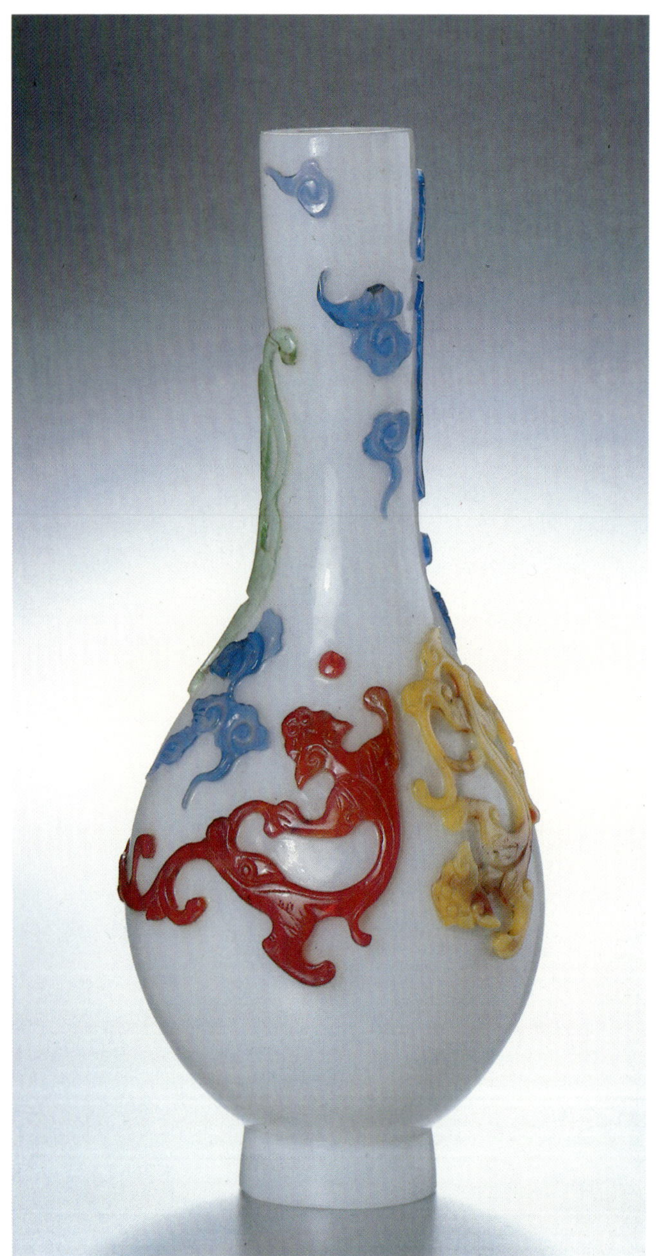

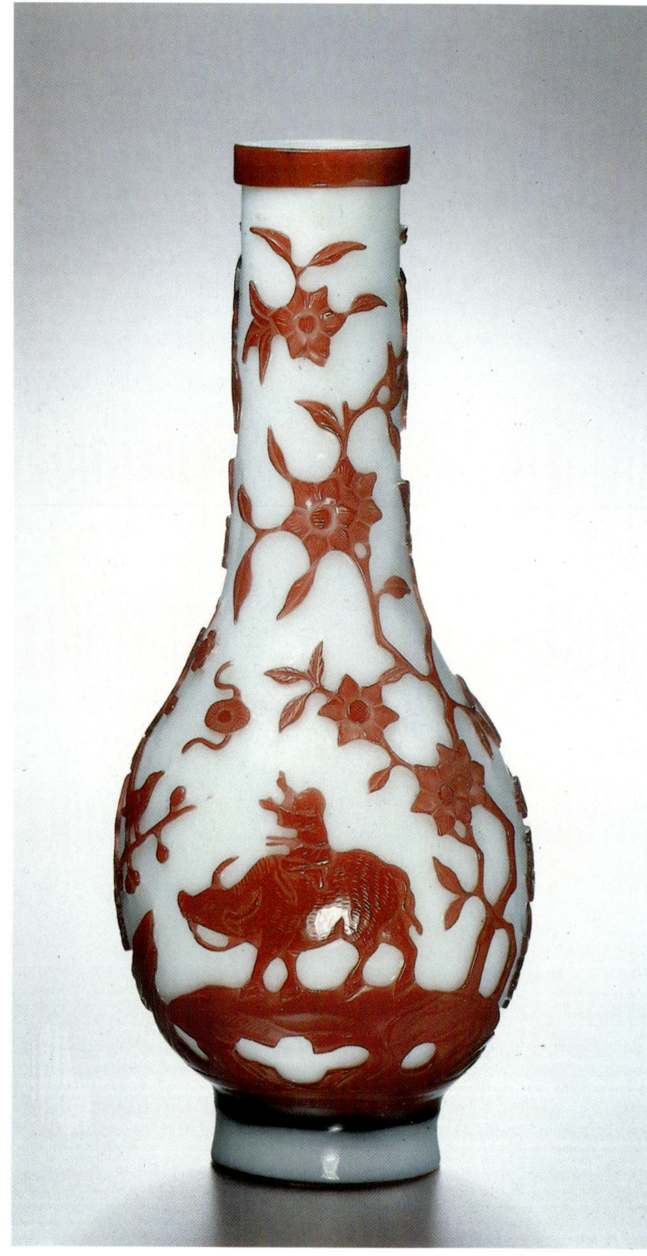

211 Vase

China
Ch'ing Dynasty
Probably 1st half of 19th c.
H 18.8, ⌀ 7.8 cm

Mold-blown or freehand-blown. Thick-walled, opaque white ground with partial overlay in red, blue, green, and marbled yellow. Decoration in gem-cutting technique: dragons and stylized clouds.

Acc. no. P 1971-1
Formerly W. Henrich Collection, Frankfurt

For Chinese glass of the 18th and 19th centuries see Ohm, Bauer, and Gabbert, Frankfurt, 1980, 277–322, esp. cat. nos. 624, 625.

Lit.: Ricke, *Museumsarbeit*, 1988, 67, fig. 26

212 Vase

China
Ch'ing Dynasty
Probably Chia-ch'ing Period (1796–1820)
H 22.6, ⌀ 9.6 cm

Mold-blown or freehand-blown. Thick-walled, opaque white ground with deep red overlay. Decoration in gem-cutting technique: boy on water buffalo, surrounded by flowering vines; on the reverse, a female deity with flower basket on clouds.

Acc. no. P 1971-10
Formerly W. Henrich Collection, Frankfurt

See Ohm, Bauer, and Gabbert, Frankfurt, 1980, no. 628.

Lit.: –

213 Bowl

China, probably Ch'ing Dynasty
1st half of 19th c.
H 16.6, ⌀ 15.8 cm

Mold-blown and shaped. Thick black overlay
on opaque white ground. Decoration in gem-
cutting technique: birds on branches with
blossoms and leaves.

Acc. no. P 1971-4
Formerly W. Henrich Collection, Frankfurt

Lit.: –

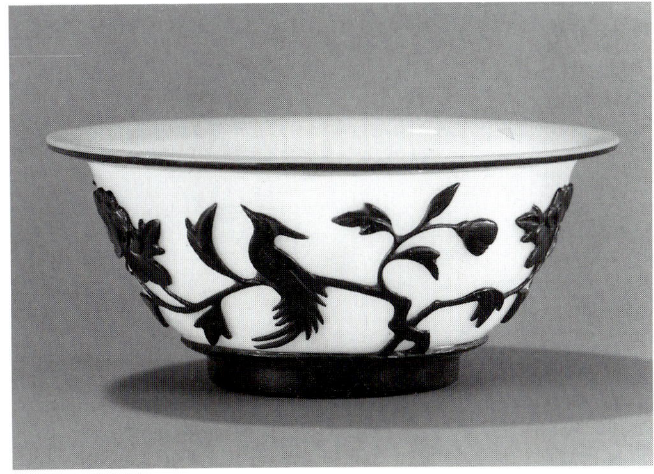

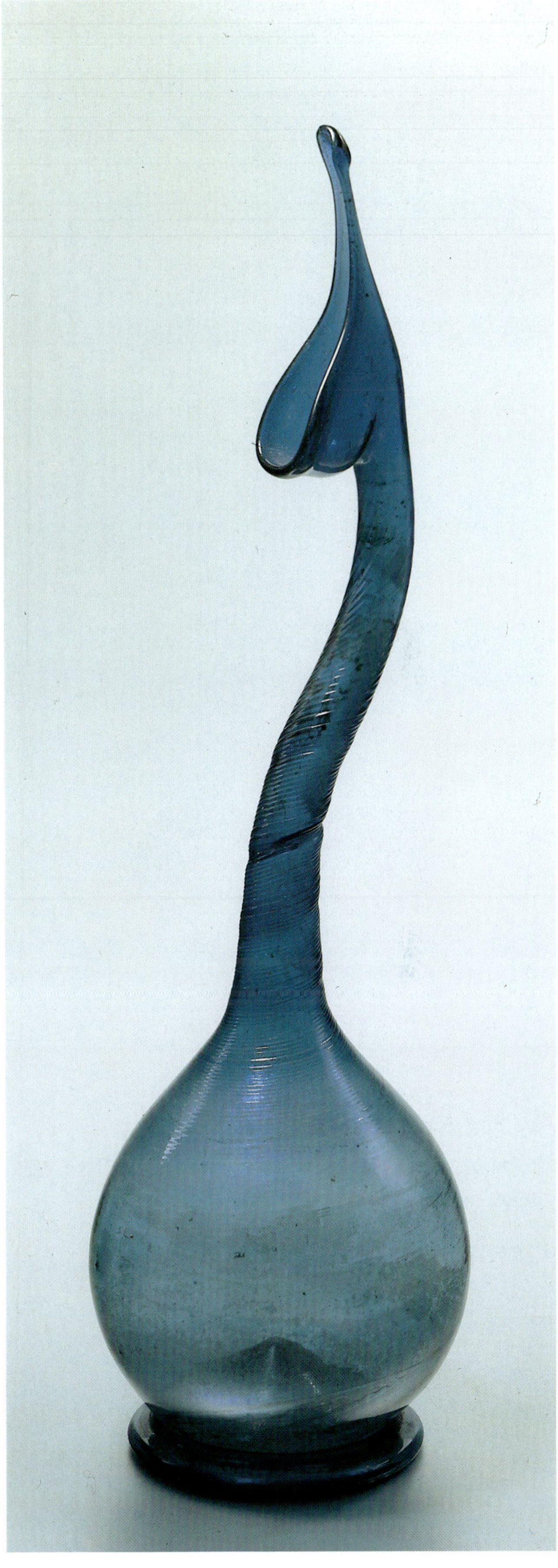

214 Rose-Water Sprinkler

Iran, Shiraz
19th c.
H 34.3, ⌀ 10.5 cm

Massive light blue glass. Optic-blown in four-
part ribbed mold; shaped. Pushed-up bottom,
foot added.

Acc. no. 12414
Formerly Franz Bock Collection, Aachen

Comparable vessels are in numerous collections. See, for example, Kämpfer, *Viertausend
Jahre*, 1966, no. 171; Klesse and Reineking,
Cologne, 1973, no. 93, 110; Fukai, *Persian
Glass*, 1977, fig. 88; Ohm, Bauer, and Gabbert, Frankfurt, 1980, no. 96. In the late
19th century, nearly every museum of applied
art in Germany acquired a large collection of
Persian glass objects, which usually dated
from the 18th and 19th centuries. Very probably, however, the largest portion of glassware represented contemporary Persian works
or pieces no more than a few decades old. In
terms of the historical development, this
glassware carried on the unbroken tradition
of Persian glass art of the 18th, in part even
of the 17th century.

Lit.: Heinemeyer, *Glas*, 1966, cat. no. 579;
Schack, *Glaskunst*, 1976, 194, fig. 25; Lötz 1,
1989, 18, fig. 7

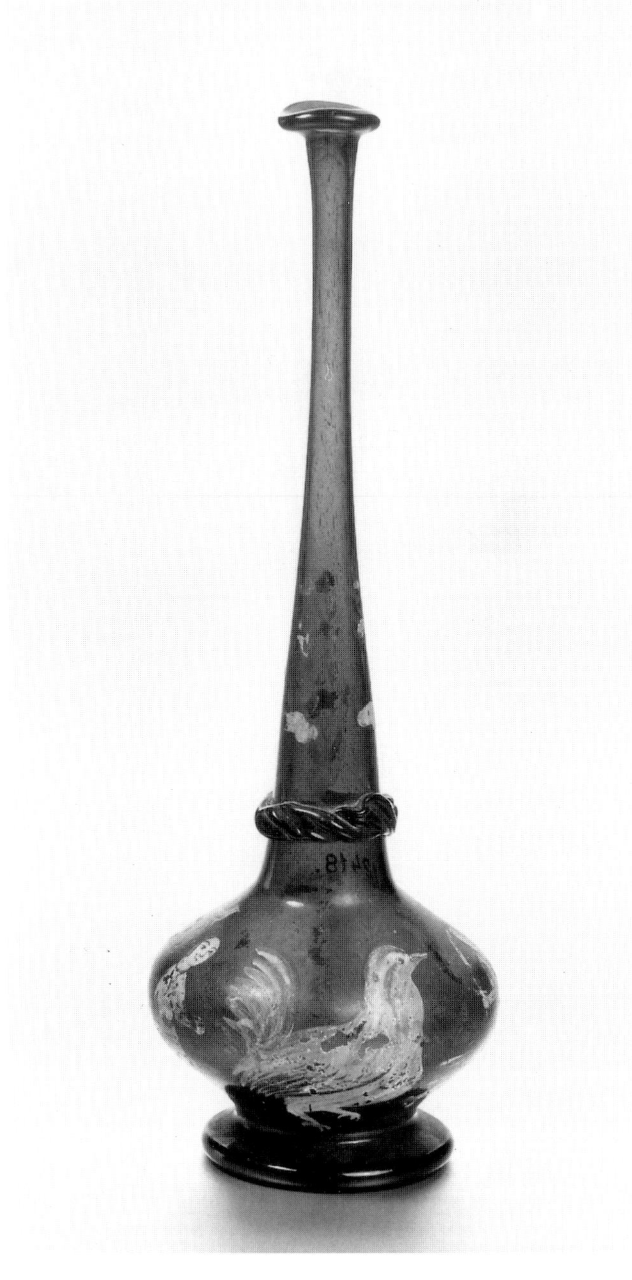

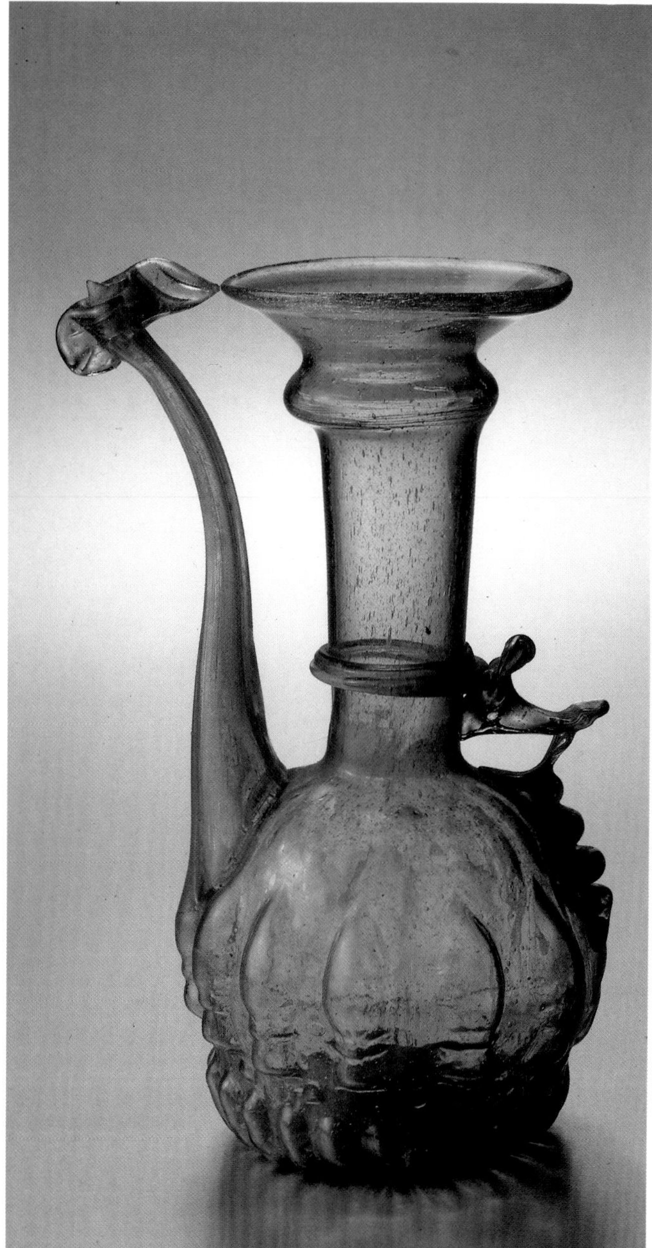

215   Perfume Sprinkler

Iran, Shiraz
19th c.
H 27.7 cm, ⌀ 9.8 cm

Dark blue glass. Free-blown and shaped. Pushed-
up bottom, foot added.
Decoration in slightly scuffed cold painting: man
with saber, two couples in conversation, large
rooster, three small birds at half-height between
the scenes; on the neck, stylized plants.

Acc. no. P 12418
Formerly Franz Bock Collection, Aachen

For similar glassware see Kämpfer, *Viertausend
Jahre*, 1966, no. 171; Schack, *Glaskunst*, 1976,
195, fig. 27; Fukai, *Persian Glass*, 1977, fig. 88.

Lit.: Heinemeyer, *Glas*, 1966, cat. no. 580

216   Pitcher

Iran, Shiraz
19th c.
H 18.1, ⌀ 11.6 cm

Green glass. Body blown in three-part mold—12
encircling almond motifs. Neck and spout shaped
freehand or added; pincered applications.

Acc. no. P 12420
Formerly Franz Bock Collection, Aachen

Common type, represented in numerous collections. See Klesse and Reineking, Cologne, 1973,
nos. 77–79; Ohm, Bauer, and Gabbert, Frankfurt,
1980, nos. 81, 82; Schack, *Glaskunst*, 1976, 195,
fig. 25; Fukai, *Persian Glass*, 1977, figs. 84, 86.

Lit.: Heinemeyer, *Glas*, 1966, cat. no. 578

Art Nouveau and Art Deco
France

The 1960s were characterized by an enthusiasm for Art Nouveau, which in its often decidedly uncritical excesses, bore the signs of a transitional fashion. To the surprise of many, the renaissance of the turn-of-the-century art form has meanwhile proved to be extraordinarily long-lived. Mere catch phrases such as "nostalgia" or "fleeing from the present" surely cannot explain this phenomenon. Looking back, the rediscovery and rehabilitation of the major art movements of around 1900 can be seen as part of the critique of a misunderstood Bauhaus ideology, its functionalism and purism, which also began in the 1960s. The growing feeling of unease towards an exclusively functional form and the renunciation of decoration and ornament, which had been raised almost to the level of dogma, was accompanied by a renewed appreciation of the qualities of an epoch in which such limitations were foreign. We learned to differentiate original artistic achievements from mass-produced objects, to distinguish what was of genuine value from a mass of trivial products. This is above all true in the realm of glass art. It fulfilled Art Nouveau intentions like no other art form and was the material of choice for the period's genuine achievements.

Moreover, Art Nouveau glass offered a variety of totally disparate forms. Even an impartial observer would find it difficult to deny that art at the turn of the century had the quality of an all-encompassing, all-embracing period style. In some countries developments that could be defined as expressions of a unified style—with limitations—took place: this is true not least of France and the United States. If, however, a marquetry glass by Emile Gallé (cat. nos. 231–33) were placed next to a "Cypriote" vase by Tiffany (cat. no. 299), or a vase designed by Ludwig Sütterlin for the Heckert refinery (cat. no. 348) next to a pitcher by Marie Kirschner (cat. nos. 312, 313) or a Josef Hoffmann glass (cat. no. 319), then the range of ideals and designs conveyed by these works proves that the term "Art Nouveau glass" is a conceptual crutch. It can hardly encompass the manifold faces of turn-of-the-century glass art. The period combined both the refinement and decadence of a late period that strove to achieve new goals.

All the period's movements share an origin in the historicist glass art of the 1860s and 1870s. In many respects Art Nouveau glass was not a rebellion against the principles of historicism, but its logical continuation, development, and fulfillment. However, proponents of Art Nouveau and Jugendstil rejected essential demands of the arts-and-crafts theoreticians—that design be true to the material, for instance—in favor of the lyrical, sensuous potential of glass.

The most important exponents of the style in glass developed their new forms after years of working in historicism. Again Gallé and Tiffany come to mind, but also the leading personalities at Lötz in Klostermühle. In France, exoticism was the point of departure. Artists studied the art of East Asia: Chinese cased glasses, jade works, and, above all, Japanese colored woodcuts. Stimulated by the completely different conception of nature evident in these prints, French artists turned to the world of flora and fauna as a source of creative inspiration.

This led to the idea of an all-encompassing synthesis of the arts based on natural forms, in which all artistic genres would have equal value and the traditional division between fine and applied arts would be abolished. This concept has to be seen against the background of the intellectual and social movements of the time. The idea of a synthesis of the arts, as it was compellingly realized in the interiors of the Ecole de Nancy, can be understood as an ideal counter image to the inadequacies of the real world, an aesthetic refuge in a world characterized by industrialization and social tensions. Art Nouveau in France was thus not only a revolutionary art of the avant-garde, but also an art of the middle classes, emerging from historicism in logical stages. The social-reform components, which played a significant role in Germany and Austria, were mostly absent in France. Unusual for the culturally centralized country is that the masterpieces of Art Nouveau did not come from Paris, the capital usually taken as a yardstick, but from the provinces. The study of East-Asian art by artists active in Paris, such as Marie François Auguste Jean or François Eugène Rousseau (cat. nos. 219, 220), had provided the decisive impulses for a new orientation in glass art. In Lorraine's capital of Nancy, however, Art Nouveau was formulated as an obligatory national style. The only task that fell upon Paris was to sanction the new style. Art critics received it enthusiastically at the Paris World Exhibitions of 1889 and 1900. And glasshouses in and around Paris could not help following the example of the Lorraine glassworks.

A central personality in this development was undoubtedly Emile Gallé. First a botanist and then a trained artist, he was able to convince the majority of designers and glass technicians working for him at his studio or at the Meisenthal glasshouse of Burgun, Schverer & Co., of his ideas. Each of these individual personalities had a different talent and Gallé was able to create something out of the sum of these achievements, described as the *genre Gallé* even in his own lifetime.

Of the works bearing his name, Gallé created only a fraction himself; the technical execution was left up to the experts at the furnace and in the decorating workshops. Yet all these glass objects demonstrate a general stylistic principle, if not a common personal style. As the studio's driving force, Gallé always kept the whole production in his hands. It was he who made the selection from a variety of newly developed models and who brought the style to a breakthrough with clever exhibition and business policies. In the finest works of the *grand genre*, form and decoration fuse in an indissoluble whole. Gallé opened up new expressive possibilities for the material. The glass vessel became a symbol of both growth and decay in nature (cat. nos. 232–46). Poetry, emotions, and atmospheric values became the object of the design (cat. nos. 230, 236) and made glass a legitimate carrier of expression in a period that is eloquently described as the "fin de siècle." The first company to take up the impulse of Gallé around 1890 was Daum Frères in Nancy (cat. nos. 247–59). For a long time the company was wrongly accused of dully emulating their glass pieces. Meanwhile this picture has been redressed. Daum Frères developed its own forms as well as new techniques. Intense research went into the potential of applied and embedded colored glass powder. In their lavish small series as well as in mass-production, the company was successful in setting itself off from the competition.

Hardly anyone in the smaller companies or amongst the independent Art-Nouveau artists could or wanted to withdraw from the influence of the Gallé-dominated Ecole de Nancy. Floral motifs remained the obligatory working basis for all (cat. nos. 260–66, 268–70, 272). The standard decoration methods used for the finest pieces, as with Gallé, were cutting and engraving. For glassware produced in larger quantities, it was etching in several layers. An exception is the painted glassware fired in a reducing atmosphere by Amédée de Caranza (cat. no. 264).

One technique deserves particular attention. At least with regard to the handling of the material, this remained largely independent of Gallé's activities and its origin lay more in ceramics than in traditional glassmaking: *pâte de verre* (cat. nos. 277–89). The works made in this manner recall eggshell porcelain. In particular the dishes and beakers of Albert Dammouse and the early pieces of François-Emile Décorchemont (cat. nos. 279, 280, 282, 283) embrace the design principle that—in contrast to that of Gallé—the work's essence is in its fragility and delicate material effect. In this respect, the early *pâte-de-verre* works are closely related to the decorative glassware of Karl Koepping, the most important German glass artist working in Jugendstil, the name given to

Art Nouveau in Germany (cat. nos. 341–43). Other artists exploited the potential of the bound glass paste as sculptural material: Henri Cros, Jean Désiré Ringel d'Illzach, and Georges Despret (cat. nos. 277, 278, 281), later increasingly also Décorchemont, Victor Amalric Walter, and Gabriel Argy-Rousseau (cat. nos. 282–89).

The transition from the design principles of Art Nouveau to those of the 1920s is fluid. The catch phrase "Art Deco"—an abbreviation of the important international arts-and-crafts exhibition in Paris in 1925—encompasses numerous design approaches. Besides the continuation of the Gallé genre in more severe, in part abstracted, stylized forms, a studio art developed. It was usually based on enamel painting and had its center in Paris (cat. no. 275).

As to manufacturers, two large, newly founded companies with completely different approaches determined the picture—René Lalique and the Verreries Schneider. The jewelry artist Lalique had already begun to make glass before the World War. Decoration having a new, highly sculptural aspect combined with a modern press-and-blow process and the eschewal of polychromy made his designs emphatically forward-looking (cat. nos. 268–70).

The designs of Charles Schneider were more deeply rooted in Art Nouveau. Instead of the restrained polychromy of Art Nouveau glassware he used the sharply contrasting tango hues of the "roaring 1920s" and realized highly unconventional, sometimes positively bizarre formal solutions (cat. nos. 271–74).

Glassware by the manufacturer Schneider marked the end of a development on a high level. Future-oriented, on the other hand, was glass by the painter Maurice Marinot (cat. nos. 290–92). He firmly believed that artists should realize their own glass designs and, in clear contrast to the Art Nouveau tradition, sought a new approach to glass art in the direct effect of the heavy transparent material. Essential impulses for contemporary glass art came from the work of Marinot and his successors Henri-Edouard Navarre and André Thuret (cat. nos. 293, 294).

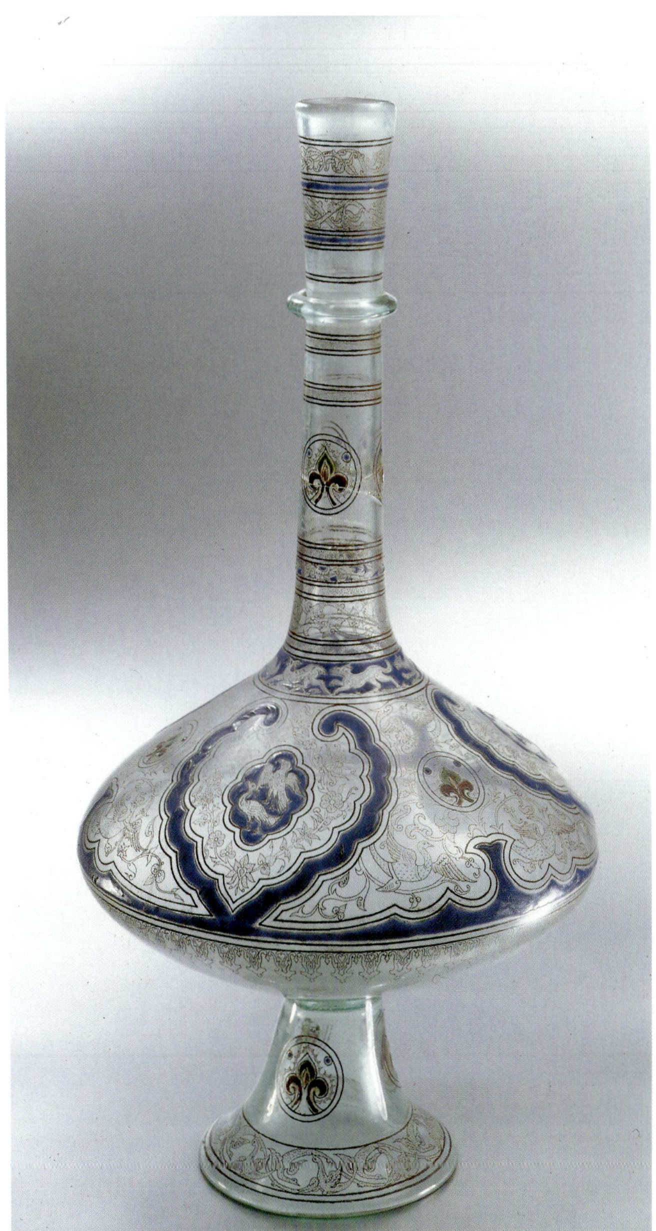

(Philippe-) Joseph Brocard
(ca. 1840–1896)

Glass artist and enamel painter

From the 1860s, ran the leading Parisian work-shop for enamel-painted glass modeled on Islamic and Indian prototypes, later also on contemporary designs.

217   Bottle

Mark in rouge enamel on wall, repeated on the foot: *Brocard à Paris 1869*
1869
H 52.2, ⌀ 26.2 cm

Light green tone. Mold-blown, shaped. Foot blown separately and attached. Enamel and gold painting.
Neck broken and glued.

Acc. no. P 1980-2
Acquired with the support of Helmut Hentrich and the Commerzbank Düsseldorf

One of the earliest glasses that can be securely attributed to Brocard, who first aroused great interest at the 1867 World Exhibition in Paris. Presumably a unique piece, emulating Syrian gold and enamel glassware of the 14th century; very likely a copy of a bottle. See C. J. Lamm, *Mittelalterliche Gläser und Steinschnittarbeiten aus dem Nahen Osten* 2 (Berlin, 1929/30), pl. 181,2.

Lit.: Hilschenz-Mlynek and Ricke, *Frankreich*, 1985, cat. no. 8

218   Decorative Goblet

Mark in rouge under the foot: *Brocard*
Ca. 1880
H 11.1, ⌀ 10.1 cm

Colorless glass. Mold-blown, shaped. Foot and node blown separately and attached.

Acc. no. P 1970-91
Gift of Helmut Hentrich

Free use of Indian and Islamic decorative motifs on a vessel form taken from the European tradition.
For dating see, for example, Polak, *Modern Glass*, 1962, fig. 14, 15 A, B.

Lit.: Hilschenz-Mlynek and Ricke, *Frankreich*, 1985, cat. no. 12; Ricke, *2500 Jahre*, 1987, cat. no. 114

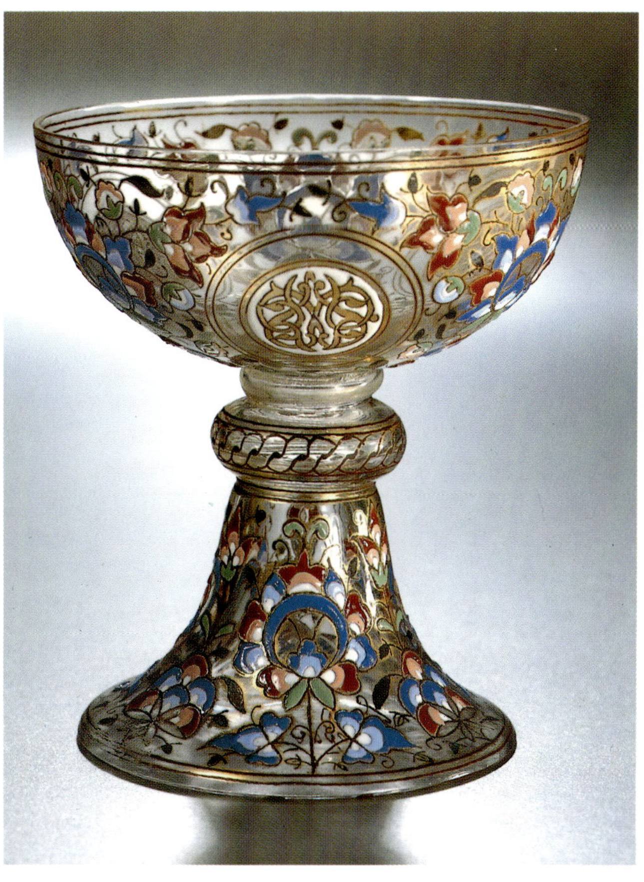

Ste. Marie François Augustin (Auguste) Jean
(1829–1896)

Entrepreneur, designer, ceramist, glass painter

Active in Paris from 1859 as ceramic and porcelain manufacturer, and from the 1870s increasingly as a glassmaker. Enamel painting in Japanizing and Orientalizing style on highly unconventional forms.

219   Jardinière

In rouge enamel in ground out pontil mark:
Jean
Ca. 1885–90
H 14.2, ⌀ 25.1 x 7.6 cm

Smoke-colored glass with blue applications. Mold-blown, shaped. Painting in gold and silver enamel, feet toned down in luster painting. Decoration on the reverse: opened book with kingfisher and plants, an ornamental ball, and serrated gold shield with butterfly.

Acc. no. P 1983-25
Gift of Helmut Hentrich

Unique piece or from small series. Japanese motifs taken from roll and lacquer painting. For Jean see Cappa, *100 ans Europe*, 1983, 172f.; Schmitt, *Sammlung Silzer*, 1989, 162ff.; Ricke and Schmitt, *Sammlung Koepff*, 1998, 308f.

Lit.: Hilschenz-Mlynek and Ricke, *Frankreich*, 1985, cat. no. 386; Ricke, *2500 Jahre*, 1987, cat. no. 115

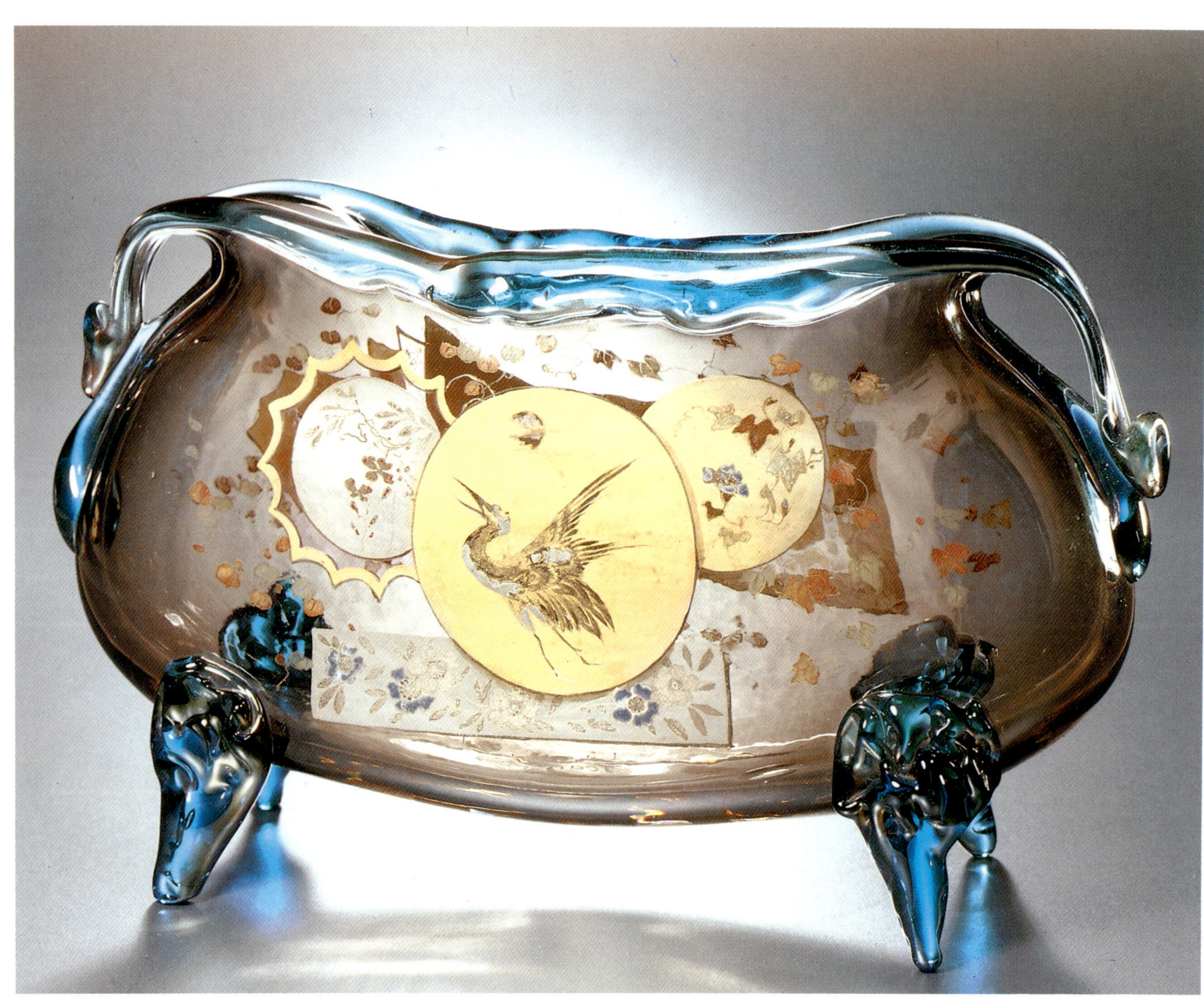

François Eugène Rousseau
(1827–1890)

Distributor of porcelain, ceramics, and glass, Paris

From 1861, made designs for porcelain and faience. Before 1869, began to sell his own glass designs, carried out by the glasshouse Appert Frères in Paris (from 1875 in Clichy). Collaborated with major glass painters and engravers.

220 Vase

Needle-etched mark on the underside of base:
E. Rousseau Paris
Ca. 1884
H 15.5, ⌀ 16.7 x 10.5 cm

Light yellow tone. Free-blown and shaped, pushed into an oval cross section. Several cased layers enclose oxide and gold foil, one layer cooled in water and crackled.
Decoration: Chinese figural scenes in stylized tree landscape etched from sealing-wax-red overlay, engraved and polished. On opposite side: bridge spanning cliffs.

Acc. no. P 1983-138
Gift of Helmut Hentrich

From small series, provable in few instances; see example exhibited in Paris in 1884: *Revue des Arts Décoratifs* 5 (1884/85), illus. p. 194. For Rousseau see also Schmitt, *Sammlung Silzer*, 1989, 302ff.; Karin Schneck, "François Eugène Rousseau (1827–1890): Keramik und Glas an der Schwelle zum Jugendstil" (mas-

ter's thesis, Berlin, 1989), esp. 50ff., n. 148, fig. 53a,b (comparable piece at Musée des Techniques, Paris); and Ricke and Schmitt, *Sammlung Koepff*, 1998, 315f.

Lit.: Hilschenz-Mlynek and Ricke, *Frankreich*, 1985, cat. no. 488

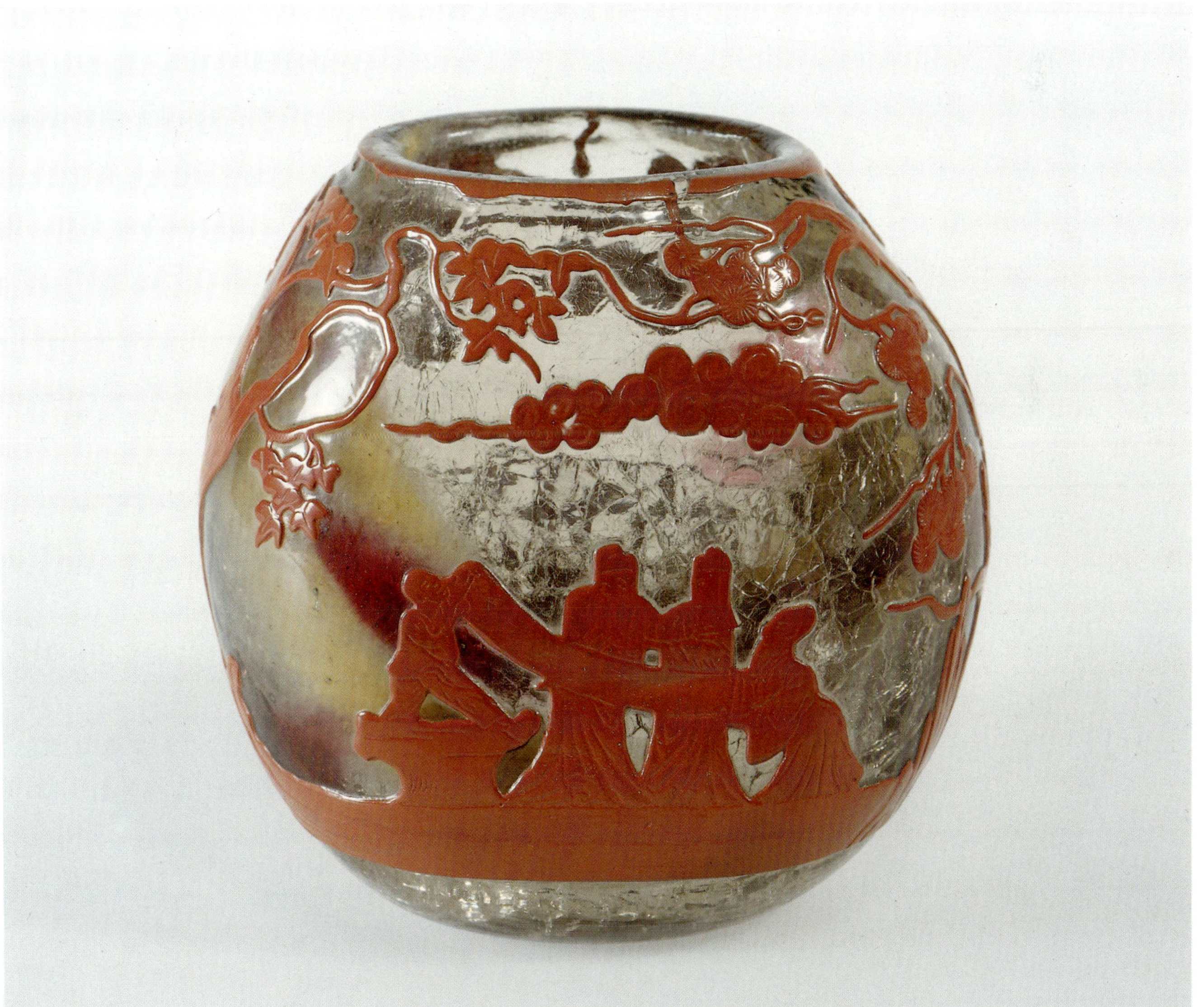

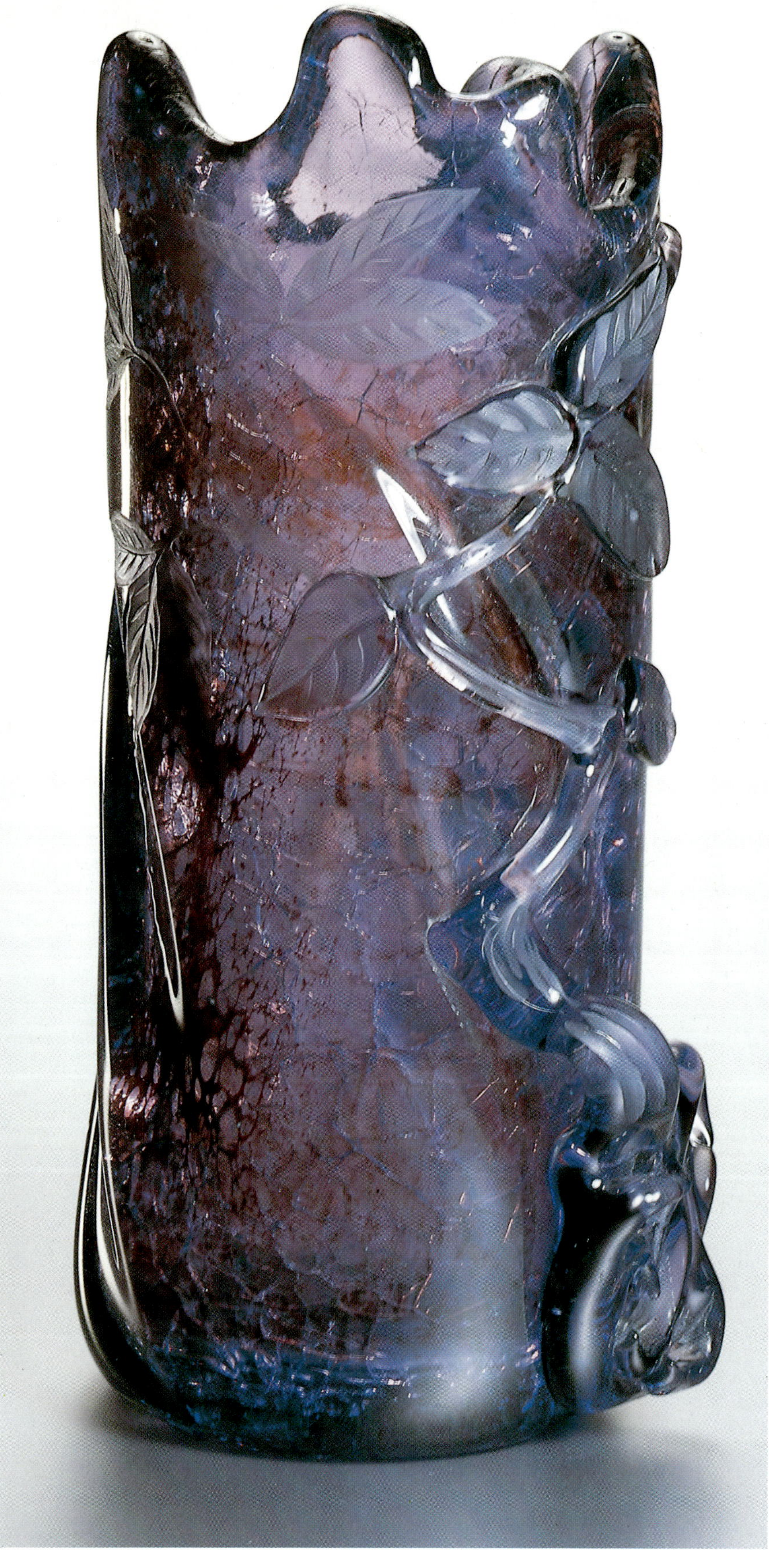

Ernest Baptiste Léveillé
(1841–1913)

Glass designer and distributor of glass and ceramics

From 1869, managed a glass and porcelain shop that he opened in Paris. In 1885, acquired the company of Eugène Rousseau and continued to run it in the spirit of the former owner. Distributed his own designs, besides glassware in the *genre Rousseau*.

221   Vase

Mark in diamond-point engraving on the underside: *E. Léveillé à Paris*
Ca. 1890
H 19.5, ⌀ 9.4 cm

Violet glass. Freehand or mold-blown; shaped. Oxide and gold-foil embedded between several overlays; one layer crackled in cold water.
Decoration: freehand sculptural applications, mat intaglio. Leaves on the wall in intaglio.

Acc. no. P 1970-279
Gift of Helmut Hentrich

Unique piece; see also ice glassware, with the same oxide pattern, by E. Rousseau. The work illustrates the close ties between early Art Nouveau glass and the art of East Asia. Chinese works of cut jade served as models. For Léveillé see Ricke and Schmitt, *Sammlung Koepff*, 1998, 311f.

Lit.: Hilschenz-Mlynek and Ricke, *Frankreich*, 1985, cat. no. 422; Ricke, *2500 Jahre*, 1987, cat. no. 116

Emile Gallé
(1846–1904)

Designer of glass, ceramics, and furniture,
entrepreneur and businessman, botanist,
chemist, and writer

1864–66, practical training in the decorating
workshops of his father's firm specialized in
glass and ceramic wares. 1865–66 studied at
the Jäde-Stegmannsche Institut für Architektur und Kunstgewerbe in Weimar. Designs for
glass and ceramics from 1867, later also for
furniture, bronze fittings, etc. In 1874, took
over the artistic direction of his father's company. 1885–96, intense collaboration with
the glass manufacturer Burgun, Schverer &
Co. in Meisenthal, Alsace, who carried out
the largest portion of Gallé glass. From the
mid-1890s, production exclusively in Gallé's
own glasshouse in Nancy. From 1884, over-
whelming successes at international exhibitions, especially the 1889 and 1990 World
Exhibitions in Paris. The *genre Gallé* became
decisive for the style of Art Nouveau in
France.

From 1904, after Gallé's death, the company
continued as Etablissments Emile Gallé. In
1931, the firm was closed down.

222 "Tête de Monstre Japonais" Vase

Mark engraved on the underside of base:
Emile Gallé Nanceiis fec'; and in black enamel
in script, scuffed: *...mile Gallé a Na...*; and
engraved on black enameled surface at base
of wall: *EG* with Cross of Lorraine
Designed in 1876
H 13.1, ⌀ 12.6 cm

Colorless glass. Mold-blown. Relief carving
and intaglio. In the lion's jaws: ornamental
frieze in relief enamel and gold contours.
Decoration: leaves and tufts of grass in black
enamel with gold. Grasshopper engraved and
partly gilded. Oriental motifs and Chinese
characters, which, translated, read: Those
who receive friendliness, but show no true
gratitude, are not real human beings.

Acc. no. P 1975-53
Gift of Helmut Hentrich

Grand genre studio piece. Dating secured by a
written statement by *Gallé*. Translation of a
concrete prototype from East Asian art into
glass: the shi-shi lion of the Japanese Bizen
ceramics. A shi-shi lion, whose form corresponds down to the smallest detail with the
glass version, was in Gallé's collection. Chinese works of rock crystal inspired the choice
of material. Several variations are documented.

Lit.: Charpentier and Thiébaut, *Gallé*, 1985,
cat. no. 66; Hilschenz-Mlynek and Ricke,
Frankreich, 1985, cat. no. 184

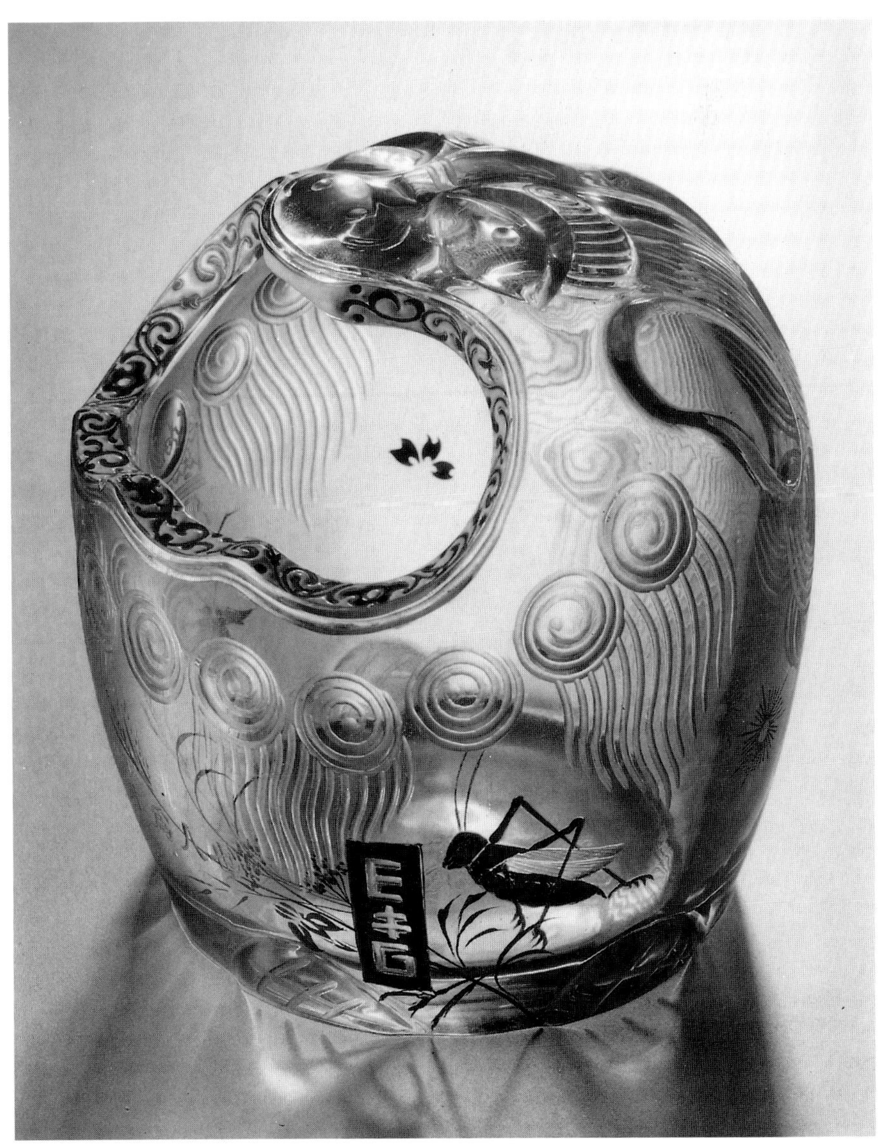

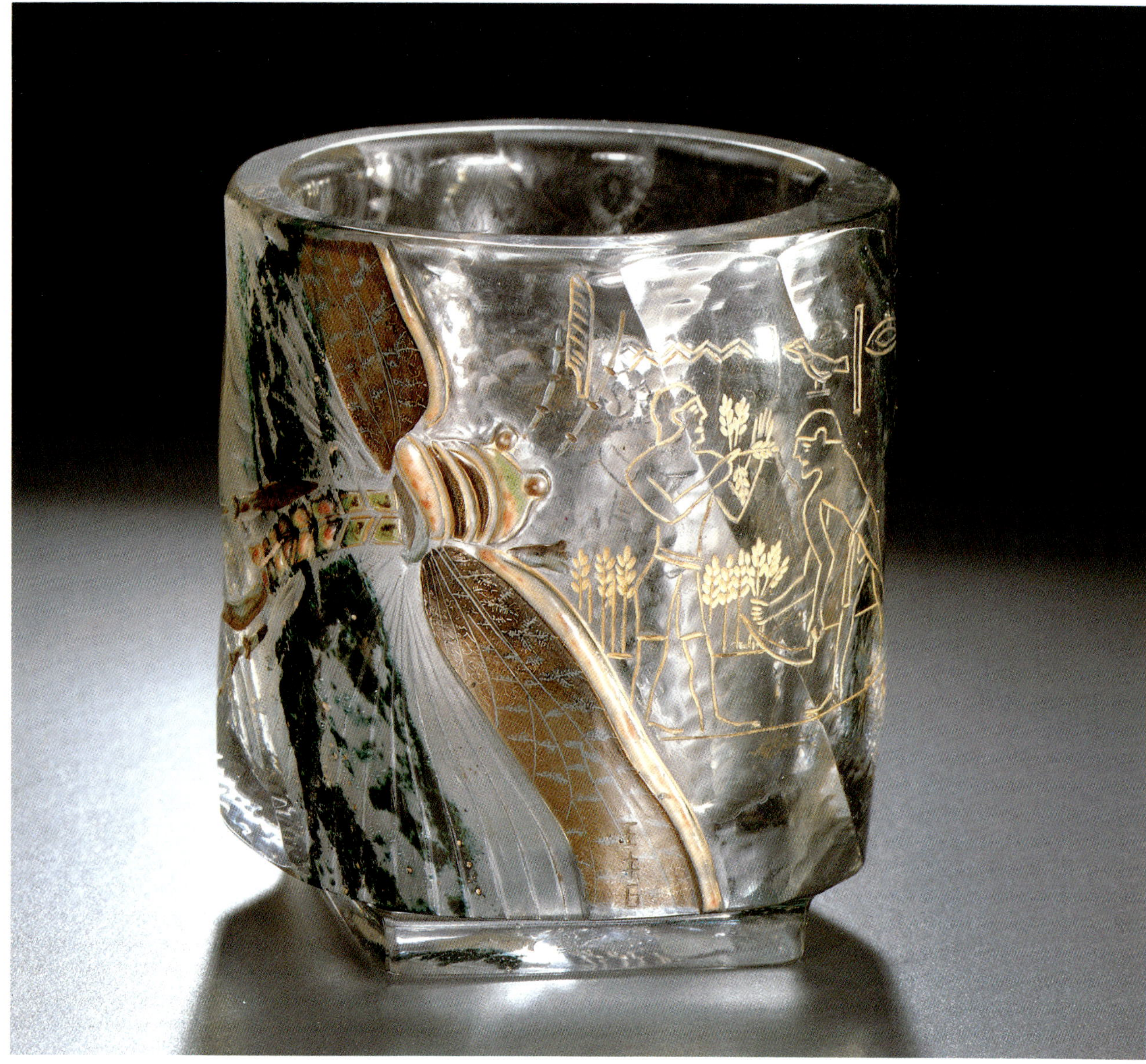

223 "Moissoneurs Egyptiens" Cigar Container

Mark engraved on the underside of base:
E. Gallé Nancy Exposition 1889;
and engraved on the wall: *EG*
Designed in 1884, executed in 1889
H 8.2, ⌀ 7.5 cm

Colorless glass with diagonal bands of
embedded powder and oxides. Mold-blown.
Cut in diagonal facets in fine *martelè* tech-
nique and polished.
Engraved and gilded decoration: Egyptians
working the fields; above, hieroglyphs.
Locusts cut, engraved, and painted in enamel.
Wings chiseled with the needle before firing.

Acc. no. P 1976-79
Gift of Helmut Hentrich

Grand genre studio piece. Gallé first showed
this early piece, which he valued highly, at
the exhibition of the *Union Centrale des Arts
Décoratifs* in 1884 and again at the 1889
World Exhibition in Paris. See Gallé, *Ecrits*,
1908, 315, with an exact description; there
also the name of the glass. For an almost
identical piece see Garner, *Gallé*, 1976, 93.

Lit.: Hilschenz-Mlynek and Ricke, *Frankreich*,
1985, cat. no. 181; Ricke, *2500 Jahre*, 1987,
cat. no. 118

224 Pitcher

Engraved mark on the underside of base:
E. Gallé Nancy—37; on the back of foot: shield in
rouge bearing the initials EG; in gold on yellow-
brown ground: Cross of Lorraine
1884
H 19.8, ⌀ 14.1 cm

Dark smoky brown glass with black glass-powder
and oxide inclusions. Free-blown and shaped.
Decoration on wall: lion cut in relief and intaglio;
engraved scrollwork and deeply etched, stylized
lilies. On the handle: heraldic fleurs-de-lis in relief
enamel with scuffed silver application on slightly
scuffed gold ground. Two cut fleurs-de-lis. On the
massive foot: ornamental gold-edged interlacing.

Acc. no. P 1970-175
Gift of Helmut Hentrich

Demi riche or *grand genre* studio piece.
Common form used with various types of decoration. For dating see an almost identical piece with
the same model number in *Kunst und Antiquitäten-
messe Hannover,* exh. cat. (Munich, 1969), illus.
p. 124. See also Gallé, *Ecrits,* 1908, 304.

Lit.: Hilschenz-Mlynek and Ricke, *Frankreich,* 1985,
cat. no. 179

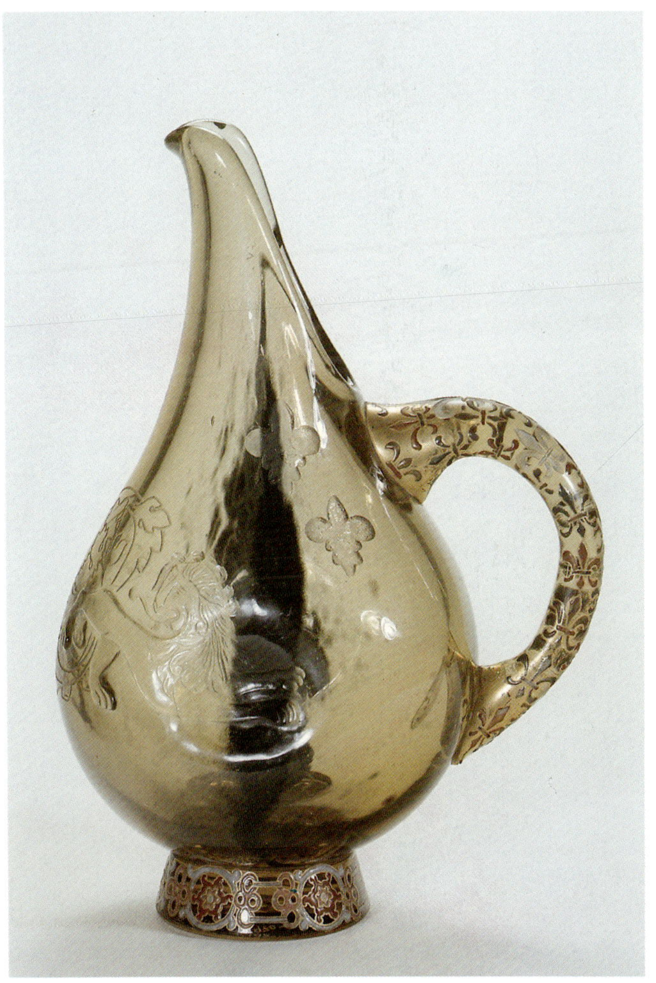

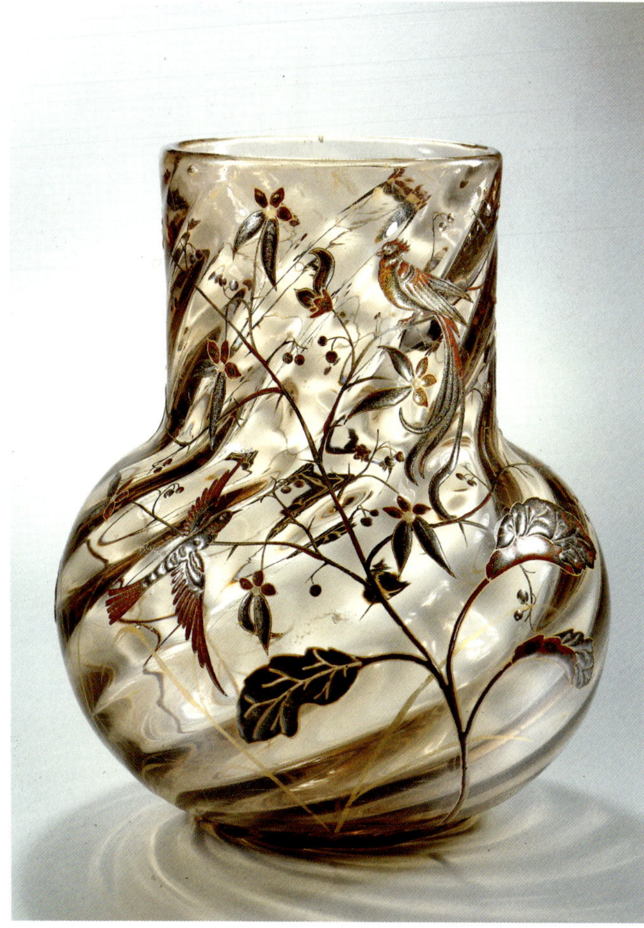

225 Vase

Mark: *EG* with Cross of Lorraine; and in black
enamel in script on the underside of base: *déposé
Emile Gallé à Nancy*
1880
H 20.8, ⌀ 17.6 cm

Smoky brown glass with a slight manganese tone.
Optic-blown.
Decoration: flowering twigs of the saxifrage and
bird of paradise in gold-edged, raised enamel,
heightened and refined with silver.

Acc. no. P 1975-44
Formerly Arnold Gehlen Collection, Aachen

Demi riche studio piece. The vase decoration is
closely related to three decoration drawings that
Gallé had copyrighted (Sotheby Monaco, 1982,
cat. no. 26, pls. 16–18, not illus.; today Corning
Museum of Glass). From 1878 until about 1900
this vessel shape was adorned with various types
of decoration.

Lit.: Hilschenz-Mlynek and Ricke, *Frankreich,* 1985,
cat. no. 174

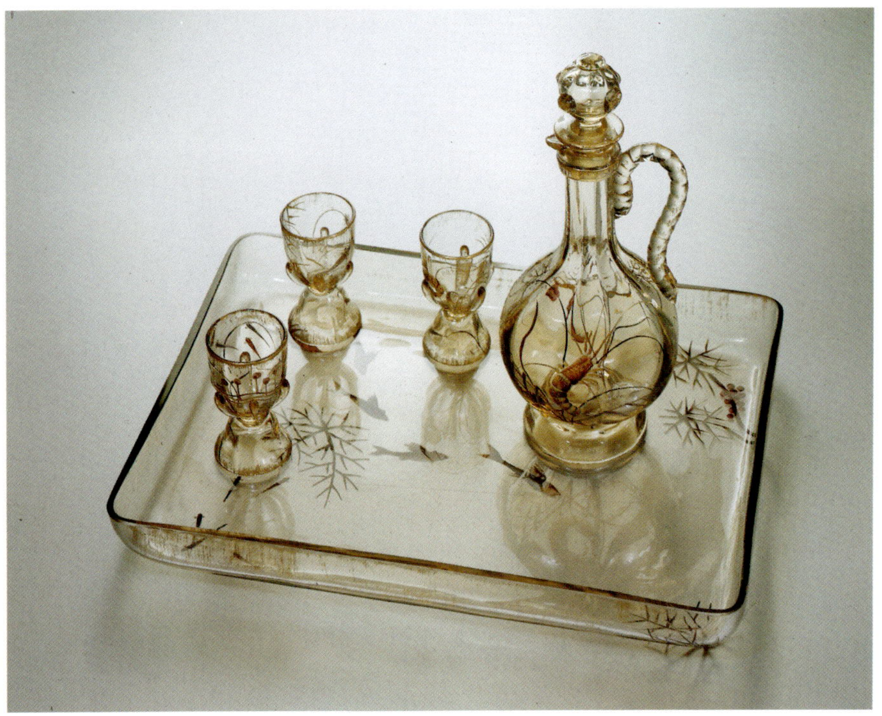

226 Pieces from a Cordial Service

Mark on the underside of the decanter's base in rouge script: *E. Gallé á Nancy*; and in diamond-point engraving: *3*
Ca. 1880–84
Decanter: H 21.2, ⌀ 9.6 cm
Tray: H 3.4, L 30.4, W 22.3 cm
Glasses: H 7, ⌀ 3.9 cm

Dark smoky brown glass. Decanter optic-blown; tray and glasses mold-blown. Applied handles, prunts, and decoration.
Cut decoration filled in with enamel, which continues freely beyond the cut contours: stylized motifs of flora and fauna of the sea. Black enamel accents. Painted and stupped gold application.

Acc. nos. P 1985-150 a–d, 151 b
Gift of Helmut Hentrich

Series ware with studio character. The decorative motifs originate from the canon of forms used by Gallé's partners Burgun, Schverer & Co. at the Meisenthal glasshouse in the 1880s. See Klesse, *Gallé*, 1982, fig. 25 (fish motifs on tray). The close stylistic affinities with F. E. Rousseau's decoration are particularly obvious in the design of the tray. Japanese colored woodcuts presumably served as models.
For 12 nearly identical glasses with two variously shaped flagons on a silver tray see Sotheby Monaco, March 1984, cat. no. 19.

Lit.: Hilschenz-Mlynek and Ricke, *Frankreich*, 1985, cat. no. 176

227 Vase

Mark in diamond-point engraving on the underside of base: *E. Gallé à Nancy*
Ca. 1889–95
H 36.6, ⌀ foot 14.2 cm

Smoky brown glass. Optic-blown and shaped. Etched decoration combined with enamel relief: star-shaped flowers with the leaves of chervil, finger grass, and other grasses. Gold contours and sparse black enamel accents.

Acc. no. P 1976-62
Gift of Helmut Hentrich

Demi riche studio piece or series ware. For a similar piece with slightly different decoration see Klesse and Mayr, *Sammlung Funke-Kaiser*, 1981, cat. no. 115.

Lit.: Hilschenz-Mlynek and Ricke, *Frankreich*, 1985, cat. no. 197

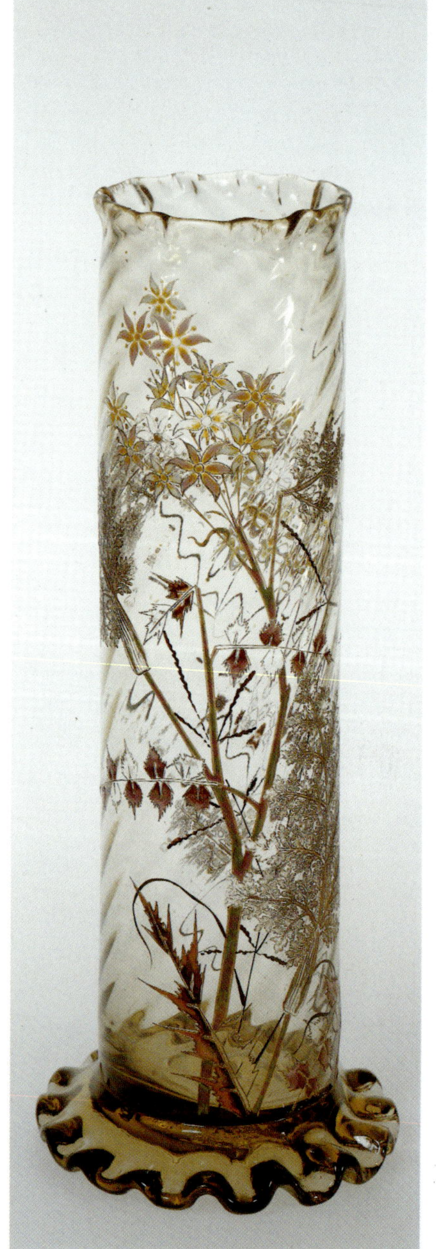

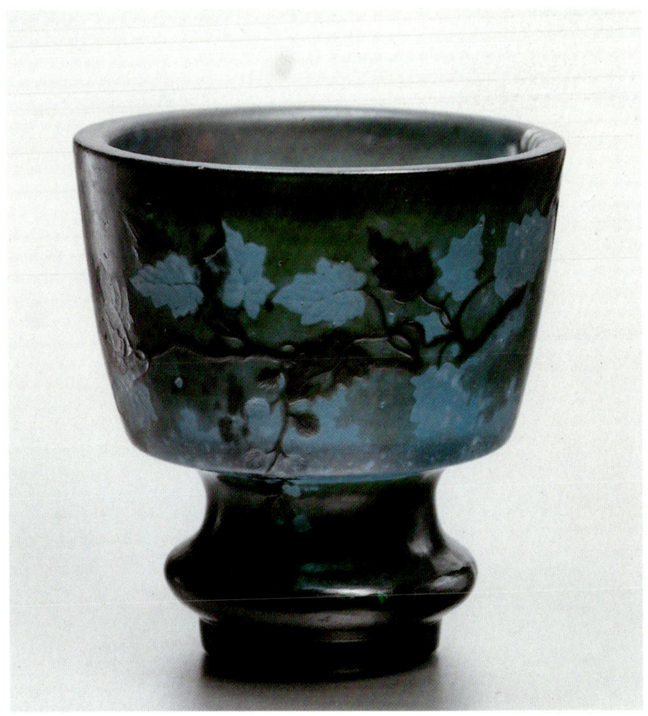

228 "La Vigne Vierge" Vase

Mark engraved on the underside of base:
Emile Gallé fecit 1894
1894
H 11.7, ⌀ 11.2 cm

On thick-walled, colorless ground, here and there applications of torn silvery metal foil, opaque dark red glass granules in two narrow vertical strips, and white dots scattered across the surface; on top of that, a thick turquoise-colored casing and a thinner brown cover layer. Mold-blown.
Decoration: vine with leaves and blossoms of wild grapes, partly worked from the turquoise surface in intaglio, partly modeled from the cover layer in relief. Surface of the vessel's interior acid-frosted; engraving and *martelé* technique cover most of the exterior, with semimat polish.

Acc. no. P 1976-66
Gift of Helmut Hentrich

Demi riche studio piece. Gallé probably created this decoration for the *Exposition de la Société Lorraine* in Nancy, the first large survey exhibition of the arts-and-crafts industry definitively influenced by Gallé in the Lorraine capital. For the same exhibition, he probably designed "Lombardy Poplar"; see, for example, Bloch-Dermant, *French Glass,*

1860–1914, 1980, illus. p. 78. All known pieces are inscribed with the date 1894. For an almost identical glass see Grover, *European Art Glass*, 1970, fig. 236. Gallé used the form over a long period of time. For a footed bowl with the same decoration, at the Musée d'Orsay in Paris, see Charpentier and Thiébaut, *Gallé*, 1985, cat. no. 110.

Lit.: Hilschenz-Mlynek and Ricke, *Frankreich,* 1985, cat. no. 202; *Meisenthal*, 1999, cat. no. 26

229 Dish

Mark on the underside of base in relief etching: *Cristallerie de Gallé*; and in needle etching: *Modèle et décor déposés*
Ca. 1895–97
H 3.8, ⌀ 17.3 cm

Colorless glass with opalescent, whitish inclusions and opaque brownish red overlay. Mold-blown.
Decoration—Turk's cap lily—etched and engraved; the worked parts lighter than the untouched surface.

Acc. no. P 1979-21
Gift of Helmut Hentrich

For dating compare the three vases in the Hentrich Collection, Hilschenz-Mlynek and Ricke, *Frankreich*, 1985, cat. nos. 211–13, and a similar vase in Stuttgart, at the Württembergisches Landesmuseum, acc. no. 3813. For lilies as decoration in general see Schmoll, *Nancy 1900*, 1980, cat. nos. 217–22, with further variations.

Lit.: Hilschenz-Mlynek and Ricke, *Frankreich*, 1985, cat. no. 214

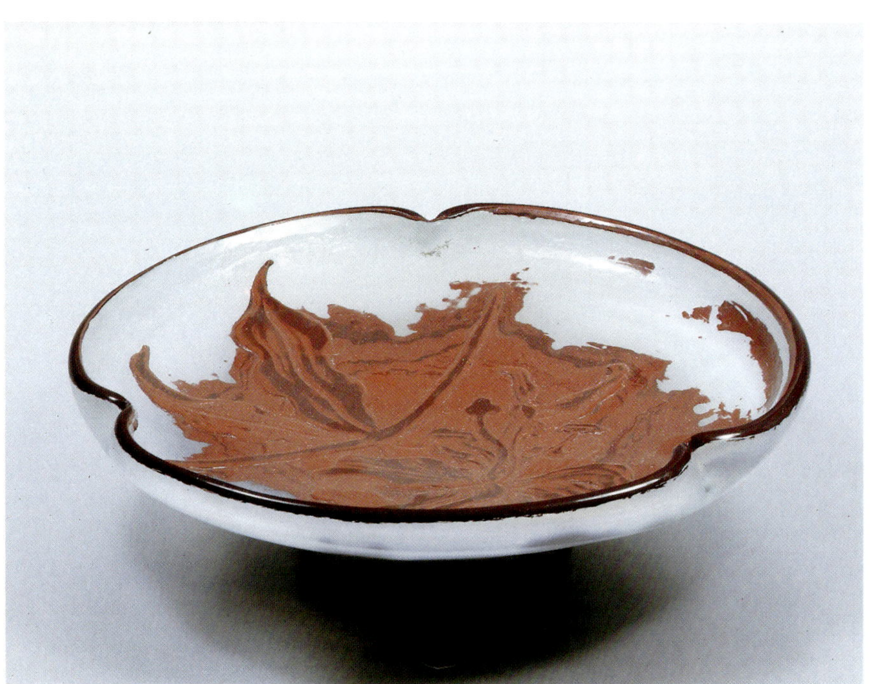

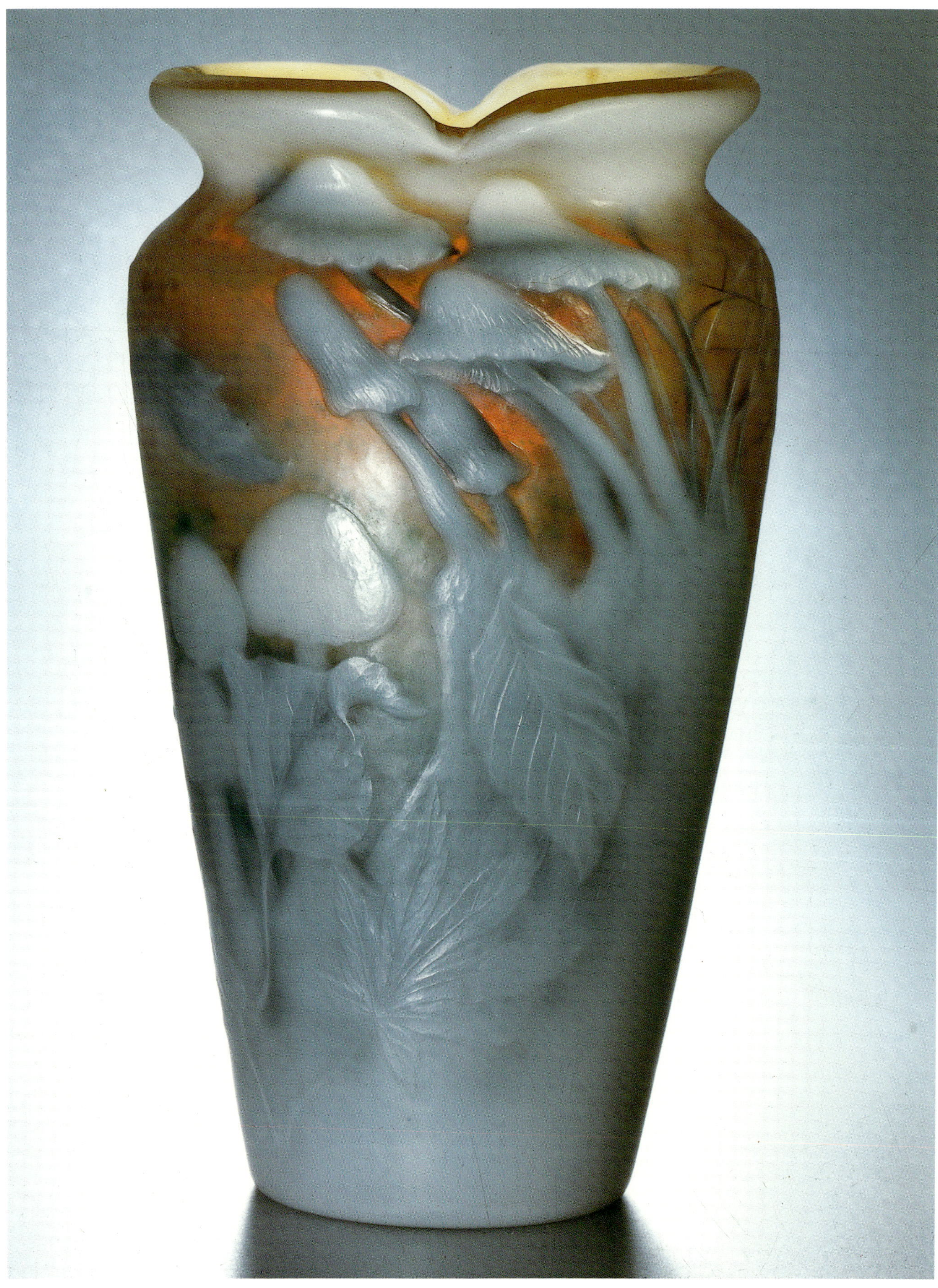

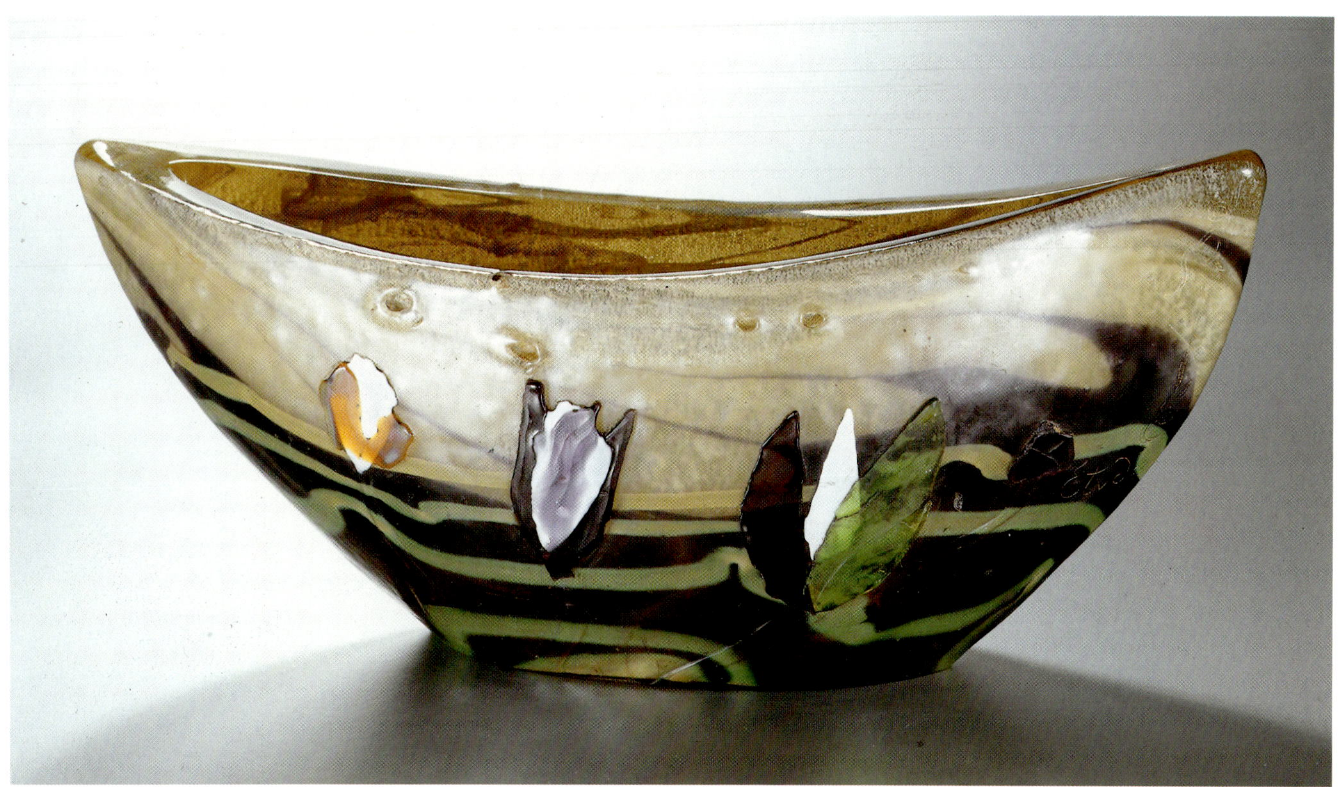

230 Vase

Engraved mark on wall: *Gallé*
Ca. 1898–1900
H 18, ⌀ 10.9 cm

On thick-walled, colorless ground with
embedded colored glass blobs: yellow-orange
casing covered by a thin, black-green layer.
Mold-blown. Shaped into an oval cross section, mouth pincered twice.
Etched decoration between the layers: grasses, clover, faded dandelion, and spider's web.
On top of that, a thick opaque white casing
with a slightly gray tone. On the surface:
falling leaves of beech, durmast oak,
sycamore, and Japanese maple, as well as two
species of mushroom, modeled in intaglio
and relief after a preparatory etching. The
remaining vessel surface has cased-glass
cutting and semimat polish.

Acc. no. P 1970-190
Gift of Helmut Hentrich

Unique piece. One of the rare glass pieces by
Gallé with etched decoration enclosed within
the wall. To do the etching, the piece had to
be cooled down during the work process.
Gallé had first introduced this process at the
1889 World Exhibition in Paris. Eugène Kremer in Meisenthal then further developed the
technique by painting between the layers.
After ending his collaboration with Burgun,
Schverer & Co., Gallé took up the technique
again and perfected it in such pieces as this.

Lit.: Hilschenz-Mlynek and Ricke, *Frankreich*,
1985, cat. no. 241; Ricke, *2500 Jahre*, 1987,
cat. no. 119

231 Boat-Shaped Vessel

Engraved and gilded mark on wall:
Gallé Etude
1898
H 11.3, L 28.9, W 8.7 cm

On thick-walled, colorless ground with a light
smoky brown tone, grainy patination with
small bubbles interspersed by a few larger
bubbles in the upper portion. In the lower
portion, dark violet cased cap drawn from the
bottom upwards. Embedded, spirally encircling thread.
Decoration: on the reverse, between the layers, plants; on the front, three-dimensional
applied tulips. Some of the leaves and stems
done in relief carving. The flower on the right
is missing one petal.

Acc. no. P 1970-202
Gift of Helmut Hentrich

Grand genre studio piece. Because some of
the bubbles on the front were broken open at
the furnace and one application lost, the
glass piece was declared an *étude* after
Gallé's death and was removed from the
glasshouse depot and put up for sale. It has
to be seen within the context of the patination and marquetry development. For a similar piece see Klesse and Mayr, *Sammlung
Funke-Kaiser*, 1981, cat. no. 159. The form is
documented as early as the 1880s.

Lit.: Charpentier and Thiébaut, *Gallé*, 1985,
cat. no. 116; Hilschenz-Mlynek and Ricke,
Frankreich, 1985, cat. no. 244

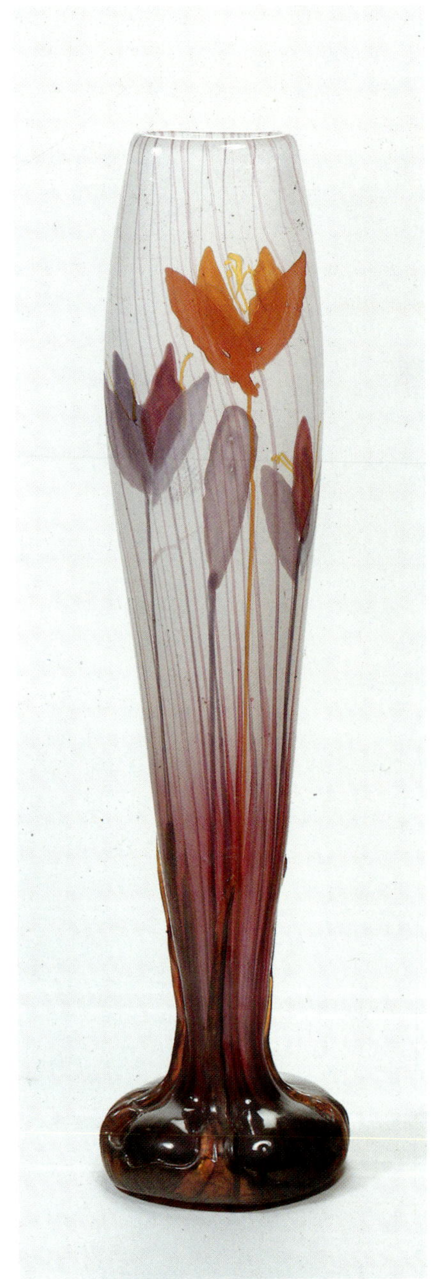

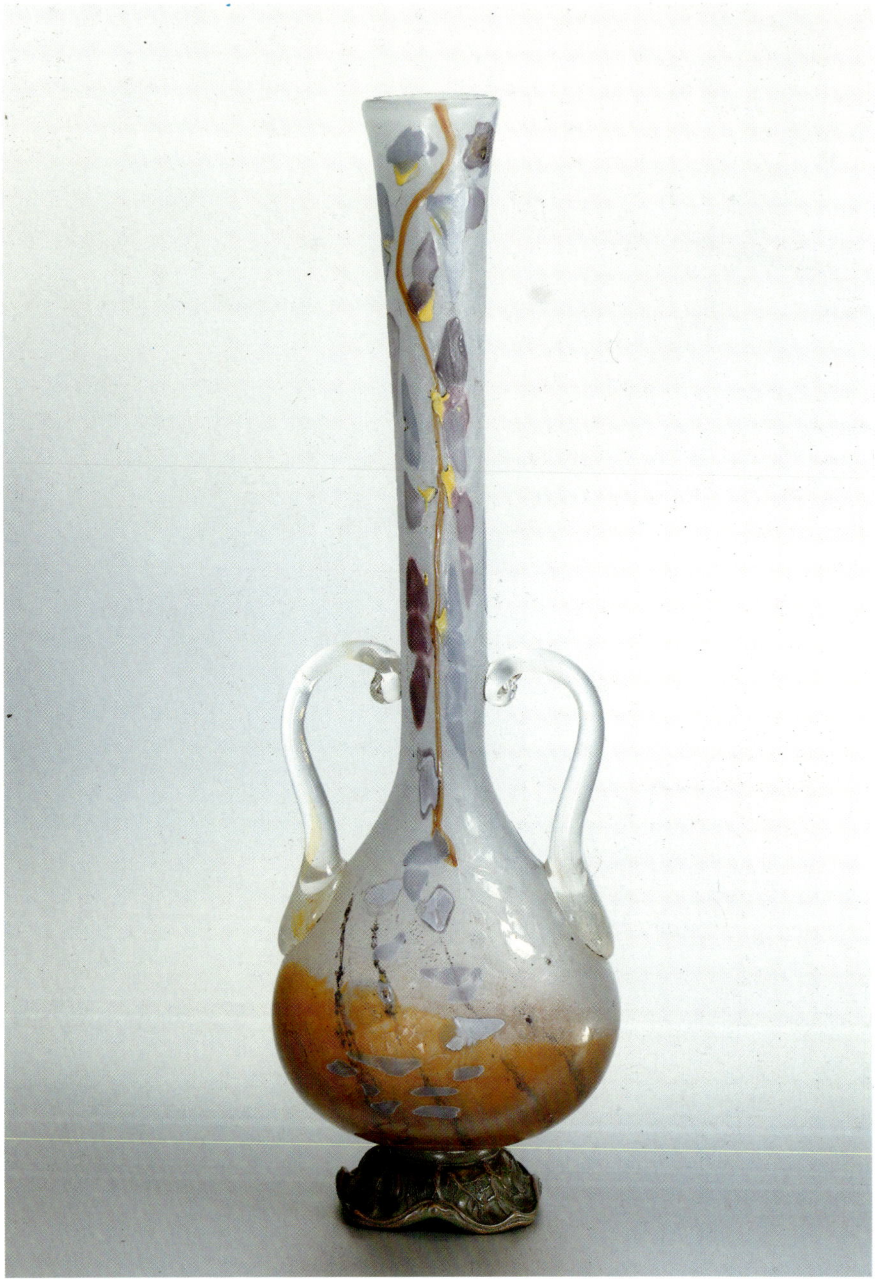

232 "Les Colchiques" Vase

Engraved mark on wall: *Gallé*
1898
H 44.3, ⌀ 11.1 cm

Patination of small bubbles embedded in thick-walled, colorless ground. At the base, partial overlays in old rose and violet, pulled into thin vertical threads. Mold-blown, body shaped in upper portion into an oval cross section. Freely applied decoration on the lower wall and on the amber-colored foot underlaid with silvery metal foil. Decoration—flowers and buds of the meadow saffron—in marquetry technique. Decoration surface modeled in relief.

Acc. no. P 1970-201
Gift of Helmut Hentrich

Grand genre studio piece. For dating compare a similar piece exhibited at the 1898 Salon: E. Gallé, "Mes envois au Salon," *Revue des Arts Décoratifs* 18, no. 6 (1898): illus. p. 146. The model was shown at the Salon in various sizes; see Gallé, *Ecrits*, 1908, 200ff. See also the variation in *La Lorraine Artiste* 23 (1905): illus. p. 20; there also the title *Les Colchiques*. Probably the most common model in *marqueterie sur verre*. Correspondingly numerous parallels and variations.

Lit.: Hilschenz-Mlynek and Ricke, *Frankreich*, 1985, cat. no. 248

233 "Les Glyzines" Vase
Engraved mark on wall: *Gallé*
1898
H 48.9, ⌀ 15.9 cm

On thick-walled, colorless ground, flaky patination with small bubbles (brochage) under a
colorless cover layer. At base, yellow-brown
cased cup. Dark violet glass-powder inclusions pulled diagonally between the layers.
Mold-blown. Body conically flattened on both
sides; handles freely applied.
Decoration: stylized bough of wisteria in
marquetry technique, the petals and surrounding ground in intaglio. The bough is
repeated, accentuated only by two-colored
leaves, in mat engraving on the reverse,
where it is overlaid with the engraved
inscription: *Humblement la nature / épand
dans la poussière / sa chevelure / parfumée /
chaque âme / peut jeter / dans le monde /
quelque fleur / de beauté.* (Modestly nature /
scatters in the dust / its foliage / fragrant /
each soul / can cast / into the world / a
flower / of beauty.) Vessel surface partly
worked in *martelé* technique.
Cast and patinated bronze foot.

Acc. no. P 1975-87
Gift of Helmut Hentrich

Grand genre studio piece. Gallé copyrighted
the bronze base together with two others on
March 5, 1898; see also cat. no. 234. Model
with a handle variation designed for the
1898 Salon; see E. Gallé, "Mes envois au
Salon," *Revue des Arts Décoratifs* 18, no. 6
(1898): illus. p. 148. One example of this
version acquired by the Museum Bellerive,
Zurich, from Gallé in 1898; see Barten and
Hakenjos, *Gallé*, 1980, cat. no. 99. A similar
piece to the present one is in Abercron, sales
cat., 1973, cat. no. 144.

Lit.: Hilschenz-Mlynek and Ricke, *Frankreich*,
1985, cat. no. 249

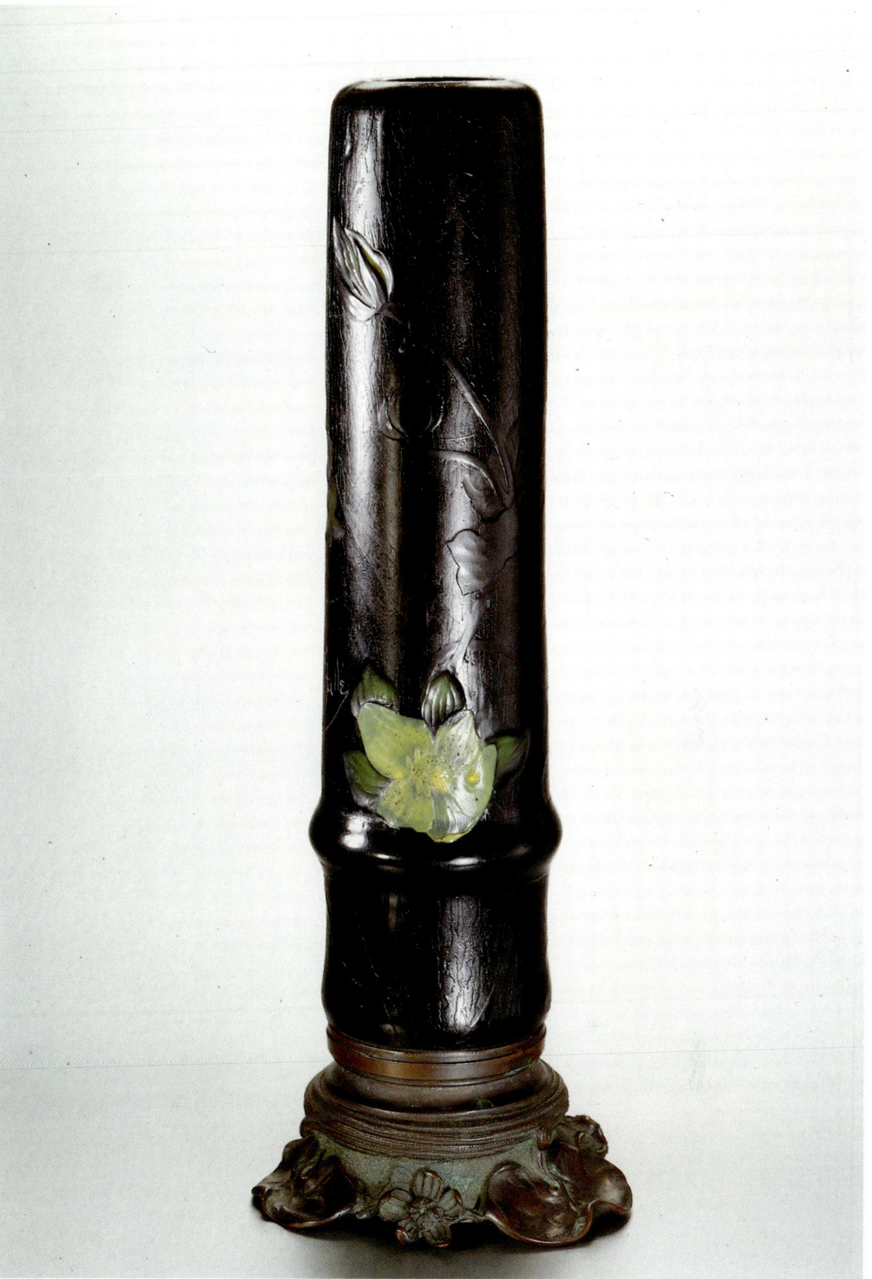

234 Vase

Engraved mark on wall, with remains of gild-
ing: *Emile Gallé* with the Cross of Lorraine
Ca. 1898
H 27.9, ⌀ without base 6.6 cm

On green-yellow ground, a thick-walled, colorless layer covered by a deep brown casing
appearing black; two applications. Surface
etched like tree bark. Mold-blown in the
shape of a bamboo stem section.
Decoration: inflorescence and leaves of a
dahlia, intaglio on the brown casing, surface
engraving on the flower-shaped applications.
Mounted on a cast and patinated bronze
base.

Acc. no. P 1970-462
Gift of Helmut Hentrich

Grand genre studio piece. Gallé copyrighted
the bronze base together with two others on
March 5, 1898; see also cat. no. 233. For an
almost identical piece see Bloch-Dermant,
French Glass, 1860–1914, 1980, illus. p. 108;
for another see Arwas, *Art Nouveau*, 1977,
illus. p. 93.

Lit.: Hilschenz-Mlynek and Ricke, *Frankreich*,
1985, cat. no. 250

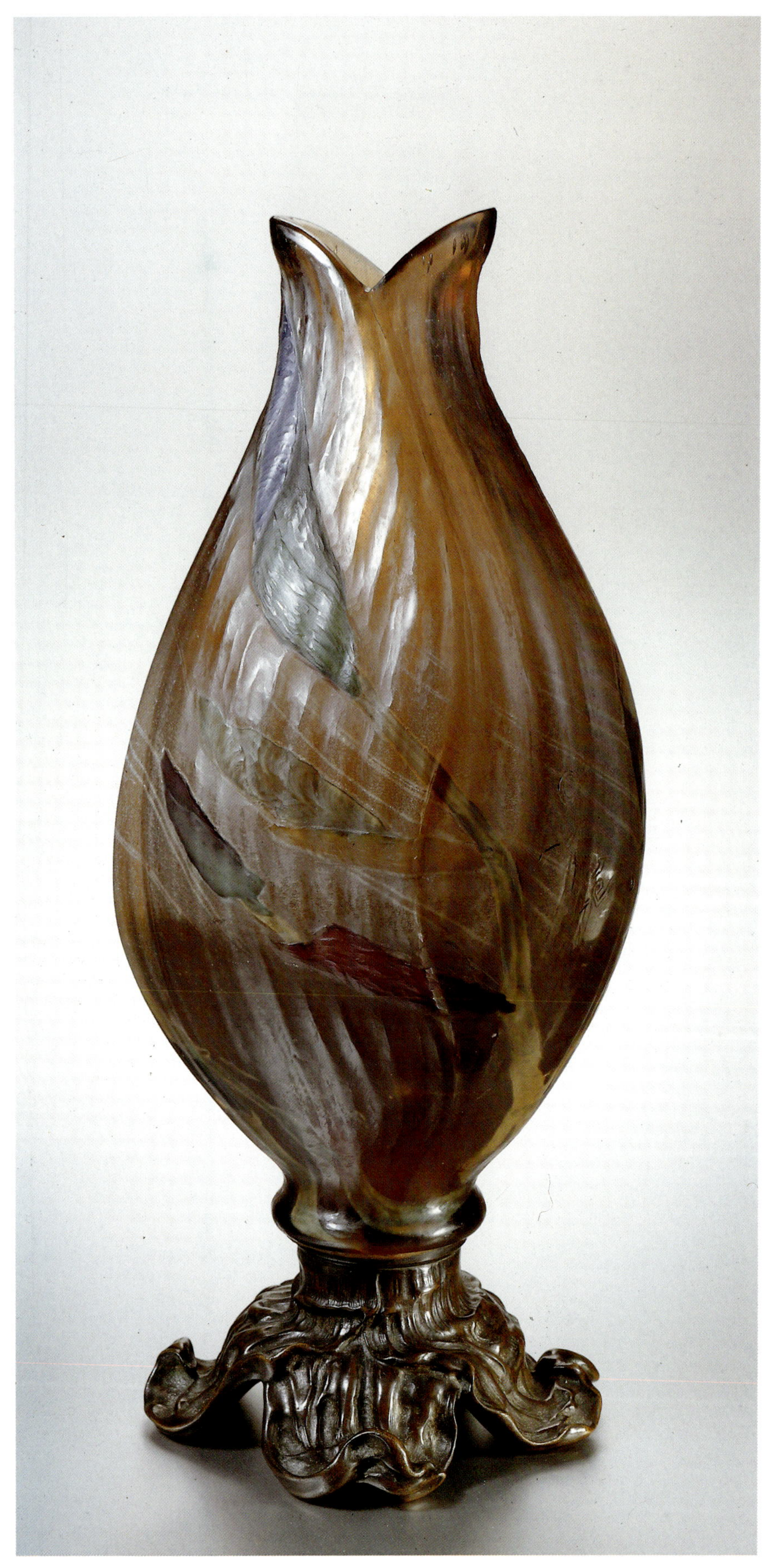

Engraved mark on wall and metal cut on the underside of the bronze foot: *Gallé*
Ca. 1898/99
H 34.7, ⌀ 15.5 cm

On thick-walled, smoky brown ground, pati-nation of small bubbles with stripes pulled diagonally; on top of that, more layers of the ground glass: in the lower zone, brown cased cup covering the patination. Mold-blown. Decoration: opening iris buds with stalks and leaves in marquetry technique, partly embed-ded in the wall, partly worked from outside; engraved. Curving flutes cut into the surface follow the shape of the body; in semimat polish.
Cast and patinated bronze base.

Acc. no. P 1970-206
Gift of Helmut Hentrich

Grand genre studio piece. Various versions made, some with a different base. At the 1900 World Exhibition in Paris, Gallé showed a variation designed for use as an electric lamp. See E. Nicolas, "M. Emile Gallé à l'Ex-position de 1900: La Verrerie," *La Lorraine Artiste* 19 (1901): 6, fig. 3. For a piece pro-duced in a similar technique and with similar decoration, but with a different base, at the Musée du Petit Palais in Paris, see Charpen-tier and Thiébaut, *Gallé*, 1985, cat. no. 117.

Lit.: Hilschenz-Mlynek and Ricke, *Frankreich*, 1985, cat. no. 261

**236 "Les Feuilles des Douleurs Passées"
Vase**

Engraved mark on wall: *Gallé*
1900
H 14.3, ⌀ 12.8 cm

On opaque gray-brown ground, thin, blue
partial flashing with silvery metal foil applications torn in many places owing to the
vessel being inflated; then a thick colorless
cover layer. Mold-blown.
Decoration: fragments of leaf-shaped colored
glass in yellow and brown tones worked into
the surface. Cracked patination in the upper
half, lower half frosted. The leaves painstakingly modeled in engraving. Engraved inscription below the mouth: *Les feuilles des*

douleurs passées / Maurice Maeterlink (The
leaves of past suffering).
On the inner edge of mouth, minor damage
smoothed by grinding.

Acc. no. P 1970-213
Gift of Helmut Hentrich

Grand genre studio piece. Gallé showed one
example of this model at the 1900 World
Exhibition in Paris, acquired by the Museum
für Kunst und Gewerbe in Hamburg. See J.
Brinckmann, *Die Ankäufe auf der Weltausstel-
lung Paris 1900* (Hamburg, 1901), 54ff. For
another example see Bloch-Dermant, *French
Glass, 1860–1914*, 1980, illus. p. 63. The
piece in the Hentrich Collection was presumably a copy made at the same time. Quota-

tions from the works of the Belgian poet
Maurice Maeterlinck (1862–1949), held in
high esteem by Gallé, are inscribed on various *verres parlants* by the artist.

Lit.: Charpentier and Thiébaut, *Gallé*, 1985,
cat. no. 127; Hilschenz-Mlynek and Ricke,
Frankreich, 1985, cat. no. 267; *L'Ecole
de Nancy*, 1999, cat. no. 113 and illus. on
p. 168

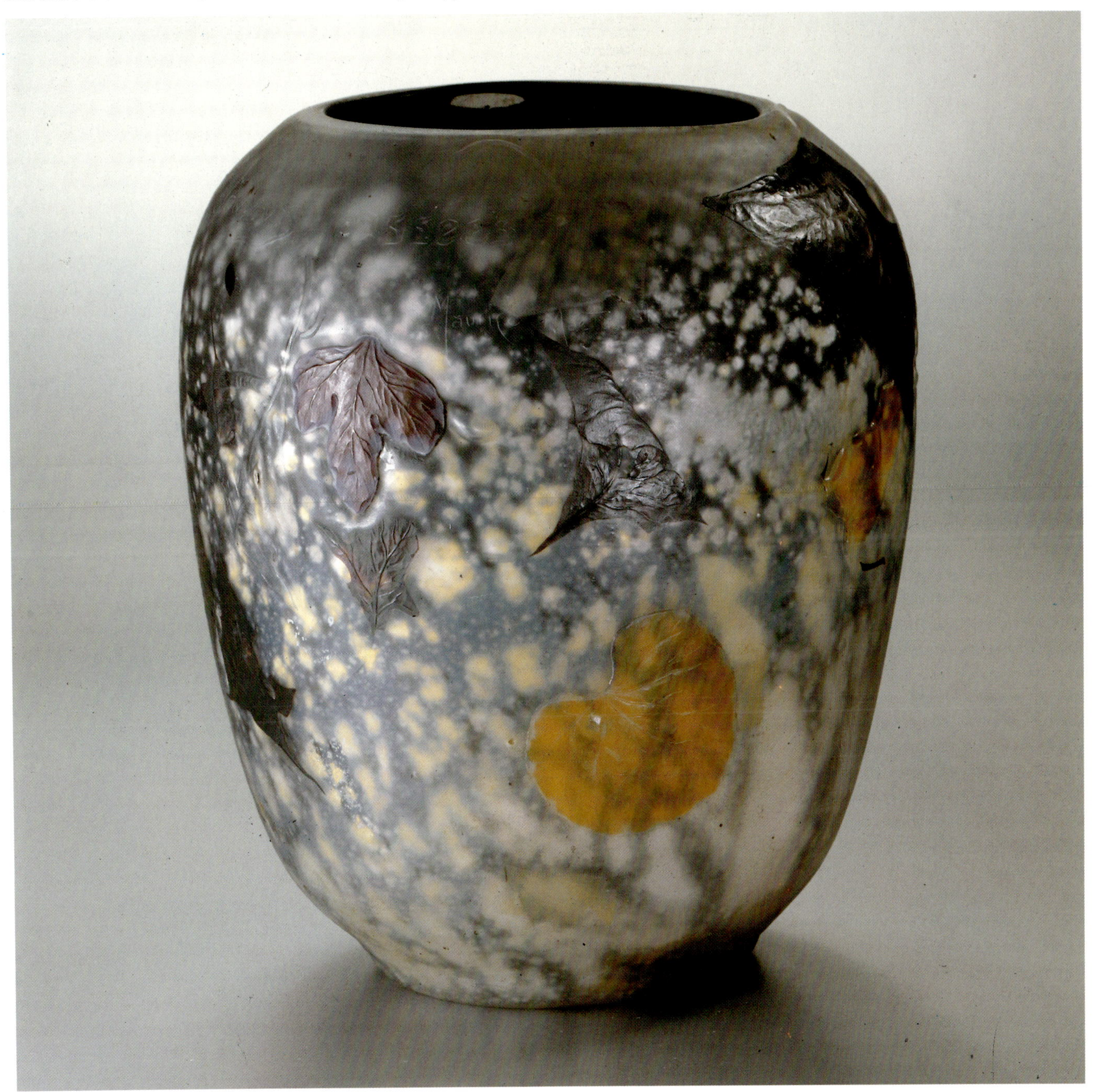

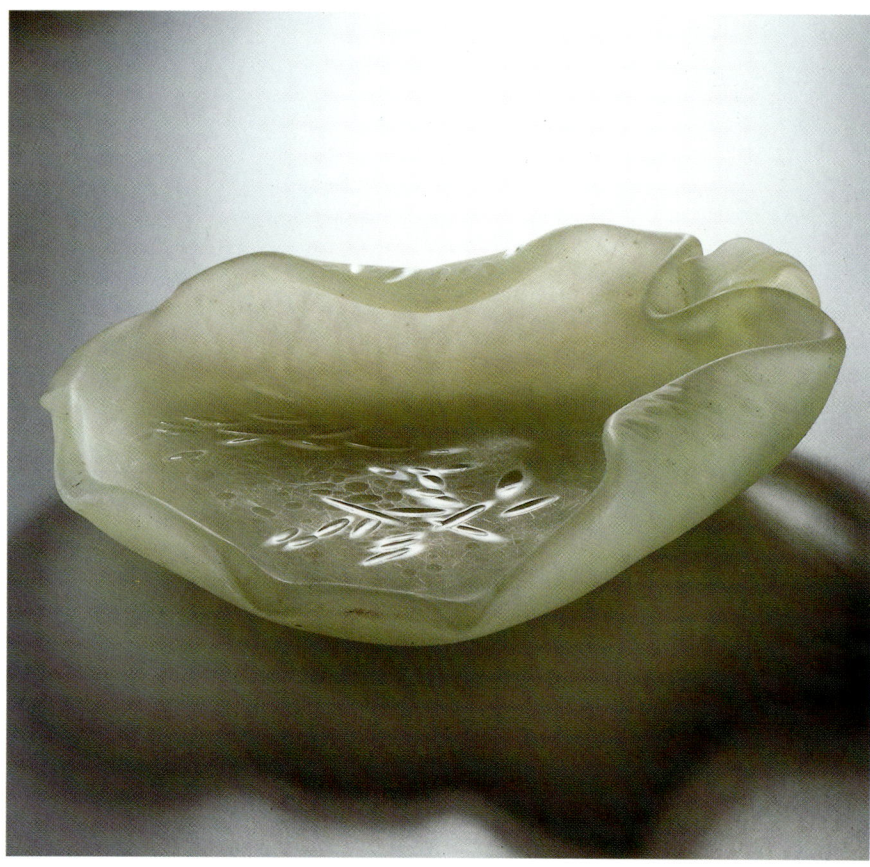

237 "Cristal Jade" Dish

Mark engraved on the outer edge of dish:
Gallé; engraved on the underside of base:
Cristal Jade Expos. 1900
1900
H 4.9, ⌀ 24.2 cm

Greenish glass with enclosed patination.
Freely shaped as leaf of a marsh marigold.
Decoration: deep cuts shaped like grains of
rice on the frosted surface; in part brightly
polished, in part left mat.

Acc. no. P 1970-210
Gift of Helmut Hentrich

Grand genre studio piece, designed for the
1900 World Exhibition in Paris. For glass imitations of semiprecious stones (from 1889)
see Gallé, *Ecrits*, 1908, 335ff., esp. 339f., on
jade imitations.

Lit.: Charpentier and Thiébaut, *Gallé*, 1985,
cat. no. 119; Hilschenz-Mlynek and Ricke,
Frankreich, 1985, cat. no. 275

238 Vase

Mark etched in relief on wall: *Gallé*
Ca. 1900
H 75.9, ⌀ 22.4 cm

Thick-walled, smoky brown ground with
opaque dark yellow overlay, in part covered
by rose. Mold-blown.
Decoration—boughs of wisteria—made in
two stages; partly mat, partly etched to a
bright polish.
One corner of mouth ground smooth after
having been slightly damaged.

Acc. no. P 1970-254
Gift of Helmut Hentrich

Demi riche studio piece. Gallé showed a large
vase having the same shape at the 1900
World Exhibition in Paris; see *Revue des Arts
Décoratifs* 21, no. 1 (1901): frontispiece. Several variations exist.

Lit.: Hilschenz-Mlynek and Ricke, *Frankreich*,
1985, cat. no. 286

239 Vase

Engraved mark on wall: *Gallé*
Ca. 1900
H 50.3, ⌀ 11.7 cm

On thick-walled, colorless ground, small-par-
ticled, silvery, metal-foil application; then a
thin yellow-green flashing and thick violet
casing. Mold-blown.
Decoration—clusters of wild oat and butterflies—etched and modeled on the entire surface in relief cut and intaglio. Background
partly in *martelé* technique. Surface semimat,
parts of the decoration brightly polished.
Above the standing base, minor damage has
been smoothed by grinding.

Acc. no. P 1976-59
Gift of Helmut Hentrich

Grand genre studio piece. Probably belongs to
a series of glass pieces on the theme of
grains made for the 1900 World Exhibition in
Paris, where the Museum für Kunst und
Gewerbe in Hamburg acquired a small vase
with a similar shape and decorated with oats.

Lit.: Hilschenz-Mlynek and Ricke, *Frankreich*,
1985, cat. no. 277

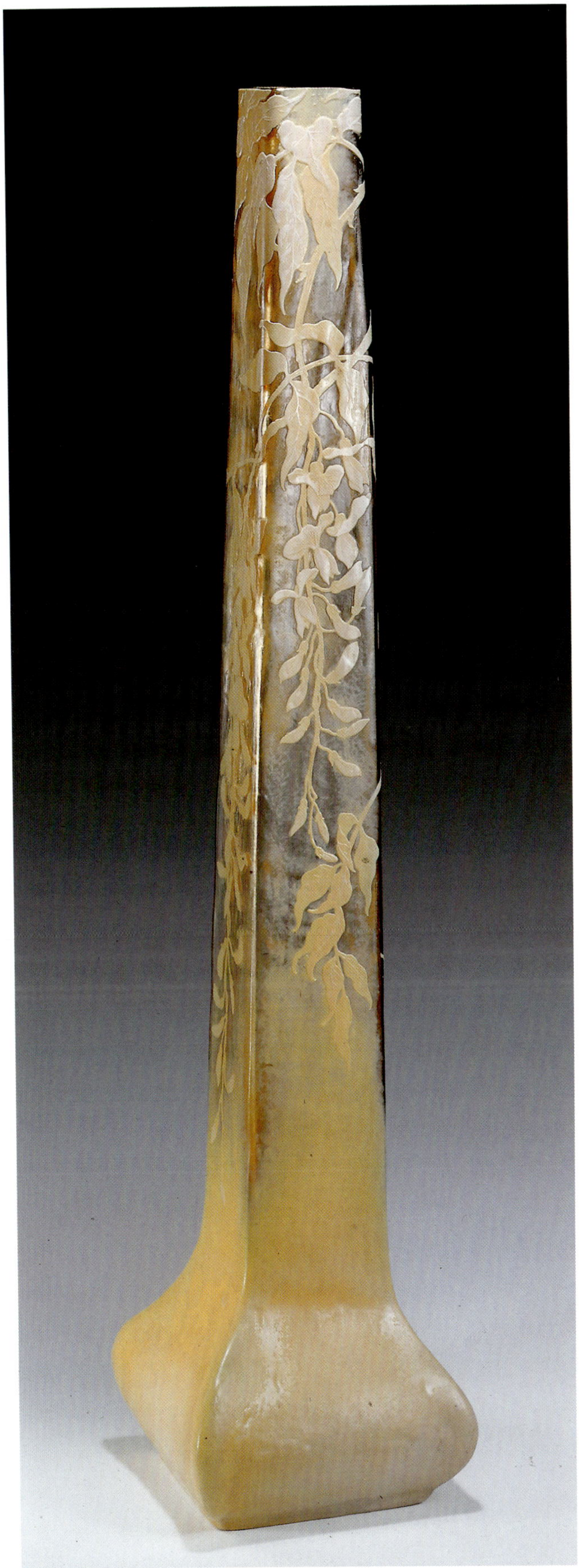

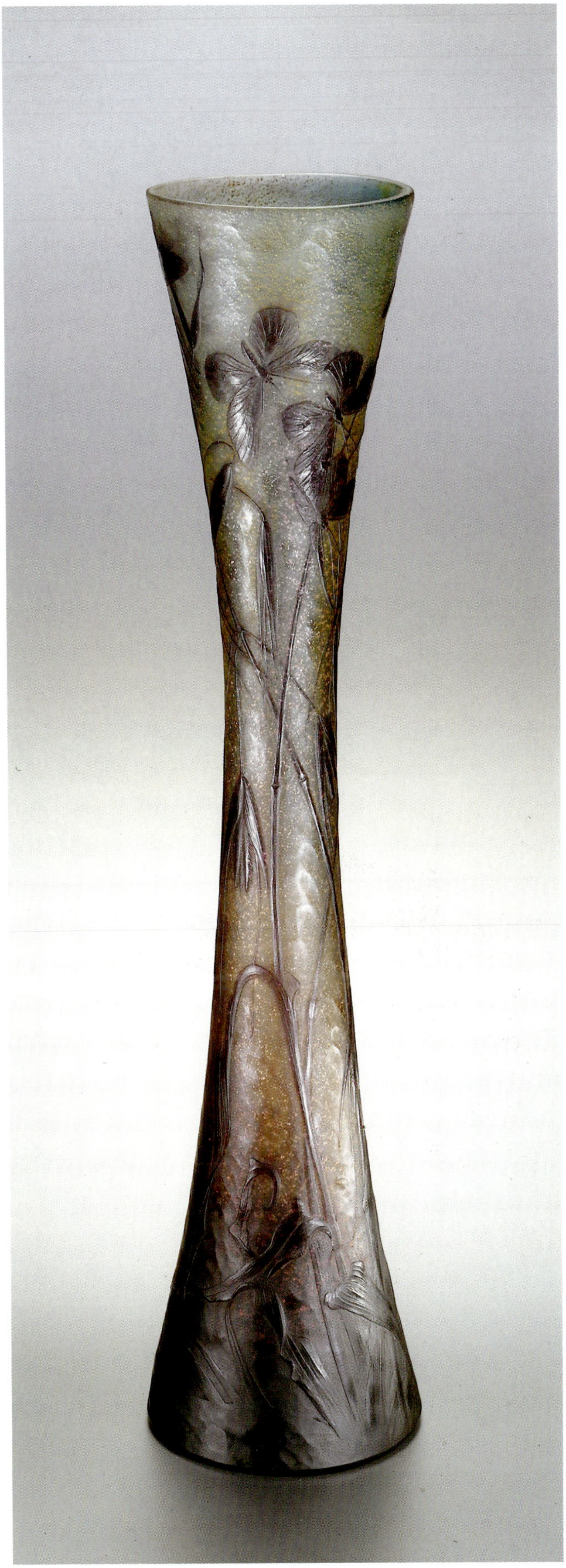

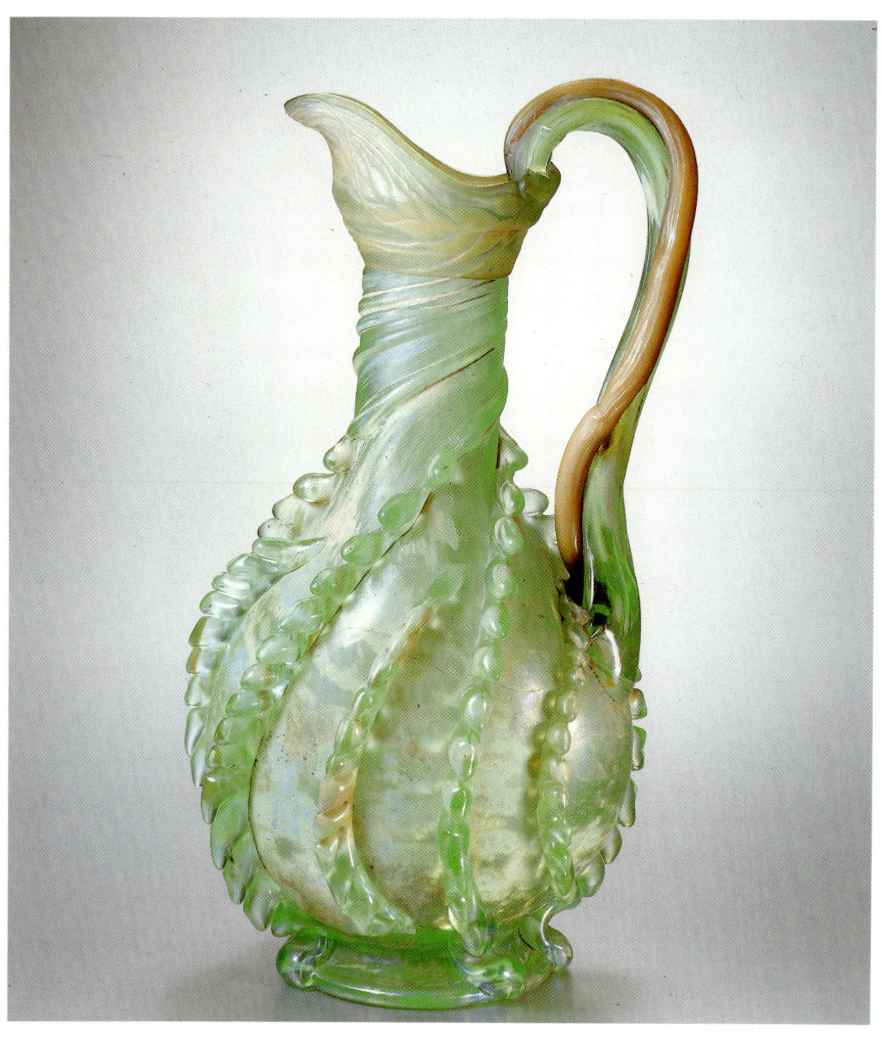

240 "L'Orge" Pitcher

Engraved mark underneath handle: *Gallé*
1900–1903
H 29.7, ⌀ 15.9 cm

Mold-blown and shaped; oval cross section. Applications run diagonally, cut with glass-maker's shears. Surface decorated with a slightly iridescent, spotted patination. The separately worked and applied pouring lip is colorless with a yellow-brown overlay. Handle freely applied.
Decoration: lip with engraved corn motif. The yellow-brown shoot running along the handle also engraved.
Strain cracks in the wall and at the base of the handle.

Acc. no. P 1976-78
Gift of Helmut Hentrich

Grand genre studio piece. The vessel symbolizes the germinating and fruit-bearing nature of grain. Gallé had shown glassware on the theme of bread grains at the 1900 World Exhibition in Paris; cf. cat. no. 239. See also a corn detail for furniture handles, copyrighted on April 8, 1899 (Sotheby Monaco, 1982, cat. no. 49, illus. p. 62). The piece from the Hentrich Collection was shown at the large survey exhibition "L'Orge broc nacré" of the Ecole de Nancy at the Louvre's Pavillon de Marsan (today Musée des Arts Decoratifs) in 1903. For an almost identical piece see Bloch-Dermant, *French Glass, 1860–1914*, 1980, illus. p. 89. Works of this type allude to Roman vessels. The particular type of patination also makes reference to these.

Lit.: Hilschenz-Mlynek and Ricke, *Frankreich*, 1985, cat. no. 279

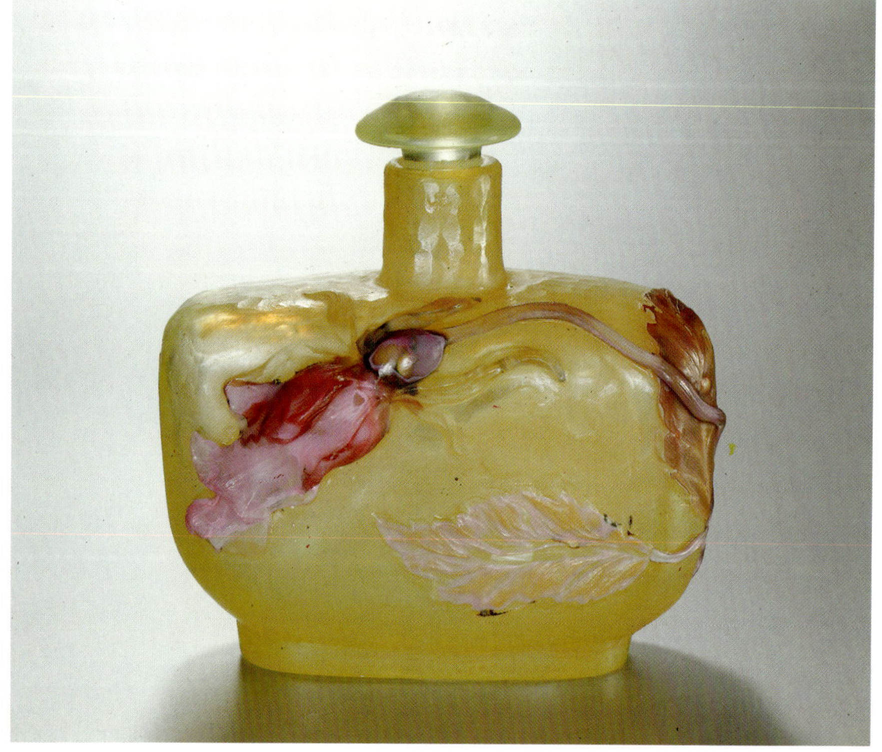

241 "Bouton de Rose" Flacon

Engraved mark on wall: *Gallé*
1902
H without stopper 9.8, ⌀ 11.2 cm

On thick-walled, colorless ground, thin milky yellow-green flashing. Mold-blown; rectangular cross section with rounded corners.
Decoration: applied rose bough with leaves and stalk. Surface relief engraved. Stylized treescape as background in relief carving; the transparent ground laid bare at some points. Vessel shoulder in *martelé* technique. Entire surface in semimat polish.
The original stopper was lost and replaced with a copy.

Acc. no. P 1970-214
Gift of Helmut Hentrich

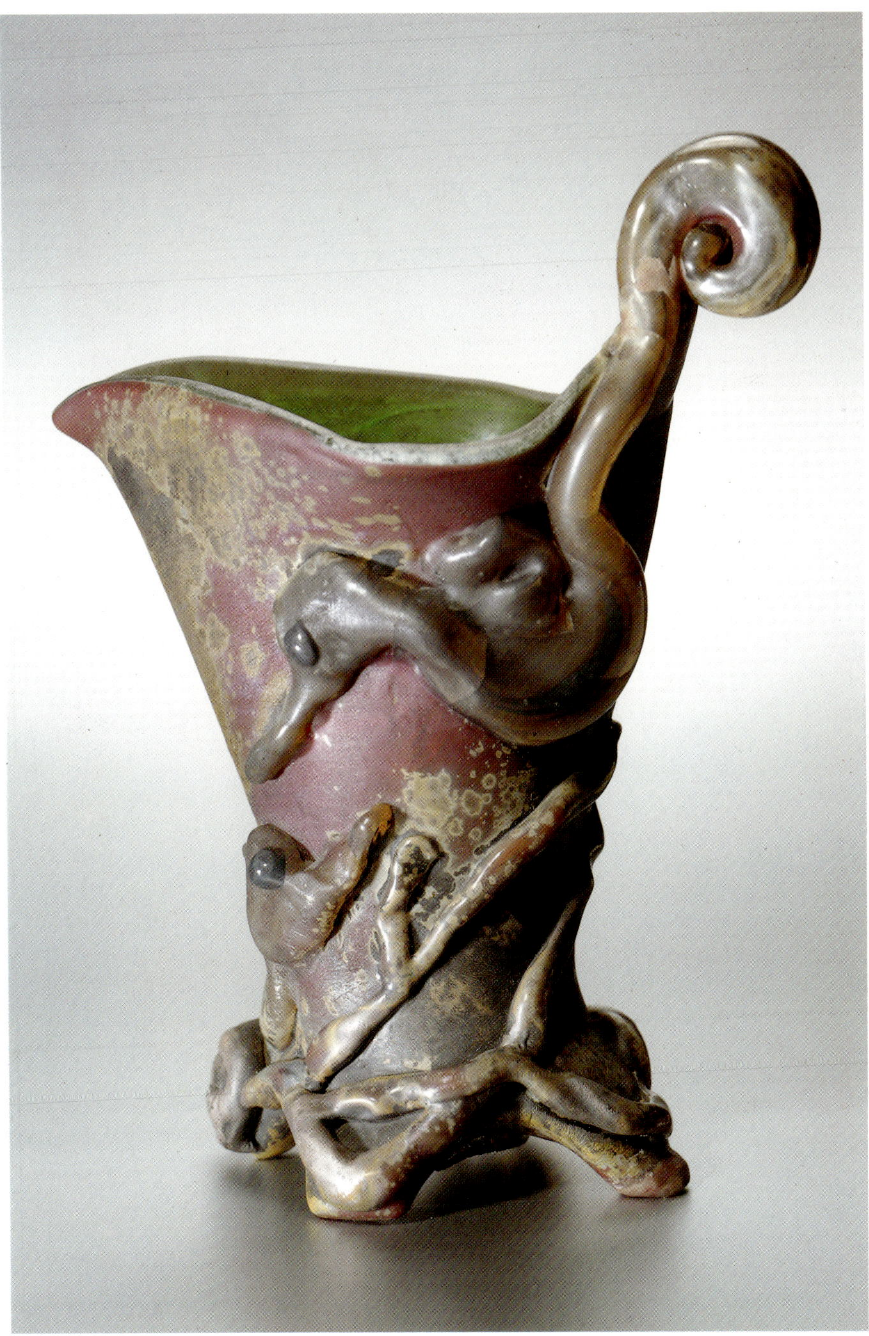

Grand genre studio piece. The model is very likely identical with the *Bouton de Rose: Flacon de senteur*, cat. no. 109.3, shown at the Salon in 1902. It belongs to a group of glassware described even in its own day as *verres sculptés*. For nearly identical examples of the flacon see Garner, *Gallé*, 1976, illus. p. 26 (with original stopper); auctioned at Christie's Geneva, May 1983, cat. no. 334 (with silver mounting). Gallé conceived the flacon shape in the late 1880s.

Lit.: Hilschenz-Mlynek and Ricke, *Frankreich*, 1985, cat. no. 306

242　"Hypocampes" Decorative Pitcher

Engraved mark on wall: *Gallé Etude*
Ca. 1901
H 18.7,　⌀ 15 cm

Thick-walled green ground. Free-blown and shaped; no other cold decorative techniques. Applied decoration—two sea horses and branches of coral—in gray-brown. Surface overlaid with irregular brown-red and metallic gray patination, partly extending into the vessel's interior.
Strain cracks in the sea-horse bodies and in the handle.

Acc. no. P 1988-64
Gift of Helmut Hentrich

Grand genre studio piece. Gallé conceived the model for engraved decoration; compare the dated piece at the Musée des Arts Décoratifs, Paris, acc. no. 24 556; illus. in Barten and Hakenjos, *Gallé*, 1980, cat. no. 137. Additional decoration was not carried out, however, owing to the frequently occurring strain problems. Numerous similar shapes and variations are known to exist; see Charpentier and Thiébaut, *Gallé*, 1985, cat. no. 133.

Lit.: Hilschenz-Mlynek and Ricke, *Frankreich*, 1985, cat. no. 308

243 Vase

Engraved mark on wall: *Gallé* with star
Ca. 1904–06
H 17.3, ⌀ 12.2 cm

Overlay glass in green and blue, with oxide
and glass-powder inclusions between the layers as well as occasional oxides baked into
the surface. Mold-blown; shaped into a trefoil
cross section.
Decoration: flowers and buds of the fringed
gentian in intaglio.

Acc. no. P 1979-24
Gift of Helmut Hentrich

Studio piece. An almost identical work is at
the Corning Museum of Glass, acc. no.
54.3.38; for another, at the Musée des Art
Décoratifs in Paris, see Charpentier and
Thiébaut, *Gallé*, 1985, cat. no. 133.

Lit.: Hilschenz-Mlynek and Ricke, *Frankreich*,
1985, cat. no. 338

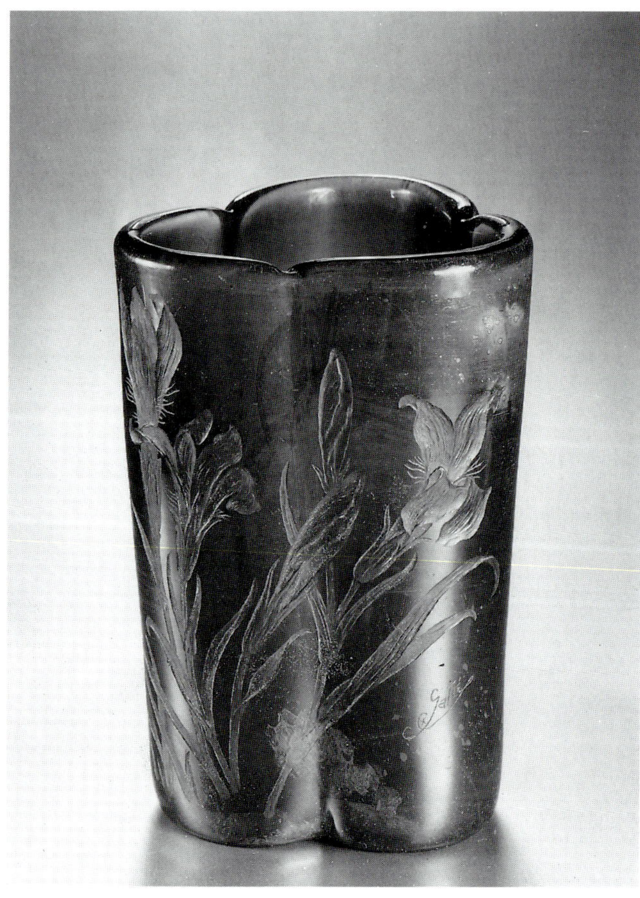

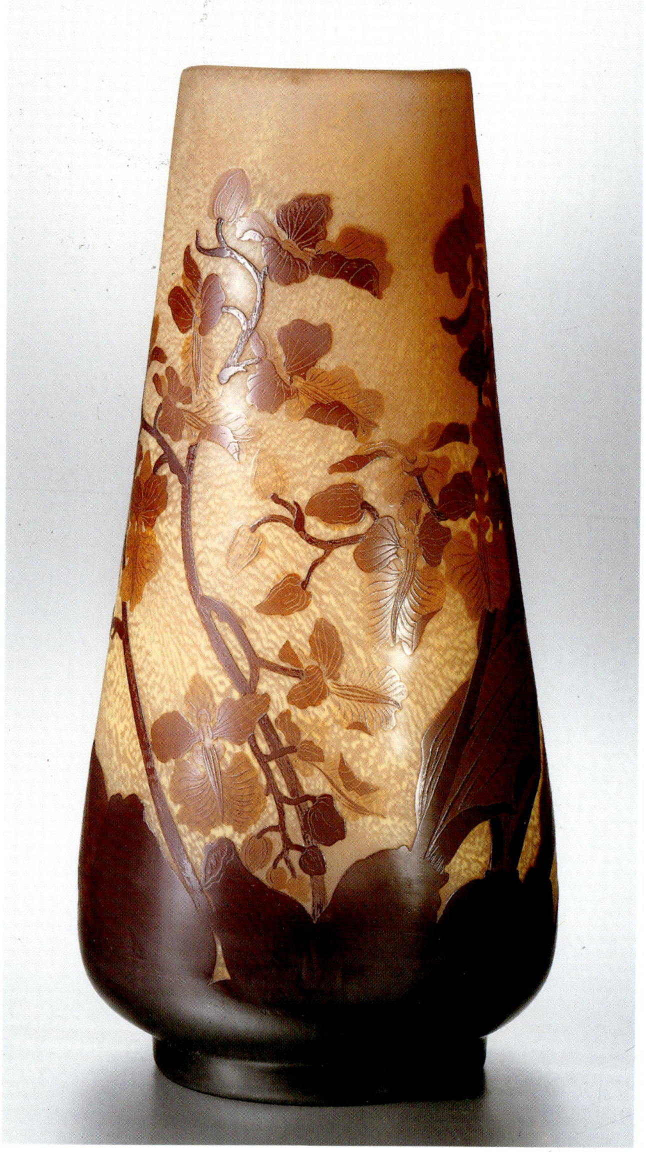

244 Vase

Mark in relief etching on wall: *Gallé*
1906–14
H 33.4, ⌀ 16.4 cm

On colorless ground, brown-rose overlay with
embedded, fine yellow glass powder. Dark
brown cover layer. Mold-blown; oval cross
section, mouth pulled slightly to the side
against the horizontal axis.
Decoration—clusters of flowering and bud-
ding orchids—etched in two stages. Interior
vessel surface acid polished, exterior ground
mat; decoration partly mat, partly polished.

Acc. no. P 1970-256
Gift of Helmut Hentrich

Studio piece or series ware. Several variations
are documented.

Lit.: Hilschenz-Mlynek and Ricke, *Frankreich*,
1985, cat. no. 351

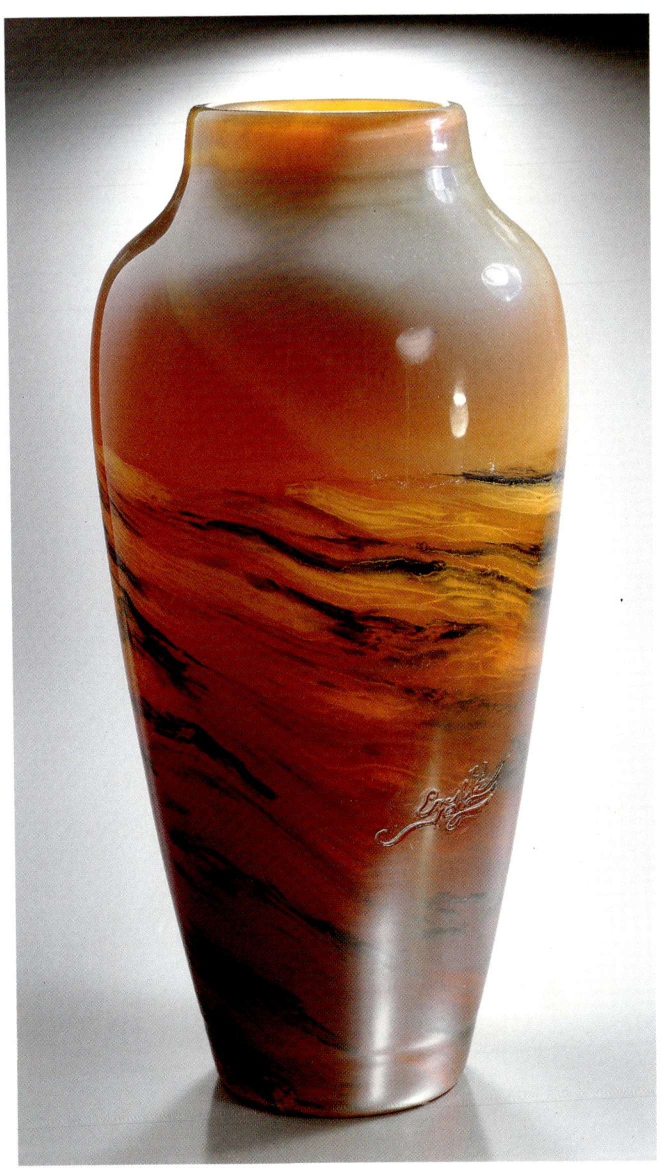

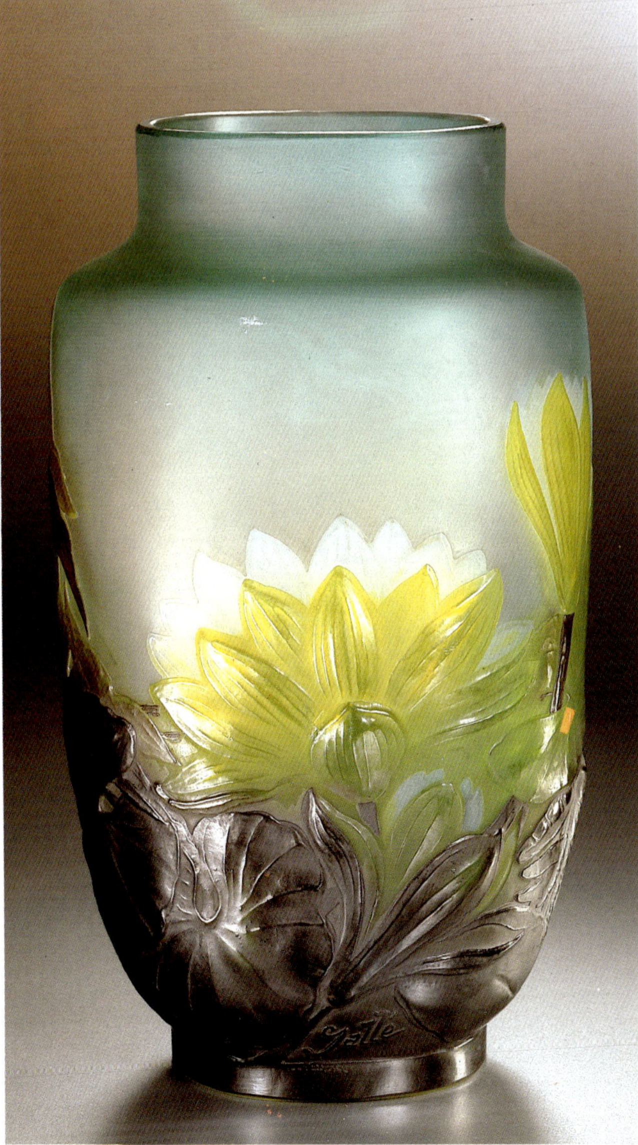

245 Vase

Deeply etched mark on wall: *Gallé*
1920s
H 36.8, ⌀ 18.2 cm

On thin brown-yellow ground partly overlaid
with yellow-white, several layers of colorless
glass. Mold-blown; made entirely at the furnace.
Vessel interior frosted.

Acc. no. P 1976-69
Gift of Helmut Hentrich

Series ware. Part of a large group produced by
the factory, this piece's appeal lies in the
colored marbled glass and in the fact that no
cold decorative techniques were used to
make it.

Lit.: Hilschenz-Mlynek and Ricke, *Frankreich*,
1985, cat. no. 371

246 Vase

Mark in relief etching on wall: *Gallé*
Ca. 1925–30
H 25.8, ⌀ 15.3 cm

On thick-walled, colorless ground, thin layers
of flashing in sea green, light green, and
dark brown. Mold-blown.
Decoration: water lilies and arrowhead floating on the surface of a pond. Etched in several stages. Surface alternatingly mat and
polished.

Acc. no. P 1984-52
Gift of Helmut Hentrich

High-quality series ware. A reaction of the
Gallé manufactory to the popular pressed
glassware models by René Lalique and others.

Lit.: Hilschenz-Mlynek and Ricke, *Frankreich*,
1985, cat. no. 379; Ricke, *2500 Jahre*, 1987,
cat. no. 168

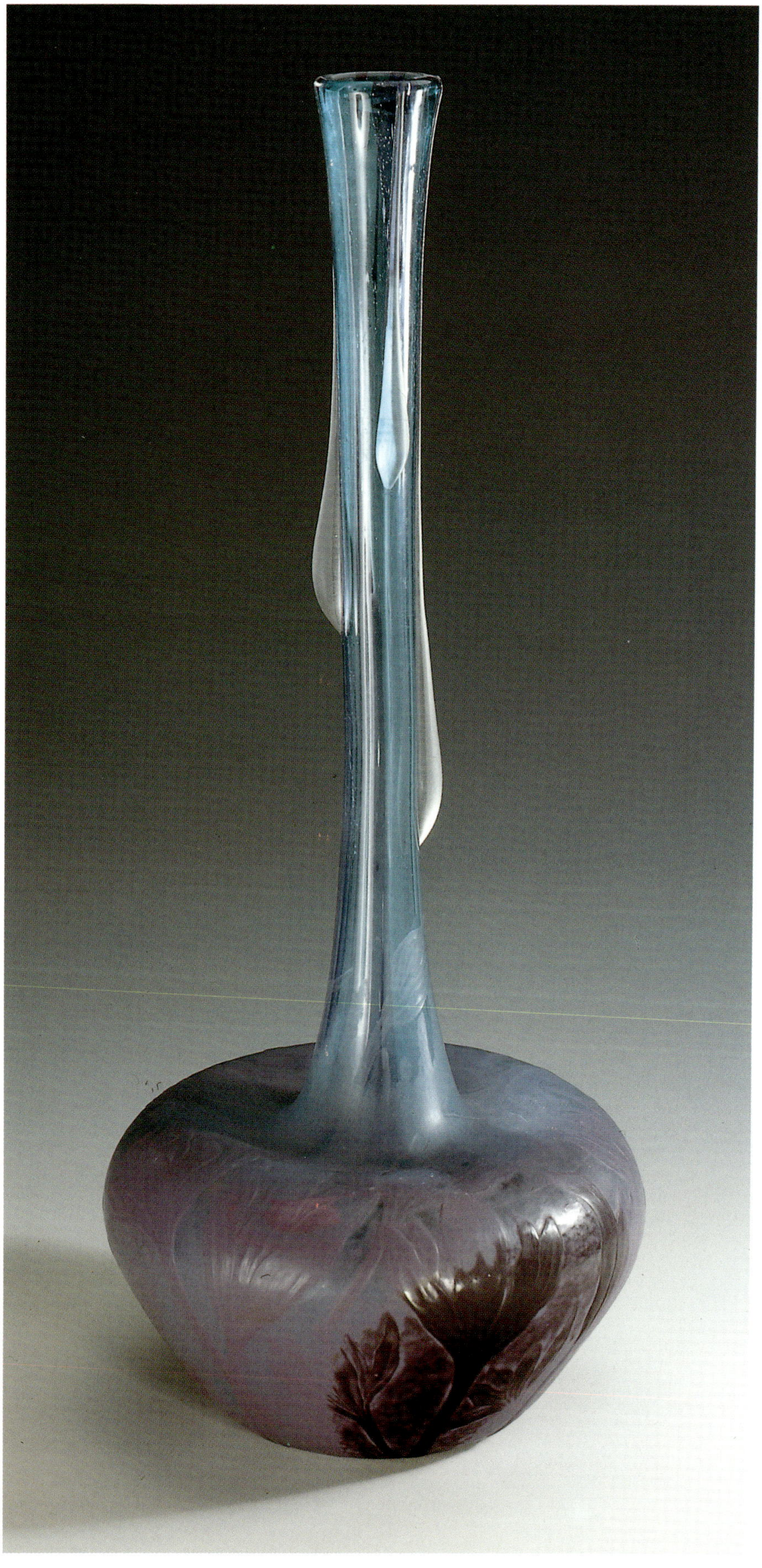

Daum Frères
Verrerie de Nancy

Glasshouse for flat and hollow glassware, decorating workshops for ornamental and utilitarian glass as well as lighting products and window glazing

Founded in 1873 by Jean Daum (1825–1885), at first for producing utilitarian ware. In 1885, his son, the jurist Jean-Louis-Auguste Daum (1853–1909), and in 1887 his youngest son, the engineer and artist Jean-Antonin Daum (1864–1930), took over the direction. Inspired by Emile Gallé's successes at the 1889 World Exhibition in Paris, the firm shifted its emphasis to the production of art glass. In 1893, first international success with glass at the World Exhibition in Chicago. At the 1900 World Exhibition in Paris, the company received international recognition with overlay objects in the Art-Nouveau style.

247 "Colchiques d'Automne" Vase

Gilded engraved mark on the underside of base: *DAUM NANCY* with Cross of Lorraine
1893
H 52, ⌀ 21,8 cm

Overlay glass with threads and pieces of broken glass embedded between the layers; mold-blown. Three colorless glass teardrops in the round, freely applied.
Decoration: meadow saffron flowers in relief engraving on ground worked in the *martelé* technique; on the shoulder, flowers in intaglio.

Acc. no. P 1975-41
Gift of Olga van Meeteren

Small series. First shown in 1893 at the Musée du Luxembourg, Paris. For a nearly identical piece, at the Brussels exhibition in 1897, see Daum Frères & Cie.'s exh. cat., *Verreries Artistiques de Nancy: Exposition de*

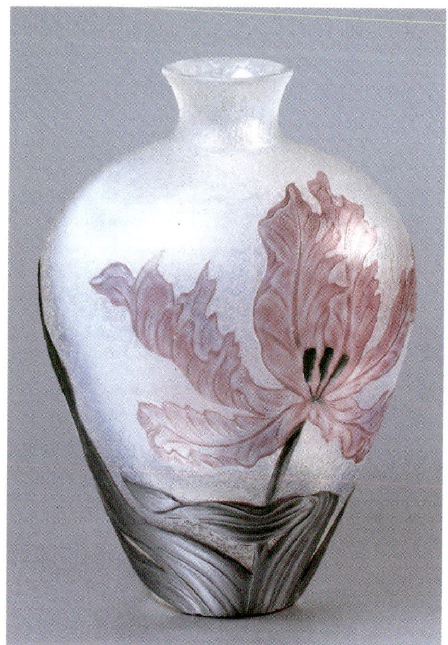

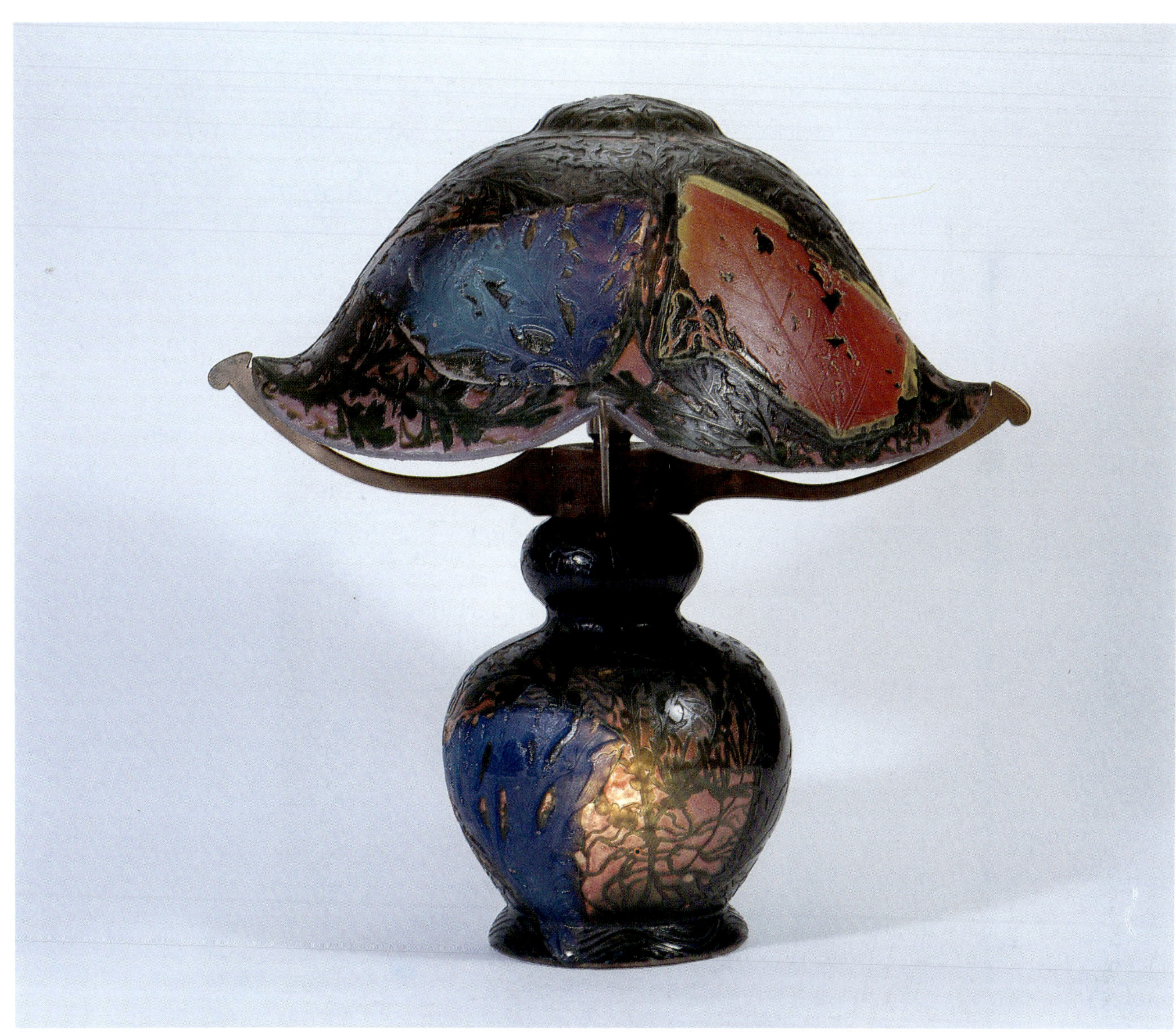

Bruxelles 1897, cat. no. 14, "Colchiques d'automne, vase à larmes," with illus.

Lit.: Hilschenz-Mlynek and Ricke, *Frankreich*, 1985, cat. no. 43

◁ **248   "Tulipe Perroquet" Vase**

Engraved mark on the underside of base: *DAUM NANCY* with Cross of Lorraine
1898
H 17.5, ⌀ 12.6 cm

Overlay glass on opalescent ground. Mold-blown.
Decoration: two red "parrot" tulips with dark green foliage in relief etching and relief carving on light, coarsely etched ground.
Slightly damaged at edge of standing base.

Acc. no. P 1979-32
Gift of Helmut Hentrich

Series ware. Model no. 1318. For a watercolor drawing of the model in Nancy see Daum Collection in Bloch-Dermant, *French Glass, 1860–1914*, 1980, illus. p. 151. A parallel is illustrated in Daum, *Mastery*, 1985, illus. p. 46. For the decoration see the preliminary sketch of 1898, ibid., illus. p. 48.

Lit.: Hilschenz-Mlynek and Ricke, *Frankreich*, 1985, cat. no. 42

△ **249   Lamp**

Engraved mark on the inside of foot: *Daum Nancy* with Cross of Lorraine
1902/03
H (with shade) 36, ⌀ 32 cm

Overlay glass with several partial applications in various colors. Foot mold-blown; shade mold-blown and shaped, pincered at four points.

Decoration: densely entwined sea plants with dark green berries and interspersed areas of blue, yellow-red, light blue, and rose on coarsely etched ground; mat and clear relief etching, in part also needle etching.
With mounting for electrical fitting. Foot and shade can be illuminated. Shade on copper mounting.

Acc. no. P 1981-423
Gift of Helmut Hentrich

Presumably a unique piece. For lamps by the Daum company see esp. W. Uecker, *Lampen und Leuchter: Art nouveau—art déco* (Herrsching am Ammersee, 1978), 67ff., and A. Duncan, *Art Nouveau and Art Deco Lighting* (London, 1978), 208.

Lit.: Hilschenz-Mlynek and Ricke, *Frankreich*, 1985, cat. no. 56

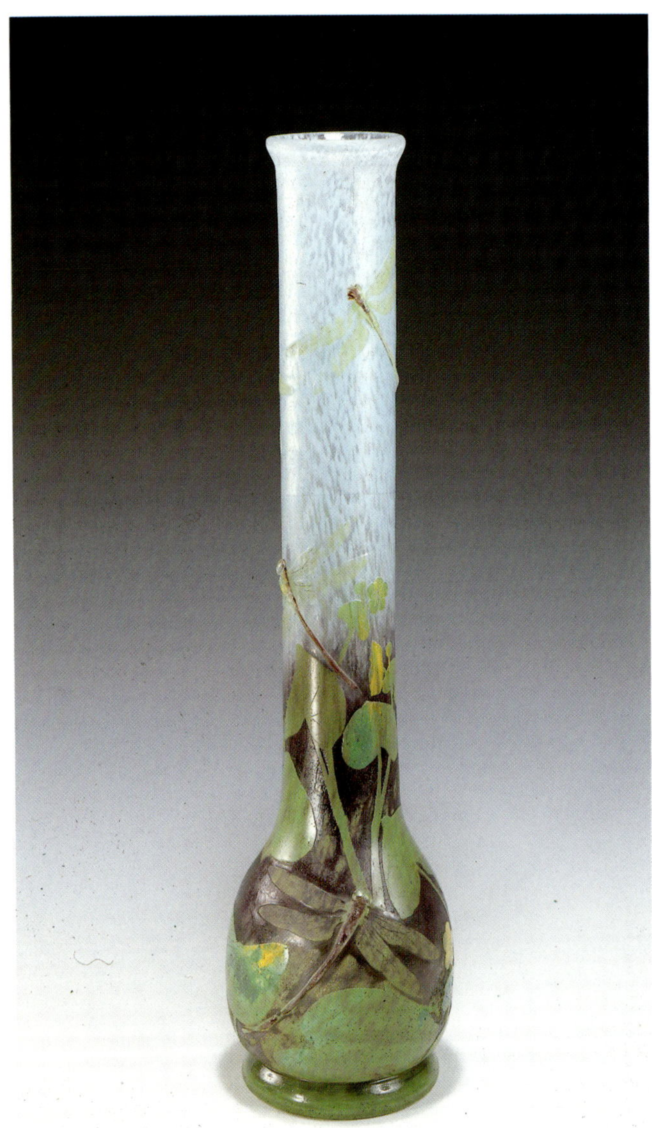

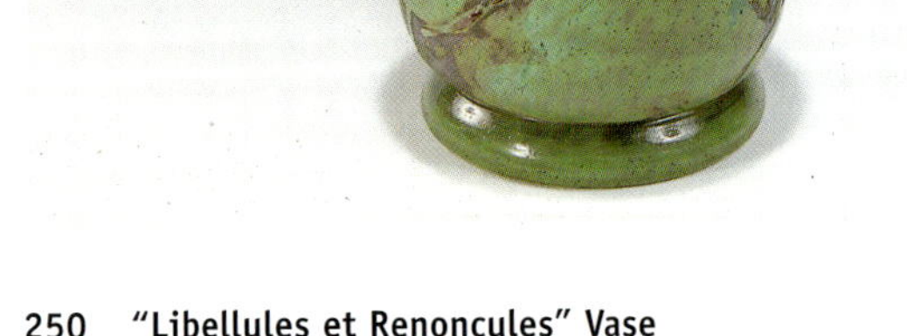

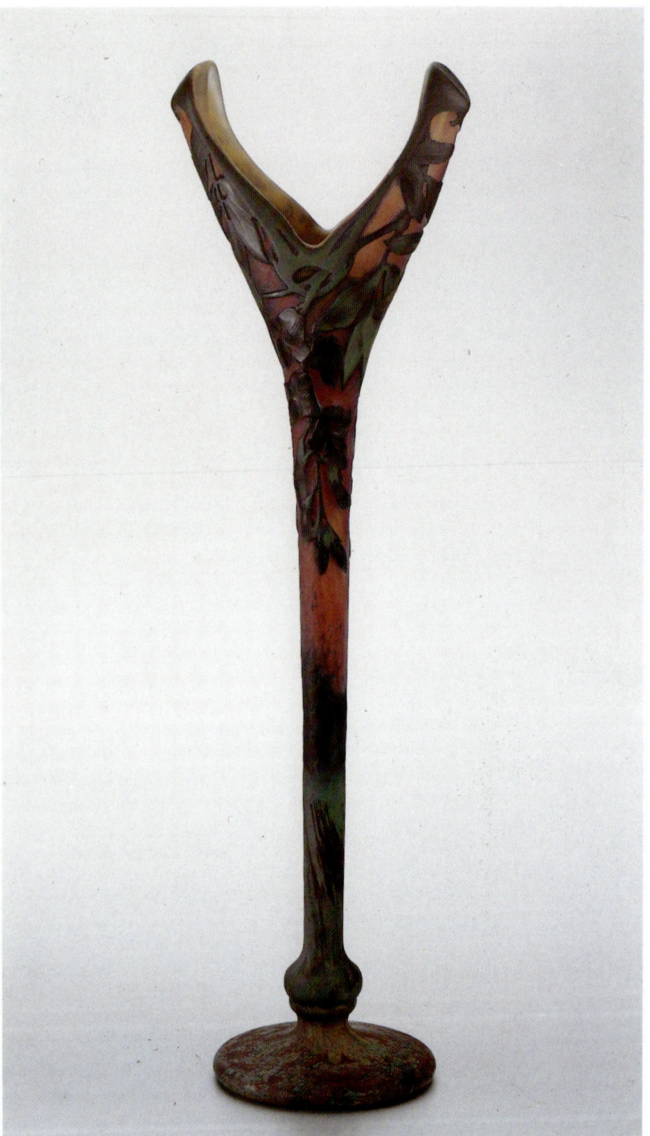

250 "Libellules et Renoncules" Vase

Engraved mark on the underside of foot: *DAUM NANCY* with Cross of Lorraine
1904
H 60.5, ⌀ 15.4 cm

Colorless glass with several overlays; between the layers and on the surface, colored glass powder. Decoration: on etched, mat ground, water plants in an opaque light green as flat relief with needle etched detailing; four three-dimensional dragon-flies in light green underlaid with red, etched and engraved; the recessed veins of the wings rubbed out darkly.

Acc. no. P 1970-117
Gift of Helmut Hentrich

High-quality series ware. Model no. 2400. For variations with the same decoration see *Art et Décoration* 7 (1905): illus. preceding p. 97.

Lit.: Hilschenz-Mlynek and Ricke, *Frankreich*, 1985, cat. no. 69

251 "Cythise" Vase

Engraved mark on foot plate: *DAUM NANCY* with Cross of Lorraine
Ca. 1913
H 39.2, ⌀ 12.1 cm

Colorless glass with several overlays. Between the layers and on the surface, colored glass powder; at the bottom spotted brown-green, pulled into stripes towards the top. Mold-blown and shaped. Decoration: entwined green boughs with dark blue flowers in relief etching and engraving on yellow-red, transparent ground.

Acc. no. P 1982-48
Gift of Helmut Hentrich

High-quality series ware.

Lit.: Hilschenz-Mlynek and Ricke, *Frankreich*, 1985, cat. no. 70

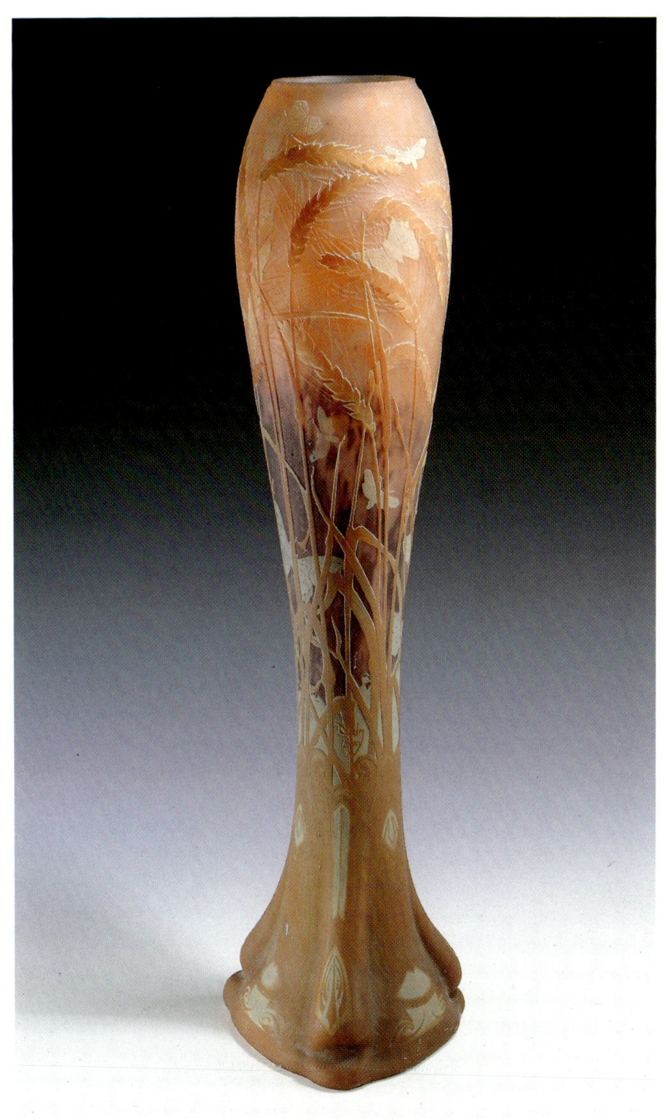

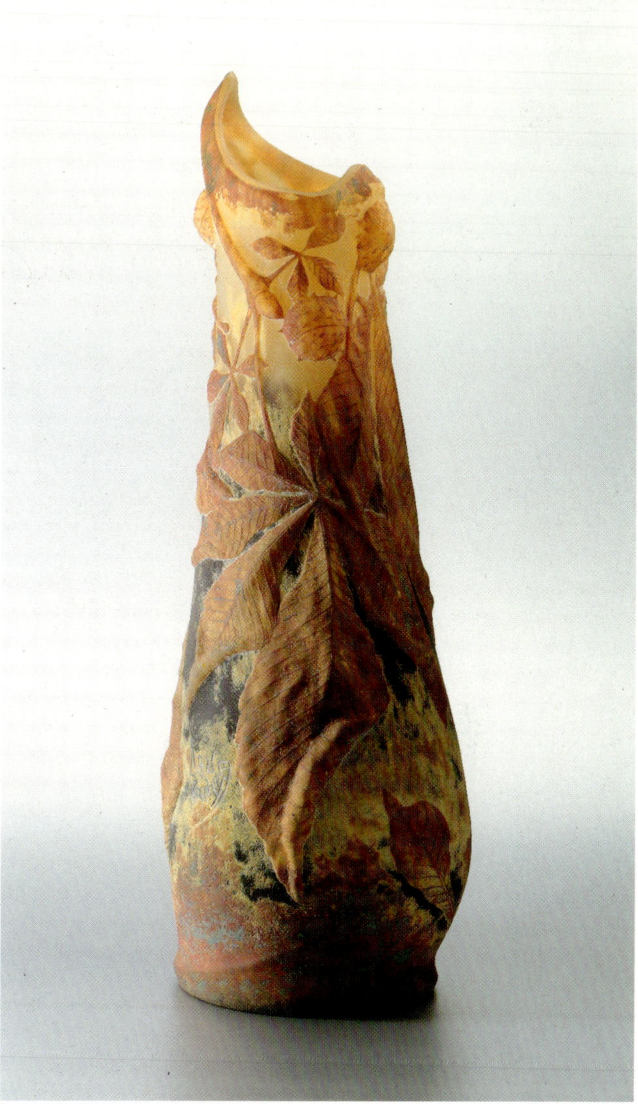

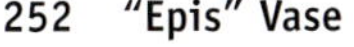

252 "Epis" Vase

Mark in relief etching on wall: *DAUM NANCY* with
Cross of Lorraine
Ca. 1905/06
H 60, ⌀ 15.2 cm

Colorless glass with multicolored, spotty powder
inclusions and opaque whitish-green and brown
overlays. Mold-blown.
Decoration: stylized ornaments and encircling
ears of corn with light green butterflies on mat
ground; interior detailing partly needle-etched.

Acc. no. P 1970-127
Gift of Helmut Hentrich

High-quality series ware.

Lit.: Hilschenz-Mlynek and Ricke, *Frankreich*,
1985, cat. no. 73

253 "Marronier" Vase

Engraved mark on wall: *DAUM NANCY* with Cross
of Lorraine
1908
H 42, ⌀ 14.4 cm

Overlay glass with multicolored embedded and
applied glass powder. Mold-blown; shaped.
Decoration on spotted ground with mat to porous
surface: three-dimensionally formed branches and
fruits of the chestnut consisting of an opaque
yellow-brownish spotty layer of powder. Surface
and interior details of the decoration frosted.

Acc. no. P 1980-94
Gift of Helmut Hentrich

Part of a large series. Model no. 3132. For a piece
blown into the same mold see Daum, *Mastery*,
1985, illus. p. 63.

Lit.: Hilschenz-Mlynek and Ricke, *Frankreich*,
1985, cat. no. 84

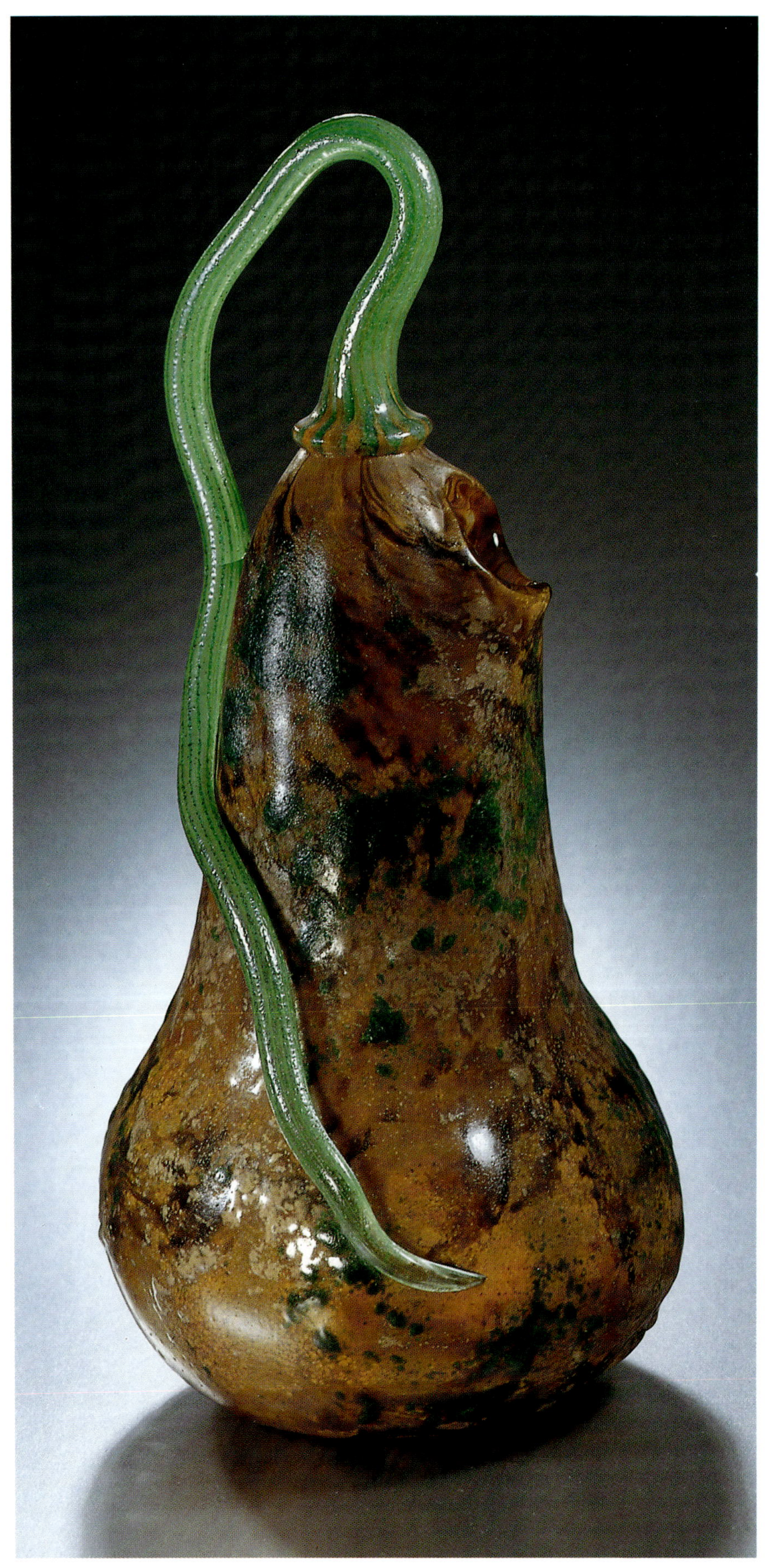

254   Decorative Vessel

Engraved mark on wall: *DAUM NANCY* with
Cross of Lorraine
Ca. 1909
H 27.5, ⌀ 13.3 cm

Overlay glass with applied, multicolored glass
powder. Free-blown and shaped into a gourd.
Vine freely applied.

Acc. no. P 1975-55
Gift of Helmut Hentrich

Small series. Several similar examples, each
slightly different, are held in public and private collections.

Lit.: Hilschenz-Mlynek and Ricke, *Frankreich*,
1985, cat. no. 87

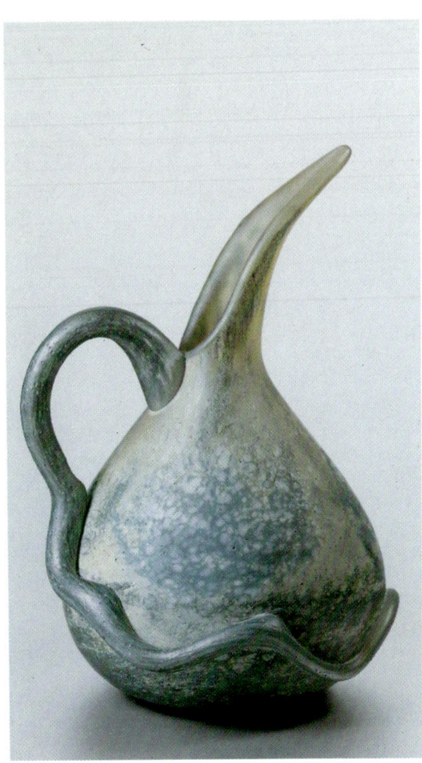

255 Pitcher

Engraved mark on wall: *DAUM NANCY* with Cross of Lorraine
Ca. 1906–13
H 19, ⌀ 12.2 cm

Colorless glass with applied, multicolored glass powder. Mold-blown. Handle freely applied. Surface frosted.

Acc. no. P 1970-142
Gift of Helmut Hentrich

Simple series ware.

Lit.: Hilschenz-Mlynek and Ricke, *Frankreich*, 1985, cat. no. 101

256 "Tabac Rouge" Vase

Engraved mark on wall: *DAUM NANCY* with Cross of Lorraine; and on foot: *253*
1912
H 58, ⌀ 13.3 cm

Colorless glass, with reddish and brown overlays on the exterior, enclosing yellow glass powder. Mold-blown.
Decoration: flowers and grasses etched, funnel-shaped flowers modeled in relief cutting. Foot slightly damaged.

Acc. no. P 1970-129
Gift of Helmut Hentrich

Series ware. Model no. 3779. For glassware with the same decoration see Blount, *French Cameo*, 1968, fig. 95, and Daum, *Mastery*, 1985, illus. p. 115.

Lit.: Hilschenz-Mlynek and Ricke, *Frankreich*, 1985, cat. no. 116

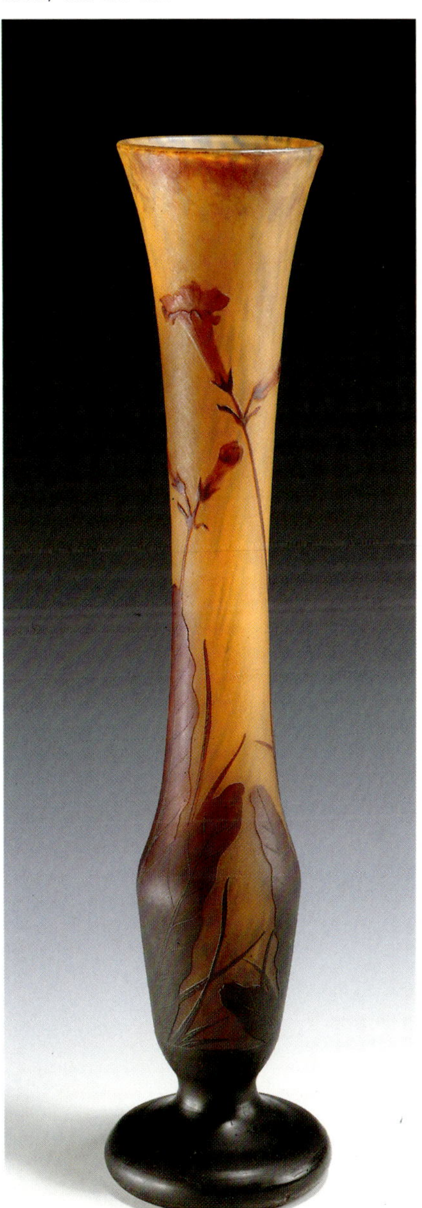

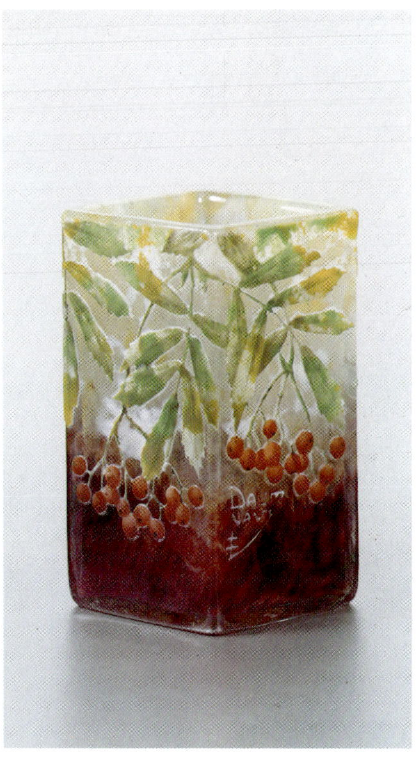

257 "Sorbier" Vase

Mark in relief etching on wall: *DAUM NANCY* with Cross of Lorraine
1910
H 11.2, ⌀ 8.4 cm

Colorless glass with opaque white overlay and multicolored glass-powder inclusions. Mold-blown.
Decoration: branches of mountain ash in relief etching; leaves and fruit painted in enamel.

Acc. no. P 1970-116
Gift of Helmut Hentrich

Lavish series ware.

Lit.: Hilschenz-Mlynek and Ricke, *Frankreich*, 1985, cat. no. 118

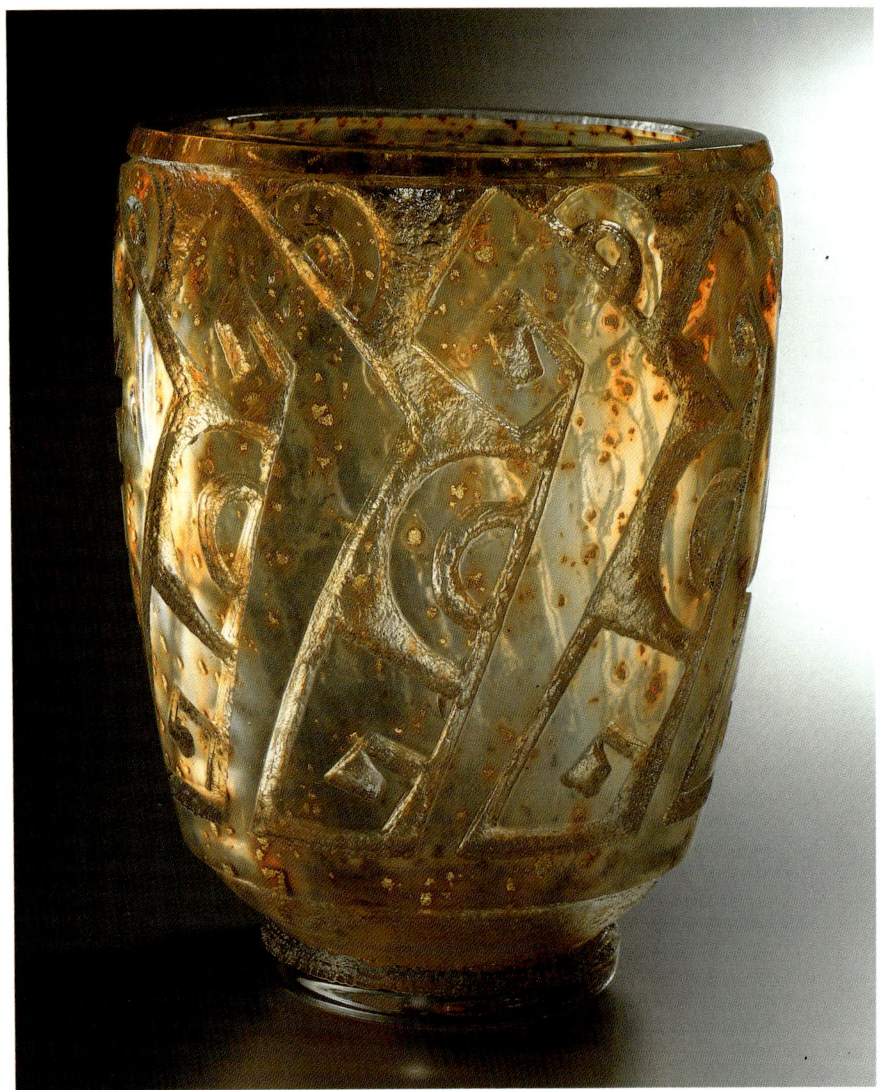

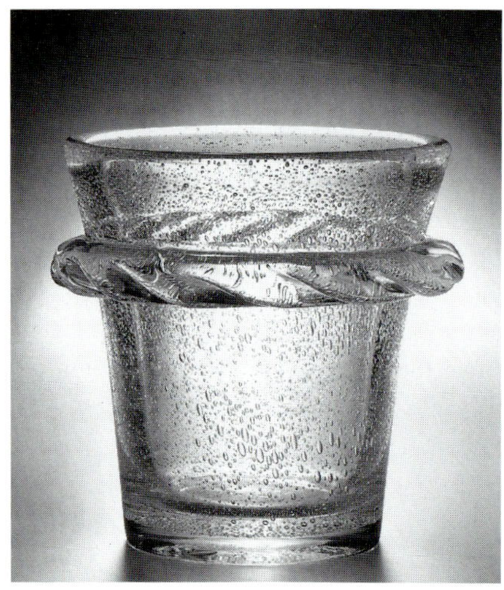

259 Pot

Engraved mark above standing base: *DAUM NANCY* with Cross of Lorraine
Ca. 1930
H 23.6, ∅ 24.3 cm

Colorless bubble glass. Mold-blown and shaped.

Acc. no. P 1989-82
Gift of Helmut Hentrich

Series ware. Daum factory's reaction to the new approach to glass design taken by Maurice Marinot and his circle.

Lit.: –

258 Vase

Engraved mark on edge of foot: *DAUM NANCY FRANCE* with Cross of Lorraine
Ca. 1930
H 23.1, ∅ 18.5 cm

Colorless, thick-walled glass with gold metal-foil inclusions in the wall; glass coloring in part owing to dissolution of metal in the hot glass. Mold-blown. Decoration crudely frosted.

Acc. no. P 1977-53
Gift of Helmut Hentrich

Series ware. For glassware with geometric motifs see *Mobilier & Décoration* 2 (1930): 233. For examples of cut glassware see *Les Echos des Industries d'Art*, no. 22 (May 1927): 28, and Daum, *Mastery*, 1985, illus. p. 169.

Lit.: Hilschenz-Mlynek and Ricke, *Frankreich*, 1985, cat. no. 133; Ricke, *2500 Jahre*, 1987, cat. no. 169

Burgun, Schverer & Co.

Glasshouse Meisenthal (Verrerie de Meisenthal)

Glasshouse for hollow ware and decorating workshop for ornamental and utilitarian glass, Meisenthal near Lemberg, Alsace

Founded in 1711 by the glassmaking family Greiner and Sebastian Burgun. From 1824, traded under the name Burgun, Schverer & Co. Under the direction of Antoine Burgun (from 1889), the company developed into the most important producer of artistic ornamental glassware and drinking-glass sets in Alsace-Lorraine. Instrumental to this success was a secret contract with Emile Gallé, who regularly made large commissions from the 1870s to 1896. In its relationship to Gallé, the Meisenthal glasshouse was not only the recipient of important impulses, but, with its competent employees, notably Eugène Kremer and Désiré Christian, also a contributing partner.

260 Vase

Mark on the Cross of Lorraine and banderole in gold imprint on the underside of base: *BS & Co. VERRERIE D'ART DE LORRAINE*; also: *deposé*
Ca. 1896–1900
H 30, ⌀ 8.5 cm

Colorless glass with a light yellow-green tone. Enamel painting and dark red threads between the layers. Mold-blown. Cloverleaf-shaped mouth pincered at three points. Decoration: painted cornflowers and daisies underneath the top colorless glass layer. The relief etching on top follows the plant outlines. Frosted ground, in part accentuated by polishing in the *martelé* technique. Details and rim of mouth gilded.

Acc. no. P 1970-21
Gift of Helmut Hentrich

High-quality series ware. Painting between the layers was a specialty of the company from 1895. Eugène Kremer contributed considerably to the technical development of this specialty; he patented the process in 1897. See Klesse, *Gallé*, 1982, 60f. Désiré Christian also used the technique of painting between layers at his Meisenthal decorating workshop after 1896; see two very similar pieces at the Hamburg Museum für Kunst und Gewerbe.

Lit.: Hilschenz-Mlynek and Ricke, *Frankreich*, 1985, cat. no. 15

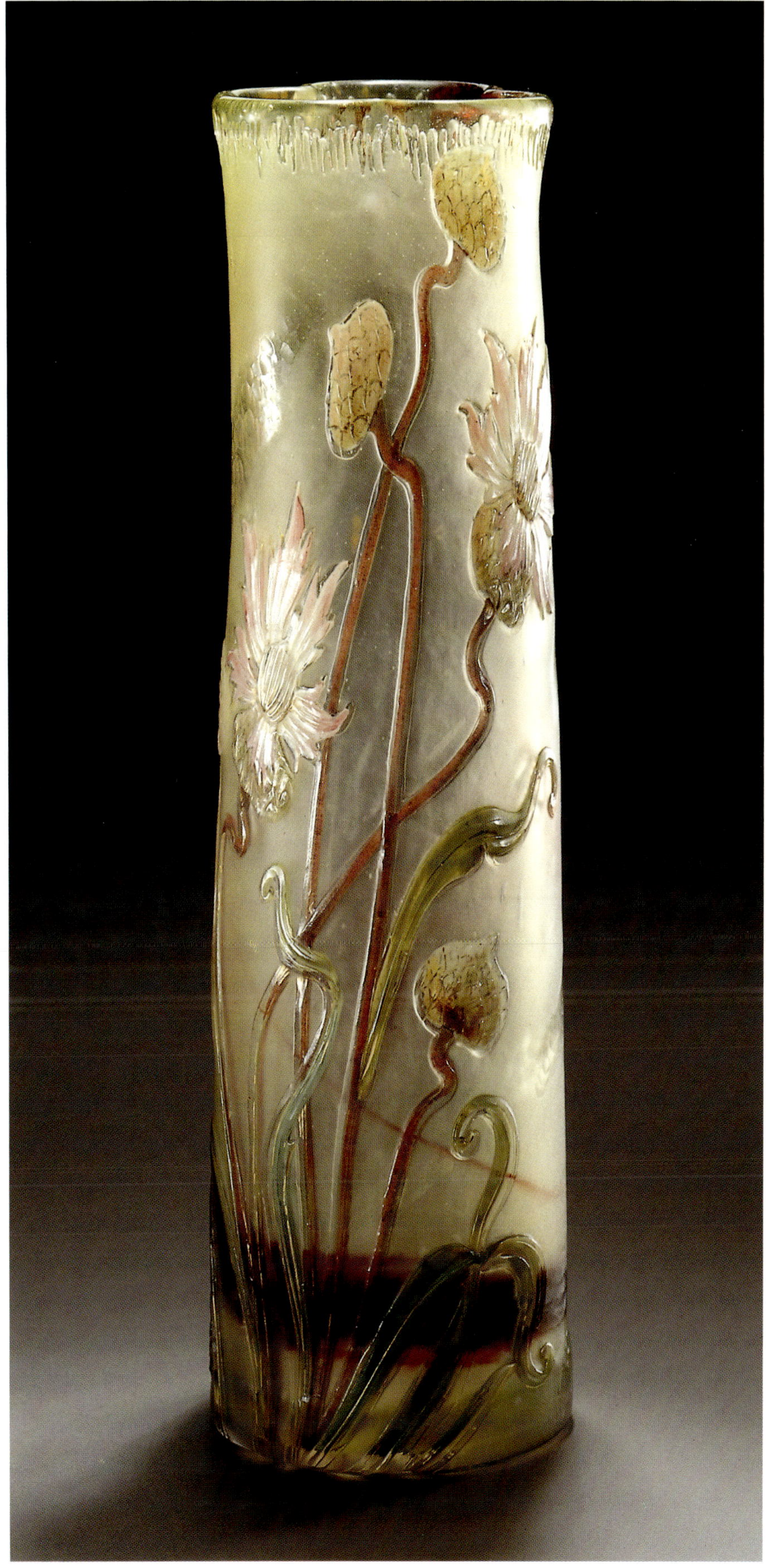

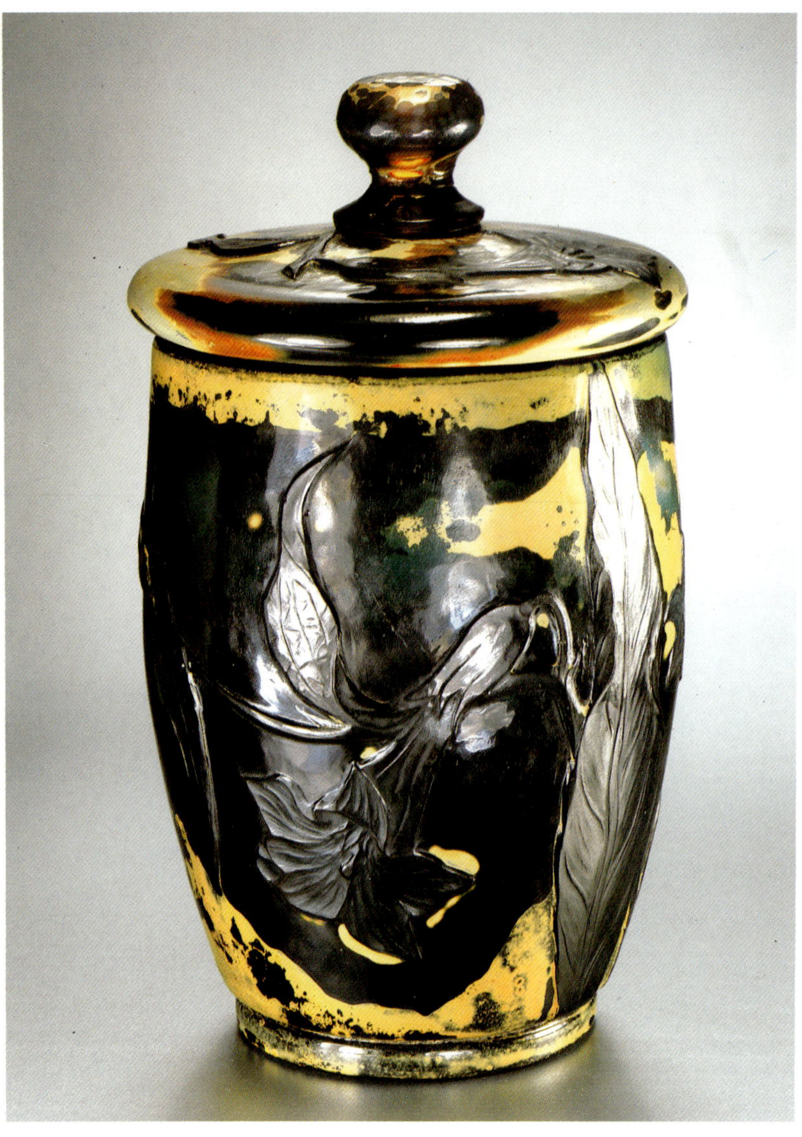

Eugène Michel
(1848–1904)

Glass engraver

After working at the Parisian decorating studios of Eugène Rousseau (from about 1867) and probably also of Ernest Léveillé (from 1885), active in Paris as an independent glass artist from the mid-1890s.

262 Vase

Engraved mark on the underside of base:
E. Michel
1895–1900
H 25.5, ⌀ 13.4 cm

Colorless glass with oxide and granular glass inclusions and a crackled layer in between; opaque green overlay. Mold-blown. Decoration: water lilies, yellow flag iris, and other aquatic plants in relief carving after preparatory etching. Ground polished, grinding lines.

Acc. no. P 1970-282
Gift of Helmut Hentrich

Unique piece. For a similar but unsigned vase see Neuwirth, *Jugendstil*, 1973, cat. no. 219. For E. Michel see also Ricke and Schmitt, *Sammlung Koepff*, 1998, 312f.

Lit.: Hilschenz-Mlynek and Ricke, *Frankreich*, 1985, cat. no. 448; Ricke, *2500 Jahre*, 1987, cat. no. 138

Désiré Christian & Sohn

Decorating workshop for ornamental and utilitarian glassware, mounted articles, as well as faience ware, Meisenthal, Alsace

Established around 1900 by Désiré Jean Baptiste Christian (1846–1907). He worked as decoration painter and glass cutter from 1864 and as director of the decoration workshops of the glasshouse Burgun, Schverer & Co., from around 1877. There he worked almost exclusively on glassware for Gallé. He began to produce his own glassware with signature in 1896.

261 "Nycotina" Covered Jar

Unsigned
Ca. 1904
H (with cover) 16.4, ⌀ 9.9 cm

Glass with several overlays and partly colored applications. Vessel and cover mold-blown. Surface in part stained yellow in a reducing atmosphere.
Decoration: on vessel wall and cover, flowers and leaves of the tobacco plant in relief etching; the entire surface of the plant modeled by engraving; at a few points, polished in the *martelé* technique.

Acc. no. P 1970-25
Gift of Helmut Hentrich

Small series. For attribution and dating see an almost identical piece, without cover, at the Württembergisches Landesmuseum, Stuttgart, acc. no. G 4172.

Lit.: Hilschenz-Mlynek and Ricke, *Frankreich*, 1985, cat. no. 24; Ricke, *2500 Jahre*, 1987, cat. no. 136; *Meisenthal*, 1999, cat. no. 91

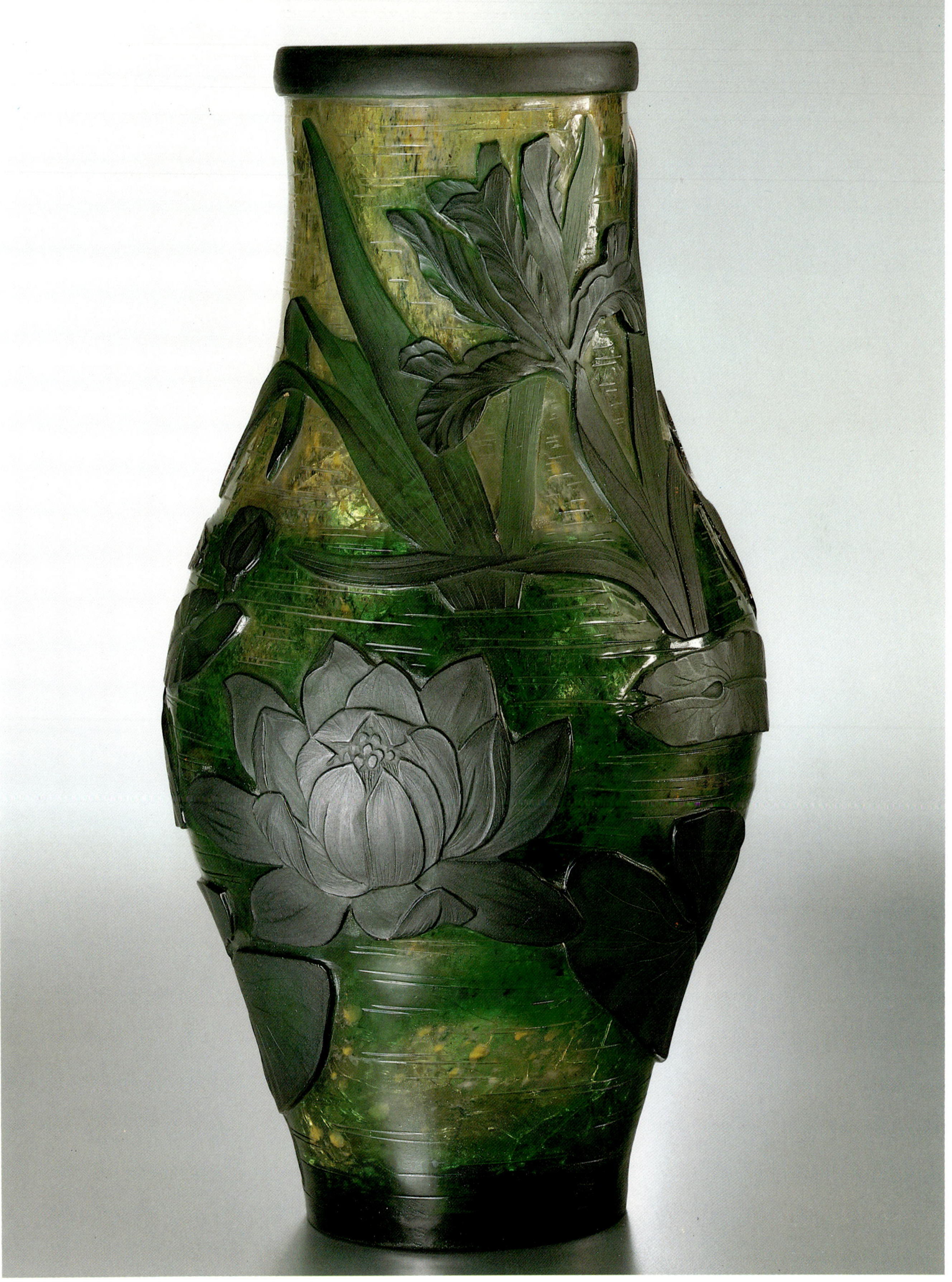

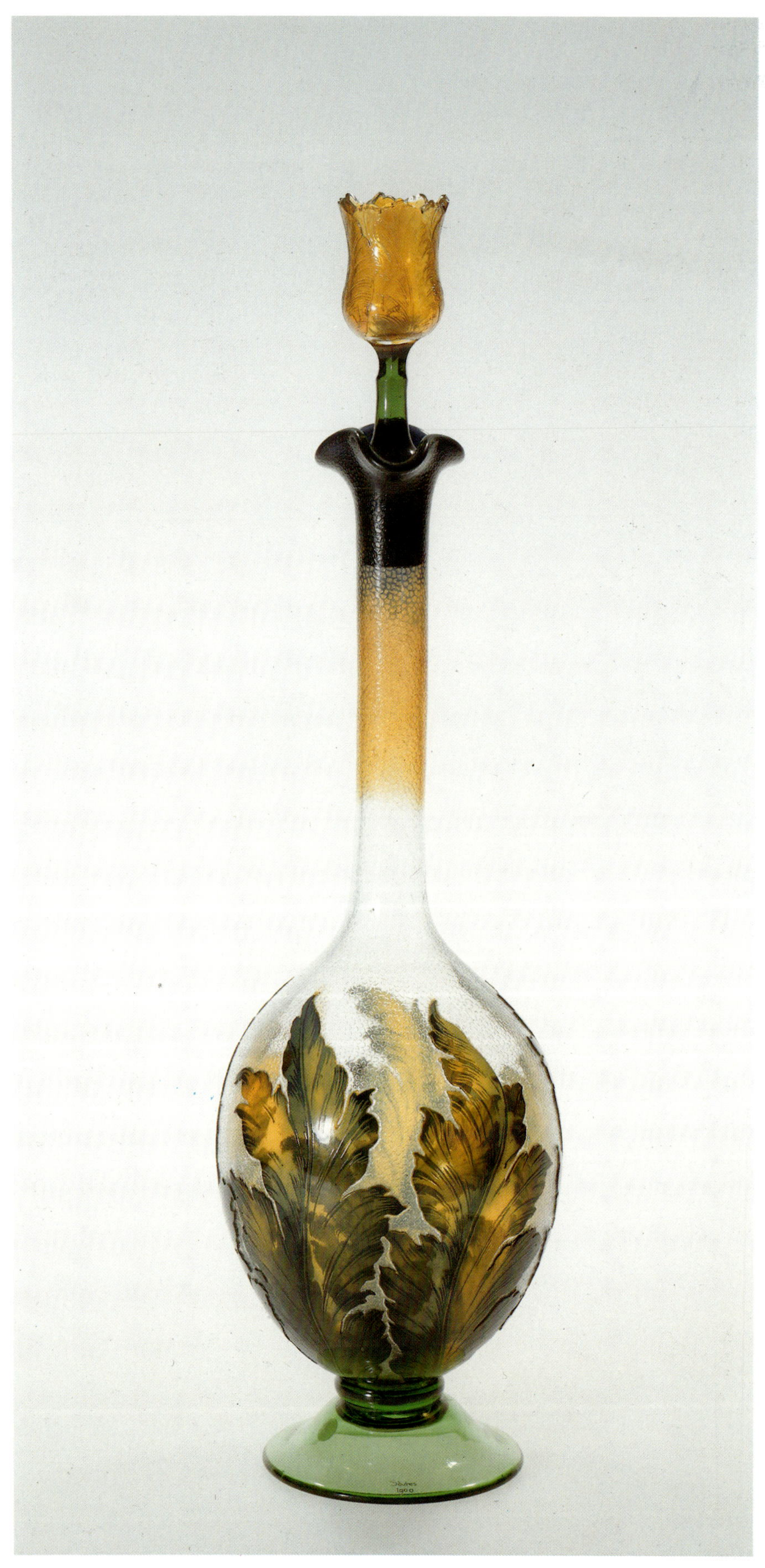

Cristalleries de Sèvres
A. Landier et Fils

Glasshouse for hollow glassware, decorating workshops for ornamental and utilitarian glass, Bas-Meudon, Seine-et-Oise

Set up in 1756 by Madame de Pompadour in a building adjacent to her palace in Meudon. After her death it was run by her brother under the name Cristalleries Royales de Sèvres until 1777. Owned by Alfred Landier and Charles Houdaille from the 1870s. At the 1900 World Exhibition in Paris under the name A. Landier et Fils, Cristalleries de Sèvres.

263 Decanter

Mark in gilded needle etching on the underside of foot: *Sèvres 1900*
Dated 1900
H (with stopper) 41, ⌀ 11.6 cm

Colorless glass, with yellow and blue-green overlays. Mold-blown and shaped. Foot attached.
Etched decoration, honeycomb patterned ground. Stopper in the shape of calyx, also relief etched. Acid polished.

Acc. no. P 1979-36
Gift of Helmut Hentrich

High-quality series ware. Presumably made for the 1900 World Exhibition in Paris; illus. in Pazaurek, *Moderne Gläser*, 1901, 100, no. 95.

Lit.: Hilschenz-Mlynek and Ricke, *Frankreich*, 1985, cat. no. 523

Amédée de Caranza

(born in Istanbul of French parents; biographical information unknown)

Ceramist, glass artist, painter, and musician

Worked as decorator at the faience factory of Longwy from about 1865/70 and from 1875, at the ceramic company Jules Vieillard & Cie. in Bordeaux, and subsequently for a short period with the ceramist Clément Massier in Vallauris. From 1903, one of the most important employees of H. Copillet in Noyen, where he carried out most of his specialized decoration by firing his glassware in a reducing atmosphere. Earliest glass dated 1895.

264 Vase

Mark in colors fired in a reducing atmosphere on wall: *A. de CARANZA*
Ca. 1900
H 29.4, ⌀ 14.7 cm

Colorless glass. Mold-blown.
Decoration: encircling branches with fruits of the horse chestnut. Colors fired in reducing atmosphere and luster painting.
In the base, strain cracks, edges slightly damaged.

Acc. no. P 1970-95
Gift of Helmut Hentrich

Unique piece. Transference of ceramic painting and firing techniques to glass design.

Lit.: Hilschenz-Mlynek and Ricke, *Frankreich*, 1985, cat. no. 21

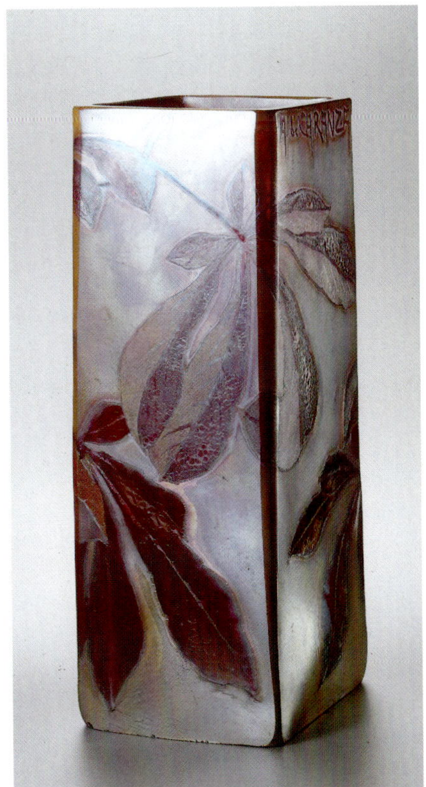

Legras & Cie.

Verreries de Saint-Denis et de Pantin Réunies

Glasshouses for hollow glassware, decorating workshops for ornamental and utilitarian glass as well as special glass, La-Plaine-Saint-Denis; sales office in Paris

Taken over from the glassmaker and technician Auguste Jean-François Legras in 1864, the company developed under his son and grandson into one of the most successful glass factories in France by 1914.

265 Vase

Unsigned
1900–1914
H 59.7, ⌀ 18.4 cm

Colorless glass on orange-red inner casing, with embedded green glass. Mold-blown, shaped.
Decoration: foliage and flower of the crown imperial, etched and partly painted in enamel. Ground with flaky, coarse frosting and stupped enamel painting. Interior details in needle etching. Gilding.

Acc. no. P 1970-275
Gift of Helmut Hentrich

High-quality series ware. For attribution see signed pieces with the same decoration but formal variations in Blount, *French Cameo*, 1968, fig. 221 D. See also variation in Schmitt, *Sammlung Silzer*, 1989, cat. no. 101.

Lit.: Hilschenz-Mlynek and Ricke, *Frankreich*, 1985, cat. no. 415

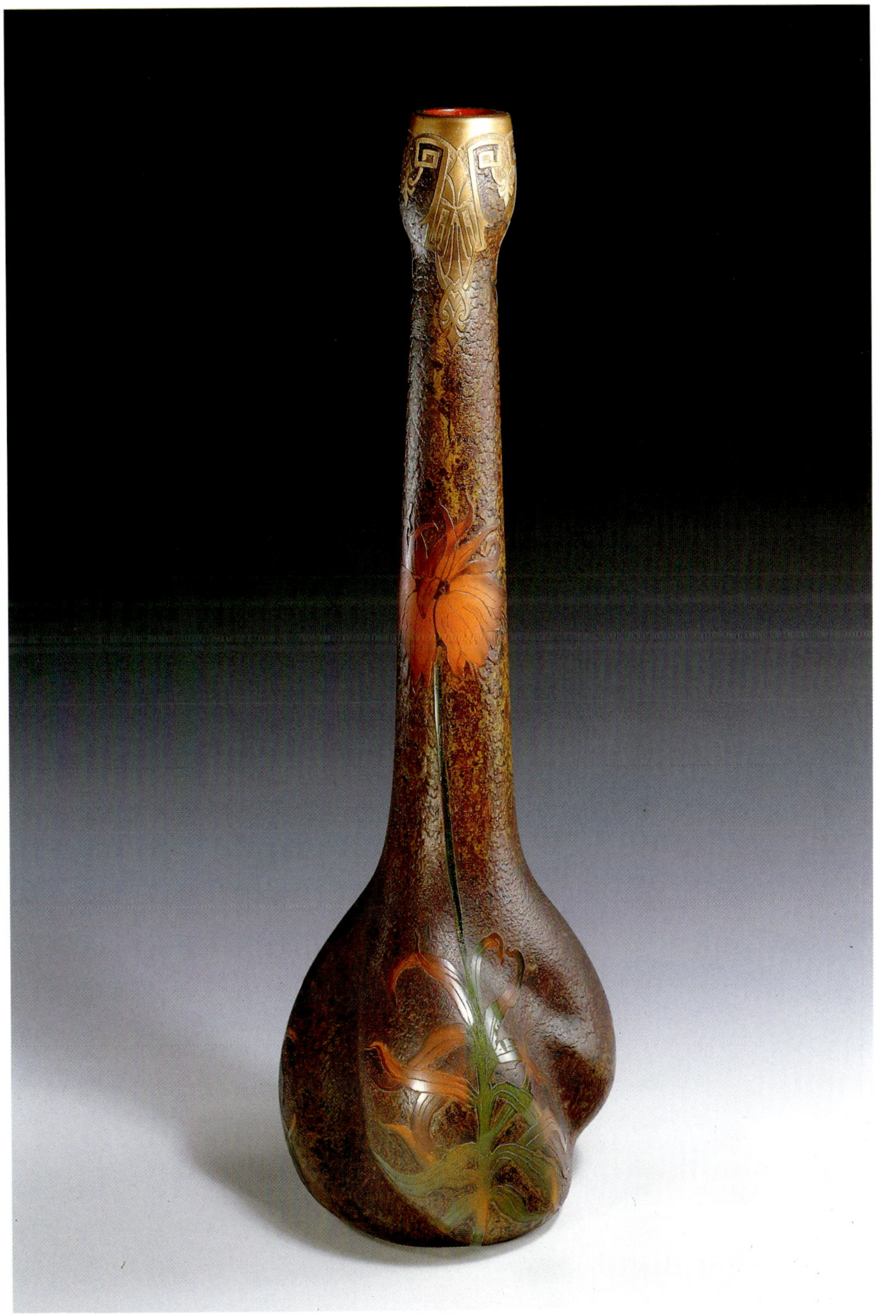

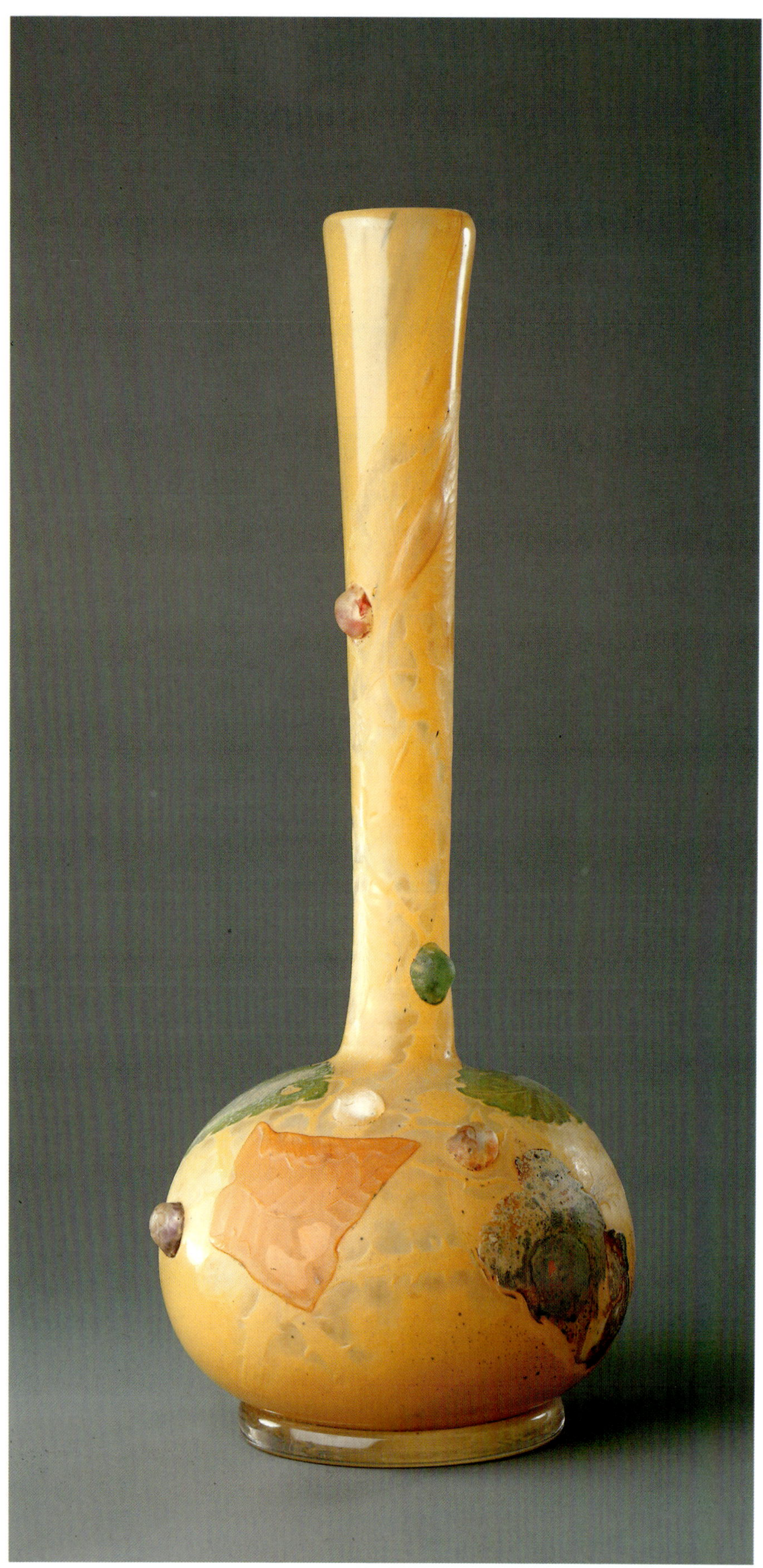

Muller Frères

Grandes Verreries de Croismare et Verrerie
d'Art Muller Frères Réunies

Glasshouse for hollow glassware, decorating
workshop for ornamental and utilitarian glass
as well as lighting products, Croismare and
Lunéville near Nancy

Founded in 1895 by the nine Muller brothers
and one sister under the direction of Henri
Muller, after he and four of the brothers had
worked as glass decorators and apprentices
at Gallé.
Emile and Eugène Muller carried out the
engraved decoration based on their own
designs. Désiré, Victor, and Auguste Muller
produced the blanks at the glasshouse
Hinzelin in Croismare, which they took over
in 1919. Between 1920 and 1927, the company was one of the most successful in the
region.
It was closed down in 1936.

266 Vase

Engraved mark on wall: *HMuller Croismare*;
ligature: *HM*
Ca. 1900–1905
H 38, ⌀ 15.4 cm

Colorless glass, yellow overlay, with applications and *cabochons* in various colors. Mold-
blown. Colorless foot.
Decoration: blackberry vine with berries and
foliage in various colors, after preparatory
etching; mat intaglio on large planes.

Acc. no. P 1970-283
Gift of Helmut Hentrich

Presumably a unique piece. Related to Gallé's
marquetry glassware, in which the decoration
also consists of colored glass fragments
worked into the glass surface.
For similar decoration see Bloch-Dermant,
French Glass, 1988, 23.

Lit.: Hilschenz-Mlynek and Ricke, *Frankreich*,
1985, cat. no. 450; *L'Ecole de Nancy*, 1999,
cat. no. 286, illus. p. 334

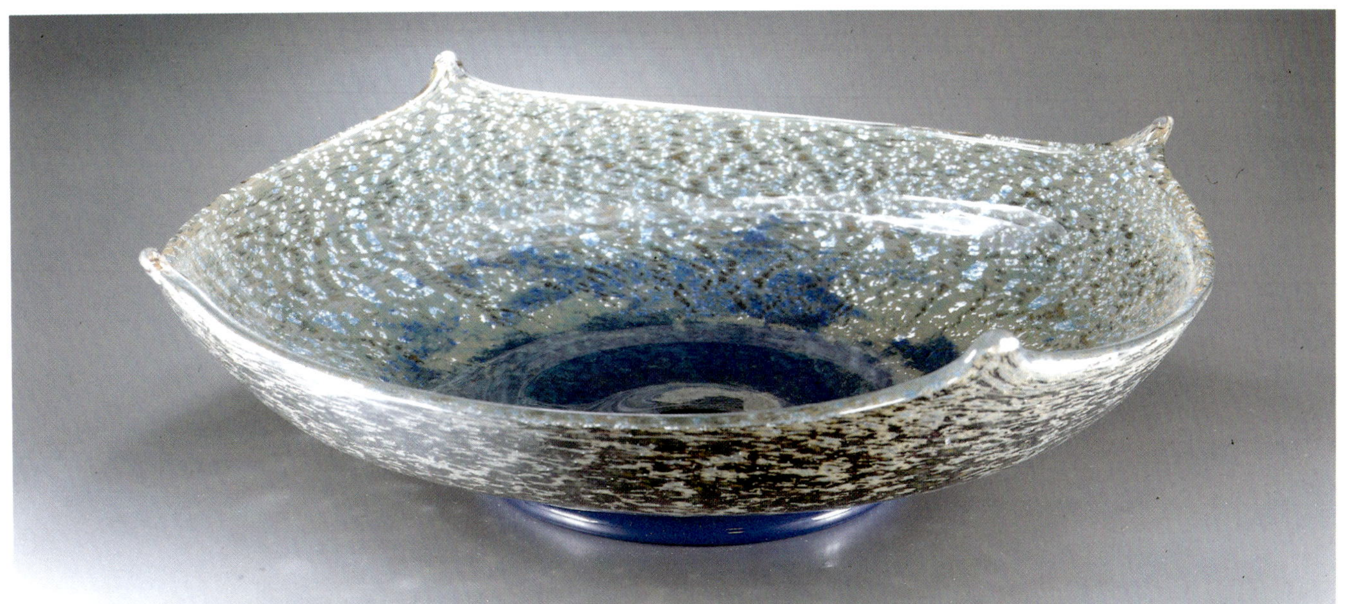

267 Dish

Diamond-engraved mark on outer wall:
MULLER FRES LUNEVILLE
1920s
H 11.8, ⌀ 44.2 cm

Colorless glass with enclosed powder decoration in greenish ocher and blue. Torn metal-foil inclusions (platinum?). Free-blown, inflated, shaped. Attached foot with blue overlay.

Acc. no. P 1990-429
Gift of Helmut Hentrich

Small series. Typical piece created during the Muller factory's heyday, in the 1920s. For a similar piece see Cappa, *100 ans Europe*, 1983, cat. no. 285.

Lit.: –

René Lalique
(1860–1945)

Goldsmith and silversmith; enamel, glass, and gemstone artist; designer for the craft industry; and painter

After working many years as a goldsmith, Lalique founded his own glasshouse in 1909, the Verrerie de Combs-la-Ville near Paris for making ornamental and utilitarian glass products. In 1912, his first glass exhibition at his Paris store. From 1921, construction of the second and larger glass factory, Verreries d'Alsace René Lalique & Cie., in Wingen-sur-Moder, for extensive mechanical mass production.

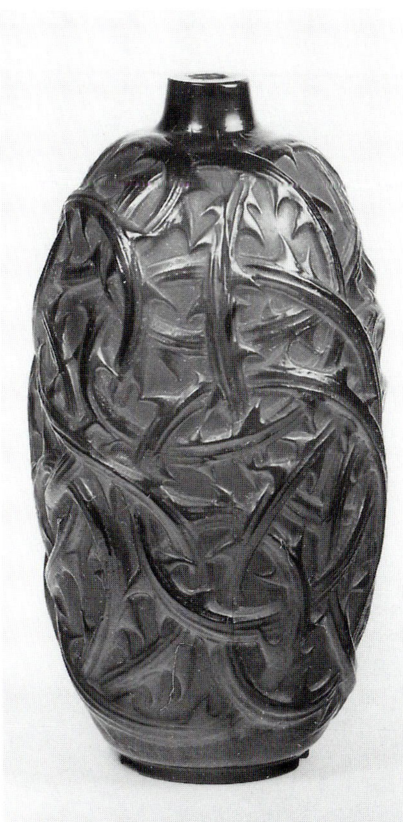

268 "Ronces" Vase

Deep-pressed mark on the underside of base:
R. LALIQUE
Designed in 1921
Produced until ca. 1932
H 23.2, ⌀ 12.7 cm

Red-brown glass. Press-and-blow process. Decoration: intertwined thorns in polished high relief. Three deep cuts at bottom (formerly used as lamp base).

Acc. no. P 1989-1
Gift of Alexander and Dorothea Mares, Düsseldorf

Large series. Compare with the 10-piece toilet set with the same decoration in *Catalogue des verreries de René Lalique* (Paris: Lalique & Cie., 1932; reprint, New York: The Corning Museum of Glass, 1981), pl. 55, model nos. 590–99. See also Marcilhac, *Lalique*, 1989, 343, nos. 590–99, "Epines" model; "Ronces" vase on p. 427, no. 946.
The model was made in various colors; see, for example, Hilschenz-Mlynek and Ricke, *Frankreich*, 1985, cat. no. 391, and Bloch-Dermant, *French Glass*, 1988, illus. p. 197.

Lit.: –

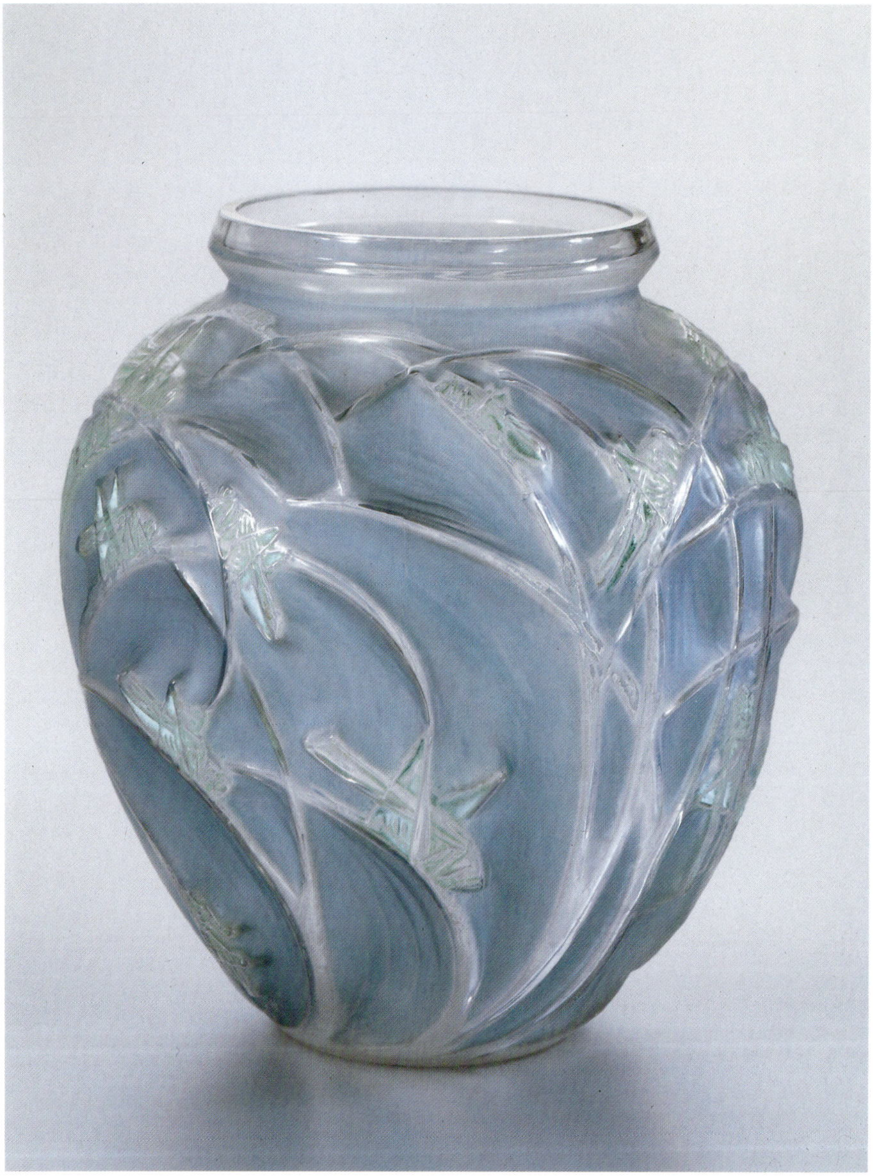

269 "Sauterelles" Vase

Engraved mark on the underside of base:
R. LALIQUE
Designed 1913
Produced until ca. 1922
H 27.3, ⌀ 25.6 cm

Colorless glass. Press-and-blow process.
Decoration on etched and patinated ground:
linear, stylized grasses with large and small
perched grasshoppers in high relief. Lower
planes mat and colored blue.

Acc. no. P 1970-262
Gift of Helmut Hentrich

Large series. No longer listed in *Catalogue
Lalique*, op. cit. See also Marcilhac, *Lalique*,
1989, 414, no. 888.

Lit.: Hilschenz-Mlynek and Ricke, *Frankreich*,
1985, cat. no. 392

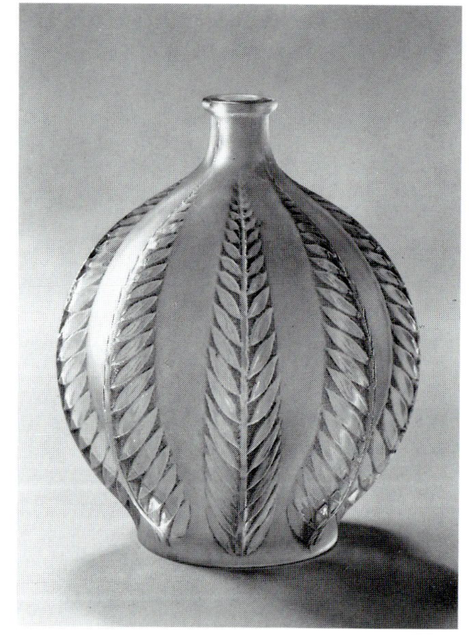

270 "Malines" Vase

Engraved mark on the underside of foot:
R. Lalique France No 957
Designed August 27, 1924
Produced until ca. 1937
H 12.4, ⌀ 10.4 cm

Colorless glass. Pressed-and-blown.
Decoration: eight encircling, vertical, polished ribs shaped like leafstalks on etched
and patinated ground matted slightly gray;
lower planes colored mat green.

Acc. no. P 1970-266
Gift of Helmut Hentrich

Large series. Listed in *Catalogue Lalique*, op.
cit., pl. 11, model no. 957. See also Marcilhac, *Lalique*, 1989, 429, no. 957.

Lit.: Hilschenz-Mlynek and Ricke, *Frankreich*,
1985, cat. no. 396

Verreries Schneider

Glasshouse for hollow ware and decorating
workshops for ornamental and utilitarian
glass as well as lighting products and stained-
glass windows

Founded in 1909/10 by Ernest Schneider
(1877–1937), former managing director of
Daum Frères, Epinay-sur-Seine.
Started producing art glass in 1918 under the
artistic direction of the younger brother,
Charles Schneider (1881–1953), who developed the whole production program of the
1920s. With this program, the company
became, together with Lalique and Daum
Frères, one of the leading French art-glass
manufacturers of its time.
Moved the factory to Lorris, Loiret, in 1962.
It was closed in 1981.

271   Decorative Goblet

Engraved mark on foot: *Schneider*
Ca. 1924/25
H 20.1, ⌀ 24.5 cm

Colorless glass, white-yellow powder inclusion on edge of cup, green in center; stem
and foot porous with a fused glass-powder
coating in green, purple-red, and white-
yellow. Mold-blown and shaped.

Acc. no. L 1983-27
On loan from the Kiffe Collection, Münster

Glassware signed with *Schneider* epitomize
Charles Schneider's artistic oeuvre. With its
daring color combination and bizarre shape,
the goblet is amongst his most striking
avant-garde creations.

Lit.: Ricke, *Schneider France*, 1981, cat.
no. 27

272   "Perlières" Vase

Needle-etched mark above base: *Le Verre
Français*
Ca. 1923–26
H 27.5, ⌀ 19.6 cm

Overlay glass with cloudy red and orange-
yellow powder inclusions, overlaid with white
spots; shiny brown layer fused onto colorless
layer in between. Mold-blown. Thread handles freely applied. Ground-out pontil mark.
Decoration: stylized berry vines, etched
twice.

Acc. no. P 1970-303
Gift of Helmut Hentrich

Series ware. The model is documented in patterns for the special production line "Le Verre
Français," which was intended for export and
to have a wide appeal. See pl. XLVI "Perlières,"
no. 1169, in Ricke, *Schneider France*, 1981,
251.

Lit.: Hilschenz-Mlynek and Ricke, *Frankreich*,
1985, cat. no. 520

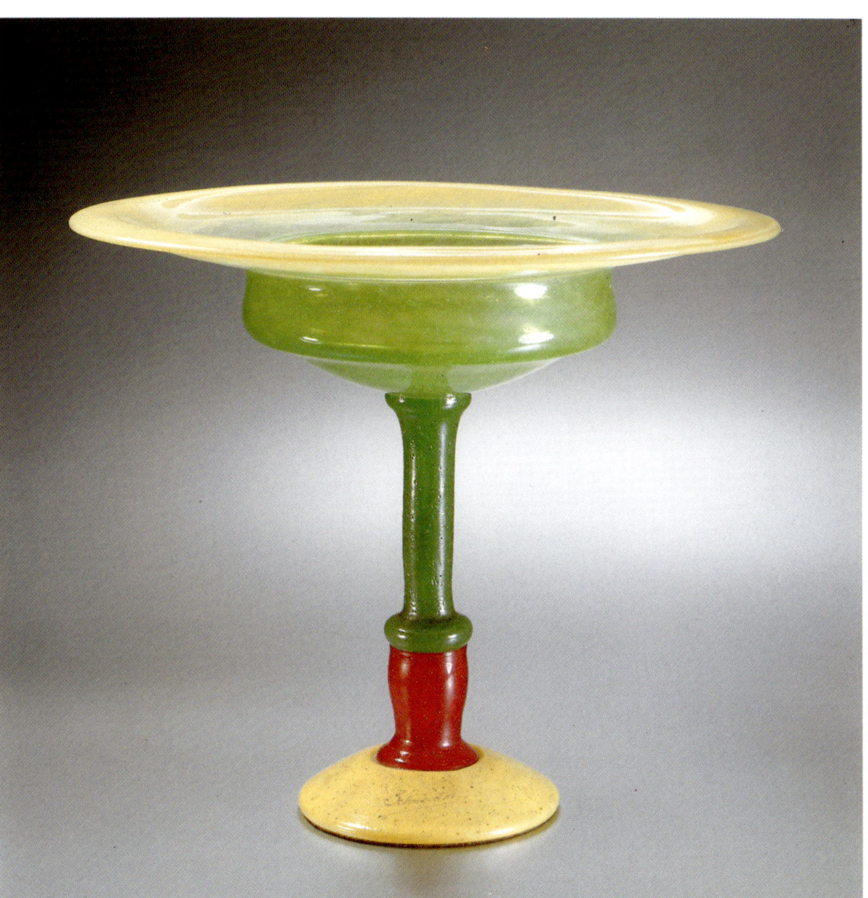

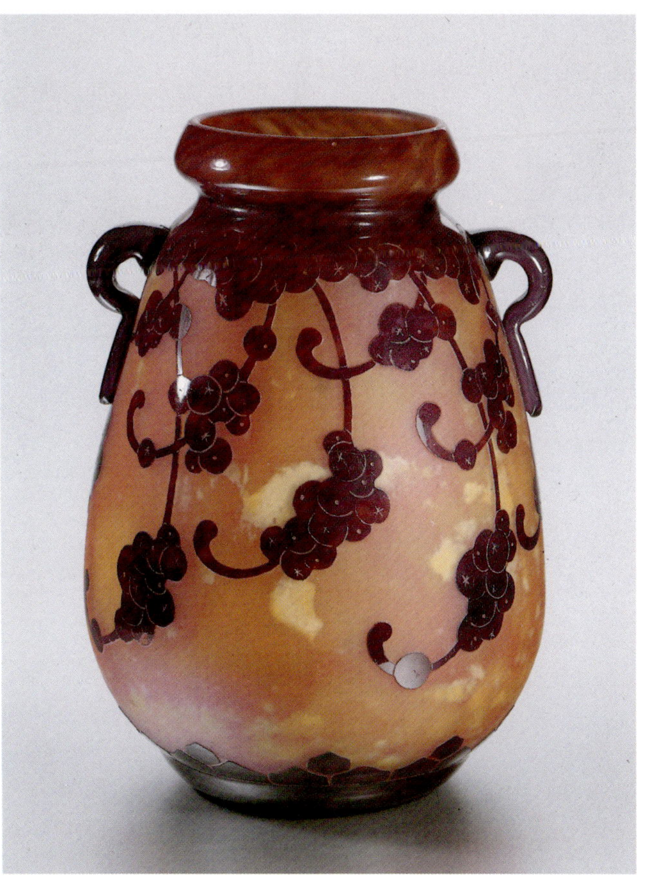

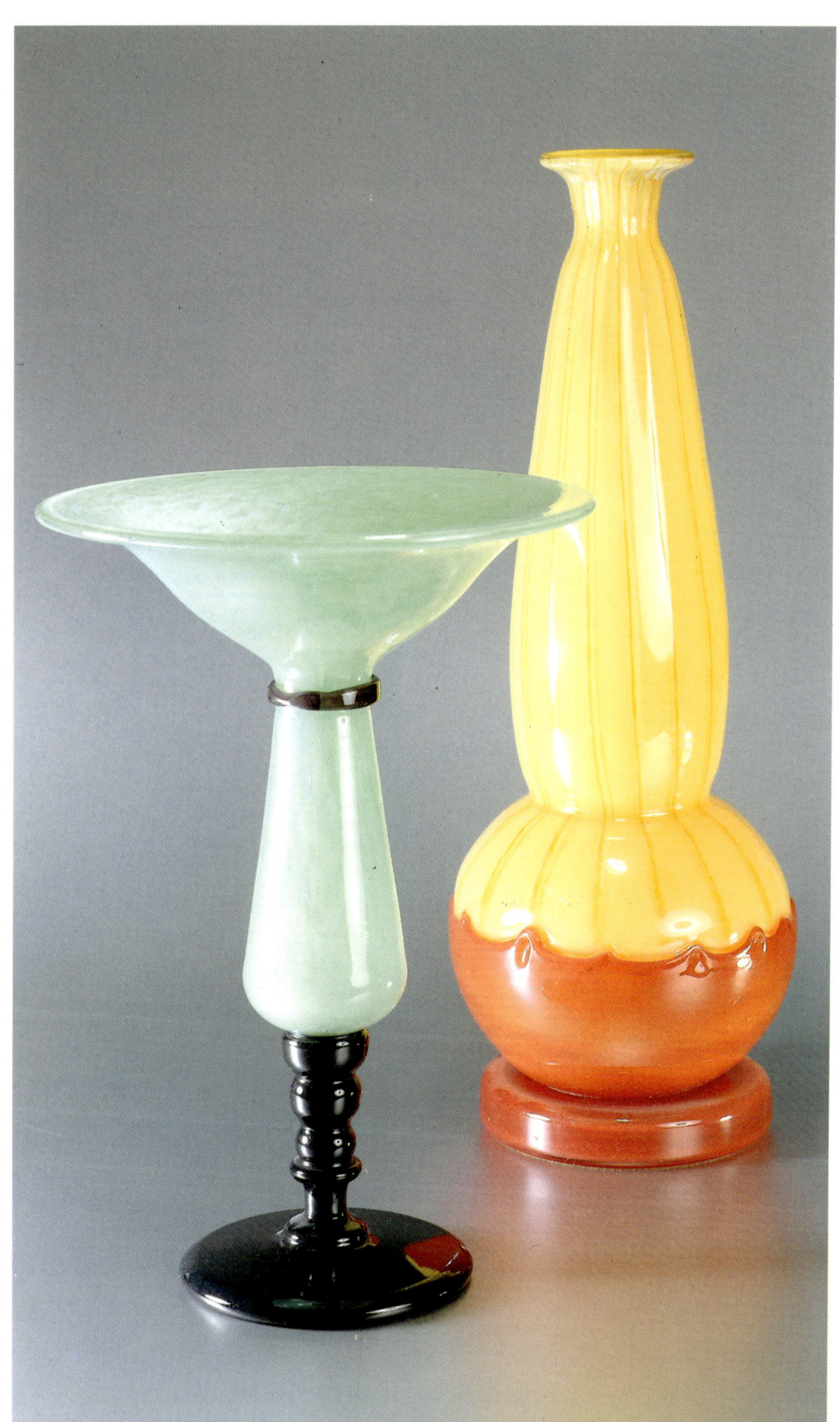

273 "Coupe Bijoux" Decorative Goblet

Mark in sandblast area on edge of foot:
SCHNEIDER
Designed ca. 1918–22; executed ca. 1926–28
H 25.1, ⌀ 18.8 cm

Colorless glass. Flaky jade green inclusions in
cup; cloudy black-violet inclusions in foot,
stem, and ring at the narrow. Mold-blown,
shaped.

Acc. no. L 1983-32
On loan from the Kiffe Collection, Münster

See the drawing on pattern sheet pl. III,
"Coupes bijoux," no. 5, of *Références Schneider*, illus. in Ricke, *Schneider France*, 1981,
208. An example from the successful series
"Coupes bijoux," which reveals a break with
Art-Nouveau ideas as well as the manufacturer's independence from the competition.

Lit.: Ricke, *Schneider France*, 1981, cat.
no. 32

274 Vase

Engraved mark on edge of foot, traces of
gilding: *Schneider*
Ca. 1927–29
H 36, ⌀ 13.1 cm

White-yellow, opalescent glass with colorless
overlay. Optic-blown in 16-part skeleton
mold, the ribs accentuated with fine lines of
applied orange-yellow glass powder. Foot and
body with vermilion and colorless overlay,
the casing cap drawn out in star shape; foot
disk somewhat darker and slightly streaky.

Acc. no. L 1983-167
On loan from the Kiffe Collection, Münster

Model not documented in *Références Schneider*.

Lit.: Ricke, *Schneider France*, 1981, cat.
no. 167

Auguste Claude Heiligenstein
(1891–1976)

Glass decorator—primarily enamel painter—
and ceramist

Trained as glass decorator at Legras & Cie. in
Saint-Denis from 1904 to 1906 and worked at
the Paris decorating studio of Cristalleries de
Baccarat. After the war, entered the decorating business of Galerie Rouard under the
direction of Marcel Goupy. In 1923, founded
his own workshop in Paris together with his
wife, the ceramist Odette Chatrousse. From
1923 to 1926, technical and artistic adviser
for the Leune establishment and, from 1926
to 1930, for the Souchon-Neuvesel group,
which had taken over the Legras factory in
1924. Drawings and models also for Daum
Frères glassware. Distribution of his work
through several renowned Parisian companies.

275   Flacon

Diamond-engraved mark on the underside of
base: *aug. heiligenstein*
Diamond-engraved diagonal stroke under vessel bottom and stopper
1928–30
H (with stopper) 21.5, ⌀ 12.3 cm

Colorless glass. Mold-blown.
Decoration: repeating pattern of branches,
flowers, and leaves on transparent yellow
ground. On front: dancing girl with veil in
translucent enamel painting. Foot-ring, rim
of mouth, stopper, and drawing in gold.

Acc. no. P 1979-26
Gift of Helmut Hentrich

Unique piece. For similar pieces see sales
catalogue *Dépôt 15* (Paris, 1972), cat. nos.
139–47.

Lit.: Hilschenz-Mlynek and Ricke, *Frankreich*,
1985, cat. no. 381; J. L. Olivier et al.,
*Auguste Heiligenstein, 1891–1976: Emailleur
sur verre et céramique*, exh. cat. (Saint-Denis,
Musée d'art et d'histoire; Paris, 1994), 10,
cat. no. 28

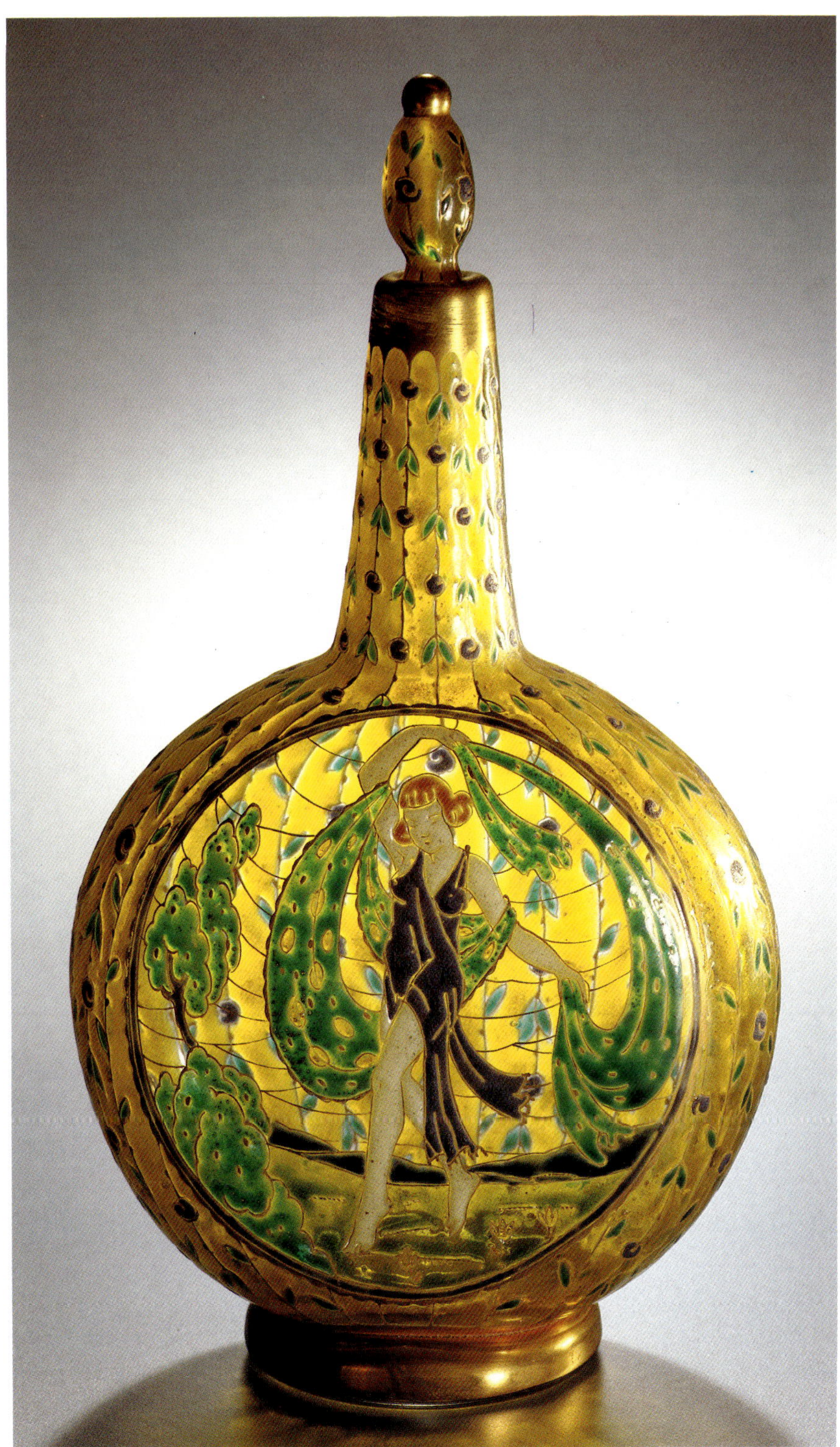

Marcel Goupy
(1886–probably 1954)

Designer and decorator—primarily enamel painter of glass and ceramics—painter, and jewelry artist

After studying at the Ecole Nationale des Arts Décoratifs in Paris, worked as goldsmith and painter. In his own studio, designed models and decoration for porcelain and faience from ca. 1914 and for ornamental and utilitarian glassware from 1918 to 1936. From 1919, close collaboration with the merchant and art dealer Georges Rouard, whose decorating studios for glass and porcelain he headed until 1954. In the 1920s and 1930s, also traded under the name of his own decoration studio.

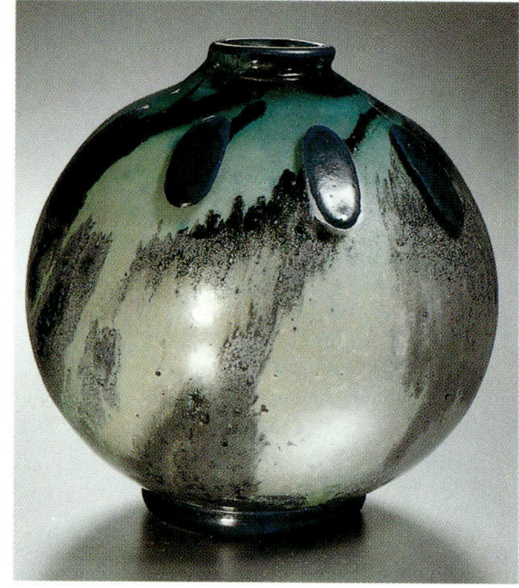

276   Vase

Mark in blue enamel on the underside of base: *M Goupy*
Ca. 1925
H 13.4, ⌀ 13.9 cm

Colorless glass, mold-blown. Eight flat applied prunts. Enamel; interior sprayed spotty opaque; mouth, prunts, and foot-ring in dark blue.

Acc. no. P 1974-41
Gift of Helmut Hentrich

Small series.

Lit.: Hilschenz-Mlynek and Ricke, *Frankreich*, 1985, cat. no. 378

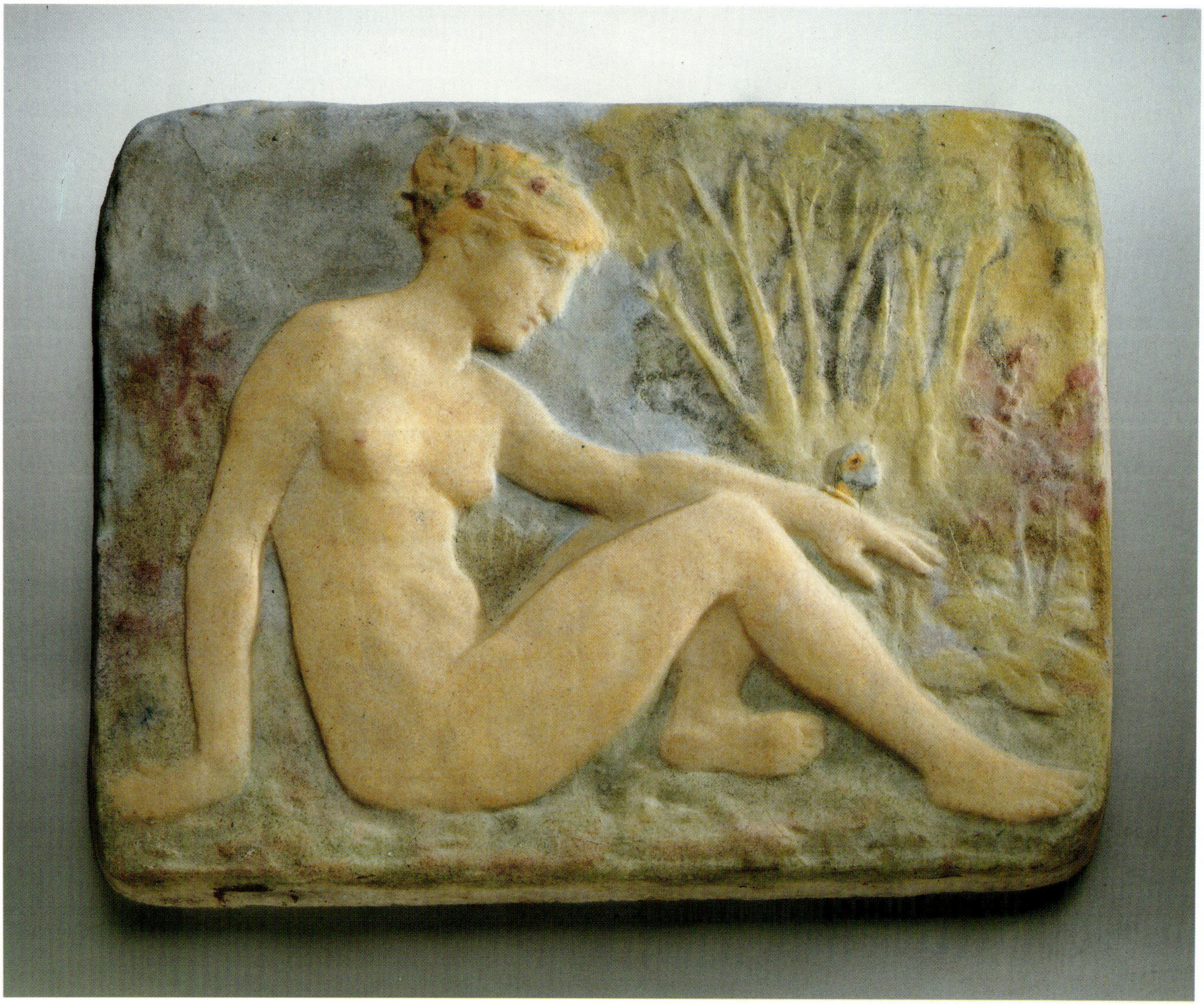

Henri Cros
(1840–1907)

Sculptor, wax modeler, glass artist, painter, and ceramist

Studied at the Ecole des Beaux-Arts in Paris. First took part as sculptor at the Salon d'Automne in 1861. Worked henceforth in various materials, preferably in polychrome wax. By studying ancient writings in the original text, he rediscovered wax and encaustic painting. Searching for a replacement for the sensitive wax, he first succeeded in making *pâte de verre* according to his own technique, which he kept secret. In 1896, his first large workshop in the old mill of the Manufacture Nationale de Porcelaine de Sèvres, followed by a studio for large-scale works in *pâte de verre* in 1903.

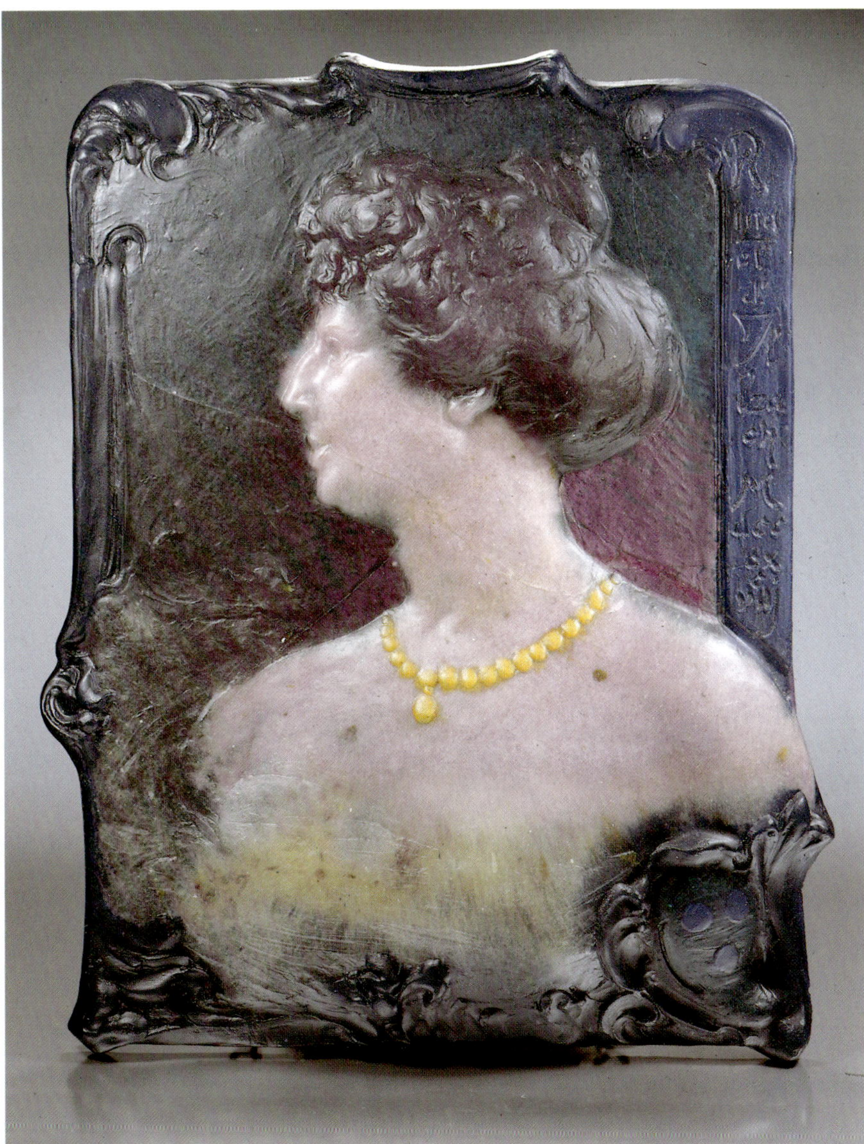

277   "Femme au Papillon" Relief

Unsigned
1890s
H 47.5, W 36.2 cm

Pâte de verre in pastel tones. Surface on the front finely structured; on the reverse coarse-grained white. Mold-melted. Clearly visible mold seams.

Acc. no. LP 1975-84
Acquired through members of the Museumsverein and with funds provided by the City of Düsseldorf

Unique piece. Numerous extant watercolor studies and sketches document Cros's love of figural scenes in an antique style. Sketches for this piece are extant in his journal of 1889/90 (private collection).

Lit.: Hilschenz-Mlynek and Ricke, *Frankreich*, 1985, cat. no. 29

Jean Désiré Ringel d'Illzach
(1847–1916)

Sculptor, medalist, ceramist, etcher, wax modeler, glass artist, and musician

After studying at the Ecole de Dessin and at the Conservatoire de Musique in Paris, took a keen interest in painting and sculpture. Worked with various materials, particularly wax. From 1882 to 1886, worked as sculptor and employee of the ceramist Ernest Chaplet in the Haviland-company studio, Paris. In 1897, first attempts with form-melted *pâte de verre* in collaboration with ceramist Albert Dammouse. After patenting the process in 1898, first introduced his *émaux agglomérés*. Other works carried out at, for example, the Glacerie de Saint-Gobain and at Burgun, Schverer & Co., Meisenthal.

278   Relief

Vertical mark on wall, as part of mold: *Ringel d'Illzach MDCCCXCVIII*; diamond-engraved on the lower right: *sala*
Dated 1898
H 41, W 34.5 cm

Pâte de verre. Mold-melted.
Depiction: bust of a woman, portrait not yet identified. Coat of arms with three blue dots. Polished in large parts.

Acc. no. P 1983-29
Gift of Helmut Hentrich

Unique piece. The model was first shown in 1910 at the Paris exhibition "La Verrerie et la Cristallerie Artistiques" at the Musée Galliera. The relief belonged for a long time to Jean Sala, who signed his name on the shield before selling it.

Lit.: Hilschenz-Mlynek and Ricke, *Frankreich*, 1985, cat. no. 486

Albert Dammouse
(1848–1926)

Sculptor, painter, ceramist, and glass artist

After studying at the Ecole Nationale des Arts Décoratifs, trained under the sculptor François Jouffroy at the Ecole Nationale des Beaux-Arts in Paris in 1868. Until 1870, trainee, later employee of ceramist Marc-Louis Solon, known as Milès. From 1871, his own porcelain studio in Sèvres. In 1897, together with Ringel d'Illzach, first attempts to create mold-melted *pâte de verre* in his own studio. In 1904, developed the technique of translucent *pâte d'émail*.

279 Dish

Stamped mark on the underside of base:
A.DAMMOUSE S (S stands for Sèvres)
Ca. 1900–1910
H 4.3, ⌀ 11.8 cm

Pâte de verre, melted in open mold. Vessel in the shape of a yellow water lily with a mat surface and veins in a low relief painted violet. Interior smoothly fused; infructescence and gynetaeom carried out in low relief. Fine hairline cracks.

Acc. no. P 1970-98
Gift of Helmut Hentrich

Unique piece. For an earlier dish in calyx shape see *Art et Décoration* 6 (1899): illus. p. 4. See also Hilschenz-Mlynek and Ricke, *Frankreich*, 1985, cat. no. 34.

Lit.: Hilschenz-Mlynek and Ricke, *Frankreich*, 1985, cat. no. 33

280 Bowl

Stamped mark on the underside of foot:
A:DAMMOUSE S
Ca. 1905–1910
H 5.9, ⌀ 10.4 cm

Pâte de verre, melted in open mold. Decoration built up in the mold with preformed parts.

Acc. no. P 1970-99
Gift of Helmut Hentrich

Unique piece. For similar pieces see Musée des Arts Décoratifs, Paris, acc. nos. D.12.039, 12.895, D.38.639; also see Klesse and Mayr, *Sammlung Funke-Kaiser*, 1981, cat. no. 37.

Lit.: Hilschenz-Mlynek and Ricke, *Frankreich*, 1985, cat. no. 35; Ricke, *2500 Jahre*, 1987, cat. no. 143

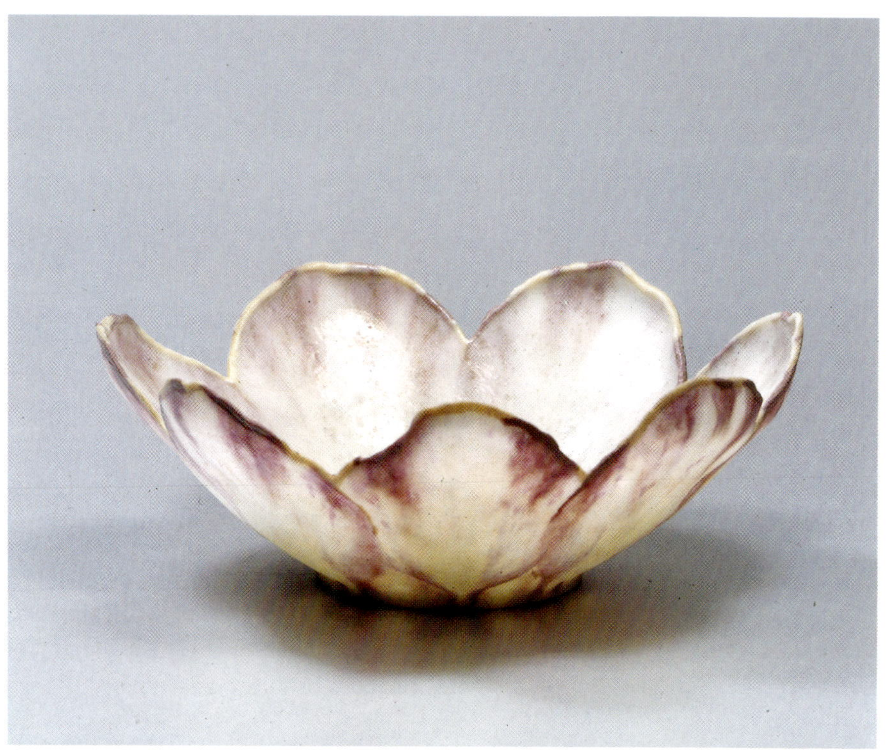

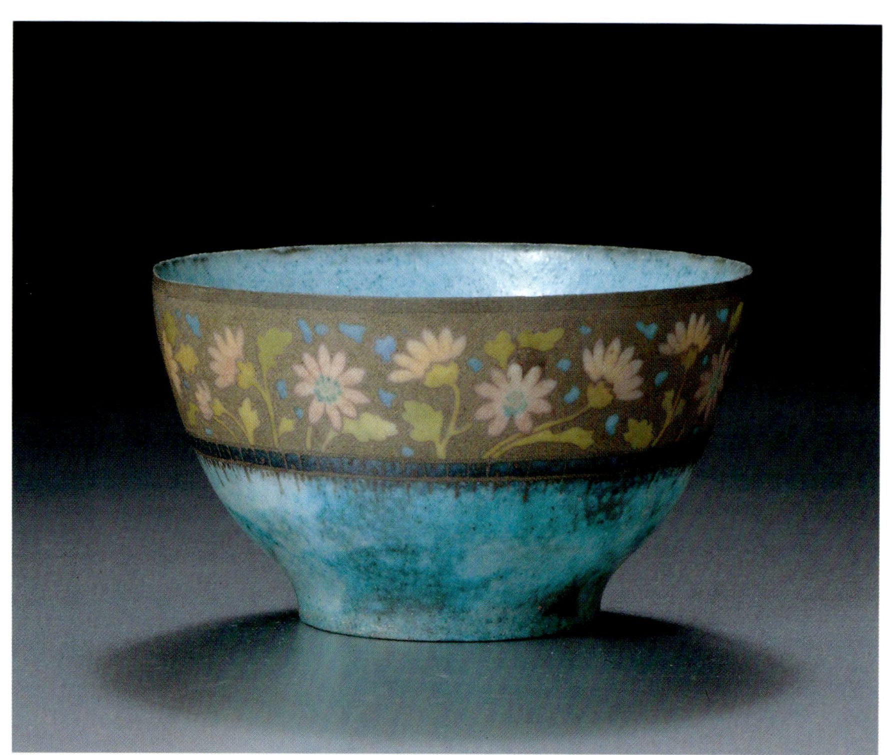

Georges Despret
(1862–1952)

Entrepreneur and artistically gifted technician

In 1884, after studying engineering, took over the management of the Glacerie Français de Jeumont founded in 1859. Production of flat glass and building glass. From about 1890, developed his own *pâte-de-verre* process. Introduced his works in the new technique at the 1900 World Exhibition in Paris. Collaborated with various artists. The factory was destroyed in World War I. The glasshouse was closed in 1937.

Yvonne Serruys (married name: Mille)
(1874–1953)

Sculptor, painter, and designer of glass

Pupil of the sculptor Egide Rombeaux and painter Emile Claus. From 1897, participated regularly with sculptures at exhibitions in Paris. Around 1905–10, designs for sculptures made of *pâte de verre* and for vessels of blown glass for the Georges Despret factory in Jeumont.

281   Fish

Mark on wall just above standing base: *Despret*; diamond-engraved and rubbed out with gold on the underside of base, the work number: *1117*
Molded shortly before 1906
Fish: H 25.7, ⌀ 18.9 cm
Base: H 5.9, ⌀ 29.8 cm

Pâte de verre, body solid, base hollow; coarse, grainy surface. Sand-molded. Fish polished.
Fish and base have different provenances.

Acc. no. P 1969-21
Gift of Firma H. Horten and Helmut Hentrich

Small series. Based on a design by Serruys for Despret; cf. *Le Goût moderne* 1, no. 1 (Nov. 1926): 11.

Lit.: Hilschenz-Mlynek and Ricke, *Frankreich*, 1985, cat. no. 165

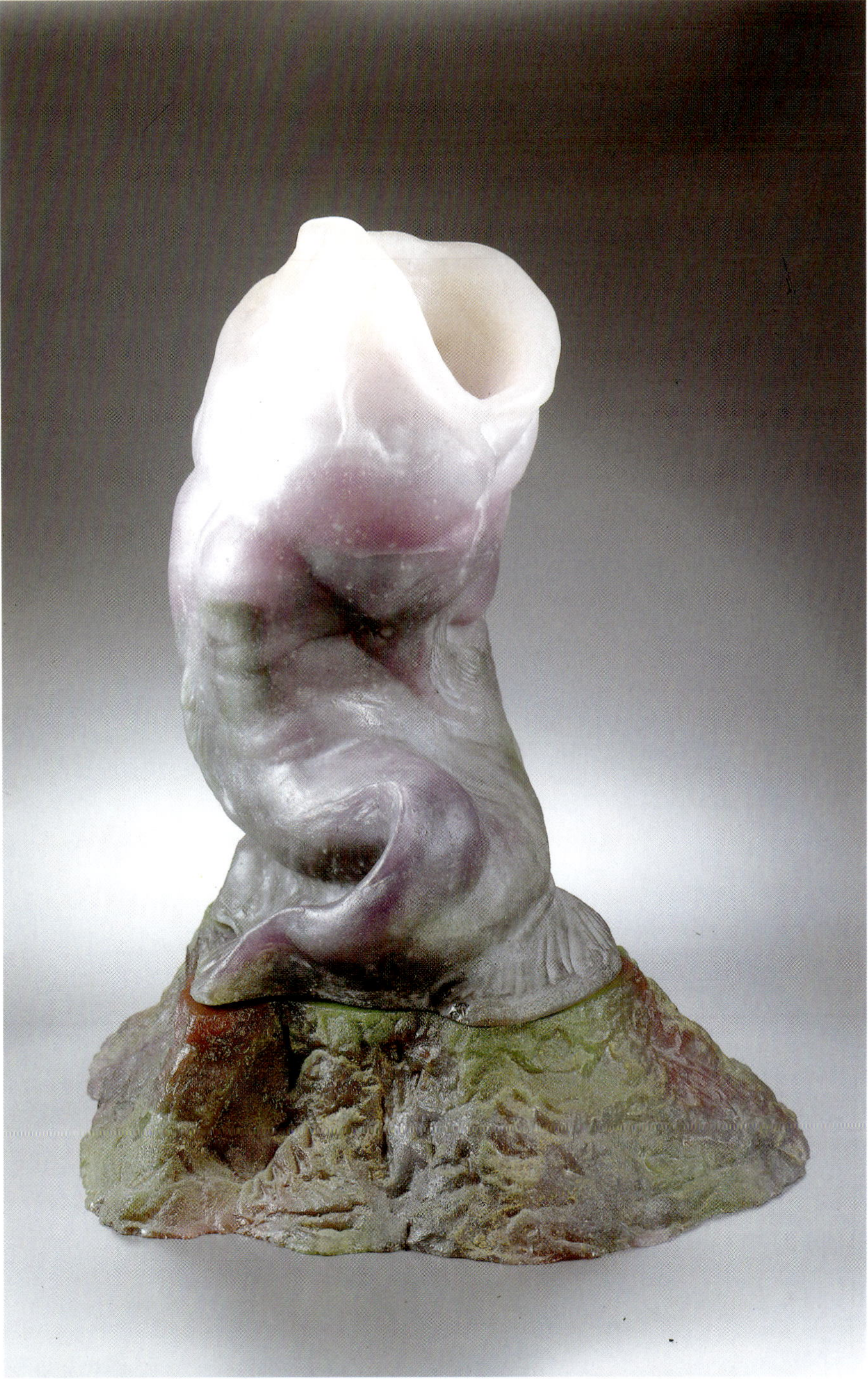

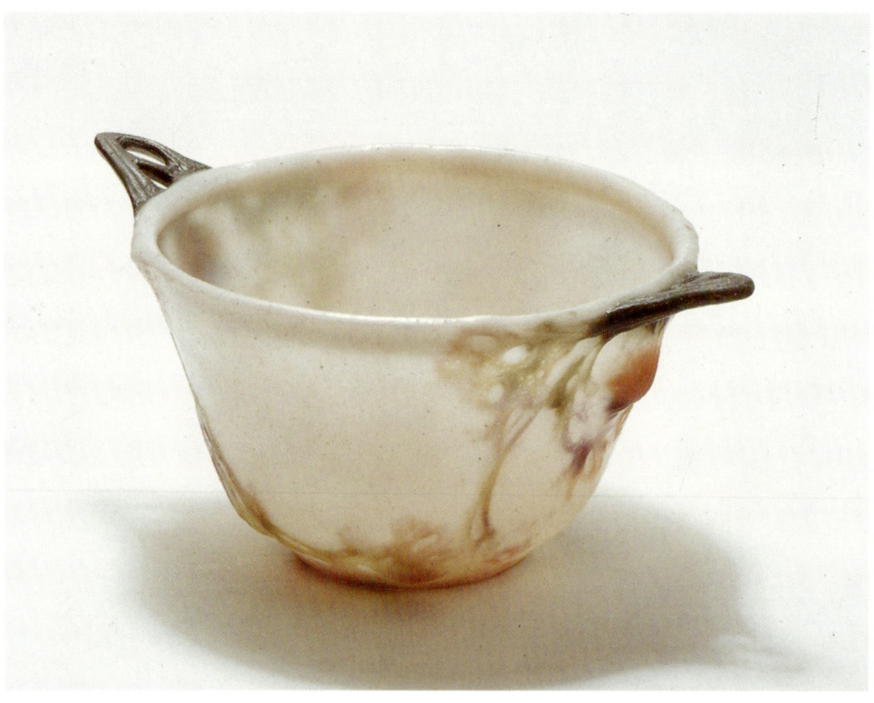

François-Emile Décorchemont
(1880–1971)

Painter, sculptor, ceramist, and glass artist

Studied at the Ecole Nationale des Arts Décoratifs in Paris from 1893 to 1900. First ceramic works around 1901–03. Inspired by Dammouse to make first *pâte-de-verre* experiments in his father's Paris studio in 1902/03; from 1907, first results in making colored *pâte de cristals*. Around 1910, his first workshop in Conches. From 1930, larger reliefs made of *pâte de cristal*; from 1932 window glazing.

282   Dish

Deeply stamped mark: *FDECORCHEMENT*; ligated: *ED*; diamond-engraved work number on the underside of base: *U 8*
Molded in 1908
H 4.7, ∅ 11.2

Pâte de verre. Fused in open mold. Two handles drawn out in shape of branches. Decoration: algae and shells in slightly pushed up relief on half opaque, whitish ground. Exterior surface mat, interior fused to a bright surface.

Acc. no. P 1970-162
Gift of Helmut Hentrich

From a small series of 11 different colored pieces. For examples of variations with similarly shaped handles see *L'Art décoratif* 9, no. 17 (1907): illus. preceding p. 216.

Lit.: Hilschenz-Mlynek and Ricke, *Frankreich*, 1985, cat. no. 143

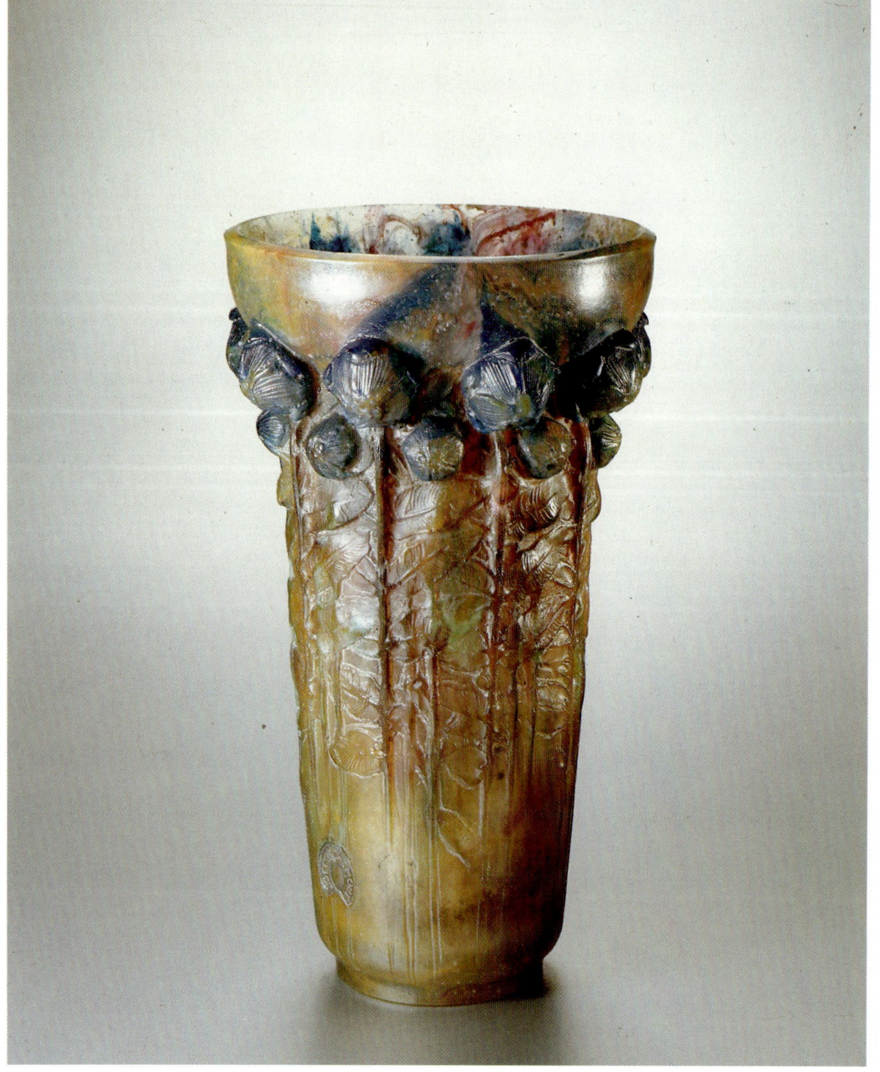

283   "Millepertius" Beaker

Deeply pressed mark: *FDECORCHEMENT*; ligated: *ED*; diamond-engraved work number on the underside of base: *no 203*
Molded in 1913
H 20.7, ∅ 12.5 cm

Pâte de cristal. Fused in two-part closed mold.
Decoration: on marbled ground, three-dimensional flower buds on long stems.
Vessel lightly polished inside and out.
Small defects on lower wall, made during firing.

Acc. no. P 1977-41
Gift of Helmut Hentrich

Model no. 47. From a small series of six known, differently colored pieces.

Lit.: Hilschenz-Mlynek and Ricke, *Frankreich*, 1985, cat. no. 144

Victor Amalric Walter

(1870–1959)

Painter, ceramist, and glass artist and technician

From 1885, studied at the Ecole Nationale de Céramique of the porcelain factory Sèvres. Worked there as porcelain painter from 1887 to 1892. In 1903, presented his first *pâte-de-verre* works. From 1906 to ca. 1914, responsible for the *pâte-de-verre* production at Daum Frères in Nancy. Models usually from other artists, especially Henri Bergé. From 1919, worked in his own workshop. Again the models were primarily by Bergé.

Henri Bergé

(1870–1930)

Sculptor, painter, and glass designer

Professor of decorative art at the Ecole professionelle de l'Est. From ca. 1897 to 1914, worked free-lance as Maître décorateur at the design studios of Daum Frères, Nancy. From ca. 1906 to 1930, models with plant and animal decoration for glass sculptures in *pâte de verre* by the painter, ceramist, and glass artist Victor Amalric Walter in Nancy.

284   Pitcher

Mark on foot, as part of mold: *AWALTER NANCY* and *HBergé sc.*, *AW* and *HB* (ligated)
1920s
H 21.5, ⌀ 16.3 cm

Pâte de verre. Fused in multipartite mold. Decoration: on both sides, vines in relief with leaves and red-brown grapes on ground colored dark blue from the foot to turquoise and light green at the top.

Acc. no. P 1985 111
Gift of Helmut Hentrich

Small series. After a model by Henri Bergé.

Lit.: Hilschenz-Mlynek and Ricke, *Frankreich*, 1985, cat. no. 555

285   Serving Platter

Mark on front of platter, as part of mold: *AWALTER NANCY* and *HBergé sc.*, *AW* and *HB* (ligated)
1920s
H 3, ⌀ 31 cm

Pâte de verre. Fused in two-part mold. Decoration: vines of the nasturtium with green foliage and yellow flowers in low relief on light yellow to violet speckled ground.

Acc. no. P 1977-48
Gift of Helmut Hentrich

Small series. After a model by Henri Bergé.

Lit.: Hilschenz-Mlynek and Ricke, *Frankreich*, 1985, cat. no. 547

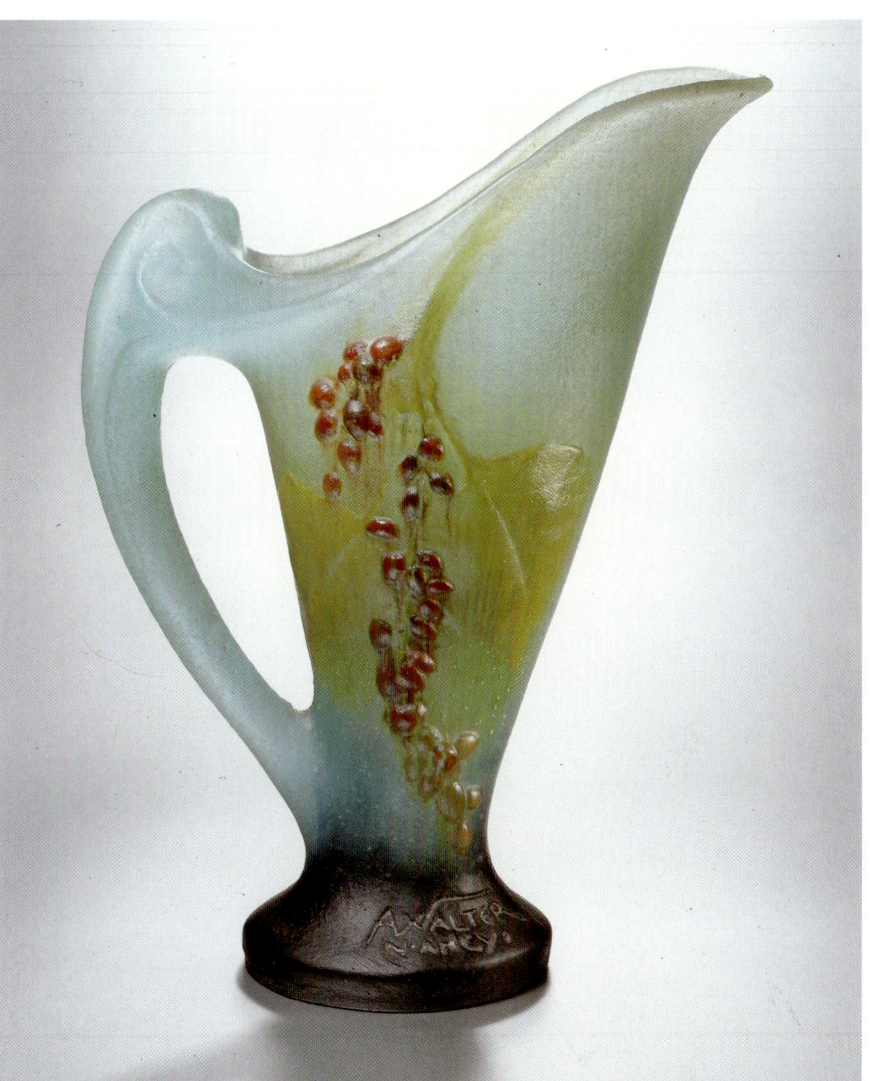

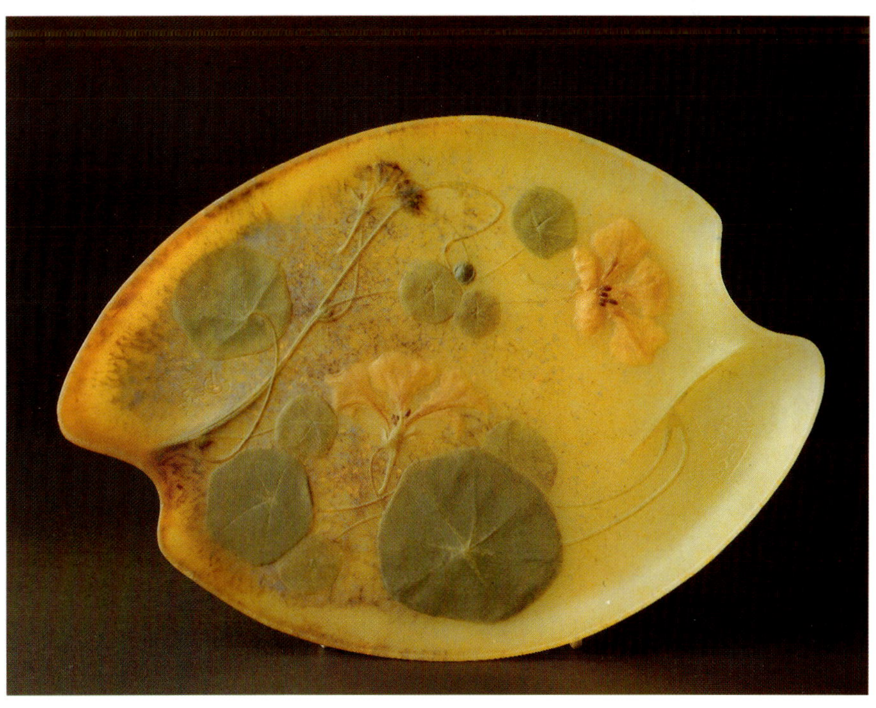

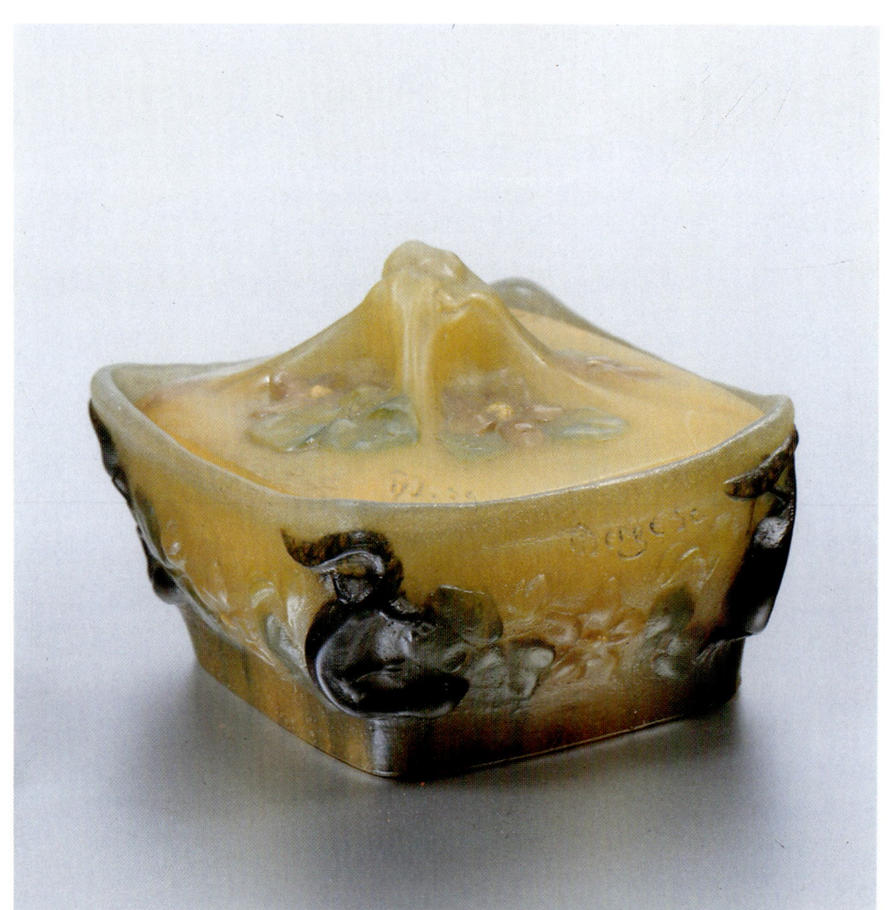

286 Covered Jar

Mark on wall as part of mold, on jar: *AWALTER NANCY* and *HBergé sc.*, *AW* and *HB* (ligated); on cover: *AW.N* and *HB.sc.*, *AW* and *HB* (ligated)
1920s
H (with cover) 7.6, ⌀ 13.8 cm

Pâte de verre. Fused in multipartite mold. Decoration on yellowish wall marbled brown towards the bottom: lizards on the four corners; in between, foliage with yellow flowers; on cover, foliage with reddish flowers; partly polished. Base slightly damaged.

Acc. no. P 1984-53
Gift of Helmut Hentrich

Small series. After a model by Henri Bergé. For another example see Klesse and Mayr, *Sammlung Funke-Kaiser*, 1981, cat. no. 387.

Lit.: Hilschenz-Mlynek and Ricke, *Frankreich*, 1985, cat. no. 546

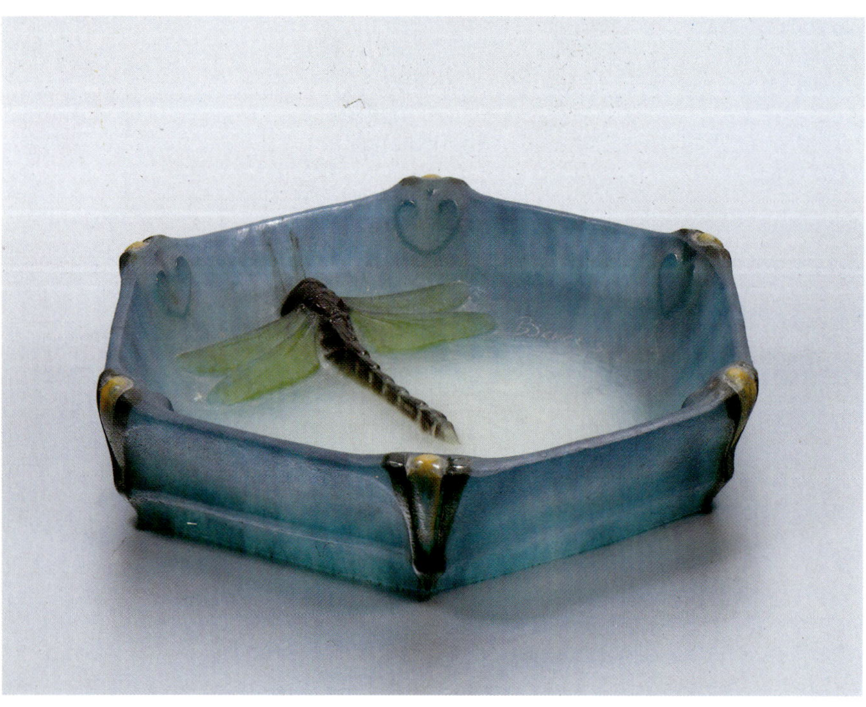

287 Dish

Mark on inside of dish, as part of mold: *AWALTER NANCY* and *HBergé sc.*, *AW* and *HB* (ligated)
1920s
H 4, ⌀ 20.9 cm

Pâte de verre. Fused in multipartite mold. Decoration on blue speckled wall, inside colorless: three-dimensional bud motifs on the six corners; dragonfly in relief in the well, partly polished.

Acc. no. P 1977-50
Gift of Helmut Hentrich

Small series. After a model by Henri Bergé.

Lit.: Hilschenz-Mlynek and Ricke, *Frankreich*, 1985, cat. no. 559

Gabriel Argy-Rousseau

Actually Joseph-Gabriel Rousseau
(1885–1953)

Ceramist, enamel painter, and glass artist

From 1902 to 1906, studied at the Ecole
Nationale de Céramique in Sèvres, then director of a laboratory for ceramic research at the
Sèvres factory. Shortly thereafter, opened his
own studio in Paris for making *pâte de verre*.
In 1913, married Marianne Argyriadès; henceforth, used the name Argy-Rousseau. In
1921, founded together with the art dealer
Gustave-Gaston Moser-Millot the joint-stock
company Les Pâtes de Verre d'Argy-Rousseau.
From 1922, collaborated with the factory
Ludwig Moser Söhne in Carlsbad, which realized some of his models. International recognition for his *pâte-de-verre* works at the large
Parisian arts-and-crafts exhibition in 1925.

288 "Monnaies du Pape" Covered Jar

Mark fused into wall, as part of mold:
G. ARGY-ROUSSEAU; and on the underside
of base: *6198*
Designed in 1920
H (with cover) 8.5, ⌀ 9.7 cm

Pâte de verre. Fused in multipartite mold.
Decoration on milky yellow wall and cover:
Judas-tree leaves in low relief, outlined in
black.

Acc. no. P 1970-85
Gift of Helmut Hentrich

Large series, produced in different color com-
binations. Bloch-Dermant, *Argy-Rousseau*,
1990, 185, no. 20.26. For similar pieces see
Klesse and Mayr, *Sammlung Funke-Kaiser*,
1981, cat. nos. 1–14 and 401.

Lit.: Hilschenz-Mlynek and Ricke, *Frankreich*,
1985, cat. no. 3

289 "Araignées et Ronces" Vase

Mark fused into wall, as part of mold:
G. ARGY-ROUSSEAU; and on the underside
of base in relief: *7848*
Designed in 1920
H (with cover) 11.3, ⌀ 13 cm

Pâte de verre. Fused in multipartite mold.
Decoration: flowering twigs and a spider's
web on both front and back.
See Bloch-Dermant, *Argy-Rousseau*, 1990,
181, no. 20.05.

Acc. no. P 1989-4
Gift of Thea Satory, Ratingen

Small series.

Lit.: *Silice e fuoco*, 1992, cat. no. 243

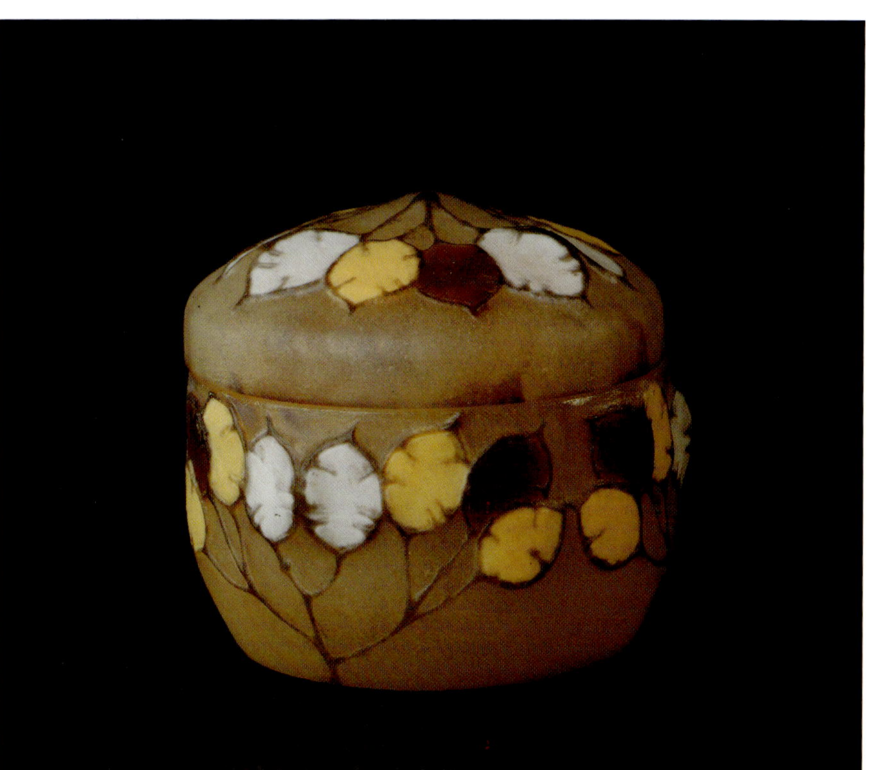

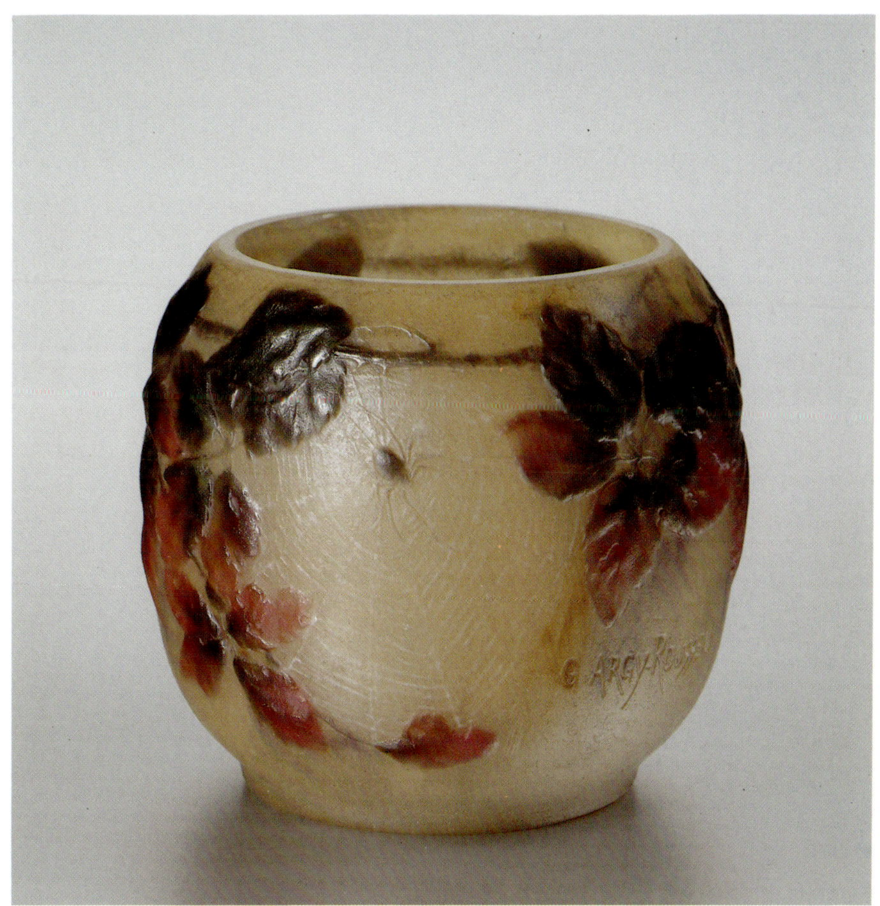

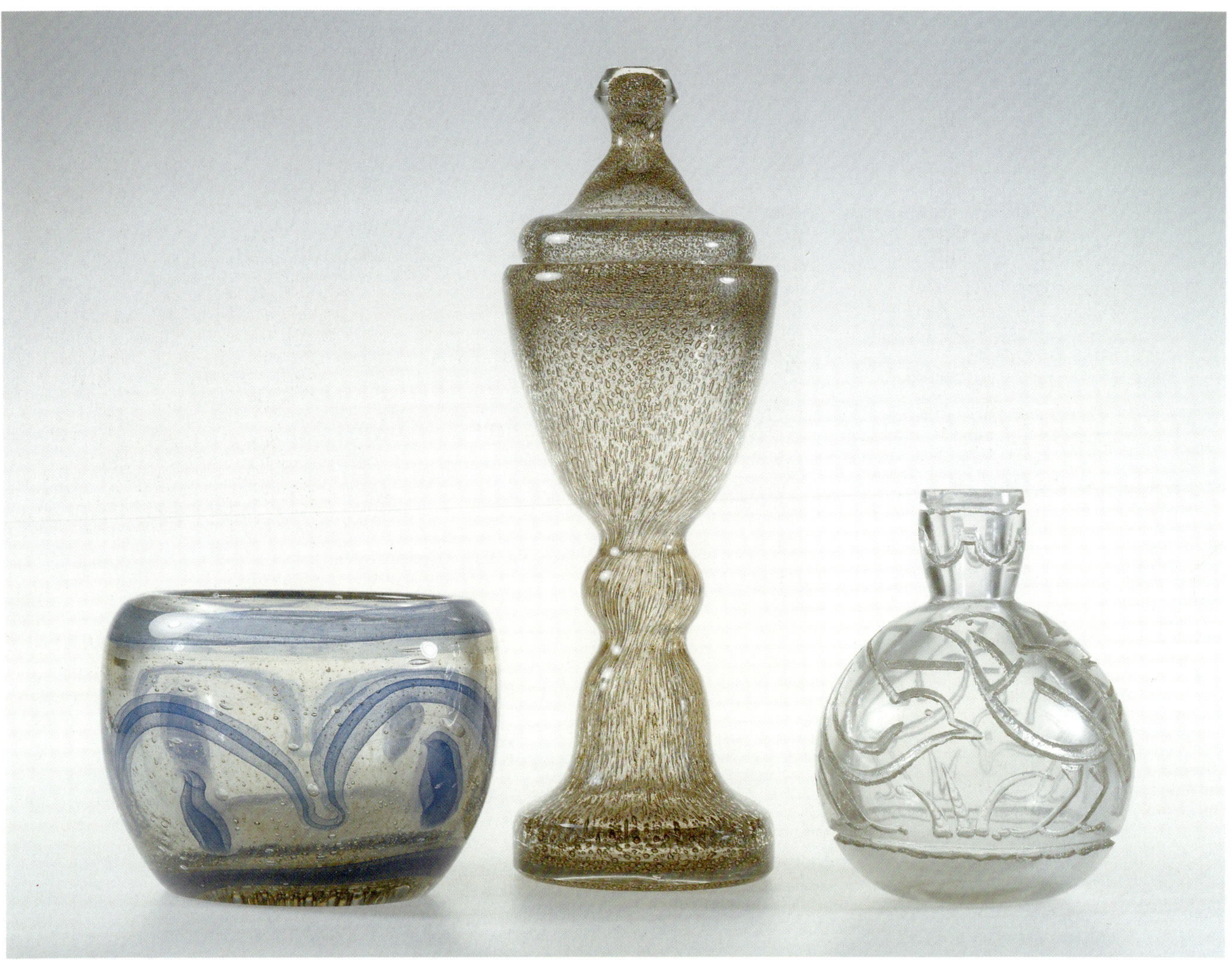

Maurice Marinot

(1882–1960)

Painter and glass artist

From 1902, studied painting at the Ecole des Beaux-Arts in Paris. Member of the Fauves. In 1905, returned to his hometown of Troyes. From 1911, took a keen interest in glass. In the coming years, opened his own workshop in the Bar-sur-Seine factory; studied production techniques and chemical recipes. Insisted that artists carry out their own glass work. From 1913 to 1923, "période d'email" with painted decoration on colorless glass. Between 1919 and 1927, translucent enamel painting, etching processes, and cut decoration. Increasing preference for pure furnace techniques, in particular that of embedding air bubbles (*technique du bullage*), which he mastered brilliantly.

290   Bowl

Needle-etched mark on the underside of base: *marinot.*; as well as model no. in ink on the paper label: *553*

1923
H 12.8, ⌀ 18 cm

Colorless, thick-walled overlay glass; between the layers irregular formation of bubbles with oxide inclusions and embedded color. Blown freehand or in mold; made entirely at the furnace.

Acc. no. P 1967-15
Gift of Florence Marinot, Troyes

Unique piece.

Lit.: Hilschenz-Mlynek and Ricke, *Frankreich*, 1985, cat. no. 435

291   Covered Goblet

Needle-etched mark on the underside of base: *marinot.*; as well as model no. in ink on paper label: *976*
1925
H (with cover) 37, ⌀ 12.8 cm

Thick-walled glass with light gray-brown tone; between the layers, dense formation of bubbles with oxide inclusions. Hollow stem opening into the bowl. Mold-blown and shaped; made entirely at the furnace.

Acc. no. P 1967-28
Gift of Florence Marinot, Troyes

Unique piece.

Lit.: Hilschenz-Mlynek and Ricke, *Frankreich*, 1985, cat. no. 446

292   Bottle

Needle-etched mark on the underside of base: *marinot.*; as well as model no. in ink on paper label: *335*
1921
H 18, ⌀ 14.1 cm

Colorless, thick-walled glass. Mold-blown. Encircling decoration: four birds in grass in deeply etched lines.

Acc. no. P 1967-20
Gift of Florence Marinot, Troyes

Unique piece.

Lit.: Hilschenz-Mlynek and Ricke, *Frankreich*, 1985, cat. no. 430

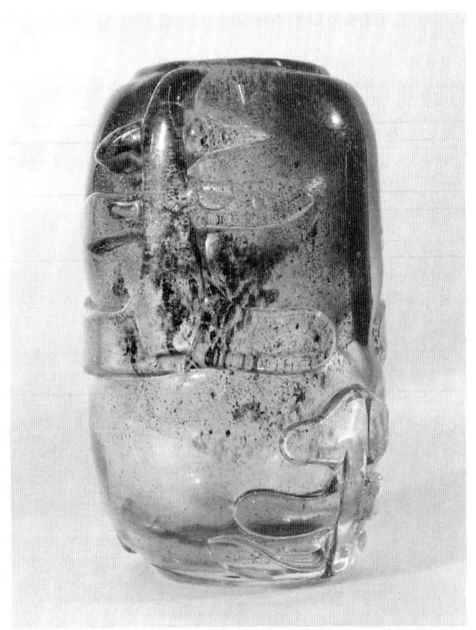

Henri-Edouard Navarre
(1885–1971)

Sculptor, medalist, draftsman, and glass and jewelry artist

After painting and working as a goldsmith, studied sculpture at the Ecole Bernard Palissy in 1903, studied at the Julian academy of drawing in 1904, as well as at the Ecole des Beaux-Arts in Paris in 1905 and 1911. At the same time, took technical courses at the Conservatoire National des Arts et Métiers. From 1905 to 1910, worked at various sculpture and chiseling workshops. After World War I, worked primarily as sculptor and successful medalist. In 1923, first glassware in collaboration with André Thuret at the glasshouse Sovirel, Bagneaux. Shortly thereafter, consultant for the glass company UMAB (Usines et Manufactures d'Art de Bezons), Bezons. Participated successfully at the Art-Deco exhibition, Paris, in 1925 (Certificate of Honor). From ca. 1932, took a keen interest in sculptural glass works.

293   Vase

Engraved mark on the underside of base:
H.NAVARRE 638
Ca. 1930
H 18.5, ⌀ 11.9 cm

Colorless, thick-walled overlay glass; between the layers, densely strewn oxide inclusions with bubble formation. Free-blown and shaped; made entirely at the furnace. Decoration: freely applied leaf or twig-shaped forms pressed flat.

Acc. no. P 1974-46
Gift of Helmut Hentrich

Unique piece. For similar glassware with three-dimensional applications see, for example, *L'Art et les Artistes* (Nov. 1934): 56, and *Mobilier et Décoration* (Feb. 1929): 70.

Lit.: Hilschenz-Mlynek and Ricke, *Frankreich*, 1985, cat. no. 470

André Thuret
(1898–1965)

Engineer and glass artist

After attending the university, from 1921 to 1924, engineer at the Verrerie de Bagneaux near Paris. Henceforth, took a scientific interest in glass technology, carrying out experiments himself. In 1923, together with Henri Navarre, first glassware at the glasshouse Sovirel, Bagneaux. From 1924 to 1926, director of the UMAB (Usines et Manufactures d'Art de Bezons), Bezons. From 1926, worked at the Conservatoire National des Arts et Métiers in Paris, at first as assistant, then as Chef de Travaux and Directeur de Laboratoire, and finally as chair of applied chemistry in the ceramic and glass industry. Realized his own glass designs until the 1950s.

294   Bowl

Diamond-engraved mark on the underside of base: *andré thuret*
1925–30
H 10, ⌀ 15 cm

Slightly yellowish, thick-walled glass. Free-blown and shaped; made entirely at furnace.

Acc. no. P 1976-16
Gift of Madame André Thuret

Unique piece.

Lit.: Hilschenz-Mlynek and Ricke, *Frankreich*, 1985, cat. no. 527

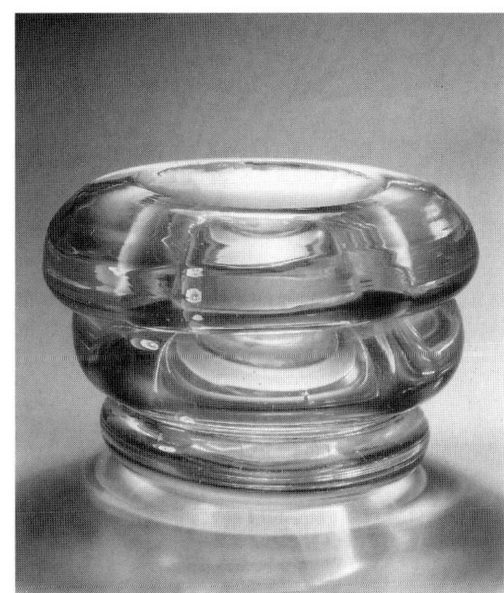

Aristide-Michel Colotte
(1885–1959)

Glass decorator, sculptor, and jewelry artist

After apprenticing at the workshops of the Cristalleries de Baccarat, from 1919, apprenticed in glass cutting and employed at the Galeries d'art des Magasins Réunis in Nancy. From 1926 to early 1940s, headed his own studio for glass works and engraved jewelry in Nancy. In 1932, founded the Société Anonyme Ateliers Colotte. Developed chiseling techniques for glass.

295   Vase

Engraved mark on wall: *A. Colotte*;
and on the underside of base: *TAILLE A LA MAIN*
Ca. 1926
H 18.6, ⌀ 16.2 cm

Colorless glass. Mold-blown.
Decoration: wide frieze with four birds in etched relief on silvery rubbed ground. In between are radiating, miter-shaped cut areas with semimat polish.

Acc. no. P 1983-139
Gift of Helmut Hentrich

Unique piece.

Lit.: Hilschenz-Mlynek and Ricke, *Frankreich*, 1985, cat. no. 26; Ricke, *2500 Jahre*, 1987, cat. no. 175; M. Mazet, *A. Colotte: Sculpteur sur verre et sur cristal* (Paris, 1994), 142, no. 33

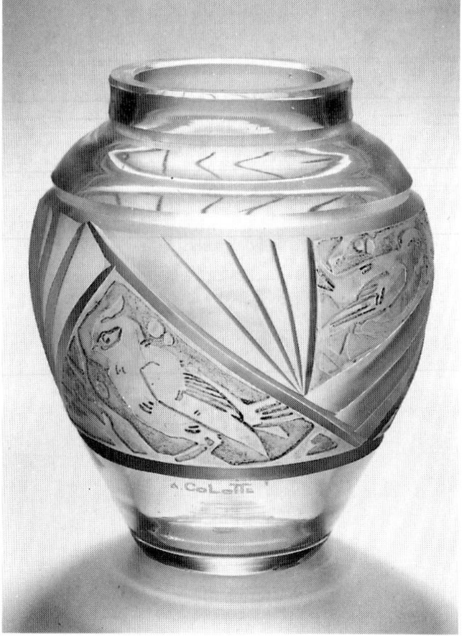

From Art Nouveau to the 1950s
North America

Besides the dominant role the *genre Gallé* played, another impulse was significant for turn-of-the-century glass art: with the glassware by Louis C. Tiffany in New York, the New World exerted for the first time a decisive influence on the development of art in Europe.

After studying painting, Tiffany enjoyed many successful years as a grand-style interior decorator and designer of widely admired stained glass and mosaics. In the early 1890s he started producing novel luxury glass in his own factories in Brooklyn and Corona, Long Island, designing most of the works himself. His most prolific period of producing decorative glassware was between 1896 and 1902, when he created his finest "Favrile" glass.

Like Gallé, Tiffany set high standards for his top products. He wanted them to be recognized as great works of art, on a par with sculpture or painting. Samuel Bing, whose Paris shop "L'Art Nouveau Bing" gave the period its name and who was one of the most committed advocates of the idea of interior decoration as a synthesis of the arts, was a strong supporter of Tiffany's work.

Even though the occasional vegetal forms and a dominating organically sinuous line linked the glass of the American with that of Art Nouveau, a fundamental conceptual difference set them apart from the works of the Ecole de Nancy. While the final appearance of Emile Gallé's glassware and that of his circle was the result of painting, cutting, engraving, or etching done in the factory's decorating workshops, most of Tiffany's pieces were completed by the glassmaker entirely at the furnace. Their often fascinating effect resulted from taking into account the behavior of hot viscous glass in the design. Its spontaneous creation in an uninterrupted process limited by time can be read from every vessel.

Tiffany drew primarily on the various possibilities of artificial iridescence to decorate his glass. In this process metallic salts were vaporized on the hot glass to create many-colored, shimmering coatings. He was inspired to this type of design by the iridescence that characterizes antique glass that has been buried underground. The copper luster of medieval Islamic ceramics also impressed him.

Techniques for creating simple iridescence were developed in Hungary and Bohemia as early as the 1850s and 1860s. Tiffany had English experts work for him in his glasshouse in Corona, perfecting the techniques and adapting them to his decorative vessels. He was primarily interested in achieving various iri-

descences on the same piece. The effect of many of the early glass works was created by this process. Linear currents, waves, and feather patterns made with hooks dragged over the surface served to evoke vegetal forms (cat. no. 297).

The approach to such glassware as the "Cypriote" (cat. no. 299) and "Lava" types was different. Their ceramic-like surfaces recall the erratic primeval forces of nature and are essentially based on the characteristic appearance of an unrefined melt solidified to a viscous state.

Tiffany's repertoire of forms ranged from being deliberately amorphous to elegant, refined, and inventive. Vessels whose appearance is determined by flowers of existing (cat. no. 304) or imaginary plant forms played a decisive role in Tiffany's oeuvre and contributed considerably to his success in Europe. Generally he deemed the vessel's plasticity and animated outline much more important than his French contemporaries. In this his ideas coincided with those of the Bohemian glass artists, whom he had provided essential impulses towards the close of the century.

Shortly after the turn of the century, a waning interest in Tiffany's decorative iridescence prompted him to develop thick-walled vessels whose embellishment evolved inside the many-layered wall. This "paperweight" technique (cat. no. 301) drew on an older process that had been developed in the mid-nineteenth century for decorative motifs embedded in the colorless glass of paperweights. In combination with enclosed iridescent veils, Tiffany achieved new effects with his usual mastery.

From about 1910, Tiffany's work increasingly lost significance. Artistic development stagnated and flourishing competition in his own country, such as from Frederick C. Carder at Steuben Glass Works, Corning, New York, or the small Quezal factory, Brooklyn, New York (cat. nos. 305, 306), weakened his company's commercial basis. In view of the many similar products offered by other manufacturers, the public was no longer willing to accept Tiffany's art demands, which now seemed unoriginal.

Louis Comfort Tiffany

(1848–1933)

Painter, designer of interior decoration, glass, and applied arts

Studied painting in New York from 1866 to 1868 and in Paris in 1869. After 1878, he devoted himself almost entirely to decorative art. In 1885, founded the Tiffany Glass Company NY in Brooklyn. In 1889, received important artistic impulses from his visit to the Paris World Exhibition. In 1892, founded a large glass factory under the name Tiffany Glass and Decorating Company NY in Corona, Long Island. Arthur J. Nash was his glasshouse master and technician. In 1893, his first big success, at the Chicago World Exhibition with decorative glassware based on his own designs. From 1894, sold his decorative glassware under the registered trade name Tiffany Favrile Glass. In 1900, worldwide success at the Paris World Exhibition.
In 1919 Tiffany withdrew from the artistic direction of his companies. In 1924, stopped glass production; in 1932, suffered bankruptcy.

296   Vase

Needle-etched in ground-out pontil mark on the underside of base: *T G C* (for *Tiffany Glass Company*)
Ca. 1890–92 (?)
H 13.6, ⌀ 13.4 cm

Milky yellow inner casing covered by colorless glass layer with olive green overlay. Silver-yellow threads, separated into rows of dots with an 18-part ribbed mold. Moldblown and shaped. Colors fired in a reducing atmosphere and iridescent.

Acc. no. P 1970-430
Gift of Helmut Hentrich

Presumably carried out in Tiffany's first glass factory in Brooklyn, NY. For dating and designation see esp. McKean, *Tiffany*, 1980, 301. A vase with similar decoration entered the Metropolitan Museum of Art, New York, in 1896; see Polak, *Modern Glass*, 1962, fig. 21B.

Lit.: Hilschenz, *Jugendstil*, 1973, cat. nos. 426f.; *Lötz* 1, 1989, 15, fig. 2

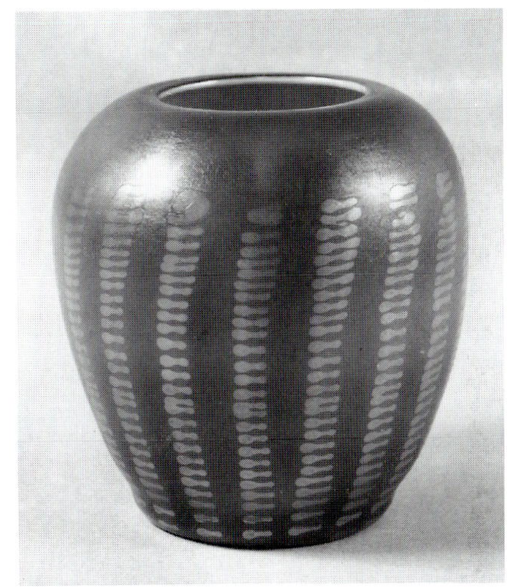

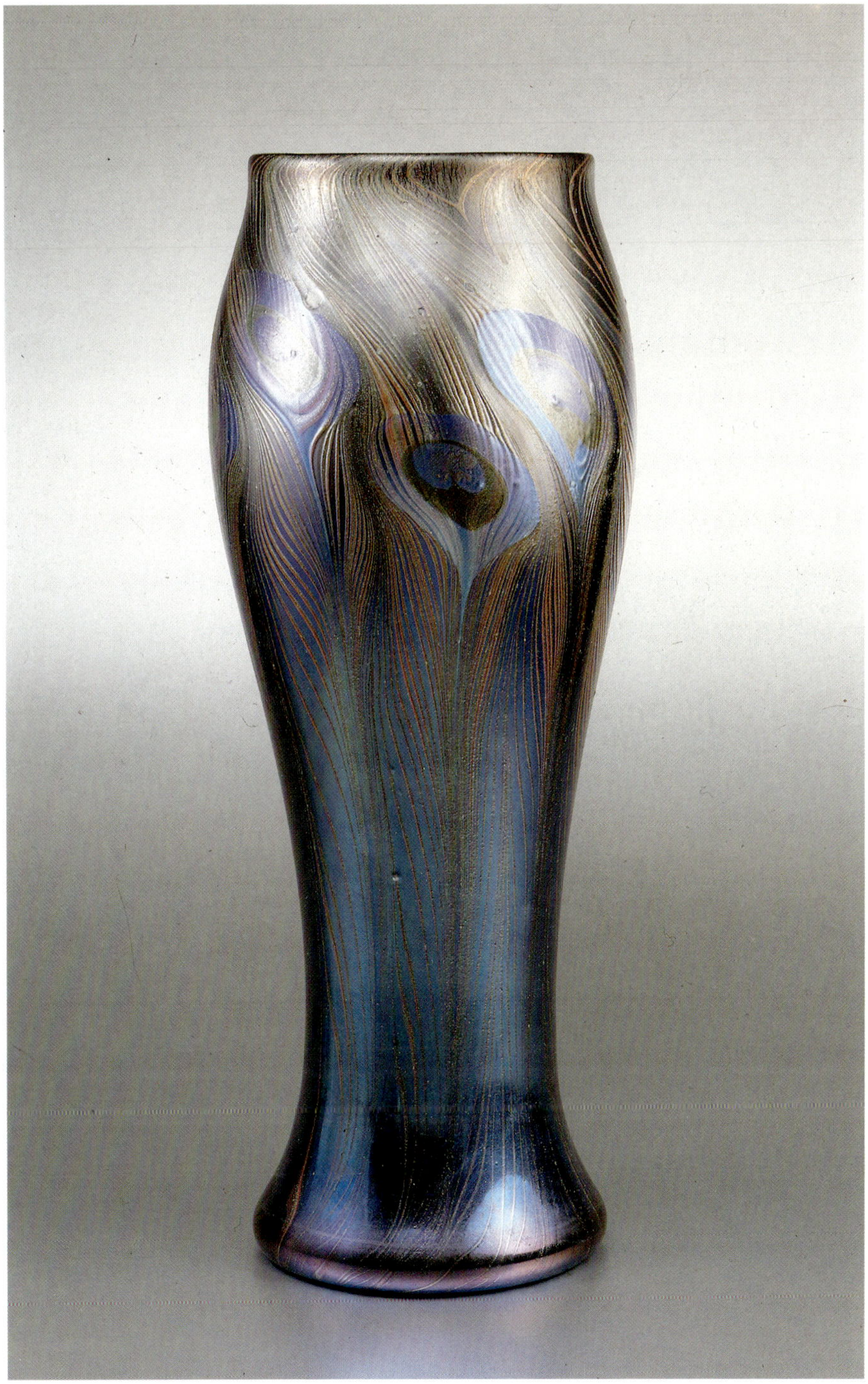

297   "Peacock-Feather" Vase

Engraved in ground-out pontil mark: *Louis C. Tiffany o 7260*
Ca. 1898
H 32.5, ⌀ 13.1 cm

Blue overlay, mold-blown and shaped. Marvered thread application in opaque rust red with aventurine and silver-yellow applications. Combed into an eight-part feather pattern. Colors fired in a reducing atmosphere and iridescent.

Acc. no. P 1970-433
Gift of Helmut Hentrich

For dating compare variations with the same decoration at the Musée des Arts Décoratifs in Paris, acc. nos. 8553, 8554, and 14229, in *Revue des Arts Décoratifs* 18 (1898), Portefeuille, after p. 248, and 19 (1899), illus. p. 324. See also, for example, Daverio, *Tiffany*, 1974, 58; Doros, Norfolk Cat., 1978, cat. nos. 96ff.

Lit.: Hilschenz, *Jugendstil*, 1973, cat. no. 430; Beard, *Modern Glass*, 1976, 81, fig. 1; *Lötz* 1, 1989, 17, fig. 5; Joppien, *Tiffany*, 1999, 145, 249, cat. no. 128

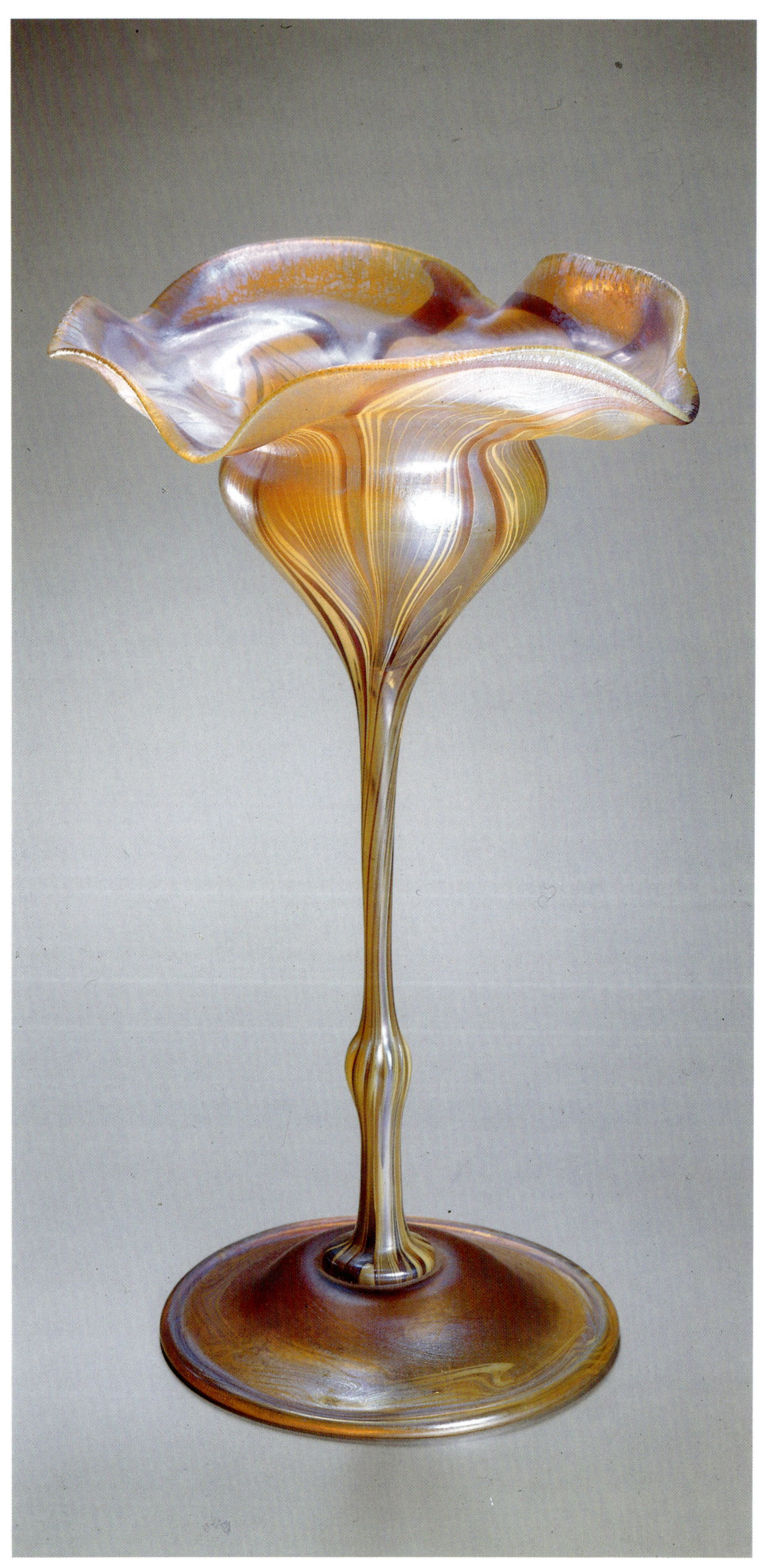

298   Decorative Glass

Engraved mark on the underside of foot:
L.C.T. o 7733
1897–1900
H 23.3, ⌀ 15.3 cm

Colorless glass with embedded yellow and
dark brown threads, combed in the shape
of a flower. Free-blown and shaped. Colors
fired in a reducing atmosphere and iridescent. Goblet subsequently slightly dilated to
achieve a delicate effect of crackled glass.

Acc. no. P 1970-437
Gift of Helmut Hentrich

Similar and almost identical flower glassware
is, for example, at the Northern Bohemian
Museum in Liberec, acc. no. 349; at the
Museum für angewandte Kunst in Vienna, acc.
nos. Gl.1984 and 1985; and, most notably,
at the Chrysler Museum in Norfolk; see Doros,
Norfolk Cat., 1978, nos. 24ff.

Lit.: Hilschenz, *Jugendstil*, 1973, cat. no. 431

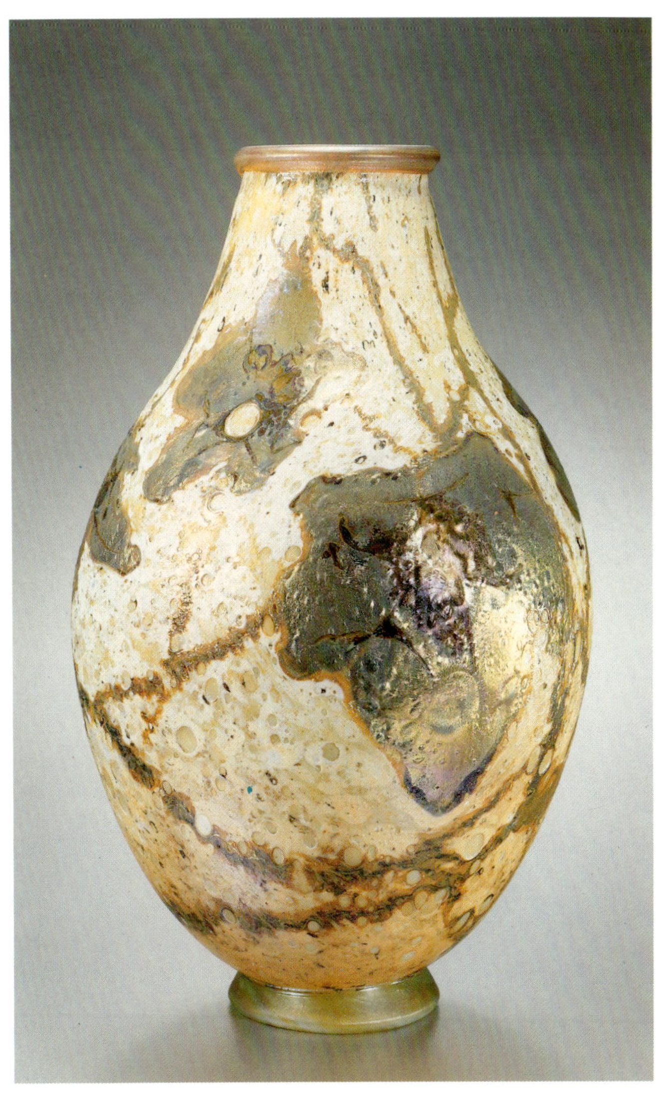

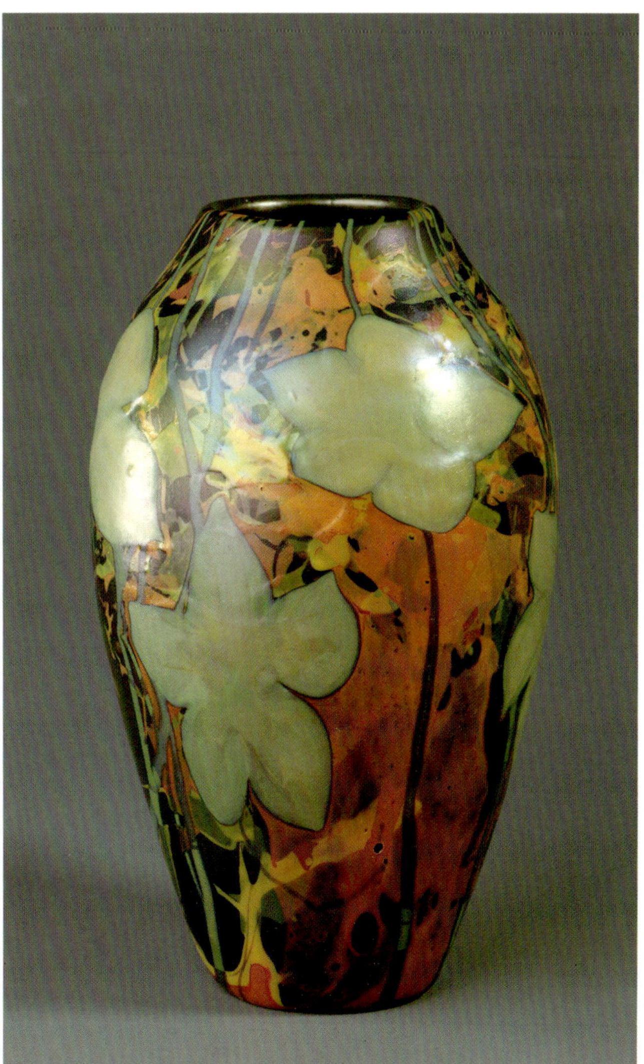

299   "Cypriote" Vase

Engraved mark on the underside of base: *L.C.T. D128
Louis C Tiffany*
Ca. 1896
H 25.6, ⌀ 15.5 cm

Massive milk glass, mold-blown. Applied glass powder and granules in opaque white with dark speckles.
Embedded blue-green threads and six preformed ivy
leaves. Bubbles and craters formed by gas-producing
elements during application of covering layer. Applied foot plate and rim thread. Colors fired in a
reducing atmosphere and iridescent.

Acc. no. P 1970-446
Gift of Helmut Hentrich

Tiffany showed vases of this type at the 1900 World
Exhibition in Paris as well; see Koch, *Tiffany*, 1976,
fig. 88; see also Revi, *Nineteenth Century*, 1964,
226, and Revi, *American Art Nouveau*, 1968, 46–49,
figs. 66–68. For a variation without foot plate see
Daverio, *Tiffany*, 1974, 67. For "Cypriote" vases generally see Doros, *Norfolk Cat.*, 1978, 50ff.

Lit.: Hilschenz, *Jugendstil*, 1973, cat. no. 444;
Schack, *Glaskunst*, 1976, 274, fig. 219; Joppien,
Tiffany, 1999, 164, 246, cat. no. 80

300   Vase

Engraved mark on the underside of base: *L.C.T. E2097*
Ca. 1897
H 18.1, ⌀ 11.3 cm

Gray-brown opaque overlay glass with embedded,
many-colored fragments, granules, and preformed
applications.
Decoration: encircling, climbing ivy with six leaves
on a mosaic-like ground. Slightly iridescent surface.

Acc. no. P 1970-447
Gift of Helmut Hentrich

For vases with similar decoration see, for example,
DKD 11 (1902/03), illus. p. 183; Revi, *American Art
Nouveau*, 1968, color plate after p. 50 (exhibition
piece at St. Louis in 1904 and Paris Salon in 1906).

Lit.: Hilschenz, *Jugendstil*, 1973, cat. no. 439; Koch,
Tiffany, 1976, fig. 121; Joppien, *Tiffany*, 1999, 133,
247, cat. no. 101

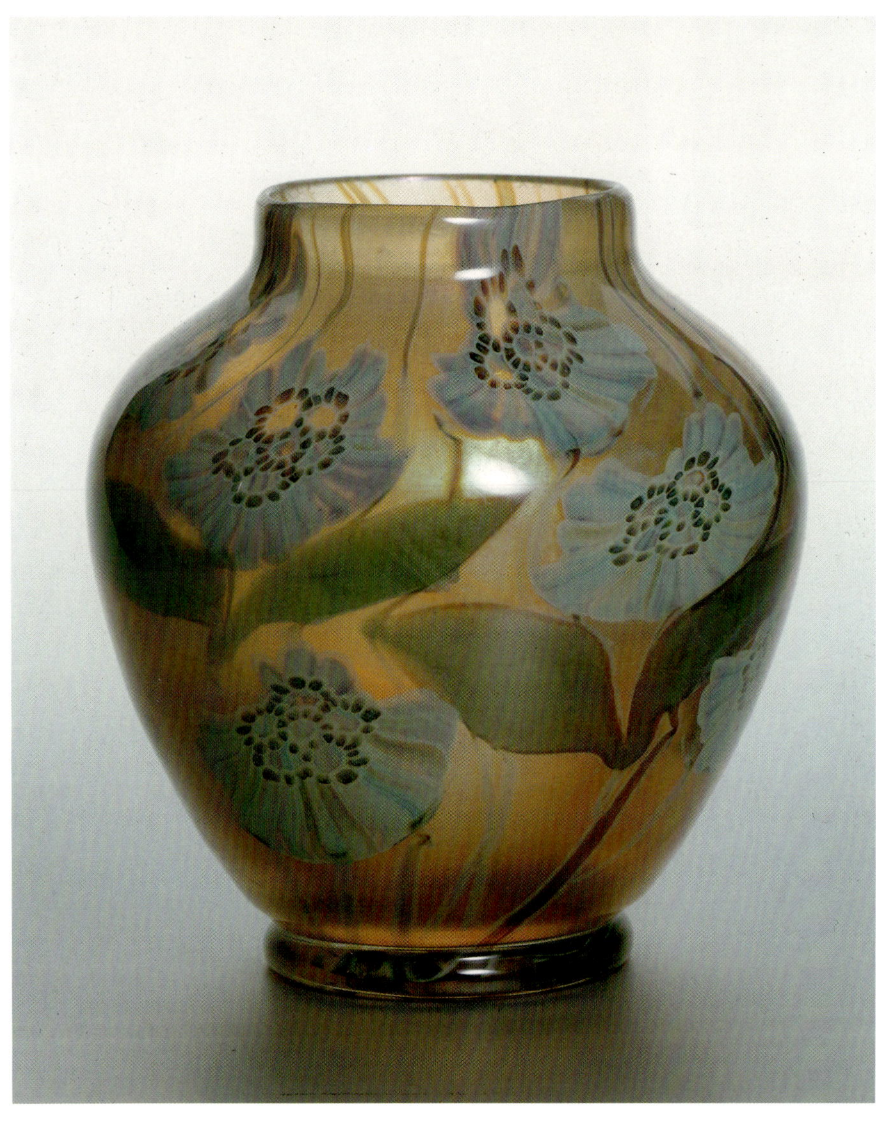

302 Vase

Engraved mark on the underside of foot:
o 10386 L.C.T.
Ca. 1900–1910
H 7, ⌀ 7.5 cm

Milky yellow inner casing, embedded overlapping thread applications in opaque white and brown-violet. Optic-blown in 16-part ribbed mold. Foot applied, rim folded downwards. Iridescent.

Acc. no. P 1970-435
Gift of Helmut Hentrich

Two similarly made glass vases in Norfolk are dated with no tenable justification to ca. 1920; see Doros, Norfolk Cat., 1978, nos. 175f.

Lit.: Hilschenz, *Jugendstil*, 1973, cat. 434

301 "Paperweight" Vase

Engraved mark on the underside of base:
8150 D L.C. Tiffany-Favrile
Ca. 1900–1902
H 14.2, ⌀ 13.4 cm

Silver-yellow ground, iridescence between the layers, colorless glass on top. Green leaves and 11 embedded flowers in millefiori technique under a strong colorless covering layer. Iridescent interior.

Acc. no. P 1970-449
Gift of Helmut Hentrich

For the "paperweight" glass see Doros, Norfolk Cat., 1978, 25ff. For similar vases shown at the large applied-arts exhibition in Turin see McKean, *Tiffany*, 1980, 177, fig. 155.

Lit.: Hilschenz, *Jugendstil*, 1973, cat. no. 446; Koch, *Tiffany*, 1976, fig. 122

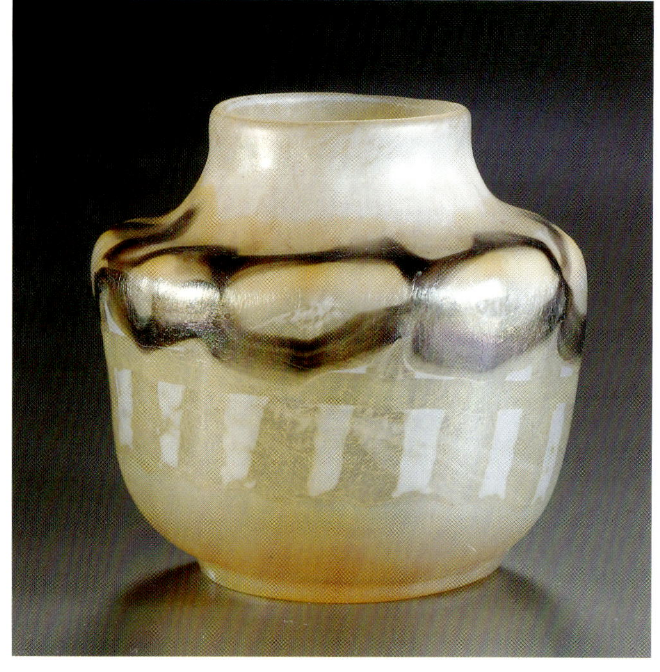

303 Vase

Engraved mark on the underside of foot:
5593 E L.C. Tiffany Favrile
1905–10
H 31, ⌀ 10.2 cm

Milk glass with red overlay. Optic-blown in
eight-part ribbed mold, embedded, dark red,
vertical threads. Colorless overlay; mold-
blown, shaped. Foot plate applied.

Acc. no. P 1970-448
Gift of Helmut Hentrich

For similarly conceived glassware, at the
Chrysler Museum, see Doros, Norfolk Cat.,
1978, nos. 164, 170.

Lit.: Hilschenz, *Jugendstil*, 1973, cat. no. 438

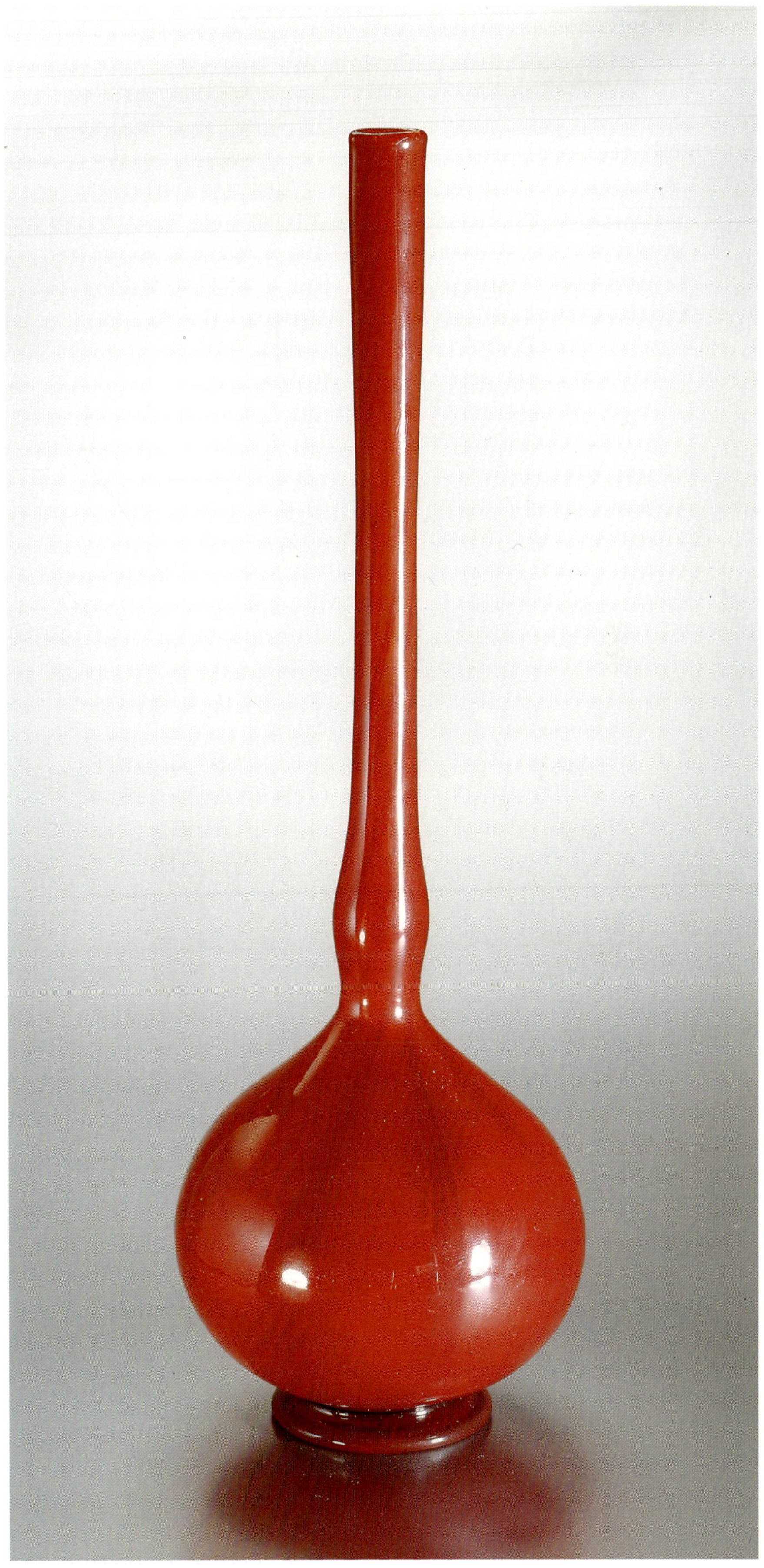

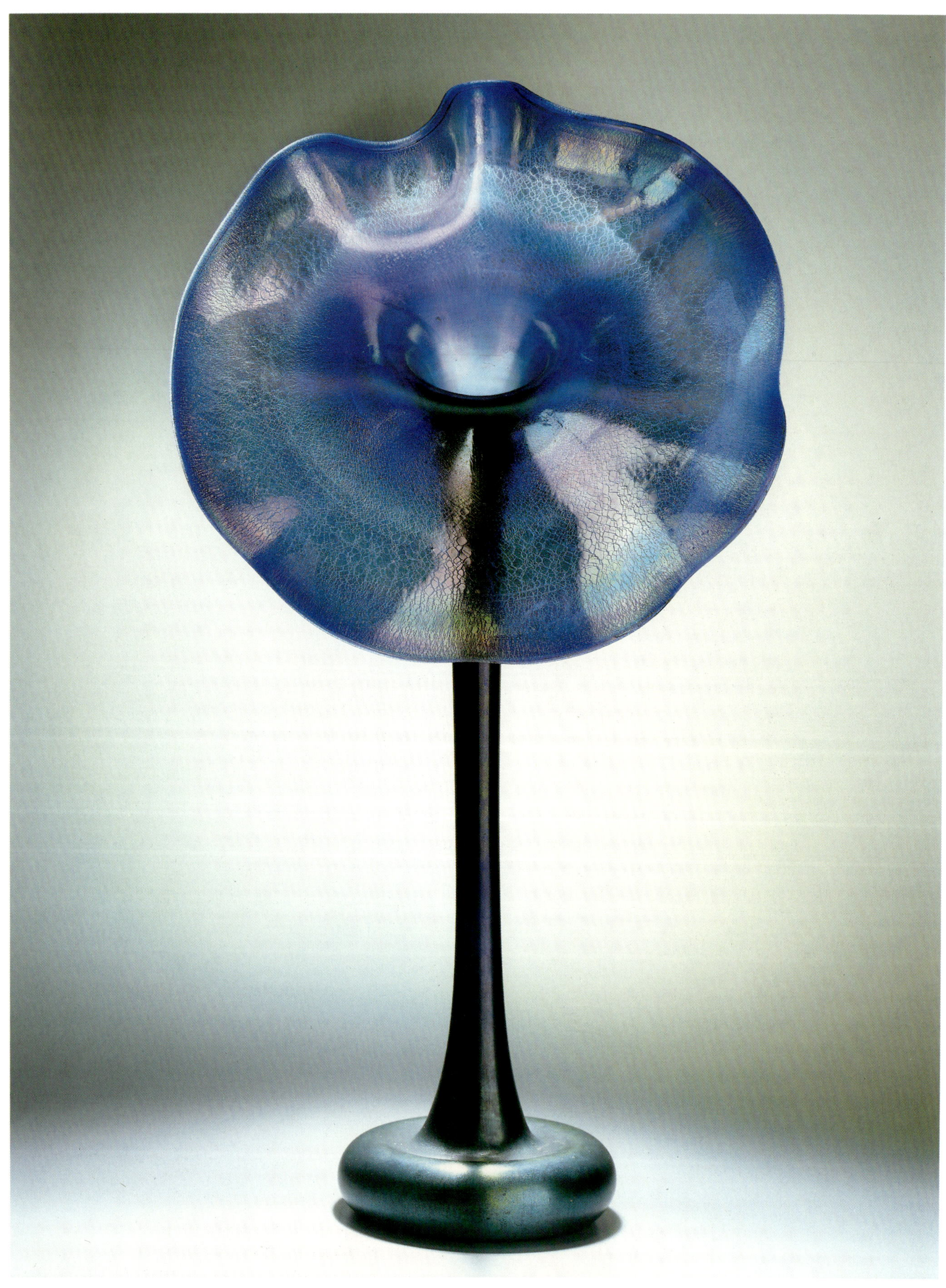

304 "Jack-in-the-Pulpit" Decorative Glass

Engraved mark on the underside of foot:
2066 G L.C. Tiffany-Favrile
Ca. 1910–12
H 52, ⌀ foot 13.1, rim 28.1 cm

Dark blue glass, free-blown and shaped. Colors fired in a reducing atmosphere and iridescent. Rim subsequently dilated, crackling the gleaming metallic, iridescent layer.

Acc. no. P 1970-440
Gift of Helmut Hentrich

Common model, named after the inflorescence of the American Indian turnip. Numerous identical examples, also in other colors, as well as variations; see Daverio, *Tiffany*, 1974, 63; Doros, Norfolk Cat., 1978, nos. 47–49.

Lit.: Hilschenz, *Jugendstil*, 1973, cat. no. 442; Ricke, *Ausgewählte Werke*, 1980, 26; Joppien, *Tiffany*, 1999, 115, 252, cat. no. 178

Frederick C. Carder

(1864–1963)

Glass technician and designer

Born in England. Before emigrating to the United States in 1902, worked for Stevens & Williams in Brierley Hill. In 1903, cofounder of the Steuben Glass Works in Corning, NY. Successfully headed the company until 1933 as director, chief designer, and glass technician, also after it was taken over by Corning Glass Works in 1918. Even after his retirement, in 1934, prolific experimental work at his company studio.

305 Fan Vase

Engraved mark on the underside of foot:
Aurene 6297
Ca. 1910/20
H 22, ⌀ foot 10.4, W 18.4 cm

Colorless glass with blue glass overlay containing silver. Ivory-colored embedded vines. Mold-blown and shaped. Colors fired in a reducing atmosphere and iridescent. Metallic layer is crackled towards the top.

Acc. no. P 1974-3

"Aurene" was Carder's registered name for lustrous, iridescent types of glass in the Tiffany genre. With these he achieved his first success. The blue variation was made between 1905 and the 1930s. See P. V. Gardner, *Frederick Carder: Portrait of a Glassmaker*, exh. cat. (Corning, NY: The Corning Museum of Glass, 1985). See also Hilschenz, *Jugendstil*, 1973, cat. nos. 468f.

Lit.: –

Quezal Art Glass & Decorating Company

Art-glass factory in Brooklyn, NY

Founded in 1901 by Martin Bach and Thomas Johnson, former employees of Tiffany, whose iridescent decoration they adopted.
Active until 1925.

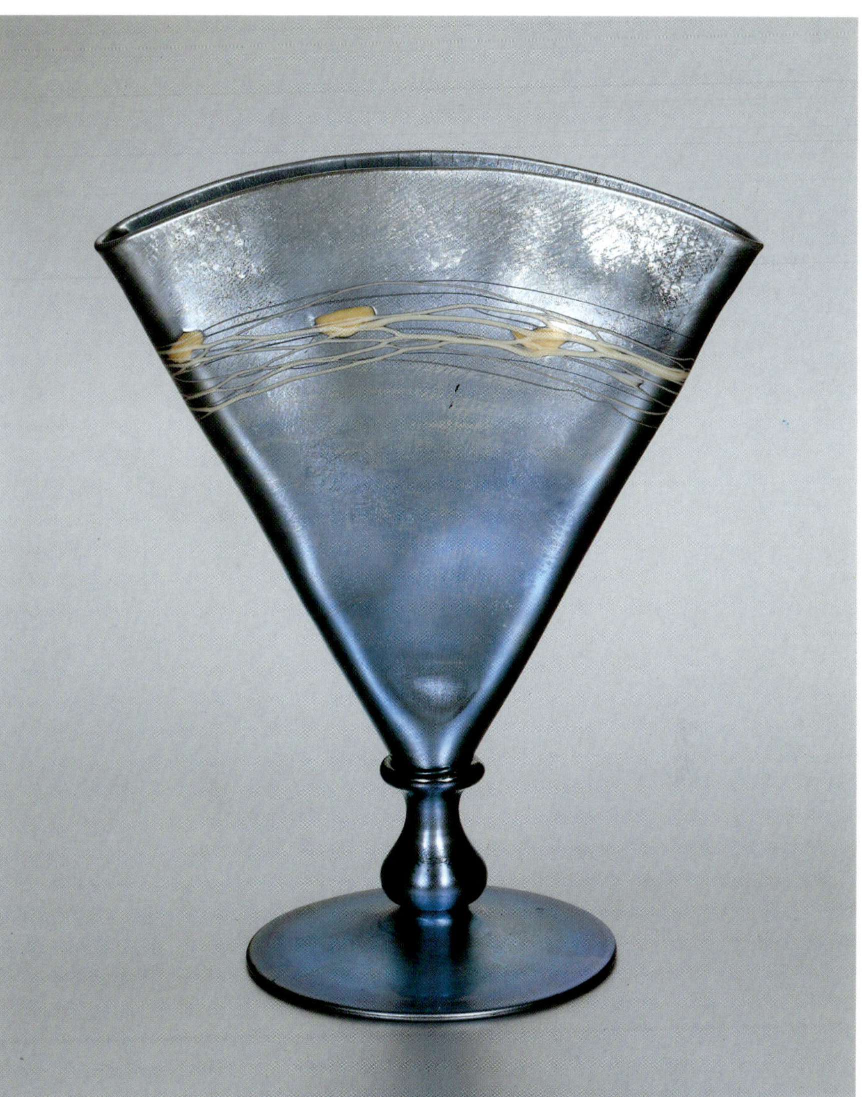

306 Vase

Engraved mark on the underside of base:
Quezal
Ca. 1910–20
H 23.8, ⌀ 12.5 cm

Slightly transparent milk glass, mold-blown. Fine green threading combed upwards into feather pattern five times. Above that a stronger silver thread combed downwards four times. Shaped. Blue thread applied around the rim. Colors fired in a reducing atmosphere and iridescent.

Acc. no. P 1988-69
Gift of Helmut Hentrich

For factory production named after the opalescent Mexican bird Quezal see Hilschenz, *Jugendstil*, 1973, 467, with earlier literature cited.

Lit.: –

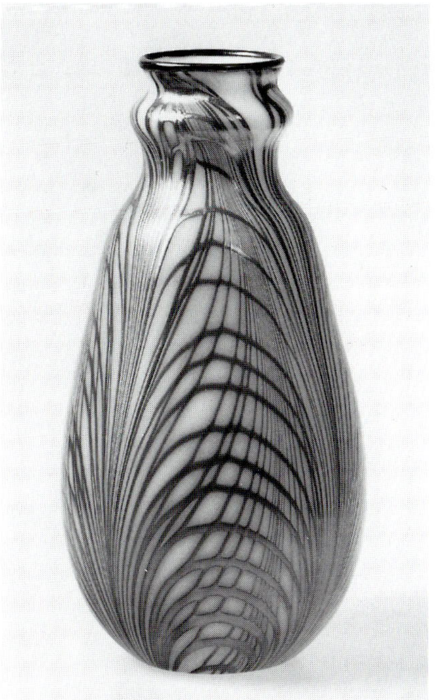

Austria and Bohemia

Glass centers with centuries of craft tradition often have difficulties keeping up with new artistic developments. Bohemia, a nucleus of European glass production in the eighteenth and nineteenth centuries, also required impulses from abroad to catch up with the major developments of the time. Once this had happened, however, the Bohemian glasshouses were able to adapt to the new movements in a very short time thanks to their excellent glassblowers and technicians. Just a few months after the first exhibition of Tiffany glassware at the museum in Reichenberg (Liberec) in 1897, the factory Johann Lötz Witwe in Klostermühle, southern Bohemia, was able to present models in the "Tiffany genre." This propelled a development leading to another highlight in the history of Art Nouveau glass. Bohemia, after France and the United States, became the third most important art-glass center around the turn of the century.

Lötz had secured a top position amongst factories working in Austria with its historicist glassware imitating semiprecious stones. It was largely made in very complex techniques at the furnace. In the 1890s the glasshouse management began to think about its contribution to the approaching 1900 World Exhibition in Paris, which was to surpass everything done previously. Lötz revived the iridescence techniques that the factory had mastered for more than two decades in different variations and now concentrated exclusively on the development of this effective method of decoration.

Following a short phase closely adhering to Tiffany's repertoire of forms and decoration (cat. no. 307), the artistic impulses received from the American led to new and original achievements within only a few months. Surface design with various types of iridescence, which Tiffany had developed, became the dominant principle of the Lötz factory's "Phänomen" decoration. Unlike Tiffany, though, Lötz in Klostermühle emphasized the body's sculpturality (cat. nos. 310, 314), which often stood in effective contrast to the delicate lines or metallically brittle surface. After 1900 decorative handles dynamically encompassing the surrounding space of the vessel's body (cat. no. 316) served to accentuate these sculptural qualities.

Naturally the factory did not achieve its extraordinary artistic development entirely of its own accord, even if the glasshouse owner Max von Spaun, the director Eduard Prochaska, and the highly skilled glassmakers played more than a minor part. Of at least equal significance were the connections the company management maintained with the art scene in Vienna. The progressive Viennese distribution company E. Bakalowits Söhne was the Lötz factory's most important client (cat. no. 308). Through the artists working for this firm, amongst them Josef Hoffmann and Kolo Moser (cat. no. 310), the glasshouse in the distant Bohemian Forest came face to face with the ideas and forms of the Viennese avant-garde. Other artists, such as the painter Franz Hofstötter (cat. no. 309), contributed considerably to the company's resounding success at the Paris World Exhibition. There Lötz, besides Gallé, Daum, and Tiffany, received a Grand Prix. The Prague painter Marie Kirschner introduced new forms into the production program of the glasshouse. In their decorative "protofunctionalism," they seem in part to anticipate the forms of the 1920s (cat. nos. 311–13). The list could be continued.

During the economically difficult years before and after World War I, the factory tried to develop new techniques and modern forms. It fell short, however, of restoring the reputation it had enjoyed around the turn of the century of being a trendsetter. Several Bohemian factories strove to imitate the successful new line of iridescent glassware at Lötz around 1900. Belonging to this circle were the glasshouse of Wilhelm Kralik Sohn in the neighboring Eleonorenhain with a formally independent, decorative glass production (cat. nos. 323–26), as well as the Harrachov Glassworks, and those of the Gebrüder Pallme-König & Habel in northern Bohemia. The latter put many of their own decorative variations on the market, mostly based on sculpturally layered net systems (cat. nos. 327–30).

Around 1910, after furnace techniques had dominated for some time, glass designers began to exploit the potential of cold work. The numerous refineries around the northern Bohemian centers of Haida and Steinschönau regained their old significance. Guided by teachers employed in the local glass schools, but usually educated in Vienna, a new type of glass design developed in northern Bohemia for which the principles of Art Nouveau were no longer binding. The refineries were supported by commissions from the large Viennese glasshouses, who worked with professors from the Wiener Kunstgewerbeschule (cat. no. 334) and designers from the Wiener Werkstätte (cat. no. 339). Thus important impulses came from northern Bohemia, affecting the subsequent development of European glass art, including French glass, in the years after World War I. Linear decoration in *Schwarzlot* painting with gold (cat. nos. 336–38), but also very colorful painting, and massive, facet-cut, colored glassware, are characteristic of these years and carry over to the glass art of the 1920s.

Johann Lötz Witwe

Factory and decorating workshop for art glassware and fine utilitarian glass, Klostermühle, southern Bohemia

Founded in 1836 by Johann Baptist Eisner. In 1851, acquired by Franz Gerstner and his wife, Susanne, Lötz's widow, who took over the direction of the glasshouse. In 1858, registered under the name Johann Lötz Witwe. In addition to utilitarian glass, fine luxury glass was made as well. In 1879, transferred to the grandson of Susanne Lötz-Gerstner, Maximilian Ritter von Spaun (1856–1909), who led it to international recognition in the area of art glass. In 1900, the company received, as did Gallé and Tiffany, the Grand Prix at the Paris World Exhibition. The lavish, iridescent "Phänomenglas" was a sensational success. After 1904, increased collaboration with artists, especially from the Viennese circle. In 1908 Max von Spaun, Jr., took over the company; in 1911, bankruptcy followed. From 1913 the company traded under the name Johann Lötz Witwe GmbH. In 1939, again bankruptcy. In 1947, production came to an end.

307   Vase

Mat-engraved mark in ground-out pontil: arrows crossed at right angles in a circle
Form and decoration: 1898, metallroth
Phänomen Gre 166
H 31.1, ⌀ 9.4 cm

Salmon-pink inner casing, the colorless cover layer with silver-yellow threads combed to four pointed feathers. Free-blown and shaped. Colors fired in a reducing atmosphere and iridescent.
The feathers outlined with engraved lines.

Acc. no. P 1970 353
Gift of Helmut Hentrich

Model from the company's first design series in Art Nouveau forms, still strongly oriented on the decorative concepts of Louis C. Tiffany.
For the paper pattern see *Lötz 2*, 1989, series 1, prod. no. 7474.

Lit.: Hilschenz, *Jugendstil*, 1973, cat. no. 343; *Lötz 1*, 1989, cat. no. 29

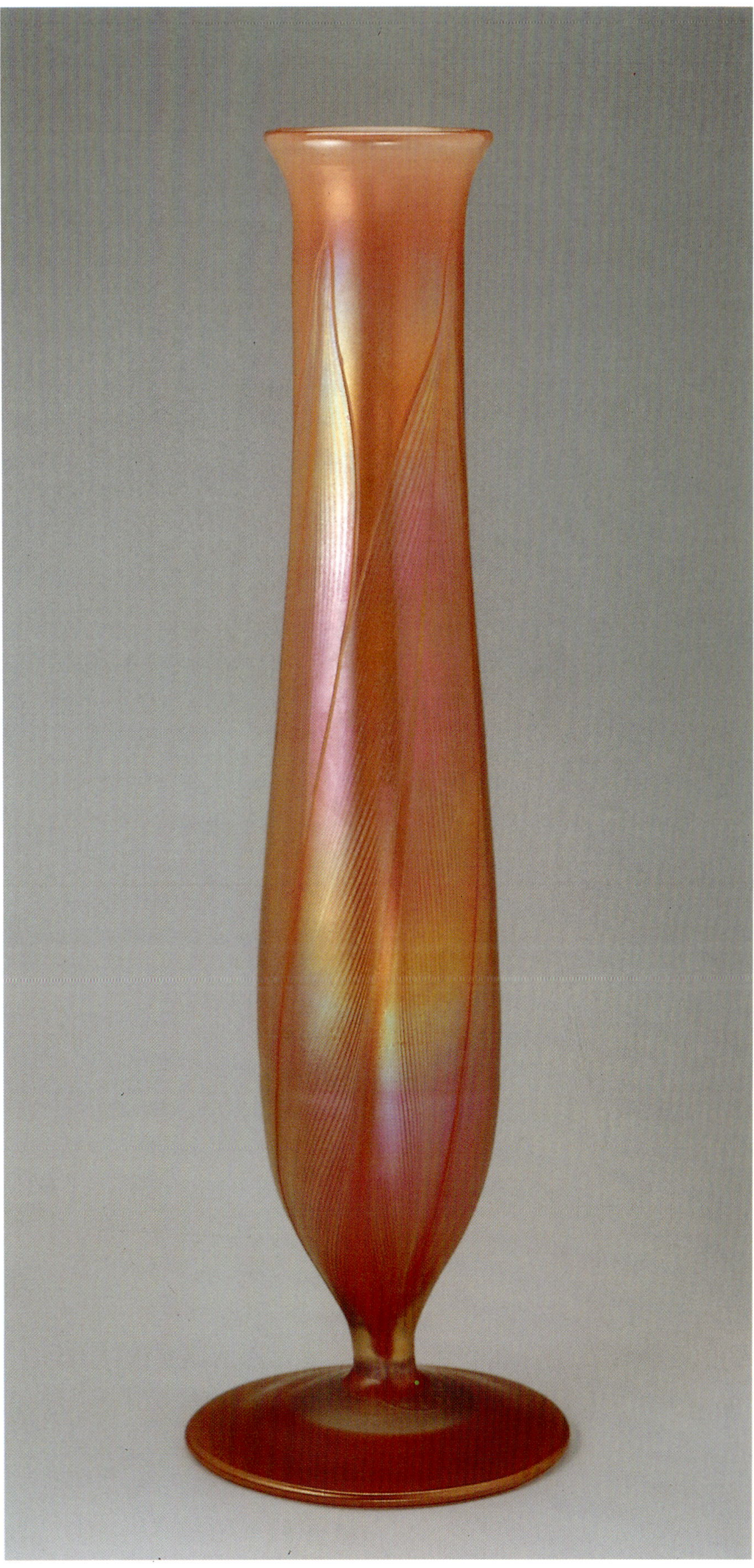

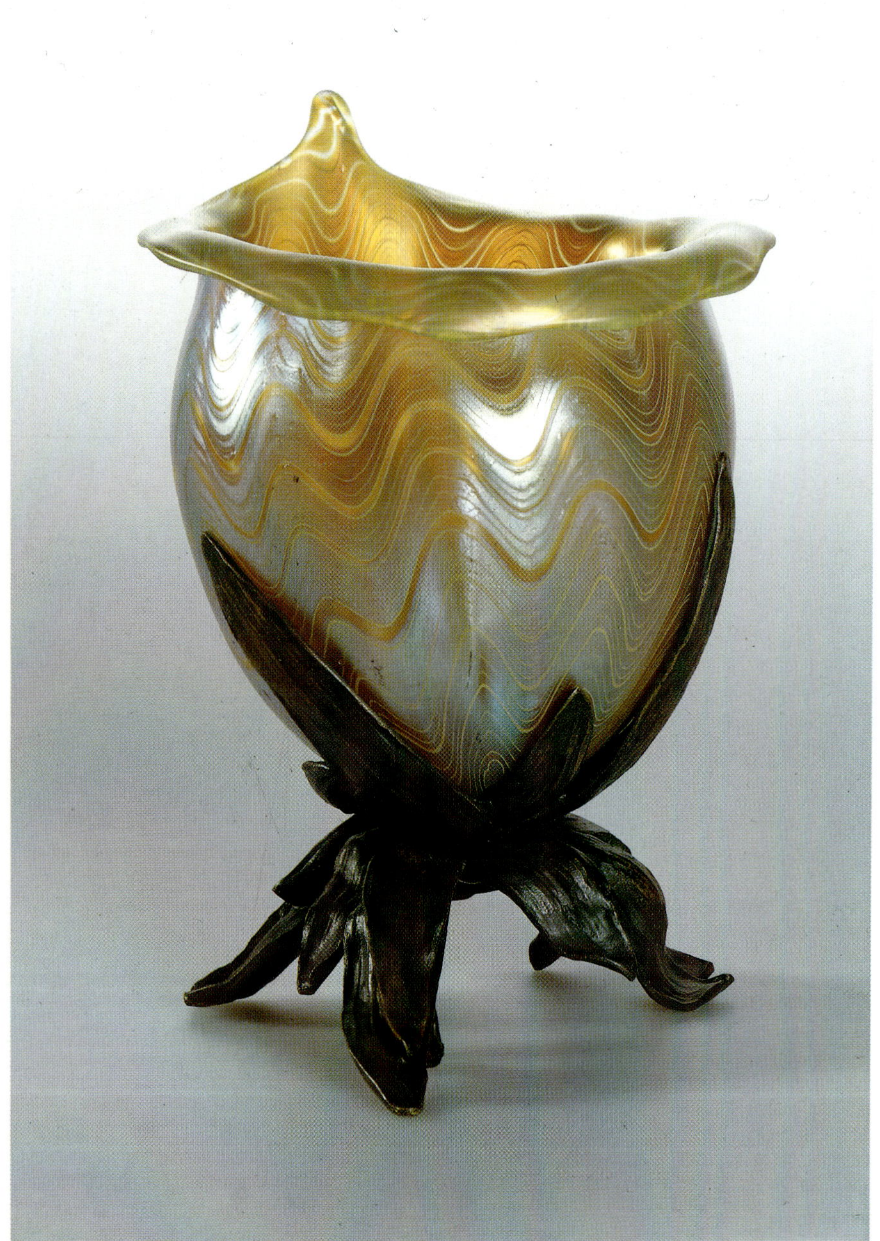

308 Vase

Unsigned
Form: 1899
Decoration: 1898, Phänomen Gre 6893
H (with mount) 24.5, ∅ 15.8 cm

Colorless foundation; widely spaced encircling threads in veined silver-yellow; drawn into waves in 12-part ribbed mold. Mold-blown and shaped. Colors fired in a reducing atmosphere and iridescent.

Acc. no. LP 1972-40
Formerly Barlach Heuer Collection; on permanent loan from the Museumsverein

Commissioned by and based on a design from the Viennese trade and distribution company E. Bakalowits Söhne, founded in 1845. Bakalowits was the Lötz factory's most important business partner and main local competition to J & L Lobmeyr. Bakalowits represented the progressive direction of the Viennese movements of the period and followed a distinctly original line in its product designs. Leading artists, such as Koloman Moser and Josef Hoffmann, were amongst the firm's designers. The model cannot presently be securely attributed to any of the artists working for Bakalowits. It shows, besides the influence of Tiffany's iridescent decoration, stylistic elements of French Art Nouveau. Gallé and Daum in Nancy had, from the early 1890s, increasingly made zoomorphic objects or vessels evoking plant forms.
The shape of this model recalls the pitcher plant's sham flower. For the paper pattern see *Lötz* 2, 1989, 272, Com. 85/3682/I.

Lit.: *Lötz* 1, 1989, cat. no. 74   •

309 Vase

Mat-engraved mark in ground-out pontil: *Loetz Austria*
Form: Franz Hofstötter, 1900
Decoration: 1900, metallgelb Phänomen Gre 356
H 21.3, ⌀ 10.2 cm

Thin yellow overlay, the colorless cover layer has broad, silver-yellow, encircling stripe. At the bottom, orange-colored cased cup is drawn out in pointed tongues. Above that, striped application in silver-yellow and brown tones, combed up and down. Mold-blown and shaped. Colors fired in a reducing atmosphere and mat iridescence.

Acc. no. LP 1972-92
Formerly Barlach Heuer Collection; on permanent loan from the Museumsverein

The vase belongs to the collection of 87 glass pieces that Lötz prepared for the Paris World Exhibition. Franz Hofstötter (1871–1958), a painter educated in Munich, certainly designed 13 of these models; a number of others are attributed to him. Hofstötter was first mentioned in connection with these designs in 1900. He remained in contact with the glasshouse and occasionally worked for Lötz in later years. For the paper pattern see *Lötz* 2, 1989, 91, series II, prod. no. 369.

Lit.: Sterner, *Sammlung Heuer*, 1972, cat. no. 87; *Lötz* 1, 1989, cat. no. 93

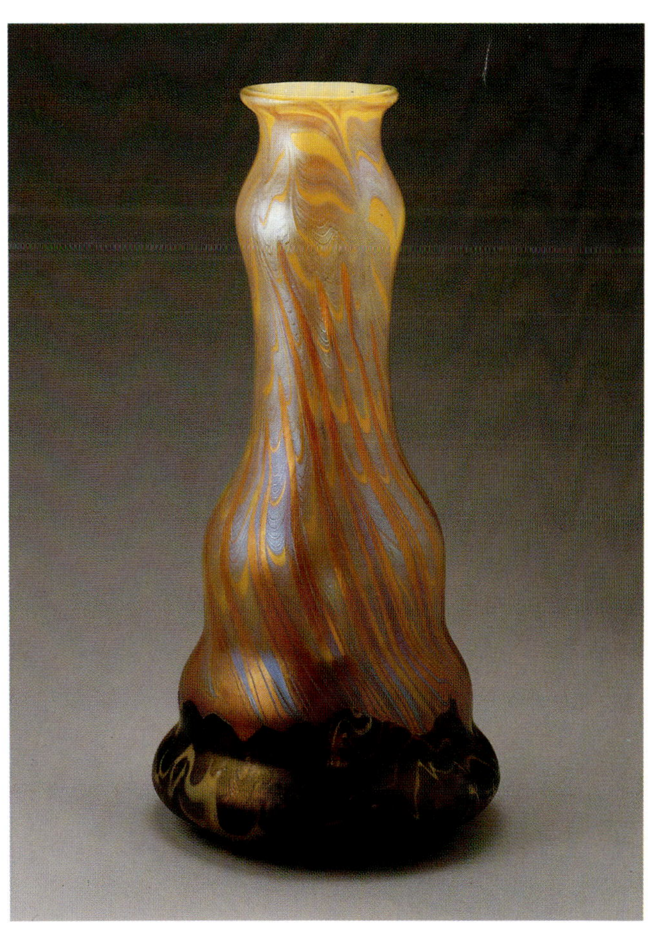

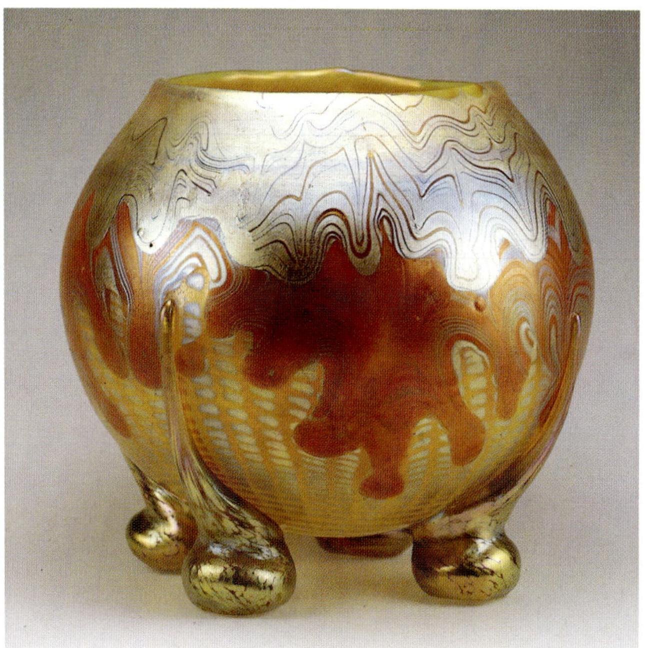

310 Vase

Mat-engraved mark in ground-out pontil:
Loetz Austria
Form: Koloman Moser, 1900, Prod.Nr.Com. 83/3785, also Nr. 2/257 (1902); commissioned by
E. Bakalowits Söhne, Vienna
Decoration: 1900, metallgelb Phänomen Gre 691
H 16.7, ⌀ 18.7 cm

Thin yellow inner casing, colorless cover layer with fine, silver-yellow, encircling threads, separated to form rows of dots in a four-part ribbed mold. Fused onto top half of vessel: orange-red glass with encircling silver-yellow threads, drawn out four times like a lambrequin. On top of that, veined silver-yellow application, combed in an irregular pattern. Mold-blown and shaped. Four massive feet with long extensions and silver-yellow glass-granule inclusions. Colors fired in a reducing atmosphere and iridescent.

Acc. no. P 1972-16
On loan from Barlach Heuer, Paris

Koloman Moser (1868–1918) was cofounder of the Wiener Sezession in 1897 and of the Wiener Werkstätte in 1903, from 1899 teacher and from 1900 professor at the Kunstgewerbeschule in Vienna. He provided the design for a "Kugelvase mit drei Füssen" (globular vase with three feet) in 1899. It was one of the commercially most successful products at Bakalowits. (For Bakalowits see cat. no. 308.) Produced at Lötz in different variations from 1900, including the version with four feet. Its basic stereometric shape made the glass the quintessence of modern glass design and was thus often used as a decorative object in modern interior design. Bakalowits had the model produced in nine decorative variations and in at least four sizes. See *DK* 4 (1901): illus. pp. 288f. For the paper pattern see *Lötz* 2, 1989, 280, Com 85/3785 and prod. no. 2/257.

Lit.: *Lötz* 1, 1989, cat. no. 190

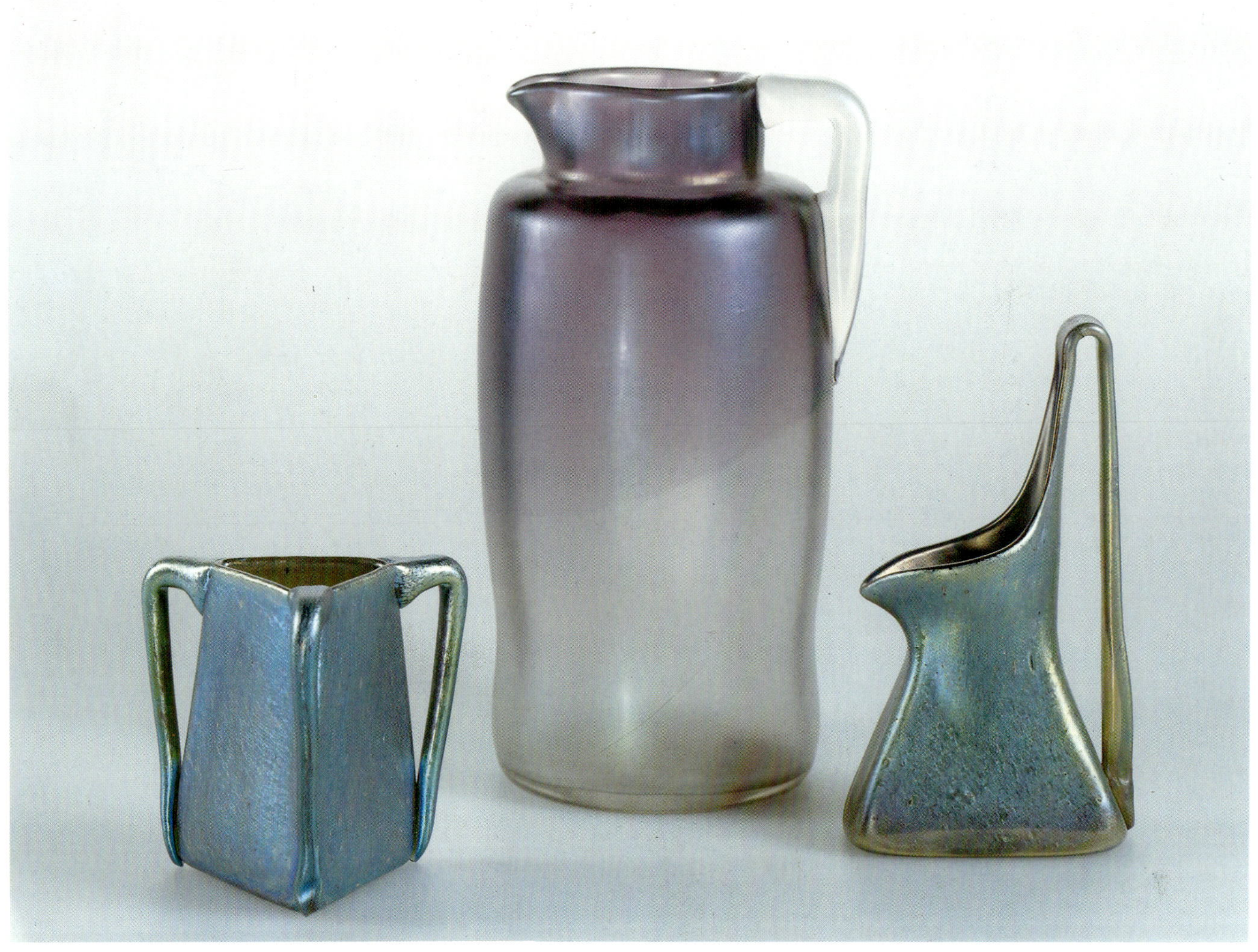

311 Vase

Engraved mark on the underside of base: *MK* (ligated) and two stars
Form: Marie Kirschner, 1903/04
Decoration: 1900, cobalt Norma mit cobalt
H 7.5, L side 6.6, ∅ (with handles) 8 cm

Colorless glass, cobalt blue inner casing, mold-blown, mat iridescence.

Acc. no. LP 1972-39
Formerly Barlach Heuer Collection; on permanent loan from the Museumsverein

Marie Kirschner (1852–1931) studied painting in Vienna, Munich, and Paris in the 1880s. Subsequently she worked primarily in applied arts and interior design. Between 1899 and 1913 she designed 279 glass pieces, which she commissioned Lötz to produce and distributed herself. (These pieces are signed *MK*.) Lötz took several of her models into its own production. (These are unsigned.)
For the pattern of this model, made in three decorative variations, see *Lötz* 2, 1989, 346, Com. 1090/120.

Lit.: *Lötz* 1, 1989, cat. no. 240

312 Pitcher

Engraved mark on the underside of base: *MK* (ligated)
Form: Marie Kirschner, 1905
Decoration: 1902, pensée verlaufend optisch matt Iris
H 18.8, ∅ 10.2 cm

Colorless glass; spreading violet inner casing. Mold-blown. Applied flat handle. Mat iridescence.

Acc. no. P 1970-384
Gift of Helmut Hentrich

According to the notation on the paper pattern, the model was produced in 11 decorative variations; see *Lötz* 2, 1989, 352, Com. 1090/185.

Lit.: Hilschenz, *Jugendstil,* 1973, cat. no. 380; *Lötz* 1, 1989, cat. no. 222

313 Small Pitcher

Engraved mark on the underside of base: *MK* (ligated) and two stars
Form: Marie Kirschner, 1901/02
Decoration: cobalt Norma
H 12.9, W 7.9, D 4.1 cm

Colorless glass, cobalt blue inner casing. Mold-blown and shaped freehand. On rectangular standing base, conically narrowing body with drawn-out handle and round, dilated mouth. Mat iridescence.

Acc. no. P 1972-38
Formerly Barlach Heuer Collection; on permanent loan from the Museumsverein

According to the notation on the paper pattern, the model was made in five decorative variations; see *Lötz* 2, 1989, 340, Com. 1090/36.

Lit.: *Lötz* 1, 1989, cat. no. 228

314 Vase

Mat-engraved mark in ground-out pontil:
Loetz Austria
Form: 1900
Decoration: 1901, cobalt Phänomen Gre
1/158
H 16.7, ⌀ 22.8 cm

On colorless ground, inner casing running
from top to bottom, yellow-green cover glass
with silver-yellow encircling threads separated to form rows of dots by a four-part ribbed
mold. Below the rim and above the base:
wide silver-yellow bands with colorless veins,
combed irregularly. Mold-blown and shaped.
Colors fired in a reducing atmosphere and
mat iridescence in a silvery luster.

Acc. no. LP 1972-91
Formerly Barlach Heuer Collection; on permanent loan from the Museumsverein

Lötz production. Compare the paper pattern,
Lötz 2, 1989, 86, series II, prod. no. 293
(variation). The model is one of a large group
of designs with two small, flat handles, prod.
nos. 284, 285, 289–99.

Lit.: Sterner, *Sammlung Heuer*, 1972, cat.
no. 86; Ricke, *Ausgewählte Werke*, 1980, 27;
Lötz 1, 1989, cat. no. 116

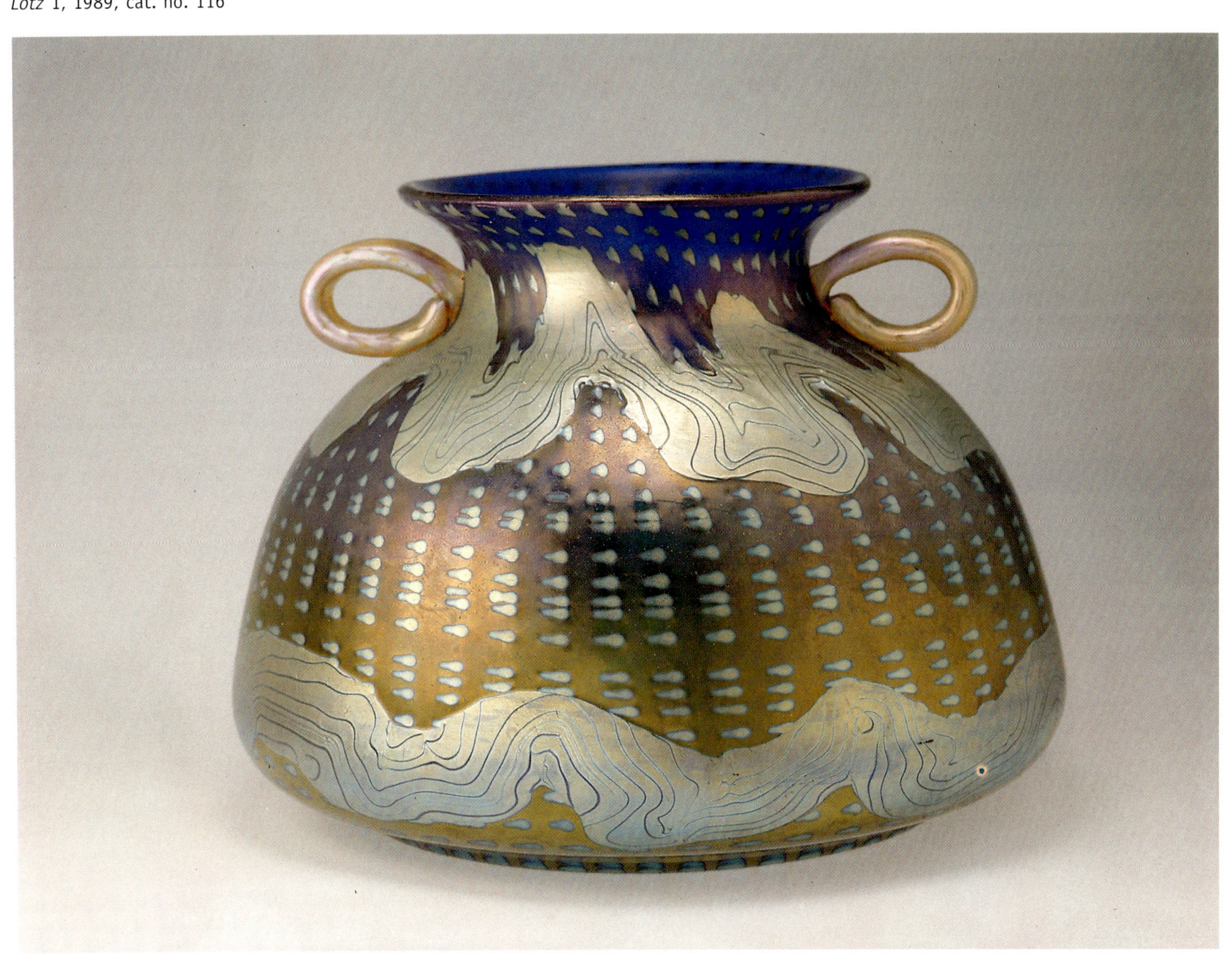

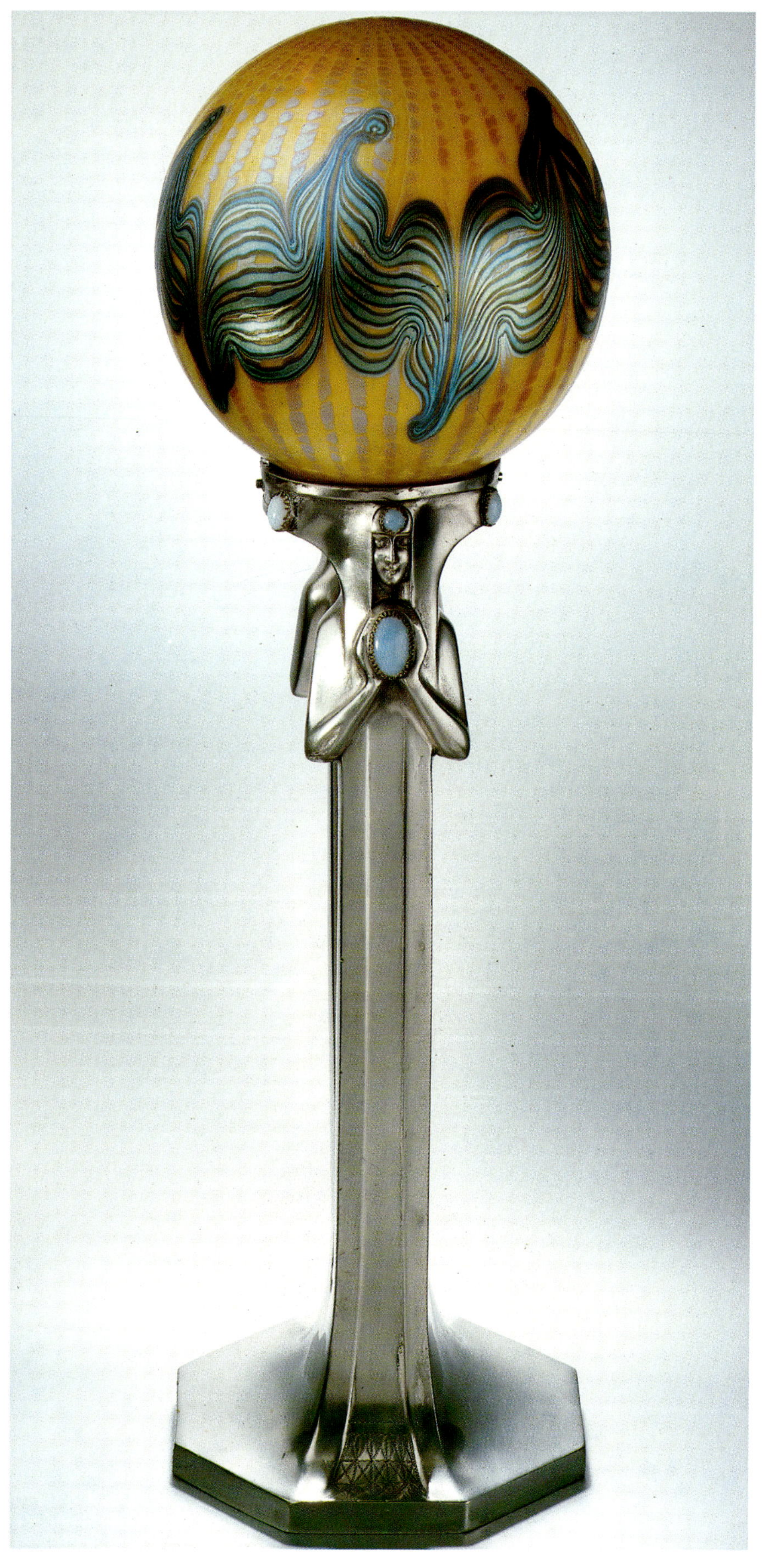

315 Lamp

Unsigned
Ca. 1901/02
Decoration: unidentified
Design for mount: Franz Pankok (?)
H (with mount) 58.1, ⌀ glass 17.8 cm

Yellow inner casing; the colorless cover layer
has densely arranged, encircling, silver-yellow
threads separated into rows of dots by a multipartite ribbed mold; on top of that, applied
encircling stripe decoration, combed up and
down 12 times. Mold-blown. Colors fired in a
reducing atmosphere and iridescent.
Mount: fine pewter; cast, soldered, and
chased. Eight moonstones.

Acc. no. LP 1992-11
Formerly Barlach Heuer Collection; on permanent loan from the Museumsverein

Franz Pankok (1874–1921), teacher at the
Kunstgewerbeschule in Barmen and designer
of furniture and applied arts, may be the
designer of the exquisite mount (kindly suggested by K. Daxl); see *Innendekoration* 16
(1905): text pp. 246–49, illus. pp. 244–54.
The illustration on p. 253 shows a salon
designed by Pankok with the lamp on a
pedestal-like, small table. As the accompanying text (p. 248) explicitly points out that
Pankok also designed lamps and as it was
customary to select accessories designed by
the respective artist for exhibition presenta-
tions or for photographs, Pankok cannot be
ruled out as artist. On the other hand, the
withdrawn, mysterious expressions of the
female figures are somewhat incongruous
with Pankok's style.
Several variations of the lamp model exist,
including some with partial gilding.

Lit.: *Lötz* 1, 1989, cat. no. 130

316 Vase

Mat-engraved mark in ground-out pontil:
Loetz Austria
Form: 1902
Decoration: 1901, rosa Phänomen Gre 1/473
H 20.2, ⌀ 14.9 cm

Silver-yellow granules embedded in transparent, light pink fond. Mold-blown and shaped.
Four decorative handles drawn from the
glass. Colors fired in a reducing atmosphere,
iridescence with a silver and gold-colored
luster.

Acc. no. L 1973-1
On loan from Barlach Heuer, Paris

Loetz production. One of the factory's most
successful models. The piece's corporeality
and sculptural quality are typical of the production between 1902 and 1904. For the
paper pattern see *Lötz* 2, 1989, 141, prod.
no. 2/619.

Lit.: Ricke, *Ausgewählte Werke*, 1980, 27;
Pazaurek and Spiegl, *20. Jahrhundert*, 1983,
45, fig. 60; *Lötz* 1, 1989, cat. no. 147

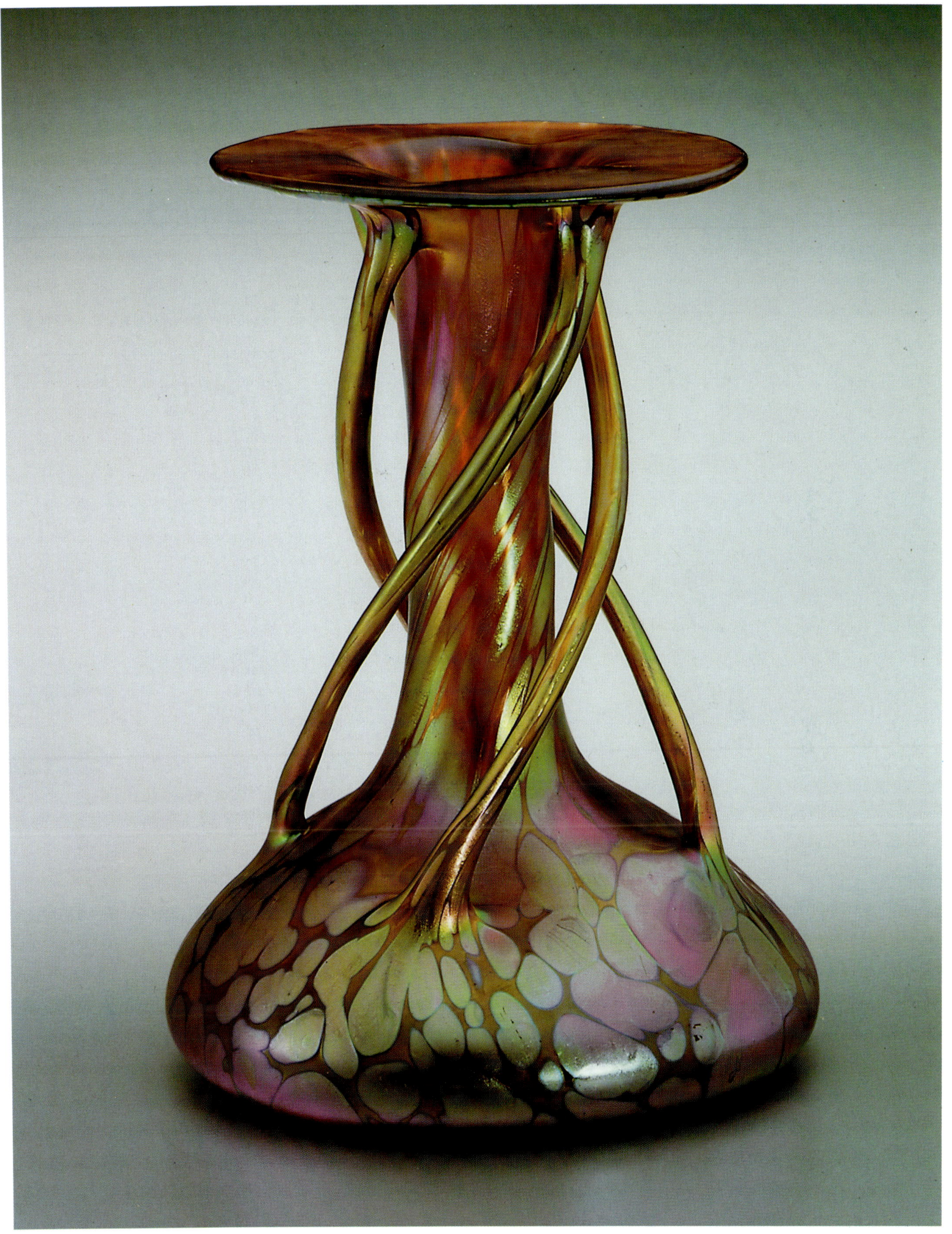

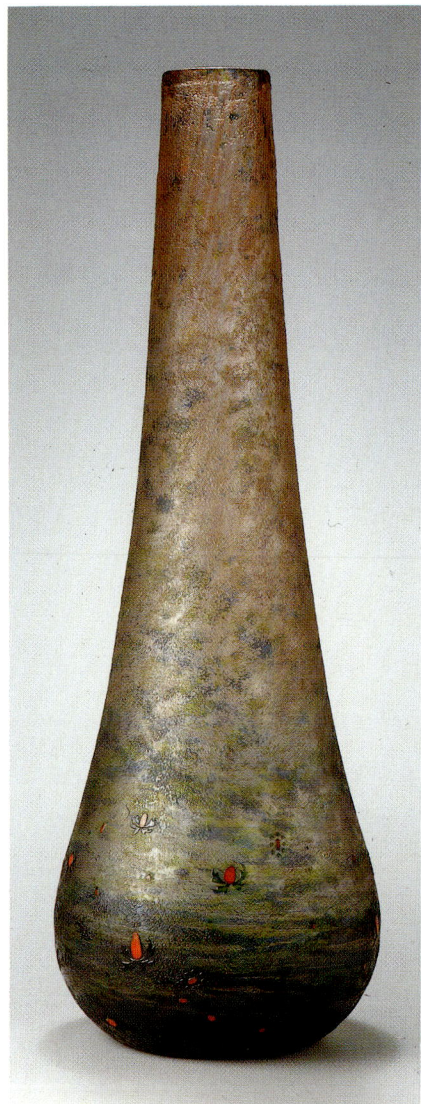

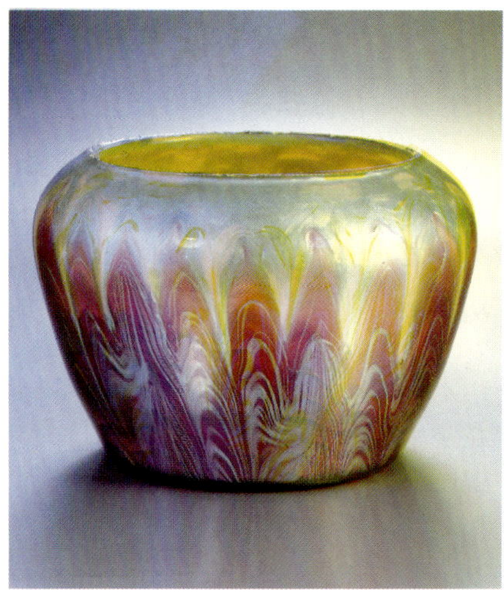

318   Vase

Unsigned
Form: 1907
Decoration: Titania, 1906/07
H 10.1, ⌀ 15 cm

Colorless layer on yellow-green inner casing.
Red-violet cased cap drawn upwards on the
lower half of the vase; silver threading
combed irregularly into 19 points. Thick,
colorless cover layer.

Acc. no. P 1980-38
Gift of Helmut Hentrich

Evidence of Lötz's efforts to find new furnace
techniques to replace the "Phänomen" glass
of around 1900, for which interest had been
waning since from about 1904.

For the paper pattern see *Lötz* 2, 1989, 178,
series II, prod. no. 4616.

Lit.: –

317   Vase

Relief-etched mark above the base, reworked
with engraving wheel: *Loetz*
Form: Franz Hofstötter, 1906
Decoration: Adolf Beckert, 1909, Ausfüh-
rung 87
H 41.1, ⌀ 14.2 cm

Salmon-pink vertical stripes in colorless
ground. Applications on vessel surface. Mold-
blown.
Decoration: etched in two stages, the red-
green plant motifs were individually retraced
by engraving.

Acc. no. P 1970-386
Gift of Helmut Hentrich

Adolf Beckert (1884–1929) studied at the
Fachschule für Glasindustrie in Haida, at the
Lehr- und Versuchsatelier für angewandte und
freie Kunst Wilhelm von Debschitz in Munich,
as well as at the School of Applied Arts in
Prague. As artistic director at the Lötz factory from mid-1909 to 1911, he sought to find

a new market by changing the production to
etched decoration. He had to give up his
position, however, owing to the company's
bankruptcy. He then taught design at the
Glasfachschule in Steinschönau and continued to advise Lötz until the 1920s.
For Franz Hofstötter see cat. no. 309.
The vase was part of the collection for the
exhibition of Austrian applied arts, Österreichisches Museum für Kunst und Industrie,
Vienna, 1909/10, cat. no. 1112.
For the paper pattern see *Lötz* 2, 1989, 163,
series II, prod. no. 3702.

Lit.: Hilschenz, *Jugendstil*, 1973, cat. no. 382;
Lötz 1, 1989, cat. no. 306

319   Vase

Relief-etched mark on wall: *Loetz*; and
engraved on the underside of base:
Prof. Hoffmann
Form and decoration: Josef Hoffmann, Vienna
1912
H 20.7, ⌀ 8.7 cm

Colorless glass, green overlay. Mold-blown. Base
and mouth rim are ground flat and polished.
Decoration etched in two stages: stylized foliated vines; surface has hoarfrost-like texture.

Acc. no. P 1986-38
Acquired with funds from the Helmut Hentrich
donation

Josef Hoffmann (1870–1956) studied architecture at the Akademie der bildenden Künste
in Vienna, worked in Otto Wagner's office,
and from 1898 was first a teacher, then professor at the Kunstgewerbeschule in Vienna.
Cofounder and until 1931 artistic director of
the Wiener Werkstätte. First glass designs for
Bakalowits in 1899 for the eighth Wiener
Sezession exhibition. Lötz carried out numerous other designs between 1906 and 1915,
for instance those commissioned by the
Österreichisches Museum für Kunst und
Industrie and the Österreichischer Werkbund.
One of more than 30 color variations. See
Lötz 1, 1989, cat. no. 316; for the paper pat-
tern see *Lötz* 2, 1989, 221, series II, prod.
no. 8127.

Lit.: –

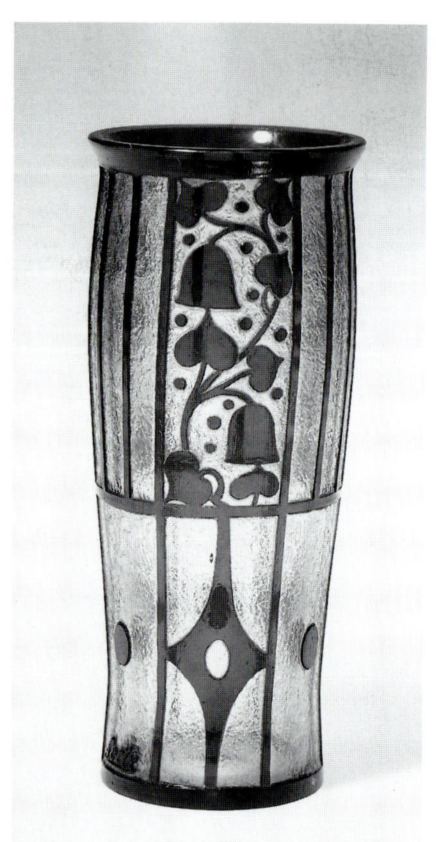

320 Footed Bowl

Unsigned
Form and decoration: Otto Prutscher
1925
H 10.1, ⌀ 11.7 cm

Bowl with opal-glass inner casing; the color-less cover layer has fine blue-green and white-yellow encircling threads. Mold-blown. Foot applied. Decoration combed up and down into feather pattern 12 times. Iridescent.

Acc. no. P 1973-1
Acquired with funds from the Helmut Hentrich donation

Otto Prutscher (1880–1949) was architect and from 1910 teacher at the Kunst-gewerbeschule in Vienna, as well as a member of the Wiener Werkstätte. He created glass designs for Bakalowits, Wiener Werkstätte, J & L Lobmeyr, as well as for himself, some of which were realized by Lötz. He maintained very close ties with the firm, especially in his late phase. From 1925 he served as artistic adviser.
The footed bowl comes from the collection for the Art-Deco exhibition in Paris, 1925; see *DK* 54 (1926): illus. p. 170. For the paper pattern see *Lötz* 2, 1989, series III, p. 249, prod. no. 2389.

Lit.: *Lötz* 1, 1989, cat. no. 381

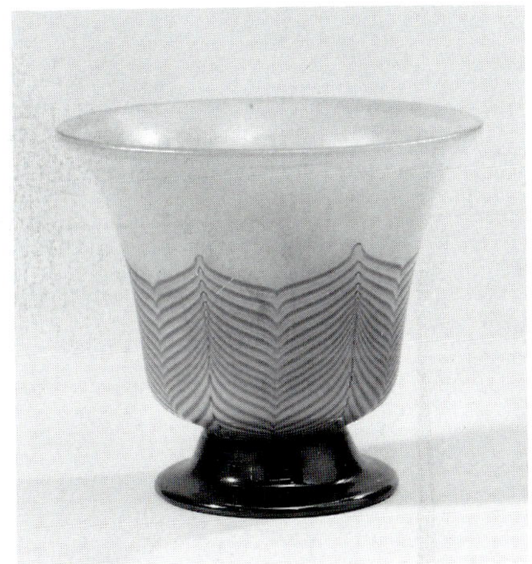

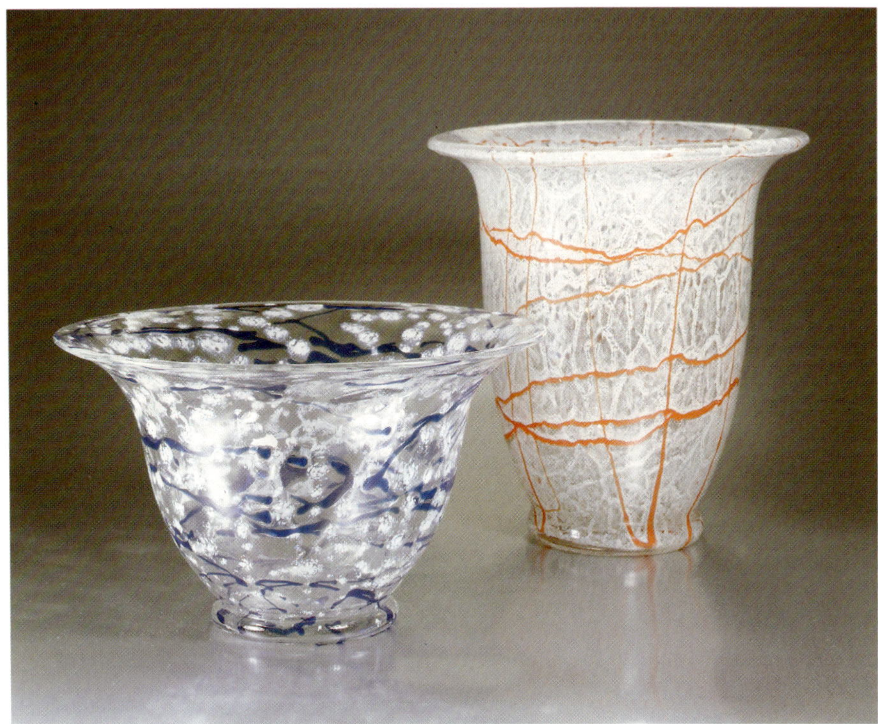

321 Bowl

Unsigned
Form and decoration: 2nd half of 1930s
16/22 Ausführung C, "Schneeflocken"
H 12.8, ⌀ 22.3 cm

Colorless glass blown in metal optic mold with irregular spherical projections, rolled in opaque white glass powder and wiped, so that only the hollows remained colored. Opaque blue threading. Fully blown and dilated.

Acc. no. P 1981-358
Gift of Helmut Hentrich

In the late production phase, revived use of steel molds with irregular "ball-optic" pattern utilized at the glasshouse by around 1900. For other examples see *Lötz* 1, 1989, cat. nos. 389, 390, and 400. See also the pattern photograph in *Lötz* 2, 1989, fig. 14.

Lit.: –

322 Vase

Unsigned
Form and decoration: 2nd half of 1930s, "Schaumglas"
H 20, ⌀ 19.8 cm

Colorless glass, crackled between the layers by submerging in salt solution, crystals outside crackles partly removed. Irregularly encircling red thread covered by a thick, colorless layer. Mold-blown and shaped.

Acc. no. P 1989-57
Gift of Helmut Hentrich

For a similar glass see *Lötz* 1, 1989, cat. no. 404. The Geislingen glassworks of the Württembergische Metallwarenfabriken used similar techniques around the same time.

Lit.: –

Wilhelm Kralik Sohn, K. K. priv. Glasfabriken

Glasshouse for hollow glassware, decorating workshops for ornamental and utilitarian glass as well as lighting products, Eleonorenhain near Wallern, southern Bohemia

Founded by Johann Meyr (1775–1841) in 1834 and soon expanded to become the largest glass factory in Bohemia. From 1841, belonged, together with the glasshouses Kaltenbach and Adolf, to Meyr's Neffe. From 1862 Wilhelm Kralik was the sole proprietor. In 1881, after the division of his estate, Eleonorenhain was taken over by Heinrich and Johann, two of Wilhelm Kralik's four sons. From 1899 to 1904/05 successful production of iridescent glassware using a special process developed by W. Kralik as early as 1875 and distributed by J & L Lobmeyr, E. Bakalowits Söhne, and L.C. Tiffany, amongst other companies.

323 Vase

Unsigned
Ca. 1902
H 19.4, ⌀ 11.5 cm

White-yellow inner casing with colorless cover layer; applied silver glass powder. Blown in two-part mold, shaped. Colors fired in a reducing atmosphere and iridescent.

Acc. no. LP 1972-107
Formerly Barlach Heuer Collection; on permanent loan from the Museumsverein

Attributed to the factory based on technical and formal similarity to verified objects. Cf. cat. nos. 324, 325.

Lit.: –

324 Vase

Unsigned, ca. 1900–1902
H 11.9, ⌀ 18.2 x 11.9

On a light salmon-pink inner casing, strong colorless cover layer, a partial greenish silver overlay at the bottom, cup drawn out in tongues. Blown in two-part mold, shaped. Colors fired in a reducing atmosphere and iridescent.

Acc. no. P 1976-34
Acquired with funds from the Helmut Hentrich donation

In the treatment of the surface related to glassware of the Lötz factory. The attribution to Kralik is verified, though, by illus. of model in H. Pudor, *Dokumente des modernen Kunstgewerbes*, series A, no. 1 (1902): 83.

Lit.: *Lötz* 1, 1989, 22, fig. 15

325 Vase

Unsigned, ca. 1900–1902
H 40.4, ⌀ 22.4 x 17.9 cm

Green glass with irregular, net-like, thread application containing silver. Blown in two-part mold, shaped. Colors fired in a reducing atmosphere and iridescent.

Acc. no. P 1970-334
Gift of Helmut Hentrich

For attribution and dating of similar glassware see H. Pudor, op. cit.

Lit.: Hilschenz, *Jugendstil*, 1973, cat. no. 330; *Lötz* 1, 1989, 22, fig. 15

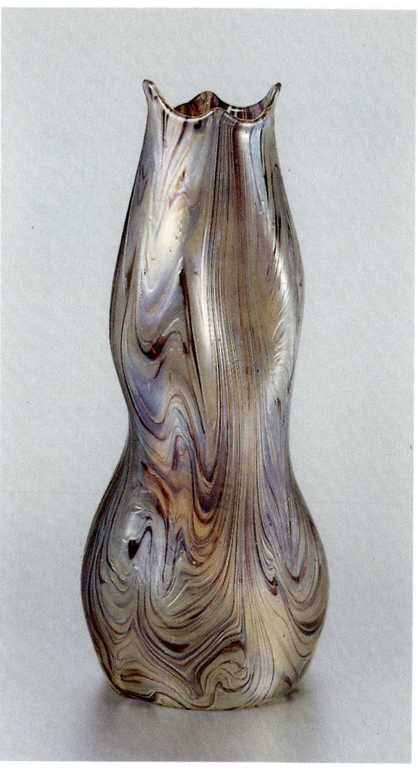

326 Vase

Unsigned
Ca. 1900–1902
H 20.9, ⌀ 9.3 x 7.6 cm

Colorless glass with brown-violet and silver-yellow embedded threads, irregularly combed, slight relief. Blown in two-part mold, shaped. Colors fired in a reducing atmosphere and iridescent.

Acc. no. P 1970-337
Gift of Helmut Hentrich

For attribution see a similar glass piece in H. Pudor, op. cit., illus. p. 115; see also cat. no. 324.

Lit.: Hilschenz, *Jugendstil*, 1973, cat. no. 333; *Lötz* 1, 1989, 22, fig. 15

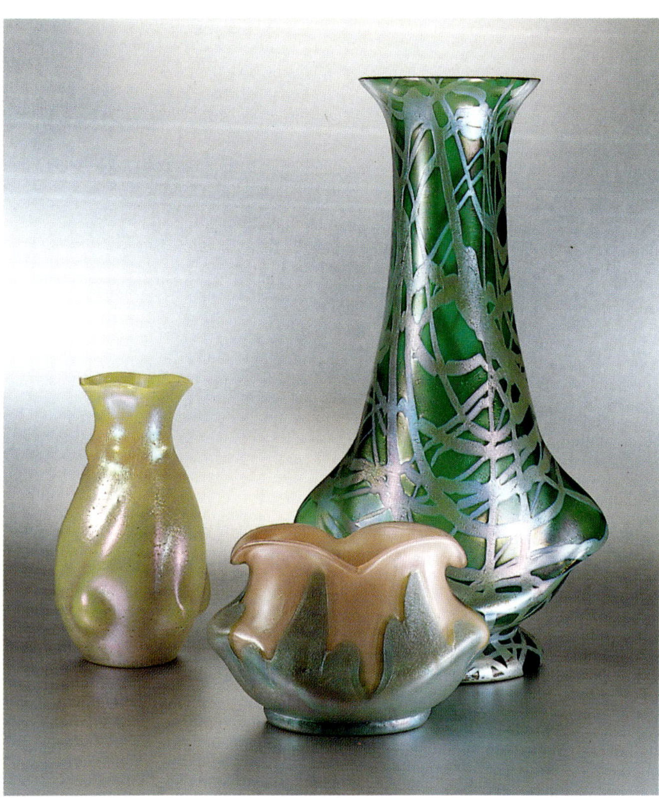

Gebrüder Pallme-König & Habel

Glasshouse for hollow glassware, decorating workshops for ornamental and utilitarian glass, lighting products, and mounts, Steinschönau and Kosten near Teplitz, northern Bohemia

Founded in 1786 by Ignaz Pallme-König in Steinschönau; in 1889, united with the Elisabethhütte in Kosten near Teplitz, which was run by Wilhelm Habel. Produced cut-crystal ware and iridescent vessels usually wrapped with applied threads.

327 Vase

Unsigned
Ca. 1900–1915
H 35.8, ⌀ 10.5 cm

Salmon-pink ground with white opal overlay; multicolored inclusions embedded in thick colorless cover layer. Mold-blown. Iridescent.

Acc. no. LP 1972-14
Formerly Barlach Heuer Collection; on permanent loan from the Museumsverein

For form and decoration variations see Bröhan, *Kunsthandwerk* 1, 1976, 188ff., as well as Passau, *Böhmisches Glas* 4, 1995, 164ff.

Lit.: Sterner, *Sammlung Heuer*, 1972, cat. no. 9

328 Vase

Unsigned
1900–1915
H 21.7, ⌀ 14.2 cm

Pink opal inner casing; silver-yellow threads combed into feather patterns are embedded in the colorless cover layer; on top of that, spiral red-brown band with vertical and horizontal stripes. Slightly iridescent.

Acc. no. P 1970-354
Gift of Helmut Hentrich

For attribution see Bröhan, *Kunsthandwerk* 1, 1976, 195f.

Lit.: Hilschenz, *Jugendstil*, 1973, cat. no. 350

329 Vase

Unsigned
Ca. 1900–1915
H 16.2, ⌀ 13.8 cm

Colorless glass, brown-violet encircling threads irregularly combed; on top of those, embedded silver glass granules. Mold-blown, shaped. Colors fired in a reducing atmosphere and iridescent.

Acc. no. P 1970-403
Gift of Helmut Hentrich

See Bröhan, *Kunsthandwerk* 1, 1976, 202, cat. nos. 294f.

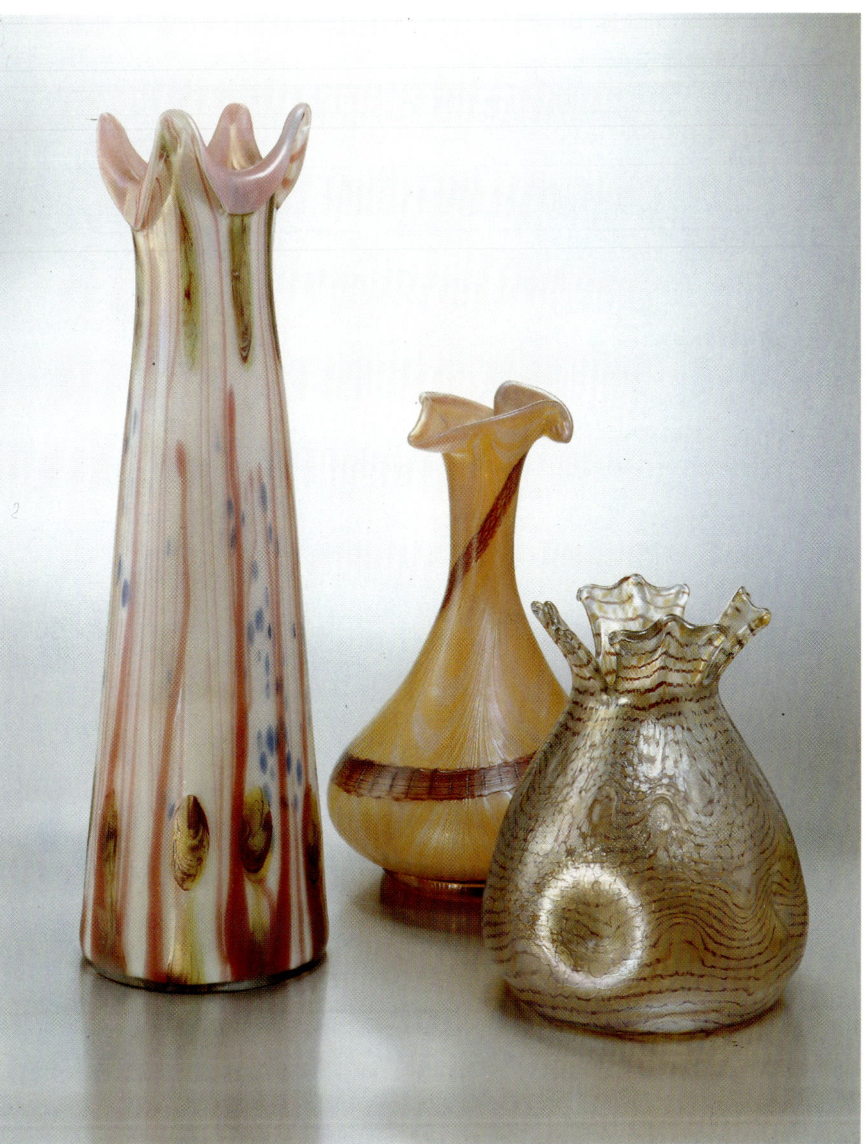

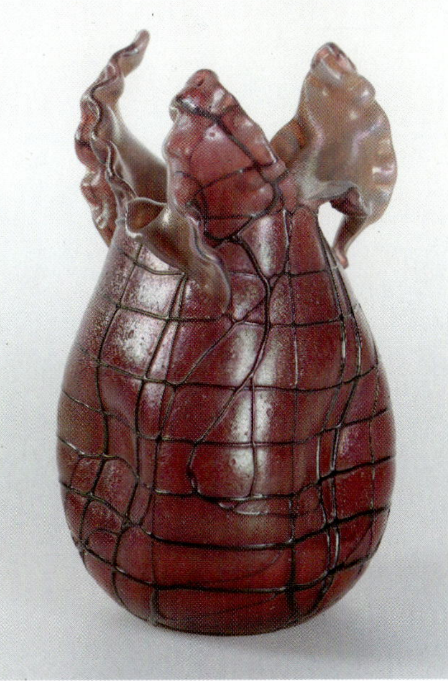

The piece may not have been made at the Kosten Elisabethhütte, but rather in Silesia (kindly suggested by Jan Mergl, Carlsbad).

Lit.: Hilschenz, *Jugendstil*, 1973, cat. no. 400

330 Vase

Unsigned
1900–1905
H 23, ⌀ 13.3 cm

Brownish white opal inner casing, strong colorless cover layer with applied brown-violet powder. Irregular net of encircling black threads. Free-blown and shaped. Iridescent.

Acc. no. P 1970-401
Gift of Helmut Hentrich

See also Bröhan, *Kunsthandwerk* 1, 1976, 191, cat. nos. 270ff., 304.

Lit.: Hilschenz, *Jugendstil*, 1973, cat. no. 398

Josef Rindskopf's Söhne

Factories for hollow glassware and decorating workshops

The glasshouse "Fanny" in Dux (founded in 1858) produced different types of luxury glass, in particular lighting products; the glasshouse "Josef" in Kosten (founded in 1890), primarily colored hollow ware. Around 1900 the two factories together had about 220 employees. According to Pazaurek, Rindskopf's Söhne was Johann Lötz Witwe factory's main competitor in iridescent glassware.

The firm's proprietors were Sidney, Albert, Edwin, and Sherman Riethof. In 1922 the central office of both factories was in Teplitz-Schönau.

331 Vase

Unsigned
Design: Peter Behrens (?) "Diluviumglas"
Kosten, ca. 1900
H 15.4, ⌀ 10 x 6.9 cm

Opaque red struck glass with yellow-greenish marbling. Mold-blown. Entire surface ground flat and polished.

Acc. no. P 1975-88
Acquired with funds from the Helmut Hentrich donation

See Pazaurek, *Moderne Gläser*, 1901, 108ff. The "Diluviumglas" is a variation of opaque red Biedermeier glassware (e.g., the red Hyalith of the Buquoy glasshouse, cat. no. 187). Pazaurek mentions in his accompanying text that Peter Behrens designed glassware of this material, without attributing any of the illustrated models to him specifically. The somewhat cumbrous floral designs shown there, however, hardly come into consideration. The attribution of the vase with the austere, functional shape illustrated here seems much more likely.

Lit.: Darmstadt, *Dokument*, 1977, vol. 4, cat. no. 19

Ludwig Moser & Söhne

Glasshouse for hollow glassware, decorating workshops for ornamental and utilitarian glass, Carlsbad, Marienbad, and Franzensbad

In 1857, founded by the glass engraver and merchant Ludwig Moser (1833–1916) as a decorating workshop in Carlsbad. From 1893, affiliated hollow-ware glasshouse in Meierhöfen near Carlsbad. In 1922, purchased the glasshouse Meyr's Neffe in Adolf near Winterberg, which had previously probably been the most important supplier of blanks.

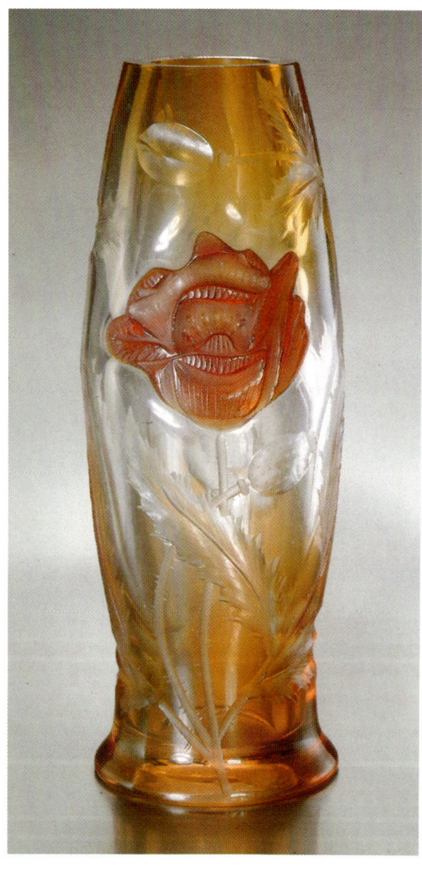

332 Vase

Engraved mark on the underside of foot: *Moser Karlsbad*; ca. 1900
H 15, ⌀ 5.7 cm

Colorless glass; at the top, brown-orange inner casing; at the bottom, overlay in the same color. Red application pressed into wall. Decoration consists of a poppy plant with five stalks, three buds, and two flowers in semimat polished intaglio; one of the flowers above red application is relief-carved. Mold-blown. Base and mouth ground flat.

Acc. no. P 1961-25

For Ludwig Moser & Söhne see Bröhan, *Kunsthandwerk* 1, 1976, 164ff., esp. cat. no. 236; Passau, *Böhmisches Glas* 6, 1995, 43ff.; J. Mergl and L. Pankova, *Moser 1857–1997* (Prague, 1997).

Lit.: Heinemeyer, *Glas*, 1966, cat. no. 534

Meyr's Neffe, K. K. priv. Kristallglasfabriken

Glasshouse for hollow and flat glassware, decorating workshops for ornamental and utilitarian glass, Adolf near Winterberg, southern Bohemia

From 1814 to 1816 Josef Meyr established the Adolfhütte, which from 1841 belonged to the firm Meyr's Neffe, together with the glasshouses Eleonorenhain and Kaltenbach. After expansion in 1862, known under the name Meyr's Neffe with sole director Wilhelm Kralik. Producer of the finest crystal glass in Bohemia. Supplier of blanks to both J & L Lobmeyr as well as E. Bakalowits Söhne; close collaboration with these firms. Until 1922 (take-over by Ludwig Moser Söhne, Carlsbad), designers were primarily artists from the Wiener Werkstätte, such as Otto Prutscher and Josef Hoffmann.

333   Stem Glass

Unsigned
Design: attr. Otto Prutscher
Adolf, ca. 1907
H 20.7, ⌀ 8.5 cm

Colorless glass, ruby red overlay. Mold-blown and shaped.
Decoration cut and polished, the stylized foliated frieze below the rim is stained yellow.

Acc. no. P 1970-390 B
Gift of Helmut Hentrich

For Otto Prutscher see cat. no. 320. For attribution and dating see similar models for the firm E. Bakalowits Söhne, such as in *DKD* 20 (1907): illus. p. 340; *DK* 18 (1908): illus. p. 542; *DK* 22 (1910): illus. p. 452; *The Studio Yearbook of Decorative Art* (1912): illus. p. 223. See also Bröhan, *Kunsthandwerk 1*, 1976, cat. nos. 334f., and Schmitt, *Sammlung Silzer*, 1989, cat. nos. 132–34.
Meyr's Neffe variously altered and adapted the decoration scheme to other forms, so that glassware of this type cannot in every case be securely attributed to Prutscher.

Lit.: Hilschenz, *Jugendstil*, 1973, cat. no. 386; Darmstadt, *Dokument*, 1977, vol. 2, cat. no. 270

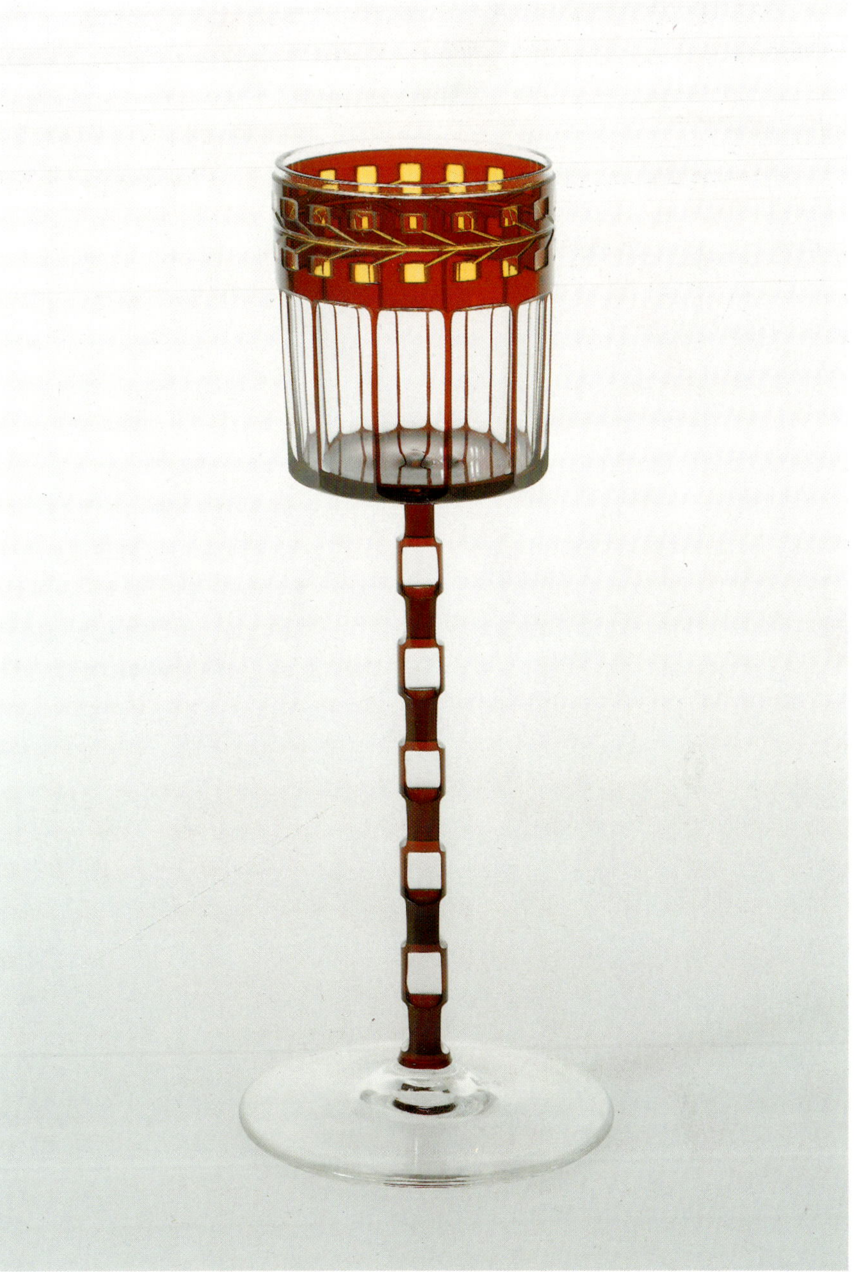

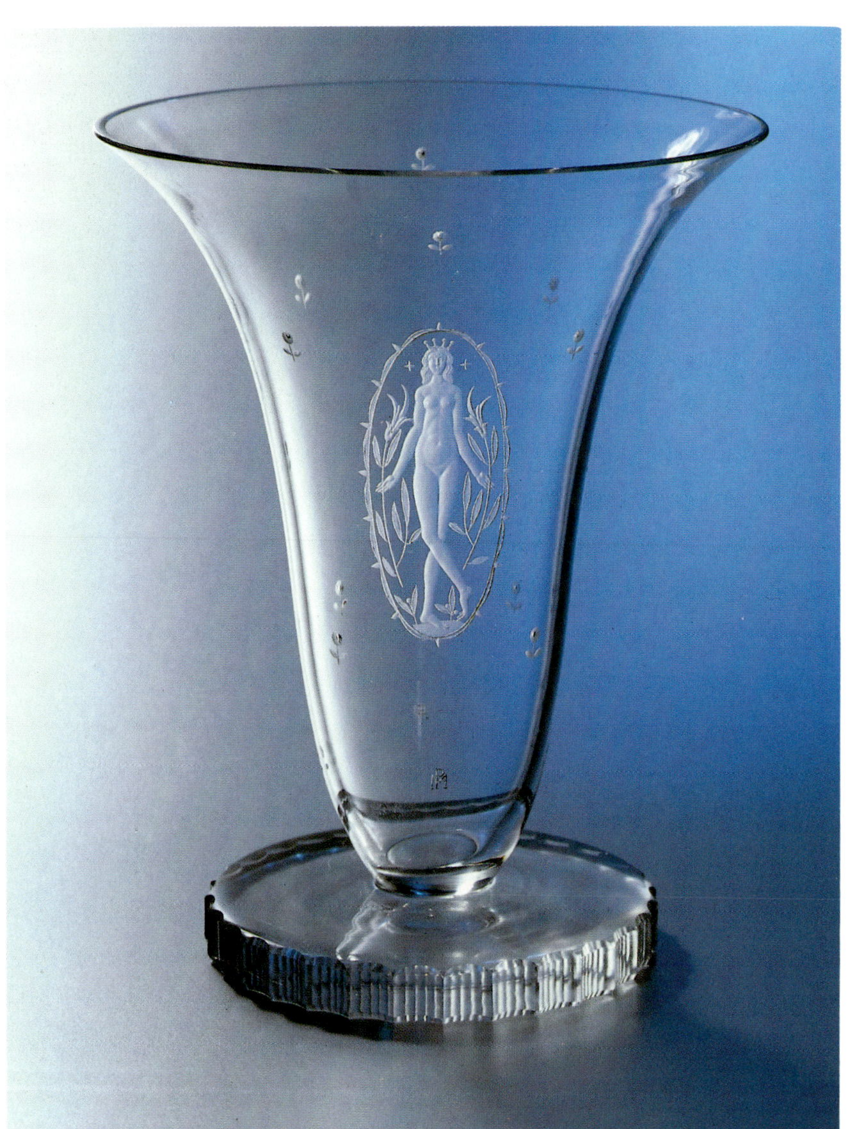

J & L Lobmeyr, Vienna

Glass distributor in Vienna

Founded in 1823 by Josef Lobmeyr in Vienna. Designs supplied by the company realized in the leading glasshouses of Bohemia. Besides firm designs, collaboration with leading Viennese artists. Meyr's Neffe in Adolf usually supplied the blanks; specialized workshops in the northern Bohemian region around Steinschönau and Haida carried out the decoration (see cat. nos. 199, 200).

334　Goblet Vase

Engraved marks on wall: *MP* and *JLLW* (ligated)
Design of form: Josef Hoffmann, ca. 1913
Decoration: Michael Powolny, ca. 1914/15
H 17.9, ⌀ 14.8 cm

Colorless glass. Mold-blown. Edge of foot cut in flutes and polished.
Decoration mat engraved.

Acc. no. P 1977-6
Acquired with funds from the Helmut Hentrich donation

For Hoffmann's design of the form (cf. here cat. no. 319) see *DKK* 34 (1914): 376, and W. Neuwirth, *Glas 1905–1925*, vol. 1 (Vienna, 1985), 70 and 79; see also Schmidt, *Lobmeyr*, 1925, pl. 18 top, and T. Bröhan, *Glaskunst der Moderne*, 1992, 183, no. 73.
Michael Powolny (1871–1954), designer of applied art, primarily ceramics, and teacher at the Wiener Kunstgewerbeschule, provided Lobmeyr and the Österreichisches Museum für Kunst und Industrie with various designs.

Lit.: Ricke and Gronert, *Glas in Schweden*, 1986, 32, fig. 13; Ricke, *2500 Jahre*, 1987, cat. no. 158

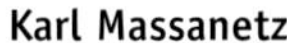

Carl Meltzer & Komp.

Glass and bronze factory with decorating workshops, Langenau near Haida

In 1822, founded under the name Focke und Meltzer in Langenau and Amsterdam. Production of glass services and metal-mounted articles. Specialized in cut decoration.

335   Flacon

Unsigned
Based on design from the Glasfachschule Haida
1914/15
H 17.6, ⌀ 9.7 cm

Colorless crystal glass, light violet overlay. Mold-blown and shaped.
Decoration in polished relief cut with rounded edges.

Acc. no. P 1987-54
Acquired with funds from the Helmut Hentrich donation

For glassware of this type see *KKh* (1915): 452f. (there the only reference to the Glasfachschule Haida); *DKD* 38 (1915/16): 278; *DK* (1916): 62. For a similar glass see Neuwirth, *Jugendstil*, 1973, cat. no. 171; see also Bröhan, *Kunsthandwerk* 1, 1976, 162ff.

Lit.: Ricke, *2500 Jahre*, 1987, cat. no. 157

Karl Massanetz

(1890–1918)

Glass painter and decoration designer

One of the most talented glass decorators in northern Bohemia before World War I. Specialized in brush and pen painting, based on his own designs, in black enamel heightened with gold.

336 a, b   Flute Glass and Plate

Unsigned
Designed for J & L Lobmeyr, Vienna
Steinschönau, 1913/14
a: H 16.3, ⌀ 8.3 cm
b: H 1.8, ⌀ 20.8 cm

Colorless glass, mold-blown, shaped.
Decoration: gold and black enamel painting with brush and pen.

Acc. no. P 1988-58
Acquired with funds from the Helmut Hentrich donation

For attribution and dating see Schmidt, *Lobmeyr*, 1925, pl. 20. For the work of Massanetz see Neuwirth, *Jugendstil*, 1973, 297ff., and Bröhan, *20er und 30er Jahre*, 1985, 391ff. (flute from the same service); see also T. Bröhan, *Glaskunst der Moderne*, 1992, 217f., nos. 93, 94.

Lit.: Pazaurek and Spiegl, *20. Jahrhundert*, 1983, 164, fig. 314

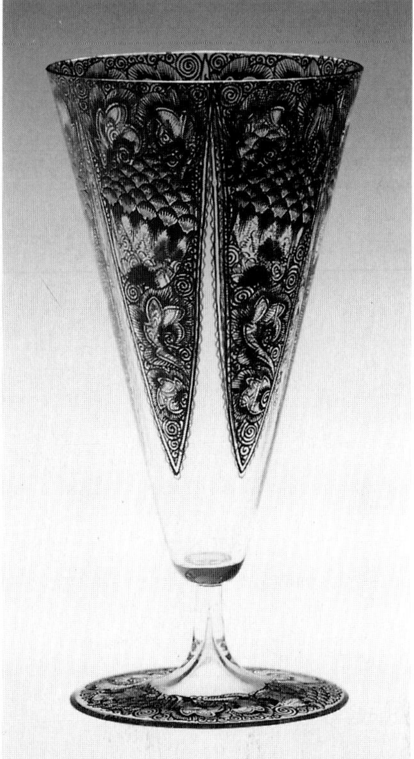

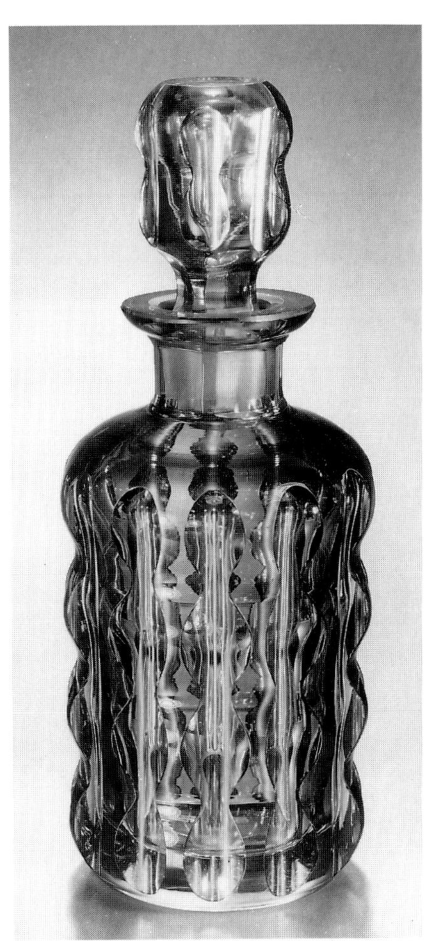

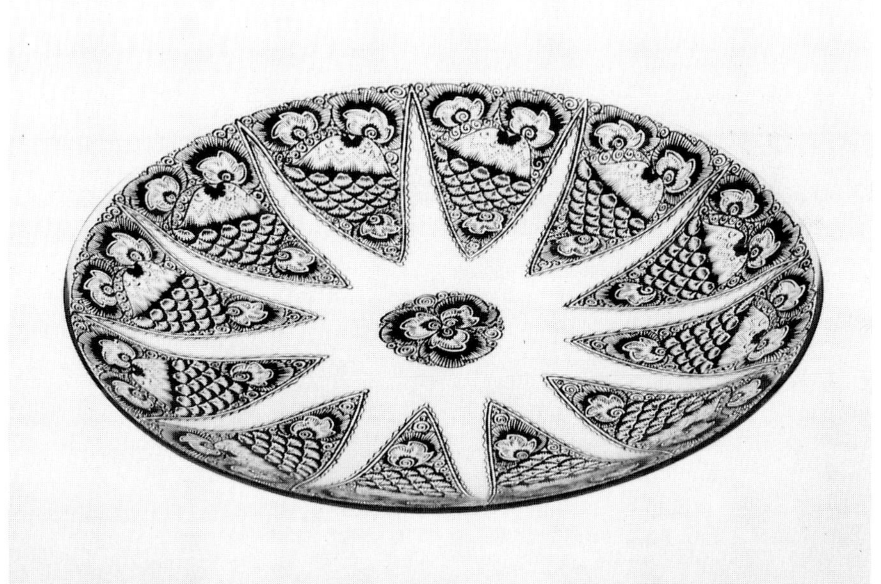

Fachschule für Glasindustrie Steinschönau

Founded in 1856 as "Fachzeichen- und Mod-
elirschule." From 1880, state school. Besides
the technical college in Haida, it was the
leading educational institution for all areas
of glass design and glass technology in
Bohemia.

337   Footed Bowl

Unsigned
Design: Alfred Walter, Fachschule Steinschönau
1913/14
H 17.7 cm, ⌀ 26.8 cm

Colorless glass. Mold-blown and shaped.
Encircling decoration: six ornamentally
framed birds of paradise. Gold and black
enamel painting with brush and pen.

Acc. no. P 1975-97
Acquired with funds from the Helmut Hentrich
donation

Alfred Walter, together with Adolf Beckert,
taught graphic subjects at the school in
Steinschönau.
The bowl was shown at the large Deutscher-
Werkbund exhibition in Cologne in 1914; see
DKK 35 (1914/15): illus. p. 166.

For further examples in various collections
see Bröhan, *Kunsthandwerk* 1, 1976, cat.
no. 310; see also T. Bröhan, *Glaskunst der
Moderne*, 1992, 197, no. 78.

Lit.: Ricke, *2500 Jahre*, 1987, cat. no. 156

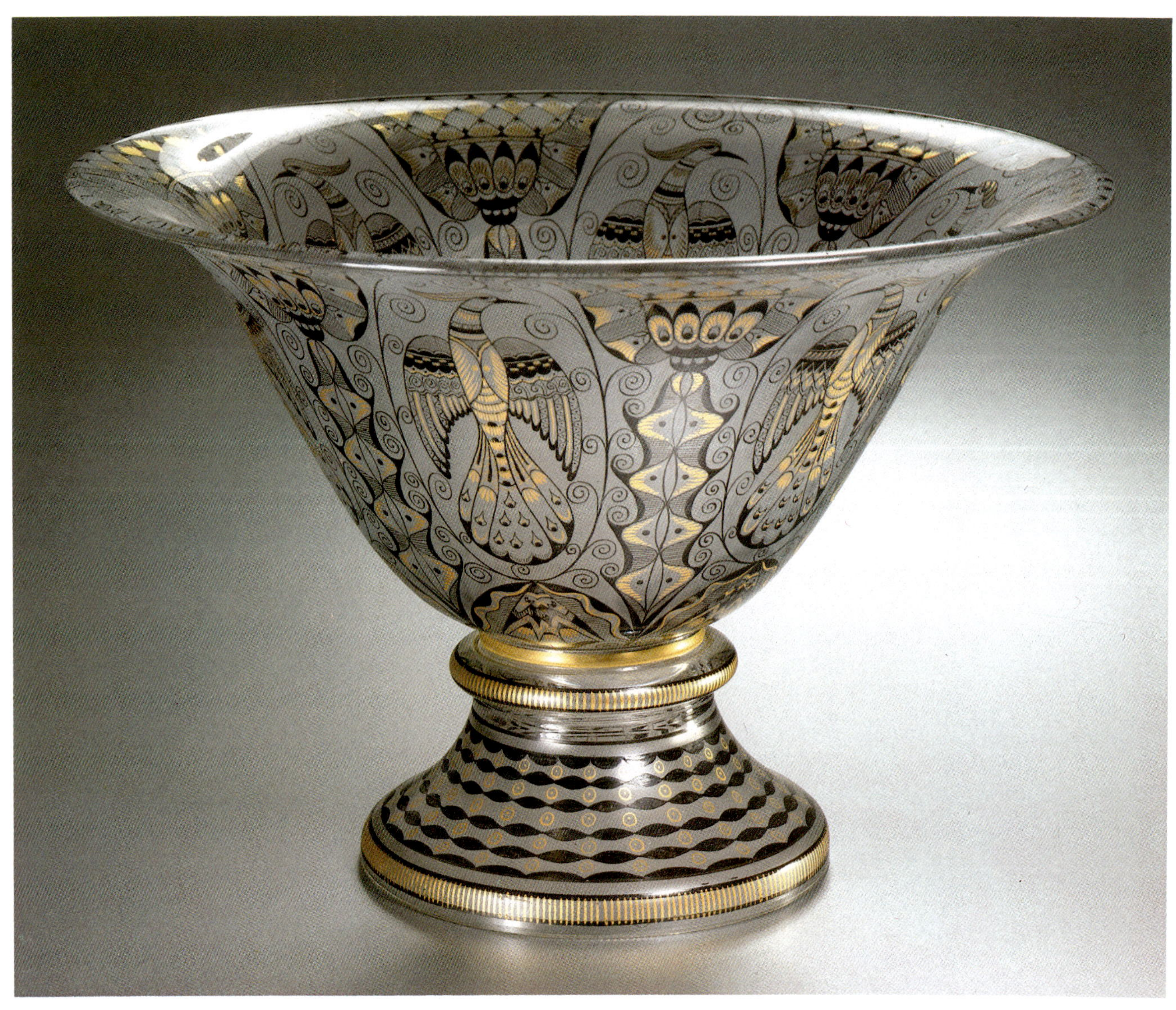

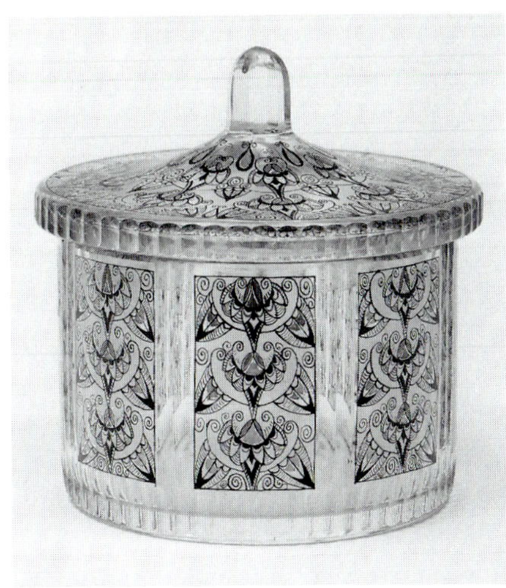

338 Covered Jar

Unsigned
Design: Adolf Beckert, Fachschule Stein-
schönau
Execution: Friedrich Pietsch, Steinschönau
Ca. 1914/15
H (with cover) 13.7, ⌀ cover 13.7 cm

Colorless glass. Mold-blown. Flute cutting.
Decoration: eight ornamental panels. Gold
and black enamel painting with brush and
pen.

Acc. no. P 1975-98
Acquired with funds from the Helmut Hentrich
donation

For Adolf Beckert see cat. no. 317. For a
taller version of the jar see Pazaurek, *Kunstgläser*, 1925, 126; see also Pazaurek and
Spiegl, *20. Jahrhundert*, 1983, 165, fig. 220.

Lit.: –

Wiener Werkstätte

Artist workshops and distributors of applied
art

Founded in 1903 by Josef Hoffmann and
Koloman Moser. From 1915, also distribution
of glassware based on designs by artists
associated with the Werkstätte. Works usually
carried out at the decorating workshops in
northern Bohemia.

339 Vase

Mark drawn with pen inside the foot: *WW*
(ligated) *HILDA JESSER*
Form: Fritzi Löw
Decoration: Hilda Jesser
Ca. 1917
Execution: Johann Oertel & Co., Haida
H 19.5, ⌀ 13.4 cm

Violet glass, appears black; mold-blown,
shaped. Acid-frosted. Painted with pen in
white: a couple on a boat; on the opposite
side, a couple next to a tree; on the ground,
a pheasant. Ornamental stars with four
points.

Acc. no. P 1982-36
Acquired with funds from the Helmut Hentrich
donation

Hilda Jesser (married name: Schmidt;
1894–1985), student, later teacher, at the
Wiener Kunstgewerbeschule. She was a member of the artist workshops at the Wiener
Werkstätte. In the design records of the
Wiener Werkstätte, the form of the vase is
associated with the name Fritzi Löw
(1891–1975) and the date 1917. For a vase
with related decoration see Pazaurek, *Kunstgläser*, 1925, 156, fig. 165.

Lit.: Ricke, *Museumsarbeit*, 1988, 76, fig. 62

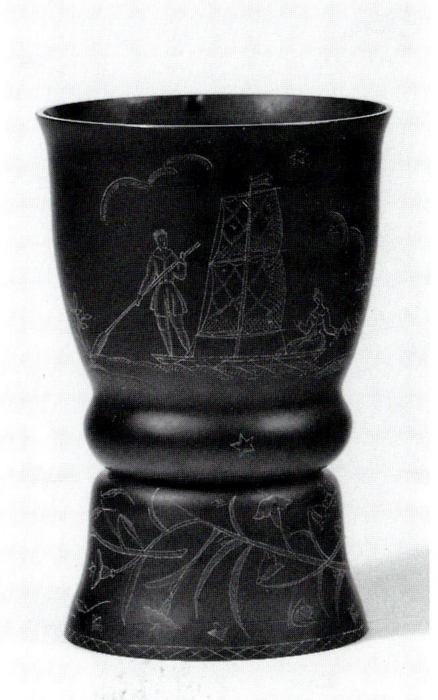

"Bimini" Werkstätte für Kunstgewerbe Ges.m.b.H.

Viennese specialty workshop for lampblown
art glass as well as ceramic and metal objects

Founded in 1923 by Fritz Lampl (1892–1955;
artistic director) and David Rosenthal (commercial director). Designs also by Josef and
Artur Berger. In 1938, the company was
closed and Lampl emigrated to London.

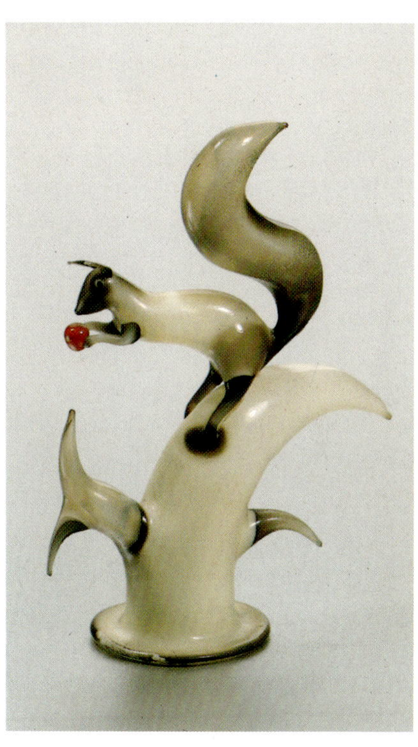

340 Small Squirrel

Unsigned
Model no. 634
Ca. 1923–25
H 12.5, W 9.7, ⌀ foot 4.3 cm

Milky glass, partly struck brown. Freely lampblown.

Acc. no. P 1979-11
Acquired with funds from the Helmut Hentrich
donation

Illustrated in an undated company production
catalogue together with several other objects
with the caption "Design Artur and Josef
Berger, Fritz Lampl." For Bimini see W.
Neuwirth, *Lampengeblasenes Glas aus Wien II:
Bimini—Wiener Glaskunst des Art Deco* (Vienna, 1992), for model no. 634 see pp. 330f.

Lit.: Ricke, *Museumsarbeit*, 1988, 76, fig. 59

Germany

In the few years of its heyday, European Art Nouveau glass developed in a field of tension created by the two poles of France and Bohemia. Germany, lying geographically between these two poles, could not avoid being influenced by both. This is illustrated particularly well by the art-glass production of the Bavarian manufacturer Ferdinand von Poschinger in Buchenau and Spiegelhütte. Besides iridescent glassware of the Lötz type or knit-wrapped vessels (cat. nos. 344, 345) similar to those of Pallme-König, he also produced etched and engraved decoration in the Gallé genre.

In Darmstadt and Munich, the chemist and glass artist Josef Emil Schneckendorf sought new forms of expression in the metallic surface that Tiffany and Lötz had introduced to glass art (cat. no. 351). In his painting with colors fired in a reducing atmosphere, however, he imitated more closely the production of the ceramists Miklós Zsolnay and Clément Massier or the glassware of Amédée de Caranza (cat. no. 264).

The decorative glassware of the Berlin graphic artist Karl Koepping (cat. nos. 341–43) was rightfully considered abroad the most original achievement of turn-of-the-century German glass art. His lampblown, extremely delicate flower designs and cordial glasses, which almost beg not to be used, show the material in its most fragile state. The emphasis on the frailty and lightness of glass shaped freehand at the lamp takes the design technically and aesthetically to an unsurpassable limit.

In the 1920s Koepping's followers in the Thuringian home workshops of Lauscha, Neuhaus, and Ilmenau (cat. nos. 361–63) returned to clear, functional vessel forms in the style of the period. The decorative element, however, corresponding to the peculiarities of work made at the lamp, always remained essential to the vessels' effect—as with decorative objects made by the Viennese company Bimini (cat. no. 340). Thuringian lamp work of the 1920s and 1930s was one of the original achievements of German glass art between the wars.

The enamel-painted glassware produced by the Silesian glass factory and the Fritz Heckert decorating firm after designs by Max Rade and Ludwig Sütterlin (cat. nos. 347, 348) was also little affected by developments beyond Germany's borders. Some of it shows direct links to graphic design, in particular book illustration. Moreover the Munich review *Die Jugend*, from which the style received its name in Germany, was the source of numerous artistic impulses around 1900.

In the area of utilitarian glass, such German designers as Peter Behrens, Richard Riemerschmid, and Hans Christiansen (cat. no. 346) were forward-looking, laying the groundwork for twentieth-century glass design. Besides the big names, a large number of designers who remained anonymous sought to produce sophisticated forms that remained true to material and function (cat. nos. 349, 350), making Germany the center of utility glass design. Thus a tradition was established, which such personalities as Richard Süssmuth (cat. no. 370) and Wilhelm Wagenfeld (cat. no. 369) carried on and which remained alive up to the 1950s.

Further major glass designers were Bruno Mauder, for many years director of the glass college in Zwiesel, and the glass artist and designer of utility glassware Alexander Pfohl. Mauder's formal idiom (cat. no. 357) influenced a whole generation of Zwiesel graduates. The same is true of Pfohl, who taught design in Haida, in the present-day Czech Republic, from 1929. In the previous decade, as director of the design studio of the Josephinenhütte in Schreiberhau, Silesia, he had determined its production program and lent it new significance (cat. nos. 358, 359). In the 1930s, besides teaching at the glass college, Pfohl worked as designer for many glass decorators in northern Bohemia and beyond (cat. no. 360). He always knew how to combine the demands of the market with his own artistic ideas.

Shortly before World War I and increasingly in the 1920s, Munich crystallized as a regional reservoir of design potential. Artists working for the Deutsche Werkstätten, such as Wolfgang von Wersin, Else Wenz-Vietor, and others, sought to link German ideas of form with Venetian techniques. Georg Carl von Reichenbach developed individually designed forms for decorative and drinking glassware (cat. no. 352) for the Debschitz-Schule, a private educational institution of high standing. Jean Beck took up the strong semiopaque tango colors introduced at Lötz in Klostermühle (cat. nos. 353–55) and developed above all in the 1920s a rich repertoire of forms in transparent colored glass, often cut.

The glasshouse of the Württembergische Metallwarenfabrik in Geislingen (cat. nos. 366–68) became another center, as did the Stuttgart Kunstgewerbeschule on account of the instructor Wilhelm von Eiff. In placing great emphasis on surface texture, von Eiff created a new design basis for cutting and engraving. With the richly differentiated engraved surface (cat. no. 364) and especially with glass cutting that appears carved (cat. no. 365), he took new paths, which continue to be influential today.

Karl Koepping
(1848–1914)

Painter, etcher, chemist, and glass designer

After graduating in chemistry and studying at
the Akademie der Bildenden Künste in
Munich, in 1890 he became director of the
master studio for copper engraving and etching at the Berliner Akademie. From 1896,
copublisher of the art journal *Pan*. From
1895, first designs of tall-stemmed, vegetal
glass creations and bottle-shaped vases. In
1896, short period of collaboration with the
art-glass blower Friedrich Zitzmann. Subsequently his glassware was realized at the
Fachschule für Glasinstrumentenmacher in
Ilmenau. From 1898, also designs for utilitarian glass.

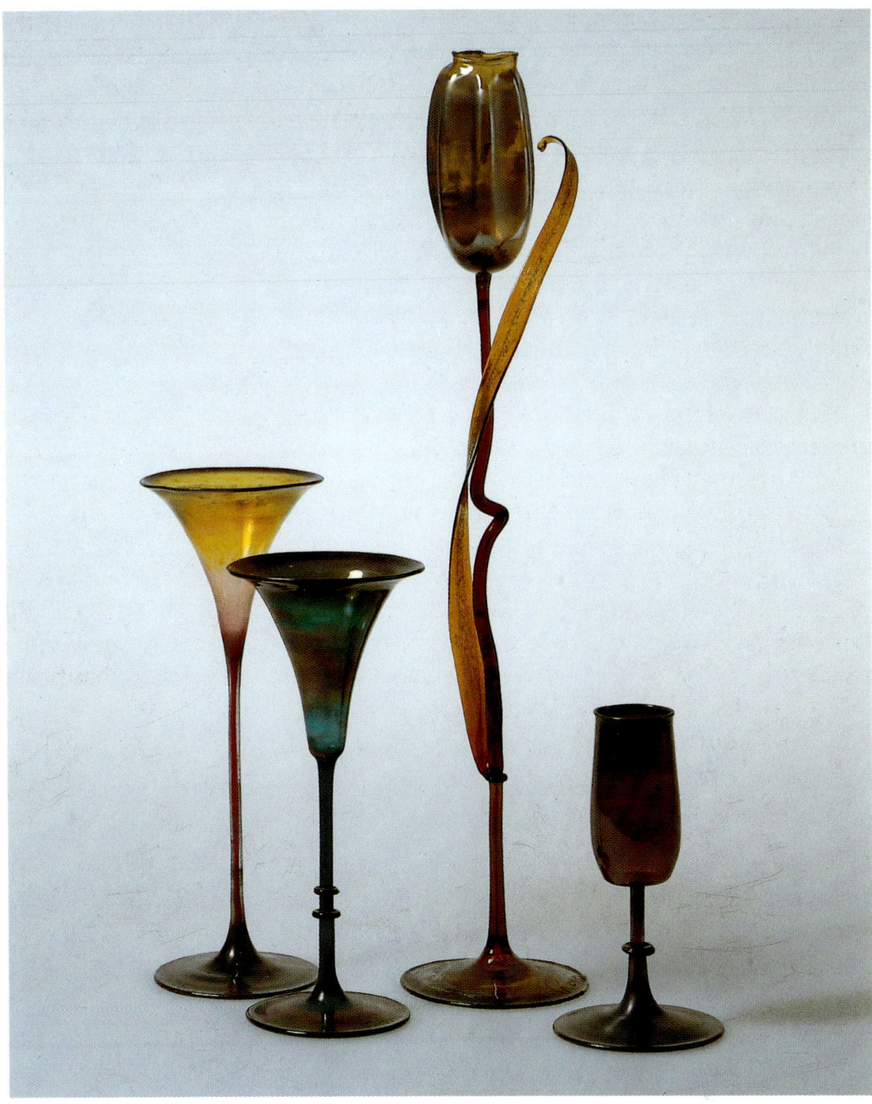

341 a, b Cordial Glasses

Fired mark on the foot: *Koepping*
Ilmenau, ca. 1899
H 17.2, 14.9; ⌀ 6.7, 6.7 cm

Freely lampblown. Iridescent with colors fired
in a reducing atmosphere.

Acc. nos. P 1970-40, 39
Gift of Helmut Hentrich

For almost identical glassware see *Dekorative
Kunst* 3 (1989): illus. p. 125; *Revue des Arts
Décoratifs* 19 (1899): illus. p. 323.

Lit.: Hilschenz, *Jugendstil*, 1973, cat. nos.
32, 33; Ricke, *Ausgewählte Werke*, 1980, 25

342 Decorative Glass

Fired mark on the foot: *CKoepping*
Ilmenau, 1896–98
H 32, ⌀ 6.7 cm

Freely lampblown. Iridescent with colors fired
in a reducing atmosphere.

Acc. no. P 1970-34
Gift of Helmut Hentrich

For glassware of this type see J. Schou-Christensen, *Glaskunst omkring år 1900* (Copenhagen: Kunstindustrimuseets Virksomhed,
1969), 168ff., with illus. For an etching with
designs for two similar glasses see *Pan*
(1896/97): pl. after p. 252. For dating see
Sprechsaal 29 (1896): 1225, and 30 (1897):
162–64. For two almost identical pieces see
Kaiser-Wilhelm-Museum in Krefeld, acc. nos.
1914/115 and 116.

Lit.: Hilschenz, *Jugendstil*, 1973, cat. no. 27;
Ricke, *Ausgewählte Werke*, 1980, 25; Pazaurek
and Spiegl, *20. Jahrhundert*, 1983, 240, fig.
458 and title page; *Lötz* 1, 1989, 21, fig. 14

343 Cordial Glass

Fired mark on foot: Koepping
Ilmenau, ca. 1899
H 10.3, ⌀ 3.7 cm

Freely lampblown. Iridescent with colors fired
in a reducing atmosphere.

Acc. no. P 1970-38
Gift of Helmut Hentrich

For almost identical glasses see *Dekorative
Kunst* 3 (1899): illus. p. 57.

Lit.: Hilschenz, *Jugendstil*, 1973, cat. no. 30;
Ricke, *Ausgewählte Werke*, 1980, 25

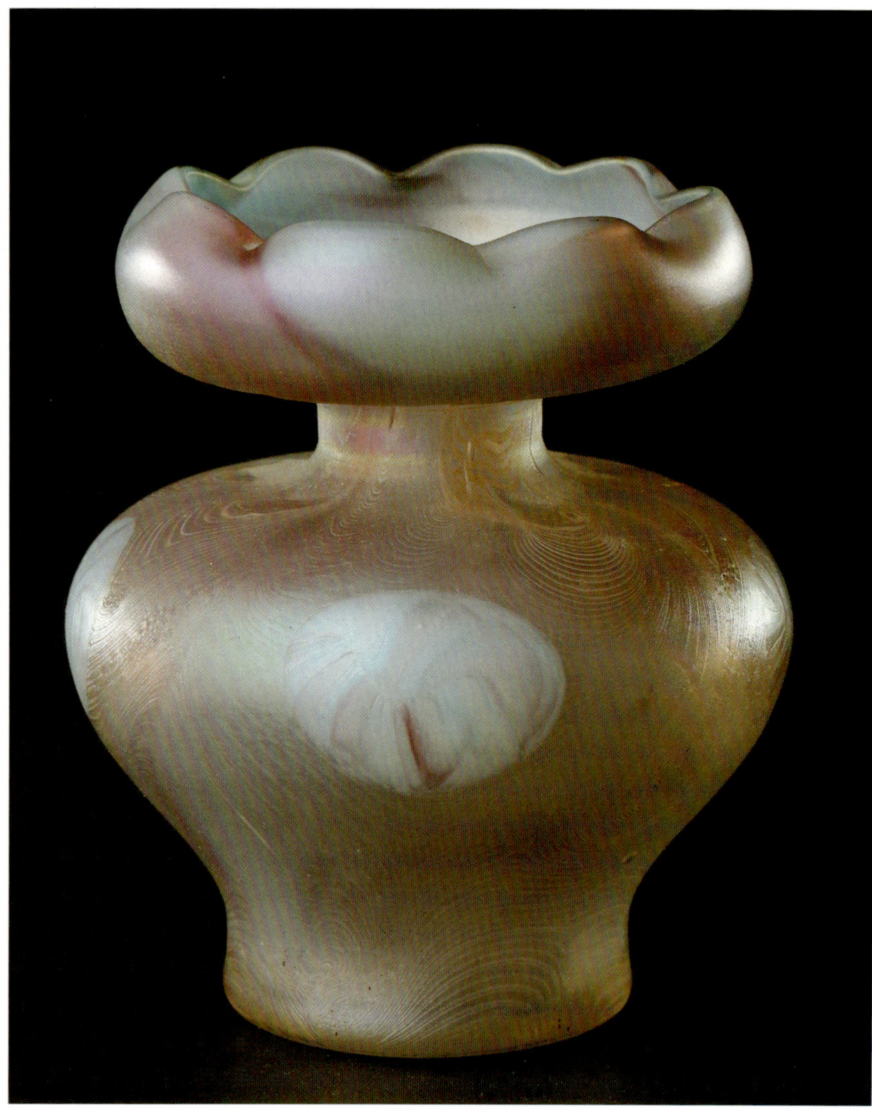

Glashüttenwerke Buchenau
Ferdinand von Poschinger

Glasshouse for hollow and flat glassware, decorating workshop for ornamental and utilitarian glass, Buchenau and Spiegelhütte near Zwiesel, Bavarian Forest

Local glass production from the 15th century. From 1568, the glasshouse belonged to the Poschinger family. In 1856, the large glassworks estate was divided, Ferdinand von Poschinger receiving Buchenau and Spiegelhütte. In Buchenau colored flat glass was produced; in Spiegelhütte, utilitarian and luxury ware. Particularly fine pieces from the Jugendstil period.
In 1933, the glasshouse was shut down.

344 Vase

Gilded needle-etched mark in ground-out pontil on the underside of base: *Ferd. von Poschinger Buchenau Bayern Glashüttenwerke Nr. 840;* also the model no. in gold: *840*
Ca. 1902

H 11.3, ⌀ 10.6 cm

On inner casing of opal glass, colorless cover layer with embedded streaks; fine, encircling, silver glass threads. On top of irregularly combed threads, four embedded, colored, marbled dots. Mold-blown, shaped. Iridescent.

Acc. no. P 1970-19; gift of Helmut Hentrich

Part of a group of some 1,000 numbered vase and dish models in the Tiffany and Gallé style, made shortly after 1900 at the Poschinger factory, Spiegelhütte. For dating see mention of "Chamäleonglas mit gezogenen Fäden" (chameleon glass with combed threads) as latest company product in *Central-Blatt für Glasindustrie und Keramik* 17 (1902): 910. For further examples of this glassware see Baumgärtner, Regensburg, 1977, 190ff., esp. cat. nos. 411, 414. For similar glassware, designed by C. Schmoll genannt Eisenwerth, see *Kunstgewerbeblatt*, n.s., 21 (1910): illus. pp. 53 and 57.

Lit.: Hilschenz, *Jugendstil*, 1973, cat. no. 12; Pazaurek and Spiegl, *20. Jahrhundert*, 1983, 51, fig. 76

345 Vase

Unsigned
F. v. Poschinger, Spiegelhütte
Ca. 1900–1905
H 31.5, ⌀ 14.5 cm

Colorless glass with opaque rusty red thread application. Mold-blown. Painted with silversalt stains, fired. Lustrous metallic surface.

Acc. no. P 1970-15
Gift of Helmut Hentrich

The chemist Maximilian Boudnik at the glasshouse of Josef Knizek in Ullersdorf, Bohemia, used this decoration method of combining stains with colors fired in a reducing atmosphere, which is technically not very complicated or unusual. Glassware with his signature is kept at the Museum of Applied Arts in Prague.
The Poschinger glasshouse in Spiegelhütte experimented on its own with this type of decoration. Various examples of such surface decoration are documented on Poschinger forms. For F. von Poschinger and M. Boudnik see Schmitt, *Sammlung Silzer*, 1989, 292ff. and 37ff., and Passau, *Böhmisches Glas 4*, 1995, 188f., and 5, 18ff.

Lit.: Hilschenz, *Jugendstil*, 1973, cat. no. 8

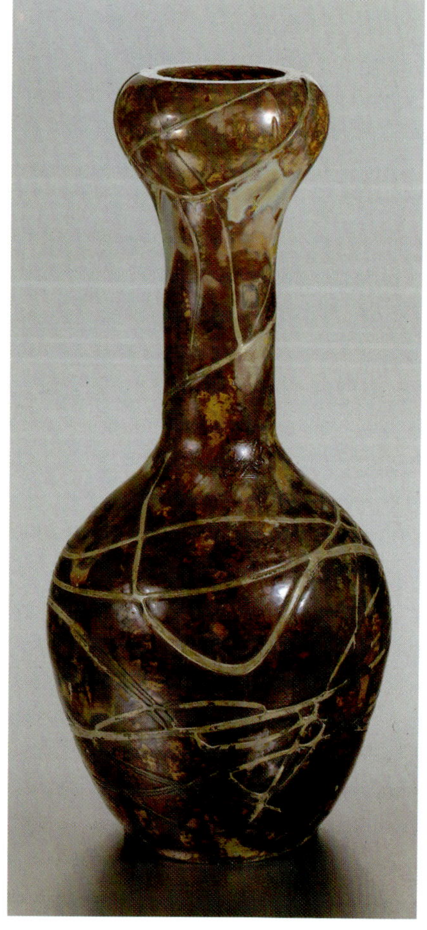

Theresienthaler Krystallglasfabrik

Glasshouse for hollow glassware and decorating workshop for utilitarian and luxury glass, Theresienthal near Zwiesel, Bavarian Forest

Founded in 1836 by Franz and Wilhelm Steigerwald. From 1861, belonged to the Poschinger family. During the late 19th century, a leading producer of historicist glassware in the old German and Venetian style. Around 1900, successful Jugendstil production, primarily drinking-glass services.

346 a–c   Glasses from a Service

Gilt-painted mark as part of decoration, ligated monogram: *HC*
Design: Hans Christiansen
Ca. 1902/03
White-wine glass: H 15.9, ⌀ 7.5 cm
Beer glass: H 17.7, ⌀ 7.3 cm
Cordial glass: H 13.1, ⌀ 5 cm

Colorless crystal glass, mold-blown and shaped. Gilt-painting.

Acc. nos. P 1985-123, 122; P 1987-39 a
Gift of Helmut Hentrich

Hans Christiansen (1866–1945), painter, graphic artist, and designer of applied art, supplied several designs to the factory in Theresienthal. See Hilschenz, *Jugendstil*, 1973, cat. no. 45.
The present service, consisting of six parts (from 1907 of eight), matches the porcelain service with the same rose decoration. See Darmstadt, *Dokument*, 1977, vol. 4, cat. nos. 103, 111; see also Pazaurek and Spiegl, *20. Jahrhundert*, 1983, 25, fig. 35.

Lit.: K.-W. Warthorst, *Die Glasfabrik Theresienthal* (Freiburg, 1996), 146f.

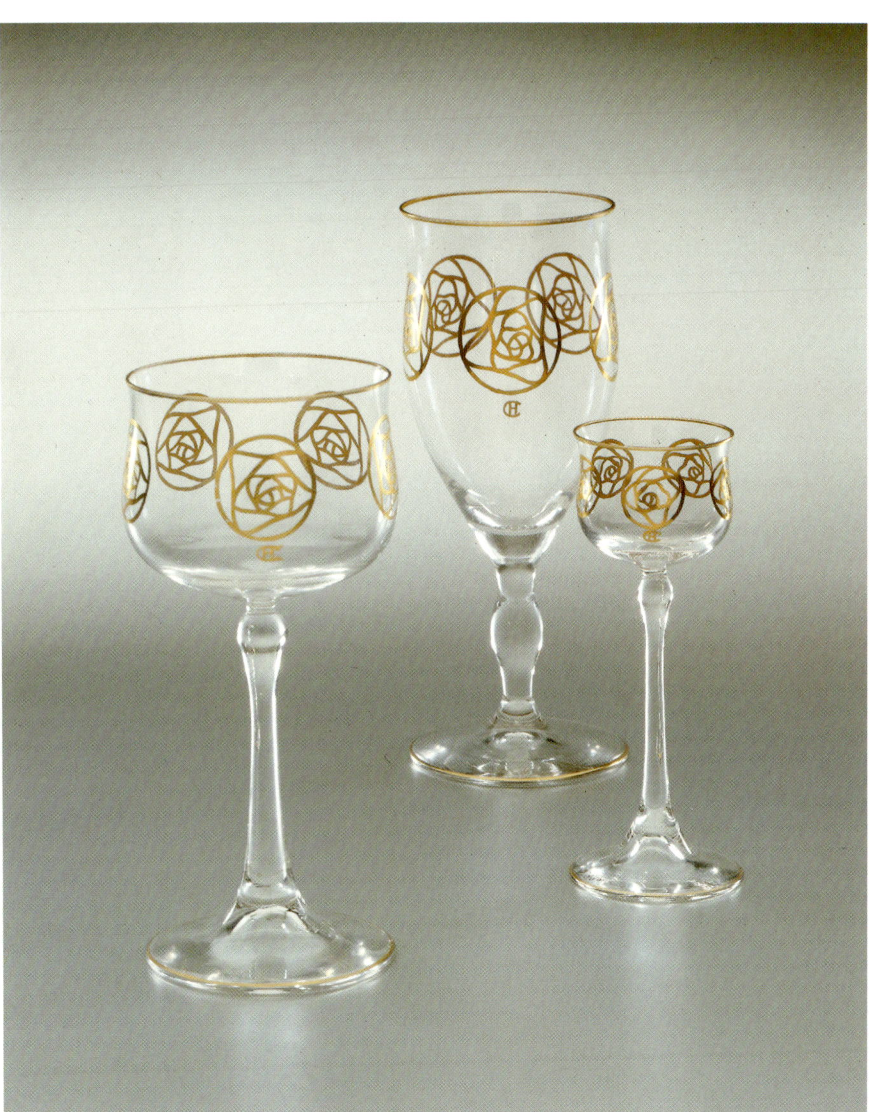

Petersdorfer Glashütte Fritz Heckert

Glasshouse for hollow glassware and decorating
workshop for ornamental and utilitarian glass,
Petersdorf in the Riesengebirge, Silesia

Founded in 1866 by Fritz Heckert (d. 1890). From
1870 to 1900, diverse glass production, above all
reproductions of ancient, old German, Oriental,
and Venetian glassware, especially enamel painted.
In 1922, merged with Josephinenhütte in
Schreiberhau and Kynast-Krystall in Harmsdorf.

347 Vase

Black mark in the ground-out pontil on the
underside of foot: *F.H. I 491/9 MR.* (F.H. for Fritz
Heckert; MR. for Max Rade)
Design: Max Rade
Ca. 1898
H 16.1, ⌀ 12.4 cm

Colorless glass. Mold-blown. Light blue-gray
toned down and matted; on top of that, decoration in opaque enamel.

Acc. no. P 1970-26
Gift of Helmut Hentrich

Max Rade (1840–1917), decoration painter and
pattern designer, was professor at the Kunstgewerbeschule in Dresden. Between 1898 and 1900,
designs for Heckert. See Pazaurek, *Moderne Gläser*,
1901, 28ff., esp. fig. 18; Schmitt, *Sammlung
Silzer*, 1989, 152ff.; Passau, *Böhmisches Glas 5*,
1995, 60ff.

Lit.: Hilschenz, *Jugendstil*, 1973, cat. no. 19

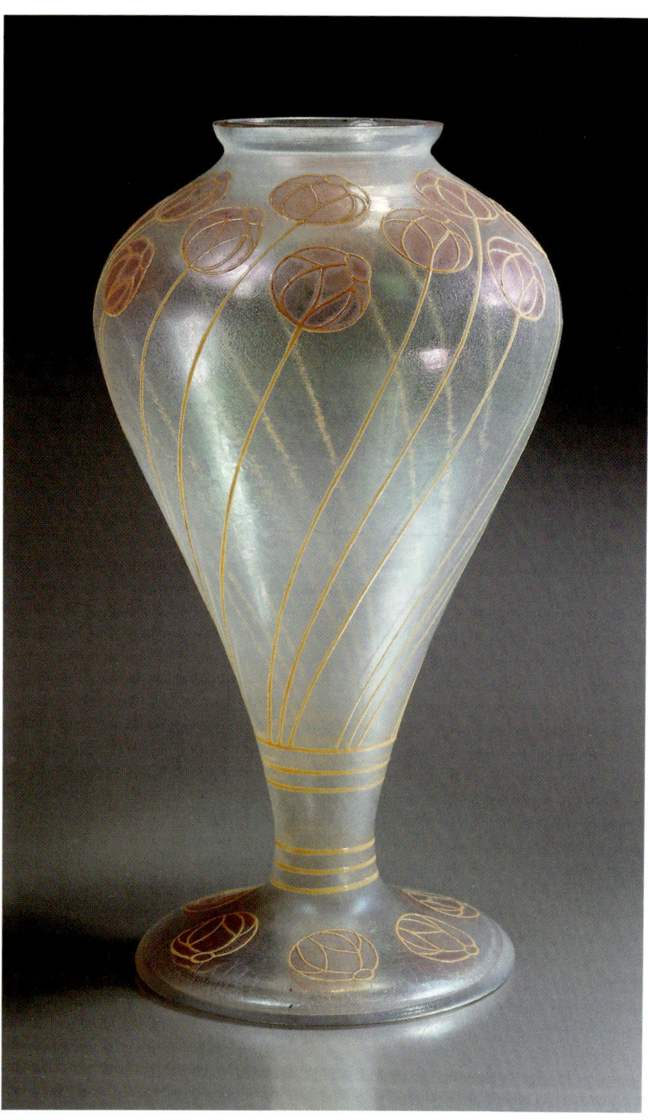

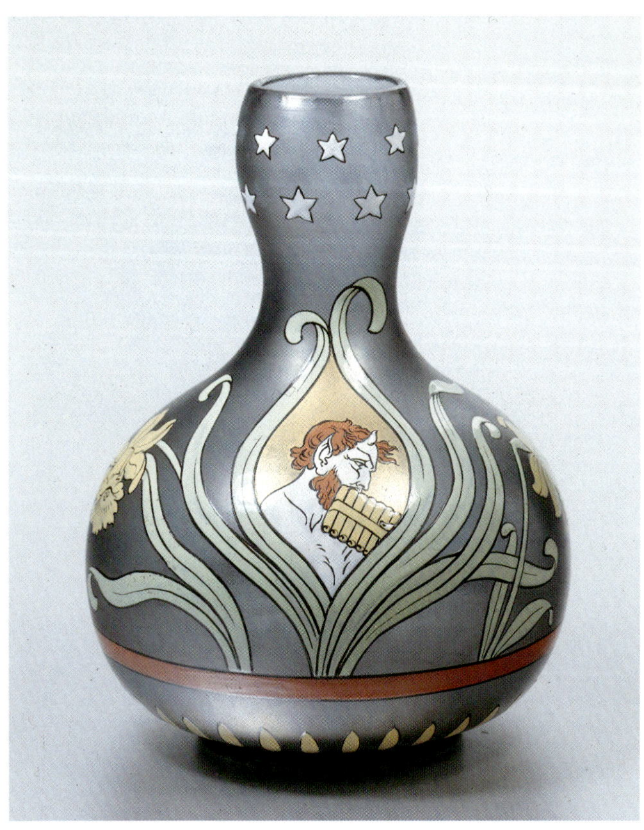

348 Vase

Design: Ludwig Sütterlin
Execution: Fritz Heckert, Petersdorf
1900/1901
H 25.3, ⌀ 14.3 cm

Colorless glass, mold-blown. Iridescent.
Mouth ground flat, no pontil mark. Decoration in yellow relief enamel and violet transparent enamel: 18 flowers encircling the
shoulder, 6 on the foot.

Acc. no. P 1961-16

Ludwig Sütterlin (1865–1917), painter, commercial artist, writer, and designer of applied
art, taught at the first Handwerkerschule für
Buchdruckerkunst in Berlin. Major type
designer. Between 1900 and 1906, glass
designs for Heckert. For dating see Pazaurek,
Moderne Gläser, 1901, 31ff., figs. 25, 26.

Lit.: Heinemeyer, *Glas*, 1966, cat. no. 536;
Schlosser, *Das alte Glas*, 1977, 405, fig. 343;
Pazaurek and Spiegl, *20. Jahrhundert*, 1983,
98, fig. 167

Gräflich Schaffgotschsche Josephinenhütte

Glasshouse for hollow ware and decorating workshop for ornamental and utilitarian glass, Schreiberhau, Riesengebirge

Founded in 1842. Under the artistic direction of Franz Pohl (1813–1884), became the most important Silesian glassworks. Around 1900, production of crystal glassware, vases, and table services with rather conservative decoration as well as iridescent reproductions of ancient glassware. During the 1920s, an artistic upswing under design-studio director Alexander Pfohl (see cat. nos. 358–60).

349 a–c   White-Wine Glasses

Printed on paper label on the underside of foot: *Josephinenhütte* with shield (factory mark)
Ca. 1900
H 29, ⌀ 8.3 cm

Colorless crystal glass; mold-blown, shaped. Stems and knops in different facet cuts. Mouth rims have double gold edging.

Acc. nos. P 1970-31a, b, c
Gift of Helmut Hentrich

Single pieces that do not belong to a table service.

Lit.: Hilschenz, *Jugendstil*, 1973, cat. no. 24; Pazaurek and Spiegl, *20. Jahrhundert*, 1983, 174, fig. 344

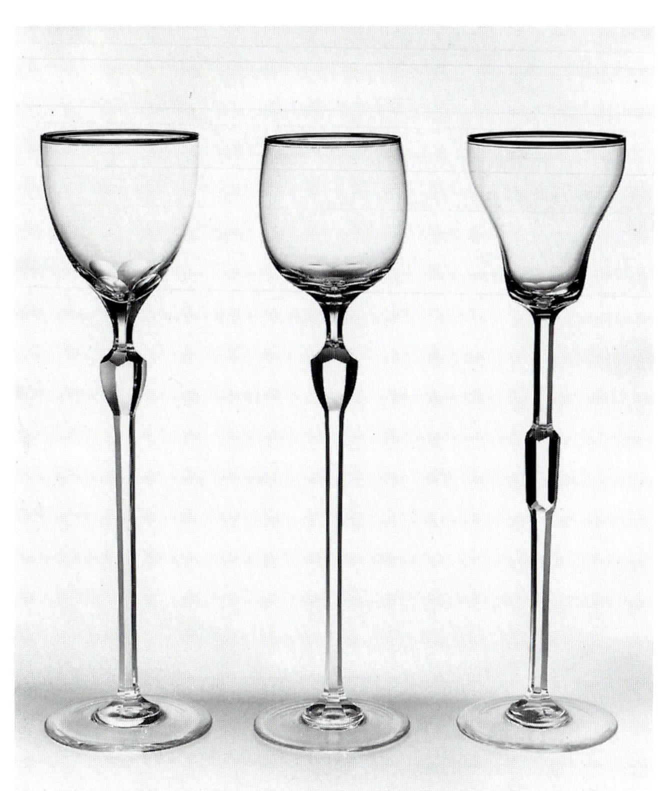

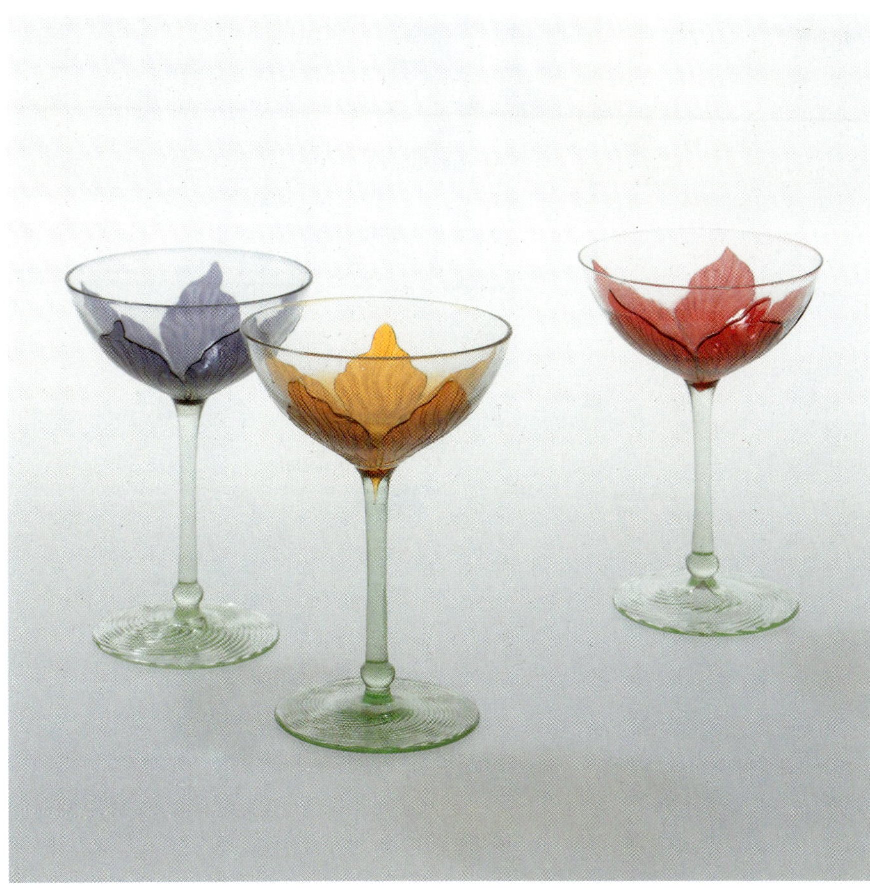

Rheinische Glashütten A.G.

Glasshouse for hollow and flat ware and decorating workshop for ornamental and utilitarian glass, Cologne-Ehrenfeld

Founded in 1864 by the entrepreneur Philipp Michel. In the last two decades of the 19th century, under the direction of Oskar Rauter, one of the most significant glasshouses in Germany; virtuoso mastery of old glass techniques. See cat. nos. 197, 198. Around 1900, efforts to make newer products in the Jugendstil style under the direction of Eduard von Kralik.

350 a–c   Flute Glasses

Unsigned
Ca. 1902
H 14.9, ⌀ 9.7 cm

Bowl of colorless crystal glass, color overlay, stem and foot light green, foot with optic ribbing. Decoration etched in two stages.

Acc. nos. P 1970-45 c, d, a
Gift of Helmut Hentrich

From a set of flute glasses. See, for example, *DK* 6 (1902): illus. p. 188.

Lit.: Hilschenz, *Jugendstil*, 1973, cat. no. 38; Ricke, *2500 Jahre*, 1987, cat. no. 151

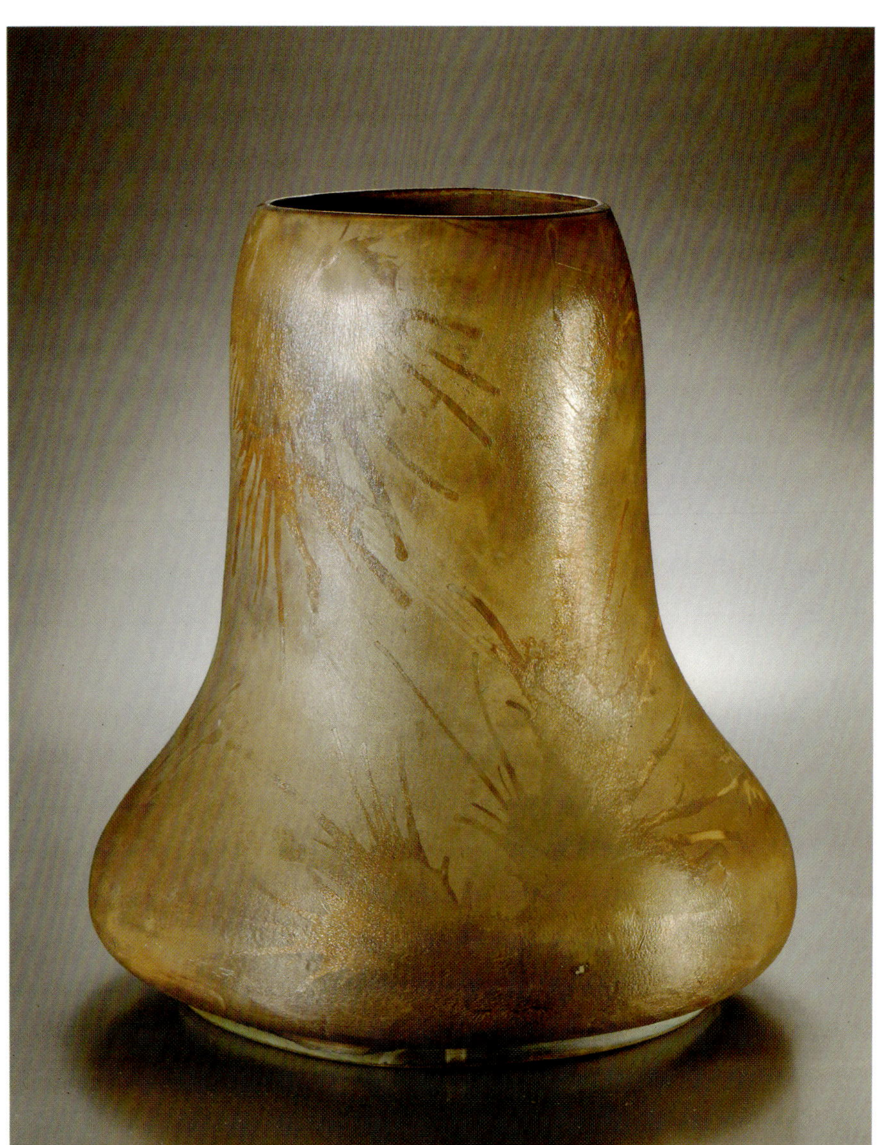

Josef Emil Schneckendorf
(1865–1949)

Sculptor, painter, glass artist, and designer of applied art

After apprenticing as sculptor and studying at the Akademie der Bildenden Künste in Munich, started making glassware in 1898. From 1907, director of the Grossherzogliche Edelglasmanufaktur Darmstadt, newly founded by Grand Duke Ernst Ludwig von Hessen und bei Rhein. After it passed into private ownership in 1910/11, Schneckendorf presumably continued to run the factory.

351 Vase

Fired mark on the underside of foot: *J.E. Sch.*
Ca. 1911
H 16.5, ⌀ 13.2 cm

Colorless glass. Mold-blown. Color fired in reducing atmosphere.

Acc. no. P 1970-51
Gift of Helmut Hentrich

For glass pieces with the same form see Vienna's Museum für angewandte Kunst, acc. no. 2188. See also *Kunst in Hessen und am Mittelrhein*, no. 5 (1966): 87, figs. 6–8; see also H. Paulus, *Josef Emil Schneckendorf 1865 bis 1949: Sein Leben und seine Bedeutung für die Edelglasschöpfung des Jugendstils* (Erlangen, 1993), 52, fig. 17.
Since there is no grand-ducal mark above Schneckendorf's monogram, the glass—in spite of its early shape—was probably made about 1911 after the company's privatization.

Lit.: Hilschenz, *Jugendstil*, 1973, cat. no. 44

Georg Carl von Reichenbach
(1872–1940)

Designer of applied art and glass

Around 1900, founded a workshop of fine and applied art. Worked with glass primarily up to World War I. From 1905, designed for the Munich Debschitz-Schule. His designs largely carried out at the Kristallglasfabrik Oberzwieselau—Benedikt von Poschinger.

352 Decorative Goblet

Unsigned
Oberzwieselau, ca. 1906
H 15.3, ⌀ 11.6 cm

Colorless glass, lower section blue inside, green overlay outside. Below the bowl, four applied button prunts. Mold-blown and shaped. The foot has four ground-out and polished oval openings.

Acc. no. P 1970-43
Gift of Helmut Hentrich

For attribution and dating compare form variations with stem conically narrowing towards the top in *DK* 14 (1906): illus. p. 354; *Kunstgewerbeblatt*, n.s., 18 (1907): illus. p. 117; *KKh* 58 (1908): fig. 48.

Lit.: Hilschenz, *Jugendstil*, 1973, cat. no. 36; Darmstadt, *Dokument*, 1977, vol. 2, cat. no. 271; Pazaurek and Spiegl, *20. Jahrhundert*, 1983, 19, fig. 22; Ricke, *2500 Jahre*, 1987, cat. no. 152

Jean Beck
(1862–1938)

Ceramist, designer of applied art, and painter. Owned an eponymous distribution company of applied arts in Munich

Founded before 1898. From 1908, concentrated increasingly on glass designs; glassware carried out in glasshouses of the Bavarian Forest, particularly in Regenhütte. Especially prolific in the 1920s.

353 Vase

Unsigned
Ca. 1910–14
H 8.7, W 4.3 cm

Strong colorless cover layer on jade green inner casing. Mold-blown. Opaque, rust red, encircling threads. Black pearl prunts. Mouth and base ground flat.

Acc. no. P 1981-335
Gift of Helmut Hentrich

Influenced by Reichenbach's designs for the Munich Debschitz-Schule; see cat. no. 352. Used strong opal colors while similar developments were taking place at Lötz in Klostermühle.

Lit.: *Lötz* 1, 1989, 23f., fig. 19

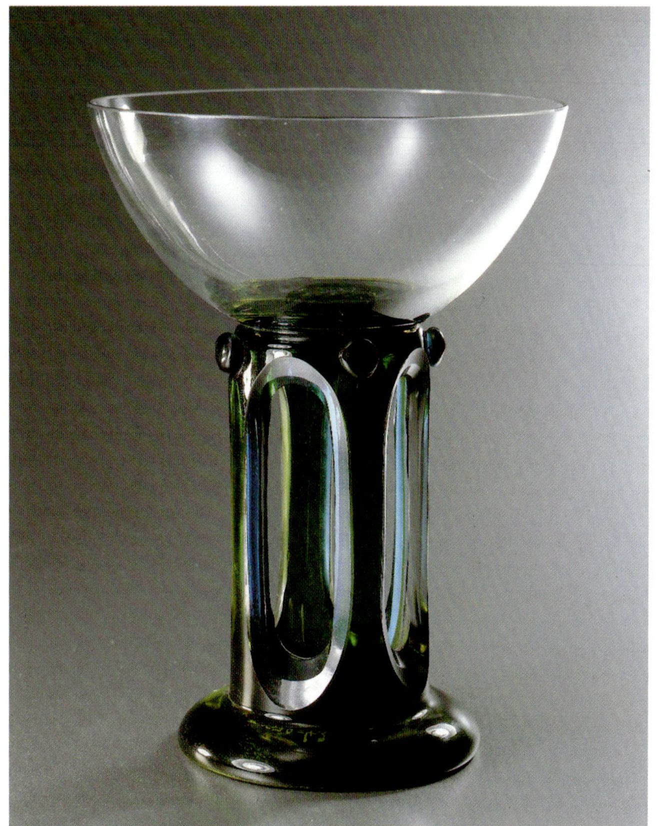

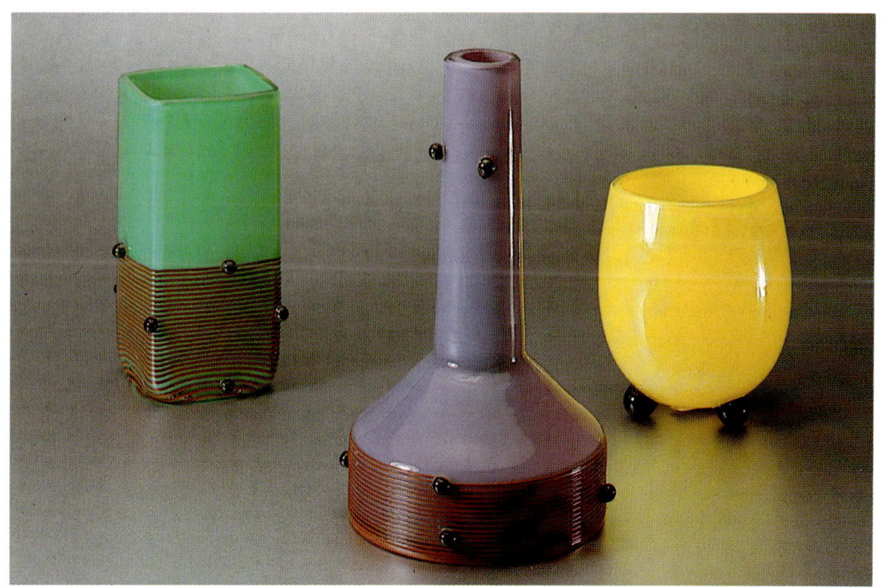

354 Vase

Encircling mark on round adhesive label: *JEAN BECK MÜNCHEN*; in the center: company mark with three shields inside one large one
Ca. 1910–14
H 11.6, ⌀ 6.8 cm

Milky violet. Like cat. no. 353.

Acc. no. P 1981-336
Gift of Helmut Hentrich

Lit.: *Lötz* 1, 1989, 23f., fig. 19

355 Vase

Unsigned
Ca. 1910–14
H 6.5, ⌀ 5.5 cm

Lemon yellow. Like cat. nos. 353, 354.

Acc. no. P 1981-334
Gift of Helmut Hentrich

Lit.: *Lötz* 1, 1989, 23f., fig. 19

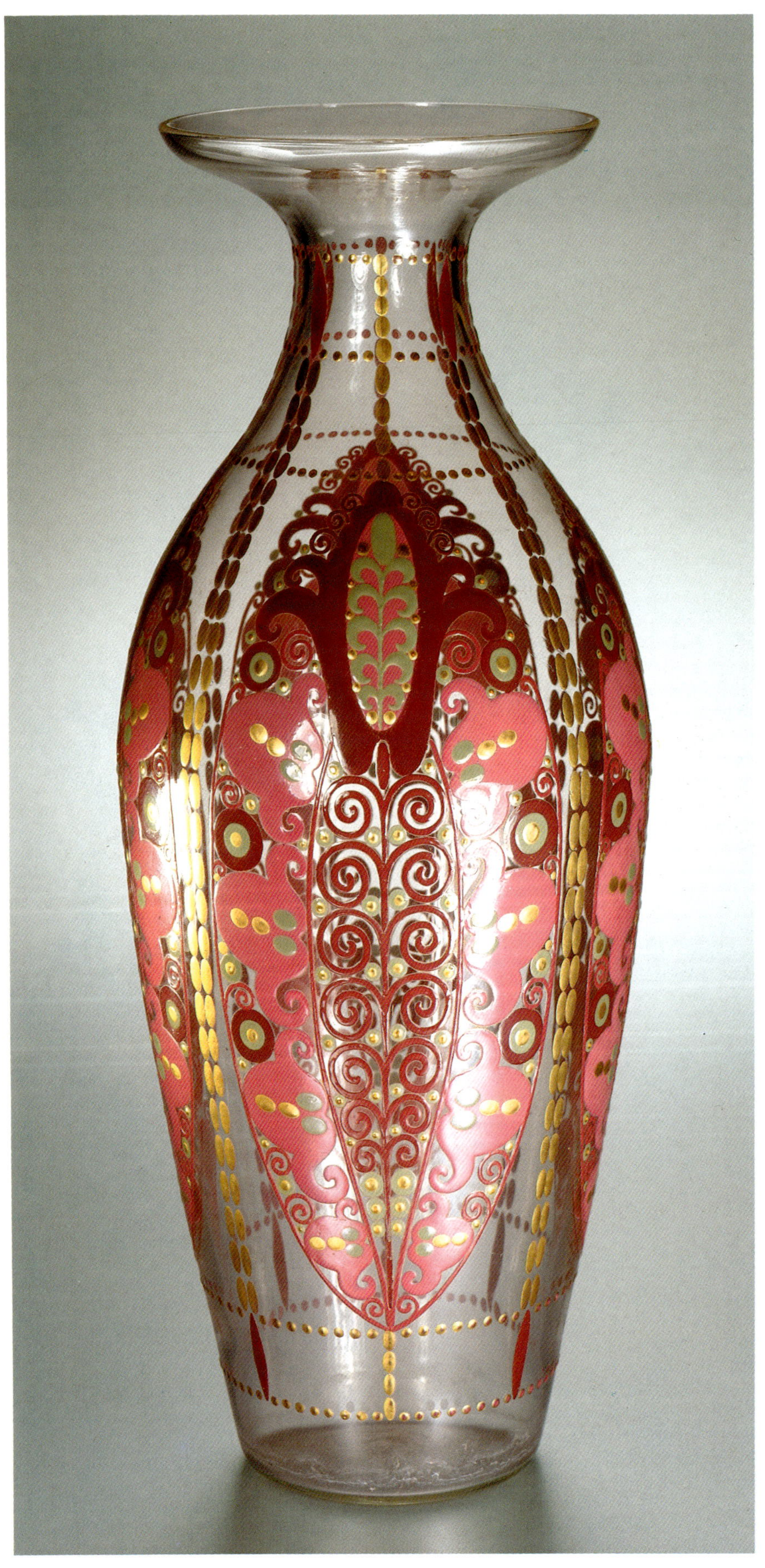

356 Vase

Unsigned
Zwiesel, ca. 1912
H 30, ⌀ 12.2 cm

Colorless glass. Mold-blown.
Encircling decoration painted in opaque enamel: four stylized floral fields. Gold beaded strings.

Acc. no. P 1970-76
Gift of Helmut Hentrich

Student work. For similar glassware see *DKD* 31 (1912/13): illus. p. 522. For decoration see also *Kunstgewerbeblatt*, n.s., 25 (1913/14): illus. p. 5, and for similar vases see *KuH* 61 (1910/11): illus. p. 199.

Lit.: Hilschenz, *Jugendstil*, 1973, cat. no. 68; Pazaurek and Spiegl, *20. Jahrhundert*, 1983, 115, fig. 210; Ricke, *2500 Jahre*, 1987, cat. no. 154; Schöne-Chotjewitz, *Zwiesel*, 1997, 130, no. 25

Bruno Mauder
(1877–1948)

Painter and designer of glass and wood carvings

From 1910 until he died, director and professor at the Glasfachschule in Zwiesel. One of the most prominent and influential glass designers in Germany during the 1920s and 1930s. Established the school's reputation as an educational center for modern design.

357   Dedication Vessel

Gold mark on the underside of base: *Entwurf: Bruno Mauder, Ausführung: Fachschule Zwiesel 1910*
H (with cover) 52, ⌀ 17.4 cm

Colorless glass. Mold-blown. Facet cut above the foot and on the finial.
Gilt-painted decoration: encircling stylized floral ornament with four fish. Encircling gold inscription: *Wanderversammlung bayerischer Landwirte in Straubing 1910, gegeben von den Bezirksfischereivereinen Kötzting, Regen, Viechtach.*

Acc. no. P 1970-74
Gift of Helmut Hentrich

For glassware with similar decoration see *KuH* 63 (1912/13): figs. 188f. For another richly decorated ceremonial goblet see *DK* 32 (1915): illus. p. 195.

Lit.: Hilschenz, *Jugendstil*, 1973, cat. no. 66; Schöne-Chotjewitz, *Zwiesel*, 1997, 126, no. 18

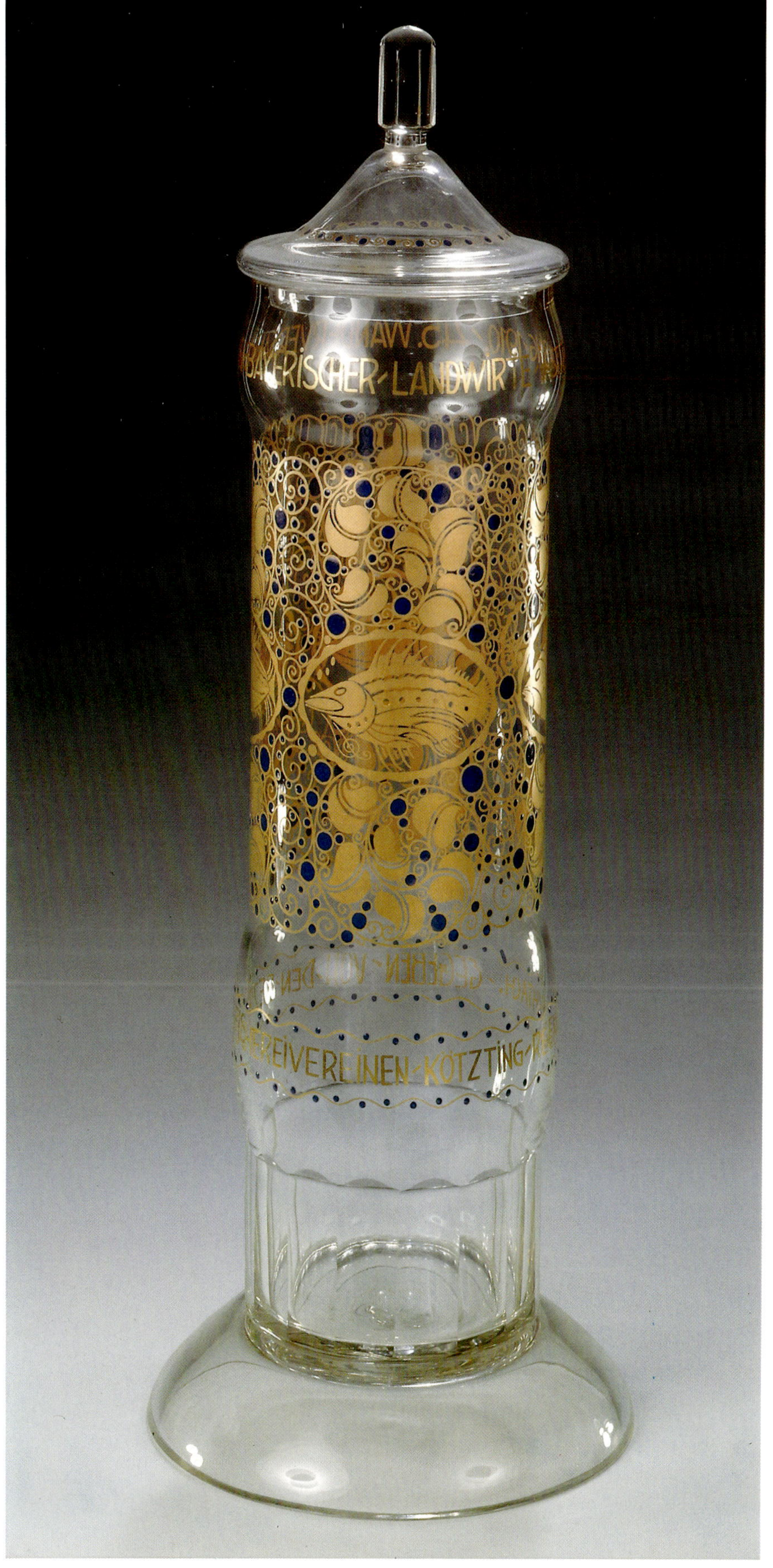

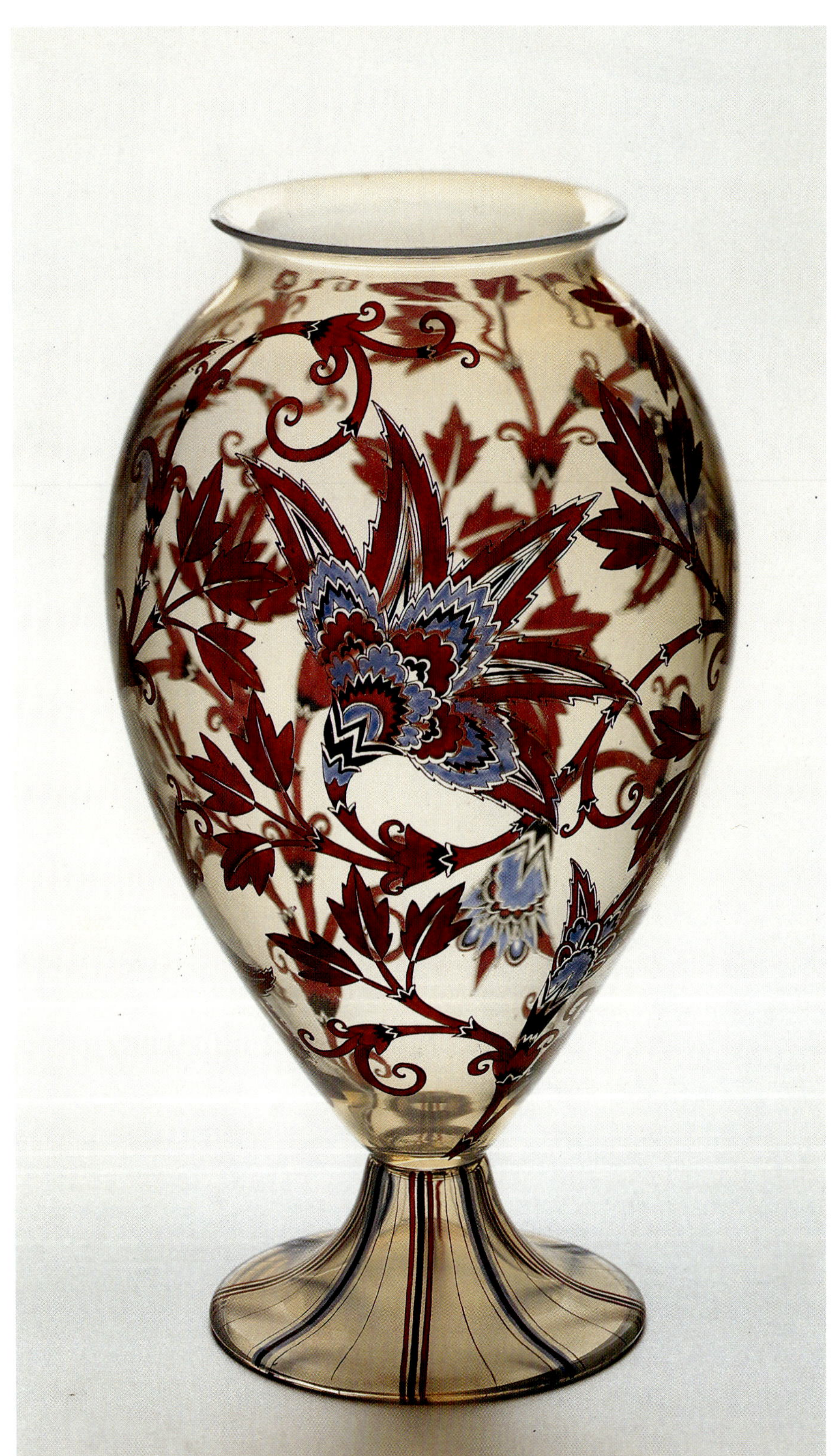

Alexander Pfohl
(1894–1953)

Glass designer, designer, painter, and design teacher

Studied at the Glasfachschule Haida and the Wiener Kunstgewerbeschule. From 1919 to 1929, responsible for design at the Gräflich Schaffgottschsche Josephinenhütte in Schreiberhau, Silesia. From 1929 to 1945, taught design at the Glasfachschule Haida; in these years numerous designs for companies in northern Bohemian glass centers. In 1949, substantially contributed to building up the Glasfachschule Hadamar in Hesse; taught there up to his death in 1953.

358   Vase

Unsigned
Ca. 1921/22
Execution: Josephinenhütte, Schreiberhau
H 26.7, ⌀ 15.7 cm

Colorless crystal glass with thin inner casing and overlay of milky opal glass. Mold-blown. Enamel-painted decoration with *Schwarzlot* outlining.

Acc. no. P 1983-7 P
On permanent loan from family estate

The decorative approach reflects the prewar development at the Wiener Kunstgewerbeschule and northern Bohemian glass schools, which strongly influenced Pfohl. See cat. nos. 336ff. and Ricke, "Pfohl," 1982, 65ff.

Lit.: Ricke, "Pfohl," 1982, 69, fig. 13; Pazaurek and Spiegl, *20. Jahrhundert*, 1983, 134, fig. 210; Scharnowski, "Pfohl," 1993, 93, no. 7; *Pfohl*, 1994, 12, fig. 3

359   Footed Bowl

Unsigned
Ca. 1920/21
Execution: Josephinenhütte, Schreiberhau
H 21.2, ⌀ 27.5 cm

Colorless crystal glass. Blue casing. Mold-
blown. Decoration in semimat miter cut.

Acc. no. P 1983-8 P
On permanent loan from family estate

Further development of the cut overlay glassware of the prewar period.
Emphasis on mat cutting structures.

Lit.: Ricke, "Pfohl," 1982, 70f., figs. 16, 17;
Scharnowski, "Pfohl," 1993, 105, no. 37;
Pfohl, 1994, 18, fig. 11

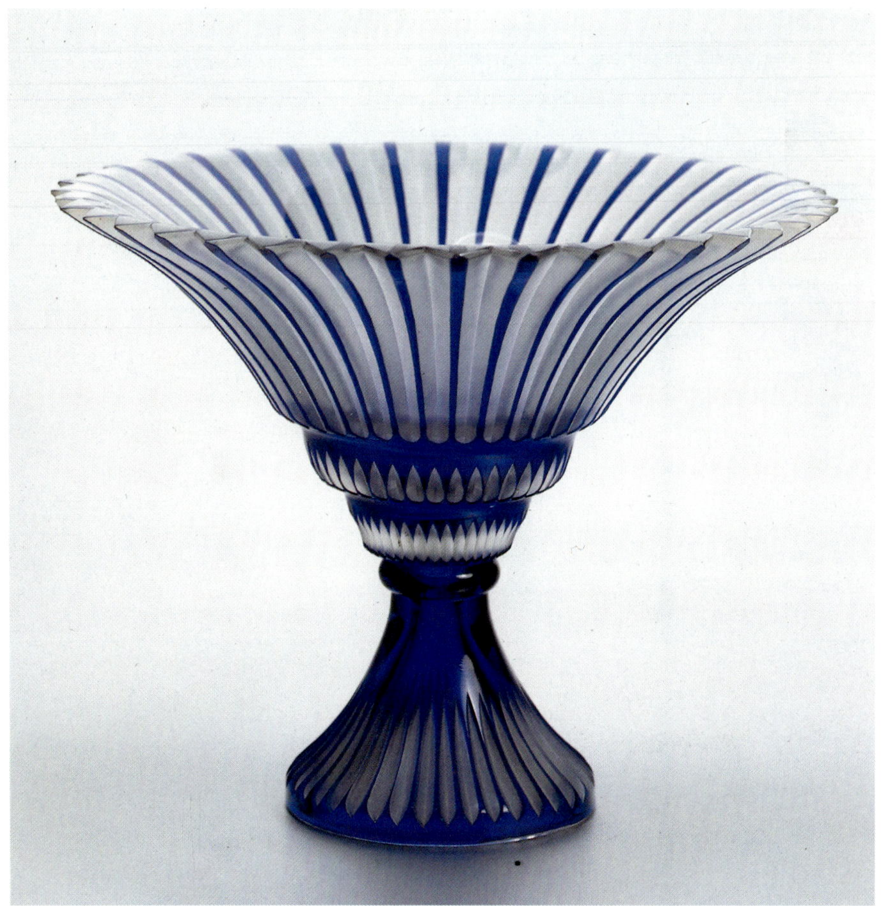

360 a, b   Beakers

Unsigned
Ca. 1931/32
Execution: Ludwig Moser & Söhne, Carlsbad
H 12.2, 12; ⌀ 8.6, 8.7 cm

Gray-blue and amber-colored crystal glass,
mold-blown. Cut and polished.

Acc. nos. L 1983-19, 20 P
On permanent loan from family estate

Adoption of Biedermeier glass traditions in
contemporary decorative forms.

Lit.: Ricke, "Pfohl," 1982, 84, fig. 36 (b);
Pfohl, 1994, 28, fig. 27

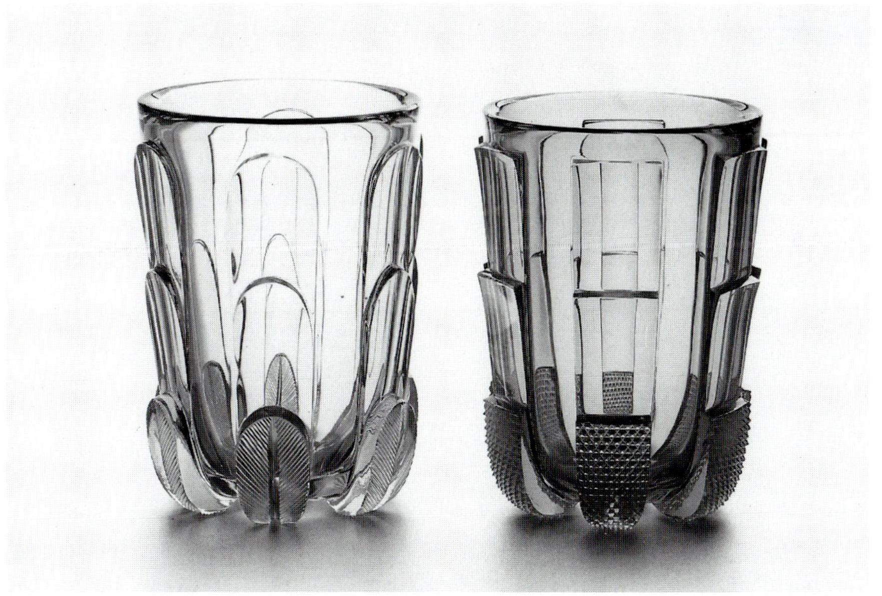

Max Grimm

Workshop for artistic lampmade glass design, Ilmenau, in the Thuringian Forest

One of the leading companies in the Thuringian art-glass region during the 1920s and 1930s.

361 Vase

Unsigned; model no. 45
Ca. 1925–27
H 31.6, ⌀ 10.2 cm

Light blue, opaquely struck soft glass. Lampblown from glass tube. Fired oxides, partial crackling and iridescent.

Acc. no. P 1970-78
Gift of Helmut Hentrich

Illustrated in the company production catalogue dated August 1928. The first two pages show 53 "Patinagläser" (patina glass pieces); see also *KuH* 77 (1927), 75.

Lit.: Hilschenz, *Jugendstil*, 1973, cat. no. 70

362 a, b   Cordial Glasses

Unsigned
Thuringian Forest
1920s
H 12.7, 8.3; ⌀ 7.9, 6.7 cm

Colored soft glass. Lampblown and shaped from canes and tubes.

Acc. nos. R 24; P 1981-285
Gift of Helmut Hentrich

Pieces from one of the numerous art-glass workshops in the Thuringian Forest. No scholarly study has been undertaken on these workshops to date.

Lit. on a: Pazaurek and Spiegl, *20. Jahrhundert*, 1983, 235, fig. 447

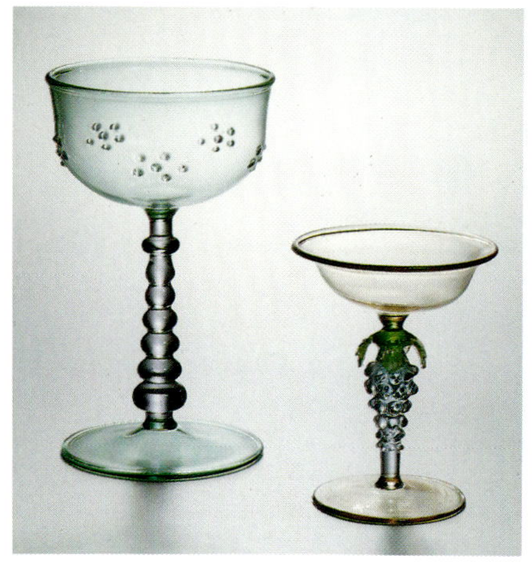

Max Traut
(1900–1970)

Art-glass blower. Proprietor and director of the Matra Werkstätten in Neuhaus am Rennsteig, Thuringian Forest

The company name Matra was formed from the first letters of the owner's names. From 1919, produced vases, utensils, and ornamental objects in the lamp technique. One of the leading companies of its kind. In 1951, newly founded in Munich. In 1954, moved to Grafrath near Munich, where glass production was stopped. Today the company produces under the name Matrau KG, Kunsthandwerk aus Bayern, under the direction of Dieter Manfred Traut.

363   Vase

Unsigned
Model no. 307
Ca. 1925–30
H 30.9, ⌀ 9.5 cm

Pink struck glass, lampblown and shaped.

Acc. no. P 1986-63
Gift of Dieter M. Traut, Grafrath

Numerous workshops in the Thuringian Forest and the Bimini company in Vienna produced vases of this type in the second half of the 1920s (see cat. no. 340). The company run by Max Traut was one of the most prominent amongst these usually anonymous art-glass workshops. The vase's provenance from the family estate secures the attribution to Traut. In addition, it was illustrated in a company catalogue of the late 1920s; it does not appear in a catalogue dated 1933.

Lit.: Ricke, *Museumsarbeit*, 1988, 76, fig. 59

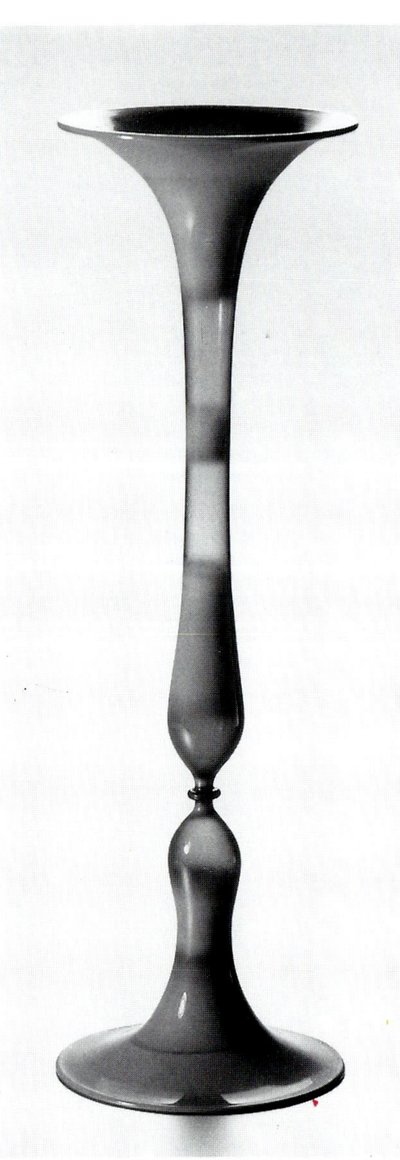

Wilhelm von Eiff
(1899–1943)

Painter, glass designer, cutter, and engraver

After studying drawing and glass engraving, worked at the engraving studio of Charles Michel, Paris, from 1909 to 1911. Then, with the support of G. E. Pazaurek, studied at the Stuttgarter Kunstgewerbeschule and worked for J & L Lobmeyr in Vienna and the Württembergische Metallwarenfabrik in Geislingen. In 1922, appointed professor at the Stuttgarter Kunstgewerbeschule, where he taught glass decoration up to his death.
Instrumental in the revival of glass engraving and cutting, and highly influential as a teacher.

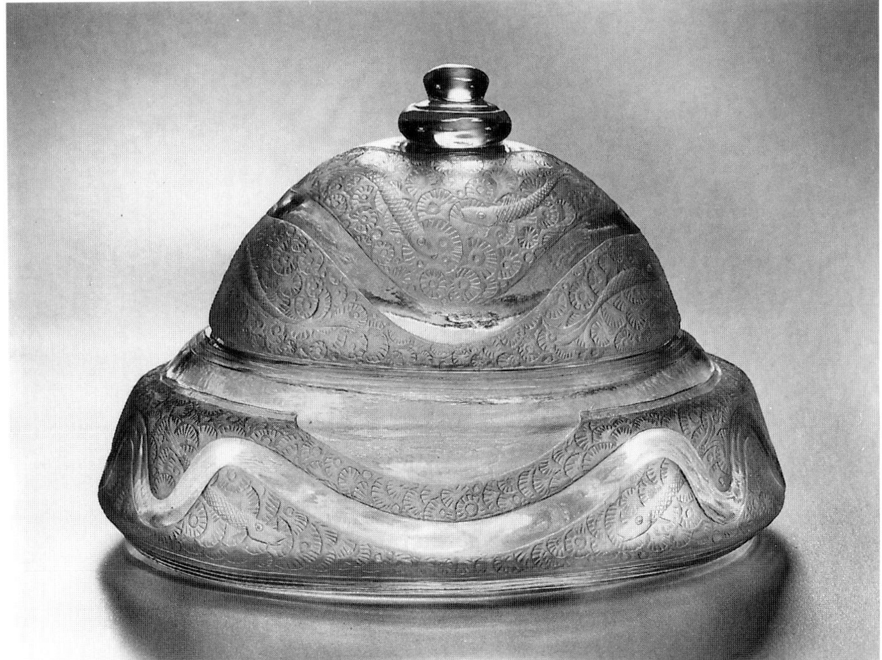

364 Covered Jar

Engraved mark on finial and on the side near base: *W. von Eiff*
Stuttgart, ca. 1921
H 12.3, ⌀ 18.6 x 12.6 cm

Colorless glass, mold-blown. Entire surface cut and engraved. Finely detailed decoration in mat relief carving, rough-polished wavy bands.

Acc. no. P 1988-23
Acquired from family estate

One of three jars of this type, which Eiff engraved around 1921. For another example from this group see Pazaurek, *Kunstgläser*, 1925, 193, fig. 210.

Lit.: Ricke, *Museumsarbeit*, 1988, 76, fig. 58; Schüly, *Eiff*, 1989, cat. no. 18

365 "Mondschale" (Moon Dish)

Engraved mark on interior edge: *K.G.S. STUTTG. ABT. PROF. v. EIFF*; and vertically engraved on the underside of base: *W v E**
Design: 1926
Execution: in a small series until 1934
H 8, ⌀ 23.5 cm

Colorless, thick-walled glass, mold-blown. In strong relief carving mostly left mat: five crescent moons with polished spheres above.

Acc. no. P 1988-21
Acquired from family estate

Typical work of the late 1920s. Emphasis on carving-like surface structures, incorporating grinding-tool marks into the design. Realized by Eiff's students at the Kunstgewerbeschule Stuttgart.

Lit.: Schüly, *Eiff*, 1989, 54, cat. no. 137

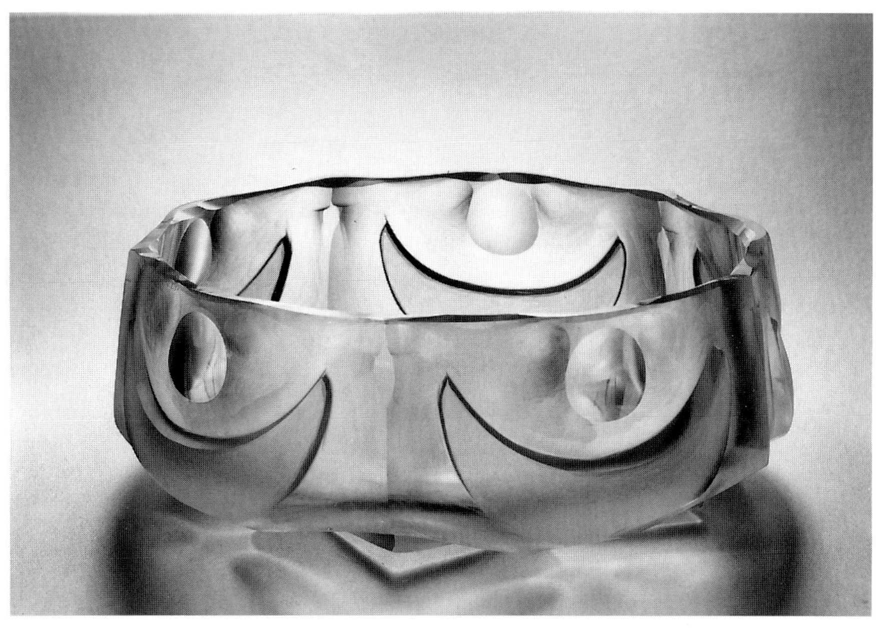

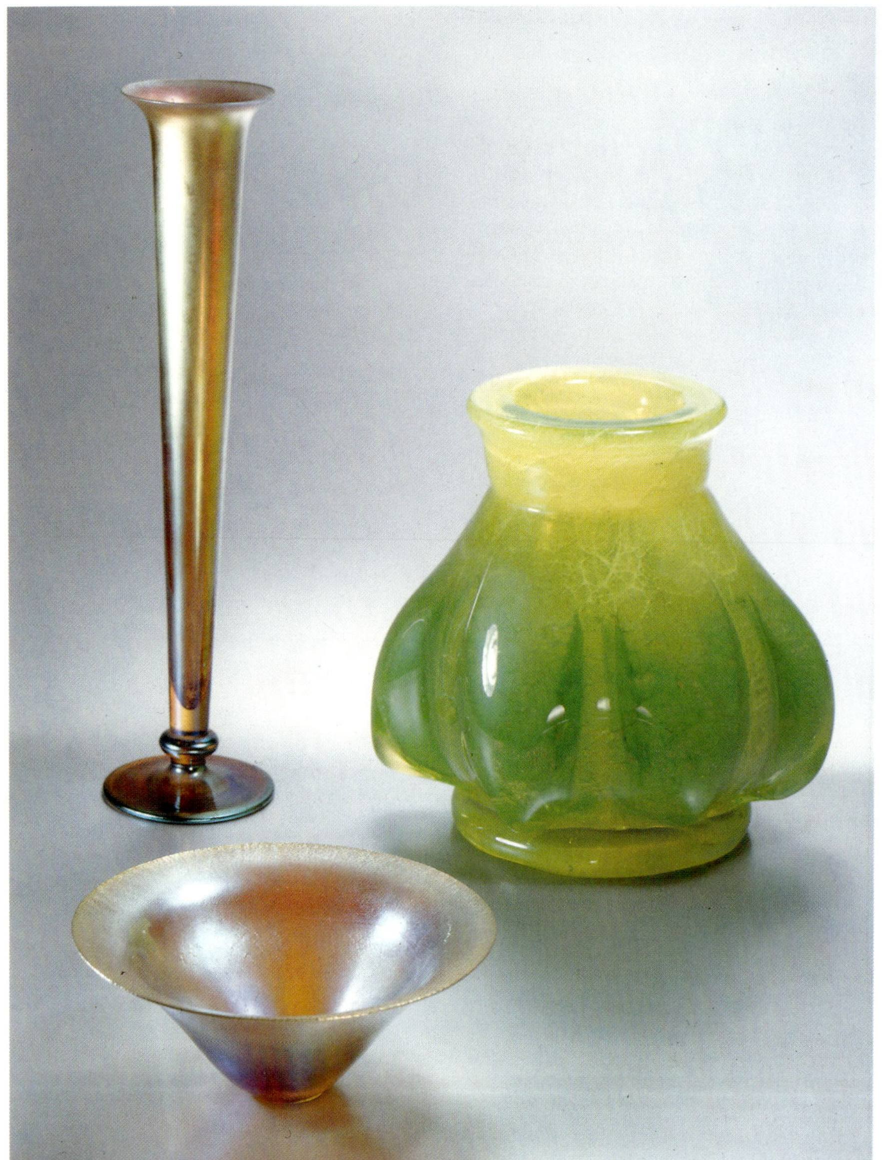

Karl Wiedmann

(1905–1992)

Glass technician and designer

After apprenticing at the Württembergische Metallwarenfabrik, Geislingen, as glass-technician with training as glassmaker, he studied cutting and engraving at the Glasfachschule in Zwiesel. From 1925, glass technician at WMF, where he developed new production techniques for art glass ("Myra," "Ikora"). From 1927 to 1951, works manager in Geislingen, then at Gral-Glas in Dürnau.

366 Bowl

Unsigned; "Myra" crystal, model no. J. 61
Ca. 1926
H 5.7, ∅ 15.8 cm

Glass with yellow tone. Mold-blown. Fired in a reducing atmosphere, iridescent. Dilated. Heavy crackling near mouth rim.

Acc. no. P 1970-64
Gift of Helmut Hentrich

Execution based on variation of the Jugendstil iridescence process developed by Wiedmann. Listed in a hand-captioned WMF pattern catalogue of 1926/27.

Lit.: Hilschenz, *Jugendstil*, 1973, cat. no. 56

367 Vase

Unsigned; "Myra" crystal, model no. J. 198
Ca. 1926
H 31.7, ∅ 8.1 cm

Like cat. no. 366.

Acc. no. P 1970-65
Gift of Helmut Hentrich

Listed in the glasshouse's handwritten pattern catalogue of 1926/27.

Lit.: Hilschenz, *Jugendstil*, 1973, cat. no. 57

368 Vase

Unsigned; "Ikora" crystal, model no. EO 683
1935
H 18.8, ∅ 21 x 16.6 cm

Light green-yellow ground crackled by sudden cooling, dark green glass-powder inclusions with small brown speckles. Optic-blown in six-part skeleton mold, thick-walled glass overlay; shaped.

Acc. no. P 1981-389
Gift of Helmut Hentrich

The Ikora techniques developed by Wiedmann in the late 1920s determined the WMF art-glass production up to the 1950s. The model is described in the catalogue as "Ikora" and "Myra" crystal. Cat. *Neuheiten* 1935/II.

Lit.: –

<table>
<tr><td>

Wilhelm Wagenfeld
(1900–1990)

Trained silversmith, industrial designer

Studied at the Staatliche Zeichenakademie Hanau
and the Bauhaus in Weimar. From 1930 to 1934, glass
designs for the Jenaer Glaswerke; from 1935 to
1947, for the Vereinigte Lausitzer Glaswerke in Weiss-
wasser; from 1950, for the Württembergische Metall-
warenfabrik in Geislingen; from 1952 to 1954, for
Rosenthal in Selb; from 1952 to 1958, for Peill &
Putzler in Düren.
Most important German designer of utilitarian glass
from the 1930s to the 1950s.

</td><td>

Richard Süssmuth
(1900–1974)

Glass cutter, designer, and manufacturer

Together with W. von Eiff, important for the renewal
of glass-cutting design in Germany. Further, trend-
setting designer of utilitarian glass forms from the
1930s to the 1950s. From 1924 to 1945, production
in Penzig, Silesia—at first just cutting workshop,
then also manufacturing of blanks. In 1946, new
factory in Immenhausen near Kassel. In 1970, with-
drew from the company management.

</td></tr>
</table>

369 Decanter of the Cordial Service "Zisterne"

Unsigned
Design: 1936
Execution: VLG, Weisswasser, Lausitz
H 18.5, ⌀ 12.6 cm

Gray-blue glass, mold-blown, shaped. Pushed-up
bottom. Massive glass stopper shaped and ground.

Acc. no. P 1981-306

Cordial glasses, 4.4 cm high, belong to the decanter;
see *Wilhelm Wagenfeld: 50 Jahre Mitarbeit in Fabriken*,
exh. cat. (Cologne: Kunstgewerbemuseum der Stadt
Köln, 1973), cat. no. 174, and G. Lueg, *Design im
20. Jahrhundert*, exh. cat. (Cologne: Museum für
angewandte Kunst Köln, 1989), cat. no. 519.

Lit.: –

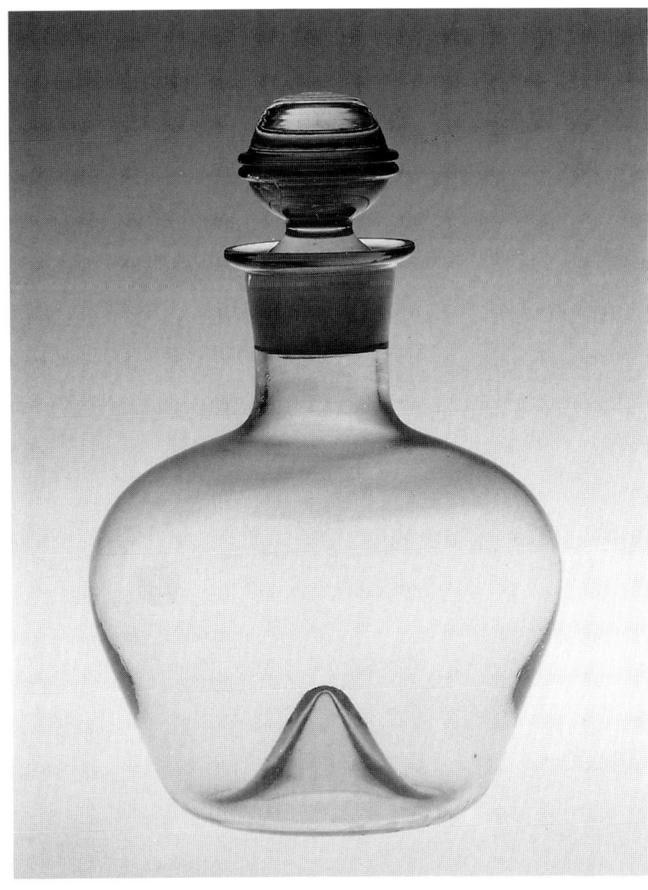

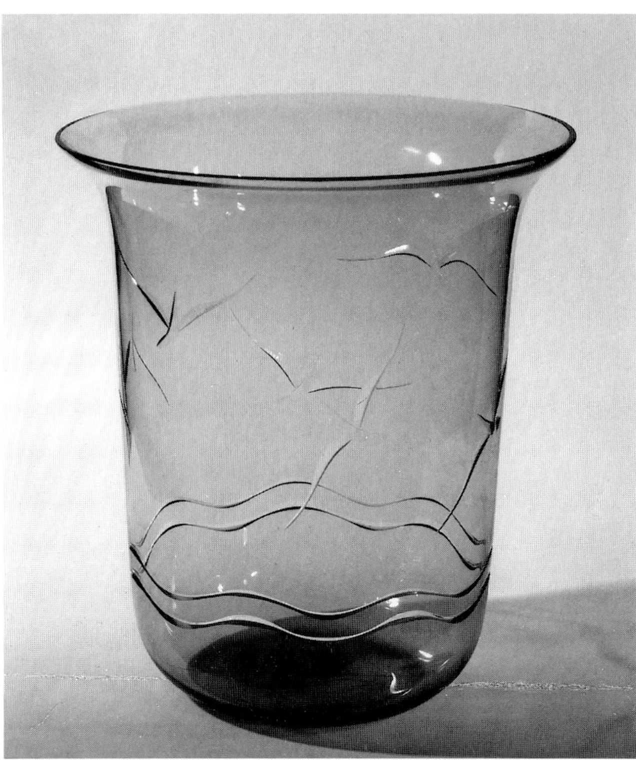

370 Vase

Unsigned
Design of form: ca. 1936/37
Design of decoration: 1928
Execution: Glashütte Richard Süssmuth
Silesia, Penzig
H 24, ⌀ 21.8 cm

Smoky brown glass, mold-blown. Base and rim
ground. Decoration in polished miter cut: six stylized
sea gulls above double wavy line.

Acc. no. P 1941-74
Acquired from the manufacturer

For form and decoration of vase see *Die Schaulade*
13A (Aug. 1937): 171, and 16A (Aug. 1940): 200.
For glassware with sea-gull decoration, dated 1928,
see R. Süssmuth, *Glas und Gläser* (Cologne, 1959),
n.p. For a similar example see Bröhan, *20er und 30er
Jahre*, 1985, cat. no. 536.

Lit.: Heinemeyer, *Glas*, 1966, cat. no. 551

Italy

Fine decoration and technical mastery were the outstanding characteristics of Venetian glass art for centuries. They were the cause of Venice's much celebrated revival during the period of historicism and nothing would have seemed more natural had this success continued in the years around the turn of the century.

Surprisingly this did not happen. Instead of the expected ascent to new heights, the self-confident Murano glassblowers had to be content sitting on the sidelines of the period's major artistic movements and leaving the front row in Europe to France and Bohemia. After a period of technical and formal differentiation taken to its extremes, the glassmakers of the traditional glass-producing island Murano, who had always concentrated more on themselves than on developments in other centers, proved to be as incapable of making a new beginning then as in the late seventeenth century.

The appeal of the decorative glass pieces made by the Artisti Barovier for Salviati lies in the material that is blown and dilated to its absolute limits, to a tenuously thin state—a non plus ultra of the freehand work possible at the furnace. They were shown at the first Venice Biennale and are justifiably deemed the precursors of the work of Karl Koepping (cat. nos. 341–43).

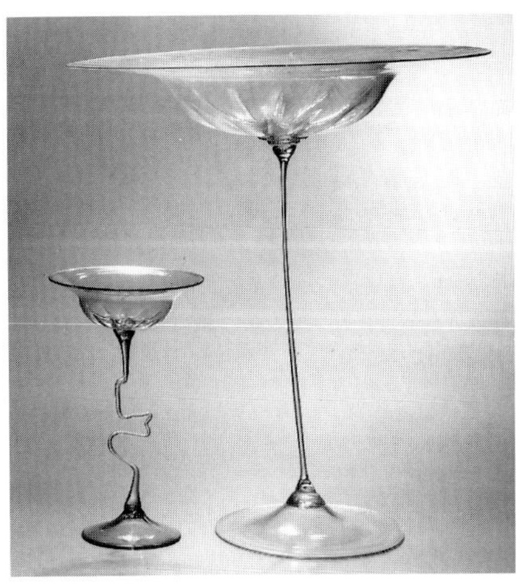

Decorative Goblets, Artisti Barovier, Murano, ca. 1895. H 10.9, 21.2 cm.

Acc. nos. P 1985-118, 119

The "Stile Liberty," as the Art Nouveau style is called in Italy, never developed a uniform face in the country's glass art. Revivals of past forms and techniques stood side by side with occasional influences of French, German, and Viennese artists. Original works appeared only after 1910, when Art Nouveau had lost its dynamism in Europe. These glass pieces reflect an approach to form that linked historical reminiscences with strengthened, usually symmetrically arranged, decorative motifs. In this they corresponded to the period's sweeping movements of European glass art, added a new, specifically Venetian note, and paved the way for the upswing in the 1920s.

The Milan attorney Paolo Venini was to become the big mover and reformer of Venetian glass art in the twentieth century. His secret to success was to combine the inexhaustible decorative potential of Venetian glass art with a contemporary formal canon. Besides designing pieces himself, Venini continued to call upon excellent designers who contributed considerably to this concept. Carlo Scarpa's designs from the 1930s and early 1940s illustrate this clearly. For his simple dishes in the mosaic-glass technique (cat. no. 378) or his famous black-and-yellow thread-glass bottle of 1940 (cat. no. 379), Scarpa did not use new techniques. Instead he employed known processes in a way that seemed simply revolutionary to his contemporaries until far into the 1950s.

Today this decade is justifiably considered one of the great periods of Venetian glass art. Before its rehabilitation, however, prevailing reservations about carefree handling of color and decoration and this period's unorthodox formal idiom had to be overcome. Against the background of the problematic 1960s and 1970s, the qualities of form design in the 1950s have meanwhile become clear. This period was characterized by an optimistic, forward-looking worldview. Today we are prepared to recognize the playful inventiveness in the ever new variations of strongly colored dot, thread, and mosaic-glass decorations as a positive aspect, as an outpouring of overflowing creativity, and not as an expression of superficiality or a lack of serious-mindedness.

Seen from this perspective, the most important names that have increasingly entered the general consciousness in recent years are, besides Venini, Archimede Seguso (cat. no. 384), Flavio Poli (cat. no. 385), and Ercole Barovier (cat. nos. 386–88). Their outstanding individual achievements—particularly those of Poli—represent a synthesis of specifically Venetian characteristics.

In its utilitarian form and as art objects Murano glass of the 1950s formed a more or less cohesive unit. However, the work of such artists as Fulvio Bianconi, Dino Martens, or Luciano Gaspari reveals clear tendencies to loosen the bond between glass design and the vessel's practical function. Design became a carrier of more far-reaching ideas. Thus Venice was the source of important impulses for the following decades.

Pauly & C.
Compagnia di Venezia e Murano

Distribution company for glassware, Venice

In 1876, founded by former partners of Antonio Salviati from England. Henceforth, main
competitor of Salviati & C. In the 19th century, dominated together with Salviati the
market of fine Venetian glass.
Almost all renowned glass artists and
glasshouses of Murano work or have worked
for Pauly & C.

371   Footed Vase

Unsigned
Ca. 1913–15
H 31.2, ⌀ 16.5 x 9.2, foot 10.9 cm

Brown-violet glass, free-blown and shaped.
Multicolored application, combed into feather
pattern. Handle, foot, and knop applied freehand.

Acc. no. P 1975-11
Acquired from Pauly & C., Venice
Gift of Udo van Meeteren, Düsseldorf

The vase combines classic Venetian forms
with Art Nouveau influences. For a similar
model, made by Giuseppe Barovier in 1913,
see Barovier Mentasti, *Murano '900*, 1977,
cat. no. 30, fig. 20; for another see Barovier
Mentasti, *Vetraria moderna*, 1977, 152, fig. 10.

Lit.: –

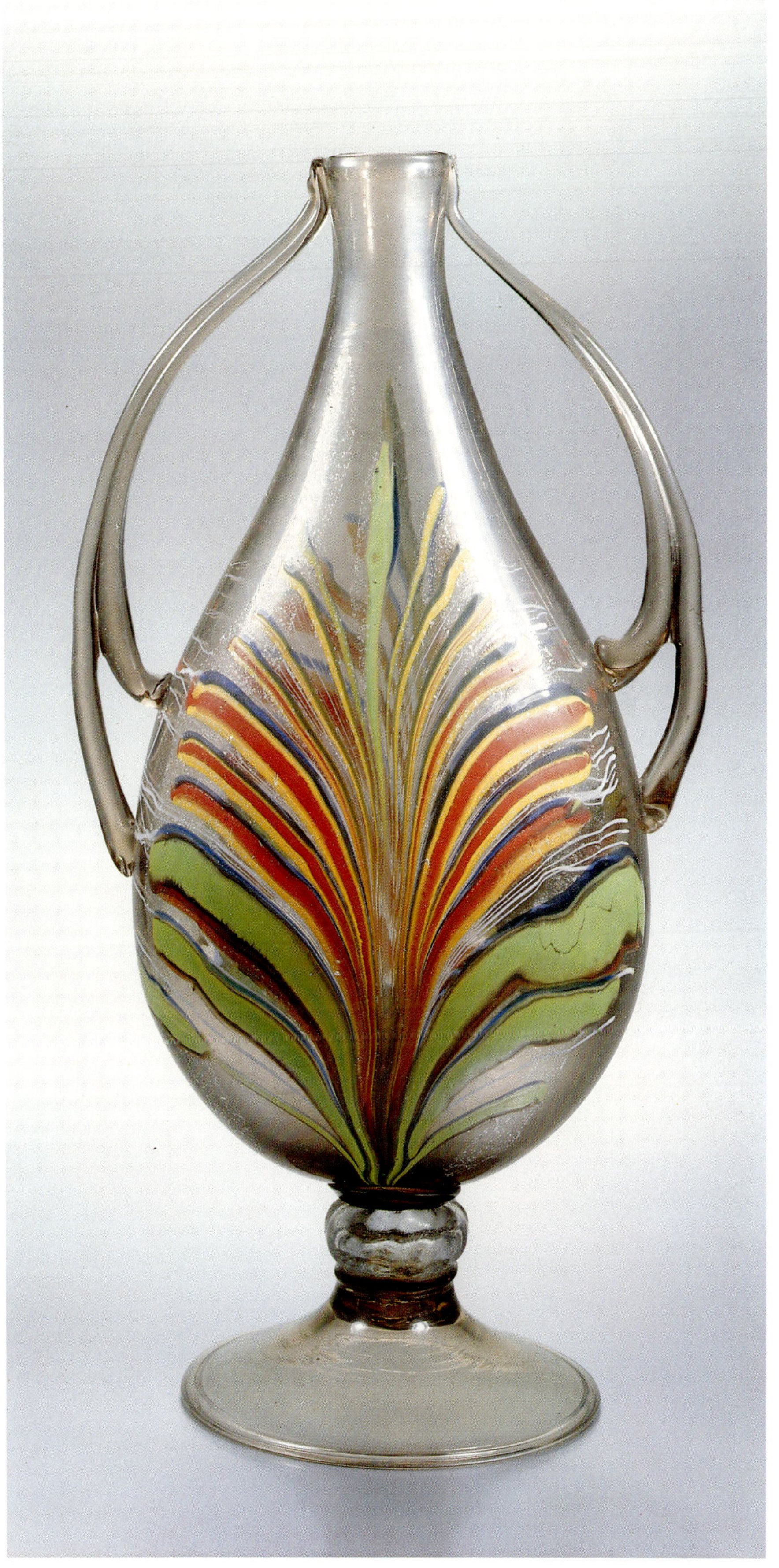

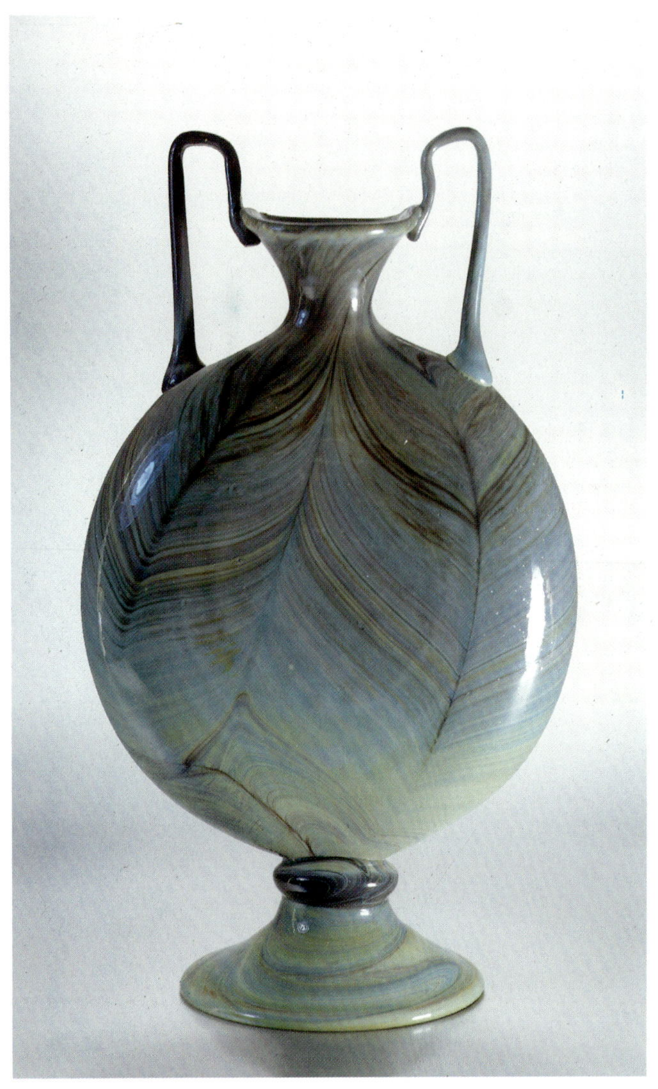

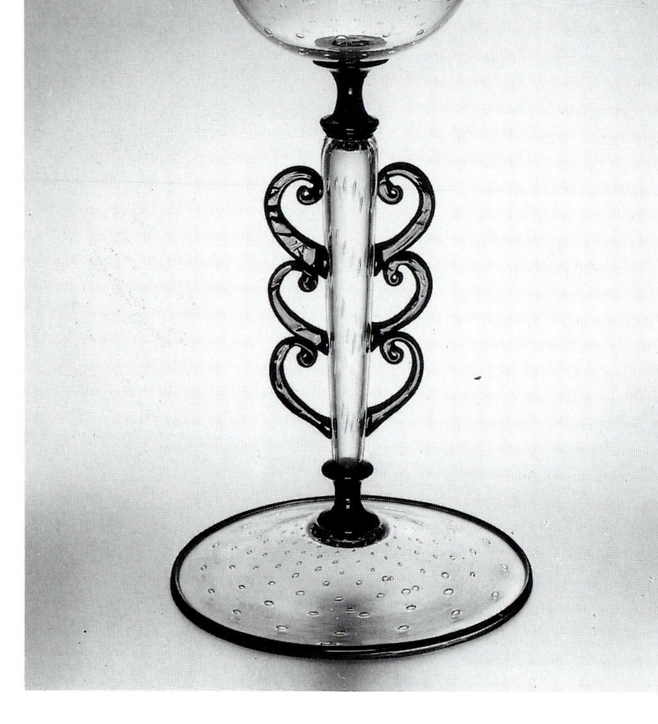

372 Footed Vase

Unsigned
1920s
H 24, ⌀ 14.2 x 5.1, foot 8.8 cm

Agate glass, free-blown and shaped, grain
combed up and down eight times. Handle and
foot with knop applied freehand.

Acc. no. P 1975-10
Acquired from Pauly & C., Venice
Gift of Udo van Meeteren, Düsseldorf

Revival of the old agate and aventurine glass
made from the 16th to the 18th century for
models in contemporary forms.

Lit.: –

373 Decorative Goblet

Design: Umberto Belotto
For Pauly & C., Venice
1927
H 35.2, ⌀ 26.5 cm

Bowl and foot blown in "quill" mold with colorless overlay. Comprises three blown parts,
fused with massive black joints. Decorative
handles applied freehand; black threads
encircle foot and mouth.

Acc. no. P 1975-16
Acquired from Pauly & C., Venice
Gift of Udo van Meeteren, Düsseldorf

For attribution and dating see Barovier Mentasti, *Vetro Veneziano*, 1982, 262, fig. 264.

Lit.: Ricke, *Museumsarbeit*, 1988, 76, fig. 54

Artisti Barovier

Art-glass factory, Murano

In 1878, founded as Fratelli Barovier & C.
Work until 1895 exclusively for Salviati Dott.
Antonio. From 1898, Artisti Barovier & C. The
owners, Giuseppe and Benvenuto Barovier,
were particularly well-known from 1911 for
their mosaic-glass designs, which they carried
out personally. Besides these, they realized
designs by such painters as Vittorio Zecchin
and Teodoro Wolf Ferrari.

Company names:
1911–19   Artisti Barovier
1920–36   Vetreria Artistica Barovier & C.
1936–39   Ferro Toso Barovier
          Vetrerie artistiche riunite S.A.
1939–42   Barovier Toso & C.
          Vetrerie artistiche riunite S.A.

See also p. 241, Barovier & Toso.

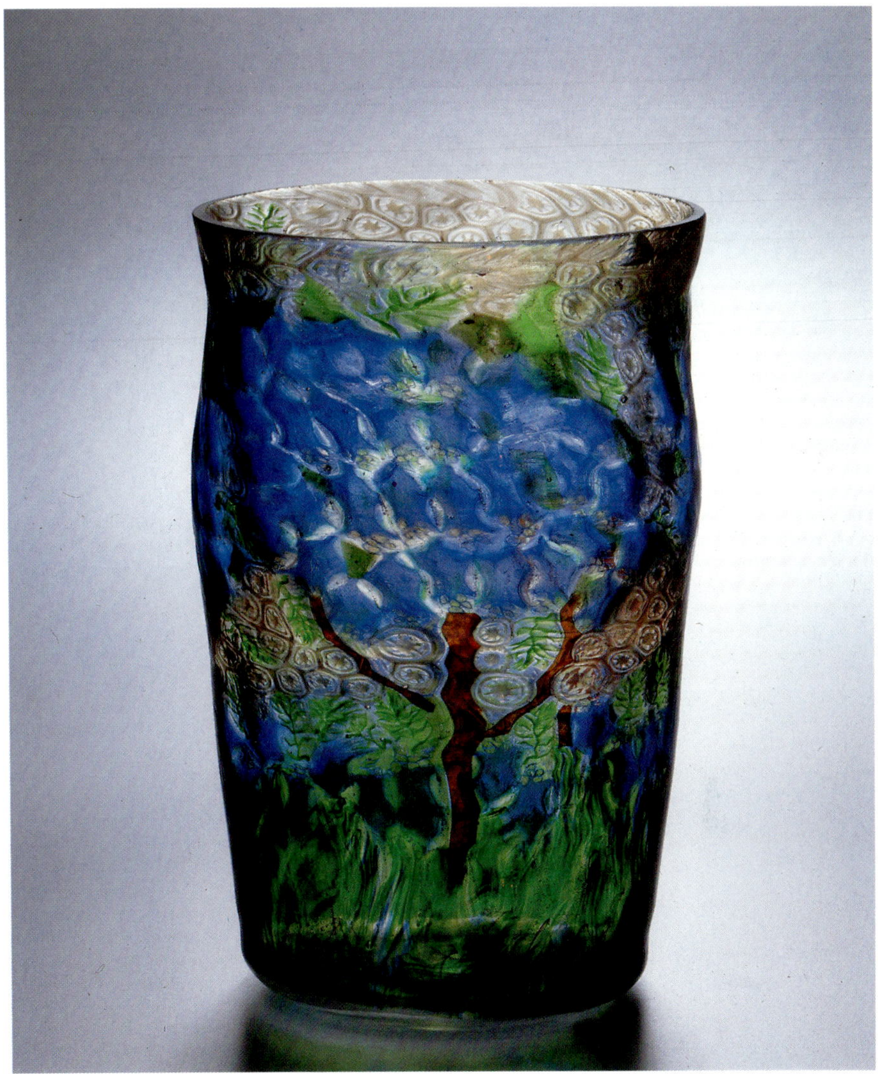

374   Vase

Mark in millefiori section on wall: *AB* (ligat-
ed) above which appears a crown, both
inside oval
Giuseppe and Benvenuto Barovier
For Artisti Barovier
Ca. 1914–19
H 17.9, ⌀ 12.3 cm

Landscape with three trees; made of millefiori sections on colorless ground.
Sections taken up with hot glass bubble;
mold-blown.

Acc. no. P 1970-458
Gift of Helmut Hentrich

In its approach, the vessel is similar to a
large vase in the Salviati-Camerino-Tedeschi
Collection, which Rosa Barovier Mentasti
attributes to Vittorio Zecchin. See Barovier
Mentasti, "Vetraria moderna," 1977, 154,
fig. 14.

Lit.: Hilschenz, *Jugendstil*, 1973, cat. no. 454

Vetri Soffiati Muranesi Cappellin-Venini & C.

Art-glass factory, Murano

Founded in 1921 by Paolo Venini (1895–1959) and Giacomo Cappellin (1887–1968) through take-over of Andrea Rioda's glasshouse. Vittorio Zecchin (1878–1947) worked as designer for the new firm. Production emphasis was placed on glassware imitating pieces shown in old master paintings (e.g., "Veronese Vase," which became Venini's trademark). In 1925, Venini and Cappellin separated, both founding their own companies.

375 "Libellula" Footed Dish

Design: Vittorio Zecchin or Napoleone Martinuzzi
For Cappellin-Venini & C., Murano
Ca. 1922–25
H 17.9, ⌀ 41.8, without handle 28.8 cm

Light blue glass, optic-blown in eight-part ribbed mold; shaped. Foot worked separately, handle applied freehand.

Acc. no. P 1982-5
Acquired with funds from the Helmut Hentrich donation

Variation of the well-known "Libellula" model of 1921, whose walls are steeper and smoother. See *DKD* 59 (1926/27): 59; see also Barovier Mentasti, *Vetro Veneziano*, 1982, 252, fig. 253. For the model shown here see *DK* 56 (1927): illus. p. 244, and *DKD* 60 (1927): 354. It cannot be ruled out that this model was made as a variation of a form by Napoleone Martinuzzi around 1926 in Venini's new firm, after he separated from Cappellin. Produced at Venini as model no. 3019 since 1926.

Lit.: Ricke and Gronert, *Glas in Schweden*, 1986, 37, fig. 18; Ricke, *Museumsarbeit*, 1988, 76, fig. 55; Venini, *Artisti*, 1996, 180, cat. no. 13

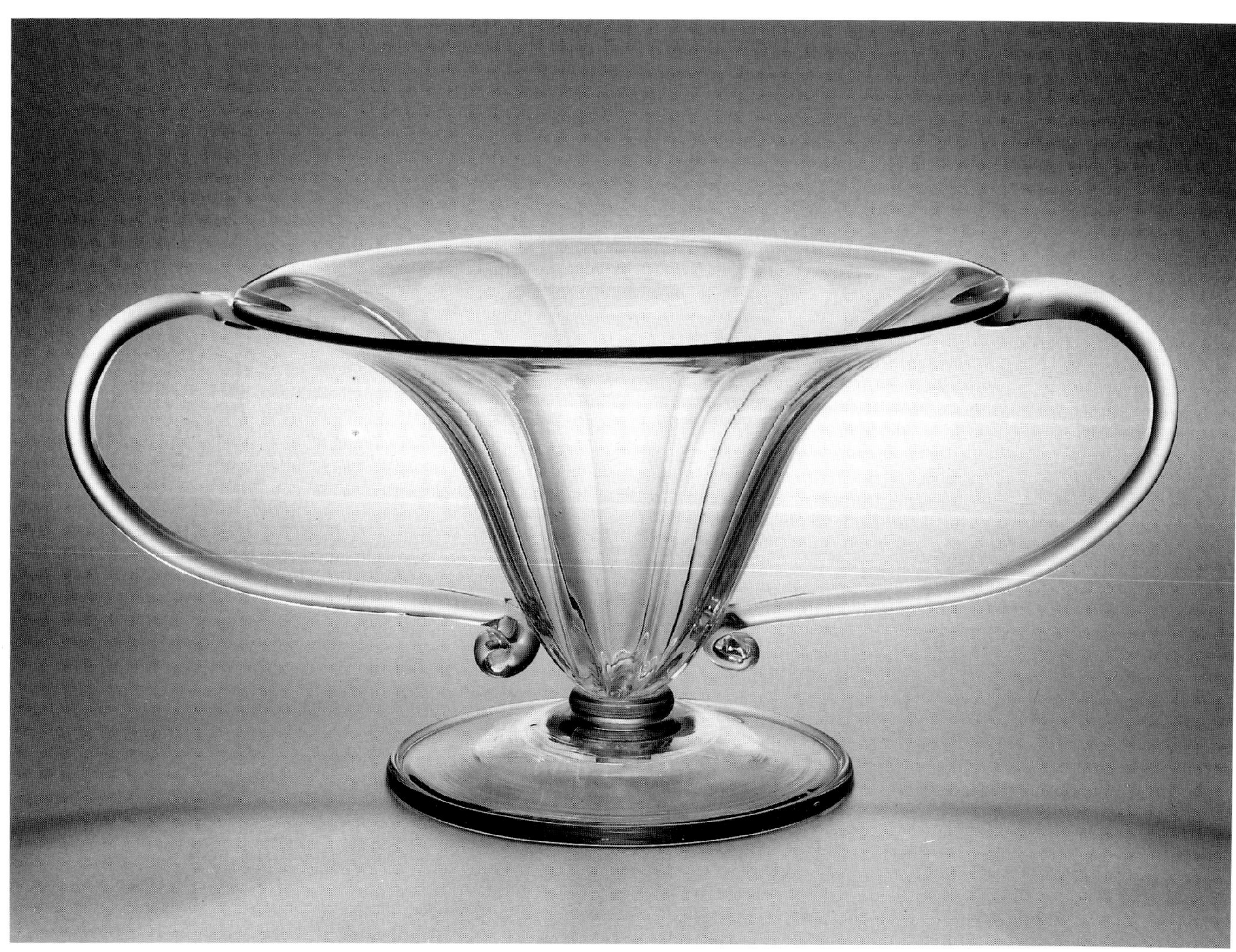

Maestri Vetrai Muranesi Cappellin & C.

Art-glass factory

Founded by Giacomo Cappellin in 1925, after separating from Venini. Artistic director was Vittorio Zecchin; from 1929/30, Carlo Scarpa. The firm was closed down in 1933.

376 Vase

Attr. Carlo Scarpa
For Maestri Vetrai Muranesi Cappellin & C., Murano (?)
Ca. 1930–33
H 21.5, ⌀ 16.7 cm

Vaporized metallic salts and applied silver foil on opal white ground; torn, crackled, and oxidized by blowing out. Free-blown and shaped. Foot and mouth in light blue glass; unfired silver-foil remains under the stand.

Acc. no. P 1975-119
Gift of Helmut Hentrich

With vases of this type, an attribution to Vittorio Zecchin, ca. 1925–30, cannot be ruled out. For attribution and dating see Barovier Mentasti, *Vetro Veneziano*, 1982, 262, fig. 263, and *Mille anni*, 1982, cat. no. 520.

Lit.: M. Barovier, *Carlo Scarpa: Glass of an Architect* (Milan, 1997), 75, 196, no. 61

S.A.L.I.R.

(Studio Ars et Labor Industrie Riunite)

Glass factory and decorating workshop, Murano

Founded in 1923. Specialized in engraving, a rather uncommon technique in Murano. The painter Guido Balsamo Stella (1882–1941) supplied designs in the 1920s, most between 1927 and 1930.

377 Decorative Goblet

Design: Guido Balsamo Stella
For S.A.L.I.R., Murano
Execution: Franz Pelzel
Ca. 1925–28
H 23, ⌀ 9.4 cm

Glass with bluish tone, mold-blown and shaped. Two parts joined by three mereses. Decoration: on the bowl, three dolphins spewing water; on the foot, waves in mat intaglio.

Acc. no. P 1988-32
Gift of Helmut Hentrich

Balsamo Stella's designs were clearly influenced by Swedish works, particularly glassware from the Orrefors factory by Simon Gate and Edward Hald. Franz Pelzel (1900–1968), who came from Bohemia and worked for S.A.L.I.R. from 1927 to 1968, carried out the engravings.

Lit.: Ricke and Gronert, *Glas in Schweden*, 1986, 38, fig. 19; V. Conedera, *I vetri d'arte della S.A.L.I.R. 1923–1987* (Venice, 1987), 106, no. 46, pl. 31

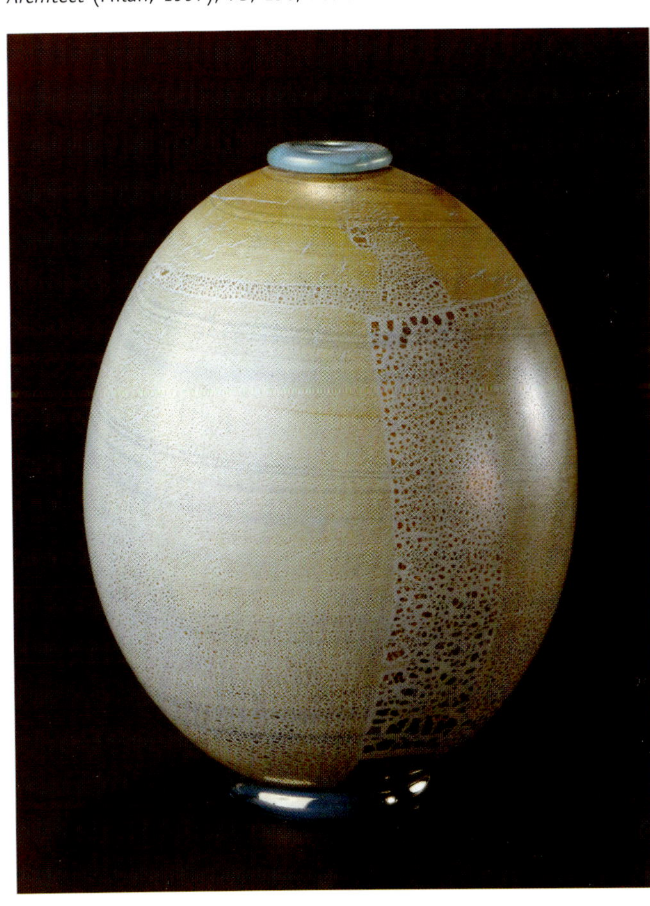

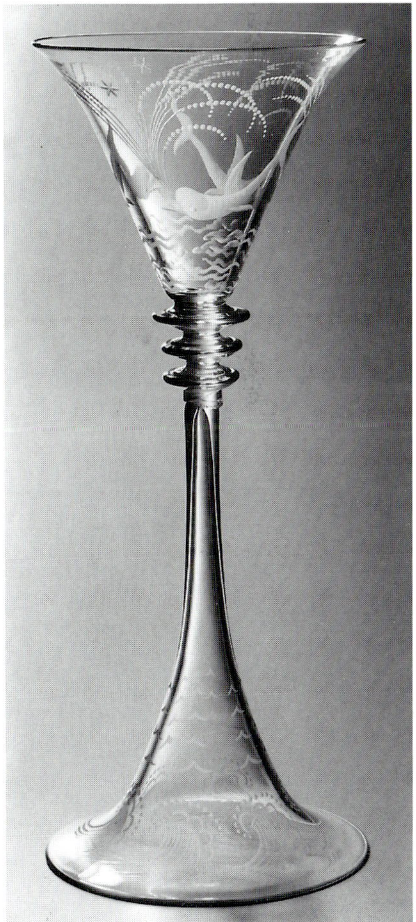

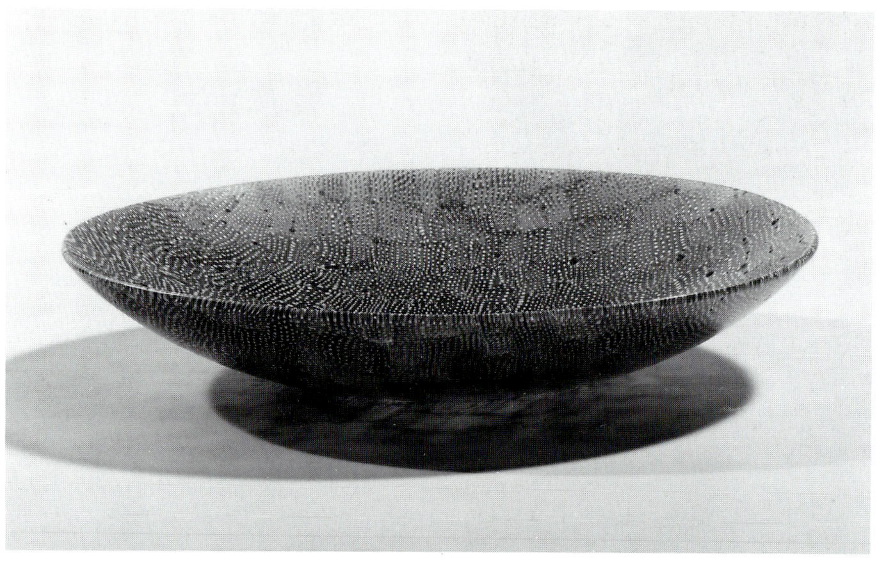

Venini & C.

Art-glass factory, Murano

Founded under the name Vetri Soffiati Venini & C. in 1925, after Paolo Venini and Giacomo Cappellin separated. Artistic director was Napoleone Martinuzzi.
With emphasis on contemporary forms, subsequently developed into the most prestigious and successful art-glass factory in Murano. Collaboration with numerous significant designers from Italy and abroad, including Carlo and Tobia Scarpa, Fulvio Bianconi, Gio Ponti, Tyra Lundgren, and Tapio Wirkkala.

378   Dish

Silver printed mark on ocher-colored ground of round adhesive label: *Venini S. A. MURANO*, Veronese vase in the center
Design: Ludovico Diaz de Santillana
For Venini & C., Murano
Ca. 1962
H 3.6, ⌀ 19.9 cm

Mosaic-glass technique, mold-melted from slices of preformed canes that have rectangular cross sections. Guinea-fowl feather pattern in opaque white and gray. Surface ground mat inside and out.

Acc. no. P 1966-297
Gift of Helmut Hentrich

For "murrine" glass of this type see Ricke and Schmitt, *Italian Glass*, 1997, 142–48.

Lit.: –

379   Bottle-Shaped "Tessuto" Vase

Diamond-engraved mark on the underside of base: *venini italia*
Design: Carlo Scarpa
For Venini & C., Murano
1940
Execution: 1950s/1960s
H 34, ⌀ 14 cm

Thread glass; one half in yellow and brown, the other half in yellow and white stripes. Free-blown and shaped.

Acc. no. P 1975-27
Gift of Udo van Meeteren, Düsseldorf

Used the traditional thread techniques for new decorative approaches. See *Venini*, 1978, n.p.; Barovier Mentasti, *Vetro Veneziano*, 1982, 284, fig. 291; *Mille anni*, 1982, cat. no. 529. See also, for example, Ricke and Schmitt, *Italian Glass*, 1997, 74, 75.

Lit.: –

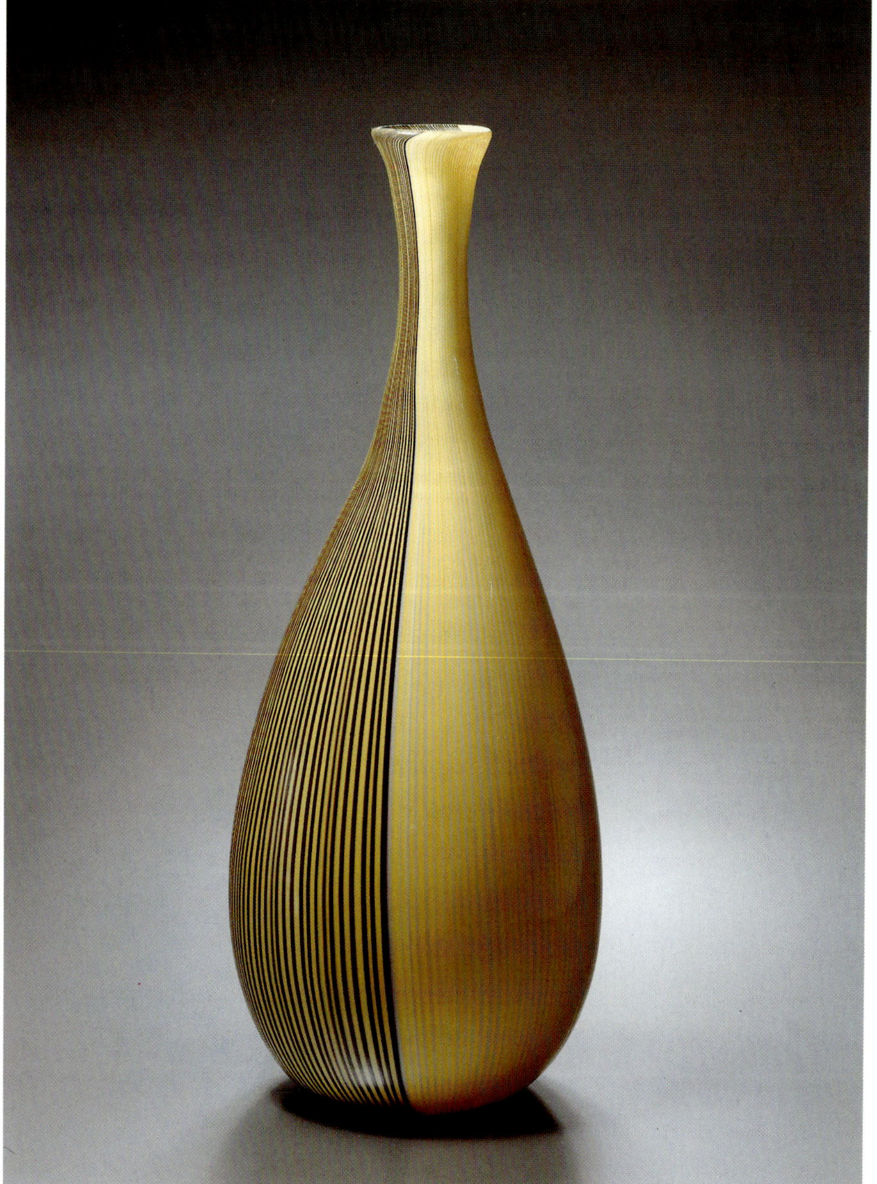

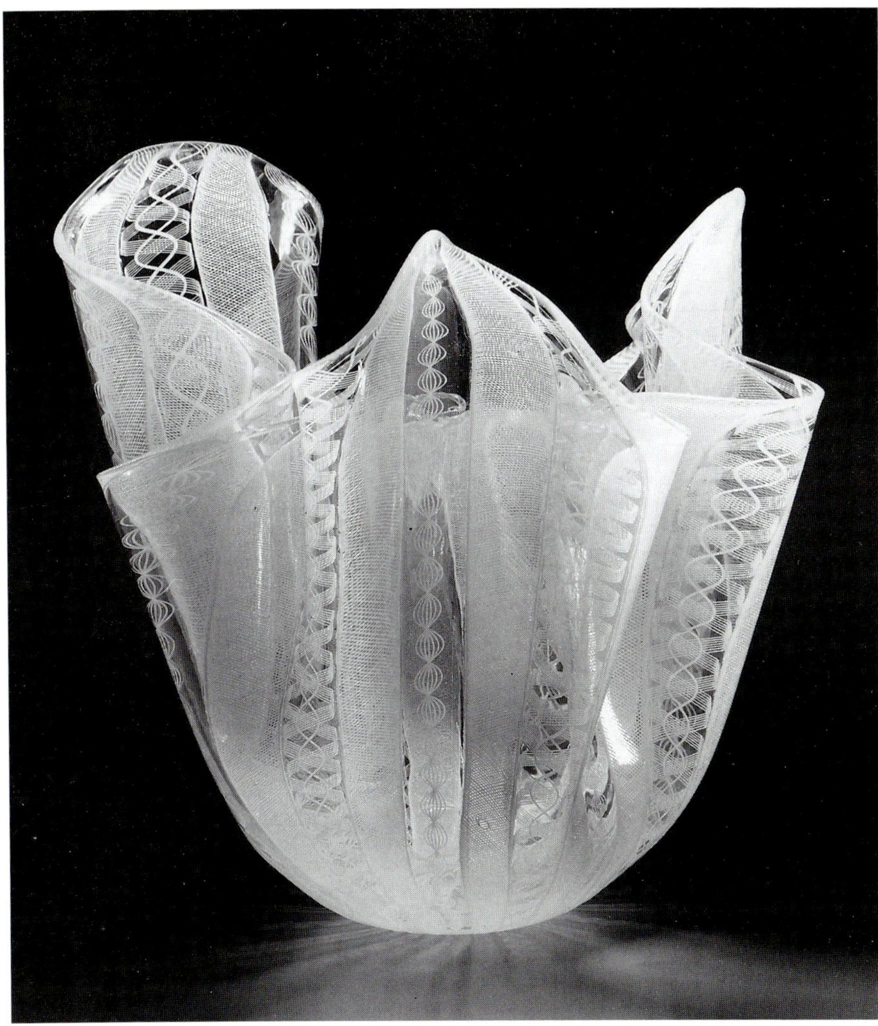

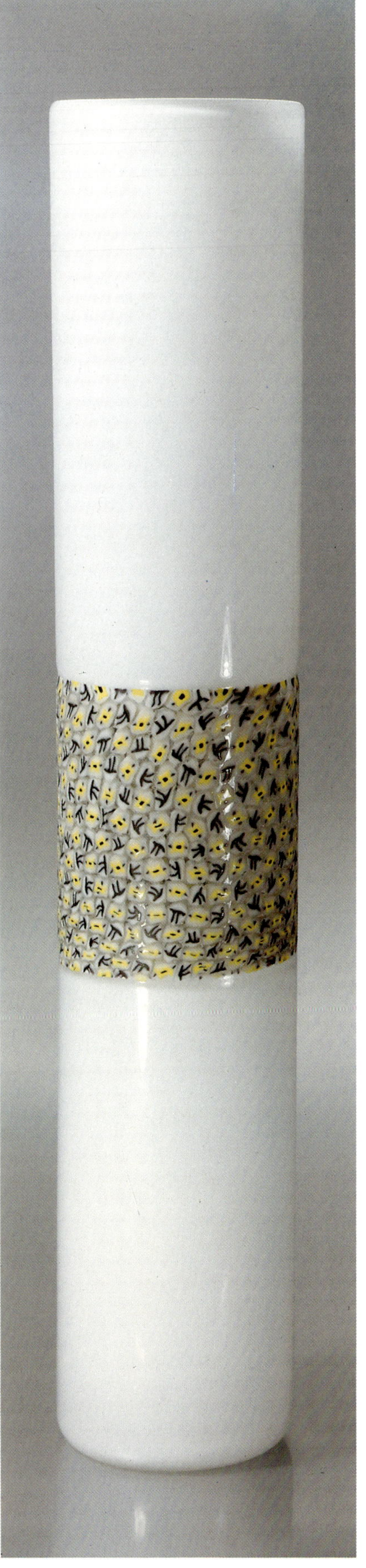

380   "Fazzoletto" Bowl

Mark as three-part acid stamp on the under-
side of base: *Venini Murano ITALIA*
Model no. 2986
Design: Fulvio Bianconi and Paolo Venini
For Venini & C., Murano
1949
Execution: 1950s
H 29.4, ⌀ 30.1 cm

Filigree-glass canes with embedded opaque
white threads in colorless glass (zanfirico lattimo Q), fused and free-formed.

Acc. no. P 1966-313
Gift of Helmut Hentrich

Venini's "Handkerchief Vase" was his most
successful model, made in several sizes and
variations over the decades. Numerous imitations by glasshouses in Italy and abroad. For
the original see *Venini/Orrefors*, 1957, cat.
no. 15; Kämpfer, *Viertausend Jahre*, 1966,
e.g., no. 206; *Venini*, 1978, n.p.; *Mille anni*,
1982, cat. no. 649; Heiremans, *Murano*,
1993, 260.

Lit.: –

381   Vase

Mark as three-part acid stamp on the underside of base: *Venini Murano ITALIA*
and adhesive label with model no.: *4137*
Design: Paolo Venini and Riccardo Licata
(*murrine*)
For Venini & C., Murano
1956
H 41.3, ⌀ 8.1 cm

Fused from separately worked pieces; white
opal inner casing, mold-blown, ring of mosaic
glass.

Acc. no. P 1957-11
Acquired from the manufacturer

For a different color combination see *Venini/
Orrefors*, 1957, cat. no. 58 (opalino bianco
fascia F); see also Heiremans, *Murano*, 1993,
281, and Ricke and Schmitt, *Italian Glass*,
1997, 150f.

Lit.: Heinemeyer, *Glas*, 1966, cat. no. 554

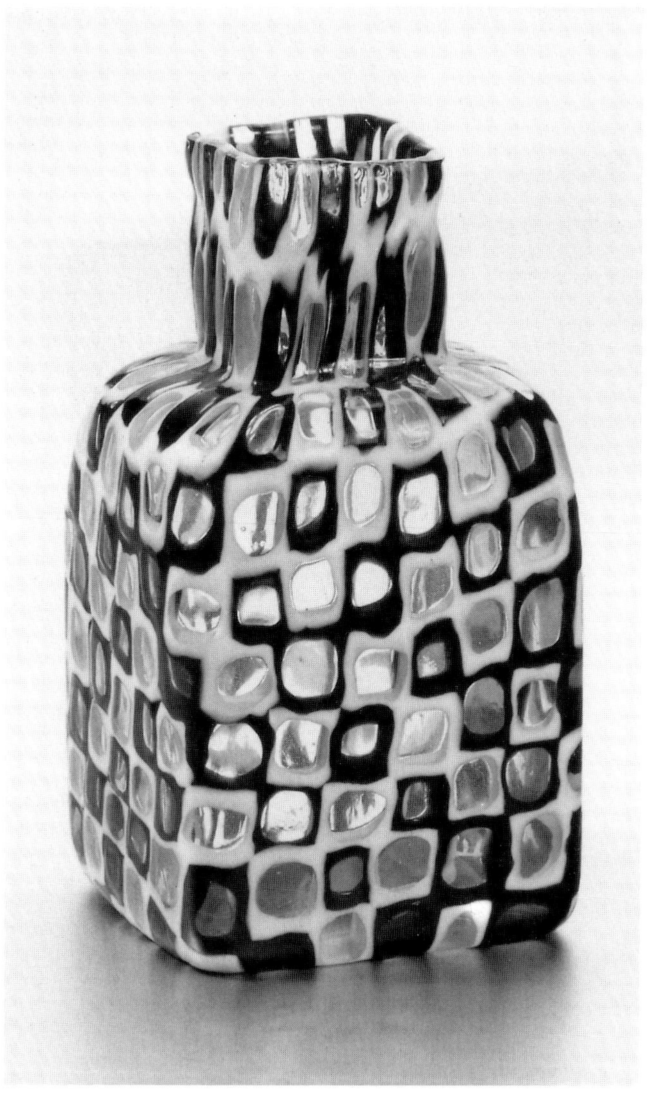

383 "Battuto" Footed Bowl

Design: Tobia Scarpa and Ludovico Diaz de Santillana
For Venini & C., Murano
1960
H 15.2, ∅ 17.2 cm

Glass with aquamarine tone, free-blown. Mat olive cut inside and out.

Acc. no. P 1966-266
Gift of Helmut Hentrich

The "Battuti" series was one of Tobia Scarpa's (b. 1935) first he designed after he began working with Venini in 1959. The basic concept was varied in several different dish forms. See *Domus* no. 361 (Dec. 1959) and no. 385 (Dec. 1961); *Venini*, 1978, n.p.; Fahr Becker-Sterner, *Fünfziger*, 1984, cat. no. 20; Heiremans, *Murano*, 1993, 285; Ricke and Schmitt, *Italian Glass*, 1997, 162.

Lit.: –

382 "Occhi" Vase

Mark as round acid stamp in ground-out pontil: *Venini ITALIA Murano*
Design: Tobia Scarpa
1959/60
H 19.5, L (of side) 10.8 cm

Slices of glass canes having a rectangular cross section in patterns of colorless/white and colorless/black-brown; fused, blown, and shaped.

Acc. no. P 1966-279
Gift of Helmut Hentrich

New decoration, usually used on variations of older forms by Carlo Scarpa or the Venini studio. For the model published in 1965 see Neuwirth, *Italienisches Glas*, 1987, 209, fig. 171; see also Ricke and Schmitt, *Italian Glass*, 1997, 165, 284.

Lit.: –

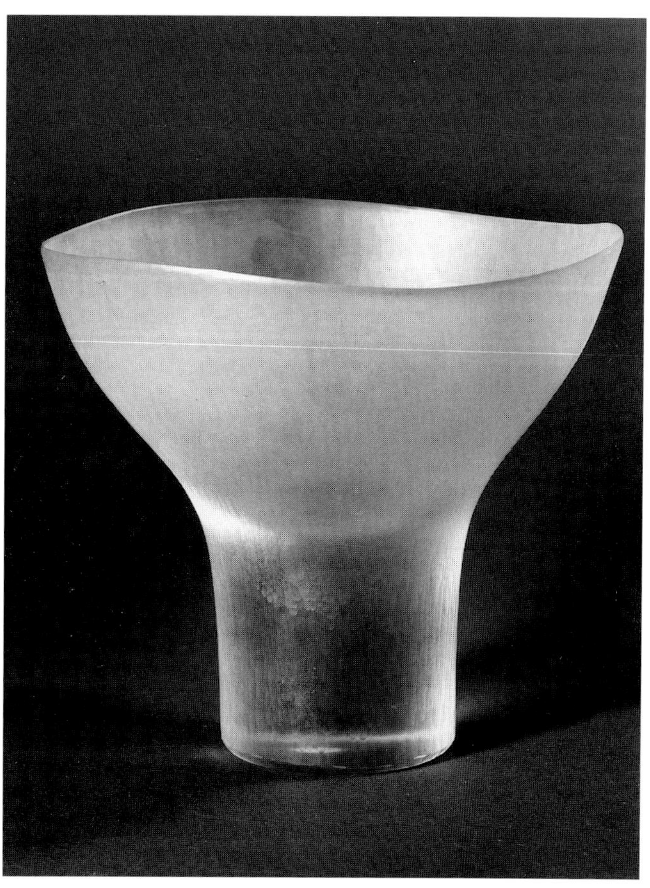

Vetreria Archimede Seguso S.a.s.
Art-glass factory, Murano

Founded in 1946 by Archimede Seguso
(1909–1999), who had worked for Venini and
Seguso Vetri d'Arte. Produced glass sculptures, vessels in thread-glass and other
Venetian techniques, most based on Seguso's
own designs.

384   Vase

Diamond-engraved mark on the underside of
base: *Seguso—Archimede Biennale 1954*
Design: Archimede Seguso
For Vetreria Archimede Seguso S.a.s., Murano
1953/54
H 27.2, ⌀ 25.2 x 10.7 cm

Opaque white and violet thread glass on colorless ground. Thick, colorless cover layer.
Free-blown and shaped.

Acc. no. P 1966-274
Gift of Helmut Hentrich

Designed for the 1954 Venice Biennale. Carried out by A. Seguso personally. See Corning, *Glass 1959*, 1959, 231. For a dish of the
same "Compositione Lattimo" group see
Barovier Mentasti, *Murano '900*, 1977, cat.
no. 109, fig. 37. For A. Seguso see Ricke and
Schmitt, *Italian Glass*, 1997, 182ff., 310f.

Lit.: Ricke and Gronert, *Glas in Schweden*,
1986, 41, fig. 24; Heiremans, *Murano*, 1993,
137

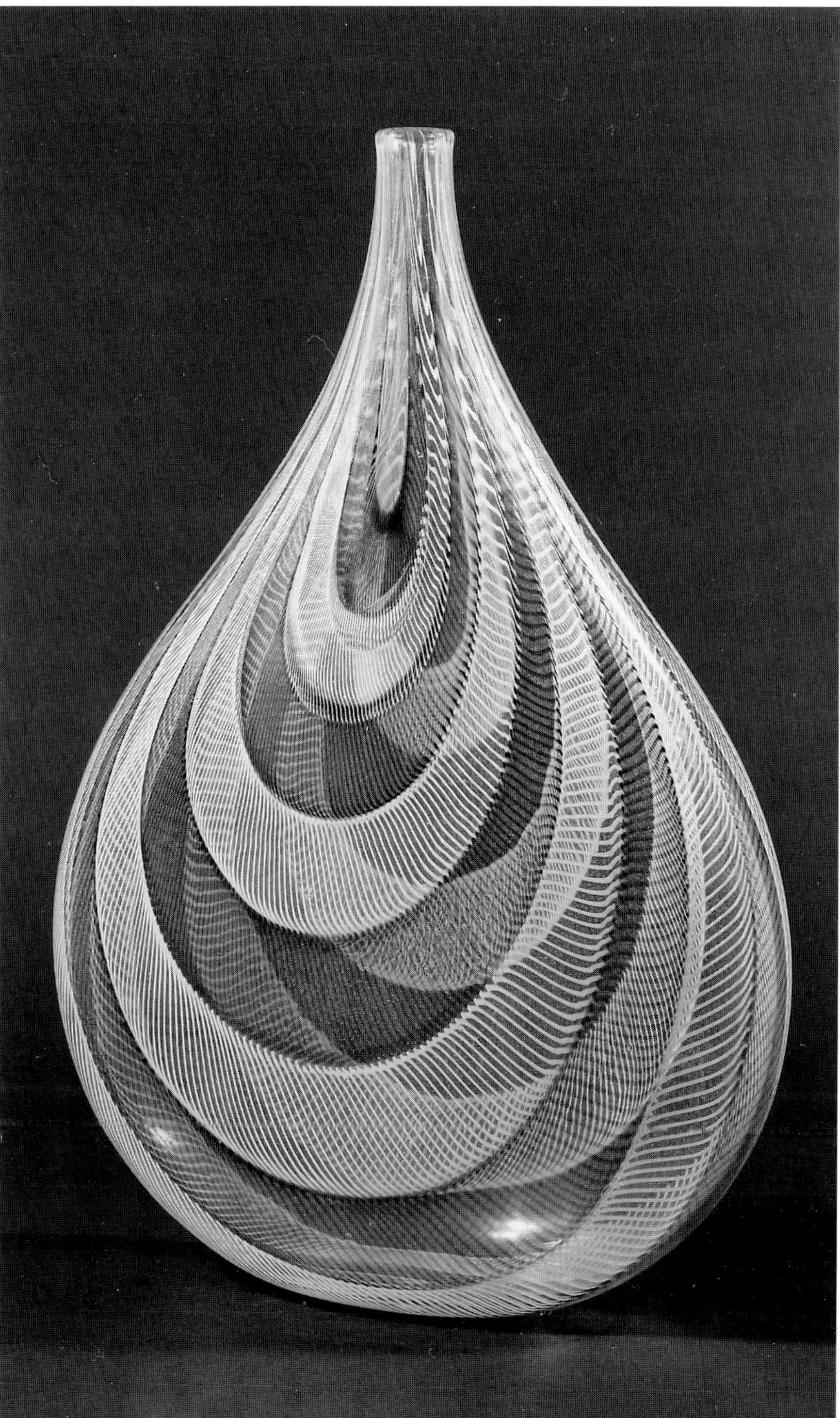

Seguso Vetri d'Arte

Art-glass factory, Murano

Founded in 1933 under the name Barovier, Seguso e Ferro by Napoleone Barovier, Antonio Seguso, and Luigi Ferro. From 1934, collaboration with Flavio Poli (1900–1984), who was artistic director of the company until 1963, followed by Mario Pinzoni until 1971. From 1937, under the name Seguso Vetri d'Arte. In 1992, sold to Gino Cenedese.

385 Bowl

Design: Flavio Poli
For Seguso Vetri d'Arte, Murano
1954
H 11.4, ⌀ 26 x 16.5 cm

Violet inner casing covered by red glass. In the upper region, thick colorless cover layer. Mold-blown. Mouth and base ground flat.

Acc. no. P 1966-309
Gift of Helmut Hentrich

Typical of the simple, clear forms that determine Poli's line at Seguso Vetri d'Arte. For this and related models see Ernst, *Moderne Gläser*, 1955, fig. 19; Corning, *Glass 1959*, 1959, 218; Kämpfer, *Viertausend Jahre*, 1966, no. 209; Neuwirth, *Italienisches Glas*, 1987, 94, cat. no. 28; Ricke and Schmitt, *Italian Glass*, 1997, 240ff., 311f.

Lit.: –

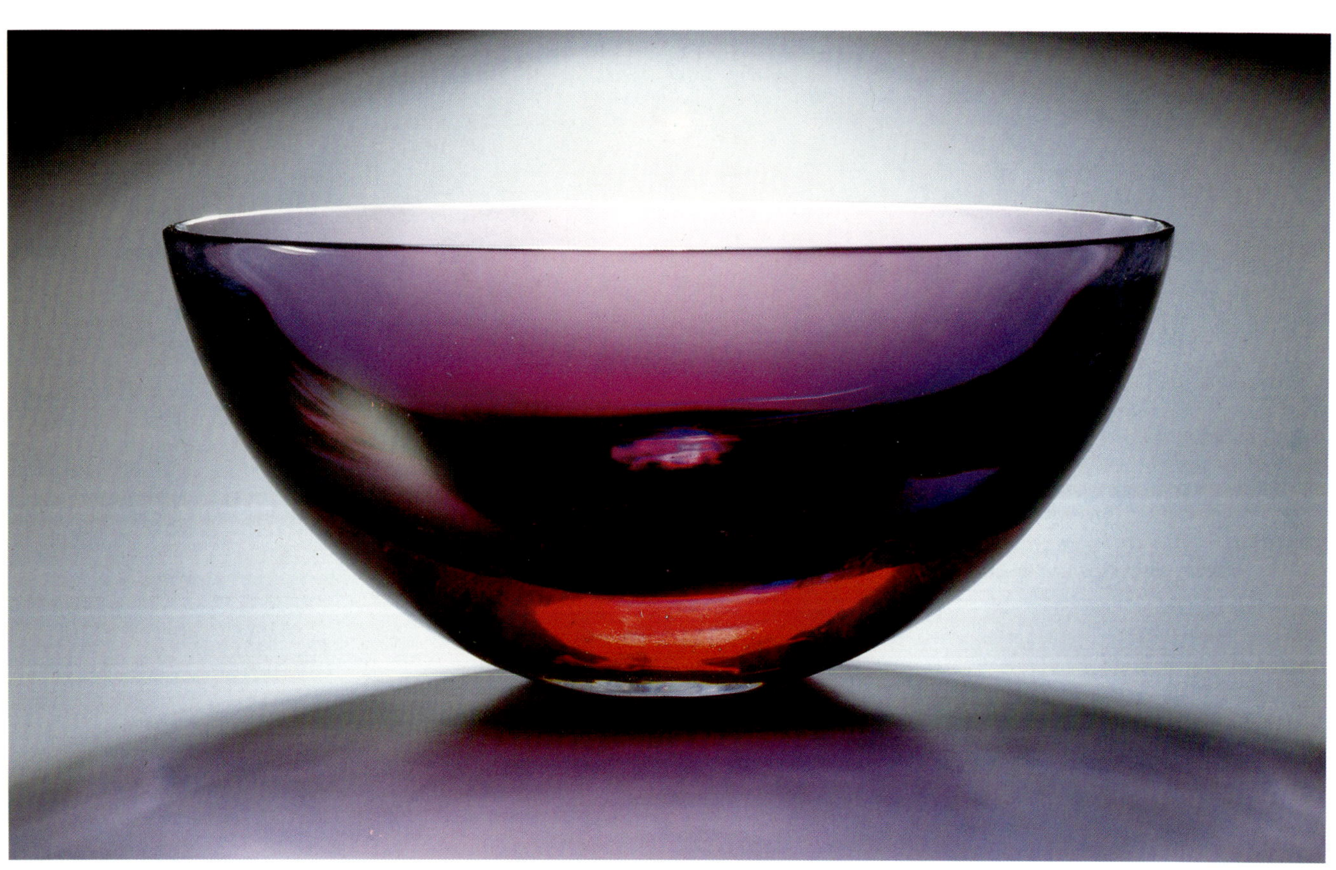

Barovier & Toso

Art-glass factory, Murano

From 1919, trading under various names (see Artisti Barovier, p. 233). From 1942, named Barovier & Toso. Production determined mostly by Ercole Barovier (1889–1974), who entered the firm in 1924 and headed it administratively and artistically from 1936 to his death. Today his son Angelo Barovier manages the firm.

386   Man Carrying Fruit Basket

Ercole Barovier
For Vetreria Artistica Barovier & C., Murano
Ca. 1933
H 34.2, W 15.3, D 10.8 cm

Massive, colorless glass, free-formed. Iridescent. Stuck feet and stand.

Acc. no. P 1982-34

Attribution and dating thanks to a company-archive photograph of the design and information kindly provided by Angelo Barovier and Jan Vicha, Munich.

Lit.: Ricke, *Museumsarbeit*, 1988, 76, fig. 56

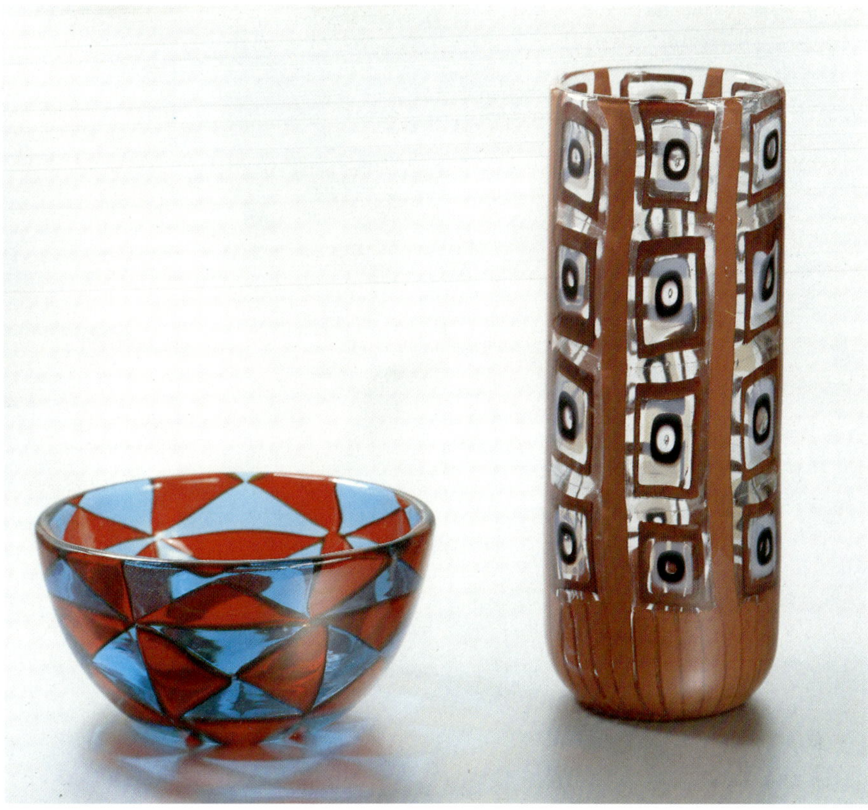

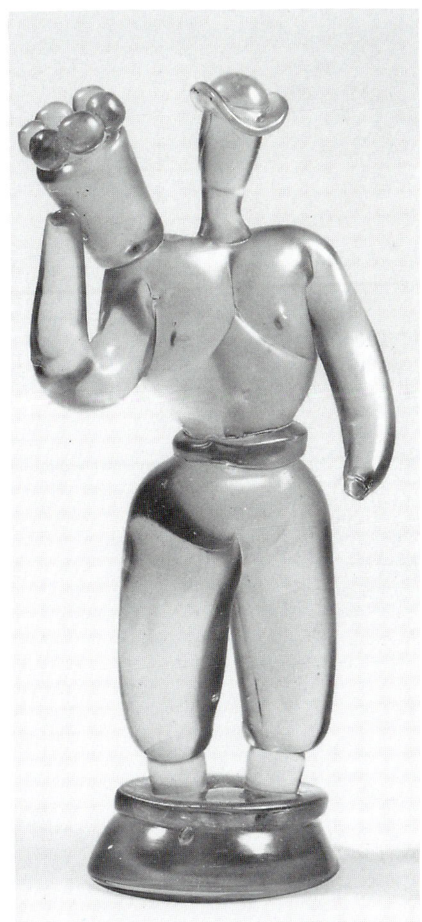

387   "Intarsio" Dish

Engraved mark on the underside of base:
Design Ercole Barovier 1962
barovier & toso murano
Design: Ercole Barovier
For Barovier & Toso, Murano
1962
H 8.6, ⌀ 16.5 cm

Red triangular forms worked into light blue ground; thick colorless cover layer. Mold-blown.

Acc. no. P 1975-34
Gift of Angelo Barovier, Murano

New expressive possibilities with old mosaic-glass techniques. For models of the same series see Barovier Mentasti, *Murano '900*, 1977, no. 45, fig. 11. For Barovier & Toso in general see Ricke and Schmitt, *Italian Glass*, 1997, 45ff., 250ff., 301ff.

Lit.: –

388   "Dorico" Vase

Engraved mark on the underside of base:
Design Ercole Barovier 1962
barovier & toso murano
Design: Ercole Barovier
For Barovier & Toso, Murano
1960
Execution: 1962
H 26.3, ⌀ 10.5 cm

Brown and milky white cane sections and ribbons embedded in colorless ground; thick colorless cover layer. Mold-blown.

Acc. no. P 1975-32
Gift of Angelo Barovier, Murano

For other pieces from the same series see Barovier Mentasti, *Murano '900*, 1977, cat. no. 44, fig. 10. Designed for the 1960 Venice Biennale together with other glassware of similar type. See *Vetri jonici: 30 Biennale di Venezia*, exh. cat. (Venice, 1960), fig. 218.

Lit.: –

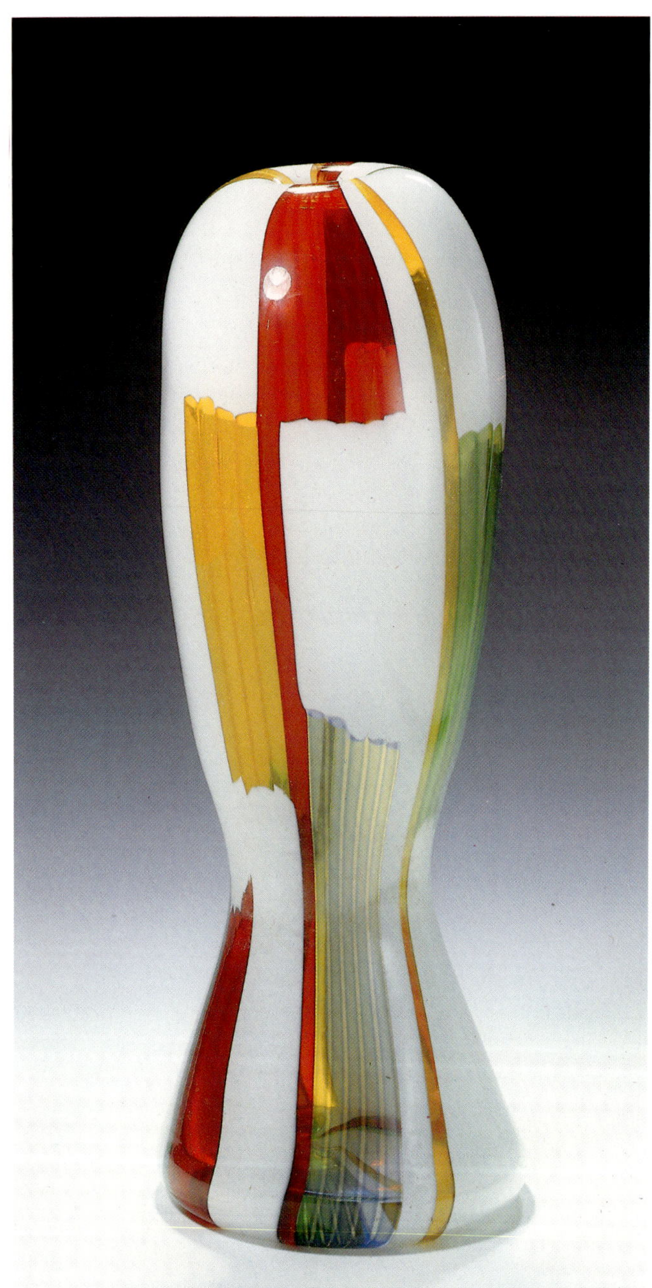

Vetreria Barbini

Art-glass factory, Murano

Founded in 1950 by Alfredo Barbini (b. 1912), who had been a partner and the first master at Vetreria Artistica Muranese Soc. An. (VAMSA), founded in 1936. From 1946, he was artistic director at Cenedese & C. Barbini's firm produced lavish art glass and superior utilitarian ware designed, amongst others, by his son Flavio Barbini.

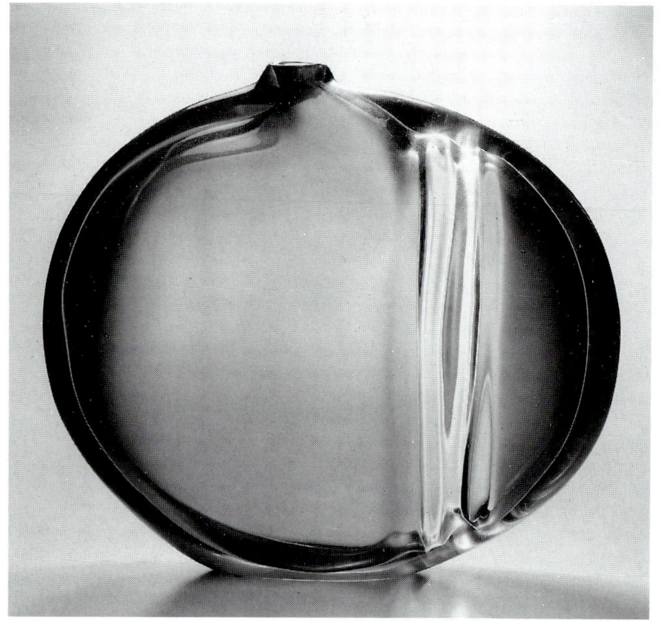

390 "Alga" Vase

Diamond-engraved mark on the underside of base: *A. Barbini 1968 Murano*
Design: Alfredo Barbini, Murano
For Vetreria Barbini, Murano
1968
H 24.7, ⌀ 29.3 x 10.8 cm

Free-blown from brown and colorless glass, fused in the *incalmo* technique.

Acc. no. P 1975-39
Gift of Alfredo Barbini

Barbini is one of Murano's most versatile artistic personalities. He often influenced development with new techniques and decoration. Free-formed glass sculptures are his particular strength.
For vases of the "Alga" series see Barovier Mentasti, *Murano '900*, 1977, cat. no. 21, fig. 17S; Barovier Mentasti, *Vetro Veneziano*, 1982, 286, fig. 293; *Mille anni*, 1982, cat. no. 573. For Barbini in general see Ricke and Schmitt, *Italian Glass*, 1997, 246ff., 300f.

Lit.: –

A.VE.M.

Arte Vetraria Muranese

Art-glass factory, Murano

Founded in 1932 by Antonio and Egidio Ferro and Emilio Nason. Collaborated in the early years with, for instance, Vittorio Zecchin and Giulio Radi, who provided most of the designs in the 1940s and 1950s.

389 Vase

Design: Anzolo Fuga
For Arte Vetraria Muranese (A.VE.M.), Murano
Execution: Luciano Ferro
1963
H 44.2, ⌀ 16.1 cm

On thin, colorless ground, opaque white glass strips and pattern of fused colored glass canes ("vaso opalina bianca decorato a geroglifici"). Thick colorless cover layer. Blown and shaped.

Acc. no. P 1989-9

In creating an intrinsically sculptural object, Fuga paved the way for developments in the late 1960s in Murano. For other works by Fuga for A.VE.M. see *Mostra del Vetro di Murano: Opera Bevilacqua la Masa*, exh. cat. (Venice: Opera Bevilacqua la Masa, 1963), n.p. Besides glass vessels, Anzolo Fuga designed primarily stained-glass windows for ecclesiastic architecture. For A.VE.M. and A. Fuga see Ricke and Schmitt, *Italian Glass*, 1997, 180ff., 300.

Lit.: –

The Nordic Countries

Everyday objects and their simple, functional shapes had a decisive impact on Scandinavian and Finnish culture over many centuries. In the vast countries of the North, the rural population had to rely on themselves to make articles of everyday life, of wood or ceramics. Thus a long tradition of functional and pleasing forms emerged. It was firmly established in the general population and remained for the most part uninfluenced by Central European styles.

With the Werkbund movement in Germany and Austria and the development of design under new principles governing utility goods made industrially or in large factories, the Scandinavian formal idiom suddenly won unexpected relevance. In the years between the wars, Sweden, Norway, Denmark, and Finland became highly acclaimed centers of the craft industry, where utensils were serially produced in exemplary fashion.

It started with glass manufacturing. The leading glasshouse, Kosta, and the smaller factory, Reijmyre, had already received recognition with fine Art-Nouveau glassware around 1900 (cat. no. 391). The Orrefors factory, founded in 1913, subsequently based its whole production program, in keeping with the ideas of the Werkbund movement, on collaboration with artists and artisans. With Simon Gate and Edward Hald, the glasshouse was able to attract two artists ideally suited to this task. In utilitarian glassware as well as in art glass, they created an unmistakable image for the glasshouse. It soon clearly influenced all other countries in the North (cat. no. 401) and left a lasting impression on Central Europe.

Utility glass based on Gate's and Hald's designs had no extraneous decoration. Its appeal lay in the animated contours, often created by optic forms, and above all in the selection of glass tones ranging from gray to smoky brown to various tones of blue. The Swedish glasshouse achieved great success with these glass pieces as well as with its engraved decorative glassware at the Art-Deco exhibition in Paris in 1925 (cat. no. 394). Expressing a feeling for life to a large extent unmarred by war experiences, hunger, and political crises, the glassware was enthusiastically received by Central European countries. Not only in the works of Bohemian glass engravers, but even in the designs of Guido Balsamo Stella in Venice (cat. 377), the influence of these glass pieces is readily discernible.

The field of tension between art glass and simple functional form characterized the 1930s in Sweden. With ornamental glass, an often spectacularly beautiful linear decoration emerged, usually made by engraving. Vicke Lindstrand became the most prominent representative of this trend (cat. no. 395). Then there were the thick-walled glass pieces with embedded creations made in the complicated Graal and Ariel techniques. Their producers carried on the tradition established by Maurice Marinot in Troyes, concentrating on decorative possibilities. Utilitarian ware returned to the colorlessness of crystal glass and in functionalism was limited to simple contours based on such elementary stereometric forms as spheres, cones, and ellipses. The most consistent designs of this type were the glasses by Gerda Strömberg for the glasshouse Eda and Strömbergshyttan (cat. no. 399).

Amongst the other artists active in the Scandinavian countries in this period, Jacob Eiler Bang must be mentioned first. In his designs for the Danish factory Holmegaard, although at first unmistakably dependent on the line followed by Orrefors (cat. no. 401), he conceived his own stylistic language in the 1930s (cat. no. 402).

Finnish factories, specifically those in Riihimäki, Iittala, and Nuutajärvi, gradually replaced the Swedish glasshouses that had dominated in the 1950s. Orrefors and his designers Nils Landberg, Edvin Öhrström (cat. no. 396), Ingeborg Lundin, and Sven Palmqvist continued to work successfully and with very high standards. Besides the decorative glassware of Murano, that made by Vicke Lindstrand at Kosta from 1950 (cat. no. 393) clearly helped shape glass art of this period. The material and design-oriented development of utility glass, however, was determined by such designers as Kaj Franck, Tapio Wirkkala, and Timo Sarpaneva at the Finnish glasshouses. Their designs received the most prestigious awards at the Milan Triennales, which functioned as a barometer for developments in the 1950s.

Kaj Franck occasionally emphasized playful elements and used bright color accents, although always based on an exact design, not on improvisation like the work of the Venetians. Wirkkala and Sarpaneva, on the other hand, were masters of highly concentrated, powerful forms. The most likely parallel to Wirkkala's early designs, in his restrained use of color with just one or two inner casings, was the work of Flavio Poli. His emphasis on the weight of simple forms has a similar significance (cat. nos. 385, 407, 408).

Kosta Glasbruk

Factory for art and utilitarian glass with decorating workshops, Kosta, Sweden

The Kosta factory, founded in 1742, is Sweden's oldest glasshouse in operation. It held particular significance around 1900 and during the 1950s. Its most important directors were Elis Bergh, from 1929 to 1950, and Vicke Lindstrand, from 1950 to 1973.

391 Vase

Needle-etched mark on the underside of base: *Kosta 353 E Wennerberg A.Bö*
Design: Gunnar Wennerberg
1900–1902
Execution: Kosta Glasbruk
H 12.6, ⌀ 13.3 cm

Blue-green glass with opaque green-yellow overlay. Encircling decoration of eight stylized flowers and vines. Etched and engraved.

Acc. no. P 1979-34
Gift of Helmut Hentrich

Swedish Art Nouveau generally maintained strong ties with its French equivalent. This is true of the vase shown here only to a certain extent. The vase designed by G. Wennerberg (1863–1911) reflects developments from northern Bohemia and Germany more than from France.

Lit.: Ricke, *2500 Jahre*, 1987, cat. no. 146

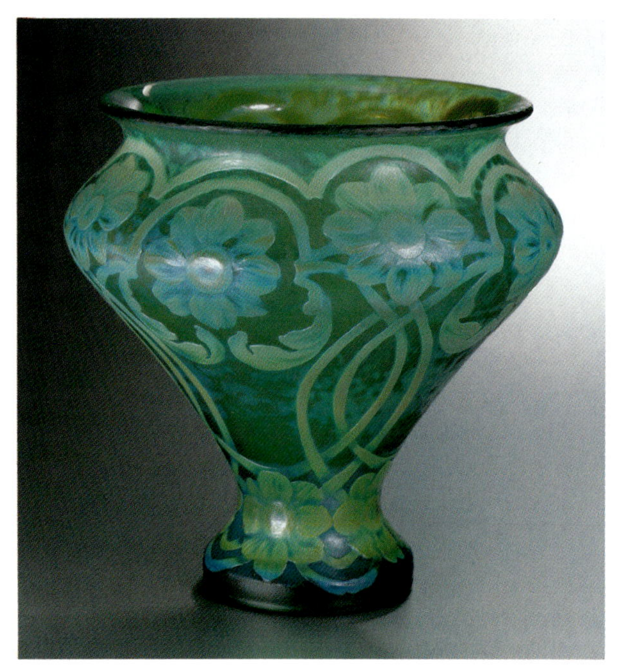

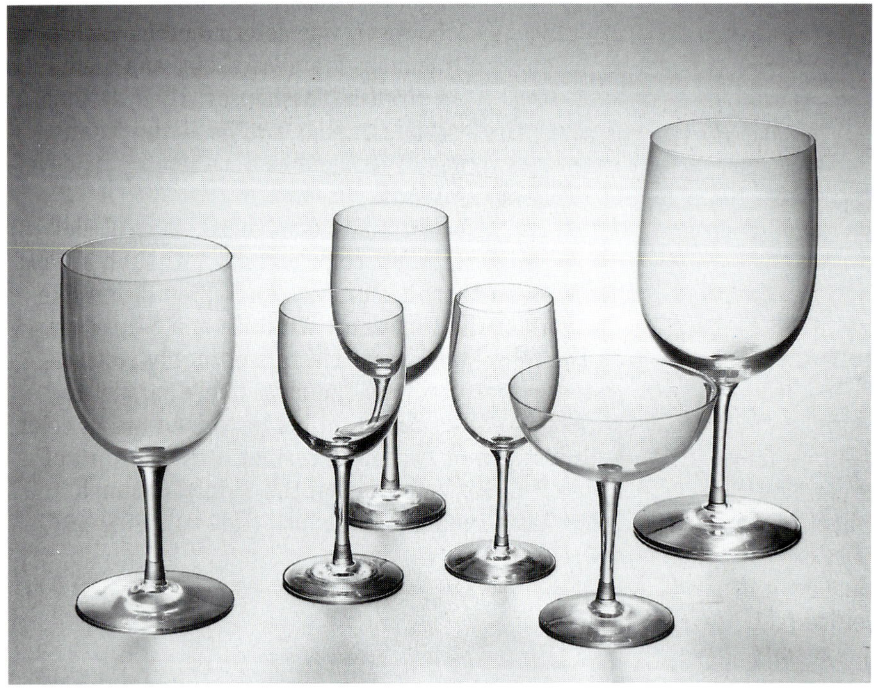

392 Glasses from the "Charm" Service

Design: Elis Bergh, April 1942
Execution: Kosta Glasbruk, 1950s/1960s
Red-wine glass: H 13.7, ⌀ 6.7 cm
Beer glass: H 16.2, ⌀ 7.7 cm
Sherry glass: H 11, ⌀ 5 cm
White-wine glass: H 12.4, ⌀ 5.1 cm
Port glass: H 10.8, ⌀ 4.4 cm
Madeira glass: H 9.3, ⌀ 8.1 cm

Colorless crystal glass, mold-blown and shaped.

Acc. nos. P 1987-13 a-f
Gift of the manufacturer

Elis Bergh's (1881–1954) special achievement lay in the design of a large number of drinking-glass sets that defined Kosta's image and set it off from its competitor Orrefors. The classic design of the "Charm" service illustrates the functional beauty of Swedish glassmaking from the 1930s.
Dating based on records in the company archives.

Lit.: Ricke and Gronert, *Glas in Schweden*, 1986, cat. no. 347

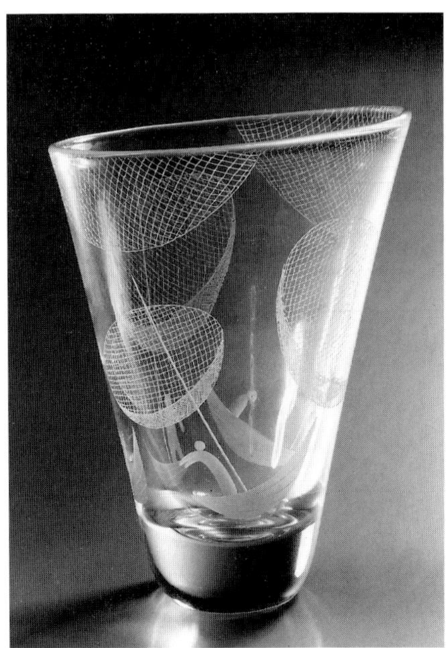

393 Vase

Diamond-engraved mark on the underside of
base: *Kosta LG 134*
Design: Vicke Lindstrand, 1951/52
Execution: Kosta Glasbruk, 1950s
H 16.8, ⌀ 12.8 cm

Colorless crystal glass, mold-blown and
shaped. Mat intaglio and diamond-point
engraved decoration: three boats carrying
one fisherman, and one carrying two.

Acc. no. P 1992-284
Formerly Städtische Galerie Schloss Oberhausen

Vicke Lindstrand worked as artistic director at
Kosta Glasbruck from 1950 to 1973. Particularly in the 1950s, his work largely determined the face of Swedish glass art.
The airy compositions of his early engravings
for Kosta are evocative. He aptly utilized the
design possibilities of transparent vessel bodies, while remaining true to the material.
For another example of the present model see
Ricke and Gronert, *Glas in Schweden*, 1986,
cat. no. 358; for the illustration in the production catalogue see Ricke and Thor,
Schwedische Glasmanufakturen, 1987, 364.

Lit.: –

Orrefors Glasbruk

Factory for art and utilitarian glassware with
decorating workshops, Orrefors, Sweden

Founded in 1913. Rose to worldwide renown
in the 1920s under artistic directors Simon
Gate (1883–1945) and Edward Hald
(1883–1980). In the 1930s, important
impulses came from the designer Vicke Lindstrand, in the 1950s/1960s from Nils Landberg, Sven Palmqvist, Edvin Öhrström, and
Ingeborg Lundin.

394 Bowl with Plate

Engraved mark on the underside of base:
Orrefors Gate 128 1923.EW.
Design: Simon Gate, 1920
Execution: Orrefors, 1923
Engraver: Emil Weidlich
H with plate 12, ⌀ bowl 22 x 16.1,
⌀ plate 21.5 x 15.9 cm

Colorless crystal glass, mold-blown, oval
cross section. Mat intaglio decoration: female
nude on a gazelle. On the other side, another
nude with a scarf-like veil, flanked by two
kneeling figures; polished sun. Base of plate
and bowl ground.

Acc. nos. P 1987-50 a, b
Acquired with funds from the Helmut Hentrich
donation

Small series, produced over several years.
Date of the design secured by extant pattern
in the company archives. See Ricke and Thor,
Schwedische Glasmanufakturen, 1987, 23.

Lit.: Ricke and Gronert, *Glas in Schweden*,
1986, cat. no. 74

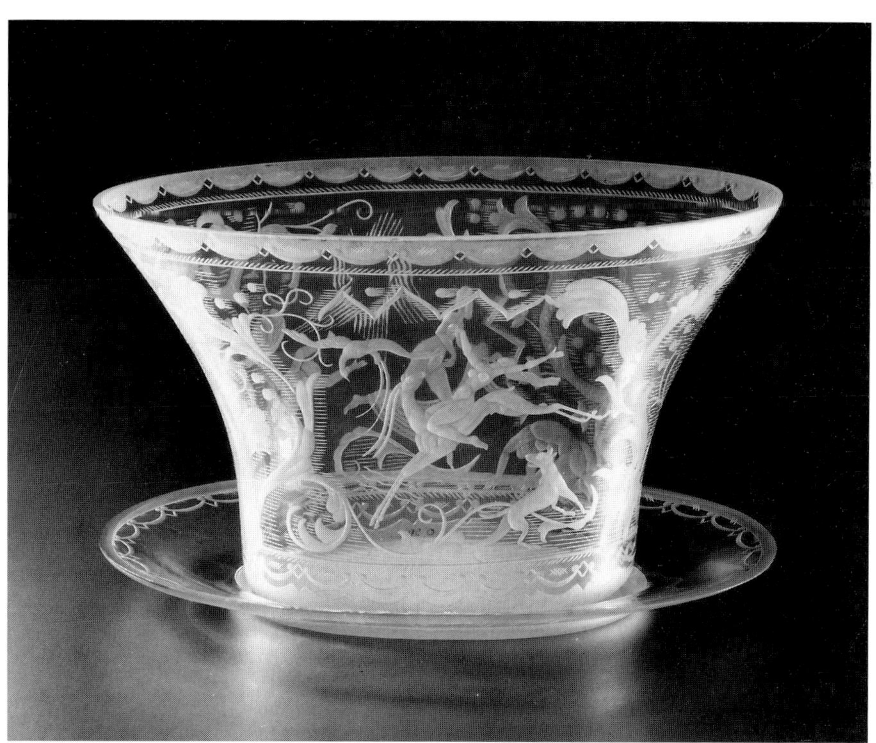

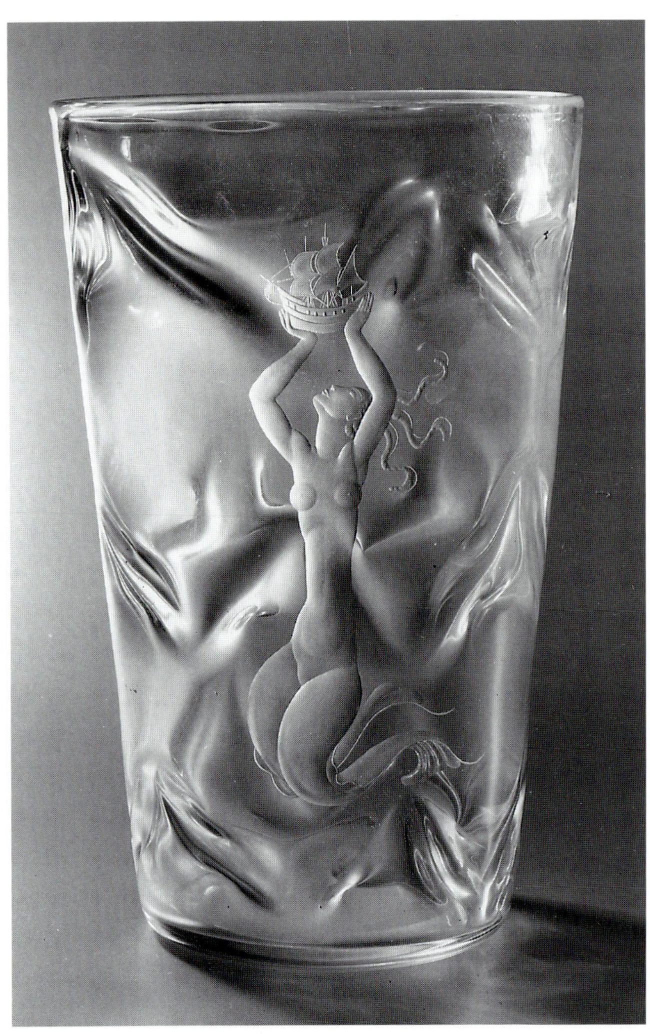

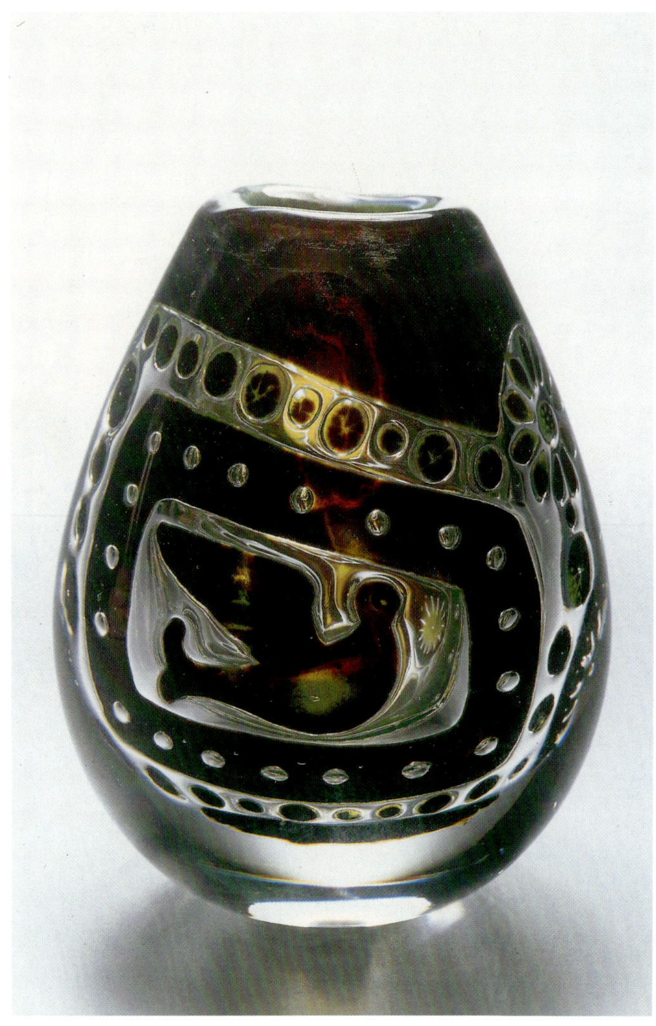

395 Vase

Engraved mark on the underside of base: *Orrefors 1265 Lindstrand A.1.G.E.*
Design: Vicke Lindstrand, 1933
Execution: Orrefors, 1935
Engraver: Gösta Elgström
H 25.1, ⌀ 16.2 cm

Colorless crystal glass, optic-blown and again fully blown in smooth-walled mold. Wall has differing thicknesses, creating the impression of waves. Decoration in rough-polished intaglio.

Acc. no. P 1986-37
Acquired with funds from the Helmut Hentrich donation

The vase was first published in the Orrefors catalogue, no. 7 (Jan. 1934); see Ricke and Thor, *Schwedische Glasmanufakturen*, 1987, 83.
Vicke Lindstrand (1904–1983), who worked for Orrefors as a designer from 1928 to 1940, concentrated on developing new types of engraving and was instrumental in devising the Ariel technique.

Lit.: –

396 "Girl and Dove" Vase

Diamond-engraved mark on the underside of base: *ORREFORS Ariel No. 458 F Edvin Öhrström*
Design: Edvin Öhrström, 1957
Execution: Orrefors
H 14.5, ⌀ 11.9 cm

Colorless crystal glass, red-brown overlay on aventurine-green. After glass was cooled down, sandblast decoration was carried out: head of girl in profile, flowers, and dove in ornamental framing. Reheated, covered with colorless, thick-walled overlay, fully blown, and shaped.

Acc. no. P 1958-3
Acquired from the manufacturer

Probably the most common and enduring decoration in the Ariel series. First design in 1937. The sculptor Edvin Öhrström (b. 1906) worked as designer for Orrefors from 1936 to 1957. Together with Lindstrand he contributed to the development of the Ariel technique.

Lit.: *Venini/Orrefors*, 1957, cat. no. 165; Heinemeyer, *Glas*, 1966, cat. no. 556; Ricke and Gronert, *Glas in Schweden*, 1986, cat. no. 242

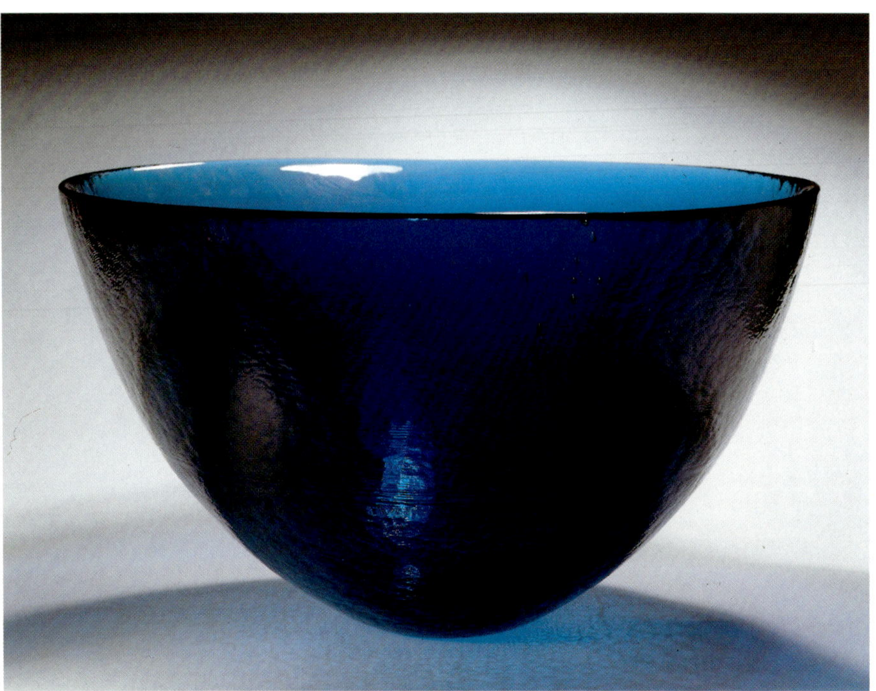

397 Fuga Bowl

Mark: *Orrefors Sven Palmqvist*
Design: Sven Palmqvist
For Orrefors Glasbruk
1962
H 31.8, ⌀ 58.3 cm

Thick-walled, dark blue glass, spun in centrifugal steel mold.

Acc. no. P 1968-6
Gift of the manufacturer

The sculptor Sven Palmqvist (1906–1984) was
associated with Orrefors as a designer from
1930 to 1973. One of his most successful
developments was the so-called Fuga technique, in which centrifugal force was used to
spin glass in rotating steel molds. See Ricke
and Gronert, *Glas in Schweden*, 1986, cat. no.
251. At first Palmqvist used it primarily for
utility glass in large series. From the mid-
1950s he created a limited number of large-
scale variations of his Fuga bowls that
impress with their sculptural power.

Lit.: –

Eda Glasbruk

Factory for art and utilitarian glassware with
decorating workshops, Eda, Sweden

Founded in Eda, Varmland, in 1833. Gerda
Strömberg (1879–1960) was artistic director
from 1927 to 1933. She was probably the
most consistent of the Swedish glass designers in the 1930s. In these years the small
glasshouse was internationally renowned.
After Gerda Strömberg left, the company fell
into decline.

398 Plate

Diamond-engraved mark on the underside of
base: *Eda '30*
Design: Gerda Strömberg, 1929/30
Execution: Eda Glasbruk, 1930
H 5.5 cm, ⌀ 40 cm

Colorless crystal glass, mold-blown and shaped.
Mat intaglio and polished cut decoration.

Acc. no. P 1988-56
Gift of Helmut Hentrich

Small series, extremely fine cutting and
engraving technique. Illustrated in the 1930
factory catalogue, model no. 3338. See Ricke
and Thor, *Schwedische Glasmanufakturen*,
1987, 417.

Lit.: Ricke and Gronert, *Glas in Schweden*,
1986, cat. no. 391

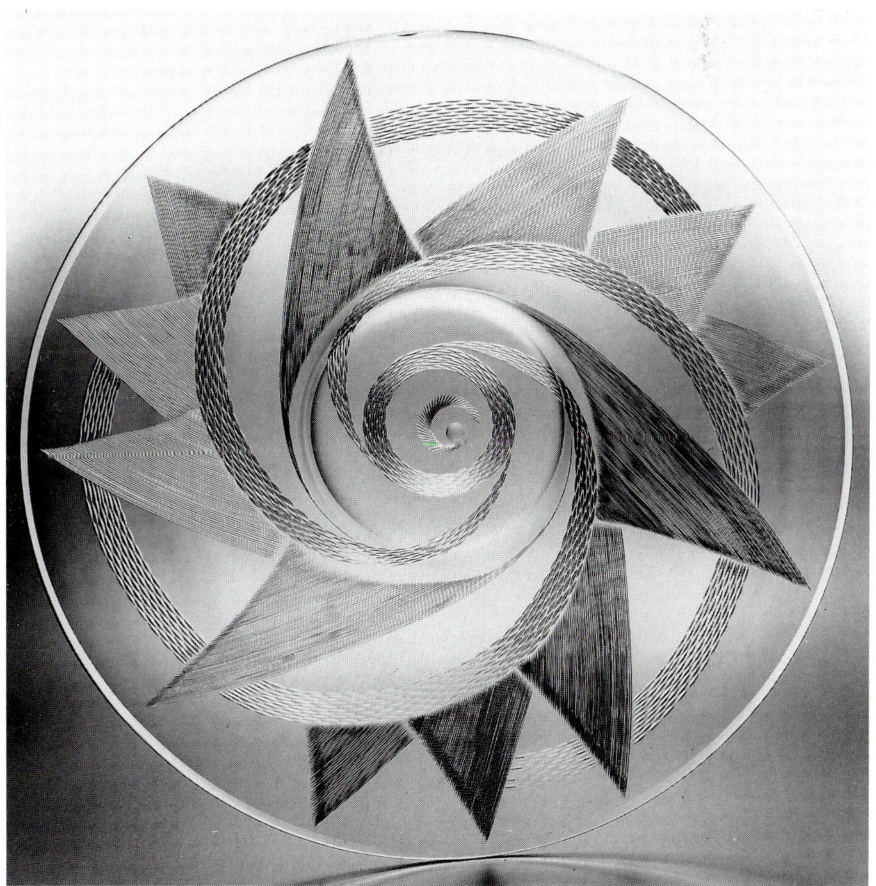

Strömbergshyttan

Art and utilitarian glass factory with decorating workshops, Hovmanstorp, Sweden

Founded in 1933 by the leading Swedish glass technician, Edvard Strömberg. His wife, Gerda Strömberg, continued the design direction she had begun at Eda. She was responsible for the factory's design up to the early 1950s. In 1979 production came to a halt.

399 Glasses of the "Sving" Service

Diamond-engraved mark on the underside of feet: *S 42*
Design: Gerda Strömberg, 1936
Execution: Strömbergshyttan
H 10.6, 15, 13.8, 11.5 cm,
⌀ 5.2, 6.3, 6.5, 11.5 cm

Colorless potash glass, mold-blown, feet worked separately and attached.

Acc. nos. L 1987-3-6
On permanent loan from the Smålands Museum Växjö

Highly regarded utility-glass design, formally pointing to the 1950s.

Lit.: Ricke and Gronert, *Glas in Schweden*, 1986, cat. no. 407

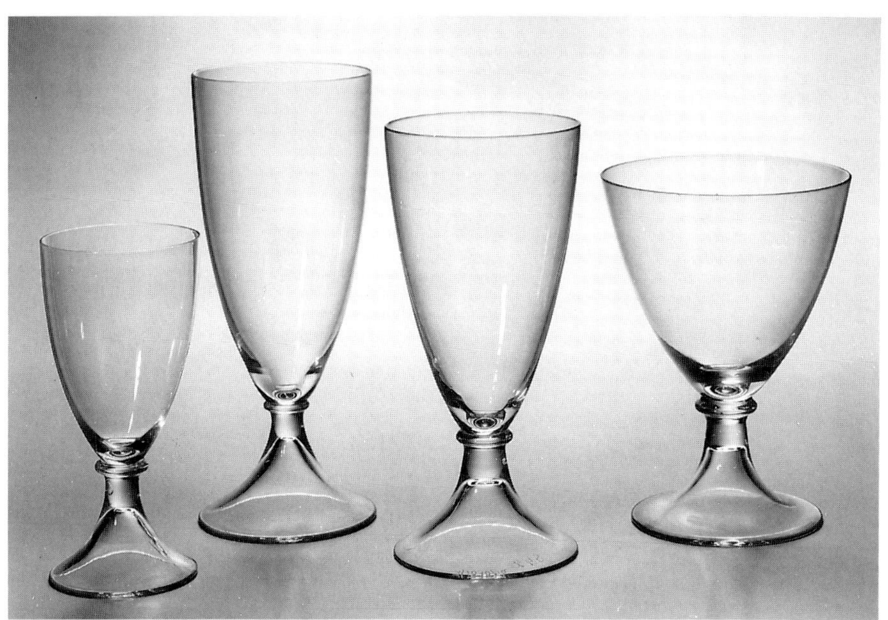

Boda Glasbruk

Art and utilitarian glass factory with decorating workshops, Boda, Sweden

Founded in 1866 by glass blowers from Kosta. International recognition after Erik Höglund (b. 1932) was hired. His designs for Boda between 1953 and 1973 gave Swedish glass art a new direction. Today the factory is merged with Kosta.

400 Vase

Engraved mark on the underside of base:
Erik Höglund 19.54
Design: Erik Höglund, 1954
Execution: Boda Glasbruk
H 25.8, ⌀ 21.4 cm

Colorless crystal glass, free-blown. Mat cut and engraved decoration, partly rough-polished: stylized heron, hippopotamus, millipede and group of people, dogs, a single man with ornamental bands and hatching.

Acc. no. P 1982-40
Acquired from the artist

Depicts a new aesthetics exploiting the expressive potential of cut structures purposely left in a rough state. For a variation of the vase see Schack, *Glaskunst*, 1976, 247, fig. 155.

Lit.: Ricke and Gronert, *Glas in Schweden*, 1986, cat. no. 445

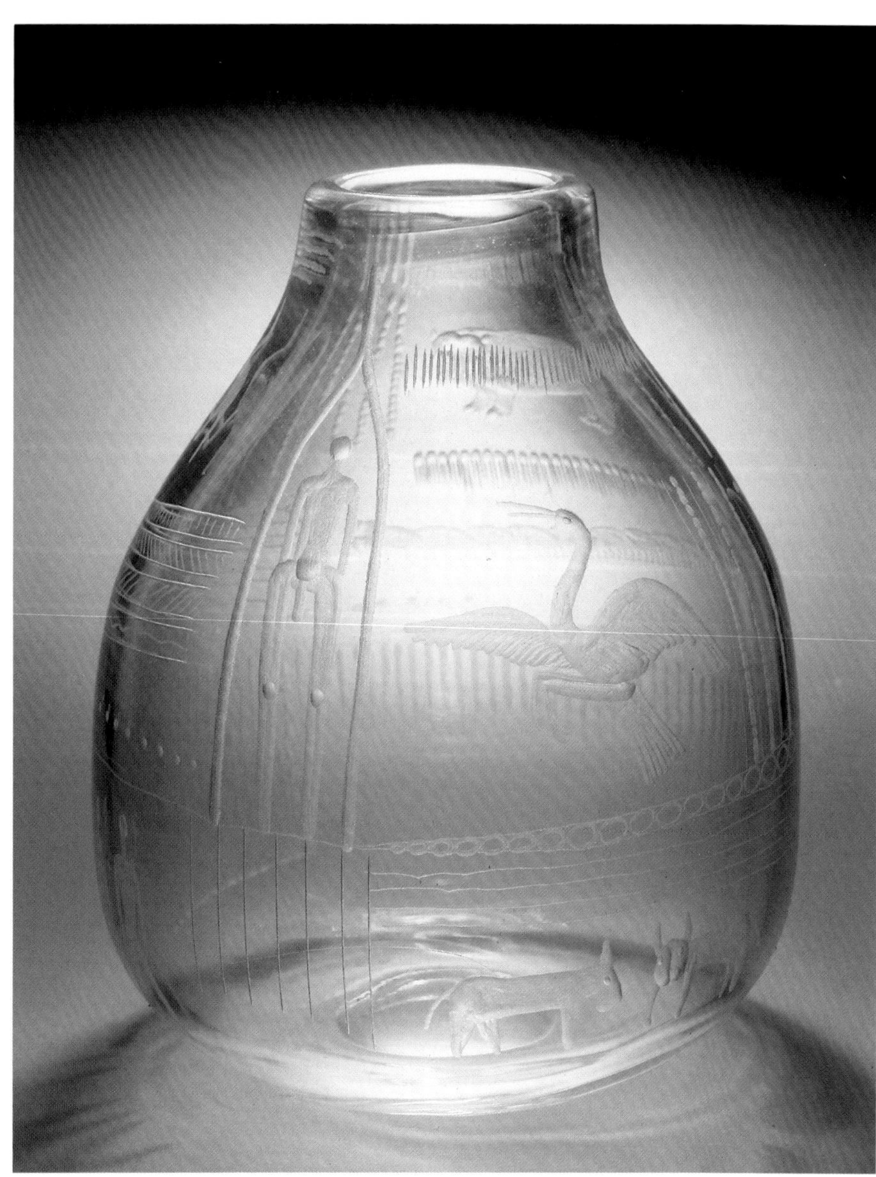

Holmegaards Glasværk

Factory for hollow glassware and decorating workshops, Næstved, Denmark

Founded in 1825. Developed into the leading Danish factory. The architect Jacob Eiler Bang (1899–1965) largely determined the production from 1926, Per Lütken (b. 1916) from 1942.

401 a–c   Glasses from the "Viol" Service

Design: Jacob Eiler Bang
1928/29
Execution: Holmegaards Glasværk, Næstved
H 8.7, 12.9, 5.6 cm, ⌀ 10.7, 8.4, 5.5 cm

Blue (a) and smoky brown (b, c) glass, optic-blown in ten (a, b) and nine-part (c) molds; shaped.

Acc. nos. P 1987-49 a-c

J. E. Bang designed utility as well as art glass. His successful "Viol" service follows the direction taken by Simon Gate and Edward Hald at Orrefors, Sandvik, from 1919. The service's appeal lies in the colored glass and animated contours, reflecting the vessels' creation in skilled craft work at the furnace. For Bang's designs and for other parts of the "Viol" service see Lassen and Schlüter, *Dansk Glas*, 1987, 21ff., figs. 31ff.

Lit.: Ricke and Gronert, *Glas in Schweden*, 1986, 36, fig. 17

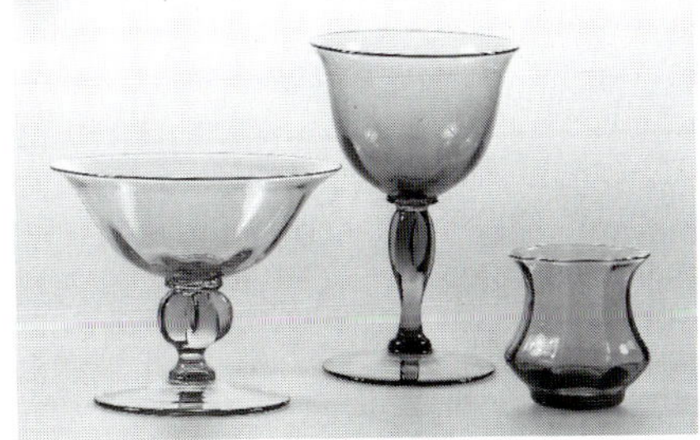

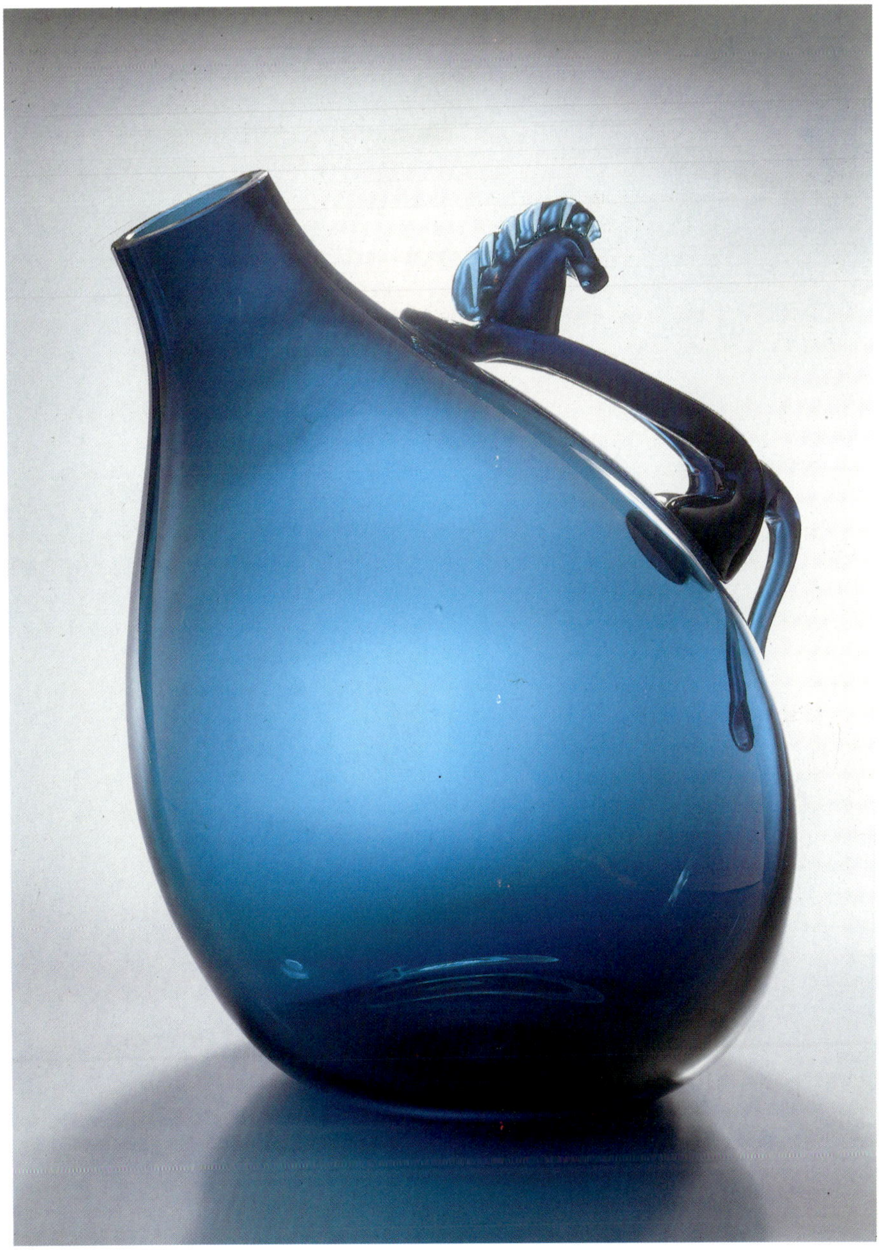

402   Pitcher

Design: Jacob Eiler Bang
1937
Execution: Holmegaards Glasværk, Næstved
H 23.7, ⌀ 19.5 cm

Massive sapphire blue glass, free-blown and shaped.

Acc. no. P 1987-42
Gift of Helmut Hentrich

Presumably designed for Holmegaard's presentation at the 1937 World Exhibition in Paris. For a model from the same series see Lassen and Schlüter, *Dansk Glas*, 1987, fig. 61.

Lit.: Ricke, *Museumsarbeit*, 1988, 76, fig. 61

403   Vase

Engraved mark on the underside of base:
HOLMEGAARD 19 PL (ligated) *55*
Design: Per Lütken
April 1955
Execution: Holmegaards Glasværk, Næstved
H 12.1, ⌀ 12.1 x 10.2 cm

Blue glass, free-blown and shaped.

Acc. no. P 1967-170
Gift of Helmut Hentrich

Per Lütken's powerful utilitarian glass designs lastingly shaped the independent appearance of Danish glass of mainly the 1950s and 1960s. For his work see Per Lütken, *Per Lütken: Glas ist Leben* (Copenhagen, 1986); for the present vase see esp. p. 92 in the appendix.

Lit.: –

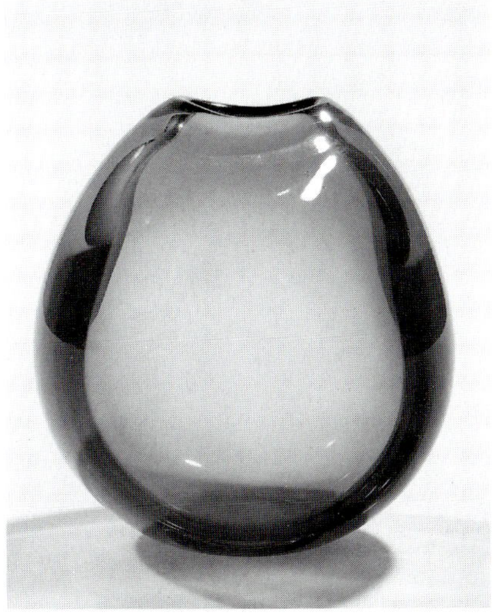

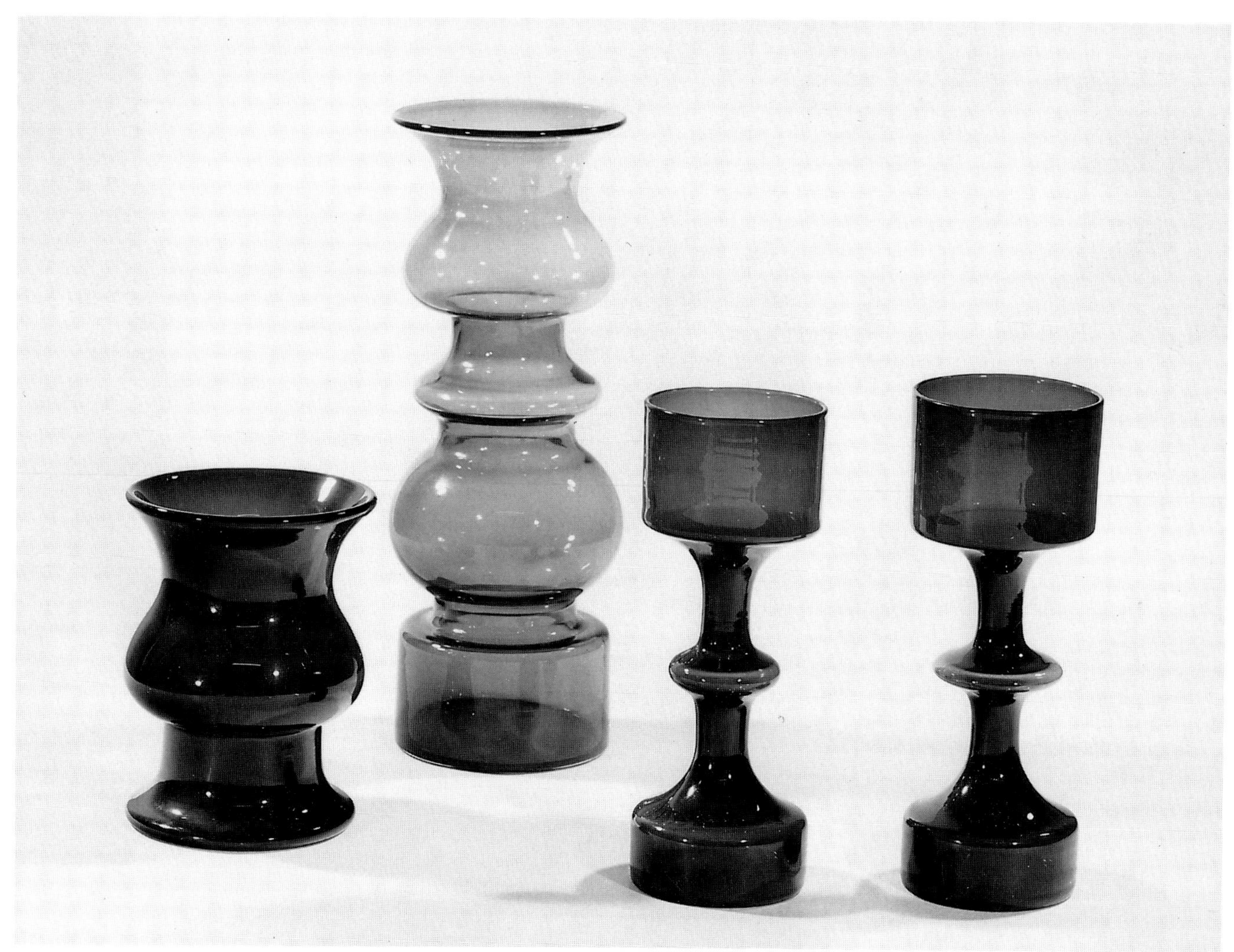

Nuutajärvi Notsjö

Hollow-glass factory with decorating work-shops, Nuutajärvi, Finland

Founded in 1793. Upswing in the 1950s through pioneering utility-glass design for large and small series as well as art glass. A definitive personality was Kaj Franck (1911–1989), who supplied the glasshouse with numerous designs between 1950 and 1980. Besides Franck, Oiva Toikka (b. 1931) was of great significance as designer from 1963, as well as Heikki Orvola (b. 1943) from 1968 and Kertuu Nurminen (b. 1943) from 1972.

404 Vase

Engraved mark on the underside of base:
K Franck   Nuutajärvi Notsjö—58
Design: Kaj Franck for Nuutajärvi
1958
H 12.1, ∅ 9.2 cm

Olive green glass, mold-blown.

Acc. no. P 1967-173
Gift of Helmut Hentrich

Lit.: –

405 Vase

Engraved mark on the underside of base:
K Franck   Nuutajärvi Notsjö—58
Design: Kaj Franck for Nuutajärvi
1958
H 24.6, ∅ 9.6 cm

Violet inner casing with a colorless cover layer, thin on the wall and thicker at the base.

Acc. no. P 1967-172
Gift of Helmut Hentrich

Lit.: –

406 a, b   Rose Vases

Engraved mark on the underside of base:
K Franck   Nuutajärvi Notsjö—58
Design: Kaj Franck for Nuutajärvi
1958
H 16.9, ∅ 6.5 cm

Gray-blue and violet glass, mold-blown.

Acc. nos. P 1967-174, 175
Gift of Helmut Hentrich

See K. Niilonen, *Finnisches Glas* (Helsinki, 1966), 58. Cat. nos. 404–6 were made following the"Kremlin Kellot" (Kremlin Bells) designs, which were introduced at the XIth Triennale in Milan. See *Die Innenarchitektur* (Essen, 1957/58): 369, and *Verrerie années 50*, 1988, 48f., nos. 3 and 4.

Lit.: –

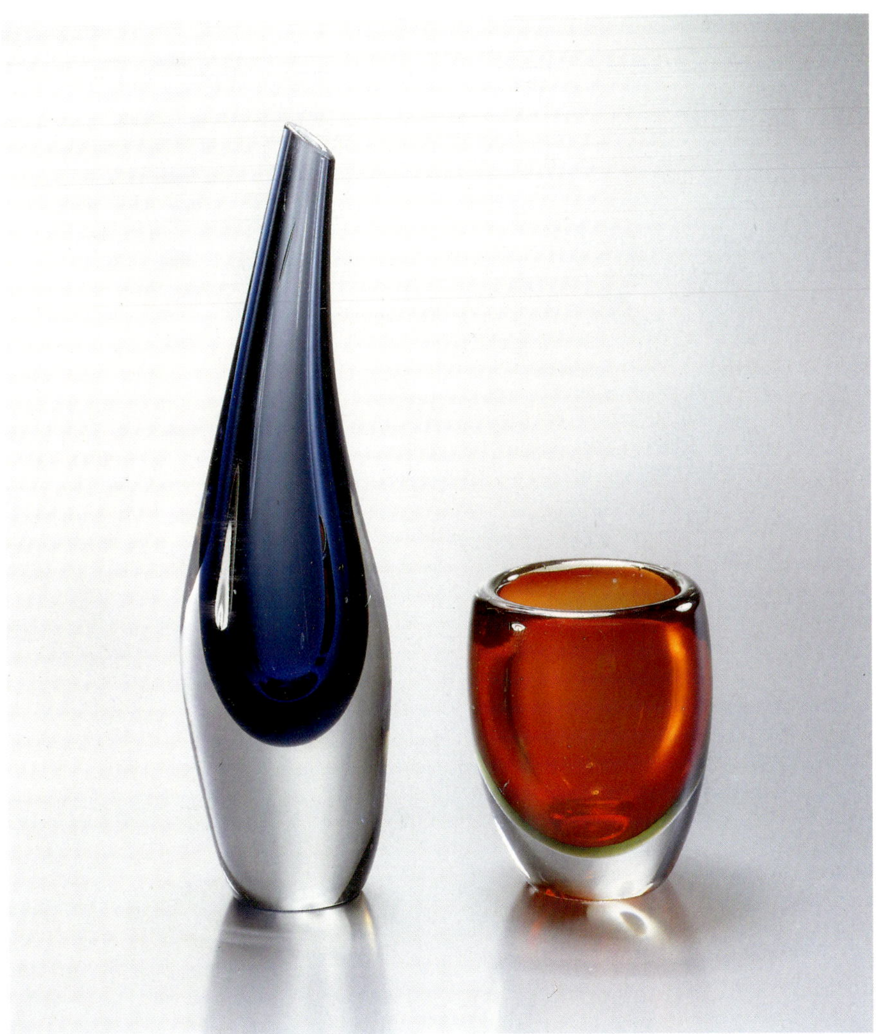

Iittala

Hollow-glass factory and decorating workshops, Iittala, Finland

Founded in 1881. From the 1940s, international success owing to fine utility glassware and exemplary design. The production was defined by Tapio Wirkkala (1915–1985) from 1947 and by Timo Sarpaneva (b. 1926) from 1950.

407 Vase

Engraved mark on the underside of base:
TAPIO WIRKKALA-IITTALA 3297
Design: Tapio Wirkkala
For Iittala
Ca. 1950/51
H 17.4, ⌀ 4.8 cm

Thick-walled, colorless glass; thin steel-blue inner casing. Mold-blown, shaped.

Acc. no. P 1966-286
Gift of Helmut Hentrich

Dating based on model numbers corresponding to those of the models for the IXth Milan Triennale; see Iittala, *Triennales*, 1987, cat. nos. 17ff. For the model itself or variations see Corning, *Glass 1959*, 1959, 124, no. 92, and Aloi and Nicodemi, *Vetri d'oggi*, 1955, 101.

Lit.: –

408 Vase

Mark: *TAPIO WIRKKALA-IITTALA*
Design: Tapio Wirkkala
For Iittala
1951
H 6.8, ⌀ 5.7 cm

Thick-walled, colorless glass, opalescent brown and transparent green inner casing. Mold-blown and shaped.

Acc. no. P 1966-287
Gift of Helmut Hentrich

For comparable glasses as early as 1949 see *Domus*, no. 4 (1949): 35. The form is similar to the small beaker-shaped vase, model no. 3507, which was shown at the IXth Milan Triennale; see Iittala, *Triennales*, 1987, cat. no. 34.

Lit.: –

409   "Iceberg" Bowl

Engraved mark on the underside of base:
TAPIO WIRKKALA 3872
Design: Tapio Wirkkala
For Iittala
1951
H 22.8, ⌀ 35.5 cm

Colorless glass, shaped in steel mold. Polished miter cuts at the edge.

Acc. no. P 1968-2
Gift of the manufacturer

Made in connection with a small series of
designs for the IXth Milan Triennale, in 1951.
See Iittala, *Triennales*, 1987, nos. 19ff. For
the present model see also Corning, *Glass
1959*, 1959, 120, no. 87.

Lit.: –

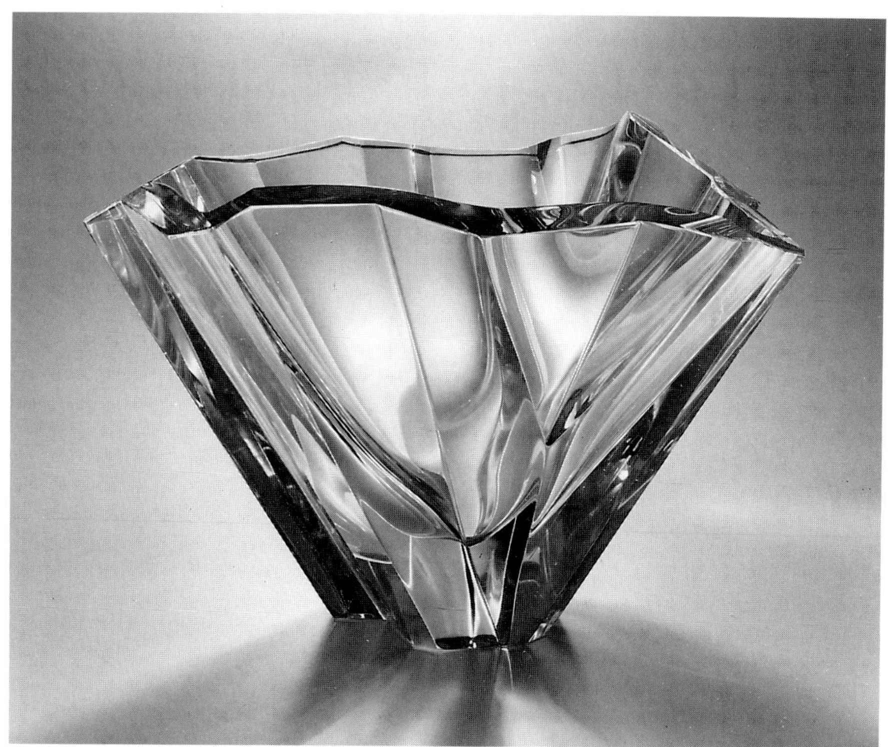

410   Glasses from the "Tapio" Service

Unsigned
Design: Tapio Wirkkala
For Iittala, model no. 2101
1954
Execution: 1980s
H 8.2, 16.9, 13.2, 8.3 cm,
⌀ 4.6, 7.4, 6.4, 7.1 cm

Colorless glass, mold-blown, shaped.

Acc. nos. P 1985-25 a-d
Acquired from the manufacturer

First shown at the Xth Milan Triennale, in
1954. See Iittala, *Triennales*, 1987, cat.
no. 75. Often referred to in the literature as
a particularly up-to-date design; see Aloi
and Nicodemi, *Vetri d'oggi*, 1955, 147; Ernst,
Moderne Gläser, 1955, e.g., fig. 3. See also
Verrerie années 50, 1988, 64f. Has been uninterruptedly produced since 1956.

Lit.: –

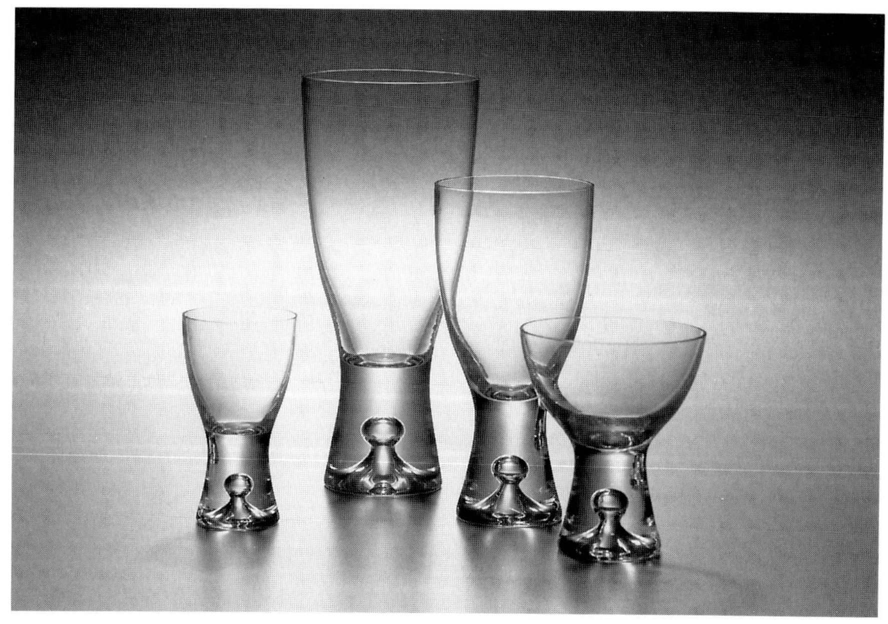

411 "Orkidea" Vase

Engraved mark on the underside of base:
TIMO SARPANEVA-IITTALA
Design: Timo Sarpaneva
For Iittala
1953
H 32, ⌀ 10.7 cm

Colorless glass, mold-blown and shaped. Cut
and polished.

Acc. no. P 1966-312
Gift of Helmut Hentrich

Introduced at the Xth Milan Triennale; see
Iittala, *Triennales*, 1987, cat. no. 56. Often
illustrated in contemporary publications; see
Aloi and Nicodemi, *Vetri d'oggi*, 1955, 115,
and Ernst, *Moderne Gläser*, 1955, 1. See also
Verrerie années 50, 1988, 58f., no. 5.
Produced from 1954 to 1972 and since 1983.

Lit.: Ricke and Gronert, *Glas in Schweden*,
1986, 41, fig. 23

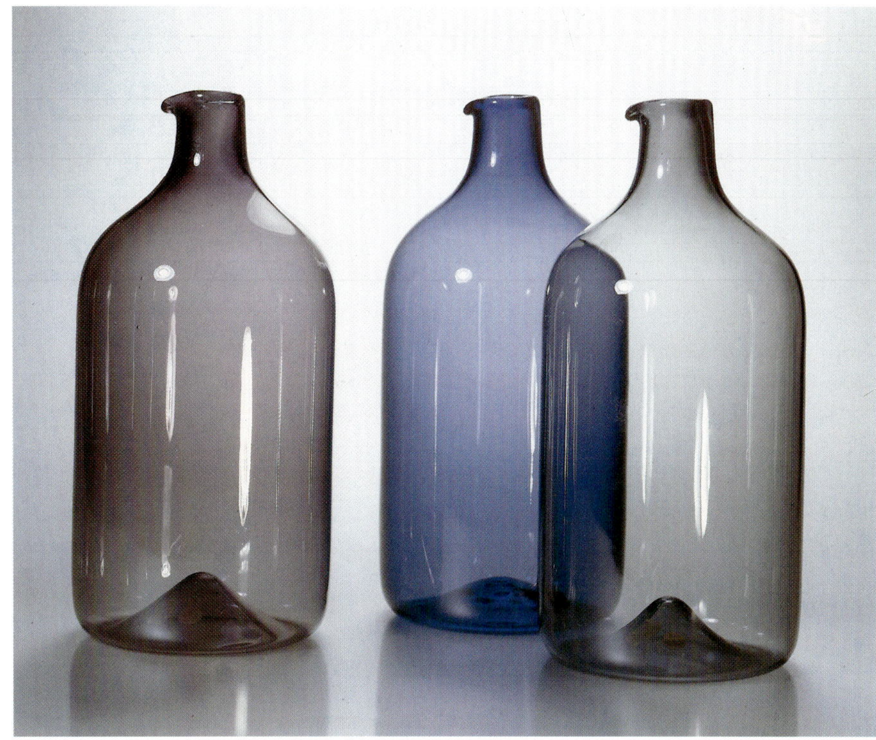

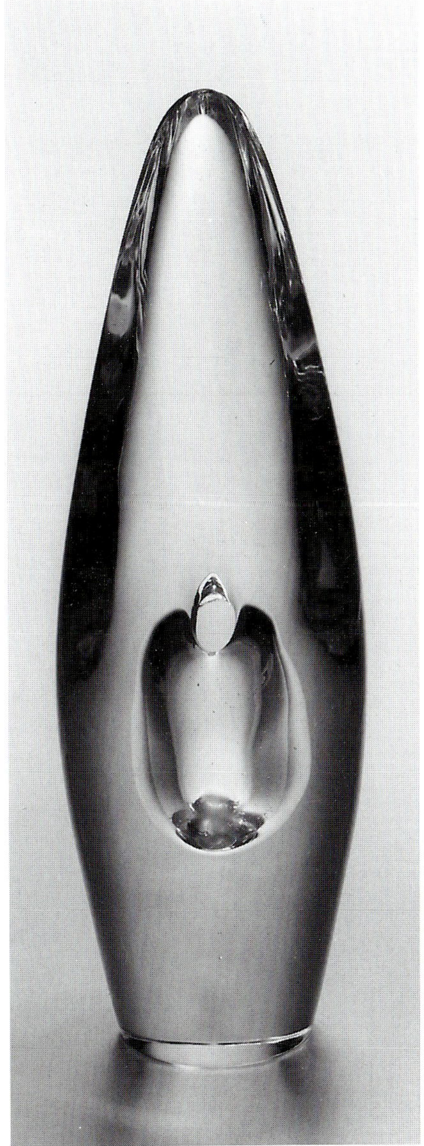

412 a–c Carafes

Engraved mark on the underside of base:
TIMO SARPANEVA IITTALA—59 (a), *—57* (b),
—58 (c)
Design: Timo Sarpaneva
For Iittala
1956
Execution: 1957–59
H 20, ⌀ 10.4 cm

Brown-violet, blue, and gray glass; mold-
blown and shaped.

Acc. nos. P 1967-150, 148, 149
Gift of Helmut Hentrich

Introduced at the XIth Milan Triennale; see
Iittala, *Triennales*, 1987, cat. no. 100. Produced from 1956 to 1964. See also *Verrerie
années 50*, 1988, 60f., cat. no. 7.

Lit.: –

The Netherlands

In contrast to Sweden and Finland, The Netherlands have a long tradition of artistic work with glass. After the period of diamond-point stippling, however, it seemed to come to an end for some time.

The new beginning, in the second decade of the twentieth century, was made with an approach similar to that in the Nordic countries. The leading factory, in Leerdam, developed a new design concept for its products, whereby, following the Werkbund example, artists played a decisive role in designing utilitarian and decorative glassware.

Andries Dirk Copier, one of the century's great designers, united at Leerdam the work of the designer and that of the glass artist on the same high level over decades. His early drinking-glass services show, in spite of all stylization typical of the times, an unmistakable individual hand (cat. no. 413). For Copier, working with the unique art object always had the function of testing new design and technical possibilities for utilitarian glass.

As at the Swedish factories, the Leerdam Unica pieces resulted from a close collaboration between glassblower and artist. Thus Copier developed in constant experimentation with the Leerdam glassmakers the multilayering crackled-glass techniques for his unique works of the 1920s. The increasingly complicated processes in the 1930s also evolved gradually.

The vases designed with subtle coloring and decorated with air bubbles embedded between the layers (cat. no. 414) show Copier at the height of his career. The powerful, simple forms of these pieces stand in contrast to the richly differentiated and atmospherically charged underwater landscapes on the inside. Besides the early Ariel glassware of Edvin Öhrström and Vicke Lindstrand for Orrefors, Copier's work belongs amongst the greatest achievements of European glass art during the late 1930s and early 1940s.

In the 1950s Leerdam showed an independent line in the designs of Floris Meydam (cat. nos. 415–17). In form and coloration it mediated between the Scandinavian and Venetian styles. The emphasis on the simple contours attests to the sophisticated design while the color of the vessel interiors is the result of chance and live matter. The smoky changes in the colored glass's appearance resulting from the oxidizing fire were deliberately incorporated into the design. Sybren Valkema also experimented with this design principle in the early 1960s.

Glasfabriek Leerdam

Hollow-glass factory with decorating workshops, Leerdam, The Netherlands

Founded in 1765. Under the direction of P. M. Cochius, the factory began a modern production in 1915 based on collaboration with artists. Pioneering designs by H. P. Berlage, K. P. C. de Bazel, and others. From 1923 to 1970 A. D. Copier (1901–1991) had a decisive influence on glass design there, particularly in the 1930s and 1940s. In the 1950s and 1960s Floris Meydam (b. 1919) and Willem Heesen (b. 1925) gradually took over his role. To this day, utility glass in large series as well as art glassware (Leerdam Unica) are made at Leerdam.

413 Glasses from the "Romanda" Service

Etched mark on the underside of base: *CL*
Design: Andries Dirk Copier
For Glasfabriek Leerdam
1924
H 10.9, 11.6, 5, 15.8, 17.3, 18.4 cm,
⌀ 6.8, 7.4, 11.9, 6.1, 7.1, 7.6 cm

Colorless glass, mold-blown and shaped.

Acc. nos. P 1986-8 a-f

The "Romanda" service is one of Copier's successful models of the 1920s. Dating based on the Leerdam factory's production catalogues. The full set is illustrated in A. van der Kley-Blekxtoon, *Leerdam glas 1878–1930* (Lochem-Ghent, 1984), 77, fig. 88.

Lit.: Ricke and Gronert, *Glas in Schweden*, 1986, 39, fig. 20

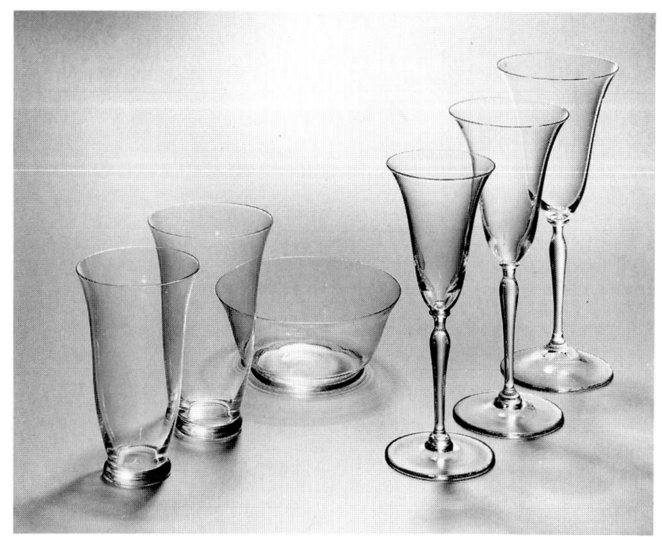

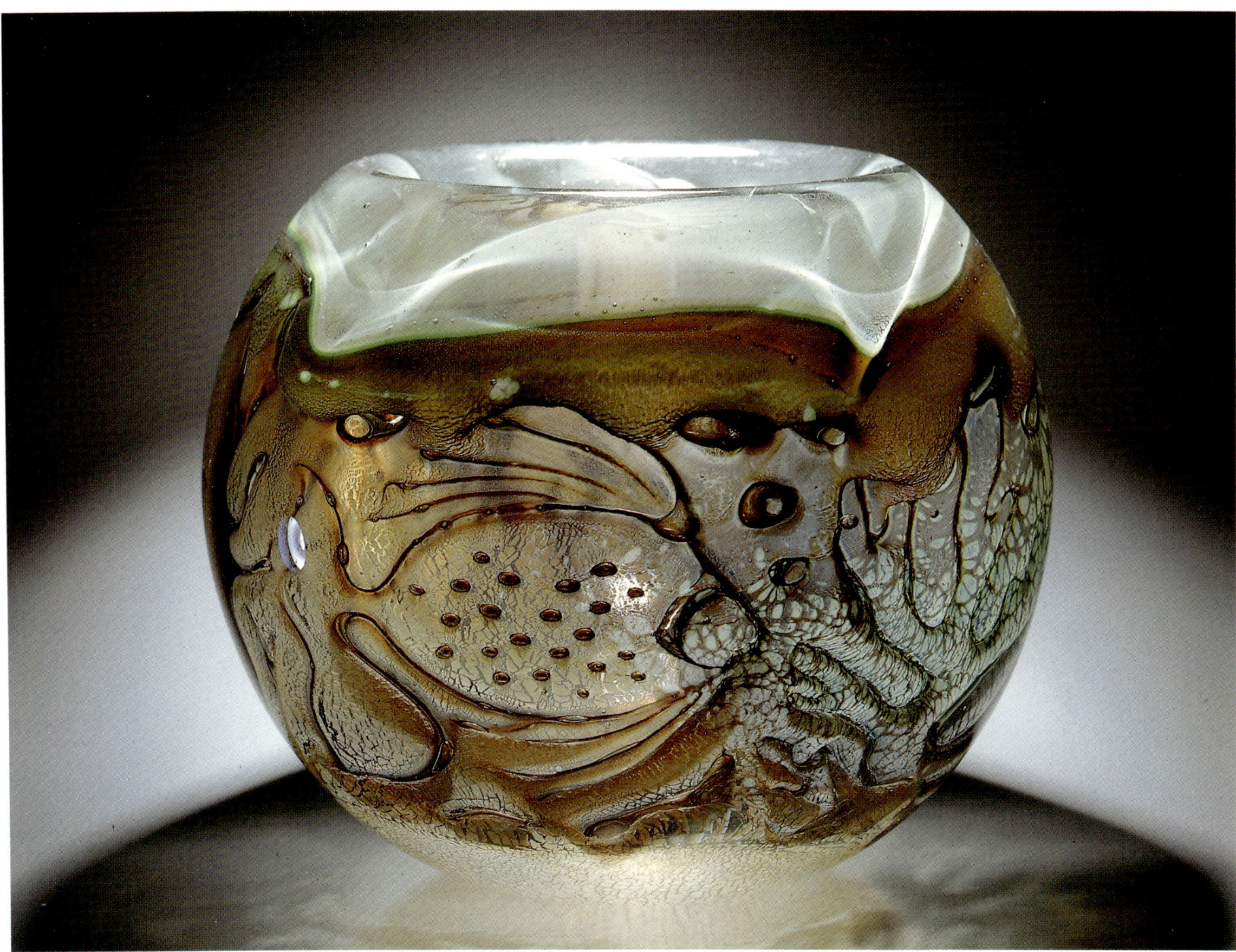

414 Vase

Diamond-engraved mark on the underside of
base: *LEERDAM UNICA V756 A D Copier*
Design: Andries Dirk Copier
For Glasfabriek Leerdam
1943
H 19.8, ⌀ 24.2 cm

On colorless ground, partial overlay in milky
turquoise and brown-violet, in part opened to
round apertures in reducing fire. Vapor-blasted with tin salt, fully blown to create crackled effect. The decoration formed by pressing
the hot glass into a mold consisting of
upright metal strips soldered in a flat box;
the embedded air was then covered with
another layer of glass creating an underglass
relief: veiltail and sea horse alternating with
eelgrass. Free-blown and shaped.

Acc. no. P 1975-115
Gift of Helmut Hentrich

Copier had experimented with figural air-bub-
ble decoration embedded in the vessel wall
from the mid-1930s. The results are similar to
the Ariel decoration used at Orrefors from
1937, but, in contrast to the Swedish works,
did not require cooling off in between or
such cold work as etching, cutting, or sandblasting. For an example of Copier's more
recent work see cat. no. 490.

Lit.: Ricke, *Leerdam*, 1977, cat. no. 98

415   Vase

Diamond-engraved mark on the underside of
base: *Leerdam Unica F Meydam MA 62*
Design: Floris Meydam
For Glasfabriek Leerdam
1957
H 9.7, ⌀ 16 cm

Opalescent green-yellow inner casing covered
in the lower zone by orange-red glass. Thick
colorless cover layer. Mold-blown; shaped.

Acc. no. P 1966-311
Gift of Helmut Hentrich

Lit.: Ricke, *Leerdam*, 1977, cat. no. 147

416   Bottle-shaped Vase

Diamond-engraved mark on the underside of
base: *Leerdam Unica F Meydam MB 892*
Design: Floris Meydam
For Glasfabriek Leerdam
1958
H 33.7, ⌀ 9 cm

Opalescent yellow inner casing with a thick,
colorless cover layer. Mold-blown; shaped.

Acc. no. P 1966-294
Gift of Helmut Hentrich

Lit.: Ricke, *Leerdam*, 1977, cat. no. 145

417   Vase

Diamond-engraved mark on the underside of
base: *Leerdam Unica F Meydam MA 2019*
Design: Floris Meydam
For Glasfabriek Leerdam
1957
H 9.6, ⌀ 9.8 cm

Red-brown inner casing drawn into a point in
the lower half, partly discolored in the fire;
on top of that a thick, colorless cover layer.
Free-blown and shaped.

Acc. no. P 1966-302
Gift of Helmut Hentrich

Cat. nos. 415–17 reflect the Netherlandish
glasshouse's response to international developments in the 1950s. Meydam's work lies
between the poles of Scandinavian and Italian glass art. For his more recent work see
cat. nos. 488 and 489.

Lit.: Ricke, *Leerdam*, 1977, cat. no. 143

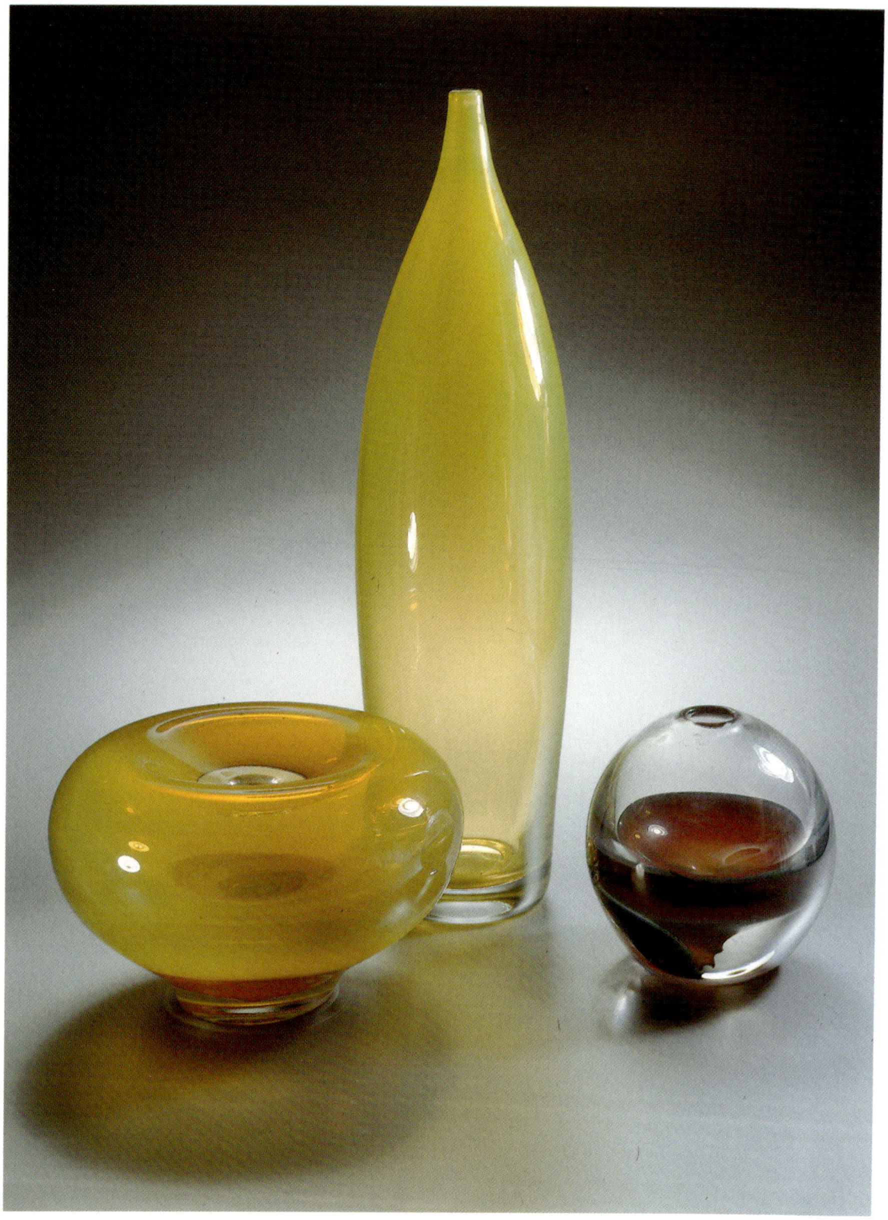

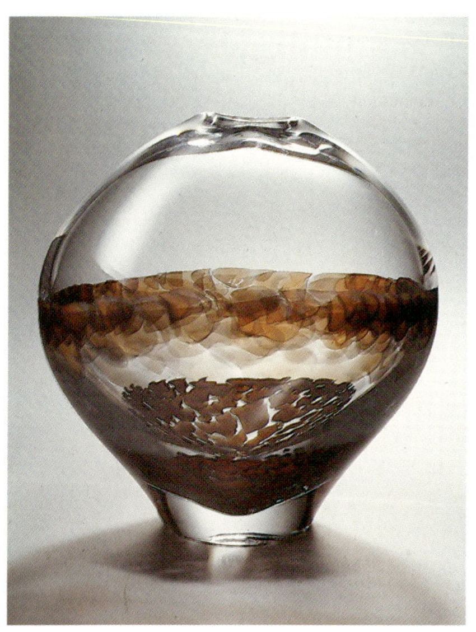

418   Vase

Diamond-engraved mark on the underside of
base: *Leerdam Unica VF 38 LL Sybren Valkema*
Design: Sybren Valkema
For Glasfabriek Leerdam
1962
Execution: L. van der Linden
H 25.7, ⌀ 26.2 x 14.5 cm

Orange-red granules embedded in colorless
ground, transformed to rust-red, ocher, gray,
and blue tones in the fire. Thick-walled,
colorless overlay. Free-blown and shaped.

Acc. no. P 1992-331
Formerly Städtische Galerie Schloss Oberhausen

S. Valkema supplied Leerdam with utilitarian
and art-glass designs in free-lance collaboration from 1948; see also cat. no. 486.

Lit.: Ricke, *Leerdam*, 1977, cat. no. 183

"New Glass"
From the 1960s to the 1990s

Just a few years ago it seemed to those concerned with glass art of the preceding three decades that the new developments around 1960 had constituted a revolution originating in North America under the motto "studio glass." In the meantime recent glass history has begun to be reevaluated and Europe's role in this development is taking clearer shape. It is becoming obvious that creative unrest and the need to hazard a new approach to glass *art* determined the thinking of progressive artists in Europe as well as in America in the 1950s. In Europe, however, this general mood showed tangible results earlier than in America. In Czechoslovakia, designers working for the large state factories began to deal intensively with non-functional, often positively sculptural, forms. This was in part an attempt to use glass to provide visual accents in an architectural context. In conventional vessel design, the familiar positions were abandoned in the 1950s as well. During these years Pavel Hlava, for instance, consistently looked beyond the vase's function as a receptacle for flowers and found artistically expressive alternatives. A case in point are his vases designed in 1959, with glass thorns pushing into the interior (cat. no. 423). He later applied this creative principle to his sculptures (cat. no. 424). At the same time Václav Cigler (cat. nos. 427, 428) worked on cut glass sculptures that he conceived as a means of transforming the environment visually. His works were emulated avidly in the 1970s, albeit in the context of other artistic ideas (cat. nos. 429, 430).

René Roubíček caused considerable excitement at the 1958 World Exhibition in Brussels with his large-scale sculptures made of free-blown and shaped glass pieces. On a small scale he also created objects having little in common with the straight and functional glass from the Czech factories (cat. nos. 421, 422).

Roubíček's playful use of the material—his humorous approach to design not yet marked by a demand for "high art"—recalls the approach taken by certain Murano glass artists of the 1950s, such as Fulvio Bianconi.

Besides the technically complicated colorful dishes and vases, which have largely shaped our idea of glass from this period, numerous experimental works taking new directions were created in Venice. Raoul Goldoni from Croatia realized non-functional sculptural concepts in glass together with Alfredo Barbini, and, from 1958, with Livio Seguso (cat. nos. 443, 444).

In Sweden, Erik Höglund strove for simplicity and originality. As early as the mid-1950s, he categorically rejected his country's famous flawless crystal in favor of thick-walled glass interspersed with bubbles, which he used in his utility-glass models for the Boda Glasshouse. Their heaviness and force stand in striking contrast to the light and elegant works designed by Nils Landberg for Orrefors, for instance. Höglund's glass art designs attest to a similar approach (cat. no. 400).

This list could easily be continued. In The Netherlands, for example, Andries Dirk Copier took completely new sculptural approaches with his one-off pieces, whereas Floris Meydam, Willem Heesen, and Sybren Valkema began to call traditional shapes into question. Erwin Eisch in Frauenau, Bavarian Forest, however, was most radical and consistent in his eschewal of the formal idiom of the 1950s (cat. nos. 449, 450). Like no other European glass artist he rejected the traditional glass vessel outright, freeing the material of incrustations, which he considered sterile and meaningless. Eisch made glass the expressive bearer of an artistic message. Transparency, for decades an indispensable and prominent feature of glass, seemed to him more of a distraction and a hindrance. An opaque, usually deep black glass melt became his material of choice. Instead of transparency and the optical weightlessness of colorless crystal, its characteristics during melting and its conduct during the process of solidifying from the fluid aggregate state were central to his design. Glass became a sculptural medium; beyond that, it allowed the artist to tell stories, to address emotions and compulsions. And in destroying familiar glass types the artist purposely invited controversy. "Provocation of form" is how Eisch has described his work (cat. no. 451).

Harvey Littleton's meeting Erwin Eisch during one of his European study trips in 1962 proved to be fruitful for subsequent developments. This occurred just before Littleton's historic seminar in Toledo, marking the beginning of the American studio-glass movement. Thus the link was forged between those forces pushing for something new in Europe and the ideas that at the same time began to be formulated in the United States. The subsequent history of modern glass art is one of a constant exchange of ideas, concepts, educational models, and technical knowledge. It was an exchange between Europe and America, in which America doubtlessly conveyed essential impulses to the Old World.

As in the United States, the 1960s in Europe remained primarily a time of experimentation and battling with technology. Possibilities opened up by working with hot glass at studio-glass furnaces—America's decisive and revolutionary innovation. In Europe, however, these new avenues were explored only very hesitantly. Studio furnaces were set up only by Erwin Eisch in Frauenau, by Volkhard Precht in the former German Democratic Republic (without knowledge of American developments), by Åsa Brandt in Sweden, and at a few academies and specialized schools. Artistically significant and pioneering works came from artists who had their pieces carried out in the traditional manner, at large glasshouses, or who continued to develop the traditional "cold" techniques.

The center of this type of work was—as it is today—the region of former Czechoslovakia. Building on centuries of tradition and supported by an excellent state educational system, highly talented artists devoted themselves to glass design. In contrast to the fine arts, in which the Eastern European states played no particular role in international developments, in glass art a socialist country was able to take the lead for Europe.

This development, however, did not yet occur in public. As in America, the breakthrough did not come until the 1970s. Museums began to organize major exhibitions in 1972, and it was only from this time that the rich landscape of galleries, which are an indispensable aspect of the glass scene in Europe today, emerged.

It is typical that some of the outstanding artist personalities of the 1970s were formerly designers at glass factories. This reflects the crisis in which European glass manufacturers found themselves during these years. In a radical process of restructuring prompted by increasing automation and wages, over 60 percent of European glasshouses working manually lost their basis of subsistence and had to close. Surviving firms were increasingly forced to use their designers to fulfill market demands instead of developing new ideas. It is understandable that particularly the good designers could not accept being mere instruments of profit strategies, instead of realizing— as had previously been the case—their own ideas in collaboration with the sales departments.

Not least because of these migrations, the number of studio furnaces in Europe increased during the 1970s. On an international level, however, their role in the general artistic development was by this time dwindling rapidly. It was acknowledged that the free and playful handling of the hot material did not suffice to fulfill the criteria for creating a work of art. Many of the young artists who approached glass with big hopes had to learn by experience that it takes years of intense effort to command the techniques of hot work, to master the material, and to make it a willing medium through which to express their ideas. Thus the workshops for cold and warm techniques became much more important for the future: for cutting and engraving, kiln forming in modified ceramic kilns, mosaic glass, painting on glass, *pâte-de-verre*,

and other techniques of fusing glass in a mold. The greatest works in glass were made by these processes and it is certainly no coincidence that these types of design reflect the working methods of the glass tradition in Europe. The impulse of the American studio-glass movement encouraged Europeans to embrace the new approaches more energetically. At the same time it made European artists aware of their inherited strengths. Meanwhile work made directly at the furnace has lost much of its significance in the United States as well.

Glass art today is astonishingly diverse. In spite of obvious internationalizing tendencies, the individual countries have retained their identities and, depending on the dynamics and the strength of their concepts, influence one another.

Japan has increasingly distinguished itself as a new force. Linking national traditions with influences from abroad, Japanese glass art has a special appeal (cat. nos. 545–58). Australia's image is also becoming more distinctive (cat. nos. 543, 544).

The goal of the 1960s to create a breakthrough in glass design has for the most part been achieved. A large number of works created today cannot be judged with the conventional criteria for evaluating crafts, for in concept and artistic quality they answer to the same demands made on sculpture. The material's intrinsic value, however, and the large proportion of complicated techniques used to make it continue to stand in the way of perceiving glass sculpture as an integral part of major contemporary art movements. In the context of modern art glass essentially leads a life of its own.

Czechoslovakia:
The Czech and Slovakian Republics

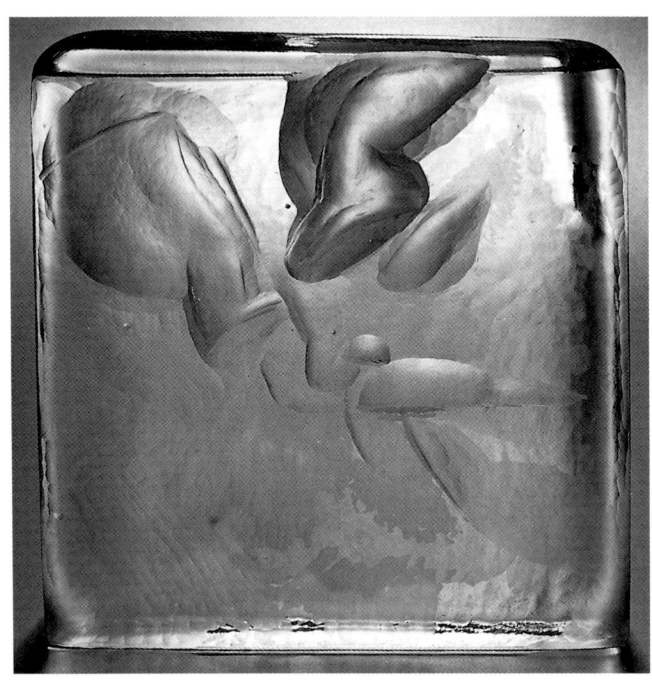

Jiří Harcuba
(b. 1928)

Education: Apprenticeship as glass engraver
at the Harrachov Glassworks; Glass School,
Nový Bor (Haida)
Lives and works in Prague

419 Vessel Object

Engraved mark on the underside of base:
J Harcuba 1958
1958
H 6.9, L 20.3, D 13.3 cm

Blown and shaped. Ground mat.

Acc. no. P 1990-379
Acquired from the artist

Blank from Moser, Carlsbad.
Created for the 1958 World Exhibition in
Brussels. A second, polished version exists.

Lit.: Ricke, *New Glass Europe*, 1991, 17

420 Portrait of Fyodor Dostoyevsky

Engraved mark above the standing base:
"Dostojevský" JHarcuba 1990
1990
H 20, W 20, D 4 cm

Colorless glass. Cut and engraved. Surface
and reverse have in part a carved texture.

Acc. no. LP 1992-15
On permanent loan from the Stadt-Sparkasse
Düsseldorf
Acquired at the exhibition "New Glass in
Europe"

Lit.: Ricke, *New Glass Europe*, 1991,
cat. no. 21

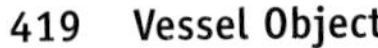

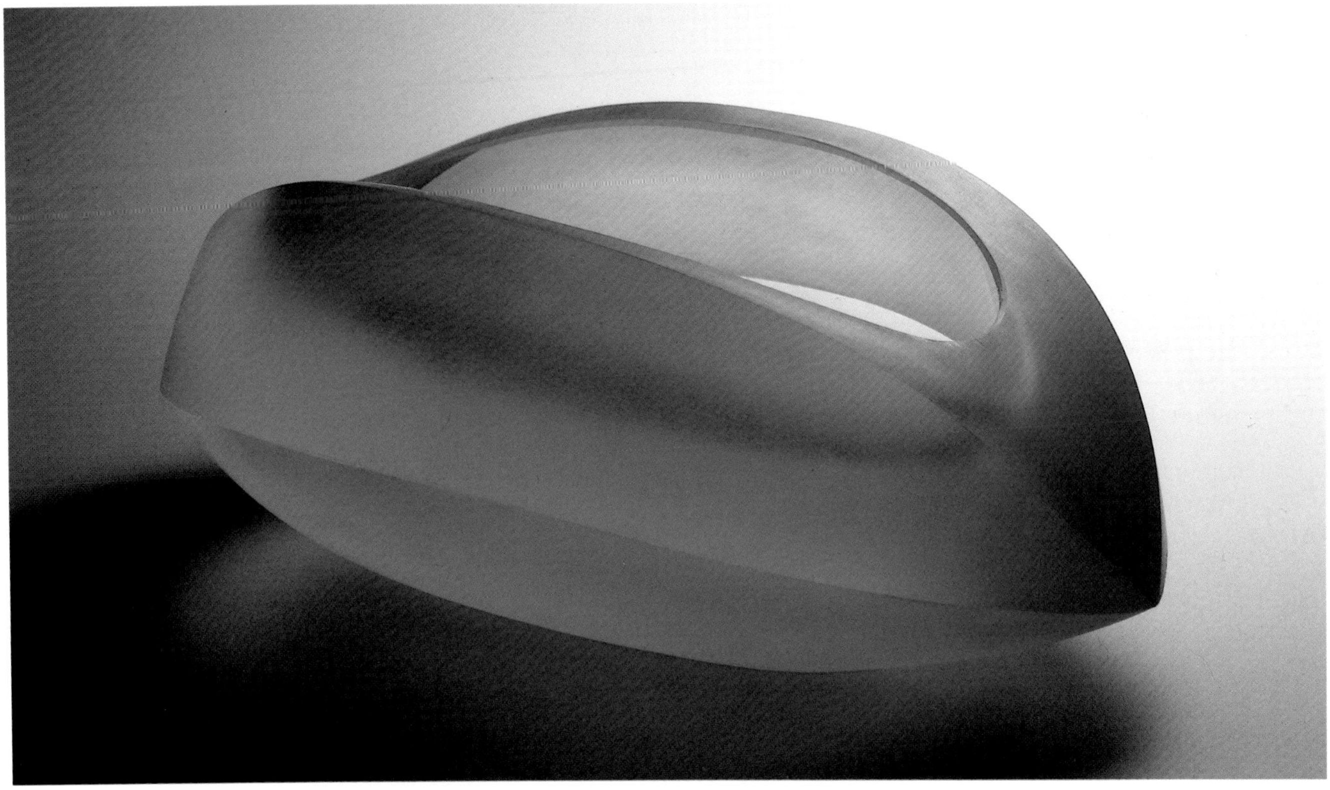

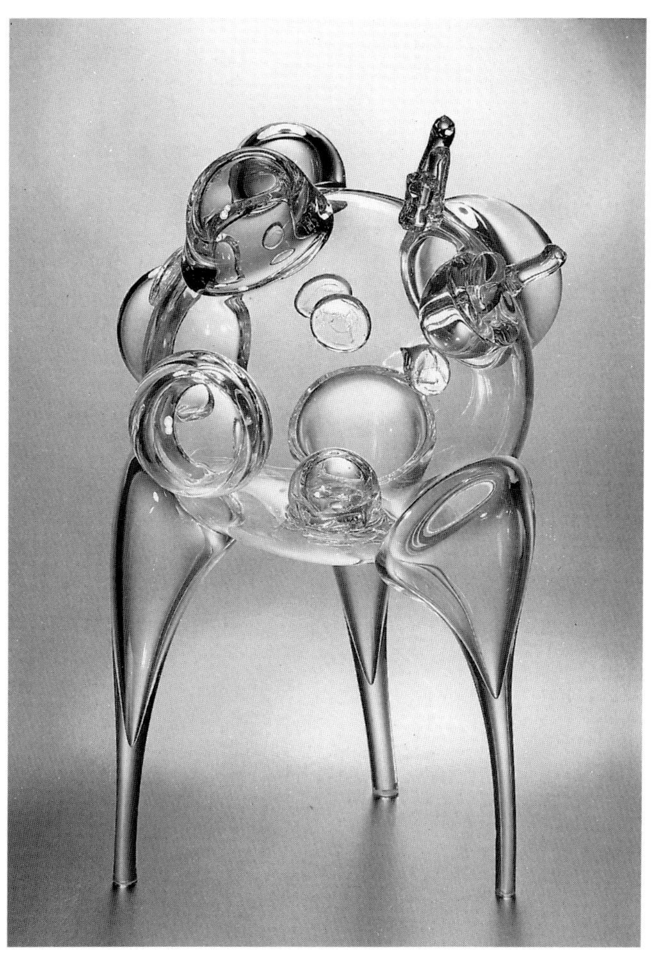

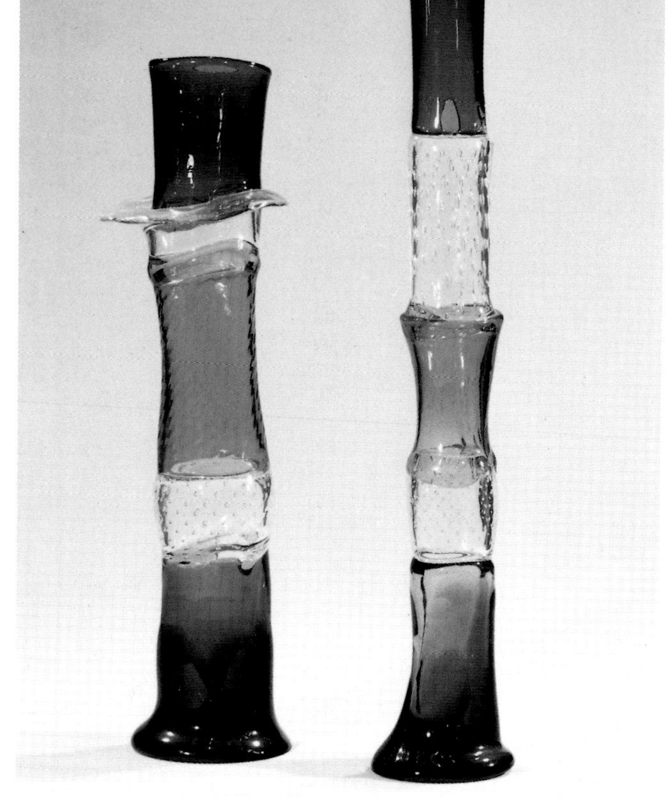

René Roubíček
(b. 1922)

Education: Academy of Applied Arts, Prague
Lives and works in Prague and Kamenický
Šenov (Steinschönau)

421 "Striding Kohlrabi II"

Diamond-engraved mark on the underside of
base: *R Roubíček*
1959
H 34.5, ⌀ 26.8 cm

Colorless crystal glass. Free-blown and
shaped.

Acc. no. P 1988-24

Part of a small series of one-off pieces; see,
for example, Schack, *Glaskunst*, 1976, 268,
fig. 205; *NG*, no. 1 (1983): 7, fig. 1; Frantz,
Contemporary Glass, 1989, 25.

Lit.: Ricke, *Museumsarbeit*, 1988, 79, fig. 72

422 a, b Vase Objects

Diamond-engraved mark on the underside of
base: *Roubíček 1973*
1973
H 52.4 and 63.3, ⌀ feet 12.2 and 10.5 cm

Fused from preformed, free-blown, and
shaped pieces. Base ground flat.

Acc. nos. P 1986-57 a, b
Gift of Helmut Hentrich
Acquired at the exhibition "Böhmisches Glas
der Gegenwart"

Executed by Josef Rozinek at the Škrdlovice
Glassworks. For a similar, but later, piece see
Schmitt, *Zürich* 1, 1992, cat. no. 156.

Lit.: Adlerová, *Böhmisches Glas Gegenwart*,
1973, nos. 122, 123

Pavel Hlava
(b. 1924)

Education: Glass School, Železný Brod (Eisenbrod), and Academy of Applied Arts, Prague
Lives and works in Prague

423 Vase

Diamond-engraved mark on the underside of
base: *PH* (ligature in circle)
1959
H 35.8, ⌀ 8.2 cm

Glass ranging in hue from red to brown,
mold-blown; freely made insertions.

Acc. no. P 1990-376

Small series. Important design, on the borderline between vessel and object. See Ricke,
New Glass Europe, 1991, 19.

Lit.: –

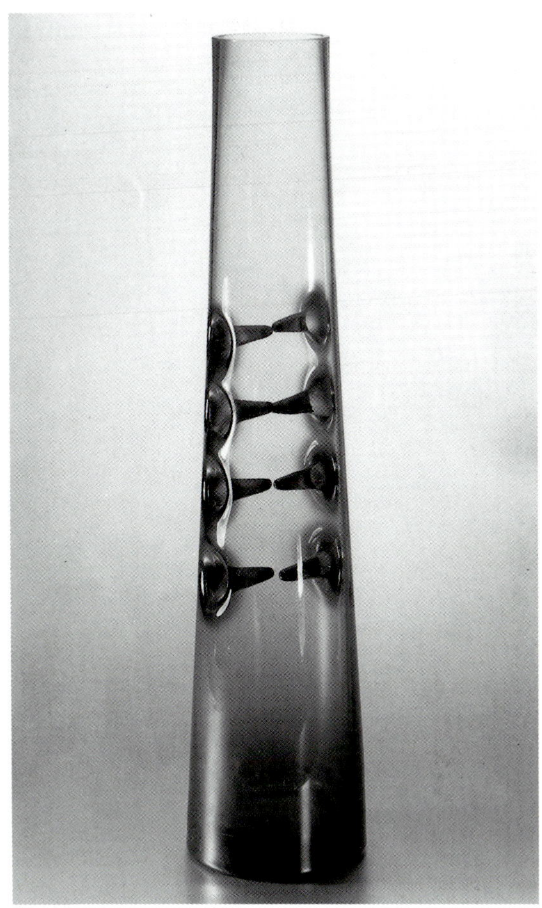

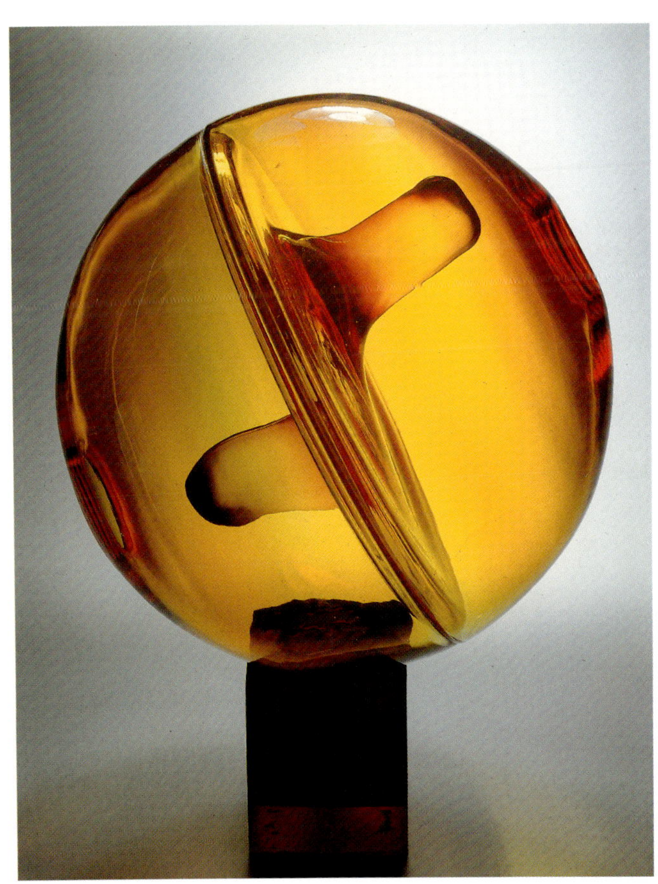

424 Sculpture

Engraved mark on the underside of pedestal:
PH (ligated) *Pavel Hlava Czechoslowakia*
1972
H 37.6, ⌀ 29 cm

Crystal glass. Red inner casing, "garnet"
glass. Mold-blown and shaped. Assembled
from two separately made pieces. Laminated
to cut and polished pedestal.
Executed by T. Lenc at Český Křištál, Chlum u
Třeboně.

Acc. no. P 1975-48
Acquired at the exhibition "Böhmisches Glas
der Gegenwart"

Lit.: Adlerová, *Böhmisches Glas Gegenwart*,
1973, cat. no. 24

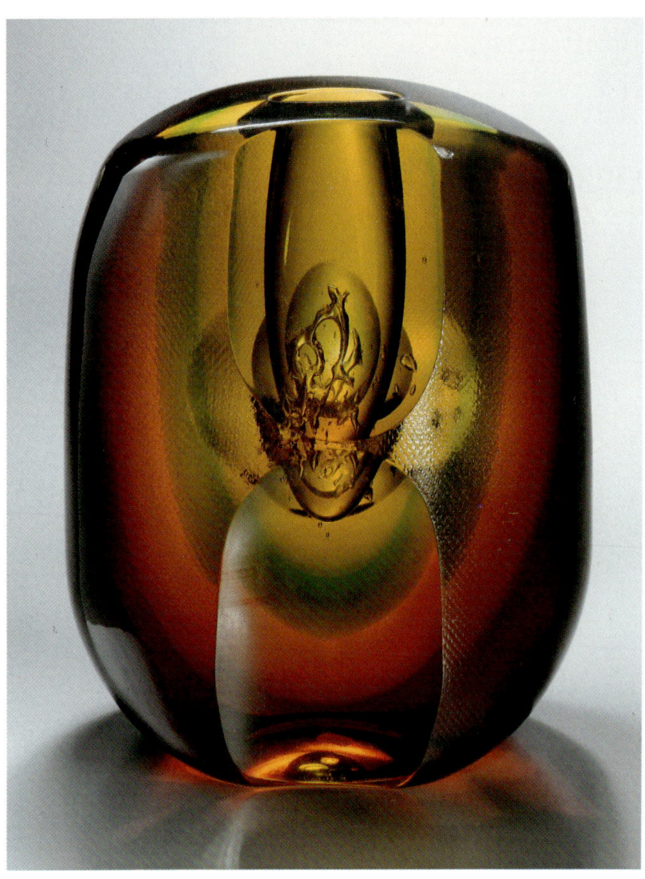

Kapka Toušková
(b. 1940)

Education: Secondary School for Fine Arts and
Academy of Fine Arts in Sofia, Bulgaria,
Academy of Applied Arts, Prague
Lives and works in Prague

426   Object

Unsigned
1973
H and ⌀ 50.5 cm

Crystal glass with partial overlays. Mold-
blown and freely shaped. Carried out by
F. Danihelka at Užitkové sklo, Nový Bor.

Acc. no. P 1974-24
Acquired at the exhibition "Böhmisches Glas
der Gegenwart"

For another example from this one-off series
see Schack, *Glaskunst*, 1976, 272, fig. 213,
and A. Adlerová, *Contemporary Bohemian
Glass* (Prague, 1979), 47.

Lit.: Adlerová, *Böhmisches Glas Gegenwart*,
1973, cat. no. 14; Ricke, *Ausgewählte Werke*,
1980, 30; J. Schou-Christensen, "Der grosse
Aufbruch: Europäische Glaskunst seit 1945,"
NG, no. 1 (1980): 11, fig. 22

Vladimír Jelínek
(b. 1934)

Education: Glass School, Kamenický Šenov
(Steinschönau), and Academy of Applied Arts,
Prague
Lives and works in Prague

425   Vase Object

Diamond-engraved mark on the underside of
base: *V. Jelínek*
1970
H 21.2, ⌀ 18.1 x 11.5 cm

Crystal glass. Several overlays, embedded air.
Impressed grid pattern. Cut and polished.

Acc. no. P 1986-61
Gift of Helmut Hentrich

See also Adlerová, *Böhmisches Glas
Gegenwart*, 1973, 46ff., and A. Adlerová,
Contemporary Bohemian Glass (Prague, 1979),
33.

Lit.: –

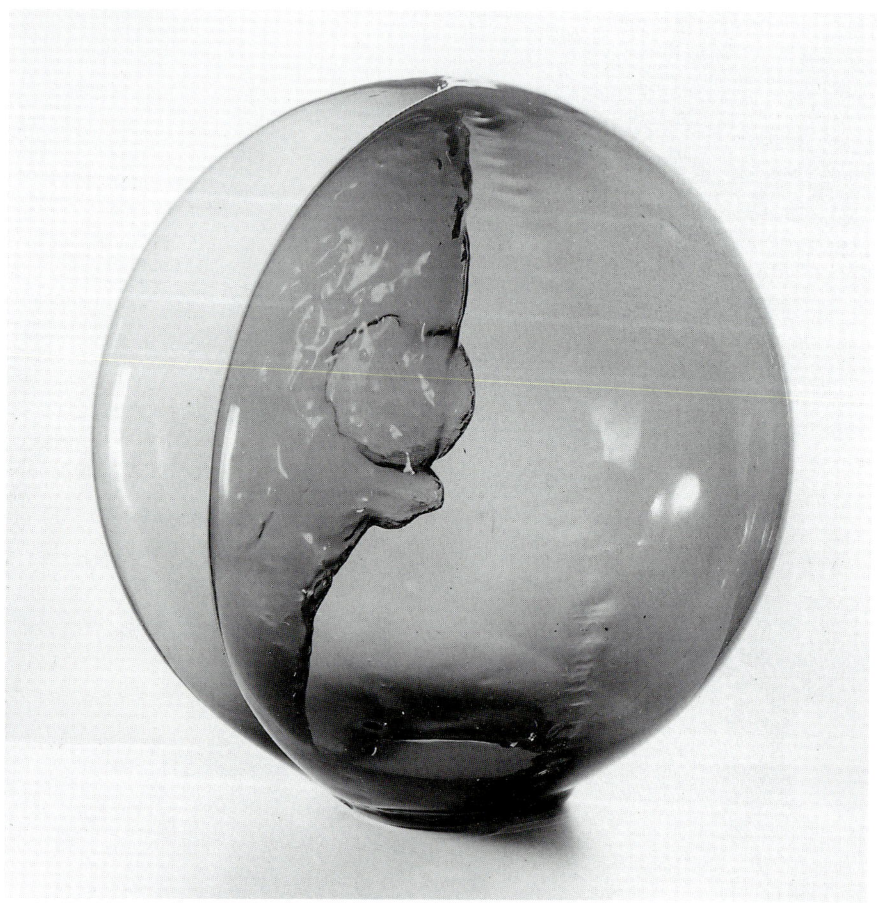

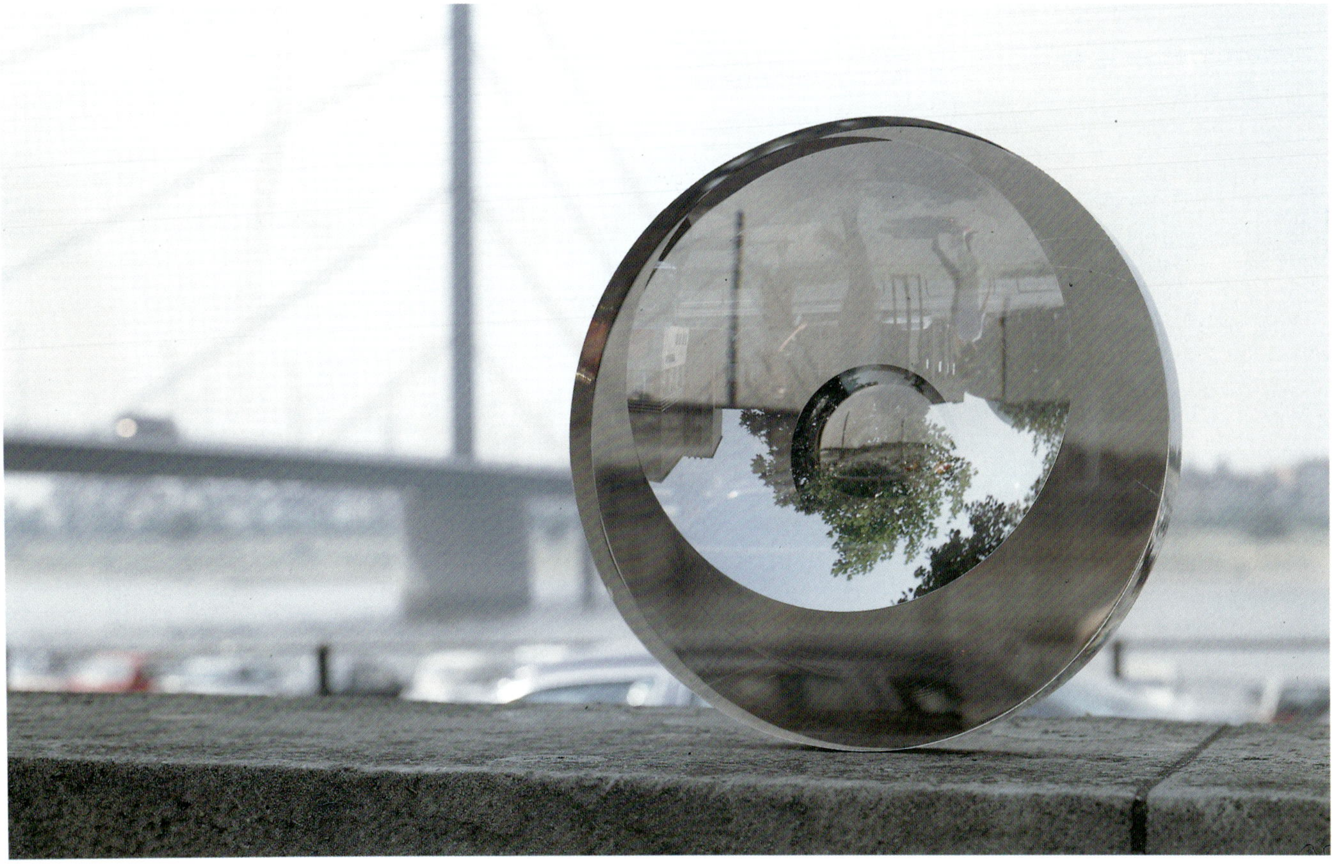

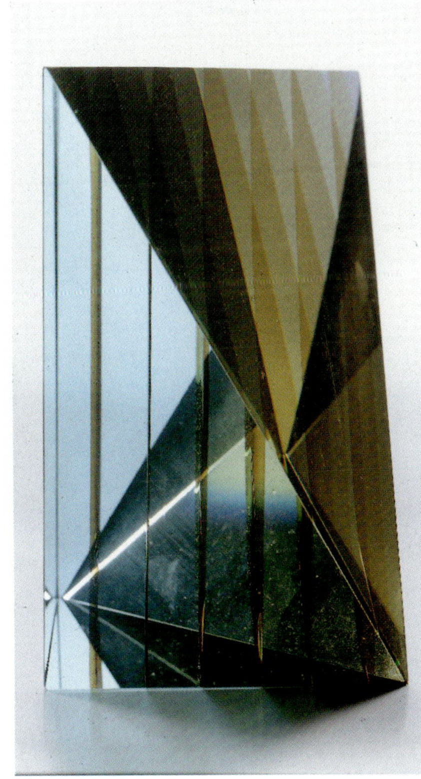

Václav Cigler
(b. 1929)

Education: Glass School, Nový Bor (Haida),
and Academy of Applied Arts, Prague
Lives and works in Prague

427   Object

Unsigned
1972, design 1967
H and ⌀ 34.7, D 5.2 cm

Lead glass. Cut and polished. Vacuum metalized.

Acc. no. P 1975-50
Acquired at the exhibition "Böhmisches Glas der Gegenwart"

See *Glasrevue* 12 (1968): 401.

Lit.: Adlerová, *Böhmisches Glas Gegenwart*,
1973, cat. no. 8; Ricke, *Licht. Form. Gestalt*,
1980, cat. no. 15

428   Object

Unsigned
Design 1978, execution 1980
13 x 13 x 7.7 cm

Constructed of fused plate glass (electrofloat
glass) vapor-blasted with gold on one side.
Sawn, cut, and polished.

Acc. no. P 1980-4
Acquired at the exhibition "Licht. Form.
Gestalt"

Lit.: Ricke, *Licht. Form. Gestalt*, 1980,
cat. no. 40

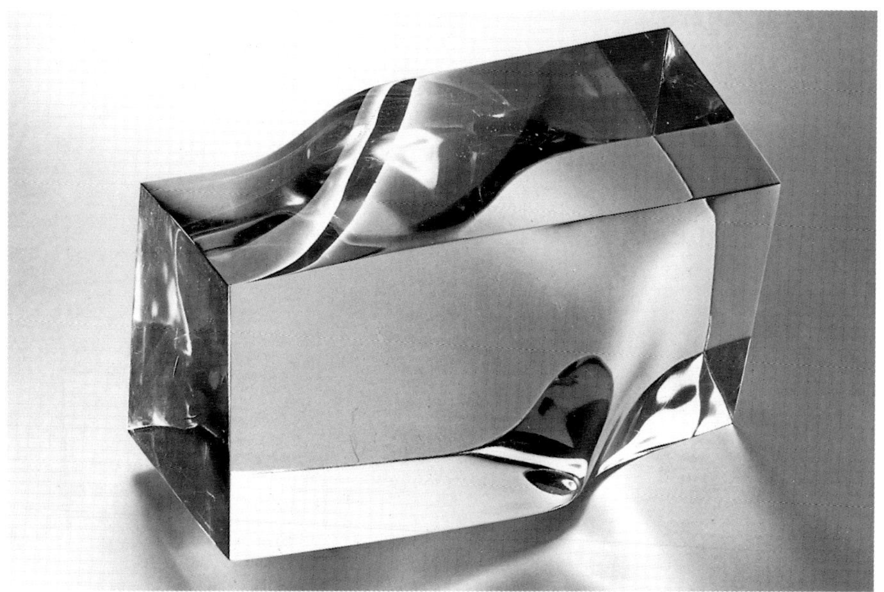

Marian Karel
(b. 1944)

Education: School for Glass and Jewelry,
Jablonec nad Nisou (Gablonz), and Academy
of Applied Arts, Prague
Lives and works in Prague

429   "Twisted Block"

Unsigned
1973
H 16, W 23, block 12.3 x 9.5 cm

Lead glass. Cut and polished.

Acc. no. P 1974-25
Acquired at the exhibition "Böhmisches Glas
der Gegenwart"

Lit.: Adlerová, *Böhmisches Glas Gegenwart*,
1973, cat. no. 54; Ricke, *Licht. Form.
Gestalt*, 1980, cat. no. 48

Aleš Vašíček
(b. 1947)

Education: Glass School, Železný Brod (Eisenbrod), and Academy of Applied Arts, Prague
Lives and works free-lance in Prague

430   Object

Diamond-engraved mark in circular form on
top, where the various parts intersect: *ALEŠ
VAŠIŽEK 1980*
1980
H 15, ∅ 30 cm

Lead glass. Three parts assembled to form
hemisphere. Not laminated. Cut and polished.

Acc. no. P 1981-290

Acquired at the exhibition "Licht. Form.
Gestalt"

Lit.: Ricke, *Licht. Form. Gestalt*, 1980,
cat. no. 106

František Vizner
(b. 1936)

Education: Glass School, Železný Brod (Eisenbrod), and Academy of Applied Arts, Prague
Lives and works in Škrdlovice

431   Plate Object

Unsigned
1978, design mid-1970s
H 3, ∅ 38 cm

Topazine crystal glass. Cut, sandblasted,
etched.

Acc. no. P 1981-291
Acquired at the exhibition "Licht. Form.
Gestalt"

For further examples of this object made in a
small series see, for example, Coburg I, 1977,
cat. no. 522, and Corning, *New Glass*, 1979,
cat. no. 259.

Lit.: Ricke, *Licht. Form. Gestalt*, 1980,
cat. no. 112

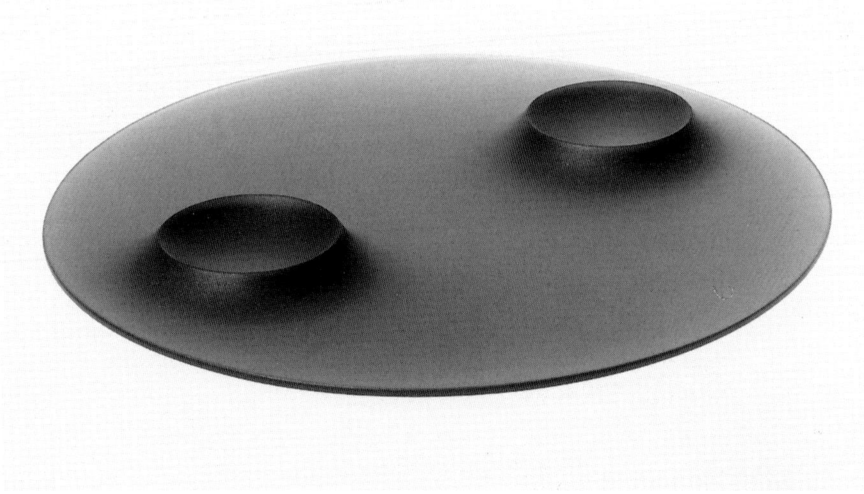

Ivo Roszypal
(b. 1942)

Education: Glass School, Kamenický Šenov
(Steinschönau), and Academy of Applied Arts,
Prague
Lives and works in Nový Bor (Haida)

432   "Music"

Diamond-engraved mark on the reverse above
mount: *IVO RUSZYPAL '79*
1979
H 43, W 63, D 17.2 cm

Colorless crystal glass. Mold-blown and freely
shaped. Chrome-plated metal mount.

Acc. no. P 1980-6

For similar pieces see Corning, *New Glass*,
1979, cat. no. 200.

Lit.: J. Schou-Christensen, "Der grosse Aufbruch: Europäische Glaskunst seit 1945," *NG*,
no. 1 (1980): 4, fig. 7; Ricke, *Museumsarbeit*,
1988, 79, fig. 77

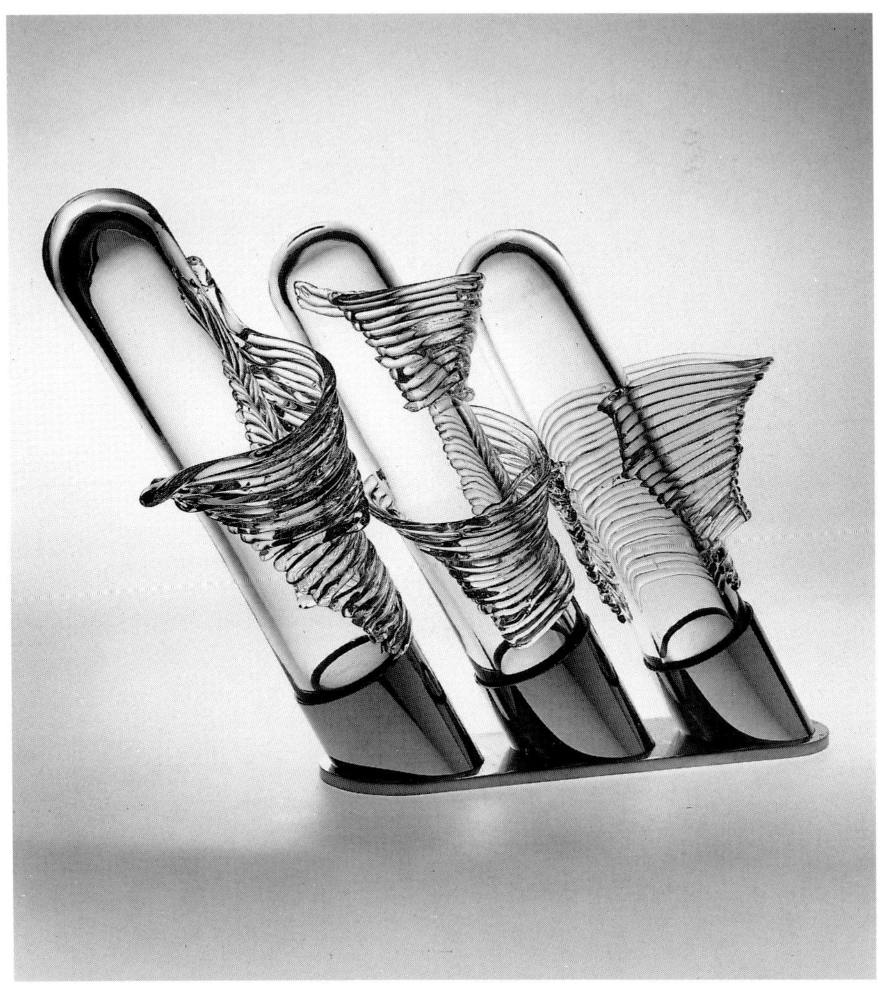

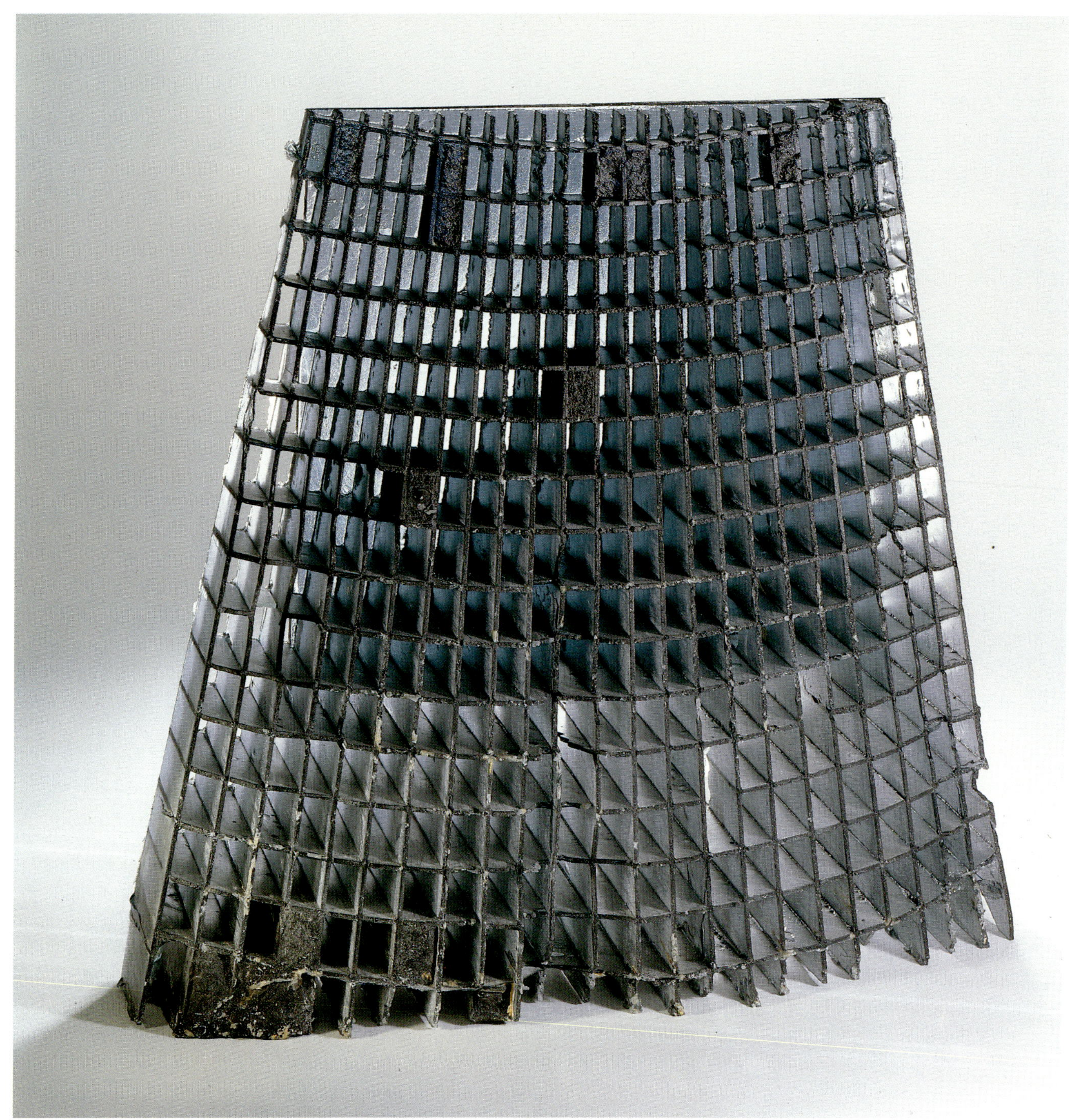

Ivan Mareš
(b. 1956)

Education: Glass School, Železný Brod (Eisenbrod), and Academy of Applied Arts, Prague
Lives and works in Prague

433   "Tower"

Unsigned
1985
H 57.5, W 61, D 16.8 cm

Gray-blue glass. Mold-melted.

Acc. no. P 1986-65

Lit.: Ricke, *Museumsarbeit*, 1988, 79, fig. 79

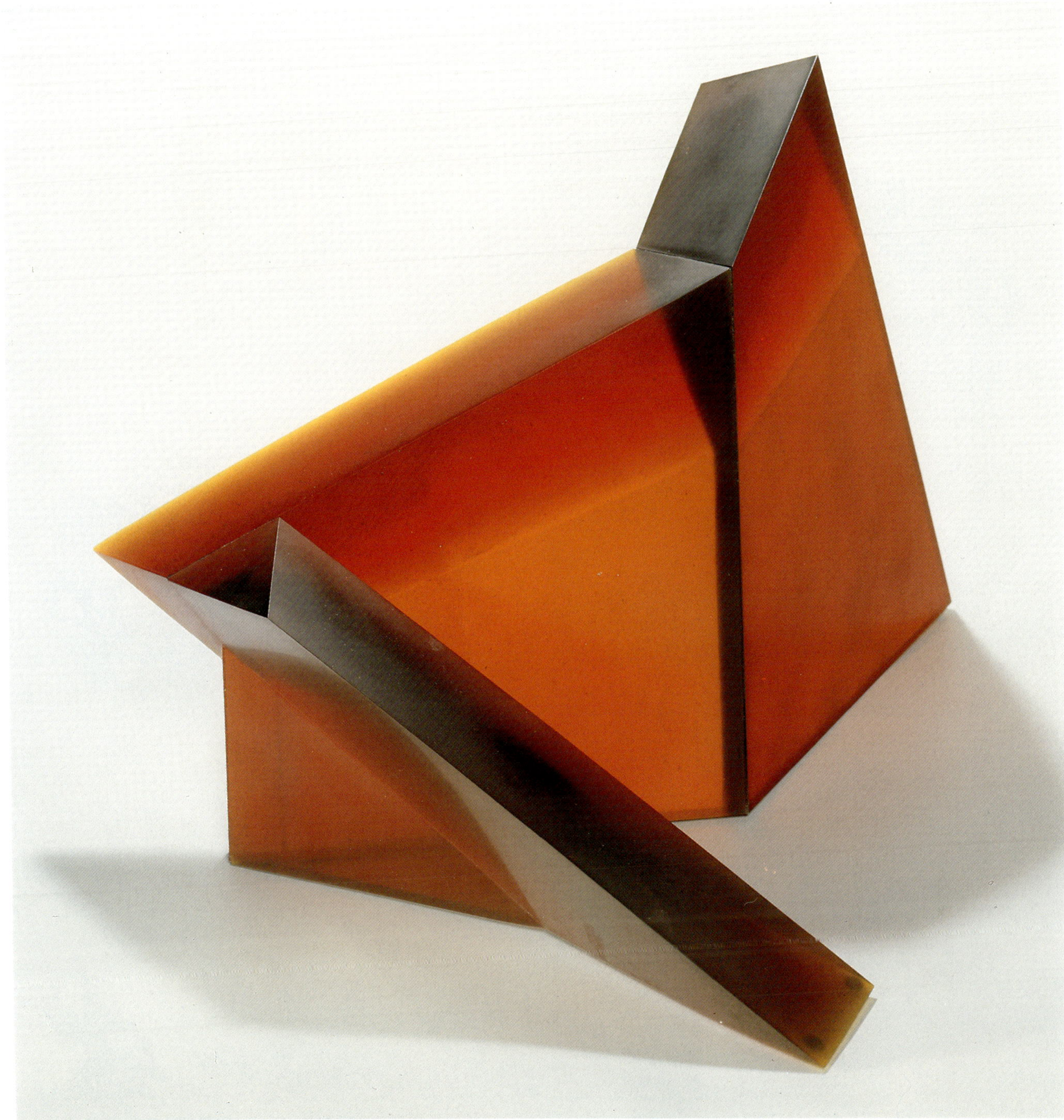

Stanislav Libenský
(1921–2002)

Education: Glass schools in Nový Bor (Haida)
and Železný Brod (Eisenbrod), and Academy
of Applied Arts, Prague

Jaroslava Brychtová
(b. 1923)

Education: Academy of Applied Arts, Prague,
and Academy of Fine Arts, Prague
The couple lives and works in Prague and
Železný Brod (Eisenbrod)

434   "Prisms in Space"

Diamond-engraved mark on the bottom on
the side: *S. LIBENSKY J. BRYCHTOVA 84*
1984
H 44, W 62.5, D 52 cm

Mold-melted in three parts, cut, semimat
polish. Laminated.

Acc. no. P 1986-64

Lit.: E. Stará, "Fünfundzwanzig Jahre päda-
gogischer Tätigkeit," *Glasrevue* 5, no. 88
(1988): 18, fig. 5; Ricke, *Museumsarbeit*,
1988, 68, fig. 27

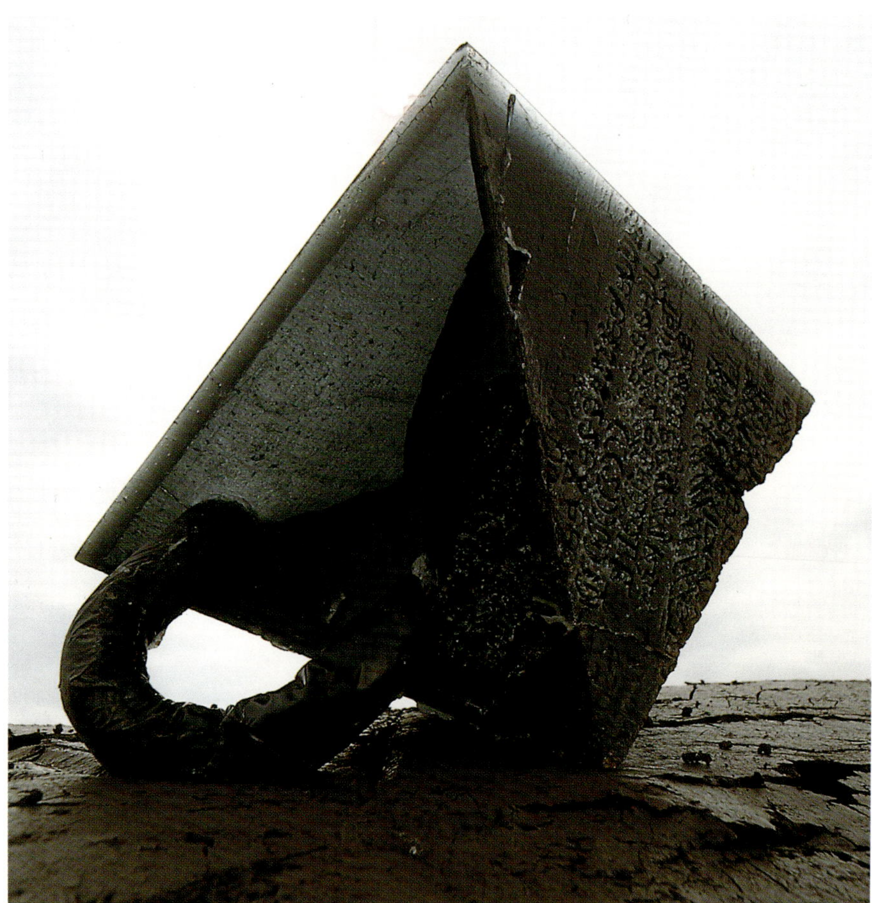

Jiří Necovář
(b. 1956)

Education: Glass School, Železný Brod (Eisenbrod), and Academy of Applied Arts, Prague
Lives and works in Pardubice

435 "Attacked Pyramid"

Vibro-engraved mark at the bottom, on the
blank side of the object: *Nekovař*
1988
H 38.5, W 39.2, D approx. 26.5 cm

Blue-gray glass, mold-melted.

Acc. no. P 1993-18
Gift of Dr. Ernst Ploil, Vienna

Lit.: –

Jaromír Rybák
(b. 1951)

Education: Glass School, Železný Brod (Eisenbrod), and Academy of Applied Arts, Prague
Lives and works in Prague

436 "Wing"

Engraved mark below the tip: *Jaromir Rybák
1990*
1990
H 37, W 50, D 50 cm

Colorless and colored crystal glass chunks
with gold foil, mold-melted. Cut and acid
polished.

Acc. no. P 1992-18
Acquired at the exhibition "New Glass in
Europe"

Lit.: Ricke, *New Glass Europe*, 1991,
cat. no. 118

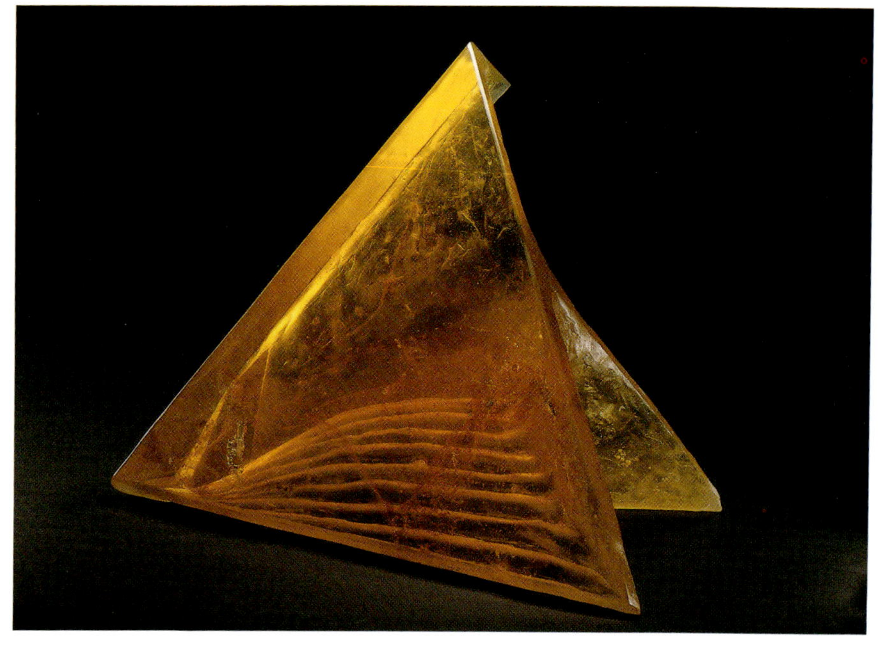

Jaroslav Matouš
(b. 1941)

Education: Glass School, Železný Brod (Eisenbrod), and Academy of Applied Arts, Prague
Lives and works in Prague

437   "Fruit Garden"

Diamond-engraved mark on the underside of
base: *Matouš 90*
1990
H 50, ⌀ 20 cm

Colorless glass, mold-blown. Enamel painted,
drilled, sandblasted. Wire and glass beads.

Acc. no. GL 2001-163
Acquired at the exhibition "New Glass in
Europe"

Lit.: Ricke, *New Glass Europe*, 1991,
cat. no. 166

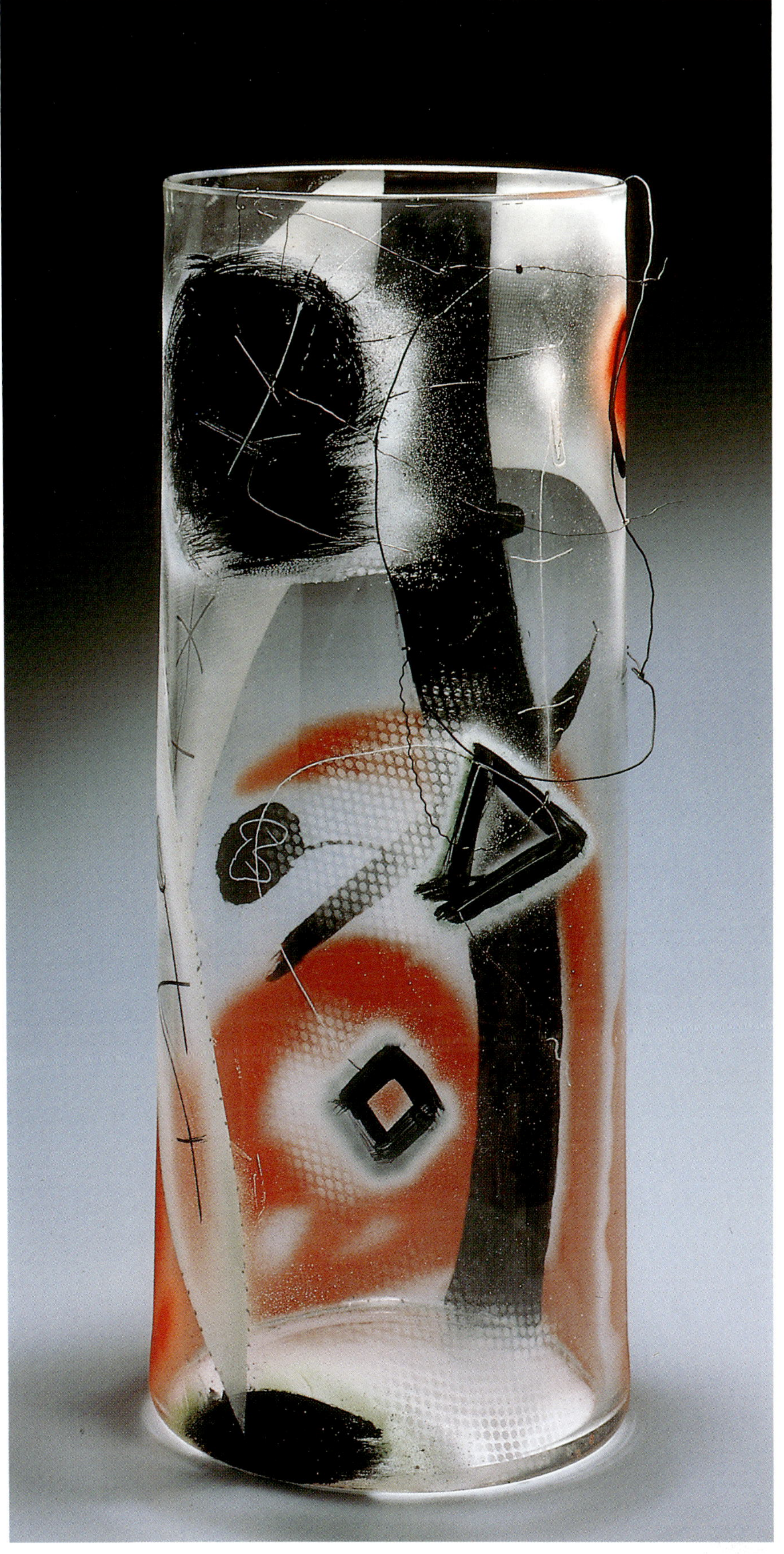

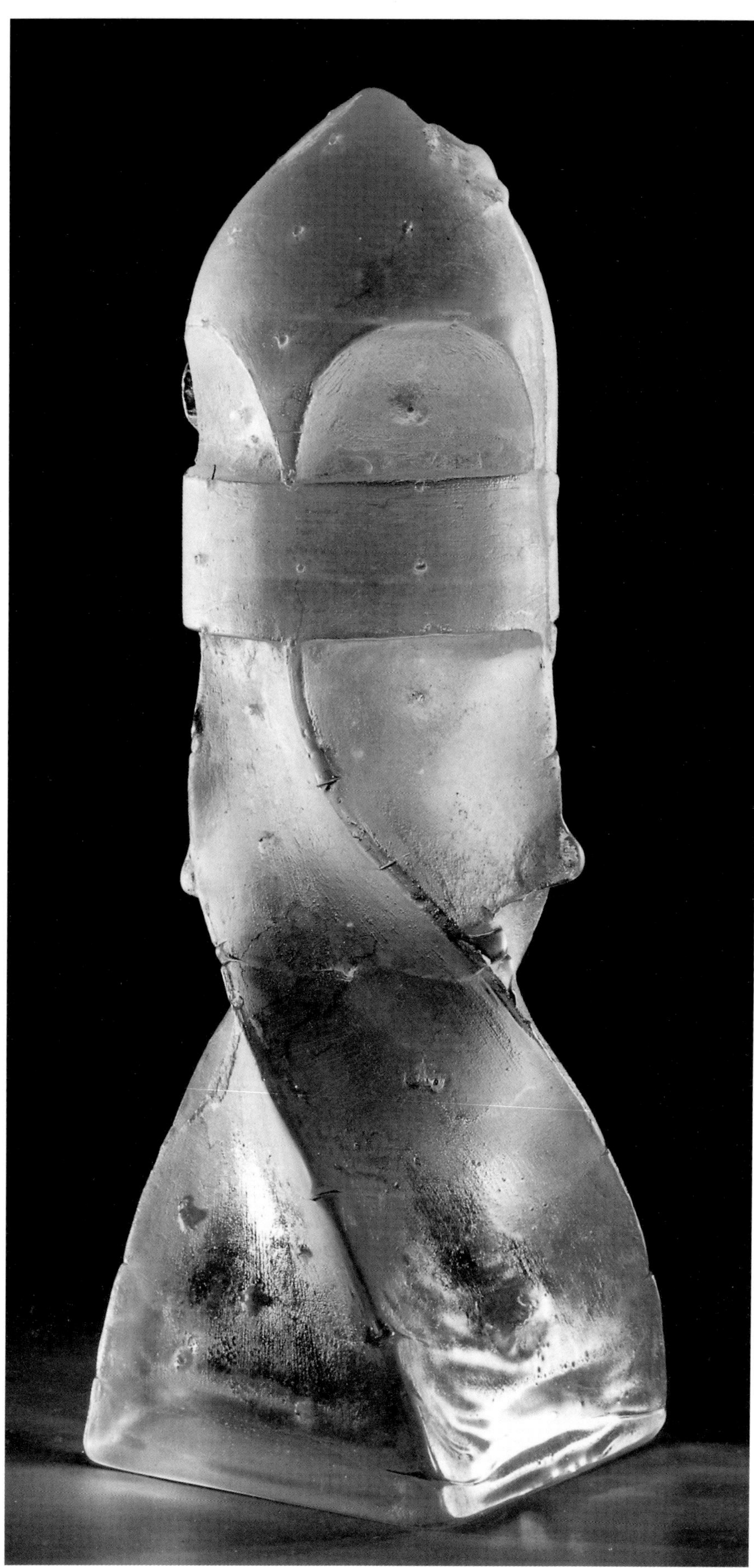

František Janák
(b. 1951)

Education: Apprenticeship at the glass company "Bohemia" in Světlá. Glass School, Kamenický Šenov (Steinschönau)
Lives and works in Prague

438   "Hommage to Antoni Gaudi I"

Diamond-engraved mark on the underside of base and engraved under the standing base:
Janák 90
1990
H 47, ⌀ 16 cm

Lead glass, mold-melted. Etched.

Acc. no. P 1992-20
Acquired at the exhibition "New Glass in Europe"

Lit.: Ricke, *New Glass Europe*, 1991, cat. no. 121

Jiřína Žertová
(b. 1932)

Education: State School of Graphic Arts and Academy of Applied Arts, Prague
Lives and works in Prague

439   "What Weather"

Diamond-engraved mark on the reverse, bottom center: *ŽERTOVÁ 85–89*
1985–89
H 90, W 72, D 38 cm

Colorless glass, mold-blown. Cold painted. Metal pedestal.

Acc. no. P 1992-19
Acquired at the exhibition "New Glass in Europe"

Lit.: Ricke, *New Glass Europe*, 1991, cat. no. 161

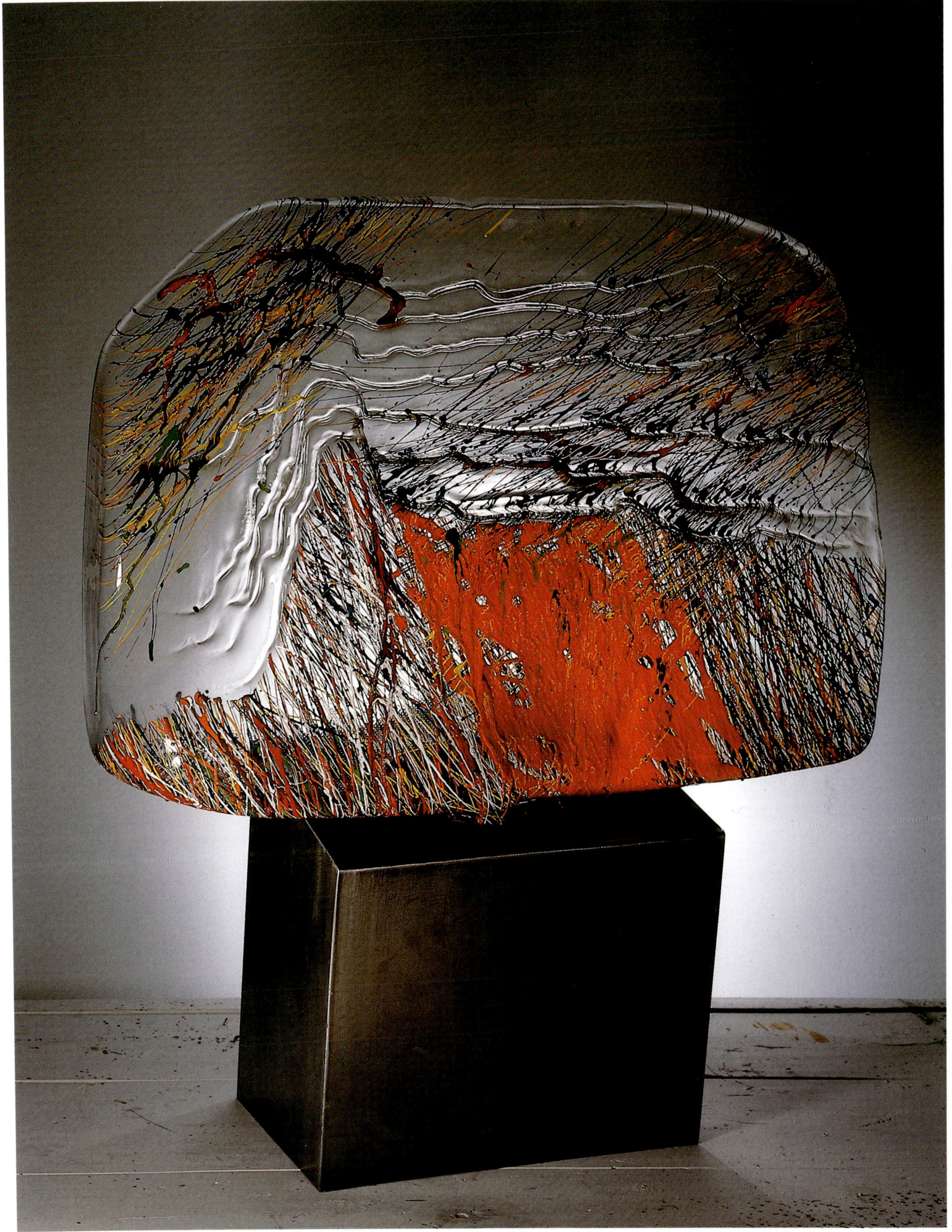

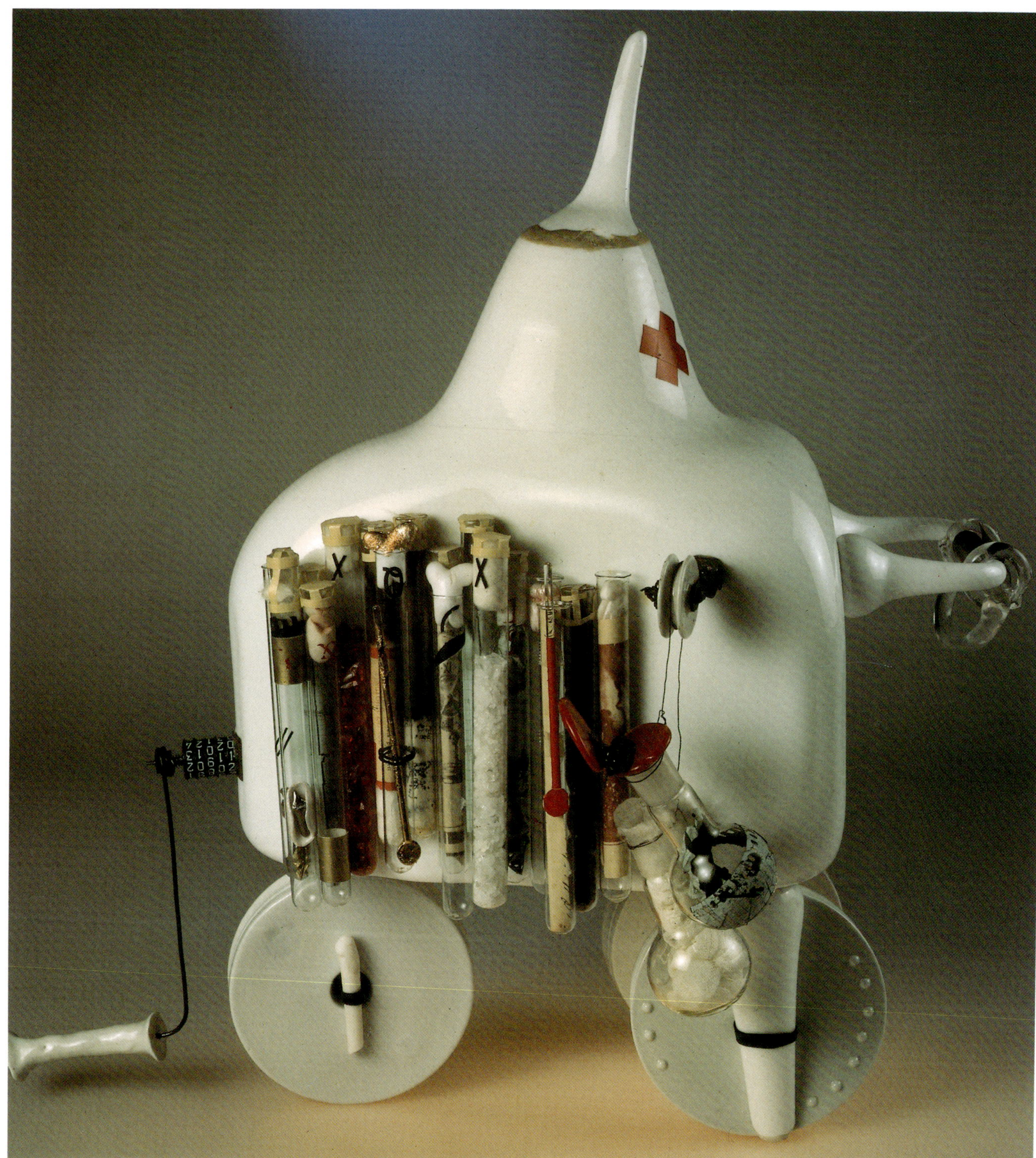

Romania

Adriana Popescu
(b. 1954)

Education: Institute of Fine Arts, Cluj-Napoca
(Klausenburg)
Lives and works in Cluj-Napoca

440   "Hospital Cart"

Engraved mark on the underside of cart:
Adriana Popescu 1989
1989
H 60, W 60, D 40 cm

Mold-blown and shaped milk glass, test
tubes, porcelain, metal, paper, rubber, string,
gold leaf on paper, fabric, sealing wax, etc.

Acc. no. P 1991-18
Acquired from the artist at the exhibition
"New Glass in Europe"

Lit.: Ricke, *New Glass Europe*, 1991,
cat. no. 40

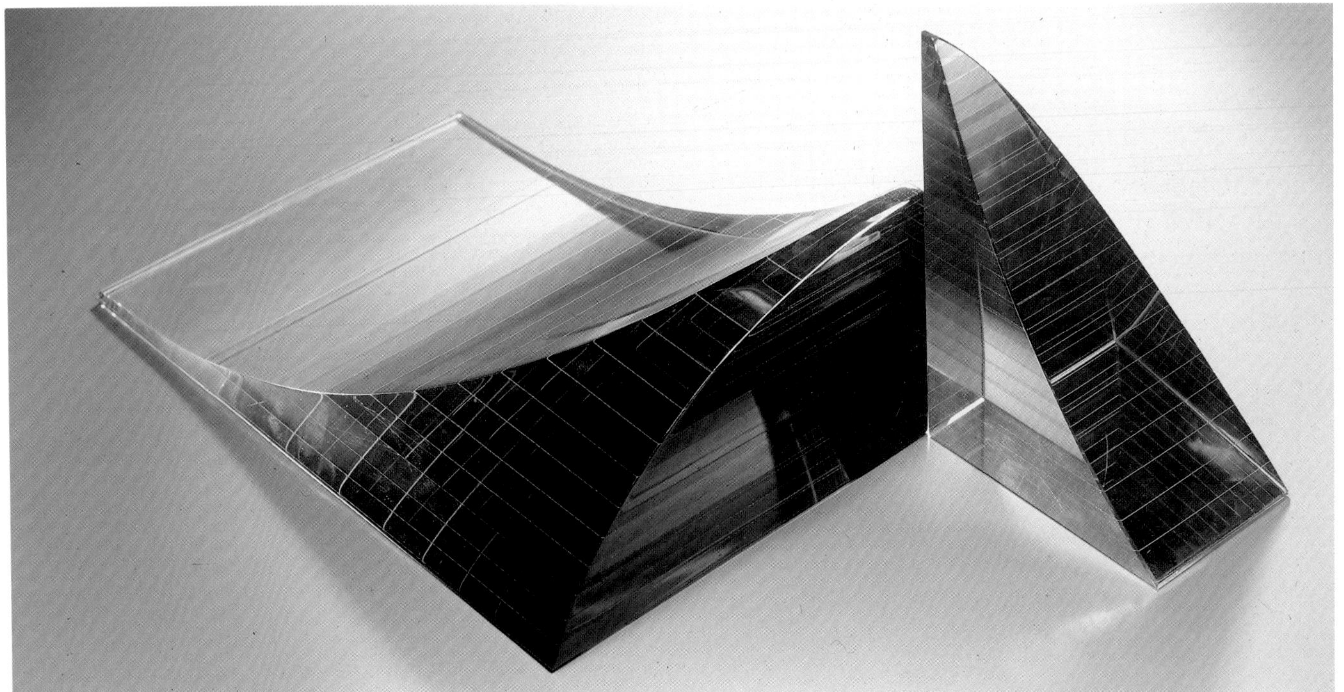

Zoltán Bohus
(b. 1941)

Education: Hungarian Academy of Applied
Arts, Budapest
Lives and works in Budapest

441   "Formula 1"

Unsigned, 1980
H 12.7, 20.6; W 21.5, 13.5; D 34.5, 8.3 cm

Greenish float glass. Laminated, cut, and
polished.

Acc. no. P 1980-26
Acquired at the exhibition "Licht. Form. Gestalt"

Lit.: Ricke, *Licht. Form. Gestalt*, 1980, cat. no.
7; I. Nagy and Maria Lugossy, "Zoltán Bohus:
Studien in Raum und Zeit," *NG*, no. 3 (1981):
89ff., fig. 7

Maria Lugossy
(b. 1950)

Education: Arts-and-Crafts School and Academy
of Applied Arts, Budapest
Lives and works in Budapest

442   "Birth of Venus"

Engraved mark on the narrow edge: *Lugossy '80*
1980
H 8, ⌀ 20 cm

Colorless optic glass. Cut and polished. Constructed from several parts like a shell. In the
hollow space of the outer, two-part shell is a
second, similarly made body.

Acc. no. P 1980-25
Acquired at the exhibition "Licht. Form. Gestalt"

Lit.: Ricke, *Licht. Form. Gestalt*, 1980, cat. no. 63

Hungary

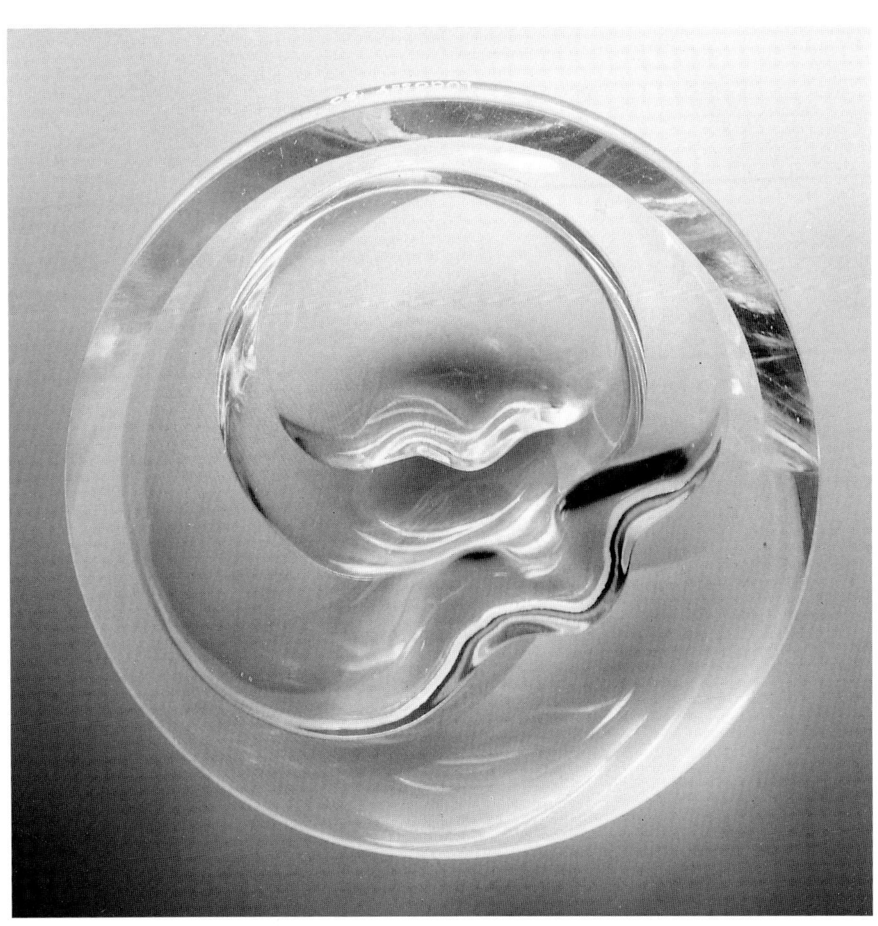

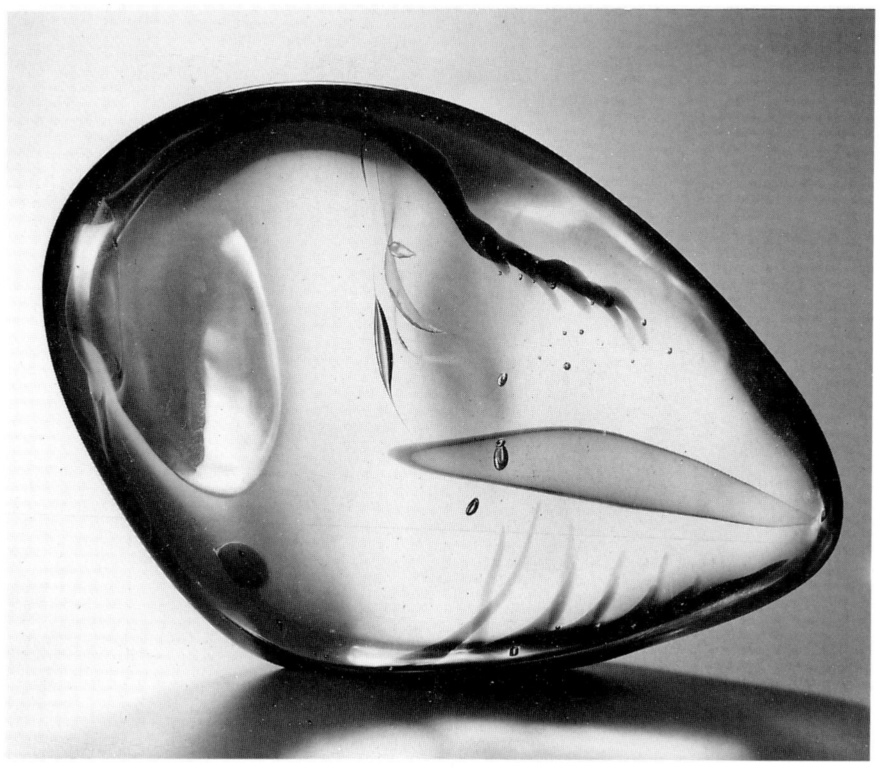

Croatia

Raoul Goldoni
(1919–1983)

Education: Academy of Fine Arts, Zagreb
Lived and worked in Zagreb, Croatia
Works carried out in Murano.

443   "Big Core III"

Diamond-engraved mark on the underside of
standing base: *Goldoni Barbini 1962*
1962
H 15.3, ⌀ 22.5 x 10.3 cm

Crystal glass with light gray-brown tone,
brown inclusions, embedded air bubbles.
Freely shaped. Carried out by Alfredo Barbini,
Murano (cf. cat. no. 390).

Acc. no. P 1974-23
Gift of Helmut Hentrich

Piece from the early years of sculptor and
designer Goldoni's work with glass (from
1958). His choice of color and manner of
working reveal that Barbini's participation
was not limited to technical execution. There
are clear parallels with his own works of the
early 1960s.

Lit.: Ricke, *Museumsarbeit*, 1988, 79, fig. 73

444   Group of Objects

Diamond-engraved mark on the underside of
each standing base: *Goldoni*
Ca. 1974/75
H 27, 25.8, 23.3; ⌀ 19.5, 25, 19.7 cm

Crystal glass, covered with several layers of
glass, fine crackling and iridescence between
the layers. Freely shaped. Carried out by Livio
Seguso (cf. cat. no. 446).

Acc. nos. P 1986-62 and 1987-20, 21
Gift of Helmut Hentrich

Lit.: –

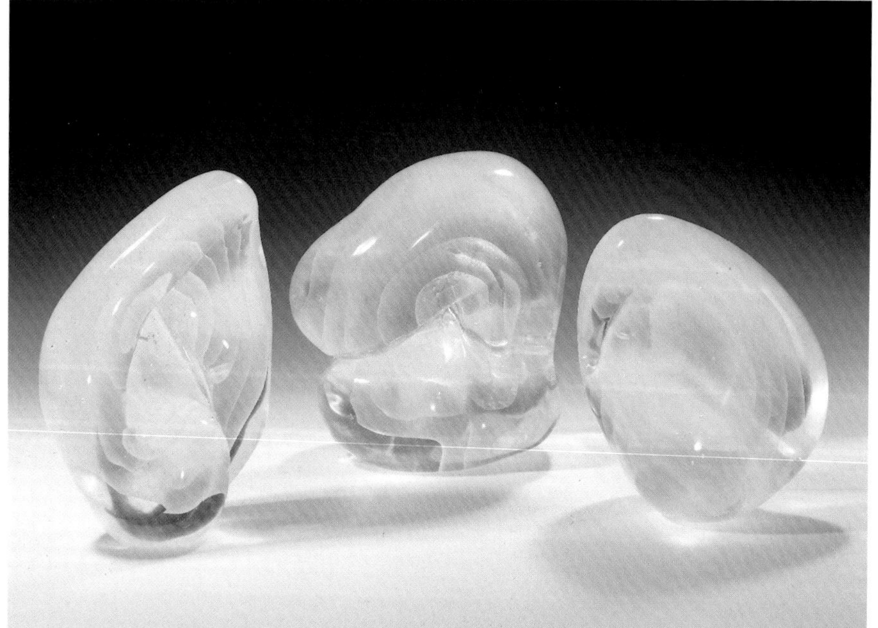

Italy

Luciano Vistosi
(b. 1931)

Education: University of Padua (chemistry);
self-taught as glass sculptor
Lives and works in Venice and Murano

445   "Due Personaggi"

Mark on foot of both pieces: –*L. Vistosi 75*–
Left: H with metal pedestal 118,
W 104, D 56 cm
Right: H 139.5, W 63, D 64 cm

Colorless crystal glass. Free-blown and
shaped. Cut open and fused.

Acc. no. P 1980-3
Anonymous donation

Lit.: G. Carandente, *Luciano Vistosi* (Venice,
1975), n.p. (6); *Luciano Vistosi and Livio
Seguso*, exh. cat. (Venice: Museo d'Arte Moderna Ca'Pesaro, 1980), 33; H. Ricke, "Murano
heute—Wege aus der Sackgasse II: Die Aussenseiter," *NG*, no. 3 (1980): 96ff., fig. 22

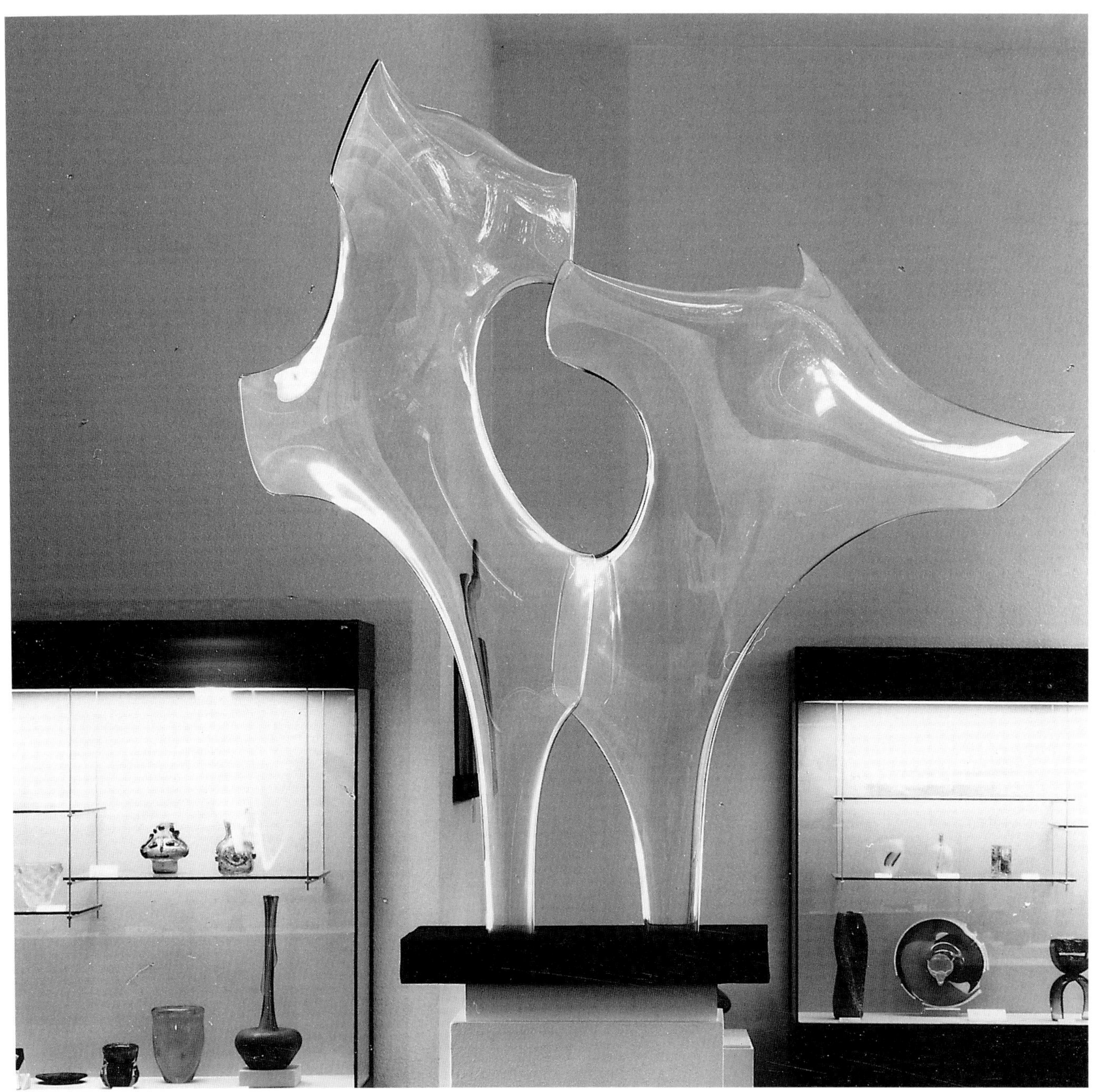

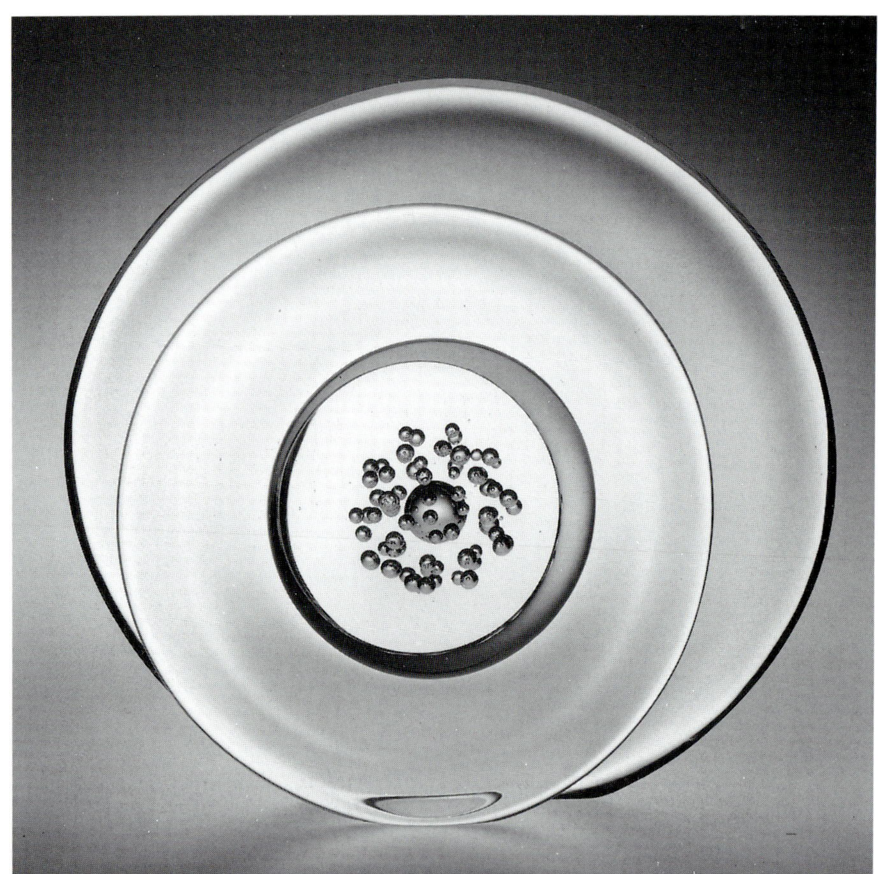

Livio Seguso
(b. 1930)

Education: Apprenticeship as glassblower,
design courses, glass technique at the
Stazione Sperimentale del Vetro, Murano
Lives and works in Murano

446   Object

Diamond-engraved on the inside, at the back,
above the standing base: *L. Seguso 78*
1978
H 37.5, W 43, D 13.2 cm

Colorless crystal glass. Freely shaped, pegged
air bubbles.

Acc. no. P 1980-5

Lit.: –

447   Object

Diamond-engraved on the underside of
standing base: *L. Seguso 83*
1983
H 19.9, ⌀ 22.3 x 15.1 cm

Glass with light smoky tone, gray-brown
inclusion, and embedded air bubble. Freely
shaped. Oval cross section.

Acc. no. P 1990-441
Gift of Helmut Hentrich

Lit.: –

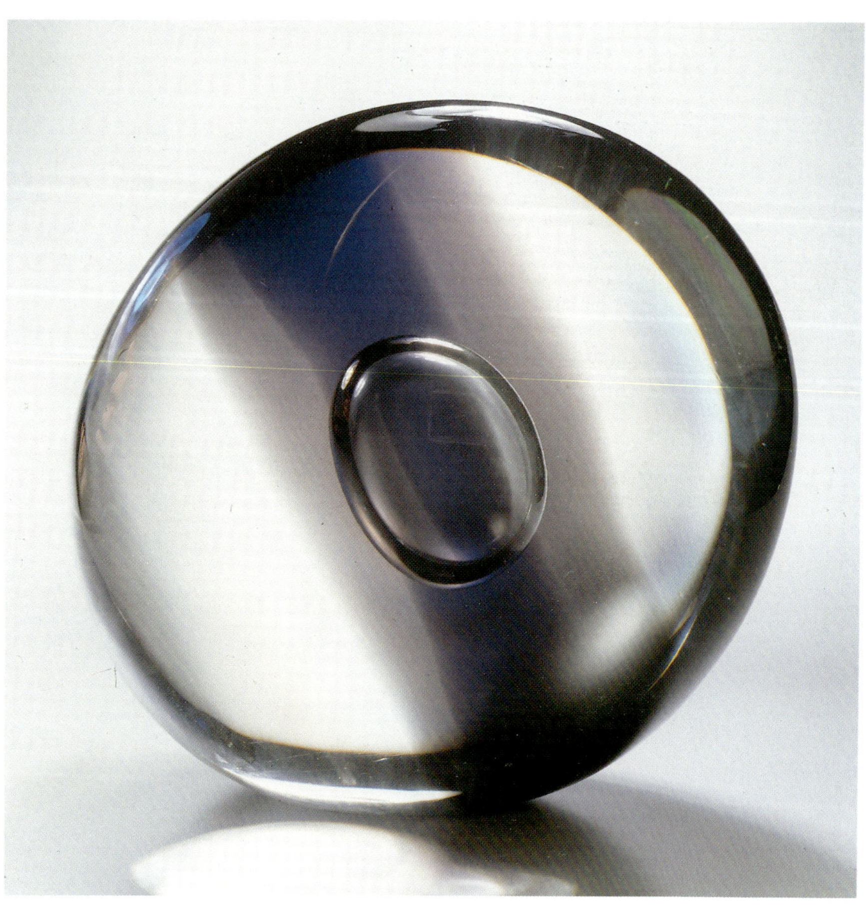

Paolo Martinuzzi
(b. 1933)

Education: Workshops of Murano; self-taught
as artist
Lives and works in Soest, Germany

448 Object

Diamond-engraved mark near the standing
base: *1978 Martinuzzi Paolo*
Hemisphere: H 13.9, ⌀ 25.2 cm
Pedestal: H 5, L 31, W 26.4 cm

Colorless. Free-blown. Diamond-engraved.

Acc. no. P 1989-16
Gift of the artist

Lit.: H. Ricke, "Murano heute—Wege aus der
Sackgasse II: Die Aussenseiter," *NG*, no. 3
(1980): 96ff., fig. 19

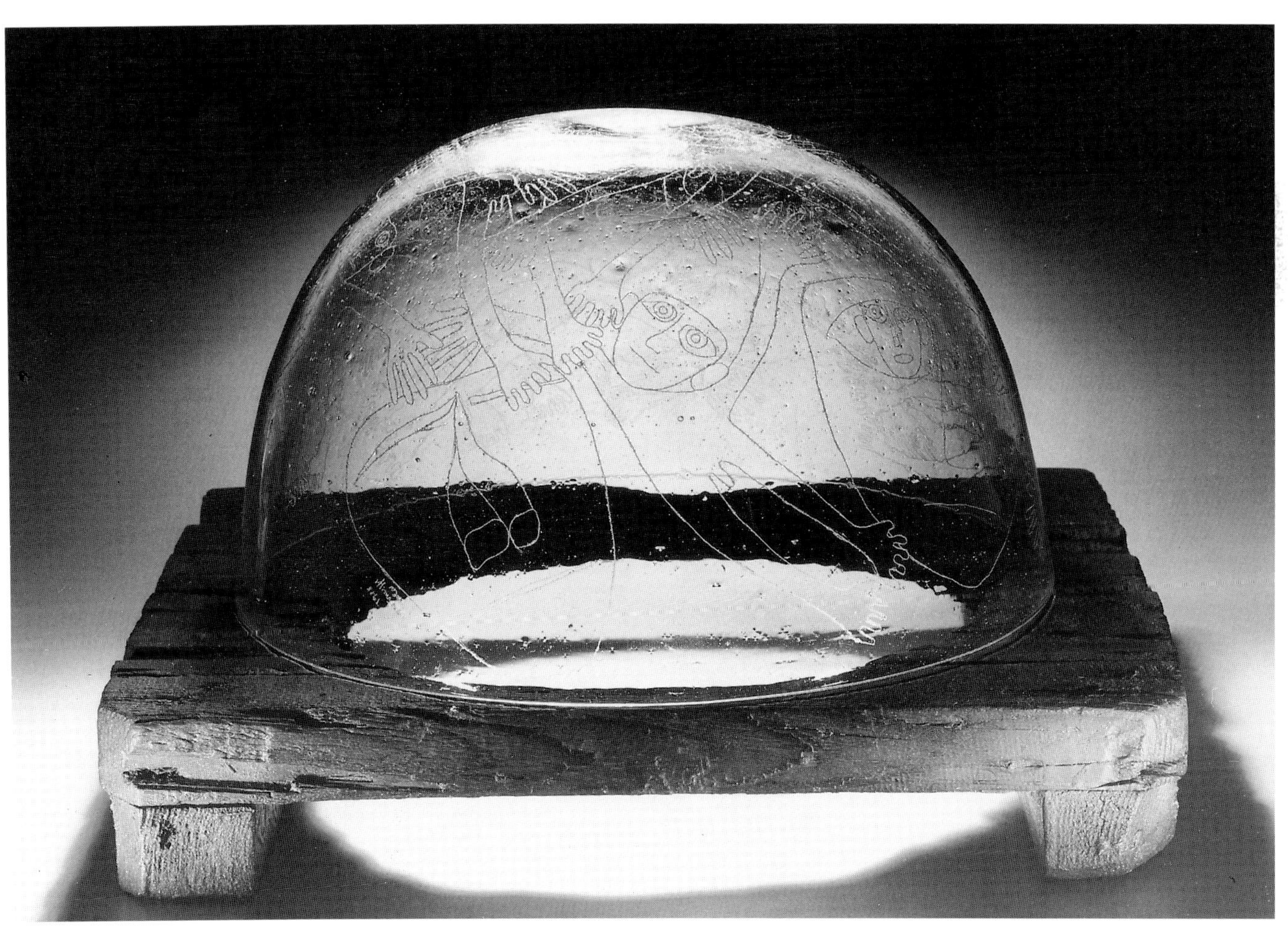

Germany

Erwin Eisch
(b. 1927)

Education: Apprenticeship as glass engraver;
Akademie der Bildenden Künste, Munich
Lives and works in Frauenau, Bavarian Forest

449 Vase Object

Diamond-engraved mark on the underside of
base: *E. Eisch*
1962
H 29.3, ⌀ 18.4 cm

Mold-blown, shaped. Partial overlay and
applications.

Acc. no. P 1992-348
Formerly Städtische Galerie Schloss Oberhausen
Acquired at Eisch's first exhibition of non-
functional glassworks, in Stuttgart, 1962

Lit.: H. Ricke, "Tendenzen in Europa: From
the Fifties to the Sixties," *NG*, no. 1 (1989):
6ff., fig. 1

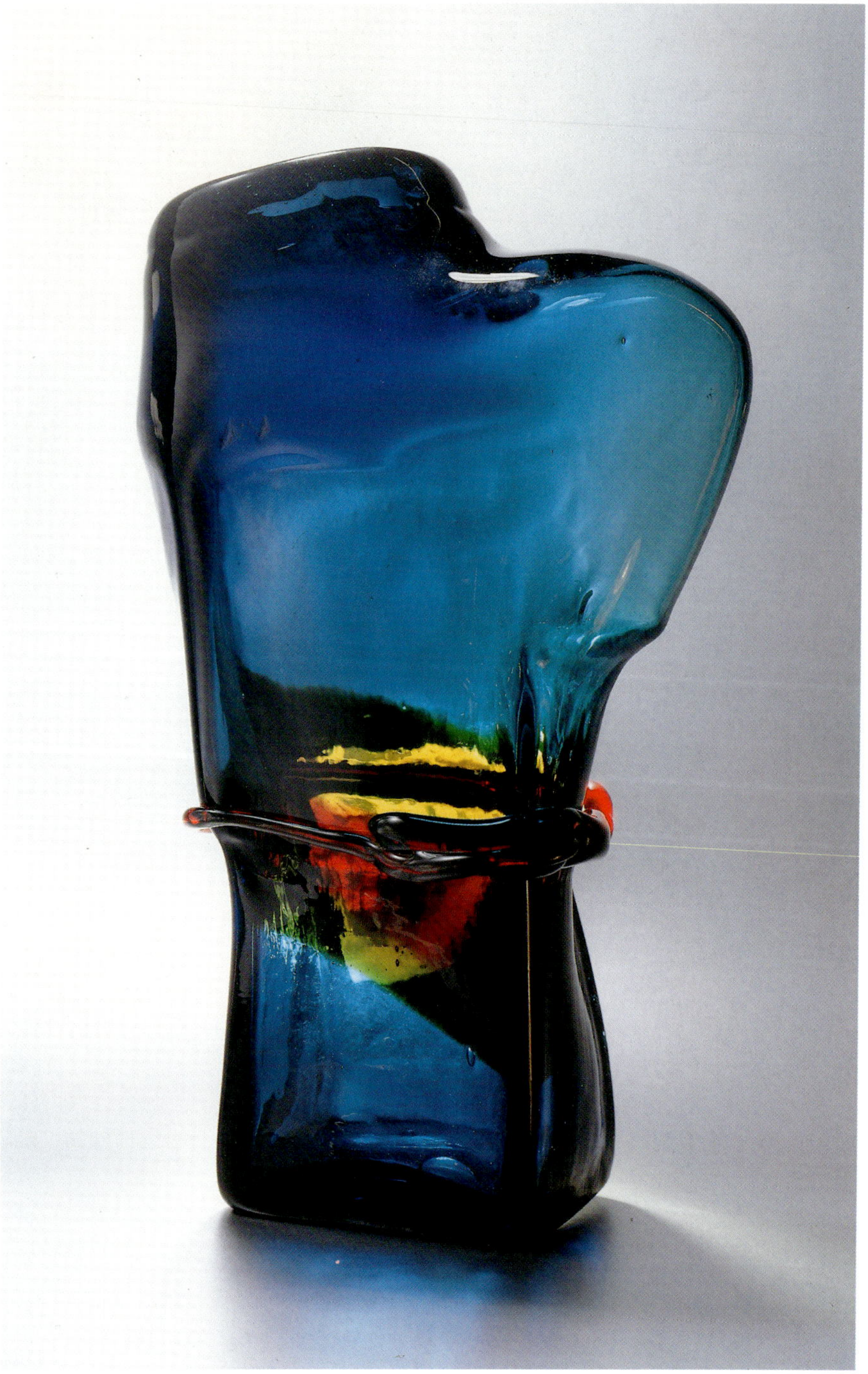

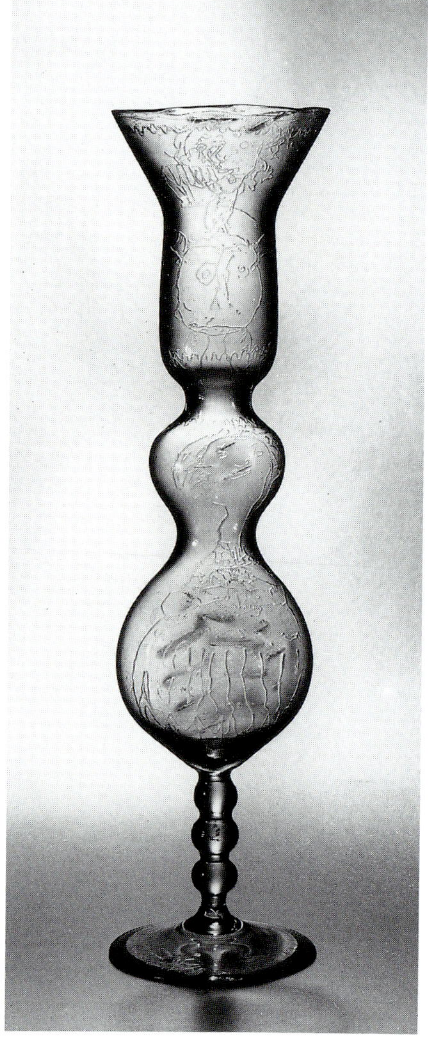

450   "Gesang der Mohren" Vase Object

Diamond-engraved mark on the underside of
foot: *Eisch 62*
1962
H 32.2, ⌀ 7.9 cm

Colorless crystal glass, free-blown and
shaped. Needle-etched drawing.

Acc. no. P 1992-349
Formerly Städtische Galerie Schloss Ober-
hausen
Acquisition as above

Lit.: H. Ricke, "Tendenzen in Europa: From
the Fifties to the Sixties," *NG*, no. 1 (1989):
6ff., fig. 8

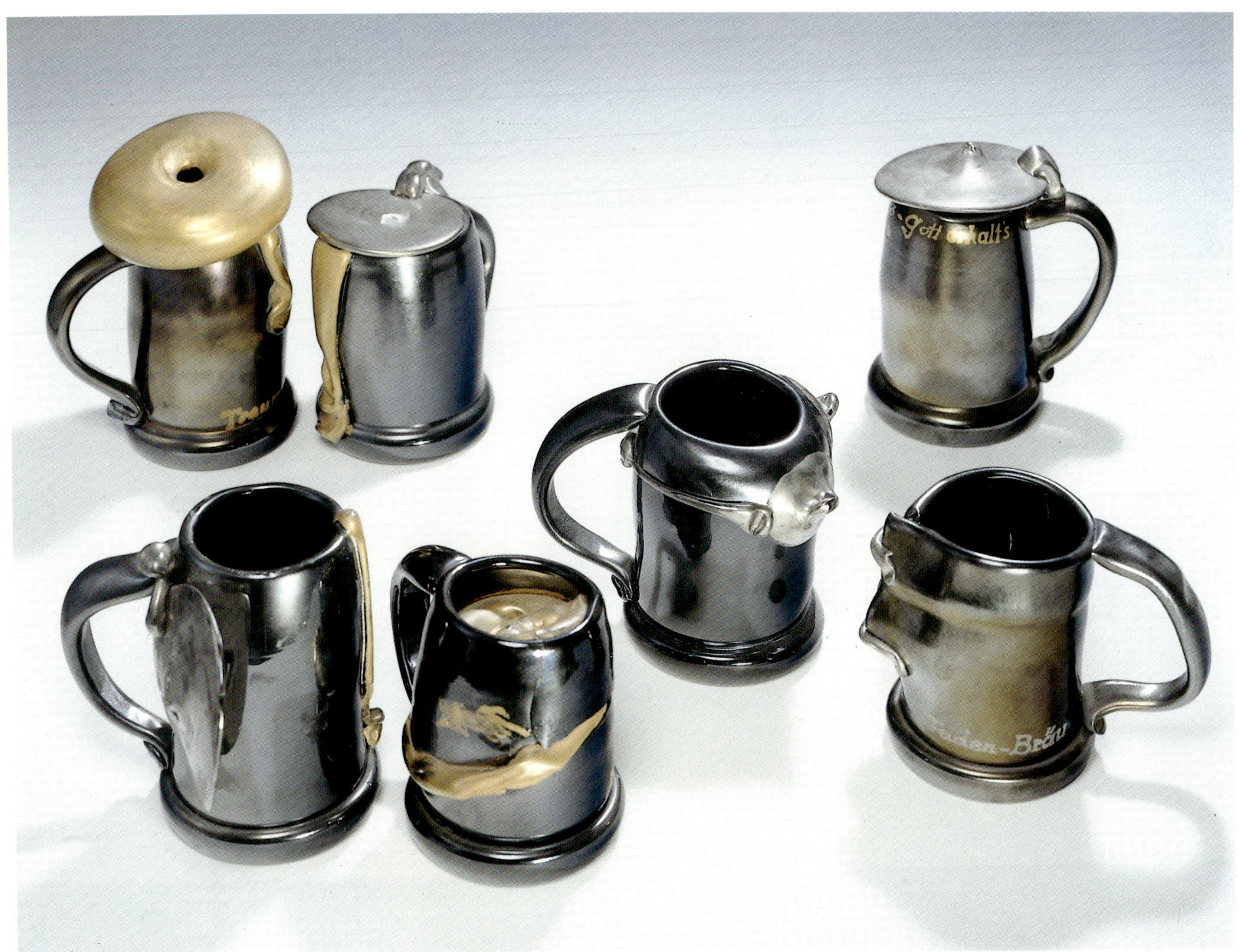

451 Beer Mugs

Engraved mark on the underside of base:
E. Eisch 76
H 12.9–19.2 cm, ⌀ 15–18.3 cm

Black glass, mold-blown, shaped, deliberately
partly broken and re-fused, applications.
Painted in gold and silver. Gold-painted
inscriptions.
Top left: *Traum-Schaum-Mass*
Bottom, 2nd from left: *Druck der Mass'n*
Middle: *Urquell Bonn* in red heart *AUS LIEBE*
Top right: *Hopfen und Malz Gott erhalt's*
Bottom right: *Faden-Bräu*.

Acc. nos. P 1976-36 a–g

Lit.: E. Eisch, "Vom Blechtrommler Oskar zur
Studio-Glas-Bewegung," *NG*, no. 1 (1980):
26ff.; Ricke, *Museumsarbeit*, 1988, 78, fig. 67

Isgard Moje-Wohlgemuth
(b. 1941)

Education: Glasfachschule Hadamar
Lives and works in Schwanewede-Meyenburg
near Bremen

452   Vase

Engraved mark on the underside of base:
Isgard Moje-Wohlgemuth HT 1982 D
1982
H 22.2, ⌀ 19.3 cm

Colorless glass. Mold-blown. Painted with dissolved metal compounds, fired several times
in a reducing atmosphere. Kiln-formed in the
last firing. Diamond-engraved and engraved
decoration: basket structure and handle.

Acc. no. P 1984-68
Acquired at the exhibition "New Glass in
Germany"

Lit.: Ricke, *New Glass Germany*, 1983,
cat. no. 122

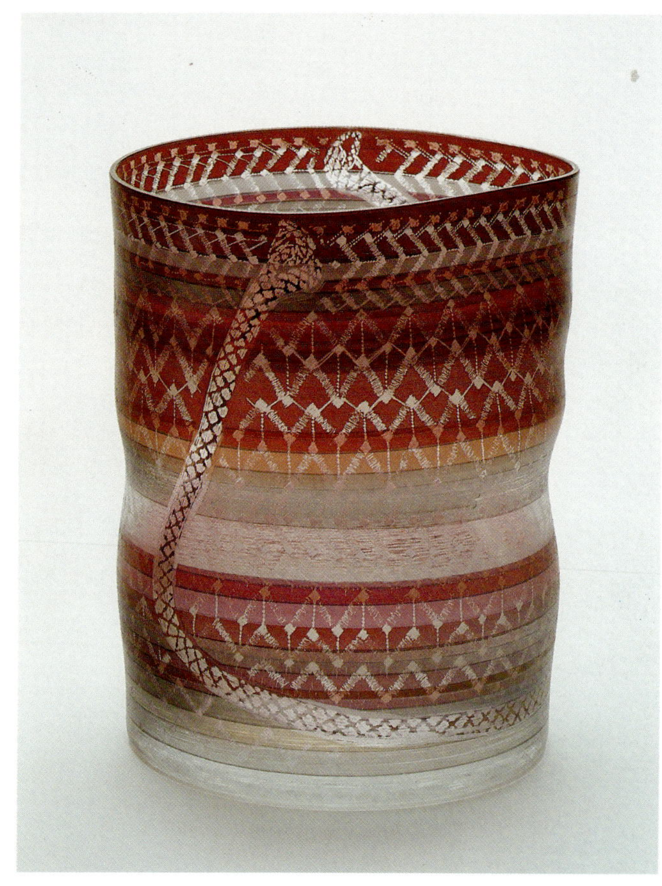

Klaus Moje
(b. 1936)

Education: Apprenticeship as glass cutter.
Glass schools in Rheinbach and Hadamar
Lives and works in Canberra, Australia

453   Dish

Engraved mark on the underside: *Klaus Moje
6-1982 38*
Hamburg, 1982
H 7.3, ⌀ 39.5 cm

Mosaic-glass technique. Preformed colored
glass ribbons fused together. Entire surface
on both sides cut with a texture, semimat
polish.

Acc. no. P 1984-69
Acquired at the exhibition "New Glass in
Germany"

Lit.: Ricke, *New Glass Germany*, 1983,
cat. no. 129

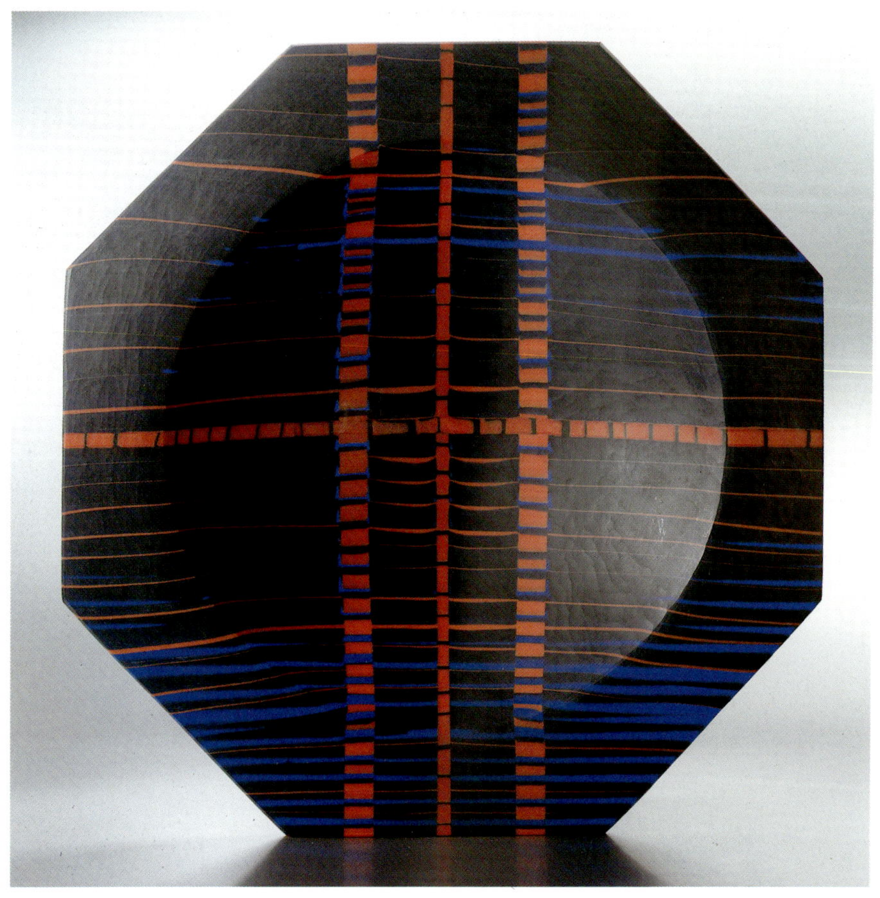

Diamond-engraved mark at the bottom, on the reverse: *CEREMONIAL DANCE FORMATION, Klaus Moje 1-1985#3*
Canberra, 1985
H without stand 61.5, W 46, D 5 cm

Mosaic-glass technique. Fused from preformed colorless and colored glass ribbons. Entire surface on both sides cut with a texture, semimat polish.

Acc. no. LP 1985-58
Acquired at the exhibition "Zweiter Coburger Glaspreis"
On permanent loan from the Museumsverein

Lit.: Coburg II, 1985, cat. no. 31 b; Klaus Moje, *Glass/Glas*, exh. cat. (Melbourne, 1995), 37, fig. 16

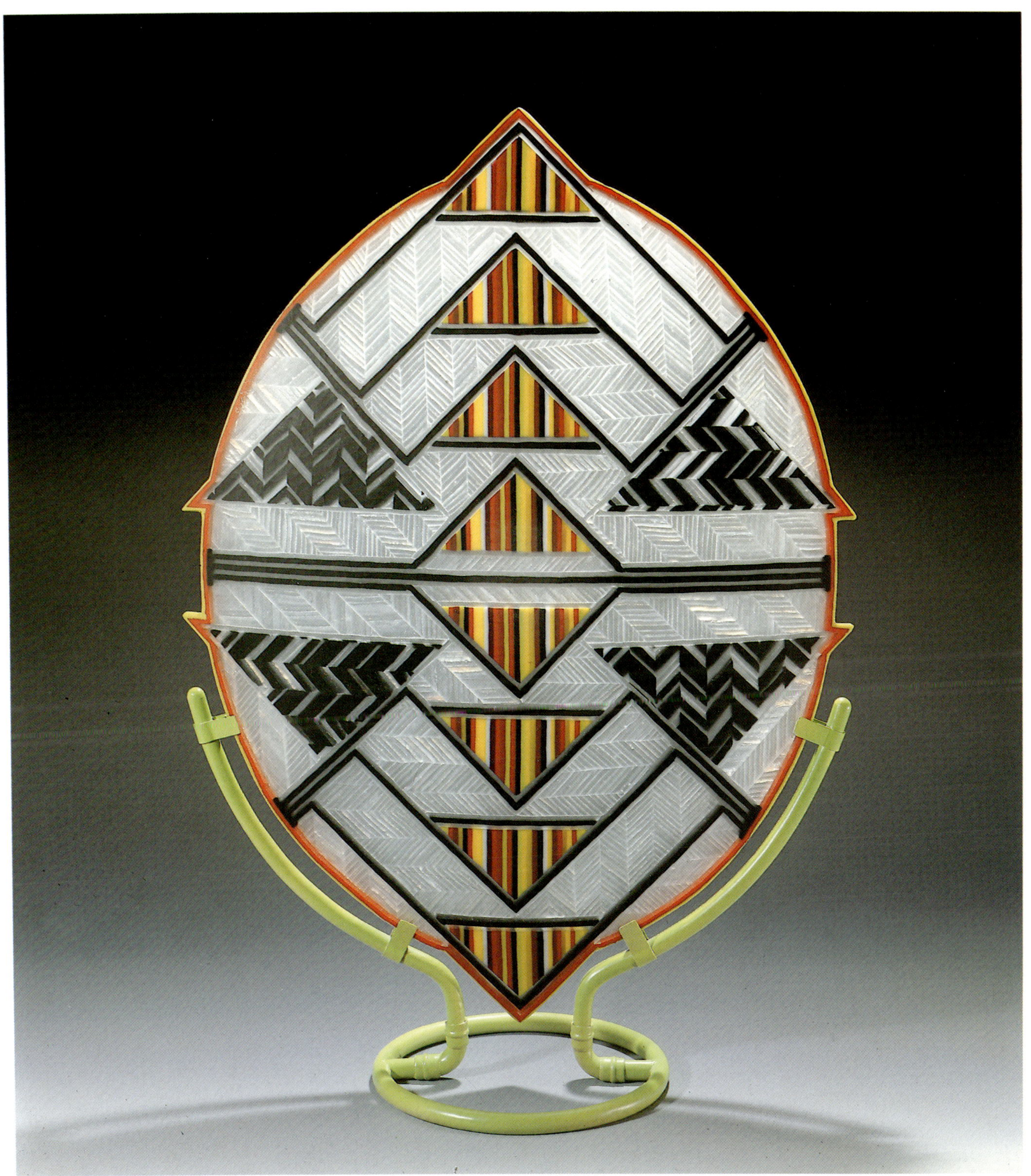

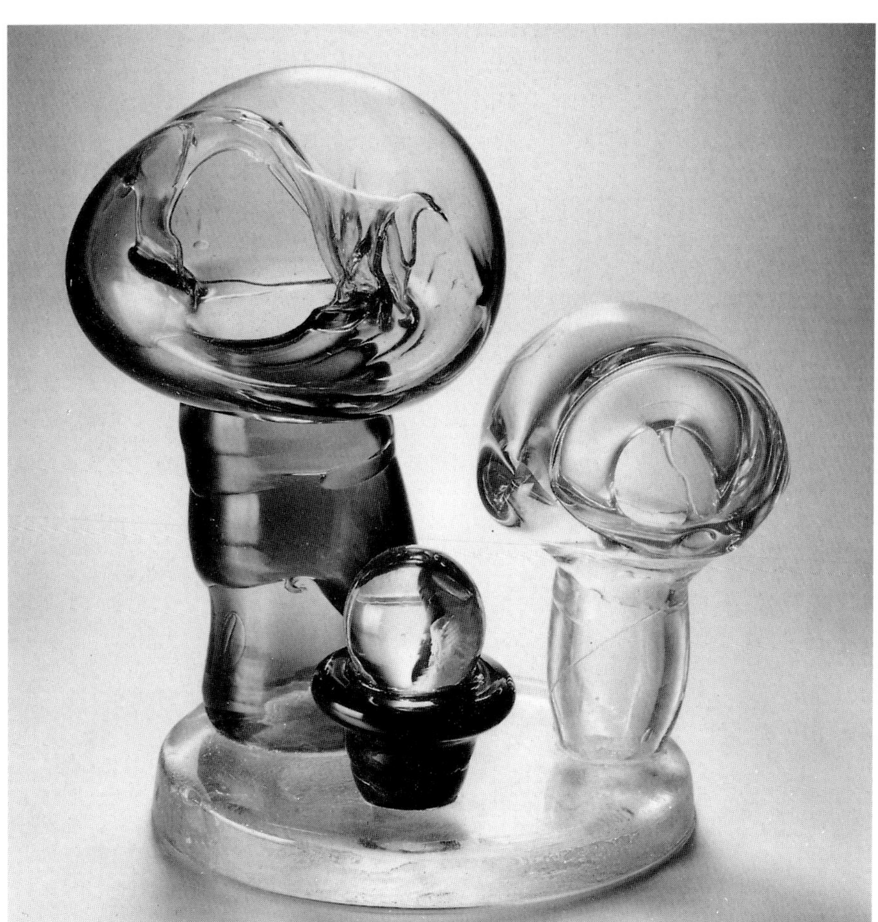

Bernhard Schagemann
(b. 1933)

Education: Akademie der Bildenden Künste, Munich
Lives and works as teacher and director at the Glasfachschule in Zwiesel

455 Object

Engraved mark on the stand on the side: *B. Schagemann 1974*
1975
Mushrooms: H a 25.2, b 8.7, c 16.4 cm
Stand: H 2, ⌀ 20 cm

Colorless and blue-gray glass. Mushrooms free-blown and shaped. Cast stand. Laminated.

Acc. no. P 1974-22

Lit.: –

Karl Berg
(b. 1943)

Education: Apprenticeship as hollow-glass finisher; Glasfachschule Zwiesel; Akademie der Bildenden Künste, Munich
Lives and works in Wegscheid near Passau

456 Object

Needle-etched mark on wall above standing base of one of the pieces: *cb 82*
1982
H 22.5, ⌀ stand 37.5 cm

Optic glass. Sawn, cut, and polished. Black, anodized aluminum pedestal.

Acc. no. P 1984-55
Acquired at the exhibition "New Glass in Germany"

Lit.: Ricke, *New Glass Germany*, 1983, cat. no. 34

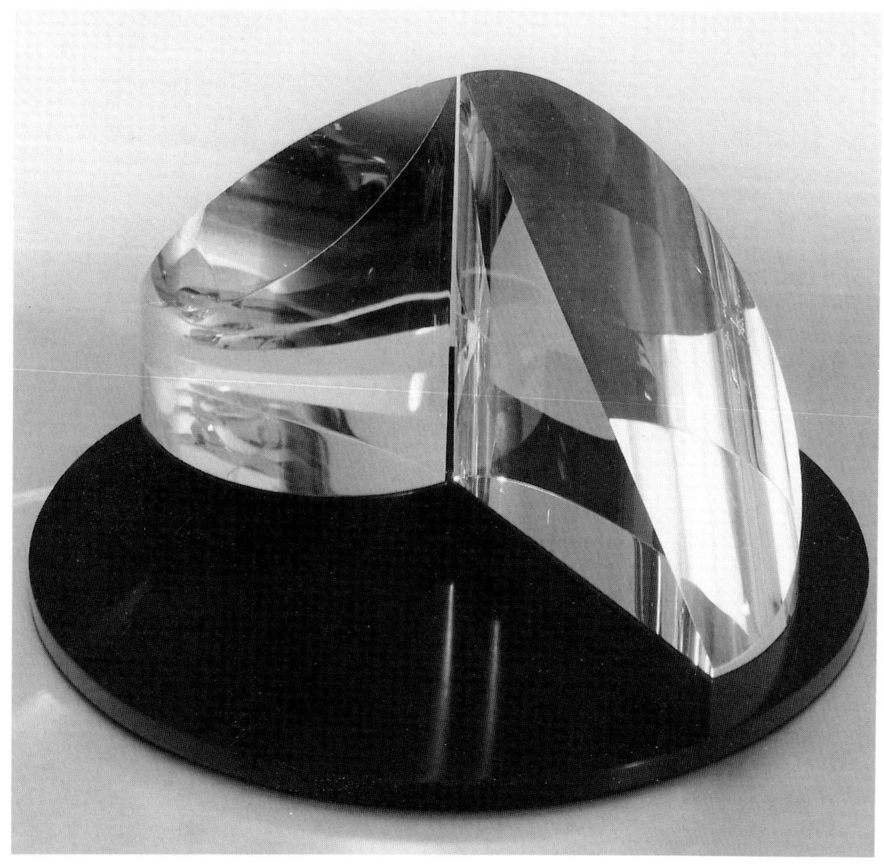

Franz Xaver Höller
(b. 1950)

Education: Apprenticeship as hollow-glass
finisher; Glasfachschule Zwiesel; Akademie
der Bildenden Künste, Munich; qualifying
examination as master; teacher training
Lives and works as specialist subject teacher
in Zwiesel

457   "Problem"

Diamond-engraved mark on the underside of
base: *Franz X. Hoeller 2/80*
Munich, 1980
H 20.4, ⌀ 22.5 cm

Colorless crystal glass. Mold-blown, shaped.
Cut and engraved, partly semimat, partly
bright polish.

Acc. no. P 1980-8

Lit.: P. Schmitt, *Glas—Silber 1980*, exh. cat.
(Karlsruhe: Badisches Landesmuseum, 1980),
no. 17

458   Variations on the Theme "Einschnitte"

Diamond-engraved mark on the underside of
each object: *fh 83*
Zwiesel, 1983
H 1.8, ⌀ 11.6 cm

Amber-colored glass. Cut and engraved. Several gradations of mat polishing.

Acc. no. P 1984-58
Acquired at the exhibition "New Glass in Germany"

Lit.: Ricke, *New Glass Germany*, 1983,
cat. no. 66

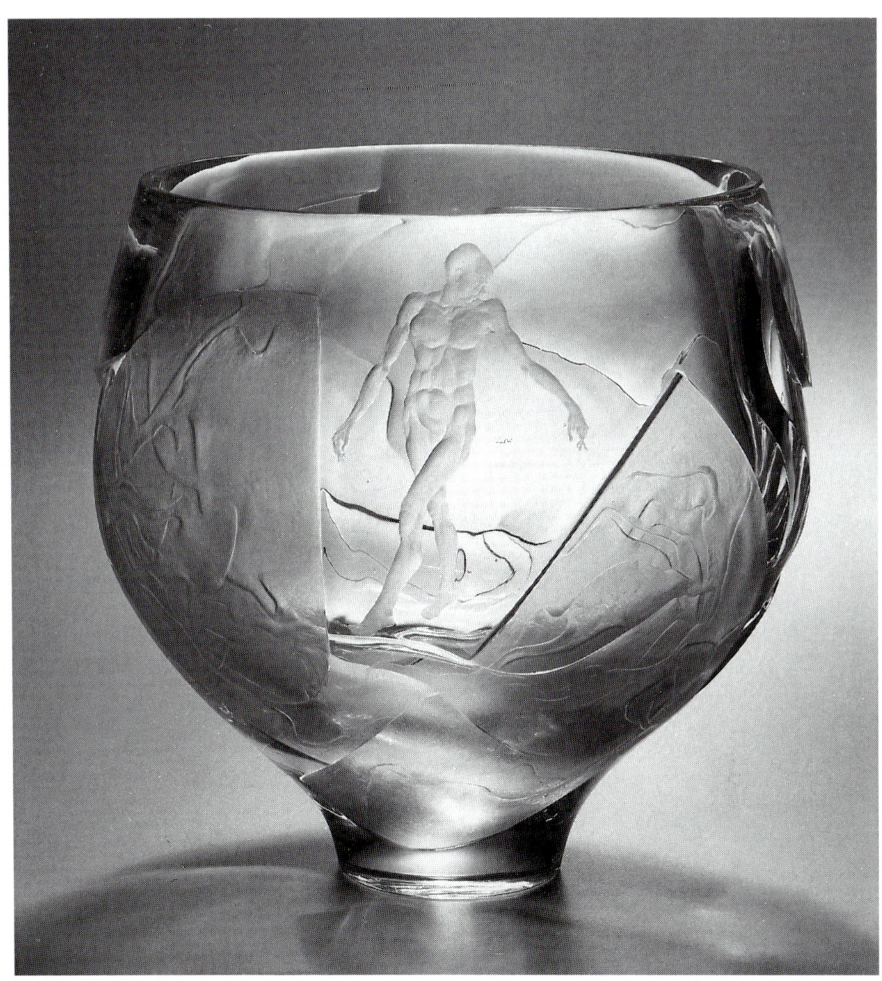

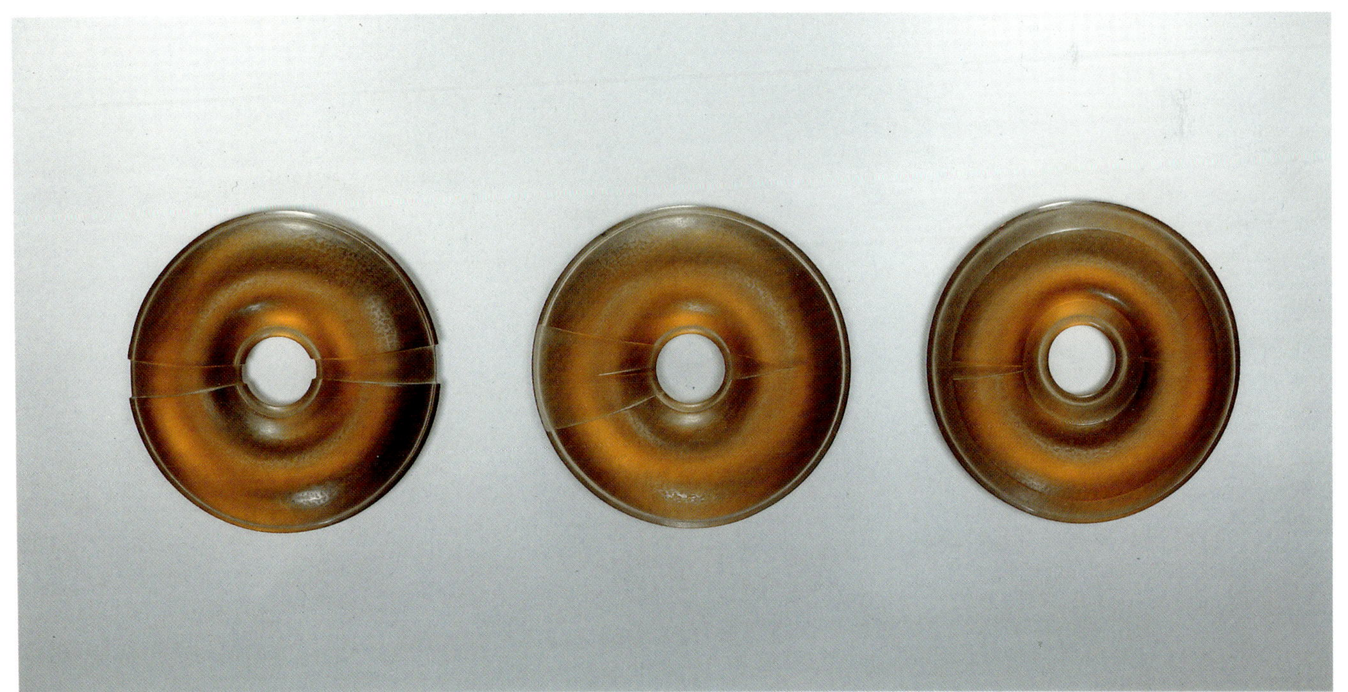

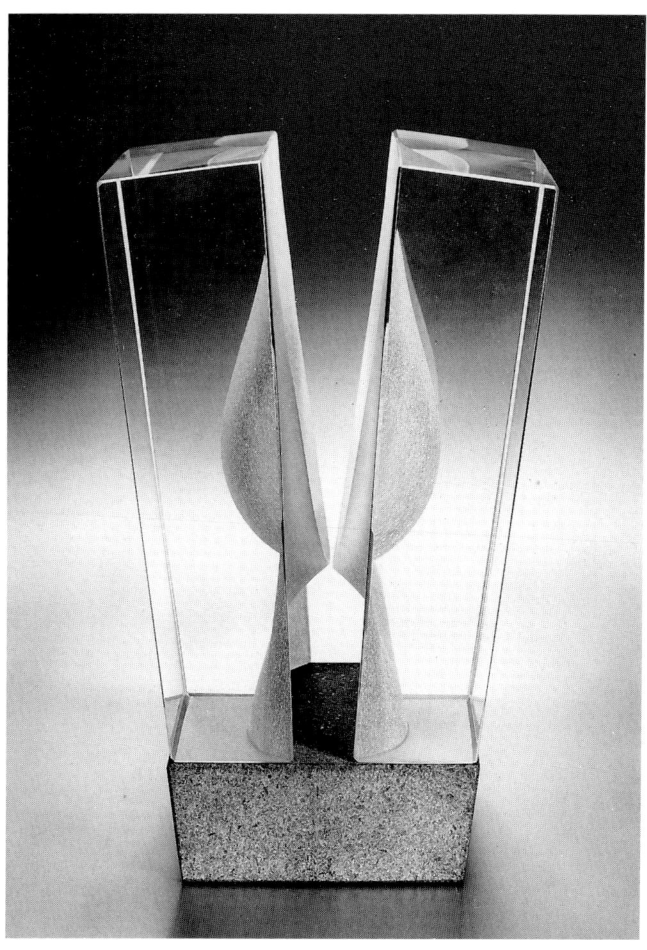

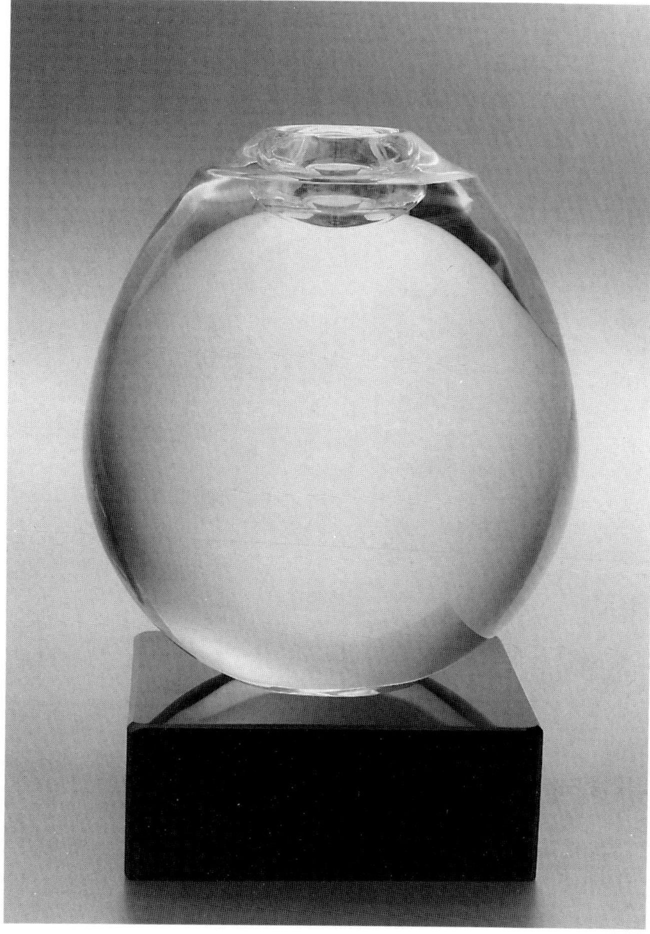

Willi Pistor
(b. 1935)

Education: Glasfachschule Hadamar; apprenticeship as hollow-glass finisher; qualifying
examination as master
Lives and works in Wilsenroth and Hadamar
(specialist teacher)

459 Object

Diamond-engraved mark on the reverse, at
the bottom: *Willi Pistor 82*
1982
H with pedestal 24.9, W 16.2, D 12.5 cm

Optic glass. Mold-melted. Interior surfaces
coarsely mat, slightly etched. Exterior surfaces polished. Granite pedestal.

Acc. no. P 1984-71
Acquired at the exhibition "Licht. Form.
Gestalt"

Lit.: Ricke, *Licht. Form. Gestalt*, 1980,
cat. no. 142

Josef Welzel
(b. 1927)

Education: Apprenticeship as glass cutter and
engraver; Glasfachschule Rheinbach; qualifying examination as master glass engraver at
the Höhere Fachhochschule, Schwäbisch
Gmünd
Lives and works as a specialist teacher in
Hadamar

460 Vase Object

Diamond-engraved mark on the underside of
base: *JW 1982*
1982
H without pedestal 15.4, $\varnothing$ 14 cm

Optic glass. Cut from the block and polished.

Acc. no. P 1984-24
Acquired at the exhibition "New Glass in Germany"

Lit.: Ricke, *New Glass Germany*, 1983,
cat. no. 179

Ernst Krebs
(b. 1939)

Education: Fachschule für Glas und Schmuck-
waren, Kaufbeuren-Neugablonz; Glasfachschule
Zwiesel; Akademie der Bildenden Künste,
Munich
Lives and works in Munich

461 "Über den Wolken"

Engraved mark on the underside of base:
E. Krebs 81
1981
H 52.4, ⌀ 17.2 cm

Colorless crystal glass. Blown in skeleton
mold. Engraved and sandblasted.

Acc. no. P 1984-65
Acquired at the exhibition "New Glass in
Germany"

Lit.: Ricke, *New Glass Germany*, 1983,
cat. no. 95

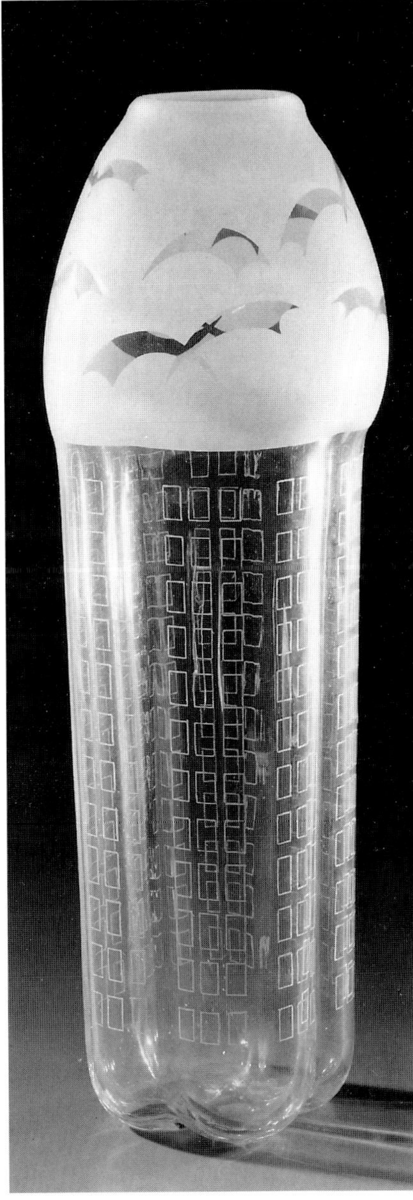

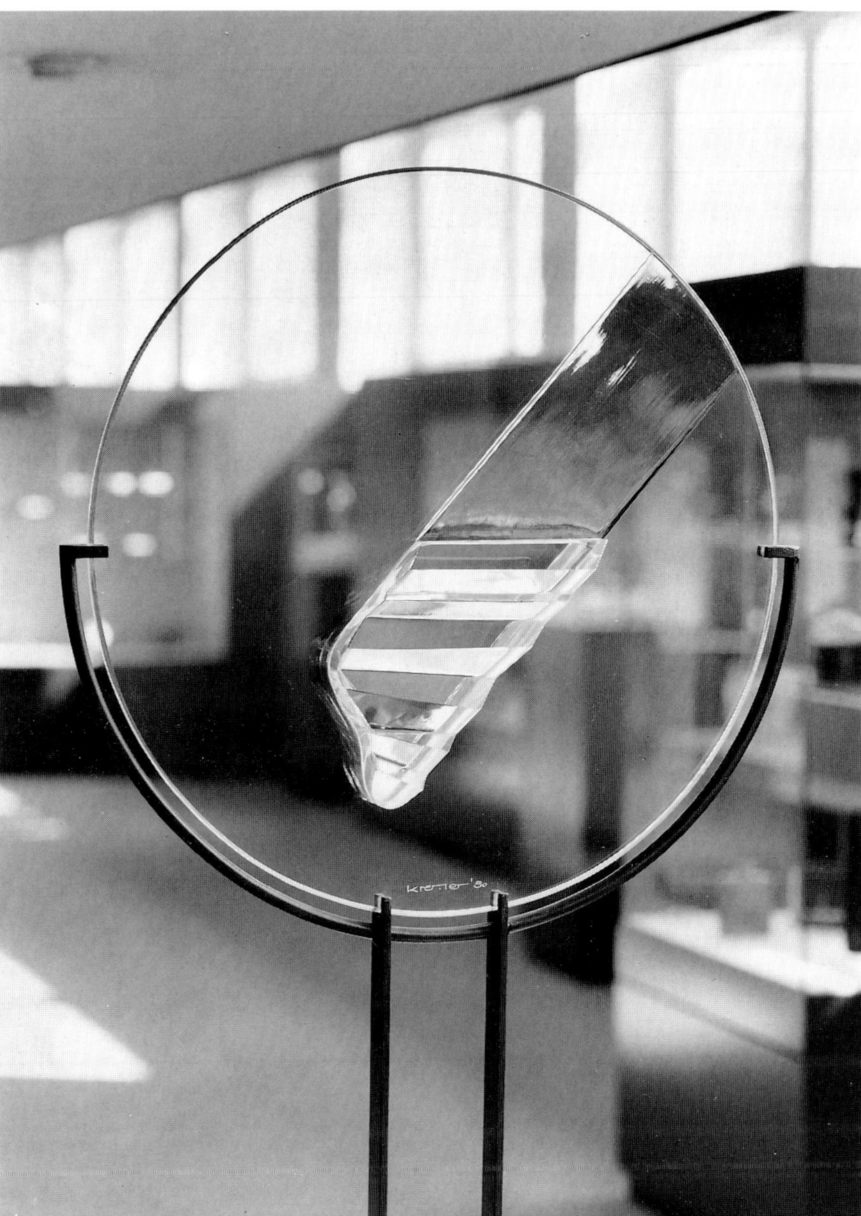

Hans Peter Kremer
(1947–1981)

Education: Apprenticeship as glass painter;
qualifying examination as master
Lived and worked in Gevelsberg

462 Standing Object

Engraved mark at the bottom of round plate:
Kremer '80
1980
H with mount 170, ⌀ 70, D 6.5 cm
Thickness of plate glass: 1.3 cm

Disk made of optic glass with deep polished
cuts. On front and back a laminated, cut, and
polished insert. Iron mount with black lacquer.

Acc. no. P 1981-294
Acquired at the exhibition "Licht. Form.
Gestalt"

Lit.: *Ricke, Licht. Form. Gestalt*, 1980, cat. no.
54; *Glaskunst: 81. Internationale Ausstellung
zur Studioglasbewegung der Gegenwart*, exh.
cat. (Kassel: Orangerie, 1981), cat. no. 141;
G. Nicola, "Glaskunst: Auf dem Weg zur
Massenkunst," *NG*, no. 4 (1981): 155ff., fig.
43

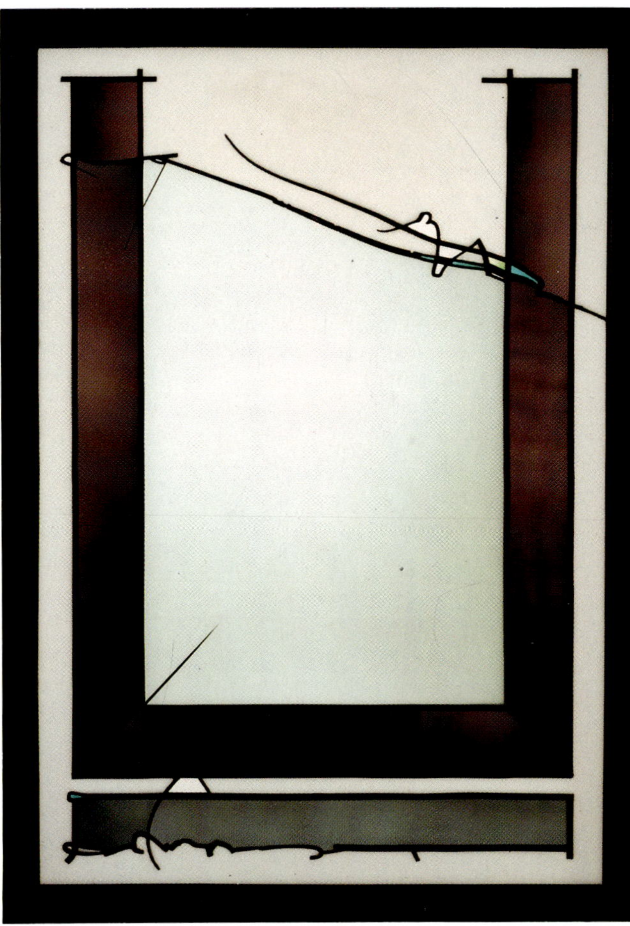

Johannes Schreiter
(b. 1930)

Education: Werkschule Münster and Landeskunstschule Mainz
Lives and works in Langen near Darmstadt

463   "Fragmentraum-Bild" 25/1982/GB

Diamond-engraved mark lower left:
Schreiter 82
1982
H 117, W 82 cm

Leaded glass. Opal overlay, opaque glass, and Plexiglas. Fired black-enamel painting. Wooden frame.

Acc. no. P 1984-20
Acquired from the artist at the exhibition "New Glass in Germany"

Carried out in collaboration with Werkstatt Wilhelm Derix, Rottweil and Taunusstein.

Lit.: Ricke, *New Glass Germany*, 1983, cat. no. 156

Jochem Poensgen
(b. 1931)

Self-taught
Lives and works in Soest

464   Pictorial Window

Unsigned
1985
H 85, W 85, D approx. 22 cm

Leaded glass in three layers: so-called antique glass with milk-glass bands, opal and blue overlay glass, and industrial flat and ornamental glass.

Acc. no. P 1985-4
Acquired from the artist

Lit.: –

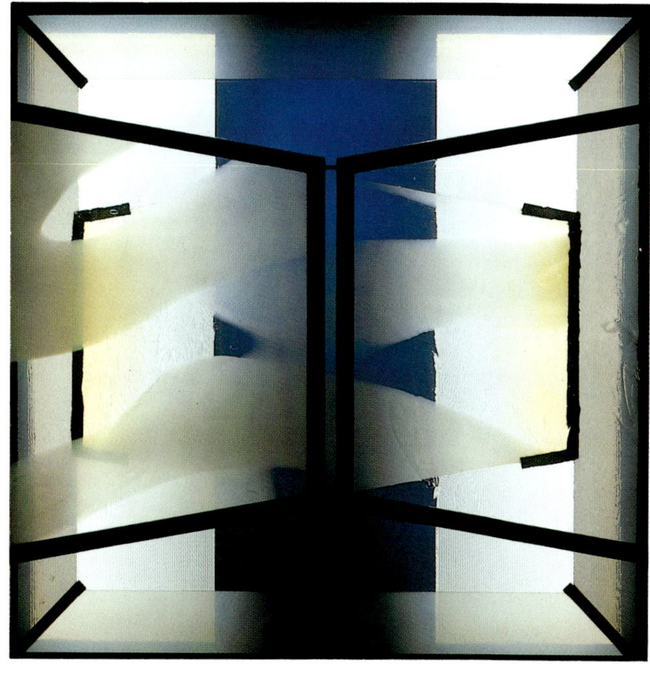

Hans Gottfried von Stockhausen
(b. 1920)

Education: Staatliche Akademie der Bildenden
Künste, Stuttgart
Lives and works in Buoch near Stuttgart

465   "Rot-Blau-Gelb"

Unsigned
1969
H 70, W 50 cm

Leaded glass. Colored overlay glass. Details
cut.

Acc. no. P 1983-142
Gift of the artist

From the "Moon" series. Background slightly
altered by artist after damaged.

Lit.: Hans Gottfried von Stockhausen, *Das
Glasbild*, texts by S. Beeh-Lustenberger,
B. Hauser, H. Ricke, P. Schmitt, and H. G. v.
Stockhausen (Munich, 1987), pl. 5

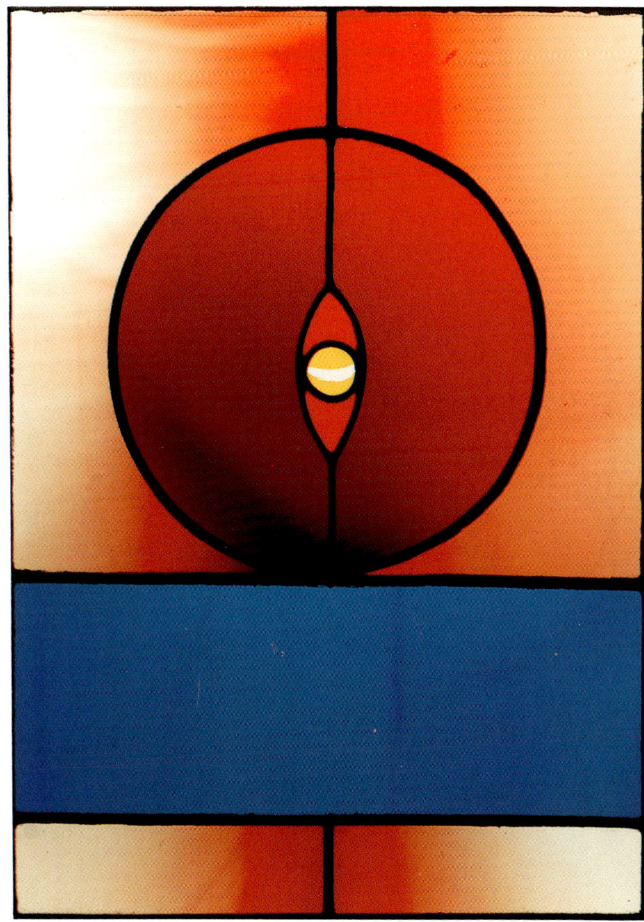

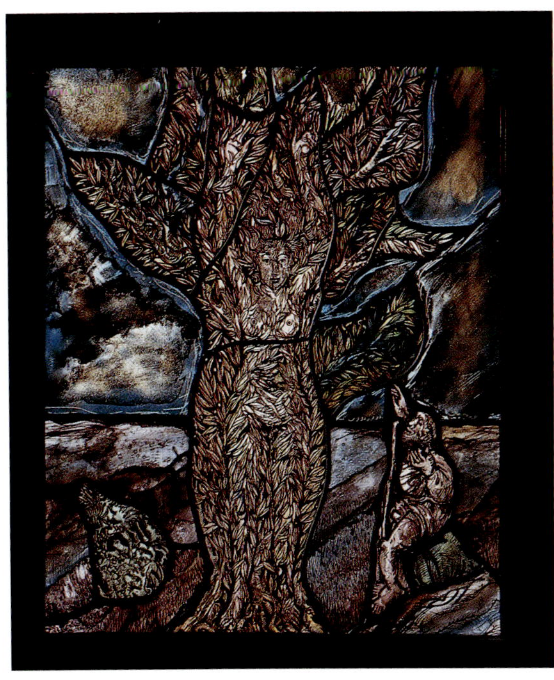

466   "Daphne"

Mark scratched into lower center and lower
right of painting: *ST 82 and ST*
1982
H 60.3, W 50.2 cm

Leaded glass. Overlay glass. Fired black-
enamel painting, in part etched before firing.
Wooden frame.

Acc. no. P 1984-29
Acquired from the artist at the exhibition
"New Glass in Germany"

Lit.: Ricke, *New Glass Germany*, 1983,
cat. no. 165

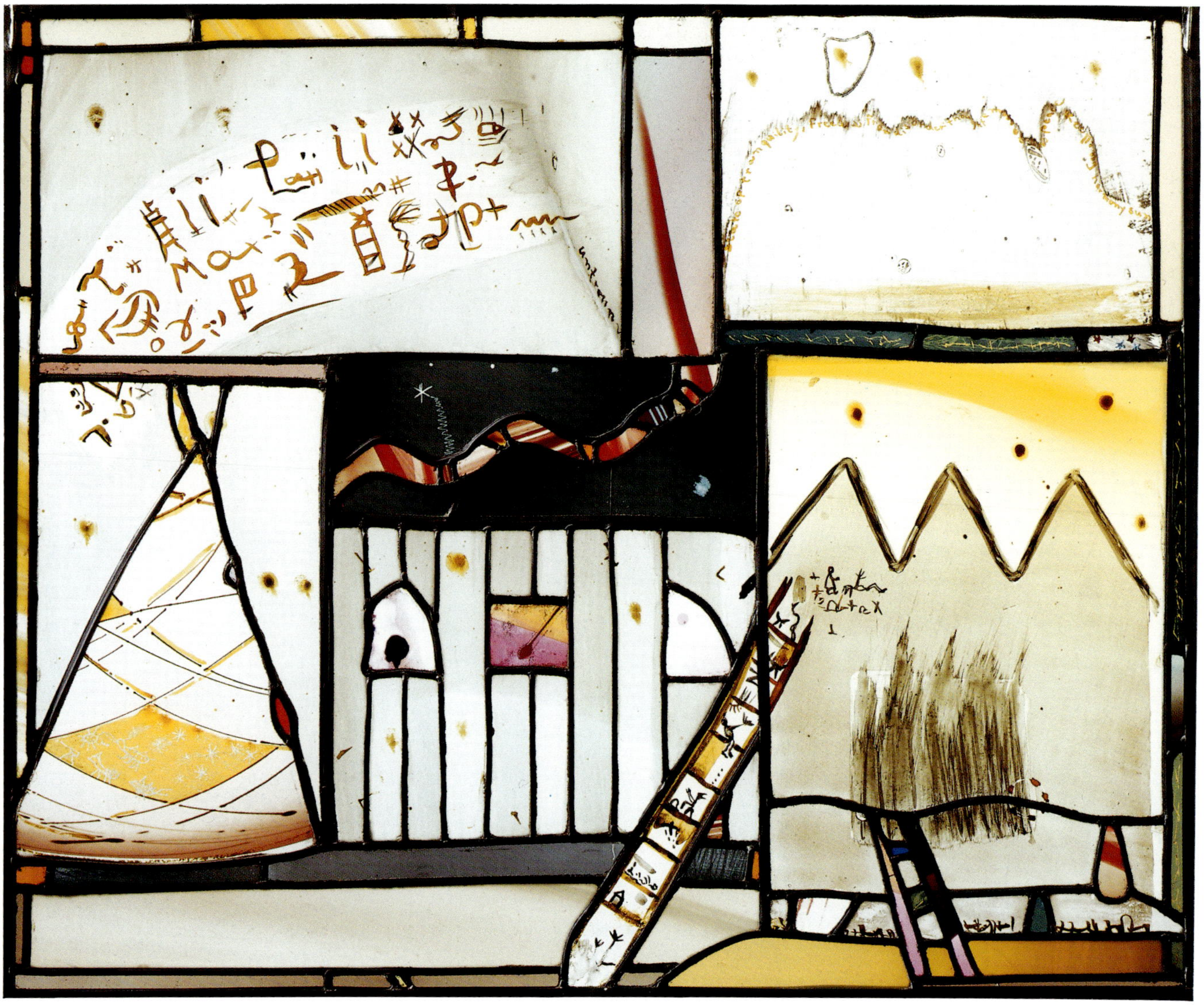

Ursula Huth
(b. 1952)

Education: Akademie der Bildenden Künste,
Stuttgart
Lives and works in Weil im Schönbuch near
Stuttgart

467 **"Ich" · "Sometimes I feel when I
kick up my heels in the sun, I'm the
happiest one"**

Mark scratched into the lead on the lower
frame profile: *Januar 1983 Ursula Huth*
1983
H 56.8, W 69.6 cm

Leaded glass. Transparent and opaque glass,
several overlays. Fired painting, engraving.

Acc. no. P 1984-62
Acquired from the artist at the exhibition
"New Glass in Germany"

Lit.: Ricke, *New Glass Germany*, 1983,
cat. nos. 23, 57, and 133

468 **Boat**

Unsigned
1991
H 18, L 49.5, W 15 cm

Pâte de verre, mold-melted. Colorless and
blue-gray tones. Three separate oars.

Acc. no. P 1992-5
Gift of the artist

The three oar-like sticks belonging to the
object can be arranged at will.

Lit.: –

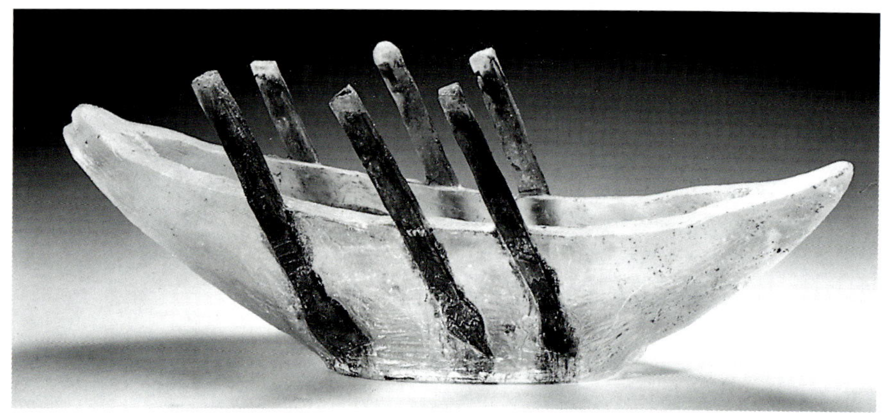

Johannes Hewel
(b. 1947)

Education: Staatliche Akademie der Bildenden
Künste, Stuttgart
Lives and works in Rot am See near Stuttgart

469   "Red Piece"

Unsigned
1988
H 60, W 50 cm

Leaded glass. Multicolored mixed glass.
Etched and fired black enameling applied to
back of glass.

Acc. no. P 1989-19
Acquired from the artist

Part of a series with a similar theme, two
others of which, *Green Piece* and *Yellow Piece*,
are also in the museum.

Lit.: –

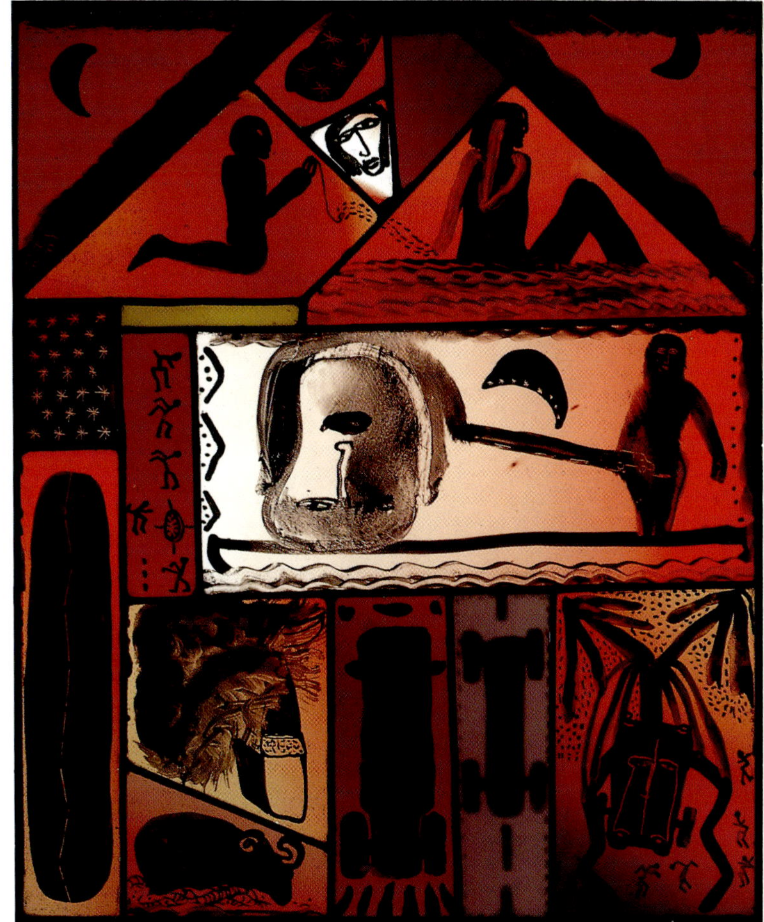

Karin Hubert
until 1986: Stöckle-Krumbein
(b. 1939)

Education: Staatliche Glasfachschule Zwiesel
and Akademie der Bildenden Künste, Munich
Lives and works in Nový Bor (Haida)

470   "Der Mondmann kommt"

Engraved mark on the right foot of the
central figure: *Karin*
1990
⌀ 74 cm

Fragments of broken glass, colorless and with
colored overlay, mat intaglio. Suspended in
iron ring with wires.

Acc. no. P 1991-17
Acquired from the artist at the exhibition
"New Glass in Europe"

Lit.: Ricke, *New Glass Europe*, 1991,
cat. no. 34

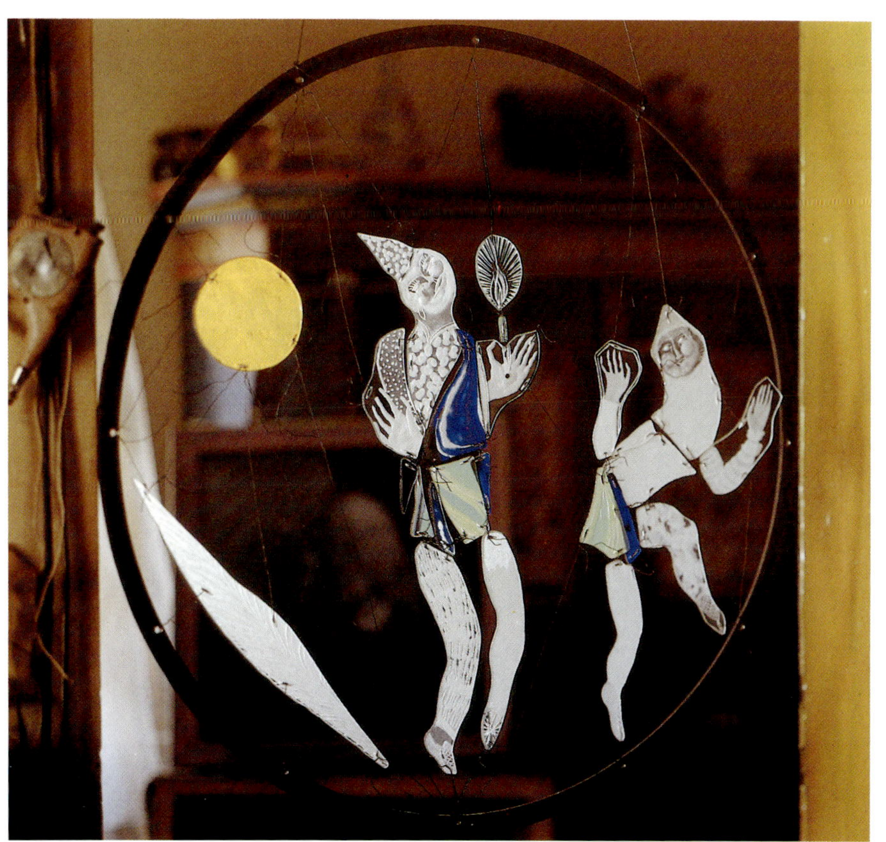

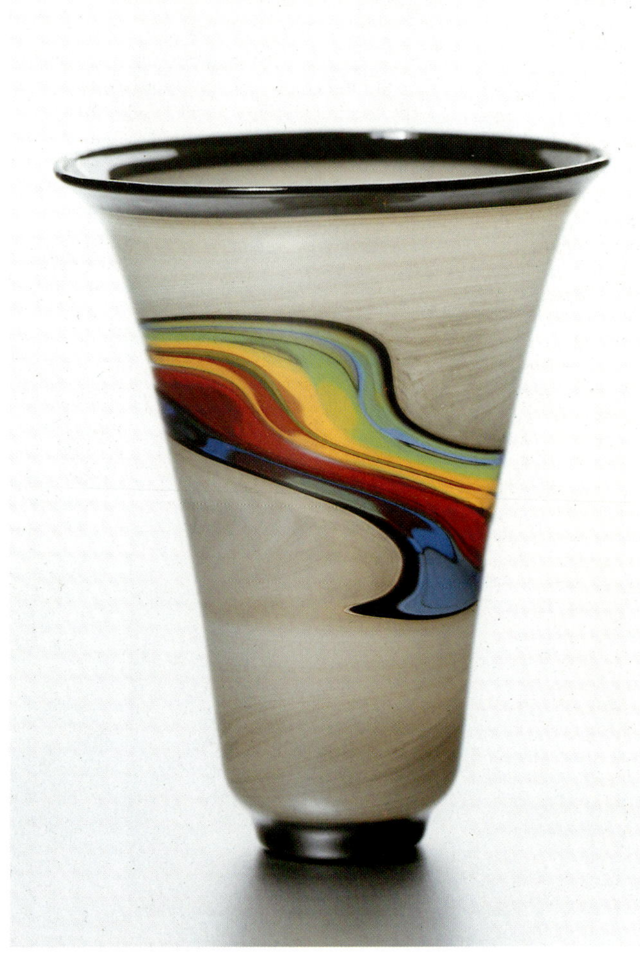 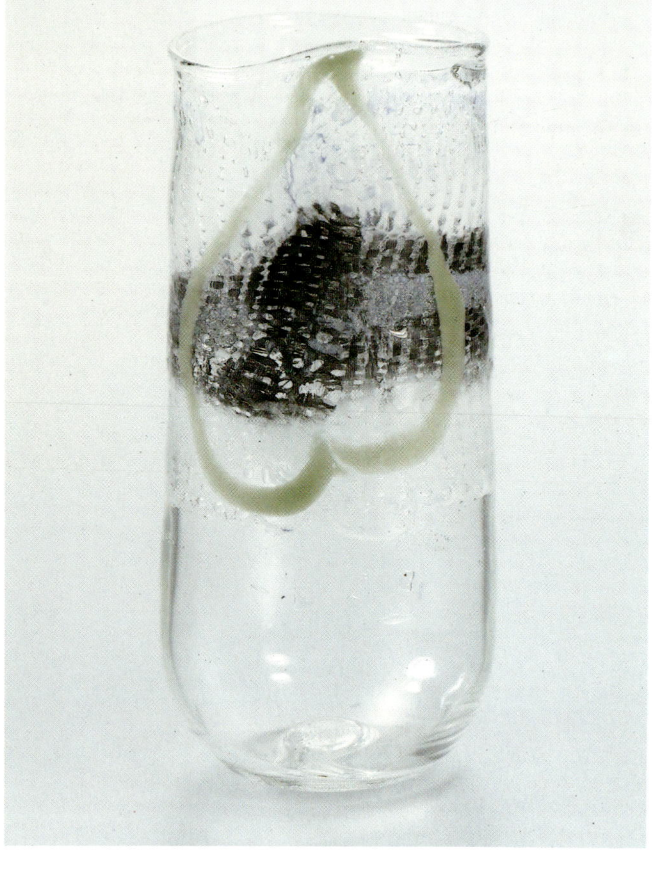

Kurt Wallstab
(b. 1920)

Education: Apprenticeship as glass-instrument maker; Fachschule für Glasinstru-
mententechnik, Ilmenau, Thuringia; qualifying examination as master
Lives and works in Griesheim near Darmstadt

471   Vase

Engraved mark on the underside of base:
Wallstab 82
1982
H 14, ⌀ 11.8 cm

Soft glass, lampblown. Montage technique
with asymmetrically staggered points in milk
glass with applied and fired bright gold leaf
and colorless overlay.

Acc. no. P 1984-23
Acquired at the exhibition "New Glass in Germany"

Lit.: Ricke, *New Glass Germany*, 1983,
cat. no. 173

Uta Majmudar
(b. 1935)

Education: Guest pupil at Glasfachschule
Hadamar; Akademie für gestaltende Hand-
werke Aachen; Pilchuck Summer School
Lives and works in Haan near Düsseldorf

472   Vase

Diamond-engraved mark on the underside of
base: *Uta Maj 86*
1986
H 12.3, ⌀ 5.5 cm

Hard glass, lampblown. Overlay technique
with embedded glass-fiber weave, oxides, and
colored glass threads.

Acc. no. P 1988-6

Lit.: –

Lubomir Hora
(b. 1946)

Education: Studied chemistry in Prague and Bratislava with a course in instrument blowing at the lamp; self-taught as artist
Lives and works in Munich

473   Vase

Mark painted on the underside of base:
Hora '83
1983
H 14.3, W 5, D 4 cm

Hard glass. Overlay technique, mold-blown and shaped at the lamp. Made iridescent with silver compounds in a reducing flame.

Acc. no. P 1984-60
Acquired at the exhibition "New Glass in Germany"

Lit.: Ricke, *New Glass Germany*, 1983, cat. no. 67

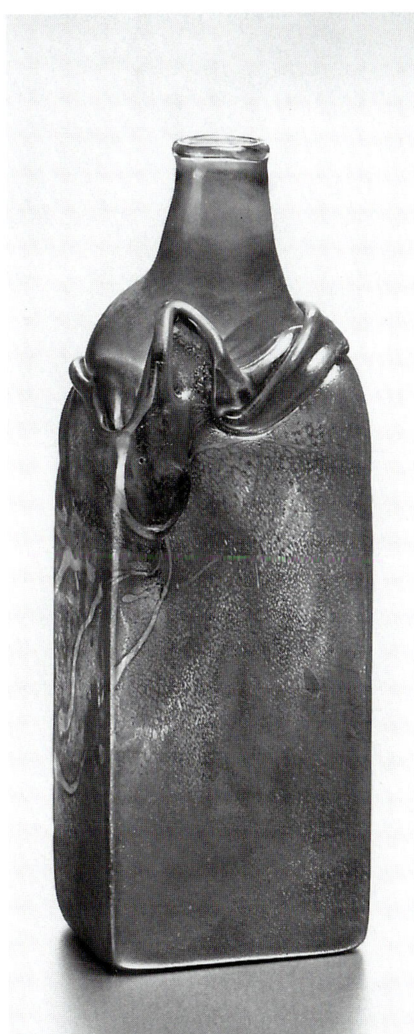

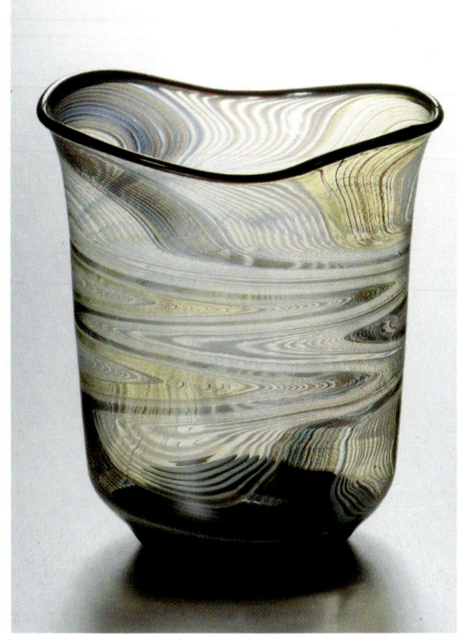

Matthias Klering
(1930–1993)

Education: Apprenticeship as glass-instrument maker; qualifying examination as master; self-taught as artist
Lived and worked in Cologne

474   Vase

Engraved mark on the underside of base:
M. Klering 82
1982
H 11.3, ⌀ 10.9 cm

Soft glass, lampblown. Thread technique, in part using individually colored, hand-drawn threads. Folded lip thread, mounted base.

Acc. no. P 1984-64
Acquired at the exhibition "New Glass in Germany"

Lit.: Ricke, *New Glass Germany*, 1983, cat. no. 84

Rosemarie Lierke
(b. 1934)

Education: Studied mathematics; took courses at the Werkkunstschule Aachen; worked at the studio glass furnace in Toledo, OH
Lives and works in Schwalbach, Taunus

475   Vase

Diamond-engraved mark on the underside of base: *Li 79*
1979
H 20.2, ⌀ 7.8 cm

Hard glass, lampblown. Overlay technique. Crackled enamel decoration between the layers.

Acc. no. P 1979-5

Lit.: Ricke, "Die Kunst der kleinen Form: Glasgestaltung vor der Lampe," *NG*, no. 1 (1980): 28ff., fig. 50

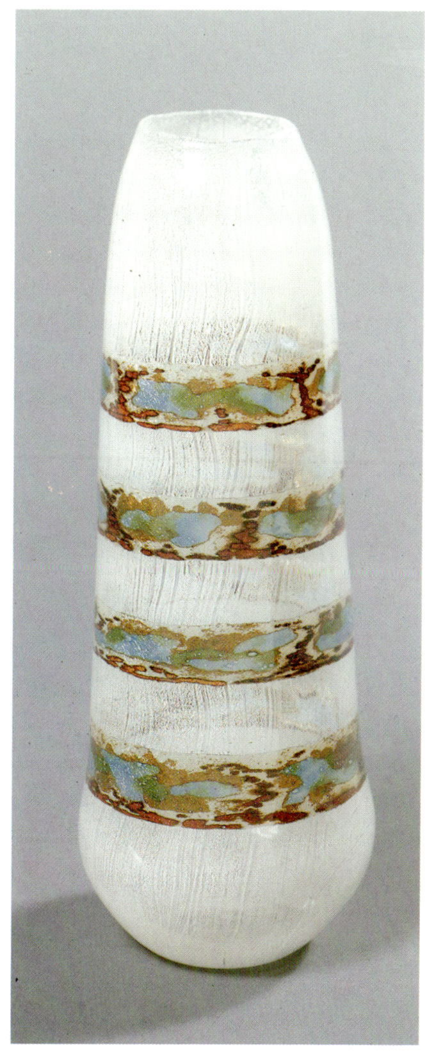

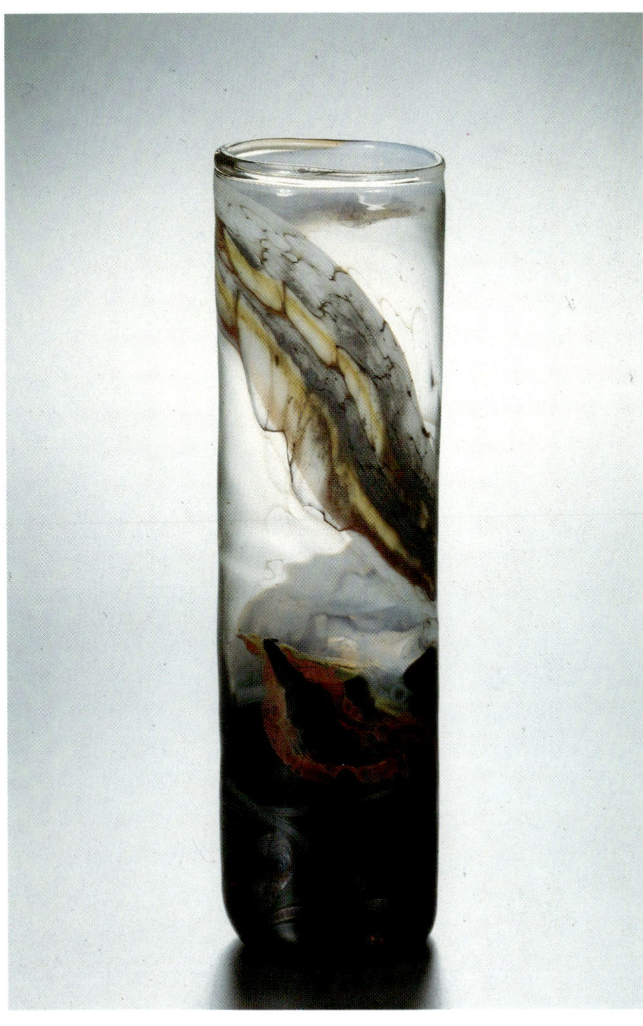

Pavel Molnar
(b. 1940)

Education: Glass School Železný Brod (Eisen-brod); course at the Akademie der Bildenden Künste, Munich
Lives and works in Barsbüttel near Hamburg

476   Vase

Engraved mark on the underside of base:
MP 79
1979
H 16.8, ⌀ 5 cm

Soft glass, lampblown. Colored glass granules embedded into the colorless wall, made by guiding the flame and shaping.

Acc. no. P 1980-18

Lit.: –

Alois Wudy
(b. 1941)

Education: Apprenticeship as hollow-glass painter and training as glass designer at the Glasfachschule Zwiesel
Lives and works as specialist teacher in Zwiesel

477   "Novembernebel" Vase

Engraved mark on the underside of base:
Alois Wudy 1982
1982
H 24.8, ⌀ 14.4 cm

Crystal glass with partial overlay blown into preheated dish painted on the inside, covered with colorless glass, final blow freehand, shaped.

Acc. no. P 1984-25
Acquired at the exhibition "New Glass in Germany"

Lit.: Ricke, *New Glass Germany*, 1983, cat. no. 185

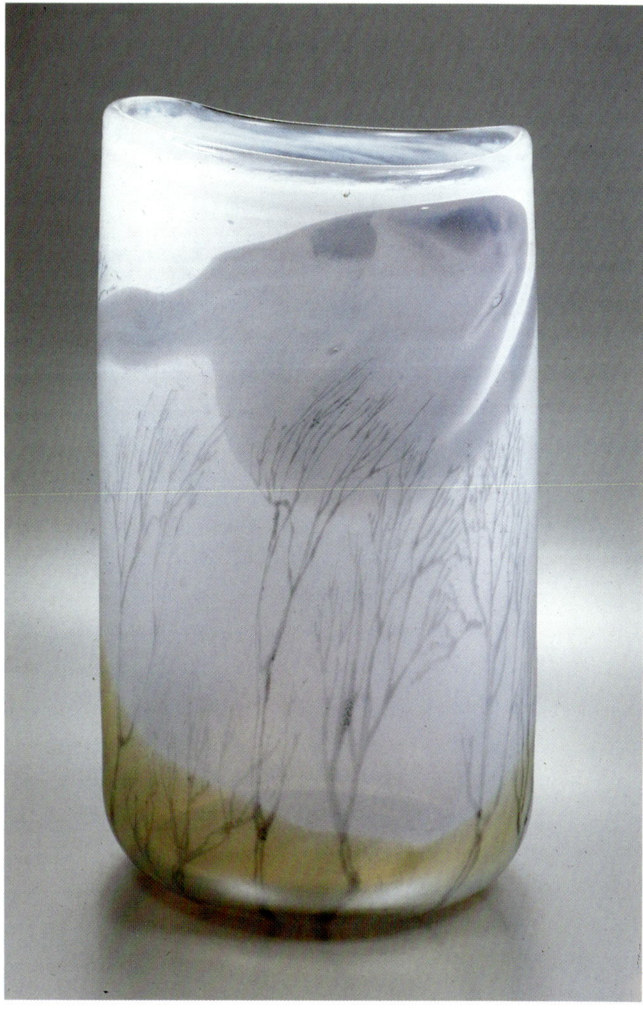

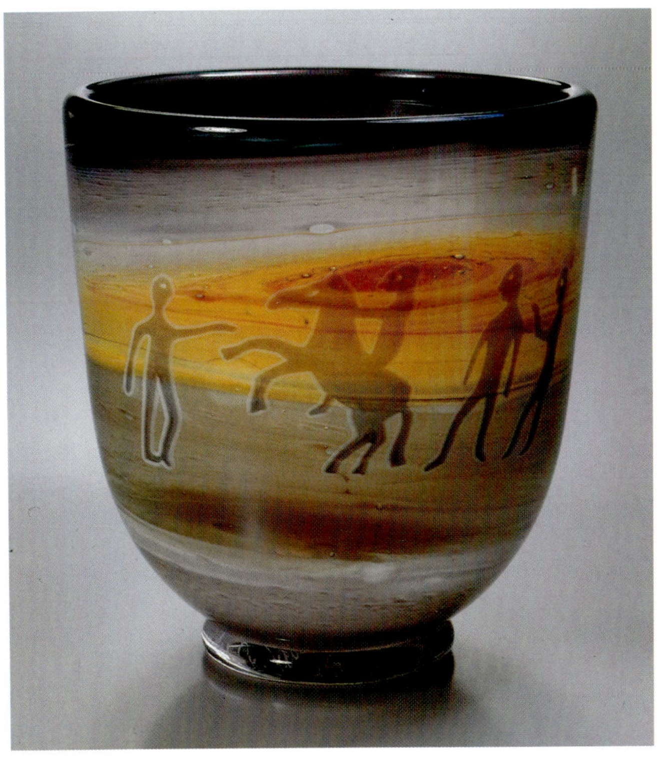

Theodor G. Sellner
(b. 1947)

Education: Apprenticeship as apparatus glassblower, Glasfachschule Zwiesel; qualifying
examination as master; self-taught as artist
Lives and works in Regenhütte, Bavarian
Forest

478   Vase

Engraved mark on the underside of base:
Th. G. Sellner 1983 Jan.
1983
H 20.9, ⌀ 19.5 cm

Combined work at the furnace and at the
lamp. Piece prepared at the lamp received
colorless flashing and two colored casings at
the furnace. Decoration made with sandblast
apparatus. Reheated, given colorless flashing,
and free-blown.

Acc. no. P 1984-22
Acquired at the exhibition "New Glass in
Germany"

Lit.: Ricke, *New Glass Germany*, 1983,
cat. no. 160

Jörg F. Zimmermann
(b. 1940)

Education: Apprenticeship as glass cutter;
Werkkunstschule Schwäbisch Gmünd; qualify-
ing examination as master
Lives and works in Uhingen

479   "Blaues Gespenst"

Engraved mark below the blowpipe's opening:
Jörg Zimmermann 1880
1984
H 24.6, ⌀ 25.3 x 22 cm

Colorless glass with blue inclusions, free-
blown through wire net, given colorless
flashing, finally blown and shaped.

Acc. no. LP 1985-60
Acquired at the exhibition "Zweiter Coburger
Glaspreis"
On permanent loan from the Museumsverein

Lit.: Coburg II, 1985, cat. no. 54a

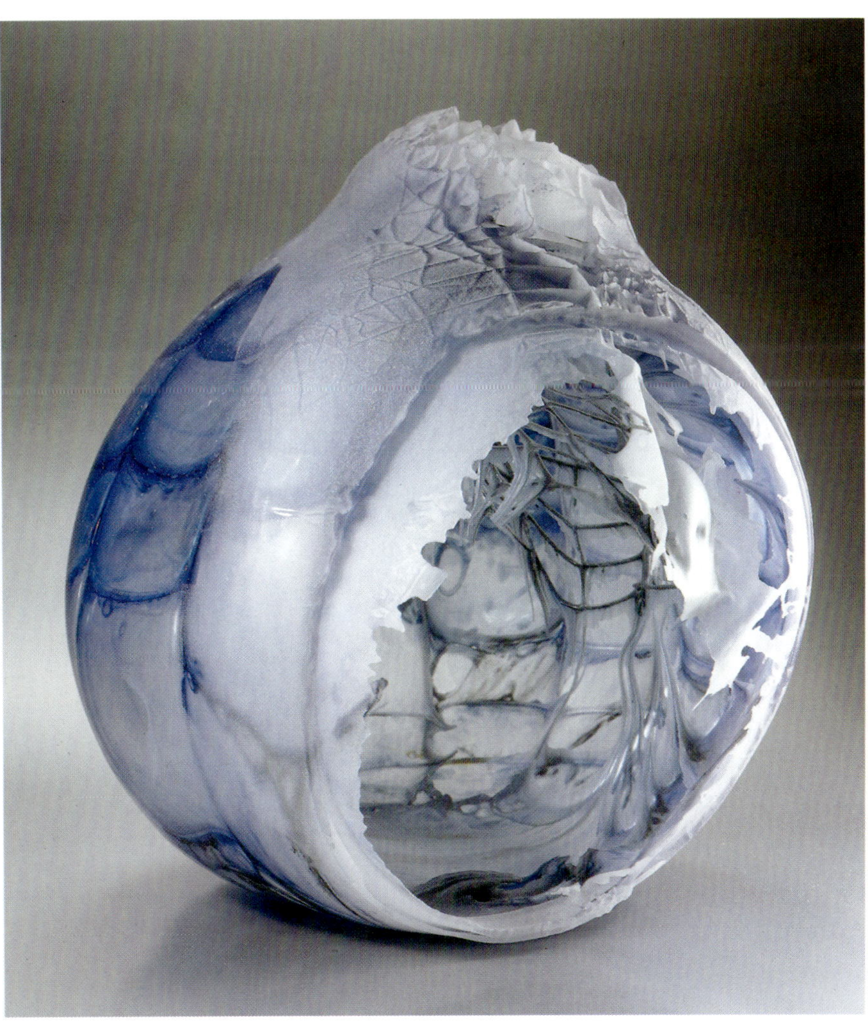

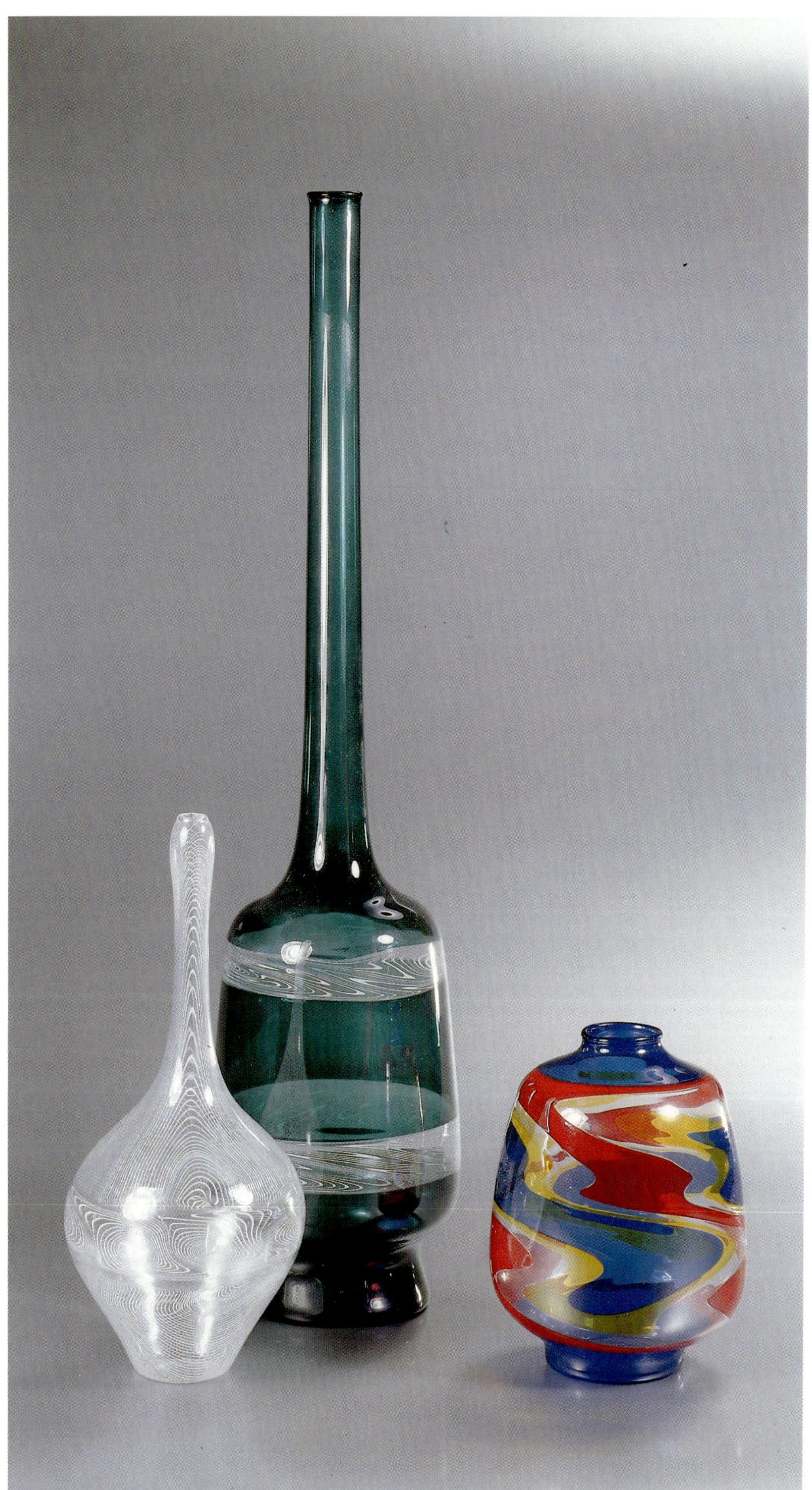

Albin Schaedel
(1905–1999)

Education: Apprenticeship as art-glass blower; qualifying examination as master
Lived and worked in Arnstadt

480   Vase

Mark: applied relief thread on the underside
of base: *S*
1965
H 17.1, ⌀ 7.7 cm

Colorless soft glass with opaque white
threads. Lampblown, montage technique.

Acc. no. P 1969-4
Gift of Helmut Hentrich

So-called shell decoration; see A. Mahnert
and M. Steffens, *Aus der Sammlung des Anger-
museums: Albin Schaedel: Glas vor der Lampe
geblasen* (Erfurt, n.d. [1979]), cat. nos. 97ff.
esp. no. 102.

Lit.: R. Lierke, "Vom heissen Glas: Ofentech-
nik—Lampentechnik," *NG*, no. 3 (1980):
106ff., fig. 30

481   Vase

Mark: applied relief thread on the underside
of base: *S*
Ca. 1965–70
H 37, ⌀ 8.5 cm

Steel blue glass with thread-glass ribbons,
colorless and opaque white. Lampblown,
montage technique.

Acc. no. P 1973-10

See H. Schönemann, *Albin Schaedel: Veröffentlichungen der Museen der Stadt Arnstadt* 5
(Weimar, n.d. [1979]), cat. no. 8 (vessel
design 1952–76), fig. 25.

Lit.: H. Ricke, "Die Kunst der kleinen Form:
Glasgestaltung vor der Lampe," *NG*, no. 1
(1980): 28–35, fig. 49; H. Ricke, "Die
Lauschaer Kunstglasbläser," *NG*, no. 2 (1983):
57ff., fig. 17

482   Vase

Mark: applied relief thread on the underside
of base: *S*
Ca. 1965–70
H 10, ⌀ 7.8 cm

Blue glass. Embedded pieces: colorless, red,
and yellow. Montage technique.

Acc. no. P 1973-11

Lit.: H. Ricke, "Die Kunst der kleinen Form:
Glasgestaltung vor der Lampe," *NG*, no. 1
(1980): 28–35, fig. 49

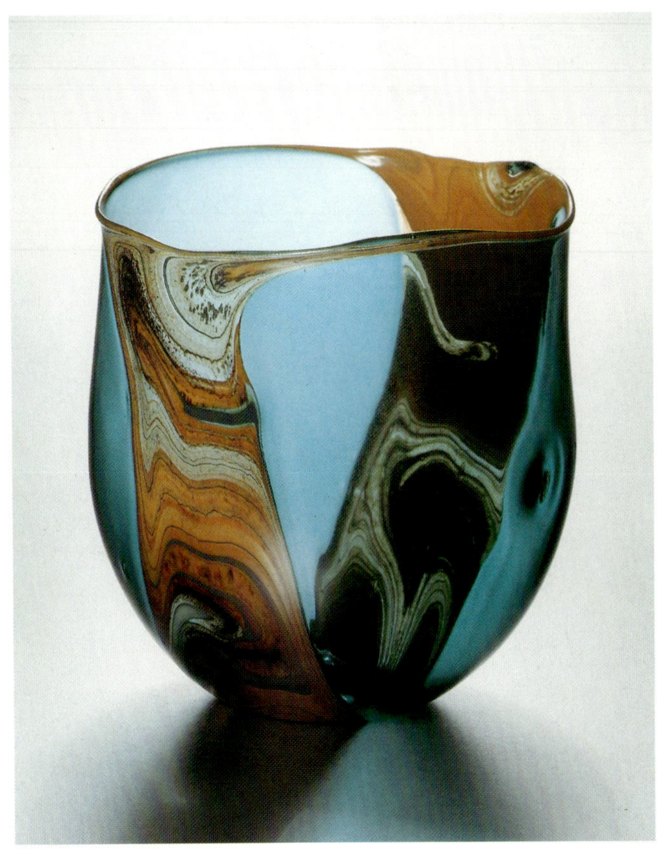

Volkhard Precht
(b. 1930)

Education: Apprenticeship as art-glass blower; guest student at the Fachschule für Keramik- und Spielzeuggestaltung in Sonneberg; qualifying examination as master
Lives and works in Lauscha, Thuringian Forest

484   "Florid" Vase

Engraved mark on the underside of base:
V. Precht 1976 II "Florid"
1976
H 13.4, ∅ 20.8 cm

Free-blown and shaped. Several partial overlays.

Acc. no. P 1977-18
Acquired at the exhibition "Coburger Glaspreis 1977"

For similar works see *Glaskunst in der DDR*, exh. cat. (Leipzig: Museum des Kunsthandwerks, 1977), nos. 27ff.

Lit.: Coburg I, 1977, cat. no. 204b

Hubert Koch
(b. 1932)

Education: Apprenticeship as art-glass blower; qualifying examination as master
Lives and works in Lauscha, Thuringian Forest

483   Vase

Mark: small glass canes applied in relief on the underside of base: *HK* (ligated)
1982
H 11.8, ∅ 11.7 cm

Lampblown. Assembled in montage technique. The embedded band is striped with colored enamel canes.

Acc. no. P 1983-9

Lit.: –

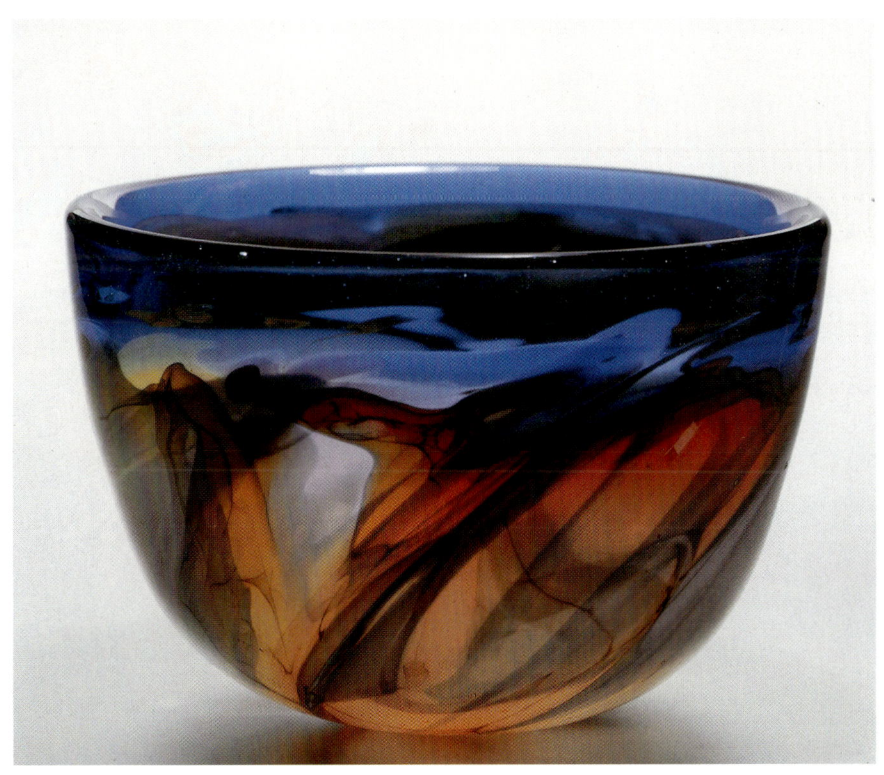

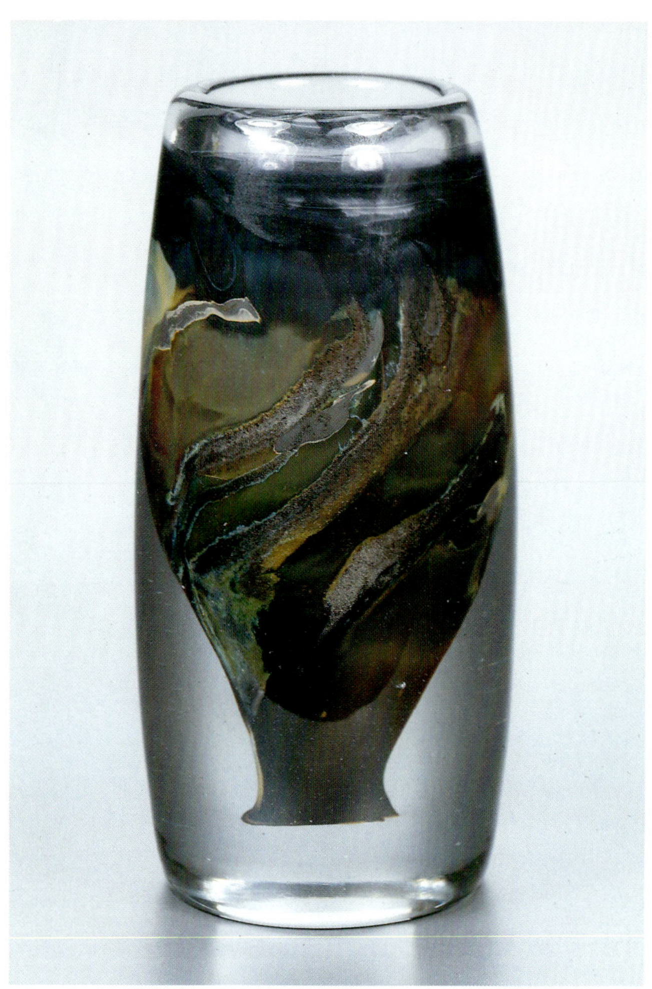

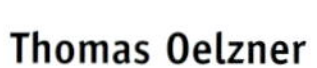

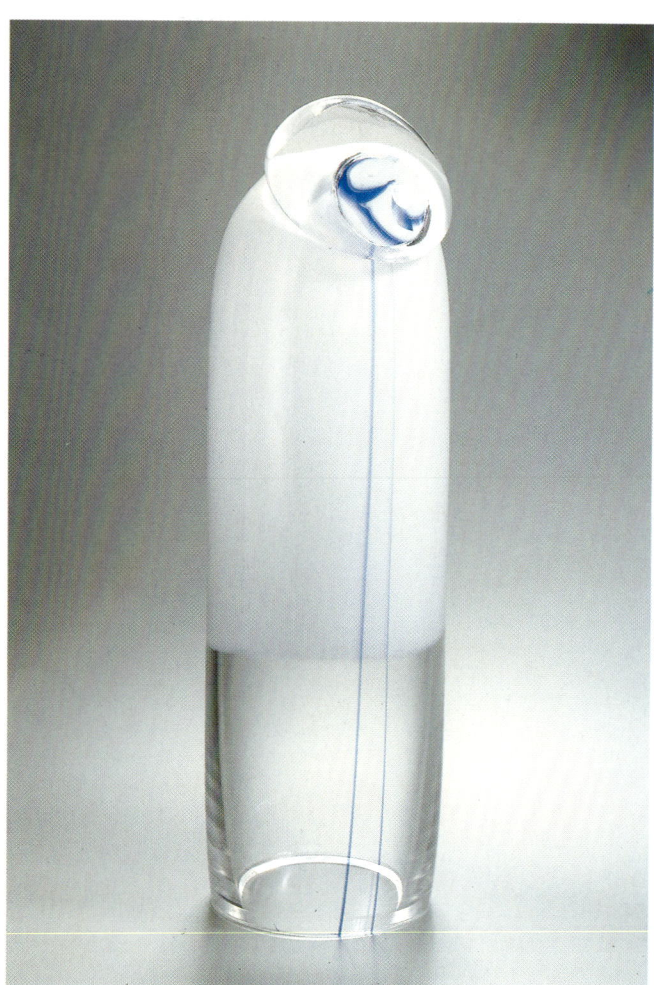

Thomas Oelzner
(b. 1939)

Education: Apprenticeship as goldsmith

Ulrike Oelzner
(b. 1939)

Education: Apprenticeship as goldsmith;
studied at the Hochschule für industrielle
Formgestaltung, Burg Giebichenstein, Halle
The couple lives and works in Leipzig

485   Vase

Engraved mark on the underside of base:
Oelzner 1978 Baden bei Wien Nr. 29
Baden near Vienna, J & L Lobmeyr—Studio
Franzensbad
1978
H 19.7, ⌀ 9.6 cm

Free-blown and shaped. Multicolored inner
casing with embedded aventurine.

Acc. no. P 1979-1

Lit.: M. Bauer, "Glasmacher in der DDR: Die
Oelzners," *NG*, no. 2 (1981): 65ff., fig. 53

The Netherlands

Sybren Valkema
(1916–1996)

Education: Art Academy, The Hague
Lived and worked in Blaaricum
(see also cat. no. 418)

486   Object

Diamond-engraved mark on the underside of
base: *Leerdam Unica VAA 1 LL Sybren Valkema*
Leerdam, 1973
H 35, ⌀ 10.6 cm

Free-blown and shaped. Opaque white inner
casing, embedded blue threads and marbling.
Ring-shaped air bubble.

Acc. no. P 1977-10

Execution: L. van der Linden. Part of a series
of one-off objects differing only in details.
See, for example, Frantz, *Contemporary Glass*,
1989, 63.

Lit.: Ricke, *Leerdam*, 1977, cat. no. 192; J.
Schou-Christensen, "Der grosse Aufbruch:
Europäische Glaskunst seit 1945," *NG*, no. 1
(1980): 10, fig. 18

Willem Heesen
(b. 1925)

Education: Glass School, Leerdam; Academy
of Fine Arts, The Hague
Lives and works in Acquoi near Leerdam

487 Object

Diamond-engraved mark on the underside of
base: *LEERDAM HAD 11 W Heesen*
Leerdam, 1976
H 33, W 23.5, D 17.7, ∅ cylinder 6.8 cm

Colorless crystal glass cylinders. Cut, polished,
laminated.

Acc. no. P 1977-14
Gift of Vereenigde Glasfabrieken Leerdam

For similar works see Coburg I, 1977,
cat. nos. 329ff.

Lit.: Ricke, *Leerdam*, 1977, cat. no. 217;
Ricke, *Licht. Form. Gestalt*, 1980, cat. no. 42

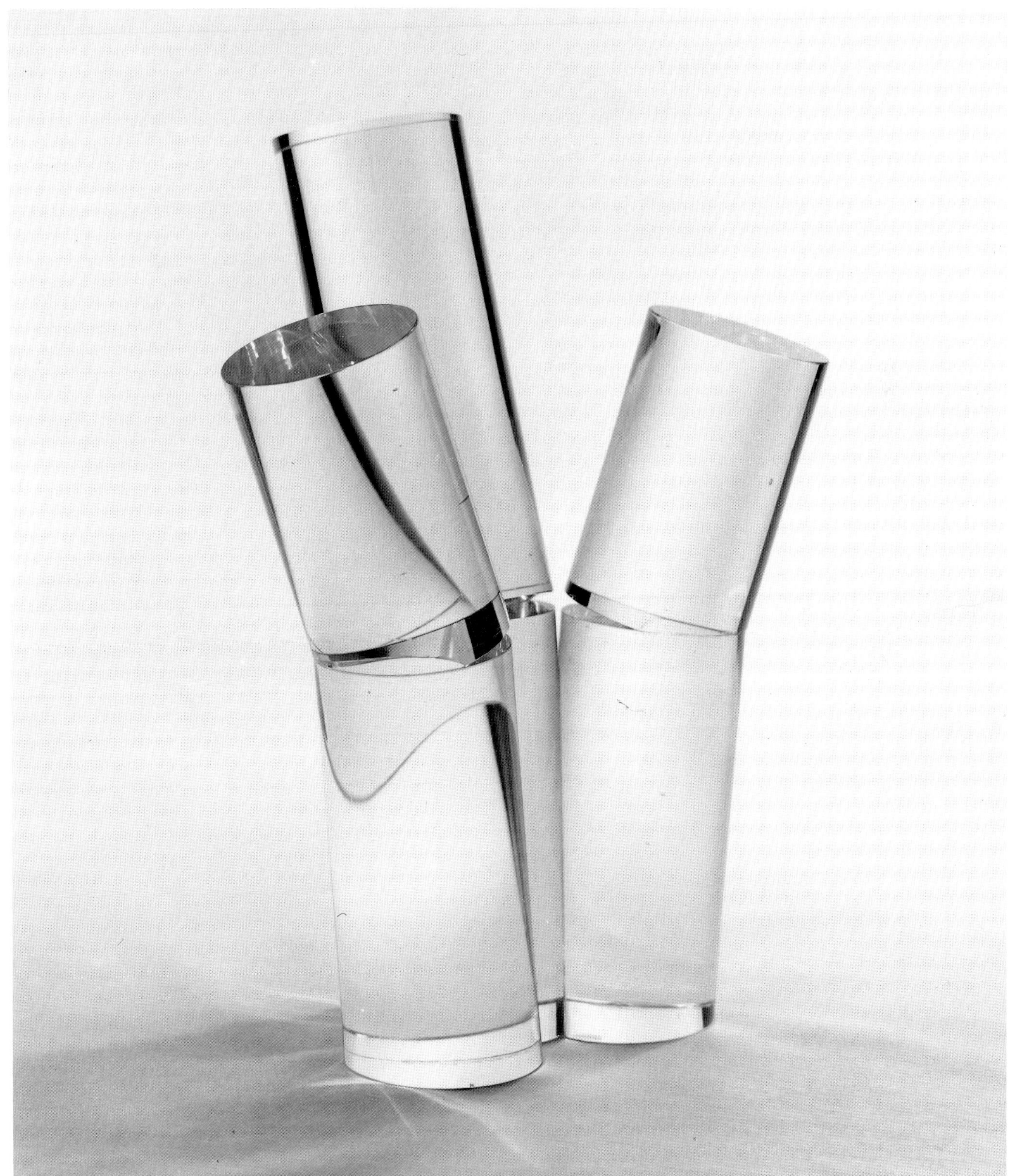

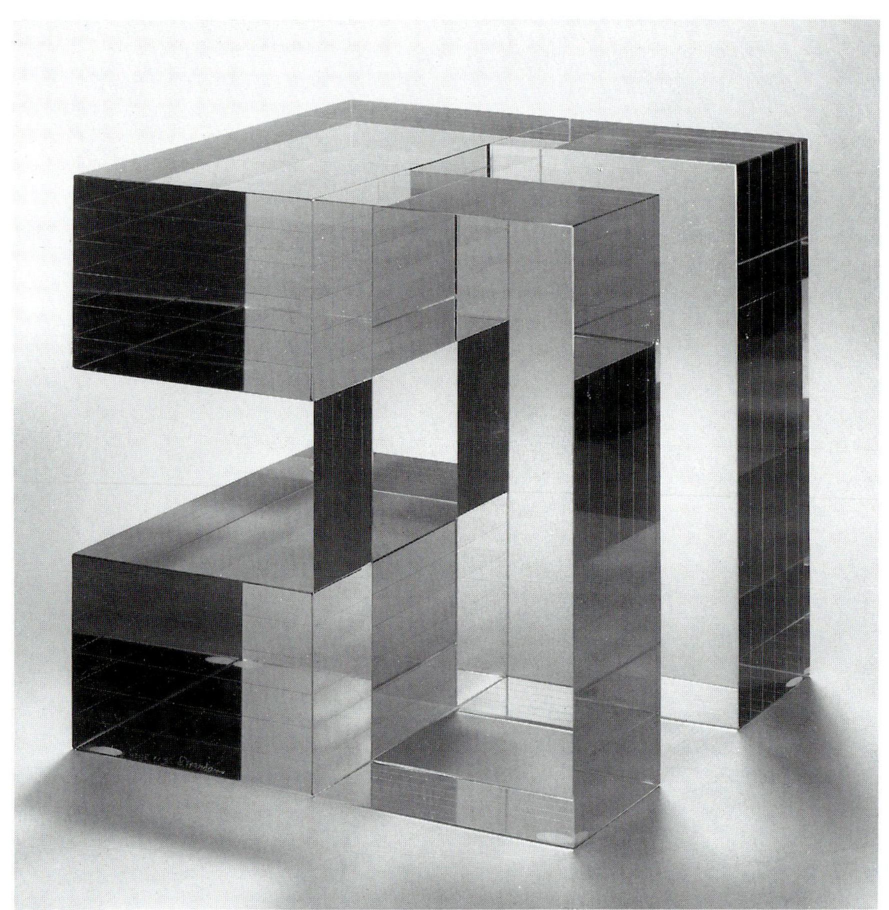

Floris Meydam
(b. 1919)

Education: Glass School, Leerdam
Lives and works in Leerdam
(see also cat. nos. 415–17)

488 Object

Diamond-engraved mark above the standing
base: *LEERDAM MAE 11 V F Meydam*
Cutting by P. W. Vermeer
1977
17.8 x 17.8 x 17.8 cm

Greenish float glass. Comprises four cubes
consisting of laminated flat glass layers.

Acc. no. P 1977-5

Lit.: Ricke, *Leerdam*, 1977, cat. no. 180;
Ricke, *Licht. Form. Gestalt*, 1980, cat. no. 66

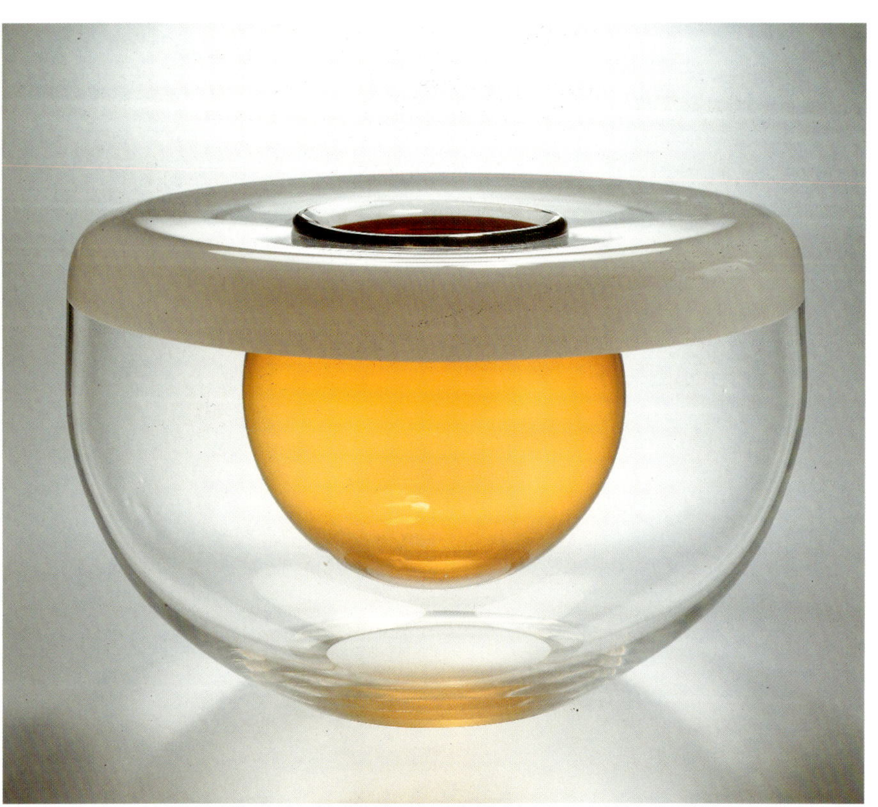

489 Vessel Object

Diamond-engraved mark on the underside of
standing base: *Leerdam Unica MAE 112 LL F
Meydam*
Execution: L. van der Linden
1977
H 19.3, ⌀ 33.5 cm

Free-blown and shaped. Exterior form partly
white, interior form has amber inner casing.

Acc. no. P 1977-15
Gift of Vereenigde Glasfabrieken Leerdam

Lit.: –

Andries Dirk Copier
(1901–1991)

Education: School of Typography in Utrecht;
evening courses at the Academy of Fine Arts,
Rotterdam
Lived in Wassenaer near The Hague; worked
at several European glassworks
(see also cat. nos. 413, 414)

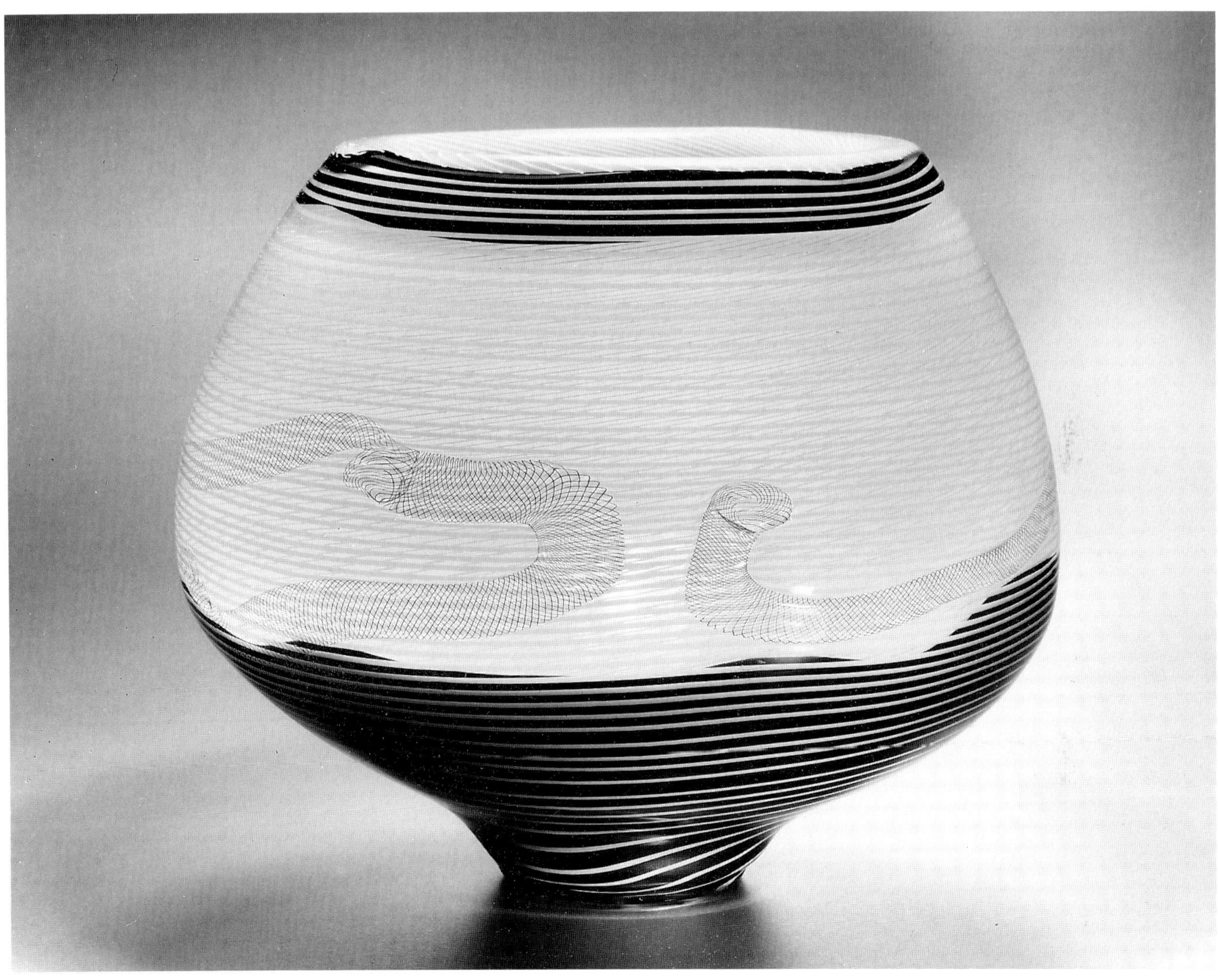

490 Vase

Diamond-engraved mark on the underside of
base: *AD Copier Lino Tagliapietra maggio 81
effetre international 8105 LT*
Execution: Lino Tagliapietra at Effetre International, Murano
1981
H 22.7, ⌀ 28.2 cm

Free-blown and shaped. Opal white inner casing. Over that: black-violet partial overlays
and white thread inclusions embedded in
several colorless layers. Glass cane made with
black threads worked into the surface.

Acc. no. P 1982-13
Acquired from the artist

For another piece from this small series of
one-offs see *World Glass Now*, 1982, 148.

Lit.: *A.D. Copier*, exh. cat. (The Hague: Haags
Gemeentemuseum, 1982), n.p.; D. U. Kuyken-
Schneider, "The Old Man: Andries Dirk Copier,"
NG, no. 2 (1982): 103, fig. 68

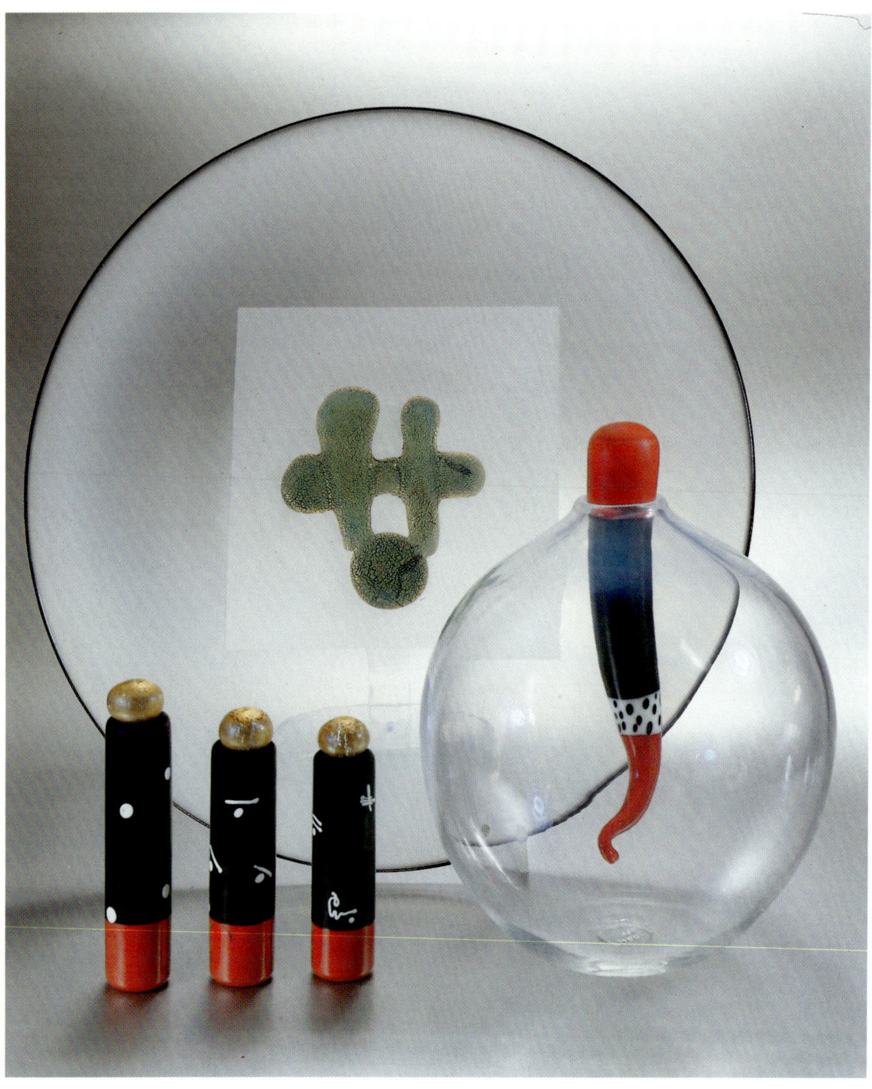

Richard Meitner
(b. 1949)

Education: University of California, Berkeley;
Gerrit Rietveld Academie, Amsterdam
Lives and works in Amsterdam

491 a–c   Flacons

Diamond-engraved mark on the underside of
each base: *R. Meitner '79*
1979
H 12.3, 11.1, 10.8; ⌀ 2.8, 2.8, 2.7 cm

Free-blown and shaped. Partial overlay, inclusions. Stoppers with torn gold leaf.

Acc. nos. P 1980-20-22

Lit.: *NG*, no. 1 (1980): cover image

492   Plate

Diamond-engraved mark on the underside of
base: *R. Meitner '79*
1979
⌀ 35.5 cm

Colorless glass with opaque white inner casing. Free-blown, dilated, embedded black
application with torn gold leaf, folded thread
at edge. Sandblasted in center.

Acc. no. P 1980-19 a

Lit.: See cat. no. 491 a–c

493   "Bottle with Penetrating Form"

Diamond-engraved mark on the underside of
base: *R. Meitner '79*
1979
H with stopper 22.7, ⌀ 18.2 cm

Colorless glass, slightly opalescent. Free-
blown and shaped. Two parts.

Acc. no. P 1980-19 b

Lit.: See cat. no. 491 a–c

494   Vessel Object

Diamond-engraved mark on the underside of
base: *R. Meitner '84*
1984
H with insert 70.7, W 22.8, D 20 cm

Colorless glass. Free-blown and shaped. Two
parts. Sprayed enamel painting. Sandblasted.

Acc. no. LP 1985-65
Acquired at the exhibition "Zweiter Coburger
Glaspreis"
On permanent loan from the Museumsverein

Lit.: Coburg II, 1985, cat. no. 136b; C. Strauss,
"Glas weckt Emotionen—Kunst von Richard
Meitner," *NG*, no. 2 (1985): 85, fig. 34; Ricke,
Museumsarbeit, 1988, 79, fig. 80 (reverse of
object)

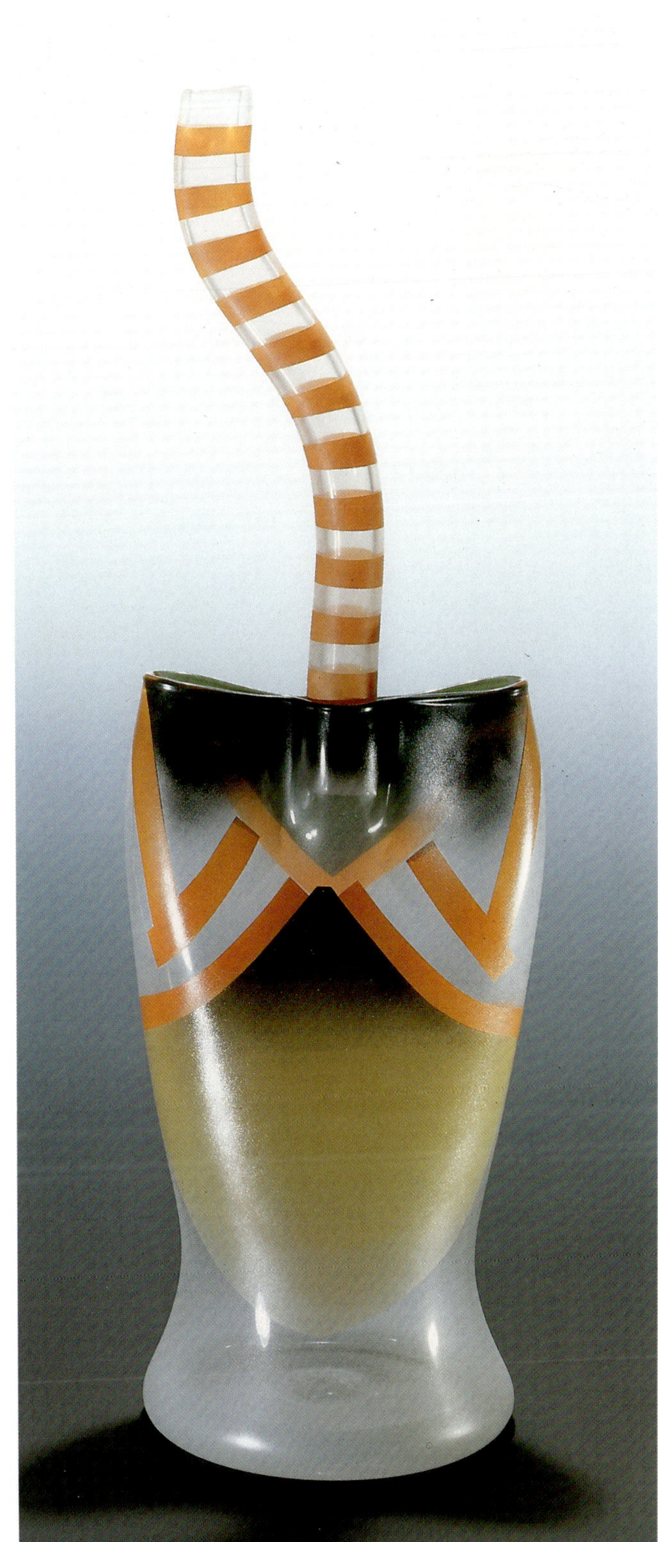

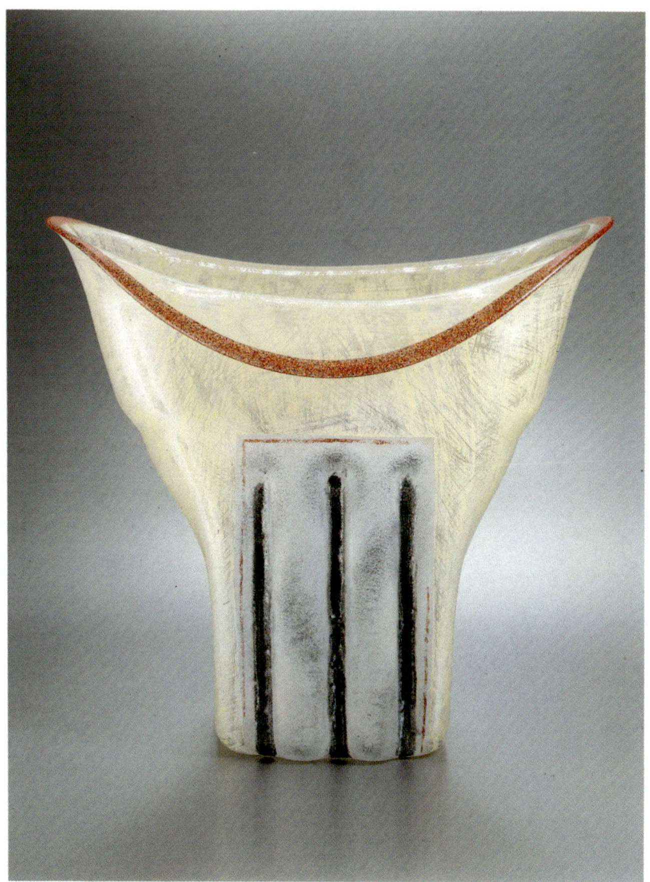

Mieke Groot
(b. 1949)

Education: Gerrit Rietveld Academie, Amsterdam; silversmith and glass designer
Lives and works in Amsterdam

495   Vase Object

Diamond-engraved mark on the underside of base: *MIEKE GROOT '84 21/11/74*
1984
H 23.9, ⌀ 26.8 cm

Colorless glass. Mold-blown, shaped. Rectangular standing base leading to an oval mouth. Colored enamel painting with scratched texture.

Acc. no. P 1985-55

For similar works see Coburg I, 1977, cat. no. 133

Lit.: –

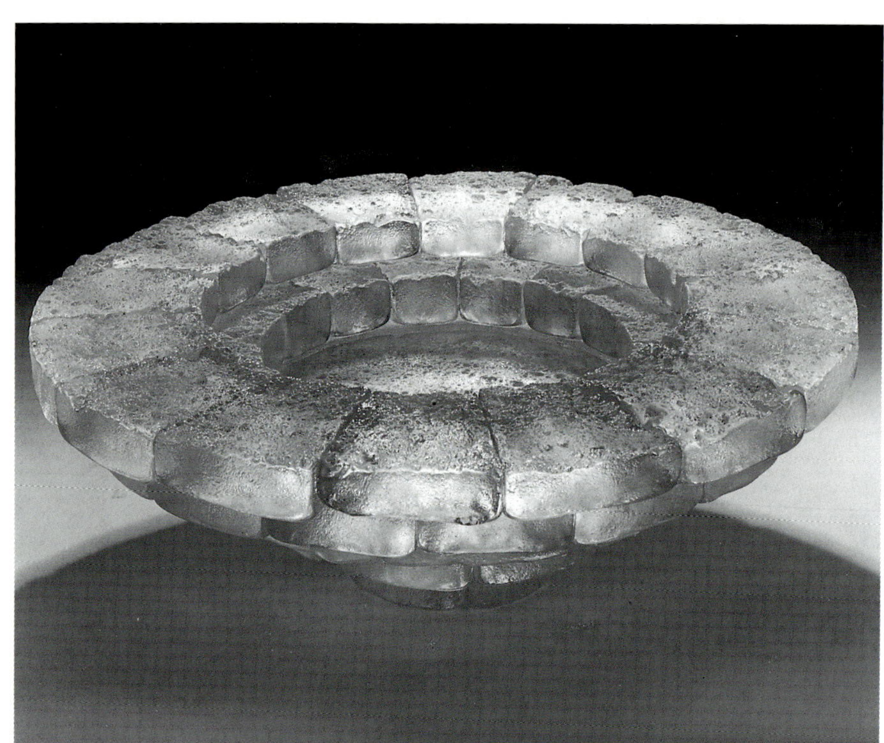

496 Untitled

Engraved mark on the underside of base:
MIEKE GROOT '90
1990
H 17.5, ⌀ 54 cm

Colorless glass, sandcast in blocks. Sandblasted, laminated.

Acc. no. P 1992-21
Acquired from the artist at the exhibition
"New Glass in Europe"

Lit.: Ricke, *New Glass Europe*, 1991,
cat. no. 127

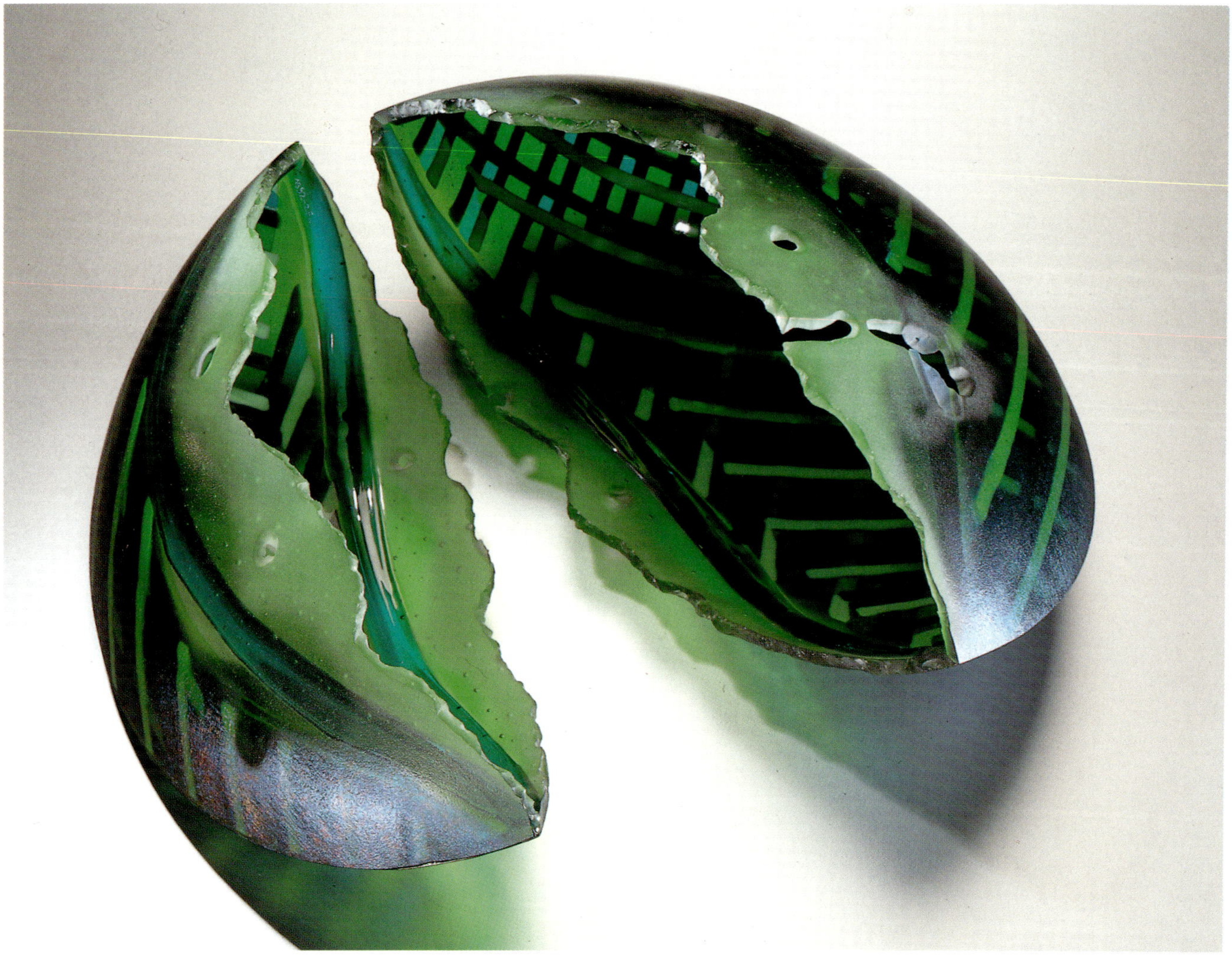

Belgium

Louis Leloup
(b. 1929)

Education: Apprenticeship as glassblower in
Val Saint Lambert; qualifying examination as
master
Lives and works in Seraing near Liège

498 "Marine"

Engraved mark at the top of pedestal:
Leloup 74
1974
H 59.7, ⌀ 23.5, H pedestal 12.6, W 10.2 cm

Colorless glass, opal blue inner casing. Two
parts fused together. Pedestal mold-blown
from black glass. Object free-blown and
shaped. Applications. Silver-salt applications
fired in a reducing atmosphere.

Acc. no. P 1976-49
Acquired at the exhibition "Modernes Glas,"
Frankfurt

Lit.: Ohm and Bauer, *Modernes Glas*, 1976,
cat. no. 64

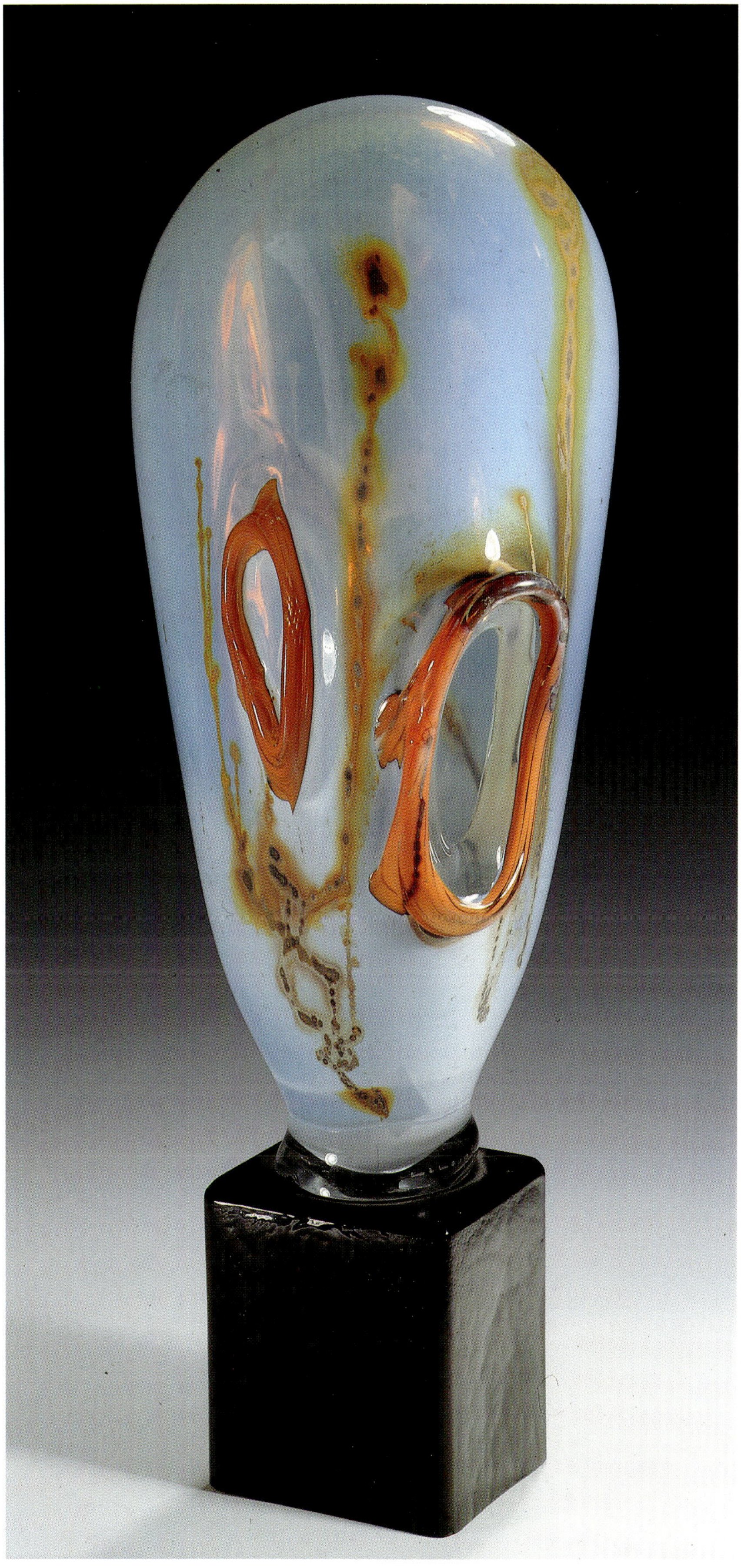

Frank van den Ham
(b. 1952)
Self-taught
Lives and works in Amsterdam

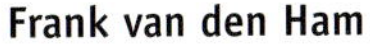 **497 "Stay with Me"**

Unsigned
1988
H 14.7, 21.5; W 35.2, 35.2; D 15.7, 22 cm

Two disks made of green glass fused with
blue, dark green, and white flat glass ribbons
and slumped into mold. Broken, sandblasted,
laminated.

Acc. no. P 1992-25
Gift of the artist

Lit.: G. Nicola, "Frank van den Ham: Think
twice," *NG*, no. 1 (1990): 20–24 and cover
image; *Frank van den Ham: Glass Fusing*, texts
by P. Dunas and U. Pietsch, exh. cat (Lübeck:
Museum für Kunst und Kulturgeschichte der
Hansestadt, 1992), 26

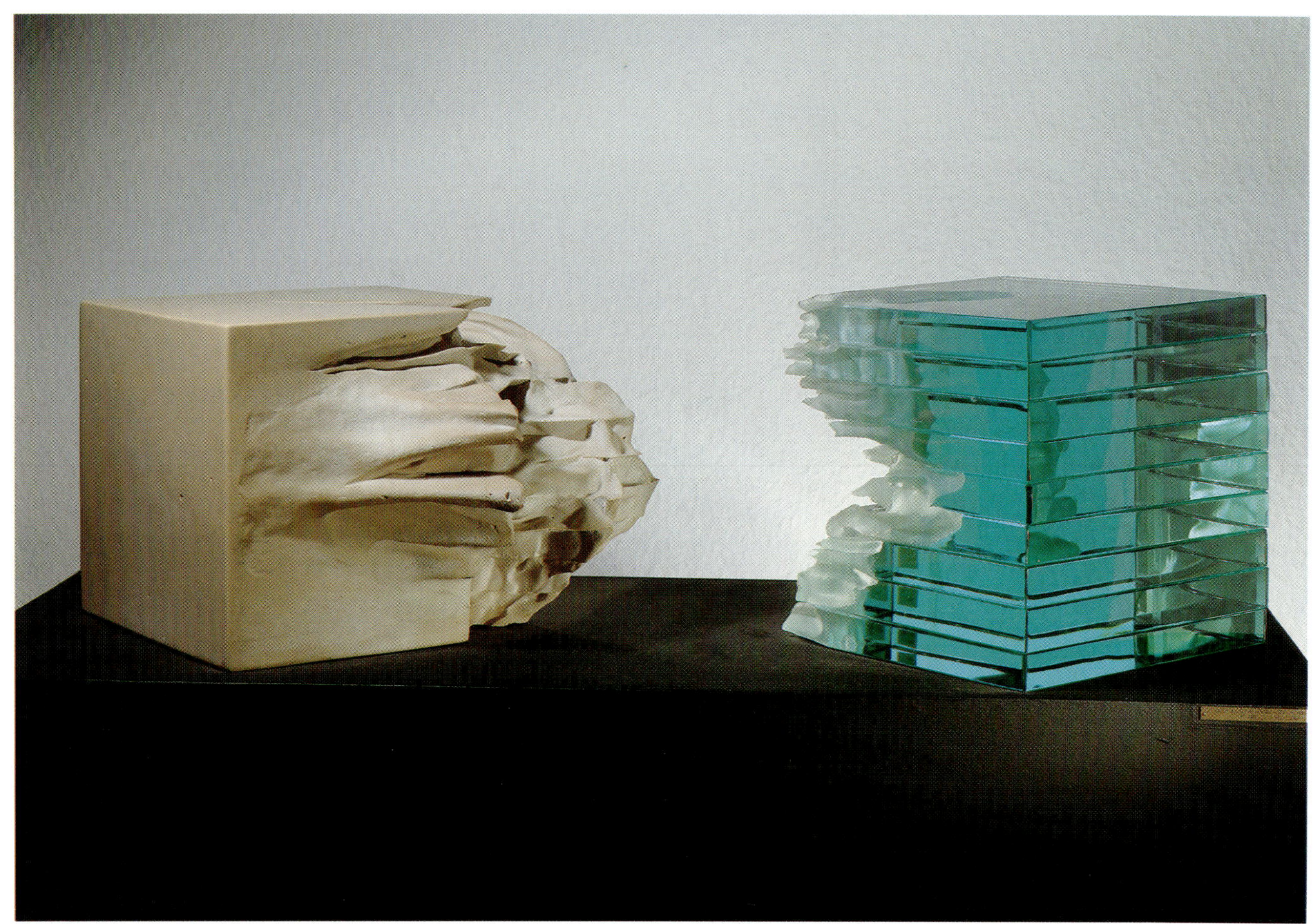

France and Austria

Jutta Cuny
(1940–1983)

Education: Studied painting and graphics
under Gerhard Swoboda; sculpture seminar at
the Internationale Sommerakademie Salzburg;
subsequently assistant to the sculptor
Francesco Somaini
Lived and worked as an Austrian in Docelle,
Vosges
Carried out her own works, mostly in the
studio of Francesco Somaini in Lomazzo, Lake
Como

499 **"Grand Affrontation—Pénétration"**
"Grosser Zusammenprall—Durch-
dringung"

Unsigned
1980
Left: H 26.4, L 51.2, D 40.9 cm
Right: H 28.3, W 39.6, D 40.9 cm
Left: polyester, cast. Right: layered non-lami-
nated plate glass; cut and polished, sandblasted.

Acc. no. P 1989-2
Gift of Dr. Ruth-Maria Franz, Vienna

For works of a similar nature see A. Bosquet
and F. Somaini, *Jutta Cuny* (Bologna, 1979),
figs. 3–5.

Lit.: J. Cuny, "Glass Sculptures by Jutta
Cuny," *NG*, no. 3 (1982): 134ff., fig. 31;
E. Crispolti and Jutta Cuny, *Sculture in Vetro
nei fotomontaggi di Cesare Somaini 1982–83*
(Bologna, 1984), pl. 3

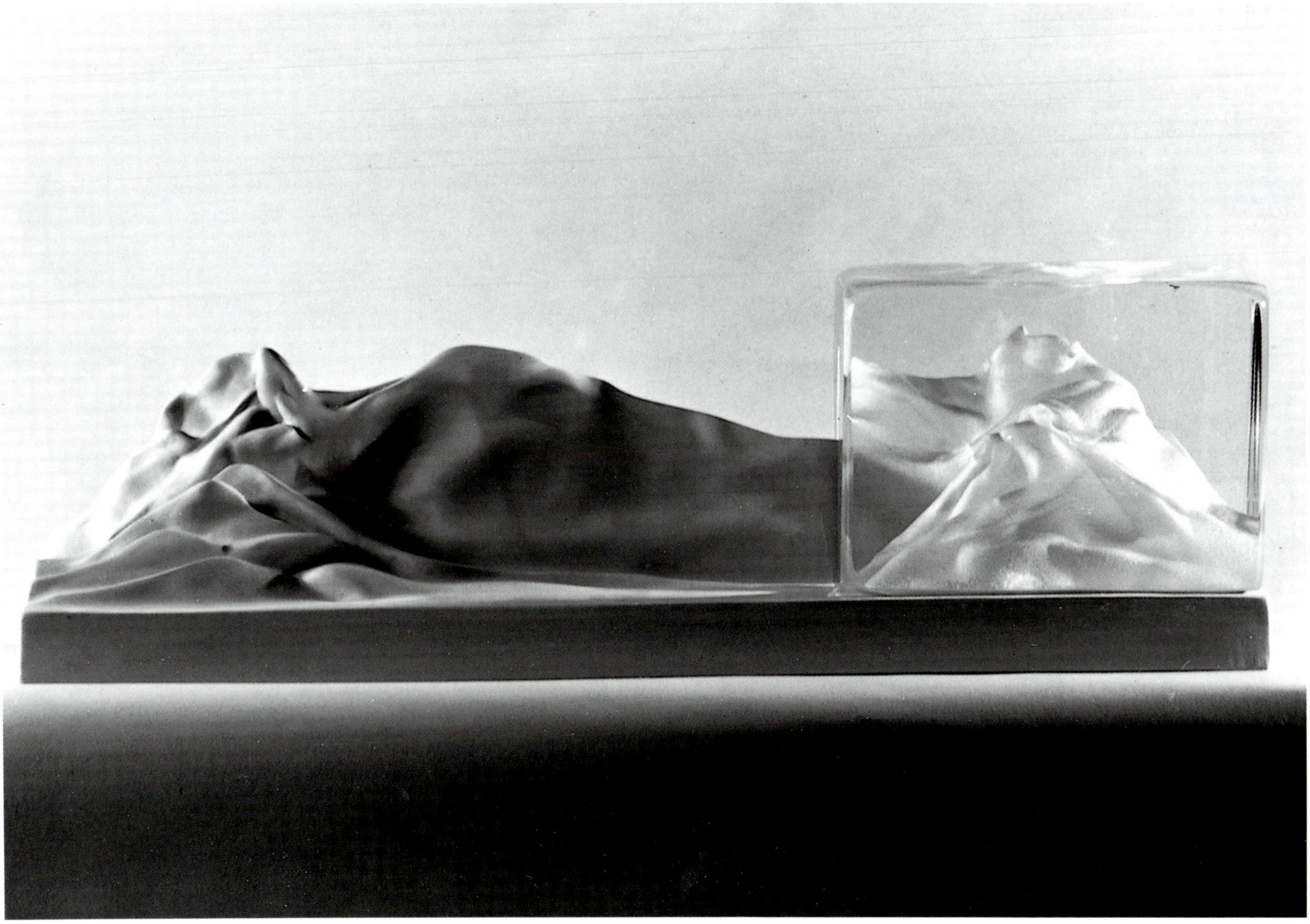

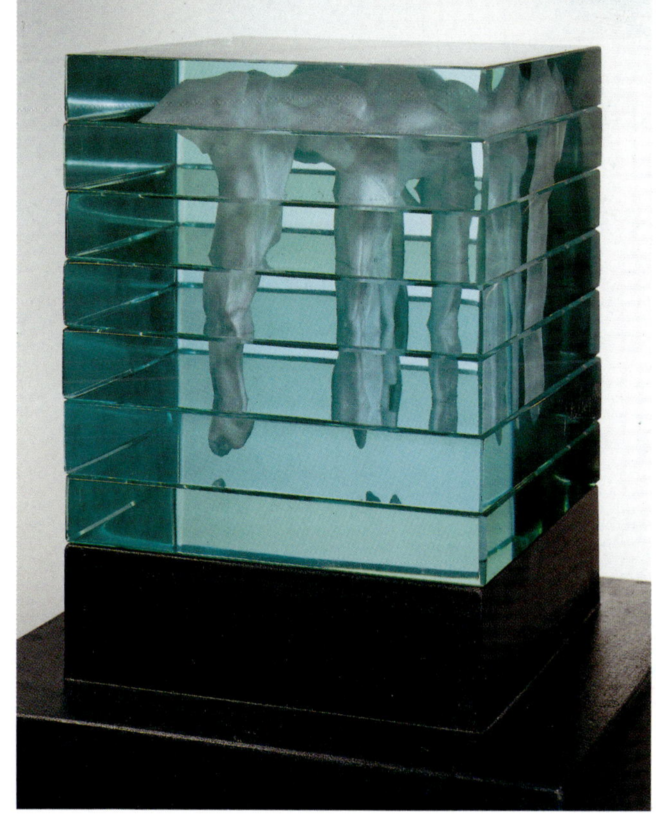

500 "Narcisse endormi"

Unsigned
1983
H 30, L 72, D 26 cm

Optic glass block, sandblasted. Sèvres biscuit
porcelain.

Acc. no. P 1993-24
Gift of Dr. Ruth-Maria Franz, Vienna

Cuny carried out the work herself in the studio
of Francesco Somaini, Lomazzo, Lake Como. The
artist's last work.

Lit.: Jutta Cuny-Franz, *Magisches Glas*, ed.
R.-M. Franz (Salzburg, 1990), 116 and fig. p. 14

501 "Projection d'une image bidimensionelle
       dans un espace vitrifié"

Diamond-engraved mark: *Jutta Cuny 1982*
1982
H 21, W 20, D 20 cm

Seven greenish glass plates, each 3 cm thick, sandblasted. Numbered 1 to 7 in diamond-engraving.

Acc. no. P 1993-23
Gift of Dr. Ruth-Maria Franz, Vienna

Carried out like cat. nos. 499 and 500.

Lit.: Jutta Cuny-Franz, *Magisches Glas*, ed.
R.-M. Franz (Salzburg, 1990), 115

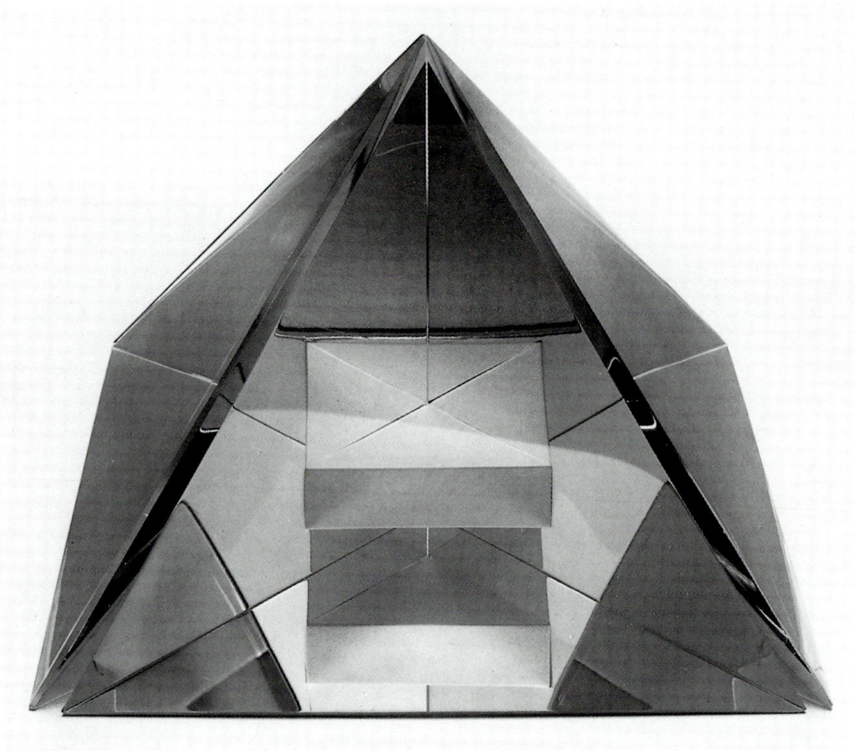

France

Yan Zoritchak
(b. 1944)

Education: Glass School, Železný Brod (Eisenbrod), and Academy of Applied Arts, Prague
Born in Slovakia, lives and works in Talloires near Annecy

502   "Dernière Demeure"

Unsigned
1980
a–c: H 21.1, W 29.6, D 14.9 cm
d: H 20, W 28.5, D 14.3 cm

Colorless, lead glass. Cut, sawn, matted, and polished.
Four-part object. Two parts have mat cuts; the other two, including the smaller one, are massive tetrahedrons.

Acc. no. P 1981-293
Acquired at the exhibition "Licht. Form. Gestalt"

The object is conceived such that it can be assembled in various ways. The illustration shows the version preferred by the artist. The two cuts on the inside supplement one another through reflection to create a closed, apparently four-sided space.

Lit.: Ricke, *Licht. Form. Gestalt*, 1980, cat. no. 114

Alain & Marisa Begou
(b. 1945, 1948)

Education: Alain—apprenticeship as fitter, then glassblower
Marisa—self-taught
Live and work in Villetelle, southern France

503   Vase

Diamond-engraved mark on the underside of base: *Begou 7.X.3* (7th month of the 10th work year, piece no. 3)
1990
H 43.5, W 30.5, D 8.1 cm

Free-blown and shaped. Several partial overlays; colored glass granules and threads embedded in colorless glass.

Acc. no. P 1991-23
Gift of the artists

Lit.: Ricke, *New Glass Europe*, 1991, cat. no. 81

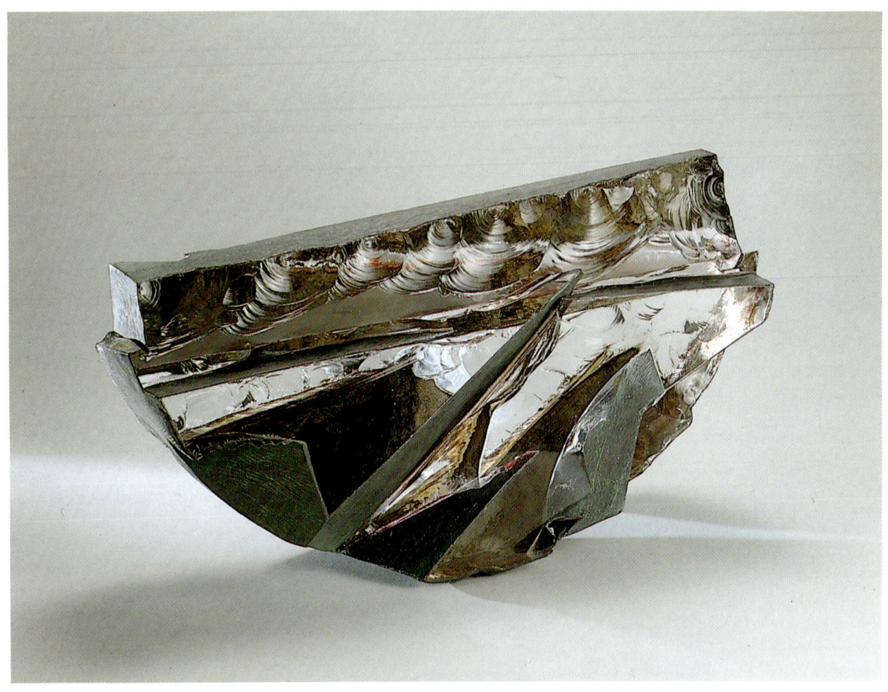

Matei Négréanu
(b. 1941)

Education: Academy of Fine Arts, Bucharest, Romania
Lives and works in Lamotte-Beuvron

504 Untitled

Engraved mark above the standing base:
Matei Négréanu 1990
1990
H 32.5, W 58.5, D 18 cm

Colorless optic glass, sawn, broken with a hammer, applied patinated lead foil; stained brown-red under the foil; sawn edge painted red.

Acc. no. GL 2001-161
Acquired from the artist at the exhibition "New Glass in Europe"

Lit.: Ricke, *New Glass Europe*, 1991, cat. no. 133

Czeslaw Zuber
(b. 1948)

Education: Art College, Wrocław, Poland
Lives and works in Paris

505 "Form and Emptiness"

Engraved mark above the standing base:
Paris '90 Zuber
1990
H 28.5, W 39.5, D 32 cm

Optic glass with yellowish tone, broken with a hammer, hammered, sandblasted, in part cut and polished. Cold painted.

Acc. no. LP 1992-14
On permanent loan from the Stadt-Sparkasse Düsseldorf
Acquired from the artist at the exhibition "New Glass in Europe"

Lit.: Ricke, *New Glass Europe*, 1991, cat. no. 4

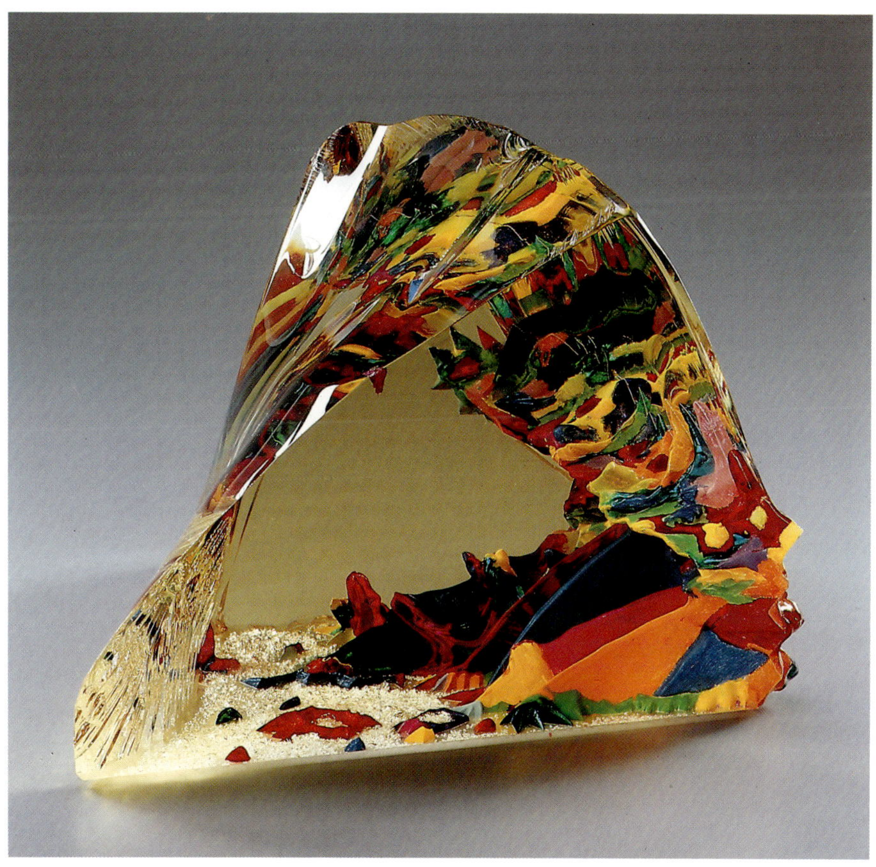

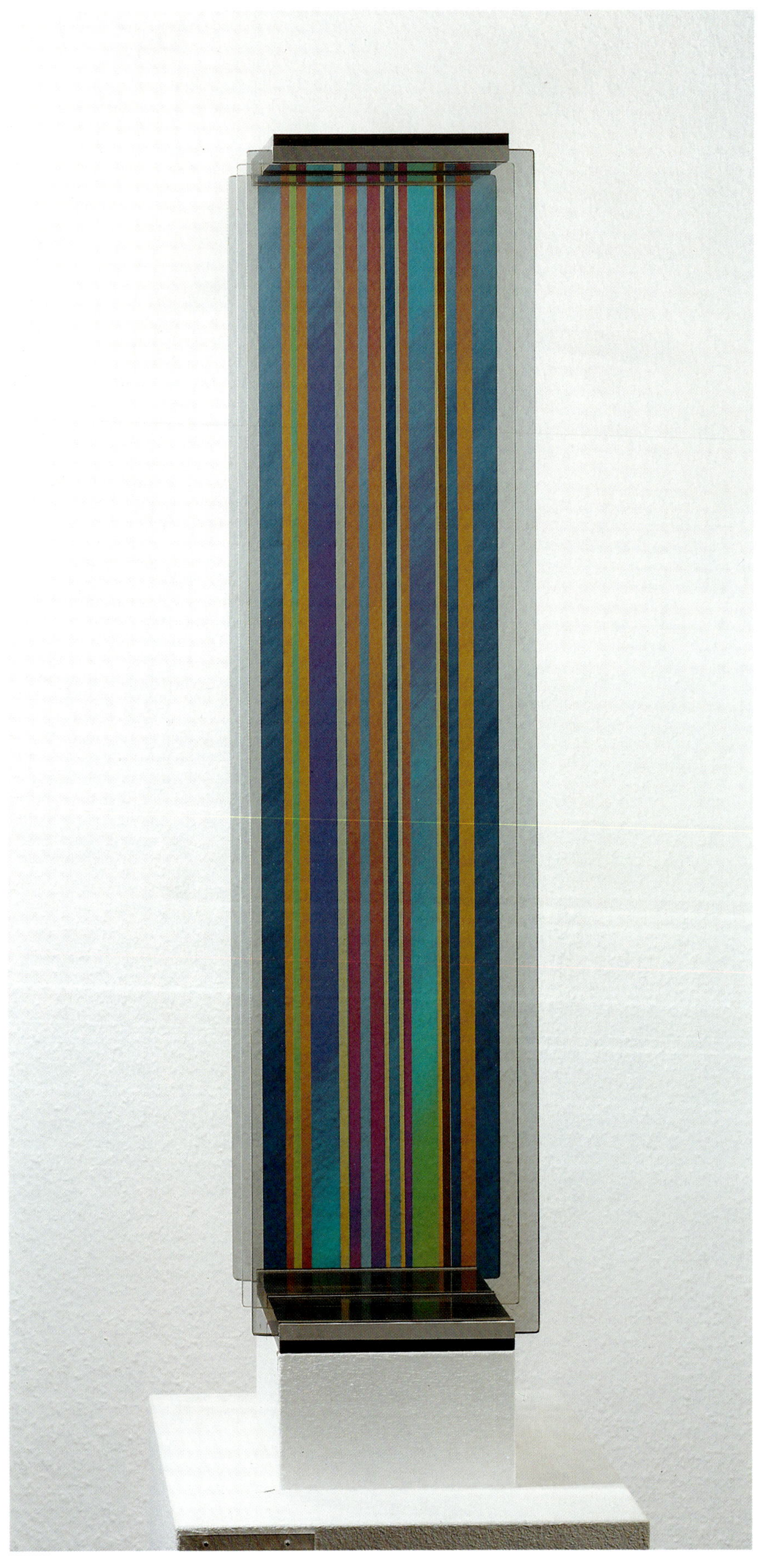

Eric H. Olson
(1909–1996)

Education: Self-taught
Lived and worked in Stockholm

506 "Optochromi"

Unsigned
1976
H 89.4, W 22, D 19 cm

Three slabs of plate glass stacked one behind
the other with a space of 8.3 cm between
them. The two outer slabs consist of three
laminated sheets each, the middle slab of
two sheets. Between the sheets are light-
refracting layers.

Acc. no. P 1978-10

Depending on where the viewer stands, various color effects, ranging from absolute
colorlessness to strong polychromicity, are
created owing to the interference of polar-
ized light. On the principle of Olson's work
see, for example, Eric H. Olson, *Edition
Galerie von Bartha* (Basel, 1980).

Lit.: –

Ann Wolff
(b. 1937)

Worked under the name Ann Wärff until 1985

Education: Meisterschule für Mode, Hamburg,
preparatory course for graphic professions;
visual communication at the Hochschule für
Gestaltung in Ulm
Lives and works in Hamburg

507 "Teekannenskulptur"

Engraved mark above the standing base:
Ann Wärff.78
1978
H 17.2, W 27.4, D 7.4 cm

Colorless crystal glass, slightly opalescent
inner casing. Blown, cast, shaped. Sandblasted on the reverse.

Acc. no. L 1985-10
On permanent loan from the artist

Made in five slightly different versions.

Lit.: H. Hilschenz and Ann Wärff, *Glass Carries
my Scattered Thoughts into the Light* (n.p.,
n.d. [1984]), 26

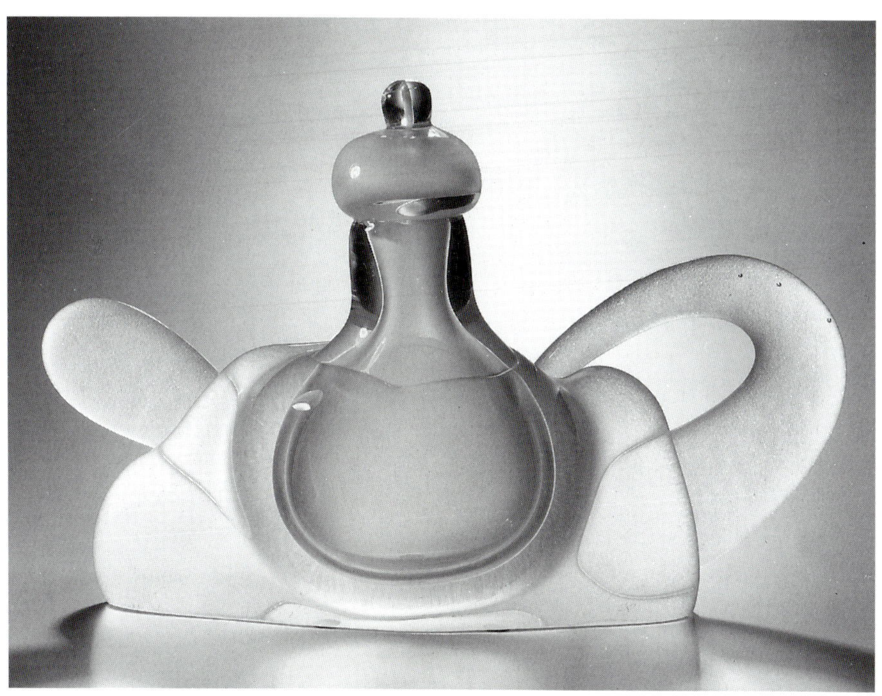

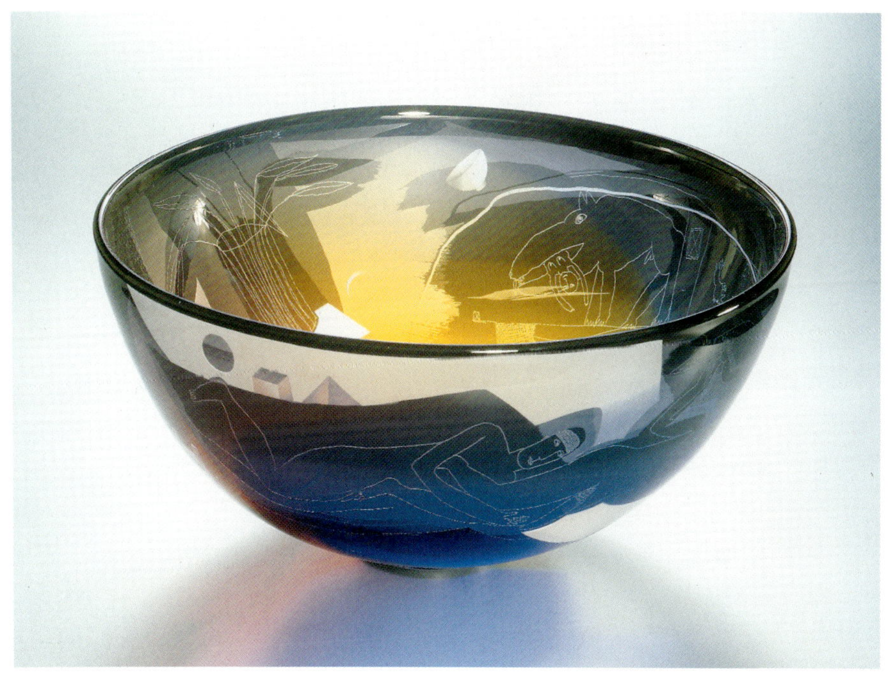

508 "somebody plays the flute in a cave"

Engraved mark on the underside of base:
Ann Wärff.WILKE 82
1982
H 16, ⌀ 31.5 cm

Colorless glass with partial overlays. Mold-
blown, shaped. Etched, sandblasted. Blank
made by Wilke Adolfsson.

Acc. no. L 1985-4
On permanent loan from the artist

Lit.: H. Hilschenz and Ann Wärff, *Glass Carries
my Scattered Thoughts into the Light* (n.p.,
n.d. [1984]), 18f.; Ricke, *Museumsarbeit*,
1988, 78, fig. 68

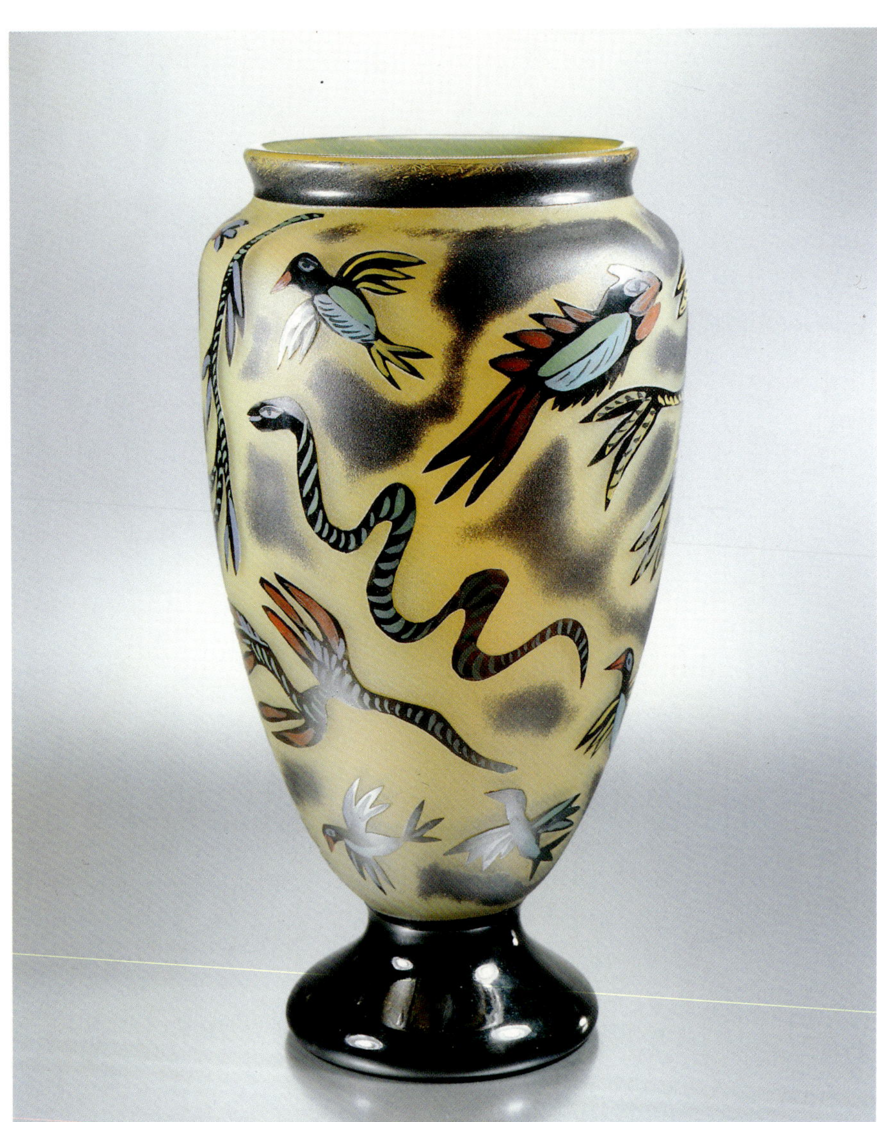

Ulrica Hydman-Vallien
(b. 1938)

Education: Art School, Stockholm
Lives and works in Åfors near Eriksmåla

509 "Jungle Night"

Engraved mark on the underside of base:
Kosta Unik B. 33 Ulrica H.V
Kosta, 1984
H 33.4, ⌀ 18.7 cm

Greenish-yellowish inner casing overlaid with
thick, colorless, brown layer. Mold-blown and
shaped. Sandblasted decoration. Enamel-
painted.

Acc. no. P 1985-102

Lit.: –

Bertil Vallien
(b. 1938)

Education: Art School, Stockholm
Lives and works in Åfors near Eriksmåla

510 "Silent Journey"

Diamond-engraved mark on top:
B. Vallien Y 230
1984
H 7.4, L 46.5, W 28.1 cm

Colorless crystal glass with colored inclusions. Sandcast. In cross section like a ship's
keel. Sandy coarse underside. The ends of
the short transverse arms ground flat and
polished.

Acc. no. P 1985-103

Lit.: –

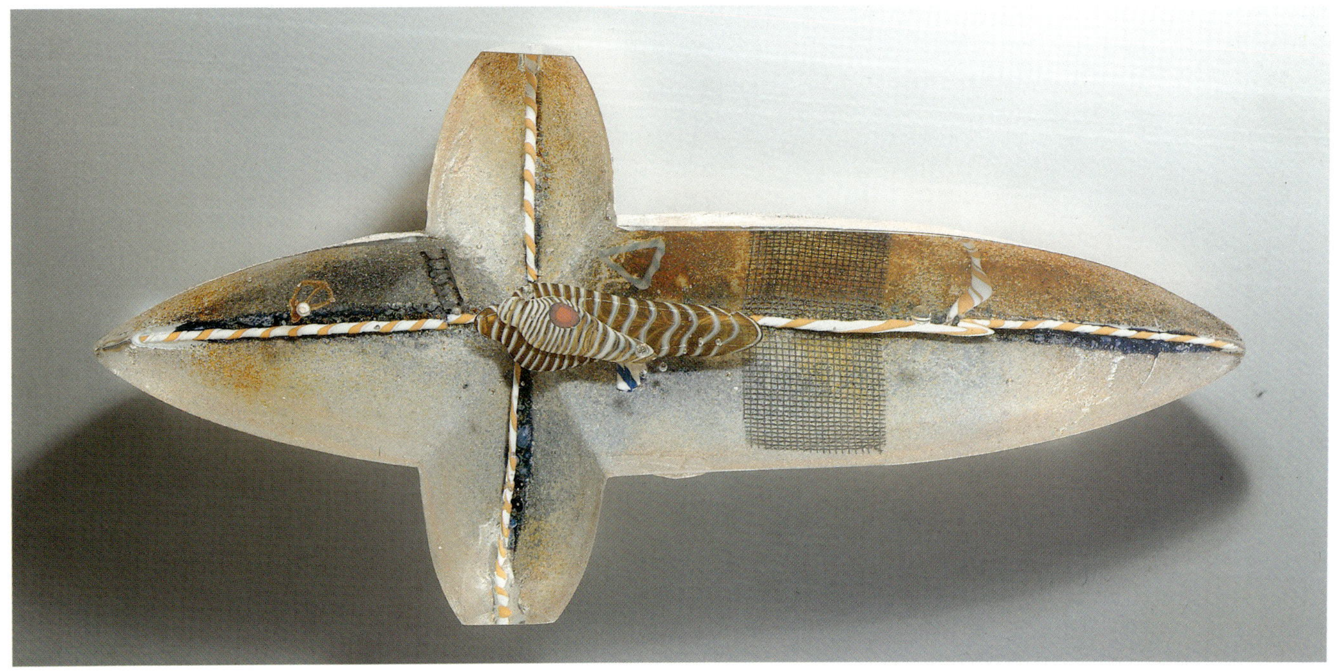

511 "Observer" Pendulum

Diamond-engraved mark on the reverse at the
bottom: *Kosta Boda Unique 1363990181 B.
Vallien*
1990
H 117, with frame 215, W 32, D 32 cm

Crystal glass, sandcast. Inclusions of colored
glass and copper previously shaped freehand.
Front in part cut and polished. Four oar-like
copper rods attached to the sides with wire.

Acc. no. LP 1992-16
On permanent loan from the Stadt-Sparkasse,
Düsseldorf
Acquired from the artist at the exhibition
"New Glass in Europe"

Lit.: Ricke, *New Glass Europe*, 1991,
cat. no. 48

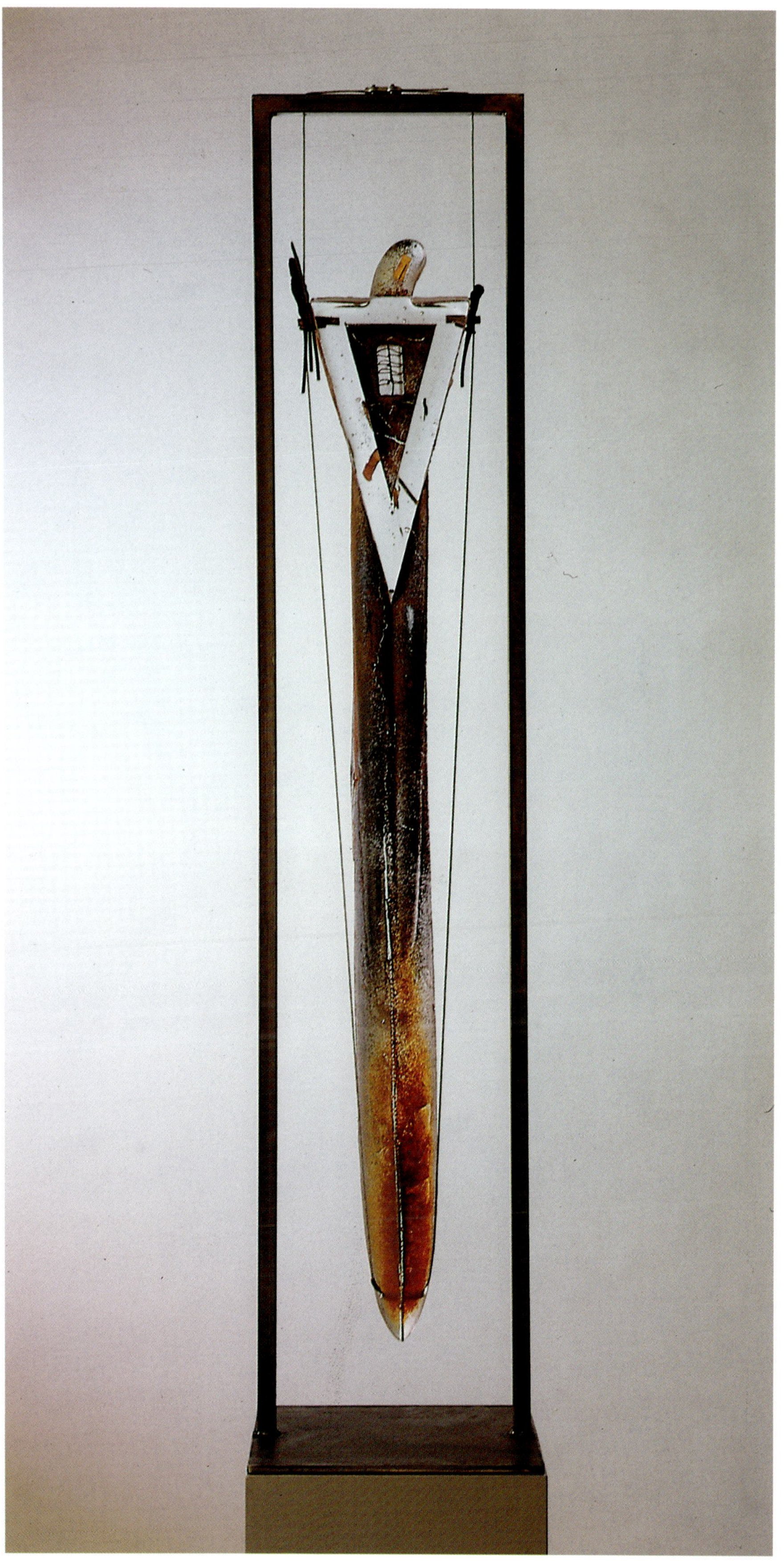

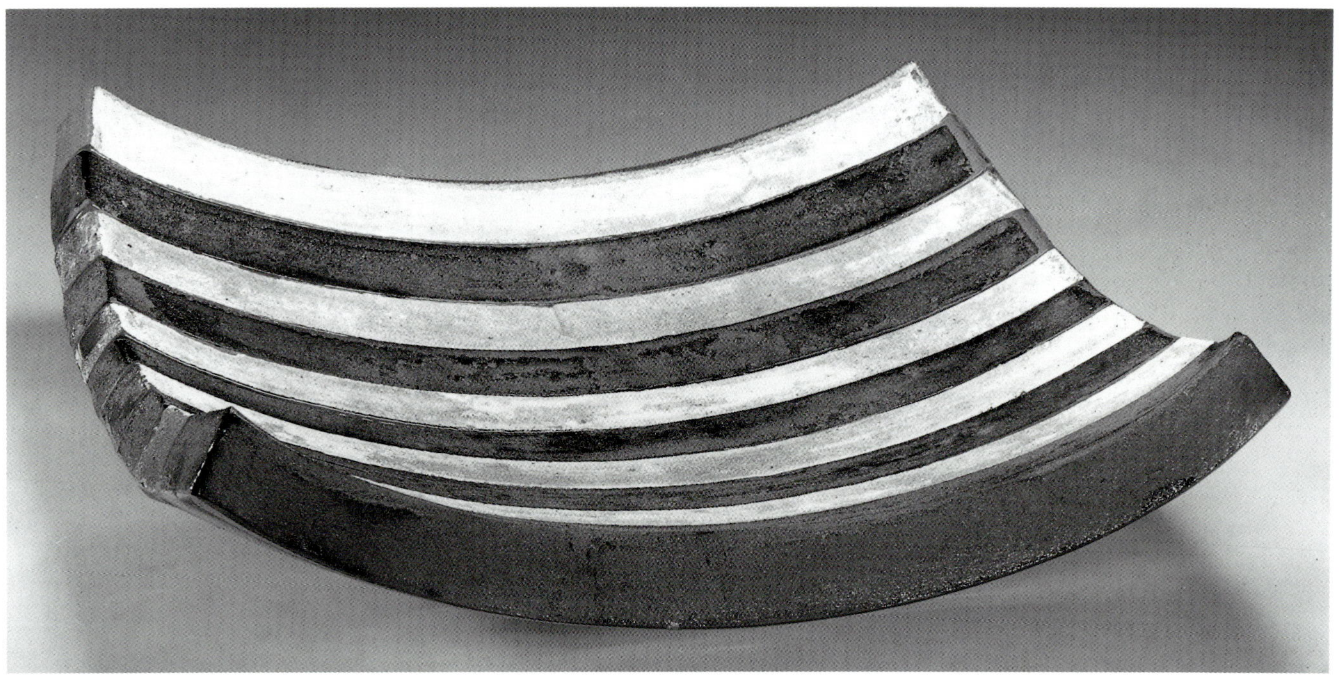

Paula Bartron
(b. 1946)

Education: College of San Matteo, CA; University of California, and Glass School, Orrefors
Lives and works in Stockholm

512   "Schwarzweiss gestreifte Platte"

Diamond-engraved mark on the underside of standing base: *Paula Bartron*
1990
H approx. 8, W 55, D 55 cm

Five strips of colorless glass with applied white enamel alternating with black enamel, sandcast. Ground flat on the sides; fused.

Acc. no. P 1991-24
Acquired from the artist at the exhibition "New Glass in Europe"

Lit.: Ricke, *New Glass Europe*, 1991, cat. no. 57

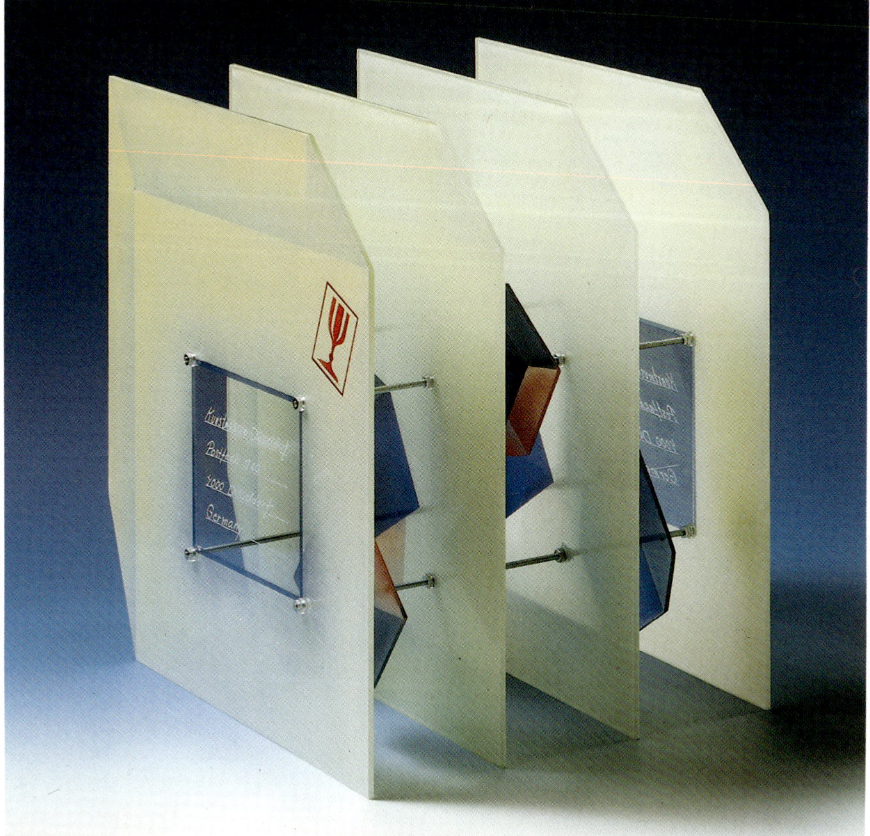

Åsa Brandt
(b. 1940)

Education: State Art School, Stockholm
Lives and works in Torshälla

513   "Zerbrechlich—Illusion eines Kastens"

Mark: *Åsa Schweden*
1990
30 x 30 x 30 cm

Four large and three small flat plate glass sheets, enamel-painted and engraved. Connected with metal rods.

Acc. no. P 1992-17
Acquired from the artist at the exhibition "New Glass in Europe"

From the front the object looks like a package with the label:
Kunstmuseum Düsseldorf
Postfach 1120
4000 Düsseldorf
Germany

Lit.: Ricke, *New Glass Europe*, 1991, cat. no. 64

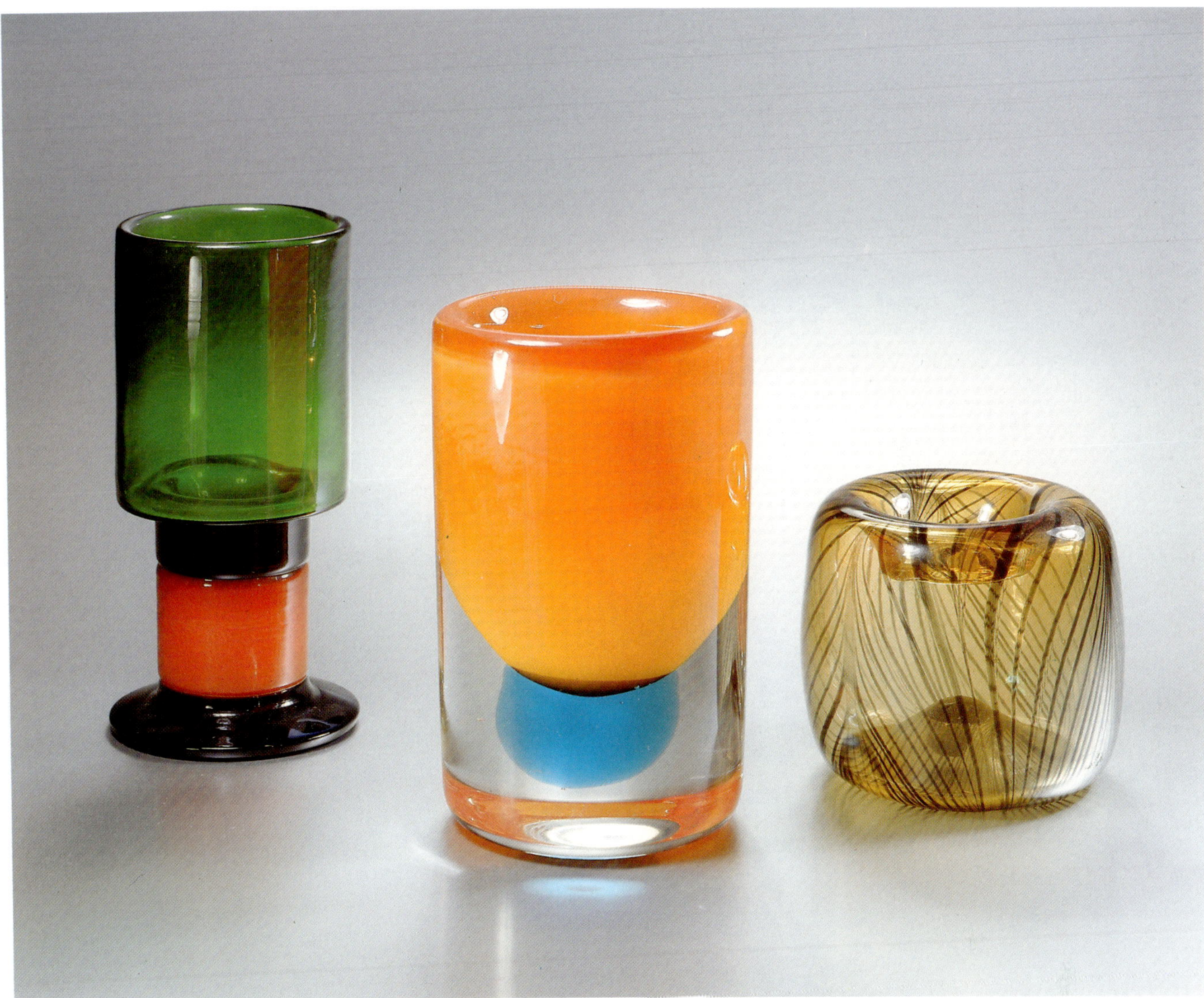

Finland

Kaj Franck
(1911–1989)

Education: Academy of Applied Arts, Helsinki
Lived and worked as a designer in Helsinki
(also see cat. nos. 404–6)

514   Decorative Goblet

Engraved inscription on the underside of
standing base: *Kaj Franck Nuutajärvi Notsjö*
Nuutajärvi, 1970
H 16.1, ∅ 7.6 cm

Mold-blown, shaped. Comprises three separately worked parts.

Acc. no. P 1979-64
Gift of Helmut Hentrich

See *The Modern Spirit: Glass from Finland*,
exh. cat. (Riihimäki: Finnish Glass Museum;
Helsinki, 1985), fig. 25.

Lit.: Ricke, *Finnische Künstler*, 1982, cat. no. 5

Inkeri Toikka
(b. 1931)

Education: Drawing School of the Turku Art
Association; Academy of Applied Arts, Helsinki
Lives and works in Nuutajärvi

515   Beaker Vase

Engraved mark on the underside of base:
Inkeri Toikka Nuutajärvi Notsjö
Ca. 1965–70
H 14.9, ∅ 9.5 cm

Colorless crystal glass, orange inner casing,
light blue inclusion. Mold-blown, shaped.

Acc. no. P 1979-59
Gift of Helmut Hentrich

Lit.: –

Heikki Orvola
(b. 1943)

Education: Academy of Applied Arts, Helsinki
Lives and works in Nuutajärvi

516   Vase

Engraved mark on the underside of base:
Heikki Orvola Nuutajärvi Notsjö
Ca. 1965–70
H 8.5, ∅ 10.2 cm

Amber-colored glass. Free-blown and shaped.
Pushed-up bottom, massive black prunt in
the middle. Combed dark-blue thread decoration.

Acc. no. P 1981-366
Gift of Helmut Hentrich

Lit.: –

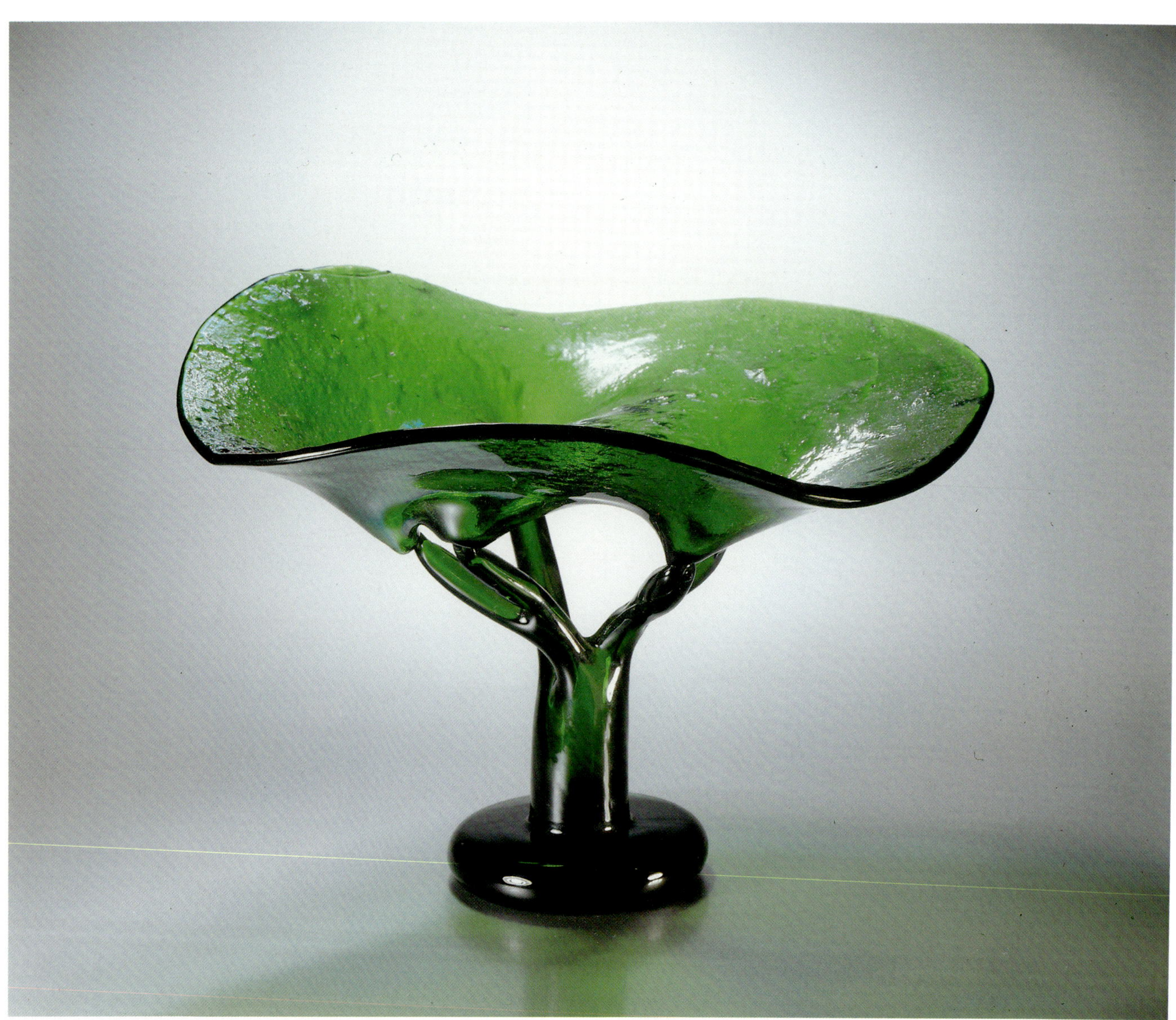

Oiva Toikka
(b. 1931)

Education: Art-and-Crafts College, Helsinki
Lives and works in Nuutajärvi

517   Dish Object

Engraved mark on the underside of standing
base: *Oiva Toikka Nuutajärvi Notsjö*
Ca. 1968–70
H 20.5, ⌀ 21.8 cm

Free-blown and shaped. Textured surface on
coarse ground.

Acc. no. P 1979-58
Gift of Helmut Hentrich

Lit.: –

314

Kertuu Nurminen
(b. 1943)

Education: Business School, Helsinki;
Academy of Applied Arts, Helsinki
Lives and works in Nuutajärvi

518   Goblet Vase

Engraved mark on the underside of foot:
Kertuu Nurminen Nuutajärvi Notsjö
1981
H 27.2, ⌀ 23.6 cm

Blown and shaped in two parts. Bowl: opaque
white and blue inner casing covered with
thick, colorless layer with air bubbles. Foot:
blue inner casing, spiral threads containing
silver in colorless cover layer, separated into
rows of dots in a ribbed mold, the dots made
iridescent in a reducing atmosphere.
Sandblasted decoration adorning the bowl's
interior.

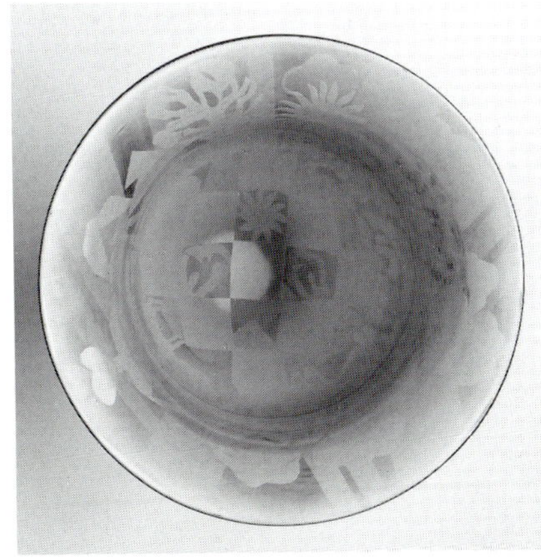

Acc. no. P 1982-12
Acquired at the exhibition "Unikate finnischer
Künstler—Glas"

Lit.: Ricke, *Finnische Künstler*, 1982,
cat. no. 26

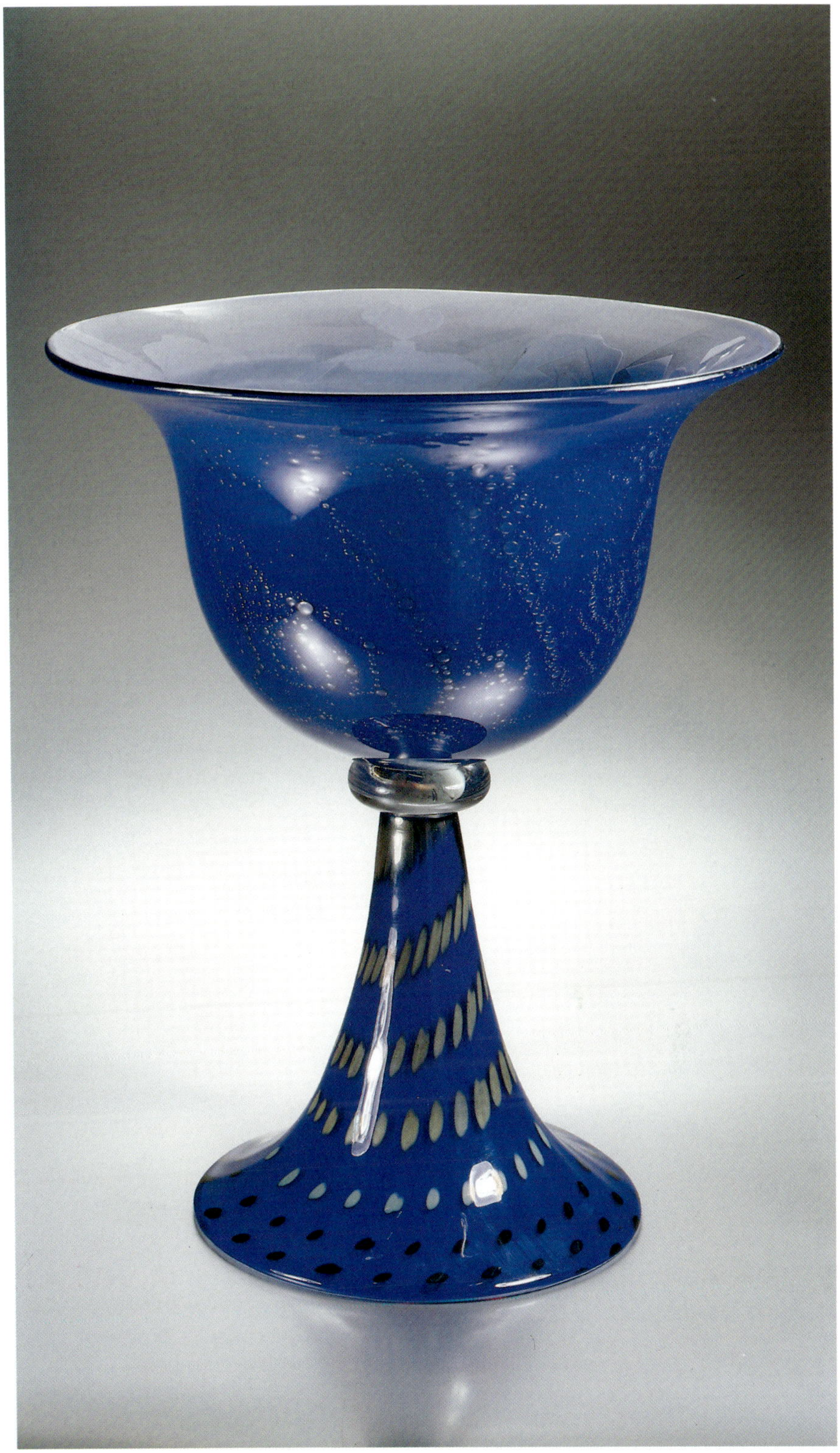

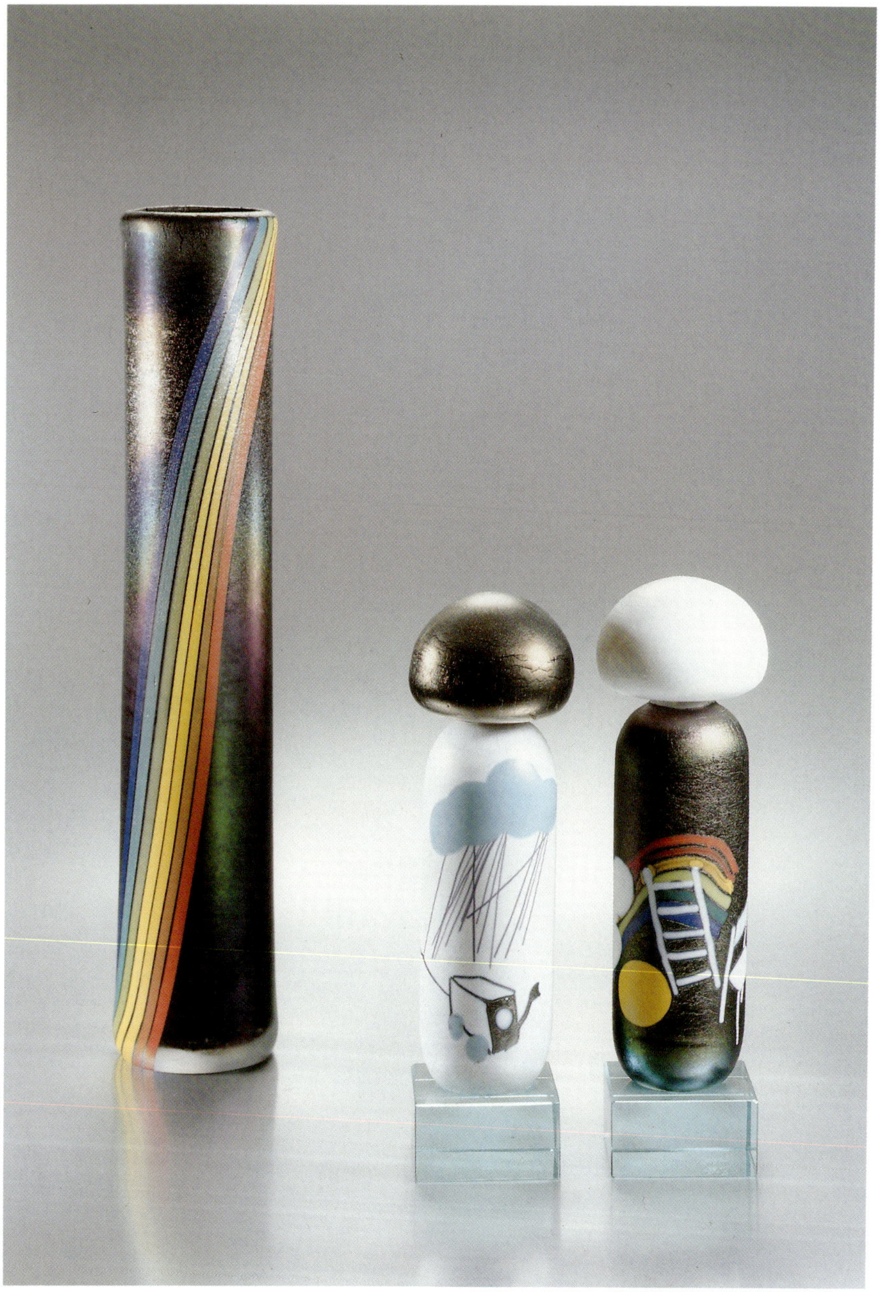

Benny Motzfeldt
(1909–1995)

Education: State Crafts and Industrial-Art
School, Oslo
Lived in Oslo

521   Vase

Diamond-engraved mark on the underside of
base: *BM 69*
Randsfjord, 1969
H 25.5, ⌀ 15.3 cm

Colorless glass with a light gray-blue tone at
the top. Mold-blown, shaped. Embedded
glass-fiber weave. Embedded oxide and air
bubbles.

Acc. no. P 1989-54
Gift of Helmut Hentrich

Lit.: –

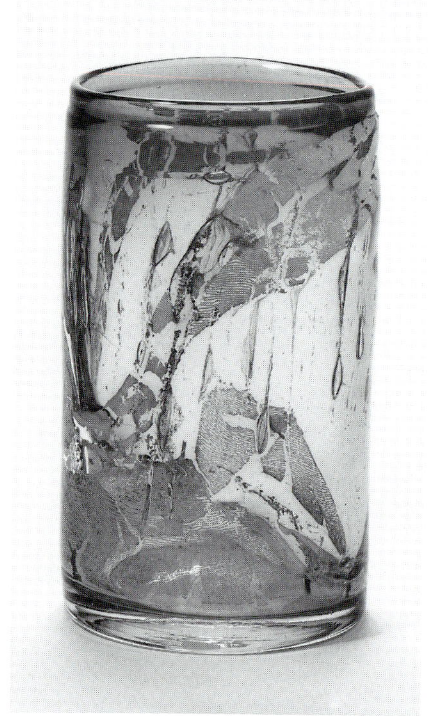

Denmark

Finn Lynggaard
(b. 1930)

Education: Academy of Fine Arts, Copenhagen
Lives and works in Ebeltoft

519   Vase

Engraved mark on the underside of base:
F.L '80 DANMARK
1980
H 31.2, ⌀ 5.6 cm

Colorless glass with black inner casing. Free-
blown and shaped. Embedded colored glass
threads.

Acc. no. P 1980-14

Lit.: –

520 a, b   Objects

Engraved mark on the pedestal: *F.L'80 DANMARK*
1980
H 18.8, 19.4; ⌀ each 5 cm

White and black overlay. Embedded decoration of colored glass threads. Colorless greenish pedestal, cut and polished.

Acc. nos. P 1980-15, 16

Lit.: –

England

Samuel J. Herman
(b. 1936)

Education: University of Wisconsin, Madison;
Edinburgh College of Art; Royal College of
Art, London
Lives and works in London

522   Vase

Diamond-engraved mark above the standing
base: *VAL Samuel J. Herman 1970 for H...(?)*
No 25
Val Saint Lambert, 1970
H 67.7, ⌀ 19.5 cm

Colorless crystal glass. Opal white inner casing. Free-blown and shaped. Applications.
Application of silver-salt solution, made iridescent in reducing atmosphere.

Acc. no. P 1974-34

Gift of Helmut Hentrich

Carried out at the glassworks Val Saint Lambert, Seraing near Liège

Lit.: –

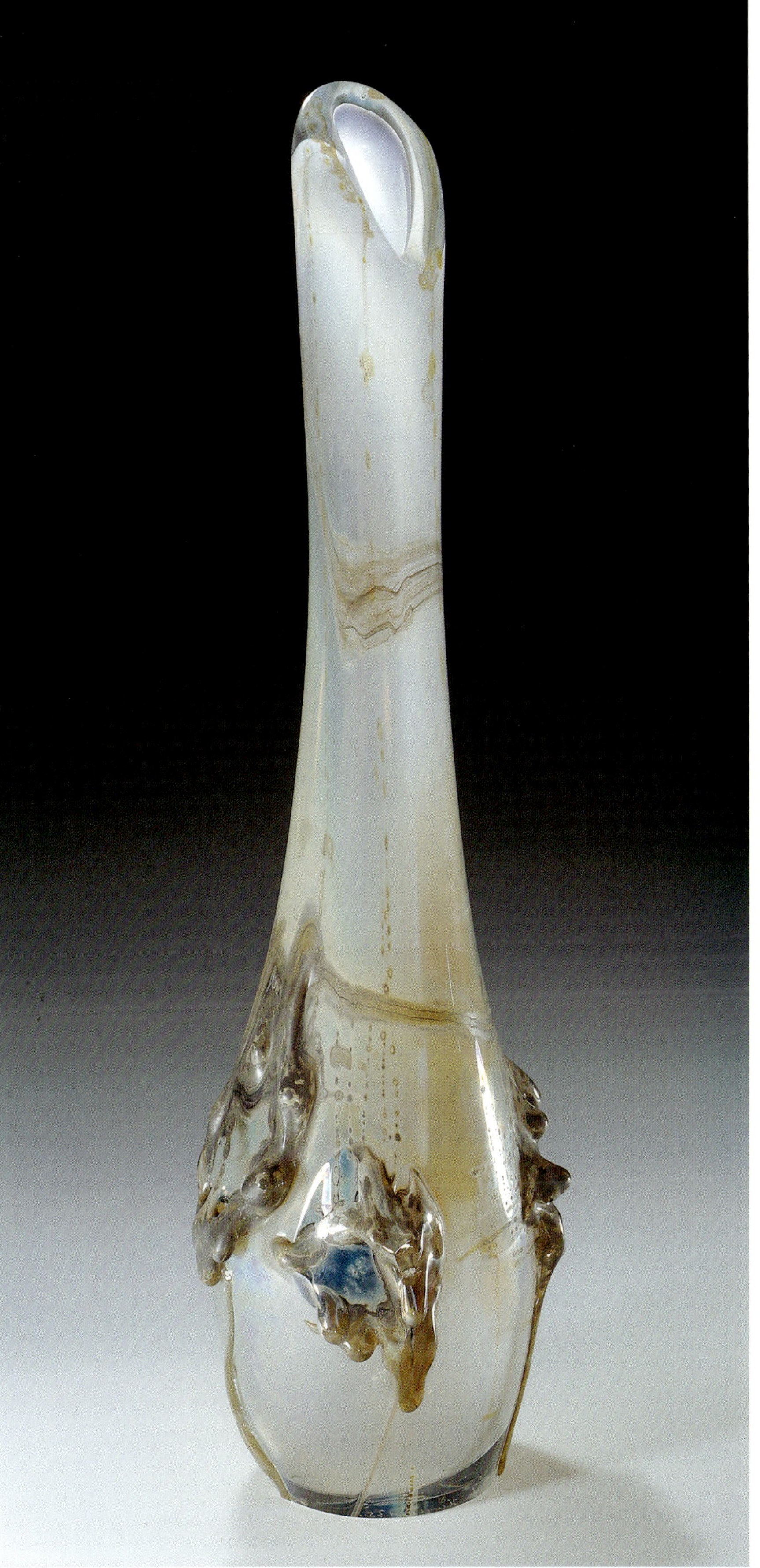

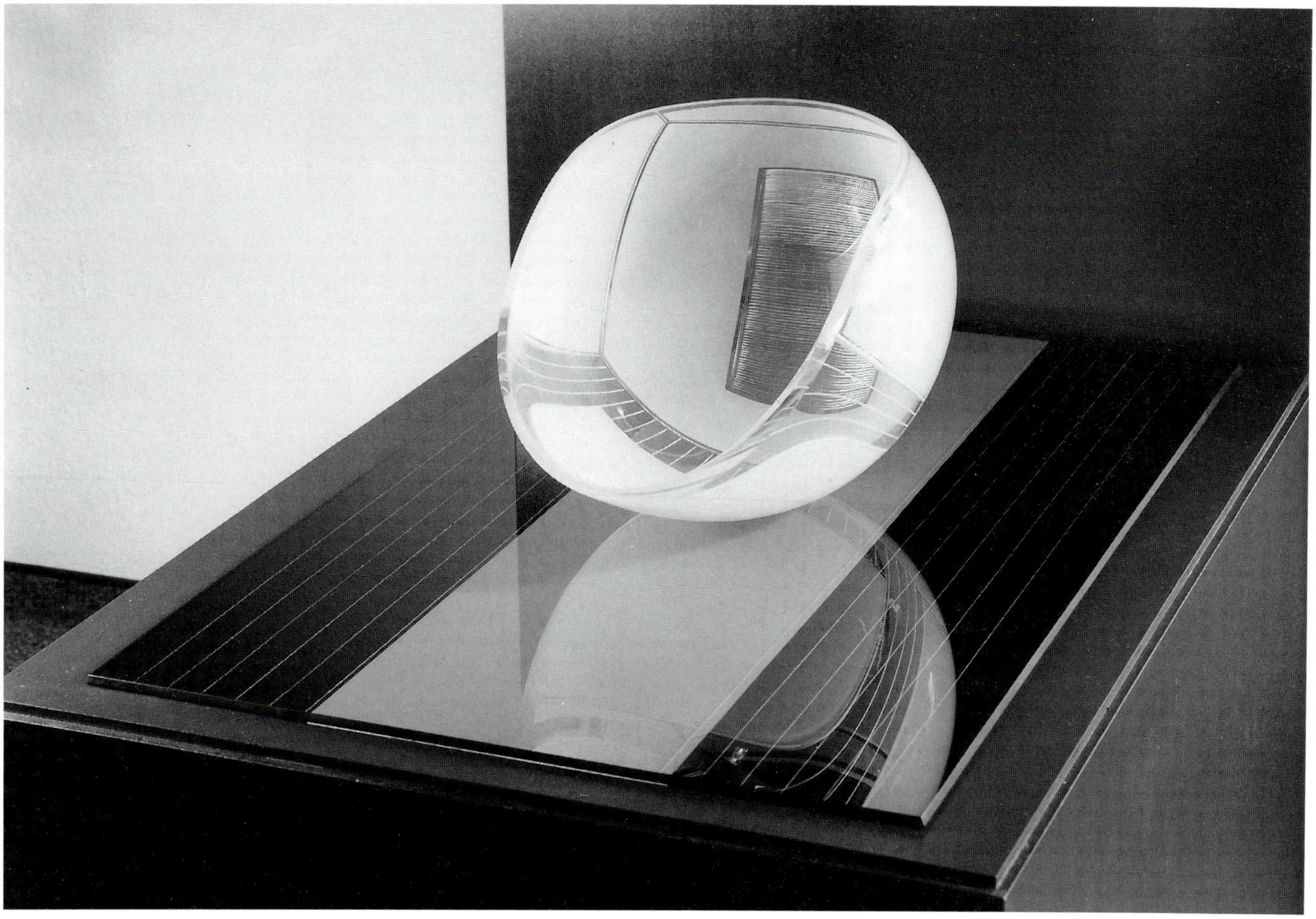

Stephen Procter
(1946–2001)

Education: Studied engineering and agricul-
ture; self-taught as artist
Lived and worked as specialist teacher in
Farnham, Surrey, and Canberra, Australia;
blanks carried out at various glassworks

523   "Changing Light"

Diamond-engraved mark on side wall:
PROCTER 84
Hergiswil, Switzerland, 1984
L 41, ⌀ 26 cm; base sheet: 85 x 58 cm

Two parts, colorless. Object can be freely
moved. Free-blown. Cut, engraved, sandblasted. Sheet of smoky brown glass, engraved
lines, paper laid beneath the center.

Acc. no. LP 1985-62
Acquired at the exhibition "Zweiter Coburger
Glaspreis"
On permanent loan from the Museumsverein

Lit.: Coburg II, 1985, cat. no. 114b; *Stephen
Procter: Thoughts about Light*, exh. cat.
(Lucerne: GLAS-GALERIE-Luzern, 1986), 48f.

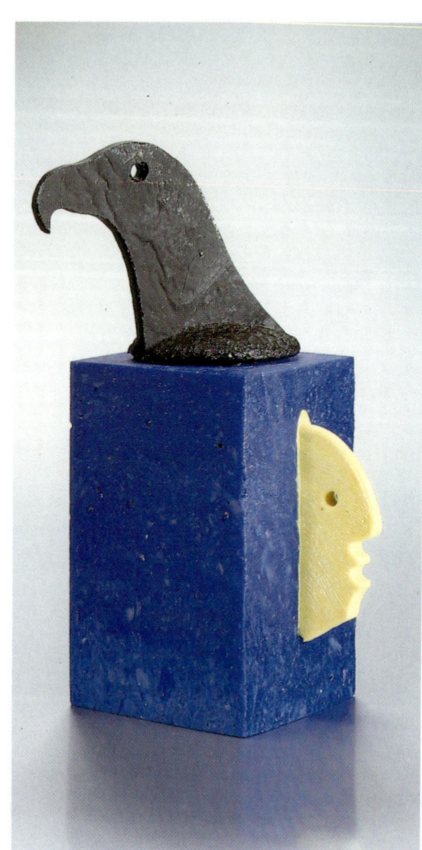

Keith Brocklehurst
(b. 1946)

Education: Leicester College of Art; Chelsea
School of Art, London; Technique of Glass
Centre in Brierley Hill
Lives and works in Yarkhill, Hereford

524   "Sky Box/Eagle Head Lid"

Diamond-engraved mark on the underside of
base: *SKY BOX 12/1984*
1984
H 15.5, W 8.6, D 5.7 cm

Pâte de verre. Mold-melted. Cut, polished
semimat.

Acc. no. LP 1985-61
Acquired at the exhibition "Zweiter Coburger
Glaspreis"
On permanent loan from the Museumsverein

Lit.: Coburg II, 1985, cat. no. 98b

525 "Caller's Bowl"

Diamond-engraved mark on one of the feet:
Keith Brocklehurst 1990
1990
H 18.1, ⌀ 14 cm

Pâte de verre, fused from four separately
worked pieces. Feet in part cut and acid-
frosted.

Acc. no. P 1991-25
Acquired from the artist at the exhibition
"New Glass in Europe"

Lit.: Ricke, *New Glass Europe*, 1991,
cat. no. 46

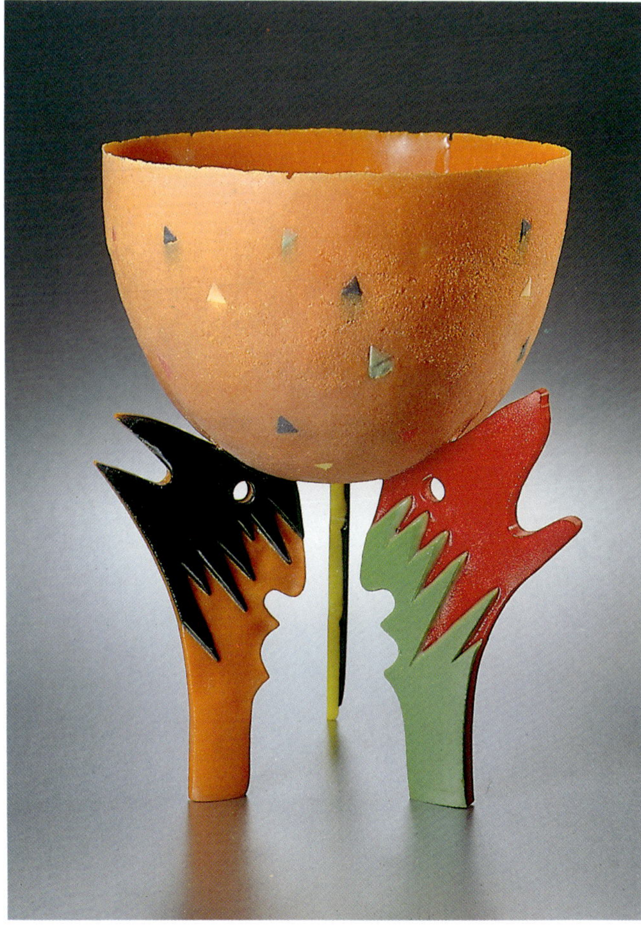

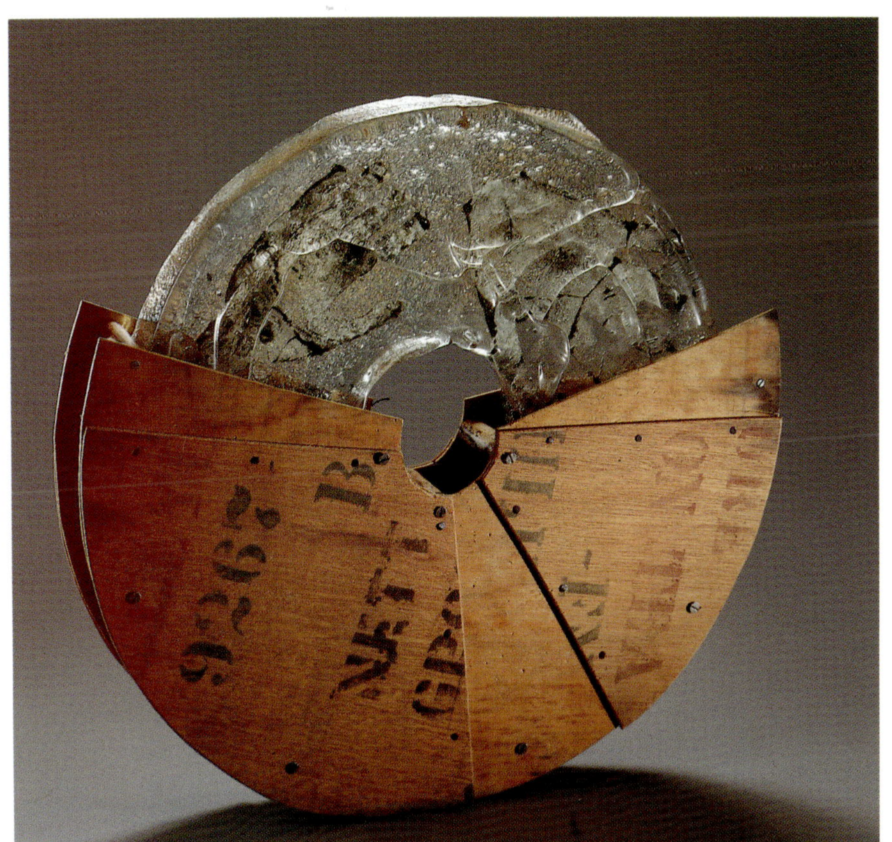

Elizabeth Swinburne
(b. 1957)

Education: Brighton Polytechnic; Middlesex
Polytechnic; Rietveld Academie Amsterdam
Lives and works in Stoke on Trent, Stafford-
shire

526 "Life Cycles # 3"

Unsigned
1992
H 49.2, ⌀ 53.2, D 7.4 cm

Colorless glass, sandcast with black inclusions. Wood from tea crates bearing numbers
and letters in black, green, and red-brown.

Acc. no. P 1993-19
Gift of Dr. Ernst Ploil, Vienna

Lit.: –

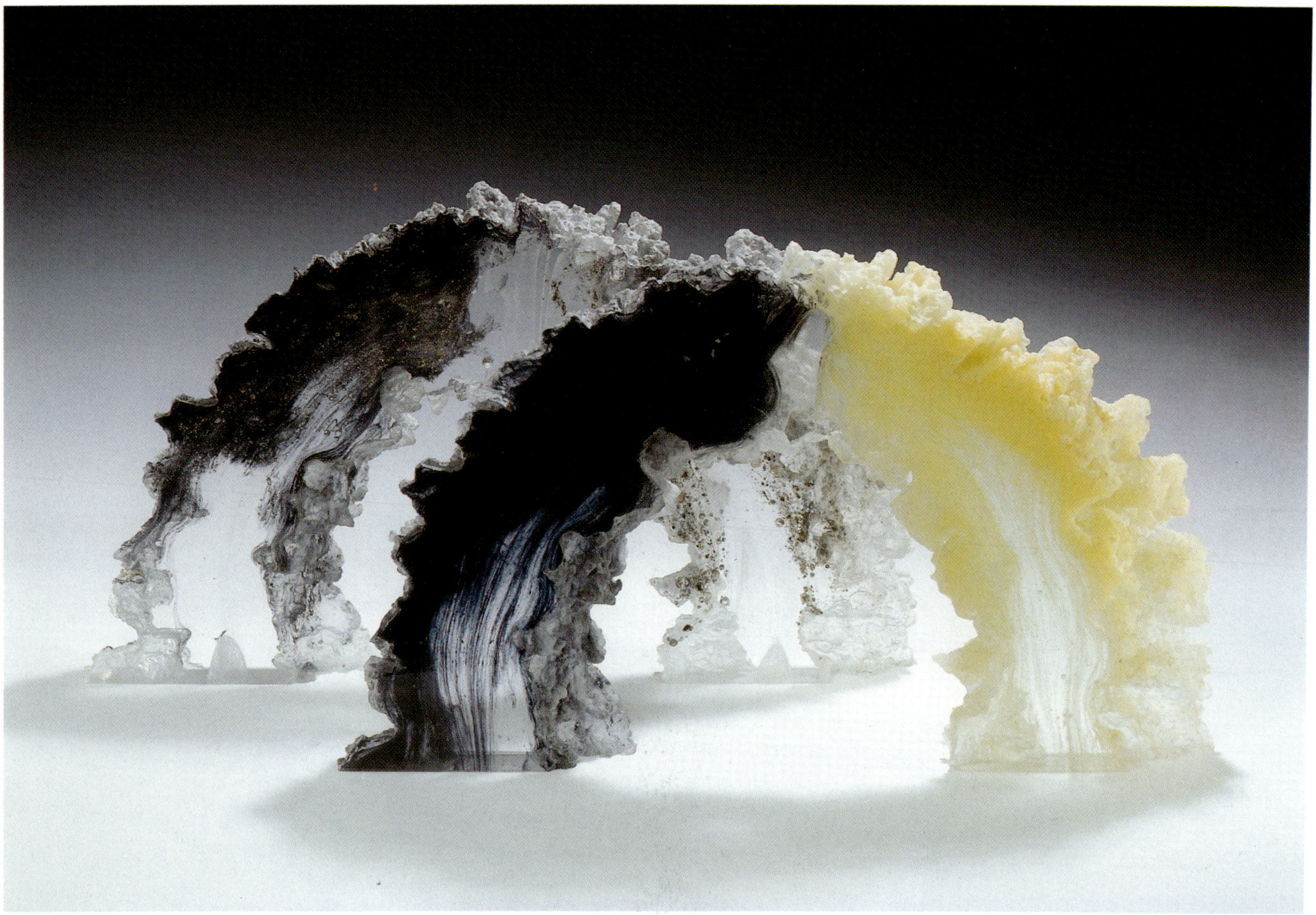

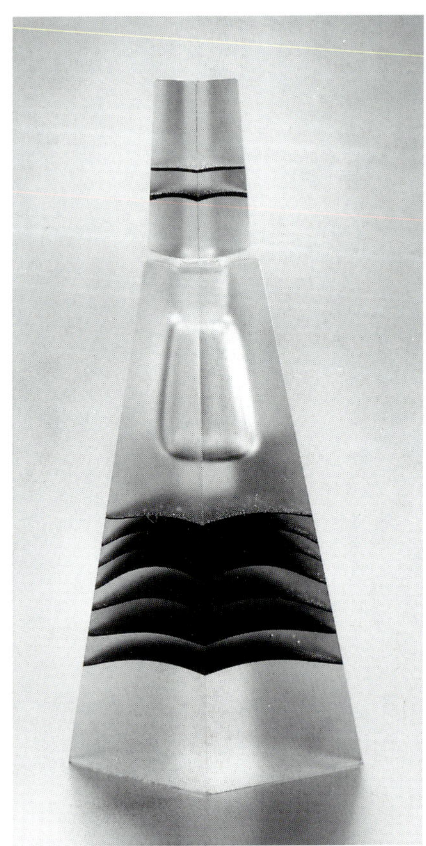

Colin Reid
(b. 1953)

Education: St. Martin's School of Art, London;
trained as scientific glassblower (lampwork);
studied at the Stourbridge College of Technology and Art
Lives and works in Stroud, Gloucestershire

527   "Twin Arch"

Diamond-engraved mark above the left,
respectively right, standing base:
first arch: *Colin Reid 1984, R 92 A*
second arch: *Colin Reid 1984, R 92 B*
1984
H each 28.1; W 48, 48.8; ⌀ 3.8 cm

Pâte de verre. Mold-melted. Cut and polished.
Narrow sides sandblasted.

Acc. no. LP 1985-63
Acquired at the exhibition "Zweiter Coburger
Glaspreis"
On permanent loan from the Museumsverein

Lit.: Coburg II, 1985, cat. no. 115c

David Taylor
(b. 1949)

Education: Central School of Art and Design,
London; Glass School, Orrefors
Lives and works in London

528   Perfume Flacon

Diamond-engraved mark on the underside
of base: *David Taylor 899 Glasshouse '84*;
on the underside of stopper: *DT 899*
1984
H 18.1, W 7.7, D 5 cm

Rhomboidal cross section. Mold-melted from
flat glass, blown. Cut, polished semimat.

Acc. no. LP 1985-64
Acquired at the exhibition "Zweiter Coburger
Glaspreis"
On permanent loan from the Museumsverein

Lit.: Coburg II, 1985, cat. no. 119a

United States of America

Harvey K. Littleton
(b. 1922)

Education: Brighton School of Art; University
of Michigan; Cranbrook Academy of Art,
Bloomfield Hills, MI
Lives and works in Spruce Pine, NC

529 "Loop"

Diamond-engraved mark on the underside of
one of the standing bases: *Harvey K. Littleton
1972 VSL*
Val Saint Lambert, 1972
H 28.4, W 31.3 cm

Colorless crystal glass with embedded threads
in blue and white. Freely shaped. Standing
bases cut and polished.

Acc. no. P 1973-7

Lit.: H. Ricke, "Unikat und Serie: Eine Orien-
tierungshilfe," *NG*, no. 1 (1980): 13ff., fig.
30b; Ricke, *Museumsarbeit*, 1988, 79, fig. 75

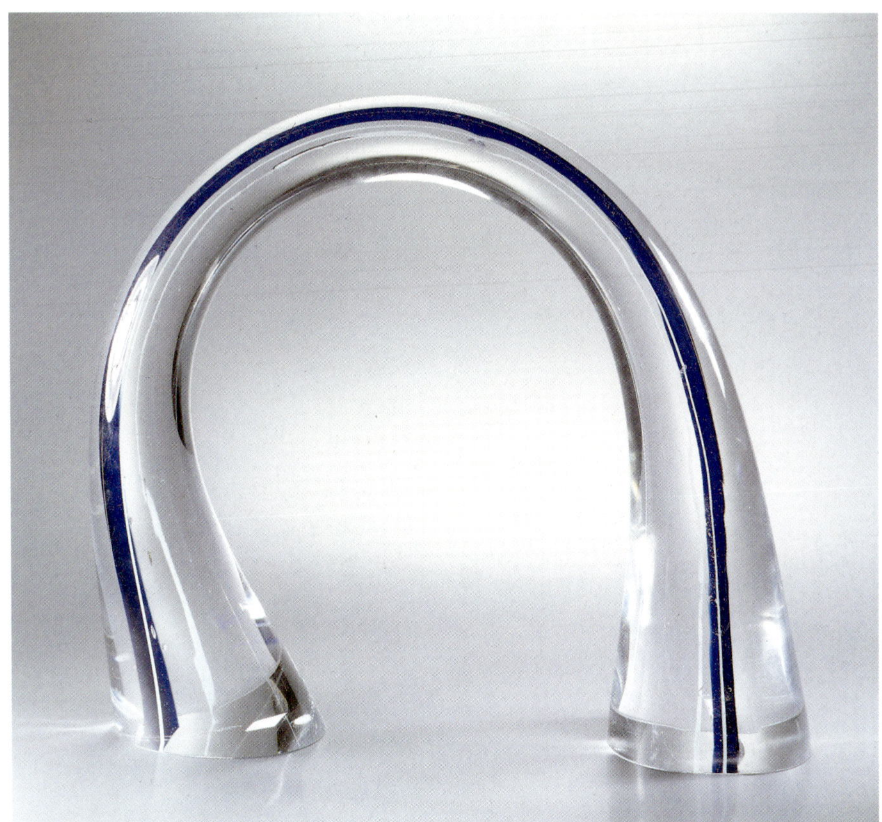

Dominick Labino
(1910–1987)

Education: Carnegie Institute of Technology,
Pittsburgh, PA; Toledo Museum of Art, School
of Design, Toledo, OH
Lived and worked in Grand Rapids, OH

530 Object

Diamond-engraved mark on the underside of
base: *Labino 9-1973*
1973
H 21.5, ⌀ 13.4 x 6.2 cm

Colorless glass, pale blue interior, built up in
several layers. Vapor-deposited iridescence
between the layers. Pegged air bubbles.
Freely shaped.

Acc. no. P 1974-6

Lit.: –

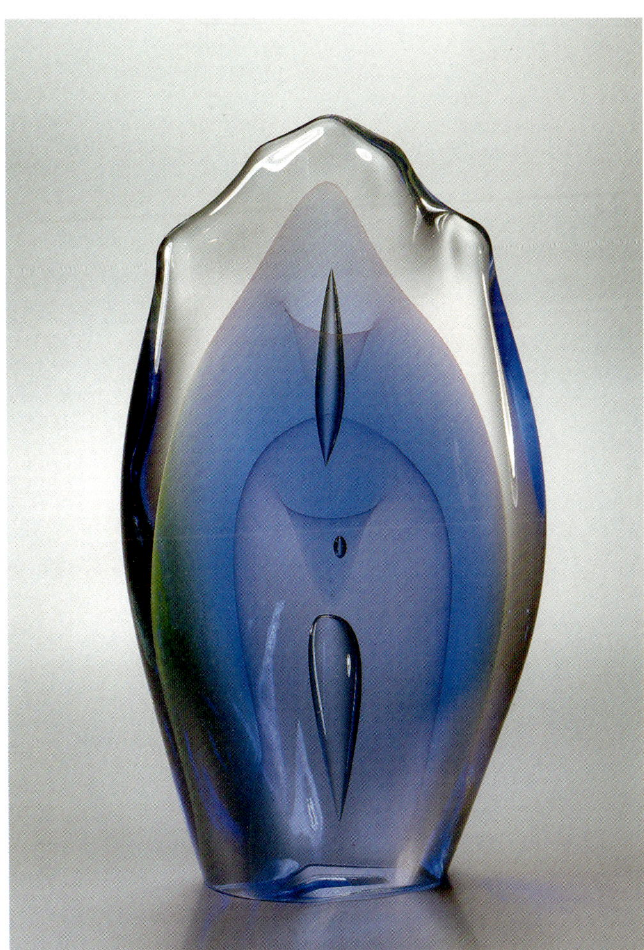

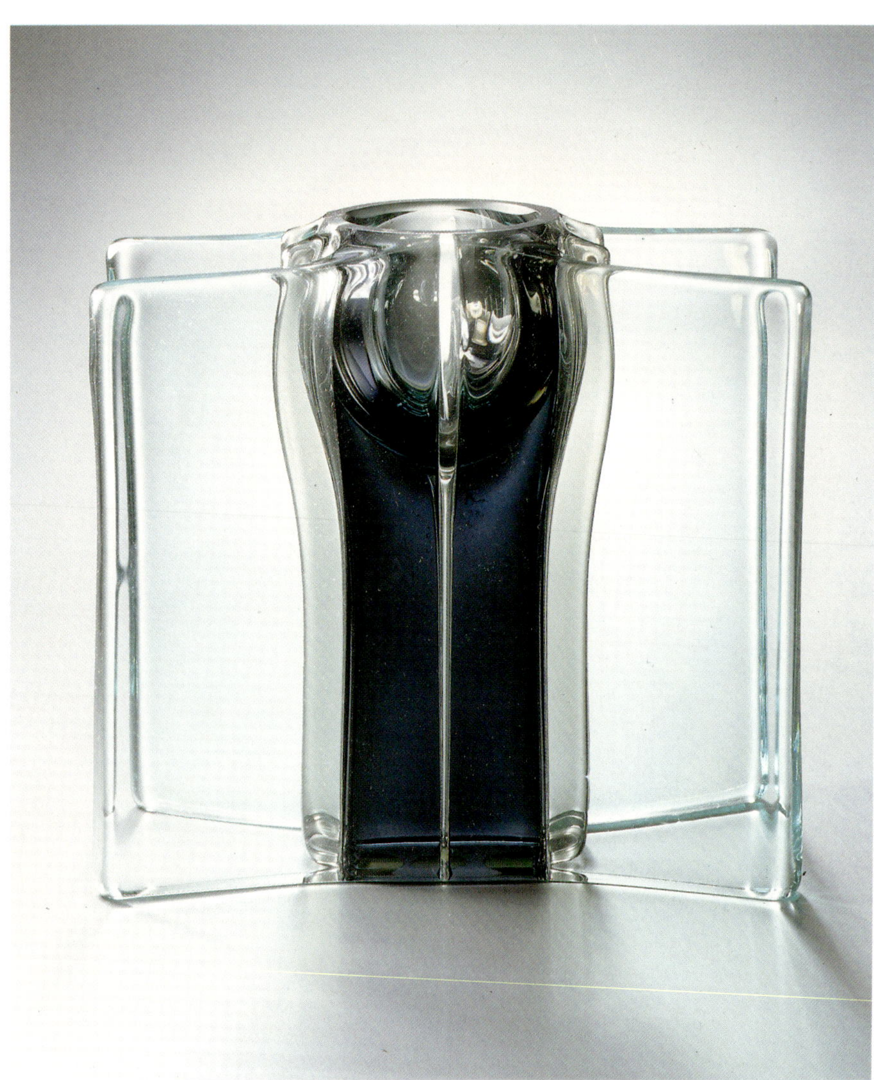

Thomas Patti
(b. 1943)

Education: Pratt Institute, Brooklyn, NY; New
School for Social Research, New York
Lives and works in Plainfield, MA

531   "Bi-axial Gray Solar Riser"

Diamond-engraved mark on the front, above
the standing base: *Patti 79*
1979
H 11.8, W 14.2, D 7.2 cm

Constructed from several sheets of flat glass
fused together. Colorless glass with light
green and gray-brown tones. Blown hollow
interior.

Acc. no. P 1980-9

Lit.: P. Hollister, "Tom Patti: The Code is in
the Glass," *NG*, no. 2 (1983): 74ff., fig. 45;
Ricke, *Museumsarbeit*, 1988, 78, fig. 70

Vernon Brejcha
(b. 1942)

Education: Fort Hays Kansas State University;
Wichita State University; University of Wis-
consin, Madison
Lives and works in Lawrence, KS

532   "Prairie Fire Dipper"

Diamond-engraved mark on the front section
of object: *"Prairie Fire Dipper" Brejcha 1981*
1981
L 41.2, H 11.1, D 10.3 cm

Colorless glass with multicolored inclusions.
Free-blown and shaped.

Acc. no. P 1982-7

Lit.: –

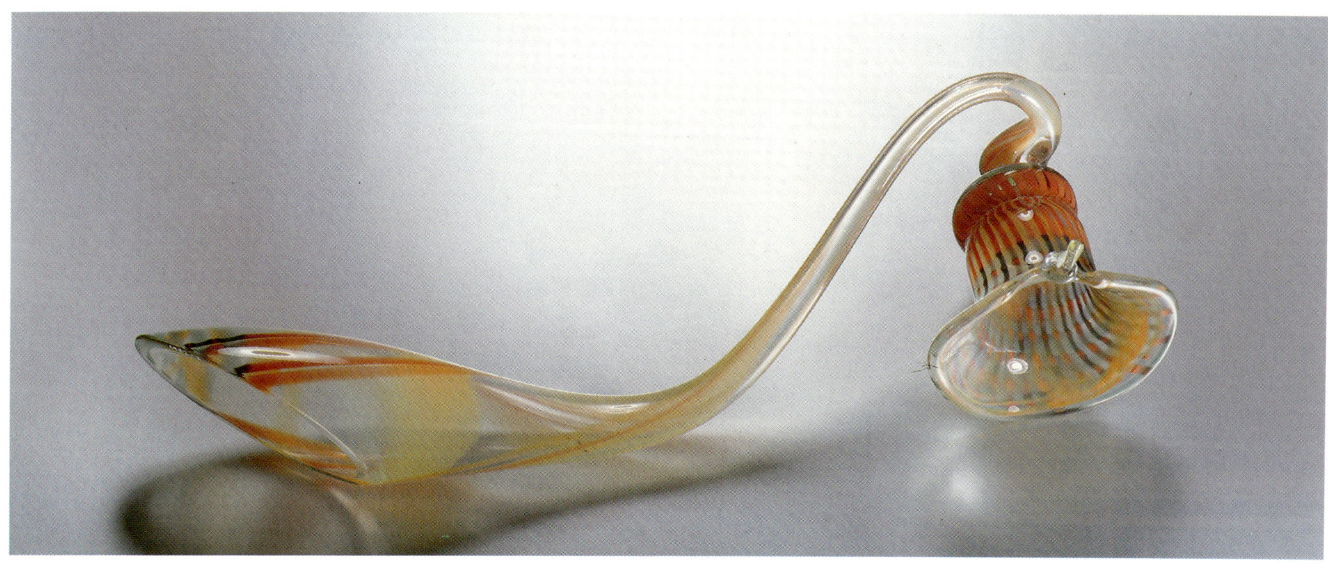

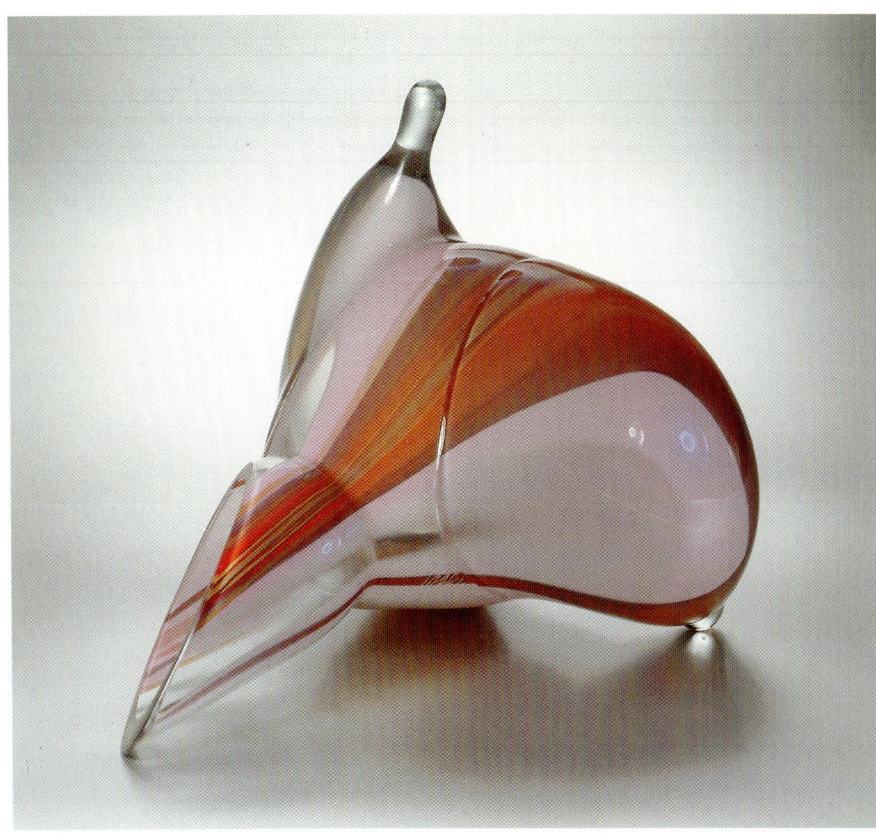

Joel Philip Myers
(b. 1934)

Education: Parsons School of Design, New York; Arts-and-Crafts School, Copenhagen (ceramics); College of Ceramics at Alfred University, Alfred, NY
Lives and works in Bloomington, IL

534   Vase

Engraved mark on wall above base:
Joel Philip Myers 1976
Baden near Vienna, J & L Lobmeyr—Studio Franzensbad
1976
H 25, ⌀ 9.8 cm

Massive, thick-walled milk glass. Free-blown and shaped. Decoration marvered into the wall. Base ground flat.

Acc. no. P 1977-4

Lit.: –

Marvin B. Lipofsky
(b. 1938)

Education: University of Illinois, Champaign-Urbana; University of Wisconsin, Madison
Lives and works in Oakland, CA

533   "Sketch"

Engraved mark on the underside of object:
M. Lipofsky 75
1975
H 20.5, W 24.7, D 19.4 cm

Colorless glass, partial multicolored overlay. Free-blown and shaped. Opening cut and polished.

Acc. no. P 1976-48
Acquired at the exhibition "Modernes Glas," Frankfurt

Lit.: Ohm and Bauer, *Modernes Glas*, 1976, cat. no. 34

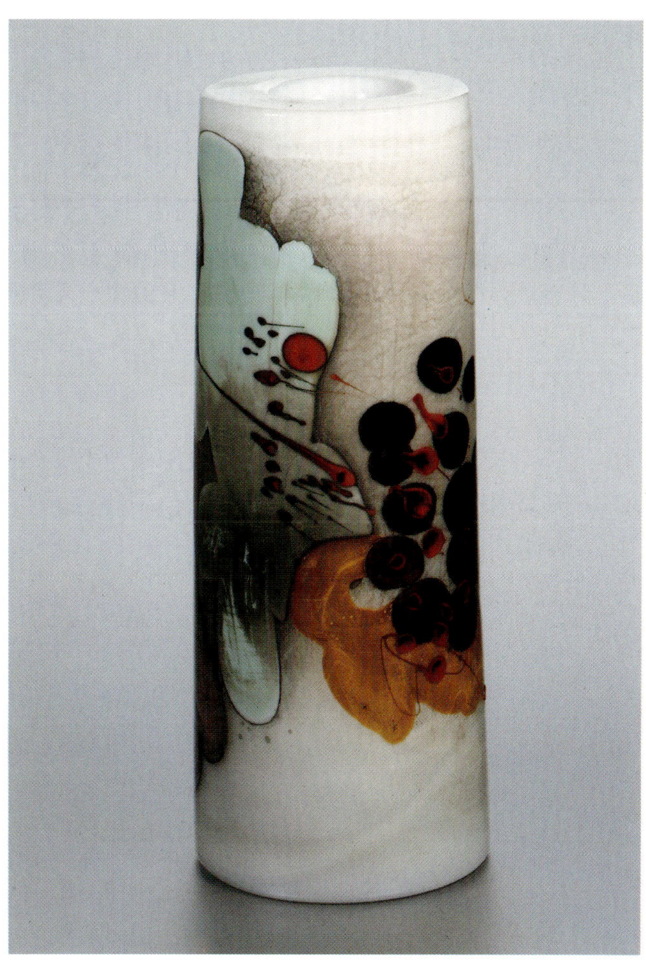

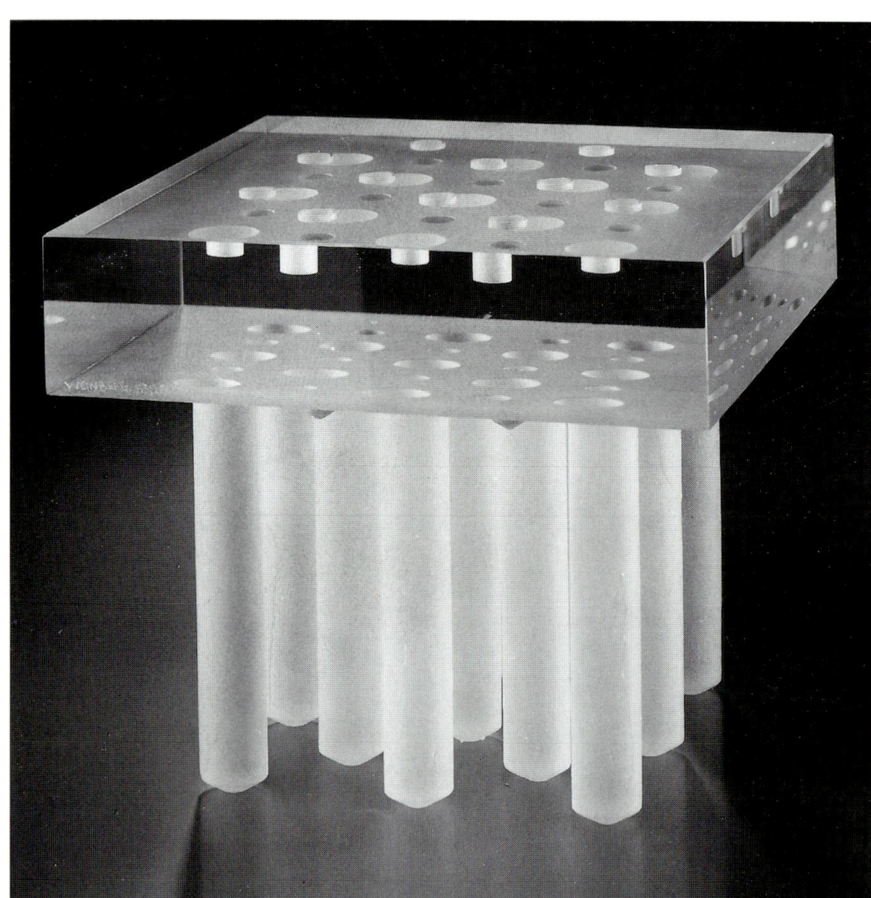

Steven I. Weinberg
(b. 1954)

Education: Rhode Island School of Design, Providence; New York College of Ceramics at Alfred University, Alfred, NY; University of Illinois, Champaign-Urbana
Lives and works in Providence, RI

535 "Untitled No. 1"

Diamond-engraved mark on the side:
WEINBERG 83/204
1983
H 16.4, L 19.5, W 19.5 cm

Colorless optic glass, mold-melted, cut, and polished. Flat block lying on 13 rods, between the rods small pink cones. Correspondingly drilled holes on top of the block.

Acc. no. P 1986-19
Acquired at the exhibition "Americans in Glass"
Gift of Stadt-Sparkasse Düsseldorf

For another example from the same series of one-offs see *Americans in Glass*, 1984, 138f.

Lit.: Ricke, *Museumsarbeit*, 1988, 79, fig. 76

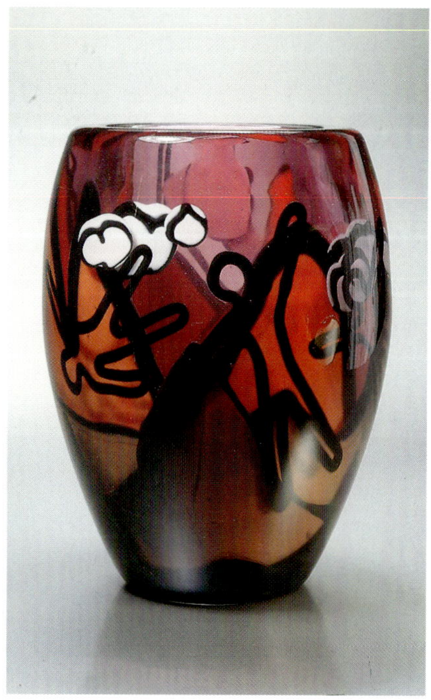

David R. Huchthausen
(b. 1952)

Education: Hochschule für Angewandte Kunst, Vienna; Illinois State University, Normal; University of Wisconsin, Madison and Wausau
Lives and works in Smithville, TN

536 Vase

Engraved mark above the standing base:
David R. Huchthausen 1977 Baden bei Wien No. 84
Baden near Vienna, J & L Lobmeyr—Studio Franzensbad
1977
H 19, ⌀ 14.9 cm

Colorless glass, several inner casings and overlays in red and orange tones. Free-blown and shaped. Opaque white dots and floating human silhouettes made of black threads between the layers.

Acc. no. P 1979-6

For another example of the same series of one-offs see Frantz, *Contemporary Glass*, 1989, 68.

Lit.: –

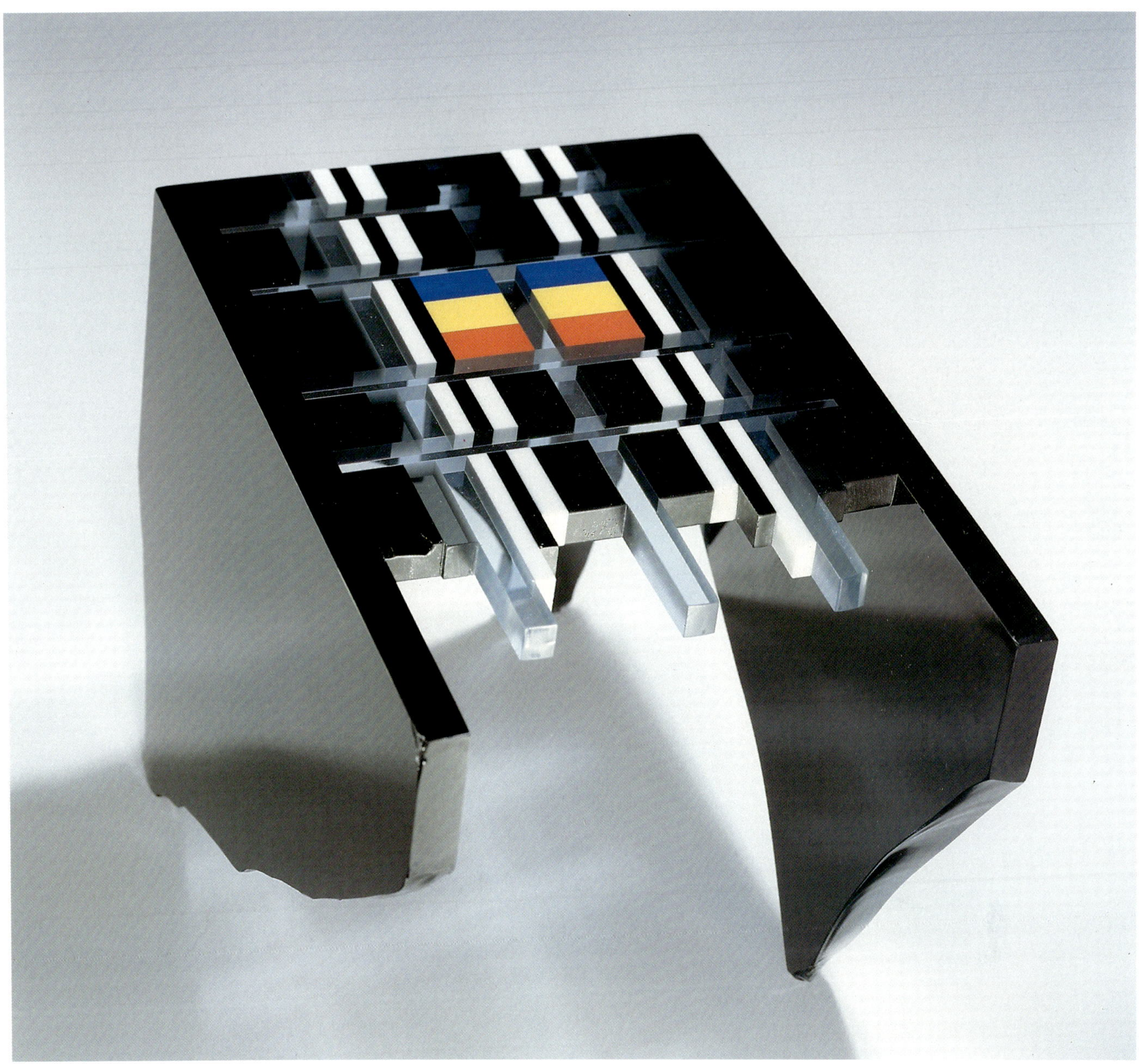

537   "Leitungsscherbe"

Sandblasted mark on the inside of object:
LS 682 DRH
1982
H 32.4, front panel 34 x 24 cm

Comprises two massive black side panels and
a middle section; each made of partly fused,
partly laminated colored glass.

Acc. no. P 1986-17
Acquired at the exhibition "Americans in
Glass"
Gift of Stadt-Sparkasse Düsseldorf

For another example of the same series of
one-offs see *Americans in Glass*, 1984, 62f.

Lit.: Ricke, *Museumsarbeit*, 1988, 79, fig. 78

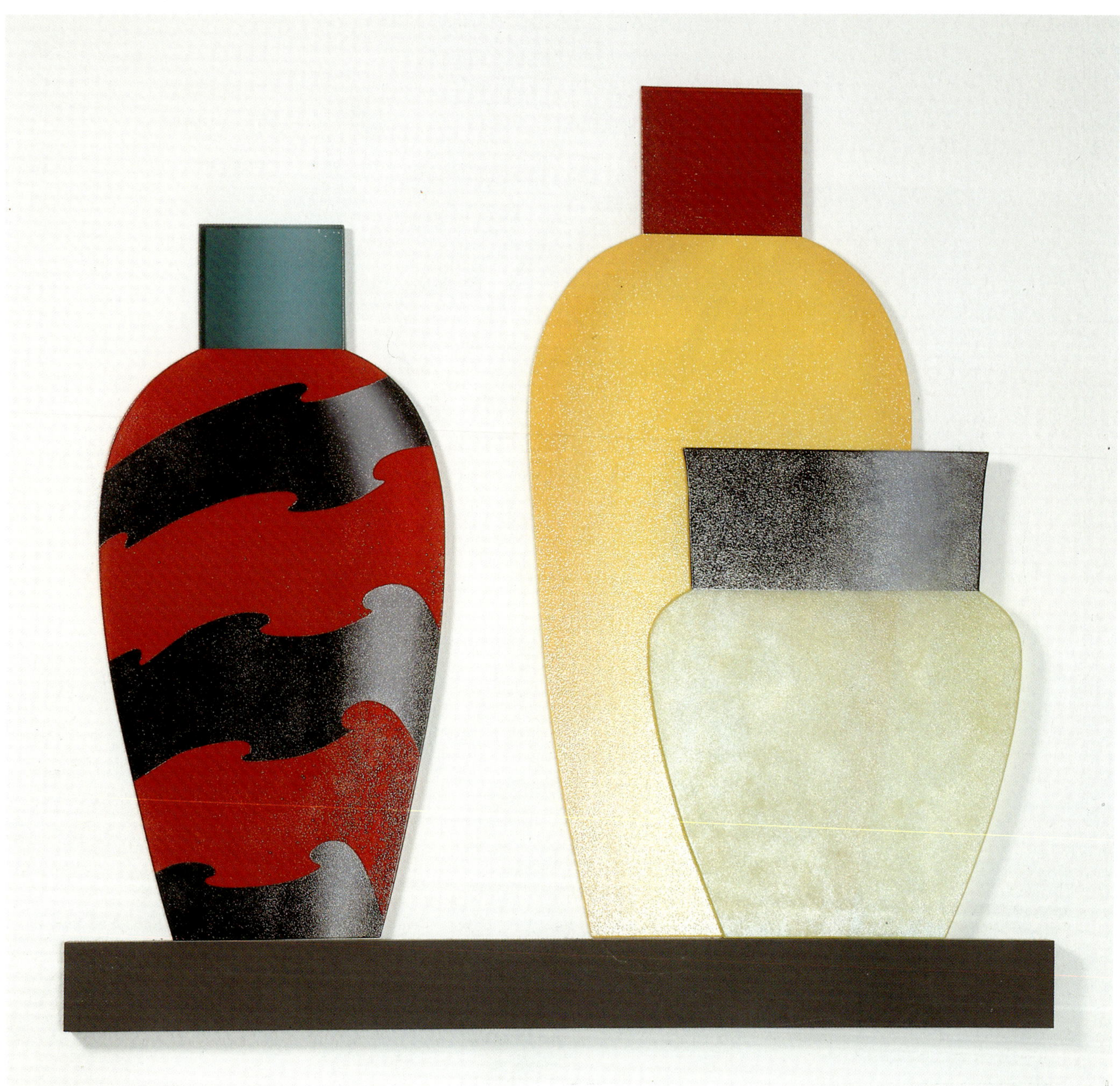

Margie Jervis
(b. 1956)

Education: Rhode Island School of Design,
Providence

Susie Krasnican
(b. 1954)

Education: Cleveland Institute of Art; Rhode
Island School of Design, Providence
Live and work in Arlington, VA

538   "Three Vases" Wall Object

Unsigned
1983
H 64, 78, 45; W 32, 37, 35 cm

Colorless plate glass. Sprayed enamel painting.

Acc. no. P 1986-18
Acquired at the exhibition "Americans in
Glass"
Gift of Stadt-Sparkasse Düsseldorf

Lit.: *Americans in Glass*, 1984, 64f.

Dale Chihuly
(b. 1941)

Education: Rhode Island School of Design,
Providence; University of Wisconsin, Madison;
University of Washington, Seattle
Lives and works in Seattle, WA

539 Dish Object from the "Macchia" Series

Engraved mark on the underside of base:
Chihuly 1984
1984
H 19.5, ⌀ 71.5 cm

Glass-granule inclusions and applied encircling
threads of colorless glass. Free-blown and
shaped.

Acc. no. P 1985-2
Gift of the artist

For Chihuly's "Macchia" series see *Americans
in Glass*, 1984, 40f.

Lit.: –

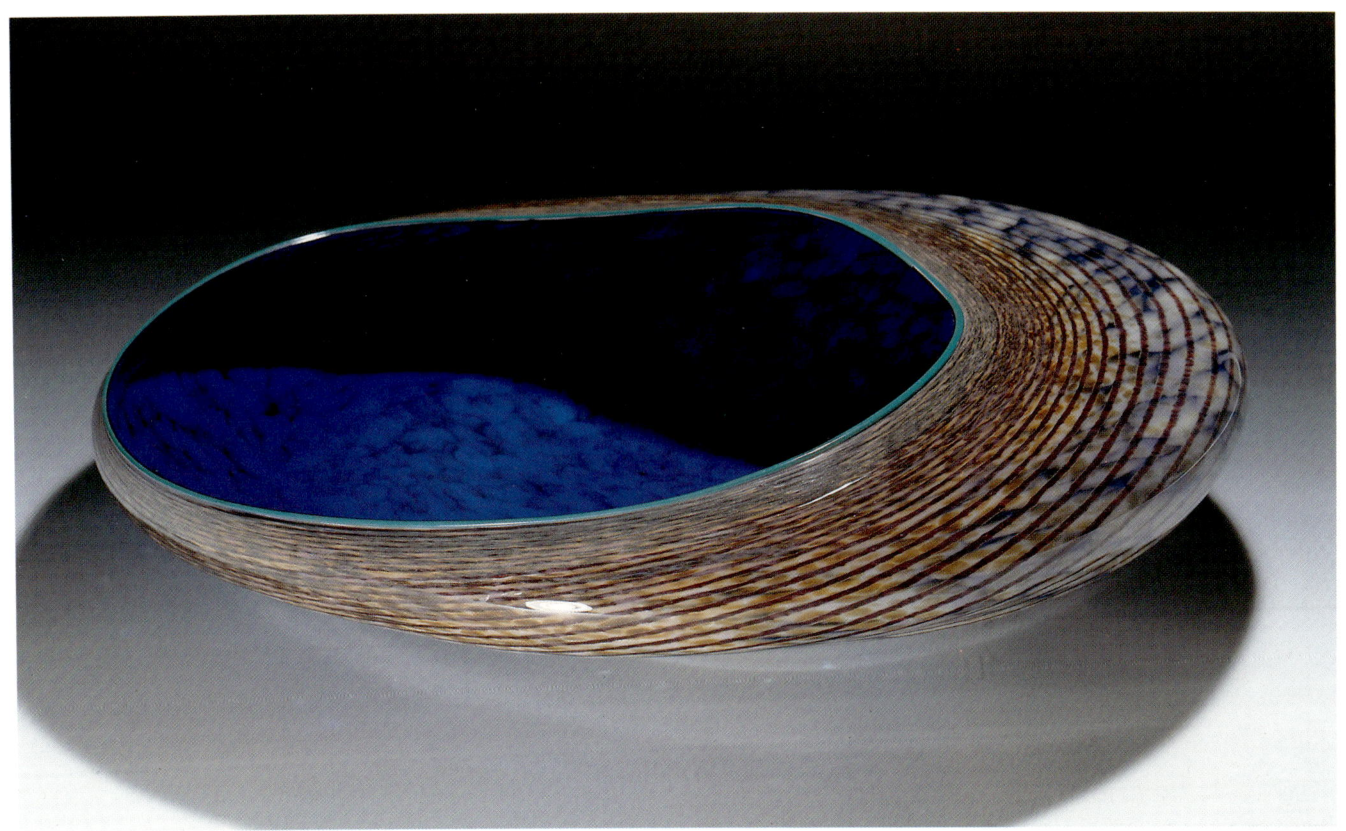

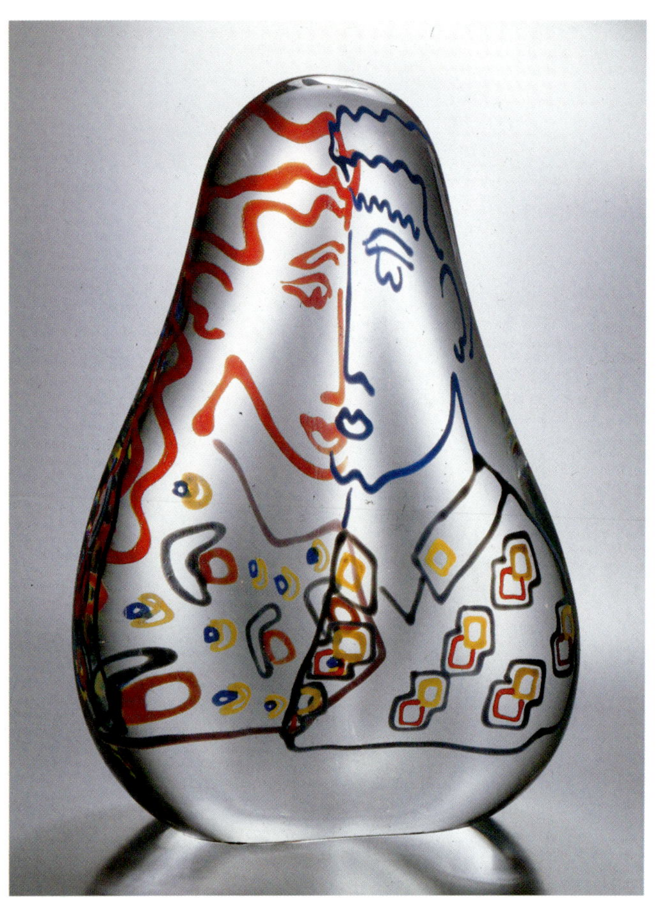

Richard Jolley
(b. 1952)

Education: Tusculum College, Greenville, TN;
George Peabody College for Teachers,
Nashville, TN; Penland School of Crafts, Pen-
land, NC
Lives and works in Knoxville, TN

540　"The Kiss"

Diamond-engraved mark on the underside of
standing base: *Richard Jolley the Kiss*
Hameln, Atelier Hoellings, 1986
H 31.5,　∅ 22 x 9.1 cm

Colorless crystal glass. Freely shaped. Figural
depiction of colored glass threads in the
wall: a male and female face in profile.

Acc. no. P 1986-14
Gift of Galerie Angela Hoellings, Hameln

For similar works see *World Glass Now*, 1988,
Special Invitation Division, cat. nos. 11, 12.

Lit.: –

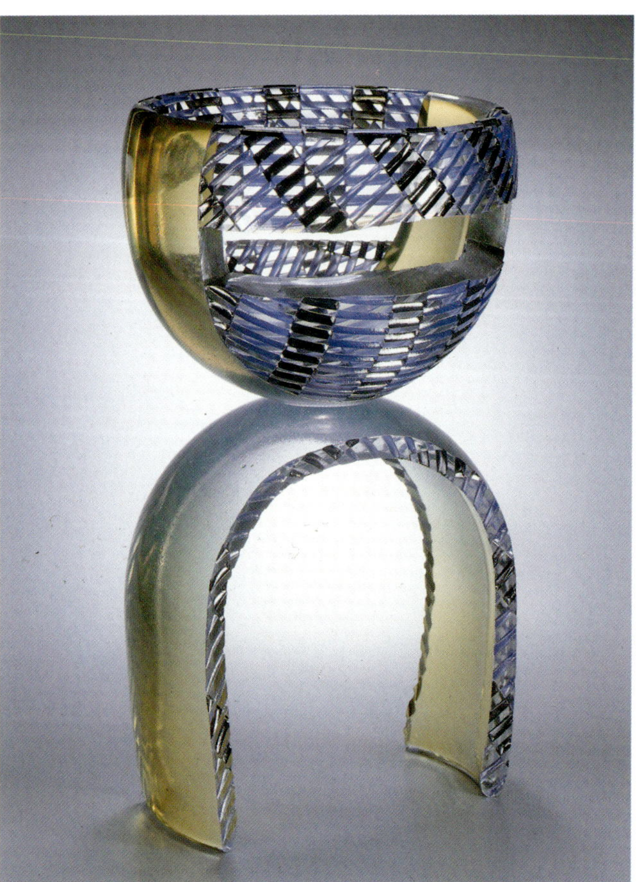

Concetta Mason
(b. 1956)

Education: Rochester Institute of Technology,
School for American Craftsmen, Rochester,
NY; Pilchuck Glass School, Stanwood, WA;
Southern Connecticut State College, New Haven
Lives and works in Rochester, NY

541　"Sea Arena"

Diamond-engraved mark on the underside of
base of bowl: *Concetta Mason c 1986 / SE
2790 "Sea Arena"*; impressed in wall of bowl,
at the bottom: *cm*
1986
H 30.5,　∅ bowl and arch each 17.8 cm

In two parts, not laminated. Colorless glass.
Free-blown and shaped. Controlled breaking,
cut, sandblasted, enameled, slightly iridescent.

Acc. no. P 1988-10

For similar pieces from the series of one-offs
see R. Bernstein, "Concetta Mason: Gefäss-
fragmente," *NG*, no. 3 (1986): 184f., and
World Glass Now, 1988, cat. nos. 74ff.

Lit.: –

Jon F. Clark
(b. 1947)

Education: Royal College of Art, London; University of Wisconsin at River Falls
Lives and works in Elkins Park, PA

542   "Dual Form, Leaning"

Diamond-engraved mark below the upper section: *Jon F. Clark 1983 "DFL"*
1983
H 99, pedestal 52 x 18.4 cm

Colorless glass; gray-blue inner casing. Mold-blown, shaped. Enamel painting. Mount of steel, pedestal of wood, painted in a copper color.

Acc. no. P 1986-16
Acquired at the exhibition "Americans in Glass"
Gift of Stadt-Sparkasse Düsseldorf

Lit.: *Americans in Glass*, 1984, 42f.

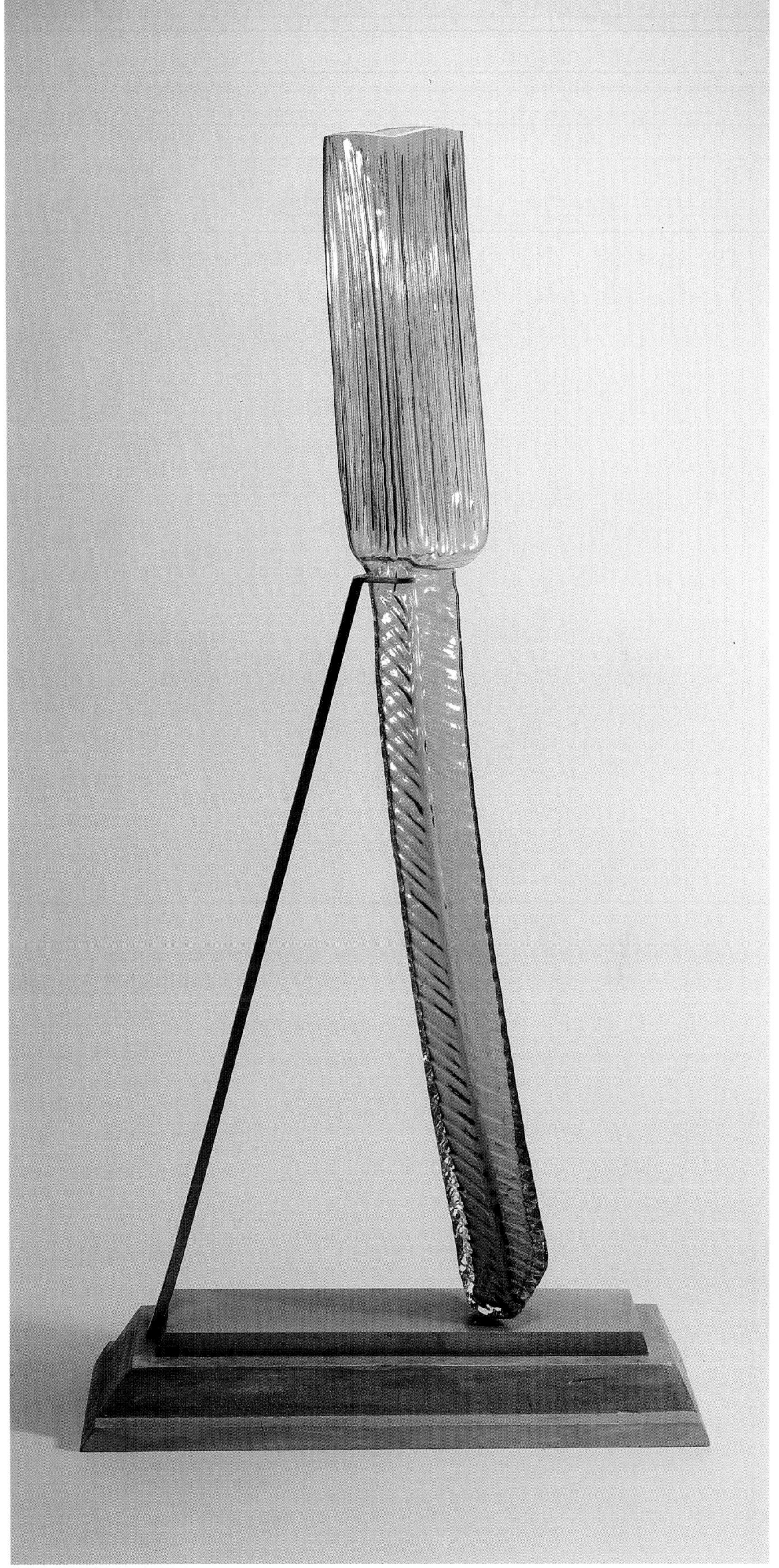

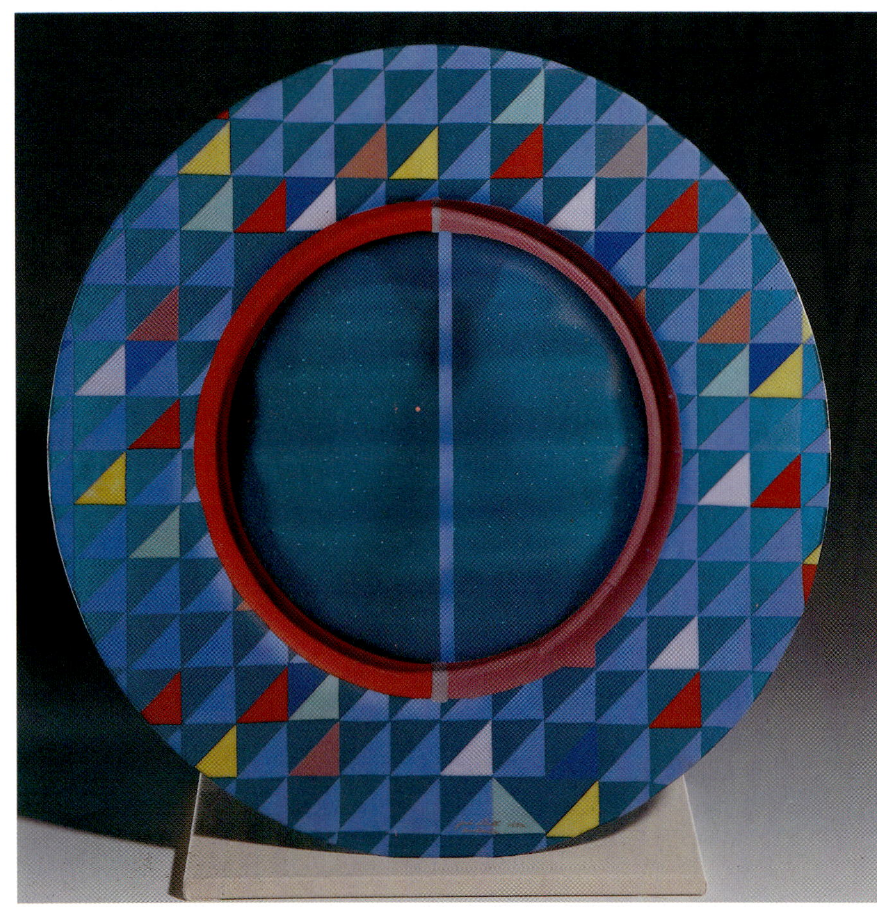

Rob Knottenbelt
(b. 1947)

Education: University of Auckland, New Zealand, and S. A. School of Art, Australia
Lives and works in Wesburn, Australia

544   "Towerzero"

Unsigned
1991
H 61, W/D 42 cm

Light green flat glass, 15 mm thick, sawn with water jet, sandblasted, etched; comprises seven laminated parts.

Acc. no. P 1993-1
Acquired from the artist
Gift of Stiftung van Meeteren, Düsseldorf

Lit.: –

Australia

Judi Elliott
(b. 1934)

Education: International Pottery School, London; Canberra School of Arts
Lives and works in Bungendore A.C.T.

543   "Nidus Messages & Qualities"

Cursive signature in gold lacquer: *judi elliott 1992 australia*
1992
H approx. 8, ⌀ 76.2 cm

Mosaic-glass technique. Numerous preformed parts in blue and turquoise tones fused and kiln-formed.

Acc. no. P 1993-2
Acquired from the artist
Gift of Stiftung van Meeteren, Düsseldorf

Lit.: –

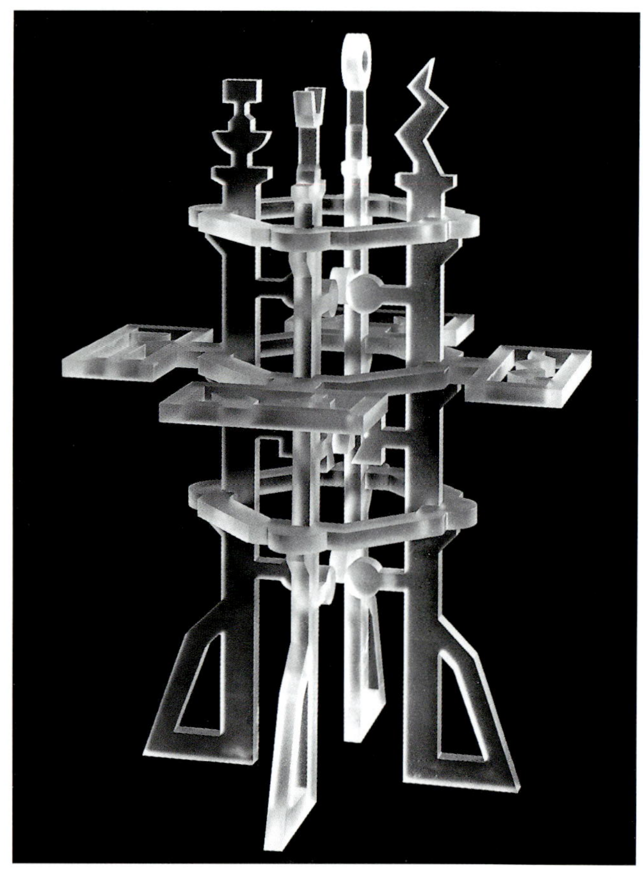

Japan

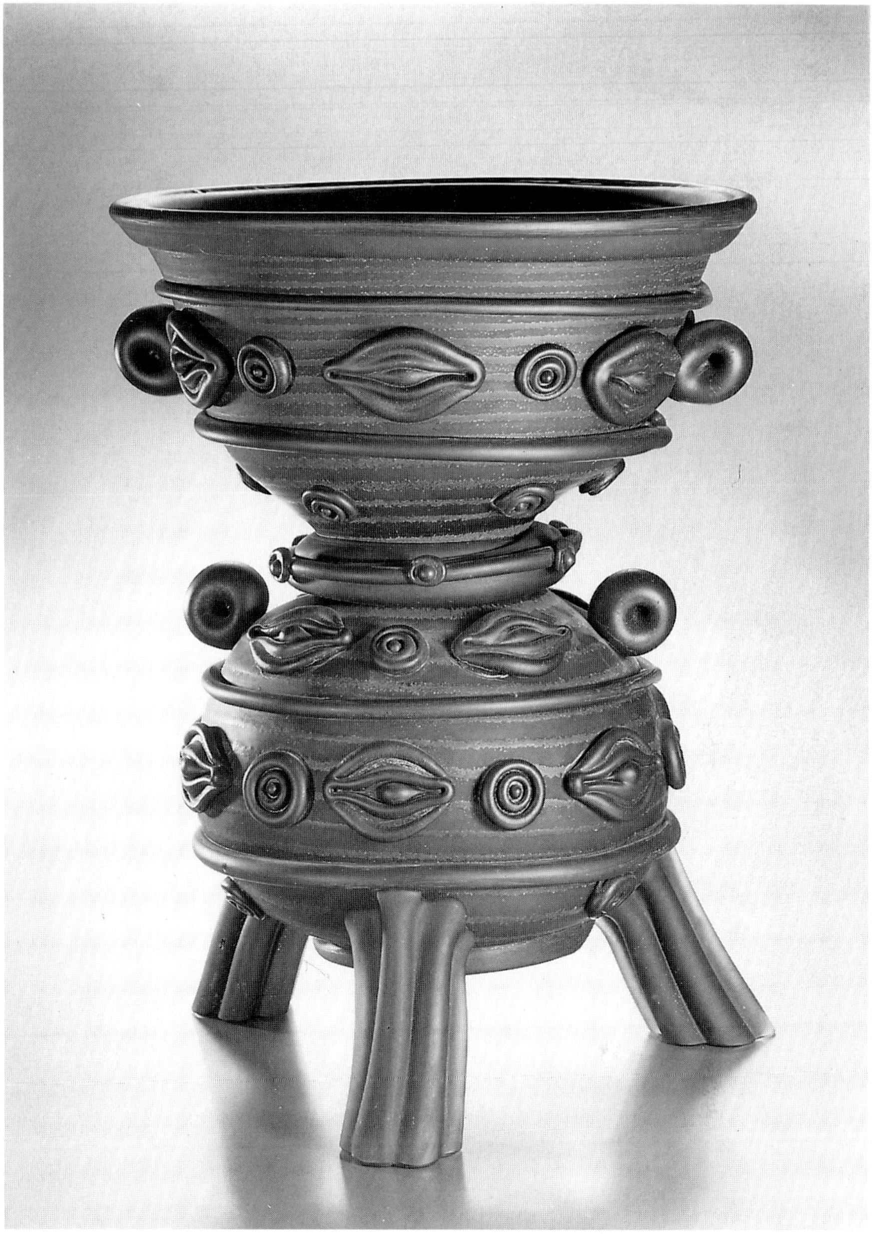

Hosatoshi Iwata
(1925–1994)

Education: Art College, Tokyo (arts-and-crafts
department)
Lived and worked in Tokyo

545   Vessel

Diamond-engraved mark on the underside of
base: *Qri Iwata*
Adhesive label bearing no. *4815*
1981
H 31.7, ⌀ 24 cm

Black glass. Free-blown and shaped. Comprising two separately worked pieces. Freely
applied decoration. Surface acid frosted.

Acc. no. P 1987-8
Gift of the artist

For similar works see *World Glass Now*, 1982,
165, cat. no. 22

Lit.: –

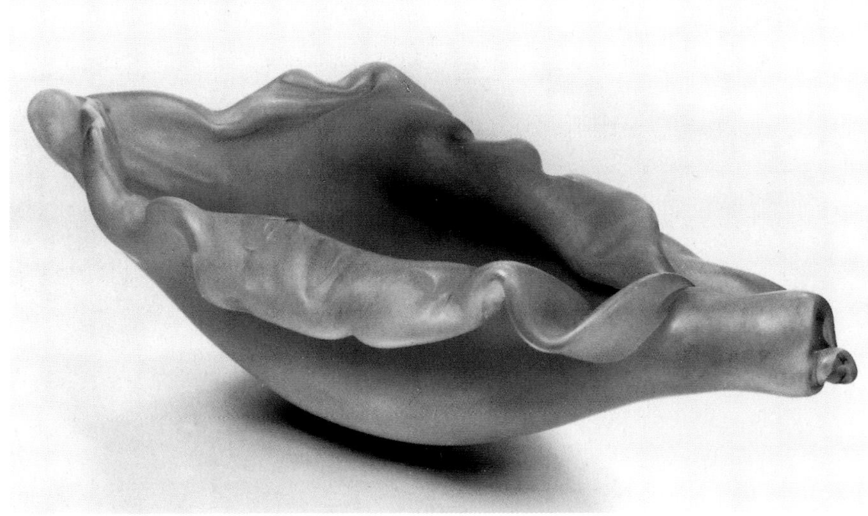

Toshichi Iwata
(1893–1980)

Education: Academy of Fine Arts, Tokyo
(metal course)
1931 founded Iwata Glass, Tokyo
Lived and worked in Tokyo

546   Shell Dish

Diamond-engraved mark on the underside of
base: *TOSHICHI IWATA*
Adhesive label: *TR 392*
1976
H 9.7, L 37, W 15.8 cm

Overlay glass covered with another layer of
colorless glass. Freely shaped.

Acc. no. P 1987-7
Gift of Iwata Glass, Tokyo

Lit.: –

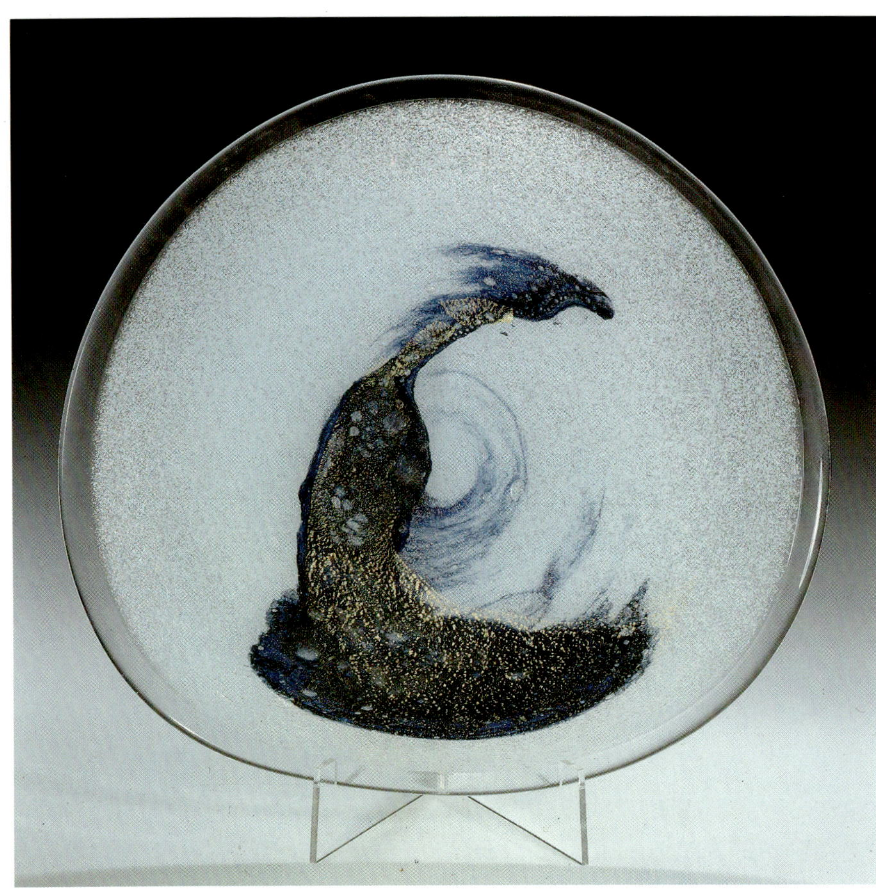

Itoko Iwata
(b. 1922)

President of Iwata Glass Company Ltd.
Lives and works in Tokyo

547   Plate

Engraved mark on the underside of base:
Itoko Iwata
1981
H 4, ⌀ 51.5 cm

Colorless glass with embedded dense bubble
decoration covered with blue glass and torn
gold foil. Free-blown, dilated, shaped; folded
rim.

Acc. no. P 1987-10
Gift of the artist

Lit.: H. Ricke, "Japans Glaskunst im Aufbruch
II," *NG* , no. 3 (1984): 122, fig. 8

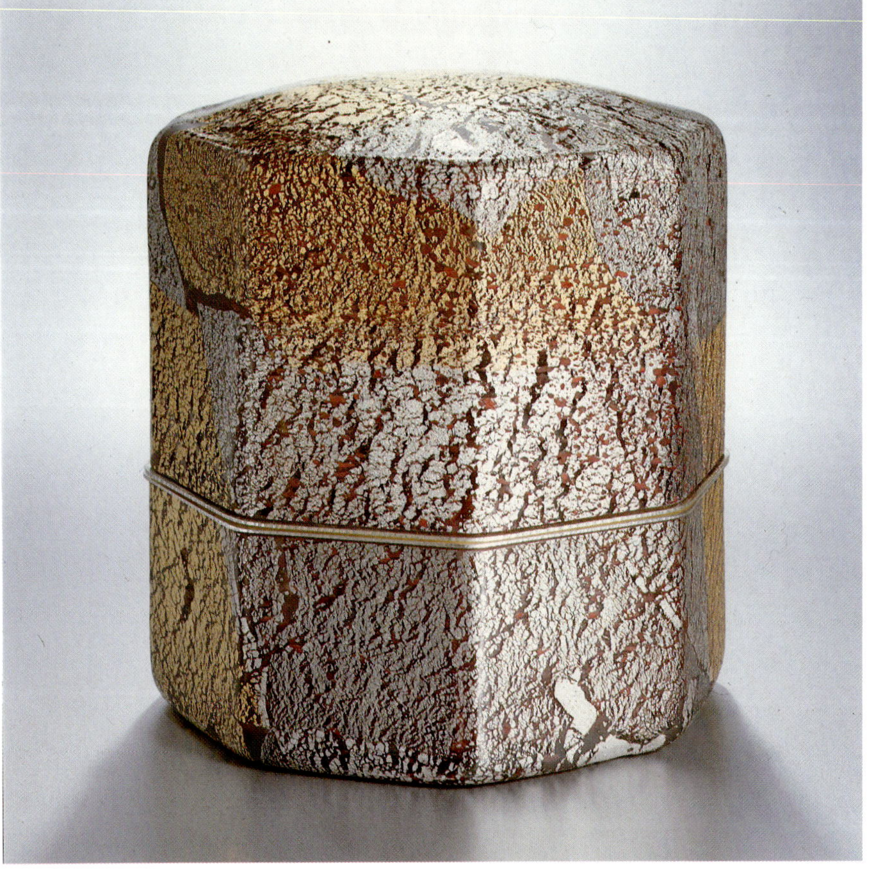

Kyohei Fujita
(b. 1921)

Education: Art College, Tokyo (metalworking
department)
Lives and works in Ichikawa, Chiba Prefecture

548   Jar

Diamond-engraved mark on the underside of
base: *Kyohei Fujita*
1986
H 20.4, ⌀ 18 cm

Irregular octagonal cross section. Glass with
dark pink overlay. Mold-blown. Embedded
colored glass granules, almost completely
covered with torn gold and platinum foil.
Surface acid-frosted.

Acc. no. P 1986-20
Gift of the artist

For Fujita's work see A. Takeda, "Kyohei Fujita and his Decorative Glass Caskets," *NG*,
no. 2 (1987): 66–72.

Lit.: *NG*, no. 2 (1987): cover image

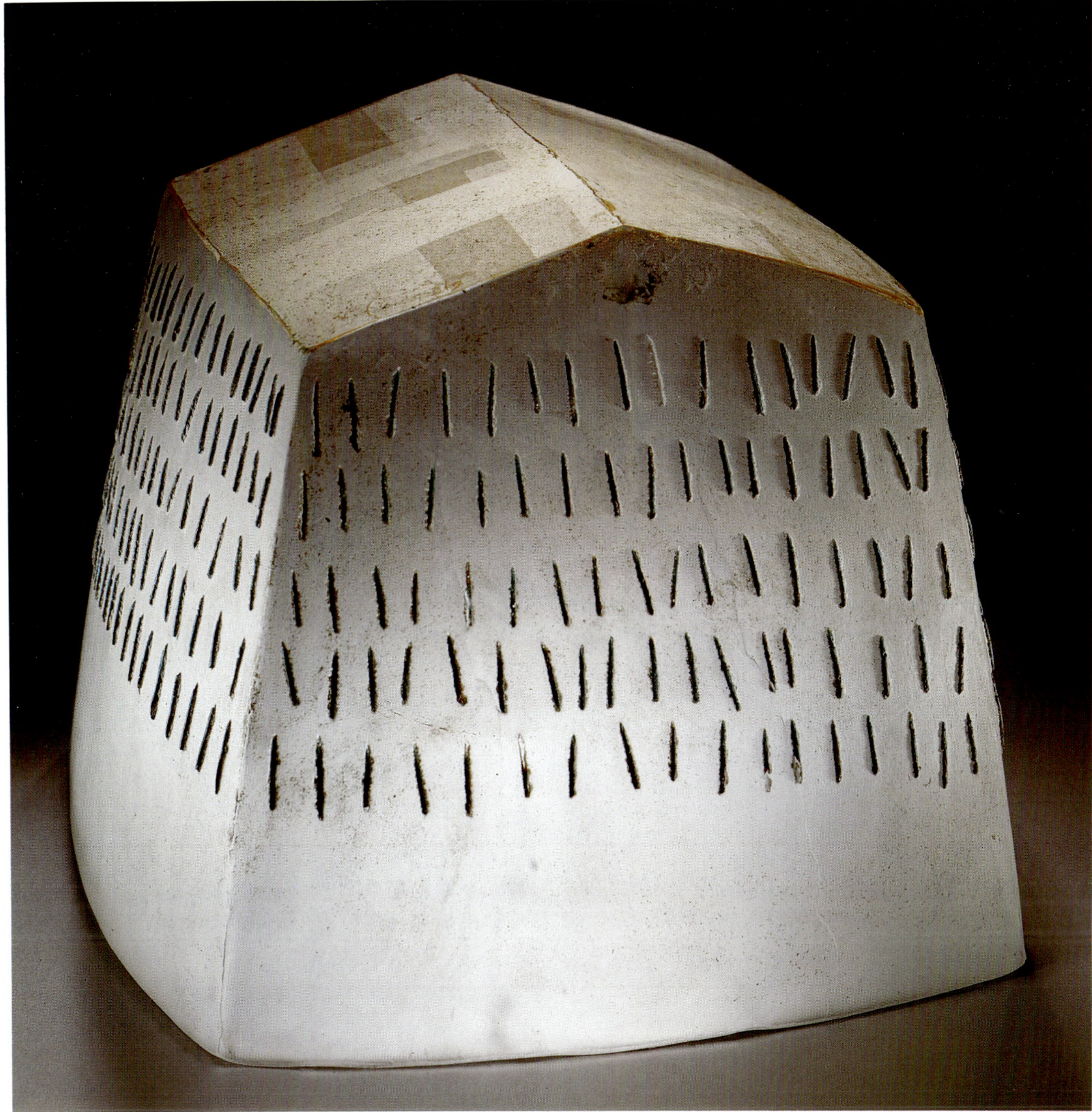

Katsuya Ogita
(b. 1957)

Education: Kanazawa College of Art and Tokyo
Glass Art Institute
Lives and works in Kanazawa

549   "Life and Time"

Engraved Kanji characters: *Katsu*
1992
H 28, W 34, D 33 cm

Mold-melted, sandblasted; covered with silver
foil, patinated.

Acc. no. P 1995-14
Acquired at the exhibition "New Glass in Japan"

Lit.: Ricke, *New Glass Japan*, 1993, cat. no. 68

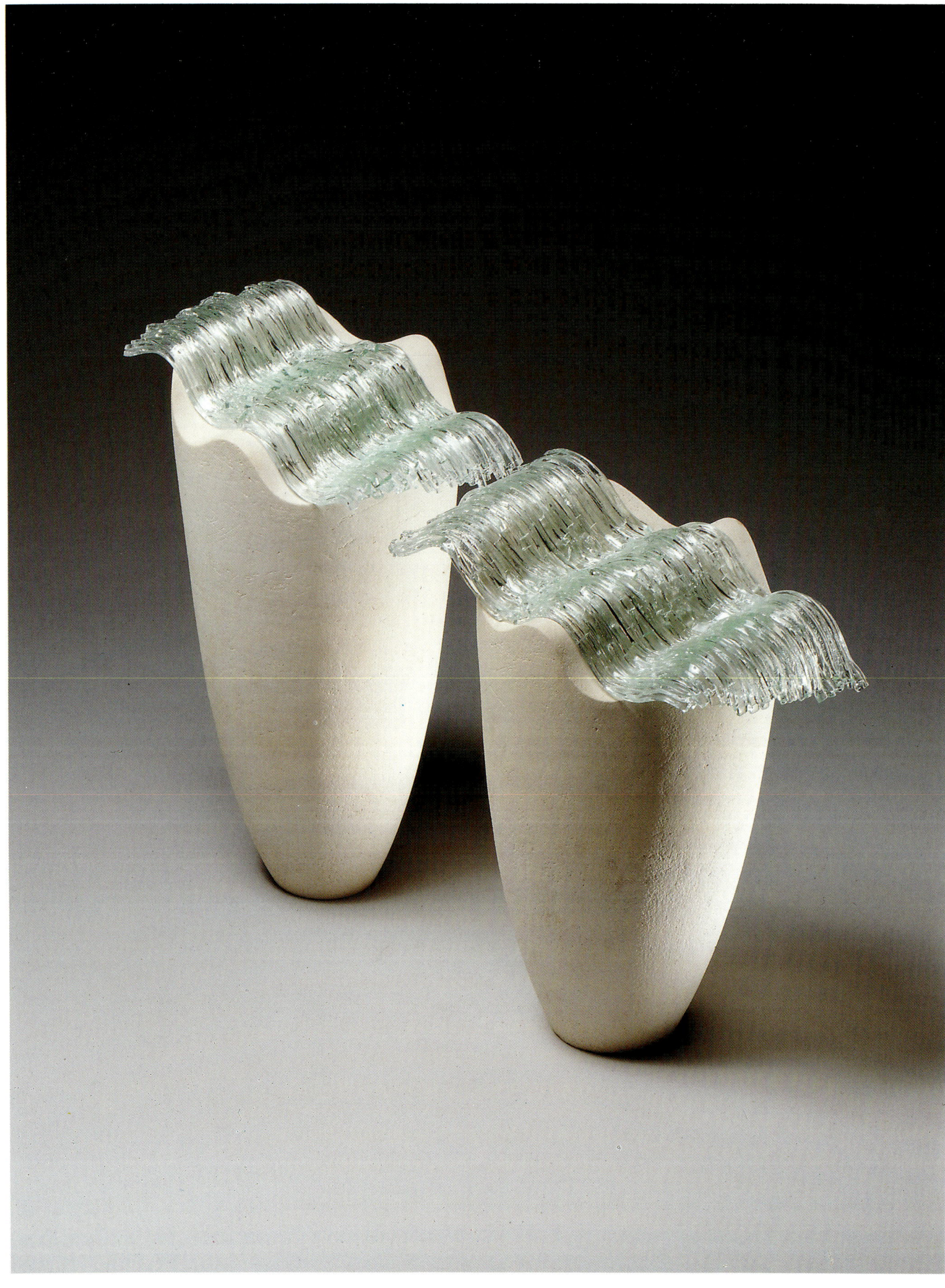

Keiko Mukaide
(b. 1954)

Education: Musashino University of Art,
Tokyo, and Edinburgh College of Art
Lives and works in Edinburgh

550 "Water Edge No. 2"

Unsigned
1993
H 36, 31.7; Ø 18.2 cm
Waves: approx. 13 x 26 cm

Two unglazed hollow ceramic vessels. On top
of these: flat glass strips fused and kiln-
formed into waves.

Acc. no. P 1995-1
Gift of Dr. Ernst Ploil, Vienna
Acquired at the exhibition "New Glass in
Japan"

Lit.: Ricke, *New Glass Japan*, 1993,
cat. no. 53

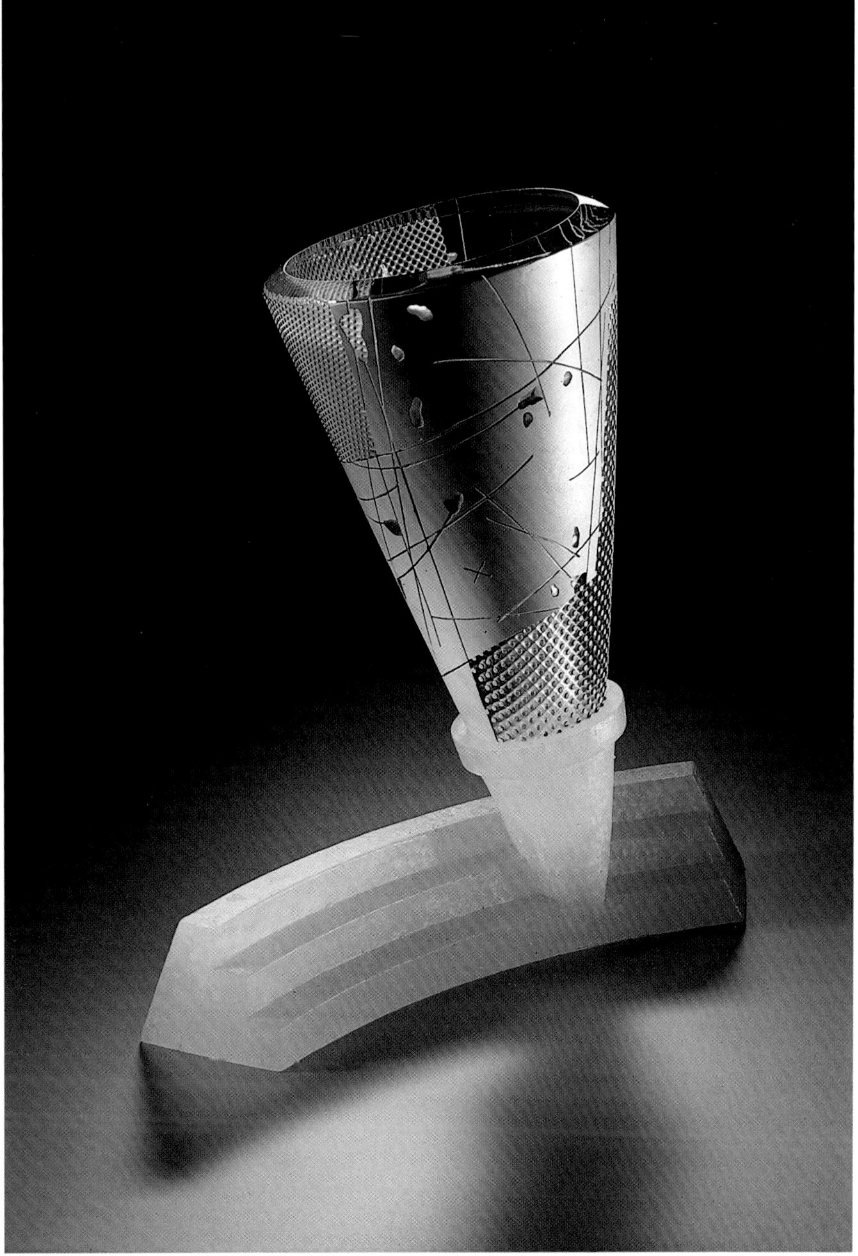

Yoshihiko Takahashi
(b. 1958)

Education: Tama University of Art, Tokyo
Lives and works in Kanagawa

551 "Arc"

Unsigned
1992
H 30.2, W 31, D 14.5 cm

Comprises two parts. The lower part mold-
melted, the upper mold-blown with double
overlay in dark blue and opaque white. Sandblasted, afterwards treated with acid. Rim of
mouth cut and polished.

Acc. no. P 1995-16
Acquired at the exhibition "New Glass in
Japan"

Lit.: Ricke, *New Glass Japan*, 1993,
cat. no. 90

Rika Kuroki
(b. 1958)

Education: California College of Arts and
Crafts, Oakland
Lives and works in Tokyo

552   "Aditi"

Unsigned
1993
H 30, ⌀ 30 x 46 cm

Blown glass body, iridescent. Paper in part
glued to glass; textile.

Acc. no. P 1995-13
Acquired at the exhibition "New Glass in
Japan"

Lit.: Ricke, *New Glass Japan*, 1993,
cat. no. 46

Yoko Hirosawa
(b. 1960)

Education: Kyoritsu Women's University and
Tokyo Glass Art Institute
Lives and works in Yamanashi

553   "Ceremonial Vessel"

Free-blown and shaped; violet-gray inner
casing, feet colorless. Silver foil application
torn by dilating. On the wall encircling
etched writing, figural and symbolic depictions.

Acc. no. P 1995-10
Acquired at the exhibition "New Glass in
Japan"

Lit.: Ricke, *New Glass Japan*, 1993,
cat. no. 12

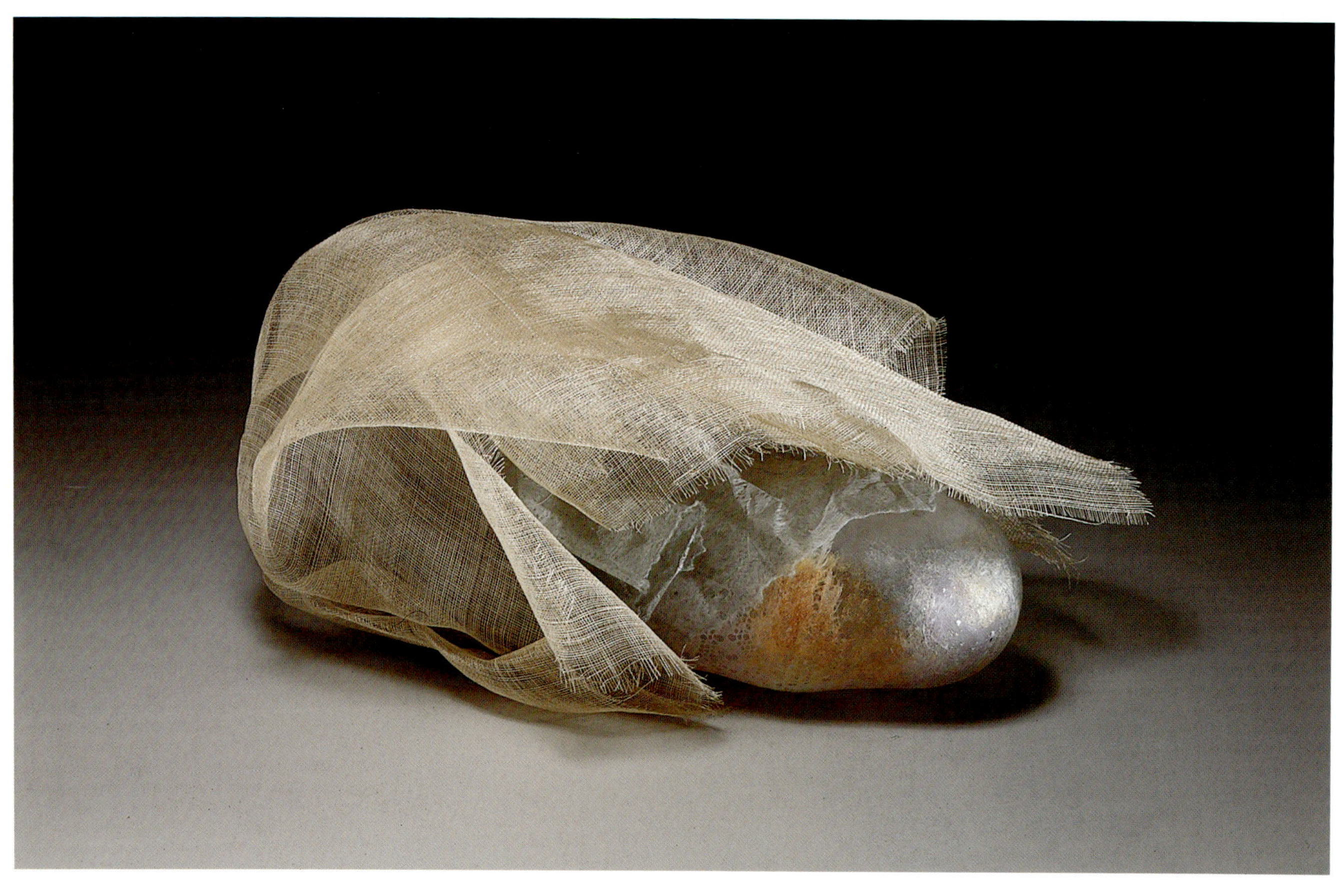

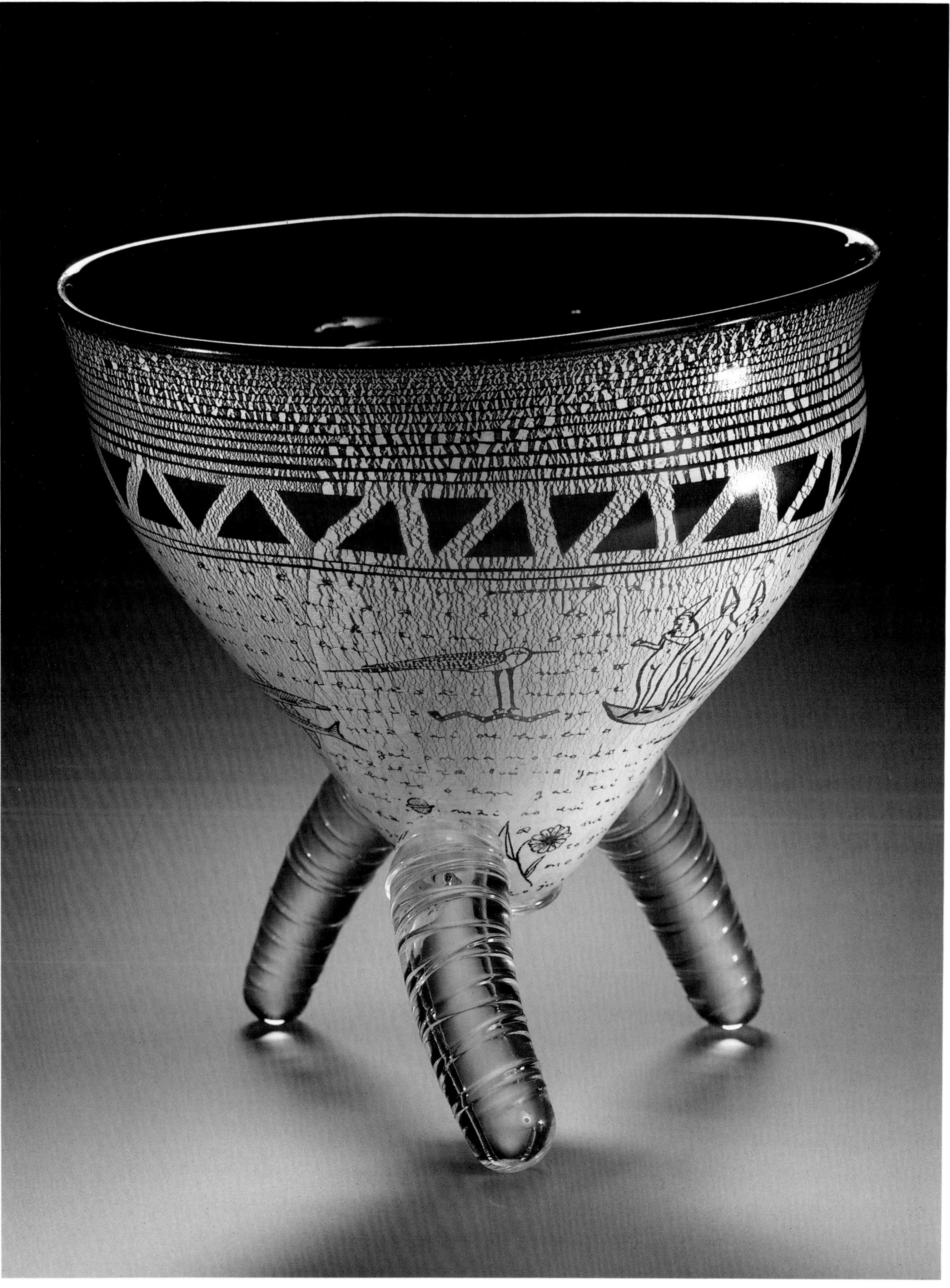

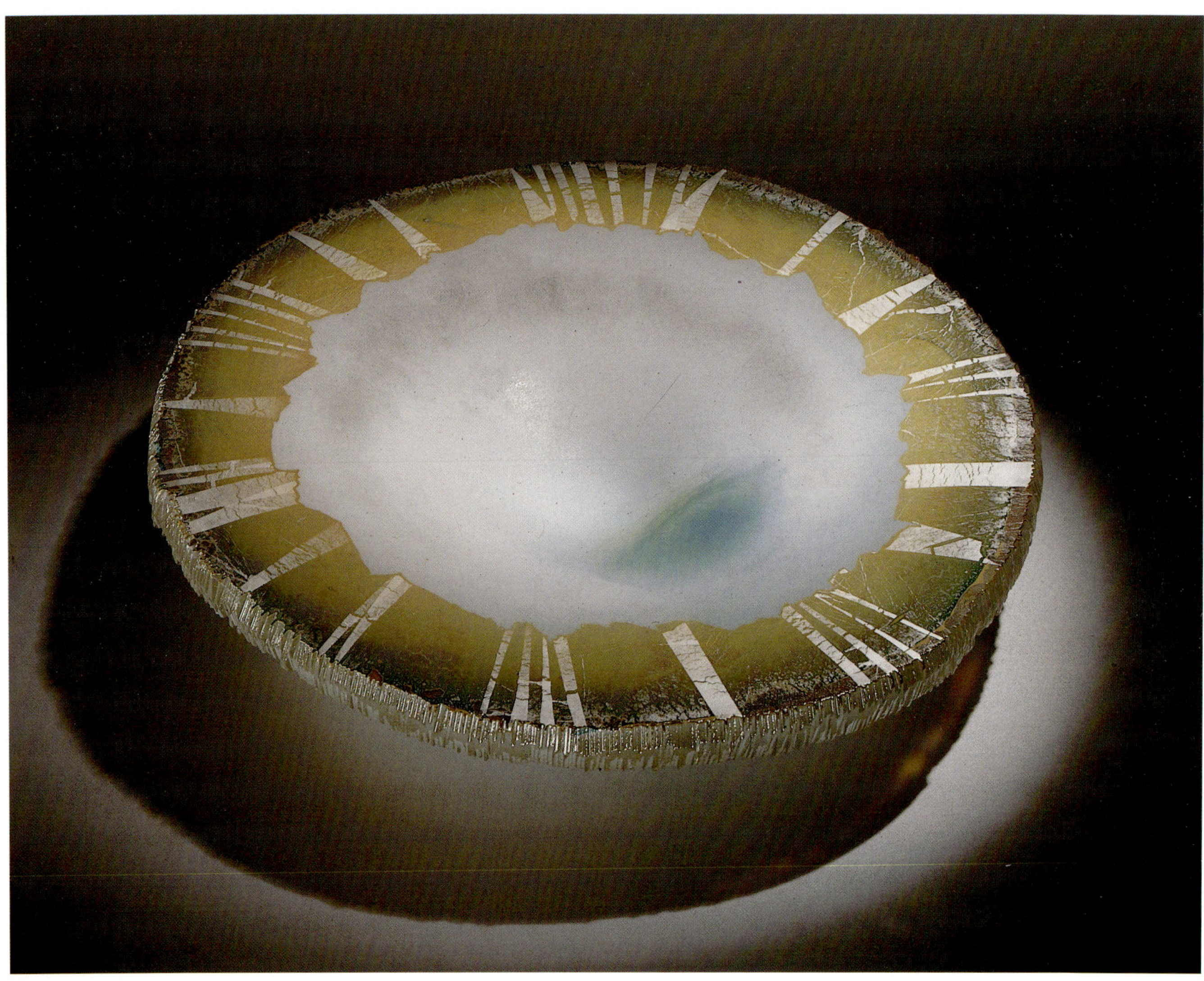

Yoko Kuramoto
(b. 1950)

Education: Musashino University of Art, Tokyo
Lives and works in Yamanashi

554   "Vessel of the Lake"

Engraved mark on the underside of base:
Yoko.K.
1993
H 7.5, ⌀ 42 cm

Cast and kiln-formed. Edge sawn and acid-
polished. Etched silver application.

Acc. no. P 1995-12
Acquired at the exhibition "New Glass in
Japan"

Lit.: Ricke, *New Glass Japan*, 1993,
cat. no. 41

Makoto Ito
(b. 1940)

Education: Tama University, Tokyo, and
apprenticeship as glassblower at Kagami
Crystal, Tokyo
Lives and works in Yamanashi and Tama near
Tokyo

555   "Businessman"

Engraved Kanji characters on the reverse:
Makoto
1993
H 48.5, ⌀ 13.5 x 6.2 cm
Pedestal: 10 x 10 x 10 cm

Kiln-formed. Embedded wires. Sandblasted,
cut, engraved. Laminated of three parts.

Acc. no. P 1995-11
Acquired at the exhibition "New Glass in
Japan"

Lit.: Ricke, *New Glass Japan*, 1993,
cat. no. 27

338

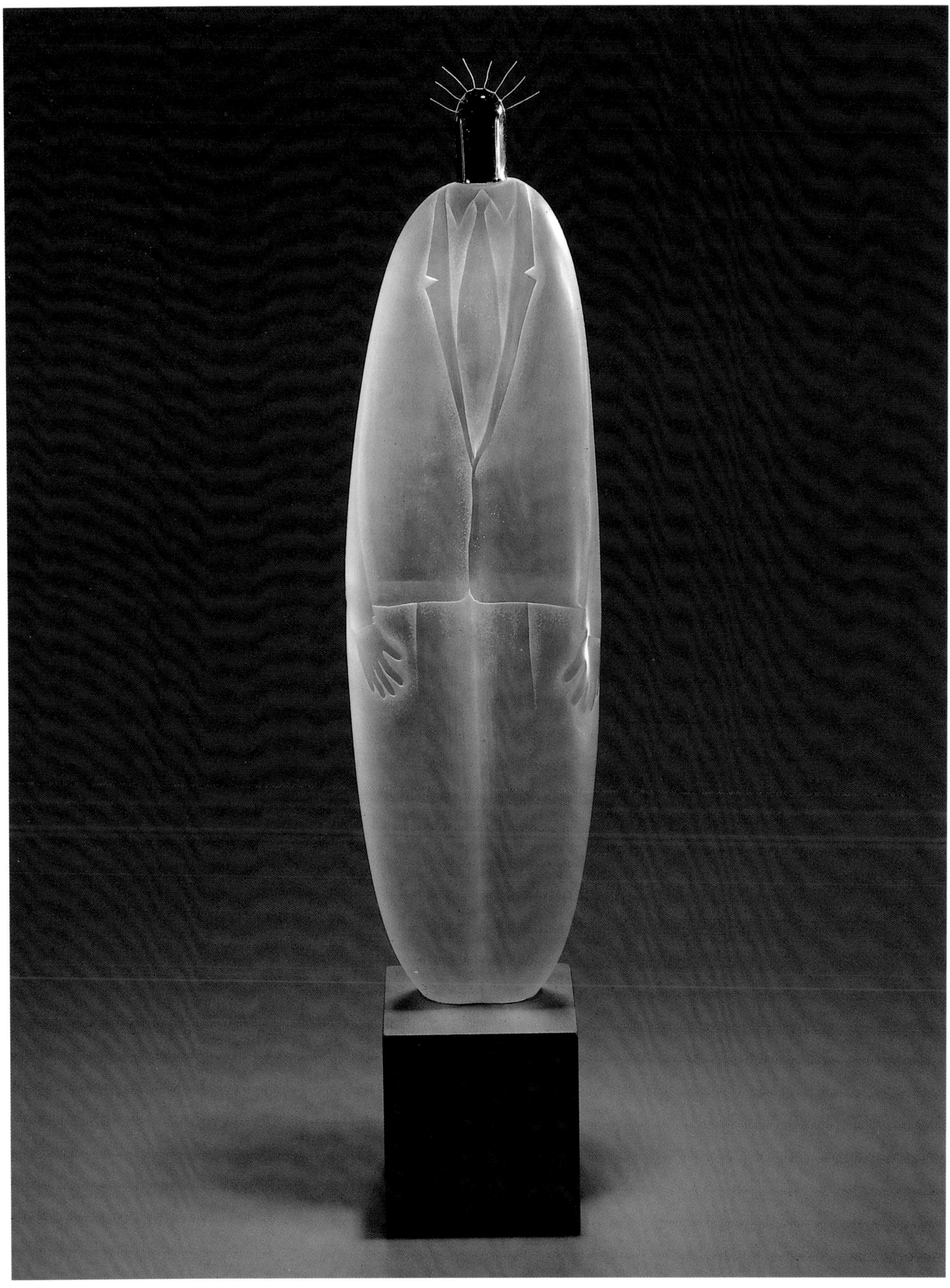

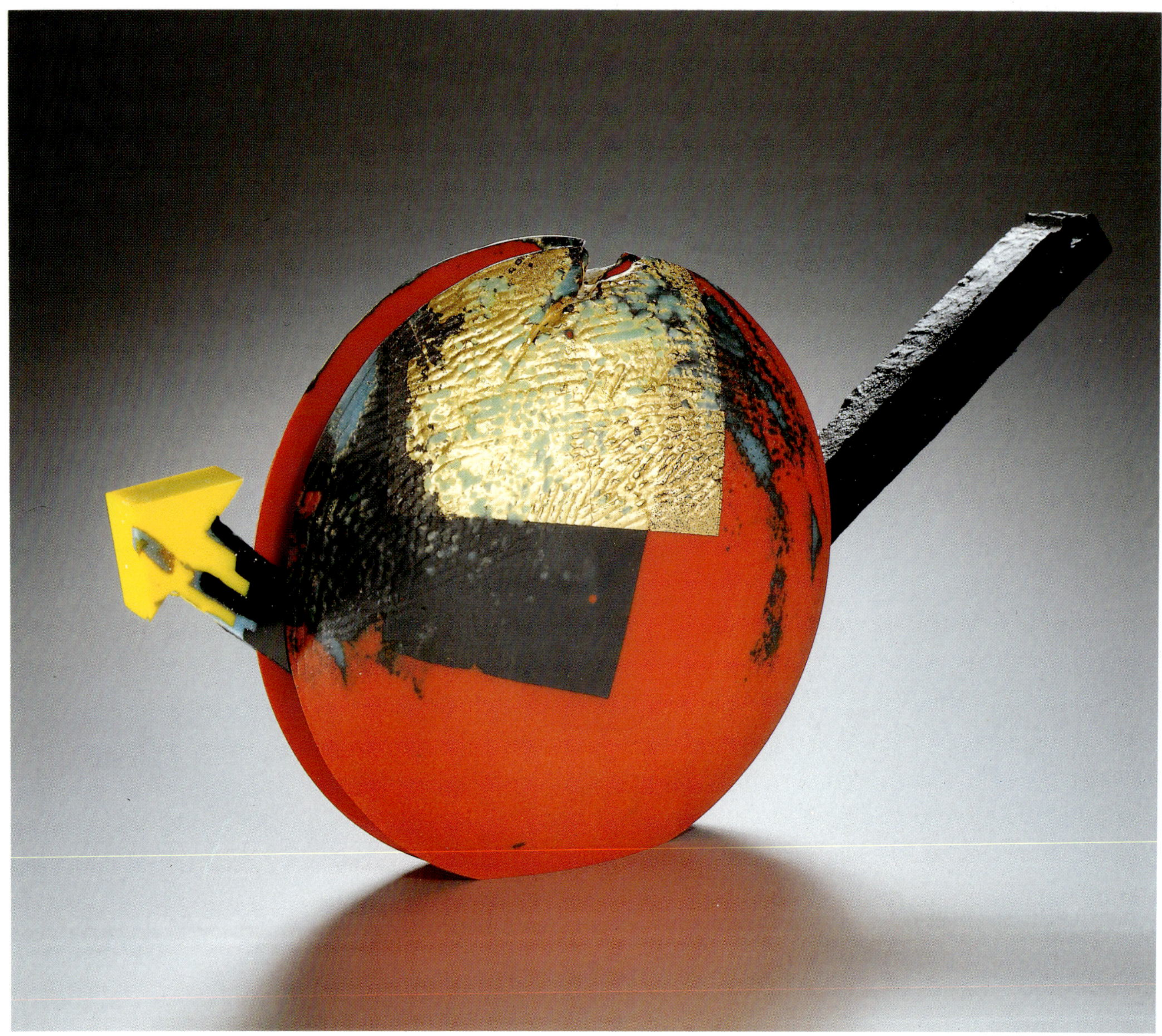

Shimpei Sato
(b. 1953)

Education: Graphic design in Japan. In 1978
studied glass at the San Francisco College of
Art
Lives and works in Tokyo

556   "Inner Portrait II"

Engraved mark on side of black bar: *Shimpei
Sato '93*
1993
H 17, ⌀ 32 x 8 cm

Pâte de verre. Applied gold leaf, cut, polished.
Comprises four laminated parts.

Acc. no. P 1995-15
Acquired at the exhibition "New Glass in
Japan"

Lit.: Ricke, *New Glass Japan*, 1993, cat. no. 77

340

Shinji Yonehara
(b. 1961)

Education: Tama University, Tokyo
Lives and works in Ebetsu, Hokkaido

557 "Line Drawing"

Engraved Kanji characters on the underside of
base: *Shin*
1993
H 29.7, ⌀ 32.3 cm

Free-blown, colored inner casing. Embedded
threads and murrine in colorless cover layer.
Frosted.

Acc. no. P 1995-18
Acquired at the exhibition "New Glass in Japan"

Lit.: Ricke, *New Glass Japan*, 1993, cat. no. 103

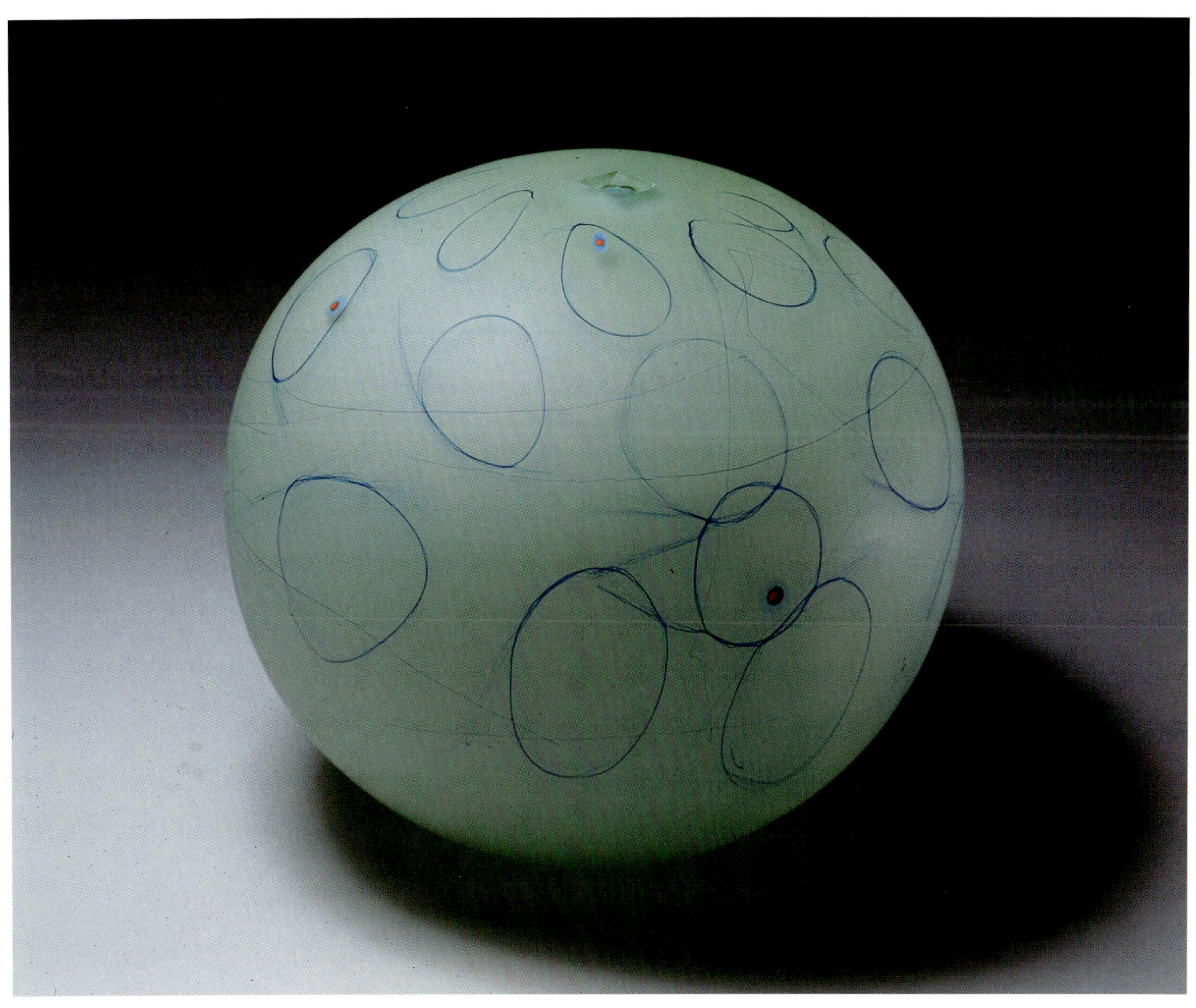

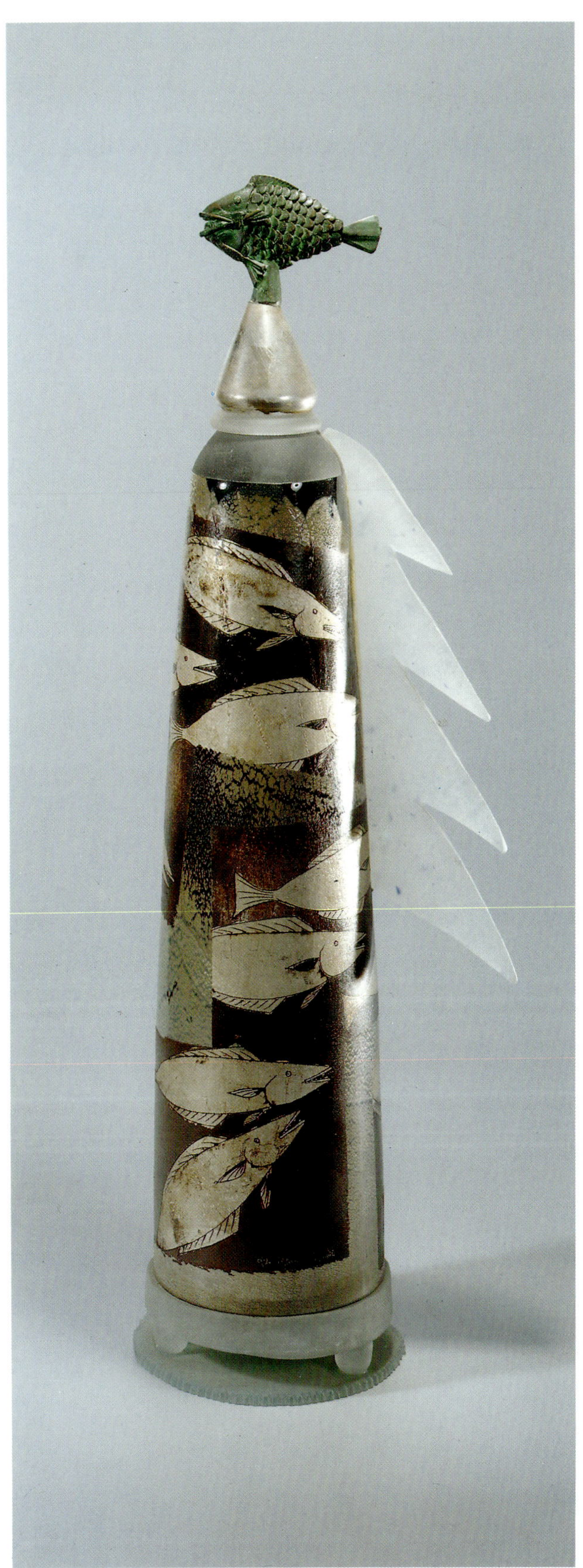

Hiroshi Yamano

(b. 1956)

Education: Chuo Bijutsu University, Tokyo
Lives and works in Yamanashi

558   "From East to West"

Engraved mark on the reverse: *92 Yamano Hiroshi
1992*
H 57.7, ⌀ foot 13.8 cm

Bluish glass, blown and shaped. Silver and
copper application, etched. Applications in
colorless *pâte de verre*. Pedestal cut, matted,
and laminated. Patinated copper fish.

Acc. no. P 1995-17
Acquired at the exhibition "New Glass in Japan"

Lit.: Ricke, *New Glass Japan*, 1993, cat. no. 99

Appendix

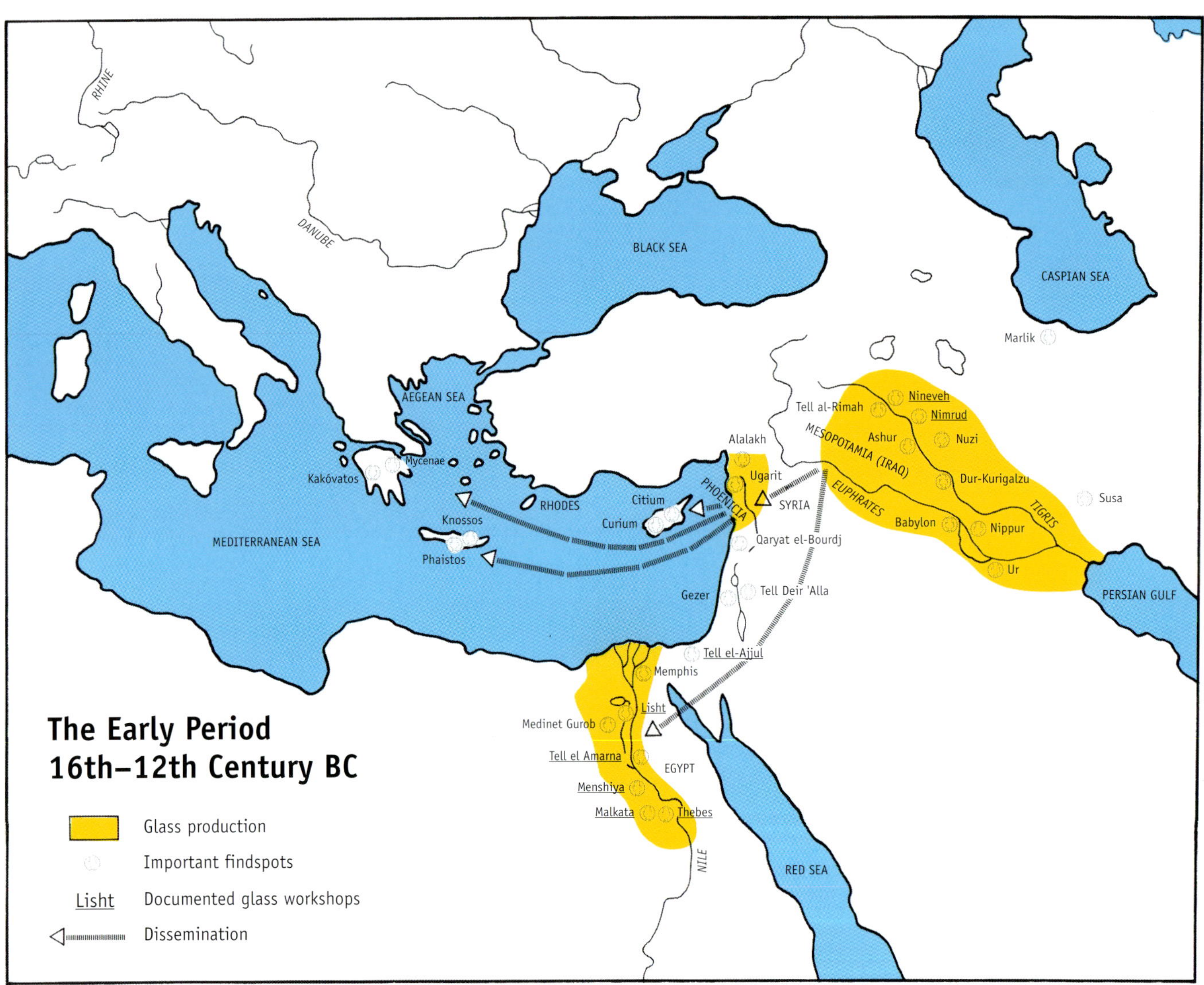

The Early Period
16th–12th Century BC

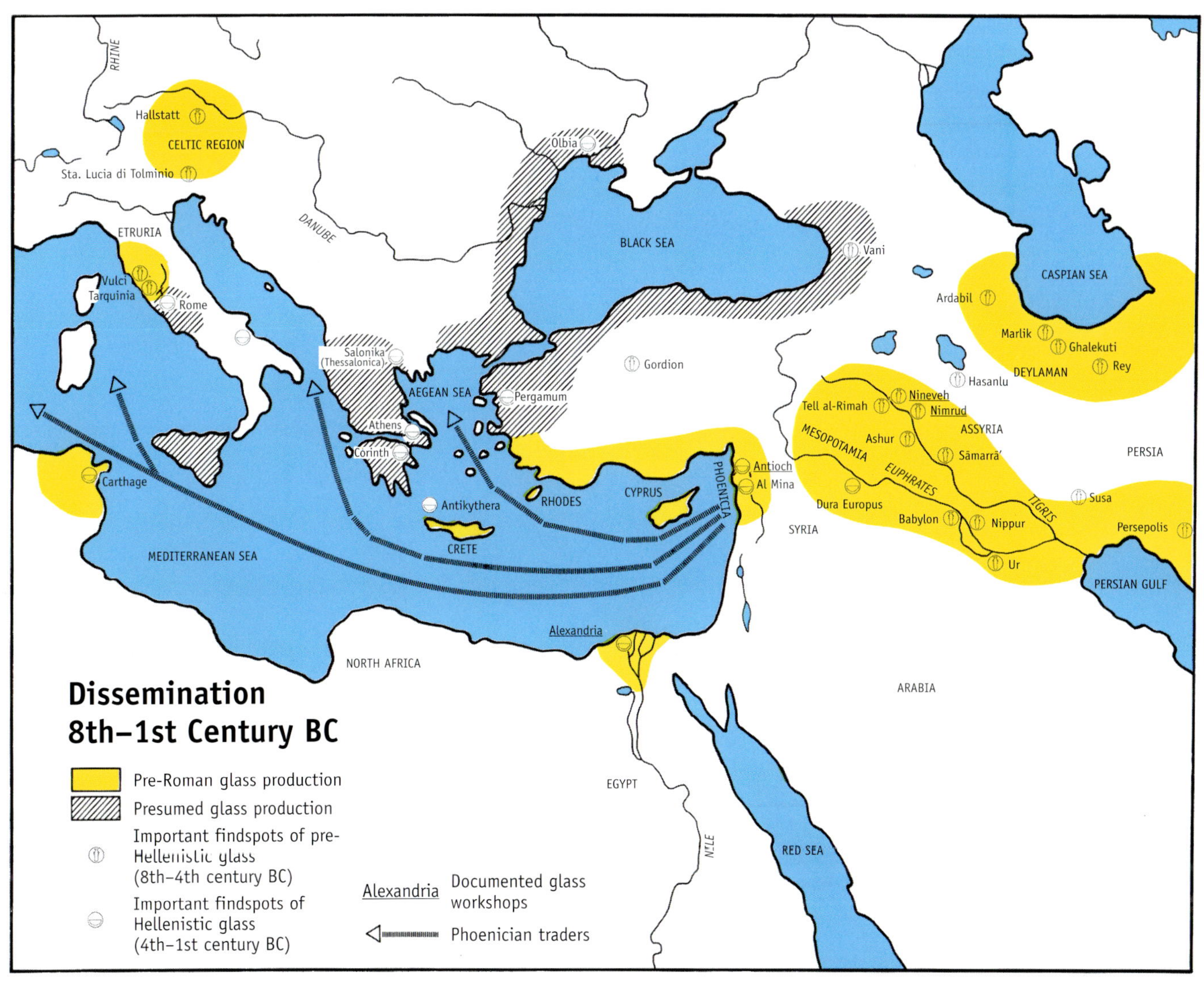

Dissemination
8th–1st Century BC

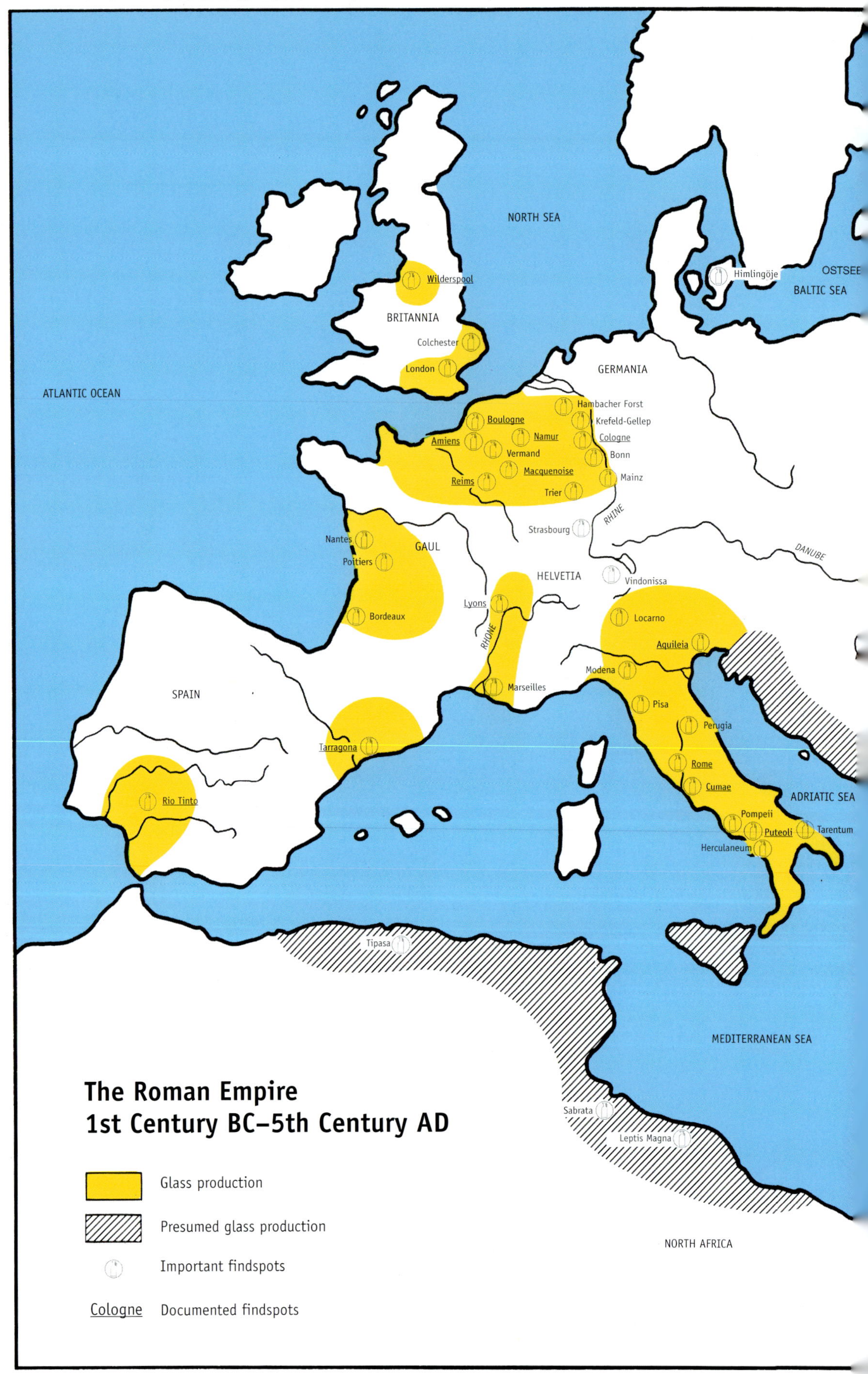

The Roman Empire
1st Century BC–5th Century AD

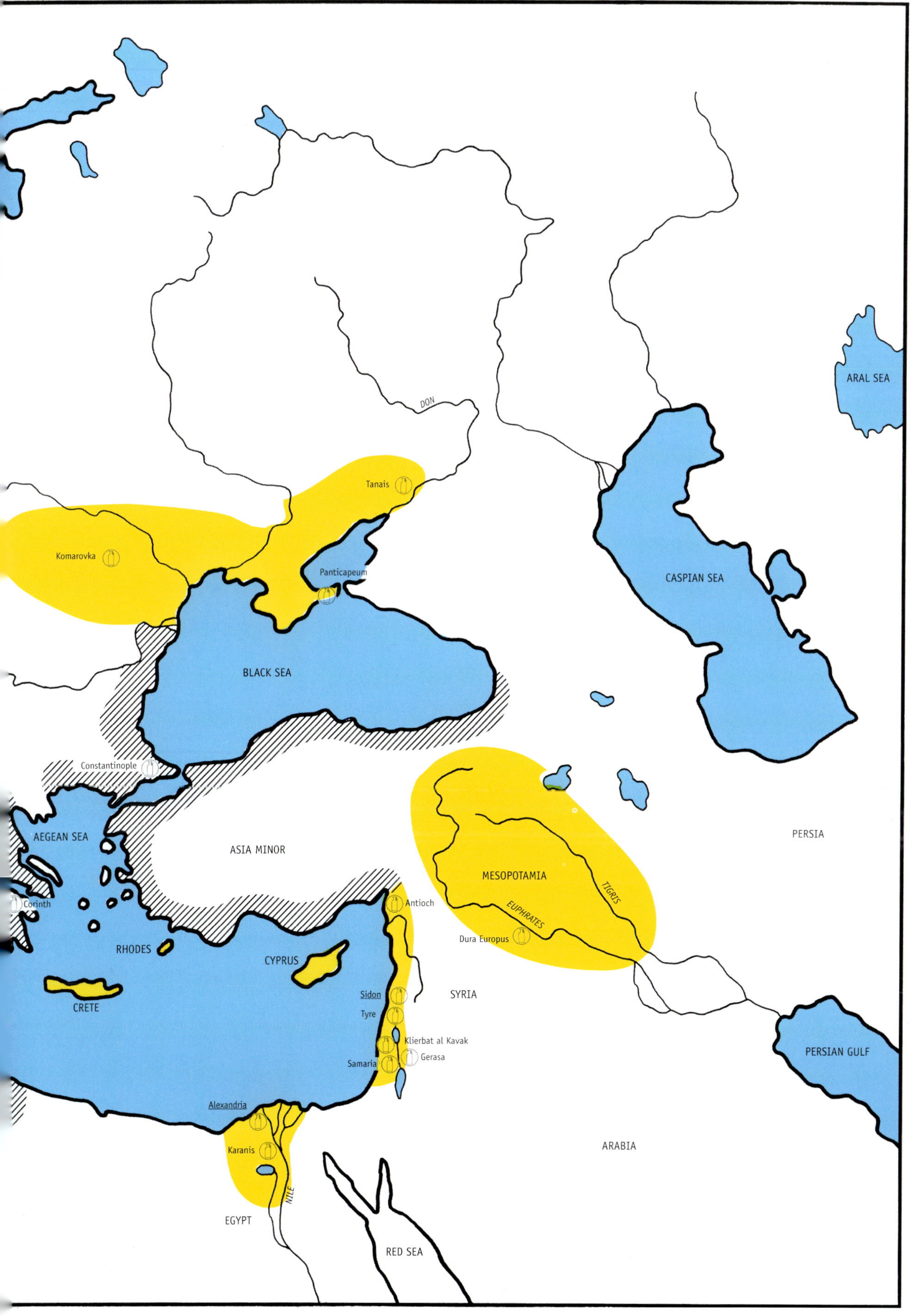

ARAL SEA
DON
Tanais
Komarovka
Panticapeum
CASPIAN SEA
BLACK SEA
Constantinople
PERSIA
AEGEAN SEA
ASIA MINOR
MESOPOTAMIA
TIGRIS
Corinth
EUPHRATES
Antioch
RHODES
CYPRUS
Dura Europus
CRETE
Sidon
SYRIA
Tyre
Klierbat al Kavak
Samaria
Gerasa
PERSIAN GULF
Alexandria
ARABIA
Karanis
NILE
EGYPT
RED SEA

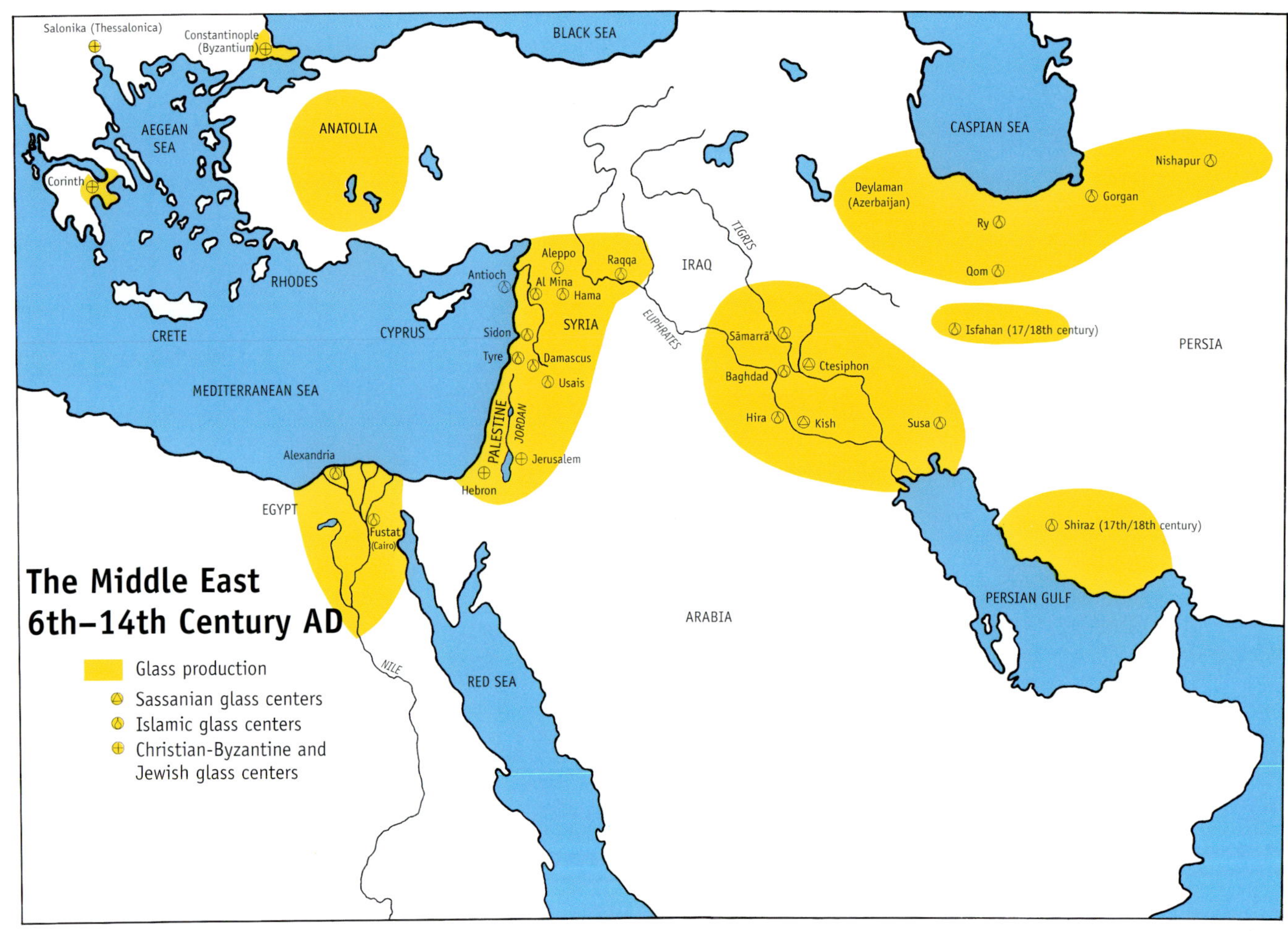

Salonika (Thessalonica)
Constantinople (Byzantium)
BLACK SEA
CASPIAN SEA
AEGEAN SEA
ANATOLIA
Nishapur
Deylaman (Azerbaijan)
Gorgan
Corinth
Ry
Aleppo
Raqqa
IRAQ
Qom
Antioch
Al Mina
Hama
RHODES
Isfahan (17/18th century)
PERSIA
CRETE
CYPRUS
SYRIA
Sidon
Sāmarrā'
Tyre
Damascus
Ctesiphon
MEDITERRANEAN SEA
Usais
Baghdad
Hira
Kish
Susa
Alexandria
PALESTINE
JORDAN
Jerusalem
EGYPT
Hebron
Shiraz (17th/18th century)
Fustat (Cairo)
PERSIAN GULF
ARABIA
NILE
RED SEA
TIGRIS
EUPHRATES
The Middle East
6th–14th Century AD
Glass production
Sassanian glass centers
Islamic glass centers
Christian-Byzantine and
Jewish glass centers

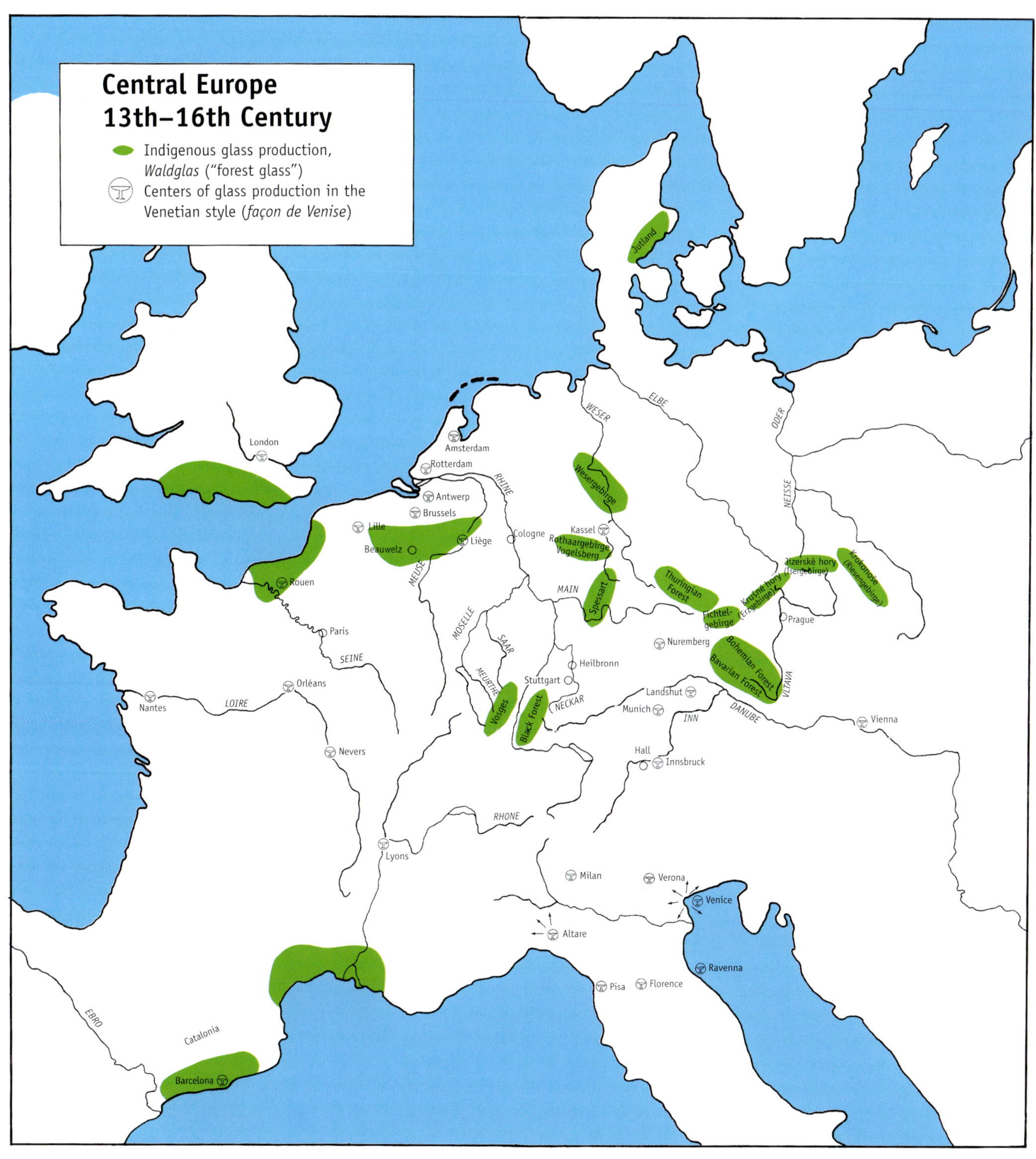

Central Europe
13th–16th Century
Indigenous glass production,
Waldglas ("forest glass")
Centers of glass production in the
Venetian style (façon de Venise)
Jutland
London
Amsterdam
Rotterdam
Antwerp
Brussels
Lille
Beauwelz
Liège
Cologne
Rouen
Paris
Weser
Elbe
Oder
Neisse
Wesergebirge
Kassel
Rothaargebirge
Vogelsberg
Rhine
Meuse
Moselle
Main
Spessart
Thuringian Forest
Jizerské hory
(Iser-birge)
Krkonoše
(Riesengebirge)
Krušné hory
(Erzgebirge)
Prague
Fichtel-
gebirge
Nuremberg
Bohemian Forest
Bavarian Forest
Vltava
Saar
Meurthe
Stuttgart
Heilbronn
Neckar
Vosges
Black Forest
Landshut
Munich
Inn
Danube
Vienna
Hall
Innsbruck
Seine
Orléans
Nantes
Loire
Nevers
Rhone
Lyons
Milan
Verona
Venice
Altare
Ravenna
Pisa
Florence
Ebro
Catalonia
Barcelona

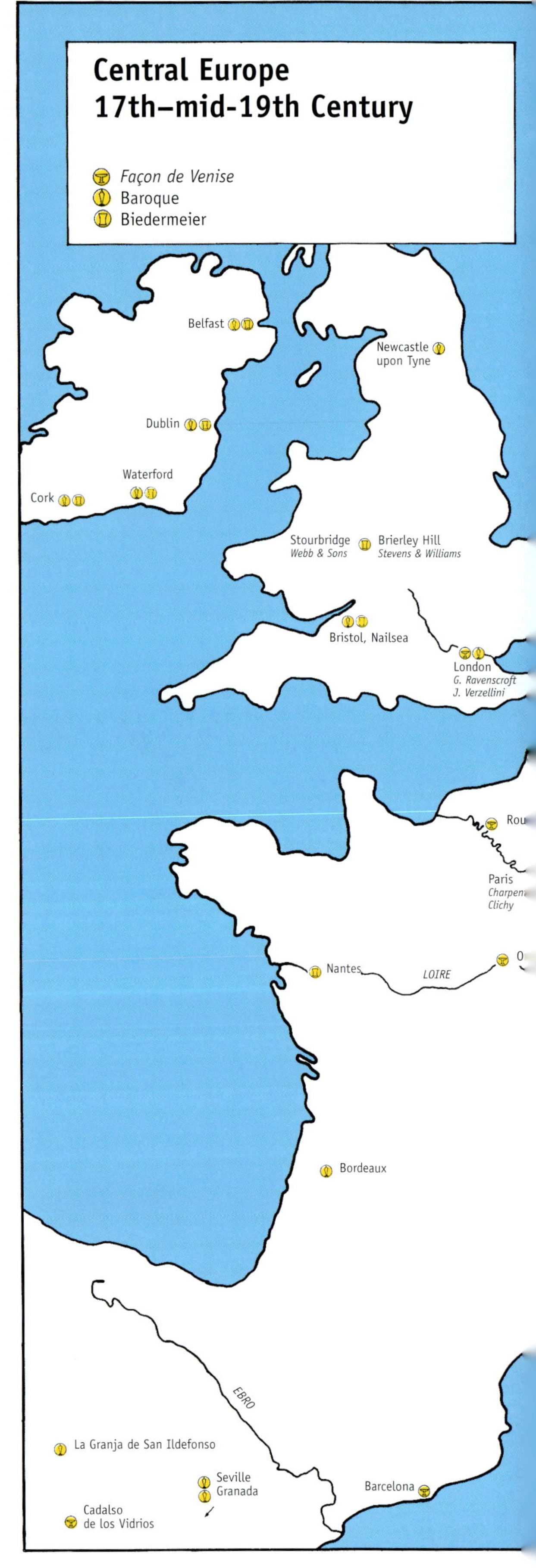

Central Europe
17th–mid-19th Century

Façon de Venise
Baroque
Biedermeier

Belfast
Newcastle upon Tyne
Dublin
Waterford
Cork
Stourbridge
Webb & Sons
Brierley Hill
Stevens & Williams
Bristol, Nailsea
London
G. Ravenscroft
J. Verzellini
Rou
Paris
Charpen
Clichy
Nantes
LOIRE
O
Bordeaux
EBRO
La Granja de San Ildefonso
Seville
Granada
Barcelona
Cadalso
de los Vidrios

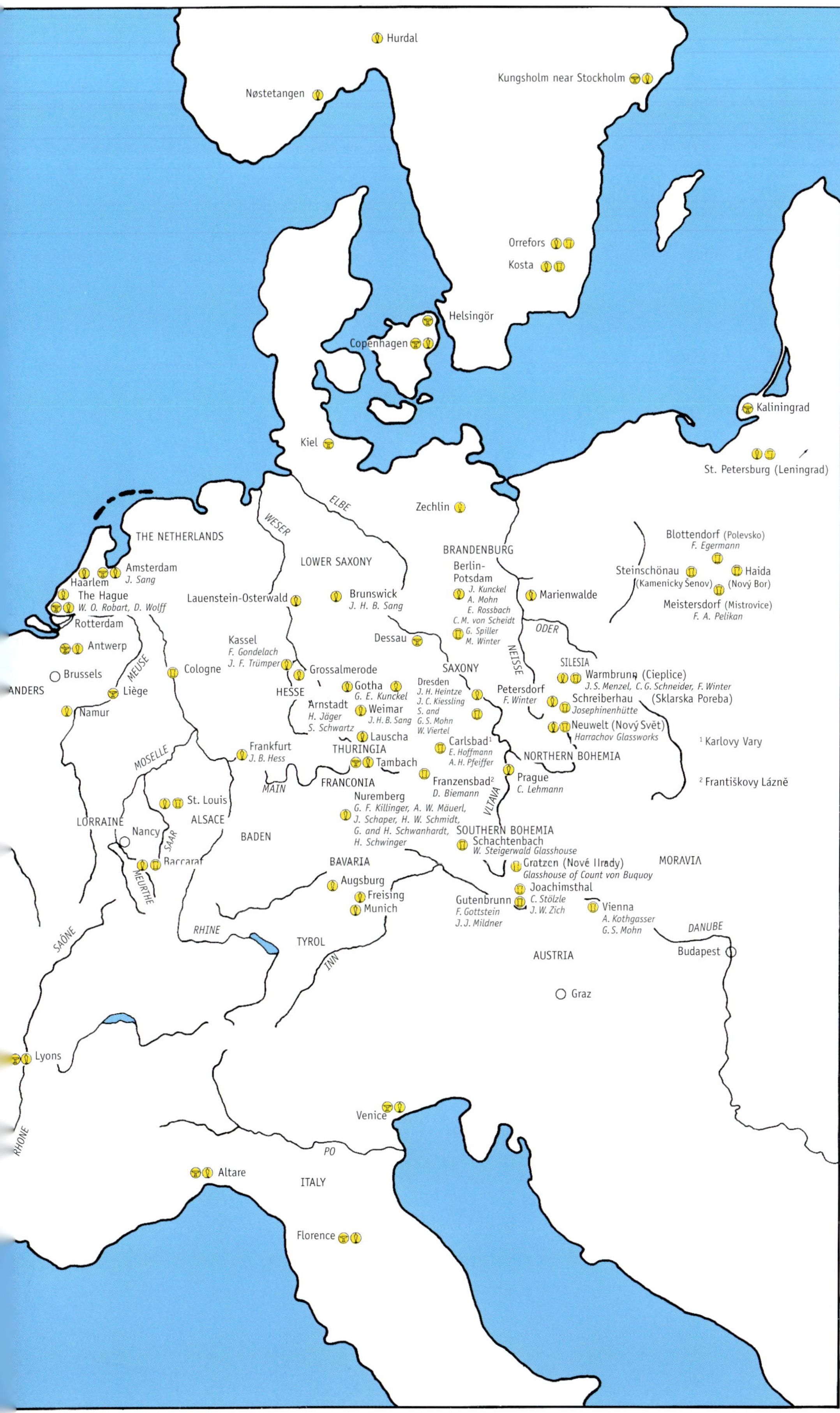

Hurdal
Nøstetangen
Kungsholm near Stockholm
Orrefors
Kosta
Helsingör
Copenhagen
Kaliningrad
Kiel
St. Petersburg (Leningrad)
ELBE
WESER
Zechlin
THE NETHERLANDS
LOWER SAXONY
BRANDENBURG
Blottendorf (Polevsko)
F. Egermann
Amsterdam
J. Sang
Berlin-
Potsdam
J. Kunckel
A. Mohn
E. Rossbach
C. M. von Scheidt
G. Spiller
M. Winter
Steinschönau
(Kamenicky Senov)
Haida
(Nový Bor)
Haarlem
The Hague
W. O. Robart, D. Wolff
Brunswick
J. H. B. Sang
Marienwalde
Meistersdorf (Mistrovice)
F. A. Pelikan
Rotterdam
Lauenstein-Osterwald
Kassel
F. Gondelach
J. F. Trümper
Dessau
ODER
NEISSE
Antwerp
SAXONY
SILESIA
Warmbrunn (Cieplice)
J. S. Menzel, C. G. Schneider, F. Winter
Brussels
MEUSE
Cologne
Grossalmerode
Gotha
G. E. Kunckel
Dresden
J. H. Heintze
J. C. Kiessling
S. and
J. H. B. Sang
G. S. Mohn
W. Viertel
Petersdorf
F. Winter
Schreiberhau
Josephinenhütte
(Sklarska Poreba)
FLANDERS
Liège
HESSE
Arnstadt
H. Jäger
S. Schwartz
Weimar
Neuwelt (Nový Svět)
Harrachov Glassworks
Namur
MOSELLE
Frankfurt
J. B. Hess
THURINGIA
Lauscha
Carlsbad[1]
E. Hoffmann
A. H. Pfeiffer
[1] Karlovy Vary
Tambach
NORTHERN BOHEMIA
MAIN
FRANCONIA
Franzensbad[2]
D. Biemann
Prague
C. Lehmann
[2] Františkovy Lázně
St. Louis
Nuremberg
G. F. Killinger, A. W. Mäuerl,
J. Schaper, H. W. Schmidt,
G. and H. Schwanhardt,
H. Schwinger
SOUTHERN BOHEMIA
VLTAVA
LORRAINE
Nancy
ALSACE
BADEN
Schachtenbach
W. Steigerwald Glasshouse
MORAVIA
SAAR
Baccarat
MEURTHE
BAVARIA
Augsburg
Freising
Munich
Gratzen (Nové Hrady)
Glasshouse of Count von Buquoy
Joachimsthal
Gutenbrunn
F. Gottstein
J. J. Mildner
C. Stölzle
J. W. Zich
Vienna
A. Kothgasser
G. S. Mohn
DANUBE
RHINE
TYROL
INN
AUSTRIA
Budapest
SAÔNE
Graz
Lyons
Venice
RHÔNE
PO
Altare
ITALY
Florence

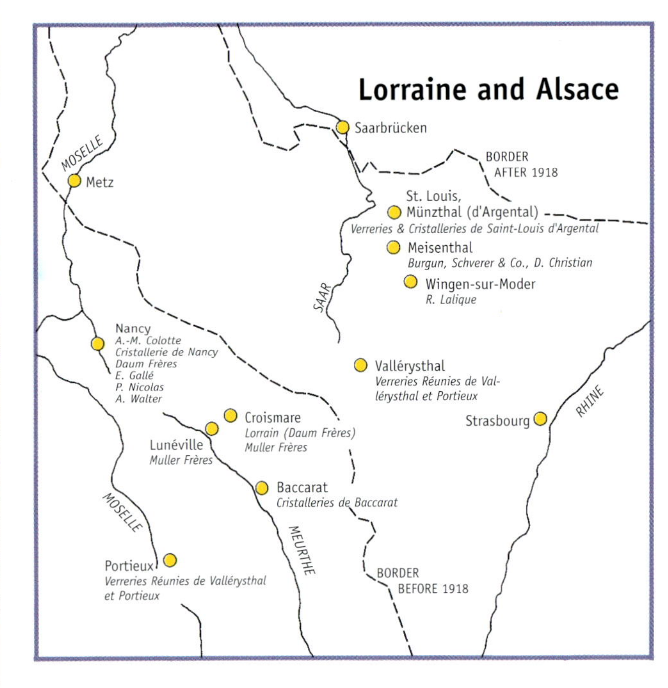

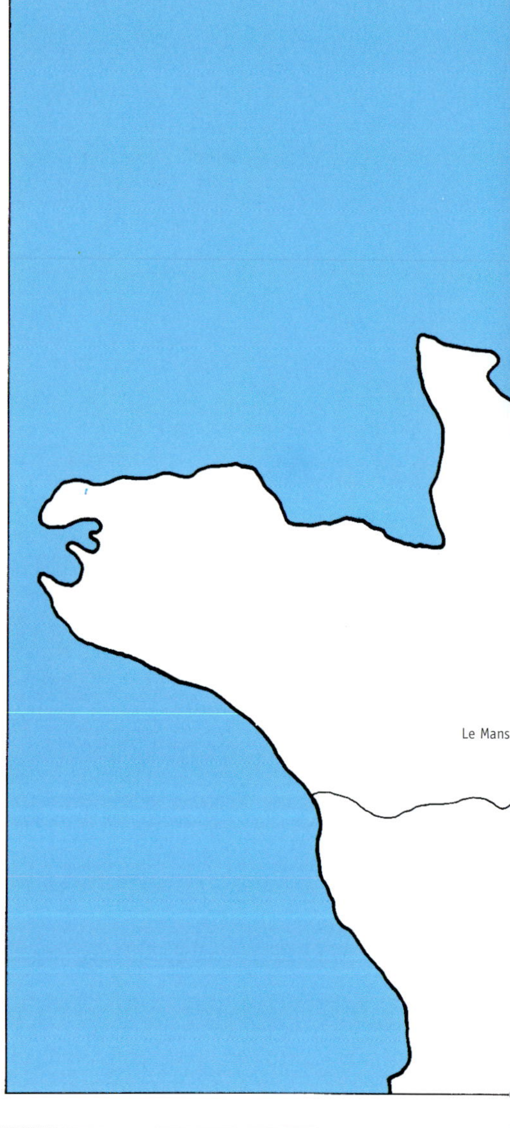

France
1870–1930

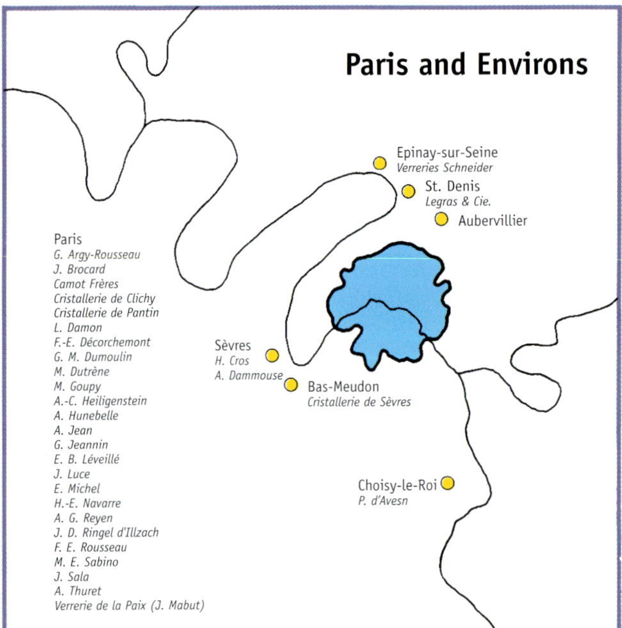

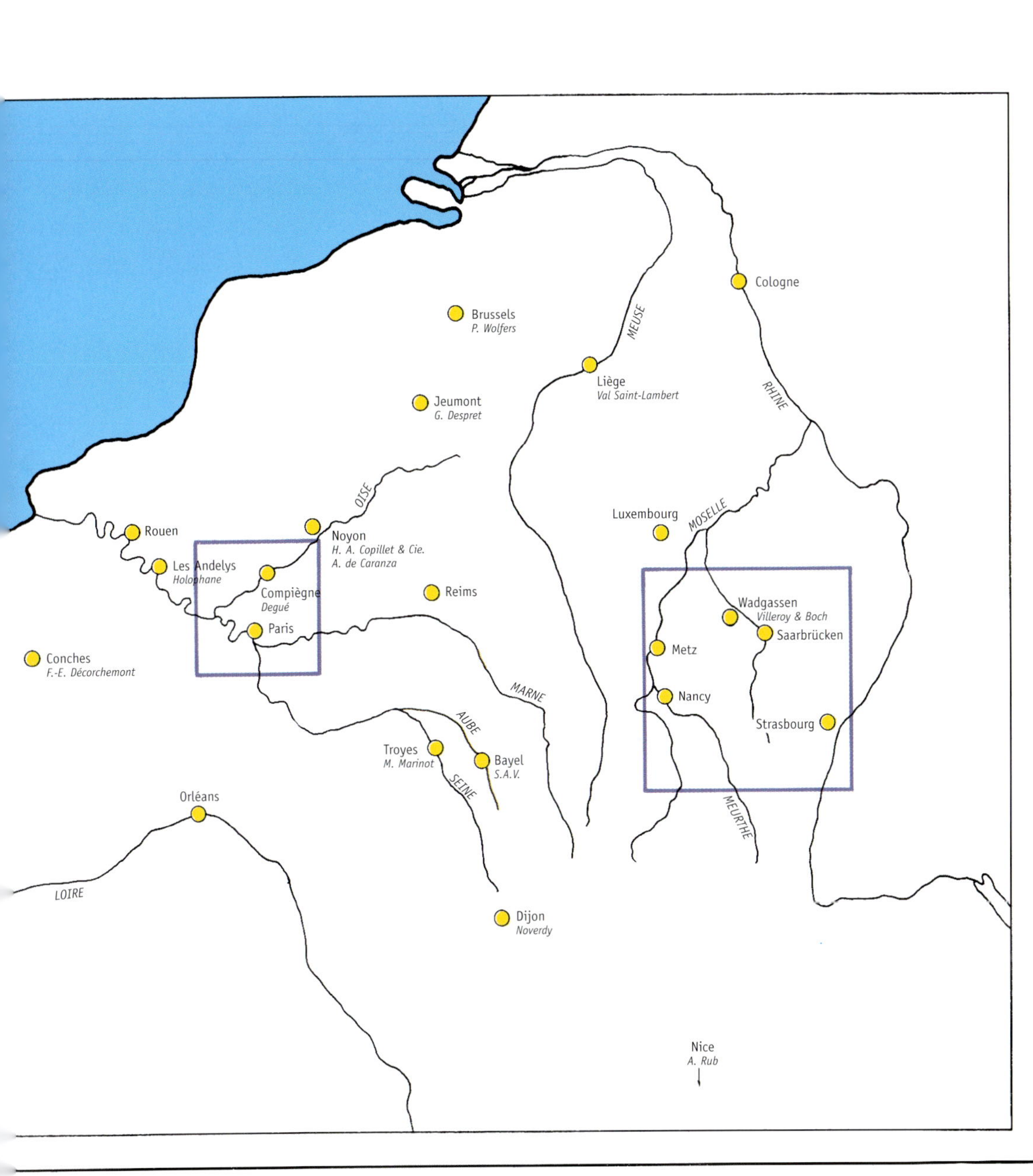

Cologne
Brussels
P. Wolfers
Liège
Val Saint-Lambert
Jeumont
G. Despret
MEUSE
RHINE
OISE
Luxembourg
MOSELLE
Rouen
Noyon
H. A. Copillet & Cie.
A. de Caranza
Wadgassen
Villeroy & Boch
Les Andelys
Holophane
Saarbrücken
Compiègne
Degué
Reims
Metz
Paris
Conches
F.-E. Décorchemont
Nancy
MARNE
Strasbourg
AUBE
MEURTHE
Troyes
M. Marinot
Bayel
S.A.V.
SEINE
Orléans
LOIRE
Dijon
Noverdy
Nice
A. Rub

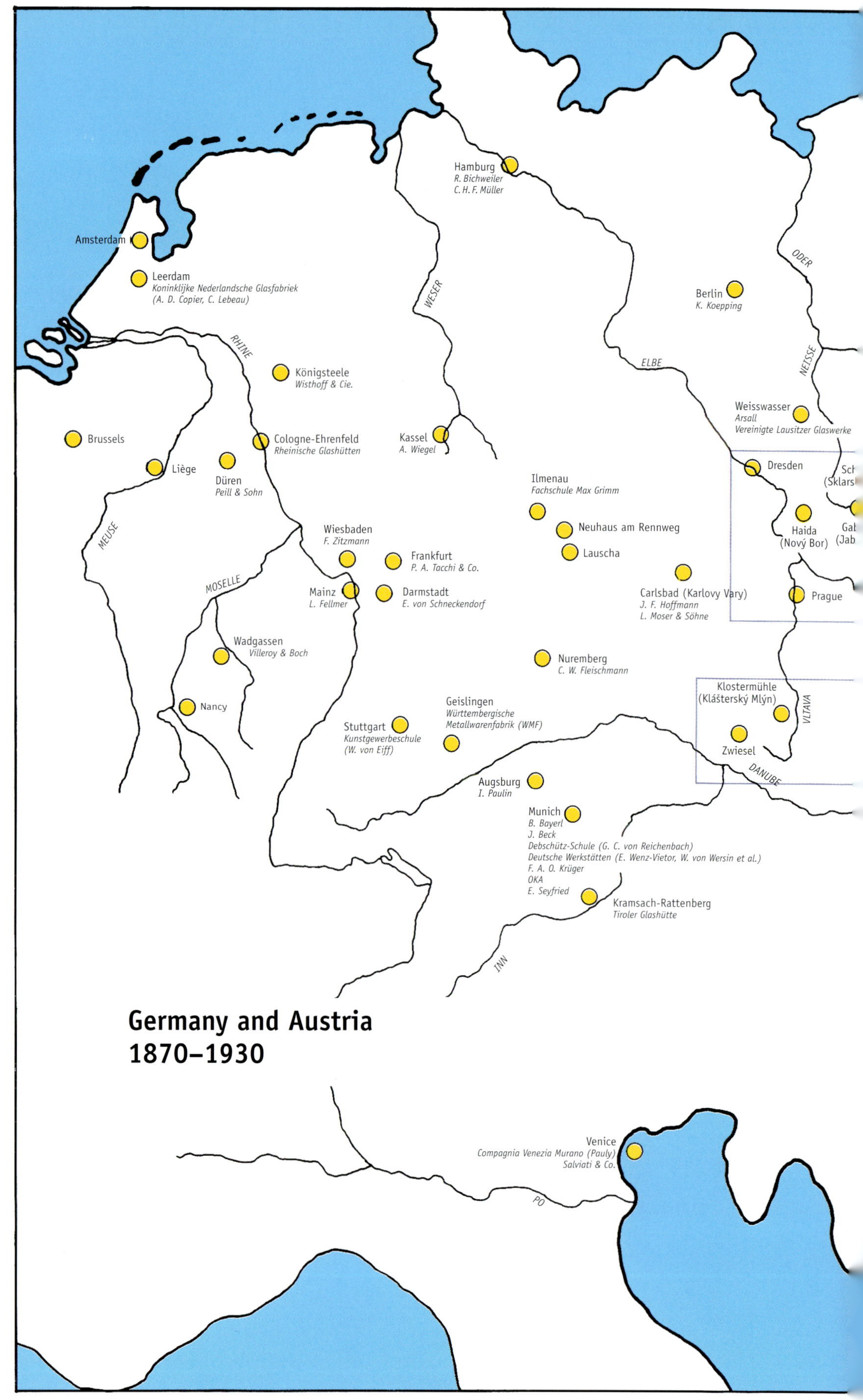

Germany and Austria
1870–1930

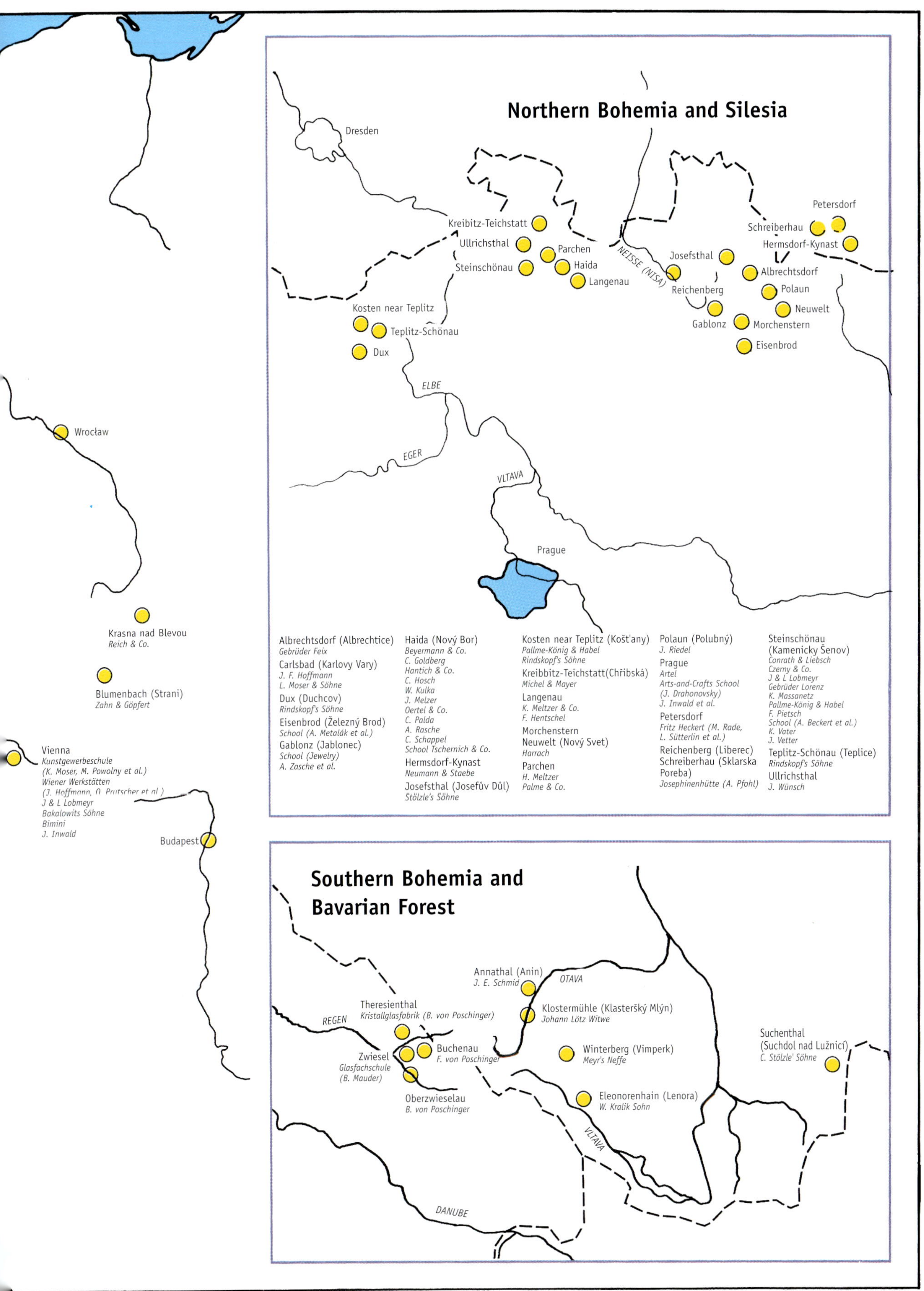

Northern Bohemia and Silesia
Dresden
Wrocław
Petersdorf
Schreiberhau
Hermsdorf-Kynast
Kreibitz-Teichstatt
Ullrichsthal
Parchen
Josefsthal
Steinschönau
Haida
Albrechtsdorf
Langenau
Polaun
Reichenberg
Neuwelt
Kosten near Teplitz
Gablonz
Morchenstern
Teplitz-Schönau
Eisenbrod
Dux
NEISSE (NISA)
ELBE
EGER
VLTAVA
Prague
Krasna nad Blevou
Reich & Co.
Carlsbad (Karlovy Vary)
J. F. Hoffmann
L. Moser & Söhne
Blumenbach (Strani)
Zahn & Göpfert
Vienna
Kunstgewerbeschule
(K. Moser, M. Powolny et al.)
Wiener Werkstätten
(J. Hoffmann, O. Prutscher et al.)
J & L Lobmeyr
Bakalowits Söhne
Bimini
J. Inwald
Budapest
Albrechtsdorf (Albrechtice)
Gebrüder Feix
Carlsbad (Karlovy Vary)
J. F. Hoffmann
L. Moser & Söhne
Dux (Duchcov)
Rindskopf's Söhne
Eisenbrod (Železný Brod)
School (A. Metalák et al.)
Gablonz (Jablonec)
School (Jewelry)
A. Zasche et al.
Haida (Nový Bor)
Beyermann & Co.
C. Goldberg
Hantich & Co.
C. Hosch
W. Kulka
J. Melzer
Oertel & Co.
C. Palda
A. Rasche
C. Schappel
School Tschernich & Co.
Hermsdorf-Kynast
Neumann & Staebe
Josefsthal (Josefův Důl)
Stölzle's Söhne
Kosten near Teplitz (Košt'any)
Pallme-König & Habel
Rindskopf's Söhne
Kreibbitz-Teichstatt(Chřibská)
Michel & Mayer
Langenau
K. Meltzer & Co.
F. Hentschel
Morchenstern
Neuwelt (Nový Svet)
Harrach
Parchen
H. Meltzer
Palme & Co.
Polaun (Polubný)
J. Riedel
Prague
Artel
Arts-and-Crafts School
(J. Drahonovsky)
J. Inwald et al.
Petersdorf
Fritz Heckert (M. Rade,
L. Sütterlin et al.)
Reichenberg (Liberec)
Schreiberhau (Sklarska
Poreba)
Josephinenhütte (A. Pfohl)
Steinschönau
(Kamenicky Šenov)
Conrath & Liebsch
Czerny & Co.
J & L Lobmeyr
Gebrüder Lorenz
K. Massanetz
Pallme-König & Habel
F. Pietsch
School (A. Beckert et al.)
K. Vater
J. Vetter
Teplitz-Schönau (Teplice)
Rindskopf's Söhne
Ullrichsthal
J. Wünsch
Southern Bohemia and
Bavarian Forest
Annathal (Anin)
J. E. Schmid
OTAVA
Theresienthal
Kristallglasfabrik (B. von Poschinger)
REGEN
Klostermühle (Klasterský Mlýn)
Johann Lötz Witwe
Buchenau
F. von Poschinger
Zwiesel
Glasfachschule
(B. Mauder)
Winterberg (Vimperk)
Meyr's Neffe
Suchenthal
(Suchdol nad Lužnicí)
C. Stölzle' Söhne
Oberzwieselau
B. von Poschinger
Eleonorenhain (Lenora)
W. Kralik Sohn
VLTAVA
DANUBE

Glossary

acid-stamped signature A simple mechanical signature. Hydrofluoric acid or etching ink is dribbled onto a piece of blotting paper and transferred with a rubber stamp to the glass. Etching ink—consisting of a mixture of barium sulphate, ammonium fluoride, and sulfuric acid—is safer for the user.
→*Zwischengoldglas*

annealing oven (or lehr) See under "Techniques," p. 359.

antique glass, so-called See under "Techniques," p. 359.

applications Decorative elements that are fused onto a glass object, such as prunts, folded threads, knops, handles, and pinched ribbons.

art glass Term used to describe glass designed by artists and carried out by technicians in glassworks.

at the flame (or lampwork or flamework) See under "Techniques," p. 359.

aventurine glass A type of glass first made in Venice, in the first half of the 17th century. By adding special copper oxide and forged scales to the melt, a brown semi-opaque glass with gold specs is created.

"ball-optic" pattern Created by using a mold with regular or irregular spherical concavities or projections. See →optic-blowing under "Techniques," p. 359.

batch The mixture of raw materials—sand (silica), lime, flux (alkali or lead compounds), and other additives—constituting glass. A certain percentage of cullet (broken scrap glass) is usually added to the batch as well. See also under "Techniques," p. 359.

black-enamel painting (or *Schwarzlot* painting) See under "Techniques," p. 359.

blowing techniques See under "Techniques," p. 359.

bowl The receptacle on stemware, goblets, vase goblets, etc.

bright gold →gilt painting

bubbles Common decorative element of work done at the furnace. Air bubbles in the wall can also be the inadvertent result of impurities or stirring the melt. They can be a deliberate effect created with →molds, the wall being subsequently cased with an additional layer of glass. Veils of bubbles and larger bubbles are made by dusting the hot glass with chemicals, e.g., soda or potash, or marvering moist sawdust into the glass, and immediately covering the surface with another glass layer. The chemical substances or moist wood transform into a gaseous state and, depending on the amount and type of substance, form variously large bubbles. By opening such bubbles in the fire, crater-like surfaces can be produced.

burnished gold →gilt painting

carving →relief-cutting

casing Covering a glass object with a thick layer of glass in a different color. →flashing, →overlay glassware

cold decoration Collective term for all decorative work done on annealed glass. →cold-working techniques

cold painting See under "Techniques," p. 359.

cold-working techniques All decorative techniques done on annealed glass, the most important of which are cutting, engraving, etching, sandblasting, and the various types of painting, even when they require subsequent firing, such as enameling.

colored glass Glass colored with the aid of metallic compounds. The basic colors and various hues in between are determined by the selection of the respective additives and different types of base glass, as well as by controlling the furnace atmosphere. As a rule metal oxides are added to the melt. Copper turns glass blue, green, or red; cobalt, an intense blue, but also pink, violet, or green; nickel, gray-brown, yellow-green, and blue to violet; vanadium, green and brown; manganese and titanium, violet; chromium, green and yellow; gold, red to pink. The so-called rare-earths neodymium and praseodymium produce red-violet or pale green hues, which look different in daylight and artificial lighting. Changes in color caused by light passing through or being cast onto the glass are also possible. In individual cases the color is created only after reheating the glass (→striking, e.g., gold ruby).

colored rods Material used as a basic ingredient of colored hollow glassware. The glassmaker breaks the required length of colored glass from colored glass rods, which he preheats at the furnace, before working with it. See also under "Techniques," p. 359.

core-forming Formerly misleadingly called sand-core technique. See under "Techniques," p. 359.

crackle glass →ice glass

crackling Cracks purposely made on the surface or in layers of the vessel. Is usually created by briefly submerging the hot glass in water or watery solutions (→ice glass). The effect can, however, also be produced by fusing different types of glass with varying coefficients of expansion to one another. See cat. no. 475. →strain crack

crucible →pot

crystal glass Fine glass melted from specially prepared, purified raw materials, thus particularly clear and characterized by a high refraction factor. The term is used today almost exclusively for →lead glass.

cutting See under "Techniques," p. 359.

decorating firms Workshops specialized in decorating glass, usually working on commission for glass companies or dealers, but also often distributing their own products. The decorating firms receive their blanks from specialized glassworks, usually providing them with the design.

diamond-point engraving See under "Techniques," p. 359.

diamond-point stippling or stipple engraving See under "Techniques," p. 359.

dilating The hot glass bubble is opened and expanded with a pair of jacks or other tools in finishing vessel mouths, dish rims, or the standing bases of blown feet.

enameling See under "Techniques," p. 359.

engraving See under "Techniques," p. 359.

etching techniques See under "Techniques," p. 359.

facet cutting See under "Techniques," p. 359.

Favrile glass A registered trade-name-like designation used by Louis C. Tiffany to distinguish his art glassware from similar products offered by other companies. The term derives from the early modern English word "fabrile," denoting hand-wrought, made by hand.

filigree glass See under "Techniques," p. 359.

flamework (or lampwork or at the flame) See under "Techniques," p. 359.

flashing Covering a glass object with a thin layer of glass in a different color. →casing, →overlay glassware

flat glass See under "Techniques," p. 359.

flux (1) (or fluxing agent) Alkali (e.g., soda, potassium, potash) or lead compounds that are mixed with the batch in order to lower the melting point.

flux (2) Soft glass with a low melting point owing to its high proportion of lead oxide and boron or bismuth compounds. Used in powdered form as a basis for enameling.

free-blowing (or offhand-blowing) See under "Techniques," p. 359.

free-forming (or tooling or hot-working) A process whereby hot glass is shaped at the furnace free-hand (offhand), that is, without the use of a →mold.

furnace work, furnace decoration →hot-working techniques

gather Glass taken from the pot in the quantity required for one work phase.

gilt painting (burnished gold) Very fine gold powder is mixed with alkali and oil until brushable. The mixture is painted onto the glass, and fired. The resulting surface is dull and must be polished. Burnished-gold surfaces created in this manner are more durable than the bright-gold coatings that do not have to be treated after firing.

glass granules Colored glass pieces in varying grain sizes, which are worked into the hot glass object after having been preheated.

glassblowing The most common way to make glass. A →gather of glass is taken from the pot with a blowpipe approx. 1.5 m long and blown to a →parison. The parison is rolled on the →marver to give it an even form and then →flashed with another layer of glass. Generally the piece is subsequently blown into a →mold or →free-blown and shaped with the help of various tools (simple woods, cracking-off irons, shears, jacks). During the finishing processes, the work is held with a →pontil.

glass-powder application and inclusion See under "Techniques," p. 359.

glory hole Special furnace used to reheat (or refire) glass during the manufacturing process. Usually gas-fired and set up to control an oxidizing or reducing flame.

hard glass The common term for heat-resistant borosilicate glass (quartz glass) with a high melting point, used in most laboratory-glass works. It is also used for art-glass blowing, but is much more difficult to color than the more frequently used →soft glass.

hollow glassware Term used to describe all three-dimensional and hollow glass objects. Usually made by blowing, in contrast to →flat glass.

hot-working →free-forming

hot-working techniques (or furnace work or furnace decoration) Work and decorative techniques performed on hot glass, that is, at the furnace.

hydrofluoric acid Hydrogen fluoride. Extremely aggressive acid. Used for etching in glass decoration.

ice glass (or crackle glass) The hot glass is briefly submerged in cold water, thus creating a fissured net of irregular, sharp-edged cracks. These are usually smoothed by a quick reheating of the glass. The effect can also be obtained by using a salt solution, which causes crystals to form on the glass surface. Subsequently covering the piece with a layer of glass produces various textures and color effects in the wall (Ikora glass of the Württembergische Metallwarenfabrik and foam glass made by Lötz in the 1930s). The term is also used for numerous other techniques that give the glass surface the look of cracked ice.

inclusions All decorative elements embedded between two glass layers. Inclusions can be colored glass, air bubbles, or such foreign materials as metal oxides, artificial impurities, etc.

inner casing Colored glass layer on the interior of the vessel.

intaglio See under "Techniques," p. 359.

intercalary, *intercalaire* →sandwich decoration

iridescence See under "Techniques," p. 359.

kiln-forming See under „Techniques." p. 359.

knop (or node) The decorative bulge on the stem of a goblet (derived from the Latin word nodus signifying "knot").

lampwork (or flamework or at the flame) See under "Techniques," p. 359.

lead glass Glass exhibiting a high refraction of light melted with lead oxide to form a →flux and stabilizer. →crystal glass

leaded glass (or stained glass) See under "Techniques," p. 359.

lehr (or annealing oven) See under "Techniques," p. 359.

luster pigments Metallic salts combined with resinic acid and dissolved in essential oils. The pigments are applied with a brush and subsequently fired in a ›muffle kiln in an oxidized atmosphere at about 600°C, producing metallic surface effects. These should be distinguished from colors fired in a →reducing atmosphere, which are more durable.

marquetry glass See under "Techniques," p. 359.

***martelé* cutting** (French, "hammered" cutting). Surface decoration resembling hammered metal and created by cutting.

marver A work surface—today usually made of iron, previously of marble—on which the glassblower preforms the →parison or rolls it into prepared pieces of glass or sprinkled glass powder.

matting Imparting the glass surface with a coarse, dull finish using hydrofluoric acid, etching ink, or sandblasting techniques.

metal-foil inclusions Heat-resistant foils, usually gold or platinum, embedded in the vessel wall. When the piece is blown out, additional effects are often achieved by crackling.

millefiori (Italian, "a thousand flowers") See under "Techniques," p. 359.

mold A form made of wood, metal, or graphite into which the hot glass is blown.

mold-blowing See under "Techniques," p. 359.

mold-melting In pre-Roman times the lost-wax process (*cire perdue*), known from bronze casting, was presumably used. Later two-part fire-resistant molds were increasingly employed. Ground or powdered glass in a mold was heated in the furnace at a relatively low temperature for a long period and fused slowly. The process was revived as *pâte de verre* in the late 19th century. Numerous variations of the mold-melting process are used in contemporary glass art.

montage See under "Techniques," p. 359.

mosaic glass See under "Techniques," p. 359.

muffle kiln A closed furnace for firing glass painting, gilding, iridescence, etc.

murrina, -e (Italian) Mosaic-glass section(s).

needle etching See under "Techniques," p. 359.

node →knop

offhand blowing (or free blowing) See under "Techniques," p. 359.

opacifier Additive used to make semiopaque and opaque opal glassware; early on usually bone ash, today tin oxide.

opal glass Colored glass melts mixed with →opacifiers to make semiopaque and opaque glass.

optic-blowing See under "Techniques," p. 359.

optic mold A mold for →optic-blowing.

overlay glassware →casing, →flashing. See under "Techniques," p. 359.

painting on glass See under "Techniques," p. 359.

paperweight technique Colored decoration applied in layers and embedded in thick-walled, colorless glass. It is characterized by the three-dimensional effects created within the glass wall. The term derives from the paperweights of the 19th century. Louis C. Tiffany, amongst others, applied the technique to hollow glassware.

parison (or paraison) The first gather taken from the furnace and blown.

pâte de verre (French, "glass paste") A type of glass made by combining glass powder with a binding agent until it is ductile. To create a vessel or a sculpture the paste is pressed into a negative mold and fused at a relatively low temperature. This method, related to ceramics, has the advantage that colors and forms can be precisely controlled. If only an exterior mold is used, the melted object will have a shiny interior and mat exterior. More thick-walled objects require multipart molds with interior and exterior forms. *Pâte de verre* can also be made by the lost-wax process.

patination Collective term for several processes for furnace-made patination and coating of glass surfaces patented by Emile Gallé in 1898. Patination can be achieved by altering the atmosphere in the furnace or by applying dust, chemicals, ashes, or minerals to the hot glass object. It can be on the glass surface or between layers and is often interspersed with small bubbles.

polishing See under "Techniques," p. 359.

pontil (or punty) An iron rod with which the glass is transferred from the blowpipe. The pontil is attached under the base of the glass object with a small amount of hot glass in order to dilate and fuse the mouth.

pontil mark A mark on the underside of glass where the →pontil was attached and then broken off during the production process. In decorated glassware since the Baroque period, it is usually ground out spherically and polished to a semimat or bright finish.

pot (or crucible) A heat-resistant ceramic vessel that is used to hold the glass melt. Depending on its size, a furnace can accommodate several pots.

pressed glassware See under "Techniques," p. 359.

prunt Round application, often in a different color from the ground and featuring a pulled-out point.

punty →pontil

"quill" mold Optic-blowing mold with projecting "quills" that leave openings in the glass. When the piece is subsequently cased with colorless glass, regular rows of air bubbles embedded in the wall are formed. →bubbles

reducing atmosphere An oxygen-deficient atmosphere created in the kiln or furnace in order to reduce the metal oxides contained in the glass melt to their original metallic state.

When color stains are painted onto the glass and fired in such an atmosphere, shiny metallic effects are created. Should be distinguished from →luster pigments and →iridescence.

refiring →reheating

reheating (or refiring) The act of reheating glass at the furnace between stages in its manufacturing process. →glory hole

relief etching See under "Techniques," p. 359.

relief-cutting (or carving) See under "Techniques," p. 359.

reticello **technique** (Italian) See under "Techniques," p. 359.

ribbed mold Mold with vertically arranged ribs into which the glass is blown. Serves not only to form ribbed surfaces, but also to facilitate various decorative techniques used on hot glass, e.g., producing a rhythmic texture on the interior wall or creating rows of dots.

rods, colored →colored rods

sandblasting See under "Techniques," p. 359.

sandwich decoration (or intercalary or *intercalaire*) Decoration—such as painting, cutting, etching—between the layers of the vessel's wall, usually under a colorless cover layer. The term is used to describe processes by which the glass is annealed between working stages, subsequently reheated, covered with another layer of colorless glass, and then blown out to its final form.

Developed in the 1890s in the studios of Emile Gallé, Burgun, Schverer & Co., and Daum Frères. Since 1916 called the "Graal" technique by the Orrefors factory in Sweden.

Schwarzlot **painting (or black-enamel painting)** See under "Techniques," p. 359.

silver glass A melt with a high silver content, producing bright iridescent glass.

silver-yellow Glass colored with silver nitrate, usually achieved with stains.

skeleton mold Mold made of wide, detached ribs. See under "Techniques," p. 359, →optic-blowing, →optic mold

soft glass Special glass with a low melting point for →lampwork. Available as tubes and rods in various colors.

stained glass (or leaded glass) See under "Techniques," p. 359.

staining See under "Techniques," p. 359.

stippling, diamond-point See under "Techniques," p. 359.

strain crack (or stress crack) A crack within the vessel wall caused by insufficient annealing or use of types of glass with too great a differential in the coefficients of expansion. Can occur long after the object was made as a result of a sudden change in temperature or by being knocked lightly.

stress crack →strain crack

striking During reheating in the furnace or when heated at certains points, some types of glass will change color or take on a new color, e.g., gold-ruby glass and special types of glass for lampwork. →soft glass

studio technology See under "Techniques," p. 359.

threading (or trailing) The application of a glass thread to a glass object. Using a simple turning mechanism, regular spiral patterns can be achieved, which are then usually dragged, combed, or blown into a →ribbed mold.

threads, applied and embedded The glass thread is pulled from a softened glass rod or a small drop of glass (→threading) and applied to the glass object in relief. It can also be embedded into the wall by rolling the glass bubble on the →marver or by enclosing it with an overlay.

tooling →free-forming

trailing →threading

transferring The act of fusing the glass to the pontil and cracking off the blowpipe to finish the mouth of the vessel.

transparent enameling See under "Techniques," p. 359.

"wave-optic" pattern Optic-blown decoration using a mold with a relief of wavy lines.

Weissglashütten (German, "white-glass" or "clear-glass" factories) Collective term for glassworks that used decolored glass in the 16th and 17th centuries. Usually in reference to glassworks *à la façon de Venise.*

Zwischengoldglas (German, "gold between glass") See under "Techniques," p. 359.

Techniques

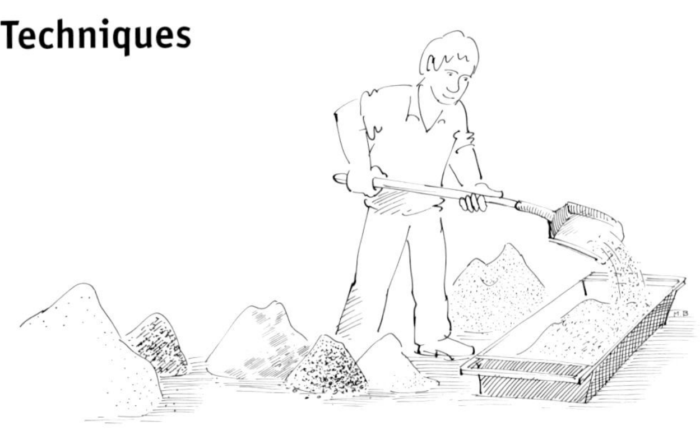

Composition

Three basic ingredients are required to make glass. The glass-forming substance is silica (silicic acid), that is, sand, quartz, or flint. Since the melting point of silica is very high, alkali (natrium, potash), a so-called fluxing agent, must be added to reduce the melting point. To ensure that the melted mass acquires the necessary hardness after cooling, calcium or lead oxide must be added. To simplify the melting process, large quantities of glass fragments are usually added to the raw materials. The illustration shows a typical batch for colorless crystal glass.

15.00 kg soda
15.00 kg marble fragments or crushed limestone
3.00 kg Na-saltpeter
18.00 kg potash
0.50 kg arsenic

100.00 kg sand

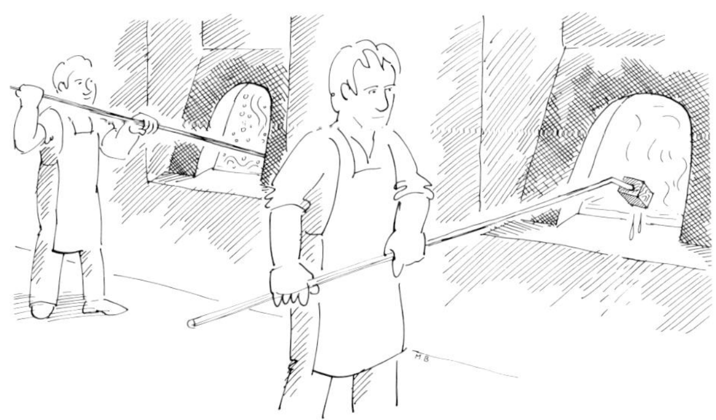

The Melt

The well-mixed batch is put into a fire-resistant pot in the furnace and melted at a temperature of about 1400°–1600°C. To fill the pot, more of the batch must be added in stages. The raw melt thus created is full of impurities and gas bubbles. To bring the bubbles to the surface, the molten glass must be brought to a boil. A piece of wood soaked in water is pushed deep into the melt (blocking). The water evaporates, forcing the small bubbles to the surface. Adding a few lumps of arsenic has the same effect. They sink into the melt and are quickly transformed into a gaseous state. It is also common to inject water vapor with an iron tube. In the pot furnaces of smaller glassworks and studios these processes are carried out sequentially; in the tank furnaces of the large factories they are done simultaneously.

After the refining process, the melt must stand off, enabling the impurities to settle at the bottom of the pot. After annealing the melt slowly, a working temperature of about 1250°C is reached.

Coloring

Since natural deposits of sand almost always contain iron oxide, simple (bottle) glass usually has a green tone. To render the glass colorless, so-called glassmaker's soap—usually manganese oxide—was added to the batch as a decolorizer from early on. The deliberate coloring of glass, however, has also been known from the beginnings of glass production. Metal oxides and salts are used in different proportions and varying temperatures to create a range of colors. Special hues are achieved with the so-called rare-earths neodymium and praseodymium: a delicate violet and a fine yellow-green.

Milk glass is made by melting together tin oxide, bone ash (phosphoric lime), cryolite, or substances containing aluminum oxide or fluorine. In smaller quantities these additives result in semitransparent, opalescent types of glass.

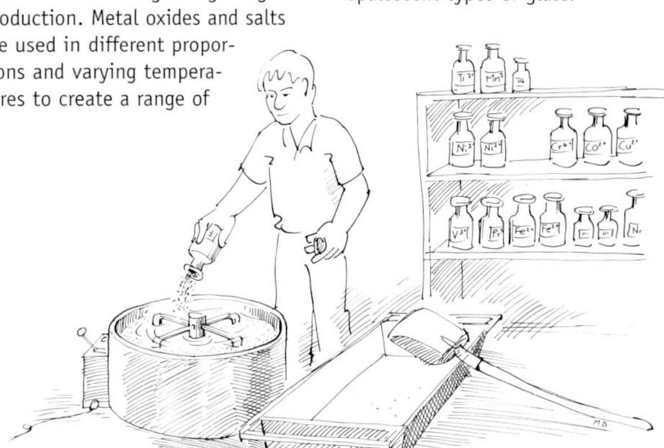

Examples include:

iron:	green, blue, yellow	nickle:	violet, brown
copper:	red, green, blue, turquoise	selenium:	pink, yellow-red
		antimony:	brown, yellow
cobalt:	light and dark blue	manganese:	violet, purple, brown
chromium:	yellow, green	silver:	yellow
uranium:	*Annagelb* and *Annagrün*	gold:	rosé, red, gold ruby

Production

Melted glass can be worked at temperatures between 900° and 1250°C. Lead and soda glass can be handled longer and are therefore easier to work with; potash glass, for a shorter time, making it more difficult. Since vessels have to be made very quickly, glassmakers usually work as a team. A helper blows the parison; the glassblower flashes it and blows the vessel into a mold or blows it out free-hand; the glassmaker finally applies the foot, handle, or decorative parts.

The tools are simple and have hardly changed over the centuries. Using them requires a good eye and excellent manual skills. Ornamentation that the glassmaker applies at the furnace is called furnace decoration; a vessel created in this manner is free-formed glass. Work done on glass after it has been cooled, for instance cutting and engraving, is called cold decoration. These methods are today simply referred to as hot and cold-working techniques.

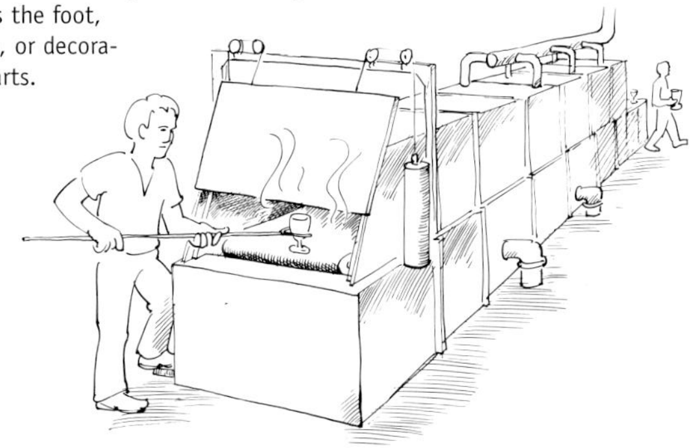

Annealing

If a glass vessel is allowed to cool in the open air, tensions, which can cause it to crack at the slightest strain, result. Specially constructed cooling furnaces (annealing oven or lehr) ensure that the cooling process is delayed. At a modern glassworks it usually takes about four hours until the glass leaves the tunnel-shaped passage; often it takes much longer, though.

Core-forming

The most common technique of making glass before the blowpipe was invented. A core usually consisting of clay and vegetal materials, approximately the size of the vessel to be created, is covered with hot glass; see cat. nos. 2–4. This can be done by wrapping the viscous glass onto the heated core or by melting powdered glass onto it in layers.

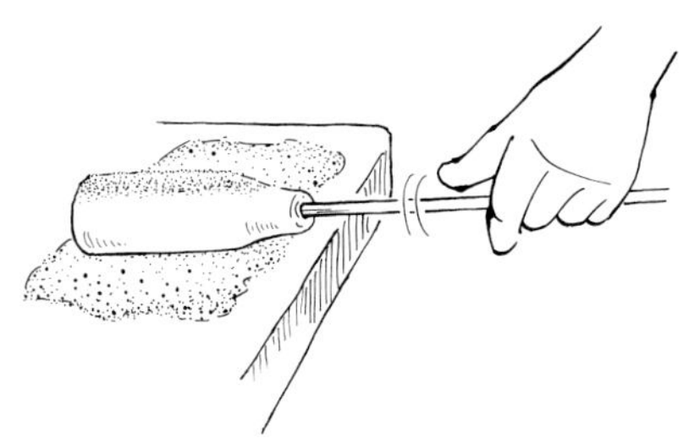
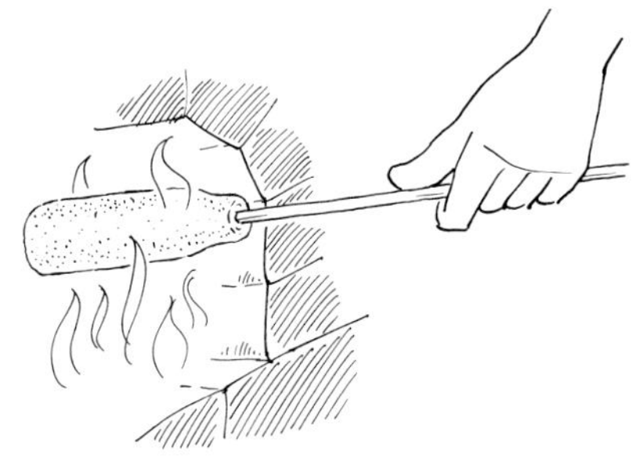

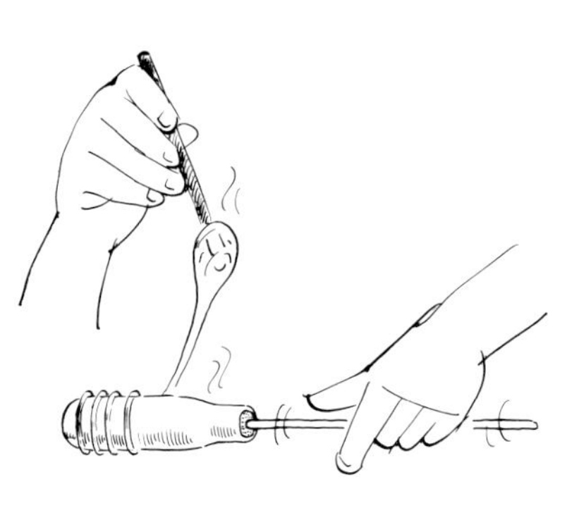
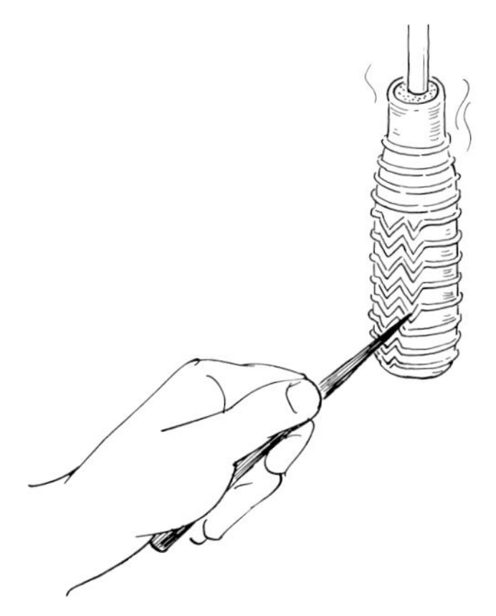
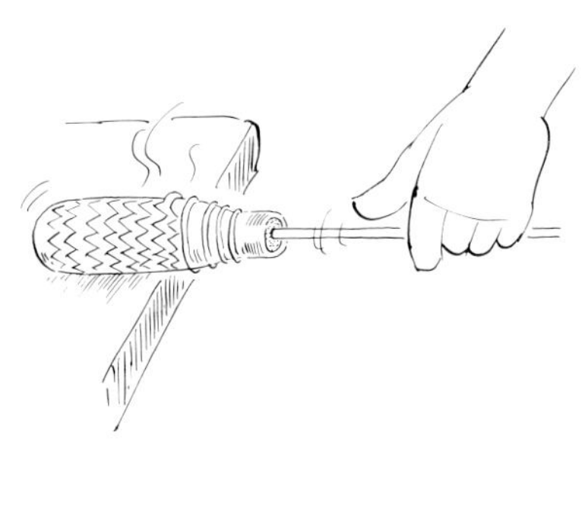

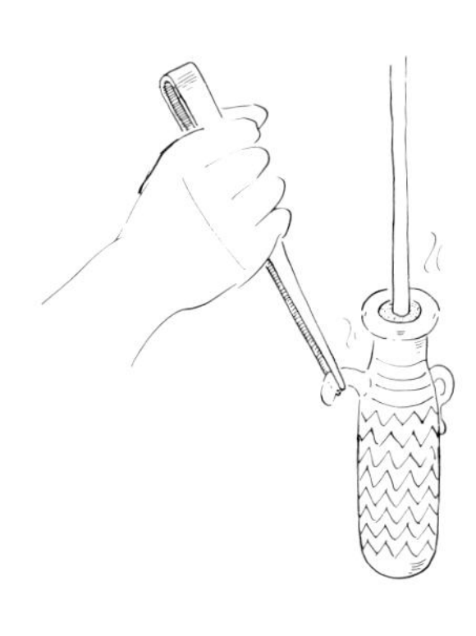
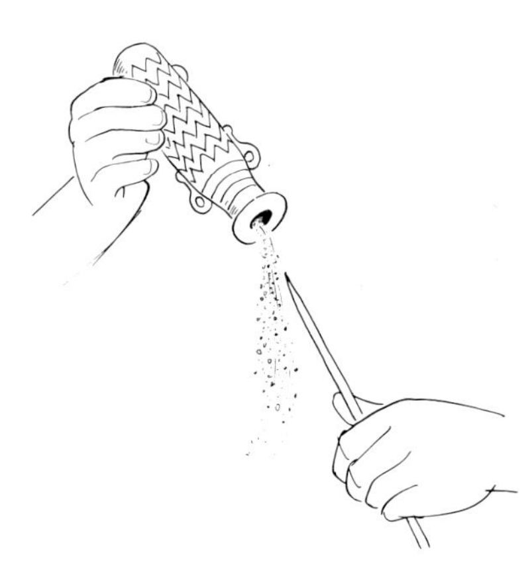
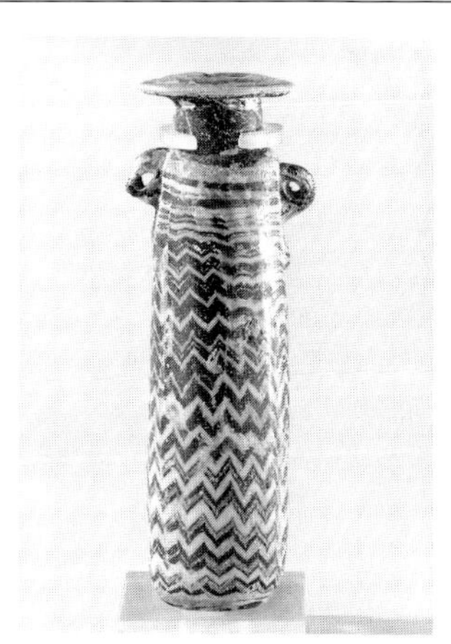

Production of a Ribbed Bowl

For many years, the production process used to make this common type of Roman bowl was thought to have been relatively complicated. The latest research makes the much simpler procedure illustrated here more plausible. See Lierke, "Rippenschalen," 1993, pp. 218–34, and Stern and Schlick-Nolte, *Early Glass*, 1994, 72–79. Many useful suggestions with regard to the drawings shown here were kindly supplied by Rosemarie Lierke, Schwalbach.

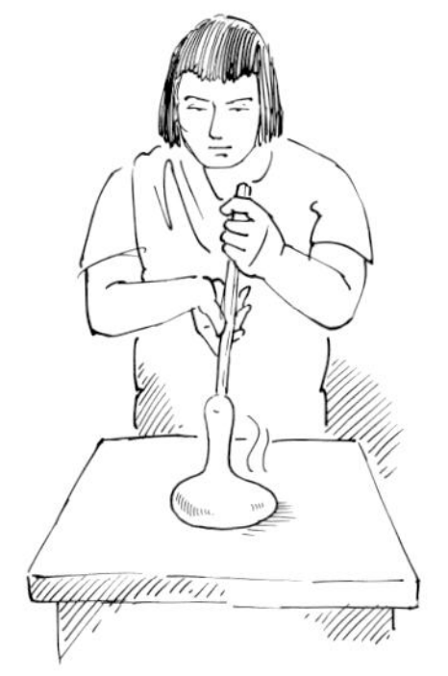
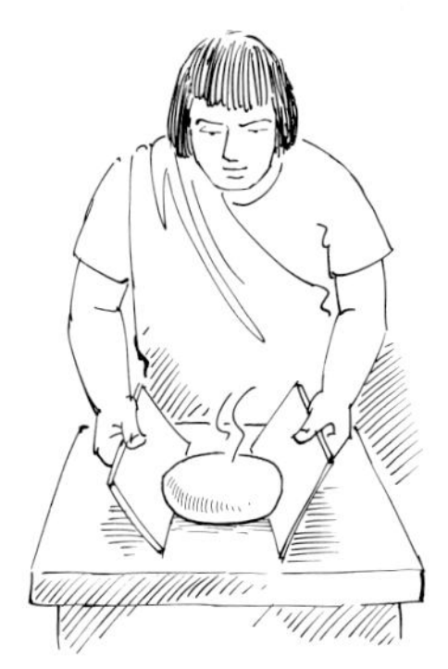

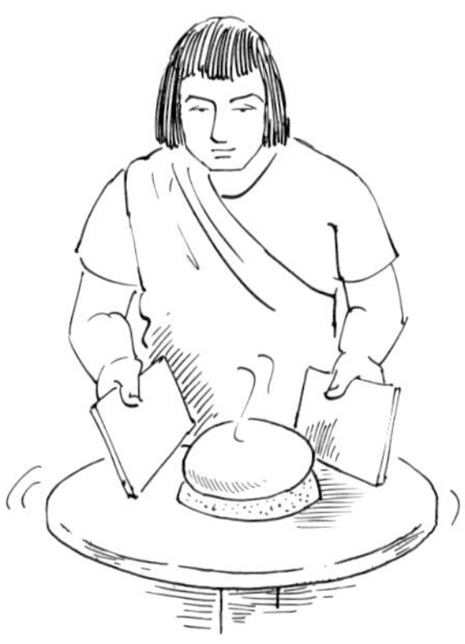 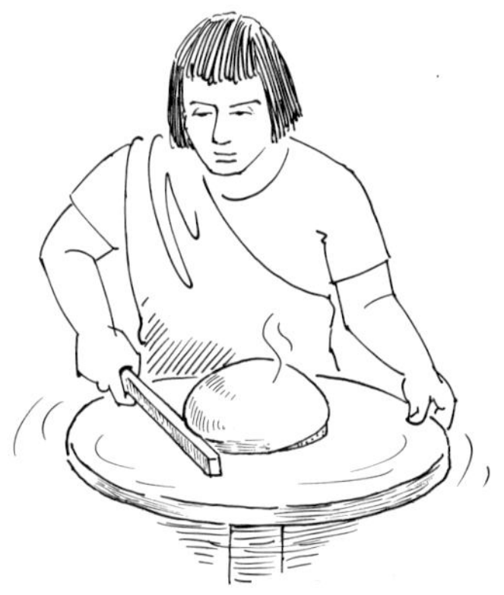 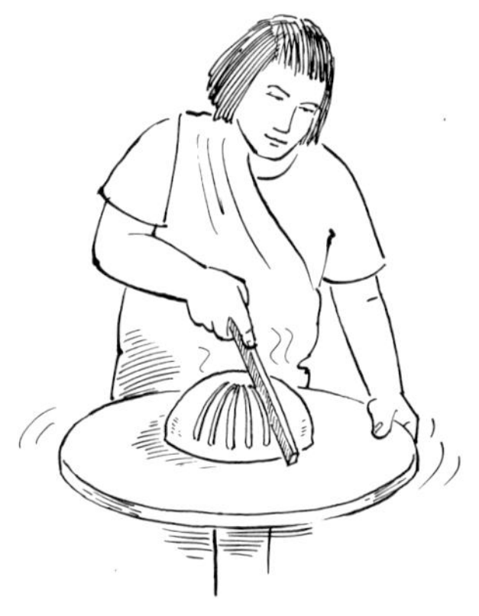

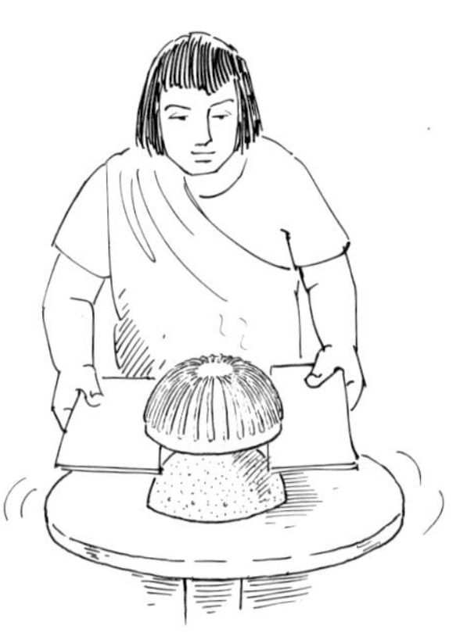 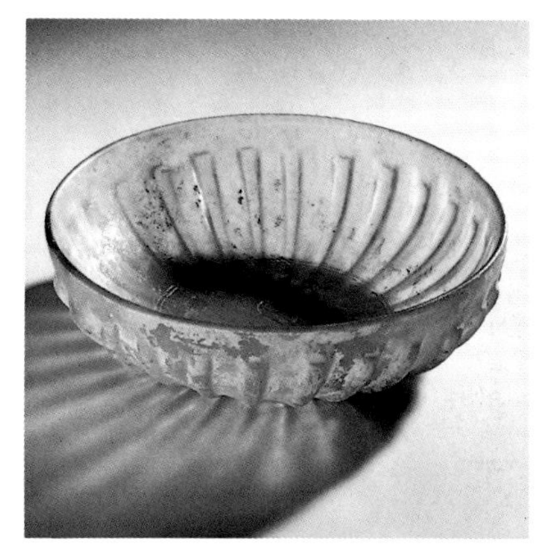

Mosaic and Millefiori Glass

In antiquity: Polychrome threads and ribbons were fused into a cane in such a way that they showed a particular design in cross section. After annealing, slices are broken off the cane and the individual sections laid out in patterns in a mold. During the slow and careful mold-melting, the sections fuse together to form a vessel. See cat. nos. 16, 20, 21, 191, 192.

A Venetian variation since the late 15th century: The sections are picked up with a hot glass bubble and can then be worked as desired. See cat. no. 374.

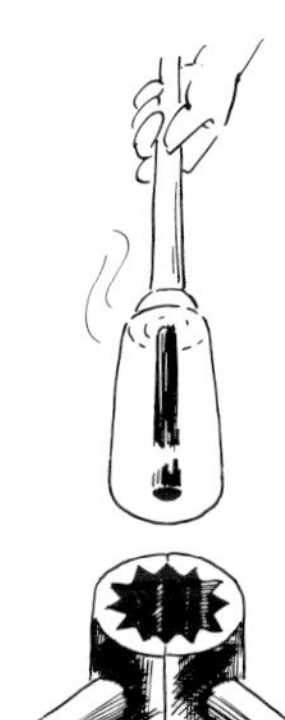 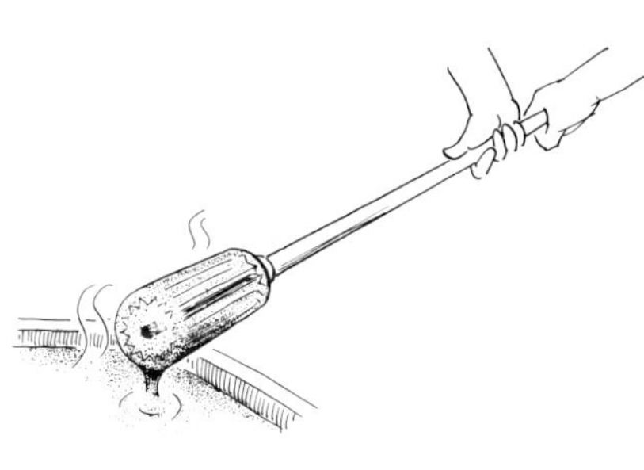

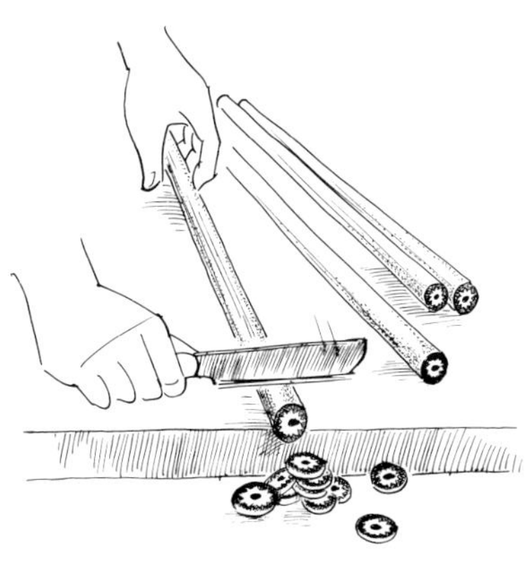 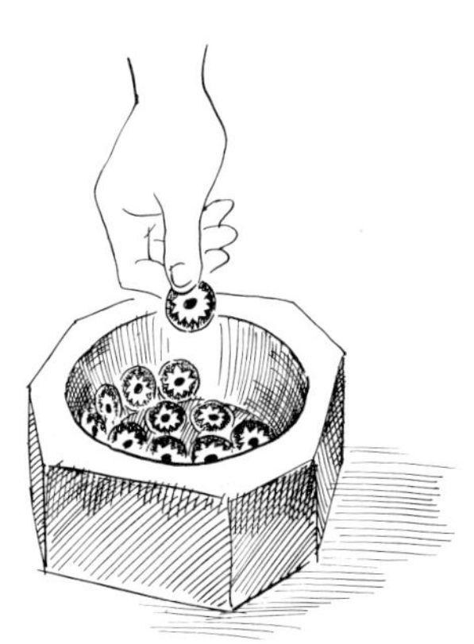 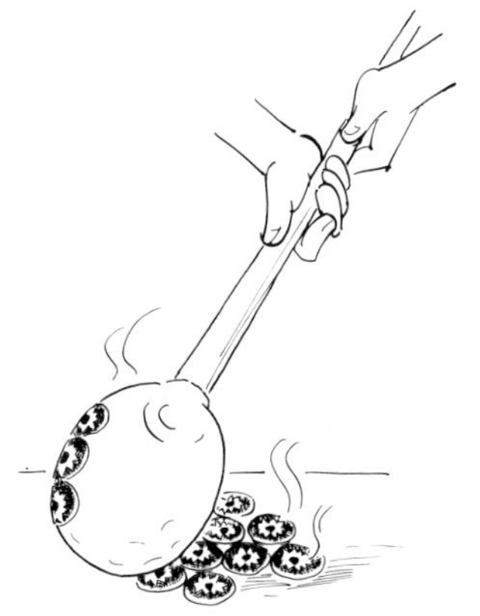

Blowing Techniques

Since the first century BC glass has been blown with the aid of pipes made of glass, clay, or wood (bamboo), their ends having been protected by clay, then increasingly of metal. There are three basic techniques.

Free-blowing: The glass is taken from the pot with the pipe and shaped with pincers and wooden tools.

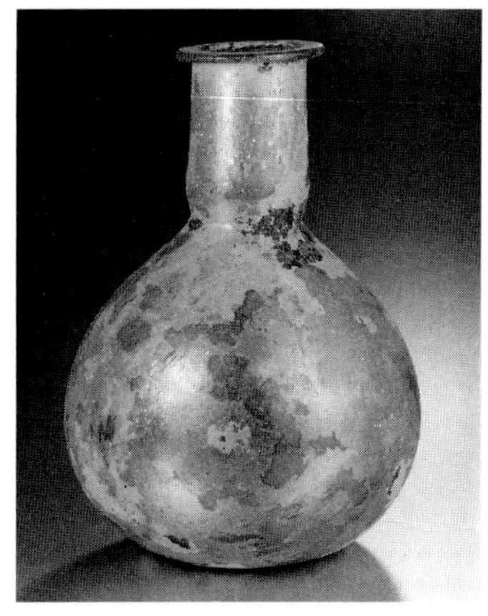

Mold-blowing: The parison is blown out in an open or closed mold consisting of several parts. Its inner pattern is visible on the surface of the vessel (so-called full mold-blowing). The seams of multipart molds usually remain visible on the glass.
On glass vessels devoid of relief surface decoration, the seams can be smoothed out by rotating the piece while blowing it out.

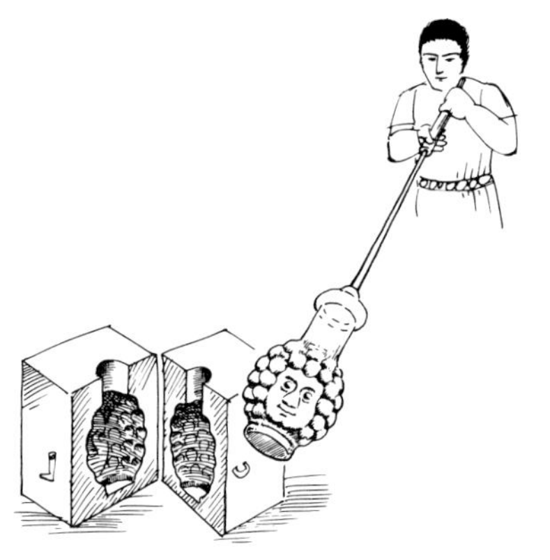

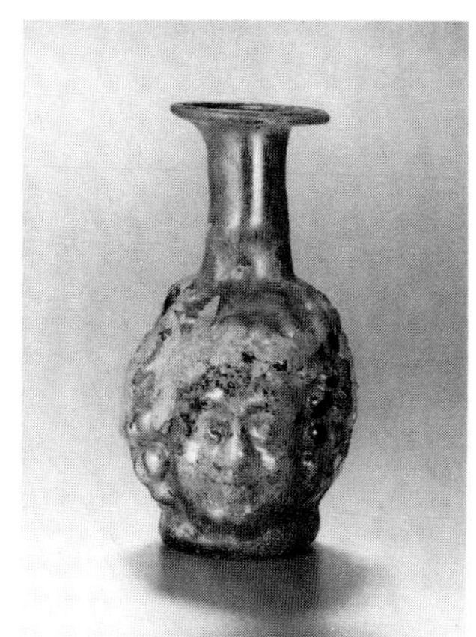

Optic-blowing: The glass bubble is given a pattern in an open mold, usually simple flutes ("rib optic" pattern). Then the vessel is freely blown out; the rib pattern can be twisted into a spiral, dilated, or otherwise transformed.

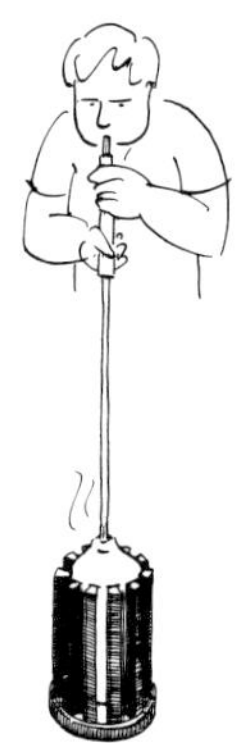

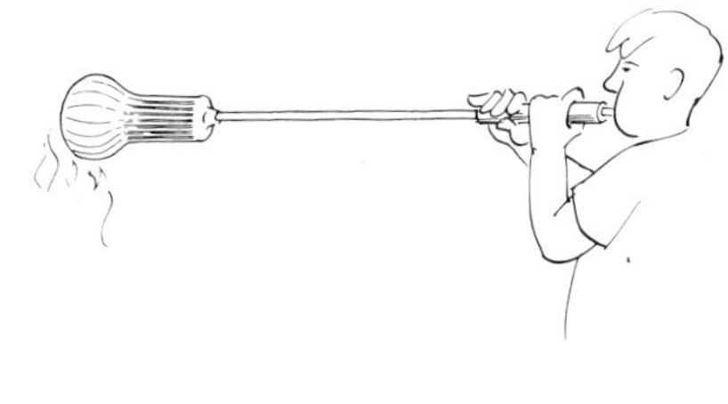

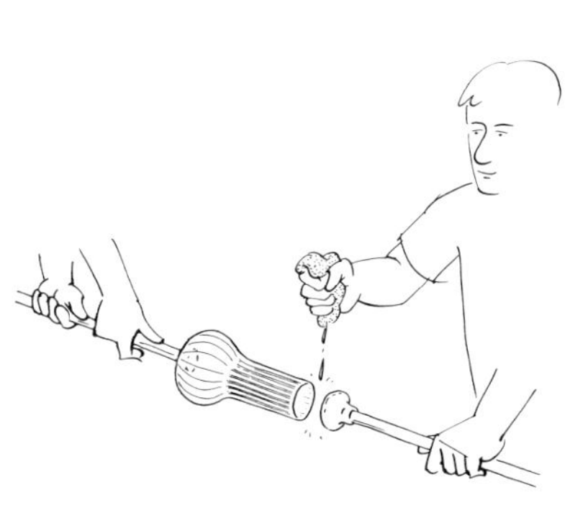

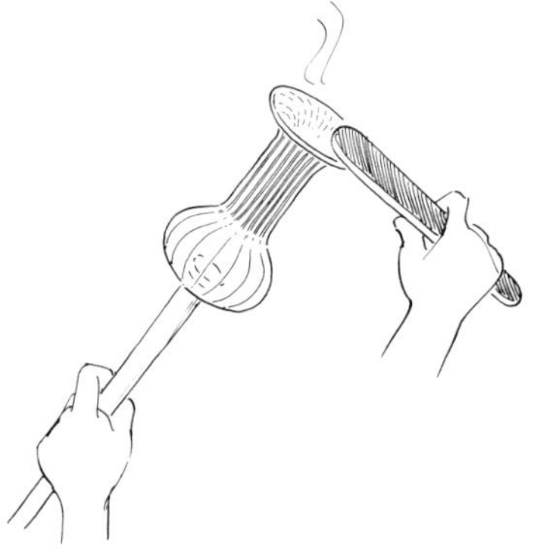

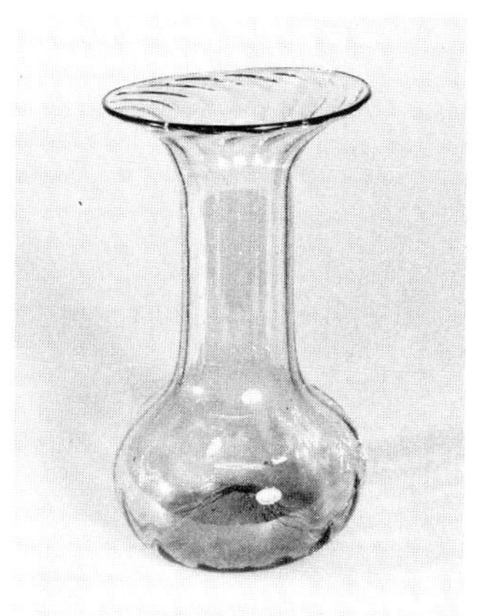

Overlay Glassware

Overlay glassware consists of two or more layers of different colored glass. The simplest method is to dip a parison into glass of another color. This process does not guarantee, however, an even distribution of the colored glass on the surface of the object. Other methods:

A length of colored glass rod is fused onto a colorless parison, distributed evenly on its surface, and then fully blown.

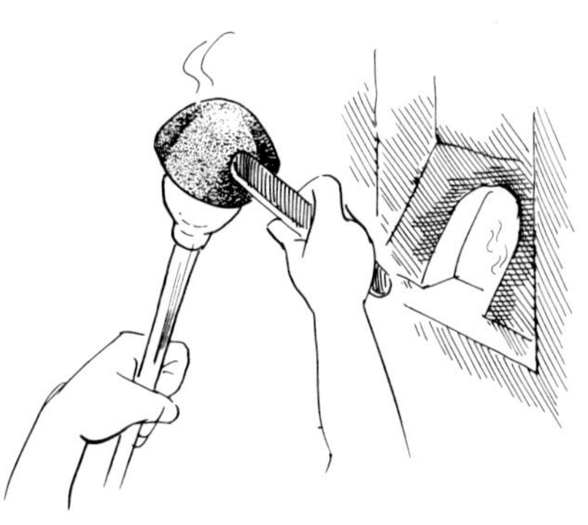

A simpler method:

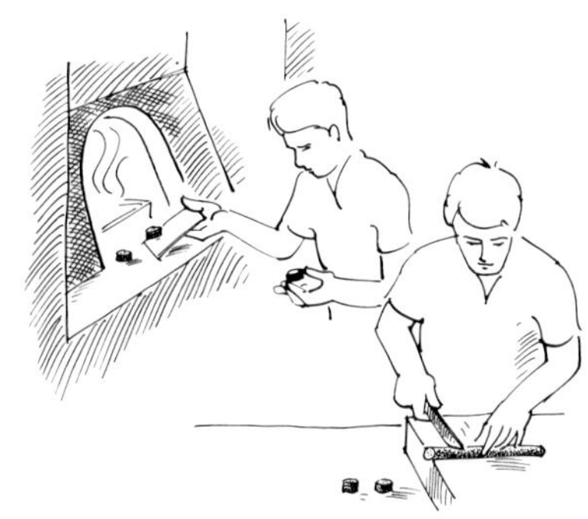
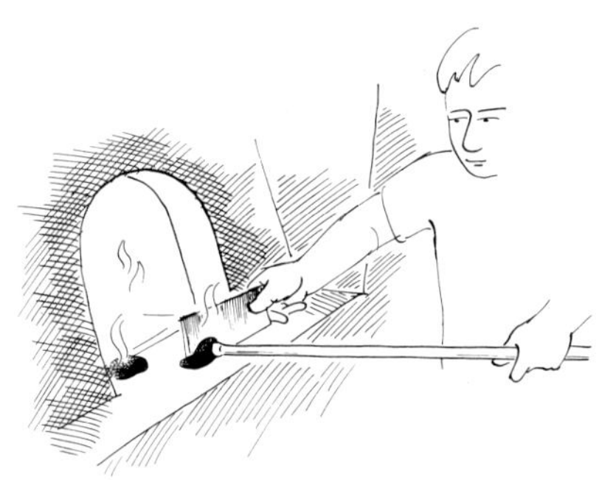

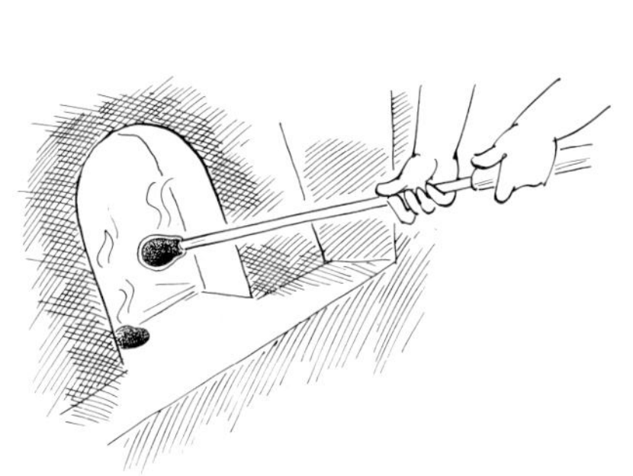
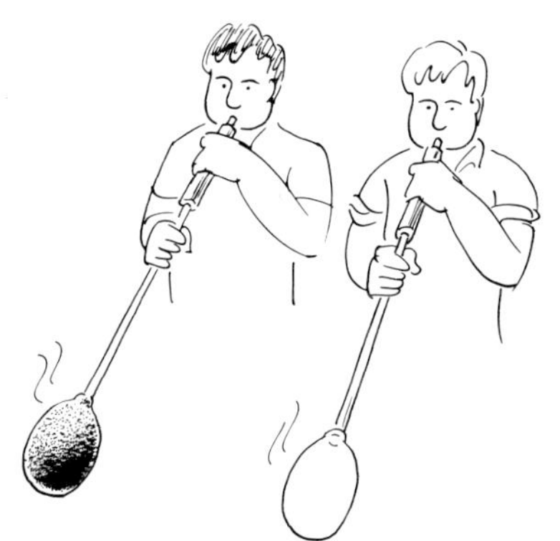
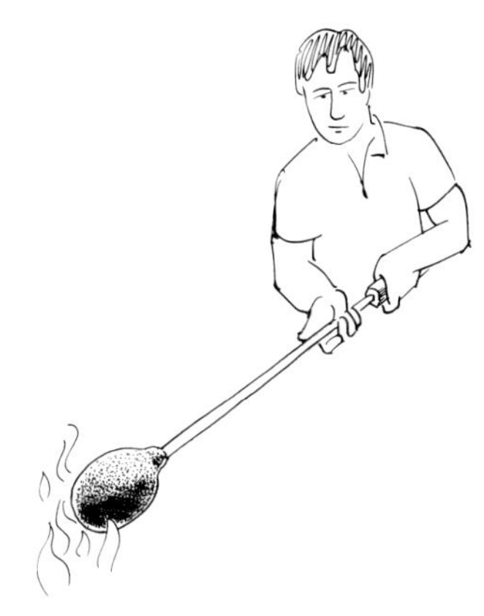

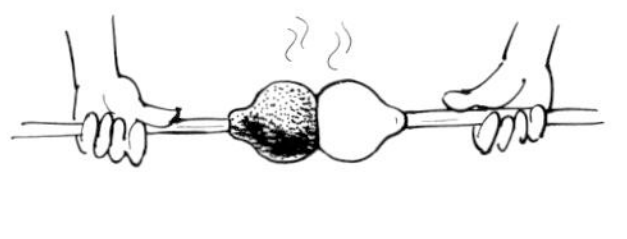

The piece is blown into a prepared colored glass cup. Used primarily for partial overlays and for goblets with a colored bowl and colorless stem.

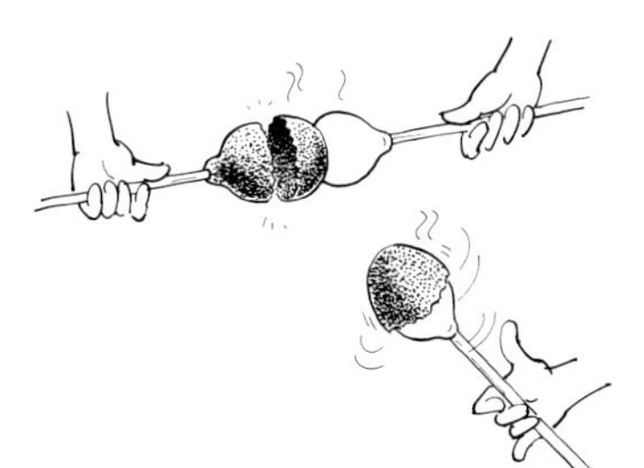
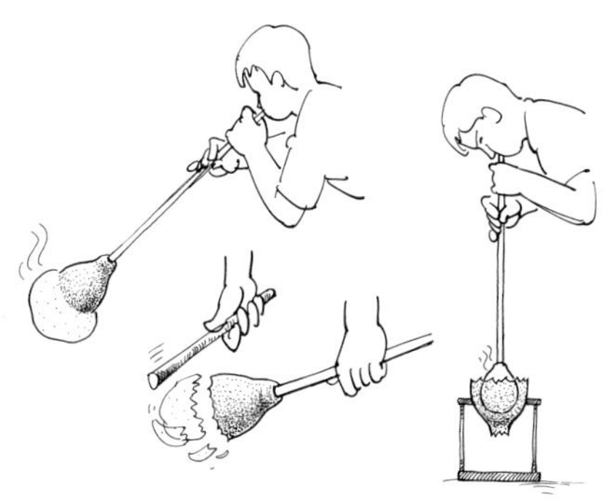

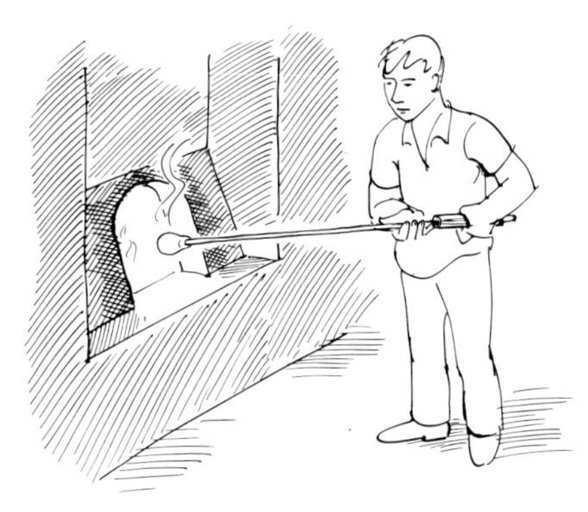
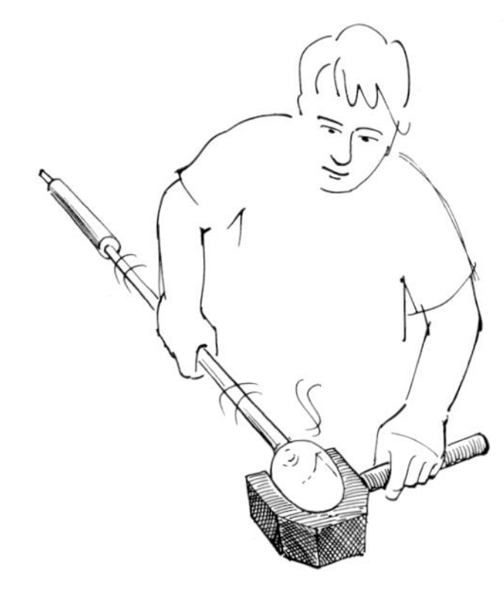

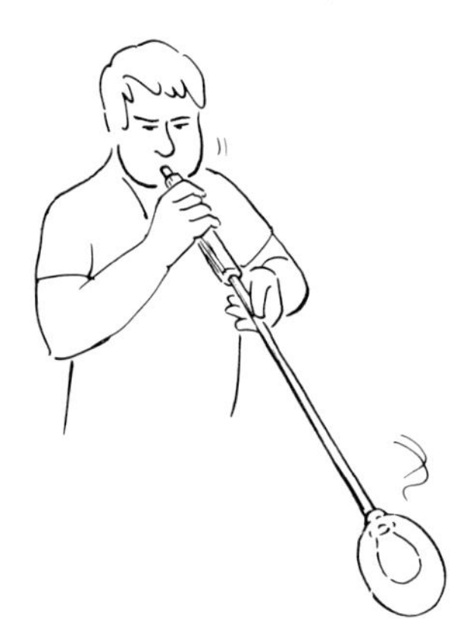
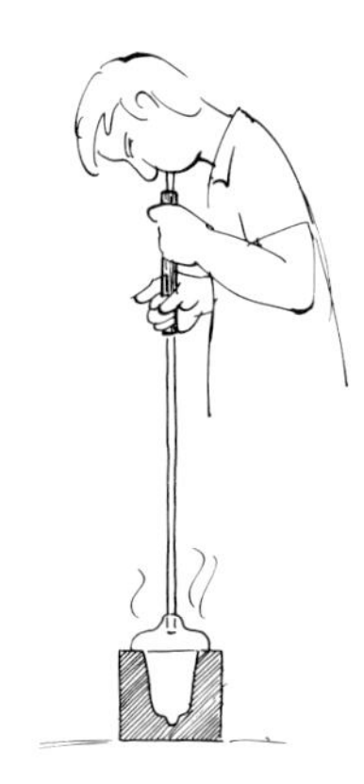
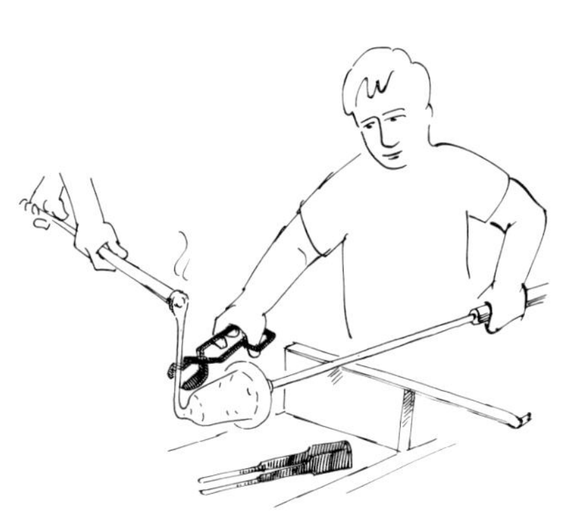

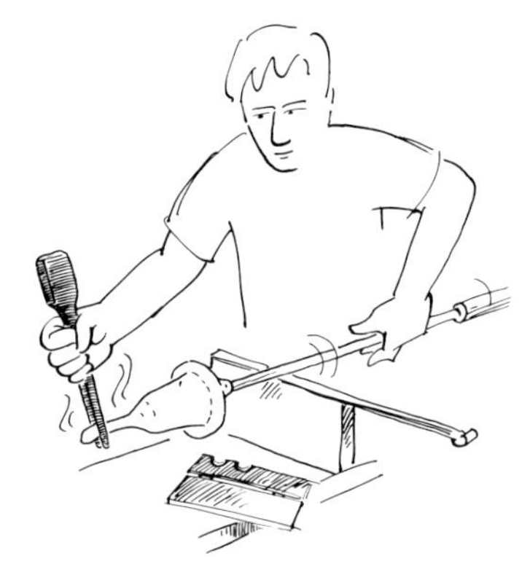
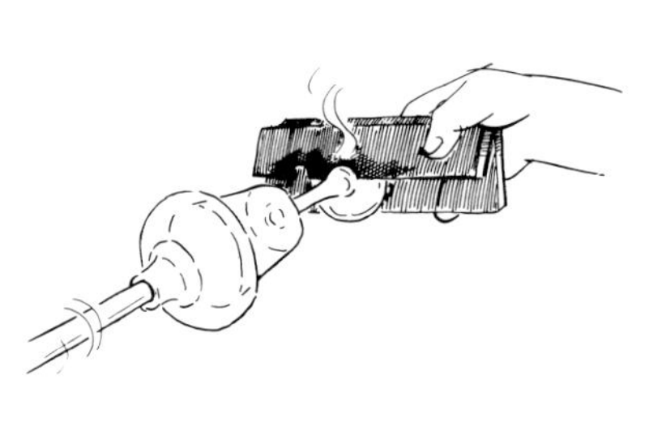
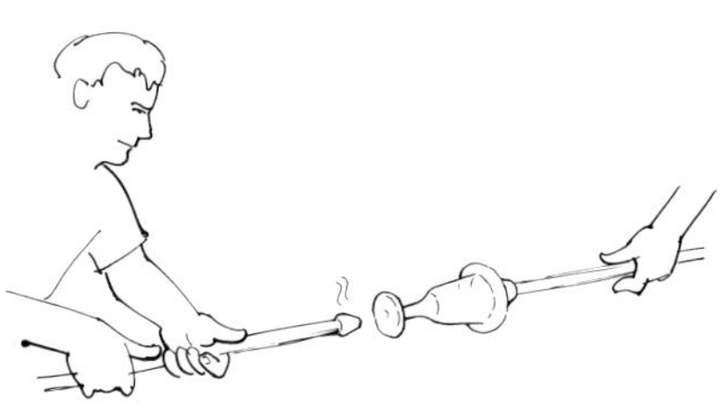

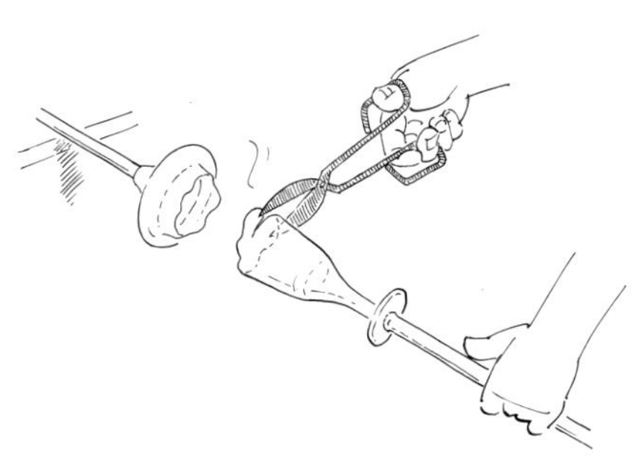
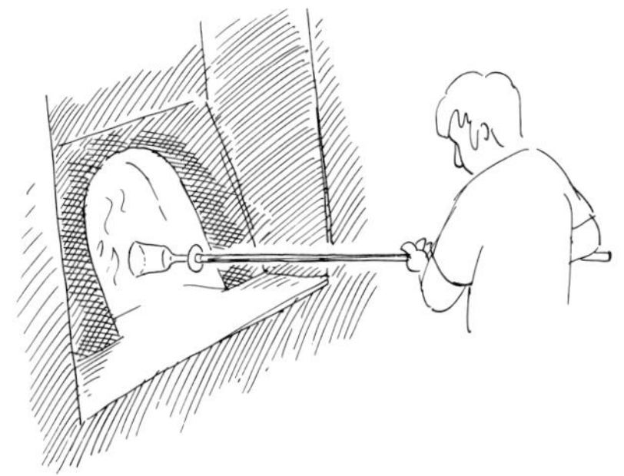

Special Furnace Techniques

Marquetry glass: Inlaid-glass work. The decoration is made of prepared pieces of colored glass that are laid out on the worktable, heated, and marvered into the surface of the glowing-red glass or fused onto it. Emile Gallé developed this technique, calling it *marqueterie de verre*. See cat. nos. 231–33, 235.

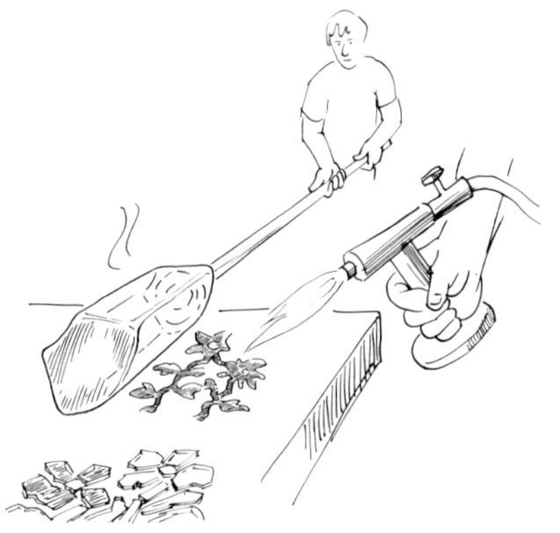

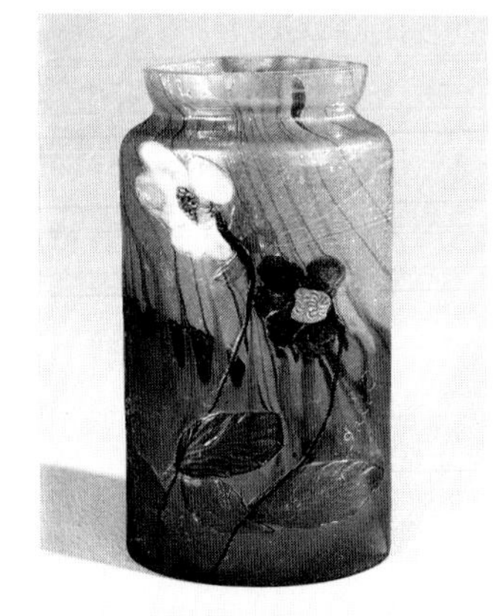

Glass-powder application and inclusion: Powdered colored glass is dusted onto the hot glass and marvered. Or it remains as a dull coating on the surface. By covering with another layer of glass, overlay effects can be achieved. Specialty of Daum Frères in Nancy and Schneider in Epinay-sur-Seine, amongst others. See cat. nos. 250–57, 271, 272.

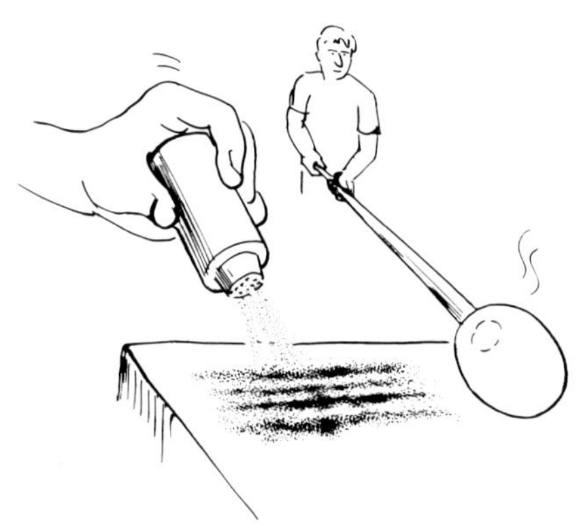

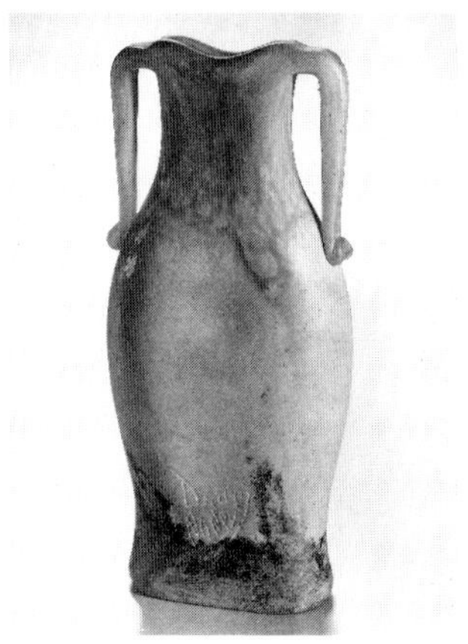

Iridescent glass: The completed glass, still hot and attached to the pontil, is placed in a small furnace (special muffle). Sprayed or vaporized metallic salts settle on the glass, forming a thin, shimmering film on the surface. Using glass types containing silver and preparing the piece in a reducing atmosphere, Tiffany in New York and Lötz in Klostermühle brought the technique to previously unattained heights. See cat. nos. 296–300, 302, 307–16.
The surface of glassware found in the ground is also iridescent.

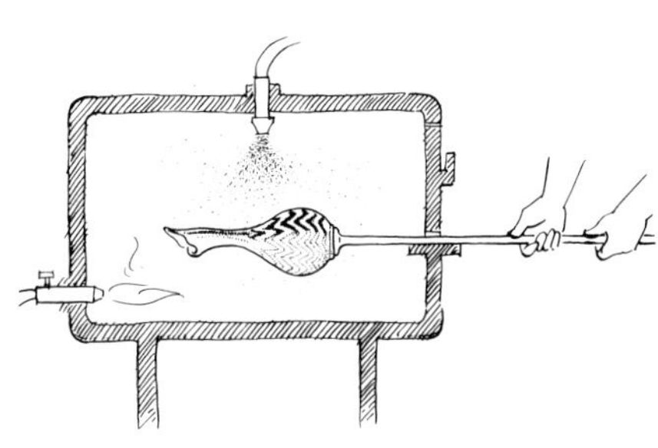

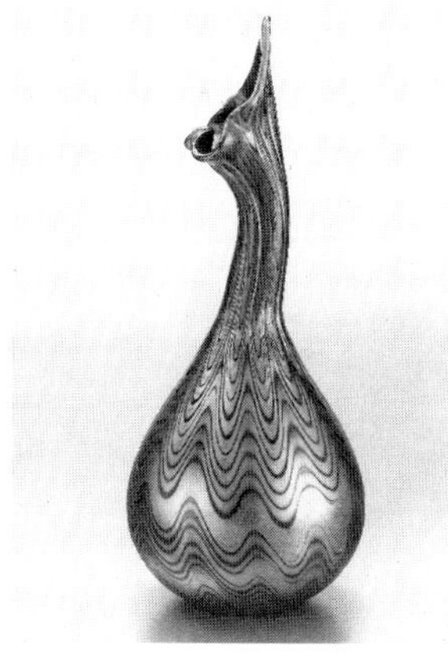

Other Hot-Working Techniques

Lampwork or flamework: Prepared glass tubes and canes are heated at the worktable with the aid of a gas burner and formed with small pincers. Welding various colored parts together (montage technique) is the most complicated form of artistic glass design at the lamp. It creates effects that are not possible at the furnace. See cat. nos. 141, 196, 341–43, 361–63, 471–76.

Pressed glassware: The hot glass is pressed into metal molds under great pressure.

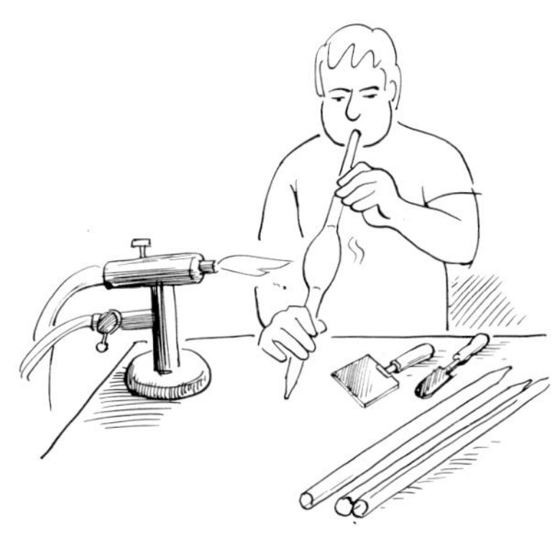

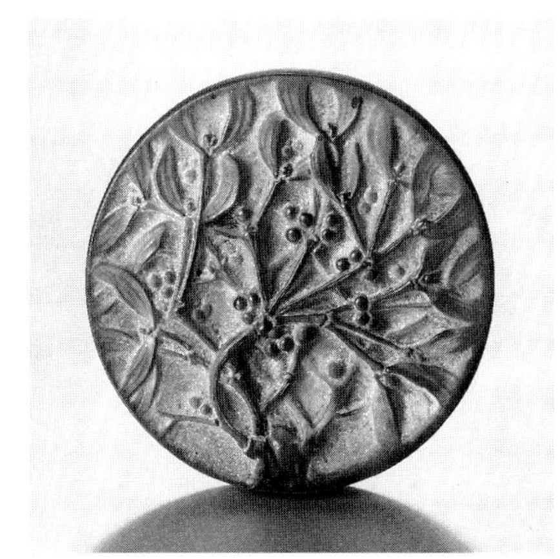

Filigree Glass

Glass vessels made with prepared glass canes, some with complicated patterns. Filigree glass canes were used to decorate vessels as early as in the pre-Roman period. The technique was revived in Venice in the 16th century and much refined. It has been considered typically Venetian ever since. See cat. nos. 132, 135–37.

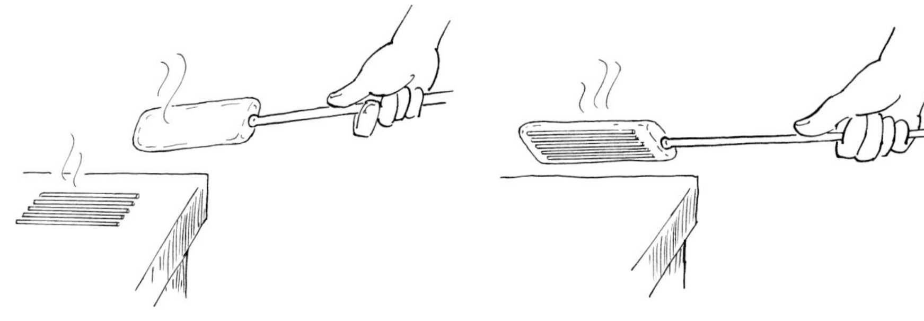

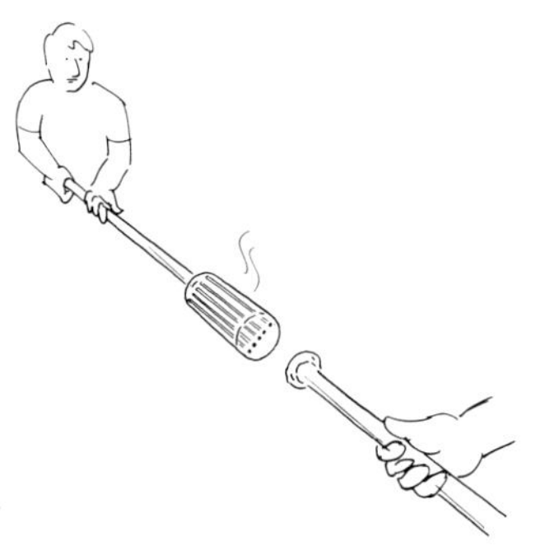

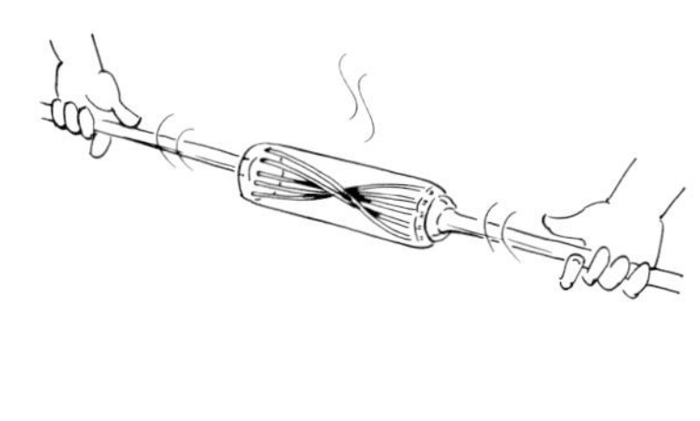

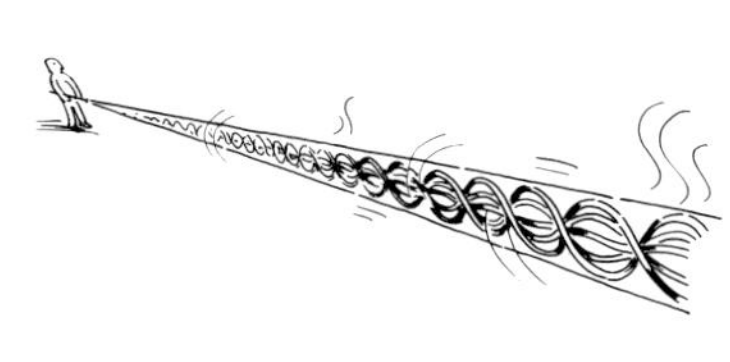

Making a Footed Bowl in *Reticello* Technique

Venetian decorative vessels with crossed milk-glass threads and embedded air bubbles (network glass) are amongst the most magnificent works of the glassmaker's art. The technique was developed in Venice in the 16th century. To make it the glassmaker must demonstrate a highly developed sense of form, technical precision, and good timing at every stage of the production process. See cat. no. 134.

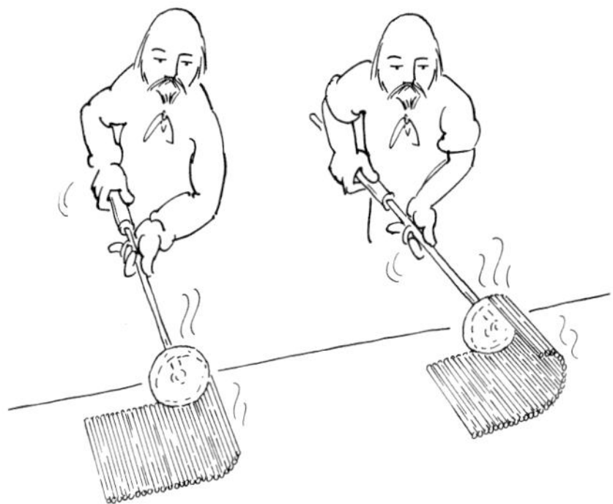

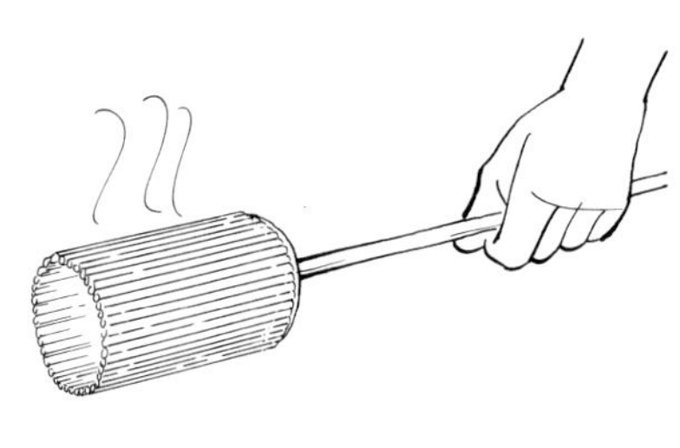

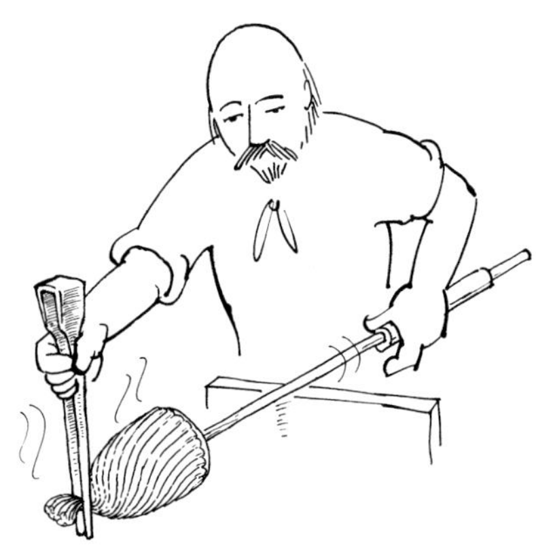

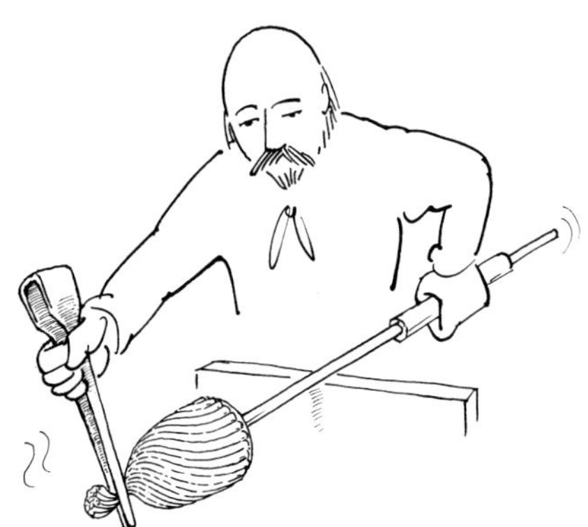

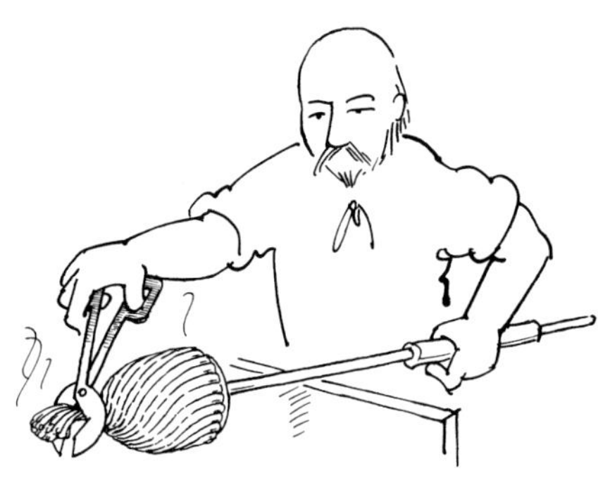

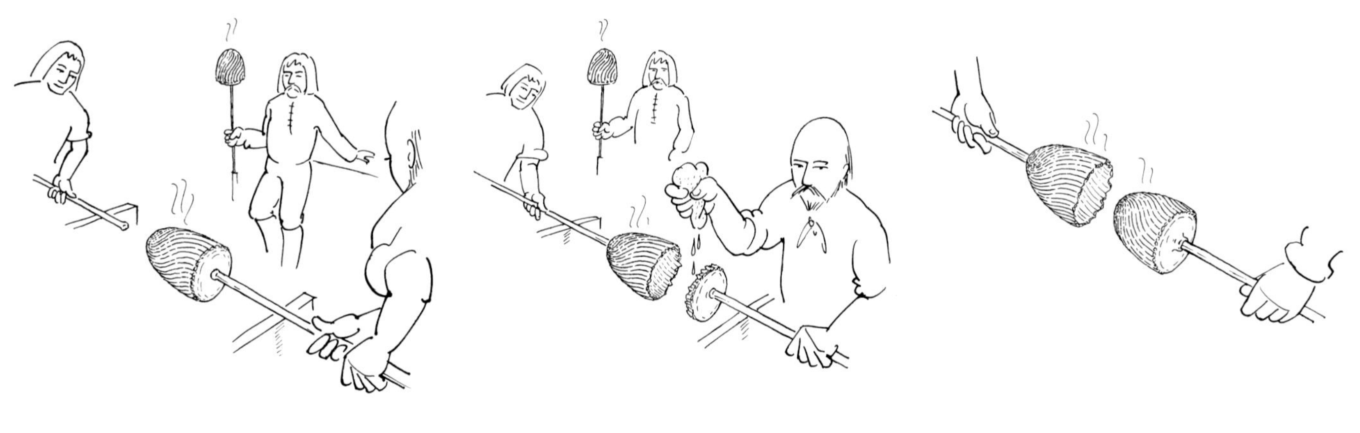

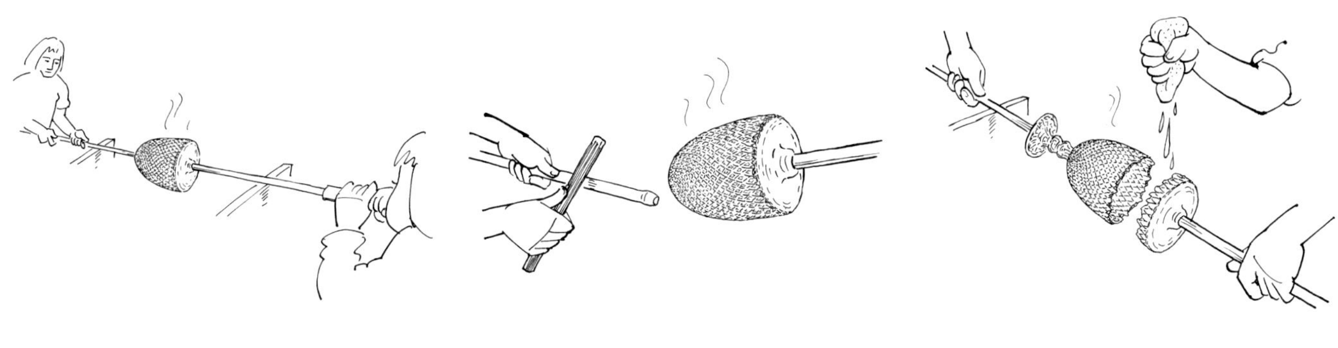

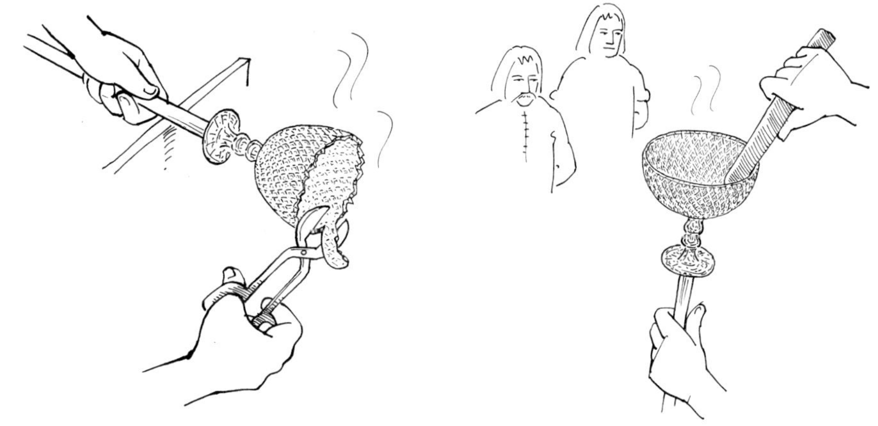

Decorative Techniques on Cold Glass

Painting on Glass

Enameling: Powdered, colored fluxes with a low melting point are mixed with a binding agent to make a paste that can be applied by brush. The painted layer is fused insolubly to the vessel at about 490°–580°C, whereby the binding agent evaporates.
A technique practiced in antiquity. Revived in Venice in the 16th and 17th centuries, it spread to Germany, where it became extremely popular. See cat. nos. 108, 109, 111–15.

Schwarzlot (German, literally "black lead"): Forged iron scales or a mixture of copper and iron oxide are added to the flux as coloring agents, creating black and gray-brown tones after firing. See cat. nos. 150, 151.

Transparent enameling: Fine painting with transparent enamel pigments. Taken over from porcelain painting. Technically developed and often used in the Biedermeier period. See cat. nos. 177, 178, 180.

Cold painting: Instead of enamel colors, lacquer or oil paints are used. They are protected merely by a layer of varnish and are thus less durable than fired enamel. See cat. no. 215.
Highly resistant printing colors have replaced enameling techniques in today's mass-produced glass.

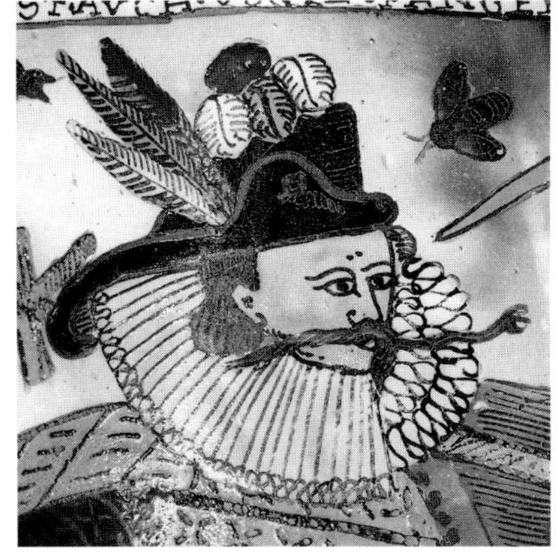
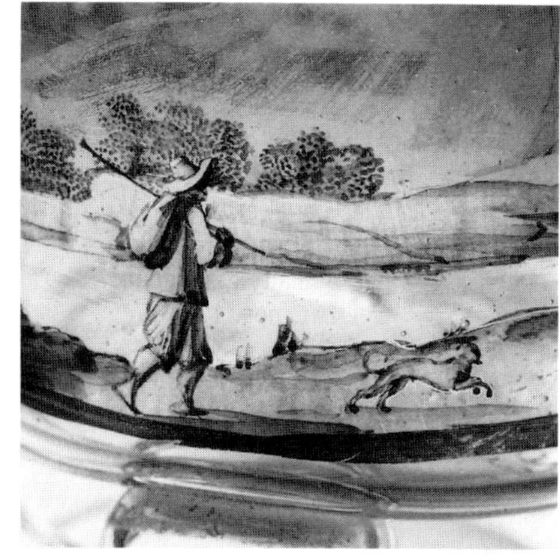
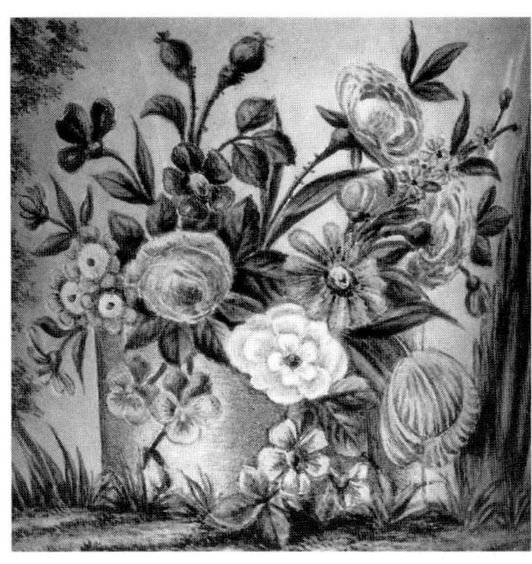
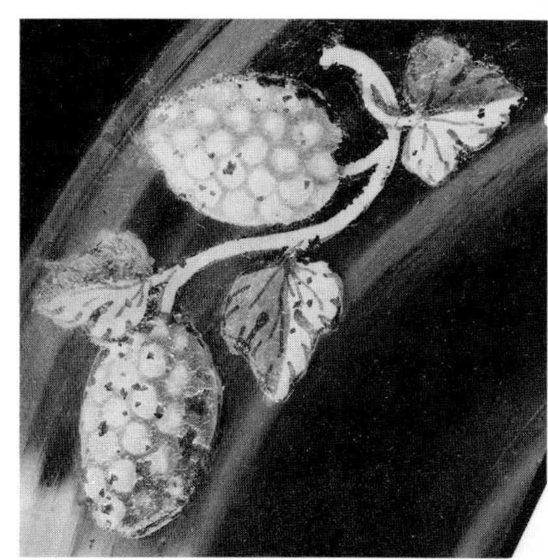

Engraving

Laborious treatment of the glass surface with small, rotating metal wheels coated with an abrasive powder in oil. The engraved decoration can be left mat or polished.
Working decorative elements into the surface of the glass is called intaglio. See cat. nos. 143–49.

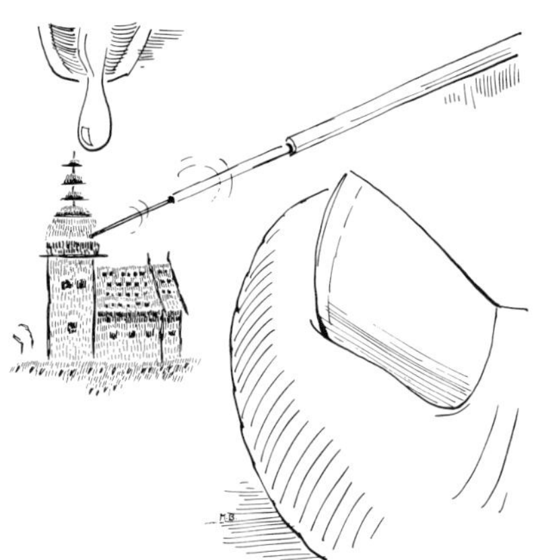
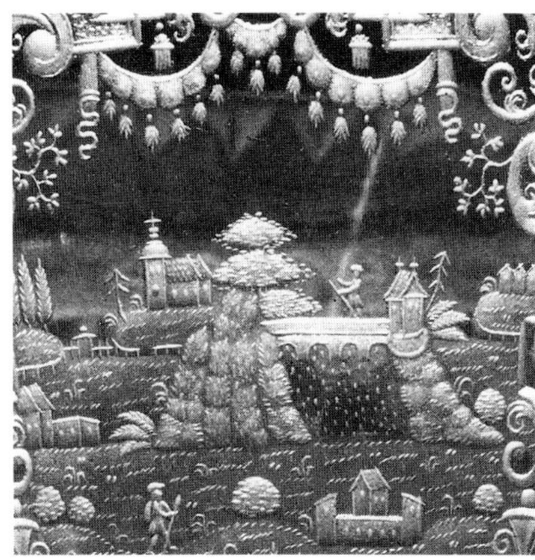

Relief-cutting (or carving): The decoration is worked on the glass surface as a three-dimensional relief with the engraving wheel. A very time-consuming technique since the entire ground surrounding the decoration must be removed.

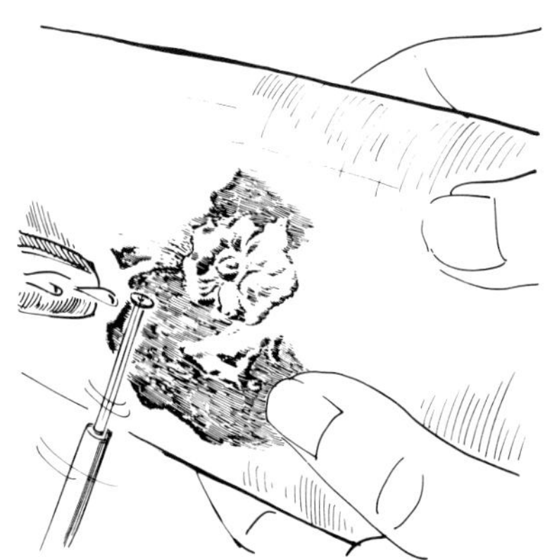
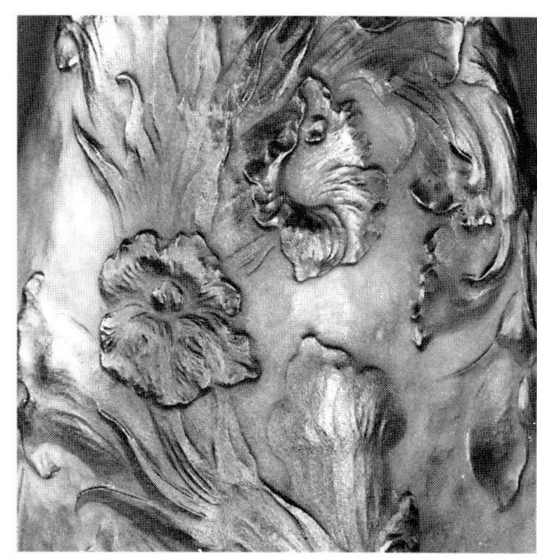

Stippling or Stipple Engraving

The depiction is created by numerous individual dots (stipples) struck against the glass surface with a diamond or steel needle. The density and varying depth of the dots produce three-dimensional effects and shading. In the second half of the 18th century, this technique was especially popular in The Netherlands. See cat. nos. 173, 174.

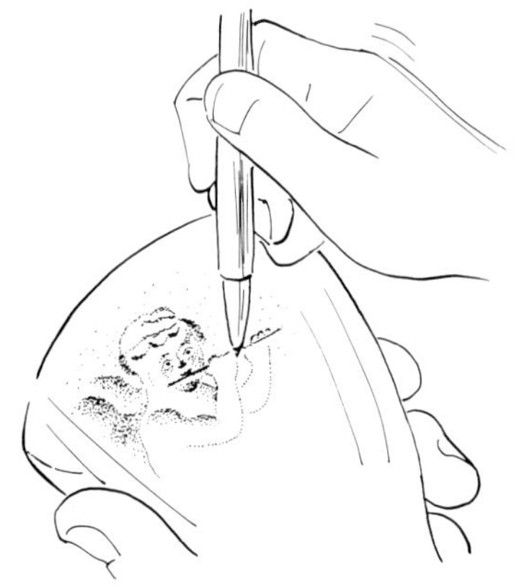

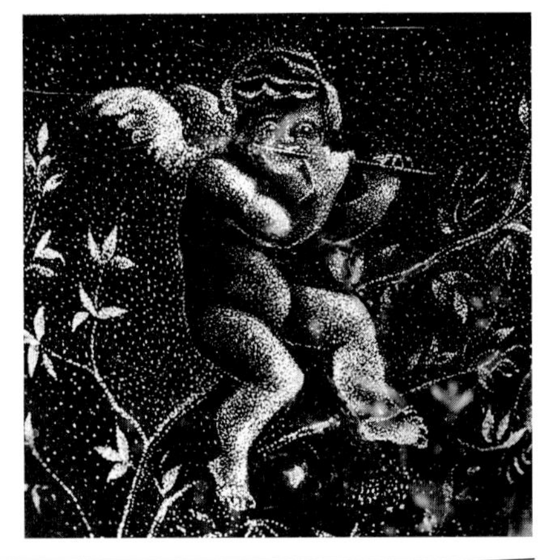

Diamond-Point Engraving

With a diamond point set into a holder, the decorator scratches ornamentation, writing, or figural depictions into the glass surface. Used in Roman and Islamic glass art. See cat. no. 64. Revived in Venice in the 16th century. See cat. no. 110, 130.

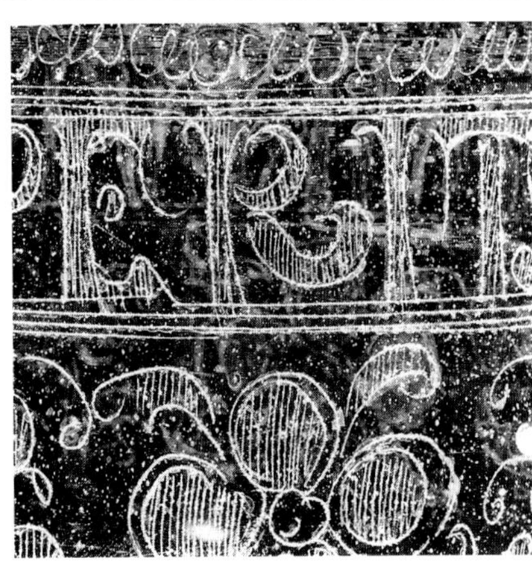

Cutting and Grinding

Working the glass surface with rotating wheels arranged vertically (cutting) or horizontally (grinding). Iron wheels are used with water and sand as an abrasive agent to roughen in the pattern, artificial or natural stone wheels with powdered pumice for smoothing. Finally the glass object can be polished by hand or with acid (with less precise results).
All evenly curved patterns and surface-grinding techniques (e.g., facets) are done on the horizontal wheel; decorative cut patterns, such as miters and circular or oval printies, on the vertical wheel.

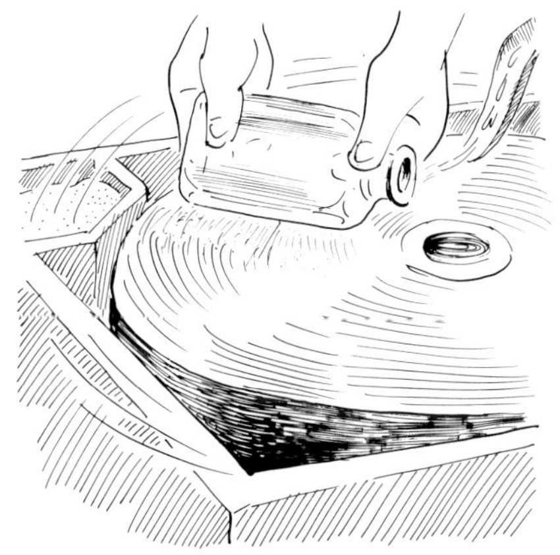

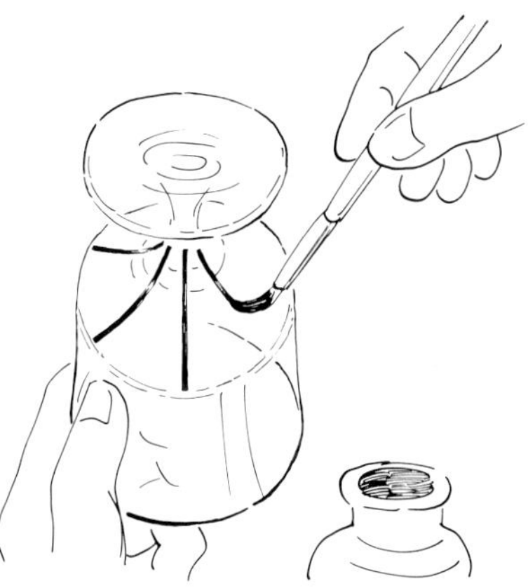

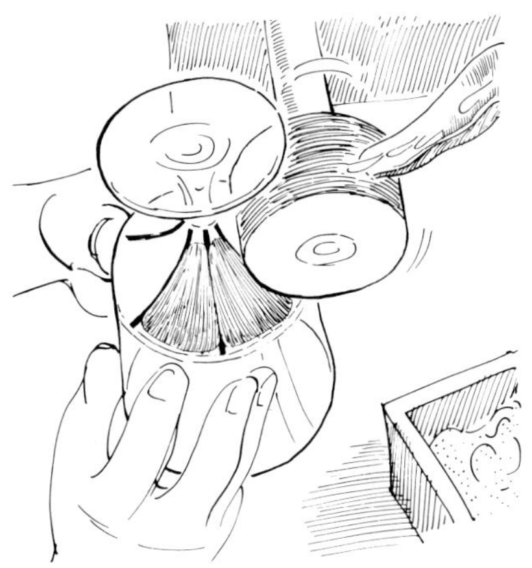

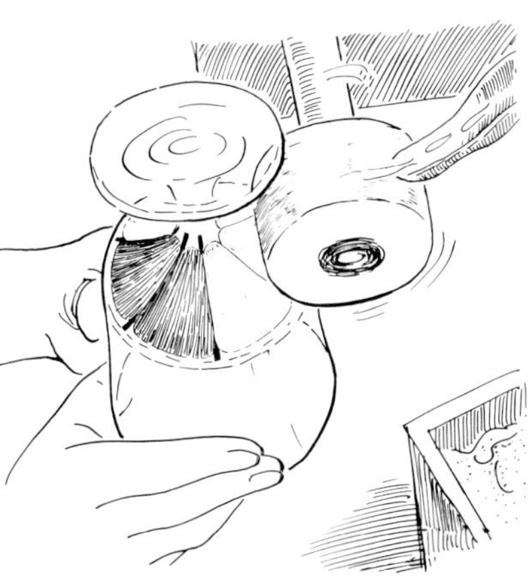

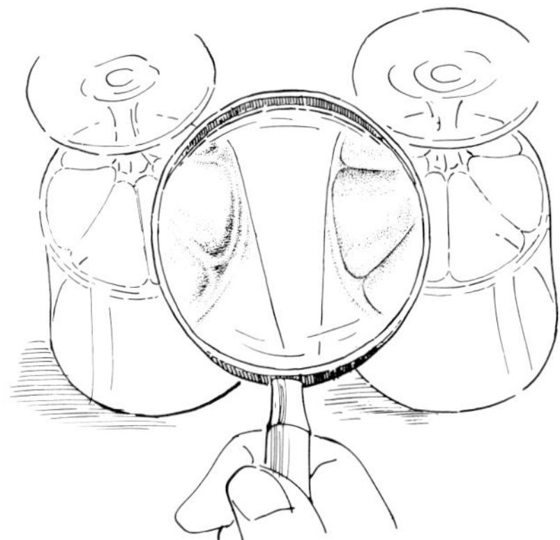

Sandblasting

Matting or incorporating decorative elements into the glass surface with the aid of a sandblasting "gun" or "pencil," which directs a stream of fine grains of sand or corundum onto the surface of the object under high pressure.

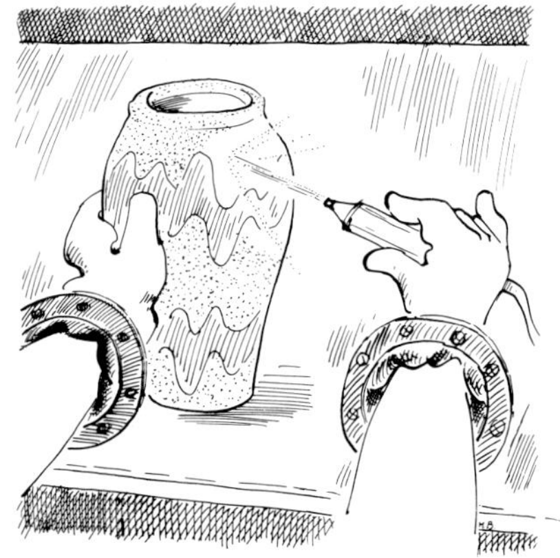

Etching Techniques

Surface treatment using hydrofluoric acid (hydrogen fluoride). Depending on the additives (sulfuric acid), etching can create mat, polished, or coarse surfaces.

Relief etching is done in several steps. At each stage, those areas not protected by asphaltic varnish, paraffin, or wax are removed.

Deep etching is carried out with particularly aggressive acid in one step.

Needle etching is created after scratching the protective lacquer with an etching needle. Only the incised line pattern emerges on the glass surface in the etching bath.
Used for signatures and interior details.

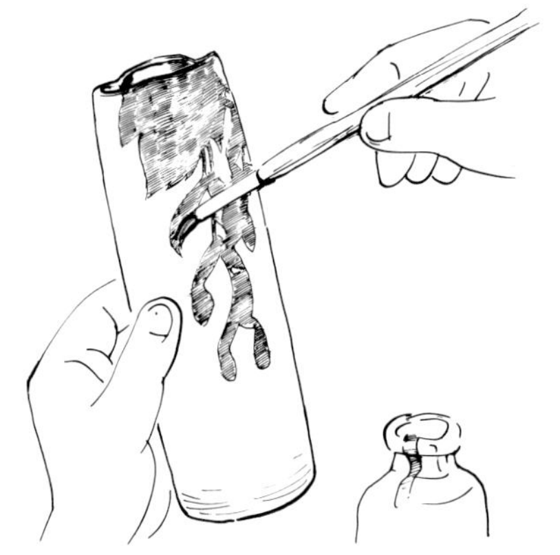

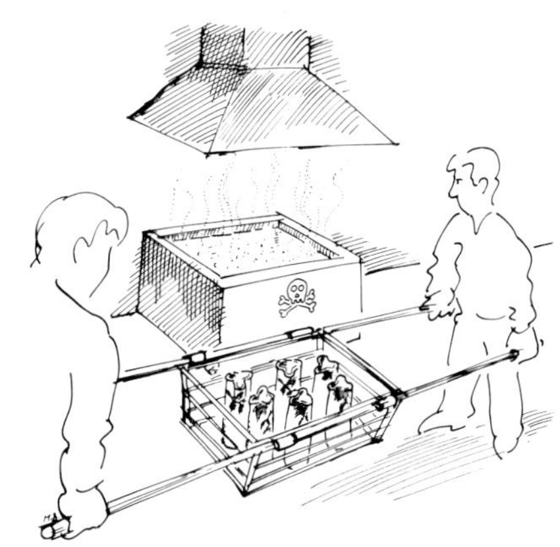

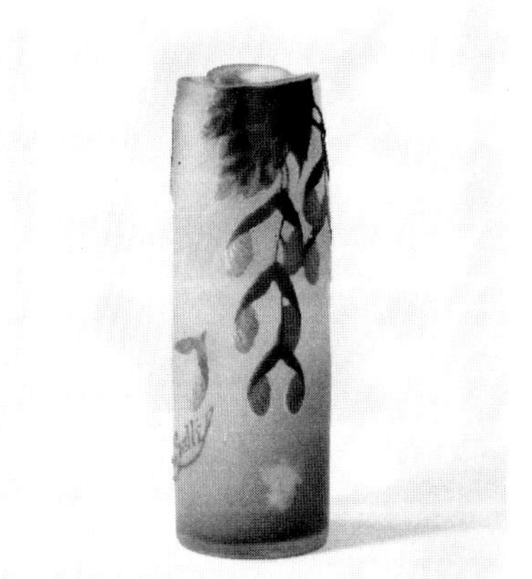

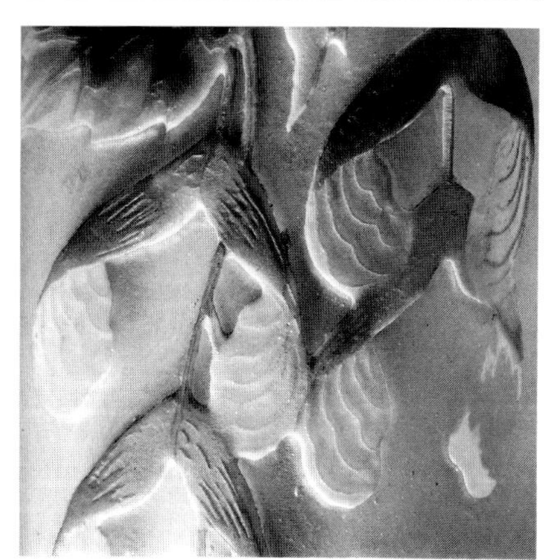

Staining

Coloring the glass surface by applying metallic salts and firing (sometimes several times). Silver salts create, for example, yellow stains, copper salts, red coloration. Redeveloped and improved in the first half of the 19th century by Friedrich Egermann.

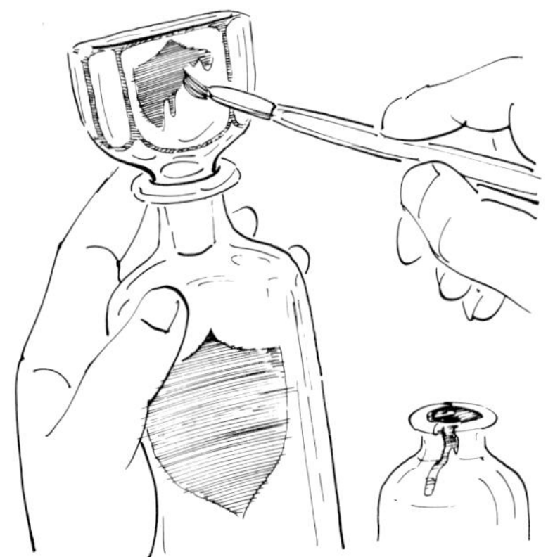

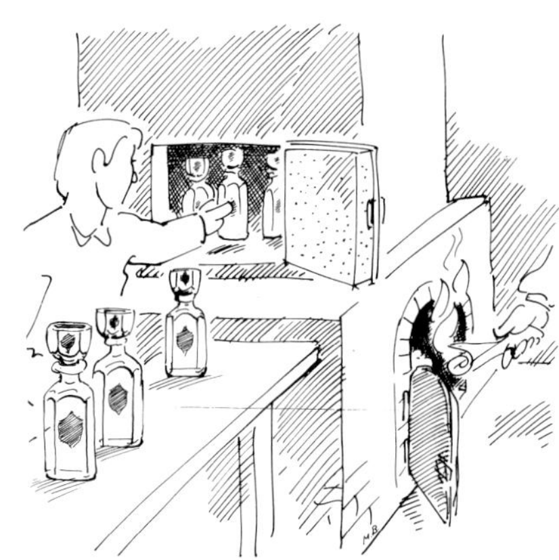

Zwischengoldglas (German, "gold between glass")

Gold leaf is applied to the glass surface and the depiction incised with scalpel and etching needle. A second glass is made to fit precisely over the first. The join is sealed. With beakers, the bottom is usually inserted separately. See cat. nos. 162, 163.
Fused *Zwischengoldglas* was made as early as in pre-Roman times.

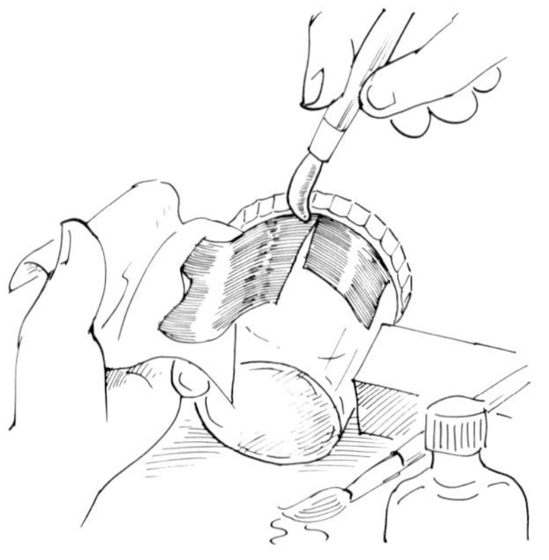
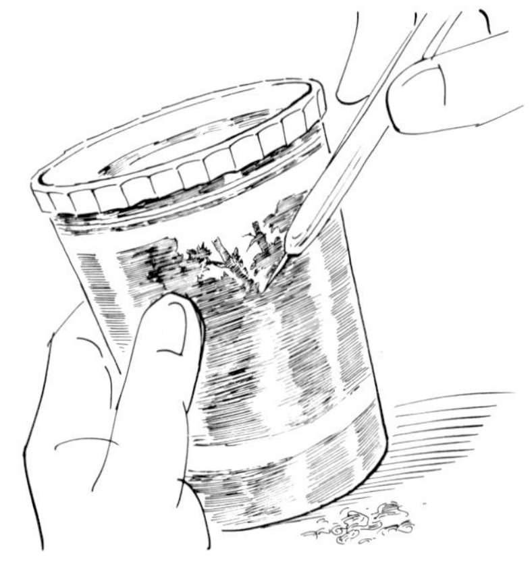

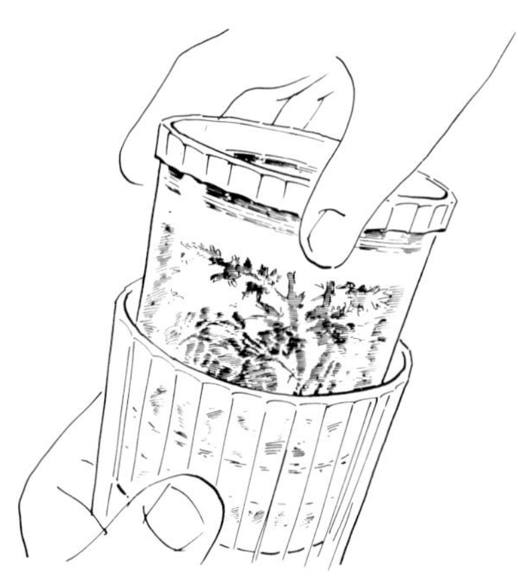
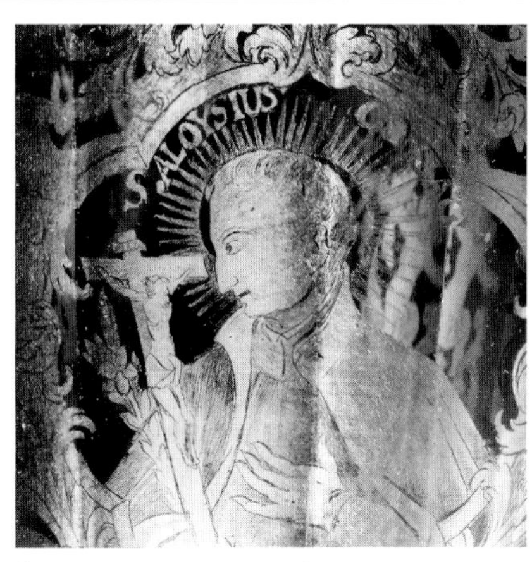

Antique Glass and Leaded Glass (Stained Glass)

The traditional artistic use of flat glass is in stained-glass windows. So-called antique glass made in a blowing and stretching process is cut out with stencils and connected with lead cames by soldering.

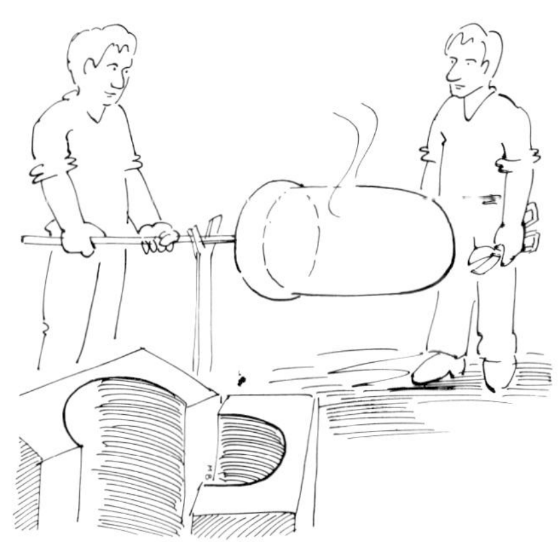
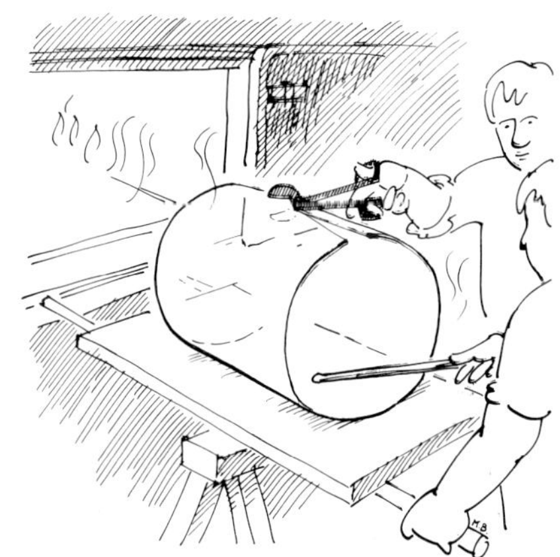

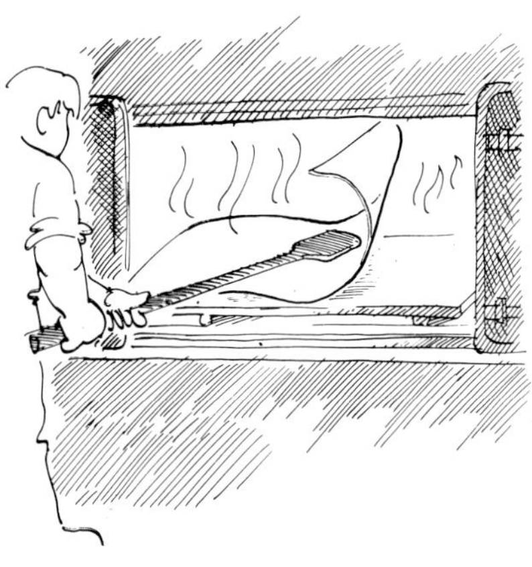
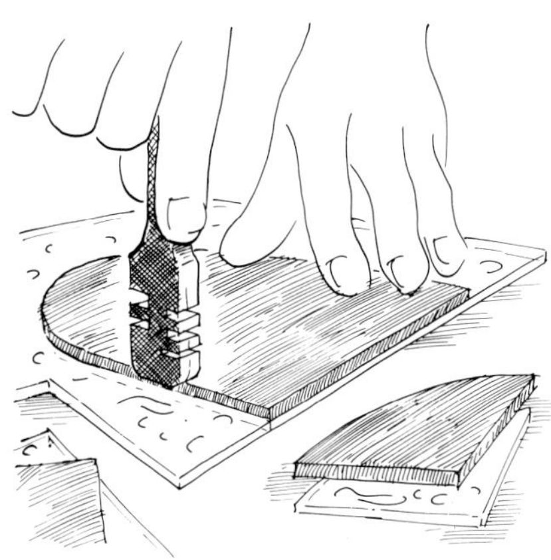
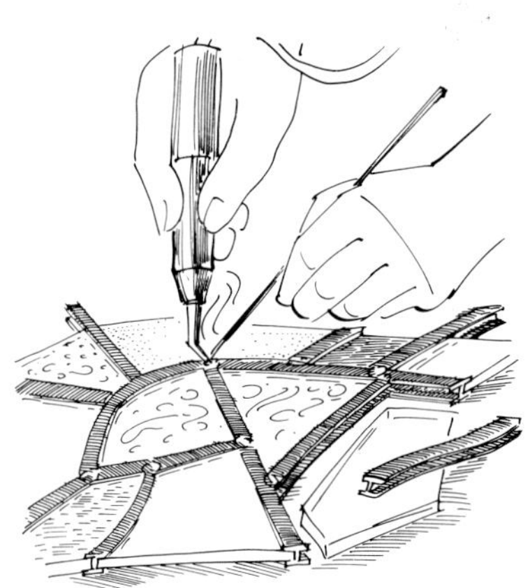

Flat Glass

Today machine-made flat glass (float glass)
and special glassware (e.g., insulating glass
vapor-blasted with metal, laminated glass)
are also used for artistic purposes—usually
by fusing or laminating several panes of glass
(see cat. nos. 428, 488) and subsequently
cutting, sandblasting, breaking, chipping,
drilling it, etc.

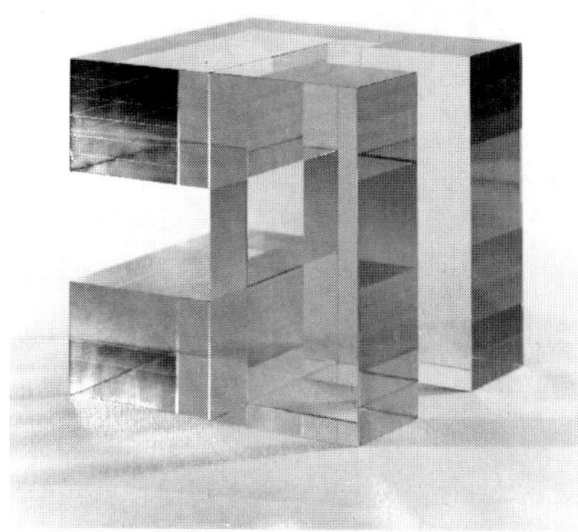

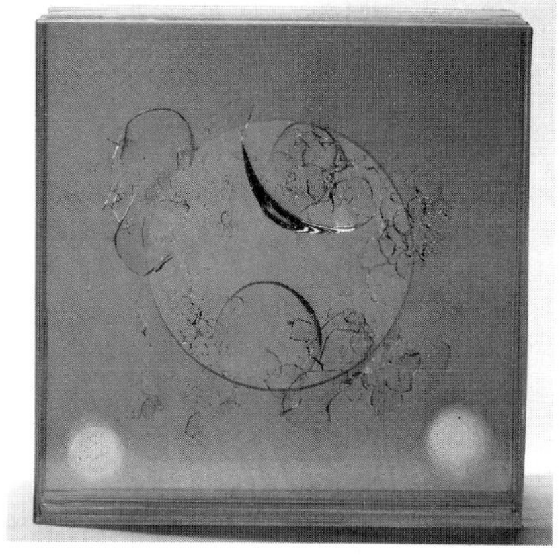

Kiln-forming: Cut panes of flat glass take the
shape in the muffle kiln of a fire-clay form.

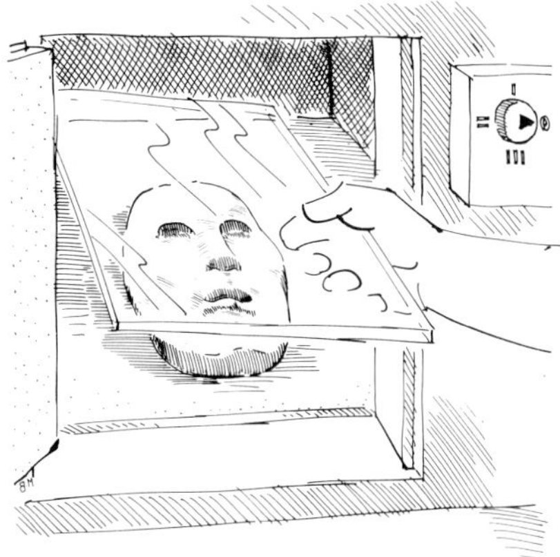

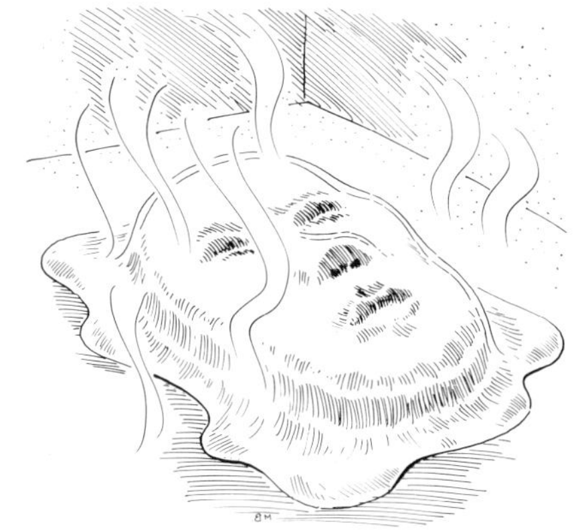

Studio Technology

The development of new types of small furnaces in the 1960s enabled artists to work in
their own studio workshops, independent of a
glassworks. These furnaces provided the basis
for the upswing of individual artistic glass
design in the 1970s and 1980s.
(Erwin Eisch at the studio furnace in the
Essener Glasgalerie.)

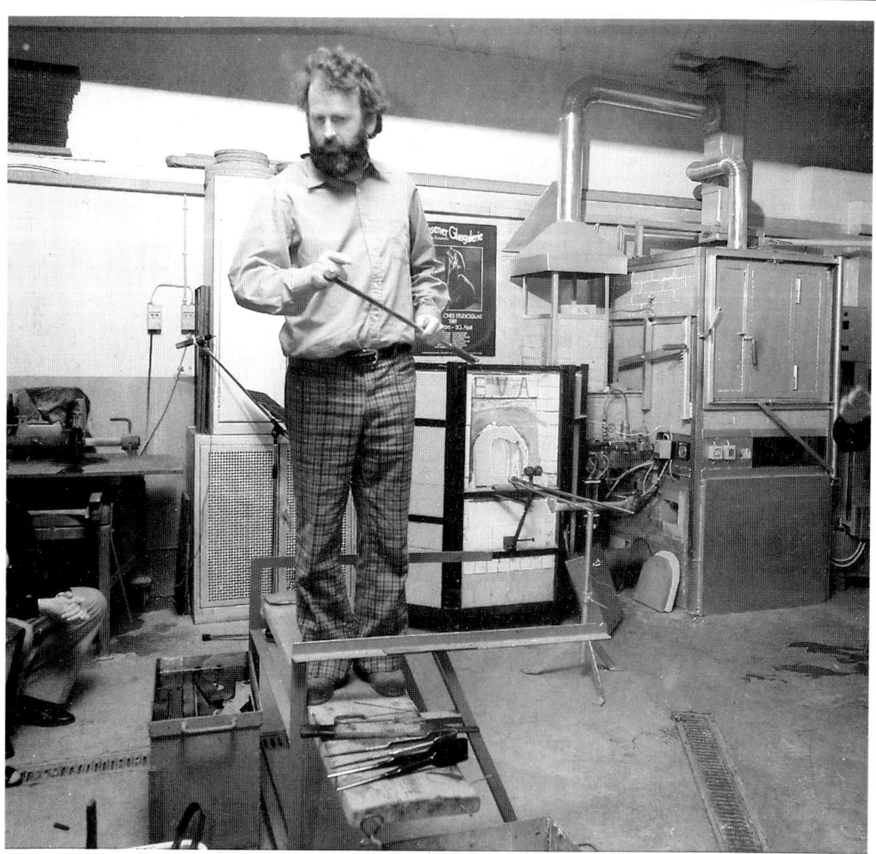

372

Reproductions Imitations Forgeries

The Glasmuseum Hentrich at the museum kunst palast has built up a publicly accessible study collection of glassware that illustrates the problem of authenticity. The terms reproduction, imitation, and forgery outline the three most important categories in classifying the material.

The term *reproduction*[1] signifies the attempt to make an identical copy of an object. The most direct means is to make a cast of the original and from that a blow mold. More common is simply to re-create the object using the same technique and materials in the most authentic way possible (F 10).

Imitations[2] attempt to approach the spirit of a period, adhering more or less closely to certain prototypes (F 1–3, 9, 12 A, B, 13 B). This can, as in historicism, be a legitimate attempt to create an artistic form, but can also have the aim to deceive. Only in this case, when the intent is fraudulent, is the term *forgery* appropriate.

A distinction must be made between *free forgeries*, which attempt to adapt the style of a certain period, but remain formally independent of a direct source (F 4, 6, 8, 13 A), and forgeries and reproductions made in historical imitation.

More common than real forgeries are *falsifications* of alleged older or newer glassware. *Objective falsification* describes all manipulations done on a piece, especially later additions of such decorative techniques as engraving, cutting, diamond-engraving, painting, gilding, staining, but also by adding, changing, or removing signatures, grinding off damaged sections, undesirable additions or mutilations, the assembling of parts that do not belong together (F 5), etc.

The term *subjective falsification* describes all false information supplied to the prospective buyer regarding the provenance of the piece, misleading assessments, etc. Another category could be the group of glass objects that have forfeited their authenticity to an unwittingly false evaluation.

The boundaries of these categories cannot be clearly delineated. Many nineteenth-century reproductions could justifiably be called imitations (F 10). It is even more difficult to make a binding distinction between imitation and forgery, since the term forgery presupposes a legal, not a formal, evaluation.

[1] Translator's note: In the original German text, the author uses the word *Kopie* and explains that it is equivalent to the word *Nachbildung* preferred in the 19th century.

[2] Translator's note: The author uses the German word *Nachahmungen* and explains that 19th-century sources usually speak of *Imitationen*.

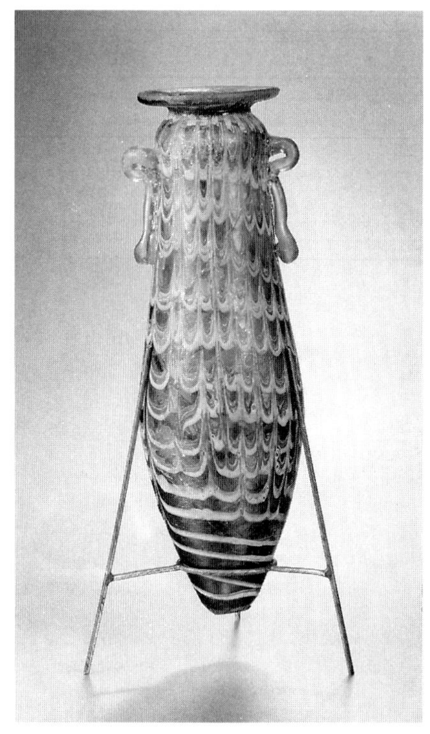

F 1 Alabastron

In the manner of pre-Roman core vessels

Murano (?), late 19th/early 20th c.
H 15.8, ⌀ 5.7 cm

Transparent manganese-violet glass, free-blown and shaped. Bluish white marvered thread decoration combed into a feather pattern.
Broken and glued.

Acc. no. L 1986-6
On loan from a private collection, Frankfurt

The vessel belongs to a large group of glassware that imitates the complicated core-forming process using the newer blowing technique.
Identifying such pieces is relatively simple. The antique ointment vessels of the sixth to third centuries BC are almost all completely opaque and show on the interior the rough surface of the clay core around which they were made. See cat. nos. 2–4 and p. 362. The pontil mark is usually visible on the blown copies—for technical reasons, a characteristic missing on authentic sandcore vessels. Attempts to grind off the pontil mark can usually be determined with a magnifying glass.

Lit.: Ricke, *Glasprobleme*, 1979, cat. no. 1 A

F 2 Fragment of a Mosaic-Glass Bowl

In the manner of the early imperial period of Roman glass

Murano, ca. 1870–90
H 11.8, ⌀ 23.1 cm

Manganese-violet and white sections of mosaic-glass canes, taken up with colorless glass and blown. Slightly iridescent. Numerous glued areas, formerly secured with five metal clamps, two of which are extant.

Acc. no. L 1986-5
On loan from a private collection, Frankfurt

The surface and color of the bowl bears an uncanny resemblance to securely attributed Roman glassware. The impression of an ancient piece is heightened by its fragmentary state and the old-fashioned type of restoration using metal clamps, a technique common for repairs made in the 17th and 18th centuries. The strong base of colorless glass onto which the mosaic-glass layer is built up proves that the bowl is a Venetian work of the 19th century. The iridescence is also clearly the result of chemicals vaporized in the furnace, not weathering underground.

Lit.: Ricke, *Glasprobleme*, 1979, cat. no. 2

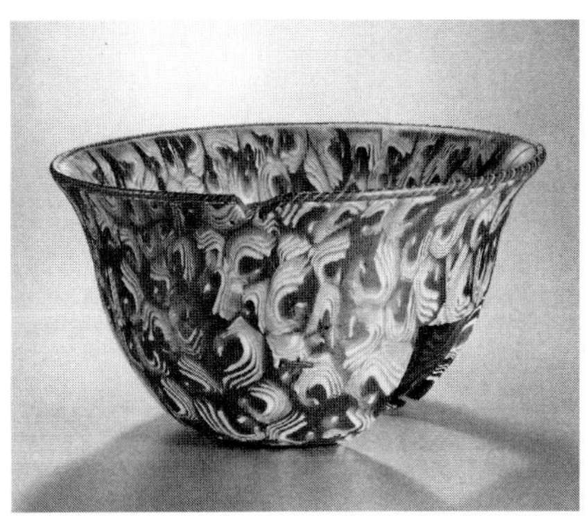

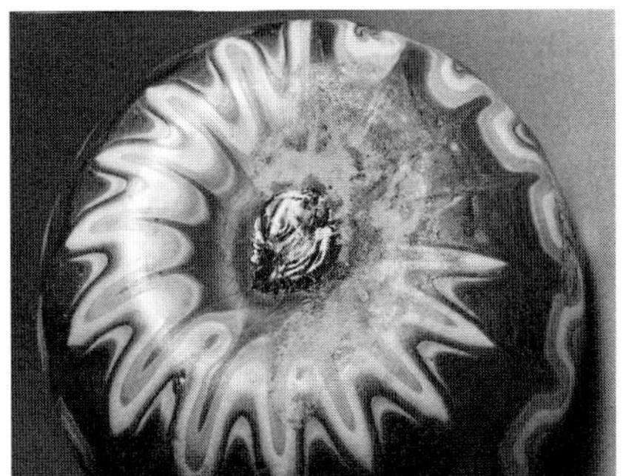

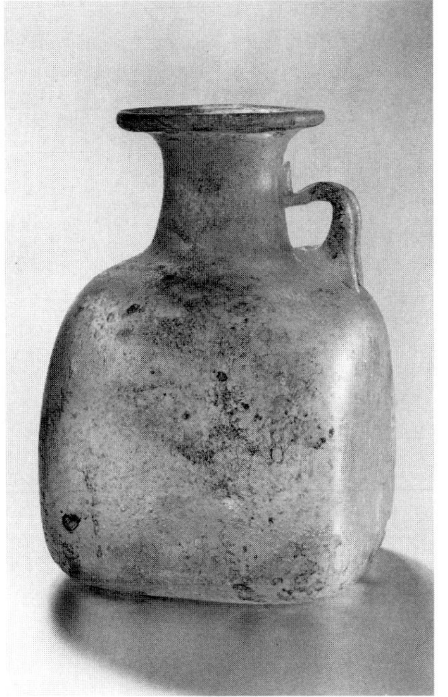

F 3 Handled Flask

In the manner of Roman vessels of the 1st and 2nd c. AD

Murano, 1970s
H 14.7, L (of side) 10.4 cm

Colorless glass interspersed with small air bubbles; mold-blown and shaped. Artificial impurities on the surface; iridescence partly mat, partly shiny.

Acc. no. P 1978-12

The bottle is an example of the imitations of historical—not only ancient—glassware still produced in Murano. The glassware is sold openly at low prices. The pieces have obviously not been produced with fraudulent intentions; they meet the tourists' demand for decorative souvenirs. Although none of these pieces was copied directly from an ancient prototype, glassware of this type has caused confusion amongst art dealers and collectors. The reason lies in the deliberately awkward technique used to produce it and in the convincing artificial aging. The iridescence on this group of glassware was achieved by dusting and fusing the glass surface with metallic salts and other chemicals with impurities. Since the piece is still attached to the pontil during this stage, there are no traces of the metallic coating at the point where the pontil was broken off.

Lit.: Ricke, *Glasprobleme*, 1979, cat. no. 4 A

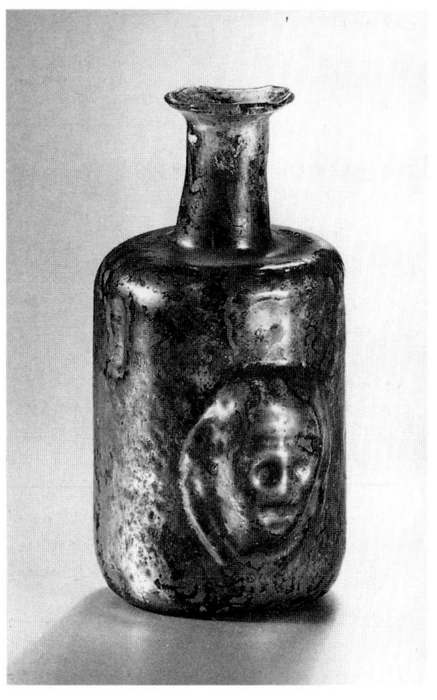

F 4 Bottle

Free forgery of a Roman vessel

Middle East (?), 1960s
H 11.3, ⌀ 7.2 cm

Colorless, slightly bubbly glass; amber stain on the interior. Artificially aged.

Acc. no. P 1965-54

Nothing comparable to the deliberately primitive face masks on this bottle is known to exist amongst securely attributed Roman glassware. Apparently the forger intended to create the impression that it is a previously unknown glass type.
The glass differs from authentic pieces primarily in its use of stains unknown in antiquity and the artificial aging. It was done on the cold piece with dissolved metallic salts, creating swaths, some of which can be seen flowing together—an effect not to be seen amongst naturally aged pieces.
The irregularly cut and insufficiently fused rim is presumably meant to give the impression of old crafts production, but stands in contrast to the evenly rounded, carefully folded mouths of comparable ancient pieces. The bottle was probably made with fraudulent intentions for the European and American markets.

Lit.: Ricke, *Glasprobleme*, 1979, cat. no. 6 A

F 5 Beaker

Conglomerate of various authentic fragments

Forgery of the 20th c.
H 7.4, ⌀ 4.3 cm

Neck: yellow-green pure glass. Base: greenish glass with small bubbles.

Acc. no. P 1965-190

The neck of a large, fine Islamic bottle was attached to a presumably Roman base, creating a new vessel for which there is no parallel in either Roman or Islamic glass art. The seam was filled in. The forger attempted to conceal it with particles of iridescence from other fragments. This retouching is no longer in evidence. The differences in the iridescence between the upper and lower sections, resulting from the different glass compositions and the different sites in which the pieces lay, are therefore all the more obvious.

Lit.: Ricke, *Glasprobleme*, 1979, cat. no. 10

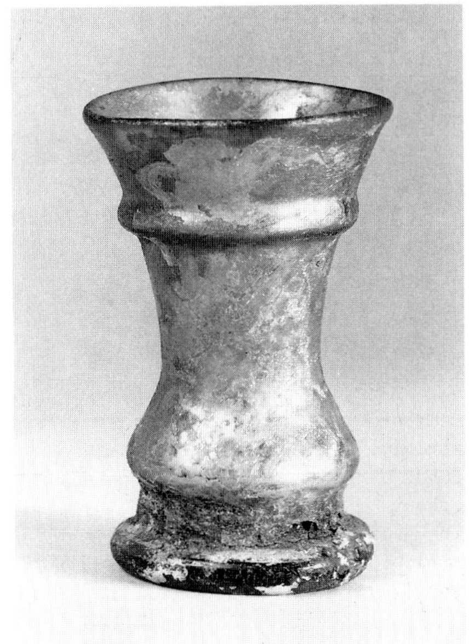

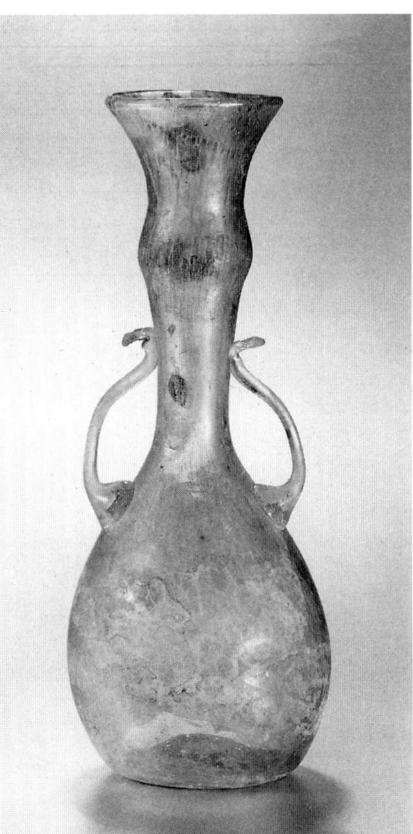

F 6 Two-handled Bottle

Free forgery of an Islamic vessel

Syria (?), 1950s/1960s
H 18.6, ⌀ 7.3 cm

Nearly colorless, slightly bluish glass. Fine glass-granule inclusions of a darker blue. Iridescence, artificial impurities.

Acc. no. P 1990-301 A
Gift of Uwe Friedleben, Hanover

This piece reveals a combination of styles. The shape of the bottle derives from Roman vessels; the details, such as the design of the bottle neck, are common to Islamic bottles. The treatment of the handles suggests Venetian vessels of the 17th century. Also unusual for ancient glass are the fine glass granules evenly embedded in the surface.
In spite of the numerous discrepancies, the vessel is convincing at first glance owing to the skillful artificial aging. Metallic iridescence was vapor-blasted onto the hot surface. After annealing the glass, an uneven mat layer of impurities was applied with acids. This work was treated with particular care at the pontil mark in order to conceal the iridescence missing at this point owing to the production method.

Lit.: Ricke, *Glasprobleme*, 1979, cat. no. 6 B

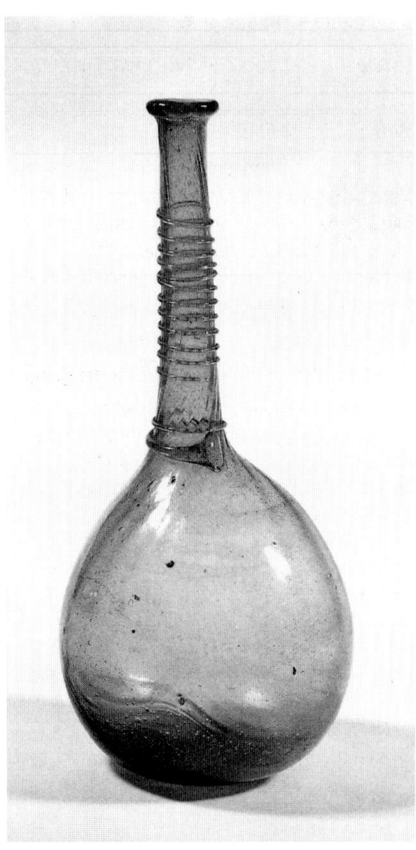

F 7 Bottle

In the manner of Islamic vessels

Middle East, 1970s/1980s
H 22.2, ⌀ 9.9 cm

Streaky, bubbly brown-green glass, optic-blown in a finely ribbed mold. Freely trailed thread. Pontil mark left visible.

Acc. no. P 1965-433

Glass craft production still exists in small glassworks in Egypt and Persia today, where unrefined glass and traditional Islamic vessel shapes are employed. Since Europeans are not familiar with these forms, this type of glassware is often misidentified and presented by dubious dealers as work of the 17th or 18th century.

Lit.: –

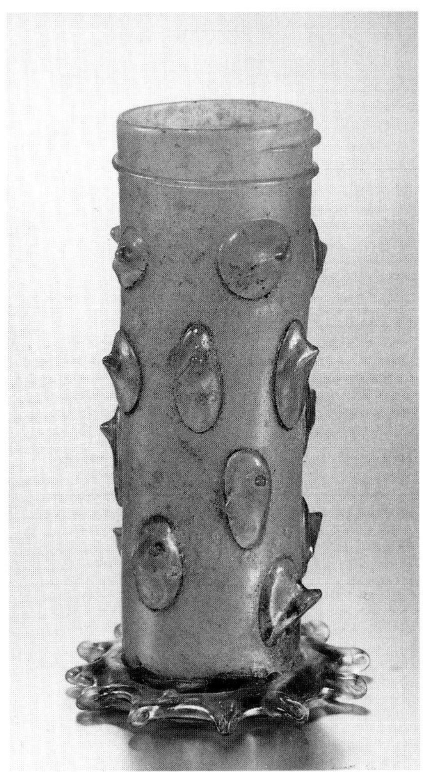

F 8 *Stangenglas*

Free forgery in the style of the early 16th c.

Germany or Murano, 1950s/1960s (?)
H 12.7, ⌀ 7.1 cm

Amber-colored glass, mold-blown and shaped.
Prunts applied and cut with shears. Drawn-out foot rim.
Iridescence, artificial impurities.

Acc. no. P 1974-7

The glass is part of a large group of carefully made forgeries of late medieval glassware.
The unusual color was deliberate and aspects of the technical execution were intended to give the impression of a rare but authentic piece.
The iridescence, vapor-blasted onto the hot glass, is visible only upon closer examination since the glass was also treated with acids. Notable is the lack of wear on the standing base of the glass. In addition, the folded foot-ring is too thick and the drawn-out points are disproportionate to the glass shape. Furthermore, it is unusual that the zigzag ring does not touch the ground. In genuine glassware of this type, the vessel normally stands on the points to create the impression of delicate lightness.
The workshop from which the glass originated also produced *Krautstrunk* glassware as reliquaries. They sometimes still appear at auctions or in galleries.

Lit.: Ricke, *Glasprobleme*, 1979, cat. no. 16

F 9 Beaker

In the manner of an early "Berkemeyer" of the 16th c.

Josef T. Böhm
Utrecht, 1950s
H 9.5, ⌀ 9.5 cm

Colorless hard glass, blown at the lamp. Artificially aged.

Acc. no. P 1980-28
Gift of Walter Spiegl, Munich

Josef Böhm produced a large collection of glassware in historicist forms, which he openly gave to dealers at an appropriate price. He never intended to deceive. In spite of this, dubious or uninformed dealers today occasionally attempt subjective falsification. Notable is the lightness of the pieces owing to the production process. Pieces that exactly reproduce prototypes are rare. Details, however, are often superbly copied.
The application of an artificial pontil mark on the underside of the vessel's base is disconcerting, since there is no technical reason for its presence in lampblown work.
The artificial aging was achieved by firing dissolved chemicals.
For other glassware by Böhm see Ricke, *Glasprobleme*, 1979, cat. nos. 17 A–C.

Lit.: –

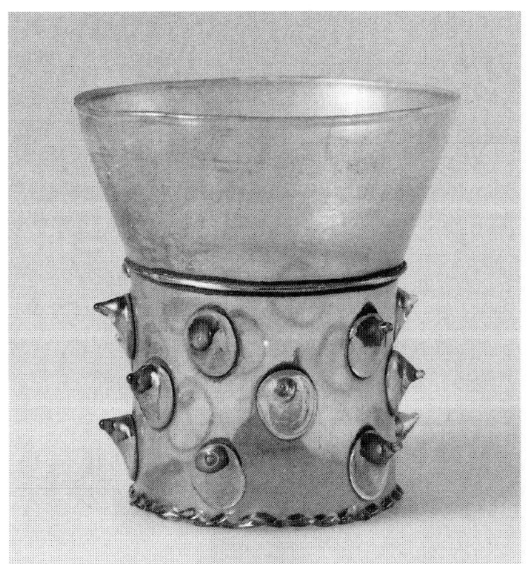

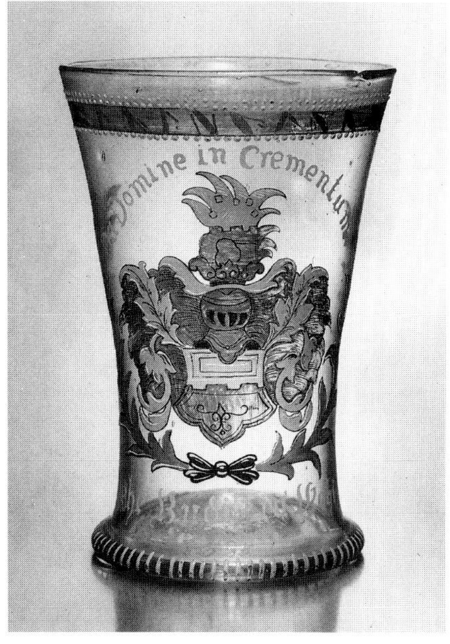

F 10 Beaker

Reproduction of an original from 1625, formerly at the Kunstgewerbemuseum Berlin

Mark: *FH 89/7.Org*
Petersdorfer Glashütte Fritz Heckert
Ca. 1880/90
H 14.9, ⌀ 10.2 cm

Colorless glass, slightly bubbly; mold-blown. Decoration: light blue coat of arms of the city of Bautzen on a gold ground, rust red opening in the helm, light green foliated vine. Inscriptions: *Da Domine in Crementum* and *Es gehe Budissin Wohl 1625*

Acc. no. P 1986-41

The enameled glass pieces of Fritz Heckert (see also p. 218) were clearly produced as historicist reproductions without dishonest intentions, but are still occasionally presented as authentic pieces.
Characteristic of Heckert's glassware is the treatment of the gold band below the mouth. It was applied with a brush in burnishing gold. Thick, diagonally applied, cross strokes were intended to give the impression of overlapping pieces of gold leaf. That was the common procedure for authentic glassware of the 17th century.
The signature *FH* can be found on numerous glasses by the company up to the early 20th century.
Many of these pieces are illustrated in a company pattern catalogue consisting of four color plates. See also A. von Saldern, *Kunst & Antiquitäten* 6 (1978): 41–44.

Lit.: Ricke, *Glasprobleme*, 1979, cat. no. 24

F 11 Goblet

Freely made in the style of the 17th century

Mallorca, Algaida, Gordiola Glassworks
1970s/1980s
H 21, ⌀ 10 cm

Amber-colored glass, comprising four parts.
Bowl and foot optic-blown in a ribbed mold
and shaped. Ornamentation freely applied
and worked with pincers. Pontil mark not
ground.

Acc. no. L 1986-2
On loan from a private collection

Similar to contemporary production in the
Middle East (cf. F 7), the craft production of
traditional glassware with national characteristics has survived at a few small glassworks
in Spain and Portugal. The growing number
of tourists in recent years has helped these
glassworks to a considerable upswing.
As these vessels are heavy and somewhat
crude they are often thought to be older than
they are.

Lit.: –

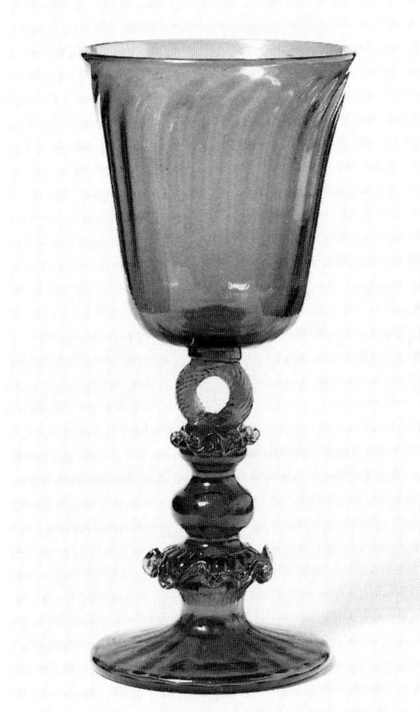

F 12 A, B Vases

In the manner of Bohemian and American
Art-Nouveau glassware

Freih. v. Poschinger'sche Krystallglasfabrik
"Axum" series, model nos. 4188, 4227
Frauenau, early 1970s
H 15.6, 25.2; ⌀ 20, 16.3 cm

A: dark red ruby glass, mold-blown, furnace-
made iridescence; free-formed crackling. B: red
overlay on milk-glass ground, mold-blown,
furnace-made iridescence—inside ocher to
salmon-colored, outside shiny gold; free-
formed crackling.

Acc. no. P 1975-89
Acc. no. P 1987-61 Gift of Uwe Friedleben,
Hanover

The pieces belong to a large group of vases
and bowls freely oriented on the forms of Art
Nouveau, which—doubtlessly without the
intention to deceive—attempted to take contemporary tastes into account. The glassware
exemplifies the revived technical possibilities
of metallic iridescence at the furnace.
Glassware from this group was, however, presented abroad as originals from around 1900.
Examples of falsification have become known,
particularly from America through the later
addition of such signatures as *L.C. Tiffany,
L.C.T., Quezal, Loetz Austria,* and others.

Lit.: Ricke, *Glasprobleme*, 1979, cat. nos. 40
A, B

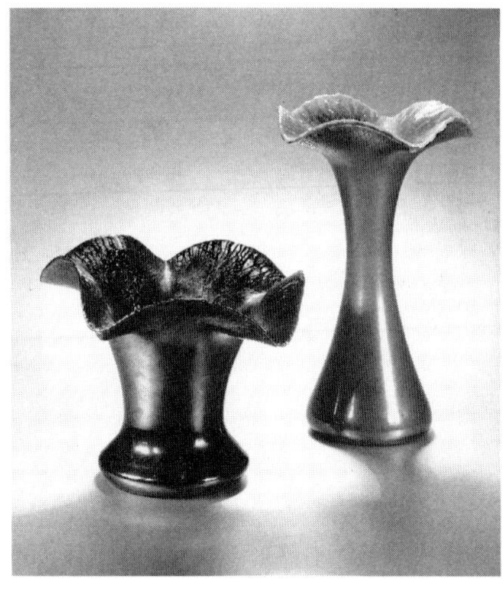

F 13 A, B Decorative Glasses

In the manner of Karl Koepping

A: mark: *F x*
Karlheinz Feldbusch, Bremen, 1976
H 22.4, ⌀ 7.5 cm

Dark red; yellow tones (fired silver chloride)
on the surface of the stem; whitish, embedded, encircling threads in the bowl; colorless
leaf with orange stripe.

B: mark: *Kö 189(0)*?
Anonymous, Germany, ca. 1970–75
H 26.7, ⌀ 5.7 cm

Dark blue; yellowish green spreading tones
(fired silver chloride); brown-orange spiral
band in the bowl; colorless leaves with
brownish-blue stripes.
Both glasses lampblown and shaped from
soft-glass tubes and canes.

Acc. no. P 1976-42; gift of the manufacturer
Acc. no. P 1987-60; gift of Uwe Friedleben,
Hanover

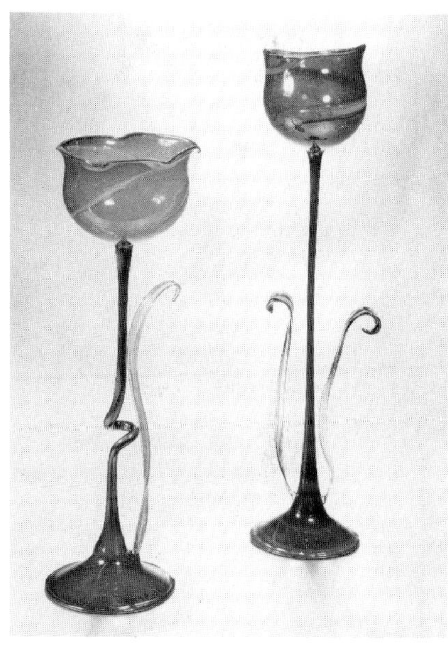

The glasses bear witness to the increased
interest in decorative Art-Nouveau glassware,
in particular the lampblown floral goblets as
they were made around 1900 after designs by
Karl Koepping (see cat. no. 342).
Works by Karlheinz Feldbusch (A) are clearly
signed *F x*, sometimes with applied thread,
sometimes by engraving.
Similar glassware without signatures or with
the abbreviation *Kö* (presumably meant as a
contraction of Koepping) below the bowl in
yellow thread application and usually with
illegible or mutilated dating (B) misled dealers and collectors in the first half of the
1970s. New pieces with such signatures have
not become known recently.

Lit.: Ricke, *Glasprobleme*, 1979,
cat. nos. 39 A, B

Literature Cited

3000 Jahre, Lucerne, 1981
   3000 Jahre Glaskunst von der Antike bis zum Jugendstil. Exh. cat. Lucerne: Kunstmuseum Luzern, 1981.

Abercron, sales cat., 1973
   W. von Abercron. *Malerei, Graphik und Kunsthandwerk um 1900*. Sales cat. Cologne, 1973.

Adlerová, *Böhmisches Glas Gegenwart*, 1973
   A. Adlerová. *Böhmisches Glas der Gegenwart*. Exh. cat. Hamburg: Museum für Kunst und Gewerbe Hamburg, 1973.

Aloi and Nicodemi, *Vetri d'oggi*, 1955
   R. Aloi and G. Nicodemi. *Esempi di decorazione moderna di tutto il mondo: Vetri d'oggi*. Milan, 1955.

Americans in Glass, 1984
   Americans in Glass. Exh. cat. Wausau, WI: The Leigh Yawkey Woodson Art Museum, 1984.

Arwas, *Art Nouveau*, 1977
   V. Arwas. *Glass: Art Nouveau to Art Déco*. London, 1977.

Barovier Mentasti, "Vetraria moderna," 1977
   R. Barovier Mentasti. "La Vetraria veneziana moderna dal 1895 al 1920." *JGS* 19 (1977): 147–59.

Barovier Mentasti, *Murano '900*, 1977
   R. Barovier Mentasti. *Vetri di Murano dell '900*. Exh. cat. Murano, Venice: Museo Vetrario, 1977.

Barovier Mentasti, *Murano '800*, 1978
   R. Barovier Mentasti. *Vetri di Murano dell '800*. Exh. cat. Murano, Venice: Museo Vetrario, 1978.

Barovier Mentasti, *Vetro Veneziano*, 1982
   R. Barovier Mentasti. *Il vetro Veneziano*. Milan, 1982.

Barovier Mentasti, *Venetian Glass*, 1992
   R. Barovier Mentasti. *Venetian Glass, 1890–1990*. Venice, 1992.

Barten and Hakenjos, *Gallé*, 1980
   S. Barten and B. Hakenjos. *Emile Gallé: Keramik, Glas und Möbel des Art Nouveau*. Exh. cat. Zurich: Museum Bellerive Zürich, 1980.

Baumgärtner, *Sammlung Heine*, 1977
   S. Baumgärtner. *Edles altes Glas: Die Sammlung Heinrich Heine Karlsruhe*. Exh. cat. 2nd ed. Karlsruhe: Badisches Landesmuseum Karlsruhe, 1977.

Baumgärtner, Regensburg, 1977
   S. Baumgärtner. *Gläser: Antike—Mittelalter—Neuere Zeit: Museum der Stadt Regensburg: Katalog der Glassammlung: Sammlung Brauser*. Coll. cat. Karlsruhe, 1977.

Baumgärtner, *Sächsisches Glas*, 1977
   S. Baumgärtner. *Sächsisches Glas: Die Glashütten und ihre Erzeugnisse*. Wiesbaden, 1977.

Baumgärtner, *Porträtgläser*, 1981
   S. Baumgärtner. *Porträtgläser: Das gläserne Bildnis aus drei Jahrhunderten*. Munich, 1981.

Baumgärtner, Bremen I, 1987
   S. Baumgärtner. *Glaskunst vom Mittelalter bis zum Klassizismus*. Coll. cat. Bremen: Bremer Landesmuseum and Focke-Museum, 1987.

Baumgärtner, Bremen II, 1988
   S. Baumgärtner. *Glaskunst vom Empire bis zum Historismus*. Coll. cat. Bremen: Bremer Landesmuseum and Focke-Museum, 1988.

Baumgartner and Krueger, *Mittelalter*, 1988
   E. Baumgartner and I. Krueger. *Phönix aus Sand und Asche: Glas des Mittelalters*. Exh. cat. Rheinisches Landesmuseum Bonn. Munich, 1988.

Beard, *Modern Glass*, 1976
   G. Beard. *International Modern Glass*. London, 1976.

Biedermeier, The Hague, 1972
   Glas Empire Biedermeier. Exh. cat. The Hague: Haags Gemeentemuseum, 1972.

Bloch-Dermant, *French Glass, 1860–1914*, 1980
   J. Bloch-Dermant. *The Art of French Glass: 1860–1914*. London, 1980.

Bloch-Dermant, *French Glass*, 1988
   J. Bloch-Dermant. *French Glass: Gallé to the Present*. Paris, 1988.

Bloch-Dermant, *Argy-Rousseau*, 1990
   J. Bloch-Dermant. *Gabriel Argy-Rousseau: Glassware as Art; With a Catalogue Raisonné of Pâtes de Verre*. London, 1990.

Blount, *French Cameo*, 1968
   B. and H. Blount. *French Cameo Glass*. Des Moines, IA, 1968.

Bosch, *Hausmaler*, 1984
   H. Bosch. *Die Nürnberger Hausmaler: Emailfarbendekor auf Gläsern und Fayencen der Barockzeit*. In collaboration with C. Kemp, I. Stahl, and R. Himpsl. Munich, 1984.

Bröhan, *Kunsthandwerk 1*, 1976
   K. H. Bröhan. *Kunst der Jahrhundertwende und der zwanziger Jahre: Sammlung Karl H. Bröhan, Berlin 2. Kunsthandwerk*, part 1: *Jugendstil. Werkbund. Art Déco. Glas, Holz, Keramik*. Berlin, 1976.

Bröhan, *20er und 30er Jahre*, 1985
   K. H. Bröhan. *Kunst der 20er und 30er Jahre: Sammlung Karl H. Bröhan, Berlin 3. Gemälde. Skulpturen, Kunsthandwerk. Industriedesign*. Berlin, 1985.

T. Bröhan, *Glaskunst der Moderne*, 1992
   T. Bröhan, ed. *Glaskunst der Moderne: Von Josef Hoffmann bis Wilhelm Wagenfeld*. Munich, 1992.

Cappa, *100 ans Europe*, 1983
   G. Cappa. *100 ans d'art verriers en Europe*. Exh. cat. Brussels: Société Génerale de Banque Bruxelles, 1983.

Charleston, *Masterpieces*, 1980
   R. J. Charleston. *Masterpieces of Glass: A World History from the Corning Museum of Glass*. New York, 1980.

Charpentier and Thiébaut, *Gallé*, 1985
   T. Charpentier and P. Thiébaut. *Gallé*. Exh. cat. Paris: Musée du Luxembourg, 1985.

Coburg I, 1977
   H. Maedebach, M. Maedebach, and E. Heller-Winter. *Coburger Glaspreis 1977*. Exh. cat. Coburg: Kunstsammlungen der Veste Coburg, 1977.

Coburg II, 1985
   J. Kruse, M. Maedebach, and S. Netzer. *Zweiter Coburger Glaspreis für moderne Glasgestaltung in Europa*. Exh. cat. Coburg: Kunstsammlungen der Veste Coburg, 1985.

Corning, *Glass 1959*, 1959
   Glass 1959: A Special Exhibition of International Glass. Exh. cat. Corning, NY: The Corning Museum of Glass, 1959.

Corning, *New Glass*, 1979
   New Glass: A Worldwide Survey. Exh. cat. Corning, NY: The Corning Museum of Glass, 1979.

Darmstadt, *Dokument*, 1977
   Ein Dokument Deutscher Kunst—Darmstadt 1901–1976. Exh. cat. Vols. 1–5. Darmstadt: Mathildenhöhe and Hessisches Landesmuseum, 1977.

Daum, *Mastery*, 1985
   N. Daum. Daum: *Mastery of Glass*. Lausanne, 1985.

Daverio, *Tiffany*, 1974
   P.-J. Daverio. *Louis Comfort Tiffany*. Lausanne, 1974.

Dikshit, *Indian Glass*, 1969
   M. G. Dikshit. *History of Indian Glass*. Bombay, 1969.

DK
   Die Kunst. Munich, 1899=1900ff. (Volumes with even numbers, and the subtitle *Angewandte Kunst*, are numbered up to 60, from 1929 they are identical with the journal *Dekorative Kunst*.)

DKD
   Deutsche Kunst und Dekoration. Darmstadt, 1897/98ff.

Doros, Norfolk Cat., 1978
   P. E. Doros. *The Tiffany Collection of the Chrysler Museum at Norfolk*. Richmond, 1978.

Dreier, *Venezianische Gläser*, 1989
   F. A. Dreier. *Venezianische Gläser und "Façon de Venise"*: Kataloge des Kunstgewerbemuseums Berlin 12. Berlin, 1989.

L'Ecole de Nancy, 1999
   L'Ecole de Nancy, 1889–1909: Art Nouveau et industries d'art. Exh. cat. Nancy: Galleries Poiret. Paris, 1999.

Ernst, *Moderne Gläser*, 1955
   H. Ernst. *Moderne Gläser*. Darmstadt, n.d. [1955]

Fahr Becker-Sterner, *Fünfziger*, 1984
G. Fahr Becker-Sterner et al. *Die Fünziger: Stilkonturen eines Jahrzehnts. Italien, Skandinavien, Frankreich, Deutschland, USA, Polen, England, Niederlande.* Exh. cat. Munich: Villa Stuck, 1984

Frantz, *Contemporary Glass*, 1989
S. K. Frantz. *Contemporary Glass: A World Survey from the Corning Museum of Glass.* New York, 1989.

Fukai, *Persian Glass*, 1977
S. Fukai. *Persian Glass.* New York, Tokyo, and Kyoto, 1977.

Gallé, *Ecrits*, 1908
E. Gallé. *Ecrits pour l'art, floriculture, art décoratif, notices d'exposition (1884–1889).* Paris, 1908. Reprint Marseilles, 1980.

Garner, *Gallé*, 1976
P. Garner. *Gallé.* London, 1976.

Glasrevue
Tschechoslowakische Glasrevue. Prague, nos. 1–22: 1946–67. *Glasrevue.* Prague, nos. 23–47: 1968–92. *Neue Glasrevue.* Prague, nos. 47ff.: 1992ff.

Glass of the Caesars, 1987
D. B. Harden, H. Hellenkemper, K. Painter, and D. Whitehouse. *Glass of the Caesars.* Exh. cat. Cologne: Römisch-Germanisches Museum der Stadt Köln; London: The British Museum; Corning, NY: The Corning Museum of Glass. Milan, 1987.

Goldstein, *Pre-Roman*, 1979
S. Goldstein. *Pre-Roman and Early Roman Glass in The Corning Museum of Glass.* Corning, NY, 1979.

Grimm, *Glück und Glas*, 1984
C. Grimm, ed. *Glück und Glas: Zur Kulturgeschichte des Spessartglases: Veröffentlichungen zur Bayerischen Geschichte und Kultur, no. 2 (1984).* Munich, 1984.

Grose, *Toledo*, 1989
D. F. Grose. *The Toledo Museum of Art: Early Ancient Glass: Core-formed, Rod-formed, and Cast Vessels and Objects from the Late Bronze Age to the Early Roman Empire: 1600 B.C. to A.D. 50.* New York, 1989.

Grover, *European Art Glass*, 1970
R. and L. Grover. *Carved and Decorated European Art Glass.* Rutland, VT, 1970.

Haase, *Sächsisches Glas*, 1988
G. Haase. *Sächsisches Glas.* Leipzig, 1988.

Heinemeyer, *Glas*, 1966
E. Heinemeyer. Kataloge des Kunstmuseums Düsseldorf I. Glas 1. Düsseldorf, 1966.

Heiremans, *Murano*, 1993
M. Heiremans. *Art Glass from Murano: Glas-Kunst aus Murano, 1910–1970.* Stuttgart, 1993.

Henkes, *Glas zonder glans*, 1994
H. E. Henkes. *Glas zonder glans: Vijf eeuwen gebruiksglas uit de bodem van de Lage Landen, 1300–1800.* Exh. cat. Text in Dutch and English. Rotterdam: Museum Boymans-van Beuningen, 1994.

Hess and Husband, *Getty*, 1997
C. Hess and T. Husband. *European Glass in The J. Paul Getty Museum.* Coll. cat. Malibu: The J. Paul Getty Museum. Los Angeles, 1997.

Hilschenz, *Jugendstil*, 1973
H. Hilschenz. *Das Glas des Jugendstils: Katalog der Sammlung Hentrich im Kunstmuseum Düsseldorf.* Munich, 1973.

Hilschenz-Mlynek and Ricke, *Frankreich*, 1985
H. Hilschenz-Mlynek and H. Ricke. *Glas: Historismus, Jugendstil, Art Déco.* Vol. 1, *Frankreich.* Die Sammlung Hentrich im Kunstmuseum Düsseldorf. Munich, 1985.

Himmelheber, *Biedermeier*, 1988
G. Himmelheber et al. *Die Kunst des Biedermeier 1815–1835: Architektur, Malerei, Plastik, Kunsthandwerk, Musik, Dichtung und Mode.* Exh. cat. Munich: Bayerisches Nationalmuseum München, 1988.

Iittala, *Triennales*, 1987
Iittala Milanon Triennaaleissa. Iittala in the Triennales of Milan. Exh. cat. Iittala: Iittala Glass Museum, 1987.

JGS
Journal of Glass Studies. Corning, NY: The Corning Museum of Glass, 1959ff.

Joppien, *Tiffany*, 1999
R. Joppien. *Louis C. Tiffany: Meisterwerke des amerikanischen Jugendstils.* Exh. cat. Hamburg: Museum für Kunst und Gewerbe Hamburg. Cologne, 1999.

Kämpfer, *Viertausend Jahre*, 1966
F. Kämpfer. *Viertausend Jahre Glas.* Munich, 1966.

Keisch and Netzer, *Preussen*, 2001
C. Keisch and S. Netzer. *Herrliche Künste und Manufacturen: Fayence, Glas und Tapisserien aus der Frühzeit Brandenburg-Preussens 1680–1720.* Exh. cat. Berlin: Kunstgewerbemuseum (part of the joint exhibition Berlin and Brandenburg "Preussen 2000"). Berlin, 2001.

KKh
Kunst und Kunsthandwerk. Vienna, 1898ff.

Klesse, *Sammlung Krug*, 1965
B. Klesse. *Glassammlung Helfried Krug* 1. Munich, 1965.

Klesse, *Sammlung Krug*, 1973
B. Klesse. *Glassammlung Helfried Krug* 2. Bonn, 1973.

Klesse and Reineking, Cologne, 1973
B. Klesse and G. Reineking-von Bock. *Kunstgewerbemuseum der Stadt Köln: Glas.* Coll. cat. Cologne, 1973.

Klesse and Saldern, *Sammlung Biemann*, 1978
B. Klesse and A. von Saldern. *500 Jahre Glaskunst: Sammlung Biemann.* Zurich, 1978.

Klesse and Mayr, *Sammlung Funke-Kaiser*, 1981
B. Klesse and H. Mayr. *Glas vom Jugendstil bis heute: Sammlung Gertrud und Dr. Karl Funke-Kaiser.* Cologne, 1981.

Klesse, *Gallé*, 1982
B. Klesse. *Auf den künstlerischen Spuren Emile Gallés: Gläser und ihre Entwürfe.* Exh. cat. Cologne: Kunstgewerbemuseum, 1982.

Klesse and Mayr, *Wolf Collection*, 1987
B. Klesse and H. Mayr. *European Glass from 1500–1800: The Ernesto Wolf Collection.* Vienna, 1987.

Koch, *Tiffany*, 1976
R. Koch. *Tiffany und seine Glaskunst.* Stuttgart, 1976.

Kroeger, *Nishapur*, 1995
J. Kroeger. *Nishapur: Glass of the Early Islamic Period.* Coll. cat. New York: The Metropolitan Museum of Art, 1995.

KuH
Kunst und Handwerk. Munich, 1851ff.

Lassen and Schlüter, *Dansk Glas*, 1987
E. Lassen and M. Schlüter. *Dansk Glas 1925–1985.* Copenhagen, 1987.

Lierke, "Rippenschalen," 1993
R. Lierke. "'aliud torno teritur': Rippenschalen und die Spuren einer unbekannten Technologie: Heisses Glas auf der Töpferscheibe," *Antike Welt* 24 (1993): 218–34.

Lierke, "Turning Wheel," 1993
R. Lierke. "It Was the Turning Wheel and not the Lathe: Mold Pressing and Mold Turning of Hot Glass in Ancient Glass Vessel Production." *Glastechnische Berichte* 66, no. 12 (1993): 321–29.

Lötz 1, Lötz 2, 1989
H. Ricke, T. Vlček, A. Adlerová, and E. Ploil, eds. *Lötz: Böhmisches Glas 1880–1940.* Coauthors: J. Mergl, D. Panenková, and W. Hennig. Vol. 1, *Werkmonographie.* Vol. 2, *Katalog der Musterschnitte.* Munich, 1989.

McKean, *Tiffany*, 1980
H. McKean. *The 'Lost' Treasures of Louis Comfort Tiffany.* New York, 1980.

Marcilhac, *Lalique*, 1989
F. Marcilhac. *René Lalique, 1860–1945. Maître verrier: Analyse de l'oeuvre et catalogue raisonné.* Paris, 1989.

Meisenthal, 1999
Meisenthal: Berceau du verre: Art nouveau. Exh. cat. Meisenthal: Musée du verre et du cristal. Strasbourg, 1999.

Meyer-Heisig, *Nürnberg*, 1963
E. Meyer-Heisig. *Der Nürnberger Glasschnitt des 17. Jahrhunderts.* Nuremberg, 1963.

Mille anni, 1982
 Mille anni del vetri Veneziano. Texts by R. Barovier-Mentasti, A. Dorigato, A. Gasparetto, and T. Toninato. Exh. cat. Venice: Palazzo Ducale, Museo Correr Venezia, 1982.

Neuwirth, *Jugendstil*, 1973
 W. Neuwirth. *Das Glas des Jugendstils: Sammlung des Österreichischen Museums für angewandte Kunst, Wien*. Munich, 1973.

Neuwirth, *Italienisches Glas*, 1987
 W. Neuwirth. *Glas. Glass. Verre. Vetri. I. 1950–1960. Italienisches Glas 1950–1960*. Vienna, 1987.

NG
 Neues Glas/New Glass. Düsseldorf and Frechen, 1980ff.

Niewöhner, *Sultan*, 1994
 E. Niewöhner, ed. *Der Sultan im Bade: Bilder und Objekte höfischen Lebens im Islam*. Exh. cat. Hanover: Kestner-Museum Hannover, 1994.

Ohm and Bauer, *Modernes Glas*, 1976
 A. Ohm and M. Bauer. *Modernes Glas aus Amerika, Europa und Japan*. Exh. cat. Frankfurt: Museum für Kunsthandwerk Frankfurt am Main, 1976.

Ohm, Bauer, and Gabbert, Frankfurt, 1980
 A. Ohm, M. Bauer, and G. Gabbert. *Europäisches und aussereuropäisches Glas*. Coll. cat. 2nd ed. Frankfurt: Museum für Kunsthandwerk Frankfurt am Main, 1980.

Passau, *Böhmisches Glas 4*, 1995
 Das Böhmische Glas 1700–1950. Vol. 4, *Jugendstil in Böhmen*. Coll. cat. Passau: Passauer Glasmuseum. Tittling, 1995.

Pazaurek, *Moderne Gläser*, 1901
 G. E. Pazaurek, *Moderne Gläser*. Leipzig, n.d. [1901].

Pazaurek, *Biedermeier*, 1923
 G. E. Pazaurek. *Gläser der Empire- und Biedermeierzeit*. Leipzig, 1923.

Pazaurek, *Kunstgläser*, 1925
 G. E. Pazaurek. *Kunstgläser der Gegenwart*. Leipzig, 1925.

Pazaurek and Philippovich, 1976
 G. E. Pazaurek and E. von Philippovich. *Gläser der Empire- und Biedermeierzeit*. Braunschweig, 1976. Rev. ed. by Pazaurek, *Biedermeier*, 1923.

Pazaurek and Spiegl, *20. Jahrhundert*, 1983
 G. E. Pazaurek and W. Spiegl. *Glas des 20. Jahrhunderts: Jugendstil. Art Déco*. Munich, 1983.

Pfohl, 1994
 W. Messner, H. Ricke, and S. Scharnowski. *Alexander Pfohl, 17.3.1894–9.8.1953: Der Glasgestalter und Maler*. Exh. cat. Hadamar, 1994.

Polak, *Modern Glass*, 1962
 A. Polak. *Modern Glass*. London, 1962.

Prohaska-Gross, "Landsknechtsglas," 1997
 C. Prohaska-Gross. "Ein Landsknechtsglas aus Durlach," *Krautstrunk und Scheisserle: Festschrift für Walter Lang zum 60. Geburtstag*. Göppingen, 1997.

Rademacher, *Mittelalter*, 1933
 F. Rademacher. *Die deutschen Gläser des Mittelalters*. Berlin, n.d. [1933].

Revi, *Nineteenth Century*, 1964
 A. C. Revi. *Nineteenth Century Glass: Its Genesis and Development*. New York, 1964.

Revi, *American Art Nouveau*, 1968
 A. C. Revi. *American Art Nouveau Glass*. Camden, NJ, 1968.

Ricke, *Leerdam*, 1977
 H. Ricke. *Leerdam Unica: 50 Jahre modernes niederländisches Glas*. Exh. cat. Düsseldorf: Kunstmuseum Düsseldorf, 1977.

Ricke, *Glasprobleme*, 1979
 H. Ricke. *Glasprobleme: Kopie, Nachahmung, Fälschung*. Exh. cat. Kunstmuseum Düsseldorf. Hanover, 1979. The same in *Glas + Steinzeug: Original, Kopie oder Fälschung, Kunst und Fälschung* 1 (Hanover, 1979): 33–91.

Ricke, *Ausgewählte Werke*, 1980
 H. Ricke. *Kunstmuseum Düsseldorf: Ausgewählte Werke, no. 5, Glas*. Coll. cat. 2nd ed. Düsseldorf, 1980.

Ricke, *Licht. Form. Gestalt*, 1980
 H. Ricke. *Licht. Form. Gestalt: Objekte aus geschliffenem Glas*. Exh. cat. Düsseldorf: Kunstmuseum Düsseldorf, 1980.

Ricke, *Schneider France*, 1981
 H. Ricke. *Schneider France: Glas des Art Deco*. Exh. cat. Düsseldorf: Kunstmuseum Düsseldorf. Hanover, 1981.

Ricke, "Rhein und Saar," *19. Jahrhundert*, 1981
 H. Ricke. "Tafelservice und Prunkpokal: Die Glasfabriken an Rhein und Saar." *Kunst des 19. Jahrhunderts im Rheinland 5, Kunstgewerbe*. Ed. Eduard Trier and Willy Weyres, pp. 205–40. Düsseldorf, 1981.

Ricke, "Pfohl," 1982
 H. Ricke. "Alexander Pfohl—Glaskünstler und Designer," *Jahrbuch des Museums für Kunst und Gewerbe Hamburg* 1 (1982): 61–100.

Ricke, *Finnische Künstler*, 1982
 H. Ricke. *Unikate finnischer Künstler: Glas*. Exh. cat. Düsseldorf: Kunstmuseum Düsseldorf, 1982.

Ricke, *New Glass Germany*, 1983
 H. Ricke. *Neues Glas in Deutschland/New Glass in Germany: Ausstellung der Deutschen Glastechnischen Gesellschaft zum XIII. Internationalen Glaskongress Hamburg 1983. Organisiert von Kunstmuseum Düsseldorf*. Düsseldorf, 1983.

Ricke, "Neue Gläser," 1985
 H. Ricke. "Neue Räume—Neue Gläser: Die Sammlung des Kunstmuseums Düsseldorf nach der Wiedereröffnung," *Kunst & Antiquitäten* 4 (1985): 44–53.

Ricke and Gronert, *Glas in Schweden*, 1986
 H. Ricke and U. Gronert, eds. *Glas in Schweden 1915–1960*. Texts by J. E. Anderbjörk, H. Dahlbäck-Luttemann, U. Gronert, A. Hald, and H. Ricke. Exh. cat. Düsseldorf: Kunstmuseum Düsseldorf. Munich, 1986.

Ricke, *2500 Jahre*, 1987
 H. Ricke. *2500 Jahre Glaskunst in Europa aus dem Besitz des Kunstmuseums Düsseldorf*. Exh. cat. Hokkaido, Sapporo: Museum of Modern Art, 1987.

Ricke and Thor, *Schwedische Glasmanufakturen*, 1987
 H. Ricke and L. Thor. *Schwedische Glasmanufakturen: Produktionskataloge 1915–1960: Orrefors, Kosta, Elme, Eda, Strömbergsrhyttan*. Munich, 1987.

Ricke, *Museumsarbeit*, 1988
 H. Ricke. "Glas," *Rückblick nach vorn: 75 Jahre Museumsarbeit*, 65–82. Düsseldorf: Kunstmuseum Düsseldorf, 1988.

Ricke, *Jugendstil/Art Déco*, 1991
 H. Ricke. Glas: *Jugendstil und Art Déco*. Exh. cat. Japan, Tokyo, Kasama, etc. Text in Japanese and German. Tokyo, 1991.

Ricke, *New Glass Europe*, 1991
 H. Ricke. *Neues Glas in Europa: 50 Künstler—50 Konzepte. New Glass in Europe: 50 Artists—50 Concepts*. Exh. cat. Text in German and English. 2nd ed. Düsseldorf: Kunstmuseum Düsseldorf im Ehrenhof—Glasmuseum Hentrich, 1991.

Ricke, *New Glass Japan*, 1993
 H. Ricke. *Neues Glas in Japan. New Glass in Japan*. Exh. cat. Texts by Y. Mizuta, B. Schmittmann, A. Takeda. Text in German and English. Düsseldorf: Kunstmuseum Düsseldorf im Ehrenhof—Glasmuseum Hentrich, 1993.

Ricke and Schmitt, *Italian Glass*, 1997
 H. Ricke and E. Schmitt. *Italian Glass: Murano–Milan 1930–1970: The Collection of the Steinberg Foundation*. Munich and New York, 1997.

Ricke and Schmitt, *Sammlung Koepff*, 1998
 H. Ricke and Eva Schmitt. *Glas des Art Nouveau: Die Sammlung Gerda Koepff*. Exh. cat. Düsseldorf: Kunstmuseum Düsseldorf. Munich, 1998.

Ritsema, Amsterdam I, 1993
 P. C. Ritsema van Eck and H. M. Zijlstra-Zweens. *Glass in the Rijksmuseum*, vol. I. (Catalogues of the Applied Arts in the Rijksmuseum Amsterdam, vol. 2, 1.) Zwolle, 1993.

Rückert, Munich, 1982
 R. Rückert. *Die Glassammlung des Bayerischen Nationalmuseums München*, vols. 1, 2. (Kataloge des Bayerischen Nationalmuseums München, vol. XVII). Munich, 1982.

Saldern, *Enameled Glass*, 1965
A. von Saldern. *German Enameled Glass: The Edwin J. Beinecke Collection and Related Pieces*. Corning, NY: The Corning Museum of Glass, 1965.

Saldern, *Alte Gläser*, 1968
A. v. Saldern. *Alte Gläser: Bildhefte des Kunstmuseums Düsseldorf* 5. Düsseldorf, 1968.

Saldern, *Meisterwerke*, 1968
Meisterwerke der Glaskunst aus internationalem Privatbesitz. Exh. cat. Text by A. von Saldern and H. Hilschenz (Jugendstil). Düsseldorf: Kunstmuseum Düsseldorf, 1968.

Saldern, "Sassanidische und islamische Gläser," 1968
A. v. Saldern. "Sassanidische und islamische Gläser in Düsseldorf und Hamburg." *Jahrbuch der Hamburger Kunstsammlungen* 13 (1968): 33–62.

Saldern et al., *Sammlung Oppenländer*, 1974
A. von Saldern, B. Nolte, P. La Baume, and T. Haevernick. *Gläser der Antike: Sammlung Erwin Oppenländer*. Exh. cat. Hamburg: Museum für Kunst und Gewerbe, 1974.

Saldern, *Antike und Islam*, 1974
A. von Saldern. *Kataloge des Kunstmuseums Düsseldorf I, Glas*. Vol. 3, *Glassammlung Hentrich: Antike und Islam*. Düsseldorf, 1974.

Saldern, *Cohn Collection*, 1980
A. von Saldern. *Glass 500 B.C. to A.D. 1900: The Hans Cohn Collection, Los Angeles, Cal.* Mainz, 1980.

Schack, *Glaskunst*, 1976
C. Schack. *Die Glaskunst: Ein Handbuch über Herstellung, Sammeln und Gebrauch des Hohlglases*. Munich, 1976.

Scharnowski, "Pfohl," 1993
S. Scharnowski. "Alexander Pfohl und die Josephinenhütte." Master's thesis, Universität Frankfurt am Main, 1993.

Schenk zu Schweinsberg, *Bildnisgläser*, 1970
E. Schenk zu Schweinsberg. *Bildnisgläser der Sammlung Heine in Karlsruhe*. Frankfurt, 1970.

Schlosser, *Das alte Glas*, 1977
J. Schlosser. *Das alte Glas: Ein Handbuch für Sammler und Liebhaber*. Munich, 1977.

Schmidt, *Lobmeyr*, 1925
R. Schmidt. *100 Jahre Österreichische Glaskunst: 1823 Lobmeyr 1925*. Vienna, 1925.

Schmitt, *Sammlung Silzer*, 1989
E. Schmitt. *Glas-Kunst-Handwerk 1870–1940: Glassammlung Silzer: Leihgabe der Deutschen Bank im Augustinermuseum Freiburg im Breisgau*. Freiburg im Breisgau, 1989.

Schmitt, *Zürich 1*, 1992
E. Schmitt. *Museum Bellerive Zürich: Glas*. Vol. 1, 1945–91. Zurich, 1992.

Schmoll, *Nancy 1900*, 1980
J. A. and H. Schmoll genannt Eisenwerth. *Nancy 1900: Jugendstil in Lothringen*. Exh. cat. Munich: Münchener Stadtmuseum, 1980.

Schöne-Chotjewitz, *Zwiesel*, 1997
K. Schöne-Chotjewitz. *Die Fachschule für Glasindustrie in Zwiesel unter der Leitung von Bruno Mauder (1910–1948)*. Vol. 2, *Schriften des Passauer Glasmuseums*. Tittling, 1997.

Schüly, *Eiff*, 1989
M. Schüly. *Wilhelm von Eiff (1890–1943) und seine Schule*. Exh. cat. Freiburg im Breisgau: Augustinermuseum Freiburg im Breisgau, 1989.

Silice e fuoco, 1992
M. Quesada, H. Ricke, and E. Tittoni, eds. *L'arte del vetro: Silice e fuoco: vetri del XIX e XX secolo*. Exh. cat. Rome: Palazzo delle Espezioni. Venice, 1992.

Sotheby Monaco, 1982
Emile Gallé: Vases, Lampes et Projets. Auction cat. Monte Carlo: Sotheby Parke Bernet Monaco S.A., 24 October 1982.

Spiegl, *Historismus*, 1980
W. Spiegl. *Glas des Historismus: Kunst- und Gebrauchsgläser des Historismus*. Braunschweig, 1980.

Spiegl, *Biedermeier*, 1981
W. Spiegl. *Biedermeier-Gläser: Kaisers Sammler Bibliothek*. Munich, 1981.

Stern and Schlick-Nolte, *Early Glass*, 1994
M. Stern and B. Schlick-Nolte. *Early Glass of the Ancient World: Ernesto Wolf Collection*. Ostfildern, 1994.

Sterner, *Sammlung Heuer*, 1972
G. Sterner. *Sammlung Barlach Heuer: Gläser des Jugendstils. Manufaktur Loetz, Klostermühle*. Exh. cat. Düsseldorf: Kunstmuseum Düsseldorf, 1972. (Expanded edition of the exh. cat. *Loetz Austria: Irisierende Farbgläser des Jugendstils*. Munich: Villa Stuck, 1972.)

Strasser, *Kothgasser*, 1977
R. von Strasser. *Die Einschreibebüchlein des Wiener Glas- und Porzellanmalers Anton Kothgasser (1769–1851)*. Karlsruhe, n.d. [1977].

Strasser and Spiegl, *Sammlung von Strasser*, 1989
R. von Strasser and W. Spiegl. *Dekoriertes Glas: Renaissance bis Biedermeier: Meister und Werkstätten: Katalog Raisonné der Sammlung Rudolf von Strasser*. Munich, 1989.

Theuerkauff-Liederwald, *Venezianisches Glas*, 1994
A.-E. Theuerkauff-Liederwald. *Venezianisches Glas der Kunstsammlungen der Veste Coburg: Die Sammlung Herzog Alfreds von Sachsen-Coburg und Gotha*. Lingen, 1994.

Venini/Orrefors, 1957
Venini Murano. Orrefors Schweden: Glas. Exh. cat. N.p. [Hanover]: Kestner Museum Hannover, 1957.

Venini, 1978
L. Massoni, ed. *Venini*. Company publication. Cermenate, 1978.

Venini, *Artisti*, 1996
A. Venini. *Gli artisti di Venini: Per una storia del vetro d'arte veneziano*. Exh. cat. Venice: Fondazione Giorgio Cini. Milan, 1996.

Verrerie années 50, 1988
La verrerie Européenne des années 50. Exh. cat. Marseilles: Musées de Marseille, 1988.

World Glass Now, 1982, 1985, 1988, 1991, 1994
World Glass Now. Exh. cats. Sapporo: Hokkaido Museum of Modern Art, 1982, 1985, 1988, 1991, 1994.

Several glass pieces of the Art Nouveau period and the 1920s to the 1940s illustrated in this volume are also included in the two exhibition catalogues: Ricke, *Jugendstil/Art Déco*, 1991, and *Silice e fuoco*, 1992. Since these publications scarcely offer more information, they are not cited in the catalogue entries.

Index of Names